Get started with your **Connected Casebook**

Redeem your code below to access the **e-book** with search, highlighting, and note-taking capabilities; **case briefing** and **outlining** tools to support efficient learning; and more.

1. Go to www.casebookconnect.com
2. Enter your access code in the box and click **Register**
3. Follow the steps to complete your registration and verify your email address

If you have already registered at CasebookConnect.com, simply log into your account and redeem additional access codes from your Dashboard.

ACCESS CODE:

Scratch off with care.

Is this a used casebook? Access code already redeemed? Purchase a digital version at **CasebookConnect.com/catalog**.

If you purchased a digital bundle with additional components, your additional access codes will appear below.

"I liked being able to search quickly while in class."

"Being able to highlight and easily create case briefs was a fantastic resource and time saver for me!"

"I loved it! I was able to study on the go and create a more effective outline."

For technical support, please visit http://support.wklegaledu.com.

TRANSNATIONAL LAW AND PRACTICE

ASPEN CASEBOOK SERIES

TRANSNATIONAL LAW AND PRACTICE

SECOND EDITION

DONALD EARL CHILDRESS III
Professor of Law
Pepperdine Caruso School of Law

MICHAEL D. RAMSEY
Hugh and Hazel Darling Foundation Professor of Law
Director, International & Comparative Law Programs
University of San Diego School of Law

CHRISTOPHER A. WHYTOCK
Vice Dean and Professor of Law and Political Science
University of California, Irvine School of Law

Wolters Kluwer

ISBN 978-1-4548-9896-2

Library of Congress Cataloging-in-Publication Data

Names: Childress, Donald Earl, 1975- author. | Ramsey, Michael D., 1964-
    author. | Whytock, Christopher A., author.
Title: Transnational law and practice / Donald Earl Childress III,
    Professor of Law, Pepperdine Caruso School of Law; Michael D.
    Ramsey, Hugh and Hazel Darling Foundation Professor of Law Director,
    Director, International & Comparative Law Programs, University of San
    Diego School of Law; Christopher A. Whytock, Vice Dean and Professor of
    Law and Political Science, University of California, Irvine School of
    Law.
Description: Second edition. | New York: Wolters Kluwer, [2021] | Series:
    Aspen casebook series | Includes bibliographical references and index. |
    Summary: "A synthesized, logical, expository treatment of the main
    principles of transnational law, litigation, and dispute resolution
    using not only cases but also primary materials—e.g., complaints,
    arbitration memorials, summary judgment briefs, discovery documents,
    motions, and appellate briefs"—Provided by publisher.
Identifiers: LCCN 2020029611 | ISBN 9781454898962 (hardback) | ISBN
    9781543817522 (ebook)
Subjects: LCSH: Civil procedure—United States—Cases | Conflict of
    laws—Civil procedure—United States. | Civil procedure.
Classification: LCC KF8839.C437 2021 | DDC 340.90973—dc23
LC record available at https://lccn.loc.gov/2020029611

About Wolters Kluwer Legal & Regulatory U.S.

Wolters Kluwer Legal & Regulatory U.S. delivers expert content and solutions in the areas of law, corporate compliance, health compliance, reimbursement, and legal education. Its practical solutions help customers successfully navigate the demands of a changing environment to drive their daily activities, enhance decision quality and inspire confident outcomes.

Serving customers worldwide, its legal and regulatory portfolio includes products under the Aspen Publishers, CCH Incorporated, Kluwer Law International, ftwilliam.com and MediRegs names. They are regarded as exceptional and trusted resources for general legal and practice-specific knowledge, compliance and risk management, dynamic workflow solutions, and expert commentary.

In loving dedication to Lisa, Jacob, Caleb, and Shana; to my parents, Donald Earl Childress, Jr. and Joan Ann Childress; and to my entire family, whose love and support has known no bounds.
Donald Earl Childress III

To Harry and Anne Ramsey, Lisa Pondrom Ramsey, and Christopher and Colin Ramsey.
Michael D. Ramsey

To my sister, Betsy, a teacher who inspires her students and inspires me.
Christopher A. Whytock

SUMMARY OF CONTENTS

CONTENTS

6 ALTERNATIVE DISPUTE RESOLUTION   541

III   HOW CAN DISPUTE RESOLUTION OUTCOMES BE ENFORCED?   595

7   COURT JUDGMENTS   597

PREFACE

The goal of this casebook is to help students learn how to solve the types of transnational legal problems they are likely to encounter in practice, regardless of their field of practice and regardless of whether they think of themselves as practicing international law. Therefore, this casebook is different from traditional public international law casebooks. Like them, it covers the sources of international law and introduces students to international courts. Unlike traditional public international law casebooks, however, this casebook urges students not to be "international law–centric" or "international court–centric" when analyzing transnational legal problems, and gives them the resources to learn how to use national law and national courts, and private norms and alternative dispute resolution methods, to solve transnational legal problems on behalf of their clients.

We believe that this casebook's approach makes it especially well suited for required courses on international or transnational law, since it focuses on problems that all students are likely to encounter in the present-day practice of law regardless of their practice area and regardless of their preexisting interest in international law. It is also well suited for both first-year and upper-division students. Much of the material deals with the transnational dimensions of first-year law courses like Civil Procedure, Contracts, Constitutional Law, and Torts, and thus will provide a less intimidating point of access to the field while also reinforcing learning across the first-year curriculum. The casebook also includes advanced material on transnational litigation in U.S. courts, making it an excellent choice for upper-division elective courses in international civil litigation. Put simply, this book is designed to prepare students for law practice in a globalized world and to equip them with the knowledge and skills they need to solve transnational legal problems, regardless of whether they plan to practice international law as such.

Donald Earl Childress III
Michael D. Ramsey
Christopher A. Whytock

July 2020

ACKNOWLEDGMENTS

We appreciate the comments and suggestions of our students as they learned from the first edition of this casebook and from professors who used the first edition in their courses.

We thank the copyright holders who kindly granted us permission to reprint excerpts from the following materials:

American Law Institute. Restatement of the Law Third, Foreign Relations Law of the United States copyrighted © 1987 by The American Law Institute. Reproduced with permission. All rights reserved.

American Law Institute. Restatement of the Law Fourth, Foreign Relations Law of the United States copyrighted © 2018 by The American Law Institute. Reproduced with permission. All rights reserved.

American Law Institute. The U.S. Law of Commercial and Investor-State Arbitration, Proposed Final Draft copyright © 2019 by The American Law Institute. Reproduced with permission. All rights reserved. (This Draft was approved by ALI membership of the 2019 Annual Meeting, subject to the discussion at the Meeting and to the usual editorial prerogative, and it may be cited as representing the Institute's position until the official text is published.)

David J. Bederman, The Spirit of International Law (2002). Reprinted by permission of the University of Georgia Press via CCC.

Duncan B. Hollis & Joshua J. Newcomber, "Political Commitments" and the Constitution, 49 Virginia Journal of International Law 507 (2009), Virginia Journal of International Law Association.

Michael McIlwrath & John Savage, International Arbitration and Mediation: A Practical Guide, Kluwer Law International, (2010).

Lucy Reed, Jan Paulsson & Nigel Blackaby, Guide to ICSID Arbitration, Kluwer Law International (2004).

Secretariat for the Voluntary Principles on Security and Human Rights, Voluntary Principles Association (2014).

UNCITRAL Model Law on International Commercial Arbitration (1985), with Amendments as Adopted in 2006. Copyright © 2008 by the United Nations Commission on International Trade Law. Reprinted with the permission of the United Nations Commission on International Trade Law via CCC.

Uniform Law Commission, Uniform Foreign-Country Money Judgments Recognition Act. Copyright © 2005 by The American Law Conference of Commissioners on Uniform State Laws. Reproduced with permission. All rights reserved.

United Nations. Draft Conclusions on Identification of Customary International Law, United Nations (2018).

World Trade Organization, Report of the Appellate Body (16 January 1998). World Trade Organization. 1998.

EDITORIAL NOTICE

We have edited the cases and other legal materials in this casebook. Where we have judged that citations, footnotes, or internal quotations are not essential for student learning, we have omitted them without indication. Otherwise, we indicate omitted text with ellipses. The formatting and style of some headings and subheadings in the edited materials have been altered to provide consistency. Footnotes in cases and other legal materials retain their original numbering. Our own footnotes appear as asterisks.

INTRODUCTION

Welcome to the world of transnational law and practice! In an increasingly globalized world, individuals, businesses, and governments are interacting more and more frequently across national borders. Individuals—tourists, businesspeople, government officials—routinely travel from one nation to another. Even when they do not travel, they engage in transactions that cross international borders. Businesses buy and sell goods and make investments all over the world. And nations, through the application of laws and regulations—and sometimes unfortunately through armed force—also participate in transnational interactions, often attempting to govern or otherwise influence activity that takes place beyond their borders. International organizations and private actors are also among today's "global governors." *See generally* WHO GOVERNS THE GLOBE? (Deborah D. Avant et al. eds., 2010). If you doubt that we live in a transnational world, pull out the smartphone in your pocket or look at the computer you are using. Both were likely designed in one nation, assembled in another, and perhaps shipped to you in yet another nation.

All of this means that you as a lawyer are increasingly likely to encounter legal problems that involve individuals, businesses, or governments of more than one nation or activity that crosses international borders. A 2007-2008 survey of lawyers who passed the bar in 2000 suggests that almost half of U.S. lawyers are called upon to solve transnational legal problems for their clients, and in some types of practice the number is considerably higher:

> Forty-four percent (44%) of attorneys reported ... work [that involved clients from outside the United States or cross-border matters]. The lawyers most likely to report doing international legal work were those in the largest law firms, where two thirds reported doing it, and inside counsel, where almost as many (65%) reported work that involved non-U.S. clients or cross-border matters. Among legal services and public defense lawyers, work that involved non-U.S. clients or non-U.S. law was also common, with 61% of attorneys reporting they had done some such work during the past year. The international work in large corporate firms mainly serves foreign corporate clients, while the work of legal services and public defense lawyers likely involves individual clients who are facing immigration issues.

THE AMERICAN BAR FOUNDATION AND THE NALP FOUNDATION FOR LAW CAREER RESEARCH AND EDUCATION, AFTER THE JD II: SECOND RESULTS FROM A NATIONAL STUDY OF LEGAL CAREERS 35 (2009). There can be little doubt that these numbers are higher today. Some lawyers will encounter transnational legal problems at a much higher rate—such as lawyers working for multinational businesses, nongovernmental human rights groups, international organizations, or a nation's foreign ministry (such as the U.S. State Department), or those specializing in fields such as international family law or immigration law. In addition, many law firms have groups of lawyers focused specifically on transnational practice, such as transnational business transactions, transnational commercial arbitration, and investor-state arbitration. But as the data suggests, you are likely to face transnational legal problems *regardless* of the focus of your practice.

Unlike traditional international law casebooks, which typically focus somewhat narrowly on international law and international courts, this casebook is designed to help you develop the knowledge and skills that you will need to solve the kinds of transnational legal problems you are most likely to encounter in practice. To be sure, this casebook will give you an excellent introduction to international law and international courts—but they are only the tip of the iceberg. For most U.S. lawyers, the most common transnational legal problems are likely to be those that arise when representing U.S. or foreign clients not in international courts, but in U.S. courts, in the courts of other nations, or in arbitration or other alternative dispute resolution processes; or when representing U.S. or foreign clients in disputes or business transactions governed not by international law, but by U.S. law or the law of another nation. Specifically, this casebook focuses on three sets of questions that pervade transnational practice:

- What are the applicable rules? Does national law, international law, or a set of private rules apply? If national law applies, *which* nation's law? Lawyers in transnational practice must be sensitive to the question of what rules apply to a given activity or dispute.
- What transnational dispute resolution methods are available and most appropriate? National courts? If so, *which* nation's courts? How does service of process and discovery work in transnational practice? And what legal doctrines apply specifically to disputes in national courts that have a transnational dimension? Beyond national courts, when are international courts available? And when might noncourt dispute resolution methods, such as mediation or arbitration, be most appropriate? A transnational lawyer must be aware of a variety of possible forums and appreciate how forum selection may influence the outcome.
- If the other party does not voluntarily comply with a dispute resolution outcome, how might that outcome be enforced? Under what circumstances will one nation enforce dispute resolution outcomes reached in another nation? How do considerations of enforcement shape other decisions about a case or a business transaction, such as the selection of a dispute resolution method?

Each set of questions entails many complexities that will be explored in this casebook. By the end of this course, we hope that you will be able to analyze these issues effectively in a wide variety of factual settings. These questions certainly do not capture all the issues that can arise in transnational law and practice. There is much more you can learn both in more specialized courses and in practice. Nevertheless, if you learn to tackle these three basic sets of pervasive issues, you will have a solid foundation for solving transnational legal problems in the real world and for furthering your study of international and transnational law. Indeed, we believe that by focusing on these questions you will be better equipped to tackle the everyday questions you will face in your law practice generally, even if you do not face transnational legal problems on a regular basis.

This casebook includes in-depth discussions of international law and international courts (Chapters 2 and 5). But a theme of the casebook is that lawyers should not be "international law–centric" or "international court–centric" when dealing with transnational legal problems. To the contrary, today's lawyers need to understand the crucial role that national law and national courts play in solving transnational legal problems (Chapters 1 and 4). This central insight was captured long ago by Philip Jessup—a lawyer, diplomat, professor, and judge on the International Court of Justice—when he coined the term "transnational law" to refer to "all law which regulates actions or events that transcend national frontiers"—not just international law, but also national law. PHILIP C. JESSUP, TRANSNATIONAL LAW 2 (1956). Yet even understanding national law and international law is not enough. Private methods of governing transnational activity, including contracting and arbitration (Chapters 3 and 6), are among the most important and fast-growing parts of transnational practice today. Thus, when we refer to transnational law, we mean not only national and international law that applies to transnational legal problems, but also the private forms of regulation and dispute resolution that lawyers and their clients use to address those problems.

No casebook can do everything. This casebook's approach—like any approach—entails trade-offs in coverage. First, we focus on issues that arise in planning for and resolving transnational disputes more than we focus on transnational business transactions. Understanding the former is, however, essential for understanding the latter. Dispute resolution provisions are an important part of almost every business agreement. More generally, expectations about the applicable legal rules and the methods by which disputes arising out of a transaction will be resolved are both major influences on the planning, negotiation, and performance of business transactions. We therefore believe that a course using this casebook can provide an excellent foundation for a subsequent course on transnational business transactions.

Second, the casebook's focus is more systemic than substantive. The national, international, and private dimensions of the transnational legal system that today's lawyers need to be familiar with are treated in depth, but we have not devoted chapters to specialized substantive fields of international law typically covered in traditional public international law courses (such as international trade, the use of force, or the law of the sea). We believe that a student who masters the fundamentals of the transnational legal system will be well equipped to learn and use particular substantive fields of international law, and that a course based on this casebook will be an excellent foundation for advanced courses in public international law—and for legal practice.

Third, this casebook's dominant perspective is U.S. legal practice. The primary reason is simple: we expect that most students using this casebook will practice primarily in the United States or advise clients based in the United States. We also have found that emphasizing the kinds of transnational problems that U.S.-based lawyers commonly encounter in practice has significant pedagogical advantages—particularly in international law courses—compared to more abstract and theoretical approaches. Nevertheless, we believe in the value of comparative perspectives. Encounters with foreign law and foreign legal systems are an important part of transnational practice. We also believe that policy perspectives can enhance student understanding. Therefore, although the casebook takes a predominantly U.S. practice perspective, we have incorporated comparative and policy material throughout.

In summary, this casebook introduces you to national law and international law, as well as private rules and nonbinding norms; to national courts, international courts, and nonlitigation dispute resolution methods such as mediation and arbitration; and to the techniques that can be used to enforce dispute resolution outcomes, including the enforcement of court judgments and arbitral awards. Unlike many courses, you will find that this course brings together your work in diverse areas such as constitutional law, statutory construction, torts, contracts, and civil procedure, and provides new twists to help you put those courses in perspective and push their boundaries.

This legal diversity can be messy—but that messiness is part of the real-world practice of law in today's globalized world. Legal scholars call this legal diversity "global legal pluralism." As one scholar puts it, "The irreducible plurality of legal orders in the world, the coexistence of domestic state law with other legal orders, the absence of a hierarchically superior position transcending the differences—all of these topics of legal pluralism [appear] on the global sphere." Ralf Michaels, *Global Legal Pluralism*, 5 ANN. REV. L. & SOC. SCI. 1 (2009). Another scholar emphasizes the "complex overlapping legal authority" that characterizes legal pluralism. Paul Schiff Berman, *Global Legal Pluralism*, 80 S. CAL. L. REV. 1155, 1162 (2007). One way of thinking about this course is as an introduction to some of the basic methods that lawyers use to grapple with legal pluralism in practice.

This introduction sets the stage for this casebook's exploration of transnational law and practice. Section A explains what this casebook means by transnational law and practice. Section B is a brief overview of the transnational legal system and its main parts, including national legal systems, international legal systems, and private ordering. Section C provides a roadmap for the rest of the casebook. Section D uses a real-world case to give you a first look at some issues that pervade transnational law and practice and to make more concrete the themes raised in this introduction.

A. What Is Transnational Law and Practice?

Let's begin with some definitions. "Transnational law" is the law that governs transnational activity and disputes arising out of transnational activity. By "transnational activity" we mean activity that involves the citizens or governments of more than one nation or takes place or has effects in the territory of more than one nation. A terminological note is important here: In international law, "state" is a term of art that is generally used instead of "nation." Specifically, "a state is an entity that has a defined territory and a permanent population, under the control of its own government, and that engages in, or has the capacity to engage in, formal relations with other such entities." RESTATEMENT (THIRD) OF FOREIGN RELATIONS LAW OF THE UNITED STATES §201 (1987). This casebook generally uses the term "nation" to avoid confusion with references to U.S. states. But throughout this course you should remember that when the term "state" is used in international law or international courts, it ordinarily refers to what this casebook calls a "nation," not to one of the 50 states of the United States.

Transnational law includes, but is not limited to, international law. "International law" is the law made among nations by treaty, through custom, or in the form of general principles common to the world's major legal systems (Chapter 2). Traditionally, international law mostly governed relationships among nations (such as diplomatic relations and the use of military force). Since World War II, however, international law has also increasingly addressed the rights and duties of individuals (as in the case of human rights law and international criminal law). But it is important not to be international law–centric, because other types of rules can also govern transnational activity: national law, contractually agreed-upon private rules, and nonbinding norms. As you will learn in Chapter 1, under some circumstances a nation's law may apply to activity outside its territory. And as you will learn in Chapter 3, parties routinely use privately negotiated contracts to govern their cross-border interactions, and nonbinding norms—like declarations of principles or corporate codes of conduct—also play an important role in governing transnational activity even though they are not legally binding.

Transnational practice refers to any work of a lawyer to help a client solve a transnational problem. For most lawyers today, transnational practice is not a distinct field of practice. Some law firms, businesses, nongovernmental organizations, international organizations, and government agencies do have groups of lawyers dedicated to transnational practice. But most lawyers called upon to help clients solve transnational legal problems are not "international lawyers" and do not perceive themselves as practicing "international law." They practice business law, family law, intellectual property law, personal injury law, criminal law, and so on. They work as solo practitioners and in small firms, as well as in large international law firms, government offices like the U.S. State Department's Office of the Legal Advisor, or international organizations like the United Nations. What they have in common is that regardless of practice area, and regardless of whether they consider themselves "international lawyers," they are likely to be called upon to help clients solve transnational legal problems.

In fact, one result of globalization is that transnational legal problems pervade virtually all fields of legal practice. U.S.-based business lawyers routinely represent U.S. clients entering into business transactions with non-U.S. parties, and vice versa. When disputes arise out of those transactions, U.S.-based lawyers help clients resolve those disputes, through litigation in U.S. courts or abroad, or through various alternative dispute resolution methods such as arbitration. U.S.-based intellectual property lawyers routinely represent clients in licensing transactions with parties in other countries, and in efforts to protect intellectual property globally. U.S.-based family lawyers represent clients in cross-border adoptions, marriages, and other relationships between citizens of different nations, and child custody, child support, or spousal support matters involving parties in different nations. U.S.-based lawyers routinely represent U.S. clients seeking compensation for injuries suffered in other nations, or non-U.S. clients seeking compensation for injuries caused by U.S. parties. For all of these activities and disputes, lawyers must confront the basic questions we posed earlier: What are the applicable rules? Where can disputes be resolved? How can dispute resolution outcomes be enforced?

To make the point as emphatically as possible: This casebook is *not* only for students interested in or expecting to practice international law. It is for *all* law students. It is designed to expose you to the sorts of transnational legal problems you are likely to encounter in real-world practice, and to help you become a better lawyer generally, *regardless* of your field of practice. Among other things, the benefit of studying transnational practice is that you will learn about a host of legal doctrines—civil procedure, antitrust law, securities law, transnational human rights, to name just a few—all within one course. You will learn how to approach these problems as a lawyer and not just as a student. To this end, practice-oriented notes and questions are included throughout the casebook.

B. The Transnational Legal System

It is important to understand the system in which transnational law is made, applied, and enforced, and in which transnational practice takes place. The transnational legal system has three basic parts: national legal systems, international legal systems, and private ordering. This section provides a brief overview of these parts. In the chapters that follow, you will learn about them in greater depth.

National legal systems are the legal systems of individual nations. National legal systems include the U.S. legal system (a "domestic" legal system, from a U.S. perspective) as well as the legal systems of other nations ("foreign" legal systems, from a U.S. perspective). Among the basic building blocks of a national legal system are institutions for lawmaking (such as legislatures), adjudication (such as courts), and law enforcement (such as regulatory agencies and police). There are more than 190 nations in the world. This means that there are more than 190 national legal systems in the world. Moreover, in some nations, there are legal subsystems—for example, in the United States, there are both state and federal legal systems.

Although there are similarities across different national legal systems, there also is considerable diversity. To try to make sense of this diversity, comparative legal scholars have long tried to categorize national legal systems. Although many different approaches to categorization have been proposed, "civil law" and "common law" are perhaps the most enduring categories for comparison. Among the differences between these two legal traditions, three stand out: history, sources, and the role of the judge. Historically, the civil law tradition has its roots in Roman law, whereas the origins of the common law tradition can be traced to England.

Regarding sources of law, in the civil law tradition, legislation, systematically organized into "codes," is the primary source of law. In the common law tradition, the "common law"—the rules that can be generalized from court decisions—is an important source of law, with the doctrine of precedent requiring courts to use rules developed in earlier cases to decide later, similar cases. This difference is significant, but it should not be overstated. Courts do cite prior decisions in civil law nations (for example, for points of legislative interpretation) and legislation is indeed an important source of law in common law systems.

In the civil law tradition, the judge plays the leading role in directing and developing litigation. There is no jury in civil trials, although some civil law nations provide for juries for serious criminal offenses. In the common law tradition, lawyers take the initiative in the development of litigation, including factual discovery, in an adversarial process overseen by the judge.

Most national legal systems today fall roughly into the common law or civil law category. England, for example, is a classic example of a common law system, and France of a civil law nation. The United States is a common law nation (although one U.S. state—Louisiana—is strongly influenced by the civil law tradition). Aside from former British colonies, most nations have civil law traditions.

Nevertheless, the common law/civil law distinction is problematic. For one thing, it is too simplistic: some civil law nations share some characteristics of ~~share characteristics~~ common law nations, and vice versa. The distinction also neglects national legal systems that do not fall neatly into either category, such as mixed systems, like India and Israel, or Islamic law systems, like Iran and Saudi Arabia. There are also features of some nations' legal systems that are not reflected by the civil law/common law distinction. For example, among the features of the U.S. legal system that distinguish it from most other legal systems is the availability of broad factual discovery backed by judicial sanctions, widely available civil juries, and punitive damages. This makes it especially important not to assume that other nations' legal systems—even other common law systems—necessarily share particular characteristics of the U.S. legal system.

Moreover, some comparative law scholars argue that the differences highlighted by the civil law/common law distinction are decreasingly pronounced—in part due to what some scholars claim is a tendency toward the convergence of national legal systems—or that the common law/civil law distinction does not capture more fundamental differences. These debates are beyond the scope of this casebook and can be explored in a course on comparative law. For our purposes, the essential point is that national legal systems are diverse. Even if you do not master the details of foreign legal systems and traditions, you will be a better lawyer if you are aware of and sensitive to their diversity and avoid assuming that a foreign legal system necessarily resembles your home legal system.

International legal systems are created by nations. Like national legal systems, international legal systems are diverse. They can be global, like the United Nations, or they can be regional, like the European Union. Moreover, they can be general in the sense that they attempt to govern a wide range of activity (again, like the United Nations or the European Union), or they can be specialized (like the system established by the U.N. Convention on the Law of the Sea, including the International Tribunal for the Law of the Sea). It is admittedly more common to refer to a single "international legal system" than to the plural "international legal systems." Not only is the singular usage traditional, it also highlights the existence of general systemic rules—rules that you will learn about in Chapter 2—that, among other things, define the sources of international law. The problem with the singular is that it suggests something more coherent and uniform than exists in reality. The plural usage is truer to the complexity of international law and the reality that the various legal institutions that operate at the international level often do so largely separately from each other—much like national legal systems do.

Some international legal systems are highly institutionalized in ways that at least formally resemble a national legal system to a certain degree, such as the European Union and arguably the World Trade Organization. Others are largely inchoate and lack the features ordinarily associated with national legal systems— such as a legislature that can enact legally binding rules, an executive that can enforce rules, and courts that can authoritatively adjudicate disputes. This has led some scholars to question whether, from the perspective of legal theory, international law is really "law." Debates about whether international law counts as law have long preoccupied legal theorists (we touch on these debates in Chapter 2), and you might learn more about them in a course on legal philosophy or public international law. From the perspective of transnational practice, however, the essential point is that international legal systems play an important role in solving many transnational legal problems. Have no doubt, what we discuss in the following chapters is law in the sense that it is (or may be) applied to govern transnational activity.

Private ordering is another important part of the transnational legal system. Nongovernmental actors, including individuals and businesses, routinely govern themselves through their own rules. For example, nongovernmental organizations—such as the International Organization for Standardization (ISO) (which you will learn about in Chapter 3) or private arbitral institutions like the International Chamber of Commerce (ICC) (which you will learn about in Chapter 6)—often develop procedural or substantive rules. Individuals or businesses engaged in business relationships routinely enter privately negotiated contracts containing detailed rules to govern those relationships. Beyond these private norms, private arbitral institutions offer dispute resolution services as alternatives to litigation in national courts. These alternative forms of dispute resolution are among the most important parts of transnational practice.

There are interesting theoretical debates about the extent to which private ordering can be autonomous from national and international legal systems. One question is whether private parties will comply with the rules they make when it becomes inconvenient to do so, and whether they will abide by the outcomes of private dispute resolution processes such as arbitration even when they are on the losing side. Some commentators argue that private ordering could not work without the existence of national legal systems willing to apply coercive force to ensure compliance. Others argue that there are alternative enforcement mechanisms that foster compliance with private rules and private dispute resolution, mechanisms that do not rely on national legal systems for support—such as retaliation, exclusion, and reputational sanctions. The reality is probably somewhere in between, with national legal systems, international legal systems, and private ordering interacting in complex ways. In any event, the willingness of national legal systems to enforce contracts and to enforce arbitral awards enhances the effectiveness of private ordering of transnational activity. *See* Christopher A. Whytock, *Private-Public Interaction in Global Governance: The Case of Transnational Commercial Arbitration*, Bus. & Pol., Vol. 12, No. 3, Article 10 (2010).

The term "system" may suggest a high degree of order and coordination. In fact, the transnational legal system is highly decentralized and only loosely coordinated. There is no centralized "transnational government" that oversees the system's parts. As a result, there is often uncertainty about whether a national legal system, international legal system, or private ordering governs particular persons or activities. Moreover, the different parts are often in conflict. For example, more than one nation may claim to govern the same transnational activity with its law or adjudicate the same transnational dispute in its courts; national law may be inconsistent with international law; and some individuals or businesses may prefer to govern their behavior not according to a particular nation's law, but rather according to contractually agreed upon rules that may or may not be consistent with national law. This question of conflict is an important one, and it is addressed in the chapters that follow.

This is part of the messiness of global legal pluralism that confronts all lawyers who encounter transnational legal problems. By learning how to determine the applicable rules (Part I), how to identify which dispute resolution methods are available and most appropriate (Part II), and how to enforce transnational dispute resolution outcomes (Part III), you will have some of the basic tools needed to deal confidently with transnational legal pluralism.

C. Roadmap

As discussed above, this casebook is organized around three groups of issues that pervade transnational practice: What rules apply to a particular transnational problem? What transnational dispute resolution methods are available and most appropriate? How can a transnational dispute resolution outcome be enforced?

First, what rules apply to a transnational legal problem? This is the focus of Part I of the casebook. It is critical to know what law governs a legal problem that you are trying to solve on behalf of a client. For transnational legal problems, the answer is often far from obvious. There is no single centralized source of transnational lawmaking. The governing law may be a mix of international law and the law of various national legal systems; the question may be even more complex because more than one nation's law may arguably cover the same set of events. For instance, U.S. law sometimes (but not always) governs the actions of U.S. citizens in a foreign nation, while foreign law (and possibly international law) may govern the same actions. Moreover, since judicial enforcement of international law takes place primarily in national courts, there is the additional question of the extent to which international law itself operates within a national legal system.

Part I introduces you to the various types of rules that might apply to a transnational problem. Chapter 1 focuses on national law. It covers the principles governing the application of the law of individual nations to transnational activity, including limits on the extraterritorial application of U.S federal law and the principles and methods of choice of law. Its basic inquiry is: Should U.S. law or the law of another nation apply to a transnational problem? Chapter 2 focuses on international law. It covers the different types of international law—including treaties, customary international law, and general principles of law—and their role as law in U.S. courts. Among other things, we will ask how litigants and courts approach finding and applying international law. Chapter 3 focuses on two other types of rules that play an important role in transnational practice: nonbinding norms and private rules. Nonbinding international norms—such as resolutions of the U.N. General Assembly—are not legally binding. Nevertheless, they can play a significant role in transnational practice. Private rules—as discussed above—are made by private actors. When included in a valid contract, they may be legally enforceable—and even if not directly enforceable they may be important considerations for transnational actors.

Part II asks: What methods are available and most appropriate for resolving a transnational dispute? As with determining the applicable rules, choosing the appropriate court (or other dispute resolution forum) may be a complex task. Just as there is no centralized transnational lawmaking authority, there is no centralized forum for transnational dispute resolution. Many transnational disputes are resolved in the same way as purely domestic disputes—in national courts. There are, in addition, a relatively small but growing number of international courts, some devoted to particular subject matter or to resolution of disputes under particular treaties. In addition, private dispute resolution methods are very important in transnational practice. Chapter 4 introduces you to the jurisdiction of national courts to hear transnational disputes, with an emphasis on U.S. federal and state courts. Among other topics, this chapter covers personal and subject matter jurisdiction, which you may have already encountered (or be concurrently encountering) in a civil procedure course—but Chapter 4 examines these jurisdictional issues in the context of transnational legal problems and also offers a comparative perspective. Chapter 5 covers international courts, such as the International Court of Justice. Chapter 6 introduces you to dispute resolution methods other than litigation in national or international courts (often called "alternative dispute resolution"). These alternatives to litigation include mediation and arbitration.

Part III asks: How can a transnational dispute resolution outcome be enforced? Just as there is no centralized structure for transnational lawmaking or transnational dispute resolution, there is no centralized method of enforcement in the transnational legal system. Most enforcement of dispute resolution outcomes depends on national courts—often the courts of nations other than the nation where the dispute was resolved. Chapter 7 covers the enforcement of national and international court judgments. Chapter 8 covers the enforcement of arbitral awards.

Part IV examines special problems in transnational dispute resolution. For example, you may have already learned about service of process. But how do you serve a defendant located in another nation? Chapter 9 gives you the background needed to answer this question by introducing you to the rules and techniques of transnational service of process. What happens if the courts of more than one nation have (or potentially have) jurisdiction over a dispute? Which nation's courts should resolve the dispute? Chapter 10, on alternative forums, examines three methods that can be used to answer this question: the *forum non conveniens* doctrine, parallel proceedings doctrines (including *lis pendens* stays and anti-suit injunctions), and forum selection clauses. What happens when a plaintiff sues a foreign nation? According to the doctrine of foreign sovereign immunity, a nation is generally immune from suit in another nation's courts. Chapter 11 examines both this general rule and the exceptions to it. What happens if a transnational dispute raises questions of foreign affairs? Should courts nevertheless resolve the dispute? Or is it more appropriate for courts to abstain in deference to the political branches of government? Chapter 12 introduces you to a variety of doctrines that courts use to answer these questions, including the act of state doctrine, foreign affairs preemption, and the political question doctrine. And you may have already learned about the discovery tools available under the Federal Rules of Civil Procedure that help litigants obtain relevant information from each other and from third parties. But how do you obtain relevant information located in foreign nations or held by foreign citizens? To help you tackle these problems, Chapter 13 introduces you to the tools of transnational discovery.

In sum, we believe this casebook's emphasis on three core issues that pervade transnational practice—determining the applicable rules, identifying which dispute resolution methods are available and most appropriate, and enforcing dispute resolution outcomes—will help you build a solid foundation for real-world practice and for the further study of international and transnational law. Such further study may include one or more courses such as public international law, comparative law, conflict of laws, and complex litigation, as well as more specialized transnational dispute resolution courses such as transnational litigation, transnational arbitration, and transnational negotiation, or specialized substantive international law courses such as human rights law, international criminal law, international business transactions, international environmental law, international trade law, or the law of the sea. And beyond serving as a foundation for practice and further study, we believe transnational law and practice provides a fruitful lens through which to consider your own national legal system. Indeed, just as transnational law and practice is all about legal problems that cross national borders, national law and practice in the United States is largely about legal problems that cross U.S. state borders. Above all, we hope that you will look forward to the interesting and challenging transnational legal problems that you are likely to encounter after law school, confident that you have the basic knowledge and skills that will help you tackle them.

D. A First Look at Transnational Law and Practice

Before continuing to Chapter 1, consider the following description of a case involving alleged harms arising from a U.S. company's activities in Ecuador. Although the case is in some ways unusual, it illustrates many of the sorts of transnational legal problems that lawyers encounter in practice.

The Chevron-Ecuador Case

In 1993, residents of the Lago Agrio region of the Amazon rainforest in the Republic of Ecuador sued Texaco, Inc., a U.S. corporation, in the U.S. District Court for the Southern District of New York. The complaint alleged extensive environmental damage and personal injuries caused by Texaco's oil extraction operations in Ecuador, as part of a joint venture with Ecuador's national oil company, Petroecuador. At Texaco's request, the U.S. court dismissed the suit, concluding that it had "everything to do with Ecuador, and nothing to do with the United States," and therefore should be brought in Ecuadorian courts. *Aguinda v. Texaco, Inc.*, 142 F. Supp. 2d 534, 537 (S.D.N.Y. 2001). The U.S. Court of Appeals for the Second Circuit affirmed. *Aguinda v. Texaco, Inc.*, 303 F.3d 470 (2d Cir. 2002). Meanwhile, Chevron Corp., also a U.S. corporation, acquired Texaco in 2001; it thereafter terminated its operations in Ecuador and no longer has a business presence there.

After the court dismissed the U.S. lawsuit, the Lago Agrio plaintiffs sued Chevron in Ecuador. Chevron argued that Texaco had entered an agreement with Ecuador and Petroecuador whereby Texaco agreed to take certain environmental remediation measures; that Ecuador and Petroecuador agreed to release Texaco from liability upon completion of those measures; and that Texaco fulfilled all of its obligations under the agreement and was therefore released from liability. The Ecuadorian court disagreed, finding Chevron liable for personal injury and environmental damage as Texaco's successor, and entered a $17.2 billion judgment against Chevron. Ecuadorian courts of appeal later affirmed the judgment (but reduced its amount to $8.6 billion).

The plaintiffs next sought to enforce the Ecuadorian judgment against Chevron in several nations, including Argentina, Brazil, and Canada (but not the United States). Chevron argued in response that the Ecuadorian judgment was invalid because the Ecuadorian legal system did not provide due process and the proceedings leading to the judgment were tainted by fraud and other improper conduct by the plaintiffs' lawyers. Chevron also brought an action in the U.S. District Court for the Southern District of New York seeking an injunction to block enforcement of the Ecuadorian judgment anywhere in the world. The district court issued the injunction, but the court of appeals reversed, finding that Chevron could not seek such an order unless the Ecuadorian plaintiffs attempted to enforce their judgment in the United States and that a U.S. court does not have the authority to determine whether another nation's courts may enforce a judgment. *Chevron Corp. v. Naranjo*, 667 F.3d 232, 234 (2d Cir. 2012).

In 2009, Chevron initiated arbitration proceedings against Ecuador pursuant to the Ecuador-U.S. Bilateral Investment Treaty. Bilateral investment treaties (BITs) are treaties between two nations that give each other's investors certain protections. For example, under the Ecuador-U.S. BIT, U.S. investors in Ecuador have rights that Ecuador must protect and Ecuadorian investors in the United States have rights that the United States must protect. These rights include a right to fair and equitable treatment, a right against arbitrary and discriminatory measures, and a right to effective means of asserting claims and enforcing rights with respect to the investment. The BIT also gives investors the right to submit investment disputes to arbitration instead of the courts of the nation where they have invested. Arbitration is a dispute resolution method whereby the disputants agree to have private third parties called "arbitrators" resolve the dispute. Typically, each party selects an arbitrator of its choice, and the two arbitrators so selected then select a third arbitrator.

In the arbitral proceedings, Chevron sought an award* releasing Chevron from liability and finding that Ecuador or Petroecuador is "exclusively liable for any judgment that may be issued in the Lago Agrio Litigation." Claimant's Notice of Arbitration, *Chevron Corp. and Texaco Petrol. Co. v. Republic of Ecuador*, PCA Case No. 2009-23 (Sept. 23, 2009), *available at* http://www.chevron.com/documents/pdf/EcuadorBITEn.pdf. The arbitral tribunal issued interim awards ordering Ecuador "to take all measures to suspend or cause to be suspended the enforcement and recognition within and without Ecuador" of the Lago Agrio judgment until the panel issues a decision on the merits. Fourth Interim Award on Interim Measures, *Chevron Corp. and Texaco Petrol. Co. v. Republic of Ecuador*, PCA Case No. 2009-23, at 25-26 (Feb. 7, 2013).

In response to the developments in the BIT arbitration proceedings, the Lago Agrio plaintiffs filed a request with the Inter-American Commission on Human Rights in February 2012, asking it to prevent Ecuador from taking steps that would impair the plaintiffs' rights under the Lago Agrio judgment. The Inter-American Commission on Human Rights is, along with the Inter-American Court of Human Rights, an organ of the Organization of American States (OAS), which is a regional international organization that includes the United States and most Latin American nations. Specifically, the plaintiffs requested the Commission "to call for precautionary measures from [Ecuador] sufficient to assure the Commission that [Ecuador] will refrain from taking any action that would contravene, undermine, or threaten the human rights [of the plaintiffs] and that to the contrary [Ecuador] will take all appropriate measures to assure the full protection and continued guarantee of those rights." Letter from Pablo Fajardo et al. to Dr. Santiago Cantón, Exec. Sec'y, Inter-Am. Comm'n on Human Rights, Org. of Am. States (Feb. 9, 2012), *available at* http://lettersblogatory.com/wp-content/uploads/2012/02/OAS-Petition.pdf.

For more information about the case, see *Chevron Corp. v. Naranjo*, 667 F.3d 232 (2d Cir. 2012), and Michael Goldhaber, Crude Awakening: Chevron in Ecuador (Kindle Single, Aug. 20, 2014). There have been a number of further developments in the Chevron-Ecuador case, some of which are described later in this casebook, and the dispute remains ongoing.

The following notes and questions explore some of the transnational legal issues raised by the *Chevron-Ecuador* case. But do not worry about providing correct legal answers at this point. For now, the goal is simply to become familiar with the issues and to grapple with them. This will help prepare you for in-depth exploration in the chapters that follow.

---

* The dispute resolution outcome in arbitration is called an "award" rather than a "judgment."

NOTES AND QUESTIONS

1. **What Are the Applicable Rules?** This issue pervades transnational law and practice. Consider the following ways that this issue can arise:
   a. If the U.S. District Court for the Southern District of New York had decided to hear the Chevron-Ecuador case, what rules do you think the court should have applied? U.S. law? Ecuadorian law? International law? Why? What considerations should guide a U.S. judge when deciding what law to apply in a transnational dispute? Should a U.S. judge ever apply a foreign nation's law? Why or why not? Consider the same questions from the perspective of an Ecuadorian judge and the arbitrators in the BIT arbitration initiated by Chevron. Would the answers be different? In 2011, Chevron sued the plaintiffs' lawyers in the U.S. District Court for the Southern District of New York alleging that they engaged in a pattern of fraudulent activity in obtaining the Ecuadorian judgment. Chevron argued that this activity violated the Racketeer Influenced and Corrupt Organizations Act (RICO), a U.S. federal statute. Should a U.S. statute apply in this case? Does it depend on where the alleged fraud occurred? Does it depend on the nationality of the plaintiffs' lawyers?
   b. Chevron argued that Ecuador violated the Ecuador-U.S. BIT. If Chevron were to make this argument in a U.S. court, should the court decide the case based on the investor rights contained in the BIT? Should a U.S. court ever apply treaties or other types of international law as binding rules of decision? Why or why not? What about an Ecuadorian court? What about the arbitrators in the BIT arbitration initiated by Chevron?
   c. Chevron's Business Conduct and Ethics Code states that "Chevron expects compliance with the letter and the spirit of applicable environmental, health and safety laws, regulations and policies" and that "[e]ach of us has the authority and responsibility to stop—or not start—any work activity if hazards or risks pose a threat to safety or the environment." *See* https://www.chevron.com/-/media/shared-media/documents/chevronbusinessconductethicscode.pdf. Do you think a judge or arbitrator should apply provisions of this code to the dispute? If not, does the code matter? Why or why not?
2. **How Can Transnational Disputes Be Resolved?** This is another pervasive issue in transnational law and practice. Consider the following from both a legal and strategic perspective:
   a. Why do you think the plaintiffs initially filed their lawsuit in the United States? What other forums may have been available, and why didn't they select one of them instead? What legal doctrines would limit the options available?
   b. What about the perspective of Texaco and Chevron? Why do you think they wanted to get the litigation out of the United States? Why might they have initially preferred to litigate in Ecuador? Why might they have hoped that the dismissal of the lawsuit by the U.S. District Court would have ended the litigation altogether? Why would they then want to file their own RICO suit in the United States?

    c.   Should the U.S. court have dismissed the plaintiffs' claim? Is it true that the case was more appropriately litigated in Ecuador? What factors might be appropriate for the court to consider when deciding which nation's courts should hear the case?

    d.   What is the role for international courts in transnational cases? Should the Lago Agrio plaintiffs have filed their suit in an international court to begin with? Why did they file with the Inter-American Commission? What other forums might have been available for the plaintiffs' claims against Ecuador? Why do you think they filed their application in the Inter-American Commission instead of an alternative forum? What would give the Inter-American Commission authority to hear a claim against Ecuador? Should the Commission (or the associated Inter-American Court of Human Rights) have authority to order Ecuador to take actions? What if Ecuador refused?

    e.   Based on the overview above, in what key respects is arbitration different from litigation? Why do you think Chevron decided to use arbitration for its claims against Ecuador? What other forums might have been available for Chevron's claims, and why do you think it decided against those alternatives? Arbitration requires the consent of the parties. What was the source of Ecuador's consent to arbitration?

3.   **How Can Transnational Dispute Resolution Outcomes Be Enforced?** If you determine the applicable legal rules and select an appropriate method for resolving a dispute, and you obtain a favorable outcome for your client, what can you do if the losing party refuses to comply with that outcome voluntarily? For example, in the *Chevron-Ecuador* case, Chevron did not voluntarily pay the plaintiffs the amount ordered by the Ecuadorian court judgment. One option is to seek a court order that seizes and sells assets of the noncomplying party and uses the proceeds to pay the prevailing party the amount owed under the judgment. To explore this issue, consider the following questions:

    a.   Why do you think the plaintiffs didn't simply seek enforcement of the Ecuadorian judgment against Chevron in the courts of Ecuador? Why do you think they instead pursued enforcement in the courts of Argentina, Brazil, and Canada? Why do you think they did not pursue enforcement in the United States?

    b.   What arguments might Chevron make to oppose enforcement of the Ecuadorian judgment against it? Who should decide whether those arguments are valid? An Ecuadorian appellate court? A U.S. court? The courts of some other nation? An international court? What considerations should be kept in mind when answering this question?

    c.   Should a court in one nation ever enforce a judgment of a court in another nation? Why or why not? The problem of enforcement can arise not only with court judgments, but also arbitral awards. Should a court ever enforce an arbitral award? Why or why not?

    d.   What alternatives to judicial enforcement might you consider to encourage a losing party to comply with a dispute resolution outcome in favor of your client?

4. **Don't Be International Law– or International Court–Centric.** As the *Chevron-Ecuador* case illustrates, international law (such as the BIT) and international organizations (such as the Inter-American Commission on Human Rights) may play a significant and sometimes very important role in solving transnational legal problems. But as this introduction has emphasized, it is important not to be international law–centric or international court–centric. As review, what sources of law other than international law, and what dispute resolution methods other than international courts, have played a role in the *Chevron-Ecuador* case?

Don't worry if you didn't understand all of the nuances of the *Chevron-Ecuador* case or if you don't have answers to all of the questions above. It is most important at this stage for you to get a preliminary taste of the kinds of transnational legal problems that you are likely to face in practice. With careful study of the materials in this casebook, we are confident that by the end of this course you will have developed the knowledge and skills you need to analyze and solve those problems and that this will make you a better lawyer regardless of your field of practice.

WHAT ARE THE APPLICABLE RULES?

In its most basic form, legal analysis involves the application of law to facts to reach a legal conclusion. These elements of legal analysis are as important in transnational law and practice as they are in purely domestic law and practice. However, determining the applicable law and relevant facts poses special challenges for lawyers and judges called upon to solve transnational legal problems. In Part I, you will learn how to determine the applicable law in the context of transnational legal problems.

Even in domestic law and practice, it can be difficult to determine what law applies to a particular problem. For example, should a U.S. federal court apply state law or federal law? This question will be familiar to you if you studied the *Erie* doctrine in a course on Civil Procedure. Or what if there is a dispute that involves persons, property, or activity with connections to more than one U.S. state, say California and Oregon? Should a court in California apply California law or Oregon law to resolve the dispute? Judges have developed "choice of law" methods to help them answer these difficult questions, and in many cases they will apply the law of a state other than their own state to resolve interstate disputes.

These issues can be especially important in the context of transnational legal problems, where the question may be whether to apply the law of one nation or the law of another nation. For example, in a dispute involving persons, property, or activity with connections to both California and Japan, should a court in California apply California law or Japanese law? Because legal differences across nations are often much more significant than legal differences across U.S. states, the stakes are often high: The outcomes of disputes may depend on which jurisdiction's law applies.

Part I has two goals. The first goal is to help you understand the different types of law that may apply to transnational legal problems, including national law (such as U.S. federal statutes, U.S. state law, or the law of a foreign nation) and international law. Part I will also briefly examine private rules and nonbinding norms, which can also play a significant role in solving transnational problems.

The second goal is to help you learn the principles that lawyers and judges use to determine what rules apply to particular transnational legal problems.

Chapter 1 introduces you to the role of national law in solving transnational legal problems. For example, U.S. state or federal law — "domestic law" from the perspective of a U.S. lawyer or judge — may be the applicable law. Alternatively, "foreign law" (again, from the perspective of a U.S. lawyer or judge), say the law of Germany, Nigeria, Japan, or Mexico, may be the applicable law. Or the laws of two or more nations may apply to different aspects of the same transnational problem. As Chapter 1 explains, just because a legal problem has a transnational dimension does not necessarily mean that international law applies. To the contrary, national law, whether domestic or foreign, will be the applicable law for many — perhaps most — transnational legal problems that you are likely to encounter in practice. Therefore, as Chapter 1 emphasizes, it is important not to be "international law–centric" when you analyze transnational legal problems.

Nevertheless, to competently analyze transnational legal problems, lawyers do need to understand the fundamentals of international law, including how it is made and how it is used in transnational disputes. Chapter 2 introduces you to these fundamentals. It begins by providing an overview of the nature and role of international law, including the three types of international law: treaties, customary international law, and general principles. It then examines treaties and customary international law in depth, from the perspectives of both the international legal system and the U.S. legal system.

Chapter 3 introduces you to nonbinding and private norms. Nonbinding norms include international declarations of principles and United Nations General Assembly resolutions. Private norms include the rules that individuals and businesses routinely agree upon to govern their relationships, and when those agreements are valid contracts, national courts will ordinarily enforce them. Unlike national law and international law, and unlike legally enforceable contracts, nonbinding norms are not legally binding. Unless the parties to a dispute have agreed that those norms will govern their activity, courts generally will not apply them as rules of decision. Nevertheless, nonbinding norms are important. As Chapter 3 explains, they may provide evidence of international law and they may eventually be adopted by states or their courts as binding law. Nonbinding norms may also provide focal points for the coordination of cross-border business and regulation and other transnational activity. Moreover, parties sometimes agree to have nonbinding norms govern their relationships — and such agreements may themselves constitute legally binding contractual obligations that are enforceable by courts.

When determining what law applies to transnational problems, the stakes are high for both client counseling and international relations. One important role of a lawyer is to help clients comply with the law and manage their exposure to legal liability — but you cannot perform this role if you do not know what laws potentially apply to your client's activity. If your client is involved in a dispute, you cannot help your client weigh whether to settle the dispute or to litigate unless you know what law applies, because that law can determine the outcome of litigation. Often, two or more legal rules may be potentially applicable, one of which may be more favorable to your client than the others — but if you do not understand the principles used to determine the applicable law, you will be unable to develop and assess arguments that might convince a judge to apply the rule that is most favorable to your client. Most fundamentally, because legal analysis requires you to apply law to the relevant facts, you cannot perform legal analysis or develop legal arguments without determining and understanding the applicable law.

Beyond client counseling, nations themselves may care about the applicable law. One way that nations regulate transnational activity is by applying their law to that activity. Therefore, whether a nation's law applies beyond its borders affects its ability to project regulatory power in the world. When more than one nation attempts to apply its law to the same transnational legal problem, the result can be international conflict. One way that nations may try to avoid this type of conflict is by creating international law to govern transnational legal problems instead of national law — but this in turn raises difficult issues about the applicability of international law in national courts, and how to handle conflicts between national law and international law. You are encouraged to keep these stakes in mind as you work through the materials that follow.

CHAPTER 1

NATIONAL LAW

Imagine that your client is a U.S. citizen who lives in Los Angeles, California and, until recently, worked in the Los Angeles office of a corporation that is incorporated in California and has its principal place of business in California. Your client alleges that the corporation wrongfully terminated her employment. Because this legal problem has connections only to California, the applicable law is most likely U.S. law (California state law and, depending on the facts, perhaps U.S. federal law).

Now imagine the same scenario, but with the following changes: Your client is a Mexican citizen, working in the corporation's Los Angeles office, but the corporation is incorporated in Canada and has its principal place of business in Vancouver, located in the Canadian province of British Columbia, where all of the corporation's business decisions are made. Now what is the applicable law? Mexican law, because your client is a Mexican citizen? California law or U.S. federal law, because California was the place of employment? Canadian law, because Canada is the employer's place of incorporation and the place where the termination decision was made? The answer is not obvious. Unlike the first example's purely domestic legal problem, this second scenario involves a transnational legal problem — that is, a legal problem with connections to more than one nation (here, Canada, Mexico, and the United States). These multinational connections raise the possibility that more than one nation's law may apply. The challenge is to determine the applicable law based on these connections in light of your client's objectives.

One way to approach the question is to focus on a particular nation's law and ask *whether* it applies to the conduct in question. Based on the principle of territorial sovereignty, you would usually conclude that a nation's law applies within its own territory, but there may be doubt whether the law applies outside the nation's territory. To be clear, nations often do apply their laws extraterritorially, but courts may be reluctant to apply law extraterritorially if the law does not clearly indicate that it has extraterritorial reach. Thus, whether a law applies extraterritorially becomes a question of statutory analysis; courts may look at the language and purpose of a law and use canons of statutory construction to decide the law's reach. For example, in the hypothetical above, a court in the United States might use extraterritoriality analysis to determine whether it should apply a U.S. federal statute to adjudicate the parties' employment dispute. As described in Section A below, U.S. courts typically use this approach in evaluating the extraterritorial reach of U.S. federal statutes.

Another approach is to think of the question as involving a choice among various potentially applicable laws, and thus to ask *which* of these laws is the right one to apply. Thus unlike extraterritoriality analysis, this approach looks not at one nation's law, but at all the nations' (or states') laws that might apply. Courts (and sometimes legislatures) have developed "choice of law" principles to guide the selection among competing laws. For example, in the above hypothetical involving contacts with Canada, Mexico, and California, a court might consider its job to choose which of the potentially applicable national laws — Canadian, Mexican, or California law — ought to govern. As described in Section B below, U.S. courts typically use this approach in claims — especially private law claims such as torts, contracts, and property — potentially involving the law of a U.S. state and a foreign nation (or, in purely domestic claims, those involving the law of multiple U.S. states).

Why there should be two approaches instead of one is something of a conceptual puzzle. As a practical matter, however, U.S. courts ordinarily use extraterritoriality analysis when a U.S. federal statute (or in some cases a state statute) potentially applies, and choice-of-law analysis when tort, contract, property, or other areas of private law are at issue.

The materials that follow are selected to help you learn these two approaches. Section A examines the extraterritorial scope of U.S. federal statutes. Section B discusses choice of law — the choice between a U.S. state's law and foreign (non-U.S.) law. Section C considers an important point of transactional strategy: to avoid the difficult project of guessing which law a court may apply, parties can specify in advance, by contract, what law governs their relationship.

A. Extraterritorial Application of National Law

How does a lawyer or a judge determine whether a nation's law applies to persons or conduct outside that nation's territory? If the law explicitly states that it does (or does not) apply extraterritorially, the task is relatively easy. But most laws do not explicitly define their geographical reach. Instead, most laws state that behavior "x" is prohibited or behavior "y" gives rise to liability. For example, as discussed in one of the cases below, the Jones Act, a U.S. federal statute, provides a cause of action for "any seaman who shall suffer personal injury in the course of his employment." Does a statute like this one, drafted in this general way and without an explicit statement about its geographical reach, apply to conduct throughout the world? The answer is often "no," but sometimes "yes," or "to some extent," depending on the facts and circumstances.

In this section, you will learn how lawyers and judges analyze these issues in the United States. This section begins by examining two rebuttable presumptions that help determine whether a U.S. federal statute will be applied extraterritorially: (1) that Congress ordinarily intends to legislate with respect to domestic, not foreign, matters (the presumption against extraterritoriality) and (2) that Congress ordinarily does not intend for a statute to violate international law (the presumption against violating international law). This section then takes a closer look at what has been a particularly contentious extraterritoriality issue: the extraterritorial application of antitrust law. As you read these materials, consider the origins of the two presumptions and whether the lower courts have reliably applied them. Also consider whether these presumptions are appropriate for their stated purposes, or whether there are other judicial or nonjudicial approaches that are more workable.

First, an important note: The cases in this section involve federal statutes, some of which are complex and may be unfamiliar to you. These statutes include Title VII of the U.S. Civil Rights Act of 1964, the Securities Exchange Act of 1934, the Racketeer Influenced and Corrupt Organizations Act (RICO), the National Labor Relations Act, the Hostage Taking Act, and the Sherman Act. You will surely encounter some of these statutes in other courses and in practice. But we include these cases *not* because we expect you to master these statutes in this course, but instead to help you understand the more general principles that determine whether a U.S. court will apply a federal statute to persons or activity outside U.S. territory. Therefore, we urge you to focus on learning those principles and the analytical steps courts use to make extraterritoriality determinations. Don't worry if you don't have a thorough understanding of the particular statutes involved.

1. *The Presumption Against Extraterritoriality*

In the three cases that follow, the U.S. Supreme Court discusses and applies a presumption against extraterritoriality. A presumption is the acceptance of a conclusion until it is shown that the conclusion is false — that is, until the presumption is rebutted. As you study the cases, focus on understanding both *what* must be presumed in extraterritoriality analysis and *how* that presumption can be rebutted.

Equal Employment Opportunity Commission v. Arabian American Oil Company

499 U.S. 244 (1991)

Chief Justice Rehnquist delivered the opinion of the Court.

These cases present the issue whether Title VII [of the U.S. Civil Rights Act of 1964, 42 U.S.C. § 2000e et seq.] applies extraterritorially to regulate the employment practices of United States employers who employ United States citizens abroad. The United States Court of Appeals for the Fifth Circuit held that it does not, and we agree with that conclusion.

Petitioner Boureslan is a naturalized United States citizen who was born in Lebanon. The respondents are two Delaware corporations, Arabian American

Oil Company (Aramco), and its subsidiary, Aramco Service Company (ASC). Aramco's principal place of business is Dhahran, Saudi Arabia, and it is licensed to do business in Texas. ASC's principal place of business is Houston, Texas.

In 1979, Boureslan was hired by ASC as a cost engineer in Houston. A year later he was transferred, at his request, to work for Aramco in Saudi Arabia. Boureslan remained with Aramco in Saudi Arabia until he was discharged in 1984. After filing a charge of discrimination with the Equal Employment Opportunity Commission (EEOC or Commission), he instituted this suit in the United States District Court for the Southern District of Texas against Aramco and ASC. He sought relief under both state law and Title VII of the Civil Rights Act of 1964, on the ground that he was harassed and ultimately discharged by respondents on account of his race, religion, and national origin.

Respondents filed a motion for summary judgment on the ground that the District Court lacked subject-matter jurisdiction over Boureslan's claim because the protections of Title VII do not extend to United States citizens employed abroad by American employers. The District Court agreed and dismissed Boureslan's Title VII claim; it also dismissed his state-law claims for lack of pendent jurisdiction and entered final judgment in favor of respondents. A panel for the Fifth Circuit affirmed. After vacating the panel's decision and rehearing the case en banc, the court affirmed the District Court's dismissal of Boureslan's complaint. Both Boureslan and the EEOC petitioned for certiorari. We granted both petitions for certiorari to resolve this important issue of statutory interpretation.

Both parties concede, as they must, that Congress has the authority to enforce its laws beyond the territorial boundaries of the United States. Cf. *Foley Bros., Inc. v. Filardo*, 336 U.S. 281, 284-285 (1949); *Benz v. Compania Naviera Hidalgo, S.A.*, 353 U.S. 138 (1957). Whether Congress has in fact exercised that authority in these cases is a matter of statutory construction. It is our task to determine whether Congress intended the protections of Title VII to apply to United States citizens employed by American employers outside of the United States.

principle It is a longstanding principle of American law "that legislation of Congress, unless a contrary intent appears, is meant to apply only within the territorial jurisdiction of the United States." *Foley Bros.*, 336 U.S., at 285. This "canon of construction . . . is a valid approach whereby unexpressed congressional intent may be ascertained." *Ibid.* It serves to protect against unintended clashes between our laws and those of other nations which could result in international discord. See *McCulloch v. Sociedad Nacional de Marineros de Honduras*, 372 U.S. 10, 20-22 (1963).

In applying this rule of construction, we look to see whether "language in the [relevant Act] gives any indication of a congressional purpose to extend its coverage beyond places over which the United States has sovereignty or has some measure of legislative control." *Foley Bros., supra*, 336 U.S., at 285. We assume that Congress legislates against the backdrop of the presumption against extraterritoriality. Therefore, unless there is "the affirmative intention of the Congress clearly expressed," *Benz, supra*, 353 U.S., at 147, we must presume it "is primarily concerned with domestic conditions." *Foley Bros., supra*, 336 U.S., at 285.

Boureslan and the EEOC contend that the language of Title VII evinces a clearly expressed intent on behalf of Congress to legislate extraterritorially. . . .

[P]etitioners argue that the statute's definitions of the jurisdictional terms "employer" and "commerce" are sufficiently broad to include United States firms that employ American citizens overseas. . . . We conclude that petitioners' evidence, while not totally lacking in probative value, falls short of demonstrating the affirmative congressional intent required to extend the protections of Title VII beyond our territorial borders.

Title VII prohibits various discriminatory employment practices based on an individual's race, color, religion, sex, or national origin. See §§ 2000e-2, 2000e-3. An employer is subject to Title VII if it has employed 15 or more employees for a specified period and is "engaged in an industry affecting commerce." An industry affecting commerce is "any activity, business, or industry in commerce or in which a labor dispute would hinder or obstruct commerce or the free flow of commerce. . . ." § 2000e(h). "Commerce," in turn, is defined as "trade, traffic, commerce, transportation, transmission, or communication among the several States; or between a State and any place outside thereof; or within the District of Columbia, or a possession of the United States; or between points in the same State but through a point outside thereof." § 2000e(g).

Petitioners argue that by its plain language, Title VII's "broad jurisdictional language" reveals Congress' intent to extend the statute's protections to employment discrimination anywhere in the world by a United States employer who affects trade "between a State and any place outside thereof." More precisely, they assert that since Title VII defines "States" to include States, the District of Columbia, and specified territories, the clause "between a State and any place outside thereof" must be referring to areas beyond the territorial limit of the United States. *broad language*

Respondents offer several alternative explanations for the statute's expansive language. They contend that the "or between a State and any place outside thereof" clause "provide[s] the jurisdictional nexus required to regulate commerce that is not wholly within a single state, presumably as it affects both interstate and foreign commerce" but not to "regulate conduct exclusively within a foreign country." They also argue that since the definitions of the terms "employer," "commerce," and "industry affecting commerce" make no mention of "commerce with foreign nations," Congress cannot be said to have intended that the statute apply overseas. In support of this argument, respondents point to Title II of the Civil Rights Act of 1964, governing public accommodation, which specifically defines commerce as it applies to foreign nations. Finally, respondents argue that while language present in the first bill considered by the House of Representatives contained the terms "foreign commerce" and "foreign nations," those terms were deleted by the Senate before the Civil Rights Act of 1964 was passed. They conclude that these deletions "[are] inconsistent with the notion of a clearly expressed congressional intent to apply Title VII extraterritorially."

We need not choose between these competing interpretations as we would be required to do in the absence of the presumption against extraterritorial application discussed above. Each is plausible, but no more persuasive than that. The language relied upon by petitioners — and it is they who must make the affirmative showing — is ambiguous, and does not speak directly to the question presented here. The intent of Congress as to the extraterritorial application of this statute must be deduced by inference from boilerplate language which can be found in any number of congressional Acts, none of which have ever been held to apply overseas. See, *e.g.*, Consumer Product Safety Act, 15 U.S.C. § 2052(a)(12); Federal Food, Drug, and Cosmetic Act, 21 U.S.C. § 321(b); Transportation Safety Act of 1974, 49 U.S.C. App. § 1802(1); Labor-Management Reporting and Disclosure Act of 1959, 29 U.S.C. § 401 et seq.; Americans with Disabilities Act of 1990, 42 U.S.C. § 12101 et seq.

Petitioners' reliance on Title VII's jurisdictional provisions also finds no support in our case law; we have repeatedly held that even statutes that contain broad language in their definitions of "commerce" that expressly refer to "foreign commerce" do not apply abroad. . . .

The EEOC places great weight on an assertedly similar "broad jurisdictional grant in the Lanham Act" that this Court held applied extraterritorially in *Steele v. Bulova Watch Co.*, 344 U.S. 280, 286 (1952). In *Steele*, we addressed whether the Lanham Act, designed to prevent deceptive and misleading use of trademarks, applied to acts of a United States citizen consummated in Mexico. The Act defined commerce as "all commerce which may lawfully be regulated by Congress." 15 U.S.C. § 1127. The stated intent of the statute was "to regulate commerce within the control of Congress by making actionable the deceptive and misleading use of marks in such commerce." *Ibid.* While recognizing that "the legislation of Congress will not extend beyond the boundaries of the United States unless a contrary legislative intent appears," the Court concluded that in light of the fact that the allegedly unlawful conduct had some effects within the United States, coupled with the Act's "broad jurisdictional grant" and its "sweeping reach into 'all commerce which may lawfully be regulated by Congress,'" the statute was properly interpreted as applying abroad. *Steele, supra*, 344 U.S., at 285, 287.

The EEOC's attempt to analogize these cases to *Steele* is unpersuasive. The Lanham Act by its terms applies to "all commerce which may lawfully be regulated by Congress." The Constitution gives Congress the power "[t]o regulate Commerce with foreign Nations, and among the several States, and with the Indian Tribes." U.S. Const., Art. 1, § 8, cl. 3. Since the Act expressly stated that it applied to the extent of Congress' power over commerce, the Court in *Steele* concluded that Congress intended that the statute apply abroad. By contrast, Title VII's more limited, boilerplate "commerce" language does not support such an expansive construction of congressional intent. . . .

. . . Without clearer evidence of congressional intent to do so . . . , we are unwilling to ascribe to that body a policy which would raise difficult issues of international law by imposing this country's employment-discrimination regime upon foreign corporations operating in foreign commerce.

This conclusion is fortified by the other elements in the statute suggesting a purely domestic focus. The statute as a whole indicates a concern that it not unduly interfere with the sovereignty and laws of the States. See, *e.g.*, 42 U.S.C. § 2000h-4 (stating that the Act should not be construed to exclude the operation of state law or invalidate any state law unless inconsistent with the purposes of the

Act); § 2000e-5 (requiring the EEOC to accord substantial weight to findings of state or local authorities in proceedings under state or local law); § 2000e-7 (providing that nothing in Title VII shall affect the application of state or local law unless such law requires or permits practices that would be unlawful under Title VII); §§ 2000e-5(c), (d), and (e) (provisions addressing deferral to state discrimination proceedings). While Title VII consistently speaks in terms of "States" and state proceedings, it fails even to mention foreign nations or foreign proceedings.

(Similarly, Congress failed to provide any mechanisms for overseas enforcement of Title VII. For instance, the statute's venue provisions,)§ 2000e-5(f)(3), are ill-suited for extraterritorial application as they provide for venue only in a judicial district in the State where certain matters related to the employer occurred or were located. And the limited investigative authority provided for the EEOC, permitting the Commission only to issue subpoenas for witnesses and documents from "any place in the United States or any Territory or possession thereof," 29 U.S.C. § 161 incorporated by reference into 42 U.S.C. § 2000e-9, suggests that Congress did not intend for the statute to apply abroad.

It is also reasonable to conclude that had Congress intended Title VII to apply overseas,(it would have addressed the subject of conflicts with foreign laws and procedures.)In amending the Age Discrimination in Employment Act of 1967 (ADEA), 81 Stat. 602, as amended, 29 U.S.C. § 621 et seq. to apply abroad, Congress specifically addressed potential conflicts with foreign law by providing that it is not unlawful for an employer to take any action prohibited by the ADEA "where such practices involve an employee in a workplace in a foreign country, and compliance with [the ADEA] would cause such employer . . . to violate the laws of the country in which such workplace is located." § 623(f)(1). Title VII, by contrast, fails to address conflicts with the laws of other nations.

. . .

Our conclusion today is buttressed by the fact that "[w]hen it desires to do so, Congress knows how to place the high seas within the jurisdictional reach of a statute." *Argentine Republic v. Amerada Hess Shipping Corp.*, 488 U.S. 428, 440 (1989).(Congress' awareness of the need to make a clear statement that a statute applies overseas is amply demonstrated by the numerous occasions on which it has expressly legislated the extraterritorial application of a statute.)See, *e.g.*, the Export Administration Act of 1979, 50 U.S.C. App. § 2415(2) (defining "United States person" to include "any domestic concern (including any permanent domestic establishment of any foreign concern) and any foreign subsidiary or affiliate (including any permanent foreign establishment) of any domestic concern which is controlled in fact by such domestic concern"); Coast Guard Act, 14 U.S.C. § 89(a) (Coast Guard searches and seizures upon the high seas); 18 U.S.C. § 7 (Criminal Code extends to high seas); 19 U.S.C. § 1701 (Customs enforcement on the high seas); Comprehensive Anti-Apartheid Act of 1986, 22 U.S.C. § 5001(5)(A) ed. Supp. V) (definition of "national of the United States" as "a natural person who is a citizen of the United States . . ."); the Logan Act, 18 U.S.C. § 953 (applying Act to "[a]ny citizen . . . wherever he may be . . ."). Indeed, after several courts had held that the ADEA did not apply overseas, Congress amended § 11(f) to provide: "The term 'employee' includes any individual who is a citizen of the United States employed by an employer in a workplace in a foreign country." 29 U.S.C. § 630(f). Congress also amended § 4(g)(1), which states: "If an employer controls a corporation whose place of incorporation is in a foreign country, any practice by such corporation prohibited under this section shall be presumed to be such practice by such employer." § 623(h)(1). The expressed purpose of these changes was to "mak[e] provisions of the Act apply to citizens of the United States employed in foreign countries by U.S. corporations or their subsidiaries." S. Rep. No. 98-467, p. 2 (1984), U.S. Code Cong. & Admin. News 1984, pp. 2974, 2975. (Congress, should it wish to do so, may similarly amend Title VII and in doing so will be able to calibrate its provisions in a way that we cannot.)

Petitioners have failed to present sufficient affirmative evidence that Congress intended Title VII to apply abroad. Accordingly, the judgment of the Court of Appeals is

Affirmed.

[An opinion by Justice Scalia, concurring in part and concurring in the judgment, is omitted.]

Justice MARSHALL, with whom Justice BLACKMUN and Justice STEVENS join, dissenting.

Like any issue of statutory construction, the question whether Title VII protects United States citizens from discrimination by United States employers abroad turns solely on congressional intent. As the majority recognizes, our inquiry into congressional intent in this setting is informed by the traditional "canon of construction which teaches that legislation of Congress, unless a contrary intent appears, is meant to apply only within the territorial jurisdiction of the United States." *Foley Bros., Inc. v. Filardo*, 336 U.S. 281, 285 (1949). But contrary to what one would conclude from the majority's analysis, this canon is not a "clear statement" rule, the application of which relieves a court of the duty to give effect to all available indicia of the legislative will. Rather, as our case law applying the presumption against extraterritoriality well illustrates, a court may properly rely on this presumption only after exhausting all of the traditional tools "whereby unexpressed congressional intent may be ascertained." Ibid. When these tools are brought to bear on the issue in this case, the conclusion is inescapable that Congress did intend Title VII to protect United States citizens from discrimination by United States employers operating overseas. Consequently, I dissent.

I

Because it supplies the driving force of the majority's analysis, I start with "[t]he canon . . . that legislation of Congress, unless a contrary intent appears, is meant to apply only within the territorial jurisdiction of the United States." *Ibid.* The majority recasts this principle as "the need to make a clear statement that a statute applies overseas." So conceived, the presumption against extraterritoriality allows the majority to derive meaning from various instances of statutory silence — from Congress' failure, for instance, "to mention foreign nations or foreign proceedings," "to provide any mechanisms for overseas enforcement," or to "addres[s] the subject of conflicts with foreign laws and procedures." At other points, the majority relies on its reformulation of the presumption to avoid the "need [to] choose between . . . competing interpretations" of affirmative statutory language that the majority concludes "does not speak directly to the question" of extraterritoriality. In my view, the majority grossly distorts the effect of this rule of construction upon conventional techniques of statutory interpretation.

Our most extensive discussion of the presumption against extraterritoriality can be found in *Foley Brothers, supra.* The issue in that case was whether the Eight Hour Law — a statute regulating the length of the workday of employees hired to perform contractual work for the United States — applied to construction projects in foreign nations. After noting "the assumption that Congress is primarily concerned with domestic conditions," the Court concluded that there was "nothing in the Act itself, as amended, nor in the legislative history, which would lead to the belief that Congress entertained any intention other than the normal one in this case." 336 U.S., at 285. The Court put particular emphasis on "[t]he scheme of the Act," including Congress' failure to draw a "distinction . . . therein between laborers who are aliens and those who are citizens of the United States." *Id.*, at 286. "The absence of any [such] distinction," the Court explained, "indicates . . . that the statute was intended to apply only to those places where the labor conditions of both citizen and alien employees are a probable concern of Congress." *Ibid.* The Court also engaged in extended analyses of the legislative history of the statute, see *id.*, at 286-288, and of pertinent administrative interpretations, see *id.*, at 288-290.

The range of factors that the Court considered in *Foley Brothers* demonstrates that the presumption against extraterritoriality is not a "clear statement" rule. . . .

(. . . Under *Foley Brothers*, a court is not free to invoke the presumption against extraterritoriality until it has exhausted all available indicia of Congress' intent on this subject.)Once these indicia are consulted and given effect in this case, I believe there can be no question that Congress intended Title VII to protect United States citizens from discrimination by United States employers abroad.

•

II

A

Title VII states: "It shall be an unlawful employment practice for an employer . . . to fail or refuse to hire or to discharge any individual, or otherwise to discriminate against any individual with respect to his compensation, terms, conditions, or privileges of employment, because of such individual's race, color, religion, sex, or national origin." 42 U.S.C. § 2000e-2(a)(1). Under the statute, "[t]he term 'employer' means a person engaged in an industry affecting commerce who has fifteen or more employees," § 2000e(b); "[t]he term 'commerce' means trade, traffic, commerce, transportation, transmission, or communication among the several States; or between a State and any place outside thereof. . . ." § 2000e(g).

(These terms are broad enough to encompass discrimination by United States employers abroad.)Nothing in the text of the statute indicates that the protection of an "individual" from employment discrimination depends on the location of that individual's workplace; nor does anything in the statute indicate that employers whose businesses affect commerce between "a State and any other place outside thereof" are exempted when their discriminatory conduct occurs beyond the Nation's borders. While conceding that it is "plausible" to infer from the breadth of the statute's central prohibition that Congress intended Title VII to apply extraterritorially, the majority goes to considerable lengths to show that this language is not sufficient to overcome the majority's clear-statement conception of the presumption against extraterritoriality. However, petitioners claim no more — and need claim no more, given additional textual evidence of Congress' intent — than that this language is consistent with a legislative expectation that Title VII apply extraterritorially, a proposition that the majority does not dispute.

Confirmation that Congress did in fact expect Title VII's central prohibition to have an extraterritorial reach is supplied by the so-called "alien exemption" provision. The alien-exemption provision states that Title VII "shall not apply to an employer with respect to the employment of aliens outside any State." 42 U.S.C. § 2000e-1.(Absent an intention that Title VII apply "outside any State," Congress would have had no reason to craft this extraterritorial exemption. And because only discrimination against aliens is exempted, employers remain accountable for discrimination against United States citizens abroad.)

The inference arising from the alien-exemption provision is more than sufficient to rebut the presumption against extraterritoriality. . . .

The history of the alien-exemption provision confirms the inference that Congress expected Title VII to have extraterritorial application. . . .

. . . The legislative history surrounding Title VII leaves no doubt that Congress had extraterritorial application in mind when it revived the alien-exemption provision from the earlier antidiscrimination bill: "In section 4 of the Act, a limited exception is provided for employers with respect to employment of aliens outside of any State. . . . The intent of [this] exemption is to remove conflicts of law which might otherwise exist between the United States and a foreign nation in the employment of aliens outside the United States by an American enterprise." H.R. Rep. No. 570, 88th Cong., 1st Sess. 4 (1963).

. . .

Notwithstanding the basic rule of construction requiring courts to give effect to all of the statutory language, see *Reiter v. Sonotone Corp.*, 442 U.S. 330, 339 (1979), the majority never advances an alternative explanation of the alien-exemption provision that is consistent with the majority's own conclusion that Congress intended Title VII to have a purely domestic focus. . . .

. . .

B

Rather than attempting to reconcile its interpretation of Title VII with the language and legislative history of the alien-exemption provision, the majority contents itself with pointing out various legislative silences that, in the majority's view, communicate a congressional intent to limit Title VII to instances of domestic employment discrimination. In particular, the majority claims that, had Congress intended to give Title VII an extraterritorial reach, it "would have addressed the subject of conflicts with foreign laws and procedures," and would have "provide[d] . . . mechanisms for overseas enforcement," including special venue provisions and extraterritorial investigatory powers for the Equal Employment Opportunity Commission (EEOC), see *ibid.* The majority also emphasizes Congress' failure to draw an express distinction between extraterritorial application of Title VII to United States employers and extraterritorial application of Title VII to foreign employers. In my view, none of these supposed omissions detracts from the conclusion that Congress intended Title VII to apply extraterritorially.

The majority is simply incorrect in its claim that Congress disregarded the subject of conflicts with foreign law. Congress addressed this concern by enacting the alien-exemption provision, the announced purpose of which was "to remove conflicts of law which might otherwise exist between the United States and a foreign nation in the employment of aliens outside the United States by an American enterprise." . . .

The majority also misrepresents the character of Title VII's venue provisions. Title VII provides that venue is proper in various districts related to the underlying charge of discrimination, but also states that "if the [employer] is not found within any such district, such an action may be brought within the judicial district in which the [employer] has his principal office." 42 U.S.C. § 2000e-5(f)(3). "Principal office" venue would extend to any United States employer doing business abroad. Identical language is found in the venue provision of the Jones Act, 46 U.S.C. App. § 688(a), which under appropriate circumstances applies to injuries occurring outside the territorial jurisdiction of the United States.

Nor can any inference be drawn from the scope of the EEOC's investigatory powers under the statute. Title VII directs the EEOC to conduct an investigation "[w]henever a charge is filed" under the statute, 42 U.S.C. § 2000e-5(b); it also states that the EEOC is to "have access to, for the purposes of examination, and the right to copy any evidence of any person being investigated," § 2000e-8(a). Far from imposing a geographic limitation on either of these powers, Title VII states that the EEOC may "exercise any or all its powers" in the District of Columbia (the site of the EEOC's principal office) or "at any other place." § 2000e-4(f).

. . .

III

The extraterritorial application of Title VII is supported not only by its language and legislative history but also by pertinent administrative interpretations. Since 1975, the EEOC has been on record as construing Title VII to apply to United States companies employing United States citizens abroad. . . .

. . .

In this case, moreover, the EEOC's interpretation is reinforced by the long-standing interpretation of the Department of Justice, the agency with secondary enforcement responsibility under Title VII. . . .

. . .

In sum, there is no reason not to give effect to the considered and consistently expressed views of the two agencies assigned to enforce Title VII.

IV

In the hands of the majority, the presumption against extraterritoriality is transformed from a "valid approach whereby unexpressed congressional intent may be ascertained," *Foley Bros.*, 336 U.S., at 285, into a barrier to any genuine inquiry into the sources that reveal Congress' actual intentions. Because the language, history, and administrative interpretations of the statute all support application of Title VII to United States companies employing United States citizens abroad, I dissent.

Morrison v. National Australia Bank Ltd.

561 U.S. 247 (2010)

Justice SCALIA delivered the opinion of the Court.

We decide whether § 10(b) of the Securities Exchange Act of 1934 provides a cause of action to foreign plaintiffs suing foreign and American defendants for misconduct in connection with securities traded on foreign exchanges.

[The term "securities" refers to financial instruments such as bonds or shares of stock. Securities are often traded on exchanges such as the New York Stock Exchange or NASDAQ or their counterparts in other nations. In order to protect investors in securities against fraud, § 10(b) of the Securities Exchange Act of 1934 (a U.S. federal statute) regulates the purchase and sale of securities. Specifically, § 10(b) provides that "[i]t shall be unlawful for any person . . . , by the use or any means or instrumentality of interstate commerce or of the mails, or of any national securities exchange, [t]o use or employ, in connection with the purchase or sale of any security registered on a national securities exchange or any security not so registered, . . . any manipulative or deceptive device or contrivance in contravention of such rules and regulations as the [U.S. Securities and Exchange] Commission [the "SEC"] may prescribe as necessary or appropriate in the public interest or for the protection of investors." Pursuant to § 10(b), the SEC promulgated Rule 10b-5, which makes it unlawful "for any person, directly or indirectly, by the use of any means or instrumentality of interstate commerce, or of the mails or of any facility of any national securities exchange, . . . [t]o make any untrue statement of a material fact or to omit to state a material fact necessary in order to make the statements made, in the light of the circumstances under which they were made, not misleading. . . ." — EDS.]

I

Respondent National Australia Bank Limited (National) was, during the relevant time, the largest bank in Australia. Its Ordinary Shares — what in America would be called "common stock" — are traded on the Australian Stock Exchange Limited and on other foreign securities exchanges, but not on any exchange in the United States. There are listed on the New York Stock Exchange, however, National's American Depositary Receipts (ADRs), which represent the right to receive a specified number of National's Ordinary Shares.

The complaint alleges the following facts, which we accept as true. In February 1998, National bought respondent HomeSide Lending, Inc., a mortgage servicing company headquartered in Florida. HomeSide's business was to receive fees for servicing mortgages (essentially the administrative tasks associated with collecting mortgage payments). The rights to receive those fees, so-called mortgage-servicing rights, can provide a valuable income stream. How valuable each of the rights is depends, in part, on the likelihood that the mortgage to which it applies will be fully repaid before it is due, terminating the need for servicing. HomeSide calculated the present value of its mortgage-servicing rights by using valuation models designed to take this likelihood into account. It recorded the value of its assets, and the numbers appeared in National's financial statements.

From 1998 until 2001, National's annual reports and other public documents touted the success of HomeSide's business, and respondents Frank Cicutto (National's managing director and chief executive officer), Kevin Race (HomeSide's chief operating officer), and Hugh Harris (HomeSide's chief executive officer) did the same in public statements. But on July 5, 2001, National announced that it was writing down the value of HomeSide's assets by $450 million; and then again on September 3, by another $1.75 billion. The prices of both Ordinary Shares and ADRs slumped. After downplaying the July write-down, National explained the September write-down as the result of a failure to anticipate the lowering of prevailing interest rates (lower interest rates lead to more refinancings, i.e., more early repayments of mortgages), other mistaken assumptions in the financial models, and the loss of goodwill. According to the complaint, however, HomeSide, Race, Harris, and another HomeSide senior executive who is also a respondent here had manipulated HomeSide's financial models to make the rates of early repayment unrealistically low in order to cause the mortgage-servicing rights to appear more valuable than they really were. The complaint also alleges that National and Cicutto were aware of this deception by July 2000, but did nothing about it.

As relevant here, petitioners Russell Leslie Owen and Brian and Geraldine Silverlock, all Australians, purchased National's Ordinary Shares in 2000 and 2001, before the write-downs. They sued National, HomeSide, Cicutto, and the three HomeSide executives in the United States District Court for the Southern District of New York for alleged violations of §§ 10(b) and 20(a) . . . of the Securities and Exchange Act of 1934, 48 Stat. 891, 15 U.S.C. §§ 78j(b) and 78t(a) . . ., and SEC Rule 10b-5, 17 CFR § 240.10b-5 (2009), promulgated pursuant to § 10(b). They sought to represent a class of foreign purchasers of National's Ordinary Shares during a specified period up to the September write-down.

---

1. Robert Morrison, an American investor in National's ADRs, also brought suit, but his claims were dismissed by the District Court because he failed to allege damages. Petitioners did not appeal that decision, and it is not before us. Inexplicably, Morrison continued to be listed as a petitioner in the Court of Appeals and here.

Respondents moved to dismiss for lack of subject-matter jurisdiction under Federal Rule of Civil Procedure 12(b)(1) and for failure to state a claim under Rule 12(b)(6). The District Court granted the motion on the former ground, finding no jurisdiction because the acts in this country were, "at most, a link in the chain of an alleged overall securities fraud scheme that culminated abroad." The Court of Appeals for the Second Circuit affirmed on similar grounds. The acts performed in the United States did not "compris[e] the heart of the alleged fraud." We granted certiorari.

II

Before addressing the question presented, we must correct a threshold error in the Second Circuit's analysis. It considered the extraterritorial reach of § 10(b) to raise a question of subject-matter jurisdiction, wherefore it affirmed the District Court's dismissal under Rule 12(b)(1). In this regard it was following Circuit precedent. The Second Circuit is hardly alone in taking this position.

But to ask what conduct § 10(b) reaches is to ask what conduct § 10(b) prohibits, which is a merits question. Subject-matter jurisdiction, by contrast, refers to a tribunal's power to hear a case. It presents an issue quite separate from the question whether the allegations the plaintiff makes entitle him to relief. The District Court here had jurisdiction under 15 U.S.C. § 78aa[3] to adjudicate the question whether § 10(b) applies to National's conduct.

In view of this error, which the parties do not dispute, petitioners ask us to remand. We think that unnecessary. Since nothing in the analysis of the courts below turned on the mistake, a remand would only require a new Rule 12(b)(6) label for the same Rule 12(b)(1) conclusion. As we have done before in situations like this, we proceed to address whether petitioners' allegations state a claim.

III

A

It is a "longstanding principle of American law 'that legislation of Congress, unless a contrary intent appears, is meant to apply only within the territorial jurisdiction of the United States.'" *EEOC v. Arabian American Oil Co.*, 499 U.S. 244, 248 (1991) (*Aramco*) (quoting *Foley Bros., Inc. v. Filardo*, 336 U.S. 281, 285 (1949)). This principle represents a canon of construction, or a presumption about a statute's meaning, rather than a limit upon Congress's power to legislate. . . . It rests on the perception that Congress ordinarily legislates with respect to domestic, not foreign matters. Thus, "unless there is the affirmative intention of the Congress clearly expressed" to give a statute extraterritorial effect, "we must

---

3. Section 78aa provides: "The district courts of the United States . . . shall have exclusive jurisdiction of violations of [the Exchange Act] or the rules and regulations thereunder, and of all suits in equity and actions at law brought to enforce any liability or duty created by [the Exchange Act] or the rules and regulations thereunder."

presume it is primarily concerned with domestic conditions." *Aramco, supra*, at 248. The canon or presumption applies regardless of whether there is a risk of conflict between the American statute and a foreign law. When a statute gives no clear indication of an extraterritorial application, it has none.

Despite this principle of interpretation, long and often recited in our opinions, the Second Circuit believed that, because the Exchange Act is silent as to the extraterritorial application of § 10(b), it was left to the court to "discern" whether Congress would have wanted the statute to apply. This disregard of the presumption against extraterritoriality did not originate with the Court of Appeals panel in this case. It has been repeated over many decades by various courts of appeals in determining the application of the Exchange Act, and § 10(b) in particular, to fraudulent schemes that involve conduct and effects abroad. That has produced a collection of tests for divining what Congress would have wanted, complex in formulation and unpredictable in application.

. . .

[T]he Second Circuit . . . excised the presumption against extraterritoriality from the jurisprudence of § 10(b) and replaced it with the inquiry whether it would be reasonable (and hence what Congress would have wanted) to apply the statute to a given situation. As long as there was prescriptive jurisdiction to regulate, the Second Circuit explained, whether to apply § 10(b) even to "predominantly foreign" transactions became a matter of whether a court thought Congress "wished the precious resources of United States courts and law enforcement agencies to be devoted to them rather than leave the problem to foreign countries." *Bersch v. Drexel Firestone, Inc.*, 519 F.2d 974, 985 (1975). . . .

The Second Circuit had thus established that application of § 10(b) could be premised upon either some effect on American securities markets or investors or significant conduct in the United States. It later formalized these two applications into (1) an "effects test," "whether the wrongful conduct had a substantial effect in the United States or upon United States citizens," and (2) a "conduct test," "whether the wrongful conduct occurred in the United States." *SEC v. Berger*, 322 F.3d 187, 192-193 (2d Cir. 2003). These became the north star of the Second Circuit's § 10(b) jurisprudence, pointing the way to what Congress would have wished. Indeed, the Second Circuit declined to keep its two tests distinct on the ground that "an admixture or combination of the two often gives a better picture of whether there is sufficient United States involvement to justify the exercise of jurisdiction by an American court." *Itoba Ltd. v. Lep Group PLC*, 54 F.3d 118, 122 (1995). The Second Circuit never put forward a textual or even extratextual basis for these tests. As early as *Bersch*, it confessed that "if we were asked to point to language in the statutes, or even in the legislative history, that compelled these conclusions, we would be unable to respond," 519 F.2d, at 993.

As they developed, these tests were not easy to administer. The conduct test was held to apply differently depending on whether the harmed investors were Americans or foreigners: When the alleged damages consisted of losses to American investors abroad, it was enough that acts "of material importance" performed in the United States "significantly contributed" to that result; whereas those acts must have "directly caused" the result when losses to foreigners abroad

prep & application

were at issue. See *Bersch*, 519 F.2d, at 993. And "merely preparatory activities in the United States" did not suffice "to trigger application of the securities laws for injury to foreigners located abroad." *Id.*, at 992. This required the court to distinguish between mere preparation and using the United States as a "base" for fraudulent activities in other countries. But merely satisfying the conduct test was sometimes insufficient without "'some additional factor tipping the scales'" in favor of the application of American law. *Interbrew v. Edperbrascan Corp.*, 23 F. Supp. 2d 425, 432 (S.D.N.Y. 1998) (quoting *Europe & Overseas Commodity Traders, S.A. v. Banque Paribas London*, 147 F.3d 118, 129 (CA2 1998)). District courts have noted the difficulty of applying such vague formulations. There is no more damning indictment of the "conduct" and "effects" tests than the Second Circuit's own declaration that "the presence or absence of any single factor which was considered significant in other cases . . . is not necessarily dispositive in future cases." *IIT v. Cornfeld*, 619 F.2d 909, 918 (1980).

Other Circuits embraced the Second Circuit's approach, though not its precise application. . . . While applying the same fundamental methodology of balancing interests and arriving at what seemed the best policy, they produced a proliferation of vaguely related variations on the "conduct" and "effects" tests. As described in a leading Seventh Circuit opinion: "Although the circuits . . . seem to agree that there are some transnational situations to which the antifraud provisions of the securities laws are applicable, agreement appears to end at that point." . . .

At least one Court of Appeals has criticized this line of cases and the interpretive assumption that underlies it. In *Zoelsch v. Arthur Andersen & Co.*, 824 F.2d 27, 32 (1987) (Bork, J.), the District of Columbia Circuit observed that rather than courts' "divining what 'Congress would have wished' if it had addressed the problem[, a] more natural inquiry might be what jurisdiction Congress in fact thought about and conferred." Although tempted to apply the presumption against extraterritoriality and be done with it, that court deferred to the Second Circuit because of its "preeminence in the field of securities law."

Commentators have criticized the unpredictable and inconsistent application of § 10(b) to transnational cases. . . .

The criticisms seem to us justified. The results of judicial-speculation-made-law — divining what Congress would have wanted if it had thought of the situation before the court — demonstrate the wisdom of the presumption against extraterritoriality. Rather than guess anew in each case, we apply the presumption in all cases, preserving a stable background against which Congress can legislate with predictable effects.

? presumption application.

B

Rule 10b-5, the regulation under which petitioners have brought suit, was promulgated under § 10(b), and "does not extend beyond conduct encompassed by § 10(b)'s prohibition." *United States v. O'Hagan*, 521 U.S. 642, 651 (1997). Therefore, if § 10(b) is not extraterritorial, neither is Rule 10b-5.

On its face, § 10(b) contains nothing to suggest it applies abroad: "It shall be unlawful for any person, directly or indirectly, by the use of any means or instrumentality of interstate commerce or of the mails, or of any facility of any national securities exchange . . . [t]o use or employ, in connection with the purchase or sale of any security registered on a national securities exchange or any security not so registered, . . . any manipulative or deceptive device or contrivance in contravention of such rules and regulations as the [Securities and Exchange] Commission may prescribe. . . ." 15 U.S.C. 78j(b).

Petitioners and the Solicitor General contend, however, that three things indicate that § 10(b) or the Exchange Act in general has at least some extraterritorial application.

First, they point to the definition of "interstate commerce," a term used in § 10(b), which includes "trade, commerce, transportation, or communication . . . between any foreign country and any State." 15 U.S.C. § 78c(a)(17). But "we have repeatedly held that even statutes that contain broad language in their definitions of 'commerce' that expressly refer to 'foreign commerce' do not apply abroad." *Aramco*, 499 U.S., at 251. The general reference to foreign commerce in the definition of "interstate commerce" does not defeat the presumption against extraterritoriality.

precedent.

Petitioners and the Solicitor General next point out that Congress, in describing the purposes of the Exchange Act, observed that the "prices established and offered in such transactions are generally disseminated and quoted throughout the United States and foreign countries." 15 U.S.C. § 78b(2). The antecedent of "such transactions," however, is found in the first sentence of the section, which declares that "transactions in securities as commonly conducted upon securities exchanges and over-the-counter markets are affected with a national public interest." § 78b. Nothing suggests that this national public interest pertains to transactions conducted upon foreign exchanges and markets. The fleeting reference to the dissemination and quotation abroad of the prices of securities traded in domestic exchanges and markets cannot overcome the presumption against extraterritoriality.

Finally, there is § 30(b) of the Exchange Act, 15 U.S.C. § 78dd(b), which does mention the Act's extraterritorial application: "The provisions of [the Exchange Act] or of any rule or regulation thereunder shall not apply to any person insofar as he transacts a business in securities without the jurisdiction of the United States," unless he does so in violation of regulations promulgated by the Securities and Exchange Commission "to prevent . . . evasion of [the Act]." (The parties have pointed us to no regulation promulgated pursuant to § 30(b).) The Solicitor General argues that "[this] exemption would have no function if the Act did not apply in the first instance to securities transactions that occur abroad." Brief for United States as Amicus Curiae 14.

We are not convinced. In the first place, it would be odd for Congress to indicate the extraterritorial application of the whole Exchange Act by means of a provision imposing a condition precedent to its application abroad. And if the whole Act applied abroad, why would the Commission's enabling regulations be limited to those preventing "evasion" of the Act, rather than all those preventing "violation"? The provision seems to us directed at actions abroad that might conceal a domestic violation, or might cause what would otherwise be a domestic violation to escape on a technicality. (At most, the Solicitor General's proposed inference is possible; but possible interpretations of statutory language do not override the presumption against extraterritoriality.) See *Aramco, supra*, at 253.

The Solicitor General also fails to account for § 30(a), which reads in relevant part as follows: ("It shall be unlawful for any broker or dealer . . . to make use of the mails or of any means or instrumentality of interstate commerce for the purpose of effecting on an exchange not within or subject to the jurisdiction of the United States) any transaction in any security the issuer of which is a resident of, or is organized under the laws of, or has its principal place of business in, a place within or subject to the jurisdiction of the United States, in contravention of such rules and regulations as the Commission may prescribe. . . ." 15 U.S.C. § 78dd(a).

(Subsection 30(a) contains what § 10(b) lacks: a clear statement of extraterritorial effect. Its explicit provision for a specific extraterritorial application would be quite superfluous if the rest of the Exchange Act already applied to transactions on foreign exchanges — and its limitation of that application to securities of domestic issuers would be inoperative.) Even if that were not true, when a statute provides for some extraterritorial application, the presumption against extraterritoriality operates to limit that provision to its terms. . . . No one claims that § 30(a) applies here.

The concurrence claims we have impermissibly narrowed the inquiry in evaluating whether a statute applies abroad, citing for that point the dissent in *Aramco*. But we do not say, as the concurrence seems to think, that the presumption against extraterritoriality is a "clear statement rule," if by that is meant a requirement that a statute say "this law applies abroad." Assuredly context can be consulted as well. But whatever sources of statutory meaning one consults to give "the most faithful reading" of the text, there is no clear indication of extraterritoriality here. The concurrence does not even try to refute that conclusion, but merely puts forward the same (at best) uncertain indications relied upon by petitioners and the Solicitor General. As the opinion for the Court in *Aramco* (which we prefer to the dissent) shows, those uncertain indications do not suffice.

In short, there is no affirmative indication in the Exchange Act that § 10(b) applies extraterritorially, and we therefore conclude that it does not.

[margin note:] Consistency of the legislation

IV

A

Petitioners argue that the conclusion that § 10(b) does not apply extraterritorially does not resolve this case. They contend that they seek no more than domestic application anyway, since Florida is where HomeSide and its senior executives engaged in the deceptive conduct of manipulating HomeSide's financial models; their complaint also alleged that Race and Hughes made misleading public statements there. This is less an answer to the presumption against extraterritorial application than it is an assertion — a quite valid assertion — that that presumption here (as often) is not self-evidently dispositive, but its application requires further analysis. For it is a rare case of prohibited extraterritorial application that lacks all contact with the territory of the United States. But the presumption against extraterritorial application would be a craven watchdog indeed if it retreated to its kennel whenever some domestic activity is involved in the case. The concurrence seems to imagine just such a timid sentinel, but our cases are to the contrary. In *Aramco*, for example, the Title VII plaintiff had been hired in Houston, and was an American citizen. See 499 U.S., at 247 (The Court concluded, however, that neither that territorial event nor that relationship was the "focus" of congressional concern, *id.*, at 255, but rather domestic employment.)

Congressional Concern.

Applying the same mode of analysis here, we think that the focus of the Exchange Act is not upon the place where the deception originated, but upon purchases and sales of securities in the United States. Section 10(b) does not punish deceptive conduct, but only deceptive conduct "in connection with the purchase or sale of any security registered on a national securities exchange or any security not so registered." 15 U.S.C. § 78j(b). Those purchase-and-sale transactions are the objects of the statute's solicitude. It is those transactions that the statute seeks to "regulate"; it is parties or prospective parties to those transactions that the statute seeks to "protec[t]." And it is in our view only transactions in securities listed on domestic exchanges, and domestic transactions in other securities, to which § 10(b) applies.

The primacy of the domestic exchange is suggested by the very prologue of the Exchange Act, which sets forth as its object "[t]o provide for the regulation of securities exchanges . . . operating in interstate and foreign commerce and through the mails, to prevent inequitable and unfair practices on such exchanges. . . ." 48 Stat. 881. We know of no one who thought that the Act was intended to "regulat[e]" foreign securities exchanges — or indeed who even believed that under established principles of international law Congress had the power to do so. The Act's registration requirements apply only to securities listed on national securities exchanges. 15 U.S.C. § 78l (a).

With regard to securities not registered on domestic exchanges, the exclusive focus on domestic purchases and sales is strongly confirmed by § 30(a) and (b), discussed earlier. The former extends the normal scope of the Exchange Act's prohibitions to acts effecting, in violation of rules prescribed by the Commission, a "transaction" in a United States security "on an exchange not within or subject to the jurisdiction of the United States." § 78dd(a). And the latter specifies that the Act does not apply to "any person insofar as he transacts a business in securities without the jurisdiction of the United States," unless he does so in violation of regulations promulgated by the Commission "to prevent evasion [of the Act]." § 78dd(b). Under both provisions it is the foreign location of the transaction that establishes (or reflects the presumption of) the Act's inapplicability, absent regulations by the Commission.

The same focus on domestic transactions is evident in the Securities Act of 1933, 48 Stat. 74, enacted by the same Congress as the Exchange Act, and forming part of the same comprehensive regulation of securities trading. . . . That legislation makes it unlawful to sell a security, through a prospectus or otherwise, making use of "any means or instruments of transportation or communication in interstate commerce or of the mails," unless a registration statement is in effect.

15 U.S.C. § 77e(a)(1). The Commission has interpreted that requirement "not to include . . . sales that occur outside the United States." 17 CFR § 230.901 (2009).

Finally, we reject the notion that the Exchange Act reaches conduct in this country affecting exchanges or transactions abroad for the same reason that *Aramco* rejected overseas application of Title VII to all domestically concluded employment contracts or all employment contracts with American employers: The probability of incompatibility with the applicable laws of other countries is so obvious that if Congress intended such foreign application "it would have addressed the subject of conflicts with foreign laws and procedures." [*Aramco*], 499 U.S., at 256 (Like the United States, foreign countries regulate their domestic securities exchanges and securities transactions occurring within their territorial jurisdiction.) And the regulation of other countries often differs from ours as to what constitutes fraud, what disclosures must be made, what damages are recoverable, what discovery is available in litigation, what individual actions may be joined in a single suit, what attorney's fees are recoverable, and many other matters. See, *e.g.*, Brief for United Kingdom of Great Britain and Northern Ireland as Amicus Curiae 16-21. The Commonwealth of Australia, the United Kingdom of Great Britain and Northern Ireland, and the Republic of France have filed amicus briefs in this case. So have (separately or jointly) such international and foreign organizations as the International Chamber of Commerce, the Swiss Bankers Association, the Federation of German Industries, the French Business Confederation, the Institute of International Bankers, the European Banking Federation, the Australian Bankers' Association, and the Association Française des Entreprises Privées (They all complain of the interference with foreign securities regulation that application of § 10(b) abroad would produce, and urge the adoption of a clear test that will avoid that consequence.) The transactional test we have adopted — whether the purchase or sale is made in the United States, or involves a security listed on a domestic exchange — meets that requirement.

. . .

(Section 10(b) reaches the use of a manipulative or deceptive device or contrivance only in connection with the purchase or sale of a security listed on an American stock exchange, and the purchase or sale of any other security in the United States.) This case involves no securities listed on a domestic exchange, and all aspects of the purchases complained of by those petitioners who still have live claims occurred outside the United States. Petitioners have therefore failed to state a claim on which relief can be granted. We affirm the dismissal of petitioners' complaint on this ground.

It is so ordered.

Justice SOTOMAYOR took no part in the consideration or decision of this case.

[An opinion by Justice Breyer, concurring in part and concurring in the judgment, is omitted.]

. . .

Justice STEVENS, with whom Justice GINSBURG joins, concurring in the judgment.

While I agree that petitioners have failed to state a claim on which relief can be granted, my reasoning differs from the Court's. I would adhere to the general approach that has been the law in the Second Circuit, and most of the rest of the country, for nearly four decades.

I

Today the Court announces a new "transactional test" for defining the reach of § 10(b) of the Securities Exchange Act of 1934 (Exchange Act), 15 U.S.C. § 78j(b), and SEC Rule 10b-5, 17 CFR § 240.10b-5(b) (2009): Henceforth, those provisions will extend only to "transactions in securities listed on domestic exchanges . . . and domestic transactions in other securities." If one confines one's gaze to the statutory text, the Court's conclusion is a plausible one. But the federal courts have been construing § 10(b) in a different manner for a long time, and the Court's textual analysis is not nearly so compelling, in my view, as to warrant the abandonment of their doctrine.

The text and history of § 10(b) are famously opaque on the question of when, exactly, transnational securities frauds fall within the statute's compass. As those types of frauds became more common in the latter half of the 20th century, the federal courts were increasingly called upon to wrestle with that question. The Court of Appeals for the Second Circuit, located in the Nation's financial center, led the effort. Beginning in earnest with *Schoenbaum v. Firstbrook*, 405 F.2d 200, *rev'd on rehearing on other grounds*, 405 F.2d 215 (1968) (en banc), that court strove, over an extended series of cases, to "discern" under what circumstances "Congress would have wished the precious resources of the United States courts and law enforcement agencies to be devoted to [transnational] transactions," 547 F.3d 167, 170 (2008). . . . [T]he Second Circuit eventually settled on a conduct-and-effects test. This test asks "(1) whether the wrongful conduct occurred in the Unites States, and (2) whether the wrongful conduct had a substantial effect in the United States or upon United States citizens." *Id.*, at 171. Numerous cases flesh out the proper application of each prong.

The Second Circuit's test became the "north star" of § 10(b) jurisprudence, not just regionally but nationally as well. With minor variations, other courts converged on the same basic approach. See Brief for United States as Amicus Curiae 15 ("The courts have uniformly agreed that Section 10(b) can apply to a transnational securities fraud either when fraudulent conduct has effects in the United States or when sufficient conduct relevant to the fraud occurs in the United States"); see also 1 Restatement (Third) of Foreign Relations Law of the United States § 416 (1986) (setting forth conduct-and-effects test). Neither Congress nor the Securities Exchange Commission (Commission) acted to change the law. To the contrary, the Commission largely adopted the Second Circuit's position in its own adjudications.

. . .

. . . The Second Circuit refined its test over several decades and dozens of cases, with the tacit approval of Congress and the Commission and with the general assent of its sister Circuits. That history is a reason we should give additional weight to the Second Circuit's "judge-made" doctrine, not a reason to denigrate it. "The longstanding acceptance by the courts, coupled with Congress' failure to reject [its] reasonable interpretation of the wording of § 10(b), . . . argues

significantly in favor of acceptance of the [Second Circuit] rule by this Court."
[*Blue Chip Stamps v. Manor Drug Stores*, 421 U.S. 723, 737 (1975).]

II

The Court's other main critique of the Second Circuit's approach — apart from what the Court views as its excessive reliance on functional considerations and reconstructed congressional intent — is that the Second Circuit has "disregard[ed]" the presumption against extraterritoriality. It is the Court, however, that misapplies the presumption, in two main respects.

First, the Court seeks to transform the presumption from a flexible rule of thumb into something more like a clear statement rule. We have been here before. In the case on which the Court primarily relies, *EEOC v. Arabian American Oil Co.*, 499 U.S. 244 (1991) (*Aramco*), Chief Justice Rehnquist's majority opinion included a sentence that appeared to make the same move. See *id.*, at 258 ("Congress' awareness of the need to make a clear statement that a statute applies overseas is amply demonstrated by the numerous occasions on which it has expressly legislated the extraterritorial application of a statute"). Justice Marshall, in dissent, vigorously objected. See *id.*, at 261 ("[C]ontrary to what one would conclude from the majority's analysis, this canon is not a 'clear statement' rule, the application of which relieves a court of the duty to give effect to all available indicia of the legislative will").

Yet even *Aramco* — surely the most extreme application of the presumption against extraterritoriality in my time on the Court — contained numerous passages suggesting that the presumption may be overcome without a clear directive. See *id.*, at 248-255 (majority opinion) (repeatedly identifying congressional "intent" as the touchstone of the presumption). And our cases both before and after Aramco make perfectly clear that the Court continues to give effect to "all available evidence about the meaning" of a provision when considering its extraterritorial application, lest we defy Congress' will. *Sale v. Haitian Centers Council, Inc.*, 509 U.S. 155, 177 (1993). Contrary to Justice Scalia's personal view of statutory interpretation, that evidence legitimately encompasses more than the enacted text. Hence, while the Court's dictum that "[w]hen a statute gives no clear indication of an extraterritorial application, it has none," makes for a nice catchphrase, the point is overstated. The presumption against extraterritoriality can be useful as a theory of congressional purpose, a tool for managing international conflict, a background norm, a tiebreaker. It does not relieve courts of their duty to give statutes the most faithful reading possible.

Second, and more fundamentally, the Court errs in suggesting that the presumption against extraterritoriality is fatal to the Second Circuit's test. For even if the presumption really were a clear statement (or "clear indication") rule, it would have only marginal relevance to this case. It is true, of course, that "this Court ordinarily construes ambiguous statutes to avoid unreasonable interference with the sovereign authority of other nations," *F. Hoffmann-La Roche Ltd. v. Empagran S.A.*, 542 U.S. 155, 164 (2004), and that, absent contrary evidence, we presume "Congress is primarily concerned with domestic conditions," *Foley Bros., Inc. v. Filardo*, 336 U.S. 281, 285 (1949). Accordingly, the presumption against extraterritoriality "provides a sound basis for concluding that Section 10(b) does not apply when a securities fraud with no effects in the United States is hatched and executed entirely outside this country." Brief for United States as Amicus Curiae 22. But that is just about all it provides a sound basis for concluding. And the conclusion is not very illuminating, because no party to the litigation disputes it. No one contends that § 10(b) applies to wholly foreign frauds.

Rather, the real question in this case is how much, and what kinds of, domestic contacts are sufficient to trigger application of § 10(b). In developing its conduct-and-effects test, the Second Circuit endeavored to derive a solution from the Exchange Act's text, structure, history, and purpose. [The Second Circuit was] well aware that United States courts "cannot and should not expend [their] resources resolving cases that do not affect Americans or involve fraud emanating from America."

The question just stated does not admit of an easy answer. The text of the Exchange Act indicates that § 10(b) extends to at least some activities with an international component, but, again, it is not pellucid as to which ones. The Second Circuit draws the line as follows: § 10(b) extends to transnational frauds "only when substantial acts in furtherance of the fraud were committed within the United States," *SEC v. Berger*, 322 F.3d 187, 193 (CA2 2003), or when the fraud was "intended to produce" and did produce "detrimental effects within" the United States, *Schoenbaum*, 405 F.2d, at 206.

This approach is consistent with the understanding shared by most scholars that Congress, in passing the Exchange Act, "expected U.S. securities laws to apply to certain international transactions or conduct." Buxbaum, Multinational Class Actions Under Federal Securities Law: Managing Jurisdictional Conflict, 46 Colum. J. Transnat'l L. 14, 19 (2007). . . . And it strikes a reasonable balance between the goals of "preventing the export of fraud from America," protecting shareholders, enhancing investor confidence, and deterring corporate misconduct, on the one hand, and conserving United States resources and limiting conflict with foreign law, on the other.[10]

Thus, while § 10(b) may not give any "clear indication" on its face as to how it should apply to transnational securities frauds, it does give strong clues that it should cover at least some of them. . . . And in my view, the Second Circuit has done the best job of discerning what sorts of transnational frauds Congress meant in 1934 — and still means today — to regulate. I do not take issue with the Court for beginning its inquiry with the statutory text, rather than the doctrine in the Courts of Appeals. I take issue with the Court for beginning and ending its inquiry with the statutory text, when the text does not speak with geographic precision, and for dismissing the long pedigree of, and the persuasive account of congressional intent embodied in, the Second Circuit's rule.

---

10. Given its focus on "domestic conditions," *Foley Bros., Inc. v. Filardo*, 336 U.S. 281, 285 (1949), I expect that virtually all "foreign-cubed" actions — in which (1) foreign plaintiffs are suing (2) a foreign issuer in an American court for violations of American securities laws based on securities transactions in (3) foreign countries — would fail the Second Circuit's test. As they generally should. Under these circumstances, the odds of the fraud having a substantial connection to the United States are low. In recognition of the Exchange Act's focus on American investors and the novelty of foreign-cubed lawsuits, and in the interest of promoting clarity, it might have been appropriate to incorporate one bright line into the Second Circuit's test, by categorically excluding such lawsuits from § 10(b)'s ambit.

Repudiating the Second Circuit's approach in its entirety, the Court establishes a novel rule that will foreclose private parties from bringing § 10(b) actions whenever the relevant securities were purchased or sold abroad and are not listed on a domestic exchange. The real motor of the Court's opinion, it seems, is not the presumption against extraterritoriality but rather the Court's belief that transactions on domestic exchanges are "the focus of the Exchange Act" and "the objects of [its] solicitude." In reality, however, it is the "public interest" and "the interests of investors" that are the objects of the statute's solicitude. And while the clarity and simplicity of the Court's test may have some salutary consequences, like all bright-line rules it also has drawbacks.

Imagine, for example, an American investor who buys shares in a company listed only on an overseas exchange. That company has a major American subsidiary with executives based in New York City; and it was in New York City that the executives masterminded and implemented a massive deception which artificially inflated the stock price — and which will, upon its disclosure, cause the price to plummet. Or, imagine that those same executives go knocking on doors in Manhattan and convince an unsophisticated retiree, on the basis of material misrepresentations, to invest her life savings in the company's doomed securities. Both of these investors would, under the Court's new test, be barred from seeking relief under § 10(b).

The oddity of that result should give pause. . . . Indeed, the Court's rule turns § 10(b) jurisprudence (and the presumption against extraterritoriality) on its head, by withdrawing the statute's application from cases in which there is both substantial wrongful conduct that occurred in the United States and a substantial injurious effect on United States markets and citizens.

III

In my judgment, if petitioners' allegations of fraudulent misconduct that took place in Florida are true, then respondents may have violated § 10(b), and could potentially be held accountable in an enforcement proceeding brought by the Commission. But it does not follow that shareholders who have failed to allege that the bulk or the heart of the fraud occurred in the United States, or that the fraud had an adverse impact on American investors or markets, may maintain a private action to recover damages they suffered abroad. Some cases involving foreign securities transactions have extensive links to, and ramifications for, this country; this case has Australia written all over it. Accordingly, for essentially the reasons stated in the Court of Appeals' opinion, I would affirm its judgment.

The Court instead elects to upend a significant area of securities law based on a plausible, but hardly decisive, construction of the statutory text. In so doing, it pays short shrift to the United States' interest in remedying frauds that transpire on American soil or harm American citizens, as well as to the accumulated wisdom and experience of the lower courts. I happen to agree with the result the Court reaches in this case. But I respectfully dissent, once again, from the Court's continuing campaign to render the private cause of action under § 10(b) toothless.

NOTES AND QUESTIONS

1. **Practice: What's at Stake?** What was at stake for the litigants in *Aramco* and *Morrison*? Specifically, why do you think the plaintiffs wanted Title VII to apply in *Aramco* and § 10(b) of the Securities Exchange Act of 1934 to apply in *Morrison*? Why do you think the defendants didn't want them to apply? What other law potentially could have applied?

2. **Practice: Litigation Strategy.** Why do you think the plaintiffs sued the defendants in *Morrison* and *Aramco* in the United States? What other forums might have potentially been available?

3. **Practice: What Kind of Motion to Dismiss?** Note Justice Scalia's procedural point in Part II of the *Morrison* opinion: If a party is seeking to dismiss a suit on the ground that a U.S. federal statute does not apply extraterritorially, the proper motion to file is a Rule 12(b)(6) motion to dismiss for failure to state a claim upon which relief can be granted, *not a Rule 12(b)(1) motion to dismiss for lack of subject matter jurisdiction.* Why do you think he insists on this procedural point? From the strategic perspective, if you were a lawyer representing the defendant, would you rather have the plaintiff's complaint dismissed for failure to state a claim or for lack of subject matter jurisdiction?

4. **Extraterritoriality Analysis.** What canon of statutory interpretation guided the Court's analysis in *Aramco*? According to the Court, what policy reasons support that canon? Beyond the Court's application of this canon, what other methods did the Court use to "fortify" and "buttress" its conclusion regarding the extraterritorial application of Title VII? How, if at all, does *Morrison* change the Supreme Court's analytical approach to the issue of whether a U.S. statute applies extraterritorially? As part of your answer to this question, outline the main analytical steps that should be taken by the lower courts after *Morrison* to determine whether or not a U.S. federal statute applies extraterritorially.

5. **Rebutting the Presumption Against Extraterritoriality.** What is necessary to rebut the presumption against extraterritoriality? The Court denies that it has announced a "clear statement rule" and insists that context may be consulted. What type of context do you think the Court is contemplating? As a plaintiff attempting to overcome the presumption, what contextual evidence might you use? Did the Court correctly determine that the presumption was not overcome for § 10(b)? For Title VII? Why or why not?

6. **Policy: Deference to the Executive Branch.** Note that the Court in *Morrison* held that § 10(b) did not apply extraterritorially even though the Solicitor General — the U.S. Department of Justice lawyer who represents the United States in the Supreme Court — filed a brief arguing that § 10(b) *did* apply extraterritorially. This illustrates that the Supreme Court may not agree with the executive branch's position on questions of extraterritoriality. Should the Supreme Court defer to the executive branch's legal positions on these questions? Why or why not?

7. **Determining a Statute's "Focus."** The Court in *Morrison* asks what the "focus" of § 10(b) is. What does the Court mean by "focus"? Why does the Court find it necessary to inquire into the statute's focus? What methods did the Court use to determine § 10(b)'s focus? Did the Court correctly identify the focus of § 10(b)? Why or why not?

8. **Policy: The Majority versus the Concurrence.** The majority in *Morrison* rejects the Second Circuit's approach as unworkable, but in his concurring opinion Justice Stevens defends it as preferable to the majority's approach. Who is right? What are the advantages and disadvantages of the two approaches to the issue of whether a U.S. federal statute applies extraterritorially? Why is Justice Stevens concurring rather than dissenting?

9. **Policy: Implications of the Presumption Against Extraterritoriality.** In *Aramco*, U.S. plaintiffs sued U.S. corporate defendants, but the Court held that U.S. law did not apply. What are the potential effects of these decisions on the ability of U.S. companies to avoid being subject to U.S. law? Are these effects desirable from a policy perspective? Why or why not? In contrast, the *Morrison* case is an example of a so-called foreign-cubed (or "f-cubed") lawsuit: It involved foreign plaintiffs, foreign defendants, and securities traded on a foreign exchange. Does this make it a more attractive application of the presumption against extraterritoriality? Or should some other presumption apply?

10. **Can § 10(b) Ever Apply in Transnational Cases?** What are the implications of the Court's holding in *Morrison* for the extraterritorial application of § 10(b)? Under what circumstances, if any, does § 10(b) apply in transnational cases after *Morrison*? Consider *Valentini v. Citigroup, Inc.*, 837 F. Supp. 2d 304 (S.D.N.Y. 2011), in which Brazilian plaintiffs sued U.S. banks for violations of § 10(b) of the Securities Exchange Act of 1934 in connection with plaintiffs' purchase of securities in Brazil. The securities purchased by plaintiffs were convertible into other securities that were traded on the New York Stock Exchange (NYSE). The court denied defendants' motion to dismiss based on *Morrison*, holding that § 10(b) was applicable:

> Defendants' . . . challenge to Plaintiffs' § 10(b) claim relies upon the Supreme Court's recent holding in *Morrison v. Nat'l Austl. Bank Ltd.* . . . that § 10(b) applies only when (1) "the purchase or sale [of a security] is made in the United States", or (2) "[the transaction] involves a security listed on a domestic exchange." Defendants argue that because the [securities] Plaintiffs purchased from them were not purchased in the United States, and not themselves listed on a domestic exchange, *Morrison* precludes their § 10(b) claim.
>
> We disagree. It is clear that the [securities] at issue in this case were not purchased in the United States. . . . Hence, we find it easy to conclude that the first prong of the *Morrison* test is not satisfied.
>
> The second prong is more complicated. Although none of the [securities purchased by Plaintiffs] were listed on a domestic exchange, they were all linked to securities listed on a domestic exchange — namely, the NYSE. . . . We are therefore confronted with a question that thus far no court appears to have addressed: does a transaction in securities that may, under certain circumstances, convert into domestically-traded stock qualify as a "transaction

involving securities listed on a domestic exchange," as the second prong of the *Morrison* test requires?

We find that it does. . . .

. . . Here, Plaintiffs purchased securities that were linked to domestically-traded . . . securities. . . . Not only [was the value of the purchased securities] linked to NYSE-traded securities, at least some of [them] were also convertible into those securities. What this means is that when Plaintiffs purchased these [securities], they were in effect purchasing a put option on those NYSE-traded stocks.

Is this an extraterritorial application of § 10(b)? Can the court's opinion be reconciled with *Morrison*? Why or why not? Also consider *City of Pontiac Policemen's & Firemen's Retirement System v. UBS AG*, 752 F.3d 173 (2d Cir. 2014). In that case, foreign plaintiffs sued foreign defendants under § 10(b) in connection with their purchase of securities on a foreign stock exchange. Plaintiffs argued that *Morrison* did not bar their suit, because the securities they purchased on the foreign exchange were also listed on the NYSE. The court rejected the plaintiffs' argument, and held that *Morrison* precluded their claim. Can this decision be reconciled with *Valentini*? Is it more consistent with *Morrison* than *Valentini*? Why or why not?

11. **What Is a Domestic Transaction?** One reason for the uncertainty regarding the scope of *Morrison* is that "[w]hile *Morrison* holds that § 10(b) can be applied to domestic purchases or sales, it provides little guidance as to what constitutes a domestic purchase or sale." *Absolute Activist Value Master Fund Ltd. v. Ficeto*, 677 F.3d 60, 67 (2d Cir. 2012). According to the Second Circuit, "to sufficiently allege a domestic securities transaction in securities not listed on a domestic exchange . . . a plaintiff must allege facts suggesting that irrevocable liability was incurred or title was transferred within the United States." *Id.* at 68. In light of *Ficeto, Valentini,* and *City of Pontiac,* what arguments would you consider making as a lawyer for a plaintiff to establish that the claim is based on a domestic transaction? What counterarguments would you consider as a lawyer for a defendant seeking to dismiss the claim based on *Morrison*?

12. **Policy: Congressional Responses to the Supreme Court's Extraterritoriality Decisions.** Shortly after the Court's *Aramco* decision, Congress amended Title VII to provide explicitly for its extraterritorial application. Civil Rights Act of 1991, § 109, 105 Stat. 1077. Does this congressional response influence your views of the Court's holding and reasoning in *Aramco*? Why or why not? Shortly after the Court's *Morrison* decision, Congress amended the Securities Exchange Act to adopt the conduct and effects tests that the Court had rejected, but only for actions brought by the U.S. Securities and Exchange Commission or the U.S. Department of Justice. Dodd-Frank Wall Street Reform and Consumer Protection Act, Title IX, § 929P(b) (2010). Does this congressional response influence your views of the Court's holding and reasoning in *Morrison*? Why or why not? Do these events suggest that the Court is doing something other than finding the intent of Congress?

13. **The Extraterritorial Reach of Other Statutes.** *Foley Bros., Inc. v. Filardo*, 336 U.S. 281 (1949), discussed in *Aramco* and *Morrison*, considered whether the U.S. "eight hour" law, limiting working hours on contracts with the U.S. government, applied to work in foreign countries. The Act provided that "Every contract made to which the United States . . . is a party . . . shall contain a provision that no laborer or mechanic doing any part of the work contemplated by the contract, in the employ of the contractor or any subcontractor . . . shall be required or permitted to work more than eight hours in any one calendar day upon such work." *Id.* at 282. The Court invoked the "canon of construction which teaches that legislation of Congress, unless a contrary intent appears, is meant to apply only within the territorial jurisdiction of the United States," which, it said, "is based on the assumption that Congress is primarily concerned with domestic conditions." *Id.* at 285. It found nothing in the Act or legislative history to overcome the presumption. In contrast, in *Steele v. Bulova Watch Co.*, 344 U.S. 280 (1952), also discussed in *Morrison* and *Aramco*, the Court held that the Lanham Act, giving federal protection to trademarks, could be applied against the defendant's watchmaking business in Mexico. The statute extended trademark protection to "all commerce which may lawfully be regulated by Congress." The Court acknowledged the presumption against extraterritorial application, and framed the question as "whether Congress intended to make the law applicable to the facts of this case." It concluded:

> In the light of the broad jurisdictional grant in the Lanham Act, we deem its scope to encompass petitioner's activities here. His operations and their effects were not confined within the territorial limits of a foreign nation. He bought component parts of his wares in the United States, and spurious "Bulovas" filtered through the Mexican border into this country; his competing goods could well reflect adversely on Bulova Watch Company's trade reputation in markets cultivated by advertising here as well as abroad.

Justice Reed, the author of *Foley Bros.*, dissented along with Justice Douglas, concluding:

> Petitioner's buying of unfinished watches in the United States is not an illegal commercial act. Nor can it be said that petitioners were engaging in illegal acts in commerce when the finished watches bearing the Mexican trade-mark were purchased from them and brought into the United States by such purchasers, all without collusion between petitioner and the purchaser. The stamping of the Bulova trade-mark, done in Mexico, is not an act within the control of Congress. It should not be utilized as a basis for action against petitioner. The Lanham Act . . . should be construed to apply only to acts done within the sovereignty of the United States. While we do not condone the piratic use of trade-marks, neither do we believe that Congress intended to make such use actionable irrespective of the place it occurred. Such extensions of power bring our legislation into conflict with the laws and practices of other nations, fully capable of punishing infractions of their own laws, and

should require specific words to reach acts done within the territorial limits of other sovereignties.

Is *Steele* consistent with *Foley Bros.*? With *Aramco*? With *Morrison*?

14. **A Comparative Perspective.** Justice Scalia makes much of the potential for the extraterritorial application of U.S. federal law to create discord with foreign countries. Since the late 1980s, however, the European Union (EU) and various foreign nations have been applying their antitrust regimes extraterritorially, often using an "effects test" approach. *See A. Ahlström Osakeyhtiö et al. v. Comm'n of the European Communities,* Joined Cases 89, 104, 114, 116, 117 & 125 to 129/85, 1988 E.C.R. 5193. Does this change your view of the correct approach? Might such an approach be appropriate where, as in the EU, actions against anticompetitive behavior are brought by government regulators and not private parties?

15. **Statutes with Clear Indication of Extraterritorial Application.** Some U.S. federal statutes clearly have extraterritorial application. For example, Congress's post-*Aramco* definition of "employee" for purposes of Title VII of the Civil Rights Act of 1964 includes the following: "With respect to *employment in a foreign country,* such term includes an individual who is a citizen of the United States." 42 U.S.C. § 2000e(f) (emphasis added). Congress's post-*Morrison* statement of jurisdiction under the Securities Exchange Act of 1934 provides as follows: "The district courts of the United States and the United States courts of any Territory shall have jurisdiction of an action or proceeding brought or instituted by the Commission or the United States alleging a violation of the antifraud provisions of this chapter involving — (1) conduct within the United States that constitutes significant steps in furtherance of the violation, *even if the securities transaction occurs outside the United States and involves only foreign investors*; or (2) *conduct occurring outside the United States that has a foreseeable substantial effect within the United States.*" 15 U.S.C. § 78aa(b) (emphasis added). *See also* Hostage Taking Act, 18 U.S.C. § 1203, excerpted below in *United States v. Yunis* (explicitly applying to conduct outside the United States if "(A) the offender or the person seized or detained is a national of the United States; (B) the offender is found in the United States; or (C) the government organization sought to be compelled is the Government of the United States").

In the following case, the Supreme Court clarifies *Morrison's* framework for analyzing the extraterritorial reach of federal statutes. The case involves the Racketeer Influenced and Corrupt Organizations Act (RICO), which is a complicated federal statute. Don't worry if you don't understand all of the complexities of RICO. Instead, we encourage you to focus on how the case sheds light on the steps that lawyers and judges must take to determine whether a given federal statute applies extraterritorially and on the reasoning that led the Court to its decision.

RJR Nabisco, Inc. v. European Community

136 S. Ct. 2090 (2016)

Justice ALITO delivered the opinion of the Court.

The Racketeer Influenced and Corrupt Organizations Act (RICO), 18 U.S.C. §§ 1961-1968, created four new criminal offenses involving the activities of organized criminal groups in relation to an enterprise. §§ 1962(a)-(d). RICO also created a new civil cause of action for "[a]ny person injured in his business or property by reason of a violation" of those prohibitions. § 1964(c). We are asked to decide whether RICO applies extraterritorially — that is, to events occurring and injuries suffered outside the United States.

I

A

RICO is founded on the concept of racketeering activity. The statute defines "racketeering activity" to encompass dozens of state and federal offenses, known in RICO parlance as predicates. These predicates include any act "indictable" under specified federal statutes, §§ 1961(1)(B)-(C), (E)-(G), as well as certain crimes "chargeable" under state law, § 1961(1)(A), and any offense involving bankruptcy or securities fraud or drug-related activity that is "punishable" under federal law, § 1961(1)(D). A predicate offense implicates RICO when it is part of a "pattern of racketeering activity" — a series of related predicates that together demonstrate the existence or threat of continued criminal activity. *H.J. Inc. v. Northwestern Bell Telephone Co.*, 492 U.S. 229, 239 (1989); see § 1961(5) (specifying that a "pattern of racketeering activity" requires at least two predicates committed within 10 years of each other).

RICO's § 1962 sets forth four specific prohibitions aimed at different ways in which a pattern of racketeering activity may be used to infiltrate, control, or operate "a[n] enterprise which is engaged in, or the activities of which affect, interstate or foreign commerce." These prohibitions can be summarized as follows. Section 1962(a) makes it unlawful to invest income derived from a pattern of racketeering activity in an enterprise. Section 1962(b) makes it unlawful to acquire or maintain an interest in an enterprise through a pattern of racketeering activity. Section 1962(c) makes it unlawful for a person employed by or associated with an enterprise to conduct the enterprise's affairs through a pattern of racketeering activity. Finally, § 1962(d) makes it unlawful to conspire to violate any of the other three prohibitions.[1]

---

1. In full, 18 U.S.C. § 1962 provides:

"(a) It shall be unlawful for any person who has received any income derived, directly or indirectly, from a pattern of racketeering activity or through collection of an unlawful debt in which such person has participated as a principal within the meaning of section 2, title 18, United States Code, to use or invest, directly or indirectly, any part of such income, or the proceeds of such income, in acquisition of any interest in, or the establishment or operation of, any enterprise which is engaged in, or the activities of which affect, interstate or foreign commerce. A purchase of securities on the open market for purposes

Violations of § 1962 are subject to criminal penalties, § 1963(a), and civil proceedings to enforce those prohibitions may be brought by the Attorney General, §§ 1964(a)-(b). Separately, RICO creates a private civil cause of action that allows "[a]ny person injured in his business or property by reason of a violation of section 1962" to sue in federal district court and recover treble damages, costs, and attorney's fees. § 1964(c).[2]

B

This case arises from allegations that petitioners — RJR Nabisco and numerous related entities (collectively RJR) — participated in a global money-laundering scheme in association with various organized crime groups. Respondents [are] the European Community and 26 of its member states. . . .

Greatly simplified, the complaint alleges a scheme in which Colombian and Russian drug traffickers smuggled narcotics into Europe and sold the drugs for euros that — through a series of transactions involving black-market money brokers, cigarette importers, and wholesalers — were used to pay for large shipments of RJR cigarettes into Europe. In other variations of this scheme, RJR allegedly dealt directly with drug traffickers and money launderers in South America and sold cigarettes to Iraq in violation of international sanctions. RJR is also said to have acquired Brown & Williamson Tobacco Corporation for the purpose of expanding these illegal activities.

---

of investment, and without the intention of controlling or participating in the control of the issuer, or of assisting another to do so, shall not be unlawful under this subsection if the securities of the issuer held by the purchaser, the members of his immediate family, and his or their accomplices in any pattern or racketeering activity or the collection of an unlawful debt after such purchase do not amount in the aggregate to one percent of the outstanding securities of any one class, and do not confer, either in law or in fact, the power to elect one or more directors of the issuer.

"(b) It shall be unlawful for any person through a pattern of racketeering activity or through collection of an unlawful debt to acquire or maintain, directly or indirectly, any interest in or control of any enterprise which is engaged in, or the activities of which affect, interstate or foreign commerce.

"(c) It shall be unlawful for any person employed by or associated with any enterprise engaged in, or the activities of which affect, interstate or foreign commerce, to conduct or participate, directly or indirectly, in the conduct of such enterprise's affairs through a pattern of racketeering activity or collection of unlawful debt.

"(d) It shall be unlawful for any person to conspire to violate any of the provisions of subsection (a), (b), or (c) of this section."

2. In full, § 1964(c) provides:

"Any person injured in his business or property by reason of a violation of section 1962 of this chapter may sue therefor in any appropriate United States district court and shall recover threefold the damages he sustains and the cost of the suit, including a reasonable attorney's fee, except that no person may rely upon any conduct that would have been actionable as fraud in the purchase or sale of securities to establish a violation of section 1962. The exception contained in the preceding sentence does not apply to an action against any person that is criminally convicted in connection with the fraud, in which case the statute of limitations shall start to run on the date on which the conviction becomes final."

The complaint alleges that RJR engaged in a pattern of racketeering activity consisting of numerous acts of money laundering, material support to foreign terrorist organizations, mail fraud, wire fraud, and violations of the Travel Act. RJR, in concert with the other participants in the scheme, allegedly formed an association in fact that was engaged in interstate and foreign commerce, and therefore constituted a RICO enterprise that the complaint dubs the "RJR Money-Laundering Enterprise."

Putting these pieces together, the complaint alleges that RJR violated each of RICO's prohibitions. RJR allegedly used income derived from the pattern of racketeering to invest in, acquire an interest in, and operate the RJR Money-Laundering Enterprise in violation of § 1962(a); acquired and maintained control of the enterprise through the pattern of racketeering in violation of § 1962(b); operated the enterprise through the pattern of racketeering in violation of § 1962(c); and conspired with other participants in the scheme in violation of § 1962(d). These violations allegedly harmed respondents in various ways, including through competitive harm to their state-owned cigarette businesses, lost tax revenue from black-market cigarette sales, harm to European financial institutions, currency instability, and increased law enforcement costs.

RJR moved to dismiss the complaint, arguing that RICO does not apply to racketeering activity occurring outside U.S. territory or to foreign enterprises. The District Court agreed and dismissed the RICO claims as impermissibly extraterritorial.

The Second Circuit reinstated the RICO claims. . . .

The lower courts have come to different conclusions regarding RICO's extraterritorial application. Compare 764 F.3d 129 (case below) (holding that RICO may apply extraterritorially) with *United States v. Chao Fan Xu*, 706 F.3d 965, 974-975 (C.A.9 2013) (holding that RICO does not apply extraterritorially . . .). Because of this conflict and the importance of the issue, we granted certiorari.

II

The question of RICO's extraterritorial application really involves two questions. First, do RICO's substantive prohibitions, contained in § 1962, apply to conduct that occurs in foreign countries? Second, does RICO's private right of action, contained in § 1964(c), apply to injuries that are suffered in foreign countries? We consider each of these questions in turn. To guide our inquiry, we begin by reviewing the law of extraterritoriality.

It is a basic premise of our legal system that, in general, "United States law governs domestically but does not rule the world." *Microsoft Corp. v. AT & T Corp.*, 550 U.S. 437, 454 (2007). This principle finds expression in a canon of statutory construction known as the presumption against extraterritoriality: Absent clearly expressed congressional intent to the contrary, federal laws will be construed to have only domestic application. *Morrison v. National Australia Bank Ltd.*, 561 U.S. 247, 255 (2010). The question is not whether we think "Congress would have wanted" a statute to apply to foreign conduct "if it had thought of the situation before the court," but whether Congress has affirmatively and unmistakably instructed that the statute will do so. *Id.*, at 261. "When a statute gives no clear indication of an extraterritorial application, it has none." *Id.*, at 255.

There are several reasons for this presumption. Most notably, it serves to avoid the international discord that can result when U.S. law is applied to conduct in foreign countries. See, *e.g.*, *Kiobel v. Royal Dutch Petroleum Co.*, 133 S. Ct. 1659, 1663-1664 (2013); *EEOC v. Arabian American Oil Co.*, 499 U.S. 244, 248 (1991) (*Aramco*); *Benz v. Compania Naviera Hidalgo, S.A.*, 353 U.S. 138, 147 (1957). But it also reflects the more prosaic "commonsense notion that Congress generally legislates with domestic concerns in mind." *Smith v. United States*, 507 U.S. 197, 204, n. 5 (1993). We therefore apply the presumption across the board, "regardless of whether there is a risk of conflict between the American statute and a foreign law." *Morrison, supra*, at 255.

Twice in the past six years we have considered whether a federal statute applies extraterritorially. In *Morrison*, we addressed the question whether § 10(b) of the Securities Exchange Act of 1934 applies to misrepresentations made in connection with the purchase or sale of securities traded only on foreign exchanges. We first examined whether § 10(b) gives any clear indication of extraterritorial effect, and found that it does not. 561 U.S., at 262-265. We then engaged in a separate inquiry to determine whether the complaint before us involved a permissible *domestic* application of § 10(b) because it alleged that some of the relevant misrepresentations were made in the United States. At this second step, we considered the "'focus' of congressional concern," asking whether § 10(b)'s focus is "the place where the deception originated" or rather "purchases and sale of securities in the United States." *Id.*, at 266. We concluded that the statute's focus is on domestic securities transactions, and we therefore held that the statute does not apply to frauds in connection with foreign securities transactions, even if those frauds involve domestic misrepresentations.

In *Kiobel*, we considered whether the Alien Tort Statute (ATS) confers federal-court jurisdiction over causes of action alleging international-law violations committed overseas. We acknowledged that the presumption against extraterritoriality is "typically" applied to statutes "regulating conduct," but we concluded that the principles supporting the presumption should "similarly constrain courts considering causes of action that may be brought under the ATS." 133 S. Ct., at 1664. We applied the presumption and held that the ATS lacks any clear indication that it extended to the foreign violations alleged in that case. Because "all the relevant conduct" regarding those violations "took place outside the United States," we did not need to determine, as we did in *Morrison*, the statute's "focus."

Morrison and *Kiobel* reflect a two-step framework for analyzing extraterritoriality issues. At the first step, we ask whether the presumption against extraterritoriality has been rebutted — that is, whether the statute gives a clear, affirmative indication that it applies extraterritorially. We must ask this question regardless of whether the statute in question regulates conduct, affords relief, or merely confers jurisdiction. If the statute is not extraterritorial, then at the second step we determine whether the case involves a domestic application of the statute, and we do this by looking to the statute's "focus." If the conduct relevant to the statute's focus occurred in the United States, then the case involves a permissible domestic application even if other conduct occurred abroad; but if the conduct relevant to the focus occurred in a foreign country, then the case involves an impermissible extraterritorial application regardless of any other conduct that occurred in U.S. territory.

What if we find at step one that a statute clearly *does* have extraterritorial effect? Neither *Morrison* nor *Kiobel* involved such a finding. But we addressed this issue in *Morrison*, explaining that it was necessary to consider § 10(b)'s "focus" only because we found that the statute does not apply extraterritorially: "If § 10(b) did apply abroad, we would not need to determine which transnational frauds it applied to; it would apply to all of them (barring some other limitation)." 561 U.S., at 267, n. 9. The scope of an extraterritorial statute thus turns on the limits Congress has (or has not) imposed on the statute's foreign application, and not on the statute's "focus."[5]

III

With these guiding principles in mind, we first consider whether RICO's substantive prohibitions in § 1962 may apply to foreign conduct. Unlike in *Morrison* and *Kiobel*, we find that the presumption against extraterritoriality has been rebutted — but only with respect to certain applications of the statute.

A

The most obvious textual clue is that RICO defines racketeering activity to include a number of predicates that plainly apply to at least some foreign conduct. These predicates include the prohibition against engaging in monetary transactions in criminally derived property, which expressly applies, when "the defendant is a United States person," to offenses that "tak[e] place outside the United States." 18 U.S.C. § 1957(d)(2). Other examples include the prohibitions against the assassination of Government officials, § 351(i) ("There is extraterritorial jurisdiction over the conduct prohibited by this section"); § 1751(k) (same), and the prohibition against hostage taking, which applies to conduct that "occurred outside the United States" if either the hostage or the offender is a U.S. national, if the offender is found in the United States, or if the hostage taking is done to compel action by the U.S. Government, § 1203(b). At least one predicate — the prohibition against "kill[ing] a national of the United States, while such national is outside the United States" — applies *only* to conduct occurring outside the United States. § 2332(a).

We agree with the Second Circuit that Congress's incorporation of these (and other) extraterritorial predicates into RICO gives a clear, affirmative indication that § 1962 applies to foreign racketeering activity — but only to the extent that the predicates alleged in a particular case themselves apply extraterritorially.

---

5. Because a finding of extraterritoriality at step one will obviate step two's "focus" inquiry, it will usually be preferable for courts to proceed in the sequence that we have set forth. But we do not mean to preclude courts from starting at step two in appropriate cases.

Put another way, a pattern of racketeering activity may include or consist of offenses committed abroad in violation of a predicate statute for which the presumption against extraterritoriality has been overcome. To give a simple (albeit grim) example, a violation of § 1962 could be premised on a pattern of killings of Americans abroad in violation of § 2332(a) — a predicate that all agree applies extraterritorially — whether or not any domestic predicates are also alleged.

We emphasize the important limitation that foreign conduct must violate "a predicate statute that manifests an unmistakable congressional intent to apply extraterritorially." 764 F.3d, at 136. Although a number of RICO predicates have extraterritorial effect, many do not. The inclusion of *some* extraterritorial predicates does not mean that *all* RICO predicates extend to foreign conduct. . . .

RJR resists the conclusion that RICO's incorporation of extraterritorial predicates gives RICO commensurate extraterritorial effect. It points out that "RICO itself" does not refer to extraterritorial application; only the underlying predicate statutes do. Brief for Petitioners 42. RJR thus argues that Congress could have intended to capture only *domestic* applications of extraterritorial predicates, and that any predicates that apply only abroad could have been "incorporated . . . solely for when such offenses are part of a broader pattern whose overall locus is domestic." *Id.,* at 43.

The presumption against extraterritoriality does not require us to adopt such a constricted interpretation. While the presumption can be overcome only by a clear indication of extraterritorial effect, an express statement of extraterritoriality is not essential. "Assuredly context can be consulted as well." *Morrison, supra,* at 265. Context is dispositive here. Congress has not expressly said that § 1962(c) applies to patterns of racketeering activity in foreign countries, but it has defined "racketeering activity" — and by extension a "pattern of racketeering activity" — to encompass violations of predicate statutes that *do* expressly apply extraterritorially. Short of an explicit declaration, it is hard to imagine how Congress could have more clearly indicated that it intended RICO to have (some) extraterritorial effect. This unique structure makes RICO the rare statute that clearly evidences extraterritorial effect despite lacking an express statement of extraterritoriality.

We therefore conclude that RICO applies to some foreign racketeering activity. A violation of § 1962 may be based on a pattern of racketeering that includes predicate offenses committed abroad, provided that each of those offenses violates a predicate statute that is itself extraterritorial. This fact is determinative as to § 1962(b) and § 1962(c), both of which prohibit the employment of a pattern of racketeering. Although they differ as to the end for which the pattern is employed — to acquire or maintain control of an enterprise under subsection (b), or to conduct an enterprise's affairs under subsection (c) — this difference is immaterial for extraterritoriality purposes.

. . .

B

RJR contends that, even if RICO may apply to foreign patterns of racketeering, the statute does not apply to foreign *enterprises.* Invoking *Morrison's* discussion of the Exchange Act's "focus," RJR says that the "focus" of RICO is the enterprise being corrupted — not the pattern of racketeering — and that RICO's enterprise element gives no clear indication of extraterritorial effect. Accordingly, RJR reasons, RICO requires a domestic enterprise.

This argument misunderstands *Morrison*. As explained above, only at the second step of the inquiry do we consider a statute's "focus." Here, however, there is a clear indication at step one that RICO applies extraterritorially. We therefore do not proceed to the "focus" step. The *Morrison* Court's discussion of the statutory "focus" made this clear, stating that "[i]f § 10(b) did apply abroad, we would not need to determine which transnational frauds it applied to; it would apply to all of them (barring some other limitation)." 561 U.S., at 267, n. 9. The same is true here. RICO — or at least §§ 1962(b) and (c) — applies abroad, and so we do not need to determine which transnational (or wholly foreign) patterns of racketeering it applies to; it applies to all of them, regardless of whether they are connected to a "foreign" or "domestic" enterprise. This rule is, of course, subject to the important limitation that RICO covers foreign predicate offenses only to the extent that the underlying predicate statutes are extraterritorial. But within those bounds, the location of the affected enterprise does not impose an independent constraint.

. . .

C

Applying these principles, we agree with the Second Circuit that the complaint does not allege impermissibly extraterritorial violations of §§ 1962(b) and (c).

The alleged pattern of racketeering activity consists of five basic predicates: (1) money laundering, (2) material support of foreign terrorist organizations, (3) mail fraud, (4) wire fraud, and (5) violations of the Travel Act. The Second Circuit observed that the relevant provisions of the money laundering and material support of terrorism statutes expressly provide for extraterritorial application in certain circumstances, and it concluded that those circumstances are alleged to be present here. 764 F.3d, at 139-140. The court found that the fraud statutes and the Travel Act do not contain the clear indication needed to overcome the presumption against extraterritoriality. But it held that the complaint alleges *domestic* violations of those statutes because it "allege[s] conduct in the United States that satisfies every essential element of the mail fraud, wire fraud, and Travel Act claims." *Id.*, at 142.

RJR does not dispute these characterizations of the alleged predicates. We therefore assume without deciding that the alleged pattern of racketeering activity consists entirely of predicate offenses that were either committed in the United States or committed in a foreign country in violation of a predicate statute that applies extraterritorially. . . . On these premises, respondents' allegations that RJR violated §§ 1962(b) and (c) do not involve an impermissibly extraterritorial application of RICO.

IV

We now turn to RICO's private right of action, on which respondents' lawsuit rests. Section 1964(c) allows "[a]ny person injured in his business or property by reason of a violation of section 1962" to sue for treble damages, costs, and attorney's fees. Irrespective of any extraterritorial application of § 1962, we conclude that § 1964(c) does not overcome the presumption against extraterritoriality. A private RICO plaintiff therefore must allege and prove a *domestic* injury to its business or property.

A

The Second Circuit thought that the presumption against extraterritoriality did not apply to § 1964(c) independently of its application to § 1962, reasoning that the presumption "is primarily concerned with the question of what *conduct* falls within a statute's purview." 764 F.3d, at 151. We rejected that view in *Kiobel*, holding that the presumption "constrain[s] courts considering causes of action" under the ATS, a "strictly jurisdictional" statute that "does not directly regulate conduct or afford relief." 133 S. Ct., at 1664. We reached this conclusion even though the underlying substantive law consisted of well-established norms of international law, which by definition apply beyond this country's borders. See *id.*, at 1664-1666.

The same logic requires that we separately apply the presumption against extraterritoriality to RICO's cause of action despite our conclusion that the presumption has been overcome with respect to RICO's substantive prohibitions. "The creation of a private right of action raises issues beyond the mere consideration whether underlying primary conduct should be allowed or not, entailing, for example, a decision to permit enforcement without the check imposed by prosecutorial discretion." *Sosa v. Alvarez-Machain*, 542 U.S. 692, 727 (2004). Thus, as we have observed in other contexts, providing a private civil remedy for foreign conduct creates a potential for international friction beyond that presented by merely applying U.S. substantive law to that foreign conduct. See, *e.g.*, *Kiobel, supra*, at 133 S. Ct., at 1665 ("Each of th[e] decisions" involved in defining a cause of action based on "conduct within the territory of another sovereign" "carries with it significant foreign policy implications").

Consider antitrust. In that context, we have observed that "[t]he application . . . of American private treble-damages remedies to anticompetitive conduct taking place abroad has generated considerable controversy" in other nations, even when those nations agree with U.S. substantive law on such things as banning price fixing. *F. Hoffmann-La Roche Ltd. v. Empagran S.A.*, 542 U.S. 155, 167 (2004). Numerous foreign countries — including some respondents in this case — advised us in *Empagran* that "to apply [U.S.] remedies would unjustifiably permit their citizens to bypass their own less generous remedial schemes, thereby upsetting a balance of competing considerations that their own domestic antitrust laws embody." *Ibid.* . . .

Allowing recovery for foreign injuries in a civil RICO action, including treble damages, presents the same danger of international friction. See Brief for United States as *Amicus Curiae* 31-34.

. . .

Respondents urge that concerns about international friction are inapplicable in this case because here the plaintiffs are not foreign citizens seeking to bypass their home countries' less generous remedies but rather the foreign countries themselves. . . . We reject the notion that we should forgo the presumption against extraterritoriality and instead permit extraterritorial suits based on a case-by-case inquiry that turns on or looks to the consent of the affected sovereign. See *Morrison, supra,* at 261 ("Rather than guess anew in each case, we apply the presumption in all cases"); cf. *Empagran,* 542 U.S., at 168. Respondents suggest that we should be reluctant to permit a foreign corporation to be sued in the courts of this country for events occurring abroad if the nation of incorporation objects, but that we should discard those reservations when a foreign state sues a U.S. entity in this country under U.S. law — instead of in its own courts and under its own laws — for conduct committed on its own soil. We refuse to adopt this double standard. "After all, in the law, what is sauce for the goose is normally sauce for the gander." *Heffernan v. City of Paterson,* 578 U.S. ___, ___ (2016).

B

Nothing in § 1964(c) provides a clear indication that Congress intended to create a private right of action for injuries suffered outside of the United States. The statute provides a cause of action to "[a]ny person injured in his business or property" by a violation of § 1962. § 1964(c). The word "any" ordinarily connotes breadth, but it is insufficient to displace the presumption against extraterritoriality. See *Kiobel,* 133 S. Ct., at 1665-1666. The statute's reference to injury to "business or property" also does not indicate extraterritorial application. If anything, by cabining RICO's private cause of action to particular kinds of injury — excluding, for example, personal injuries — Congress signaled that the civil remedy is not coextensive with § 1962's substantive prohibitions. The rest of § 1964(c) places a limit on RICO plaintiffs' ability to rely on securities fraud to make out a claim. This too suggests that § 1964(c) is narrower in its application than § 1962, and in any event does not support extraterritoriality.

The Second Circuit did not identify anything in § 1964(c) that shows that the statute reaches foreign injuries. Instead, the court reasoned that § 1964(c)'s extraterritorial effect flows directly from that of § 1962. Citing our holding in *Sedima, S.P.R.L. v. Imrex Co.,* 473 U.S. 479 (1985), that the "compensable injury" addressed by § 1964(c) "necessarily is the harm caused by predicate acts sufficiently related to constitute a pattern," *id.,* at 497 the Court of Appeals held that a RICO plaintiff may sue for foreign injury that was caused by the violation of a predicate statute that applies extraterritorially, just as a substantive RICO violation may be based on extraterritorial predicates. 764 F.3d, at 151. Justice GINSBURG advances the same theory. This reasoning has surface appeal, but it fails to appreciate that the presumption against extraterritoriality must be applied separately to both RICO's substantive prohibitions and its private right of action. It is not enough to say that a private right of action must reach abroad because the underlying law governs conduct in foreign countries. Something more is needed, and here it is absent.

. . .

C

Section 1964(c) requires a civil RICO plaintiff to allege and prove a domestic injury to business or property and does not allow recovery for foreign injuries. The application of this rule in any given case will not always be self-evident, as disputes may arise as to whether a particular alleged injury is "foreign" or "domestic." But we need not concern ourselves with that question in this case. As this case was being briefed before this Court, respondents filed a stipulation in the District Court waiving their damages claims for domestic injuries. The District Court accepted this waiver and dismissed those claims with prejudice. Respondents' remaining RICO damages claims therefore rest entirely on injury suffered abroad and must be dismissed.

The judgment of the United States Court of Appeals for the Second Circuit is reversed, and the case is remanded for further proceedings consistent with this opinion.

So ordered.

Justice SOTOMAYOR took no part in the consideration or decision of this case.

Justice GINSBURG, with whom Justice BREYER and Justice KAGAN join, concurring in Parts I, II, and III and dissenting from Part IV and from the judgment.

. . .

I

. . .

[T]he Court concludes, when the predicate crimes underlying invocation of § 1962 thrust extraterritorially, so too does § 1962. I agree with that conclusion.

I disagree, however, that the private right of action authorized by § 1964(c) requires a domestic injury to a person's business or property and does not allow recovery for foreign injuries. One cannot extract such a limitation from the text of § 1964(c), which affords a right of action to "[a]ny person injured in his business or property by reason of a violation of section 1962." Section 1962, at least subsections (b) and (c), all agree, encompasses foreign injuries. How can § 1964(c) exclude them when, by its express terms, § 1964(c) is triggered by "a violation of section 1962"? To the extent RICO reaches injury abroad when the Government is the suitor pursuant to § 1962 (specifying prohibited activities) and § 1963 (criminal penalties) or § 1964(b) (civil remedies), to that same extent, I would hold, RICO reaches extraterritorial injury when, pursuant to § 1964(c), the suitor is a private plaintiff.

II

·A

I would not distinguish, as the Court does, between the extraterritorial compass of a private right of action and that of the underlying proscribed conduct. Instead, I would adhere to precedent addressing RICO, linking, not separating, prohibited activities and authorized remedies. See *Sedima, S.P.R.L. v. Imrex Co.*, 473 U.S. 479, 495 (1985) ("If the defendant engages in a pattern of racketeering activity in a manner forbidden by [§ 1962], and the racketeering activities injure the plaintiff in his business or property, the plaintiff has a claim under § 1964(c)."); *ibid.* (refusing to require a "distinct 'racketeering injury'" for private RICO actions under § 1964(c) where § 1962 imposes no such requirement).[2]

To reiterate, a § 1964(c) right of action may be maintained by "[a]ny person injured in his business or property by reason of a violation of *section 1962*" (emphasis added). "[I]ncorporating one statute . . . into another," the Court has long understood, "serves to bring into the latter all that is fairly covered by the reference." *Panama R. Co. v. Johnson*, 264 U.S. 375, 392 (1924). RICO's private right of action, it cannot be gainsaid, expressly incorporates § 1962, whose extraterritoriality, the Court recognizes, is coextensive with the underlying predicate offenses charged. See *ante*, at 2101-2106. See also *ante*, at 2102 ("[I]t is hard to imagine how Congress could have more clearly indicated that it intended RICO to have (some) extraterritorial effect."). The sole additional condition § 1964(c) imposes on access to relief is an injury to one's "business or property." Nothing in that condition should change the extraterritoriality assessment. In agreement with the Second Circuit, I would hold that "[i]f an injury abroad was proximately caused by the violation of a statute which Congress intended should apply to injurious conduct performed abroad, [there is] no reason to import a domestic injury requirement simply because the victim sought redress through the RICO statute." 764 F.3d 149, 151 (2014).

. . .

This very case illustrates why pinning a domestic-injury requirement onto § 1964(c) makes little sense. All defendants are U.S. corporations, headquartered in the United States, charged with a pattern of racketeering activity directed and managed from the United States, involving conduct occurring in the United States. In particular, according to the complaint, defendants received in the United States funds known to them to have been generated by illegal narcotics trafficking and terrorist activity, conduct violative of § 1956(a)(2); traveled using the facilities of interstate commerce in furtherance of unlawful activity, in violation of

---

2. Insisting that the presumption against extraterritoriality should "apply to § 1964(c) independently of its application to § 1962," ante, at 2105-2106, the Court cites *Kiobel v. Royal Dutch Petroleum Co.*, 133 S. Ct. 1659 (2013). That decision will not bear the weight the Court would place on it. As the Court comprehends, the statute there at issue, the Alien Tort Statute, 28 U.S.C. § 1350, is a spare jurisdictional grant that itself does not "regulate conduct or afford relief." *Kiobel*, 133 S. Ct., at 1664. With no grounding for extraterritorial application in the statute, *Kiobel* held, courts have no warrant to fashion, on their own initiative, claims for relief that operate extraterritorially. See ibid. ("[T]he question is not what Congress has done but instead what courts may do.").

§ 1952; provided material support to foreign terrorist organizations "in the United States and elsewhere," in violation of § 2339B; and used U.S. mails and wires in furtherance of a "scheme or artifice to defraud," in violation of §§ 1341 and 1343. In short, this case has the United States written all over it.

B

The Court nevertheless deems a domestic-injury requirement for private RICO plaintiffs necessary to avoid international friction. When the United States considers whether to initiate a prosecution or civil suit, the Court observes, it will take foreign-policy considerations into account, but private parties will not. It is far from clear, however, that the Court's blanket rule would ordinarily work to ward off international discord. Invoking the presumption against extraterritoriality as a bar to *any* private suit for injuries to business or property abroad, this case suggests, might spark, rather than quell, international strife. Making such litigation available to domestic but not foreign plaintiffs is hardly solicitous of international comity or respectful of foreign interests. Cf. *Pfizer*, 434 U.S., at 318-319 ("[A] foreign nation is generally entitled to prosecute any civil claim in the courts of the United States upon the same basis as a domestic corporation or individual might do. To deny him this privilege would manifest a want of comity and friendly feeling." (internal quotation marks omitted)).

RICO's definitional provisions exclude "[e]ntirely foreign activity." 783 F.3d 123, 143 (Lynch, J., dissenting from denial of rehearing en banc). Thus no suit under RICO would lie for injuries resulting from "[a] pattern of murders of Italian citizens committed by members of an Italian organized crime group in Italy." *Ibid.* That is so because "murder is a RICO predicate only when it is 'chargeable under state law' or indictable under specific federal statutes." *Ibid.* (citing § 1961(1)(A), (G)).

To the extent extraterritorial application of RICO could give rise to comity concerns not present in this case, those concerns can be met through doctrines that serve to block litigation in U.S. courts of cases more appropriately brought elsewhere. Where an alternative, more appropriate forum is available, the doctrine of *forum non conveniens* enables U.S. courts to refuse jurisdiction. See *Piper Aircraft Co. v. Reyno*, 454 U.S. 235 (1981) (dismissing wrongful-death action arising out of air crash in Scotland involving only Scottish victims); Restatement (Second) of Conflict of Laws § 84 (1969). Due process constraints on the exercise of general personal jurisdiction shelter foreign corporations from suit in the United States based on conduct abroad unless the corporation's "affiliations with the [forum] in which suit is brought are so constant and pervasive 'as to render it essentially at home [there].'" *Daimler AG v. Bauman*, 134 S. Ct. 746, 751 (2014) (quoting *Goodyear Dunlop Tires Operations, S.A. v. Brown*, 564 U.S. 915, 919 (2011); alterations omitted). These controls provide a check against civil RICO litigation with little or no connection to the United States. . . .

The Court hems in RICO out of concern about establishing a "double standard." But today's decision does exactly that. U.S. defendants commercially engaged here and abroad would be answerable civilly to U.S. victims of their criminal activities, but foreign parties similarly injured would have no RICO remedy. "Sauce for the goose" should indeed serve the gander as well. I would resist reading into § 1964(c) a domestic-injury requirement Congress did not prescribe. Instead, I would affirm the Second Circuit's sound judgment:

> "To establish a compensable injury under § 1964(c), a private plaintiff must show that (1) the defendant 'engage[d] in a pattern of racketeering activity in a manner forbidden by' § 1962, and (2) that these 'racketeering activities' were the proximate cause of some injury to the plaintiff's business or property."

Because the Court overturns that judgment, I dissent.

Justice BREYER, concurring in part, dissenting in part, and dissenting from the judgment.

I join Parts I through III of the Court's opinion. But I do not join Part IV. The Court there holds that the private right of action provision in the Racketeer Influenced and Corrupt Organizations Act (RICO), 18 U.S.C. § 1964(c), has no extraterritorial application. Like Justice GINSBURG, I believe that it does.

. . .

Unlike the Court, I cannot accept as controlling the Government's argument as *amicus curiae* that "[a]llowing recovery for foreign injuries in a civil RICO action . . . presents the . . . danger of international friction." The Government does not provide examples, nor apparently has it consulted with foreign governments on the matter. By way of contrast, the European Community and 26 of its member states tell us "that the complaint in this case, which alleges that American corporations engaged in a pattern of racketeering activity that caused injury to respondents' businesses and property, comports with limitations on prescriptive jurisdiction under international law and respects the dignity of foreign sovereigns." In these circumstances, and for the reasons given by Justice GINSBURG, I would not place controlling weight on the Government's contrary view.

Consequently, I join Justice GINSBURG's opinion.

NOTES AND QUESTIONS

1. **Practice: What's at Stake?** What was at stake for the litigants in *RJR Nabisco*? Specifically, why do you think the plaintiffs wanted U.S. federal law to apply? Why do you think the defendants didn't want U.S. federal law to apply? What other law potentially could have applied?
2. **Practice: Litigation Strategy.** Why do you think the plaintiffs sued the defendants in the United States? What other forums might have potentially been available? Why didn't the plaintiffs sue there instead?
3. **Clarifying the *Morrison* Framework.** In what ways does the Court in *RJR Nabisco* clarify the *Morrison* framework for analyzing the extraterritorial reach of federal statutes? In particular, what is the relationship between the presumption against extraterritoriality and a statute's "focus"? Is the "focus"

analysis always necessary? And what light does the Court's opinion in *RJR Nabisco* shed on what the *Morrison* Court meant when, in confirming that the presumption against extraterritoriality is not a "clear statement rule," it stated that "[a]ssuredly context can be consulted as well"? Specifically, what "context" did the Court find important in *RJR Nabisco*?

In *WesternGeco LLC v. ION Geophysical Corporation*, 138 S. Ct. 2129 (2018), the Supreme Court decided an extraterritoriality issue without doing the first analytical step at all. That case involved the federal Patent Act. Under § 271(f)(2) of that Act, a company is liable for patent infringement if it ships components of a patented invention overseas to be assembled there. Under § 284, a patent owner who proves infringement is entitled to recover lost-profits damages. The trial court ruled in favor of WesternGeco, the patent owner, awarding it damages for profits it lost outside the United States. The issue was whether the award of damages for foreign lost profits was an impermissible extraterritorial application of § 284. *Id.* at 2134. The Court explained its approach as follows:

> We resolve this case at step two. While "it will usually be preferable" to begin with step one, courts have the discretion to begin at step two "in appropriate cases." One reason to exercise that discretion is if addressing step one would require resolving "difficult questions" that do not change "the outcome of the case," but could have far-reaching effects in future cases. That is true here. WesternGeco argues that the presumption against extraterritoriality should never apply to statutes, such as § 284, that merely provide a general damages remedy for conduct that Congress has declared unlawful. Resolving that question could implicate many other statutes besides the Patent Act. We therefore exercise our discretion to forgo the first step of our extraterritoriality framework.

Id. at 2136-37. The Court proceeded to conclude that the focus of § 284 was on the act of infringement. The Court accordingly held that "[t]he conduct in this case that is relevant to that focus clearly occurred in the United States, as it was ION's domestic act of supplying the components that infringed WesternGeco's patents. Thus, the lost-profits damages that were awarded to WesternGeco were a domestic application of § 284." *Id.* at 2138.

4. **Applying *Morrison* to RICO.** Why did the majority in *RJR Nabisco* separately analyze the extraterritorial reach of RICO's substantive provisions in § 1962 and its private right of action in § 1964(c)? Why did it reach different conclusions about the extraterritorial reach of these two sections?

5. **What Counts as "Domestic Injury"?** The Court in *RJR Nabisco* held that "Section 1964(c) requires a civil RICO plaintiff to allege and prove a domestic injury to business or property and does not allow recovery for foreign injuries," commenting that "[t]he application of this rule in any given case will not always be self-evident, as disputes may arise as to whether a particular alleged injury is 'foreign' or "domestic.'" But the plaintiffs in *RJR Nabisco* waived their damages claims for domestic injuries, so the Court did not need to decide whether given injuries were indeed domestic. How should courts

decide what counts and doesn't count as domestic injury? *Compare Tatung Company, Ltd. v. Shu Tze Hsu*, 217 F. Supp. 3d 1138 (C.D. Cal. 2016) (holding that foreign plaintiff's inability to enforce a domestic judgment due to defendant's alleged conspiracy to avoid enforcement was a "domestic injury") *with Bascuñan v. Daniel Yarur Elsaca*, 2016 WL 5475998 (S.D.N.Y. 2016) (holding that an economic injury is suffered in the place where the plaintiff resides and sustains the economic impact of the loss; where defendants caused funds in New York to be fraudulently siphoned from plaintiff's share of his parents' estate, and plaintiff was a Chilean citizen and resident, the injury was suffered in Chile and thus was foreign injury).

6. **Extraterritoriality and International Relations.** Why does the majority believe that the extraterritorial application of RICO's private right of action provision would present a "danger of international friction"? Why are Justices Ginsburg and Breyer skeptical about whether there is such a danger in this case? What do you think? More broadly, is it appropriate for concerns about international relations to influence a court's legal analysis? Why or why not?

7. **Policy: The Desirability of the Presumption Against Extraterritoriality.** Do you think the presumption against extraterritoriality is the best principle to apply to determine whether a U.S. federal statute applies extraterritorially? Why or why not? If not, what alternatives would be more appropriate?

2. The Presumption Against Violating International Law

Even if the presumption against extraterritoriality is rebutted for a particular U.S. federal statute, a court may nevertheless decline to apply the statute extraterritorially and dismiss a plaintiff's claim by employing another presumption: the presumption that Congress does not intend for a statute to apply in a way that violates international law.

This raises two basic questions. First, what is international law? Chapter 2 provides an in-depth examination of international law (traditionally called the "law of nations"). For now, it is sufficient to understand that international law is law made among nations (rather than by a single nation) by treaty, through custom, or in the form of general principles common to the world's national legal systems. A rule of customary international law exists when a sufficiently large number of nations follow that rule out of a sense of legal obligation.

Second, which rules of international law might the United States or another nation violate by applying its laws outside its territory? The relevant rules are rules of customary international law that govern *jurisdiction to prescribe*. "Jurisdiction to prescribe is the authority of a state to make law applicable to persons, property, or conduct. Legislative bodies exercise prescriptive jurisdiction when they enact statutes, but so does the executive branch when it adopts generally applicable orders or regulations, and so do courts when they make generally applicable common law." RESTATEMENT (FOURTH) OF FOREIGN RELATIONS LAW OF THE UNITED STATES, Part IV, Introductory Note (2018). (Remember: In the language of international law used by the *Restatement*, "state" refers to a nation, such as Japan, Nigeria, or the United States, *not* to a U.S. state, such as California.) Under customary international law, there are a limited number of specified grounds for asserting prescriptive jurisdiction. If a nation applies its law extraterritorially in the absence of any applicable grounds for doing so, it violates the customary international law limits on jurisdiction to prescribe.

Under the customary international law of prescriptive jurisdiction, a nation generally has the authority to apply its law to persons, things, and activity located solely within its own territory. As the materials in this section illustrate, the issue is more complicated in the context of transnational activity. Because such activity is not limited to the territory of a single nation, a nation may have to apply its law extraterritorially in order to regulate that activity effectively. But through the nineteenth century, the customary international law of prescriptive jurisdiction generally authorized a nation to apply its law only within its own territory, subject to narrow exceptions. As the U.S. Supreme Court put it in *The Apollon*, 22 U.S. 362, 369 (1824), "The laws of no nation can justly extend beyond its own territory, except so far as regards its own citizens." In the twentieth century, however, customary international law evolved to provide additional bases for prescriptive jurisdiction.

The following excerpts from the *Restatement (Fourth)* provide a summary of the customary international law rules of prescriptive jurisdiction. Like other Restatements, the *Restatement (Fourth) of Foreign Relations Law* is not a source of law, but rather an expert statement of the law. However, lawyers and judges look to the *Restatement* for guidance on questions about international law and its relationship to the U.S. legal system.

Restatement (Fourth) of the Foreign Relations Law of the United States (2018)

§ 407 Customary International Law Governing Jurisdiction to Prescribe

Customary international law permits exercises of prescriptive jurisdiction if there is a genuine connection between the subject of the regulation and the state seeking to regulate. The genuine connection usually rests on a specific connection between the state and the subject being regulated, such as territory, effects, active personality, passive personality, or protection. In the case of universal jurisdiction, the genuine connection rests on the universal concern of states in suppressing certain offenses.

§ 408 Jurisdiction Based on Territory

International law recognizes a state's jurisdiction to prescribe law with respect to persons, property, and conduct within its territory.

§ 409 Jurisdiction Based on Effects

International law recognizes a state's jurisdiction to prescribe law with respect to conduct that has a substantial effect within its territory.

§ 410 Jurisdiction Based on Active Personality

International law recognizes a state's jurisdiction to prescribe law with respect to the conduct, interests, status, and relations of its nationals outside its territory.

§ 411 Jurisdiction Based on Passive Personality

International law recognizes a state's jurisdiction to prescribe law with respect to certain conduct outside its territory that harms its nationals.

§ 412 Jurisdiction Based on the Protective Principle

International law recognizes a state's jurisdiction to prescribe law with respect to certain conduct outside its territory by persons not its nationals that is directed against the security of the state or against a limited class of other fundamental state interests, such as espionage, certain acts of terrorism, murder of government officials, counterfeiting of the state's seal or currency, falsification of official documents, perjury before consular officials, and conspiracy to violate immigration or customs laws.

§ 413 Universal Jurisdiction

International law recognizes a state's jurisdiction to prescribe law with respect to certain offenses of universal concern, such as genocide, crimes against humanity, war crimes, certain acts of terrorism, piracy, the slave trade, and torture, even if no specific connection exists between the state and the persons or conduct being regulated.

NOTES AND QUESTIONS

1. **Restatements of Law.** What are Restatements, and where do they come from? Are they law? Why do judges and lawyers cite Restatements such as the *Restatement (Fourth) of Foreign Relations Law*? As a lawyer, how would you advise a client whose litigating position appeared to be supported by a Restatement?

2. **Customary International Law Bases for Prescriptive Jurisdiction.** The *Restatement* sets forth various customary international law bases for prescriptive jurisdiction — that is, bases upon which a nation may argue that an application of its law to particular persons or activity is permitted by international law. These bases have commonly used labels: the territorial principle (§ 408), the effects principle (§ 409), the nationality principle (also known as the active personality principle) (§ 410), the passive personality principle (§ 411), the protective principle (§ 412), and universal jurisdiction (§ 413). As the *Restatement* indicates regarding the passive personality principle: "A state may exercise prescriptive jurisdiction with respect to certain conduct

committed outside its territory by a person who is not its national, if the victim of the conduct was its national. Some states exercise passive-personality jurisdiction over crimes committed against residents, in addition to nationals. . . . Passive-personality jurisdiction historically has been more controversial than jurisdiction based on territory or active personality. Despite this, states increasingly have exercised this form of prescriptive jurisdiction, particularly with respect to terrorist offenses." RESTATEMENT (FOURTH) § 411, cmt. a.

3. **Applying Customary International Law Bases for Prescriptive Jurisdiction.** Which bases for prescriptive jurisdiction, if any, might justify application of U.S. law in the following situations? Explain your analysis. (1) The application of U.S. state or federal criminal law to a U.S. citizen accused of committing a crime in California. (2) The application of U.S. state or federal criminal law to a U.S. citizen accused of committing a crime in Canada. (3) The application of Title VII in *Aramco*, § 10(b) in *Morrison* and *Valenti*, and RICO in *RJR Nabisco*. (4) War crimes committed outside U.S. territory by non-U.S. citizens against non-U.S. citizens.

4. **Policy: Evaluating the Bases for Prescriptive Jurisdiction from the Perspective of Nations.** Consider the various bases for prescriptive jurisdiction set forth in the *Restatement (Fourth)*. Which of them would you expect to be most widely accepted by nations? Which of them would you expect to be the most controversial? Why do you think so? Why would nations want to limit their ability to exercise jurisdiction extraterritorially?

The following cases illustrate how U.S. courts apply the presumption that Congress does not intend for a statute to violate international law. As you read the cases, pay close attention to the role that customary international law bases for prescriptive jurisdiction plays in the parties' arguments and the courts' reasoning.

McCulloch v. Sociedad Nacional de Marineros de Honduras

372 U.S. 10 (1963)

Mr. Justice CLARK delivered the opinion of the Court.

These companion cases, involving the same facts, question the coverage of the National Labor Relations Act. . . . A corporation organized and doing business in the United States beneficially owns seagoing vessels which make regular sailings between United States, Latin American, and other ports transporting the corporation's products and other supplies; each of the vessels is legally owned by a foreign subsidiary of the American corporation, flies the flag of a foreign nation, carries a foreign crew, and has other contacts with the nation of its flag. The question arising is whether the Act extends to the crews engaged in such a maritime operation. The National Labor Relations Board, in a representation proceeding on the application of the National Maritime Union [N.M.U.], held that it does and ordered an election. . . . The vessels' foreign owner sought to enjoin the Board's Regional Director from holding the election. . . .

We have concluded that the jurisdictional provisions of the Act do not extend to maritime operations of foreign flag ships employing alien seamen.

. . .

I.

The National Maritime Union of America, AFL-CIO, filed a petition in 1959 with the National Labor Relations Board seeking certification under § 9(c) of the Act [that it should be named] . . . as the representative of the unlicensed seamen employed upon certain Honduran flag vessels owned by Empresa Hondurena de Vapores, S.A., a Honduran corporation. The petition was filed against United Fruit Company, a New Jersey corporation which was alleged to be the owner of the majority of Empresa's stock. Empresa intervened, and, on hearing, it was shown that United Fruit owns all of its stock and elects its directors, though no officer or director of Empresa is an officer or director of United Fruit, and all are residents of Honduras. In turn, the proof was that United Fruit is owned by citizens of the United States, and maintains its principal office at Boston. Its business was shown to be the cultivation, gathering, transporting and sale of bananas, sugar, cacao and other tropical produce raised in Central and South American countries and sold in the United States.

United Fruit maintains a fleet of cargo vessels which it utilizes in this trade. A portion of the fleet consists of 13 Honduran-registered vessels operated by Empresa and time chartered to United Fruit, which vessels were included in National Maritime Union's representation proceeding. The crews on these vessels are recruited by Empresa in Honduras. They are Honduran citizens (save one Jamaican), and claim that country as their residence and home port. The crew are required to sign Honduran shipping articles, and their wages, terms and condition of employment, discipline, etc., are controlled by a bargaining agreement between Empresa and a Honduran union, Sociedad Nacional de Marineros de Honduras. Under the Honduran Labor Code only a union whose "juridic personality" is recognized by Honduras and which is composed of at least 90% of Honduran citizens can represent the seamen on Honduran-registered ships. The N.M.U. fulfills neither requirement. Further, under Honduran law, recognition of Sociedad as the bargaining agent compels Empresa to deal exclusively with it on all matters covered by the contract. The current agreement, in addition to recognition of Sociedad, provides for a union shop, with a "no strike or lockout" provision, and sets up wage scales, special allowances, maintenance and cure provisions, hours of work, vacation time, holidays, overtime, accident prevention, and other details of employment as well.

United Fruit, however, determines the ports of call of the vessels, their cargoes and sailings, integrating the same into its fleet organization. While the voyages are, for the most part, between Central and South American ports and those of the United States, the vessels each call at regular intervals at Honduran ports for the purpose of taking on and discharging cargo and, where necessary, renewing the ship's articles.

II.

The Board concluded from these facts that United Fruit operated a single, integrated maritime operation within which were the Empresa vessels, reasoning that United Fruit was a joint employer with Empresa of the seamen covered by N.M.U.'s petition. [I]t concluded that the maritime operations involved substantial United States contacts, outweighing the numerous foreign contacts present. The Board held that Empresa was engaged in "commerce" within the meaning of § 2(6) of the Act[3] and that the maritime operations "affected commerce" within § 2(7),[4] meeting the jurisdictional requirement of § 9(c)(1). It therefore ordered an election to be held among the seamen signed on Empresa's vessels to determine whether they wished N.M.U., Sindicato Maritimo Nacional de Honduras, or no union to represent them.

. . .

[An] overriding consideration is that the Board's assertion of power to determine the representation of foreign seamen aboard vessels under foreign flags has aroused vigorous protests from foreign governments and created international problems for our Government. Important interests of the immediate parties are of course at stake. [T]he presence of public questions particularly high in the scale of our national interest because of their international complexion is a uniquely compelling justification for prompt judicial resolution of the controversy over the Board's power. . . .

III.

Since the parties all agree that the Congress has constitutional power to apply the National Labor Relations Act to the crews working foreign flag ships, at least while they are in American waters, . . . we go directly to the question whether Congress exercised that power.

. . . Petitioners say that the language of the Act may be read literally as including foreign flag vessels within its coverage. But . . . they have been unable to point to any specific language in the Act itself or in its extensive legislative history that reflects such a congressional intent. Indeed, the opposite is true . . . [in] the language of Chairman Hartley characterizing the Act as "a bill of rights both for American workingmen and for their employers.". . . [I]f the sponsors of the original Act or of its amendments conceived of the application now sought by the Board, they failed to translate such thoughts into describing the boundaries of the

---

3. 29 U.S.C. § 152(6): "The term 'commerce' means trade, traffic, commerce, transportation, or communication among the several States, or between the District of Columbia or any Territory of the United States and any State or other Territory, or between any foreign country and any State, Territory, or the District of Columbia, or within the District of Columbia or any Territory, or between points in the same State but through any other State or any Territory or the District of Columbia or any foreign country."

4. 29 U.S.C. § 152(7): "The term 'affecting commerce' means in commerce, or burdening or obstructing commerce or the free flow of commerce, or having led or tending to lead to a labor dispute burdening or obstructing commerce or the free flow of commerce."

Act as including foreign flag vessels manned by alien crews. . . . In addition, our attention is called to the well established rule of international law that the law of the flag state ordinarily governs the internal affairs of a ship. See . . . Colombos, The International Law of the Sea (3d rev. ed. 1954), 222-223. The possibility of international discord cannot therefore be gainsaid. Especially is this true on account of the concurrent application of the Act and the Honduran Labor Code that would result with our approval of jurisdiction. Sociedad, currently the exclusive bargaining agent of Empresa under Honduran law, would have a head-on collision with N.M.U. should it become the exclusive bargaining agent under the Act. This would be aggravated by the fact that, under Honduran law, N.M.U. is prohibited from representing the seamen on Honduran flag ships even in the absence of a recognized bargaining agent. . . .

The presence of such highly charged international circumstances brings to mind the admonition of Mr. Chief Justice Marshall in *The Charming Betsy*, 2 Cranch 64 (1804), that "an act of congress ought never to be construed to violate the law of nations if any other possible construction remains. . . ." We therefore conclude . . . that for us to sanction the exercise of local sovereignty under such conditions in this delicate field of international relations there must be present the affirmative intention of the Congress clearly expressed. Since neither we nor the parties are able to find any such clear expression, we hold that the Board was without jurisdiction to order the election. This is not to imply, however, any impairment of our own sovereignty, or limitation of the power of Congress in this field. . . . [W]e conclude here that the arguments should be directed to the Congress, rather than to us.

. . .

United States v. Yunis

924 F.2d 1086 (D.C. Cir. 1991)

MIKVA, Chief Judge:

Appellant Fawaz Yunis challenges his convictions on conspiracy, aircraft piracy, and hostage-taking charges stemming from the hijacking of a Jordanian passenger aircraft in Beirut, Lebanon. . . .

Yunis appeals . . . from the district court's denial of his motion to dismiss for lack of subject matter and personal jurisdiction. Appellant's principal claim is that, as a matter of domestic law, the federal hostage taking and air piracy statutes do not authorize assertion of federal jurisdiction over him. Yunis also suggests that a contrary construction of these statutes would conflict with established principles of international law, and so should be avoided by this court. . . .

The Hostage Taking Act provides, in relevant part:

(a) [W]hoever, whether inside or outside the United States, seizes or detains and threatens to kill, to injure, or to continue to detain another person in order to compel a third person or a governmental organization to do or to abstain from any act . . . shall be punished by imprisonment by any term of years or for life.

(b) (1) It is not an offense under this section if the conduct required for the offense occurred outside the United States unless —

(A) the offender or the person seized or detained is a national of the United States;

(B) the offender is found in the United States; or

(C) the governmental organization sought to be compelled is the Government of the United States.

18 U.S.C. § 1203. . . . Since two of the passengers on [the hijacked fight] were U.S. citizens, section 1203(b)(1)(A), authorizing assertion of U.S. jurisdiction where "the offender or the person seized or detained is a national of the United States," is satisfied. . . .

Appellant's argument that we should read the Hostage Taking Act differently to avoid tension with international law falls flat. . . .

The district court concluded that two jurisdictional theories of international law, the "universal principle" and the "passive personal principle," supported assertion of U.S. jurisdiction to prosecute Yunis on hijacking and hostage-taking charges. Under the universal principle, states may prescribe and prosecute "certain offenses recognized by the community of nations as of universal concern, such as piracy, slave trade, attacks on or hijacking of aircraft, genocide, war crimes, and perhaps certain acts of terrorism," even absent any special connection between the state and the offense. See RESTATEMENT (THIRD) OF THE FOREIGN RELATIONS LAW OF THE UNITED STATES §§ 404, 423 (1987) [hereinafter Restatement]. Under the passive personal principle, a state may punish non-nationals for crimes committed against its nationals outside of its territory, at least where the state has a particularly strong interest in the crime. See id. at § 402 comment g; United States v. Benitez, 741 F.2d 1312, 1316 (11th Cir. 1984) (passive personal principle invoked to approve prosecution of Colombian citizen convicted of shooting U.S. drug agents in Colombia).

Relying primarily on the Restatement, Yunis argues that hostage taking has not been recognized as a universal crime and that the passive personal principle authorizes assertion of jurisdiction over alleged hostage takers only where the victims were seized because they were nationals of the prosecuting state. Whatever merit appellant's claims may have as a matter of international law, they cannot prevail before this court. Yunis seeks to portray international law as a self-executing code that trumps domestic law whenever the two conflict. That effort misconceives the role of judges as appliers of international law and as participants in the federal system. Our duty is to enforce the Constitution, laws, and treaties of the United States, not to conform the law of the land to norms of customary international law. See U.S. Const. art. VI. As we said in Committee of U.S. Citizens Living in Nicaragua v. Reagan, 859 F.2d 929 (D.C. Cir. 1988): "Statutes inconsistent with principles of customary international law may well lead to international law violations. But within the domestic legal realm, that inconsistent statute simply modifies or supersedes customary international law to the extent of the inconsistency." Id. at 938. See also Federal Trade Comm'n v. Compagnie de Saint-Gobain-Pont-a-Mousson, 636 F.2d 1300, 1323 (D.C. Cir. 1980) (U.S. courts "obligated to give effect to an unambiguous exercise by Congress of its jurisdiction to prescribe even if such an exercise would exceed the limitations imposed by international law").

To be sure, courts should hesitate to give penal statutes extraterritorial effect absent a clear congressional directive. *See Foley Bros. v. Filardo*, 336 U.S. 281, 285 (1949). . . . Similarly, courts will not blind themselves to potential violations of international law where legislative intent is ambiguous. *See Murray v. The Schooner Charming Betsy*, 6 U.S. (2 Cranch) 64, 118, (1804) ("[A]n act of congress ought never to be construed to violate the law of nations, if any other possible construction remains. . . ."). But the statute in question reflects an unmistakable congressional intent, consistent with treaty obligations of the United States, to authorize prosecution of those who take Americans hostage abroad no matter where the offense occurs or where the offender is found. Our inquiry can go no further.

NOTES AND QUESTIONS

1. **The *Charming Betsy* Canon.** As described in *McCulloch*, the presumption against reading statutes to violate customary international law is associated with Chief Justice Marshall's opinion for the Supreme Court in *Murray v. The Schooner Charming Betsy*, 6 U.S. 64 (1804). The question in that case was whether a U.S. statute should extend to the trading activities of a Danish citizen in the Caribbean (and thus allow seizure of his ship, *The Charming Betsy*, for noncompliance). The Court held that, because such a regulation and seizure would violate the international law of jurisdiction (which would not allow U.S. regulation of a non-U.S. citizen outside the United States), the statute should not be read to cover the activity. Although there are indications that the presumption was a recognized canon of statutory interpretation before the *Charming Betsy* case, *e.g.*, *Talbot v. Seeman*, 5 U.S. 1 (1801), it has taken the name of its most famous enunciation — hence, the "Charming Betsy" canon.

    The *Restatement (Fourth)* states the canon as follows: "Where fairly possible, courts in the United States construe federal statutes to avoid conflict with international law governing jurisdiction to prescribe. If a federal statute cannot be so construed, the federal statute is controlling as a matter of federal law." RESTATEMENT (FOURTH) OF FOREIGN RELATIONS LAW § 406 (2018). The *Restatement's* predecessor, the *Restatement (Third)* (cited in *Yunis*), had a similar description of the canon.

2. **Policy: Should There Be a Presumption Against Violating International Law?** What is the rationale for the presumption against statutes violating international law? Is it a belief that Congress does not want to violate international law? Or that international law should not be violated? Or that courts should not violate international law? Should the courts apply this presumption? How is this presumption different than the presumption against extraterritoriality discussed above? Does it have the same goals? Implications

of the canon beyond the topic of prescriptive jurisdiction are discussed in Chapter 2.

3. **Congressional Violations of International Law.** As in *Yunis*, courts generally hold that Congress can legislate in violation of the international law of jurisdiction if it does so clearly. Was it clear in *Yunis*? Was it clear in *McCulloch*?

   The *Restatement (Fourth)* § 406, cmt. b, explains:

   > As a matter of federal law, Congress has authority to override international law governing jurisdiction to prescribe, although a self-executing provision of a later-in-time treaty would supersede an earlier statute. If Congress were to violate international law governing jurisdiction to prescribe, the United States would not be relieved of its obligations under international law or of the consequences of a violation of those obligations.

   Does that make sense? Why does Congress have power to violate international law? Should Congress have this power? Why isn't the correct conclusion that Congress is acting illegally? In such a case, should courts strike down a law as beyond Congress's powers? If not, what good is this presumption if in the end it does not constrain Congress?

4. **The Jones Act and International Law.** In *Lauritzen v. Larsen*, 345 U.S. 571 (1953), the Court considered the applicability of the Jones Act, a federal statute, to injuries suffered by a Danish seaman, employed on a Danish-flagged ship, in Cuban waters. The seaman had signed on as crew while in New York. The Jones Act stated that "[a]ny seaman who shall suffer personal injury in the course of his employment may, at his election, maintain an action for damages" in which U.S. law would apply. The Court acknowledged that the Act "makes no explicit requirement that either the seaman, the place of employment or the injury have the slightest connection with the United States." The Court nonetheless read the statute to conform to the choice of law rules of international maritime law, which (it said) turned on seven factors related to the extent of contacts with the relevant country, and concluded on the facts that the Jones Act should not apply. The seven factors were (1) the place of the wrongful act; (2) the law of the flag; (3) the allegiance or domicile of the injured; (4) the allegiance of the defendant shipowner; (5) the place of contract; (6) the inaccessibility of the foreign forum; and (7) the law of the forum. *Id.* at 583-90. Should the Court have used the presumption against extraterritoriality here? Should it have used that presumption in *McCulloch*? In *Yunis*?

5. **The Impact of International Law on National Law.** Note that through application of the *Charming Betsy* canon, international law can influence the interpretation of U.S. federal statutes. Chapter 2 explores the circumstances in which international law can have an even more direct impact in the U.S. legal system: the application of treaties and customary international law as rules of decision in U.S. courts.

3. *Extraterritorial Economic Regulation: The Example of Antitrust*

One field of U.S. federal law — antitrust law — has given rise to its own approach to extraterritoriality, one that has developed somewhat differently from the approach reflected in *Aramco* and *Morrison*. We therefore treat antitrust separately in this section. Antitrust law aims "to maximize consumer welfare by encouraging firms to behave competitively while yet permitting them to take advantage of every available economy that comes from internal or jointly created production efficiencies, or from innovation producing new processes or new or improved products." P.E. AREEDA & H. HOVENKAMP, ANTITRUST LAW: AN ANALYSIS OF ANTITRUST PRINCIPLES AND THEIR APPLICATION 4 (3d ed. 2006). The premise of antitrust policy is that "competition presses producers to satisfy customer wants at the lowest price while using the fewest resources." E. GELLHORN, W.E. KOVACIC & S. CALKINS, ANTITRUST LAW AND ECONOMICS 57 (5th ed. 2004). The primary U.S. antitrust rules are found in a variety of statutes, including the Sherman Act, 15 U.S.C. §§ 1-7. Section 1 of the Sherman Act prohibits "every contract, combination . . . or conspiracy in restraint of trade or commerce among the several states."* Section 2 provides that "[e]very person who shall monopolize, or attempt to monopolize, or combine or conspire with any other person or persons, to monopolize any part of the trade or commerce among the several States, or with foreign nations, shall be deemed guilty of a felony. . . ."

A challenge for national antitrust regulators is that while antitrust law is primarily national, markets are global. Anticompetitive behavior in one nation may have effects — such as price increases — in another nation. Regulators in one nation may therefore seek to apply its antitrust law to activity taking place in another nation's territory — but the other nation may not approve of this. For this reason, the extraterritorial application of antitrust law has been an especially contentious issue. As the cases below illustrate, the approach of U.S. courts regarding the extraterritorial reach of U.S. antitrust law has undergone considerable evolution, at various times applying a strong presumption against extraterritoriality and at other times allowing broad extraterritorial scope. Consider the text of §§ 1 and 2 of the Sherman Act above: Does the text indicate whether these sections of the Sherman Act should apply extraterritorially? And consider the broader question: Should the Sherman Act apply extraterritorially? Is antitrust unique or should it be a model for approaching extraterritoriality in other areas?

---

* The U.S. courts have held that certain practices are per se illegal under § 1, including price-fixing, bid-rigging, and customer and market allocations. Other restraints are assessed using a "rule of reason" to determine whether the practice's pro-competitive effects outweigh its anticompetitive effects. D. BRODER, U.S. ANTITRUST LAW AND ENFORCEMENT: A PRACTICE INTRODUCTION 17-18 (2d ed. 2011).

American Banana Company v. United Fruit Company

213 U.S. 347 (1909)

Mr. Justice HOLMES delivered the opinion of the court:

This is an action brought to recover threefold damages under the [Sherman Antitrust] [A]ct. The circuit court dismissed the complaint upon motion, as not setting forth a cause of action. This judgment was affirmed by the circuit court of appeals, and the case then was brought to this court by writ of error.

. . .

[Both plaintiff and defendant were U.S. corporations engaged in the banana trade. Plaintiff, who had purchased a fruit plantation in Panama, alleged that defendant had conspired with others in Panama, Costa Rica, and Colombia to drive plaintiff's plantation out of business, so that defendant could prevent competition and control and monopolize the banana trade. Plaintiff claimed that defendant thereby violated the Sherman Antitrust Act.]

. . .

It is obvious that, however stated, the plaintiff's case depends on several rather startling propositions. In the first place, the acts causing the damage were done, so far as appears, outside the jurisdiction of the United States, and within that of other states. It is surprising to hear it argued that they were governed by the act of Congress.

No doubt in regions subject to no sovereign, like the high seas, or to no law that civilized countries would recognize as adequate, such countries may treat some relations between their citizens as governed by their own law, and keep, to some extent, the old notion of personal sovereignty alive. They go further, at times, and declare that they will punish anyone, subject or not, who shall do certain things, if they can catch him, as in the case of pirates on the high seas. In cases immediately affecting national interests they may go further still and may make, and, if they get the chance, execute, similar threats as to acts done within another recognized jurisdiction. An illustration from our statutes is found with regard to criminal correspondence with foreign governments. And the notion that English statutes bind British subjects everywhere has found expression in modern times and has had some startling applications. But the general and almost universal rule is that the character of an act as lawful or unlawful must be determined wholly by the law of the country where the act is done. . . . For another jurisdiction, if it should happen to lay hold of the actor, to treat him according to its own notions rather than those of the place where he did the acts, not only would be unjust, but would be an interference with the authority of another sovereign, contrary to the comity of nations, which the other state concerned justly might resent. . . .

Law is a statement of the circumstances, in which the public force will be brought to bear upon men through the courts. But the word commonly is confined to such prophecies or threats when addressed to persons living within the power of the courts. A threat that depends upon the choice of the party affected to bring himself within that power hardly would be called law in the ordinary sense. . . .

The foregoing considerations would lead, in case of doubt, to a construction of any statute as intended to be confined in its operation and effect to the territorial limits over which the lawmaker has general and legitimate power. "All legislation is prima facie territorial." . . . Words having universal scope, such as "every contract in restraint of trade," "every person who shall monopolize," etc., will be taken, as a matter of course, to mean only everyone subject to such legislation, not all that the legislator subsequently may be able to catch. In the case of the present statute, the improbability of the United States attempting to make acts done in Panama or Costa Rica criminal is obvious, yet the law begins by making criminal the acts for which it gives a right to sue. We think it entirely plain that what the defendant did in Panama or Costa Rica is not within the scope of the statute so far as the present suit is concerned. Other objections of a serious nature are urged, but need not be discussed.

. . .

[N]ot only were the acts of the defendant in Panama or Costa Rica not within the Sherman act, but they were not torts by the law of the place, and therefore were not torts at all, however contrary to the ethical and economic postulates of that statute. . . .

. . .

Judgment affirmed.

Mr. Justice HARLAN concurs in the result.

NOTES AND QUESTIONS

1. **Practice: What's at Stake?** What was at stake for the litigants in *American Banana*? Specifically, why do you think the plaintiff wanted the Sherman Act to apply? Why do you think the defendant didn't want the Sherman Act to apply? What other law potentially could have applied? What was the likely impact of the Court's decision on the plaintiff's attempt to recover from the defendant? If you were the lawyer representing American Banana, what would you advise your client about its options in this dispute after the Court held that the Sherman Act did not apply?

2. **Practice: Litigation Strategy.** Why do you think the plaintiff sued the defendant in the United States? What other forums might have potentially been available, and why do you think the plaintiff didn't sue the defendant in such an alternative forum instead?

3. **Policy: Extraterritoriality and International Relations.** What implications, if any, might the Court's decision regarding the applicability of the Sherman Act have had on international relations — including relations between the United States and Costa Rica and Panama? What might the implications have been if the Court had held that the Sherman Act did apply?

4. **Customary International Law Bases for Prescriptive Jurisdiction.** What are the principles of prescriptive jurisdiction as described by the Court in

American Banana? Would the outcome of the case have been different if the Court had instead applied principles such as those stated in the *Restatement (Fourth) of Foreign Relations Law* (discussed in Section A.2 above)?

5. **Prescriptive Jurisdiction and Statutory Interpretation.** What canon of statutory interpretation did the Court announce in *American Banana*? What relationship do you think there is, if any, between this canon of construction and the Court's statement of the principles of prescriptive jurisdiction? To what extent is the Court's approach similar to the presumption against extraterritoriality (discussed in Section A.1 above)?

6. **Policy: Evaluating Strict Territoriality.** What policy reasons does the Court in *American Banana* give to support the rule that "the character of an act as lawful or unlawful must be determined wholly by the law of the country where the act is done"? Do you find these reasons convincing? Why or why not?

7. **The Evolution of Antitrust Extraterritoriality.** In the decades following the Court's decision in *American Banana*, the courts began applying the Sherman Act extraterritorially. In *United States v. Sisal Sales Corp.*, 274 U.S. 268 (1927), for example, the Court applied the Sherman Act to a conspiracy to monopolize the market for sisal (a plant used for fiber) in Mexico. Even though the sisal market was located entirely in Mexico and the monopolization was approved by the Mexican government, the Court unanimously found the situation "radically different" from *American Banana*: "Here we have a contract, combination and conspiracy entered into by parties within the United States and made effective by acts done therein. The fundamental object was control of both importation and sale of sisal and a complete monopoly of both internal and external trade and commerce therein." *Id.* at 276. In *United States v. Aluminum Co. of America (Alcoa)* (2d Cir. 1945), the U.S. Court of Appeals for the Second Circuit in an influential opinion by Judge Learned Hand applied the Sherman Act to extraterritorial activity by an international aluminum cartel. The court acknowledged that

> it is quite true that we are not to read general words, such as those in this Act, without regard to the limitations customarily observed by nations upon the exercise of their powers. . . . We should not impute to Congress an intent to punish all whom its courts can catch, for conduct which has no consequences within the United States [citing *American Banana*].

But, the court continued, "it is settled law . . . that any state may impose liabilities, even upon persons not within its allegiance, for conduct outside its borders that has consequences within its borders which the state reprehends." *Id.* at 443. On this basis, the Second Circuit stated what has become known as the "effects test": A U.S. federal statute may be applied to regulate a defendant's extraterritorial conduct if the defendant intended to cause an effect inside U.S. territory and the conduct in fact had such an effect. "Where both conditions are satisfied, the situation certainly falls within such decisions as [*Sisal Sales*]." *Id.* at 444. The Supreme Court thereafter adopted *Alcoa*'s effects test in a series of cases, notably *Continental Ore Co. v. Union Carbide*

& *Carbon Co.*, 370 U.S. 690 (1962). The extraterritorial application of the antitrust laws led to substantial friction with foreign governments, some of which were less concerned about the effects of monopolies than the United States. Both Britain and Australia, for example, enacted statutes directly limiting the enforcement of U.S. antitrust claims. Possibly in response, some U.S. federal courts began refining the effects test to limit its scope. For example, in another Sherman Act case, *Timberlane Lumber Co. v. Bank of America,* the U.S. Court of Appeals for the Ninth Circuit observed that "[t]he effects test by itself is incomplete because it fails to consider other nations' interests," and it adopted the following tripartite analysis incorporating a "jurisdictional rule of reason": "The problem should be addressed in three parts: Does the alleged restraint [on competition] affect, or was it intended to affect, the foreign commerce of the United States? Is it of such a type and magnitude so as to be cognizable as a violation of the Sherman Act? As a matter of international comity and fairness, should the extraterritorial jurisdiction of the United States be asserted to cover it?" 549 F.2d 597, 615 (9th Cir. 1976).

The question of limits on the antitrust laws' extraterritorial reach again came to the Supreme Court in the following cases: *Hartford Fire Ins. Co. v. California* and *F. Hoffmann-La Roche Ltd. v. Empagran S.A.* As you read these cases, keep in mind the following important point: In contrast to *American Banana* and consistent with the evolution of antitrust extraterritoriality discussed in the notes above, courts now take as a given that the Sherman Act can apply extraterritorially. The problem faced by the Supreme Court in the cases that follow is therefore not whether the presumption against extraterritoriality has been overcome, but instead what limits on extraterritorial application exist even though that presumption has been overcome. Has the Supreme Court answered this question consistently?

Hartford Fire Insurance Co. v. California

509 U.S. 764 (1993)

Justice SOUTER announced the judgment of the Court and delivered the opinion of the Court with respect to Parts I, II-A, III, and IV. . . .

The Sherman Act makes every contract, combination, or conspiracy in unreasonable restraint of interstate or foreign commerce illegal. 26 Stat. 209, as amended, 15 U.S.C. § 1. These consolidated cases present questions about the application of that Act to the insurance industry, both here and abroad. The plaintiffs (respondents here) allege that both domestic and foreign defendants (petitioners here) violated the Sherman Act by engaging in various conspiracies to affect the American insurance market. . . . [A] group of foreign defendants argues that the principle of international comity requires the District Court to refrain from exercising jurisdiction over certain claims against it. We hold . . . that, even assuming it applies, the principle of international comity does not preclude District Court jurisdiction over the foreign conduct alleged.

I

The two petitions before us stem from consolidated litigation comprising the complaints of 19 States and many private plaintiffs alleging that the defendants, members of the insurance industry, conspired in violation of § 1 of the Sherman Act to restrict the terms of coverage of commercial general liability (CGL) insurance[1] available in the United States. Because the cases come to us on motions to dismiss, we take the allegations of the complaints as true.

A

According to the complaints, the object of the conspiracies was to force certain primary insurers (insurers who sell insurance directly to consumers) to change the terms of their standard CGL insurance policies to conform with the policies the defendant insurers wanted to sell. . . .

[P]rimary insurers themselves usually purchase insurance to cover a portion of the risk they assume from the consumer. This so-called "reinsurance" may serve at least two purposes, protecting the primary insurer from catastrophic loss, and allowing the primary insurer to sell more insurance than its own financial capacity might otherwise permit. Thus, "[t]he availability of reinsurance affects the ability and willingness of primary insurers to provide insurance to their customers." Insurers who sell reinsurance themselves often purchase insurance to cover part of the risk they assume from the primary insurer; such "retrocessional reinsurance" does for reinsurers what reinsurance does for primary insurers. Many of the defendants here are reinsurers or reinsurance brokers, or play some other specialized role in the reinsurance business; defendant Reinsurance Association of America (RAA) is a trade association of domestic reinsurers.

. . .

C

Nineteen States and a number of private plaintiffs filed 36 complaints against the insurers involved in this course of events, charging that the conspiracies described above violated § 1 of the Sherman Act, 15 U.S.C. § 1. After the actions had been consolidated for litigation in the Northern District of California, the defendants moved to dismiss for failure to state a cause of action, or, in the alternative, for summary judgment. The District Court . . . dismissed the three claims that named only certain London-based defendants, invoking international comity and applying the Ninth Circuit's decision in *Timberlane Lumber Co. v. Bank of America, N.T. & S.A.*, 549 F.2d 597 (1976).

The Court of Appeals reversed. . . . [A]s to the three claims brought solely against foreign defendants, the court applied its Timberlane analysis, but

---

1. CGL insurance provides "coverage for third party casualty damage claims against a purchaser of insurance (the 'insured')."

concluded that the principle of international comity was no bar to exercising Sherman Act jurisdiction.

We granted certiorari . . . to address the application of the Sherman Act to the foreign conduct at issue. We now affirm [as to the extraterritorial claims]. . . .

. . .

III

[W]e [now] take up the question . . . whether certain claims against the London reinsurers should have been dismissed as improper applications of the Sherman Act to foreign conduct. The Fifth Claim for Relief in the California Complaint alleges a violation of § 1 of the Sherman Act by certain London reinsurers who conspired to coerce primary insurers in the United States to offer CGL coverage on a claims-made basis, thereby making "occurrence CGL coverage . . . unavailable in the State of California for many risks." The Sixth Claim for Relief in the California Complaint alleges that the London reinsurers violated § 1 by a conspiracy to limit coverage of pollution risks in North America, thereby rendering "pollution liability coverage . . . almost entirely unavailable for the vast majority of casualty insurance purchasers in the State of California." The Eighth Claim for Relief in the California Complaint alleges a further § 1 violation by the London reinsurers who, along with domestic retrocessional reinsurers, conspired to limit coverage of seepage, pollution, and property contamination risks in North America, thereby eliminating such coverage in the State of California.

At the outset, we note that the District Court undoubtedly had jurisdiction of these Sherman Act claims, as the London reinsurers apparently concede. Although the proposition was perhaps not always free from doubt, see *American Banana Co. v. United Fruit Co.*, 213 U.S. 347 (1909), it is well established by now that the Sherman Act applies to foreign conduct that was meant to produce and did in fact produce some substantial effect in the United States. See *Matsushita Elec. Industrial Co. v. Zenith Radio Corp.*, 475 U.S. 574, 582, n. 6 (1986); *United States v. Aluminum Co. of America*, 148 F.2d 416, 444 (CA2 1945) (L. Hand, J.). Such is the conduct alleged here: that the London reinsurers engaged in unlawful conspiracies to affect the market for insurance in the United States and that their conduct in fact produced substantial effect.

According to the London reinsurers, the District Court should have declined to exercise such jurisdiction under the principle of international comity.[24] The Court of Appeals agreed that courts should look to that principle in deciding whether to exercise jurisdiction under the Sherman Act. This availed the London reinsurers nothing, however. To be sure, the Court of Appeals believed that

---

24. Justice Scalia contends that comity concerns figure into the prior analysis whether jurisdiction exists under the Sherman Act. . . . This contention is inconsistent with the general understanding that the Sherman Act covers foreign conduct producing a substantial intended effect in the United States, and that concerns of comity come into play, if at all, only after a court has determined that the acts complained of are subject to Sherman Act jurisdiction. . . . In any event, the parties conceded jurisdiction at oral argument . . . and we see no need to address this contention here.

"application of [U.S.] antitrust laws to the London reinsurance market 'would lead to significant conflict with English law and policy,'" and that "[s]uch a conflict, unless outweighed by other factors, would by itself be reason to decline exercise of jurisdiction." But other factors, in the court's view, including the London reinsurers' express purpose to affect United States commerce and the substantial nature of the effect produced, outweighed the supposed conflict and required the exercise of jurisdiction in this litigation.

[E]ven assuming that in a proper case a court may decline to exercise Sherman Act jurisdiction over foreign conduct (or, as Justice Scalia would put it, may conclude by the employment of comity analysis in the first instance that there is no jurisdiction), international comity would not counsel against exercising jurisdiction in the circumstances alleged here.

The only substantial question in this litigation is whether "there is in fact a true conflict between domestic and foreign law." The London reinsurers contend that applying the Act to their conduct would conflict significantly with British law, and the British Government, appearing before us as amicus curiae, concurs. They assert that Parliament has established a comprehensive regulatory regime over the London reinsurance market and that the conduct alleged here was perfectly consistent with British law and policy. But this is not to state a conflict. "[T]he fact that conduct is lawful in the state in which it took place will not, of itself, bar application of the United States antitrust laws," even where the foreign state has a strong policy to permit or encourage such conduct. RESTATEMENT (THIRD) FOREIGN RELATIONS LAW § 415, Comment j; see *Continental Ore Co., supra*, 370 U.S., at 706-707. . . . No conflict exists, for these purposes, "where a person subject to regulation by two states can comply with the laws of both." RESTATEMENT (THIRD) FOREIGN RELATIONS LAW § 403, Comment e. Since the London reinsurers do not argue that British law requires them to act in some fashion prohibited by the law of the United States, or claim that their compliance with the laws of both countries is otherwise impossible, we see no conflict with British law. We have no need in this litigation to address other considerations that might inform a decision to refrain from the exercise of jurisdiction on grounds of international comity.

IV

The judgment of the Court of Appeals is affirmed [as to the extraterritoriality issue]. . . .

It is so ordered.

Justice SCALIA [joined by Justices O'CONNOR, KENNEDY, and THOMAS]. . . .

I dissent from the Court's ruling concerning the extraterritorial application of the Sherman Act. . . .

II

Petitioners . . . , various British corporations and other British subjects, argue that certain of the claims against them constitute an inappropriate extraterritorial application of the Sherman Act. It is important to distinguish two distinct questions raised by this petition: whether the District Court had jurisdiction, and whether the Sherman Act reaches the extraterritorial conduct alleged here. On the first question, I believe that the District Court had subject-matter jurisdiction over the Sherman Act claims against all the defendants (personal jurisdiction is not contested). Respondents asserted nonfrivolous claims under the Sherman Act, and 28 U.S.C. § 1331 vests district courts with subject-matter jurisdiction over cases "arising under" federal statutes. . . . [T]hat is sufficient to establish the District Court's jurisdiction over these claims. . . .

The second question — the extraterritorial reach of the Sherman Act — has nothing to do with the jurisdiction of the courts. It is a question of substantive law turning on whether, in enacting the Sherman Act, Congress asserted regulatory power over the challenged conduct. If a plaintiff fails to prevail on this issue, the court does not dismiss the claim for want of subject-matter jurisdiction — want of power to adjudicate; rather, it decides the claim, ruling on the merits that the plaintiff has failed to state a cause of action under the relevant statute.

There is, however, a type of "jurisdiction" relevant to determining the extraterritorial reach of a statute; it is known as "legislative jurisdiction," or "jurisdiction to prescribe," 1 RESTATEMENT (THIRD) OF FOREIGN RELATIONS LAW OF THE UNITED STATES 235 (1987) (hereinafter RESTATEMENT (THIRD)). This refers to "the authority of a state to make its law applicable to persons or activities," and is quite a separate matter from "jurisdiction to adjudicate," see id., at 231. There is no doubt, of course, that Congress possesses legislative jurisdiction over the acts alleged in this complaint: Congress has broad power under Article I, § 8, cl. 3, "[t]o regulate Commerce with foreign Nations," and this Court has repeatedly upheld its power to make laws applicable to persons or activities beyond our territorial boundaries where United States interests are affected. But the question in this litigation is whether, and to what extent, Congress has exercised that undoubted legislative jurisdiction in enacting the Sherman Act.

Two canons of statutory construction are relevant in this inquiry. The first is the "longstanding principle of American law 'that legislation of Congress, unless a contrary intent appears, is meant to apply only within the territorial jurisdiction of the United States.'" Aramco, supra, 499 U.S., at 248 (quoting Foley Bros., Inc. v. Filardo, 336 U.S. 281, 285 (1949)). Applying that canon in Aramco, we held that the version of Title VII of the Civil Rights Act of 1964 then in force did not extend outside the territory of the United States even though the statute contained broad provisions extending its prohibitions to, for example, "'any activity, business, or industry in commerce.'" We held such "boilerplate language" to be an insufficient indication to override the presumption against extraterritoriality. The Sherman Act contains similar "boilerplate language," and if the question were not governed by precedent, it would be worth considering whether that presumption controls the outcome here. We have, however, found the presumption to be overcome with respect to our antitrust laws; it is now well established that the Sherman Act applies extraterritorially.

But if the presumption against extraterritoriality has been overcome or is otherwise inapplicable, a second canon of statutory construction becomes relevant: "[A]n act of congress ought never to be construed to violate the law of nations if any other possible construction remains." *Murray v. Schooner Charming Betsy*, 2 Cranch 64, 118 (1804) (Marshall, C.J.). This canon is "wholly independent" of the presumption against extraterritoriality. *Aramco*, 499 U.S., at 264. . . . It is relevant to determining the substantive reach of a statute because " the law of nations," or customary international law, includes limitations on a nation's exercise of its jurisdiction to prescribe. See RESTATEMENT (THIRD) §§ 401-416. Though it clearly has constitutional authority to do so, Congress is generally presumed not to have exceeded those customary international-law limits on jurisdiction to prescribe.

Consistent with that presumption, this and other courts have frequently recognized that, even where the presumption against extraterritoriality does not apply, statutes should not be interpreted to regulate foreign persons or conduct if that regulation would conflict with principles of international law. For example, in *Romero v. International Terminal Operating Co.*, 358 U.S. 354 (1959), the plaintiff, a Spanish sailor who had been injured while working aboard a Spanish-flag and Spanish-owned vessel, filed a Jones Act claim against his Spanish employer. The presumption against extraterritorial application of federal statutes was inapplicable to the case, as the actionable tort had occurred in American waters. See *id.*, at 383. The Court nonetheless stated that, "in the absence of a contrary congressional direction," it would apply "principles of choice of law that are consonant with the needs of a general federal maritime law and with due recognition of our self-regarding respect for the relevant interests of foreign nations in the regulation of maritime commerce as part of the legitimate concern of the international community." *Id.*, at 382-383. "The controlling considerations" in this choice-of-law analysis were "the interacting interests of the United States and of foreign countries." *Id.*, at 383.

Romero referred to, and followed, the choice-of-law analysis set forth in *Lauritzen v. Larsen*, 345 U.S. 571 (1953). . . . *Lauritzen* also involved a Jones Act claim brought by a foreign sailor against a foreign employer. The *Lauritzen* Court recognized the basic problem: "If [the Jones Act were] read literally, Congress has conferred an American right of action which requires nothing more than that plaintiff be 'any seaman who shall suffer personal injury in the course of his employment.'" *Id.*, at 576. The solution it adopted was to construe the statute "to apply only to areas and transactions in which American law would be considered operative under prevalent doctrines of international law." *Id.*, at 577 (emphasis added). To support application of international law to limit the facial breadth of the statute, the Court relied upon — of course — Chief Justice Marshall's statement in *Schooner Charming Betsy*. It then set forth "several factors which, alone or in combination, are generally conceded to influence choice of law to govern a tort claim." 345 U.S., at 583; see *id.*, at 583-593 (discussing factors). See also *McCulloch v. Sociedad Nacional de Marineros de Honduras*, 372 U.S. 10, 21-22 (1963) (applying *Schooner Charming Betsy* principle to restrict application of National Labor Relations Act to foreign-flag vessels).

Lauritzen, *Romero*, and *McCulloch* were maritime cases, but we have recognized the principle that the scope of generally worded statutes must be construed in light of international law in other areas as well. More specifically, the principle was expressed in *United States v. Aluminum Co. of America*, 148 F.2d 416 (CA2 1945), the decision that established the extraterritorial reach of the Sherman Act. In his opinion for the court, Judge Learned Hand cautioned "we are not to read general words, such as those in [the Sherman] Act, without regard to the limitations customarily observed by nations upon the exercise of their powers; limitations which generally correspond to those fixed by the 'Conflict of Laws.'" *Id.*, at 443.

More recent lower court precedent has also tempered the extraterritorial application of the Sherman Act with considerations of "international comity." The "comity" they refer to is not the comity of courts, whereby judges decline to exercise jurisdiction over matters more appropriately adjudged elsewhere, but rather what might be termed "prescriptive comity": the respect sovereign nations afford each other by limiting the reach of their laws. That comity is exercised by legislatures when they enact laws, and courts assume it has been exercised when they come to interpreting the scope of laws their legislatures have enacted. It is a traditional component of choice-of-law theory. See J. Story, Commentaries on the Conflict of Laws § 38 (1834) (distinguishing between the "comity of the courts" and the "comity of nations," and defining the latter as "the true foundation and extent of the obligation of the laws of one nation within the territories of another"). Comity in this sense includes the choice-of-law principles that, "in the absence of contrary congressional direction," are assumed to be incorporated into our substantive laws having extraterritorial reach. *Romero, supra,* 358 U.S., at 382-383; *see also Lauritzen, supra,* 345 U.S., at 578-579. . . . Considering comity in this way is just part of determining whether the Sherman Act prohibits the conduct at issue.

In sum, the practice of using international law to limit the extraterritorial reach of statutes is firmly established in our jurisprudence. In proceeding to apply that practice to the present cases, I shall rely on the Restatement (Third) for the relevant principles of international law. Its standards appear fairly supported in the decisions of this Court construing international choice-of-law principles (*Lauritzen, Romero,* and *McCulloch*) and in the decisions of other federal courts, especially *Timberlane*. Whether the Restatement precisely reflects international law in every detail matters little here, as I believe this litigation would be resolved the same way under virtually any conceivable test that takes account of foreign regulatory interests.

Under the Restatement, a nation having some "basis" for jurisdiction to prescribe law should nonetheless refrain from exercising that jurisdiction "with respect to a person or activity having connections with another state when the exercise of such jurisdiction is unreasonable." Restatement (Third) § 403(1). The "reasonableness" inquiry turns on a number of factors including, but not limited to: "the extent to which the activity takes place within the territory [of the regulating state]," *id.*, § 403(2)(a); "the connections, such as nationality, residence, or economic activity, between the regulating state and the person principally responsible for the activity to be regulated," *id.*, § 403(2)(b); "the character of the activity to be regulated, the importance of regulation to the regulating state, the extent to which other states regulate such activities, and the degree to which the desirability of such regulation is generally accepted," *id.*, § 403(2)(c); "the extent to which another state may have an interest in regulating the activity," *id.*, § 403(2)(g); and "the likelihood of conflict with regulation by another state," *id.*, § 403(2)(h). Rarely would these factors point more clearly against application of United States law. The activity relevant to the counts at issue here took place primarily in the United Kingdom, and the defendants in these counts are British corporations and British subjects having their principal place of business or residence outside the United States. Great Britain has established a comprehensive regulatory scheme governing the London reinsurance markets, and clearly has a heavy "interest in regulating the activity," *id.*, § 403(2)(g). Finally, § 2(b) of the McCarran-Ferguson Act allows state regulatory statutes to override the Sherman Act in the insurance field, subject only to the narrow "boycott" exception set forth in § 3(b) — suggesting that "the importance of regulation to the [United States]," Restatement (Third) § 403(2)(c), is slight. Considering these factors, I think it unimaginable that an assertion of legislative jurisdiction by the United States would be considered reasonable, and therefore it is inappropriate to assume, in the absence of statutory indication to the contrary, that Congress has made such an assertion.

It is evident from what I have said that the Court's comity analysis, which proceeds as though the issue is whether the courts should "decline to exercise . . . jurisdiction," rather than whether the Sherman Act covers this conduct, is simply misdirected. . . . [I]f one erroneously chooses, as the Court does, to make adjudicative jurisdiction (or, more precisely, abstention) the vehicle for taking account of the needs of prescriptive comity, the Court still gets it wrong. It concludes that no "true conflict" counseling nonapplication of United States law (or rather, as it thinks, United States judicial jurisdiction) exists unless compliance with United States law would constitute a violation of another country's law. That breathtakingly broad proposition, which contradicts the many cases discussed earlier, will bring the Sherman Act and other laws into sharp and unnecessary conflict with the legitimate interests of other countries — particularly our closest trading partners.

In the sense in which the term "conflic[t]" was used in *Lauritzen*, 345 U.S., at 582, and is generally understood in the field of conflicts of laws, there is clearly a conflict in this litigation. The petitioners here, like the defendant in *Lauritzen*, were not compelled by any foreign law to take their allegedly wrongful actions, but that no more precludes a conflict-of-laws analysis here than it did there. See *id.*, at 575-576 (detailing the differences between foreign and United States law). Where applicable foreign and domestic law provide different substantive rules of decision to govern the parties' dispute, a conflict-of-laws analysis is necessary.

. . .

I would reverse the judgment of the Court of Appeals on this issue, and remand to the District Court with instructions to dismiss for failure to state a claim. . . .

1. **The Sherman Act's Extraterritorial Reach.** According to the Court in *Hartford*, under what circumstances does the Sherman Act apply to foreign conduct? What customary international law principles of prescriptive jurisdiction might provide a basis for applying the Sherman Act in those circumstances?

2. **The Principle of Comity.** In *Hartford*, what does the Court mean by "the principle of international comity"? According to the Court, assuming that a court may in a proper case decline to exercise jurisdiction on international comity grounds, under what circumstances does this principle "counsel against exercising jurisdiction"? Why did the Court conclude that the principle of international comity would not counsel against exercising jurisdiction in this case? What type of jurisdiction is the Court referring to in its discussion of comity? Prescriptive jurisdiction? Some other type of jurisdiction? How does Justice Scalia's understanding of comity, expressed in his dissenting opinion, differ from that expressed in Justice Souter's majority opinion? Who do you think has the better understanding?

3. **Justice Scalia's Dissent.** In his *Hartford* dissent, Justice Scalia concedes that "it is now well established that the Sherman Act applies extraterritorially." Why, then, does he conclude that it doesn't apply in this case?

4. **The Relationship Between the Presumption Against Extraterritoriality and the Presumption Against Violating International Law.** In his *Hartford* dissent, Justice Scalia identifies two canons of statutory interpretation that are relevant to inquiries about the extraterritorial application of a U.S. federal statute: the presumption against extraterritoriality (discussed in Section A.1 above) and the *Charming Betsy* canon (the presumption against violating international law, discussed in Section A.2 above). Why do you think Justice Scalia believes it is necessary to apply the second canon if the presumption against extraterritoriality is overcome or does not apply? Are the two canons redundant or different?

5. **The Sherman Act and Customary International Law Bases for Prescriptive Jurisdiction.** In *Hartford*, the facts alleged by the plaintiffs indicated that the defendants' conduct "was meant to produce and did in fact produce some substantial effect in the United States." According to Justice Scalia, why aren't these facts sufficient for establishing prescriptive jurisdiction under the customary international law principles of prescriptive jurisdiction contained in the *Restatement (Third) of Foreign Relations*? Do you agree with his analysis?

F. Hoffmann-La Roche Ltd. v. Empagran S.A.

542 U.S. 155 (2004)

Justice BREYER delivered the opinion of the Court.

The Foreign Trade Antitrust Improvements Act of 1982 (FTAIA) excludes from the Sherman Act's reach much anticompetitive conduct that causes only foreign injury. It does so by setting forth a general rule stating that the Sherman Act "shall not apply to conduct involving trade or commerce . . . with foreign nations." 96 Stat. 1246, 15 U.S.C. § 6a. It then creates exceptions to the general rule, applicable where (roughly speaking) that conduct significantly harms imports, domestic commerce, or American exporters.

We here focus upon anticompetitive price-fixing activity that is in significant part foreign, that causes some domestic antitrust injury, and that independently causes separate foreign injury. We ask two questions about the price-fixing conduct and the foreign injury that it causes. First, does that conduct fall within the FTAIA's general rule excluding the Sherman Act's application? That is to say, does the price-fixing activity constitute "conduct involving trade or commerce . . . with foreign nations"? We conclude that it does.

Second, we ask whether the conduct nonetheless falls within a domestic-injury exception to the general rule, an exception that applies (and makes the Sherman Act nonetheless applicable) where the conduct (1) has a "direct, substantial, and reasonably foreseeable effect" on domestic commerce, and (2) "such effect gives rise to a [Sherman Act] claim." §§ 6a(1)(A), (2). We conclude that the exception does not apply where the plaintiff's claim rests solely on the independent foreign harm.

To clarify: The issue before us concerns (1) significant foreign anticompetitive conduct with (2) an adverse domestic effect and (3) an independent foreign effect giving rise to the claim. In more concrete terms, this case involves vitamin sellers around the world that agreed to fix prices, leading to higher vitamin prices in the United States and independently leading to higher vitamin prices in other countries such as Ecuador. We conclude that, in this scenario, a purchaser in the United States could bring a Sherman Act claim under the FTAIA based on domestic injury, but a purchaser in Ecuador could not bring a Sherman Act claim based on foreign harm.

I

The plaintiffs in this case originally filed a class-action suit on behalf of foreign and domestic purchasers of vitamins under, inter alia, § 1 of the Sherman Act, 26 Stat. 209, as amended, 15 U.S.C. § 1, and §§ 4 and 16 of the Clayton Act, 38 Stat. 731, 737, as amended, 15 U.S.C. §§ 15, 26. Their complaint alleged that petitioners, foreign and domestic vitamin manufacturers and distributors, had engaged in a price-fixing conspiracy, raising the price of vitamin products to customers in the United States and to customers in foreign countries.

As relevant here, petitioners moved to dismiss the suit as to the foreign purchasers (the respondents here), five foreign vitamin distributors located in Ukraine, Australia, Ecuador, and Panama, each of which bought vitamins from petitioners for delivery outside the United States. Respondents have never asserted that they purchased any vitamins in the United States or in transactions in United States commerce, and the question presented assumes that the relevant "transactions occurr[ed] entirely outside U.S. commerce." The District Court dismissed their claims. . . .

A divided panel of the Court of Appeals reversed. The panel concluded that the FTAIA's general exclusionary rule applied to the case, but that its domestic-injury exception also applied. It basically read the plaintiffs' complaint to allege that the vitamin manufacturers' price-fixing conspiracy (1) had "a direct, substantial, and reasonably foreseeable effect" on ordinary domestic trade or commerce, i.e., the conspiracy brought about higher domestic vitamin prices, and (2) "such effect" gave "rise to a [Sherman Act] claim," i.e., an injured domestic customer could have brought a Sherman Act suit, 15 U.S.C. §§ 6a(1), (2). Those allegations, the court held, are sufficient to meet the exception's requirements.

The court assumed that the foreign effect, i.e., higher prices in Ukraine, Panama, Australia, and Ecuador, was independent of the domestic effect, i.e., higher domestic prices. But it concluded that, in light of the FTAIA's text, legislative history, and the policy goal of deterring harmful price-fixing activity, this lack of connection does not matter. The District of Columbia Circuit denied rehearing en banc by a 4-to-3 vote.

We granted certiorari to resolve a split among the Courts of Appeals about the exception's application. . . .

IV

We turn now to the basic question presented, that of the exception's application. Because the underlying antitrust action is complex, potentially raising questions not directly at issue here, we reemphasize that we base our decision upon the following: The price-fixing conduct significantly and adversely affects both customers outside the United States and customers within the United States, but the adverse foreign effect is independent of any adverse domestic effect. In these circumstances, we find that the FTAIA exception does not apply (and thus the Sherman Act does not apply) for two main reasons.

First, this Court ordinarily construes ambiguous statutes to avoid unreasonable interference with the sovereign authority of other nations. See, *e.g.*, *McCulloch v. Sociedad Nacional de Marineros de Honduras*, 372 U.S. 10, 20-22 (1963) (application of National Labor Relations Act to foreign-flag vessels); *Romero v. International Terminal Operating Co.*, 358 U.S. 354, 382-383 (1959) (application of Jones Act in maritime case); *Lauritzen v. Larsen*, 345 U.S. 571, 578 (1953) (same). This rule of construction reflects principles of customary international law — law that (we must assume) Congress ordinarily seeks to follow. See Restatement (Third) of Foreign Relations Law of the United States §§ 403(1), 403(2) (1986) (hereinafter Restatement) (limiting the unreasonable exercise of prescriptive jurisdiction with respect to a person or activity having connections with another State); *Murray v. Schooner Charming Betsy*, 2 Cranch 64, 118 (1804) ("[A]n act of congress ought never to be construed to violate the law of nations if any other possible construction remains"); *Hartford Fire Ins. Co. v. California*, 509 U.S. 764, 817 (1993) (Scalia, J., dissenting) (identifying rule of construction as derived from the principle of "'prescriptive comity'").

This rule of statutory construction cautions courts to assume that legislators take account of the legitimate sovereign interests of other nations when they write American laws. It thereby helps the potentially conflicting laws of different nations work together in harmony — a harmony particularly needed in today's highly interdependent commercial world.

No one denies that America's antitrust laws, when applied to foreign conduct, can interfere with a foreign nation's ability independently to regulate its own commercial affairs. But our courts have long held that application of our antitrust laws to foreign anticompetitive conduct is nonetheless reasonable, and hence consistent with principles of prescriptive comity, insofar as they reflect a legislative effort to redress domestic antitrust injury that foreign anticompetitive conduct has caused.

But why is it reasonable to apply those laws to foreign conduct insofar as that conduct causes independent foreign harm and that foreign harm alone gives rise to the plaintiff's claim? Like the former case, application of those laws creates a serious risk of interference with a foreign nation's ability independently to regulate its own commercial affairs. But, unlike the former case, the justification for that interference seems insubstantial. See *Restatement* § 403(2) (determining reasonableness on basis of such factors as connections with regulating nation, harm to that nation's interests, extent to which other nations regulate, and the potential for conflict). Why should American law supplant, for example, Canada's or Great Britain's or Japan's own determination about how best to protect Canadian or British or Japanese customers from anticompetitive conduct engaged in significant part by Canadian or British or Japanese or other foreign companies?

We recognize that principles of comity provide Congress greater leeway when it seeks to control through legislation the actions of American companies, see *Restatement* § 402; and some of the anticompetitive price-fixing conduct alleged here took place in America. But the higher foreign prices of which the foreign plaintiffs here complain are not the consequence of any domestic anticompetitive conduct that Congress sought to forbid, for Congress did not seek to forbid any such conduct insofar as it is here relevant, i.e., insofar as it is intertwined with foreign conduct that causes independent foreign harm. Rather Congress sought to release domestic (and foreign) anticompetitive conduct from Sherman Act constraints when that conduct causes foreign harm. Congress, of course, did make an exception where that conduct also causes domestic harm. See House Report, at 13, U.S. Code Cong. & Admin. News 1982, 2487, 2498 (concerns about American firms' participation in international cartels addressed through "domestic injury" exception). But any independent domestic harm the foreign conduct causes here has, by definition, little or nothing to do with the matter.

We thus repeat the basic question: Why is it reasonable to apply this law to conduct that is significantly foreign insofar as that conduct causes independent foreign harm and that foreign harm alone gives rise to the plaintiff's claim? We can find no good answer to the question.

. . .

Respondents reply that many nations have adopted antitrust laws similar to our own, to the point where the practical likelihood of interference with the relevant interests of other nations is minimal. Leaving price fixing to the side, however, this Court has found to the contrary. See, *e.g., Hartford Fire*, 509 U.S., at 797-799 (noting that the alleged conduct in the London reinsurance market, while illegal under United States antitrust laws, was assumed to be perfectly consistent with British law and policy). . . .

Regardless, even where nations agree about primary conduct, say, price fixing, they disagree dramatically about appropriate remedies. The application, for example, of American private treble-damages remedies to anticompetitive conduct taking place abroad has generated considerable controversy. And several foreign nations have filed briefs here arguing that to apply our remedies would unjustifiably permit their citizens to bypass their own less generous remedial schemes, thereby upsetting a balance of competing considerations that their own domestic antitrust laws embody. *E.g.*, Brief for Government of Federal Republic of Germany et al. as Amici Curiae 2 (setting forth German interest "in seeing that German companies are not subject to the extraterritorial reach of the United States' antitrust laws by private foreign plaintiffs — whose injuries were sustained in transactions entirely outside United States commerce — seeking treble damages in private lawsuits against German companies"); Brief for Government of Canada as Amicus Curiae 14 ("treble damages remedy would supersede" Canada's "national policy decision"); Brief for Government of Japan as Amicus Curiae 10 (finding "particularly troublesome" the potential "interfere[nce] with Japanese governmental regulation of the Japanese market").

These briefs add that a decision permitting independently injured foreign plaintiffs to pursue private treble-damages remedies would undermine foreign nations' own antitrust enforcement policies by diminishing foreign firms' incentive to cooperate with antitrust authorities in return for prosecutorial amnesty.

Respondents alternatively argue that comity does not demand an interpretation of the FTAIA that would exclude independent foreign injury cases across the board. Rather, courts can take (and sometimes have taken) account of comity considerations case by case, abstaining where comity considerations so dictate. Cf., *e.g.*, *Hartford Fire, supra*, at 797, n.24.

In our view, however, this approach is too complex to prove workable. The Sherman Act covers many different kinds of anticompetitive agreements. Courts would have to examine how foreign law, compared with American law, treats not only price fixing but also, say, information-sharing agreements, patent-licensing price conditions, territorial product resale limitations, and various forms of joint venture, in respect to both primary conduct and remedy. The legally and economically technical nature of that enterprise means lengthier proceedings, appeals, and more proceedings — to the point where procedural costs and delays could themselves threaten interference with a foreign nation's ability to maintain the integrity of its own antitrust enforcement system. Even in this relatively simple price-fixing case, for example, competing briefs tell us (1) that potential treble-damages liability would help enforce widespread anti-price-fixing norms (through added deterrence) and (2) the opposite, namely, that such liability would hinder antitrust enforcement (by reducing incentives to enter amnesty programs). How could a court seriously interested in resolving so empirical a matter — a matter potentially related to impact on foreign interests — do so simply and expeditiously?

We conclude that principles of prescriptive comity counsel against the Court of Appeals' interpretation of the FTAIA. Where foreign anticompetitive conduct plays a significant role and where foreign injury is independent of domestic effects, Congress might have hoped that America's antitrust laws, so fundamental a component of our own economic system, would commend themselves to other nations as well. But, if America's antitrust policies could not win their own way in the international marketplace for such ideas, Congress, we must assume, would not have tried to impose them, in an act of legal imperialism, through legislative fiat.

Second, the FTAIA's language and history suggest that Congress designed the FTAIA to clarify, perhaps to limit, but not to expand in any significant way, the Sherman Act's scope as applied to foreign commerce. See House Report, at 2-3, U.S. Code Cong. & Admin. News 1982, 2487, 2487-2488. And we have found no significant indication that at the time Congress wrote this statute courts would have thought the Sherman Act applicable in these circumstances.

. . .

Taken together, these two sets of considerations, the one derived from comity and the other reflecting history, convince us that Congress would not have intended the FTAIA's exception to bring independently caused foreign injury within the Sherman Act's reach.

V

[R]espondents point to policy considerations, namely, that application of the Sherman Act in present circumstances will (through increased deterrence) help protect Americans against foreign-caused anticompetitive injury. Petitioners, however, have made important experience-backed arguments (based upon amnesty-seeking incentives) to the contrary. We cannot say whether, on balance, respondents' side of this empirically based argument or the enforcement agencies' side is correct. But we can say that the answer to the dispute is neither clear enough, nor of such likely empirical significance, that it could overcome the considerations we have previously discussed and change our conclusion.

For these reasons, we conclude that petitioners' reading of the statute's language is correct. That reading furthers the statute's basic purposes, it properly reflects considerations of comity, and it is consistent with Sherman Act history.

VI

We have assumed that the anticompetitive conduct here independently caused foreign injury; that is, the conduct's domestic effects did not help to bring about that foreign injury. Respondents argue, in the alternative, that the foreign injury was not independent. Rather, they say, the anticompetitive conduct's domestic effects were linked to that foreign harm. Respondents contend that, because vitamins are fungible and readily transportable, without an adverse domestic effect (i.e., higher prices in the United States), the sellers could not have maintained their international price-fixing arrangement and respondents would not have suffered their foreign injury. They add that this "but for" condition is sufficient to bring the price-fixing conduct within the scope of the FTAIA's exception.

The Court of Appeals, however, did not address this argument, and, for that reason, neither shall we. Respondents remain free to ask the Court of Appeals to consider the claim. The Court of Appeals may determine whether respondents properly preserved the argument, and, if so, it may consider it and decide the related claim.

For these reasons, the judgment of the Court of Appeals is vacated, and the case is remanded for further proceedings consistent with this opinion.

It is so ordered.

Justice O'CONNOR took no part in the consideration or decision of this case.

Justice SCALIA, with whom Justice THOMAS joins, concurring in the judgment.

I concur in the judgment of the Court because the language of the statute is readily susceptible of the interpretation the Court provides and because only that interpretation is consistent with the principle that statutes should be read in accord with the customary deference to the application of foreign countries' laws within their own territories.

NOTES AND QUESTIONS

1. **Policy: Implications for the United States and Other Nations.** What was at stake for U.S. antitrust regulators in *Empagran*? And what was at stake for foreign nations? What concerns did foreign nations raise in the briefs they filed with the court? Do the principles used to determine extraterritoriality issues properly balance the interests of the United States and foreign nations in the field of antitrust?

2. **Statutory Interpretation.** What canon of statutory interpretation guided the Court's holding in *Empagran* that the Sherman Act did not apply? How, if at all, does this canon differ from the *Charming Betsy* canon applied by Justice Scalia in his *Hartford* dissent? Is there tension between the reasoning in *Hartford* and *Empagran*, or can they be read as consistent in approach?

3. **Comity (Revisited).** According to the Court, what is the role of comity in determining whether a U.S. statute applies extraterritorially? How does the Court's understanding of comity in *Empagran* differ from its understanding of comity in *Hartford*?

4. **Policy: Reasons for and Against Extraterritorial Application of Antitrust Law.** What policy concerns are raised by the Court to support its holding in *Empagran*? What policy reasons might support a different holding — that is, that the Sherman Act should apply in circumstances like those in the *Empagran* case? The Court concludes in *Empagran* that "in this scenario, a purchaser in the United States could bring a Sherman Act claim . . . based on domestic injury, but a purchaser in Ecuador could not bring a Sherman Act claim based on foreign harm." From a policy perspective, is this a desirable outcome? Why or why not?

5. **Reconciling *Hartford* and *Empagran*.** Can the Court's holding in *Empagran* be reconciled with its holding in *Hartford*? Why or why not? How might the cases be factually distinguished? In light of the Court's opinions, what does a plaintiff have to show factually for the Sherman Act to apply?

REVIEW NOTES AND QUESTIONS

1. Carefully review the materials on extraterritoriality analysis presented in this section. As you do so, keep in mind three basic steps in analyzing whether the presumption against extraterritoriality would bar a plaintiff's claim under a U.S. federal statute:

   - Always begin by carefully reading the statute. Does it clearly indicate that it applies extraterritorially? In other words, is the presumption against extraterritoriality overcome? How does the answer to this question affect your analysis?
   - Identify the "focus" of the statute. Under the facts of the case, did the activity that is the focus of the statute occur inside U.S. territory? How does the answer to this question affect your analysis?
   - Would extraterritorial application of the statute violate customary international law limits on jurisdiction to prescribe? If so, then under the *Charming Betsy* doctrine, can the statute be interpreted to avoid such a violation? If it cannot be interpreted to avoid a violation of international law, how would this affect your analysis?

2. Think about the broader implications of the cases in Section A for real-world lawyering:

   - If you represent a defendant arguing that a suit should be dismissed because the plaintiff's claim would require an impermissible extraterritorial application of a U.S. federal statute, what type of motion to dismiss would you file?
   - If you represent a plaintiff suing a defendant for violations of a U.S. federal statute, what will you need to demonstrate in order to convince a judge that the statute applies to a particular transnational legal problem? What will the defendant's lawyer need to demonstrate to convince the judge otherwise?
   - If you represent a plaintiff suing a defendant for violations of a U.S. statute, and it has already been established (as it has for § 10(b) of the Securities Exchange Act) that the statute does not apply extraterritorially, what arguments might you explore to convince a judge that the statute nevertheless should apply in your lawsuit?
   - If you represent a defendant who has been sued by a plaintiff for violations of a U.S. federal statute, and it has already been established (as it has for the Sherman Act) that the presumption against extraterritoriality has been overcome for that statute, what alternative arguments might you make to avoid application of the statute?

- Why is the issue of whether a U.S. federal statute applies extraterritorially so important for the litigants in disputes arising out of transnational activity? Is the issue also important from the perspective of international relations? Why or why not?

3. Why should there be a presumption against the extraterritorial application of U.S. federal statutes? What policy reasons support this presumption? What policy reasons might be used to challenge the presumption? In your view, is there a better approach? What would it be?

B. Choice of Law: Determining Which Nation's Law Applies to Transnational Activity

Extraterritoriality analysis addresses *whether* a particular nation's law applies to a given transnational legal problem. For example, as discussed in Section A of this chapter, U.S. courts apply two presumptions — a presumption against extraterritoriality and a presumption against violating international law — to analyze whether U.S. federal statutes apply extraterritorially. If a plaintiff's claim depends on the application of a U.S. federal statute outside U.S. territory, the claim may proceed only if the statute applies extraterritorially. Otherwise, the claim will be dismissed.

This section introduces you to a different type of analysis that is used to determine what law applies to a transnational legal problem: *choice-of-law analysis.* Two practical points merit emphasis at the outset. First, extraterritoriality analysis is used when the issue involves a U.S. federal statute; choice-of-law analysis is used when the issue involves tort law, contract law, property law, or other types of so-called private law.* Second, extraterritoriality analysis determines *whether* a U.S. federal statute applies; choice-of-law analysis determines *which* nation's law applies. For example, if a plaintiff files a tort claim in a U.S. court and the tort arises out of activity with connections to both Mexico and California, choice-of-law analysis determines whether the court will apply Mexican tort law or California tort law. If the choice-of-law analysis points to Mexican tort law, the suit may proceed with the U.S. court applying Mexican (rather than California) law to decide the tort issue. In contrast, extraterritoriality analysis never results in the application of foreign law — instead, either the U.S. federal statute is applied or the plaintiff's claim is dismissed. The result is what is sometimes called the "public law taboo." U.S. courts using choice-of-law analysis may apply foreign *private* law (e.g., foreign tort or contract law) to decide a case, but U.S. courts generally do not apply foreign *public* law (e.g., foreign criminal, tax, antitrust, or securities

---

* "Private law" is generally understood as referring to law that governs relationships between individuals or businesses.

law).* To summarize, choice-of-law analysis is used to determine which nation's private law applies (and based on that analysis, a U.S. court may apply foreign law to decide a claim), and extraterritoriality analysis is used to determine whether a U.S. federal statute applies (and based on that analysis, a U.S. court will either apply U.S. law or dismiss the claim).

As you study the following materials, keep in mind these five points: First, choice-of-law issues are important. Whether a party wins or loses a case, how much a party can recover, and how a party must conduct itself to comply with the law are all issues that can be affected by choice of law. As you read the cases, always ask yourself: What is at stake for the parties? Why are they paying their lawyers to litigate choice-of-law issues?

Second, to analyze choice-of-law issues, courts apply choice-of-law principles — principles crafted to help courts determine whether an issue before them should be governed by the law of the forum or the law of a foreign nation. These principles are separate from the substantive principles of tort law or contract law. For lawyers to make convincing arguments about what law a court should apply, they must understand not only the potentially applicable rules of tort or contract law, but also the choice-of-law principles that will determine which nation's rules of tort or contract law will be applied. In general, the choice-of-law principles that U.S. courts apply to analyze choice-of-law issues involving U.S. states (e.g., whether California or Nevada law applies) are the same ones they apply to analyze choice-of-law issues involving foreign nations (e.g., whether California or French law applies).

Third, there are diverse choice-of-law principles in the United States (and around the world). Choice-of-law principles are forum law — that is, a court in a particular jurisdiction will generally apply that jurisdiction's choice-of-law principles. For example, a Costa Rican court will apply Costa Rica's choice-of-law principles. Likewise, a California court will apply California's choice-of-law principles (and, as explained later in this section, a federal court in California sitting in diversity will likewise apply California's choice-of-law principles). A messy, difficult, but fascinating reality of choice of law in the United States is that different U.S. states have different choice-of-law principles. Some states apply the traditional principles embodied in the *Restatement (First) of Conflict of Laws*; others apply the more modern principles embodied in the *Restatement (Second) of Conflict of Laws*; and still others, such as California and New York, apply their own distinctive choice-of-law principles.

The practical implication of the diversity of choice-of-law principles in the United States is that to develop arguments about which law a U.S. court should apply to a transnational legal problem, you first need to identify that forum's choice-of-law principles. But there is an interesting historical question, too: Why

---

* According to one definition, "public law" is "[t]he body of law dealing with the relations between private individuals and the government, and with the structure and operation of the government itself; constitutional law, criminal law, and administrative law taken together." BLACK'S LAW DICTIONARY (11th ed. 2019). For a discussion and critique of the public law taboo, see William S. Dodge, *Breaking the Public Law Taboo*, 43 HARV. INT'L L.J. 161 (2002).

is there a patchwork of choice-of-law principles in the United States instead of a uniform federal approach? Congress could in theory pass federal legislation imposing a single set of choice-of-law principles for state and federal courts to use, but it has so far declined to do so. In the meantime, an implication of the *Erie* doctrine is that choice of law is a matter of state law when a case is filed in federal court based on diversity jurisdiction. *Klaxon Co. v. Stentor Elec. Mfg. Co.*, 313 U.S. 487 (1941).

Until the middle of the twentieth century, courts throughout the United States applied the traditional principles contained in the *First Restatement*. These principles are often referred to as "jurisdiction selecting" and "territorial" because they select the law of a particular jurisdiction where a particular key event or thing was located — for example, very generally speaking, the law of the place of the wrong applies to a tort claim (*lex loci delicti*), the law of the place of contracting applies to a contract claim (*lex loci contractus*), and the law of the place of property applies to claims regarding that property (*lex situs*). One benefit of such an approach is that it provides (in theory) clarity. For instance, under this approach a California domiciliary bringing suit in tort for an injury in Mexico would expect a court to apply the substantive tort law of Mexico, wherever the case is filed.

The traditional approach, however, was criticized for leading to arbitrary and unjust results, and for requiring various ad hoc "escape devices" to avoid such results. So, for instance, if the California domiciliary brings suit in California and the court in that state believes that the application of Mexican law is unjust, it might decide that California public policy requires the application of California law. In part based on a movement in legal theory known as Legal Realism, a "choice of law revolution" ensued in the United States in the 1950s and 1960s, producing a variety of alternative choice-of-law approaches. These "modern methods," including the *Second Restatement*, California's approach, and New York's approach — all of which are examined below — take into account multiple factors, including state interests and policy considerations. These choice-of-law methods are supposed to more transparently take account of the policy reasons that led courts in the traditional framework to "escape" the *First Restatement*'s jurisdiction-selecting rules. For this reason, modern methods are sometimes labeled "policy selecting" — and they are sometimes criticized as being unpredictable. A full discussion of the history of choice of law in the United States is well beyond the scope of this chapter. For a thorough account, see SYMEON C. SYMEONIDES, THE AMERICAN CHOICE-OF-LAW REVOLUTION IN THE COURTS: PAST, PRESENT AND FUTURE (2006). The point here is simply to provide a very basic understanding of the origins of the messiness of choice of law in the United States.

Fourth, choice-of-law principles generally operate based on connections between particular nations or other jurisdictions and the parties and the occurrences giving rise to a dispute. These connections can be legal connections (such as nationality), territorial connections (such as the place where various relevant events occurred), or both. As you read the cases that follow, pay close attention to the different types of connections that are relevant to different choice-of-law methods, and how these connections are evaluated.

Fifth, you will notice that in some of the cases that follow, the court refers to choice-of-law issues as "conflict of laws" issues. Technically, however, conflict of laws (often called "private international law" outside the United States) refers to a bigger set of issues that arise from multinational (or multistate) legal problems. These issues include not only choice of law, but also jurisdiction and the recognition and enforcement of foreign court judgments, both of which are discussed in other parts of this casebook. Thus, choice of law — which is the focus of this section — is part of the broader field of conflict of laws.

This section begins by introducing you to a variety of choice-of-law problems and the various choice-of-law methods that judges and lawyers in different U.S. states use to analyze them. It then examines an issue that arises if foreign law applies: How does a lawyer attempt to prove, and how does a judge determine, exactly what foreign law requires?

1. *Choice-of-Law Methods*

As mentioned above, there are diverse choice-of-law principles in the United States (and around the world). In the United States, different U.S. states take different approaches to choice-of-law problems. The following materials introduce you to some of the more common choice-of-law methods used by lawyers and judges in the United States, including the traditional approach of the *First Restatement*, New York's approach, California's approach, and the approach of the *Second Restatement*. As you study these materials, ask yourself: Which methods are the most likely to lead to clear conclusions about whether forum law or foreign law applies? Should clarity be the goal of choice of law methods? Which methods are most flexible? Is flexibility a good or bad thing in choice-of-law? Would it be better to have one choice-of-law method that judges in all U.S. courts would use? If you were crafting a choice-of-law system, which methods would you prefer?

Raskin v. Allison

57 P.3d 30 (Kan. App. 2002)

PADDOCK, S.J.

This is an interlocutory appeal by the plaintiffs from the partial summary judgment granted to defendants on a choice-of-law question. The trial court found the substantive law of Mexico would govern the claims in this personal injury action where the injuries occurred in Mexico although all parties were Kansas residents. We affirm.

The facts are brief and uncontroverted. Kaley Raskin and Jenna Turnbaugh, both minors, received personal injuries resulting from a collision of the water craft they occupied and a water craft operated by Chad Leathers in the ocean waters off Cabo San Lucas, Mexico.

Kaley's and Jenna's parents filed this action individually and as next friends to their minor daughters against Ken and Karen Allison individually and as guardians ad litem for their minor son and stepson, Chad Leathers. Plaintiffs' claims were framed on the theories of negligence and negligent entrustment.

. . .

Kansas follows the rule that the law of the state where the tort occurred, lex loci delicti, should apply. *Ling v. Jan's Liquors*, 237 Kan. 629, 634 (1985).

Here, plaintiffs do not dispute the injuries were sustained in Mexican waters and that under the rule of *lex loci delicti*, Mexican law would normally control. However, plaintiffs argue the rule should not apply in this case because (1) all the parties are residents of Kansas, (2) Kansas has never invoked the rule in a case where a foreign country's law would apply, and (3) the rule of comity requires that Kansas protect its own residents and apply Kansas law.

Kansas Residents

Plaintiffs argue that because all the parties are Kansas residents, Kansas has the greater interest in applying its substantive law; therefore, the case should be governed by Kansas law.

However, the Kansas Supreme Court has repeatedly applied the law of the place of the injury, even when all the parties were residents of Kansas. In each of those cases, the law of the place of injury was less favorable to the plaintiffs than Kansas law.

For example, in *Kokenge v. Holthaus*, 165 Kan. 300 (1948), Kansas residents were traveling together in Iowa when an automobile accident occurred. The Kansas passenger sued the Kansas driver in a Kansas court. The Supreme Court held that because the accident happened in Iowa and the injuries were sustained there, the Iowa guest statute applied. 165 Kan. at 307. Under that Iowa statute, the passenger was required to show reckless operation of the vehicle by the driver in order to recover. 165 Kan. at 307.

In *McDaniel v. Sinn*, 194 Kan. 625 (1965), all the parties were Kansas residents. The plaintiffs' decedent was killed in an accident in Missouri while traveling with the defendant. The Supreme Court rejected the plaintiffs' arguments that when all the parties are from Kansas, *lex loci delicti* should be rejected and Kansas law should control. 194 Kan. at 626.

Because the Kansas Supreme Court has consistently applied the rule of *lex loci delicti* in tort cases, even when all parties are Kansas residents, plaintiffs' first argument fails.

Application to Foreign Countries

Plaintiffs also contend that because Kansas courts have never applied the *lex loci delicti* rule to apply the law of a foreign country, the rule should be rejected in this case. Plaintiffs are correct in asserting that neither of the Kansas appellate courts have applied the law of a foreign country in a tort case. This court, however, recently applied Canadian law in a contract case where the contract was made in Canada by applying the rule of lex loci contractus [*i.e.*, the law of the place of contracting]. See *Layne Christensen Co. v. Zurich Canada*, 30 Kan. App. 2d 128, (2002).

Plaintiffs have not cited compelling authority that the rule of lex loci delicti does not apply in cases involving foreign countries. Kansas follows traditional choice of law principles largely reflected in the original *Restatement of Conflict of Laws* (1934). . . . We have no hesitation in finding that the lex loci delicti rule would apply in tort cases notwithstanding the injuries were incurred in a foreign country.

   . . .

Public Policy Exception

Actually, the thread that weaves through all of the plaintiffs' arguments is that damage limitations purportedly contained in Mexico's law are contrary to Kansas public policy and should not be enforced by Kansas courts. Plaintiffs seem to argue that public policy is defined by Kansas legislative enactments and since the Kansas Legislature had not enacted statutes with damage limitations similar to those in Mexico, Mexican laws are therefore contrary to Kansas public policy. Plaintiffs cite no authority establishing what damage limitations exist in Mexico. However, a recent case cited by defendants appeared to support the conclusion that Mexico recognizes that contributory negligence is a complete defense in a tort claim. *Spinozzi v. ITT Sheraton Corp.*, 174 F.3d 842, 844 (7th Cir. 1999). Also, Mexican law apparently limits recovery of damages in tort cases to the amount of the injured party's medical and rehabilitative expense and lost wages at the minimum wage rate. See *Hernandez v. Burger*, 102 Cal. App. 3d 795, 799 (1980) (citing Civ. Code of the State of Baja California [Norte], art. 1793; Ley Federal del Trabajo, arts. 487, 491, and 495). Plaintiffs assert these damage limitations in their brief.

Kansas cases consistently hold that a Kansas court will not apply the law of another state to a claim if that other state's law is contrary to Kansas public policy. . . .

In *Brenner v. Oppenheimer & Co., Inc.*, 273 Kan. 525 (2002), the Supreme Court invalidated a contractual choice-of law provision finding that its reference to New York law was contrary to "strong public policy" in Kansas and would not be enforced. In its discussion, the Supreme Court held that a "strong public policy" is one "so thoroughly established as a state of public mind so united and so definite and fixed that its existence is not subject to any substantial doubt." The *Brenner* court found a strong public policy in the fact that the incorporation of New York law into the contract between a Kansas resident and a securities broker evaded Kansas' securities law prohibiting the sale of unregistered securities.

   . . .

   . . . Kansas appears to be following the prevailing view that the public policy exception in conflict of law theory should be narrowly limited. See 16 Am. Jur. 2d, Conflict of Laws § 25; see also *Pool v. Day*, 141 Kan. 195, 200 (1935) (Oklahoma common law liability rules not a violation of Kansas public policy despite Kansas' guest statute requiring proof of gross and wanton conduct by the driver). As previously noted, the plaintiffs here appear to contend that if the law of another jurisdiction is different than Kansas law, it is contrary to Kansas public policy.

The Kansas Supreme Court has repeatedly upheld the application of the law of other states in tort cases even when those laws impose a higher burden of proof on plaintiffs before they can recover damages. . . . The Supreme Court has even upheld the application of another State's wrongful death statute even though that statute excluded some types of damages allowed under Kansas law. See *McDaniel v. Sinn*, 194 Kan. at 625-26.

Thus, Kansas cases indicate the "public policy" exception in the choice-of-law context is limited and generally not triggered because of limitations on damages or higher burdens of proof.

Finally, plaintiffs cannot seriously contend that the application of Mexican law is unfair when they voluntarily vacationed there. As the Tenth Circuit once stated:

> "It is a firmly established principle of American jurisprudence that the laws of one state have no extra-territorial effect in another state. The forum state will give effect to foreign law as long as the foreign law is not repugnant to the moral sense of the community. The mere fact that the law of the foreign state differs from the law of the state in which recognition is sought is not enough to make the foreign law inapplicable. . . . Indeed, this Court is reminded of the oft-paraphrased advice of St. Ambrose, Catholic bishop of Milan in the fourth century, to St. Augustine. 'When you are at Rome, live in the Roman style; when you are elsewhere, live as they do elsewhere.'" *Brennan v. University of Kansas*, 451 F.2d 1287, 1289-90 (10th Cir. 1971).

The record before the court fails to establish a sound basis to refuse to apply Mexican law in this case based on the public policy exception. The limitations on damages allegedly contained in Mexican law do not appear to violate a "strong public policy" as defined by prior Kansas Supreme Court decisions.

The trial court correctly determined that the substantive law of Mexico would govern the claims in this personal injury action.

Affirmed.

NOTES AND QUESTIONS

1. **Practice: What's at Stake?** The issue in this case is whether a Kansas state court should apply the tort law of Kansas or the tort law of Mexico to the plaintiffs' tort claims. Why do the parties care what law applies?
2. **Identifying the Applicable Choice-of-Law Principles.** What choice-of-law principle did the court apply to determine whether to apply the law of Kansas or the law of Mexico? Upon what legal authority did the court rely to apply that choice-of-law principle?
3. **The Public Policy Exception.** What is the public policy exception? Why didn't the exception apply in this case? Should it have applied? What reasons might there be for having a public policy exception to the traditional *First Restatement* choice-of-law method? What might be some reasons against having this exception?

4. **Policy: Law of Kansas or Law of Mexico?** In this case, a Kansas state court applied the law of Mexico to personal injury claims brought by one Kansas resident against another Kansas resident. Is this a fair and appropriate choice of law from the perspective of the parties? From the perspective of Kanas and Mexico? Why or why not?

5. **Choice of Law and Choice of Forum.** As this and other cases in this section illustrate, the answer to the "which law" question is *not* necessarily the same as the answer to the "which court" question. Even if a U.S. state court has jurisdiction and decides to exercise it, the court may apply the law of another state or the law of a foreign nation, depending on its choice-of-law analysis. Conversely, a particular U.S. state court does not necessarily have jurisdiction even if, according to a choice-of-law analysis, that state's law would govern. Simply put, *choice of law and jurisdiction are separate issues, and they are governed by different rules*: Choice-of-law issues are governed by choice-of-law principles, and jurisdictional issues are governed by jurisdictional principles (including subject matter jurisdiction and personal jurisdiction principles).

6. **The *First Restatement*.** The court states that Kansas's choice-of-law principles are based on "traditional choice of law principles largely reflected in the original Restatement of Conflict of Laws (1934)." The reference is to the *Restatement (First) of Conflict of Laws*, which restates choice-of-law principles as well as principles governing jurisdiction and judgments. Section 382 of the *First Restatement* provides that "the law of the place of the wrong" determines whether a person is liable in tort, and § 379 provides that "[t]he place of wrong is in the state where the last event necessary to make an actor liable for an alleged tort takes place." That event is generally understood to be the place of the plaintiff's injury, because the defendant is not liable for a tort unless the plaintiff suffers an injury. *See* RESTATEMENT (FIRST) OF CONFLICT OF LAWS § 379, Note 1 ("Except in the case of harm from poison, when a person sustains bodily harm, the place of wrong is the place where the harmful force takes effect upon the body."). As discussed earlier, a Restatement is not binding legal authority, but courts often adopt principles contained in a Restatement. The Kansas courts, as well as the courts of a number of other U.S. states, continue to use the traditional choice-of-law principles reflected in the *First Restatement*. As noted above, the traditional approach to choice of law is only one of many approaches, and different states take different approaches. We will explore some of these other approaches later in this section.

7. **Place of Injury versus Place of Conduct.** As just indicated, under the *First Restatement*, the "place of the wrong" is generally understood to be the place of the plaintiff's injury. Why should the focus be on the place of the injury? Sometimes the place of the injury is different from the place of the defendant's tortious conduct (for example, if the defendant negligently manufactures a product in one nation, and the product injures the plaintiff in another nation). In that situation, should the law of the place of the conduct govern instead? Why or why not?

8. **Characterization and Choice of Law.** Note that while the court refers to its method for tort cases as *lex loci delicti*, it refers to its method for contract cases as *lex loci contractus* (a reference to the principle that the law governing contract issues is generally the law of the place of contracting). This illustrates another important point: *Different choice-of-law principles are applied to different types of choice-of-law issues.* For example, according to the traditional principles of the *First Restatement*, the law of the place of the wrong generally governs tort issues, and the law of the place of contracting generally governs contract issues. This means that to determine which choice-of-law principle applies to a particular issue, the issue must be "characterized" — for example, characterized as a tort issue or a contract issue.

9. **Choice of Law Across the United States.** As of 2019, 9 states apply the traditional *First Restatement* approach in tort cases (Alabama, Georgia, Kansas, Maryland, New Mexico, North Carolina, South Carolina, Virginia, and West Virginia) and 11 apply it in contract cases (Alabama, Florida, Georgia, Kansas, Maryland, New Mexico, Oklahoma, Rhode Island, South Carolina, Tennessee, and Virginia). Symeon C. Symeonides, *Choice of Law in the American Courts in 2019: Thirty-Third Annual Survey*, 68 Am. J. Comp. L. (forthcoming 2020).

10. **Practice: A Look at the Briefs.** For a look at how lawyers briefed the choice-of-law issues in the *Raskin* case, you may wish to examine the following: Brief of Appellants (2002 WL 34576891), Brief of Appellees (2002 WL 34576892), and Reply Brief of Appellants (2002 WL 34576893).

Edwards v. Erie Coach Lines Co.

17 N.Y.3d 306 (2011)

READ, J.

Near Geneseo, New York on January 19, 2005 a charter bus carrying members of an Ontario[, Canada] women's hockey team plowed into the rear end of a tractor-trailer parked on the shoulder of the highway. Three bus passengers and the tractor-trailer's driver died; several bus passengers were seriously hurt. We are called upon to decide the choice-of-law issue presented by these six lawsuits, which were brought to recover damages for wrongful death and/or personal injuries.

I.

Nearly a half-century ago, in *Babcock v. Jackson*, 12 N.Y.2d 473 (1963), we abandoned what had long been our choice-of-law rule whereby the law of the place of the tort invariably governed. Because "in nearly all such cases, the conduct causing injury and the injury itself occurred in the same jurisdiction," this rule offered "the advantages of certainty, ease of application and predictability," but at the expense of "the interest which [other] jurisdictions . . . [might] have in the resolution of particular issues." [S]ee *Cooney v. Osgood Mach.*, 81 N.Y.2d 66 (1993) (place-of-the-tort theory "failed to accord any significance to the policies underlying the conflicting laws of other jurisdictions").

To "accom[m]odat[e] the competing interests in tort cases with multi-State contacts," we adopted the "center of gravity" or "grouping of contacts" approach, which gave the "controlling effect to the law of the jurisdiction which, because of its relationship or contact with the occurrence or the parties ha[d] the greatest concern with the specific issue raised in the litigation." This new method of analysis, however, was limited to competing loss-allocation — not conduct-regulating — rules.[1] As we explained in *Babcock*,

> "[w]here the defendant's exercise of due care in the operation of his automobile is in issue, the jurisdiction in which the allegedly wrongful conduct occurred will usually have a predominant, if not exclusive, concern. In such a case, it is appropriate to look to the law of the place of the tort so as to give effect to that jurisdiction's interest in regulating conduct within its borders, and it would be almost unthinkable to seek the applicable rule in the law of some other place." 12 N.Y.2d at 483.

The facts of *Babcock* illustrate how "grouping of contacts" worked. In that case, a New York passenger in a car operated by a New York driver was injured in an automobile accident that occurred in Ontario during a weekend trip to Canada. We noted that the trip began and was to end in New York, where the car was garaged, licensed and insured, and where the driver-passenger relationship arose. The "guest" passenger sued the "host" driver in New York for negligence. At the time, the Ontario guest statute barred the passenger from recovering damages from the driver, while New York law did not.

Looking to the "grouping of contacts," we decided that New York — not Ontario, the place of the tort — possessed "the dominant contacts and the superior claim for application of its law" as to whether the passenger should "recover[ ] for damages for a wrong concededly committed." We commented that, in this context,

> "[a]lthough the rightness or wrongness of [the driver's] conduct may depend upon the law of the particular jurisdiction through which the automobile passes, the rights and liabilities of the parties which stem from their guest-host relationship should remain constant and not vary and shift as the automobile proceeds from place to place. Indeed, such a result . . . accords with the interests of the host in procuring liability insurance adequate under the applicable law, and the interests of his insurer in reasonable calculability of the premium."

Over time, the "grouping of contacts" approach put into place by *Babcock* evolved into a more explicit "interest analysis." This method of deciding

---

1. Loss-allocation rules "prohibit, assign, or limit liability after the tort occurs," whereas conduct-regulating rules "have the prophylactic effect of governing conduct to prevent injuries from occurring" in the first place. . . .

choice-of-law issues "reject[ed] a quantitative grouping of contacts" because "[c]ontacts obtain significance only to the extent that they relate to the policies and purposes sought to be vindicated by the conflicting laws."

We refined our "interest analysis" so as "to assure a greater degree of predictability and uniformity" in *Neumeier v. Kuehner*, 31 N.Y.2d 121 (1972), a case where a domiciliary of Ontario was killed when the automobile in which he was a passenger collided with a train in Ontario. The vehicle was owned and driven by a resident of New York, who was also killed in the accident. The passenger's wife and administratrix, a citizen of Canada and a domiciliary of Ontario, brought an action for wrongful death in New York against the driver's estate and the railway company, both of which interposed affirmative defenses involving the Ontario guest statute.[3] The wife, asserting that the Ontario statute was unavailable, moved to dismiss the affirmative defenses, and Supreme Court denied the motion. The Appellate Division reversed, and asked us if its order was properly made. We answered, "No."

Neumeier set up a three-rule framework for resolving choice of law in conflicts settings involving guest statutes, which by definition allocate losses after the tort occurs rather than regulate primary conduct. Under the first *Neumeier* rule, when the driver and passenger are domiciled in the same state, and the vehicle is registered there, the law of their shared jurisdiction controls.

The second rule addresses the situation where the [defendant-]driver and the [plaintiff-]passenger are domiciled in different states, and [each state's law] favors its domiciliary. When the driver's conduct occurs in the state where he is domiciled, [and that state's law] would not impose liability, [then] that state's law applies [and the driver should not be exposed to liability under the law of the passenger's state of domicile]. Conversely, [when the passenger's injury occurs in the state where she is domiciled, and that state's law] permits the injured passenger to recover, then [that state's law applies and] the driver . . . may not interpose a conflicting law of his state as a defense.

In other situations, when the passenger and the driver are domiciled in different states, the rule is necessarily less categorical. Thus, under the third *Neumeier* rule, the law of the state where the accident occurred governs unless it can be shown that displacing that normally applicable rule will advance the relevant substantive law purposes without impairing the smooth working of the multi-state system or producing great uncertainty for litigants.

Since the passenger in *Neumeier* was domiciled in Ontario, where the guest statute did not allow recovery, and the driver in New York, the third rule — the law of the place of the tort (i.e., Ontario) — would normally control. We saw no reason to apply the third rule's proviso since the wife "failed to show that [New York's] connection with the controversy was sufficient to justify displacing" *lex loci delicti*, the law of the place of the wrong. The wife did not show that ignoring Ontario's guest statute in a case "involv[ing] an Ontario-domiciled guest at the expense

---

3. When we handed down *Neumeier*, the Ontario guest statute provided that the owner or driver of a motor vehicle was not liable for damages for the injury or death of a guest-passenger in the absence of gross negligence. . . .

of a New Yorker . . . further[ed] the substantive law purposes of New York"; and "failure to apply Ontario's law would impair . . . the smooth working of the multistate system [and] produce great uncertainty for litigants by sanctioning forum shopping and thereby allowing a party to select a forum [countenancing] a larger recovery than [that party's] own domicile."

We have routinely applied the *Neumeier* framework to conflicts in loss-allocation situations not involving guest statutes. . . .

II.

The charter bus's driver (Ryan A. Comfort), his employer (Erie Coach Lines Company), and the company that leased the bus (Trentway-Wagar, Inc.) are Ontario[, Canada] domiciliaries, as are (or were) all the injured and deceased passengers. The tractor-trailer driver (Ernest Zeiset) was a Pennsylvania domiciliary, as are his employer (Joseph French, doing business as J & J Trucking) and the companies that hired the trailer (Verdelli Farms, Inc. and V.F. Transportation, Inc.). The injured passengers and the representatives of those who died (collectively, plaintiffs) filed multiple wrongful death and personal injury lawsuits in Supreme Court.

These split-domicile lawsuits presented an obvious choice-of-law issue because Ontario caps noneconomic damages where negligence causes catastrophic personal injury, while New York does not cap such damages in a no-fault case involving serious injury. Following extensive discovery, Erie Coach, Trentway and Comfort (collectively, the bus defendants) and J & J Trucking, the administratrix of Zeiset's estate, Verdelli Farms and V.F. Transportation (collectively, the trailer defendants) moved for orders from Supreme Court determining that, under New York's choice-of-law principles, Ontario law applied to "all loss allocation issues" in these cases.

On March 23, 2009, Supreme Court granted both motions. . . .

The trial of these cases was bifurcated, and, during the course of the jury trial on liability, the parties reached a settlement of that issue. In the stipulation of settlement, placed on the record on June 17, 2009, the bus defendants agreed to 90% and the trailer defendants to 10% liability. Meanwhile, plaintiffs had appealed Supreme Court's orders determining that Ontario law would govern any award of noneconomic damages to be made at a damages trial. The Appellate Division affirmed.

. . . [The Appellate Division] rejected plaintiffs' argument that the Ontario cap was procedural rather than substantive. . . .

The Appellate Division agreed with Supreme Court's bottom-line conclusion that the Ontario cap applied to damages recovered from the bus and trailer defendants, but conducted separate choice-of-law analyses. With respect to the bus defendants, the court looked to the first *Neumeier* rule, which directs that the law of the parties' common domicile — here, Ontario — governs. The court observed that applying the law of a shared domicile reduced the risk of forum shopping; rebutted the charge of local bias; and served "the concepts of mutuality and reciprocity," which are "support[ed by the] consistent application of the common domicile law."

As between plaintiffs and the trailer defendants, the Appellate Division applied the third *Neumeier* rule, which prefers the law of the place of the tort. Invoking the proviso to the third rule, the court decided, however, that Ontario law should govern, reasoning that "while applying Ontario law [might] not affirmatively advance the substantive law purposes of New York, it [would] not frustrate those interests because New York has no significant interest in applying its own law to this dispute." The court also commented that New York law created great uncertainty for the litigants because the trailer defendants were only 10% liable for the accident pursuant to the parties' settlement. If the trailer defendants' exposure to noneconomic damages was unlimited while the bus defendants' liability for this item of damages was capped, the trailer defendants might end up paying far more than their stipulated share.

Finally, the Appellate Division concluded that plaintiffs failed to meet the "heavy burden of establishing that the application of Ontario law violate[d] the public policy of New York." The court pointed out that "resort to the public policy exception should be reserved for those foreign laws that are truly obnoxious," which was not the case here. In any event, the Appellate Division decided that the parties' contacts were too few and limited in scope to implicate New York's public policy.

The Appellate Division granted plaintiffs permission to appeal, and asked us whether its orders were properly made. For the reasons that follow, we answer "No" with respect to the trailer defendants.

III.

. . .

[P]laintiffs press for what they call a "single, joint analysis" in cases, such as this one, with multiple tortfeasors. As a result, the Edwards plaintiffs argue, the trial judge "properly analyzed both sets of Defendants — those related to the bus and those related to the tractor trailer — together," although he reached the wrong conclusion. In our view, however, the correct way to conduct a choice-of-law analysis is to consider each plaintiff vis-à-vis each defendant, which is essentially the approach taken by the Appellate Division. . . . The rules in the *Neumeier* framework, in fact, by their very nature call for a plaintiff-by-defendant inquiry.

Here, the Ontario cap controls any award of noneconomic damages against the bus defendants because they share an Ontario domicile with plaintiffs. We described the relevant choice-of-law principle and its rationale in *Cooney*:

> "Under the first *Neumeier* rule, when [the plaintiff and the defendant] share a common domicile, that law should control. Indeed, when both parties are from the same jurisdiction, there is often little reason to apply another jurisdiction's loss allocation rules. The domiciliary jurisdiction, which has weighed the competing considerations underlying the loss allocation rule at issue, has the greater 'interest in enforcing the decisions of both parties to accept both the benefits and the burdens of identifying with that jurisdiction and to submit themselves to its authority'. . . . Moreover, this rule reduces opportunities for forum shopping because the same law will apply whether the suit is brought in the locus jurisdiction or in the common domicile, the two most likely forums."

We had earlier made the same point at least as forcefully in *Schultz*, where we stressed that "the locus jurisdiction has at best a minimal interest in determining the right of recovery or the extent of the remedy in an action by a foreign domiciliary for injuries resulting from the conduct of a codomiciliary that was tortious under the laws of both jurisdictions." . . .

In sum, Ontario has weighed the interests of tortfeasors and their victims in cases of catastrophic personal injury, and has elected to safeguard its domiciliaries from large awards for nonpecuniary damages. In lawsuits brought in New York by Ontario-domiciled plaintiffs against Ontario-domiciled defendants, New York courts should respect Ontario's decision, which differs from but certainly does not offend New York's public policy.

Finally, we look to the third *Neumeier* rule to decide whether the Ontario cap controls with respect to the trailer defendants. Critically, the third rule establishes the place of the tort — here, New York — as the "normally applicable" choice in a conflicts situation such as this one, where the domicile of plaintiffs, the domicile of the trailer defendants and the place of the tort are different. . . .

The trailer defendants contend that . . . the law of New York should not govern, even though the accident occurred there. We do not agree. While New York employs "interest analysis" rather than "grouping of contacts," the number and intensity of contacts is relevant when considering whether to deviate from *lex loci delicti* under the third *Neumeier* rule, i.e., whether even to analyze if displacing this "normally applicable" choice would "advance the relevant substantive law purposes without impairing the smooth working of the multi-state system or producing great uncertainty for litigants."

. . .

Here, . . . there was no cause to contemplate a jurisdiction other than New York, the place where the conduct causing injuries and the injuries themselves occurred. The trailer defendants did not ask Supreme Court to consider the law of their domicile, Pennsylvania, and they had no contacts whatsoever with Ontario other than the happenstance that plaintiffs and the bus defendants were domiciled there.

Accordingly, [Ontario's cap on noneconomic damages controls any award of noneconomic damages against the bus driver, his employer, and the lessor of the bus, but New York law applies to tort claims against the driver of the tractor-trailer, his employer, and the companies that hired the trailer].

NOTES AND QUESTIONS

1. **Practice: What's at Stake?** The issue in the *Edwards* case is whether a New York state court should apply the tort law of New York or the tort law of Ontario, Canada to the plaintiffs' tort claims. Why do the parties care about this choice-of-law issue?

2. **Determining the Applicable Choice-of-Law Principles.** What choice-of-law principles did the court use to determine whether to apply the law of

New York or the law of Ontario, Canada? How do these principles differ from those of the *First Restatement*'s traditional place-of-the-wrong approach?

3. **Conduct-Regulating versus Loss-Allocating Rules.** Note that according to New York's approach to choice-of-law problems in tort cases, it is important to characterize the choice-of-law issue as either conduct-regulating or loss-allocating. As the Court of Appeals of New York (New York's high court) explains: "[A] distinction [is] drawn between laws that regulate primary conduct (such as standards of care) and those that allocate losses after the tort occurs (such as vicarious liability rules). If conflicting conduct-regulating laws are at issue, the law of the jurisdiction where the tort occurred will generally apply because that jurisdiction has the greatest interest in regulating behavior within its borders. But if competing 'postevent remedial rules' [that is, loss-allocating rules] are at stake other factors are taken into consideration, chiefly the parties' domiciles" [as set forth in the *Neumeier* rules]. *Cooney v. Osgood Machinery, Inc.*, 81 N.Y.2d 66, 72 (Ct. App. N.Y. 1993).

4. **Different Outcomes for Different Parties.** The court in *Edwards* applied Ontario, Canada law to plaintiffs' claim against the bus defendants, but it applied New York law to plaintiffs' claims against the trailer defendants. Why did New York's choice-of-law principles lead to these different outcomes in the same case? Is this a fair result?

5. **Policy: Advantages and Disadvantages of Traditional Choice-of-Law Principles.** Why did New York abandon the traditional "place of the tort" method for choice of law? What are the advantages and disadvantages of the traditional method and New York's method? Which method do you think is better?

6. **Characterization: Substance or Procedure?** As the *Edwards* court notes, the lower court rejected plaintiffs' argument that Ontario's cap on damages was "procedural" rather than "substantive." Generally, procedural issues are governed by the law of the forum rather than subjected to choice-of-law analysis. What might be the reason for this rule? In the *Edwards* case, why do you think the plaintiff argued that the Ontario cap on noneconomic damages was procedural rather than substantive? Why do you think the Appellate Division rejected plaintiff's argument? As these questions suggest, in addition to tort/contract and conduct-regulating/loss-allocating characterization (discussed above), substance/procedure characterization can also affect how choice-of-law issues are resolved.

7. **Practice: A Look at the Briefs.** For a look at how lawyers briefed the choice-of-law issues in the *Edwards* case, you may wish to examine the following: Brief for Plaintiffs-Appellants (2010 WL 7768951); Brief for Defendants-Respondents Trentway-Wagar, Inc., Erie Coach Lines Company and Ryan A. Comfort (2010 WL 7768952); and Brief for Defendants-Respondents Coach USA, Inc., Coach Canada, Inc., Erie Coach Lines Company, Trentway-Wagar, Inc., Trentway-Wagar (PROPERTIES), Inc., and Ryan A. Comfort (2011 WL 5007849).

Tucci v. Club Mediterranee, S.A.

89 Cal. App. 4th 180 (2001)

ALDRICH, J.

Introduction

After she was injured while at work in the Dominican Republic, plaintiff Gina Tucci brought a personal injury action in California against her employer, defendant Club Med [then a French corporation]. [T]he parties filed competing motions for summary judgment. In her motion, Tucci relied on the provision in the California workers' compensation law (Lab. Code, § 3200 et seq.) allowing her to avoid the law's exclusivity to sue for damages in tort. Tucci claimed she was entitled to summary judgment on the issue of her employer's negligence. In its motion, Club Med acknowledged the jurisdiction of the California courts but contended that under applicable choice of law principles, the law of the Dominican Republic governed and precluded Tucci's tort action against her employer. Ruling that the law of the Dominican Republic applied, the trial court granted Club Med summary judgment and denied Tucci's motion. We conclude, pursuant to established choice of law principles, that the trial court was correct. Accordingly, we affirm the judgment.

Factual and Procedural Background

The facts are undisputed. Tucci, a California resident, accepted by telephone the offer to work for four months as an aerobics instructor for the Club Med resort in Punta Cana, the Dominican Republic.

While at work in Punta Cana, Tucci injured her eye. On April 18, 1996, on her ride back from an eye doctor's office in Santo Domingo, in a truck owned by Club Med and driven by a Club Med employee, she suffered pelvic injuries. After being treated locally, she was airlifted to a United States hospital for further treatment.

Pursuant to Dominican Republic law, Club Med maintained workers' compensation insurance for its employees with AXA Courtage (a French insurance company). AXA Courtage is not authorized to write compensation insurance in California. Club Med had not secured a workers' compensation policy with an insurer licensed in California. AXA Courtage paid Tucci in excess of $110,000 in medical benefits. She rejected all additional benefits offered by Club Med and its insurer.

Tucci filed for benefits with the Workers' Compensation Appeals Board (WCAB), which action is not part of this lawsuit. Simultaneously, she brought this personal injury suit in superior court seeking declaratory relief and damages for breach of Club Med's statutory duty to carry workers' compensation according to California law, and for negligent operation, maintenance, and entrustment of a motor vehicle.

In due course, Tucci moved for summary judgment on the grounds, because she was a resident of California at the time of her injury and the employment contract was entered into in California, that she was entitled to workers' compensation benefits from California. She then asserted, because Club Med failed to carry a workers' compensation policy with an insurer "duly authorized [and licensed] to write compensation insurance in this state" (§ 3700, subd. (a); see § 5305), that she was entitled further to avoid the exclusivity of the workers' compensation law and sue Club Med in tort for damages (§§ 3706, 3700, subd. (a)), including attorney fees, and to invoke the applicable presumption of employer negligence.

Club Med opposed Tucci's motion and claimed its entitlement to summary judgment on the ground of an absolute defense. Rather than . . . contest jurisdiction, Club Med urged that choice of law principles required application of the law of the Dominican Republic whose workers' compensation and social security systems provided the exclusive remedy for Tucci's work-related injury.

The trial court granted Club Med's summary judgment motion and denied Tucci's motion. Applying California choice of law rules, the trial court concluded that Dominican Republic law governed this case. In particular, the court found while Club Med did not have a "California policy," as defined under the Labor Code, the AXA Courtage insurance policy provided Tucci "with proper coverage under Dominican law." That is, the court noted, all medical treatment that plaintiff had undergone by the time of the judgment, totaling well over $110,000, was fully paid for by AXA Courtage pursuant to the worker's compensation policy purchased by Tucci's employer. The court noted that Tucci did not claim that her employer had failed to provide her coverage or that the benefits were inadequate. Rather, the court observed, Tucci's position was that she should be allowed to sue her employer for tort damages because Club Med did not purchase a California workers' compensation insurance policy. After all of her claims were dismissed, Tucci filed her appeal.

Discussion

. . .

3. Applicable Legal Principles and the Parties' Contentions.

. . . Nearly every workers' compensation statute in this country contains "an exclusive remedy provision" under which an employee who receives "an award of statutory benefits [is] foreclose[d from] any other type of compensation for the [work-related] injury, including damages in tort. Employees trade their tort remedies 'for a system of compensation without contest, thus sparing [them] the cost, delay and uncertainty of a claim in litigation.' Conversely, workers' compensation statutes typically allow a damages remedy against employers who fail to assume the statutory compensation burdens." (*Garcia v. American Airlines, Inc.*, 12 F.3d 308, 310 (1993).) The employer "who avoids sharing the burdens of the system is not entitled to enjoy its primary benefit, the immunity from non-statutory liability." (*Garcia v. American Airlines, Inc., supra*, 12 F.3d at p. 310.) This is the workers' compensation quid pro quo. (*Id.* at p. 311.)

This quid pro quo works thusly for a California resident injured elsewhere: An employee, who was hired here and who suffered accidental injury in the course of employment outside this state, is entitled to seek California workers' compensation benefits. (§ 3600.5, subd. (a).) The injured employee may also avoid the workers' compensation exclusivity provision and seek damages at common law, against the employer who fails to assume the statutory burdens by "fail[ing] to secure the payment of compensation." (§ 3706.) As applicable here, employers obtain security for payment of compensation pursuant to section 3700, subdivision (a), by obtaining insurance through an insurer that is "duly authorized to write compensation insurance in this state."

By contrast, the Dominican Republic's workers' compensation law provides the exclusive remedy for an employee injured there. The workers' compensation insurer in the Dominican Republic is obligated, upon receipt of proof of an injury, to disburse funds irrespective of negligence. Additionally, all employees in the Dominican Republic have access to the state social security system, which operates as a pension plan and state-sponsored health care provider. Otherwise, employees in the Dominican Republic may not file a negligence action against the employer independent from an action to recover workers' compensation insurance. Punitive or exemplary damages are also unavailable to employees there.

Tucci's position is essentially, because she was hired in California and injured in the course of employment outside of this state, that California law governs and she is entitled to California's compensation benefits. Continuing, she argues, because Club Med was not insured by a company licensed to write insurance in California (§ 3700, subd. (a)), section 3706 allows her to avoid the workers' compensation exclusivity provision and to seek additional recovery in tort. Stated differently, even though she may obtain all California workers' compensation benefits that exceed her recovery under Dominican Republic law, Tucci aims additionally to render inapplicable the exclusivity of the California Workers' Compensation Act on the ground that AXA Courtage is not an insurance company "duly authorized to write compensation insurance in this state." (§ 3700, subd. (a).)

Club Med argues, under applicable choice of law rules, that the law of the Dominican Republic governs and prohibits Tucci from obtaining any recovery beyond worker's compensation benefits and that country's social security system.

Thus, our task is to determine which law applies.

4. Conflict of Laws Analysis.

When it is the forum, California resolves choice-of-law questions in disputes arising out of a tort using the "governmental interest analysis," which balances the interests of the involved states and parties. (*Offshore Rental Co. v. Continental Oil Co.* (1978) 22 Cal. 3d 157, 161 [applying Louisiana law in tort action].) "California applies its own rule of decision unless a party litigant properly invokes the law of a foreign state. . . ."

This governmental interest analysis involves three steps. (1) The court determines whether the foreign law differs from that of the forum. (2) If there is a difference, the court examines each jurisdiction's interest in the application of its own law to determine whether a "true conflict" exists. . . . When both jurisdictions have a legitimate interest in the application of its rule of decision, (3) the court analyzes the "comparative impairment of the interested jurisdictions." . . . The court applies "the law of the state whose interest would be the more impaired if its law were not applied." With these rules in mind, we turn to a comparison of the laws of these two jurisdictions.

a. The Laws of California and the Dominican Republic Differ.

With respect to the exclusivity of workers' compensation, the laws of California and the Dominican Republic are clearly different. As explained above, under California law, when an employer is not insured by a company authorized to write insurance in California, the injured employee may obtain compensation benefits and also sue for damages in tort. By contrast, an employee in the Dominican Republic may not file a negligence claim independent of an action to recover workers' compensation benefits.

b. A True Conflict Exists Between California's Interests and Those of the Dominican Republic.

Turning to the respective interests of California and the Dominican Republic in providing recovery under each state's laws, we conclude they are divergent, although both jurisdictions have recognized "substantial interests . . . in the welfare and subsistence of disabled workers."

California has clearly expressed its interest in swiftly compensating its own residents for work-related injuries (*State Comp. Ins. Fund v. Ind. Acc. Com.* (1942) 20 Cal. 2d 264, 272), in triggering industrial safety, encouraging employers to obtain adequate insurance, and in shifting the cost of injury onto the cost of goods rather than onto society. (*S. G. Borello & Sons, Inc. v. Department of Industrial Relations* (1989) 48 Cal. 3d 341, 354.)[11] More important, California has a strong interest in assuring that its employers are adequately insured. (Cal. Const., art. XIV, § 4.)[12] The quid pro quo, above described, allowing an injured employee to avoid the workers' compensation exclusivity, provides an incentive for employers to secure adequate insurance. . . .

The Dominican Republic's interest in applying its laws lies not only in making certain (1) that workers are adequately insured for workplace injuries, as in California, but also in (2) assuring that businesses in that country face limited

---

11. The goals of California's Workers' Compensation Act are "(1) to ensure that the cost of industrial injuries will be part of the cost of goods rather than a burden on society, (2) to guarantee prompt, limited compensation for an employee's work injures, regardless of fault, as an inevitable cost of production, (3) to spur increased industrial safety, and (4) in return, to insulate the employer from tort liability for his employees' injuries." (*S. G. Borello & Sons, Inc. v. Department of Industrial Relations, supra,* 48 Cal. 3d at p. 354.)

12. The California Constitution has granted the Legislature plenary power to establish "full provision for adequate insurance coverage against liability to pay or furnish compensation; full provision for regulating such insurance coverage in all of its aspects . . . [and] full provision for otherwise securing the payment of compensation. . . ." (Cal. Const., art. XIV, § 4; *Rideaux v. Torgrimson* (1939) 12 Cal. 2d 633, 637.)

and predictable financial liability for work-related injuries, and in (3) predictably defining the duties and liabilities of an employer doing business within its borders, all with the goal of encouraging business investment and development there. The Dominican Republic has a particular interest in applying its law to incidents occurring within its borders, where claims are based largely on the alleged acts of the employer in that country. . . . In short, both of the jurisdictions have legitimate interests in applying their own laws.

c. The Dominican Republic's Interests Will Be More Impaired by Not Applying Its Laws.

We next look at whose interest would be most impaired if its law were not applied. In workers' compensation law, the United States Supreme Court has long recognized that the state where an injury occurs, the state where an employment relationship is created, and the state where an injured employee resides all have the significant contacts necessary to justify application of their own workers' compensation laws. Hence, both the Dominican Republic where the injury occurred, and California where Tucci resides and the employment relationship was created, have sufficient connection to this case to justify Tucci's receipt of workers' compensation benefits.

However, California's interest in assuring that Tucci receive maximum workers' compensation benefits because she is a resident and the contract of hire was created here (§§ 5305, 3600.5), does not in and of itself justify applying California law to enable her to seek additional recovery in tort.

Applying California law to provide Tucci with a common law remedy would both contravene the quid pro quo around which American workers' compensation systems are designed, and defeat the Dominican Republic's policy of providing limited and predictable legal liability and financial responsibility for employers. Under the quid pro quo, employees secure a practical and expeditious remedy for their industrial accidents, while employers secure a limited and determinate liability. When a worker's second claim is for common-law damages rather than additional benefits, however, most states, on grounds of comity and policy, will respect the other jurisdiction's exclusive remedy provisions immunizing the employer from non-statutory liability. The rationale underlying this uniform treatment is compelling. The central purpose of compensation acts is to substitute a limited but certain remedy for the former remedy in tort — a compromise benefiting both employer and employee. When an employee who has received benefits under such a compensation scheme later tries to get back into the common-law damage system, he is essentially un-doing this fundamental quid pro quo. Given that Tucci will receive all compensation benefits to which she may be entitled under either jurisdiction, and can also partake of the Dominican Republic's social security system's benefits, a holding allowing her also to sue for tort damages under California law would seriously undermine California's workers' compensation bargain and flout the guarantee of predictable and limited liability for Dominican Republic employers.

Moreover, application of California law would not advance the purpose of the section 3706 penalty provision. Tucci seeks to avail herself of the penalty of a common law damages action simply because Club Med was not insured by a company authorized to write insurance in California as required by section 3700, subdivision (a). However, the objective of section 3700 appears to be to ensure that employers are adequately insured by a solvent company.[13] Tucci does not claim she was inadequately reimbursed. Nor can she given that AXA Courtage has paid all of her medical bills and she remains entitled to the Dominican Republic's social security system's benefits, and possibly any California benefits that exceed her Dominican Republic benefits. Therefore, California has little interest in penalizing Club Med for providing adequate workers' compensation through a solvent French, rather than Californian company.

. . .

The goals behind California's workers' compensation scheme would not be harmed by applying Dominican Republic law. The aims of the California system to encourage employers to obtain adequate insurance and to place the cost of injury on the cost of goods rather than on society are met here. Club Med had adequate insurance and the burden of this injury was assumed by it and not by the California public. Moreover, California's interest in making certain that California residents, such as Tucci, receive the maximum workers' compensation benefits allowed by law is satisfied even if this state's laws are not applied because Tucci may seek all workers' compensation benefits afforded by California law that exceed those to which she is entitled in the Dominican Republic. California's interests would not be impaired if they were not applied.

Turning to the Dominican Republic's interests, its critical goal of fostering business investment and development, its legitimate interest in seeing that its law determines the consequences of actions within its borders causing injury to people there and its interest in predictably and finally limiting liability predominate and would be significantly undermined if its laws were not applied. . . .

Finally, application of Dominican Republic's law to limit Tucci's recovery to workers' compensation benefits comports with California's long-held preference for workers' compensation exclusivity. The rule of liberal construction [of the workers' compensation law] is not altered because a plaintiff believes that [she] can establish negligence on the part of [her] employer and brings a civil suit for damages. It requires that we liberally construe the [Workers' Compensation] Act in favor of awarding work[ers] compensation, not in permitting civil litigation.

On balance, California's interest will not be impaired if its laws do not govern, whereas the goals of the Dominican Republic's workers' compensation scheme will be greatly undermined if its laws are not applied in this case. This is especially true where Club Med was insured by a solvent company that paid Tucci all of her medical benefits, and she remains entitled to seek benefits under the Dominican

---

13. At oral argument, we requested that the parties submit additional briefing about the legislative history behind the requirement in subdivision (a) of section 3700, that employers obtain compensation with an insurer "duly authorized to write compensation insurance in this state." It appears from the legislative history of the section, that the motivation for the italicized language was the failure in 1916 of the Commonwealth Casualty Company that forced the state to shoulder the cost of that company's losses.

social security system and is also pursuing any California workers' compensation benefits to which she may be entitled. Therefore, the trial court was correct, as a matter of law, in ruling that the law of the Dominican Republic governs the substantive issues of this case.

Disposition

The judgment is affirmed.

NOTES AND QUESTIONS

1. **Practice: What's at Stake?** The issue in *Tucci* is whether a California state court should apply the workers' compensation law of California or the workers' compensation law of the Dominican Republic to the plaintiff's claims. Why do the parties care about this choice-of-law issue?

2. **Choice-of-Law Principles.** What choice-of-law principles did the court use to determine whether to apply the law of California or the law of the Dominican Republic? How do these principles differ from those used in the *Raskin* and *Edwards* cases?

3. **"True" and "False" Conflicts.** According to California's approach to choice-of-law issues in tort cases, if California law and foreign law are different, the court must determine whether there is a "true conflict" between the two jurisdictions over the applicable law. The distinction between "true" and "false" conflicts comes from "interest analysis," which is a choice-of-law theory developed by Professor Brainerd Currie. According to Currie, a court faced with a choice-of-law issue should identify the governmental policies of the forum state expressed in its law, and determine whether, in light of those policies and given the facts of the case, the forum state has an interest in applying its law as the rule of decision. The court should do the same for the foreign state or foreign nation. If based on this analysis, both states have an interest in having their law applied as the rule of decision in the case, there is a "true conflict." Otherwise, there is a "false conflict" — even if the laws are different — because only one state has such an interest. *See* Brainerd Currie, *Notes on Methods and Objectives in the Conflict of Laws*, 1959 DUKE L.J. 171. For an overview of Currie's interest analysis theory, see WILLIAM M. RICHMAN, WILLIAM L. REYNOLDS & CHRISTOPHER A. WHYTOCK, UNDERSTANDING CONFLICT OF LAWS § 78 (4th ed. 2013).

4. **Identifying State Policies and Interests.** In *Tucci*, how did the court determine what California's and the Dominican Republic's respective policies and interests were? Are you convinced by the court's analysis? How would the analysis have been different if the plaintiff had been a resident of the Dominican Republic rather than California? Or if plaintiff's injuries occurred in California rather than the Dominican Republic? As a lawyer, when you face choice-of-law

issues, what type of research will you do to develop and support your claims about the policies and interests of the forum state and a foreign nation?

5. **Comparative Impairment versus Currie's Interest Analysis.** According to Currie's interest analysis theory, if there is a false conflict, then a court should apply the law of the interested jurisdiction, regardless of whether that is the forum or the foreign state or nation. However, if there is a true conflict, the court should apply the law of the forum. Currie, *supra*, at 178. California's version of interest analysis is commonly referred to as the "comparative impairment" method to distinguish it from Currie's approach. How is California's approach to true conflicts different from Currie's approach? Which approach do you think is better, and why?

6. **Practice: Raising Choice-of-Law Issues.** What would have happened in this case if Club Med's lawyers didn't raise the choice-of-law issue, and why? Consider both the implications for the outcome of the case and the implications for the lawyers.

7. **Practice: A Look at the Briefs.** For a look at how lawyers briefed the choice-of-law issues in the *Tucci* case, you may wish to examine the following: Appellant's Opening Brief (2000 WL 34228858), Appellant's Reply Brief (2000 WL 34228857), Appellant's Supplemental Brief (2000 WL 34024938), and Respondent's Supplemental Brief (2000 WL 34024941).

Ortega v. Yokohama Corporation of North America

2010 WL 1534044 (Del. Super. 2010)

Jurden, J.

I. Introduction

Before the Court is Yokohama Corporation of North America (hereinafter "YCNA") and Yokohama Tire Corporation's (hereinafter "YTC")[1] Choice of Law Motion (hereinafter "Defendants' Motion"). Defendants' Motion is filed pursuant to Superior Court Civil Rule 44.1.[2]

Defendants argue that the substantive law of Mexico should apply to all of Plaintiffs' claims.[3] In the alternative, they argue that California law

---

1. YCNA and YTC are hereinafter collectively referred to as "Defendants."

2. Superior Court Civil Rule 44.1 provides: A party who intends to raise an issue concerning the law of a foreign country shall give notice in the party's pleadings or other reasonable written notice. The Court, in determining foreign law, may consider any relevant material or source, including testimony, whether or not submitted by a party or admissible under the Delaware Rules of Evidence. The Court's determination shall be treated as a ruling on a question of law.

3. Defendants argue specifically that the law of the Mexican State of Michoacán should apply.

should apply to all of Plaintiffs' claims. If the Court rejects these arguments, Defendants argue that Virginia law should apply to Plaintiffs' claims of defective design and manufacture, California law should apply to Plaintiffs' marketing defect claims, and Mexican law should apply to Plaintiffs' damages claims.

For the reasons that follow, Defendants' Choice of Law Motion is GRANTED IN PART and DENIED IN PART.

II. Background

The Parties

Plaintiffs are residents of [Estado de México], a state within the Republic of Mexico. YCNA is a Delaware corporation with its principal place of business in California. YTC is incorporated in California with its principal place of business in California.

The Accident

This suit stems from a motor vehicle accident that occurred on June 8, 2005 in the Mexican State of Michoacán. Nelson Flores Hernandez (hereinafter "Decedent"), was driving his 1998 Ford Explorer. Marcelino Valdez was his passenger. Plaintiffs claim the right rear tire of the Explorer suffered a sudden catastrophic tread separation which caused the Explorer to lose control and roll over. Decedent suffered fatal injuries.

Plaintiffs filed suit on June 7, 2007 alleging, inter alia: (1) strict liability; (2) breach of warranty; and (3) that Defendants negligently designed, tested, manufactured, and marketed an unsafe tire.

The Product

The tire is identified as a Yokohama Prodigy Radial A/T, DOT CCD6USH1902 (hereinafter "the Tire"). It is undisputed that the Tire was designed and manufactured in Virginia and tested in Ohio. No other information about the Tire is known by the parties.

III. Discussion

Delaware Courts apply the "most significant relationship" test of the Restatement (Second) of Conflict of Laws in order to determine choice of law. The significant relationship test is a flexible one and "requires each case to be decided on its own facts." "Pursuant to Section 145[(1)] of the Second Restatement, the local law of the state which 'has the most significant relationship to the occurrence and the parties under the principles stated in § 6 [of the Restatement]' will govern the rights of litigants in a tort suit."

Section 145[(2)] lists contacts which should be considered when determining the law applicable to an issue. These contacts include:

(1) the place where the injury occurred,
(2) the place where the conduct causing the injury occurred,
(3) the domicil, residence, nationality, place of incorporation and place of business of the parties, and
(4) the place where the relationship, if any, between the parties is centered.

Each of the aforementioned contacts must be weighed in light of § 6 of the Restatement (Second) Conflict of Laws, which requires consideration of the following:

(1) the needs of the interstate and international systems,
(2) the relevant policies of the forum,
(3) the relevant policies of other interested states and the relative interests of those states in the determination of the particular issue,
(4) the protection of justified expectations,
(5) the basic policies underlying the particular field of law,
(6) certainty, predictability and uniformity of result, and
(7) ease in the determination and application of the law to be applied.

Section 146 of the Restatement (Second) Conflict of Laws directs the Court to apply the law of the state where the injury occurred in an action for a personal injury unless "some other state has a more significant relationship under the principles stated in § 6 to the occurrence and the parties, in which event the local law of the other state will be applied." A place of injury does not play an important role in the selection of the applicable law "when the place of injury can be said to be fortuitous or when for other reasons it bears little relation to the occurrence and the parties with respect to the particular issue."[27]

Place of Injury

The place of injury in this case is fortuitous. The motor vehicle accident occurred in the Mexican State of Michoacán. However, neither of the parties has significant ties with that state. Neither Plaintiffs nor Defendants are residents of Michoacán.[28] Because Michoacán has no connection to the claim other than the fact that it was the location of the accident, it is considered fortuitous and, thus, accorded less weight than the other factors.

---

27. [Restatement (Second) of Conflict of Laws § 145, cmt. e.]
28. Plaintiffs are all residents of the State of Mexico. YCNA is a Delaware corporation with its principal place of business in California. YTC is incorporated in California with its principal place of business in California.

Place Where Conduct That Caused the Injury Occurred

The wrongful conduct alleged by Plaintiffs in their lawsuit occurred within the United States. Although there are many facts unknown about the Tire, it is undisputed that it was designed and manufactured in Virginia, and tested in Ohio.

Domicil, Residence, Nationality, Place of Incorporation and Place of Business of the Parties

As noted above, at all relevant times Plaintiffs were residents of the State of Mexico. YTC is incorporated in California and YCNA is incorporated in Delaware. Both YTC and YNCA have principal places of business in California.

Defendants argue that California has the most significant contacts over any other United States jurisdiction[30] because it is where YTC is incorporated and where YTC and YNCA have principal places of business.[31] However, the most significant relationship test does not allow a court to simply add up all of the contacts as listed in Section 145 and § 6 and apply the law of the state with the most contacts. The Court must weigh and consider the significance of each of the contacts.

The Place Where the Relationship Between the Parties Is Centered

The relationship between the parties in this case is centered in the State of Virginia, the place where the Tire was designed and manufactured. Although the State of California has several contacts, and quantitatively more contacts perhaps than Virginia,[33] Section 145 has a qualitative element. "[Section 145] clearly states that the 'contacts are to be evaluated according to their relative importance with respect to the particular issue.'"

Because much is unknown about the Tire, the choice of law determination is a bit more challenging in this case. First, it is not known when or where the Tire was placed into the stream of commerce.[36] It is also not known how the Tire arrived in Mexico or when or how Decedent obtained the Tire. Finally, and perhaps most importantly, it is not known where the Tire was marketed. Modern choice of law considerations suggest that the jurisdiction where a product is marketed has a greater interest than a jurisdiction where a product is manufactured, developed, or tested.

---

30. Defendants argue this in the alternative in the event the Court does not find Mexican law to apply.

31. Defendants further suggest that California is where the tire was marketed because California is the location of Yokohama's marketing headquarters.

33. As previously noted, California is YTC's place of incorporation and both YTC and YCNA's principal place of business is in California.

36. After designed and manufactured, the subject tire was tested in Ohio. There is no evidence as to where the tire entered the stream of commerce.

If the Court rejects the application of Mexican law, Defendants argue in the alternative that California is "the place where all corporate decisions pertaining to the subject tires marketing, advertising, instructions, labeling, warnings, warranties, distribution, and sales are made[,]" and thus, California law should apply to marketing claims. While Defendants' "marketing headquarters" may very well be located in California, "the jurisdiction where a product is marketed" is to be considered, not the location of a company's marketing headquarters or the state in which marketing decisions take place. Plaintiffs argue that Virginia law should apply to the warranty, marketing and consumer claims because Virginia is the place where the Tire was designed, manufactured, and placed into the stream of commerce. In making this argument, Plaintiffs offer no support for their assertion that the Tire was placed in the stream of commerce in Virginia. Here, there is no way to ascertain where the Tire was marketed or where it was placed into the stream of commerce.[41]

Based on what is known about the Tire, the Court concludes the state where the relationship between the parties is centered is Virginia. Virginia is where the Tire came into existence, where it was both designed and made.

Factors — Section 6 Restatement (Second) Conflict of Laws

After weighing each of the aforementioned contacts in light of the factors set forth in § 6 of the Restatement, the Court finds that Virginia law shall apply to all claims and damages[42] in this case.

The laws of Mexico severely limit the amount of damages a plaintiff can recover in a wrongful death action and do not provide for a survival cause of action. The purpose of those laws would seem to be to protect resident defendants from being accountable for large monetary damages associated with such actions. Because Defendants in this case are from the United States, neither the Country of Mexico nor any Mexican State has a strong policy interest in the application of its laws. Here, the State of Virginia has a stronger interest because, presumably, it would want to protect the public from any wrongful and/or harmful conduct allegedly caused by product designers and/or product manufacturers which conduct business within the state.

In addition, although the accident occurred in Michoacán, a foreign plaintiff has come to the U.S. . . . in order to hold defendants accountable for alleged wrongful conduct which occurred solely in the U.S. It therefore does not offend fundamental fairness to allow for the suit to proceed under United States law. Furthermore, it seems fair to hold Defendants to the laws of the country in which

---

41. It is also known that Yokohama does not sell tires in the Country of Mexico.

42. Defendants argue that damages should be decoupled from the underlying claims, that the Court must undergo an independent choice of law analysis regarding damages, and that Mexican law should apply to damages. Having considered the issue of damages, the Court finds that Virginia has the most significant relationship to that issue as well because Plaintiffs claim that the design and manufacturing of the Tire caused Plaintiffs' damages — conduct that occurred in Virginia.

they are incorporated and the country in which they conduct extensive business, rather than have Defendants comply with the laws of a foreign country.

Although the States of Delaware and California may have some interest in the application of their respective laws, these interests are not as significant as those of Virginia. As discussed supra, Defendants are incorporated in Delaware and California and have principal places of business in California. But today, it is common for businesses to incorporate in one state, have a principal place of business in another, and conduct business both nationally or internationally. All contacts must be considered and weighed in terms of significance to the issues of the particular case. And Defendants should reasonably expect to be held accountable under the laws of a state in which they conduct business.

Finally, application of Virginia law will foster certainty, predictability, uniformity and ease in determination in this case. The application of Mexican law could be more costly and complicated for both the parties and the Court.

IV. Conclusion

Based on the foregoing, because Virginia has the most significant relationship to the occurrence and parties in this case, Virginia law shall apply to the Plaintiffs' claims and damages.

It Is So Ordered.

NOTES AND QUESTIONS

1. **Practice: What Are the Stakes?** The issue in *Ortega* was whether a Delaware state court should apply the tort law of Mexico (specifically, the law of the Mexican State of Michoacán) or the tort law of Virginia to decide this case. Why do the parties care about this choice-of-law issue?
2. **Choice-of-Law Principles.** What choice-of-law principles did the court use to determine whether to apply the law of Mexico or the law of Virginia? How do they differ from the traditional *First Restatement*, New York, and California approaches?
3. **Structuring a *Second Restatement* Analysis.** The *Second Restatement* has several different elements (§ 6, § 145(1), § 145(2), and § 146), but it does not provide clear instructions about the order in which these elements should be applied. For this reason, one challenge — for lawyers, judges, and students — is how to structure a *Second Restatement* choice-of-law analysis. Do you think the court structured its analysis properly? If you were a clerk for the judge in this case, how would you have suggested that the analysis be structured?
4. **Policy: Evaluating the Outcome.** Is it fair and appropriate for a plaintiff who is not a U.S. citizen to sue a U.S. business based on U.S. state law that is more favorable to plaintiffs than the law of the plaintiff's own nation, when the U.S. business allegedly caused plaintiff to suffer an injury in the plaintiff's nation? Why or why not?

5. **Practice: Choice-of-Law and Forum Shopping.** Would the outcome in *Ortega* be different if the plaintiffs had sued (and were able to obtain jurisdiction over) defendants in a state like Kansas that applies the *First Restatement* method to decide choice-of-law issues in tort cases? Why or why not? In what ways might differences in states' choice-of-law methods create incentives for forum shopping?

6. **The Spread of the *Second Restatement*.** As the *Ortega* court indicates, Delaware courts apply the choice-of-law principles of the *Restatement (Second) of Conflict of Laws* to decide choice-of-law issues. The *Restatement (Second)* was adopted by the American Law Institute in 1969 as the successor to the *Restatement (First) of Conflict of Laws*. Today, the *Restatement (Second)* represents the most common choice-of-law approach in the United States: As of 2019, 25 U.S. jurisdictions apply it in tort cases and 24 apply it in contract cases. Symeon C. Symeonides, *Choice of Law in the American Courts in 2019: Thirty-Third Annual Survey*, 68 Am. J. Comp. L. (forthcoming 2020). However, as noted above, some states continue to apply the *First Restatement* method, and California and New York take yet different approaches in tort cases. Beyond these methods, there are still other methods used by U.S. courts that are not covered in this section, but which you would learn about in a specialized course on conflict of laws.

Naghiu v. Inter-Continental Hotels Group, Inc.

165 F.R.D. 413 (D. Del. 1996)

Murray M. Schwartz, Senior District Judge.

I. Introduction

Plaintiffs Leslie and Laverne Naghiu, citizens of Virginia, have filed suit in this diversity action against the Inter-Continental Hotels Group, Inc. ("Inter-Continental" or "defendant"), a Delaware corporation. Plaintiffs aver that during Leslie Naghiu's ("Naghiu" or "plaintiff") stay as a guest of defendant's hotel in Zaire,* Africa in March, 1993, he was attacked in his room, causing him to suffer personal bodily injury and a loss of $146,000 in property. Laverne Naghiu claims a loss of consortium flowing from her husband's injuries.

Inter-Continental has moved for dismissal under Rule 12(b)(6) of the Federal Rules of Civil Procedure, arguing that plaintiff is not the real party in interest in this case as to the loss of personal property. In addition, Inter-Continental has moved for summary judgment under Rule 56 on the issue of whether it is liable in tort for the events that allegedly occurred on its premises.

---

* Zaire is now known as the Democratic Republic of Congo. — Eds.

Jurisdiction is invoked pursuant to 28 U.S.C. § 1332. For the reasons stated below, the Court will grant defendant's motions as to both issues.

II. Factual Background

The Court views the facts in this case, which are rich with intrigue, in the light most favorable to the plaintiffs. Naghiu, an employee of the Christian Broadcast Network, Inc. ("CBN"), serves as the director of executive protection for Dr. Pat Robertson ("Robertson").[1] In this capacity, Naghiu coordinates security arrangements for Robertson on his trips abroad. Naghiu is an employee of CBN but is not an officer or director of CBN; he has no ownership or voting control in the affairs of CBN. Naghiu's employment with CBN is based out of Virginia Beach, Virginia.

In March 1993, on behalf of Robertson, Naghiu traveled to Zaire to purchase diamonds and render humanitarian aid. To that end, Naghiu estimates that he carried on his person approximately $100,000 in cash, kept in an attaché case. He describes the "street" environment in Zaire as follows:

> There is very little street crime in Zaire. The crime in Zaire is perpetrated nine out of ten times by the military. But that doesn't keep CBN away from performing the humanitarian tasks and the businesses that [Robertson] is there for. As CBN likes to put it, if you don't like the heat in the kitchen you can leave.

Naghiu further delineated the risks of travel abroad to Zaire:

> [I]t is a risk to anyone who is involved in the international arena from the standpoint of a security person. We are not talking about a security guard at the K-Mart. We are talking about someone that works the international arena and knows what the circumstances and consequences can be in a volatile continent. I am not trying to earmark Zaire. I happen to enjoy working in Zaire. What I am saying is that the continent itself, today there are 23 countries in that continent that are under military strife.

From 1992-93, Naghiu traveled numerous times to Zaire on behalf of CBN. Out of concern for Robertson's safety and welfare, Naghiu twice recommended that Robertson not personally travel to Zaire when Naghiu perceived conditions as too dangerous. Robertson followed Naghiu's advice on those occasions.

As of the March, 1993 CBN expedition to Zaire, Robertson's corporation had rendered approximately two million dollars in humanitarian aid to that country. With this legacy of prior aid, CBN's March, 1993 return to Zaire was covered by the Zaire media, including television. During all of this, Naghiu was charged with the security of the attaché case containing the money. The Robertson entourage booked its stay at defendant's Inter-Continental Hotel Kinshasa ("hotel"), the only suitable lodging for business travelers in Kinshasa, Zaire. Inter-Continental

---

1. Dr. Robertson is an internationally-known televangelist, humanitarian, and former United States presidential candidate. 2 Who's Who in America 2897 (1994).

admits that it routinely advised all paying guests to give their valuables, including cash, to the hotel staff for safe-keeping.

Upon arrival at the Inter-Continental Kinshasa, Naghiu asked the night personnel to procure a safe deposit box for the cash. The night clerk told Naghiu there were no accessible boxes available until the following morning. From his vantage point at the registration desk, Naghiu could see the boxes and perceived them to be in a state of "disarray."

Naghiu claims that the following morning he again approached Inter-Continental's front desk clerk and requested a safe deposit box, but was told to "come back later." Naghiu retained the attaché case containing the cash. A short time later in his stay, Naghiu complained to the hotel's General Manager that there were prostitutes roaming the hotel's elevators and corridors soliciting business from the hotel's guests. Although he had the opportunity, Naghiu did not mention to the General Manager about his inability to obtain a safe deposit box for his valuables. At some point during the CBN trip, $46,000 was added to the attaché as proceeds of a diamond transaction.

On the evening of March 23, 1993, Naghiu supped at a private residence that was ". . . 45 minutes outside of Kinshasa in an area where soldiers and military types have stopped vehicles, accosted foreigners and even Zaireans, manhandled them. Shot them." Consequently, as Naghiu has testified, he left the attaché case and its contents in his hotel room while he left the premises. He did not consider making another effort at obtaining a hotel safe deposit box. Naghiu hid the attaché case behind a couch and set of heavy drapes in his hotel room on the 19th floor.

According to Naghiu, he returned from dinner to his hotel door and used his key to enter his room. He remembers now that the door appeared to have been unlocked, although it did not strike him at the time as out of the ordinary. Upon gaining entry, he attempted to turn on the overhead light, without success. Naghiu finally located a floor lamp that lit and then immediately witnessed a man going through his large suitcase, strewing clothing on the floor. Naghiu yelled at the man, who brandished a "long, very thin bladed Belgian sabre" and lunged at Naghiu. The man missed Naghiu and instead impaled the hotel room wall, leaving "a tremendous indentation." Naghiu then claims the man assaulted him with the knife, cutting him above the ear on the left side of his head and on the right forearm. Naghiu says he fought his assailant when another man approached from the bathroom; that is the last thing Naghiu remembers before being knocked unconscious.

Naghiu's companions found him unconscious in his room and brought him to another site for medical attention. Inter-Continental refused to allow Naghiu's fellow security officer into the room to perform an immediate investigation. According to plaintiff, within 24 hours of the attack, the holes in the wall made by the attacker's knife were filled in, the room had been painted and the carpet had been replaced. Naghiu subsequently filed criminal charges with the Zairean authorities. When he returned stateside, Naghiu claims that Robertson expected reimbursement of the stolen money. Robertson later told Naghiu, however, not "to worry about [the money], that [Naghiu] was bonded."

III. Discussion

. . .

C. Real Party in Interest — Loss of Personal Property

Defendants first argue that plaintiff may not recover for the alleged loss of the $146,000 because plaintiff is not the real party in interest as required by the Federal Rules of Civil Procedure. Fed. R. Civ. P. 17(a) requires that "[e]very action shall be prosecuted in the name of the real party in interest." Unless a party is "[a]n executor, administrator, guardian, bailee,* trustee of an express trust, a party with whom or in whose name a contract has been made for the benefit of another, or a party authorized by statute," a litigant cannot sue in his "own name without joining the party for whose benefit the action is brought." Fed. R. Civ. P. 17(a). The underlying aim of the rule is to ensure fairness to the defendant by protecting the defendant against a subsequent action by the party actually entitled to relief, and by ensuring that the judgment will have proper res judicata effect. . . .

Choice of Law

Naghiu argues that he was a bailee of the money and as such, is a real party in interest as explicitly enumerated by Fed. R. Civ. P. 17. In analyzing plaintiff's status as bailee vel non, the Court looks to the substantive law creating the right being sued upon to ascertain whether plaintiff possesses a substantive right to relief. As a threshold matter, the Court must decide which jurisdiction's law controls the issue of whether plaintiff is to be considered a bailee of the $146,000.

Where, as here, the jurisdiction of a federal court is founded upon the diversity statute, 28 U.S.C. § 1332, the Court applies the substantive law, including the choice of law provisions of the state in which the federal court sits. . . . [*Klaxon Co. v. Stentor Elec. Mfg. Co.*, 313 U.S. 487 (1941)]. This Court therefore will look to Delaware choice of law rules to determine the substantive law that governs the dispute between Naghiu and Inter-Continental.

For choice of law questions sounding in contract,[2] Delaware courts follow the "most significant relationship" approach of the *Restatement (Second) of Conflict of Laws. Travelers Indem. Co. v. Lake*, 594 A.2d 38, 41 (Del. 1991). . . . Under Restatement section 188, the rights and duties of the parties with respect to an issue in contract are determined by the local law of the state with the most significant relationship to the transaction and the parties by reference to the following principles: a) the place of contracting, b) the place of negotiation of the contract, c) the place of performance, d) the location of the subject matter of the contract, and e) the domicile, residence, or place of incorporation and

---

* A "bailee" is "[s]omeone who receives personal property from another, and has possession of but not title to the property. A bailee is responsible for keeping the property safe until it is returned to the owner." BLACK'S LAW DICTIONARY (11th ed. 2019). — EDS.

2. Delaware courts have determined that a bailment arrangement is by nature a contractual relation. . . .

place of business of the parties. Restatement (Second) of Conflicts § 188 (1971). Considering plaintiff as a putative bailee of CBN based in Virginia, the Court finds that factors a, b, c, d and part of e of the Restatement approach point to Virginia. Accordingly, the Court holds that Virginia has the most significant relationship to the occurrence and the parties with respect to whether plaintiff was a bailee of the cash and thus satisfies Rule 17's real party in interest requirement. Thus, Virginia law shall control as to whether plaintiff was in fact a bailee.

The Supreme Court of Virginia has ruled that "[a] bailment has been broadly defined as 'the rightful possession of goods by one who is not the owner.'" *K-B Corp. v. Gallagher*, 218 Va. 381 (1977) (quoting 9 S. Williston, Contracts § 875 (3d ed. 1967)). In addition, to be considered a bailee, one must have both physical control of the goods and an intent to exercise that control. *K-B Corp.*, 237 S.E.2d at 185.

Although there may be superficial similarity, a master and servant (or employer and employee) do not stand in the relationship of a bailor and bailee to one another. Unlike the employer's relationship with his employee, the bailor has no control over the bailee. The bailment relation is concerned only with personal property, and the bailee is not subject to direction in carrying out the purposes of the bailment, except as the bailment contract provides, but occupies rather the position of an independent contractor. On the other hand, employment imports control and direction of the employee's acts within the scope of the employment relationship. "[W]here an owner of a chattel delivers it to another to perform work in respect to or by means of it, the relationship of the parties is that of bailor and bailee where the owner parts with control over it and is that of master and servant where he retains control thereof." *Payne v. Kinder*, 147 W. Va. 352 (1962).

As an employee of CBN, Naghiu was charged with safekeeping the cash as a duty of his master-servant relationship. In reality, Naghiu had only custodial possession of the money; others in the CBN party exercised control over how the money or diamonds were to be transacted. Thus, contrary to plaintiff's assertions, he could not be considered a bailee to satisfy Rule 17's real party in interest requirement. In sum, Naghiu has not demonstrated any legal interest in the cash allegedly stolen from his hotel room on March 23, 1993. He has testified under oath that he has no ownership interest in the money, and has no written authorization to seek its recovery. In addition, he has never claimed to be suing on Pat Robertson's or anyone else's behalf. Thus, as to defendant's liability for the stolen cash, plaintiff has proffered no theory supporting his status as a real party in interest to this action.

. . .

D. Naghiu's Personal Injuries — Premises Liability

The Court sitting in diversity must also determine what substantive law governs the tort claims in this case. Again, the Court first looks to the forum state's choice of law rules for guidance. Similar to its approach for analyzing choice of law questions for contract issues, Delaware adheres to the "most significant relationship" approach of the *Restatement (Second) of Conflict of Laws* for tort issues. *Travelers Indem. Co.*

v. Lake, 594 A.2d at 47. Under section 145 of the Restatement, the local law of the state which "has the most significant relationship to the occurrence and the parties under the principles stated in section 6" will govern the rights and liabilities of the parties in a tort action. *Id.* (quoting Restatement (Second) of Conflict of Laws § 145(1) (1971)). Section [6] delineates the following considerations:

> (a) the needs of the interstate and international systems,
> (b) the relevant policies of the forum,
> (c) the relevant policies of other interested states and the relative interests of those states in the determination of the particular issue,
> (d) the protection of justified expectations,
> (e) the basic policies underlying the particular field of law,
> (f) certainty, predictability, and uniformity of result,
> (g) ease in the determination and application of the law to be applied.

Id. at § 6. Section 145[(2)] speaks directly to the relevant contacts the Court must consider when applying section six:

> (a) the place where the injury occurred,
> (b) the place where the conduct causing the injury occurred,
> (c) the domicile, residence, nationality, place of incorporation, and place of business of the parties, and
> (d) the place where the relationship, if any, between the parties is centered.

Id. at § 145. If the tort case involves personal injury, as this one does, the Court is directed by Restatement section 146 "to apply the law of the state where the injury occurred in a 'personal injury case' unless the forum state has a 'more significant relationship' under section Six principles to the 'occurrence and the parties.'"

With these principles in mind, the Court concludes that the Supreme Court of Delaware would apply Zairean law to Naghiu's claims for personal injury against Inter-Continental. As the forum wherein his alleged personal injury occurred, under section 146, Zaire has the most significant relationship to the occurrence and to the issues raised by Naghiu. Zaire is also at the heart of the parties' relationship to one another, as the Inter-Continental Hotel Kinshasa is located in that forum and it is the hotel's conduct that is at issue in this case. Thus, the majority of the Restatement factors point to Zairean law as the source of the substantive rule of decision in this case.[4]

[In a discussion excerpted in the next subsection, the court found that Naghiu had not shown facts to support his negligence claim under Zairean law, and thus granted summary judgment for the defendants on both claims.]

---

4. The Supreme Court of Delaware has held that different choice of law rules under the Restatement (Second) of Conflicts apply to different causes of action, differentiating between actions in contract and tort. *Travelers Indem. Co. v. Lake*, 594 A.2d 38, 41, 47 (Del. 1991). Because the choice of law analysis is issue-specific, this Court's determination that Virginia law controlled the bailment issue is considered separately from the question of what law controls the negligence issue in this case. This process of applying the rules of different states to discrete issues within the same case is known as "dépeçage."

NOTES AND QUESTIONS

1. **Choice-of-Law Principles.** In the *Naghiu* case, a federal court — the U.S. District Court for the District of Delaware — had to determine whether the law of Virginia or the law of Zaire governed a contract issue and a tort issue. What choice-of-law principles did the court use to determine these choice-of-law issues, and why?

2. *Dépeçage.* As the court explains in footnote 4, the choice-of-law process of "applying the rules of different states to discrete issues within the same case is known as 'dépeçage.'" Terminology aside, the important point is that when courts are faced with multiple choice-of-law issues, they may apply the law of the forum to decide some of those issues and apply the law of one or more foreign states or nations to decide the others. For an overview of *dépeçage*, see WILLIAM M. RICHMAN, WILLIAM L. REYNOLDS & CHRISTOPHER A. WHYTOCK, UNDERSTANDING CONFLICT OF LAWS § 61 (4th ed. 2013).

3. **Second Restatement Analysis: Torts versus Contracts.** In the *Naghiu* case, the court decided what law to apply to a contract issue and a tort issue. Even though the court applied the *Second Restatement* to decide both choice-of-law issues, it decided that the law of Virginia governed the contract issue and the law of Zaire governed the tort issue. Why did the court reach these different outcomes? More generally, why can the outcome of a choice-of-law analysis depend on how the choice-of-law issue is characterized (for example, whether it is characterized as a tort or contract choice-of-law issue)?

4. **Relevant Contacts in Contract Cases.** According to § 188(1) of the *Second Restatement*, "[t]he rights and duties of the parties with respect to an issue in contract are determined by the local law of the state which, with respect to that issue, has the most significant relationship to the transaction and the parties under the principles stated in § 6." You are familiar with the § 6 principles from *Ortega*, and these principles are also set forth in the court's opinion in *Naghiu*. The § 6 principles are part of a proper *Second Restatement* analysis in both tort and contract cases. However, the contacts to be taken into account for contract issues, which are set forth in the court's opinion (and contained in § 188(2)), are different from the contacts to be taken into account for tort issues, which are also set forth in the court's opinion (and contained in § 145(2)). How are the § 188(2) contacts different from the § 145(2) contacts?

5. **Specific Choice-of-Law Principles.** According to § 188(3) of the *Second Restatement*, "[i]f the place of negotiating the contract and the place of performance are in the same state, the local law of this state will usually be applied, except as otherwise provided in §§ 189-199 and 203." These and other provisions of the *Second Restatement* contain specific principles to be applied to particular types of contracts and particular contract issues. For

example, according to § 206, "[i]ssues relating to details of performance of a contract are determined by the local law of the place of performance" — such as "whether the debtor shall be allowed days of grace, and the exact time and place at which performance is due" and "the manner in which presentment and protest shall be made and notice given, and the kind of currency in which payment shall be made." § 206, cmt. b. Whenever you analyze a choice-of-law issue under the *Second Restatement*, you should carefully examine not only the general provisions, but also specific provisions such as those mentioned in this note.

6. **Proper Application of the Second Restatement.** In your view, did the court properly apply the *Second Restatement* in *Naghiu*? Is anything missing analytically? What might a more thorough *Second Restatement* choice-of-law analysis have looked like? Why might courts find it difficult to apply the *Second Restatement*'s choice-of-law rules in a thorough and systematic manner? How can you help as a lawyer?

7. **The CISG and the Applicable Law in Contract Cases.** The U.N. Convention on Contracts for the International Sale of Goods (CISG) is a treaty that was developed by the U.N. Commission on International Trade Law (UNCITRAL). The CISG governs matters such as formation of contracts, the obligations of the seller and buyer, and contractual remedies. Currently, 93 nations, including the United States, are parties to the CISG (https://uncitral.un.org/en/texts/salegoods/conventions/sale_of_goods/cisg/status). The following are the key provisions governing the CISG's scope of application:

Article 1

(1) This Convention applies to contracts of sale of goods between parties whose places of business are in different States:*

(a) when the States are [Parties to this Convention]; or
(b) when the rules of private international law lead to the application of the law of a [Party to the Convention].

(2) The fact that the parties have their places of business in different States is to be disregarded whenever this fact does not appear either from the contract or from any dealings between, or from information disclosed by, the parties at any time before or at the conclusion of the contract.

(3) Neither the nationality of the parties nor the civil or commercial character of the parties or of the contract is to be taken into consideration in determining the application of this Convention.

---

* Remember once again that in the technical language of international law, the term "state" refers to a nation (such as Japan, Nigeria, or the United States), not a U.S. state (such as California).

Article 2

This Convention does not apply to sales:

(a) of goods bought for personal, family or household use, unless the seller, at any time before or at the conclusion of the contract, neither knew nor ought to have known that the goods were bought for any such use;
(b) by auction;
(c) on execution or otherwise by authority of law;
(d) of stocks, shares, investment securities, negotiable instruments or money;
(e) of ships, vessels, hovercraft or aircraft;
(f) of electricity.

Article 3

(1) Contracts for the supply of goods to be manufactured or produced are to be considered sales unless the party who orders the goods undertakes to supply a substantial part of the materials necessary for such manufacture or production.

(2) This Convention does not apply to contracts in which the preponderant part of the obligations of the party who furnishes the goods consists in the supply of labour or other services.

A very important legal and practical point is that the CISG governs contracts covered by these provisions *unless* the parties to the contract opt out of the CISG. *See* Article 6 ("The parties may exclude the application of this Convention. . . ."). Therefore, as a lawyer advising a client considering a contract that might be covered by the CISG, unless you want the CISG's provisions to govern, you must be very careful to include language in the contract that explicitly states that the parties exclude application of the CISG, and you should consider a choice-of-law clause that indicates an alternative source of governing law.

2. Comparative Perspective

In the United States, choice-of-law principles are primarily a product of common law. In contrast, in the European Union and most civil law systems, choice of law is governed primarily by rules reflected in a code or regulation. For example, Article 4 of Regulation (EC) No. 593/2008 of the European Parliament and of the Council of 17 June 2008 on the Law Applicable to Contractual Obligations (also called the Rome I Regulation) provides as follows:

1. To the extent that the law applicable to the contract has not been chosen [by the parties, subject to specified exceptions], the law governing the contract shall be determined as follows:

(a) a contract for the sale of goods shall be governed by the law of the country where the seller has his habitual residence;

(b) a contract for the provision of services shall be governed by the law of the country where the service provider has his habitual residence;

(c) a contract relating to a right in rem in immovable property or to a tenancy of immovable property shall be governed by the law of the country where the property is situated;

(d) notwithstanding point (c), a tenancy of immovable property concluded for temporary private use for a period of no more than six consecutive months shall be governed by the law of the country where the landlord has his habitual residence, provided that the tenant is a natural person and has his habitual residence in the same country;

(e) a franchise contract shall be governed by the law of the country where the franchisee has his habitual residence;

(f) a distribution contract shall be governed by the law of the country where the distributor has his habitual residence;

(g) a contract for the sale of goods by auction shall be governed by the law of the country where the auction takes place, if such a place can be determined; . . .

(h) a contract concluded within a multilateral system which brings together or facilitates the bringing together of multiple third-party buying and selling interests in financial instruments . . . , in accordance with nondiscretionary rules and governed by a single law, shall be governed by that law.

2. Where the contract is not covered by paragraph 1 or where the elements of the contract would be covered by more than one of points (a) to (h) of paragraph 1, the contract shall be governed by the law of the country where the party required to effect the characteristic performance of the contract has his habitual residence.

3. Where it is clear from all the circumstances of the case that the contract is manifestly more closely connected with a country other than that indicated in paragraphs 1 or 2, the law of that other country shall apply.

4. Where the law applicable cannot be determined pursuant to paragraphs 1 or 2, the contract shall be governed by the law of the country with which it is most closely connected.

Additional rules cover carriage contracts, consumer contracts, insurance, and employment.

With regard to noncontractual disputes, Article 4 of Regulation (EC) No. 864/2007 of the European Parliament and of the Council of 11 July 2007 on the Law Applicable to Non-Contractual Obligations (also called the Rome II Regulation) provides the following general rules:

1. Unless otherwise provided for in this Regulation, the law applicable to a non-contractual obligation arising out of a tort/delict shall be the law of the country in which the damage occurs irrespective of the country in which the event giving rise to the damage occurred and irrespective of the country or countries in which the indirect consequences of that event occur.

2. However, where the person claimed to be liable and the person sustaining damage both have their habitual residence in the same country at the time when the damage occurs, the law of that country shall apply.

3. Where it is clear from all the circumstances of the case that the tort/ delict is manifestly more closely connected with a country other than that indicated in paragraphs 1 or 2, the law of that other country shall apply. A manifestly closer connection with another country might be based in particular on a pre-existing relationship between the parties, such as a contract, that is closely connected with the tort/delict in question.

Do the EU regulations adopt a more sensible system than the U.S. approach? Do they provide clear rules? Are they too inflexible? Can you say with confidence how the prior cases would have been decided under the EU regulations? Why hasn't this approach been adopted in the United States?

3. *Determining Foreign Law*

A judge in the United States will be familiar with U.S. federal law and the law of his or her U.S. state. But as we have seen, choice-of-law analysis may require U.S. judges to apply the law of a foreign nation. When this happens, how is a judge supposed to determine what foreign law requires? Rule 44.1 of the Federal Rules of Civil Procedure provides basic guidance: "A party who intends to raise an issue about a foreign country's law must give notice by a pleading or other writing. In determining foreign law, the court may consider any relevant material or source, including testimony, whether or not submitted by a party or admissible under the Federal Rules of Evidence. The court's determination must be treated as a ruling on a question of law." The cases in this section illustrate how judges have applied Rule 44.1 to determine foreign law.

Naghiu v. Inter-Continental Hotels Group, Inc.

165 F.R.D. 413 (D. Del. 1996)

MURRAY M. SCHWARTZ, Senior District Judge.

[In the excerpt in the prior subsection, the court found that the law of Zaire governed plaintiff's tort claims for injury suffered in a hotel in Kinshasa, Zaire.]

1. The Zairean Civil Code

Under the Federal Rules of Civil Procedure, "[t]he court, in determining foreign law, may consider any relevant material or source." Fed. R. Civ. P. 44.1. Here, the Court accepts the parties' proffer of opinion letters expounding Zairean law authored by individuals with expertise in the relevant provisions of the Zairean Civil Code. See *id.* Advisory Committee Note (the Court may rely on presentation by counsel in applying foreign law). Each side has argued for application of the same provisions of Zairean law.

Zaire Civil Code Articles 258 and 259 speak to general tort liability of those who commit injury to others:

Article 258. Any act of a man which causes damages to another obliges him by whose fault it occurred to make reparation.

Article 259. Each person is liable for the damages he causes not only by his act but by his negligence or imprudence.

Citing these provisions, defendant argues that if any reparations are due plaintiff, they are owed by his assailants. However, in direct contrast to defendant's argument, its Zairean attorney "expert" opined in his letter that these provisions of Zairean code allow Naghiu, as a hotel guest who has sustained injury, to file suit against the hotel for negligence. One of plaintiff's opinion letters also paraphrased Zairean Civil Code Article 19 as "provid[ing] that no persons foreign to the hotel can get access to the premises and rooms assigned to the guests except if they were duly authorized by the innkeeper or his agent."

Naghiu argues that Inter-Continental failed to take the necessary measures in order to maintain the premises free from hazards and dangerous conditions and was thus negligent in allowing the criminals to victimize plaintiff. Although the Court accepts the general principle that under Zairean law, Inter-Continental could be liable under a negligence theory, neither party has supplied the Court with the necessary provisions of Zairean law for the Court to make an informed decision. For example, the Court is uninformed as to the standard of care to which the Inter-Continental hotel is held under circumstances such as these, and whether defendant is held to be an absolute insurer of its guests' safety. Defendant has argued that the "incident involving Naghiu was the first and only incident of a burglary or assault" on record. However, the Court does not know whether the lack of prior notice of such attacks to the hotel is significant under Zairean law.

The Court recognizes that the Zairean Civil Code may not explicitly address every aspect of innkeeper liability. In that instance, Article 1 of the Zairean Code directs that where the Zairean law is silent, other sources of law may be considered, especially provisions of French or Belgian law. 6A Modern Systems Legal Encyclopedia § 1.4(C)(2) (1990). . . . However, the parties have not supplied the Court with any Belgian or French law to fill in the analytical chasm left gaping in this case.

Fed. R. Civ. P. 44.1 does not address the effect of the parties' failure to supply foreign law. When such a failure has occurred, "the party who has the affirmative on an issue of foreign law loses if he fails to prove that law." 9 WRIGHT & MILLER at § 2447 (collecting cases). To avoid this harsh result, other courts, including the Court of Appeals for the Third Circuit, have looked to their own forum's substantive law to fill in any gaps. See *Walter v. Netherlands Mead N.V.*, 514 F.2d 1130, 1137 n.4 (3d Cir.). . . . The Court will therefore look to Delaware tort law.

2. Delaware Law

The rule in Delaware, similar to the analogous Zairean Civil Code provision, is that a proprietor of a public place, such as a hotel, may be subject to liability to its invitee for the harm sustained while the invitee is on the land within the scope of his invitation. *DiOssi Maroney*, 548 A.2d 1361, 1366 (Del. 1988) (quoting

Restatement (Second) of Torts § 332 comment e (1965)). However, such a proprietor is not an insurer against all personal injuries inflicted on its premises. *Jardel Co. v. Hughes*, 523 A.2d 518, 525 (Del. 1987) (citing Restatement (Second) of Torts § 344 (1965)). Possessors of land are under a "residual obligation of reasonable care to protect business invitees from the acts of third persons." *Id.* If prior incidents of criminal conduct have occurred on the premises, Delaware courts have held a proprietor to a duty to foresee specific criminal conduct and take reasonable measures for security protection. *Id.* Mindful of these standards, and viewing the facts in the light most favorable to the plaintiff, the Court turns to the evidentiary record in this case.

Plaintiff's briefing on the tort issue in this case consisted of a factual narrative similar to that outlined above and a reiteration of the conclusory allegations of negligence contained in his complaint. At the summary judgment stage, Naghiu's burden is to make a showing sufficient to establish the existence of the essential elements of negligence on the part of Inter-Continental: duty, breach of that duty, and injury proximately caused by the breach. *Naidu v. Laird*, 539 A.2d 1064, 1072 (Del. 1988). . . . Unfortunately, Naghiu has failed to marshal enough evidence to support his bare subjective assertions of negligence. Although it is clear that the hotel owed Naghiu a duty of reasonable care, Naghiu has not placed any facts into the record demonstrating a breach of that duty. He has not shown that there were prior assaults on Inter-Continental Kinshasa guests or that the hotel knew or should have known of such attacks but failed to take reasonable security precautions. While the Court is sensitive to the difficulties of proof plaintiff must surmount due to distance and the passage of time, he must nevertheless surmount them to survive summary judgment. On the current record, this he has not done. Naghiu has merely relied upon his self-serving assertions, conclusory allegations and suspicions and has thus failed to establish a prima facie case of negligence. Accordingly, the Court will grant summary judgment in favor of defendant as to plaintiff's tort claim and his spouse's derivative loss of consortium claim. . . .

Bodum USA Inc. v. La Cafetière, Inc.

621 F.3d 624 (7th Cir. 2010)

EASTERBROOK, Chief Judge.

From the mid-1950s through 1991, Société des Anciens Etablissements Martin S.A. ("Martin") distributed a successful French-press coffee maker known as the Chambord. A French-press coffee maker (called a cafetière à piston in France) is a carafe in which hot water is mixed with coffee grounds. When the brewing is complete, a mesh screen attached to a rod drives the grounds to the bottom of the carafe. Clear coffee then can be poured from the top. In 1991 Bodum Holding purchased all of Martin's stock. Today subsidiaries of Bodum Holding sell throughout the world coffee makers that use the Chambord design and name.

Martin's principal investor and manager was Louis-James de Viel Castel, who had other businesses. One of these, the British firm Household Articles Ltd., sold a French-press coffee maker that it called La Cafetière, which closely resembles the Chambord design. Viel Castel wanted to continue Household's business after Bodum bought Martin. So Viel Castel and Jørgen Jepsen Bodum, the main investor in Bodum Holding, negotiated. An early draft agreement provided that Household could sell the Chambord design in the United Kingdom, but nowhere else. After several rounds of revisions, however, the agreement provided that Household would never sell a French-press coffee maker in France, that it would not use the trade names Chambord or Melior, and that for four years it would not distribute through the importers, distributors, or agents that Martin employed during 1990-91. The agreement was signed, and Bodum Holding acquired Martin.

La Cafetière, Inc., was incorporated in Illinois in 2006 to serve as the distributor of Household's products in the United States. One of these is the La Cafetière model, which carries the name "Classic" in this country. . . . Bodum Holding's U.S. distributor (Bodum USA, Inc.) filed this suit under federal and state law, contending that the sale of any coffee maker similar to the Chambord design violates Bodum's common-law trade dress. Trade dress, a distinctive appearance that enables consumers to identify a product's maker, is a form of trademark. Household contends that the 1991 agreement permits it to sell the La Cafetière design anywhere in the world, except France, provided that it does not use the words Chambord or Melior — and Household has never used either of those marks. The district court agreed with this contention and granted summary judgment in Household's favor. . . .

The Chambord design and the La Cafetière design are indeed similar, and although they are not identical a casual coffee drinker (or purchaser) would have trouble telling them apart. . . .

Here is the critical language, from Article 4 of the contract:

> In consideration of the compensation paid to Stockholder [Viel Castel] for the stocks of [Martin,] Stockholder guarantees, limited to the agreed compensation, see Article 2, that he shall not — for a period of four (4) years — be engaged directly or indirectly in any commercial business related to manufacturing or distributing [Martin's] products. . . . Notwithstanding Article 4 [Bodum Holding] agrees that Stockholder through Household . . . can manufacture and distribute any products similar to [Martin's] products outside of France. It is expressly understood that Household [] is not entitled, directly or indirectly, to any such activity in France, and that Household [] furthermore is not entitled, directly or indirectly, globally to manufacture and/or distribute coffee-pots under the trade marks and/or brand names of "Melior" and "Chambord," held by [Martin]. Stockholder agrees that Household [] is not entitled to use for a period of four (4) years the importers, distributors, and agents which [Martin] uses and/or has used the last year. Any violation of these obligations will constitute a breach of Stockholder's obligation according to Article 4.

The parties agree that this is an accurate translation of the French original, and that French substantive law governs its interpretation. The district judge thought that the contract is clear and that Household can sell its La Cafetière outside of France, if it does not use the Chambord or Melior names. Even if the

La Cafetière or Classic model is identical to the Chambord model (which it is not, as a glance at the illustrations shows), a thing identical to something else also is "similar" to it.

Bodum contends that, under French law, the parties' intent prevails over the written word. Article 1156 of the French Civil Code provides: "One must in agreements seek what the common intention of the contracting parties was, rather than pay attention to the literal meaning of the terms." (Again this is an agreed translation, as are all other translations in this opinion.) Jørgen Bodum has submitted an affidavit declaring that he understood the contract to limit Household's sales of the La Cafetière model to the United Kingdom and Australia. This means, Bodum Holding insists, that there must be a trial to determine the parties' intent. It supports this position with the declaration of Pierre-Yves Gautier, a Professor of Law at Université Panthéon-Assas Paris II, who Bodum tenders as an expert on French law. Household has replied with declarations from two experts of its own.

Although Fed. R. Civ. P. 44.1 provides that courts may consider expert testimony when deciding questions of foreign law, it does not compel them to do so — for the Rule says that judges "may" rather than "must" receive expert testimony and adds that courts may consider "any relevant material or source." Judges should use the best of the available sources. The Committee Note in 1966, when Rule 44.1 was adopted, explains that a court "may engage in its own research and consider any relevant material thus found. The court may have at its disposal better foreign law materials than counsel have presented, or may wish to reexamine and amplify material that has been presented by counsel in partisan fashion or in insufficient detail."

Sometimes federal courts must interpret foreign statutes or decisions that have not been translated into English or glossed in treatises or other sources. Then experts' declarations and testimony may be essential. But French law, and the law of most other nations that engage in extensive international commerce, is widely available in English. Judges can use not only accepted (sometimes official) translations of statutes and decisions but also ample secondary literature, such as treatises and scholarly commentary. It is no more necessary to resort to expert declarations about the law of France than about the law of Louisiana, which had its origins in the French civil code, or the law of Puerto Rico, whose origins are in the Spanish civil code. No federal judge would admit "expert" declarations about the meaning of Louisiana law in a commercial case.

Trying to establish foreign law through experts' declarations not only is expensive (experts must be located and paid) but also adds an adversary's spin, which the court then must discount. Published sources such as treatises do not have the slant that characterizes the warring declarations presented in this case. Because objective, English-language descriptions of French law are readily available, we prefer them to the parties' declarations.

[Using English translations of the French Civil Code and French court decisions, as well as English-language law review articles and books, the court analyzed the meaning of Article 1156. The court concluded, contrary to Bodum's argument, that Article 1156 did not require a trial to determine the parties' intent and held that the agreement permitted La Cafetière, Inc., to distribute its "Classic" La Cafetière coffee maker in the United States.]

. . .

The judgment is affirmed.

POSNER, Circuit Judge, concurring.

I join the majority opinion, and write separately merely to express emphatic support for, and modestly to amplify, the court's criticism of a common and authorized but unsound judicial practice. That is the practice of trying to establish the meaning of a law of a foreign country by testimony or affidavits of expert witnesses, usually lawyers or law professors, often from the country in question.

The contract in this case is in writing and unambiguously entitles the defendant to continue to sell its "Classic" coffee maker in the United States, because, although it is a product "similar" to the plaintiff's coffee maker, only in France is the defendant forbidden to sell products "similar" to the plaintiff's products. The plaintiff argues that nevertheless it is entitled to a trial at which Jørgen Bodum, its principal, would testify that part of the deal the parties *thought* they were making, although it is not reflected in the written contract, was that the defendant would be barred from selling its "Classic" coffee maker in the United States because it is identical rather than merely "similar" to the plaintiff's "Chambord" coffee maker. (Yet the plaintiff concedes in its reply brief that "it may certainly be true that all identical products are similar.") The issue of contractual interpretation is governed by French law.

Rule 44.1 of the Federal Rules of Civil Procedure provides that a federal court, "in determining foreign law, . . . may consider any relevant material or source, including testimony, whether or not submitted by a party or admissible under the Federal Rules of Evidence." The committee note explains that the court "may engage in its own research and consider any relevant material thus found. The court may have at its disposal better foreign law materials than counsel have presented, or may wish to reexamine and amplify material that has been presented by counsel in partisan fashion or in insufficient detail." Thus the court doesn't *have* to rely on testimony; and in only a few cases, I believe, is it justified in doing so. This case is not one of them.

The only evidence of the meaning of French law that was presented to the district court or is found in the appellate record is an English translation of brief excerpts from the French Civil Code and affidavits by three French law professors (Pierre-Yves Gautier for the plaintiff and Christophe Caron and Jérôme Huet for the defendant, with Huet's affidavit adding little to Caron's). The district court did no research of its own, but relied on the parties' submissions.

When a court in one state applies the law of another, or when a federal court applies state law (or a state court federal law), the court does not permit expert testimony on the meaning of the "foreign" law that it has to apply. This is true even when it's the law of Louisiana, which is based to a significant degree on the *Code Napoléon* (curiously, adopted by Louisiana after the United States acquired Louisiana from France).

Yet if the law to be applied is the law of a foreign country, even a country such as the United Kingdom, Canada, or Australia in which the official language is English and the legal system derives from the same source as ours, namely the English common law, our courts routinely rely on lawyers' testimony about the meaning of the foreign law. Not only rely but sometimes suggest, incorrectly in light of Rule 44.1, that testimony is *required* for establishing foreign law.

Lawyers who testify to the meaning of foreign law, whether they are practitioners or professors, are paid for their testimony and selected on the basis of the convergence of their views with the litigating position of the client, or their willingness to fall in with the views urged upon them by the client. These are the banes of expert testimony. When the testimony concerns a scientific or other technical issue, it may be unreasonable to expect a judge to resolve the issue without the aid of such testimony. But judges are experts on law, and there is an abundance of published materials, in the form of treatises, law review articles, statutes, and cases, all in English (if English is the foreign country's official language), to provide neutral illumination of issues of foreign law. I cannot fathom why in dealing with the meaning of laws of English-speaking countries that share our legal origins judges should prefer paid affidavits and testimony to published materials.

It is only a little less perverse for judges to rely on testimony to ascertain the law of a country whose official language is not English, at least if is a major country and has a modern legal system. Although most Americans are monolingual, including most judges, there are both official translations of French statutes into English . . . and abundant secondary material on French law, including French contract and procedural law, published in English. . . . Neither party cited *any* such material, except translations of statutory provisions; beyond that they relied on the affidavits of their expert witnesses.

Because English has become the international *lingua franca*, it is unsurprising that most Americans, even when otherwise educated, make little investment in acquiring even a reading knowledge of a foreign language. But our linguistic provincialism does not excuse intellectual provincialism. It does not justify our judges in relying on paid witnesses to spoon feed them foreign law that can be found well explained in English-language treatises and articles. I do not criticize the district judge in this case, because he was following the common practice. But it is a bad practice, followed like so many legal practices out of habit rather than reflection. It is excusable only when the foreign law is the law of a country with such an obscure or poorly developed legal system that there are no secondary materials to which the judge could turn. The French legal system is obviously not of that character. The district court could — as this court did in *Abad v. Bayer Corp.*, 563 F.3d 663, 670-71 (7th Cir. 2009), with respect to the law of Argentina — have based his interpretation of French contract law on published writings as distinct from paid testimony.

. . .

The parties' reliance on affidavits to establish the standard for interpreting their contract has produced only confusion. They should have relied on published analyses of French commercial law.

Wood, Circuit Judge, concurring.

While I endorse without reservation the majority's reading of the 1991 contract that is at the heart of this case, I write separately to note my disagreement with the discussion of Fed. R. Civ. P. 44.1 in both the majority opinion and in Judge Posner's concurring opinion. Rule 44.1 itself establishes no hierarchy for sources of foreign law, and I am unpersuaded by my colleagues' assertion that expert testimony is categorically inferior to published, English-language materials. Exercises in comparative law are notoriously difficult, because the U.S. reader is likely to miss nuances in the foreign law, to fail to appreciate the way in which one branch of the other country's law interacts with another, or to assume erroneously that the foreign law mirrors U.S. law when it does not. As the French might put it more generally, apparently similar phrases might be *faux amis*. A simple example illustrates why two words might be "false friends." A speaker of American English will be familiar with the word "actual," which is defined in Webster's Third New International Dictionary as "existing in act, . . . existing in fact or reality: really acted or acting or carried out — contrasted with *ideal* and *hypothetical*. . . ." Webster's Third New International Dictionary 22 (1993). So, one might say, "This is the actual chair used by George Washington." But the word "actuel" in French means "present" or right now. Le Robert & Collins Compact Plus Dictionnaire 7 (5th ed. 2003). A French person would thus use the term "les événements actuels" or "actualité" to refer to current events, not to describe something that really happened either now or in the past.

There will be many times when testimony from an acknowledged expert in foreign law will be helpful, or even necessary, to ensure that the U.S. judge is not confronted with a "false friend" or that the U.S. judge understands the full context of the foreign provision. Some published articles or treatises, written particularly for a U.S. audience, might perform the same service, but many will not, even if they are written in English, and especially if they are translated into English from another language. It will often be most efficient and useful for the judge to have before her an expert who can provide the needed precision on the spot, rather than have the judge wade through a number of secondary sources. In practice, the experts produced by the parties are often the authors of the leading treatises and scholarly articles in the foreign country anyway. In those cases, it is hard to see why the person's views cannot be tested in court, to guard against the possibility that he or she is just a mouthpiece for one party. Prominent lawyers from the country in question also sometimes serve as experts. That too is perfectly acceptable in principle, especially if the question requires an understanding of court procedure in the foreign country. In many places, the academic branch of the legal profession is entirely separate from the bar. Academic writings in such places tend to be highly theoretical and removed from the day-to-day realities of the practice of law.

To be clear, I have no objection to the use of written sources of foreign law. Rule 44.1 permits the court to consider "any relevant material or source, including testimony, whether or not submitted by a party or admissible under the Federal Rules of Evidence." The written sources cited by both of my colleagues throw useful light on the problem before us in this case, and both were well within their rights to conduct independent research and to rely on those sources. There is no need, however, to disparage oral testimony from experts in the foreign law. That kind of testimony has been used by responsible lawyers for years, and there will be many instances in which it is adequate by itself or it provides a helpful gloss on the literature. The tried and true methods set forth in Fed. R. Evid. 702 for testing the depth of the witness's expertise, the facts and other relevant information on which the witness has relied, and the quality of the witness's application of those principles to the problem at hand, suffice to protect the court against self-serving experts in foreign law, just as they suffice to protect the process for any other kind of expert.

Finally, my colleagues see no material difference between a judge's ability to research the laws of Louisiana or Puerto Rico and her ability to research the laws of France, Australia, or Indonesia. With respect, I cannot agree with them. Like the laws of the other 49 states, the law of Louisiana is based on many sources. One important such source is the Code Napoléon, but it is not the only source. Louisiana has legislation on the usual topics, it is part of the federal system, and its courts function much like the courts of other states.

Puerto Rico's system is somewhat less accessible for non-Spanish-speaking Americans. Interestingly, one finds Puerto Rican materials under the "International/ Worldwide Materials" database in Westlaw, not under the U.S. database. This is so even though Congress has expressly defined Puerto Rico as a "state" for purposes of the diversity jurisdiction statute. See 28 U.S.C. § 1332(e) (2010). There is no denying the fact, however, that Puerto Rico is far more integrated into the U.S. legal system than any foreign country is. Since Puerto Rico falls within the jurisdiction of the First Circuit, see 28 U.S.C. § 41 (2010), the judges of that court regularly hear cases implicating Puerto Rican law. Furthermore, American law has greatly influenced the Puerto Rican legal system. . . . As a practical matter, therefore, the Supreme Court was on firm ground when it assumed, in the text of Rule 44.1, that only the law of a "foreign country" would be subject to the rule's procedures, not the law of a U.S. state, territory, or commonwealth.

For these reasons, although I join the majority's reasoning in all other respects, I do not share their views about the use of expert testimony to prove foreign law. I therefore concur in the judgment to that extent.

NOTES AND QUESTIONS

1. **Practice: Determining Foreign Law.** How do lawyers show a judge what legal rule governs a particular issue? And if a rule's meaning is unclear, how do lawyers support arguments about what the rule means? In the purely domestic context, U.S. lawyers do this by citing to U.S. state or federal statutes and court cases, and perhaps secondary sources such as treatises or law review articles. How might these tasks be more complicated when the rule is a rule of a foreign nation? What materials might you use to show a court what the law of a foreign nation says about an issue and to clarify the meaning of that

law? What materials did the court refer to in the *Naghiu* case to determine what the law of Zaire provided with respect to the plaintiff's personal injury claims? What materials did the court refer to in the *Bodum* case to determine what the law of France provided with respect to interpretation of the parties' contract? For a thorough review of the issues surrounding proof of foreign law, see Peter Hay, *The Use and Determination of Foreign Law in Civil Litigation in the United States*, 62 AM. J. COMP. L. 213 (2014).

2. **Practice: Providing Evidence of Foreign Law.** In *Naghiu*, the court held that the law of Zaire provided the applicable tort standard. Yet the court ultimately applied the law of the forum — Delaware — to decide whether the defendant was liable. Why? If you were the lawyer for one of the parties, and you believed that the law of Zaire would have been more favorable to your client on the tort issue, what could you have done to lead the court to apply the law of Zaire? If a party does not prove foreign law, why shouldn't the court just dismiss the complaint for failure to state a claim?

3. **Rule 44.1.** Rule 44.1 of the Federal Rules of Civil Procedure reads as follows in its entirety: "A party who intends to raise an issue about a foreign country's law must give notice by a pleading or other writing. In determining foreign law, the court may consider any relevant material or source, including testimony, whether or not submitted by a party or admissible under the Federal Rules of Evidence. The court's determination must be treated as a ruling on a question of law." Many states have adopted similar rules governing the determination of foreign law. Rule 44.1 has three principal elements:

   • First, Rule 44.1 requires that a party give notice of its intent to raise an issue about a foreign country's law. As the Notes of Advisory Committee on Rules (1966) explain, the purpose of the rule's first sentence is "[t]o avoid unfair surprise." The Notes further explain that the notice "may, but need not be, incorporated in the pleadings," and they explain the following regarding the timing of notice: "The new rule does not attempt to set any definite limit on the party's time for giving the notice of an issue of foreign law; in some cases the issue may not become apparent until the trial and notice then given may still be reasonable. The stage which the case has reached at the time of the notice, the reason proffered by the party for his failure to give earlier notice, and the importance to the case as a whole of the issue of foreign law sought to be raised, are among the factors which the court should consider in deciding a question of the reasonableness of a notice." The Notes also explain that the Advisory Committee deemed it "best to permit a written notice to be given outside of and later than the pleadings, provided the notice is reasonable." If a party fails to give notice of its intent to raise an issue of foreign law, a court may nevertheless raise the issue on its own accord, but the party risks waiving the right to raise the issue. *See In re Magnetic Audiotape Antitrust Litigation*, 334 F.3d 204, 209 (2d Cir. 2003) (barring party from raising foreign law issue due to its failure to give reasonable notice of the issue as required by Rule 44.1).

   • Second, Rule 44.1 allows courts determining foreign law to "consider any relevant material or source, including testimony, whether or not

submitted by a party or admissible under the Federal Rules of Evidence."
While a court may seek these materials on its own, it is advisable for lawyers to take the initiative to research and present the materials and sources
necessary to establish foreign law and its meaning. As the *Naghiu* court
notes, failure of a party to do so may lead to the "harsh result" that the
party loses on the foreign law issue; or, alternatively, the court may assume
for purposes of its decision that the law of the forum is the same as the
foreign country's law, and then proceed to decide the issue under the law
of the forum. The court in *Naghiu* took the second approach to plaintiff's
personal injury claim, applying Delaware tort law to issues on which the
parties failed to sufficiently explain the law of Zaire. As the *Bodum* case
indicates, however, some judges neither insist upon (nor welcome) expert
testimony — at least when there is adequate English language material
available to determine the meaning of foreign law.

- Third, Rule 44.1 states that "[t]he court's determination must be treated
as a ruling on a question of law." As such, a determination of a question of
foreign law is for the court, not for the finder of fact, and a district court's
determination of foreign law is subject to de novo review on appeal.

4. **Policy: The Appropriate Evidence for Determining Foreign Law.** Who has
the better of the arguments among the judges in the *Bodum* case regarding
the materials and sources that should be considered in determining foreign
law? What are the problems with expert testimony? What are the problems
with judges assessing foreign legal materials on their own? Are the sources
relied on by the majority and concurrence reliable? Are the problems different in proving the law of France, as compared to proving the law of Zaire?
What can an attorney do to respond to these problems when making arguments based on foreign law?

5. **Information Provided by Foreign Governments About Foreign Law.** Are
U.S. courts bound to defer to foreign governments when determining the
meaning of foreign law? In a unanimous opinion in *Animal Science Products,
Inc. v. Hebei Welcome Pharmaceutical Co. Ltd.*, 138 S. Ct. 1865 (2018), the
U.S. Supreme Court held that deference is not required.

Animal Science involved price-fixing claims against the respondents,
who were Chinese producers of vitamin C. The respondents did not deny
that their behavior violated U.S. antitrust law. Instead, they raised several
defenses — including foreign sovereign compulsion and the doctrine of international comity — each of which depended on a conclusion that Chinese law
required them to fix vitamin C export prices. In support of the respondents,
the Ministry of Commerce of the People's Republic of China filed an amicus
brief asserting that Chinese law indeed required respondents to set prices and
reduce quantities of vitamin C sold abroad.

The district court "respectfully decline[d] to defer" to the Ministry's interpretation and rejected respondents' defenses, concluding that Chinese law
did not compel the respondents' anticompetitive conduct. In reaching its
conclusion, the district court considered not only the ministry's brief, but
also the testimony of the petitioner's expert witness, the text of the relevant

government directives, and other sources of information about Chinese law. The case went to trial, and judgment was entered in favor of petitioners.

The Second Circuit reversed, holding that "when a foreign government . . . directly participates in U.S. court proceedings by providing a sworn evidentiary proffer regarding the construction and effect of its laws and regulations, which is reasonable under the circumstances presented, a U.S. court is bound to defer to those statements."

The Supreme Court vacated the Second Circuit's decision, holding that "[a] federal court should accord respectful consideration to a foreign government's submission, but is not bound to accord conclusive effect to the foreign government's statements." The Supreme Court reasoned that the Second Circuit's "unyielding rule is inconsistent with Rule 44.1 [of the Federal Rules of Civil Procedure]," which provides that "[i]n determining foreign law, the court may consider any relevant material or source, including testimony, whether or not submitted by a party or admissible under the Federal Rules of Evidence" and that "[t]he court's determination must be treated as a ruling on a question of law." It also pointed out that the Second Circuit's rule was inconsistent with international practice, as reflected in two treaties dealing with the determination of foreign law.

What does it mean to give "respectful consideration" to foreign government statements? The Supreme Court stated that "no single formula or rule will fit all cases in which a foreign government describes its own law." It did, however, identify a number of considerations that are relevant when determining how much weight to give to a foreign government's interpretation, including "the statement's clarity, thoroughness, and support; its context and purpose; the transparency of the foreign legal system; the role and authority of the entity or official offering the statement; and the statement's consistency with the government's past positions." Regarding context, the Court emphasized that when the foreign government offers the interpretation "in the context of litigation, there may be cause for caution in evaluating the foreign government's submission." On the other hand, under the Supreme Court's approach it would seem that a prior decision of a foreign country's independent court about the meaning of its own law would ordinarily deserve substantial weight.

Is the Supreme Court's approach a sensible one? Why do you think the Second Circuit insisted on a different approach? In practical terms, what does the *Animal Science* decision mean for how lawyers make arguments about the meaning of foreign law?

C. Choice-of-Law Clauses

As the choice-of-law materials presented so far may suggest, it can be difficult to determine — not to mention to predict — what law a court will apply to resolve a transnational dispute. This uncertainty can, in turn, make it difficult for individuals and businesses to figure out which legal rules should guide their conduct, and also can make it difficult for lawyers to give them advice about the law governing their transnational activity. In the cases that follow, how did the parties attempt to mitigate this uncertainty? To what extent were they successful in doing so?

Johnson v. Ventra Group, Inc.

191 F.3d 732 (6th Cir. 1999)

GILMAN, Circuit Judge.

John Johnson became the United States sales representative for Manutec Steel Industries, Inc., a Canadian corporation, in 1985. He filed suit in the Province of Ontario, Canada against Manutec when his employment was terminated in 1988, claiming damages under the terms of his contract. The Supreme Court of Ontario awarded him damages of approximately $1,500,000 in February of 1990. He now seeks to enforce this judgment against Ventra Group, Inc. and Ventratech Limited, Manutec's alleged successor corporations. The district court granted summary judgment in favor of the defendants. For the reasons set forth below, we AFFIRM the judgment of the district court.

I. Background

Manutec and Johnson entered into a sales representation contract on September 10, 1985, according to which he was to open and develop Manutec's stamping business in the automotive industry. Johnson was to be the exclusive sales representative for Manutec in the United States in exchange for a five percent commission on all sales. The contract's termination clause provided as follows:

> The initial term of this agreement shall be three (3) years. At the end of the first year and at the end of each year thereafter, this agreement shall be automatically extended for an additional year unless either party gives notice to the other of termination, for the purposes of providing, in effect, a two (2) year termination notice.

According to Johnson, he proceeded to develop a substantial amount of business with Chrysler and General Motors. On April 7, 1988, however, Manutec terminated Johnson's contract without notice. Between the time that Johnson entered into the contract in 1985 and the time that the contract was terminated in 1988, Manutec became the wholly-owned subsidiary of Ventra Manufacturing, Ltd. through a stock purchase that occurred on September 30, 1987.

Johnson filed suit against Manutec in the Ontario trial court (known as the Supreme Court of Ontario) on May 25, 1988. Ventra Manufacturing was not made a party to the lawsuit. Johnson alleged that Manutec terminated his contract to avoid paying him commissions without the requisite two years' notice. On February 26, 1990, Johnson obtained a default judgment in the amount of approximately $1,500,000 against Manutec from the Supreme Court of Ontario.

Between the time that Johnson filed his lawsuit and the time that he won his judgment, however, various corporate changes had occurred. First, Manutec and its parent corporation, Ventra Manufacturing, had gone through another transformation. On January 13, 1989, ITL Industries Limited, a publicly traded Canadian corporation, acquired 100 percent of the outstanding shares of Ventra Manufacturing. ITL then changed its name to Ventra Group, Inc., one of the named defendants in the present action. Manutec thus became a wholly-owned subsidiary of Ventra Group. Second, in mid-December of 1989, the secured creditors of Manutec placed the company into receivership because of its insolvency. The secured creditors appointed two receiver-managers, Price Waterhouse and Richter & Partners, Inc., who controlled Manutec's operations during the period of its receivership. It was during this period that Johnson obtained the default judgment against Manutec.

In order to maximize the value obtained from the sale of Manutec's secured property, the receivers sold at auction all of Manutec's assets located at its plant in Brampton, Ontario to Chrysler and various third parties. On November 23, 1990, approximately one year after Manutec had been placed in receivership, Ventra Group and its wholly-owned, newly incorporated subsidiary Ventratech (the other named defendant in the instant action) purchased certain assets from one of Manutec's other plants in Ridgetown, Ontario.

On January 13, 1994, Johnson filed his First Amended Complaint against Ventra Group and Ventratech in the <u>Circuit Court of Wayne County, Michigan</u> to enforce the judgment that he had obtained against Manutec from the Supreme Court of Ontario. . . . On June 7, 1995, the court issued an opinion granting the motion for a determination of [foreign] law, ruling that Ontario law applied to the action. . . .

On October 1, 1997 Johnson filed his Second Amended Complaint [against Ventra Group and Ventratech], alleging the following causes of action: (1) enforcement of a foreign judgment based on successor liability, (2) breach of contract and fraud, (3) intentional interference with contractual, business, or financial relations, (4) fraudulent conveyance, (5) oppression or unfair conduct, (6) unjust enrichment, and (7) violation of the Michigan Sales Representative Statute. Ventra Group and Ventratech moved for summary judgment as to all of Johnson's claims. Johnson sought summary judgment only as to his causes of action regarding the enforcement of a foreign judgment and his unjust enrichment theory. On March 6, 1998, the district court . . . denied Johnson's motion for partial summary judgment and granted summary judgment in favor of Ventra Group and Ventratech. . . .

Johnson has appealed . . . the district court's grant of the motion for a determination of foreign law entered on June 7, 1995 . . . [and] the district court's order denying Johnson's motion for summary judgment and granting summary judgment in favor of Ventra Group and Ventratech entered March 6, 1998. . . .

II. Analysis

A. Choice of Law

[Johnson argued that defendants Ventra Group and Ventratech were liable as Manutec's successors under the default judgment entered against Manutec by the

Ontario court, and that he could therefore enforce the judgment against them. The choice-of-law issue in this case was whether the court should apply the law of Ontario or the law of Michigan (the forum state) to resolve this successor liability issue. As the court found, "[U]nder Ontario law, successor liability does not follow the purchase of assets; an assumption of liability may be conveyed only by an express transfer of the obligation at the time of sale." Ontario law also did not recognize Johnson's alternative theory that Ventra Group and Ventratech were liable because they were the "mere continuation" of Manutec's business. In contrast, the court concluded that Michigan law recognized successor liability in a variety of situations, including either express or implied assumption of a selling corporation's liabilities, transactions that amount to a merger of the two corporations, mere continuation, and fraudulent avoidance of liability.]

A federal court's determination of foreign law is "treated as a ruling on a question of law." Fed. R. Civ. P. 44.1. Accordingly, the district court's determination that Ontario law applies and its interpretation of that law is subject to de novo review.

The parties dispute whether the instant action is governed by Michigan law or Ontario law. To resolve this dispute, a federal court whose jurisdiction is based on diversity of citizenship must apply the conflict of law rules of the forum state. See *Klaxon Co. v. Stentor Elec. Mfg. Co.*, 313 U.S. 487, 490 (1941). Because Johnson filed suit in a federal district court in Michigan, we must look to Michigan's conflict of law rules to determine whether Michigan law or Ontario law governs this dispute.

Michigan has adopted the approach set forth in the Restatement (Second) of Conflict of Laws. . . . According to this approach, a contractual choice of law provision will be binding unless either:

> (a) [t]he chosen state has no substantial relationship to the parties or the transaction and there is no other reasonable basis for the parties' choice, or
> (b) application of the law of the chosen state would be contrary to a fundamental policy of a state which has a materially greater interest than the chosen state in the determination of the particular issue and which, under the rule of [§] 188, would be the state of the applicable law in the absence of an effective choice of law by the parties.

Restatement (Second) of Conflict of Laws § 187(2) (1988). In the instant action, Johnson's sales representative contract states that "[t]his agreement shall be interpreted and governed by the laws of the Province of Ontario." . . .

2. Neither of the Two Exceptions Set Forth in [the Restatement] Apply

Having determined that Michigan's contractual choice of law rule applies to the present case, we turn to the question of whether either of the exceptions stated in the *Restatement* applies. The first exception clearly does not apply because the [the state whose law was] chosen . . . , Ontario, has a substantial relationship to Manutec, Johnson, and the transactions between them. Specifically, Manutec was incorporated and operated in Ontario, Johnson's prior lawsuit against Manutec was filed and concluded in Ontario, both Ventra Group and Ventratech are Ontario corporations, certain of Manutec's assets were acquired by them in Ontario, and the negotiations with Manutec's receivers occurred in Ontario.

. . .

Johnson . . . argues that the application of Ontario law is contrary to Michigan's fundamental policy in favor of successor liability. The fact, however, that a different result might be achieved if the law of the chosen forum is applied does not suffice to show that the foreign law is repugnant to a fundamental policy of the forum state. . . . If the situation were otherwise, and foreign law could automatically be ignored whenever it differed from the law of the forum state, then the entire body of law relating to conflicts would be rendered meaningless.

. . .

We find . . . persuasive the case of *Moses v. Business Card Express, Inc.*, 929 F.2d 1131 (6th Cir. 1991), where an Alabama franchisee brought suit in a federal court in Alabama against a Michigan franchisor. The case was then transferred to Michigan and Michigan law was applied pursuant to the choice of law clause contained in the franchise agreement. One of the issues on appeal was whether it would offend the public policy interests of Alabama, the original forum state, not to allow the Alabama franchisee to recover punitive damages for fraud or misrepresentation. Alabama law allows such a recovery, whereas Michigan law does not. The court held that "this was the state of the law when the plaintiffs entered into the contract" and "[t]hey cite no case in which it has been held that a state's dominating public interest is violated by requiring its citizens and residents to try a lawsuit in another jurisdiction with a different rule on punitive damages where the parties have agreed that the other state's substantive law is controlling." *Id.* at 1139. In the instant case, Johnson expressly agreed to have Ontario's law control his contract and the state of Ontario law on the issue of successor liability has not changed since the time of the agreement.

Johnson, citing the Michigan Sales Representative Statute, also argues that Michigan has "a long common law history of protecting procuring agents and a recent statutory history of protecting sales representatives by statutory mandate." This statute imposes sanctions on any "principal" who fails to make timely commission payments to a terminated "sales representative." See Mich. Comp. Laws § 600.2961 (1996). Johnson, however, has already received legal redress from his "principal" by obtaining a default judgment against Manutec. In the present case, he is trying to enforce that judgment against separate legal entities on the theory of successor liability. Because this theory involves an entirely different body of law that is not covered by the Michigan Sales Representative Statute, the statute is not relevant to this issue.

We thus conclude that the contractual choice of law provision governs and that neither of the two exceptions set forth in the Restatement applies.

3. *The Scope of the Choice of Law Provision*

The next question is whether the choice of law provision governs all of Johnson's claims. Johnson's contractually based claims are clearly covered. In addition, this court has held that a similar provision governed claims for fraud and misrepresentation in *Moses*, 929 F.2d at 1139. Moreover, Michigan's choice of law rules governing contract actions have also been applied to the quasi-contractual claim of unjust enrichment. . . . The choice of law provision set forth in the contract is therefore broad enough to govern all of Johnson's claims.

. . .

[Applying Ontario law, the court affirmed the district court's grant of summary judgment in favor of Ventra Group and Ventratech, and its denial of Johnson's motion for partial summary judgment.]

III. Conclusion

For all of the reasons set forth above, we AFFIRM the judgment of the district court.

Cooper v. Meridian Yachts, Ltd.

575 F.3d 1151 (11th Cir. 2009)

TRAGER, District Judge:

This case concerns an injury to a sea captain and the subsequent settlement of his claims by the third-party plaintiffs[-appellants]. The present appeal arises out of the third-party plaintiffs' attempt to recover the sums paid to settle the maritime personal injury action. Specifically, the third-party plaintiffs seek indemnity, contribution and equitable subrogation from the third-party defendants[-appellees], who allegedly constructed, designed or maintained the defective foodlift that caused the injury. The crucial question below was whether Dutch law or federal maritime law applied to the third-party action. The district court, finding in favor of Dutch law, dismissed the action, determining on summary judgment that the third-party claims were barred by a ten-year statute of repose [under Dutch law].

The first set of issues presented before this Court revolve around a shipbuilding agreement entered into between the shipowner third-party plaintiff and the shipbuilder third-party defendant. [One of the] provisions within the shipbuilding agreement [that is] particularly relevant [is] a Dutch choice of law clause. . . . We first look at whether [this] provision[] govern[s] any of the third-party claims. If so, we then determine the effects the applicable provision has on those claims.

. . .

A review of Dutch law indicates that the third-party claims that are based on a strict liability theory are barred by the Dutch statute of repose. However, the third-party plaintiffs also allege general tort claims. For these claims, Dutch law provides a separate statute of limitations. That statute of limitations allows the general tort claims to proceed. [However, a separate limitation of liability provision in the agreement bars all of the claims.]

. . .

Factual Background

On the 28th or 29th of July 2005, Jameson Cooper ("Cooper"), the captain of a 198-foot motor yacht named the M/Y MEDUSE (the "MEDUSE"), was injured when the ship's dumbwaiter or foodlift (referred to by the parties as the "foodlift") landed on his leg, causing severe injuries. According to Cooper, the accident occurred while he was attempting to retrieve some of his clean laundry that had become lodged in a space between the floor of the foodlift and the ship's deck. In an effort to free the clothes, Cooper placed his left foot on the floor of the foodlift and his right foot on the deck of the MEDUSE. At the moment that he was able to free the articles of clothing, the foodlift fell, injuring his leg. The MEDUSE was located somewhere in the Red Sea at the time of the accident.

[Third-party defendant-appellee] De Vries Scheepsbow B.V. ("De Vries") is the entity that constructed the MEDUSE for [third-party plaintiff-appellant] Meridian Yachts, Ltd. ("Meridian"). . . . De Vries and Meridian entered into a shipbuilding agreement (the "agreement") on January 31, 1994, which governed the purchase and manufacture of the vessel. The agreement, which was written in English, was executed by Meridian as buyer and De Vries as builder. The ship was built in the Netherlands and was delivered to Meridian on January 24, 1997. The delivery, according to appellees, took place at a Dutch seaport. . . .

. . . Article 13 [of the agreement] has a choice of law provision:

> This Agreement, and all disputes arising out of or in connection with it, shall be construed in accordance with and shall be governed by the Dutch law.

The agreement also contains a limitation of liability provision in Article 10. Its critical language provides:

> [T]he Builder shall have no liability whatsoever for any loss or damage directly arising from the defectiveness or deficiency of parts . . . except if resulting from intentional conduct or gross negligence of the Builder or his servants. Liability of the Builder for loss of business, loss of profits, consequential damages or other (indirect) damage, however, is always excluded. . . .

. . .

Procedural History

On October 27, 2006, Cooper filed suit in The United States District Court for the Southern District of Florida (the "district court") seeking damages for the injuries he suffered onboard the MEDUSE. . . .

On July 5, 2007, . . . appellants [including Meridian] filed a third-party complaint against [appellees, including] De Vries, the shipbuilder. . . . [Appellants] sought to hold [appellees] liable for any damages that could potentially be awarded to Cooper. The amended third-party complaint alleges that the foodlift that injured Cooper was "designed, installed, constructed, manufactured and inspected by one or more of the [appellees]." The . . . appellants claim that by negligently placing the defective foodlift in the stream of commerce, appellees breached an independent duty they owed to Cooper, making them liable to the . . . appellants for indemnity, contribution and equitable subrogation under federal maritime law. The third-party complaint, however, does not commit itself to a particular theory of liability, referencing both negligence and strict liability.

On November 30, 2007, the ... appellants settled Cooper's personal injury action and the case remained pending only with respect to the ... appellants' claims against [appellees]. Following settlement, the ... appellants filed an amended third-party complaint seeking recovery of the sums paid to Cooper. ...

On November 28, 2007, appellees moved for summary judgment. On June 3, 2008, the district court held that because the agreement between Meridian and De Vries governed the construction of the MEDUSE, including the allegedly defective foodlift, Meridian's claims, which arose out of or in connection with the agreement, were subject to the agreement's Dutch choice of law provision contained in Article 13. Therefore, claims brought by Meridian, the only one of the ... appellants who was a signatory to the agreement, were barred by the ten-year Dutch statute of repose. The decision neither discussed whether Dutch law actually contained a ten-year statute of repose or whether the statute of repose was applicable to Meridian's claims because the four appellants never contested the substance of appellees' presentation of Dutch law. In the alternative, the district court found that Meridian's third-party claims were also barred by the limitation of liability clause in Article 10 of the agreement.

. . .

Discussion

. . .

The only two parties in this action that signed the agreement were Meridian, the shipowner, and De Vries, the shipbuilder. As a signatory, Meridian's third-party claims against De Vries are governed by both the Dutch choice of law provision and the limitation of liability provision.

With respect to the issue of what law governs, Meridian does not argue that the agreement's choice of law provision is invalid. Instead, the shipowner asserts that, because its claims for indemnity, contribution and equitable subrogation are not "disputes arising out of or in connection with" the agreement, the choice of law provision does not apply to those causes of action. In determining whether a choice of law clause contained in a contract between two parties also governs tort claims between those parties, a court must first examine the scope of the provision. *See Green Leaf Nursery v. E.I. DuPont De Nemours & Co.*, 341 F.3d 1292, 1300-01 (11th Cir. 2003). A choice of law provision that relates only to the agreement will not encompass related tort claims. *Id.* at 1300. For example, a provision providing that "[t]his release shall be governed and construed in accordance with the laws of the State of [X]," will be construed narrowly as it only purports to govern the agreement itself and does not refer "to any and all claims or disputes arising out of the" agreement. *Id.*

The provision at issue here, however, is clearly meant to be read broadly. The provision provides that "all disputes arising out of or in connection with" the agreement "shall be construed in accordance with and shall be governed by the Dutch law." Such a provision purports to govern "all disputes" having a connection to the agreement and not just the agreement itself. Although pursued as an indemnity/

contribution action, Meridian's claims are based on its allegation that the foodlift constructed by De Vries, as part of the agreement, was negligently or defectively manufactured. Such an action is necessarily connected to the agreement. *See Int'l Underwriters AG & Liberty Re-Insurance Corp., S.A. v. Triple I: Int'l Invs., Inc.*, 533 F.3d 1342, 1348-49 (11th Cir. 2008) ("[W]here the dispute occurs as a fairly direct result of the performance of contractual duties . . . , then the dispute can fairly be said to arise out of or relate to the contract in question."). Accordingly, Meridian's third-party claims against De Vries fall under the choice of law provision and are therefore governed by Dutch law.

Before the district court, however, the parties were less than helpful in explicating the content of Dutch law. The . . . appellants argue that the evidence introduced by appellees concerning the Dutch statute of repose was insufficient to demonstrate the untimeliness of their third-party claims. In support of their summary judgment motion, appellees presented the affidavit of a Netherlands attorney that stated:

> [U]nder Dutch law any product liability claim would have become timebarred by virtue of Article 6:191, Paragraph 2 providing for an absolute extinction of such claim after the lapse of 10 years after the day the product came into circulation. Accordingly, such claim would have become timebarred in any case by January 24, 2007, as M/Y MEDUSE was delivered on January 24, 1997.

The affidavit, however, is incomplete. Specifically, it failed to apprise the district court of the separate statute of limitations that Dutch law creates for negligence claims as opposed to claims on the basis of strict liability. Our independent review of Dutch law confirms that, while a strict products liability action is untimely when brought more than ten years after the defective product was first put into circulation, there is a separate five-year limitations period from the date of injury for negligence claims. This research confirms the untimeliness of Meridian's claims against De Vries, to the extent that such claims allege strict liability under Article 6:185 of the Dutch Civil Code. Specifically, Article 6:190, paragraph 1 of the Dutch Civil Code provides that "[t]he liability referred to in Article 185, paragraph 1 extends to (a) damage caused by death or personal injuries. . . ." The Civil Code of the Netherlands 687 (Hans Warendorf, Richard Thomas & Ian Curry-Sumner, trans., Kluwer Law International 2009). The current action falls squarely within this definition because it seeks to recover damages caused by Cooper's injuries resulting from the allegedly defective foodlift. Furthermore, Article 6:191, paragraph 2 provides a statu[t]e of repose for all strict products liability actions brought pursuant to Article 6:185, including a third-party action for indemnity and contribution:

> The right to damages of the injured person against the producer pursuant to Article 185, paragraph 1 is extinguished on expiry [sic] of ten years from the beginning of the day following that on which the producer put the thing which caused the damage into circulation. The same applies to the right of a third person who is also liable for the damage, with respect to his right of recourse against the producer.

Id. at 688. Thus, Meridian's strict products liability claim was extinguished under Dutch law because the third-party complaint was filed more than ten years after the delivery of the MEDUSE.

Moreover, the . . . appellants presented no evidence on the Dutch law statute of repose that would demonstrate the timeliness of an action for strict products liability brought under Article 6:185. If they had a contrary view of Dutch law, it was their duty to present such law to this court. *Cf. Cont'l Technical Servs., Inc. v. Rockwell Int'l Corp.*, 927 F.2d 1198, 1199 (11th Cir. 1991) (stating that "having the power to take notice of state law [does not] mean that federal courts must scour the law of a foreign state for possible arguments a claimant — particularly a claimant with counsel — might have made."). Having failed to do so, we rely on our research of foreign law for this point, which indicates that Meridian is time-barred from bringing a third-party claim under a strict liability theory.

Although appellees have established that Meridian's strict products liability claim is time-barred, they have failed to explain why Meridian cannot take advantage of the separate limitations period recognized under Dutch law for general tort claims. Dutch law further indicates that the statute of limitations for actions brought under the general tort provisions, pursuant to Article 6:162 of the Dutch Civil Code, expires five years from the day after Cooper sustained his injuries. Klaas Bisschop & Sjoerd Meijer, "Netherlands," The International Comparative Legal Guide to: Product Liability 243 § 5.2 (Global Legal Group 2008) ("A cause of action for damages on the basis of an unlawful act cannot be brought after a lapse of five years after the commencement of the day following the day on which the aggrieved party became aware of both the damage and of the person or legal entity liable. In any event an action cannot be brought after a lapse of twenty years following the event that caused the damage."). Accordingly, Meridian's third-party claims are not time-barred if brought as general tort claims, i.e. negligence. DENNIS CAMPBELL & CHRISTIAN CAMPBELL, INTERNATIONAL PRODUCT LIABILITY I/373 (2006) ("Under [Dutch] common tort rules, the general extinction period is twenty years after the damage causing event. Therefore, if a victim can no longer file a claim based on strict products liability, he can submit a claim based on the general tort provisions. However, in that event, he is not able to benefit from the strict liability imposed on the producer and is then — in principle — required to prove fault.").

. . .

In any event, we conclude that the limitation of liability clause in Article 10 precludes all of Meridian's claims against the shipbuilder. . . . [Based on the choice-of-law provision, the court interpreted Article 10 under Dutch principles of contract interpretation.]

NOTES AND QUESTIONS

1. **Practice: What Are the Stakes?** The issue in *Johnson* was whether a federal court sitting in Michigan should apply the law of Michigan or the law of Ontario, Canada. Why do the parties care about this choice-of-law issue?

What was the choice-of-law issue in *Meridian Yachts*, and why did the parties in that case care about the choice-of-law issue?

2. **Choice-of-Law Principles.** What choice-of-law principles did the court use to decide the choice-of-law issue in *Johnson*, and why?

3. **The *Second Restatement* and Choice-of-Law Provisions.** Section 188 of the *Second Restatement*, relied upon by the court in *Naghiu*, states choice-of-law principles for contract issues "[i]n the absence of an effective choice of law by the parties." In contrast, Section 187 of the *Second Restatement*, relied upon by the court in *Johnson*, states choice-of-law principles for contract issues when the parties have themselves chosen the state or nation that will provide the applicable law. What law did the parties to the sales representative contract at issue in *Johnson* choose, and how did they express that choice?

4. **Practice: Choice-of-Law Clauses.** A provision of a contract in which the parties choose the applicable law is called a "choice-of-law clause" or "choice-of-law provision." Choice-of-law clauses are frequently included in contracts. Indeed, many practitioners would say that it is a mistake not to include a choice-of-law clause in a contract. Why do you think choice-of-law clauses are so widely used and so widely viewed as essential?

5. **Practice: Drafting the Choice-of-Law Clause in *Johnson*.** Focus on the language of the choice-of-law clause included in the plaintiff's sales representative contract in *Johnson*. The court held that the choice-of-law clause clearly covered the plaintiff's contract claims. The court also held that it was broad enough to govern the plaintiff's other claims (for example, his fraud and unjust enrichment claims). Is the court's interpretation of the choice-of-law clause too broad? Why or why not? If you were the lawyer who drafted the contract, and the parties agreed that Ontario law should govern not only contract claims but also quasi-contractual claims and tort claims arising out of the parties' relationship, how would you have written the choice-of-law clause? If the parties agreed that Ontario law should govern only contractual claims and not other claims, how would you have written the choice-of-law clause so as to minimize the likelihood of the court interpreting the clause the way it did in *Johnson*? Write both versions of your choice-of-law clause.

6. **Practice: Drafting the Choice-of-Law Clause in *Meridian Yachts*.** Now focus closely on the choice-of-law clause in *Meridian Yachts*. The court held that the clause meant that Dutch law would be applied not only to contract claims, but also to tort claims. Why did the court reach this conclusion? If you were the lawyer drafting the contract, and you wanted the choice-of-law clause to cover contract claims only, how would you have drafted it? If you wanted the choice-of-law clause to cover both contract and tort claims, and you wanted to ensure that a court would interpret it that way, how would you have drafted it? Write both versions of your choice-of-law clause.

7. **Practice: Sample Choice-of-Law Clauses.** Consider the following real-world choice-of-law clauses. Why do you think some of them exclude choice-of-law principles? Why might the parties to an agreement end up with law other than their intended law if choice-of-law principles were not excluded? Would you draft any of these clauses differently? Why or why not?

- "This Agreement shall be governed by and construed and interpreted in accordance with the laws of the Province of Ontario and the laws of Canada applicable therein."
- "This Agreement and the other Loan Documents and any claims, controversy, dispute or cause of action (whether in contract or tort or otherwise) based upon, arising out of or relating to this Agreement or any other Loan Document (except, as to any other Loan Document, as expressly set forth therein) and the transactions contemplated hereby and thereby will be governed by, and construed and enforced in accordance with, the law of the State of California, without reference to conflicts or choice of law principles thereof."
- "[This Agreement] shall be governed by, and construed in accordance with, the laws of the State of California (except its choice-of-law provisions)."

8. **Policy: The Desirability of Enforcing Choice-of-Law Clauses.** The general principle that parties should be able to select the law to govern their contractual relationships is often called the principle of "party autonomy." Although widely accepted today, courts were once hesitant to allow parties to choose their own law. What might have explained the earlier skepticism? Is party autonomy a good idea? Why or why not?

9. **Practice: A Look at the Briefs.** For a look at how lawyers briefed the choice-of-law issues in the *Johnson* case, you may wish to examine the following: Plaintiff-Appellant's Final Brief on Appeal (1999 WL 34845008); Defendants-Appellees Ventra Group, Inc. and Ventratech Limited's Brief on Appeal (1999 WL 34845007); and Plaintiff-Appellant's Reply Brief (1999 WL 34845006).

Richards v. Lloyd's of London

135 F.3d 1289 (9th Cir. 1998) (en banc)

GOODWIN, Circuit Judge:

The primary question this case presents is whether the antiwaiver provisions of the Securities Act of 1933 and the Securities Exchange Act of 1934 void choice of law and choice of forum clauses in an international transaction. The district court found that they do not. . . . [W]e affirm the district court.

Background

Appellants, all citizens or residents of the United States, are more than 600 "Names" who entered into underwriting agreements. The Names sued four defendants: the Corporation of Lloyd's, the Society of Lloyd's, the Council of Lloyd's, (collectively, "Lloyd's") and Lloyd's of London, (the "unincorporated association").

Lloyd's is a market in which more than three hundred Underwriting Agencies compete for underwriting business. Pursuant to the Lloyd's Act of 1871-1982, Lloyd's oversees and regulates the competition for underwriting business in the Lloyd's market. The market does not accept premiums or insure risks. Rather, Underwriting Agencies, or syndicates, compete for the insurance business. Each Underwriting Agency is controlled by a Managing Agent who is responsible for the financial status of its agency. The Managing Agent must attract not only underwriting business from brokers but also the capital with which to insure the risks underwritten.

The Names provide the underwriting capital. The Names become Members of the Society of Lloyd's through a series of agreements, proof of financial means, and the deposit of an irrevocable letter of credit in favor of Lloyd's. To become a Name, one must travel to England to acknowledge the attendant risks of participating in a syndicate and sign a General Undertaking. The General Undertaking is a two page document containing choice of forum and choice of law clauses (collectively the "choice clauses"), which form the basis for this dispute. The choice clauses read:

> 2.1 The rights and obligations of the parties arising out of or relating to the Member's membership of, and/or underwriting of insurance business at, Lloyd's and any other matter referred to in this Undertaking shall be governed by and construed in accordance with the laws of England.
>
> 2.2 Each party hereto irrevocably agrees that the courts of England shall have exclusive jurisdiction to settle any dispute and/or controversy of whatsoever nature arising out of or relating to the Member's membership of, and/or underwriting of insurance business at, Lloyd's. . . .

By becoming a Member, the Names obtain the right to participate in the Lloyd's Underwriting Agencies. The Names, however, do not deal directly with Lloyd's or with the Managing Agents. Instead, the Names are represented by Members' Agents who, pursuant to agreement, stand in a fiduciary relationship with their Names. Upon becoming a Name, an individual selects the syndicates in which he wishes to participate. In making this decision, the individual must rely to a great extent on the advice of his Members' Agent. The Names generally join more than one underwriting agency in order to spread their risks across different types of insurance. When a Name undertakes an underwriting obligation, that Name is responsible only for his share of an agency's losses; however, his liability is unlimited for that share.

In this case, the risk of heavy losses has materialized and the Names now seek shelter under United States securities laws and the Racketeer Influenced and Corrupt Organizations Act ("RICO"), 18 U.S.C. § 1961 et seq. The Names claim that Lloyd's actively sought the investment of United States residents to fill an urgent need to build up capital. According to the Names, Lloyd's concealed information regarding the possible consequences of the risks undertaken and deliberately and disproportionately exposed the Names to massive liabilities for which sufficient underwriting capital or reinsurance was unavailable.

This appeal does not address the merits of the underlying claims. It addresses only the Names' contention that their disputes with Lloyd's should be litigated in the United States despite contract clauses binding the parties to proceed in England under English law. It also addresses whether default should have been entered against the unincorporated association.

Standard of Review

We review the district court's decision to enforce the choice clauses for abuse of discretion. *Argueta v. Banco Mexicano, S.A.*, 87 F.3d 320, 323 (9th Cir. 1996). As we are reviewing a Rule 12(b)(3) motion decision, we need not accept the pleadings as true. *Id.* at 324.

Whether the securities laws void the choice clauses is a question of law that we review de novo. *Pinal Creek Group v. Newmont Mining Corp.*, 118 F.3d 1298, 1300 (9th Cir. 1997).

Discussion

The Names make three arguments for repudiating the choice clauses. They contend (1) that the antiwaiver provisions of the federal securities laws void such clauses, (2) that the choice clauses are invalid because they offend the strong public policy of preserving an investor's remedies under federal and state securities law and RICO and (3) that the choice clauses were obtained by fraud. We will address each of these in turn.

I

We analyze the validity of the choice clause under *The Bremen v. Zapata Off-Shore Co.*, 407 U.S. 1 (1972), where the Supreme Court stated that courts should enforce choice of law and choice of forum clauses in cases of "freely negotiated private international agreement[s]."

A

The Names dispute the application of *Bremen* to this case. They contend that *Bremen* does not apply to cases where Congress has spoken directly to the immediate issue — as they claim the antiwaiver provisions do here.

The Securities Act of 1933 provides that:

> Any condition, stipulation, or provision binding any person acquiring any security to waive compliance with any provision of this subchapter or of the rules and regulations of the Commission shall be void.

15 U.S.C. § 77n. The 1934 Securities Exchange Act contains a substantially similar provision. 15 U.S.C. § 78cc(a). The Names seize on these provisions and claim that they void the choice clauses in their agreement with Lloyd's.

Certainly the antiwaiver provisions are worded broadly enough to reach this case. They cover "*any* condition, stipulation, or provision binding *any* person acquiring *any* security to waive compliance with *any* provision of this subchapter. . . ." Indeed, this language is broad enough to reach any offer or sale of anything that could be alleged to be a security, no matter where the transaction occurs.

Nevertheless, this attempt to distinguish *Bremen* fails. . . . [I]n *Scherk v. Alberto-Culver Co.*, 417 U.S. 506 (1974), the Supreme Court explicitly relied on *Bremen* in a case involving a securities transaction. Echoing the language of *Bremen*, the Court found that "[a] contractual provision specifying in advance the forum in which disputes shall be litigated and the law to be applied is . . . an almost indispensable precondition to achievement of the orderliness and predictability essential to any international business transaction." *Id.* at 516. This passage should leave little doubt as to the applicability of *Bremen* to the case at hand.

B

Having determined that *Bremen* governs international contracts specifying forum and applicable law, we turn to the question whether the contract between Lloyd's and the Names is international. Not surprisingly, the Names contend that these were purely domestic securities sales. They claim that Lloyd's solicited the Names in the United States and that the trip the Names made to England was a mere ritual without legal significance.

We disagree. The Names signed a contract with English entities to participate in an English insurance market and flew to England to consummate the transaction. That the Names received solicitations in the United States does not somehow erase these facts. Moreover, Lloyd's insistence that individuals travel to England to become a Name does not strike us as mere ritual. Lloyd's likely requires this precisely so that those who choose to be the Names understand that English law governs the transaction. Entering into the Lloyd's market in the manner described is plainly an international transaction.

II

. . .

A

The Names' strongest argument for escaping their agreement to litigate their claims in England is that the choice clauses contravene a strong public policy embodied in federal and state securities law and RICO.

We follow our six sister circuits that have ruled to enforce the choice clauses. We do so because we apply *Scherk* and because English law provides the Names with sufficient protection.

. . .

[T]he Supreme Court has explained that, in the context of an international agreement, there is "no basis for a judgment that only United States laws and United States courts should determine this controversy in the face of a solemn agreement between the parties that such controversies be resolved elsewhere." [*Scherk.*] To require that "'American standards of fairness' must . . . govern the controversy demeans the standards of justice elsewhere in the world, and unneces-sarily exalts the primacy of United States law over the laws of other countries." *Id.*

These passages from *Scherk*, we think, resolve the question whether public policy reasons allow the Names to escape their "solemn agreement" to adjudi-cate their claims in England under English law. . . . As the Supreme Court has explained, "'[w]e cannot have trade and commerce in world markets and interna-tional waters exclusively on our terms, governed by our laws, and resolved in our courts.'" *Id.* (quoting *Bremen*, 407 U.S. at 9).

Relying on *Mitsubishi Motors Corp. v. Soler Chrysler-Plymouth, Inc.*, 473 U.S. 614, 634 (1985), the Names argue that federal and state securities laws are of "fundamental importance to American democratic capitalism." They claim that enforcement of the choice clauses will deprive them of important remedies provided by our securities laws. The Supreme Court disapproved of such an out-come, the Names contend, when it stated that "in the event the choice-of-forum and choice-of-law clauses operated in tandem as a prospective waiver of a party's right to pursue statutory remedies for antitrust violations, we would have little hesitation in condemning the agreement as against public policy." *Id.* at 637 n.19.

Without question this case would be easier to decide if this footnote in *Mitsubishi* had not been inserted. Nevertheless, we do not believe dictum in a footnote regarding antitrust law outweighs the extended discussion and holding in *Scherk* on the validity of clauses specifying the forum and applicable law. The Supreme Court repeatedly recognized in *Scherk* that parties to an international securities transaction may choose law other than that of the United States. . . .

B

Of course, were English law so deficient that the Names would be deprived of any reasonable recourse, we would have to subject the choice clauses to another level of scrutiny. In this case, however, there is no such danger. *See Haynsworth*, 121 F.3d at 969 ("English law provides a variety of protections for fraud and mis-representations in securities transactions."). *Cf. British Midland Airways Ltd. v. International Travel, Inc.*, 497 F.2d 869, 871 (9th Cir. 1974) (This court is "hardly in a position to call the Queen's Bench a kangaroo court.").

We disagree with the dramatic assertion that "[t]he available English remedies are not adequate substitutes for the firm shields and finely honed swords pro-vided by American securities law." *Richards v. Lloyd's of London*, 107 F.3d 1422, 1430 (9th Cir. 1997). The Names have recourse against both the Member and Managing Agents for fraud, breach of fiduciary duty, or negligent misrepresenta-tion. Indeed, English courts have already awarded substantial judgments to some of the other Names. *See Arubuthnott v. Fagan and Feltrim Underwriting Agencies Ltd.*, 3 Re LR 145 (H.L. 1994); *Deeny v. Gooda Walker Ltd.*, Queen's Bench Division (Commercial Court), The Times 7 October 1994.

While it is true that the Lloyd's Act immunizes Lloyd's from many actions possible under our securities laws, Lloyd's is not immune from the consequences of actions committed in bad faith, including fraud. Lloyd's Act of 1982, Ch. 14(3) (e)(i). The Names contend that entities using the Lloyd's trade name willfully and fraudulently concealed massive long tail liabilities in order to induce them to join syndicates. If so, we have been cited to no authority that Lloyd's partial immunity would bar recovery.

C

The addition of RICO claims does not alter our conclusion. . . .

D

The Names also argue that the choice clauses were the product of fraud. They claim that at the time of signing the General Undertaking, Lloyd's knew that the Names were effectively sacrificing valid claims under U.S. law by signing the choice clauses and concealed this fact from the Names. Had the Names known this fact, they contend, they never would have agreed to the choice clauses. The Names never allege, however, that Lloyd's misled them as to the legal effect of the choice clauses. Nor do they allege that Lloyd's fraudulently inserted the clauses without their knowledge. Accordingly, we view the allegations made by the Names as going only to the contract as a whole, with no allegations as to the inclusion of the choice clauses themselves.

Absent such allegations, these claims of fraud fail. The Supreme Court has noted that simply alleging that one was duped into signing the contract is not enough. *Scherk*, 417 U.S. at 519 n.14 (The fraud exception in *Bremen* "does not mean that any time a dispute arising out of a transaction is based upon an allegation of fraud . . . the clause is unenforceable."). For a party to escape a forum selection clause on the grounds of fraud, it must show that "the *inclusion of that clause in the contract* was the product of fraud or coercion." *Id.* . . .

Affirmed.

THOMAS, Circuit Judge, with whom Judge PREGERSON and Judge HAWKINS join, dissenting.

The majority espouses a reasonable foreign policy, but one which emanates from the wrong branch of government. Congress has already explicitly resolved the question at hand. In the Securities Act of 1933 and the Securities Exchange Act of 1934 (the "Acts"), Congress expressly provided that investors cannot contractually agree to disregard United States securities law. Thus, in applying the "reasonableness" policy-weighing approach of *M/S Bremen v. Zapata Off-Shore Co.*, 407 U.S. 1 (1972), the majority displaces Congress' specific statutory directive. Furthermore, even assuming that the *Bremen* analysis applies here, the circumstances surrounding this dispute compel the conclusion that enforcement of the choice clauses would be unreasonable. Accordingly, I respectfully dissent.

I.

. . . [T]he [Securities] Acts do not merely declare "a strong public policy" against the waiver of compliance with United States securities laws. Rather, the

Acts explicitly and unconditionally prohibit such a waiver. The language of the Securities Act of 1933 is clear and unambiguous:

> Any condition, stipulation, or provision binding any person acquiring any security to waive compliance with any provision of this subchapter or of the rules and regulations of the Commission shall be void.

15 U.S.C. § 77n. The Securities Exchange Act of 1934 contains a similar restriction. *See* 15 U.S.C. § 78cc(a).

. . . With adoption of those sections, Congress announced a per se rule that American laws cannot be ignored in this context. Courts should not employ amorphous public policy to emasculate plain statutory language. "Under our constitutional framework, federal courts do not sit as councils of revision, empowered to rewrite legislation in accord with their own conceptions of prudent public policy." *United States v. Rutherford*, 442 U.S. 544, 555 (1979). Rather, "[o]nly when a literal construction of a statute yields results so manifestly unreasonable that they could not fairly be attributed to congressional design will an exception to statutory language be judicially implied." *Id.* Because Congress quite reasonably intended that our securities laws be enforced even when a salesperson managed to obtain an investor's waiver, we "have no license to depart from the plain language" of the Acts. *Id.*

. . .

NOTES AND QUESTIONS

1. **Policy: The Limits of Party Autonomy.** Why do the plaintiffs and the dissent argue that the parties' choice of law should not be recognized? Is that persuasive? Why shouldn't parties be able to choose whatever law they want to govern their relationships?

2. **Antitrust Law and Securities Law.** As discussed in *Richards*, the Supreme Court in *Mitsubishi Motors Corp. v. Soler Chrysler-Plymouth, Inc.*, 473 U.S. 614, 637 n.19 (1985), strongly implied that a choice-of-law clause could not displace U.S. antitrust laws. Is *Richards* consistent with that view? To what extent are antitrust and securities laws different?

3. **Other Areas of Law.** What other laws are arguably not affected by choice-of-law clauses? One common rule in state contract law, for example, limits or prohibits covenants not to compete (that is, contractual agreements that one party will not engage in a business that competes with the other party for a defined period). Would a choice-of-law clause selecting the law of a state or nation that did not have such a limit be enforceable? How would you advise a client considering signing such a contract?

4. **Choice of Law versus Choice of Forum.** Note that choice-of-law clauses are not the same as choice-of-forum clauses. Choice-of-law clauses select the law that will govern disputes arising out of a contract. In contrast, choice-of-forum clauses select the forum that will resolve such a dispute. In the General

Undertaking in the *Richards* case, the parties included both types of clauses, and they both pointed to England. However, parties may select the law of one nation to govern disputes, and select the courts of a different nation to resolve disputes in accordance with the selected law. For now, the essential point is that choice-of-law and choice-of-forum clauses serve different functions and need not select the same nation. Chapter 10 explores choice-of-forum clauses in more detail.

5. **The CISG.** As discussed in detail above, the CISG is a treaty that governs matters such as formation of contracts, the obligations of the seller and buyer, and contractual remedies. Recall that the CISG governs transnational sales contracts between parties in CISG countries *unless the parties to the contract opt out of the CISG. See* Article 6 ("The parties may exclude the application of this Convention. . . ."). Therefore, as a lawyer advising a client considering a contract that might be covered by the CISG, unless you want the CISG's provisions to govern, you must be very careful to include language in the contract that explicitly states that the parties exclude application of the CISG, and you should consider a choice-of-law clause that indicates an alternative source of governing law.

6. **Comparative Perspective.** Consider how European Union law deals with choice-of-law clauses. Regulation (EC) No. 593/2008 of the European Parliament and of the Council of 17 June 2008 on the Law Applicable to Contractual Obligations (the *Rome I Regulation*) provides as follows:

Article 3

Freedom of choice

1. A contract shall be governed by the law chosen by the parties. The choice shall be made expressly or clearly demonstrated by the terms of the contract or the circumstances of the case. . . .

. . .

3. Where all other elements relevant to the situation at the time of the choice are located in a country other than the country whose law has been chosen, the choice of the parties shall not prejudice the application of provisions of the law of that other country which cannot be derogated from by agreement.

. . .

Article 9

Overriding mandatory provisions

1. Overriding mandatory provisions are provisions the respect for which is regarded as crucial by a country for safeguarding its public interests, such as its political, social or economic organisation, to such an extent that they are applicable to any situation falling within their scope, irrespective of the law otherwise applicable to the contract under this Regulation.

2. Nothing in this Regulation shall restrict the application of the overriding mandatory provisions of the law of the forum.

3. Effect may be given to the overriding mandatory provisions of the law of the country where the obligations arising out of the contract have to be or have been performed, in so far as those overriding mandatory provisions render the performance of the contract unlawful. In considering whether to give effect to those provisions, regard shall be had to their nature and purpose and to the consequences of their application or non-application.

How would *Richards* be decided under the *Rome I Regulation*? Is the answer clear? Is it a better result?

REVIEW NOTES AND QUESTIONS

1. Carefully review the materials presented in this section. As you do so, keep in mind these basic steps in choice-of-law analysis:

   - First, remember that choice-of-law principles are determined by the law of the forum. For example, in a lawsuit filed in a California state court, the court would apply California choice-of-law principles. Different states have adopted different choice-of-law principles, ranging from the traditional approach of the *First Restatement* to the *Second Restatement*. Some states have unique choice-of-law methods, such as California and New York. In general, choice-of-law principles are a matter of state common law. However, some choice-of-law rules are embodied in statutes, and in two states — Louisiana and Oregon — choice-of-law principles are extensively codified by statute. Therefore, choice-of-law research entails a combination of common law and statutory research. Also remember that a federal court applies the choice-of-law principles of the state in which it sits if its jurisdiction is based on diversity of citizenship. In other cases, federal common law provides the applicable choice-of-law principles. In general, these federal common law principles follow the *Second Restatement*. In some specific areas of the law, federal courts apply other principles. For example, for maritime torts, the federal courts apply a multifactor choice-of-law method set forth in *Lauritzen v. Larsen*, 345 U.S. 571 (1953).
   - Second, characterize the choice-of-law issue to be decided in order to determine the applicable choice-of-law principles. Remember that one characterization problem is whether an issue is procedural or substantive. Generally speaking, procedural issues are decided based on the law of the forum. If the issue is substantive, remember that the applicable choice-of-law principles depend on the substantive area of the law at issue — for example, different choice-of-law principles apply to tort and contract issues. In addition, remember that in New York, the choice-of-law principles

applicable to tort issues further depend on whether the issue involves a conduct-regulating or loss-allocating rule.

- Third, apply the applicable choice-of-law principles to the facts of the case to determine which nation's law applies.
- Fourth, if you intend to argue that foreign law applies, provide the notice required by Rule 44.1, assemble the materials you will use to provide proof of foreign law under Rule 44.1, and consider retaining an expert witness.

2. Remember that choice of law is not just a litigation issue, but also a planning issue. Whenever you draft a contract on behalf of a client, consider including a choice-of-law clause and draft it carefully. In addition, you should determine whether the contract is covered by the CISG and, if it is, you should consider whether to include a contract clause opting out of the CISG's provisions.

3. Choice of law is important not only in transnational litigation, but also in purely domestic litigation in the United States. For example, in a contract dispute between a business in Oregon and a business in California, would Oregon or California contract law govern a contract dispute? The materials in this section provide only a small sampling of choice-of-law issues and choice-of-law methods. For a more thorough treatment of this important area of law, you may wish to consider taking a course on conflict of laws, which includes extensive treatment of choice-of-law issues.

CHAPTER 2

INTERNATIONAL LAW

As Chapter 1 describes, national law is often a source of rules that may apply to transnational legal problems. This chapter focuses on another source of potentially applicable rules: international law. As you will see, one challenge when studying international law and using it in practice is that international law operates at two levels. First, it operates at the international level, when nations together make international legal rules (for example, when they make treaties) or apply international law to make legal claims against each other (for example, when one nation sues another before an international court, as discussed in Chapter 5, or raises diplomatic objections to another nation's conduct). Second, international law can operate within national legal systems (for example, when national courts apply international law to decide an issue). In many legal systems, including the U.S. legal system, national courts may not automatically enforce international law as binding rules of decision. The challenge, then, is to understand the circumstances in which international law has what is called "domestic effect."

Another challenge is that it often is unclear whether a purported rule of international law is really a rule of international law at all. In practice lawyers invoking a rule of international law typically need to prove that the rule is indeed a rule of international law — and the opposing lawyer will often argue that it is not. As we will see, this dynamic introduces difficulties because the sources of international law are themselves contested. Although this may seem different from national law, be careful not to exaggerate the difference. After all, in the U.S. legal system and other common law systems, lawyers routinely make arguments about what is or is not a common law rule. And, of course, lawyers and nonlawyers alike frequently disagree about what is or is not an individual right or a governmental power under the U.S. Constitution. Therefore, instead of worrying about international law seeming less coherent or more amorphous than national law, we urge you to think of international law as an opportunity to use and hone the abilities you have already started to develop in your "noninternational" law courses to perform complex legal analysis and make convincing legal arguments.

With these challenges in mind, this chapter's basic goals are twofold. The first goal is to help you understand the different types of international law, including international agreements, customary international law, and general principles of law. The second goal is to help you understand the role of international law in the U.S. legal system. The chapter proceeds as follows: Section A provides an introduction to the nature, sources, and role of international law. Section B focuses on treaties and other types of international agreements. Section C focuses on customary international law.

A. Introduction: The Nature and Role of International Law

1. Overview

As traditionally understood, international law is law among nations — namely, the body of rules that nations recognize as legally binding in their relations with one another. It does not arise from any single nation's legal system, and, at least in some senses, it is superior to the legal system of any particular nation. Although once viewed as principally addressing interactions among nations, international law has important implications for private parties as well. It can govern relations between nations and private parties (including relations between national governments and their own citizens), and it can govern relations between private parties. Even when international law does not directly govern a legal dispute, it may serve as a backdrop for decision making.

In an era of globalization, it is natural to think that international law is gaining importance, and it is. But despite much recent growth of international law and international organizations, the basic building blocks of the modern international legal system remain sovereign nations, each exercising supreme authority over a defined geographic area. As the *Restatement (Third) of the Foreign Relations Law of the United States* describes (pp. 16-17):

> The international political system is loose and decentralized. Its principal components — "sovereign" states — retain their essential autonomy. There is no "world government" as the term "government" is commonly understood. There is no central legislature with general law-making authority; the General Assembly and other organs of the United Nations influence the development of international law but only when their product is accepted by states. There is no executive institution to enforce law; the United Nations Security Council has limited executive power to enforce the provisions of the [U.N.] Charter and to maintain international peace and security, but it has no authority to enforce international law generally; within its jurisdiction, moreover, the Council is subject to the veto power of its five permanent members . . . [the] People's Republic of China, France, [Russia], the United Kingdom and the United States. There is no international judiciary with general, comprehensive and compulsory jurisdiction; the International Court of Justice decides cases submitted to it and renders advisory opinions but has only limited compulsory jurisdiction.

One might add that international organizations such as the United Nations lack their own standing military or police forces, and thus depend on nations, directly or indirectly, to supply enforcement power.

As a result, international law's practical force is highly dependent upon nations' willingness to comply with it voluntarily and, in some instances, to enforce it against nations that do not. It is important to note that much international law enforcement can and often does take place outside of courts. Nations enforce international law informally, in their diplomatic relations; through economic sanctions and other informal forms of reward, punishment, or retaliation; and even through military force. Nonetheless, judicial enforcement of international law is a potential way that international law can be given practical effect.

As the international legal system is currently configured, the greatest potential for judicial enforcement of international law is through national courts. There are relatively few international fora for the adjudication of international law claims, and, in particular, there are very few available to private parties and very few that have any means to enforce their own judgments. Chapter 5 provides an in-depth examination of international courts. The point here is that because international courts generally have limited jurisdiction, international law cannot primarily rely on them for implementation and enforcement. For example, the International Court of Justice (ICJ), mentioned in the excerpt above, is an arm of the United Nations that was created after World War II with the idea that it would be a "world court" (it is still sometimes called the World Court) to peacefully resolve disputes among nations. But the ICJ only has jurisdiction over cases between nations, not between nations and individuals. It can only issue binding decisions where all the disputing nations have agreed to its jurisdiction, and in practice most nations have not agreed to its jurisdiction for most disputes. Most importantly, the ICJ has no ability to enforce its own judgments. In practice, this means that the ICJ depends heavily on nations to abide by its decisions voluntarily.

More recently, various new international courts (or court-like entities called tribunals or dispute settlement bodies) have been established. For example, various criminal tribunals, such as the International Criminal Tribunal for the Former Yugoslavia (ICTY) and the International Criminal Tribunal for Rwanda (ICTR) — established in the 1990s — have tried and imprisoned violators of international human rights law in particular conflicts; other specialized criminal tribunals have been established in the aftermath of particular conflicts; and the International Criminal Court (ICC) seeks to expand the model of the ICTY and ICTR to punish "the most serious crimes of concern to the international community as a whole." Rome Statute of the International Criminal Court, Art. 5.1. However, most of these courts are limited to particular issues and specific geographic areas. The ICC remains a somewhat tentative venture: Some important nations, including China, India, Russia, and the United States, are not part of it, and so far it has issued only a handful of judgments. In trade and investment, the World Trade Organization (WTO) has a dispute settlement mechanism that functions much like a court to resolve trade disputes among member nations on the basis of international law. But again, the WTO only hears disputes among nations (not individuals), and only on specified trade matters; and like the ICJ it depends on disputants to comply voluntarily with its judgments or on its member nations to enforce its judgments. Regional courts and multinational institutions have been established in particular geographic areas — most notably, the European

Union — that enjoy broad jurisdiction and legal authority, but the United States and many other countries are for the most part outside such institutions.

None of this means that international courts are unimportant. But they are primarily important in particular geographic and subject matter areas; and they do not obviate the need for enforcement of international law at the national level.*

It is also true that enforcement of international law and international judgments at the national level can be done by various organs of government, not just the judiciary. As noted, much international law enforcement is informal and done through diplomacy. Further, much enforcement is voluntary, as when a nation complies with an international judgment by, for example, amending its trade laws in response to a determination of a WTO dispute settlement panel. Thus enforcement of international law can occur in the executive branch, in the legislative branch, and even (as we will see) at the subnational level as in the States of the United States.

As a result, the role of international law in national courts (including U.S. courts) is only a small part of the picture. It is, though, an important part of the picture for lawyers, as well as for people and entities that may prefer to vindicate their claims through (hopefully) neutral, independent, and law-oriented courts rather than through the political branches of national governments.

2. *Types of International Law*

International law does not mean simply any law that applies to cross-border activities. Indeed, most cross-border activity, including much of the world's commerce, communications, and travel, is regulated by the national laws of one or more nations. Extraterritoriality analysis and choice-of-law analysis, discussed in Chapter 1, help determine which nation's national law should govern transnational problems. Transnational law — the law that governs transnational activity and disputes arising out of transnational activity — thus includes, but is much broader than, international law. What distinguishes international law from other types of transnational law is that it arises separately from, and is not made by, the legal system of any single nation.

There are various ways to categorize international law. It is sometimes divided between public international law (the law of relations among nations) and private international law (the law of relations among private individuals and businesses). This is often not a useful division, because it is sometimes unclear how a particular set of laws should be classified and because it is unclear that the resolution of many practical legal issues depends on the distinction. Further, international law is sometimes classified as consensual and nonconsensual (that is, whether particular nations have agreed to abide by it). This is an important distinction that we will take up shortly, but also a difficult one, and thus not a good starting point. Instead, a better way to think about international law is according to its sources or "types."

---

* As noted, Chapter 5 provides a more detailed look at international courts.

As the following materials show, international law is generally described in three main categories of sources: (1) treaties and other agreements among nations, (2) customary international law, and (3) general principles of law.

Restatement (Third) of the Foreign Relations Law of the United States (1987)

Section 102. Sources of International Law

(1) A rule of international law is one that has been accepted as such by the international community of states
    (a) in the form of customary law;
    (b) by international agreement; or
    (c) by derivation from general principles common to the major legal systems of the world.

(2) Customary international law results from a general and consistent practice of states followed by them from a sense of legal obligation.

(3) International agreements create law for the states parties thereto and may lead to the creation of customary international law when such agreements are intended for adherence by states generally and are in fact widely accepted.

(4) General principles common to the major legal systems, even if not incorporated or reflected in customary law or international agreement, may be invoked as supplementary rules of international law where appropriate.

Statute of the International Court of Justice, Article 38(1)

33 U.N.T.S. 993 (June 26, 1945)

The Court, whose function is to decide in accordance with international law such disputes as are submitted to it, shall apply:

    a. international conventions, whether general or particular, establishing rules expressly recognized by the contesting states;
    b. international custom, as evidence of a general practice accepted as law;
    c. the general principles of law recognized by civilized nations;
    d. . . . judicial decisions and the teachings of the most highly qualified publicists of the various nations, as subsidiary means for the determination of rules of law.

a. Treaties

Treaties and similar instruments (also called conventions, covenants, compacts, or international agreements) are express agreements among nations, usually written, that are intended by their signatories to be legally binding. For most people, a treaty is the definitive type of international law, causing the least conceptual difficulty. In its purest form, a treaty is like a contract between two nations, each of which agrees to take (or refrain from taking) specified actions. Based on our understanding of contracts as legally binding instruments enforceable by courts, it is natural to think of treaties in a similar way.

As we will see, the contract analogy is imprecise. Some treaties look much like ordinary contracts, but others do not. In modern practice, many of the most important treaties are not "bilateral" (between two nations) but "multilateral," involving dozens or even over one hundred nations. Some treaties, such as the U.N. Charter, encompass almost every nation in the world. Some treaties are "constitutional" in that they create international organizations with specified powers (for example, the agreements establishing the United Nations, the International Criminal Court, or the World Trade Organization). Some treaties are "regulatory," in that they establish legal relations among private parties. For example, the Convention on Contracts for the International Sale of Goods (CISG) regulates cross-border sales transactions among private parties, and the Warsaw Convention on international air transport establishes the scope of liability of international air carriers to their passengers. Some treaties function as a sort of global "bill of rights." Most notably, the International Covenant on Civil and Political Rights (ICCPR) lists basic generally applicable rights — such as freedom of speech — that each nation agrees to respect.

Some treaties regulate specific topics, such as the Hague Service Convention, which addresses service of process in transnational civil suits (discussed in Chapter 9); other treaties address topics that are usually outside the ordinary judicial workload, such as the decision to use military force (for example, portions of the U.N. Charter) or the conduct of war (for example, the Geneva Conventions on the treatment of prisoners of war). Some treaties (or parts of treaties) contain very specific terms while others may be more abstract, open-ended, or aspirational. Thus, some treaties look like contracts, but others (or parts of others) may look like constitutions, bills of rights, statutes or administrative regulations, diplomatic arrangements, or statements of goals or objectives.

Even a casual glance at a list of treaties and other international agreements reveals that there are an enormous number of them, covering many transnational activities (and even some activities that do not seem transnational at all). That does not mean that all or even most transnational disputes are necessarily governed by treaty law. It does mean, however, that lawyers called upon to solve their clients' transnational legal problems must understand how to consult and apply treaty law — and in particular, must understand the extent to which treaty law forms a source of law within the relevant national legal systems.

b. Customary International Law

In most descriptions of international law, the second major category after treaties is customary international law. Most basically, customary international law is unwritten law to which nations may have (at most) only tacitly agreed. Compared to treaties, customary international law is a more difficult concept on at least two grounds: the way in which customary international law obligations arise and the ways the existence of such obligations can be proved. This section briefly addresses these conceptual difficulties.

1. **Custom and Consent.** One way to think about customary international law is that is reflects unwritten agreement among nations on legal rules, shown by common practices. According to Section 102 of the *Restatement (Third) of Foreign Relations Law*, quoted above, customary international law "results from a general and consistent practice of states followed by them from a sense of legal obligation." The great eighteenth-century international law scholar Emer de Vattel observed:

> Certain maxims and customs consecrated by long use, and observed by nations in their mutual intercourse with each other as a kind of law, form the customary law of nations, or the custom of nations. This law is founded on tacit consent, or, if you please, on a tacit convention of the nations that observe it towards each other.
> . . .
> When a custom or usage is generally established, either between all the civilised nations in the world, or only between those of a certain continent, as of Europe, for example, or between those who have a more frequent intercourse with each other . . . it becomes obligatory on all the nations in question, who are considered as having given their consent to it, and are bound to observe it toward each other, as long as they have not expressly declared their resolution of not observing it in the future.

EMER DE VATTEL, THE LAW OF NATIONS, prelim., §§ 25-26 (1758). One example of custom, prior to its codification by treaty in the Vienna Convention on Diplomatic Relations (1961), is diplomatic immunity. By longstanding tradition, nations gave diplomatic immunity to the ambassadors of other nations (that is, they exempted ambassadors from civil and criminal process in their domestic courts). Nations came to recognize this immunity as a legal principle long before it was adopted in a treaty and even where it was not part of the nation's formal domestic law. This conception of immunity arising from custom is reflected, for example, in Chief Justice John Marshall's opinion for the U.S. Supreme Court in *The Schooner Exchange v. McFaddon*, 11 U.S. 116, 138-39 (1812), which noted "the immunity which all civilized nations allow to foreign ministers." This immunity, Marshall continued,

> is granted by the governing power of the nation to which the minister is deputed. [It] . . . could not be erected and supported against the will of the sovereign of the territory. He is supposed to assent to it.
> This consent is not expressed. It is true that in some countries . . . a special law is enacted for the case. But the law obviously proceeds on the idea of prescribing the punishment of an act previously unlawful, not of granting to a foreign minister a privilege which he would not otherwise possess.
> The assent of the sovereign to the very important and extensive exemptions from territorial jurisdiction which are admitted to attach to foreign ministers is implied from the considerations that without such exemption, every sovereign would hazard his own dignity by employing a public minister abroad. His minister would owe temporary and local allegiance to a foreign prince, and

would be less competent to the objects of his mission. A sovereign committing the interests of his nation with a foreign power to the care of a person whom he has selected for that purpose cannot intend to subject his minister in any degree to that power, and therefore a consent to receive him implies a consent that he shall possess those privileges which his principal intended he should retain — privileges which are essential to the dignity of his sovereign and to the duties he is bound to perform.

In *The Schooner Exchange*, Marshall went on to find that a similar immunity from judicial process applied to foreign warships as a result of the customary practices of nations. Note that in this conception of customary international law, nations' consent is essential. This approach is typically labeled "positivism," from the idea that the law must be "posited" by some act of a lawmaker (in this case, multiple lawmakers in the form of the nations of the international community). As one leading scholar has explained,

> One of the leading conjectures for a positivist basis for international legal obligation is consent. Under this theory, the rules of international law become positive law when the will of the state consents to being bound by them, either expressly or by implication. The doctrine of consent generally teaches that the common consent of states voluntarily entering the international community gives international law its validity. States — and presumably other international actors — are said to be bound by international law because they have given their consent. . . . [T]he majority view . . . is that state consent to international law norms need not be made in reference to written treaties but may be also manifested in regard to customary obligations.

DAVID J. BEDERMAN, THE SPIRIT OF INTERNATIONAL LAW 14 (2002). Thinking of customary international law as arising from each nation's tacit consent permits an analogy to treaties; in each case the obligation arises from sovereign consent, express in one case and implicit in the other. Thus it is often said that customary international law contains two elements: (a) state practice and (b) the state's acceptance of the practice as reflecting a legal obligation (called "opinio juris").

2. **Positivist and Naturalist International Law.** While customary law based on tacit consent is widely accepted as *one* basis for non-treaty-based international law, a core question is whether it is the *only* appropriate basis. As Professor Bederman puts it, "The debate today . . . is whether law for the international community is exclusively the product of consent by the participants in the system (however manifested) or also includes enduring truths that somehow reflect the fundamental values of that community. Put another way, are all rules in a legal community internally generated by means and institutions chosen by the participants, or is there also a metaphysic of first principles that govern the system?" BEDERMAN, *supra*, at 19. In the early history of international law (then called the "law of nations") consent was secondary at best. "The earliest, 'classic' scholars of international law writing before and during the Thirty Years War [of the early seventeenth century] . . . tended to emphasize the moral imperatives of law between nations and were part of a

larger natural law tradition — a 'common law' of states backed up by religious and philosophical principles of good faith and goodwill between men and nations." *Id.* at 5. By the eighteenth century, the rise of Enlightenment thinking in Europe replaced international law's quasi-religious inspiration with deductive reasoning; law formed by state consent was recognized, but it was not thought central or exclusive:

> The eighteenth-century view [of international law] was more complex [than pure positivism], and more openly based on natural law identified by reason. As Vattel put it, "the Law of Nations is in its origin merely the Law of Nature applied to Nations." [William] Blackstone . . . said that the law of nations "depends upon the rules of natural law, or upon mutual compacts, treaties, leagues, and agreements between these several communities." Vattel even subtitled his work "Principles of Natural Law Applied to the Conduct and to the Affairs of Nations and of Sovereigns."
>
> The overriding impulse in eighteenth-century law was not positivism but rationalism. Much of the idea, at least, was that principles of international relations could be discovered through reason, from the nature and needs of the international system. [The German scholar Christian von] Wolff called his 1749 work "The Law of Nations Treated According to a Scientific Method"; as the title indicated, it was methodologically deductive rather than descriptive, deriving rules logically from universally accepted first principles. The law of nations, Vattel explained, is "the law which ought to prevail between Nations or sovereign States"; as he quoted Wolff: "the law of nations is certainly connected with the Law of Nature. Hence we call it the natural Law of Nations, by reference to its origins; and by reference to its binding force we call it the necessary law of nations. This law is common to all nations, and that nation which does not act according to it violates the common law of all mankind." It was, Vattel said, "founded on the nature of things, and particularly on the nature of man. . . ."

Michael D. Ramsey, The Constitution's Text in Foreign Affairs 344-45 (2007). Indeed, Vattel argued that the "natural" law of nations overrode mere agreements among sovereigns, so that agreements or tacit consent contrary to natural justice would not be binding. Vattel, *supra*, prelim., § 26. By the nineteenth century, though, naturalism and rationalism began to recede as the basis of international law, ultimately to be replaced by a strict positivism. In an early manifestation, Chief Justice Marshall refused to find that the slave trade violated international law, even though it might violate the law of nature:

> Whatever might be the answer of a moralist to this question [i.e., the legality of the slave trade], a jurist must search for its legal solution, in those principles of action which are sanctioned [i.e., approved] by the usages, the national acts, and the general assent, of that portion of the world of which he considers himself to be a part, and to whose law the appeal is made. If we resort to this standard as the test of international law, the question, as has already been observed, is decided in favour of the legality of the trade. Both Europe and America embarked on it; and for nearly two centuries, it was carried out without opposition, and without censure.

The Antelope, 23 U.S. 66, 120 (1825). At the end of the nineteenth century, Justice Horace Gray wrote for the U.S. Supreme Court that in determining international law,

> where there is no treaty and no controlling executive or legislative act or judicial decision, resort must be had to the customs and usages of civilized nations, and, as evidence of these, to the works of jurists and commentators who by years of labor, research, and experience have made themselves peculiarly well acquainted with the subjects of which they treat. Such works are resorted to by judicial tribunals not for the speculations of their authors concerning what the law ought to be, but for trustworthy evidence of what the law really is.

The Paquete Habana, 175 U.S. 677, 700 (1900). The twentieth century, however, saw a revival of naturalist influences in international law, reflected most strongly in the international law of human rights. Positivist international law tends to affirm the actions of nations (since nations create it and consent to it); but the horrors of the Holocaust and World War II suggested the need for law not bound to state practice, so that state practice could be condemned. In particular, the trials of the top Nazi leaders at Nuremberg

> marked an important milestone in customary international law's shift away from pure positivism and back toward conceptions of natural law that had prevailed in early American history. . . . Nuremberg laid the foundations for modern human rights law. . . .
>
> There is real doubt that the [law applied at Nuremberg] accurately reflected the positive law of the time. Those who defended the Nuremberg Tribunal often couched their arguments in natural law terms. Professor Quincy Wright, for example, noted that "[t]he assumptions underlying . . . the Charter of the Nuremberg Tribunal are far removed from the positivistic assumptions which generally influenced the thought of international jurists of the nineteenth century." But Wright argued that pure positivism was not practicable in a system without centralized legislative authority. "In such a situation," Wright wrote, "the law must have within itself the means of its own change, and that element is what the seventeenth century jurists called 'natural law' and which in modern terminology can perhaps better be expressed by the word 'justice' as interpreted by predominant world opinion.". . .
>
> Out of Nuremberg grew the modern law of international human rights. As Professor Louis Sohn has observed, "The modern rules of international law concerning human rights are the result of a silent revolution of the 1940s."

William S. Dodge, *Customary International Law in the Supreme Court, 1946-2000, in* INTERNATIONAL LAW IN THE U.S. SUPREME COURT: CONTINUITY AND CHANGE 356-57 (David L. Sloss, Michael D. Ramsey & William S. Dodge eds., 2011). In Professor Bederman's description:

> [The modern] vision is not exclusively one of state power and a positive grant of rights by nations to people. Instead, it is at least partly premised on a natural law notion of the inherent worth of human beings and is manifested in the creation of rules by which a state must treat its own citizens. Therefore, the pendulum of natural and positive approaches to international obligations has swung back

to a more neutral position in which the international community recognizes values separate and apart from state sovereignty.

BEDERMAN, *supra,* at 9. At the same time, it is important to note that the (partial) revival of naturalism remains controversial; customary international law based on state practice continues to be the dominant paradigm, and many scholars, policymakers, and judges insist that state consent is the touchstone of international legal obligation. For the practitioner, the most evident implication of this debate is the scope of customary international law. If customary international law depends upon nations' consent (and especially if it depends on the consent of all nations) its scope may be quite limited, because consent may be difficult to achieve or to prove for all but the most basic rules of international interaction. If customary international law arises more broadly from fundamental principles, its rules can be found (or argued for) in much wider circumstances.

3. **Determining Custom.** Even among those who focus on state practice and consent as the sole or primary basis of customary international law, there are sharp disagreements about the appropriate evidence to establish custom. We will explore this question in greater detail later, but for now it can be quickly summarized as follows. Almost everyone who accepts the basic premise of customary international law would accept the actual conduct of nations as evidence of international law's content. (Justice Gray's opinion in *The Paquete Habana,* quoted above and excerpted in greater length in Section C below, contains a lengthy example of establishing an international rule by painstaking examination of actual state practice.) The difficult question is the extent to which actual practice is required, or rather what additional evidence may be offered. To highlight some key areas of disagreement:

   a.   Must customary law be based on the conduct of *all* nations, or only a subset? What if most nations have never encountered the particular issue, or their conduct regarding it is inconclusive or inconsistent?

   b.   What if most nations act in one way but others disregard the general practice, either openly or covertly? What if nations say they will act one way and yet act another?

   c.   Can rules of customary international law be derived from actions other than actual conduct — for example, diplomatic statements or U.N. General Assembly resolutions (which U.N. member nations approve by majority vote)?

   d.   Can rules of customary international law be derived from international materials that emanate from bodies other than nations — for example, U.N. commissions or reports, judgments of international courts, or other acts or reports of international bodies on which states have input (and which they may or may not tacitly seem to accept)?

   e.   Can rules of international law be found by analogy or similar processes of legal reasoning that derive concrete rules from abstract statements of principle or from conduct or statements regarding similar but distinct facts?

Professor Bederman observed:

> How, then, is it proven that a norm of international conduct is really a "general practice" that qualifies it as a binding rule of customary international law? States rarely oblige by disclosing and handily collecting all of their relevant international practices in one location, and customary practices often are not formally recorded at all. Furthermore, what states do should matter a lot more than what they say. International lawyers necessarily rely on written evidence of state practice (such as diplomatic correspondence, official manuals, or newspaper accounts of contemporary events). . . . [I]t is vital for customary international law's legitimacy that it be based on empirically observed state practice and not merely on the aspirations of policy makers and commentators. . . .

BEDERMAN, *supra*, at 14. Of course, the more that "naturalistic" elements are admitted into the determination of customary international law, the more difficult and less objective the inquiry may appear. While these questions may appear abstract or theoretical, they have great significance in practice, where the core customary international law issue is often *whether* a claimed rule of customary international law exists. Suppose, for example, the question is whether a multinational corporation that does business with an oppressive government is responsible for the human rights violations that government commits. (We will take up that question directly later in this chapter.) How should a court (or the corporation's management or lawyers) investigate whether a rule of customary international law addresses this matter?

4. *Jus Cogens.* The naturalistic impulse in international law finds expression in the concept of *jus cogens* (sometimes called peremptory norms or mandatory law). According to Article 53 of the Vienna Convention on the Law of Treaties, a *jus cogens* norm is "a norm accepted and recognized by the international community of States as a whole as a norm from which no derogation is permitted and which can be modified only by a subsequent norm of general international law having the same character." Thus, a rule of customary international law that has *jus cogens* status has priority over other rules of international law and can only be modified by a later rule that has *jus cogens* status and not, for example, by treaty. *Jus cogens* norms thus may be thought of as fundamental first principles of the international community. As we will see, several core principles of international human rights law, including prohibitions on slavery, genocide, and torture, are labeled *jus cogens*. But the phrase may raise more questions than it answers. For a norm to be deemed "accepted and recognized by the international community of States as a whole" as having *jus cogens* status, must all nations consent to that status? Or is it sufficient that most nations consent? If the consent of all nations is not required, should nations that do not consent be barred from derogating from the norm? If so, on what basis other than consent? Can *jus cogens* norms be based on fundamental moral principles that do not depend on nations at all? How does one determine whether a norm has, or does not have, *jus cogens* status in the absence of a world lawmaker?

What norms are recognized as having *jus cogens* status? For one expert's perspective, consider the following:

> Without prejudice to the existence of other peremptory norms of general international law (jus cogens), the most widely recognized examples of peremptory norms of general international law (jus cogens) are: (a) the prohibition of aggression or aggressive force; (b) the prohibition of genocide; (c) the prohibition of slavery; (d) the prohibition of apartheid and racial discrimination; (e) the prohibition of crimes against humanity; (f) the prohibition of torture; (g) the right to self-determination; and (h) the basic rules of international humanitarian law.

United Nations International Law Commission, Fourth Report on Peremptory Norms of General International Law (jus cogens), Draft Conclusion 24 (2019) (Dire Tladi, Special Rapporteur) (https://legal.un.org/docs/?symbol=A/CN.4/727).

c. General Principles of Law

A third type of international law is called general principles of law. General principles of law are defined as principles recognized by the world's major legal systems.

> These are not, as some commentators have suggested, metaphysical "first principles" of [the] international legal order. Rather, the emphasis is on general principles of domestic law (sometimes called municipal law) as recognized in the legal systems of "civilized nations." The point here is that the international legal system remains primitive and unformed and that often recourse must be had to "borrowing" legal rules from domestic law.
>
>   . . .
>
> How does a legal rule become a general principle? . . . The language of Article 38 [of the ICJ statute] suggests that a principle would have to be recognized not just in one legal system but rather in most of the world's legal cultures . . . [that is], jurisdictions embracing the common law tradition, the civil law, significant religious legal cultures (including Islamic law), and ideological legal systems (including socialist law as practiced in China and elsewhere).

BEDERMAN, *supra*, at 30.

Although there is some debate about the appropriate role of general principles of law, it is usually understood that they are "gap fillers" that may be used when the two main types of international law — treaties and customary international law — do not provide an applicable rule. As Section 102 of the *Restatement (Third) of Foreign Relations Law* puts it, they "may be invoked as supplementary rules of international law where appropriate." Commonly cited examples include limitations periods within which a claim must be brought, the obligation to act in good faith, and the right of self defense. *See* BEDERMAN, *supra*, at 31 (giving these examples).

3. Is International Law Really Law?

A final introductory point, of particular relevance to judicial enforcement, is whether international law actually counts as law. Unlike most of national law, the idea of international law prompts extreme skepticism on the part of some commentators and at least nagging doubt in others. How is it possible to have law that arises outside of a sovereign lawmaker? The *Restatement (Third) of Foreign Relations Law, supra*, at 17, acknowledges:

> The absence of central legislative and executive institutions ha[s] led to skepticism about the legal quality of international law. Many observers consider international law to be only series of precepts of morality or etiquette, of cautions and admonitions lacking in both specificity and binding quality. Governments, it is sometimes assumed, commonly disregard international law and observe it only when they deem it to be in their interest to do so.

It is true, of course, that there is no "sovereign" international government that can issue commands, in the way national governments do. Thus law cannot arise, ordinarily at least, in the international arena in the same way that national law does. This has led some writers to deny the very possibility of international law. John Austin, a nineteenth-century English legal writer and one of international law's best-known detractors, wrote:

> [T]he law obtaining between nations is not positive law: for every positive law is set by a given sovereign to a person or persons in a state of subjection to its author. As I have already intimated, the law obtaining between nations (improperly so called) is set by general opinion. The duties which it imposes are enforced by moral sanctions: by fear on the part of nations, or by fear on the part of sovereigns, of provoking general hostility, and incurring its probable evils, in case they shall violate maxims generally received and respected.

JOHN AUSTIN, THE PROVINCE OF JURISPRUDENCE DETERMINED 208 (1832). On this ground, Austin described international law as really just "international morality." *Id.* at 201.

More recently, another great English jurisprudential writer, H.L.A. Hart, similarly questioned whether international law was a legal system because it lacks "a unifying rule of recognition, specifying 'sources' of law and providing general criteria for the identification of its rules" as well as "the secondary rules of change and adjudication which provide for legislatures and courts." H.L.A. HART, THE CONCEPT OF LAW 214 (2d ed. 1994) (originally published 1961). "Reduced to their essentials, both Austin and Hart's jurisprudence regard international law as devoid of the elements that confer order, predictability, structure, and validity on any legal system." BEDERMAN, *supra*, at 2.

The *Restatement (Third)*, pp. 17, 19, responds in part as follows:

> International law is law like other law, promoting order, guiding, restraining, regulating behavior. States, the principal addressees of international law, treat it as law, consider themselves bound by it, attend to it with a sense of legal obligation and with concern for the consequences of violation. Some states refer to international law in their constitutions; many incorporate it into their domestic legal systems; all take account of it in their governmental institutional arrangements and in their international relations.
>
> . . .
>
> A principal weakness perceived in international law is the lack of effective police authority to enforce it. That is indeed a weakness, but the criticism

reflects misplaced emphasis. Effective police authority deters violations of law, but there are other inducements to compliance. In the international system, law is observed because of a combination of forces, including the unarticulated recognition by states generally of the need for order, and of their common interest in maintaining particular norms and standards, as well as every state's desire to avoid the consequences of violation, including damage to its "credit" and the particular reactions by the victim of a violation. There are occasional, sometimes flagrant, violations, but all nations generally observe their obligations under international law, and an international legal system exists and functions as a working reality. That states (governments) make law, interpret law for their own guidance, and respond to interpretations and actions by others, makes for a complex legal-political-diplomatic process, but it is no less "legal" even if it is less structured than domestic law. . . .

4. International Law in Domestic Courts

Because international courts are infrequently available to resolve transnational disputes, enforcement of international law often depends upon national courts. This raises a question: To what extent are national courts willing and able to use international law as a source of law? On the one hand, one might think that national courts should always apply international law because international law, which is binding on the nation as a whole, is superior to all national law. On the other hand, one might think that national courts, created by the national sovereign, exist to enforce national laws, and thus would not enforce international law unless a rule of the national sovereign directed them to. These two positions are sometimes called, respectively, "monism" and "dualism" — referring to the conception of international law as either aspects of a single system of law or reflective of two distinct systems of law. As one scholar puts it:

> In international law scholarship, the terms "monism" and "dualism" are sometimes used to describe possible relationships between international law and domestic law. Although there is much uncertainty surrounding these terms, in essence the distinction is as follows: The monist view is that international law and domestic law are part of the same legal order, and that international law is automatically incorporated into each nation's legal system. By contrast, the dualist view is that international law and domestic law are distinct, and that each nation determines for itself when and to what extent international law is incorporated into its legal system. It is not clear how useful these categories are. In a sense, every nation is dualistic, in that one must consult the nation's domestic law in order to determine international law's status within that system. At most, the terms "monism" and "dualism" describe tendencies within particular legal systems.

Curtis A. Bradley, International Law in the U.S. Legal System xii (2013).

For the practicing lawyer, the most important observation is that national legal systems vary significantly in the way domestic judges treat international law. As a prominent example, in the British legal system (and some other systems derived from it) treaties are generally not enforceable by domestic courts at all; there must be (and typically is) domestic implementing legislation through which the national legislature directs how treaties are enforced. In contrast, the U.S.

Constitution, Article VI, declares that treaties are the "supreme Law of the Land" of their own force; as a result, treaties are often (though as we will see, not always) regarded as part of U.S. law by U.S. courts even without implementing legislation. National legal systems are sufficiently diverse and complex in their approach to this matter that very few generalizations are possible. The practicing lawyer must consult the specific national law of the jurisdiction in which international law is to be enforced before reaching any conclusions.

NOTES AND QUESTIONS

1. **The Law of Sources.** Article 38 of the Statute of the International Court of Justice (ICJ Statute) is widely considered an authoritative statement of the "sources" of international law: treaties, customary international law, and general principles of law. Around this basic statement of the types of international law has developed a body of international law that governs the creation and proof of international law. This body of law is often called the "law of sources."

2. **Making Treaties.** As discussed in Section B below, treaty-making and many other aspects of treaties are governed by both international law and national law. As a prelude to studying the law of treaties, consider these questions: Why do nations make treaties in the first place? Even in situations where there are good reasons for making a treaty, why might nations nevertheless be reluctant to do so? What barriers — national and international, political and otherwise — might make it difficult to make treaties?

3. **Proving Customary International Law.** As indicated by Article 38(1) of the ICJ Statute and reflected in Section 102 of the *Restatement (Third) of Foreign Relations Law*, a rule of customary international law is created when nations follow that rule in practice and do so out of a sense of legal obligation. In the law of sources, these two elements of customary international law are typically referred to as "state practice" (the so-called objective element) and "opinio juris" (or sense of legal obligation, the so-called subjective or psychological element). As discussed above, there are significant debates about the nature and extent of state practice necessary to prove a rule of customary international law (for example, although it is generally agreed that state practice need not be universal for a rule of customary international law to exist, it is debated how widespread that practice must be). There is also debate about the relative weight that should be placed on state practice on the one hand and *opinio juris* on the other hand when determining whether a rule of customary international law exists. These debates aside, as a practical matter lawyers relying on a rule of customary international law need to assemble evidence to convince a judge or other legal actor that there is in fact widespread state practice and *opinio juris* — that is, evidence of what nations actually do and evidence that they do so out of a sense of legal obligation. Evidence of *opinio juris* may include, among other things,

official government statements or press releases, diplomatic correspondence, national court decisions, opinions of government legal advisors, or votes of nations on resolutions of international organizations. This evidence is often difficult to gather, because nations often act without announcing their reasons (legal or otherwise).

Recent work of the U.N. International Law Commission may provide some guidance:

Conclusion 2

Two constituent elements

To determine the existence and content of a rule of customary international law, it is necessary to ascertain whether there is a general practice that is accepted as law (opinio juris).

Conclusion 3

Assessment of evidence for the two constituent elements

1. In assessing evidence for the purpose of ascertaining whether there is a general practice and whether that practice is accepted as law (opinio juris), regard must be had to the overall context, the nature of the rule, and the particular circumstances in which the evidence in question is to be found.

2. Each of the two constituent elements is to be separately ascertained. This requires an assessment of evidence for each element.

. . .

Conclusion 4

Requirement of practice

1. The requirement of a general practice, as a constituent element of customary international law, refers primarily to the practice of States that contributes to the formation, or expression, of rules of customary international law.

2. In certain cases, the practice of international organizations also contributes to the formation, or expression, of rules of customary international law.

3. Conduct of other actors is not practice that contributes to the formation, or expression, of rules of customary international law, but may be relevant when assessing the practice referred to in paragraphs 1 and 2.

Conclusion 5

Conduct of the State as State practice

State practice consists of conduct of the State, whether in the exercise of its executive, legislative, judicial or other functions.

Conclusion 6

Forms of practice

1. Practice may take a wide range of forms. It includes both physical and verbal acts. It may, under certain circumstances, include inaction.

2. Forms of State practice include, but are not limited to: diplomatic acts and correspondence; conduct in connection with resolutions adopted by an international organization or at an intergovernmental conference; conduct in connection with treaties; executive conduct, including operational conduct "on the ground"; legislative and administrative acts; and decisions of national courts.

3. There is no predetermined hierarchy among the various forms of practice.

Conclusion 7

Assessing a State's practice

1. Account is to be taken of all available practice of a particular State, which is to be assessed as a whole.

2. Where the practice of a particular State varies, the weight to be given to that practice may, depending on the circumstances, be reduced.

Conclusion 8

The practice must be general

1. The relevant practice must be general, meaning that it must be sufficiently widespread and representative, as well as consistent.

2. Provided that the practice is general, no particular duration is required.

. . .

Conclusion 9

Requirement of acceptance as law (opinio juris)

1. The requirement, as a constituent element of customary international law, that the general practice be accepted as law (opinio juris) means that the practice in question must be undertaken with a sense of legal right or obligation.

2. A general practice that is accepted as law (opinio juris) is to be distinguished from mere usage or habit.

Conclusion 10

Forms of evidence of acceptance as law (opinio juris)

1. Evidence of acceptance as law (opinio juris) may take a wide range of forms.

2. Forms of evidence of acceptance as law (opinio juris) include, but are not limited to: public statements made on behalf of States; official publications; government legal opinions; diplomatic correspondence; decisions of national courts; treaty provisions; and conduct in connection with resolutions adopted by an international organization or at an intergovernmental conference.

3. Failure to react over time to a practice may serve as evidence of acceptance as law (opinio juris), provided that States were in a position to react and the circumstances called for some reaction.

U.N. International Law Commission, Draft Conclusions on Identification of Customary International Law (2018) (https://legal.un.org/ilc/texts/instruments/english/draft_articles/1_13_2018.pdf).

Is this helpful?

4. **Persistent Objectors.** In general, if a customary international law rule exists, all nations are legally bound by it. However, if a nation persistently objects to an emerging rule before the rule comes into existence — that is, before there has been sufficient state practice and evidence of *opinio juris* to establish it as a rule of customary international law — then the persistent objector will not be bound by it. The persistent objector rule can be understood as one way in which the law of sources accounts for the importance of consent in the formation of international law. The International Law Commission's Draft Conclusions on the Identification of Customary International Law provide the following guidance:

Conclusion 15

Persistent objector

1. Where a State has objected to a rule of customary international law while that rule was in the process of formation, the rule is not opposable to the State concerned for so long as it maintains its objection.

2. The objection must be clearly expressed, made known to other States, and maintained persistently.

3. The present draft conclusion is without prejudice to any question concerning peremptory norms of general international law (jus cogens).

5. **Proving General Principles of Law.** Because general principles of law are principles of law common to the world's major legal systems, some experts argue that determining whether a putative general principle of law exists involves an exercise in comparative legal analysis. *See* MARK WESTON JANIS, INTERNATIONAL LAW 59 (5th ed. 2008) (referring to the "search for general principles of law as an exercise in comparative law"). Others, however, caution that "[i]t would be incorrect to assume that tribunals have in practice adopted a mechanical system of borrowing from domestic law after a census of domestic systems." IAN BROWNLIE, PRINCIPLES OF PUBLIC INTERNATIONAL LAW 16 (7th ed. 2008). The fact remains that persuasive arguments about the existence (or not) of a general principle of law require, at a minimum, an examination of the domestic law of national legal systems.

6. **General Principles of Law in Practice.** For a real-world example of efforts to prove and disprove a general principle of law, read paragraphs 374-80 of Mexico's memorial and paragraphs 8.27-8.34 of the United States' memorial filed with the ICJ in *Avena and Other Mexican Nationals (Mexico v. United*

States of America) (the memorials are available on the ICJ's website: http://
www.icj-cij.org/docket/index.php?p1=3&p2=3&k=11&case=128&code=
mus&p3=1).* (A "memorial" is a brief filed with the ICJ.) What rule did
Mexico's lawyers try to establish as a general principle of law? How did Mexico's
lawyers try to convince the court that this rule existed as a general principle of
law? What sort of research did this entail, what evidence did Mexico present,
and what was Mexico's strategy? How did the U.S. lawyers try to show that it
was not a general principle of law? What sort of research did this entail, what
evidence did the United States present, and what was the United States' strategy?
In your opinion, did Mexico's lawyers or the United States' lawyers make the
stronger argument? How can you (or a judge) tell? How could each side have
improved its argument? How does the method of demonstrating the existence
(or nonexistence) of a general principle of law differ from the method of demonstrating the existence of a rule of customary international law? Ultimately, the
ICJ did not rule on the issue.

7. **Judicial Decisions and the Teachings of Publicists.** In addition to the three
    types of international law introduced above — treaties, customary interna-
    tional law, and general principles of law — Article 38 of the ICJ Statute refers
    to "judicial decisions and the teachings of the most highly qualified publicists
    of the various nations, *as subsidiary means for the determination of interna-
    tional law*" (emphasis added). Judicial decisions may include the decisions
    of national courts, international courts (including earlier decisions of the
    ICJ itself or its predecessor, the Permanent Court of International Justice),
    or arbitral tribunals. The teachings of "publicists" includes work of leading
    scholars of international law as well as the work of organizations such as the
    U.N. International Law Commission or the International Committee of the
    Red Cross that attempt to codify customary international law. As the italicized
    phrase indicates, however, it is important to note that judicial decisions and the
    works of publicists are *not* international law. They are instead merely sources
    of evidence — or, in the language of the ICJ Statute, "subsidiary means for the
    determination" — of what international law is. Therefore (at least in theory),
    the most persuasive subsidiary means are those that carefully analyze and state
    what the rules of international law *are*, rather than what those rules should be.

8. **International Law as "Law."** Is international law "law"? Might lawyers and
    judges answer this question differently than legal philosophers? What criteria
    should one use to answer this question? Is this an important question to ask?
    With regard to John Austin's assessment quoted above, could his description
    not also apply to much national constitutional law — such as U.S. constitu-
    tional principles governing the separation of powers among the executive,
    legislative, and judicial branches, the federalism principles reserving power

---

* To find these materials, go to the ICJ's homepage at http://www.icj-cij.org/homepage/index
.php; click on "List of All Cases"; click on "More" under the *Avena* case under year 2003; then click
on "Written Proceedings" to find the memorials.

to the states, or individual rights against the government? Just as there is no higher "sovereign government" that sits above nations to compel them to comply with international law, there is no higher "sovereign government" that sits above the branches of the U.S. federal government to force them not to infringe on each other's powers, or to compel the federal government to respect states' rights or individual rights. Yet few lawyers and scholars would assert that U.S. constitutional law is not really law. *See generally* Christopher A. Whytock, *Thinking Beyond the Domestic-International Divide: Toward a Unified Concept of Public Law*, 36 Geo. J. Int'l L. 155 (2004). Why is international law different? Or is it?

The next two sections address how U.S. courts have grappled with the two most important types of international law: treaties and customary international law. Of course, this focus gives only a part of the picture. International law is applied by international courts and tribunals, by parts of the U.S. government other than the courts (principally the executive branch), and by national courts and executives in other nations. Each brings particular institutional biases and concerns to the project of applying international law. For most lawyers in the United States, however, the perspective of the U.S. courts has the most immediate importance.

As you read the materials in the next sections, consider the following questions. Is international law a type of law that national courts can apply in the same way they apply statutes and constitutions? What are the potential differences that might pose challenges for courts? What are some strategies for overcoming (or at least mitigating) these challenges? Are some types of international law more appropriate for judicial enforcement than others? Further, even assuming international law can be applied easily by national courts, should it be? Why might some people feel very strongly that it should not, and how might their concerns be addressed? Are these concerns more weighty for some types of international law than others?

B. Treaties and Other International Agreements

This section introduces you to treaties and other international agreements. It first provides an overview of the international law of treaties. The central focus, however, is the status of treaties in the U.S. legal system — including their enforcement and interpretation in U.S. courts, the relationship between treaties and statutes, and the relationship between treaties and the U.S. Constitution. As you study these materials, consider not only how you would view these issues as a litigant or a U.S. judge, but also how your view might change if you were instead a lawyer for the U.S. Department of State or a judge on an international court.

1. *The International Law of Treaties*

What is a treaty? How are treaties made, what effect do they have, and how are they interpreted? A field of international law called the "law of treaties" itself provides answers to these questions. Much of the international law of treaties has been codified in the 1969 Vienna Convention on the Law of Treaties (VCLT) — the so-called treaty on treaties — which entered into force in 1980. The United States is not a party to the VCLT,* but it considers most of the VCLT's provisions to be legally binding customary international law. *See* RESTATEMENT (THIRD) OF THE FOREIGN RELATIONS LAW OF THE UNITED STATES, at 144-45. As you read the excerpts from the VCLT and the *Restatement (Third)* below, focus on understanding, under the international law of treaties, how treaties are made, what effect they have, and how they are interpreted, and what terminology is used in this field of international law.

Restatement (Third) of the Foreign Relations Law of the United States (1987)

Section 102, comment f

International agreement as source of law. An international agreement creates obligations binding between the parties under international law. See Section 321. Ordinarily, an agreement between states is a source of law only in the sense that a private contract may be said to make law for the parties under the domestic law of contracts. Multilateral agreements open to all states, however, are increasingly used for general legislation, whether to make new law, as in human rights . . . , or for codifying and developing customary law, as in the Vienna Convention on the Law of Treaties.

Section 321

Every international agreement in force is binding upon the parties to it and must be performed by them in good faith.

Comment [a]:

. . . *Pacta sunt servanda*. This section states the doctrine of *pacta sunt servanda*,** which lies at the core of the law of international agreements and is perhaps the most important principle of international law. It includes the implication that international law obligations survive restrictions imposed by domestic law.

---

* A dispute between the U.S. President and the Senate regarding how the United States may become bound to international agreements has prevented the United States from becoming a party to the VCLT. The dispute does not reflect disagreement with the vast majority of the VCLT's provisions.

** In Latin, "agreements must be kept." — EDS.

Vienna Convention on the Law of Treaties

1155 U.N.T.S. 331 (May 23, 1969)

. . .

Article 2. Use of Terms

1. For the purposes of the present Convention:

(a) "treaty" means an international agreement concluded between States in written form and governed by international law, whether embodied in a single instrument or in two or more related instruments and whatever its particular designation;

(b) "ratification", "acceptance", "approval" and "accession" mean in each case the international act so named whereby a State establishes on the international plane its consent to be bound by a treaty;

. . .

(d) "reservation" means a unilateral statement, however phrased or named, made by a State, when signing, ratifying, accepting, approving or acceding to a treaty, whereby it purports to exclude or to modify the legal effect of certain provisions of the treaty in their application to that State;

(e) "negotiating State" means a State which took part in the drawing up and adoption of the text of the treaty;

(f) "contracting State" means a State which has consented to be bound by the treaty, whether or not the treaty has entered into force;

(g) "party" means a State which has consented to be bound by the treaty and for which the treaty is in force;

. . .

Article 11. Means of expressing consent to be bound by a treaty

The consent of a State to be bound by a treaty may be expressed by signature, exchange of instruments constituting a treaty, ratification, acceptance, approval or accession, or by any other means if so agreed.

. . .

Article 19. Formulation of reservations

A State may, when signing, ratifying, accepting, approving or acceding to a treaty, formulate a reservation unless:

(a) the reservation is prohibited by the treaty;

(b) the treaty provides that only specified reservations, which do not include the reservation in question, may be made; or

(c) in cases not falling under sub-paragraphs (a) and (b), the reservation is incompatible with the object and purpose of the treaty.

Article 24. Entry into force

1. A treaty enters into force in such manner and upon such date as it may provide or as the negotiating States may agree.

2. Failing any such provision or agreement, a treaty enters into force as soon as consent to be bound by the treaty has been established for all the negotiating States.

Article 26. Pacta sunt servanda

Every treaty in force is binding upon the parties to it and must be performed by them in good faith.

Article 27. Internal law and observance of treaties

A party may not invoke the provisions of its internal law as justification for its failure to perform a treaty.

. . .

Article 53. Treaties conflicting with a peremptory norm of general international law (jus cogens)

A treaty is void if, at the time of its conclusion, it conflicts with a peremptory norm of general international law. For the purposes of the present Convention, a peremptory norm of general international law is a norm accepted and recognized by the international community of States as a whole as a norm from which no derogation is permitted and which can be modified only by a subsequent norm of general international law having the same character.

Article 54. Termination of or withdrawal from a treaty under its provisions or by consent of the parties

The termination of a treaty or the withdrawal of a party may take place:

(a) in conformity with the provisions of the treaty; or

(b) at any time by consent of all the parties after consultation with the other contracting States.

. . .

Article 60. Termination or suspension of the operation of a treaty as a consequence of its breach

1. A material breach of bilateral treaty by one of the parties entitles the other to invoke the breach as a ground for terminating the treaty or suspending its operation in whole or in part.

2. A material breach of a multilateral treaty by one of the parties entitles:

(a) the other parties by unanimous agreement to suspend the operation of the treaty in whole or in part or to terminate it either:

(i) in the relations between themselves and the defaulting State, or

(ii) as between all the parties;

(b) a party specially affected by the breach to invoke it as a ground for suspending the operation of the treaty in whole or in part in the relations between itself and the defaulting State;

(c) any party other than the defaulting State to invoke the breach as a ground for suspending the operation of the treaty in whole or in part with respect to itself if the treaty is of such a character that a material breach of its provisions by one party radically changes the position of every party with respect to the further performance of its obligations under the treaty.

. . .

Article 62. Fundamental change of circumstances

1. A fundamental change of circumstances which has occurred with regard to those existing at the time of the conclusion of a treaty, and which was not foreseen by the parties, may not be invoked as a ground for terminating or withdrawing from the treaty unless:

(a) the existence of those circumstances constituted an essential basis of the consent of the parties to be bound by the treaty; and

(b) the effect of the change is radically to transform the extent of obligations still to be performed under the treaty.

. . .

NOTES AND QUESTIONS

1. **Definition of "Treaty."** How does the VCLT define a "treaty"? Note that under the VCLT's definition, a document's status as a treaty does not depend on its designation. Thus, if a document meets the definition, it is a "treaty" for purposes of the VCLT even if it is called something else — such as "convention," "compact," or "agreement." As a result, for international law purposes, the designation ordinarily lacks significance. As we will see later, the United States often makes "executive agreements" or "congressional-executive agreements," as well as "treaties," that have different meanings as a matter of U.S. constitutional law. Even though they are not called "treaties" as a matter of U.S. law, they count as treaties under international law if they meet the VCLT's definition of treaty. Although the VCLT applies only to agreements "between States in written form," under some circumstances the unilateral declaration of a nation or an unwritten agreement between nations may nevertheless be binding under international law — but the VCLT would not apply.

2. **Consent to Be Bound.** A central concept in the international law of treaties is "consent to be bound." A "negotiating state" is not legally bound by a treaty unless it has expressed its consent to be bound by it. Articles 11 through 15 of the VCLT provide rules to determine how a negotiating state may express its consent to be bound. The methods of expressing consent to be bound may include "signature, exchange of instruments constituting a treaty, ratification, acceptance, approval or accession. . . ." VCLT Article 11. Ordinarily, the treaty itself will specify what a negotiating state must do to express its consent to be bound and, under the VCLT, those treaty provisions govern. Often a negotiating state will authorize a representative to sign a treaty for purposes of adopting its text; but unless the treaty so provides (or, absent a treaty provision, unless the VCLT so provides), becoming a signatory is insufficient to express consent to be bound. Instead, a subsequent step, such as ratification, is frequently required (especially for multilateral treaties). A nation ratifies a treaty by declaring in a written document called an "instrument of ratification" that the nation considers itself bound by the treaty, and either exchanging the instrument of ratification with other nations or depositing it

with a depository for the treaty. ANTHONY AUST, HANDBOOK OF INTERNATIONAL LAW 60 (2d ed. 2010). Do not confuse ratification, which is an international act, with the steps required by a national legal system for treaty approval (such as the Senate's advice and consent under the U.S. Constitution). The term "accession" refers to a method by which a nation may express its consent to be bound that is analogous to ratification, except that the nation did not originally sign the treaty.

3.   **Historical Perspective.** In the days of slow communication, the separate steps of signature and ratification allowed a representative (usually an ambassador) to sign on behalf of the nation, after which the nation's ruler (usually the monarch) confirmed through "ratification" that the ambassador had acted according to the ruler's will. In modern times the two-step process allows the legislative branch (or a part of it) to approve the executive branch's decision to sign the treaty, in countries where such a requirement is imposed by national law. For example, under Article II, Section 2 of the U.S. Constitution, the President must have the consent of two-thirds of the Senate to make a treaty. In modern U.S. practice, this produces a three-step process: (a) the President (or a delegate) signs the treaty; (b) the President seeks and receives the Senate's advice and consent; (c) the President ratifies the treaty on behalf of the United States, thus making the United States a party. Note that while it is often colloquially said in the United States that the Senate "ratifies" treaties, that is incorrect, at least as a matter of international law terminology. It is a common mistake, though, made even by the U.S. Supreme Court. *E.g.*, *Wilson v. Girard*, 354 U.S. 524, 528 (1957) ("In light of the Senate's ratification of the Security Treaty. . . ."). The proper terminology for U.S. Senate approval of a treaty is "advice and consent" (or just "consent").

4.   **Entry into Force.** A treaty is not legally binding until it enters into force. Ordinarily, the treaty itself sets forth the requirements that must be satisfied for it to enter into force. For example, some treaties provide that they do not become effective until a certain date, or (in the case of multilateral treaties) until a certain number of nations have ratified the treaty or otherwise expressed their consent to be bound. If the treaty does not specify the requirements for entry into force, Article 24(2) of the VCLT provides that a treaty enters into force only when all of the negotiating nations have expressed their consent to be bound. Once a treaty does enter into force, it legally binds those nations that have expressed consent to be bound by it. Those nations are then called "parties." *See* VCLT Article 2(1)(g) (defining "party" as "a State which has consented to be bound by the treaty and for which the treaty is in force"). Common usage (even among lawyers) may employ the term "signatories" to indicate states that have become bound to a treaty, but this is incorrect because, as discussed above, signature does not necessarily indicate consent to be bound and even nations that have expressed consent to be bound are not bound until the treaty has also entered into force. Once a treaty enters into force, it remains "in force" with respect to the parties until it expires or is properly terminated.

5. **Obligation Not to Defeat Object and Purpose.** Note that under Article 18 of the VCLT, even before a treaty enters into force, nations that have signed the treaty are obligated to "refrain from acts which would defeat the object and purpose of a treaty." What do you think this requires a signatory to do or refrain from doing?

6. **Termination of Treaties.** Many treaties allow parties to terminate their obligations upon appropriate notice (sometimes without limitation, and sometimes upon the occurrence of particular events). Customary international law also may allow termination, for example under the principle of changed circumstances ("rebus sic stantibus"). *See* VCLT Articles 54-64. In addition, nations will sometimes announce that they no longer intend to comply with a treaty, even if the treaty does not by its terms allow them to do so. In common usage these situations are sometimes called "termination" of a treaty (or a "withdrawal" from the treaty), but it is important to keep them separate because they have very different consequences. If a nation declares itself no longer bound by a treaty in accordance with the treaty's terms or with customary international law, no violation of international law occurs. If a nation declares itself no longer bound where the treaty does not permit it to do so, the nation has violated international law and may be subject to penalties or other consequences. Although terminology is not completely standard on this point, it is best to use "termination" or "withdrawal" to refer only to the former situation, and to use "abrogation" to refer to the latter.

7. **Reservations.** A nation generally may make "reservations" to a treaty (meaning that it will not be bound by a particular provision or part of a provision of the treaty). The exceptions to this general rule, as well as provisions governing the legal effect of reservations, are contained in Articles 19 through 23 of the VCLT. The important practical point is that when invoking a treaty provision with respect to a particular nation, one must determine whether or not that nation has made a reservation that relates to that treaty provision and, if so, the effect of that reservation. For a brief overview of the rules governing treaty reservations, see AUST, *supra*, at 64-73.

8. **Nonbinding Agreements.** A core requirement of a treaty is that the parties consider it legally binding. Nations also make nonbinding agreements (sometimes called "political commitments") which are diplomatic arrangements but do not have the force of law.

> Political commitments have a long history. They are not simply "scraps of paper"; political commitments include some of the most significant texts of the last century. The United States regards the Atlantic Charter, which formed the basis for the Allied Powers' coordinated efforts during World War II, as a political commitment. President Richard Nixon and China's Chairman Mao Zedong used the same mechanism to establish a new Sino-U.S. relationship via the "Shanghai Communiqué." Perhaps the most renowned political commitment came in 1975, when nation-states competing in the Cold War concluded the Helsinki Accords. The Accords established an organizational forum — the forerunner of today's Organization for Security and Co-operation in Europe (OSCE) — to host dialogue on issues ranging from human rights

to security. More recently, on July 8, 2008, the Group of Eight (G8) issued a Declaration on Environment and Climate Change, in which the United States (for the first time) committed to seek fifty-percent reductions in global greenhouse gas emissions by 2050. Alongside these more prominent examples, bilateral and multilateral political commitments have been employed in almost every field of international relations.

The popularity of political commitments reflects their utility to nation-states. They serve as alternatives for normative commitments where states cannot (or do not want to) create legal obligations, whether as a matter of international law via treaty or national law via contract. Beyond substance, political commitments may establish processes for interstate communication on a range of topics, projects, and problems. And, whether political commitments involve substance, process, or both, states can and do rely on them. When a state undertakes a political commitment, other participating states tailor their conduct accordingly. At times, compliance with the political norm or participation in the agreed process serves as its own end; or, it can presage or supplement legal agreements. In any case, if a state violates its political commitment, other states can sanction it, albeit through political instead of legal means. . . .

Duncan B. Hollis & Joshua J. Newcomer, *"Political" Commitments and the Constitution*, 49 VA. J. INT'L L. 507, 510-12 (2009). Given the difficulties of formal (judicial) enforcement of treaties in the international legal system, what are the practical differences between treaties and "nonbinding" agreements? When might nations choose a "binding" agreement over a "nonbinding" agreement?

In June 2015, the Obama administration announced a Joint Comprehensive Plan of Action (JCPOA) among the United States, Russia, China, Great Britain, France, Germany, and Iran regarding Iran's nuclear program. Among other things, Iran agreed to certain limits on its nuclear program designed to prevent its acquisition of a nuclear bomb, and the Obama administration agreed to lift U.S. economic sanctions against Iran. After some initial uncertainty, the U.S. State Department clarified that it understood the JCPOA (which was not signed by the parties nor approved by Congress or the Senate) as a nonbinding agreement. Why might a nonbinding agreement be preferred in this situation? Are there any practical differences between a binding and nonbinding agreement in this situation? President Obama had preexisting statutory authority to lift the Iran sanctions. Why does that matter?

Also in 2015, President Obama signed the Paris Agreement on climate change, a multilateral agreement whose goal is to reduce carbon emissions. He did not seek Senate advice and consent, principally on the argument that the material provisions of the agreement are nonbinding. President Obama then ratified the Agreement on behalf of the United States in 2016. Why do you think the President took this approach?

In 2017, newly elected President Donald Trump announced the withdrawal of the United States from the Paris Agreement. Subsequently, in 2018, President Trump also announced U.S. withdrawal from the JCPOA. Does the President have this power to withdraw in these circumstances? What are the relevant considerations? Based on this sequence of events, what do you think are the advantages and disadvantages of President Obama's approval of the Paris Agreement and the JCPOA on his own authority rather seeking Senate approval?

2. *Enforcing Treaties in U.S. Courts*

This section addresses the use of treaties as law in U.S. courts. We focus here on U.S. courts to provide a concrete practical context in which to consider issues of treaty enforcement. Of course, each national legal system views treaties in its own way (as do international courts and dispute resolution bodies), and their approaches may differ sharply from the U.S. approach. Nonetheless, many of the issues that arise in U.S. treaty enforcement may have counterparts in other fora, even if their resolution may be quite different.

You might think of the question in terms of choice of law. A court has a transnational dispute to resolve; what law will it use to resolve it? One possible source of law is a treaty. But there may be others, including constitutional law, domestic statutes, common law, or foreign law. Will the court use the rules contained in the treaty? The answer, in the United States, is complex: Often it will, but for various reasons it may not.

The starting point for understanding the effect of treaties in the U.S. legal system is the text of the U.S. Constitution. Under Article II, Section 2, the President has power to make treaties with the advice and consent of two-thirds of the Senate. According to Article VI, all treaties made under the authority of the United States are "supreme Law of the Land." Under Article III, U.S. federal courts have jurisdiction over disputes "arising under" treaties. As explored in later reading, however, U.S. practice is somewhat more complicated than what these provisions on their face may suggest.

U.S. Constitution

Article II, Section 2

The President . . . shall have Power, by and with the Advice and Consent of the Senate, to make Treaties, provided two-thirds of the Senators present concur. . . .

Article III, Section 2

The judicial power of the United States shall extend to all Cases, in Law and Equity, arising under this Constitution, the Laws of the United States, and Treaties made, or which shall be made, under their Authority. . . .

Article VI

This Constitution, and the Laws of the United States which shall be made in Pursuance thereof; and all Treaties made, or which shall be made, under the Authority of the United States, shall be the supreme Law of the Land; and the

Judges in every State shall be bound thereby, any Thing in the Constitution or Laws of any State to the Contrary notwithstanding.

———————————

Since the early years of the Constitution, U.S. courts have relied on Article VI to enforce treaty obligations directly as binding domestic law. *E.g., Ware v. Hylton,* 3 U.S. 199 (1796) (applying Article 4 of the 1783 Treaty of Peace between the United States and the United Kingdom to override a contrary Virginia state law). Of course, cases involving treaty obligations are subject to procedural requirements applicable to cases generally — for example, that the court have jurisdiction over the litigants and the subject matter, that the litigants have standing as required by Article III of the Constitution, that proper notice be provided to the defendant, etc. In addition, cases involving treaty obligations may face procedural barriers that arise generally in transnational cases (such as foreign sovereign immunity or *forum non conveniens* — matters considered in Chapters 10 and 11). Treaty cases involve their own particular considerations as well, however. In particular, a U.S. court may decline to enforce a treaty obligation if it concludes that the treaty obligation was not meant to be judicially enforced. As you will see, this involves two distinct but related questions: (1) whether the treaty is "self-executing" and (2) whether it provides a private right of action.

a. Self-Execution and Non-Self-Execution

As quoted above, Article VI of the U.S. Constitution provides that treaties, along with the Constitution and U.S. federal statutes, are "the supreme Law of the Land." Explaining this provision, Alexander Hamilton wrote, "The treaties of the United States, to have any force at all, must be considered as part of the law of the land. Their true import, as far as respects individuals, must, like all other laws, be ascertained by judicial determination." *The Federalist,* No. 22, at 182 (1787) (Isaac Kramnick ed., 1987). That suggests that treaties have the same legal status as statutes. However, in modern practice only "self-executing" treaties are applied directly as law by U.S. courts in the manner of statutes. Thus, one of the first questions faced when litigating a question of treaty law is whether the treaty on its own has any legal effect in U.S. courts.

Medellín v. Texas

552 U.S. 491 (2008)

[José Medellín, a Mexican citizen, challenged his death sentence imposed by Texas courts under Texas law. When arrested, Medellín was not informed of his right under the Vienna Convention on Consular Relations to contact the Mexican consulate to assist in his defense. Medellín argued that his sentence should be reconsidered in light of this violation and a related judgment of the International Court of Justice. The Texas courts refused to reconsider the sentence, and Medellín appealed.]

Chief Justice ROBERTS delivered the opinion of the Court.

The International Court of Justice (ICJ), located in the Hague, is a tribunal established pursuant to the United Nations Charter to adjudicate disputes between member states. In the *Case Concerning Avena and Other Mexican Nationals (Mex. v. U.S.)*, 2004 I.C.J. 12 (Judgment of Mar. 31) . . . [t]he ICJ held that, based on violations of the Vienna Convention, 51 named Mexican nationals were entitled to review and reconsideration of their state-court convictions and sentences in the United States.* . . .

Petitioner José Ernesto Medellín . . . is one of the 51 Mexican nationals named in the *Avena* decision. . . . We granted certiorari to decide . . . [whether] the ICJ's judgment in *Avena* [is] directly enforceable as domestic law in a state court in the United States. . . . We conclude that . . . *Avena* [does not] . . . constitute[] directly enforceable federal law that pre-empts state limitations on the filing of successive habeas petitions. We therefore affirm the decision below.

I

A

In 1969, the United States, upon the advice and consent of the Senate, ratified the Vienna Convention on Consular Relations . . . and the Optional Protocol Concerning the Compulsory Settlement of Disputes to the Vienna Convention. . . . Article 36 of the Convention . . . provides that if a person detained by a foreign country "so requests, the competent authorities of the receiving State shall, without delay, inform the consular post of the sending State" of such detention, and "inform the [detainee] of his righ[t]" to request assistance from the consul of his own state.

The Optional Protocol provides . . . [that] disputes arising out of the interpretation or application of the Vienna Convention . . . "shall lie within the compulsory jurisdiction of the International Court of Justice" and "may accordingly be brought before the [ICJ] . . . by any party to the dispute being a Party to the present Protocol."**

. . .

Under Article 94(1) of the U.N. Charter, "[e]ach Member of the United Nations undertakes to comply with the decision of the [ICJ] in any case to which it is a party.". . . By ratifying the Optional Protocol . . . , the United States consented to the specific jurisdiction of the ICJ with respect to claims arising out of the Vienna Convention.

. . .

B

. . . Medellín, a Mexican national, has lived in the United States since preschool. A member of the "Black and Whites" gang, Medellín was convicted of

---

* The *Avena* decision is excerpted in Chapter 5. — EDS.

** After the *Avena* decision, the United States withdrew from the Optional Protocol. — EDS.

capital murder and sentenced to death in Texas for the gang rape and brutal murders of two Houston teenagers. . . .

Medellín was arrested . . . [and] was given *Miranda* warnings; he then signed a written waiver and gave a detailed written confession. Local law enforcement officers did not, however, inform Medellín of his Vienna Convention right to notify the Mexican consulate of his detention. Medellín was convicted of capital murder and sentenced to death; his conviction and sentence were affirmed on appeal. Medellín first raised his Vienna Convention claim in his first application for state postconviction relief. The state trial court held that the claim was procedurally defaulted because Medellín had failed to raise it at trial or on direct review. The trial court also rejected the Vienna Convention claim on the merits, finding that Medellín had "fail[ed] to show that any non-notification of the Mexican authorities impacted on the validity of his conviction or punishment." The Texas Court of Criminal Appeals affirmed. . . .

[After] the ICJ issued its decision in *Avena* . . . Medellín . . . filed a second application for habeas relief in state court. . . . The Texas Court of Criminal Appeals subsequently dismissed Medellín's second state habeas application as an abuse of the writ. . . .

II

Medellín . . . contends that the ICJ's judgment in *Avena* constitutes a "binding" obligation on the state and federal courts of the United States. He argues that "by virtue of the Supremacy Clause, the treaties requiring compliance with the *Avena* judgment are *already* the 'Law of the Land' by which all state and federal courts in this country are 'bound.'" Accordingly, Medellín argues, *Avena* is a binding federal rule of decision that pre-empts contrary state limitations on successive habeas petitions.

No one disputes that the *Avena* decision . . . constitutes an *international* law obligation on the part of the United States. But not all international law obligations automatically constitute binding federal law enforceable in United States courts. The question we confront here is whether the *Avena* judgment has automatic *domestic* legal effect such that the judgment of its own force applies in state and federal courts.

This Court has long recognized the distinction between treaties that automatically have effect as domestic law, and those that — while they constitute international law commitments — do not by themselves function as binding federal law. The distinction was well explained by Chief Justice Marshall's opinion in *Foster v. Neilson*, 2 Pet. 253, 315 (1829), overruled on other grounds, *United States v. Percheman*, 7 Pet. 51 (1833), which held that a treaty is "equivalent to an act of the legislature," and hence self executing, when it "operates of itself without the aid of any legislative provision." When, in contrast, "[treaty] stipulations are not self-executing they can only be enforced pursuant to legislation to carry them into effect." *Whitney v. Robertson*, 124 U.S. 190, 194 (1888). In sum, while treaties may comprise international commitments . . . they are not domestic law unless Congress has either enacted implementing statutes or the treaty itself conveys an intention that it be "self-executing" and is ratified on these terms.[2]

A treaty is, of course, "primarily a compact between independent nations." *Head Money Cases*, 112 U.S. 580, 598 (1884). It ordinarily "depends for the enforcement of its provisions on the interest and the honor of the governments which are parties to it." . . . Only "[i]f the treaty contains stipulations which are self-executing, that is, require no legislation to make them operative, [will] they have the force and effect of a legislative enactment." *Whitney, supra*, at 194.[3]

A

. . .

The obligation on the part of signatory nations to comply with ICJ judgments derives . . . from Article 94 of the United Nations Charter. . . . Article 94(1) provides that "[e]ach Member of the United Nations *undertakes to comply* with the decision of the [ICJ] in any case to which it is a party." (emphasis added). The Executive Branch contends that the phrase "undertakes to comply" is not "an acknowledgement that an ICJ decision will have immediate legal effect in the courts of U.N. members," but rather "a *commitment* on the part of U.N. Members to take *future* action through their political branches to comply with an ICJ decision."

We agree with this construction of Article 94. The Article is not a directive to domestic courts. It does not provide that the United States "shall" or "must" comply with an ICJ decision, nor indicate that the Senate that ratified the U.N. Charter intended to vest ICJ decisions with immediate legal effect in domestic courts. Instead, the words of Article 94 . . . call upon governments to take certain action. See also *Foster*, 2 Pet., at 314, 315 (holding a treaty non-self executing because its text — " 'all . . . grants of land . . . shall be ratified and confirmed' " — did not "act directly on the grants" but rather "pledge[d] the faith of the United States to pass acts which shall ratify and confirm them"). . . .

The remainder of Article 94 confirms that the U.N. Charter does not contemplate the automatic enforceability of ICJ decisions in domestic courts. Article 94(2) — the enforcement provision — provides the sole remedy for noncompliance: referral to the United Nations Security Council by an aggrieved state. The U.N. Charter's provision of an express diplomatic — that is, nonjudicial — remedy

---

2. The label "self-executing" has on occasion been used to convey different meanings. What we mean by "self-executing" is that the treaty has automatic domestic effect as federal law upon ratification. Conversely, a "non-self-executing" treaty does not by itself give rise to domestically enforceable federal law. Whether such a treaty has domestic effect depends upon implementing legislation passed by Congress.

3. Even when treaties are self-executing in the sense that they create federal law, the background presumption is that "[i]nternational agreements, even those directly benefiting private persons, generally do not create private rights or provide for a private cause of action in domestic courts." 2 Restatement (Third) of Foreign Relations Law of the United States § 907, Comment *a*, p. 395 (1986). Accordingly, a number of the Courts of Appeals have presumed that treaties do not create privately enforceable rights in the absence of express language to the contrary. . . .

is itself evidence that ICJ judgments were not meant to be enforceable in domestic courts. . . .

Second, as the President and Senate were undoubtedly aware in subscribing to the U.N. Charter and Optional Protocol, the United States retained the unqualified right to exercise its veto of any Security Council resolution. This was the understanding of the Executive Branch when the President agreed to the U.N. Charter and the declaration accepting general compulsory ICJ jurisdiction. See, *e.g.*, The Charter of the United Nations for the Maintenance of International Peace and Security: Hearings before the Senate Committee on Foreign Relations, 79th Cong., 1st Sess. (1945), . . . at 286 (statement of Leo Paslovsky, Special Assistant to the Secretary of State for International Organizations and Security Affairs) ("[W]hen the Court has rendered a judgment and one of the parties refuses to accept it, then the dispute becomes political rather than legal. It is as a political dispute that the matter is referred to the Security Council"); A Resolution Proposing Acceptance of Compulsory Jurisdiction of International Court of Justice: Hearings on S. Res. 196 before the Subcommittee of the Senate Committee on Foreign Relations, 79th Cong., 2d Sess., 142 (1946) (statement of Charles Fahy, State Dept. Legal Adviser) (while parties that accept ICJ jurisdiction have "a moral obligation" to comply with ICJ decisions, Article 94(2) provides the exclusive means of enforcement).

If ICJ judgments were instead regarded as automatically enforceable domestic law, they would be immediately and directly binding on state and federal courts pursuant to the Supremacy Clause. Mexico or the ICJ would have no need to proceed to the Security Council to enforce the judgment in this case. Noncompliance with an ICJ judgment through exercise of the Security Council veto — always regarded as an option by the Executive and ratifying Senate during and after consideration of the U.N. Charter, Optional Protocol, and ICJ Statute — would no longer be a viable alternative. There would be nothing to veto. In light of the U.N. Charter's remedial scheme, there is no reason to believe that the President and Senate signed up for such a result.

In sum, Medellín's view that ICJ decisions are automatically enforceable as domestic law is fatally undermined by the enforcement structure established by Article 94. His construction would eliminate the option of noncompliance contemplated by Article 94(2), undermining the ability of the political branches to determine whether and how to comply with an ICJ judgment. Those sensitive foreign policy decisions would instead be transferred to state and federal courts charged with applying an ICJ judgment directly as domestic law. And those courts would not be empowered to decide whether to comply with the judgment — again, always regarded as an option by the political branches — any more than courts may consider whether to comply with any other species of domestic law.

This result would be particularly anomalous in light of the principle that "[t]he conduct of the foreign relations of our Government is committed by the Constitution to the Executive and Legislative — 'the political' — Departments." *Oetjen v. Central Leather Co.*, 246 U.S. 297, 302 (1918). . . .

It is, moreover, well settled that the United States' interpretation of a treaty "is entitled to great weight." *Sumitomo Shoji America, Inc. v. Avagliano*, 457 U.S.

176, 184-185 (1982). The Executive Branch has unfailingly adhered to its view that the relevant treaties do not create domestically enforceable federal law. . . .

B

. . .

[T]he dissent proposes a multifactor, judgment-by-judgment analysis that would "jettiso[n] relative predictability for the open-ended rough-and-tumble of factors." *Jerome B. Grubart, Inc. v. Great Lakes Dredge & Dock Co.*, 513 U.S. 527, 547 (1995). The dissent's novel approach to deciding which (or, more accurately, when) treaties give rise to directly enforceable federal law is arrestingly indeterminate. Treaty language is barely probative. Determining whether treaties themselves create federal law is sometimes committed to the political branches and sometimes to the judiciary. Of those committed to the judiciary, the courts pick and choose which shall be binding United States law — trumping not only state but other federal law as well — and which shall not. They do this on the basis of a multifactor, "context specific" inquiry. Even then, the same treaty sometimes gives rise to United States law and sometimes does not, again depending on an ad hoc judicial assessment.

Our Framers established a careful set of procedures that must be followed before federal law can be created under the Constitution — vesting that decision in the political branches, subject to checks and balances. They also recognized that treaties could create federal law, but again through the political branches, with the President making the treaty and the Senate approving it. The dissent's understanding of the treaty route, depending on an ad hoc judgment of the judiciary without looking to the treaty language — the very language negotiated by the President and approved by the Senate — cannot readily be ascribed to those same Framers.

. . .

C

Our conclusion that *Avena* does not by itself constitute binding federal law is confirmed by the postratification understanding of signatory nations. There are currently 47 nations that are parties to the Optional Protocol and 171 nations that are parties to the Vienna Convention. Yet neither Medellín nor his *amici* have identified a single nation that treats ICJ judgments as binding in domestic courts. . . .

Even the dissent flinches at reading the relevant treaties to give rise to self-executing ICJ judgments in all cases. It admits that "Congress is unlikely to authorize automatic judicial enforceability of *all* ICJ judgments, for that could include some politically sensitive judgments and others better suited for enforcement by other branches." Our point precisely. But the lesson to draw from that insight is hardly that the judiciary should decide which judgments are politically sensitive and which are not.

. . .

D

. . . Contrary to the dissent's suggestion, neither our approach nor our cases require that a treaty provide for self-execution in so many talismanic words; that is a caricature of the Court's opinion. Our cases simply require courts to decide whether a treaty's terms reflect a determination by the President who negotiated it and the Senate that confirmed it that the treaty has domestic effect. . . .

. . .

The judgment of the Texas Court of Criminal Appeals is affirmed.

[Justices Scalia, Kennedy, Thomas, and Alito joined the opinion of the Court. Justice Stevens filed an opinion concurring in the judgment.]

JUSTICE BREYER, with whom Justice SOUTER and Justice GINSBURG join, dissenting:

The Constitution's Supremacy Clause provides that "all Treaties . . . which shall be made . . . under the Authority of the United States, shall be the supreme Law of the Land; and the Judges in every State shall be bound thereby." The Clause means that the "courts" must regard "a treaty . . . as equivalent to an act of the legislature, whenever it operates of itself without the aid of any legislative provision." *Foster v. Neilson*, 2 Pet. 253, 314 (1829). . . .

In the *Avena* case the International Court of Justice (ICJ) (interpreting and applying the Vienna Convention on Consular Relations) issued a judgment that requires the United States to reexamine certain criminal proceedings in the cases of 51 Mexican nationals. The question here is whether the ICJ's *Avena* judgment is enforceable now as a matter of domestic law, *i.e.*, whether it "operates of itself without the aid" of any further legislation.

I

. . .

A

Supreme Court case law stretching back more than 200 years helps explain what, for present purposes, the Founders meant when they wrote that "all Treaties . . . shall be the supreme Law of the Land." In 1796, for example, the Court decided the case of *Ware v. Hylton*, 3 Dall. 199. A British creditor sought payment of an American's Revolutionary War debt. The debtor argued that he had, under Virginia law, repaid the debt by complying with a state statute enacted during the Revolutionary War that required debtors to repay money owed to British creditors into a Virginia state fund. The creditor, however, claimed that this state-sanctioned repayment did not count because a provision of the 1783 Paris Peace Treaty between Britain and the United States said that "the creditors of either side should meet with no lawful impediment to the recovery of the full value . . . of all bona fide debts, theretofore contracted"; and that provision, the creditor argued, effectively nullified the state law. The Court, with each Justice writing separately, agreed with the British creditor, held the Virginia statute invalid, and found that the American debtor remained liable for the debt.

The key fact relevant here is that Congress had not enacted a specific statute enforcing the treaty provision at issue. Hence the Court had to decide whether the provision was (to put the matter in present terms) "self-executing.". . . *Before* adoption of the U.S. Constitution, all such provisions would have taken effect as domestic law *only if* Congress on the American side, or Parliament on the British side, had written them into domestic law. But . . . *after* the Constitution's adoption, while further parliamentary action remained necessary in Britain . . . further legislative action in respect to the treaty's debt-collection provision *was no longer necessary* in the United States. The ratification of the Constitution with its Supremacy Clause means that treaty provisions that bind the United States may (and in this instance did) also enter domestic law without further congressional action and automatically bind the States and courts as well. . . .

. . .

[T]his Court has frequently held or assumed that particular treaty provisions are self-executing, automatically binding the States without more. . . . As far as I can tell, the Court has held to the contrary only in two cases: *Foster, supra*, which was later reversed, and *Cameron Septic Tank Co. v. Knoxville*, 227 U.S. 39 (1913), where specific congressional actions indicated that Congress thought further legislation necessary.

. . .

B

The case law provides no simple magic answer to the question whether a particular treaty provision is self-executing. But the case law does make clear that, insofar as today's majority looks for language about "self-execution" in the treaty itself and insofar as it erects "clear statement" presumptions designed to help find an answer, it is misguided.

. . .

The many treaty provisions that this Court has found self-executing contain no textual language on the point. Few, if any, of these provisions are clear. . . . Those that displace state law in respect to such quintessential state matters as, say, property, inheritance, or debt repayment, lack the "clea[r] state[ment]" that the Court today apparently requires. . . . These many Supreme Court cases finding treaty provisions to be self-executing cannot be reconciled with the majority's demand for textual clarity.

. . .

. . . In a word, for present purposes, the absence or presence of language in a treaty about a provision's self-execution proves nothing at all. At best the Court is hunting the snark. At worst it erects legalistic hurdles that can threaten the application of provisions in many existing commercial and other treaties and make it more difficult to negotiate new ones.

. . .

C

. . . I would find the relevant treaty provisions self-executing as applied to the ICJ judgment before us (giving that judgment domestic legal effect) for the following reasons, taken together.

First, the language of the relevant treaties strongly supports direct judicial enforceability, at least of judgments of the kind at issue here. . . . [I]n accepting Article 94(1) of the Charter, "[e]ach Member . . . undertakes to comply with the decision" of the ICJ "in any case to which it is a party." And the ICJ Statute (part of the U.N. Charter) makes clear that . . . a decision of the ICJ between parties that have consented to the ICJ's compulsory jurisdiction has *"binding force . . .* between the parties and in respect of that particular case." Art. 59, *id.*, at 1062 (emphasis added). Enforcement of a court's judgment that has "binding force" involves quintessential judicial activity.

True, neither the Protocol nor the Charter explicitly states that the obligation to comply with an ICJ judgment automatically binds a party as a matter of domestic law without further domestic legislation. But how could the language of those documents do otherwise? The treaties are multilateral. . . . [S]ome signatories follow British further-legislation-always-needed principles, others follow United States Supremacy Clause principles, and still others, *e.g.*, the Netherlands, can directly incorporate treaty provisions into their domestic law in particular circumstances. Why, given national differences, would drafters, seeking as strong a legal obligation as is practically attainable, use treaty language that requires all signatories to adopt uniform domestic-law treatment in this respect? . . .

I recognize, as the majority emphasizes, that the U.N. Charter uses the words "undertakes to comply," rather than, say, "shall comply" or "must comply." But what is inadequate about the word "undertak[e]"? A leading contemporary dictionary defined it in terms of "lay[ing] oneself under obligation . . . to perform or to execute." Webster's New International Dictionary 2770 (2d ed. 1939). And that definition is just what the equally authoritative Spanish version of the provision (familiar to Mexico) says directly: The words "compromete a cumplir" indicate a present obligation to execute, without any tentativeness of the sort the majority finds in the English word "undertakes." See *Carta de las Naciones Unidas*, Articulo 94, 59 Stat. 1175 (1945); Spanish and English Legal and Commercial Dictionary 44 (1945) (defining "comprometer" as "become liable"); *id.*, at 59 (defining "cumplir" as "to perform, discharge, carry out, execute"). . . .

The upshot is that treaty language says that an ICJ decision is legally binding, but it leaves the implementation of that binding legal obligation to the domestic law of each signatory nation. In this Nation, the Supremacy Clause, as long and consistently interpreted, indicates that ICJ decisions rendered pursuant to provisions for binding adjudication must be domestically legally binding and enforceable in domestic courts at least sometimes. And for purposes of this argument, that conclusion is all that I need.

Second, the Optional Protocol here applies to a dispute about the meaning of a Vienna Convention provision that is . . . about an individual's "rights," namely, his right upon being arrested to be informed of his separate right to contact his nation's consul. The provision language is precise. The dispute arises at the intersection of an individual right with ordinary rules of criminal procedure; it consequently concerns the kind of matter with which judges are familiar.

Third, logic suggests that a treaty provision providing for "final" and "binding" judgments that "settl[e]" treaty-based disputes is self-executing insofar as the judgment in question concerns the meaning of an underlying treaty provision that is itself self-executing. . . .

. . .

Fourth, the majority's very different approach has seriously negative practical implications. The United States has entered into at least 70 treaties that contain provisions for ICJ dispute settlement similar to the Protocol before us. . . . If the Optional Protocol here, taken together with the U.N. Charter and its annexed ICJ Statute, is insufficient to warrant enforcement of the ICJ judgment before us, it is difficult to see how one could reach a different conclusion in any of these other instances. And the consequence is to undermine longstanding efforts in those treaties to create an effective international system for interpreting and applying many, often commercial, self-executing treaty provisions. . . .

Fifth, other factors, related to the particular judgment here at issue, make that judgment well suited to direct judicial enforcement. The specific issue before the ICJ concerned "'review and reconsideration'" of the "possible prejudice" caused in each of the 51 affected cases by an arresting State's failure to provide the defendant with rights guaranteed by the Vienna Convention. This review will call for an understanding of how criminal procedure works, including whether, and how, a notification failure may work prejudice. As the ICJ itself recognized, "it is the judicial process that is suited to this task." Courts frequently work with criminal procedure and related prejudice. Legislatures do not. . . .

Sixth, to find the United States' treaty obligations self-executing as applied to the ICJ judgment (and consequently to find that judgment enforceable) does not threaten constitutional conflict with other branches; it does not require us to engage in nonjudicial activity; and it does not require us to create a new cause of action. . . .

Seventh, neither the President nor Congress has expressed concern about direct judicial enforcement of the ICJ decision. To the contrary, the President favors enforcement of this judgment.* . . .

For these seven reasons, I would find that the United States' treaty obligation to comply with the ICJ judgment in *Avena* is enforceable in court in this case without further congressional action beyond Senate ratification of the relevant treaties. The majority reaches a different conclusion because it looks for the wrong thing (explicit textual expression about self-execution) using the wrong standard (clarity) in the wrong place (the treaty language). Hunting for what the text cannot contain, it takes a wrong turn. It threatens to deprive individuals, including businesses, property owners, testamentary beneficiaries, consular officials, and others,

---

* The President argued that while the *Avena* judgment was itself non-self-executing, the President had the power to execute it by issuing a directive to Texas. In a part of the opinion omitted here, the Court's majority rejected the latter view and held that only Congress can give a non-self-executing treaty the status of judicially enforceable federal law. — EDS.

of the workable dispute resolution procedures that many treaties, including commercially oriented treaties, provide. In a world where commerce, trade, and travel have become ever more international, that is a step in the wrong direction.

. . .

For the reasons set forth, I respectfully dissent.

NOTES AND QUESTIONS

1. **The Domestic Effect of Treaties.** What are the implications of the distinction between a self-executing treaty and a non-self-executing treaty? How is your answer different if you are speaking as a U.S. judge, a lawyer for a private party, a lawyer for the U.S. executive branch, or a judge on an international court? What would have happened if the Court in *Medellín* had found Article 94 to be self-executing?

2. **Distinguishing Between Self-Executing and Non-Self-Executing Treaties.** According to the court in *Medellín*, how does one determine whether a treaty is self-executing or non-self-executing? Why does the majority find the treaty in *Medellín* to be non-self-executing? Why does the dissent disagree? Who has the better argument? Is Chief Justice Roberts's test for self-execution too categorical? Is Justice Breyer's test too indeterminate? Which approach is better in this regard? Can you predict how each would deal with non-self-execution claims in future cases?

3. **The Origins of Article VI.** Under the Articles of Confederation, the United States' governing document prior to ratification of the Constitution, U.S. States persistently refused to abide by treaty commitments made by the national government, causing extreme foreign policy difficulties. As Justice Breyer's dissent discusses, the 1783 Treaty of Peace with Britain, which was generally very favorable to the United States, provided that British creditors would meet "no lawful impediment" in collecting pre-war debts from American debtors. However, States continued to impose "impediments" to protect their citizens, and the matter became a major issue in U.S.-British relations in the 1780s. Among other things, Britain refused to evacuate military posts in the frontier regions of the United States, although it had promised to do so in the Treaty. State noncompliance with treaties became a theme of the Articles' critics in the years leading to the Constitution Convention in Philadelphia in 1787. At the Convention, Virginia Governor Edmund Randolph began by listing the problems of the Articles, including that the national government "could not cause infractions of treaties . . . to be punished." The drafters' inclusion of treaties in Article VI of the new Constitution was a direct response to the difficulties under the Articles. *See* INTERNATIONAL LAW IN THE U.S. SUPREME COURT: CONTINUITY AND CHANGE 9-13 (David L. Sloss, Michael D. Ramsey & William S. Dodge eds., 2011). Do the historical origins of Article VI undermine the Court's conclusion in *Medellín*? Why does Justice Breyer think so, and why is Chief Justice Roberts not persuaded?

4. ***Foster v. Neilson* and the Beginning of Non-Self-Execution.** The Supreme Court's first major treaty case was *Ware v. Hylton* in 1796, discussed in Justice Breyer's *Medellín* dissent. Applying the provision of the Treaty of Peace regarding British creditors, the Court in *Ware* held that a Virginia law limiting the rights of British creditors was invalid. In the years following *Ware*, the Court routinely held treaties to override inconsistent state law (and in at least one case, inconsistent federal law) — what would later be called "self-execution." *E.g., United States v. Schooner Peggy*, 5 U.S. 103 (1801); *Owings v. Norwood's Lessee*, 9 U.S. 344 (1809); *Chirac v. Chirac's Lessee*, 15 U.S. 259 (1817). As indicated in *Medellín*, Chief Justice Marshall's opinion in *Foster v. Neilson* in 1829 is considered the beginning of the judicial doctrine of non-self-executing treaties. The case involved the validity of a Spanish land grant in what is now Louisiana (at one point part of Spanish Florida). In the treaty acquiring Florida from Spain, the United States agreed that Spanish grants "shall be ratified and confirmed." Marshall argued:

> Our constitution declares a treaty to be the law of the land. It is, consequently, to be regarded in courts of justice as equivalent to an act of the legislature, whenever it operates of itself without the aid of any legislative provision. But when the terms of the stipulation import a contract, when either of the parties engages to perform a particular act, the treaty addresses itself to the political, not the judicial department; and the legislature must execute the contract before it can become a rule for the court.

Because the U.S. Congress had not acted to ratify the land grants in question, Marshall and one other Justice thought they were not binding on the Court. (The rest of the Court thought the grants were invalid in any event because the land was not part of the Florida territory covered by the treaty.) Interestingly, Marshall later changed his mind about the particular treaty, concluding — after reading the Spanish version — that the provision did not need legislative implementation. *United States v. Percheman*, 32 U.S. 51 (1832). But the idea that some treaties needed congressional implementation to become law was repeated in later cases, including *Whitney v. Robertson*, 124 U.S. 190 (1888). What might explain the Court's recourse to non-self-execution?

5. **The Meaning of Self-Execution and Non-Self-Execution.** The possible effects of self-execution include (a) treaties may override ("preempt") inconsistent state law; (b) treaties may give private parties a right to sue the government or another private party; (c) treaties may provide a defense against a claim brought by a government or private party; and (d) treaties may override inconsistent federal statutes. Are some of these effects more or less problematic than others? Is the doctrine of non-self-execution designed to protect federalism and separation of powers, or is something more or different at work as a background principle? What does it mean to say that a treaty is non-self-executing? How is that consistent with Article VI? As an example of a self-executing treaty preempting state law, consider the U.N. Convention on Contracts for the International Sale of Goods (CISG), which contains provisions similar to (but not identical to) the Uniform Commercial Code (UCC).

In *VLM Food Trading Int'l, Inc. v. Illinois Trading Company*, 748 F.3d 780 (7th Cir. 2013), the question was whether the CISG or the Illinois UCC applied to a contact between a U.S. and a Canadian corporation. The court found that the CISG applied to the contract and was self-executing, thus overriding inconsistent provisions of the UCC-based state law. What would have happened if the CISG was not self-executing?

6.   **Pre-*Medellín* Examples of Non-Self-Executing Treaties.** Before *Medellín*, the modern Supreme Court had not considered the question of non-self-execution, but lower federal courts had held numerous treaty provisions to be non-self-executing. *See, e.g., Diggs v. Richardson*, 555 F.2d 848 (D.C. Cir. 1976); *United States v. Postal*, 589 F.2d 862 (5th Cir. 1979). In *Diggs*, the court explained:

> This suit seeks judicial enforcement of a U.N. Security Council resolution which calls upon member states to have no dealings with South Africa which impliedly recognize the legality of that country's occupation of the former U.N. territory of Namibia.* The plaintiffs . . . seek declaratory and injunctive relief prohibiting our government from continuing to deal with the South Africans concerning the importation of seal furs from Namibia.

The court rejected the claim, concluding:

> In determining whether a treaty is self-executing courts look to the intent of the signatory parties as manifested by the language of the instrument, and, if the instrument is uncertain, recourse must be had to the circumstances surrounding its execution. . . .
>
> Applying this kind of analysis to the particular Security Council Resolution on which plaintiffs rely, we find that the provisions here in issue were not addressed to the judicial branch of our government. They do not by their terms confer rights upon individual citizens; they call upon governments to take certain action. The provisions deal with the conduct of our foreign relations, an area traditionally left to executive discretion. The Resolution does not provide specific standards. The "entrenchment" standard of the Resolution, while possibly of such a nature that it might be elaborated by an international tribunal, is essentially the kind of standard that is rooted in diplomacy and its incidents, rather than in conventional adjudication, and is foreign to the general experience and function of American courts. In the absence of contrary indication in the international legislative history, and in the absence of domestic legislation evincing an intention for judicial enforcement, we conclude that the provisions of Resolution 301 involved here do not confer on individual citizens rights that are judicially enforceable in American domestic courts.

7.   **Examples of Self-Executing Treaties.** In the modern era prior to *Medellín*, lower federal courts frequently found treaties to be self-executing. *E.g., People of Saipan v. U.S. Department of the Interior*, 502 F.2d 90 (9th Cir. 1974).

---

* Article 25 of the U.N. Charter requires U.N. members to "accept and carry out the decisions of the Security Council." — EDS.

The *Saipan* case involved a claim premised on the Trusteeship Agreement for the Pacific Islands, under the auspices of the United Nations; the plaintiffs, inhabitants of an island governed by the United States pursuant to the Trusteeship Agreement, sought to block a development project approved by the United States. As the court explained,

> Specifically, Article 6 of the Trusteeship Agreement requires the United States to "promote the economic advancement and self-sufficiency of the inhabitants, and to this end . . . regulate the use of natural resources" and to "protect the inhabitants against the loss of their lands and resources. . . ."
>
> Defendants contend, though, that provisions of the Trusteeship Agreement, including Article 6, can be enforced only before the Security Council of the United Nations. We disagree, concluding that the Trusteeship Agreement can be a source of rights enforceable by an individual litigant in a domestic court of law.
>
> The extent to which an international agreement establishes affirmative and judicially enforceable obligations without implementing legislation must be determined in each case by reference to many contextual factors: the purposes of the treaty and the objectives of its creators, the existence of domestic procedures and institutions appropriate for direct implementation, the availability and feasibility of alternative enforcement methods, and the immediate and long-range social consequences of self- or non-self-execution.
>
> The preponderance of features in this Trusteeship Agreement suggests the intention to establish direct, affirmative, and judicially enforceable rights. The issue involves the local economy and environment, not security; the concern with natural resources and the concern with political development are explicit in the agreement and are general international concerns as well; the enforcement of these rights requires little legal or administrative innovation in the domestic fora; and the alternative forum, the Security Council, would present to the plaintiffs obstacles so great as to make their rights virtually unenforceable.
>
> Moreover, the Trusteeship Agreement constitutes the plaintiffs' basic constitutional document. For all these reasons, we believe that the rights asserted by the plaintiffs are judicially enforceable.

Similarly, in *Diggs v. Shultz*, 470 F.2d 461 (D.C. Cir. 1972), the court found a U.N. Security Council resolution that barred trade with Rhodesia (modern Zimbabwe) to be self-executing. Are these cases consistent with *Diggs v. Richardson*?

8. **The Future of Self-Execution.** What remains of self-execution after *Medellín*? How would you argue in a subsequent case that a treaty is self-executing? In *Brzak v. United Nations*, 597 F.3d 107 (2d Cir. 2010), a post-*Medellín* case, the court found the Convention on Privileges and Immunities of the United Nations, which provides that "[t]he United Nations . . . shall enjoy immunity from every form of legal process except insofar as in any particular case it has expressly waived its immunity," to be self-executing under *Medellín's* test. The court accordingly dismissed plaintiffs' claim for sex discrimination against the United Nations on the basis of immunity. Is that consistent

with *Medellín*? Can you predict how the pre-*Medellín* cases discussed above (*Diggs v. Richardson, People of Saipan*) would have come out if decided after *Medellín*?

9. **Senate Declarations of Non-Self-Execution.** In giving its advice and consent to treaties, the U.S. Senate sometimes includes Reservations, Understandings, and Declarations (RUDs) setting forth the Senate's views on particular aspects of the treaty. Starting in the 1990s, the Senate began including declarations of non-self-execution along with its consent to a number of human rights treaties. For example, in consenting to the International Covenant on Civil and Political Rights (ICCPR) in 1992 the Senate stated: "[T]he provisions of Article 1 through 27 of the Covenant are not self-executing." The Supreme Court has not directly considered the effect of non-self-executing declarations. Lower courts have consistently assumed that treaties subject to non-self-executing declarations cannot be invoked judicially as a source of law. *But see Igartua v. United States*, 626 F.3d 592, 625 (1st Cir. 2010) (Torruella, J., dissenting) (arguing that courts are not bound by the Senate's declaration of non-self-execution regarding the ICCPR). Why would the Senate adopt these declarations? Does the practice of Senate declarations of non-self-execution support or undermine an aggressive judicial use of non-self-execution doctrine?

10. **The Role of Executive Branch.** As discussed more extensively below, courts afford deference to executive branch interpretations of treaties. In *More v. Intelcom Support Services, Inc.*, 960 F.2d 466 (5th Cir. 1992), the court found it largely conclusive that the executive branch thought a treaty was non-self-executing. *See also Brzak v. United Nations, supra* (relying heavily on executive branch statements of self-execution during the Senate approval process). In *Medellín*, the Supreme Court referred to the executive branch's position that the treaty was non-self-executing, but only after the Court had closely examined the treaty language itself. How important should the executive branch's current view be? How important should it be if the executive branch at the time the treaty was ratified thought it was non-self-executing? What should a court do if the executive branch has changed positions?

11. **British and Commonwealth Practice.** As discussed in *Medellín*, the long-standing British practice is that treaties are non-self-executing. "Within the British Empire there is a well-established rule that the making of a treaty is an executive act, while the performance of its obligations, if they entail alternation of the existing domestic law, requires legislative action. . . . Once [treaties] are created, while they bind the state as against the other contracting parties, Parliament may refuse to perform them and so leave the state in default." *Attorney-General for Canada v. Attorney-General for Ontario*, [1937] A.C. 326, 347-48 (opinion of Atkin, L.J.). This approach is followed in most British Commonwealth countries as well. Often these countries pass implementing legislation in parliament before they ratify the treaty. Is this a better approach? What are the advantages (if any) of having some — but not all — treaties be self-executing? In the United States, Congress also frequently passes statutes that incorporate treaties into domestic law,

thus eliminating the self-execution question. *See, e.g., Swarna v. al-Awadi,* 622 F.3d 123 (2d Cir. 2010) (finding it unnecessary to decide whether the Vienna Convention on Diplomatic Relations was self-executing because a federal statute required courts to dismiss any action in which the defendant was entitled to immunity under the Convention).

12. **Presumptions.** The *Restatement (Third) of Foreign Relations Law,* Section 111, states that "[a]n international agreement of the United States is 'non-self-executing' (a) if the agreement manifests an intention that it shall not become effective as domestic law without the enactment of implementing legislation, (b) if the Senate in giving consent to a treaty, or Congress by resolution, requires implementing legislation, or (c) if implementing legislation is constitutionally required." The notes add that "if the Executive Branch has not requested implementing legislation and Congress has not enacted such legislation, there is a strong presumption that the treaty has been considered self-executing by the political branches, and should be considered self-executing by the courts." (Section 111, Reporters' Note 5). It does not appear that the Supreme Court applied this presumption in *Medellín*; arguably it applied the opposite presumption, suggesting that a treaty that is silent on its status is non-self-executing. Which is the right approach?

13. **Aftermath.** As a result of the *Medellín* case, José Medellín was executed by the State of Texas, an outcome that placed the United States in violation of international law. Does that suggest a problem with the Court's decision? Can it really be the case that the United States was required under international law to recognize the ICJ decision, and yet Texas was not required to? What steps might have been taken to prevent an international law violation? Are any of them realistic?

b. Treaties and Private Rights

Even if a treaty is self-executing, U.S. courts may not think it allows private litigants to sue to enforce it. This subsection considers how to approach that question, which is usually phrased as whether the treaty creates "private rights" or a "private right of action."

McKesson Corp. v. Islamic Republic of Iran

539 F.3d 485 (D.C. Cir. 2008)

GRIFFITH, Circuit Judge:

[McKesson Corp. sued Iran for loss of McKesson's interest in a dairy operation located in Iran, which was taken over by the Iranian government after the 1979 revolution. McKesson based its claim on the 1955 Treaty of Amity, Economic Relations, and Consular Rights between the United States and Iran, which provides protection for investments by the nationals of each party within the territory

[handwritten margin note: Mck v. Iran / Trea of Amity]

of the other. Previous opinions in the case held Iran not entitled to foreign sovereign immunity.]

. . .

We must determine whether the Treaty of Amity provides a private cause of action. . . . If it does not, and if a cause of action cannot otherwise be found, then McKesson's complaint must be dismissed. . . .

To determine whether a treaty creates a cause of action, we look to its text. . . . The Treaty of Amity, like other treaties of its kind, is self-executing. As such, it "operates of itself without the aid of any legislative provision," *Foster v. Neilson*, 27 U.S. 253, 314 (Marshall, C.J.), and its text is "the supreme Law of the Land," U.S. Const. art. VI, cl. 2, on par with that of a statute, *Whitney v. Robertson*, 124 U.S. 190, 194 (1888). That the Treaty of Amity is self-executing begins but does not end our search for a treaty-based cause of action, because "[w]hether a treaty is self-executing is a question distinct from whether the treaty creates private rights or remedies." RESTATEMENT (THIRD) OF FOREIGN RELATIONS LAW OF THE UNITED STATES § 111 cmt. h (1986). . . . "Even when treaties are self-executing in the sense that they create federal law, the background presumption is that '[i]nternational agreements, even those directly benefiting private persons, generally do not create private rights or provide for a private cause of action in domestic courts.'" *Medellín*, 128 S. Ct. at 1357 n.3 (quoting RESTATEMENT, *supra*, § 907 cmt. a).

We find nothing in the Treaty of Amity that overcomes this presumption. To be sure, article IV(2) of the Treaty of Amity directly benefits McKesson by declaring that "property shall not be taken except for a public purpose, nor shall it be taken without the prompt payment of just compensation." McKesson contends that the Treaty of Amity creates a right ("property shall not be taken") and provides a remedy ("just compensation"), and that together these make a cause of action. Not so. The Treaty of Amity tells us what McKesson will receive — money — but leaves open the critical question of how McKesson is to secure its due. For a federal court trying to decide whether to interject itself into international affairs, the Treaty of Amity's silence on this point makes all the difference. A treaty that "only set[s] forth substantive rules of conduct and state[s] that compensation shall be paid for certain wrongs . . . do[es] not create private rights of action for foreign corporations to recover compensation from foreign states in United States courts." *Argentine Republic v. Amerada Hess Shipping Corp.*, 488 U.S. 428, 442 (1989). And without a cause of action, McKesson cannot invoke federal judicial authority to pursue its desired remedy. *Cf.* HENRY M. HART, JR. & ALBERT M. SACKS, THE LEGAL PROCESS 137 (William N. Eskridge, Jr. & Philip P. Frickey eds., 1994) ("A right of action is a species of power — of remedial power. It is a capacity to invoke the judgment of a tribunal of authoritative application upon a disputed question about the application of preexisting arrangements and to secure, if the claim proves to be well-founded, an appropriate official remedy.").

It would be one thing if the Treaty of Amity explicitly called upon the courts for enforcement, as the Warsaw Convention does. See Convention for the Unification of Certain Rules Relating to International Transportation by Air, Oct. 12, 1929 (declaring that "carrier[s] shall be liable for damage" to passengers and baggage (arts. 17, 18(1)); that "action[s] for damages" must be brought before certain courts (art. 28(1)); that "[t]he right to damages" lasts for two years (art. 29(1)); and that "passenger[s] or consignor[s] shall have a right of action" in cases of successive carriers (art. 30(3))); . . . Federal court participation is appropriate where the President, by and with the advice and consent of the Senate, makes a treaty declaring that money should change hands by way of judicial compulsion rather than executive negotiation. But unlike the Warsaw Convention, with its explicit references to "right[s] of action" and "action[s] for damages," the Treaty of Amity reflects no such determination.

Reasoning by analogy to the Takings Clause of the Fifth Amendment, McKesson next asks us to use our federal common law power to recognize an implied cause of action. The phrase "just compensation" appears in both the Treaty of Amity and the Takings Clause. . . . McKesson urges us to infer a cause of action from the former, as the Supreme Court has from the latter.

This attempt to draw an analogy between a treaty and the Constitution is unsound. When it comes to implied causes of action, the Constitution stands apart from other texts. See *Davis v. Passman*, 442 U.S. 228 (1979) (explaining that "the question of who may enforce a statutory right is fundamentally different from the question of who may enforce a right that is protected by the Constitution"); . . . Inferring a cause of action from the Constitution squares with the "presum[ption] that justiciable constitutional rights are to be enforced through the courts." *Davis*, 442 U.S. at 242. By contrast, inferring a treaty-based cause of action embroils the judiciary in matters outside its competence and authority. *See Medellín*, 128 S. Ct. at 1357 n.3 (noting presumption against finding treaty-based causes of action); *Sosa v. Alvarez-Machain*, 542 U.S. 692, 727 (2004) (noting that "a decision to create a private right of action is one better left to legislative judgment in the great majority of cases," and that "the possible collateral consequences of making international rules privately actionable argue for judicial caution"). . . .

Our conclusion that the Treaty of Amity does not create an implied cause of action accords with the prevailing sentiment against recognition of implied causes of action. *See, e.g., Cort v. Ash*, 422 U.S. 66 (1975); *Alexander v. Sandoval*, 532 U.S. 275, 286 (2001) ("Like substantive federal law itself, private rights of action to enforce federal law must be created by Congress."); . . .

In the absence of a textual invitation to judicial participation, we conclude the President and the Senate intended to enforce the Treaty of Amity through bilateral interaction between its signatories. We give "'great weight'" to the fact that the United States shares this view. *Medellín*, 128 S. Ct. at 1361 (quoting *Sumitomo Shoji Am., Inc. v. Avagliano*, 457 U.S. 176, 184-85 (1982)); see United States Amicus Br. at 5-11 (arguing that the Treaty of Amity does not create a cause of action). This interpretation is in keeping with traditional assumptions about how treaties operate. As the Supreme Court declared in *The Head Money Cases*:

> A treaty is primarily a compact between independent nations. It depends for the enforcement of its provisions on the interest and the honor of the governments which are parties to it. If these fail, its infraction becomes the subject of international negotiations and reclamations, so far as the injured party chooses to seek redress, which may in the end be enforced by actual war. It is obvious that with all this the judicial courts have nothing to do and can give no redress.

Edye v. Robertson (The Head Money Cases), 112 U.S. 580, 598 (1884). The Treaty of Amity does not provide a cause of action. We must leave to the political branches the implementation of its just compensation guarantee. . . .*

NOTES AND QUESTIONS

[handwritten: Test for private right of action]

1. **Treaty Self-Execution and Private Rights of Action.** If a treaty is self-executing, why is there also a need to find a private right of action? If a person has standing (that is, an injury that can be remedied), why should the law (treaty) not give a remedy? Does it make sense to have a broad category of treaties that are self-executing but do not convey private rights? What differences, if any, are there between the test for self-execution and the test for a private right of action? Does this suggest the need for two separate doctrines, or not? Consider pre-*Medellín* cases that found a treaty to be self-executing, such as *People of Saipan* and *Diggs v. Schultz*, discussed above. Should these cases also have considered whether there was a private cause of action to enforce them? Should they have found one?

2. **Statutes and Causes of Action.** The need to find a private cause of action is not unique to treaties; it also arises with respect to federal statutes and regulations. For example, in *Cort v. Ash*, 422 U.S. 66 (1975), cited in *McKesson*, a federal statute, 18 U.S.C. § 610, prohibited certain corporate contributions to political campaigns. Ash, a stockholder in a corporation, sued the corporation's board of directors for violating the statute. The Supreme Court unanimously held that § 610 did not provide for private suit, and that Congress intended the statute to be enforced only by the government. Likewise, in *Alexander v. Sandoval*, 532 U.S. 275 (2001), the U.S. Department of Justice issued regulations, pursuant to a federal statute, prohibiting any state agency receiving federal funding from "utiliz[ing] criteria or methods of administration which have the effect of subjecting individuals to discrimination because of their race, color, or national origin." Alabama, pursuant to a state English-only law, began administering drivers' license examinations only in English. Sandoval sued, claiming his rights under the regulations had been violated. In a 5-4 decision by Justice Scalia, the Supreme Court held that no private remedy existed. The majority explained: "Like substantive federal law itself, private rights of action to enforce federal law must be created by Congress. . . . The judicial task is to interpret the statute Congress has passed to determine whether it displays an intent to create not just a private right but also a private

---

* The court of appeals remanded to the district court to determine if McKesson had other sources of a cause of action. The district court found causes of action under customary international law and Iranian law. On further appeal, the court of appeals rejected the international law cause of action but affirmed the finding of a cause of action under Iranian law. *McKesson Corp. v. Islamic Republic of Iran*, 672 F.3d 1066 (D.C. Cir. 2012). — EDS.

remedy." The majority went on to find that Congress intended the prohibition to be enforced administratively rather than through private suit. Why should this rationale be applied in the treaty context?

3. **The Origins of the Private Rights Doctrine.** Like the doctrine of non-self-execution, the idea that treaties may not grant privately enforceable rights has its judicial origins in the nineteenth century. *The Head Money Cases*, 112 U.S. 580 (1884), quoted in *McKesson*, noted that treaties often are simply agreements between governments that do not concern individuals. However, the Court there went on to say:

> But a treaty may also contain provisions which confer certain rights upon the citizens or subjects of one of the nations residing in the territorial limits of the other, which partake of the nature of municipal law and which are capable of enforcement between private parties in the courts of the country. . . . And when such rights are of a nature to be enforced in a court of justice, the court resorts to the treaty for a rule of decision for the case before it as it would to a statute.

The Head Money Cases involved a claim that certain duties imposed on immigrants by federal law violated U.S. treaty obligations. The Court did not determine whether the treaty provided private rights, as it ruled that the federal statute superseded the treaty. An academic study of nineteenth-century treaty cases found that the Court typically assumed treaties relied on by litigants were sources of private rights enforceable in court. INTERNATIONAL LAW IN THE U.S. SUPREME COURT: CONTINUITY AND CHANGE 14-15, 66-67 (David L. Sloss, Michael D. Ramsey & William S. Dodge eds., 2011). What do you think accounts for this shift in judicial approach?

4. **Overlap Between Private Rights and Self-Execution Analysis.** Note that *Medellín* and *McKesson* contemplate a two-step process in which self-execution and the existence of a private right of action are separate inquiries. Some decisions may seem to conflate the two. For example, in *Goldstar (Panama) S.A. v. United States*, 967 F.2d 965 (4th Cir. 1992), the plaintiff, Goldstar, claimed that the United States had violated the 1907 Hague Convention Respecting the Law and Customs of War on Land by allowing its property to be destroyed in the U.S. invasion of Panama. The court rejected the claim, arguing:

> International treaties are not presumed to create rights that are privately enforceable [citing *The Head Money Cases* and *Foster v. Neilson*]. Courts will only find a treaty to be self-executing if the document, as a whole, evidences an intent to provide a private right of action. The Hague Convention does not explicitly provide for a privately enforceable cause of action. Moreover, we find that a reasonable reading of the treaty as a whole does not lead to the conclusion that the signatories intended to provide such a right.
> . . . Article 1 of the Hague Convention states, "[t]he Contracting Powers shall issue instructions to their armed land forces which shall be in conformity with the Regulations. . . ." This language must be taken as further evidence that the Hague Convention is not self-executing, and that, instead, the

signatories contemplated that individual nations would take subsequent executory actions to discharge the obligations of the treaty

In sum, we hold that the Hague Convention is not self-executing and, therefore, does not, by itself, create a private right of action for its breach.

In *Argentine Republic v. Amerada Hess Shipping Corp.*, 488 U.S. 428 (1989), cited in both *Goldstar* and *McKesson*, the Supreme Court rejected a claim against Argentina for violating two treaties regarding the conduct of warfare on the high seas. The Court observed: "These [treaties], however, only set forth substantive rules of conduct and state that compensation shall be paid for certain wrongs. They do not create private rights of action for foreign corporations to recover compensation from foreign states in United States courts." For this proposition the Court cited both *Foster v. Neilson* and *The Head Money Cases*, leaving some doubt as to whether the Court meant that the treaties were non-self-executing or that the treaties did not convey private rights (or both).

5. **Private Rights and Defendants.** *McKesson* discusses private rights in terms of the existence or nonexistence of a cause of action (a requirement for a plaintiff). Stated more broadly, the idea of private rights implicates defendants as well, where a defendant invokes a treaty provision as a defense. For example, in numerous cases prior to *Medellín*, alien criminal defendants argued that failure to notify their consulates after their arrest violated their rights and entitled them to various remedies including suppression of evidence or a new trial. While many of these cases sidestepped the question of private rights, a few held directly that the Convention did not create a private right. E.g., *United States v. Emuegbunam*, 268 F.3d 377, 391-93 (6th Cir. 2001) ("[W]e hold that the Vienna Convention does not create a right for a detained foreign national to consult with the diplomatic representatives of his nation that the federal courts can enforce. A contrary conclusion risks aggrandizing the power of the judiciary and interfering in the nation's foreign affairs, the conduct of which the Constitution reserves for the political branches."). In a somewhat different context, another court of appeals held that the Convention does create a private right for foreign defendants to consult with their consulates. *Jogi v. Voges*, 480 F.3d 822 (7th Cir. 2007).

6. **Express Disclaimer of Private Rights.** Some treaties expressly state that they do not create private rights. For example, the Mutual Legal Assistance Treaty (MLAT) between the United States and the United Kingdom, Article 1, para. 3, states: "This treaty is intended solely for mutual legal assistance between the Parties. The provisions of this Treaty shall not give rise to a right on the part of any private person to obtain, suppress, or exclude any evidence, or to impede the execution of a request." Unsurprisingly, courts have held that the U.S.-U.K. MLAT and others like it do not create private rights. E.g., *In re Request from the United Kingdom*, 685 F.3d 1, 11-13 (1st Cir. 2012).

7. **Effect of a Self-Executing Treaty with No Private Rights.** A treaty that does not grant private rights might still have effect in court. One example is if a

government or international organization invokes the treaty. *E.g., In re the Matter of the Search of the Premises Located at 840 140th Avenue*, 634 F.3d 557 (9th Cir. 2011) (U.S. government successfully relied on an MLAT with Russia to grant authority to conduct certain investigations); *Brzak v. United Nations, supra* (United Nations successfully relied on a treaty to provide immunity from suit).

8. **Finding Self-Execution and Private Rights of Action.** Consider whether private rights of action should be found in the following situations:

   a. The International Covenant on Civil and Political Rights (ICCPR) sets forth basic rights, such as the freedom of speech, that nations agree to guarantee to their own citizens. As noted previously, in giving its consent to the ICCPR the U.S. Senate declared that it is not self-executing. Would it be self-executing if the Senate had not made a declaration? If it were self-executing, would it provide a cause of action? What additional facts about the Covenant might you want to know to answer these questions? Why do you think the Senate wanted the ICCPR not to be a source of judicially enforceable rights?

   b. The U.N. Charter imposes various obligations on members of the United Nations. One well-known set of provisions in the Charter, Articles 4(2) and 51, prohibit nations from using armed force except in self-defense or as authorized by the U.N. Security Council. Are these provisions self-executing? Do they provide a cause of action, such that claims could be brought in U.S. court against the United States, for example in regard to the 2003 invasion of Iraq, on the grounds that the invasion violated the U.N. Charter? What would it mean to say that the obligation is self-executing but that it does not provide a cause of action?

   c. The U.N. Charter has provisions relating to human rights. Article 55, for example, provides:

   > With a view to the creation of conditions of stability and well-being which are necessary for peaceful and friendly relations among nations based on respect for the principle of equal rights and self-determination of peoples, the United Nations shall promote:
   >
   > a. higher standards of living, full employment, and conditions of economic and social progress and development;
   >
   > b. solutions of international economic, social, health, and related problems; and international cultural and educational cooperation; and
   >
   > c. universal respect for, and observance of, human rights and fundamental freedoms for all without distinction as to race, sex, language, or religion.

   Could any of these provisions serve as the basis for a suit in U.S. court? *Compare Sei Fujii v. State*, 217 P.2d 481, 488 (Cal. App. 1950) (U.N. Charter precludes California from discriminating against Japanese aliens regarding land ownership), *with Sei Fujii v. State*, 242 P.2d 617, 620-22 (Cal. 1952) (U.N. Charter is non-self-executing). How would this issue be analyzed under *Medellín* and *McKesson*?

3. *Treaties and Statutes*

If a treaty is part of domestic law, a further question is how treaties interact with statutes. We have already seen that sometimes treaties and statutes are complementary — that is, statutes implement treaties by incorporating them into domestic law and providing supporting legislation to assure compliance. But sometimes treaties and statutes may appear to conflict. This section considers how such conflicts may be resolved.

The Fund for Animals, Inc. v. Kempthorne

472 F.3d 872 (D.C. Cir. 2006)

KAVANAUGH, Circuit Judge:

. . .

I

[The United States is a party to international conventions with Canada and Mexico for the protection of migratory birds.] The Canada and Mexico conventions expressly cover the family *Anatidae.* That family includes the mute swan, thought to be a European species originally brought to the United States for ornamental purposes. . . .

[The Migratory Bird Treaty Act is a U.S. statute implementing the migratory bird conventions.] Starting in the 1970s, the Secretary of the Interior regularly published a list of species protected under the Act. The list did not include the mute swan. A citizen eventually challenged the Secretary's decision not to protect the mute swan. In [*Hill v. Norton*, 275 F.3d 98 (D.C. Cir. 2001)], we concluded that the Secretary's interpretation of the Migratory Bird Treaty Act was not reasonable when measured against the statutory text: The statute covers birds "included in the terms of the conventions" themselves, and we stated that the Canada convention "undisputably include[s] mute swans." *Hill,* 275 F.3d at 104. Although the Secretary argued that the mute swan was not protected because it was not native to the United States, we stated that the Secretary pointed to "nothing in the statute, applicable treaties, or administrative record" to support an exclusion for non-native species. The text of the Migratory Bird Treaty Act and the Canada convention's references to "swans" weighed against such an exclusion and meant that the Secretary's interpretation was not reasonable. . . .

In 2004, after the *Hill* decision, Congress passed and President Bush signed the Migratory Bird Treaty Reform Act. The Reform Act amended the Migratory Bird Treaty Act's prohibition on killing or hunting migratory birds so that the statute "applies only to migratory bird species that are native to the United States or its territories." 16 U.S.C. § 703(b)(1). . . . And subject to certain exceptions not relevant here, the Reform Act provided that "a migratory bird species that occurs in the United States or its territories solely as a result of intentional or unintentional human-assisted introduction shall not be considered native to the United States or its territories. . . ."

. . .

The Maryland Department of Natural Resources then [announced] its intention to begin killing adult mute swans in the Chesapeake Bay in the spring of 2005. Maryland had previously concluded that such killing was necessary because the mute swan population . . . posed a danger to the bay ecosystem.

The Fund for Animals, Inc., [and other plaintiffs] . . . sued the Secretary [of the Interior, Dirk Kempthorne] under the Administrative Procedure Act. Plaintiffs conceded that the mute swan was not native to the United States or its territories. The complaint nonetheless challenged the [Secretary's] decision not to list the mute swan as protected, asserting that the statute continues to require protection of the mute swan. . . .

III

. . . As the Secretary determined and the parties here agree, the mute swan is not a native migratory bird species.

It follows, therefore, that the Migratory Bird Treaty Act does not protect the mute swan. Plaintiffs argue that this approach is too straightforward, contending in essence that this provision of the Reform Act does not mean what it says. Their argument relies on the separate "sense of Congress" provision in the Reform Act, which states:

> "It is the sense of Congress that the language of this section is consistent with the intent and language of the 4 bilateral treaties implemented by this section."

. . .

Given the apparent conflict between the conventions and the amended statute, together with Congress's stated belief that there is no such conflict, plaintiffs contend that the statute must be deemed ambiguous. And plaintiffs argue that we must therefore apply the canon of construction that ambiguous statutes should not be interpreted to abrogate a treaty (namely, the conventions' protection of the mute swan).

. . . Read most naturally, the sense of Congress provision indicates nothing more than Congress's disagreement with this Court's 2001 decision in *Hill* (which had concluded that the Canada convention "undisputably include[s] mute swans"). The sense of Congress provision makes clear that the Reform Act was not an attempt to limit or back away from America's treaty obligations, but rather was a correction of what Congress believed to be an erroneous judicial interpretation of a treaty. In any event, Congress may or may not be correct in its interpretation of the conventions' original scope, but that is of no moment in this case. The sense of Congress provision does not in any way alter the plain text of the Reform Act's other provisions, which clearly and unambiguously provide that the Migratory Bird Treaty Act does not protect non-native species such as the mute swan.

[P]laintiffs cite the canon of construction that ambiguous statutes should not be construed to abrogate treaties. That argument lacks merit. The canon applies only to ambiguous statutes (and as we have just explained, this statute is not ambiguous).

The Constitution establishes that statutes enacted by Congress with the concurrence of the President (or over his veto) have no less weight than treaties made by the President with the advice and consent of two-thirds of the Senate. *See* U.S. CONST. art. II, § 2, cl. 2; U.S. CONST. art. VI, cl. 2. . . .

Consistent with this doctrine, the Supreme Court has long recognized that a later-enacted statute trumps an earlier-enacted treaty to the extent the two conflict. This is known as the last-in-time rule. *See Whitney v. Robertson*, 124 U.S. 190, 194 (1888) (if self-executing treaty and statute "are inconsistent, the one last in date will control the other"); . . . At the same time, the Supreme Court also has stated that an ambiguous statute should be construed where fairly possible not to abrogate a treaty. *See Trans World Airlines, Inc. v. Franklin Mint Corp.*, 466 U.S. 243, 252 (1984); *see also Roeder v. Islamic Republic of Iran*, 333 F.3d 228, 237 (D.C. Cir. 2003). . . . The combination of the last-in-time rule and the canon against abrogation has produced a straightforward practice: Courts apply a statute according to its terms even if the statute conflicts with a prior treaty (the last-in-time rule), but where fairly possible, courts tend to construe an *ambiguous* statute not to conflict with a prior treaty (the canon against abrogation).

The canon against construing ambiguous statutes to abrogate prior treaties does not help plaintiffs here, however, because the amended Migratory Bird Treaty Act is unambiguous, as we concluded above. To accept plaintiffs' argument with respect to the canon, we would have to *distort* the plain meaning of a statute in an attempt to make it consistent with a prior treaty. The Supreme Court has not extended the canon that far, and for good reason: Distorting statutory language simply to avoid conflicts with treaties would elevate treaties above statutes in contravention of the Constitution.

[Affirmed.]

Roeder v. Islamic Republic of Iran

333 F.3d 228 (D.C. Cir. 2003)

RANDOLPH, Circuit Judge:

Americans taken hostage in Iran in 1979 and held for 444 days brought a class action on behalf of themselves, and their spouses and children, against the Islamic Republic of Iran and its Ministry of Foreign Affairs. [The district court dismissed the complaint.] . . . Among the several issues presented on appeal, the principal question is whether legislation specifically directed at this lawsuit, and enacted while the case was pending in the district court, provided a cause of action for the hostages and their families.

. . . In order to secure the hostages' release, . . . the United States [and Iran] entered into the Algiers Accords, [an executive agreement] settling a broad range of disputes between this country and Iran. As part of the Accords, the United States agreed to "bar and preclude the prosecution against Iran of any claim of a United States national arising out of the events related to (A) the seizure of the 52

United States nationals on November 4, 1979, [and] (B) their subsequent detention." The hostages were released the next day. . . .

. . . The authority of the President to settle claims of American nationals
through executive agreements is clear. There is no doubt that laws passed after the
President enters into an executive agreement may abrogate the agreement. The
question here is whether legislation enacted while the case was pending abrogated
the Algiers Accords.

The [Foreign Sovereign Immunities Act (FSIA)] provides generally that a foreign state is immune from the jurisdiction of the United States courts unless one
of the exceptions listed in 28 U.S.C. § 1605(a) applies. [Iran did not appear to contest the claims, and in August 2001 the district court entered a default judgment.]
At the time plaintiffs filed their complaint and up to entry of the default judgment
of liability, none of the [FSIA] exceptions applied to this case. . . . [The United
States government then intervened in the dispute, arguing that Iran had sovereign
immunity under the FSIA and that the Algiers Accords blocked the suit.] After
the United States moved to intervene and vacate the default judgment, Congress
amended the FSIA. A provision in an appropriations act stated that . . . the immunity of the foreign state would not apply . . . if "the act is related to Case Number
1:00CV03110(ESG) [sic] in the United States District Court for the District of
Columbia." Six weeks later, Congress corrected an error in the case number by
striking 1:00CV03110(ESG) and inserting 1:00CV03110(EGS).

Together, these amendments created an exception, for this case alone, to Iran's
sovereign immunity, which would otherwise have barred the action. The evident
purpose was to dispose of the government's argument, in its motion to vacate, that
plaintiffs' action should be dismissed because Iran [had sovereign immunity]. . . .

The question remained whether the Algiers Accords, on which the United
States had relied as a second ground for dismissal, survived the amendments. [The
district court agreed with the United States, vacated the default judgment, and
dismissed the complaint for failure to state a claim. Plaintiffs appealed.] . . . The
amendments do not, on their face, say anything about the Accords. They speak only
to the antecedent question of Iran's immunity from suit in United States courts.
Plaintiffs therefore urge us to consider statements in the "Conference Report" on
the second appropriations act, which made the technical correction to the case
number. These statements, plaintiffs say, show that Congress expressly recognized
a conflict between their lawsuit and the Accords and passed the amendments to
resolve the conflict in plaintiffs' favor.

Some words about conference reports are in order. After the House and the
Senate pass different versions of legislation, each body appoints conferees to resolve
disagreements between the House and Senate bills. If a majority of the conferees
from each body agree, they submit two documents to their respective houses: a
conference report presenting the formal legislative language and a joint explanatory statement that explains the legislative language and how the differences
between the bills were resolved. Each body must vote on approving the conference
report in its entirety and may not approve it only in part or offer any amendments.

. . . The statements [plaintiffs] think important are in the joint explanatory statement. . . . While both the conference report and the joint explanatory

statement are printed in the same document, Congress votes only on the conference report. . . . The point is that . . . the explanatory remarks in the "conference report" do not have the force of law.

. . . The joint explanatory statement relating to [the second Act], which corrected the typographical error in [the first Act], declares that the earlier amendment "quashed" the "Department of State's motion to vacate" and mentions that, in the intervening weeks, the "Department of State" continued to argue that the judgment should be vacated. It then explains the meaning of [the first Act]: "The provision acknowledges that, *notwithstanding any other authority*, the American citizens who were taken hostage by the Islamic Republic of Iran in 1979 have a claim against Iran under the Antiterrorism Act of 1996."

. . . This statement, and the italicized language in particular, is the type of language that might abrogate an executive agreement — if the statement had been enacted. But Congress did not vote on the statement and the President did not sign a bill embodying it.[6]

There is thus no clear expression in anything Congress enacted abrogating the Algiers Accords. Yet neither a treaty nor an executive agreement will be considered "abrogated or modified by a later statute unless such purpose on the part of Congress has been clearly expressed." *Trans World Airlines v. Franklin Mint Corp.*, 466 U.S. 243, 252 (1984). . . . The way Congress expresses itself is through legislation. While legislative history may be useful in determining intent, the joint explanatory statements here go well beyond the legislative text of [the second Act], which did nothing more than correct a typographical error. Moreover, the explanatory statements, rather than explain the language of [the second Act], deal with the [previous Act]. Such legislative history alone cannot be sufficient to abrogate a treaty or an executive agreement.

. . .

Executive agreements are essentially contracts between nations, and like contracts between individuals, executive agreements are expected to be honored by the parties. Congress (or the President acting alone) may abrogate an executive agreement, but legislation must be clear to ensure that Congress — and the President — have considered the consequences. The requirement of clear statement assures that the legislature has in fact faced, and intended to bring into issue, the critical matters involved in the judicial decision. The kind of legislative history offered here cannot repeal an executive agreement when the legislation itself is silent.

As against this, plaintiffs say that we should not presume that Congress, in passing the amendments, did "a futile thing." . . . The amendments were not futile acts. [T]he amendments had the effect of removing Iran's sovereign immunity, which the United States had raised in its motion to vacate. This enabled plaintiffs to argue that the Accords were not a valid executive agreement. . . . That

---

6. Upon signing the first appropriations act, President [George W.] Bush stated: "the Executive Branch will act, and encourage the courts to act, . . . in a manner consistent with the obligations of the United States under the Algiers Accords." In signing the bill containing the technical correction, the President issued a similar statement.

the district court rejected the argument is of no moment. Plaintiffs' opportunity to have it decided resulted directly from the amendments.

Affirmed.

NOTES AND QUESTIONS

1. **Origins of the "Later-in-Time Rule."** The judicial rule that a later-in-time statute overrides an earlier treaty dates from a series of nineteenth-century cases. For example, in *Whitney v. Robertson*, 124 U.S. 190 (1888), cited in *Kempthorne*, plaintiffs were importing sugar from the Dominican Republic. A treaty between the Dominican Republic and the United States specified that duties on Dominican sugar would not be higher than duties on sugar from other nations. A congressional act established duties on Dominican sugar higher than duties on sugar from Hawaii (then an independent country). Plaintiffs claimed they were entitled to the lower duty under the Treaty. In an often-cited passage, the Court ruled otherwise:

> The act of Congress under which the duties were collected authorized their exaction. . . . It was passed after the treaty with the Dominican Republic, and, if there be any conflict between the stipulations of the treaty and the requirements of the law, the latter must control. . . . By the Constitution, a treaty is placed on the same footing, and made of like obligation, with an act of legislation. Both are declared by that instrument to be the supreme law of the land, and no superior efficacy is given to either over the other. When the two relate to the same subject, the courts will always endeavor to construe them so as to give effect to both, if that can be done without violating the language of either; but if the two are inconsistent, the one last in date will control the other, provided always the stipulation of the treaty on the subject is self-executing. If the country with which the treaty is made is dissatisfied with the action of the legislative department, it may present its complaint to the executive head of the government and take such other measures as it may deem essential for the protection of its interests. The courts can afford no redress. Whether the complaining nation has just cause of complaint or our country was justified in its legislation are not matters for judicial cognizance.

2. **Policy and the Later-in-Time Rule.** The later-in-time rule is well entrenched in the courts but has been criticized in academic commentary. Note that the result of a statute superseding a treaty is ordinarily that the treaty remains a binding legal obligation of the United States in international law, with the statute putting the United States in violation of its international obligation. Is that a sensible result? Isn't the point of Article VI of the Constitution to assure that the United States' domestic law matches its international obligations? How might these considerations affect the courts in *Kempthorne* and *Roeder*?

3. **Later-in-Time Treaties.** If the later-in-time rule arises from the constitutional provision placing treaties and statutes "on the same footing," that implies that

a later treaty overrides a prior statute. The Supreme Court so held in *Cook v. United States*, 288 U.S. 102 (1933): "The Treaty, being later in date than the Act . . . superseded . . . the authority which had been conferred by [the Act] upon officers of the Coast Guard to board, search and seize beyond our territorial waters [citing *Whitney*]." Does that make sense? Is there a problem with having in effect two legislative bodies — Congress as a whole for statutes and two-thirds of the Senate for treaties — acting on the same subject matter?

4. **Presumption Against Violating Treaties.** Around the same time as *Whitney*, the Court developed the idea that statutes should not be construed to violate treaties if another reading of the statute was available. In *Chew Heong v. United States*, 112 U.S. 536 (1884), the plaintiff was a Chinese citizen who had been a resident of the United States. An 1880 treaty with China provided that U.S.-resident Chinese citizens could return freely to the United States after traveling abroad. Chew Heong traveled outside the United States starting in 1881. In 1882, Congress passed substantial restrictions on Chinese immigration to the United States. When Chew Heong tried to return to the United States in 1884, immigration authorities refused to admit him, which he argued violated the treaty. The Court began by observing:

> [T]he court should be slow to assume that Congress intended to violate the stipulations of a treaty, so recently made with the government of another country. "There would no longer be any security," says Vattel, "no longer any commerce between mankind, if they did not think themselves obliged to keep faith with each other, and to perform their promises." Vattel, Book 2, ch. 12. . . . A treaty that operates of itself without the aid of legislation is equivalent to an act of Congress, and while in force constitutes a part of the supreme law of the land. . . . [T]he court cannot be unmindful of the fact, that the honor of the government and people of the United States is involved in every inquiry whether rights secured by such stipulations shall be recognized and protected. And it would be wanting in proper respect for the intelligence and patriotism of a co-ordinate department of the government were it to doubt, for a moment, that these considerations were present in the minds of its members when the legislation in question was enacted.

The Court then applied a rule developed earlier for conflicting statutes:

> [E]ven in the case of statutes, whose repeal or modification involves no question of good faith with the government or people of other countries, the rule is well settled that repeals by implication are not favored, and are never admitted where the former can stand with the new act. Mr. Justice Story, speaking for the court upon a question of the repeal of a statute by implication, said: "That it has not been expressly or by direct terms repealed is admitted; and the question resolves itself into the narrow inquiry, whether it has been repealed by necessary implication. We say by necessary implication, for it is not sufficient to establish that subsequent laws cover some, or even all, of the cases provided for by it, for they may be merely affirmative, or cumulative, or auxiliary. But there must be a positive repugnancy between the provisions of the new laws and those of the old, and even then the old law is repealed by implication only *pro tanto*, to the extent of the repugnancy."

Applying this rule, the Court held that the statute provided an exception for Chinese laborers who had been in the United States at the time the treaty was adopted.

5. ***Chew Heong* as a Clear Statement Rule?** In *United States v. Palestine Liberation Organization*, 695 F. Supp. 1456 (S.D.N.Y. 1988), the court faced an apparent conflict between the United Nations Headquarters Agreement, a treaty establishing the U.N. headquarters in New York, and the Anti-terrorism Act of 1987 (ATA), a U.S. statute. The Headquarters Agreement appeared to allow all members and invitees of the United Nations to establish offices at the Headquarters. The United Nations had invited the Palestine Liberation Organization (PLO) to attend its sessions as an observer, and the PLO had established a "Mission" in New York for this purpose. The ATA specifically forbade the PLO from establishing any "office, headquarters, premises or other facilities or establishments within the jurisdiction of the United States." The court rejected a suit to close the PLO's U.N. Mission:

> [O]nly where a treaty is irreconcilable with a later enacted statute and Congress had clearly evinced an intent to supersede a treaty by enacting a statute does the later enacted statute take precedence. . . . The principles enunciated and applied in *Chew Heong* and its progeny . . . require the clearest of expressions on the part of Congress. . . . Congress' failure to speak with one clear voice on this subject requires us to interpret the ATA as inapplicable to the Headquarters Agreement.
>
> First, neither the Mission nor the Headquarters Agreement is mentioned in the ATA itself. . . . Second, the ATA . . . does not purport to apply notwithstanding any treaty. . . . Third, no member of Congress expressed a clear and unequivocal intent to supersede the Headquarters Agreement by passage of the ATA.
>
> It is nevertheless contended by the United States that the [ATA] requires the closing of the Mission. . . . The government argues that its position is supported by the provision that the ATA would take effect "notwithstanding any provision of law to the contrary" . . . suggesting that Congress thereby swept away any inconsistent international obligations of the United States. In effect, the government urges literal application of the maxim that in the event of conflict between two laws, the one of later date will prevail.
>
> We cannot agree. . . .

Why isn't the ATA unambiguous? Does this case ask too much of Congress?

6. **Finding Congressional Override of a Treaty.** Based on the foregoing cases, what is required for Congress to override a treaty? Unambiguous language? Or a clear statement? What is the difference? If there is a difference, which is the better rule? Are the cases reconcilable? Compare the statutory language in *Kempthorne, Roeder,* and the *PLO* case. Is there a clear statement in *Kempthorne*? Why isn't there a clear statement in *Roeder* or *PLO*?

7. **Subsequent History of the *Roeder* Litigation.** After the D.C. Circuit's decision in the *Roeder* case excerpted above, in 2008 Congress passed yet another amendment to the FSIA that provided an express cause of action

to sue countries designated as state sponsors of terrorism (as Iran was) for terrorist acts (including hostage-taking). 28 U.S.C. § 1605A(a). The amendment also specified that a court "shall hear a claim" under this section if it is "related to" Roeder's prior claim (which the statute specifically identified by case number). However, the amendment did not refer to the Algiers Accords. The *Roeder* plaintiffs re-filed their claim under this provision, arguing that it showed a clear intent to override the Algiers Accords' bar on suit for the 1979 hostage-taking episode. The district court again dismissed the claim, and the D.C. Circuit affirmed in another opinion by Judge Randolph. *Roeder v. Islamic Republic of Iran*, 646 F.3d 56 (D.C. Cir. 2011). The court observed:

> We do not deny the force of Roeder's argument. In the end it may well represent the best reading of [the applicable provisions]. But our focus is not on the best reading. Legislation abrogating international agreements "must be clear to ensure that Congress — and the President — have considered the consequences." *Roeder I*, 333 F.3d at 238. An ambiguous statute cannot super[s]ede an international agreement if an alternative reading is fairly possible. *Fund for Animals, Inc. v. Kempthorne*, 472 F.3d 872, 879 (D.C. Cir. 2006). This clear statement requirement — common in other areas of federal law, *see Roeder I*, 333 F.3d at 238 — "assures that the legislature has in fact faced, and intended to bring into issue, the critical matters involved in the judicial decision." *Gregory v. Ashcroft*, 501 U.S. 452, 461 (1991).

The court also observed: "In *Roeder I* we gave an example of language that might suffice to abrogate even without an express reference to the Accords, but the 2008 amendments contain no such language or anything comparable."

8. ***Chew Heong* and Non-Self-Executing Treaties.** A number of the early cases, including *Whitney* and *Chew Heong*, found a duty to reconcile statutes and treaties in the case of self-executing treaties. In a concurrence in *Kempthorne*, Judge Kavanaugh, writing only for himself, specifically argued that there is no such obligation for non-self-executing treaties:

> Like statutes, self-executing treaties automatically become part of domestic American law. By contrast, non-self-executing treaties have no effect or force as a matter of domestic law. . . . The canon against interpreting ambiguous statutes to abrogate treaties applies with respect to self-executing treaties which have the force of American law. The canon is quite similar to the familiar doctrine against implied repeal of statutes — under which courts will not interpret an ambiguous statute to repeal a prior statute.
>
> There is little authority squarely analyzing whether those interpretive principles should extend to *non-self-executing* treaties, which have no force as a matter of domestic law.
>
> Courts have reason to be cautious about taking that step, however. When the Legislative and Executive Branches have chosen not to incorporate certain provisions of a non-self-executing treaty into domestic law, we must assume that they acted intentionally. Given such a deliberate decision by the Legislative and Executive Branches, basic principles of judicial restraint counsel courts to refrain from bringing the non-self-executing treaty into domestic law through the back door (by using the treaty to resolve questions of American

law). In other words, because non-self-executing treaties have no legal status in American courts, there seems to be little justification for a court to put a thumb on the scale in favor of a non-self-executing treaty when interpreting a statute. Doing so would not reflect the appropriate judicial deference to the Legislative and Executive Branches in determining if, when, and how to incorporate treaty obligations into domestic law. . . .

To be sure, the canon has been referenced in passing in some cases that may involve non-self-executing treaties. And some have expressly concluded that the canon should apply even with respect to non-self-executing treaties. *See Ma v. Ashcroft*, 257 F.3d 1095, 1114 (9th Cir. 2001). . . . But that conclusion is questionable in light of the principles of judicial restraint outlined above. . . .

In *Ma v. Ashcroft*, cited in Judge Kavanaugh's concurrence, the court construed an immigration statute not to give the executive branch authority to indefinitely detain certain aliens who were not entitled to enter the United States but could not be returned to their home countries. The court relied in part on Article 9 of the ICCPR, a non-self-executing treaty, providing that "[n]o one shall be subjected to arbitrary arrest and detention." The court, with little analysis of the non-self-execution issue, invoked the general proposition (discussed in later sections) that an ambiguous statute should not be construed to violate international law.

9. **Note on Executive Agreements.** The international agreement in *Roeder* was an executive agreement (that is, an agreement signed only by the President without the consent of the Senate). As discussed in a subsequent section, executive agreements have been found constitutional under certain circumstances, in particular for claims settlements, and there is no doubt that they can constitute binding international obligations. Note that the court did not comment on whether the Algiers Accords' status as an executive agreement rather than a treaty for U.S. constitutional purposes mattered in deciding whether Congress had overridden it. Should it? What are the possible sources of the courts' duty to construe statutes not to override treaties? What do the possibilities suggest about their application to non-self-executing treaties or executive agreements?

10. **A Re-invigoration of the Later-in-Time Rule?** *Breard v. Greene*, 523 U.S. 371 (1998), was the first case in the Supreme Court's long-running confrontation with the Vienna Convention on Consular Relations (which continued in *Medellín*, discussed above). As in *Medellín*, Breard was a foreign national who had been arrested, tried, and sentenced to death in state court in the United States without being told of a right to contact his country's consulate, and as in *Medellín*, Breard did not object to this lack of notification during his trial. Breard then brought a federal habeas corpus petition challenging his sentence, arguing for the first time that he had been sentenced in violation of the Convention. The Court, denying the petition, wrote:

We have held "that an Act of Congress . . . is on a full parity with a treaty, and that when a statute which is subsequent in time is inconsistent with a treaty, the statute to the extent of conflict renders the treaty null." *Reid v. Covert*, 354 U.S. 1, 18 (1957) (plurality opinion); *see also Whitney v. Robertson*, 124 U.S. 190, 194 (1888) (holding that if a treaty and a federal statute conflict, "the one last in date will control the other"). The Vienna Convention — which arguably confers on an individual the right to consular assistance following arrest — has continuously been in effect since 1969. But in 1996, before Breard filed his habeas petition raising claims under the Vienna Convention, Congress enacted the Antiterrorism and Effective Death Penalty Act (AEDPA), which provides that a habeas petitioner alleging that he is held in violation of "treaties of the United States" will, as a general rule, not be afforded an evidentiary hearing if he "has failed to develop the factual basis of [the] claim in State court proceedings."

In what sense was AEDPA inconsistent with the Vienna Convention? Should the Court have tried to reconcile the two?

4. International Agreements and the U.S. Constitution

In addition to the issues examined so far, international agreements raise a number of important questions of U.S. constitutional law. Three are discussed here. First, to what extent may the United States make international agreements other than through the treaty-making clause of Article II, Section 2? Second, can treaties and other international agreements change or modify the scope of constitutional rights? Third, what is the relationship between treaty making and the federal structure of Congress's limited and enumerated powers?

a. Executive and Congressional-Executive Agreements

In modern U.S. practice, most international agreements are not made with Senate's advice and consent, as Article II, Section 2 seems to require (although some important treaties continue to be made that way). Many international agreements are made by the President with the approval of majorities of both houses of Congress — either through statutes authorizing the President to make future agreements on particular subjects or through statutes specifically approving agreements already signed by the President. These agreements are called "congressional-executive agreements." As the cases below describe, the President also sometimes makes agreements under the President's own constitutional authority, without statutory approval by Congress. These agreements are called "sole executive agreements," or just "executive agreements." The following cases consider their constitutionality and domestic effect.

United States v. Belmont

301 U.S. 324 (1937)

Mr. Justice SUTHERLAND delivered the opinion of the Court.

This is an action at law brought by petitioner [the United States] against respondents in a federal district court to recover a sum of money deposited by a Russian corporation (Petrograd Metal Works) with August Belmont, a private banker doing business in New York City. . . . A motion to dismiss the complaint for failure to state facts sufficient to constitute a cause of action was sustained by the district court, and its judgment was affirmed by the court below. . . .

The corporation had deposited with Belmont, prior to 1918, the sum of money which petitioner seeks to recover. In 1918, [after the Russian Revolution] the Soviet Government duly enacted a decree by which it dissolved, terminated and liquidated the corporation (together with others), and nationalized and appropriated all of its property and assets of every kind and wherever situated, including the deposit account with Belmont. As a result, the deposit became the property of the Soviet Government, and so remained until November 16, 1933, at which time the Soviet Government released and assigned to petitioner all amounts due to that government from American nationals, including the deposit account of the corporation with Belmont. Respondents failed and refused to pay the amount upon demand duly made by petitioner.

The assignment was effected by an exchange of diplomatic correspondence between the Soviet Government and the United States. The purpose was to bring about a final settlement of the claims and counterclaims between the Soviet Government and the United States, and it was agreed that the Soviet Government would take no steps to enforce claims against American nationals. . . . The assignment . . . [is part] of the larger plan to bring about a settlement of the rival claims of the [U.S. and Soviet governments]. The continuing and definite interest of the Soviet Government in the collection of assigned claims is evident, and the case, therefore, presents a question of public concern, the determination of which well might involve the good faith of the United States in the eyes of a foreign government. . . .

[The district court] took the view that . . . the nationalization decree, if enforced, would put into effect an act of confiscation. And it held that a judgment for the United States could not be had, because, in view of that result, it would be contrary to the controlling public policy of the State of New York.

[W]e are of opinion that no state policy can prevail against the international compact here involved.

We take judicial notice of the fact that, coincident with the assignment set forth in the complaint, the President recognized the Soviet Government, and normal diplomatic relations were established between that government and the Government of the United States, followed by an exchange of ambassadors. The effect of this was to validate, so far as this country is concerned, all acts of the Soviet Government here involved from the commencement of its existence. The recognition, establishment of diplomatic relations, the assignment, and agreements with respect thereto, were all parts of one transaction, resulting in an international compact between the two governments. That the negotiations, acceptance of the assignment, and agreements and understandings in respect thereof were within the competence of the President may not be doubted. Governmental power over internal affairs is distributed between the national government and the several states. Governmental power over external affairs is not distributed, but is vested exclusively in the national government.

And in respect of what was done here, the Executive had authority to speak as the sole organ of that government. The assignment and the agreements in connection therewith did not, as in the case of treaties, as that term is used in the treaty-making clause of the Constitution (Art. II, § 2), require the advice and consent of the Senate.

A treaty signifies "a compact made between two or more independent nations with a view to the public welfare." *Altman & Co. v. United States*, 224 U.S. 583. But an international compact, as this was, is not always a treaty which requires the participation of the Senate. There are many such compacts, of which a protocol, a *modus vivendi*, a postal convention, and agreements like that now under consideration are illustrations. *See* 5 Moore, Int. Law Digest, 210-221. The distinction was pointed out by this court in the *Altman* case, *supra*, which arose under § 3 of the Tariff Act of 1897, authorizing the President to conclude commercial agreements with foreign countries in certain specified matters. We held that, although this might not be a treaty requiring ratification by the Senate, it was a compact negotiated and proclaimed under the authority of the President, and as such was a "treaty" within the meaning of the Circuit Court of Appeals Act, the construction of which might be reviewed upon direct appeal to this court.

Plainly, the external powers of the United States are to be exercised without regard to state laws or policies. The supremacy of a treaty in this respect has been recognized from the beginning. Mr. Madison, in the Virginia Convention, said that, if a treaty does not supersede existing state laws as far as they contravene its operation, the treaty would be ineffective. "To counteract it by the supremacy of the state laws, would bring on the Union the just charge of national perfidy, and involve us in war." 3 Elliot's Debates 515. And see [*Ware v. Hylton*]. And while this rule in respect of treaties is established by the express language of cl. 2, Art. VI, of the Constitution, the same rule would result in the case of all international compacts and agreements from the very fact that complete power over international affairs is in the national government, and is not and cannot be subject to any curtailment or interference on the part of the several states. In respect of all international negotiations and compacts, and in respect of our foreign relations generally, state lines disappear. As to such purposes, the State of New York does not exist. Within the field of its powers, whatever the United States rightfully undertakes it necessarily has warrant to consummate. And when judicial authority is invoked in aid of such consummation, state constitutions, state laws, and state policies are irrelevant to the inquiry and decision. It is inconceivable that any of them can be interposed as an obstacle to the effective operation of a federal constitutional power.

It results that the complaint states a cause of action, and that the judgment of the court below to the contrary is erroneous. . . .

Judgment reversed.

[An opinion of Chief Justice Stone, joined by Justices Brandeis and Cardozo, concurring in the result, is omitted.]

Dames & Moore v. Regan

453 U.S. 654 (1981)

Justice REHNQUIST delivered the opinion of the Court.

I

On November 4, 1979, the American Embassy in Tehran was seized and our diplomatic personnel were captured and held hostage. In response to that crisis, President Carter, acting pursuant to the International Emergency Economic Powers Act (hereinafter IEEPA), . . . blocked the removal or transfer of [Iranian property in the United States]. . . .

On December 19, 1979, petitioner Dames & Moore filed suit in [federal court] . . . against the Government of Iran. . . . [Dames & Moore claimed it was owed over $3 million by Iran in connection with a contract to assist in building a nuclear power plant]. The District Court issued orders of attachment directed against property of the defendants. . . . On January 20, 1981, the Americans held hostage were released by Iran pursuant to an Agreement entered into the day before [known as the Algiers Accords]. . . . The Agreement stated that

> "[i]t is the purpose of [the United States and Iran] . . . to terminate all litigation as between the Government of each party and the nationals of the other, and to bring about the settlement and termination of all such claims through binding arbitration."

In furtherance of this goal, the Agreement called for the establishment of an Iran-United States Claims Tribunal which would arbitrate any claims not settled within six months. Awards of the Claims Tribunal are to be "final and binding," and "enforceable . . . in the courts of any nation in accordance with its laws." Under the Agreement, the United States is obligated "to terminate all legal proceedings in United States courts involving claims of United States persons and institutions against Iran and its state enterprises, to nullify all attachments and judgments obtained therein, to prohibit all further litigation based on such claims, and to bring about the termination of such claims through binding arbitration."

In addition, the United States must "act to bring about the transfer" by July 19, 1981, of all Iranian assets held in this country by American banks. One billion dollars of these assets will be deposited in a security account in the Bank of England, to the account of the Algerian Central Bank, and used to satisfy awards rendered against Iran by the Claims Tribunal.

On January 19, 1981, President Carter issued a series of Executive Orders implementing the terms of the agreement. . . . Moreover, he "suspended" all "claims which may be presented to the . . . Tribunal," and provided that such claims "shall have no legal effect in any action now pending in any court of the United States."

Meanwhile, on January 27, 1981, petitioner moved for summary judgment in the District Court against the Government of Iran. . . . The District Court granted petitioner's motion and awarded petitioner the amount claimed under the contract, plus interest. Thereafter, petitioner attempted to execute the judgment by obtaining writs of garnishment and execution in state court in the State of Washington, and a sheriff's sale of Iranian property in Washington was noticed to satisfy the judgment. However, . . . the District Court stayed execution of its judgment pending appeal by the Government of Iran [and] . . . ordered that all prejudgment attachments obtained against the Iranian defendants be vacated, and that further proceedings . . . be stayed in light of the Executive Orders discussed above.

[P]etitioner filed this action in the District Court for declaratory and injunctive relief against the United States and the Secretary of the Treasury, seeking to prevent enforcement of the Executive Orders and Treasury Department regulations implementing the Agreement with Iran. In its complaint, petitioner alleged that the actions of the President and the Secretary of the Treasury . . . were beyond their statutory and constitutional powers. . . . [The district court dismissed the complaint]. Arguing that this is a case of "imperative public importance," petitioner then sought a writ of certiorari before judgment. Because the issues presented here are of great significance and demand prompt resolution, we granted the petition for the writ, [and] adopted an expedited briefing schedule. . . .

II

The parties and the lower courts, confronted with the instant questions, have all agreed that much relevant analysis is contained in *Youngstown Sheet & Tube Co. v. Sawyer*, 343 U.S. 579 (1952). Justice Black's opinion for the Court in that case, involving the validity of President Truman's effort to seize the country's steel mills in the wake of a nationwide strike, recognized that "[t]he President's power, if any, to issue the order must stem either from an act of Congress or from the Constitution itself." Justice Jackson's concurring opinion elaborated in a general way the consequences of different types of interaction between the two democratic branches in assessing Presidential authority to act in any given case. When the President acts pursuant to an express or implied authorization from Congress, he exercises not only his powers but also those delegated by Congress. In such a case, the executive action

> "would be supported by the strongest of presumptions and the widest latitude of judicial interpretation, and the burden of persuasion would rest heavily upon any who might attack it."

When the President acts in the absence of congressional authorization, he may enter "a zone of twilight in which he and Congress may have concurrent authority, or in which its distribution is uncertain." In such a case, the analysis becomes more complicated, and the validity of the President's action, at least so far as separation of powers principles are concerned, hinges on a consideration of all the circumstances which might shed light on the views of the Legislative Branch toward such action, including "congressional inertia, indifference or quiescence." Finally, when the President acts in contravention of the will of Congress, "his power is at its lowest ebb," and the Court can sustain his actions "only by disabling the Congress from acting upon the subject."

[I]t is doubtless the case that executive action in any particular instance falls not neatly in one of three pigeonholes, but rather at some point along a spectrum running from explicit congressional authorization to explicit congressional prohibition. This is particularly true as respects cases such as the one before us, involving responses to international crises the nature of which Congress can hardly have been expected to anticipate in any detail.

III

[The Court held that the termination of the attachments was authorized by Congress in the IEEPA.]

IV

Although we have concluded that the IEEPA constitutes specific congressional authorization to the President to nullify the attachments and order the transfer of Iranian assets, there remains the question of the President's authority to suspend claims pending in American courts. . . .

We conclude that, although the IEEPA authorized the nullification of the attachments, it cannot be read to authorize the suspension of the claims. [The Court also concluded that a related statute, the Hostage Act, did not authorize suspension.] . . .

Concluding that neither the IEEPA nor the Hostage Act constitutes specific authorization of the President's action suspending claims, however, is not to say that these statutory provisions are entirely irrelevant to the question of the validity of the President's action. We think both statutes highly relevant in the looser sense of indicating congressional acceptance of a broad scope for executive action in circumstances such as those presented in this case. . . . [T]he IEEPA delegates broad authority to the President to act in times of national emergency with respect to property of a foreign country. The Hostage Act similarly indicates congressional willingness that the President have broad discretion when responding to the hostile acts of foreign sovereigns. . . .

Although we have declined to conclude that the IEEPA or the Hostage Act directly authorizes the President's suspension of claims for the reasons noted, we cannot ignore the general tenor of Congress' legislation in this area in trying to determine whether the President is acting alone, or at least with the acceptance of Congress. As we have noted, Congress cannot anticipate and legislate with regard to every possible action the President may find it necessary to take, or every possible situation in which he might act. Such failure of Congress specifically to delegate authority does not, "especially . . . in the areas of foreign policy and national security," imply "congressional disapproval" of action taken by the Executive. On the contrary, the enactment of legislation closely related to the question of the President's authority in a particular case which evinces legislative intent to accord the President broad discretion may be considered to "invite" "measures on independent presidential responsibility," *Youngstown*, 343 U.S. at 637 (Jackson, J., concurring). At least this is so where there is no contrary indication of legislative intent and when, as here, there is a history of congressional acquiescence in conduct of the sort engaged in by the President. It is to that history which we now turn.

Not infrequently in affairs between nations, outstanding claims by nationals of one country against the government of another country are "sources of friction" between the two sovereigns. To resolve these difficulties, nations have often entered into agreements settling the claims of their respective nationals. As one treatise writer puts it, international agreements settling claims by nationals of one state against the government of another "are established international practice reflecting traditional international theory." L. Henkin, Foreign Affairs and the Constitution 262 (1972). Consistent with that principle, the United States has repeatedly exercised its sovereign authority to settle the claims of its nationals against foreign countries. Though those settlements have sometimes been made by treaty, there has also been a longstanding practice of settling such claims by executive agreement, without the advice and consent of the Senate.[8] Under such agreements, the President has agreed to renounce or extinguish claims of United States nationals against foreign governments in return for lump-sum payments or the establishment of arbitration procedures. To be sure, many of these settlements were encouraged by the United States claimants themselves, since a claimant's only hope of obtaining any payment at all might lie in having his Government negotiate a diplomatic settlement on his behalf. But it is also undisputed that the United States has sometimes disposed of the claims of its citizens without their consent, or even without consultation with them, usually without exclusive regard for their interests, as distinguished from those of the nation as a whole. . . . Since 1952, the President has entered into at least 10 binding settlements with foreign nations, including an $80 million settlement with the People's Republic of China.

Crucial to our decision today is the conclusion that Congress has implicitly approved the practice of claim settlement by executive agreement. This is best demonstrated by Congress' enactment of the International Claims Settlement Act of 1949. The Act had two purposes: (1) to allocate to United States nationals funds received in the course of an executive claims settlement with Yugoslavia, and (2) to provide a procedure whereby funds resulting from future settlements could be distributed. To achieve these ends Congress created the International Claims Commission, now the Foreign Claims Settlement Commission, and gave it jurisdiction to make final and binding decisions with respect to claims by United States nationals against settlement funds. By creating a procedure to implement future settlement agreements, Congress placed its stamp of approval

---

8. At least since the case of the "Wilmington Packet" in 1799, Presidents have exercised the power to settle claims of United States nationals by executive agreement. In fact, during the period of 1817-1917, no fewer than eighty executive agreements were entered into by the United States looking toward the liquidation of claims of its citizens.

on such agreements. Indeed, the legislative history of the Act observed that the United States was seeking settlements with countries other than Yugoslavia, and that the bill contemplated settlements of a similar nature in the future.

Over the years, Congress has frequently amended the International Claims Settlement Act to provide for particular problems arising out of settlement agreements, thus demonstrating Congress' continuing acceptance of the President's claim settlement authority. . . .

In addition to congressional acquiescence in the President's power to settle claims, prior cases of this Court have also recognized that the President does have some measure of power to enter into executive agreements without obtaining the advice and consent of the Senate. . . .

. . .

In light of all of the foregoing — the inferences to be drawn from the character of the legislation Congress has enacted in the area, such as the IEEPA and the Hostage Act, and from the history of acquiescence in executive claims settlement — we conclude that the President was authorized to suspend pending claims pursuant to Executive Order No. 12294. As Justice Frankfurter pointed out in *Youngstown*, "a systematic, unbroken, executive practice, long pursued to the knowledge of the Congress and never before questioned. . .may be treated as a gloss on 'Executive Power' vested in the President by § 1 of Art. II." Past practice does not, by itself, create power, but "long-continued practice, known to and acquiesced in by Congress, would raise a presumption that the [action] had been [taken] in pursuance of its consent. . . ." *United States v. Midwest Oil Co.*, 236 U.S. 459 (1915). Such practice is present here, and such a presumption is also appropriate. In light of the fact that Congress may be considered to have consented to the President's action in suspending claims, we cannot say that action exceeded the President's powers.

. . . Just as importantly, Congress has not disapproved of the action taken here. Though Congress has held hearings on the Iranian Agreement itself, Congress has not enacted legislation, or even passed a resolution, indicating its displeasure with the Agreement. Quite the contrary, the relevant Senate Committee has stated that the establishment of the Tribunal is "of vital importance to the United States." We are thus clearly not confronted with a situation in which Congress has in some way resisted the exercise of Presidential authority.

Finally, we reemphasize the narrowness of our decision. We do not decide that the President possesses plenary power to settle claims, even as against foreign governmental entities. . . . But where, as here, the settlement of claims has been determined to be a necessary incident to the resolution of a major foreign policy dispute between our country and another, and where, as here, we can conclude that Congress acquiesced in the President's action, we are not prepared to say that the President lacks the power to settle such claims.

[Affirmed.]

[Separate opinions of Justice Stevens, concurring in part, and Justice Powell, concurring in part and dissenting in part, are omitted.]

1. **History and Practice of Non-Treaty Agreements.** As the Court indicated in *Dames & Moore*, international agreements not approved by a supermajority of the Senate date to the eighteenth century; initially they were used infrequently and typically for claims settlements and other minor matters. Michael D. Ramsey, *Executive Agreements and the (Non)Treaty Power*, 77 N.C. L. REV. 133 (1998). Since World War II they have become increasingly common. One study calculates that between 1990 and 2000 the United States entered into 249 treaties and 2,857 non-treaty agreements. Oona A. Hathaway, *Treaties' End: The Past, Present and Future of International Lawmaking in the United States*, 117 YALE L.J. 1236, 1287 (2008). What do you think accounts for this shift?

2. **Congressional-Executive Agreements.** In the area of tariff and trade regulation, in modern practice major international agreements are typically approved by a majority of the House and the Senate, in the manner of statutes. For example, the North American Free Trade Agreement (NAFTA) was approved in this manner in 1993, as was the agreement establishing the World Trade Organization (WTO) in 1994, the Dominican Republic-Central America-United States Free Trade Agreement (DR-CAFTA) in 2005, along with various bilateral free trade agreements. Approval of such agreements is typically accompanied by implementing legislation. As such, while they are subject to substantial academic debate as to their constitutionality, they typically do not raise practical litigation issues because in effect they have the status of statutes. In *Made in the USA Foundation v. United States*, 242 F.3d 1300 (11th Cir. 2001), an industry group challenged NAFTA on the ground that it had not been approved by two-thirds of the Senate. After the district court rejected the challenge, the court of appeals affirmed on the ground that the claim was a non-justiciable political question (see Chapter 12). Why do you think Congress and the President would opt for the congressional-executive agreement process over approval as a treaty? Does this process violate constitutional separation of powers? In addition to agreements with express congressional approval (as with NAFTA), the President makes many international agreements with implied or indirect statutory approval. These typically — but not always — involve relatively minor diplomatic matters. Are these agreements more problematic as a matter of constitutional separation of powers?

3. **Sole Executive Agreements.** In *United States v. Belmont*, the agreement had not been approved by either Congress as a whole or a supermajority of the Senate. *Belmont* indicated that at least some sole executive agreements may have the same constitutional status as treaties even though sole executive agreements are not mentioned in Article VI. That holding was reaffirmed in *United States v. Pink*, 315 U.S. 203 (1942), also involving President Roosevelt's agreement settling Soviet claims. Both *Pink* and *Belmont* involved executive agreements preempting state law. In *Roeder v. Islamic Republic of Iran, supra*,

the court of appeals treated the Algiers Accords (the executive agreement upheld in *Dames & Moore*) as equivalent to a treaty for purposes of the canon against abrogation. Whether executive agreements have the legal status of treaties in other respects (for example, the later-in-time rule or the ability to provide a cause of action) is unclear.

4. **The Scope of Executive Agreements.** The Supreme Court's principal cases on sole executive agreements involved claims settlements. In addition, the agreement in *Pink* and *Belmont* involved diplomatic recognition of the Soviet Union, a power thought to be a unilateral presidential power as a result of the President's power to receive ambassadors in Article II, Section 3 of the Constitution. The extent to which sole executive agreements may have domestic legal status outside of the settlement context remains unclear. In *Medellín v. Texas, supra*, in a discussion unrelated to the self-execution issue, the Court described its prior cases as "involv[ing] a narrow set of circumstances: the making of executive agreements to settle civil claims between American citizens and foreign governments or foreign nationals." Is that the right way to read *Belmont* and *Dames & Moore*? Is it the best result?

5. **The Law and Policy of Executive Agreements.** Does *Dames & Moore* follow *Belmont* or take a different approach? What seems most important to the Court in *Belmont*? What seems most important to the Court in *Dames & Moore*? How would you argue for a narrow reading of each of the decisions? What are the advantages of giving the President power to enter into executive agreements or congressional-executive agreements? What are the disadvantages? What would have happened if the Court ruled against the President in *Belmont* or *Dames & Moore*? What does that suggest about the need for executive agreement power?

6. **Executive Agreements and Prior Congressional Approval.** Some major congressional-executive agreements, including NAFTA, the WTO Agreement, and DR-CAFTA, have received express congressional approval after they were negotiated and signed, in the manner of treaties (except without a requirement of a Senate supermajority). But in many cases, the executive branch has argued that Congress's delegation of power to the President in a particular area implicitly includes power to make international agreements. For example, in 2011, President Obama's administration signed the Anti-Counterfeiting Trade Agreement (ACTA), a multilateral agreement on intellectual property rights enforcement. Initially, the executive branch argued that the agreement could be done on the President's independent authority as a sole executive agreement. After substantial objections, including from members of Congress, the administration shifted ground to argue that Congress previously had approved the agreement implicitly in statutes generally authorizing the President to take action to prevent copyright abuse. How would you argue, under *Belmont* and *Dames & Moore*, that the ACTA did or did not require further approval from Congress or the Senate? Are presidential agreements with (arguable) prior congressional approval more or less problematic, constitutionally or practically, than sole executive agreements?

b. Treaties and Constitutional Rights

A second important constitutional issue is whether treaties are subject to the individual rights protections of the U.S. Constitution. Recall that as a matter of international law, generally the domestic law of a treaty party does not excuse noncompliance with the treaty; thus, in asking whether the Constitution invalidates treaty provisions, the question is only one of U.S. domestic law, not of international law.

Reid v. Covert

354 U.S. 1 (1956)

Mr. Justice BLACK announced the judgment of the Court and delivered an opinion, in which THE CHIEF JUSTICE, Mr. Justice DOUGLAS, and Mr. Justice BRENNAN join.

These cases raise basic constitutional issues of the utmost concern. They call into question the role of the military under our system of government. They involve the power of Congress to expose civilians to trial by military tribunals, under military regulations and procedures, for offenses against the United States, thereby depriving them of trial in civilian courts, under civilian laws and procedures and with all the safeguards of the Bill of Rights. These cases are particularly significant because, for the first time since the adoption of the Constitution, wives of soldiers have been denied trial by jury in a court of law and forced to trial before courts-martial.

. . . Mrs. Clarice Covert killed her husband, a sergeant in the United States Air Force, at an airbase in England. Mrs. Covert, who was not a member of the armed services, was residing on the base with her husband at the time. She was tried by a court-martial for murder under Article 118 of the Uniform Code of Military Justice (UCMJ). The trial was on charges preferred by Air Force personnel, and the court-martial was composed of Air Force officers. The court-martial asserted jurisdiction over Mrs. Covert under Article 2(11) of the UCMJ. . . .

Counsel for Mrs. Covert contended that she was insane at the time she killed her husband, but the military tribunal found her guilty of murder and sentenced her to life imprisonment. . . . [H]er counsel petitioned the District Court for a writ of habeas corpus to set her free on the ground that the Constitution forbade her trial by military authorities. [The District Court granted the writ, and the United States appealed.]

[The opinion first concluded that Covert was protected by the Constitution and the Bill of Rights, even though tried abroad. The opinion further found that Covert's military trial violated Article III, Section 2 of the Constitution and the Fifth and Sixth Amendments.]

At the time of Mrs. Covert's alleged offense, an executive agreement was in effect between the United States and Great Britain which permitted [the] United States' military courts to exercise exclusive jurisdiction over offenses committed in Great Britain by American servicemen or their dependents. For its part, the United States agreed that these military courts would be willing and able to try and to punish all offenses against the laws of Great Britain by such persons. . . . Even though a court-martial does not give an accused trial by jury and other Bill of Rights protections, the Government contends that . . . [the court-martial procedures are valid] under the international agreements made with those countries. The obvious and decisive answer to this, of course, is that no agreement with a foreign nation can confer power on the Congress, or on any other branch of Government, which is free from the restraints of the Constitution.

. . . There is nothing in [Article VI of the Constitution] which intimates that treaties and laws enacted pursuant to them do not have to comply with the provisions of the Constitution. Nor is there anything in the debates which accompanied the drafting and ratification of the Constitution which even suggests such a result. . . . It would be manifestly contrary to the objectives of those who created the Constitution, as well as those who were responsible for the Bill of Rights — let alone alien to our entire constitutional history and tradition — to construe Article VI as permitting the United States to exercise power under an international agreement without observing constitutional prohibitions. In effect, such construction would permit amendment of that document in a manner not sanctioned by Article V. The prohibitions of the Constitution were designed to apply to all branches of the National Government, and they cannot be nullified by the Executive or by the Executive and the Senate combined.

There is nothing new or unique about what we say here. This Court has regularly and uniformly recognized the supremacy of the Constitution over a treaty. For example, in *Geofroy v. Riggs*, 133 U.S. 258, it declared:

> "The treaty power, as expressed in the Constitution, is in terms unlimited except by those restraints which are found in that instrument against the action of the government or of its departments, and those arising from the nature of the government itself and of that of the States. It would not be contended that it extends so far as to authorize what the Constitution forbids, or a change in the character of the government, or in that of one of the States, or a cession of any portion of the territory of the latter, without its consent."

This Court has also repeatedly taken the position that an Act of Congress, which must comply with the Constitution, is on a full parity with a treaty, and that, when a statute which is subsequent in time is inconsistent with a treaty, the statute to the extent of conflict renders the treaty null. [*Whitney v. Robertson.*] It would be completely anomalous to say that a treaty need not comply with the Constitution when such an agreement can be overridden by a statute that must conform to that instrument.

. . .

Affirmed.

[Justices Frankfurter and Harlan concurred in the result, limiting it to capital cases, without materially discussing the treaty issue. Justices Clark and Burton dissented on the ground that Congress's power to make rules for the government and regulation of the armed forces (Article I, Section 8) included the power to create courts-martial for military dependents. Justice Whittaker did not participate.]

Boos v. Barry

485 U.S. 312 (1988)

[A District of Columbia law made it illegal to display any sign that tends to bring a foreign government into "public odium" or "public disrepute" within 500 feet of that nation's embassy. Petitioners, who wished to protest in front of the Soviet and Nicaraguan embassies, filed suit in federal district court against respondent city officials, asserting a First Amendment challenge. The court granted respondents' motion for summary judgment, and the court of appeals affirmed.]

Justice O'CONNOR delivered the opinion of the Court.

. . .

Our cases indicate that as a content-based restriction on political speech in a public forum, [the D.C. law] must be subjected to the most exacting scrutiny. Thus, we have required the [government] to show that the "regulation is necessary to serve a compelling state interest and that it is narrowly drawn to achieve that end." . . .

We first consider whether the display clause serves a compelling governmental interest in protecting the dignity of foreign diplomatic personnel. Since the dignity of foreign officials will be affronted by signs critical of their governments or governmental policies, we are told, these foreign diplomats must be shielded from such insults in order to fulfill our country's obligations under international law.

As a general matter, we have indicated that, in public debate, our own citizens must tolerate insulting, and even outrageous, speech in order to provide adequate breathing space to the freedoms protected by the First Amendment. A "dignity" standard . . . is so inherently subjective that it would be inconsistent with our longstanding refusal to punish speech because the speech in question may have an adverse emotional impact on the audience.

We are not persuaded that the differences between foreign officials and American citizens require us to deviate from these principles here. The dignity interest is said to be compelling in this context primarily because its recognition and protection is part of the United States' obligations under international law. The Vienna Convention on Diplomatic Relations . . . imposes on host states

> "[the] special duty to take all appropriate steps to protect the premises of the mission against any intrusion or damage and to prevent any disturbance of the peace of the mission or impairment of its dignity."

As a general proposition, it is of course correct that the United States has a vital national interest in complying with international law. The Constitution itself attempts to further this interest by expressly authorizing Congress "[t]o define and punish Piracies and Felonies committed on the high Seas, and Offenses against the Law of Nations." U.S. Const., Art. I, § 8, cl. 10. Moreover, protecting foreign emissaries has a long history and noble purpose. . . .

The need to protect diplomats is grounded in our Nation's important interest in international relations. As a leading commentator observed in 1758,

> "[i]t is necessary that nations should treat and hold intercourse together, in order to promote their interests, — to avoid injuring each other, — and to adjust and terminate their disputes."

E. Vattel, The Law of Nations 452 (J. Chitty ed. 1844) (translation). This observation is even more true today, given the global nature of the economy and the extent to which actions in other parts of the world affect our own national security. Diplomatic personnel are essential to conduct the international affairs so crucial to the wellbeing of this Nation. In addition, in light of the concept of reciprocity that governs much of international law in this area, we have a more parochial reason to protect foreign diplomats in this country. Doing so ensures that similar protections will be accorded those that we send abroad to represent the United States, and thus serves our national interest in protecting our own citizens. Recent history is replete with attempts, some unfortunately successful, to harass and harm our ambassadors and other diplomatic officials. These underlying purposes combine to make our national interest in protecting diplomatic personnel powerful indeed.

At the same time, it is well established that

> "no agreement with a foreign nation can confer power on the Congress, or on any other branch of Government, which is free from the restraints of the Constitution."

Reid v. Covert, 354 U.S. 1 (1957). *See* 1 Restatement of Foreign Relations Law of the United States § 131, Comment a, p. 53 (Tent. Draft No. 6, Apr. 12, 1985) ("[R]ules of international law and provisions of international agreements of the United States are subject to the Bill of Rights and other prohibitions, restrictions or requirements of the Constitution, and cannot be given effect in violation of them").

Thus, the fact that an interest is recognized in international law does not automatically render that interest "compelling" for purposes of First Amendment analysis. We need not decide today whether, or to what extent, the dictates of international law could ever require that First Amendment analysis be adjusted to accommodate the interests of foreign officials. Even if we assume that international law recognizes a dignity interest and that it should be considered sufficiently "compelling" to support a content-based restriction on speech, we conclude that [the D.C. law] is not narrowly tailored to serve that interest.

[Reversed.]

[Justices Brennan, Marshall, Stevens, and Scalia joined Justice O'Connor's opinion, although Justices Brennan and Marshall concurred separately to disagree on a different point. Chief Justice Rehnquist, joined by Justices White and Blackmun, dissented, stating: "For the reasons stated by Judge Bork in his majority opinion below, I would uphold [the law.]" In the lower court opinion, a divided panel had upheld the restriction, relying heavily on the international law requiring protection of diplomats. After reviewing the extensive history of laws enacted to protect diplomats and emphasizing the requirements of the Vienna Convention, Judge Bork concluded:

> The obligations of the United States under international law, reaffirmed by treaty, do not, of course, supersede the first amendment. Neither, however, has it ever

been suggested that the first amendment is incompatible with the United States' most basic obligations under the law of nations. The two must be accommodated and [the District Columbia law under review] accomplishes an accommodation well within the range of the permissible.

Judge Wald dissented. *Finzer v. Barry*, 798 F.2d 1450 (D.C. Cir. 1986).]

NOTES AND QUESTIONS

1. **Treaties and the Constitution.** Is the question in *Reid* a hard one? Is it obvious that a treaty can't override the Constitution? Why can't the President and Congress pursuant to the treaty power change the constitutional rules applicable to persons on a military base abroad?

2. **Complying with International Law as a "Compelling" Interest.** Is the result in *Boos* compelled by the decision in *Reid*? How does Judge Bork in the lower court opinion argue it is not? Does the decision in *Boos* foreclose any limits on free speech arising from international law? Article 20 of the ICCPR requires that "[a]ny propaganda for war shall be prohibited by law" and "[a]ny advocacy of national, racial or religious hatred that constitutes incitement to discrimination, hostility or violence shall be prohibited by law." Could these provisions be used to justify U.S. laws that otherwise violate the First Amendment?

3. **Implications for Treaty Compliance.** If the United States is unable to comply with a treaty provision because doing so would violate the U.S. Constitution, can the United States use this as an excuse for noncompliance? This question draws attention once again to the distinction between domestic and international effect. The Constitution may prevent the United States from giving effect to a treaty provision. However, according to Article 27 of the Vienna Convention on the Law of Treaties, "[a] party may not invoke the provisions of its internal law as justification for its failure to perform a treaty." Therefore, a nation's noncompliance with a treaty — even if necessary to comply with its constitution (or other parts of its national law) — may lead to a violation of international law. What would be the violation of international law in *Boos* and *Reid*?

---

c. Treaties and Federalism

If treaties cannot override the Constitution's individual rights protections, can they change the Constitution's allocations of power between the States and the national government? The following case addresses this question in the context of a prosecution under federal law of a local offense that might not have been within the federal government's power but for a treaty.

Bond v. United States
572 U.S. 844 (2014)

Chief Justice ROBERTS delivered the opinion of the Court.

. . .

I

A

In 1997, the President of the United States, upon the advice and consent of the Senate, ratified the Convention on the Prohibition of the Development, Production, Stockpiling, and Use of Chemical Weapons and on Their Destruction. The nations that ratified the Convention had bold aspirations for it: "general and complete disarmament under strict and effective international control, including the prohibition and elimination of all types of weapons of mass destruction." This purpose traces its origin to World War I, when "[o]ver a million casualties, up to 100,000 of them fatal, are estimated to have been caused by chemicals . . . , a large part following the introduction of mustard gas in 1917." Kenyon, Why We Need a Chemical Weapons Convention and an OPCW, in The Creation of the Organisation for the Prohibition of Chemical Weapons 1, 4 (I. Kenyon & D. Feakes eds. 2007). . . .

The Convention provides:

> "(1) Each State Party to this Convention undertakes never under any circumstances:
>> "(a) To develop, produce, otherwise acquire, stockpile or retain chemical weapons, or transfer, directly or indirectly, chemical weapons to anyone;
>> "(b) To use chemical weapons;
>> "(c) To engage in any military preparations to use chemical weapons;
>> "(d) To assist, encourage or induce, in any way, anyone to engage in any activity prohibited to a State Party under this Convention." Art. I.

"Chemical Weapons" are defined in relevant part as "[t]oxic chemicals and their precursors, except where intended for purposes not prohibited under this Convention, as long as the types and quantities are consistent with such purposes." Art. II(1)(a). "Toxic Chemical," in turn, is defined as "Any chemical which through its chemical action on life processes can cause death, temporary incapacitation or permanent harm to humans or animals. This includes all such chemicals, regardless of their origin or of their method of production, and regardless of whether they are produced in facilities, in munitions or elsewhere." Art. II(2). "Purposes Not Prohibited Under this Convention" means "[i]ndustrial, agricultural, research, medical, pharmaceutical or other peaceful purposes," Art. II(9)(a). . . .

Although the Convention is a binding international agreement, it is not self-executing. That is, the Convention creates obligations only for State Parties and "does not by itself give rise to domestically enforceable federal law" absent "implementing legislation passed by Congress." *Medellín v. Texas*, 552 U.S. 491, 505, n.2 (2008). It instead provides that "[e]ach State Party shall, in accordance with its constitutional processes, adopt the necessary measures to implement its obligations under this Convention." Art. VII(1). "In particular," each State Party shall "[p]rohibit natural and legal persons anywhere . . . under its jurisdiction . . . from undertaking any activity prohibited to a State Party under this Convention, including enacting penal legislation with respect to such activity." Art. VII(1)(a).

Congress gave the Convention domestic effect in 1998 when it passed the Chemical Weapons Convention Implementation Act. The Act closely tracks the text of the treaty: It forbids any person knowingly "to develop, produce, otherwise acquire, transfer directly or indirectly, receive, stockpile, retain, own, possess, or use, or threaten to use, any chemical weapon." 18 U.S.C. § 229(a)(1). It defines "chemical weapon" in relevant part as "[a] toxic chemical and its precursors, except where intended for a purpose not prohibited under this chapter as long as the type and quantity is consistent with such a purpose." § 229F(1)(A). "Toxic chemical," in turn, is defined in general as "any chemical which through its chemical action on life processes can cause death, temporary incapacitation or permanent harm to humans or animals. . . ." § 229F(8)(A). Finally, "purposes not prohibited by this chapter" is defined as "[a]ny peaceful purpose related to an industrial, agricultural, research, medical, or pharmaceutical activity or other activity," and other specific purposes. § 229F(7). A person who violates section 229 may be subject to severe punishment: imprisonment "for any term of years," or if a victim's death results, the death penalty or imprisonment "for life." § 229A(a).

B

Petitioner Carol Anne Bond is a microbiologist from Lansdale, Pennsylvania. In 2006, Bond's closest friend, Myrlinda Haynes, announced that she was pregnant. When Bond discovered that her husband was the child's father, she sought revenge against Haynes. Bond stole a quantity of 10-chloro-10H-phenoxarsine (an arsenic-based compound) from her employer, a chemical manufacturer. She also ordered a vial of potassium dichromate (a chemical commonly used in printing photographs or cleaning laboratory equipment) on Amazon.com. Both chemicals are toxic to humans and, in high enough doses, potentially lethal. It is undisputed, however, that Bond did not intend to kill Haynes. She instead hoped that Haynes would touch the chemicals and develop an uncomfortable rash.

Between November 2006 and June 2007, Bond went to Haynes's home on at least 24 occasions and spread the chemicals on her car door, mailbox, and doorknob. These attempted assaults were almost entirely unsuccessful. The chemicals that Bond used are easy to see, and Haynes was able to avoid them all but once. On that occasion, Haynes suffered a minor chemical burn on her thumb, which she treated by rinsing with water. Haynes repeatedly called the local police to report the suspicious substances, but they took no action. When Haynes found powder on her mailbox, she called the police again, who told her to call the post office. Haynes did so, and postal inspectors placed surveillance cameras around her home. The cameras caught Bond opening Haynes's mailbox, stealing an envelope, and stuffing potassium dichromate inside the muffler of Haynes's car.

Federal prosecutors naturally charged Bond with two counts of mail theft, in violation of 18 U.S.C. § 1708. More surprising, they also charged her with two counts of possessing and using a chemical weapon, in violation of section 229(a). Bond moved to dismiss the chemical weapon counts on the ground that section 229 exceeded Congress's enumerated powers and invaded powers reserved to the States by the Tenth Amendment. The District Court denied Bond's motion. She then entered a conditional guilty plea that reserved her right to appeal. The District Court sentenced Bond to six years in federal prison plus five years of supervised release, and ordered her to pay a $2,000 fine and $9,902.79 in restitution.

. . .

The Third Circuit . . . rejected Bond's constitutional challenge to her conviction, holding that section 229 was necessary and proper to carry the Convention into effect. The Court of Appeals relied on this Court's opinion in *Missouri v. Holland*, 252 U.S. 416 (1920), which stated that "[i]f the treaty is valid there can be no dispute about the validity of the statute" that implements it "as a necessary and proper means to execute the powers of the Government," *id.*, at 432.

We . . . granted certiorari. . . .

II

In our federal system, the National Government possesses only limited powers; the States and the people retain the remainder. The States have broad authority to enact legislation for the public good — what we have often called a "police power." *United States v. Lopez*, 514 U.S. 549, 567 (1995). The Federal Government, by contrast, has no such authority and "can exercise only the powers granted to it," *McCulloch v. Maryland*, 4 Wheat. 316, 405 (1819), including the power to make "all Laws which shall be necessary and proper for carrying into Execution" the enumerated powers, U.S. Const., Art. I, § 8, cl. 18. . . .

The Government frequently defends federal criminal legislation on the ground that the legislation is authorized pursuant to Congress's power to regulate interstate commerce. In this case, however, . . . the Government . . . explicitly disavowed that argument before the District Court. As a result, in this Court the parties have devoted significant effort to arguing whether section 229, as applied to Bond's offense, is a necessary and proper means of executing the National Government's power to make treaties. Bond argues that the lower court's reading of *Missouri v. Holland* would remove all limits on federal authority, so long as the Federal Government ratifies a treaty first. She insists that to effectively afford the Government a police power whenever it implements a treaty would be contrary to the Framers' careful decision to divide power between the States and the National Government as a means of preserving liberty. To the extent that *Holland* authorizes such usurpation of traditional state authority, Bond says, it must be either limited or overruled.

The Government replies that this Court has never held that a statute implementing a valid treaty exceeds Congress's enumerated powers. To do so here, the Government says, would contravene another deliberate choice of the Framers: to avoid placing subject matter limitations on the National Government's power to make treaties. And it might also undermine confidence in the United States as an international treaty partner.

Notwithstanding this debate, it is "a well-established principle governing the prudent exercise of this Court's jurisdiction that normally the Court will not decide a constitutional question if there is some other ground upon which to dispose of the case." *Escambia County v. McMillan*, 466 U.S. 48, 51 (1984) *(per curiam)*; . . . Bond argues that section 229 does not cover her conduct. So we consider that argument first.

III

Section 229 exists to implement the Convention, so we begin with that international agreement. As explained, the Convention's drafters intended for it to be a comprehensive ban on chemical weapons. But even with its broadly worded definitions, we have doubts that a treaty about *chemical weapons* has anything to do with Bond's conduct. The Convention, a product of years of worldwide study, analysis, and multinational negotiation, arose in response to war crimes and acts of terrorism. There is no reason to think the sovereign nations that ratified the Convention were interested in anything like Bond's common law assault.

Even if the treaty does reach that far, nothing prevents Congress from implementing the Convention in the same manner it legislates with respect to innumerable other matters — observing the Constitution's division of responsibility between sovereigns and leaving the prosecution of purely local crimes to the States. . . .

Fortunately, we have no need to interpret the scope of the Convention in this case. Bond was prosecuted under section 229, and the statute — unlike the Convention — must be read consistent with principles of federalism inherent in our constitutional structure.

A

In the Government's view, the conclusion that Bond "knowingly" "use[d]" a "chemical weapon" in violation of section 229(a) is simple: The chemicals that Bond placed on Haynes's home and car are "toxic chemical[s]" as defined by the statute, and Bond's attempt to assault Haynes was not a "peaceful purpose." §§ 229F(1), (8), (7). The problem with this interpretation is that it would "dramatically intrude[ ] upon traditional state criminal jurisdiction," and we avoid reading statutes to have such reach in the absence of a clear indication that they do. *United States v. Bass*, 404 U.S. 336, 350 (1971).

Part of a fair reading of statutory text is recognizing that Congress legislates against the backdrop of certain unexpressed presumptions. . . . For example, . . . we presume, absent a clear statement from Congress, that federal statutes do not apply outside the United States. *Morrison v. National Australia Bank Ltd.*, 561 U.S. 247, 255 (2010). So even though section 229, read on its face, would cover a chemical weapons crime if committed by a U.S. citizen in Australia, we would not apply the statute to such conduct absent a plain statement from Congress. The notion that some things "go without saying" applies to legislation just as it does to everyday life.

Among the background principles of construction that our cases have recognized are those grounded in the relationship between the Federal Government and the States under our Constitution. [Multiple citations are omitted.]

[W]hen legislation "affect[s] the federal balance, the requirement of clear statement assures that the legislature has in fact faced, and intended to bring into issue, the critical matters involved in the judicial decision." *Bass, supra*, at 349.

. . .

These precedents make clear that it is appropriate to refer to basic principles of federalism embodied in the Constitution to resolve ambiguity in a federal statute. In this case, the ambiguity derives from the improbably broad reach of the key statutory definition given the term — "chemical weapon" — being defined; the deeply serious consequences of adopting such a boundless reading; and the lack of any apparent need to do so in light of the context from which the statute arose — a treaty about chemical warfare and terrorism. We conclude that, in this curious case, we can insist on a clear indication that Congress meant to reach purely local crimes, before interpreting the statute's expansive language in a way that intrudes on the police power of the States.

B

We do not find any such clear indication in section 229. "Chemical weapon" is the key term that defines the statute's reach, and it is defined extremely broadly. But that general definition does not constitute a clear statement that Congress meant the statute to reach local criminal conduct.

In fact, a fair reading of section 229 suggests that it does not have as expansive a scope as might at first appear. To begin, as a matter of natural meaning, an educated user of English would not describe Bond's crime as involving a "chemical weapon." Saying that a person "used a chemical weapon" conveys a very different idea than saying the person "used a chemical in a way that caused some harm." The natural meaning of "chemical weapon" takes account of both the particular chemicals that the defendant used and the circumstances in which she used them.

When used in the manner here, the chemicals in this case are not of the sort that an ordinary person would associate with instruments of chemical warfare. . . .

The Government would have us brush aside the ordinary meaning and adopt a reading of section 229 that would sweep in everything from the detergent under the kitchen sink to the stain remover in the laundry room. Yet no one would ordinarily describe those substances as "chemical weapons." . . . That the statute *would* apply so broadly, however, is the inescapable conclusion of the Government's position: Any parent would be guilty of a serious federal offense — possession of a chemical weapon — when, exasperated by the children's repeated failure to clean the goldfish tank, he considers poisoning the fish with a few drops of vinegar. We are reluctant to ignore the ordinary meaning of "chemical weapon" when doing so would transform a statute passed to implement the international Convention on Chemical Weapons into one that also makes it a federal offense to poison goldfish. . . .

The Government's reading of section 229 would alter sensitive federal-state relationships, convert an astonishing amount of traditionally local criminal conduct into a matter for federal enforcement, and involve a substantial extension of federal police resources. It would transform the statute from one whose core concerns are acts of war, assassination, and terrorism into a massive federal anti-poisoning regime that reaches the simplest of assaults. As the Government reads section 229, hardly a poisoning in the land would fall outside the federal statute's domain. Of course Bond's conduct is serious and unacceptable — and against the laws of Pennsylvania. But the background principle that Congress does not normally intrude upon the police power of the States is critically important. In light of that principle, we are reluctant to conclude that Congress meant to punish Bond's crime with a federal prosecution for a chemical weapons attack.

. . .

It is also clear that the laws of the Commonwealth of Pennsylvania (and every other State) are sufficient to prosecute Bond. Pennsylvania has several statutes that would likely cover her assault. . . .

The Government objects that Pennsylvania authorities charged Bond with only a minor offense based on her harassing telephone calls and letters, and declined to prosecute her for assault. But we have traditionally viewed the exercise of state officials' prosecutorial discretion as a valuable feature of our constitutional system. And nothing in the Convention shows a clear intent to abrogate that feature. Prosecutorial discretion involves carefully weighing the benefits of a prosecution against the evidence needed to convict, the resources of the public fisc, and the public policy of the State. . . .

In sum, the global need to prevent chemical warfare does not require the Federal Government to reach into the kitchen cupboard, or to treat a local assault with a chemical irritant as the deployment of a chemical weapon. There is no reason to suppose that Congress — in implementing the Convention on Chemical Weapons — thought otherwise.

The judgment of the Court of Appeals is reversed, and the case is remanded for further proceedings consistent with this opinion.

. . .

Justice SCALIA, with whom Justice THOMAS joins, and with whom Justice ALITO joins as to Part I, concurring in the judgment.

Somewhere in Norristown, Pennsylvania, a husband's paramour suffered a minor thumb burn at the hands of a betrayed wife. The United States Congress . . . has made a federal case out of it. What are we to do?

It is the responsibility of "the legislature, not the Court, . . . to define a crime, and ordain its punishment." *United States v. Wiltberger*, 5 Wheat. 76, 95 (1820) (Marshall, C.J., for the Court). And it is "emphatically the province and duty of the judicial department to say what the law [including the Constitution] is." *Marbury v. Madison*, 1 Cranch 137, 177 (1803) (same). Today, the Court shirks its job and performs Congress's. As sweeping and unsettling as the Chemical Weapons Convention Implementation Act of 1998 may be, it is clear beyond doubt that it covers what Bond did; and we have no authority to amend it. So we are forced to decide — there is no way around it — whether the Act's application to what Bond did was constitutional.

I would hold that it was not. . . .

I. The Statutory Question

A. Unavoidable Meaning of the Text

The meaning of the Act is plain. No person may knowingly "develop, produce, otherwise acquire, transfer directly or indirectly, receive, stockpile, retain, own, possess, or use, or threaten to use, any chemical weapon." 18 U.S.C. § 229(a)(1). A "chemical weapon" is "[a] toxic chemical and its precursors, except where intended for a purpose not prohibited under this chapter as long as the type and quantity is consistent with such a purpose." § 229F(1)(A). A "toxic chemical" is "any chemical which through its chemical action on life processes can cause death, temporary incapacitation or permanent harm to humans or animals. The term includes all such chemicals, regardless of their origin or of their method of production, and regardless of whether they are produced in facilities, in munitions or elsewhere." § 229F(8)(A). A "purpose not prohibited" is "[a]ny peaceful purpose related to an industrial, agricultural, research, medical, or pharmaceutical activity or other activity." § 229F(7)(A).

Applying those provisions to this case is hardly complicated. Bond possessed and used "chemical[s] which through [their] chemical action on life processes can cause death, temporary incapacitation or permanent harm." Thus, she possessed "toxic chemicals." And, because they were not possessed or used only for a "purpose not prohibited," § 229F(1)(A), they were "chemical weapons." Ergo, Bond violated the Act. End of statutory analysis, I would have thought.

The Court does not think the interpretive exercise so simple. But that is only because its result-driven antitextualism befogs what is evident.

. . .

[A section disputing the Court's finding of ambiguity is omitted.]

II. The Constitutional Question

Since the Act is clear, the *real* question this case presents is whether the Act is constitutional as applied to petitioner. An unreasoned and citation-less sentence from our opinion in *Missouri v. Holland*, 252 U.S. 416 (1920), purported to furnish the answer: "If the treaty is valid" — and no one argues that the Convention is not — "there can be no dispute about the validity of the statute under Article I, § 8, as a necessary and proper means to execute the powers of the Government." *Id.*, at 432. Petitioner and her *amici* press us to consider whether there is anything to this *ipse dixit*. The Constitution's text and structure show that there is not.

A. Text

Under Article I, § 8, cl. 18, Congress has the power "[t]o make all Laws which shall be necessary and proper for carrying into Execution the foregoing Powers and all other Powers vested by this Constitution in the Government of the United States, or in any Department or Officer thereof." One such "other Powe[r]" appears in Article II, § 2, cl. 2: "[The President] shall have Power, by and with the Advice and Consent of the Senate, to make Treaties, provided two thirds of the Senators present concur." Read together, the two Clauses empower Congress to pass laws "necessary and proper for carrying into Execution . . . [the] Power . . . to make Treaties."

It is obvious what the Clauses, read together, do *not* say. They do not authorize Congress to enact laws for carrying into execution "Treaties," even treaties that do not execute themselves, such as the Chemical Weapons Convention. . . .

. . . A treaty is a contract with a foreign nation *made*, the Constitution states, by the President with the concurrence of "two thirds of the Senators present." . . . So, because the President and the Senate can enter into a non-self-executing compact with a foreign nation but can never by themselves (without the House) give that compact domestic effect through legislation, the power of the President and the Senate "to make" a Treaty cannot possibly mean to "enter into a compact with a foreign nation and then give that compact domestic legal effect." . . . Upon the President's agreement and the Senate's ratification, a treaty — no matter what kind — has been *made* and is not susceptible of any more making.

How might Congress have helped "carr[y]" the power to make the treaty — here, the Chemical Weapons Convention — "into Execution"? . . . It could have appropriated money for hiring treaty negotiators, empowered the Department of State to appoint those negotiators, formed a commission to study the benefits and risks of entering into the agreement, or paid for a bevy of spies to monitor the treaty-related deliberations of other potential signatories. . . .

But a power to help the President *make* treaties is not a power to *implement* treaties already made. See generally Rosenkranz, *Executing the Treaty Power*, 118 Harv. L. Rev. 1867 (2005). Once a treaty has been made, Congress's power to do what is "necessary and proper" to assist the making of treaties drops out of the picture. To legislate compliance with the United States' treaty obligations, Congress must rely upon its independent (though quite robust) Article I, § 8, powers.

B. Structure

"[T]he Constitutio[n] confer[s] upon Congress . . . not all governmental powers, but only discrete, enumerated ones." *Printz v. United States*, 521 U.S. 898, 919 (1997). And, of course, "enumeration presupposes something not enumerated." *Gibbons v. Ogden*, 9 Wheat. 1, 195 (1824). But in *Holland*, the proponents of unlimited congressional power found a loophole: "By negotiating a treaty and obtaining the requisite consent of the Senate, the President . . . may endow Congress with a source of legislative authority independent of the powers enumerated in Article I." L. Tribe, American Constitutional Law § 4-4, pp. 645-646 (3d ed. 2000). . . .

. . .

If that is true, then the possibilities of what the Federal Government may accomplish, with the right treaty in hand, are endless and hardly farfetched. It could begin, as some scholars have suggested, with abrogation of this Court's constitutional rulings. For example, the holding that a statute prohibiting the carrying of firearms near schools went beyond Congress's enumerated powers, *United States v. Lopez*, 514 U.S. 549, 551 (1995), could be reversed by negotiating a treaty with Latvia providing that neither sovereign would permit the carrying of guns near schools. . . .

But reversing some of this Court's decisions is the least of the problem. Imagine the United States' entry into an Antipolygamy Convention, which called for — and Congress enacted — legislation providing that, when a spouse of a man with more than one wife dies intestate, the surviving husband may inherit no part of the estate. Constitutional? The Federalist answers with a rhetorical question: "Suppose by some forced constructions of its authority (which indeed cannot easily be imagined) the Federal Legislature should attempt to vary the law of descent in any State; would it not be evident that . . . it had exceeded its jurisdiction and infringed upon that of the State?" The Federalist No. 33, at 206 (A. Hamilton). Yet given the Antipolygamy Convention, *Holland* would uphold it. Or imagine that, to execute a treaty, Congress enacted a statute prohibiting state inheritance taxes on real property. Constitutional? Of course not. Again, The Federalist: "Suppose . . . [Congress] should undertake to abrogate a land tax imposed by the authority of a State, would it not be equally evident that this was an invasion of that concurrent jurisdiction in respect to this species of tax which its constitution plainly supposes to exist in the State governments?" No. 33, at 206. *Holland* would uphold it. As these examples show, *Holland* places Congress only one treaty away from acquiring a general police power.

The Necessary and Proper Clause cannot bear such weight. . . . No law that flattens the principle of state sovereignty, whether or not "necessary," can be said to be "proper."

. . .

Justice THOMAS, with whom Justice SCALIA joins, and with whom Justice ALITO joins as to Parts I, II, and III, concurring in the judgment.

. . .

I write separately to suggest that the Treaty Power is itself a limited federal power. . . . The Constitution does not . . . comprehensively define the proper bounds of the Treaty Power, and this Court has not yet had occasion to do so. As a result, some have suggested that the Treaty Power is boundless — that it can reach any subject matter, even those that are of strictly domestic concern. See, *e.g.*, Restatement (Third) of Foreign Relations Law of the United States, § 302, Comment *c* (1986). A number of recent treaties reflect that suggestion by regulating what appear to be purely domestic affairs. See, *e.g.*, Bradley, The Treaty

Power and American Federalism, 97 Mich. L. Rev. 390, 402-409 (1998) (citing examples).

Yet to interpret the Treaty Power as extending to every conceivable domestic subject matter — even matters without any nexus to foreign relations — would destroy the basic constitutional distinction between domestic and foreign powers. It would also lodge in the Federal Government the potential for "a police power over all aspects of American life." *Lopez, supra*, at 584 (Thomas, J., concurring). . . .

I doubt the Treaty Power creates such a gaping loophole in our constitutional structure. Although the parties have not challenged the constitutionality of the particular treaty at issue here, in an appropriate case I believe the Court should address the scope of the Treaty Power as it was originally understood. Today, it is enough to highlight some of the structural and historical evidence suggesting that the Treaty Power can be used to arrange intercourse with other nations, but not to regulate purely domestic affairs. . . .

[Extensive historical discussion is omitted.]

. . . I acknowledge that the distinction between matters of international intercourse and matters of purely domestic regulation may not be obvious in all cases. But this Court has long recognized that the Treaty Power is limited, and hypothetical difficulties in line-drawing are no reason to ignore a constitutional limit on federal power.

The parties in this case have not addressed the proper scope of the Treaty Power or the validity of the treaty here. The preservation of limits on the Treaty Power is nevertheless a matter of fundamental constitutional importance, and the Court ought to address the scope of the Treaty Power when that issue is presented. . . .

[An opinion of Justice Alito, concurring in the judgment, is omitted.]

NOTES AND QUESTIONS

1. **The Opinions in *Bond*.** Note that the Court in *Bond* was unanimous in its judgment, but the opinions take very different approaches. What views do they share? How are they different? What message do they send for future litigation?

2. **Missouri v. Holland.** As indicated in *Bond*, the leading case regarding treaties and federalism is *Missouri v. Holland*, 252 U.S. 416 (1920), in which the Court upheld the Migratory Bird Treaty Act (the Act that, as amended, later became the focus of *Kempthorne, supra*). Prior to the treaty, two lower courts held unconstitutional an earlier act of Congress regulating migratory birds because it exceeded Congress's enumerated powers under the Constitution. Without deciding whether those decisions were correct, the Court in *Missouri v. Holland* upheld the Act as a valid implementation of the treaty. As described in *Bond*, the Court principally addressed the question whether the treaty exceeded the powers of the federal government as a whole; it assumed that "if the treaty is valid there can be no dispute about the validity of the statute under Article I, Section 8, as a necessary and proper means to execute

the powers of the Government." Is that assumption correct? Why does Justice Scalia think otherwise? Is this still an open issue after *Bond*?

3. **Justice Thomas's Concurrence.** What does Justice Thomas mean by insisting that a treaty must involve matters of "international concern"? What treaties might not do so? How would you argue that a treaty regarding internal matters, such as how a nation treats its own citizens, addresses matters of international concern? In *United States v. Park*, 938 F.3d 354 (D.C. Cir. 2019), the court upheld a conviction under a federal statute implementing the Optional Protocol on the Sale of Children, Child Prostitution and Child Pornography (an international treaty protecting children from sexual exploitation) as applied to the activities of a U.S. citizen in Vietnam. Does that involve a matter of "international concern"? What if the activities had been by a U.S. citizen entirely within the United States?

5. Interpreting Treaties

To enforce a treaty (or even to determine if the treaty is self-executing), a U.S. court will need to determine what the treaty says. As with a statute, determining meaning may be straightforward or not, depending on the clarity of the treaty's language. An important question to consider is what materials should be used to interpret treaties, and in particular how these materials might differ from materials used to interpret statutes. This section considers some key issues relating to treaty interpretation, first in the context of treaties regulating private behavior and second in the more complicated context of enforcing treaties against the U.S. government. Notably, unlike the other issues considered in prior sections, treaty interpretation is also highly relevant for international courts and other international bodies. The international law of treaties, reflected in the Vienna Convention on the Law of Treaties (VCLT) and other international sources, contains rules and guidelines for interpreting treaties. As you study these sections, consider the similarities and differences between the interpretive methods used by U.S. courts and those embodied in the provisions of the VCLT. Should the U.S. methods be the same as the international methods? Should international interpretations be binding on or persuasive to U.S. interpreters?

a. Basic Approaches to Treaty Interpretation

Vienna Convention on the Law of Treaties
1155 U.N.T.S. 331 (May 23, 1969)

Article 31. General rule of interpretation

1. A treaty shall be interpreted in good faith in accordance with the ordinary meaning to be given to the terms of the treaty in their context and in the light of its object and purpose.

2. The context for the purpose of the interpretation of a treaty shall comprise, in addition to the text, including its preamble and annexes:

(a) any agreement relating to the treaty which was made between all the parties in connexion with the conclusion of the treaty;

(b) any instrument which was made by one or more parties in connexion with the conclusion of the treaty and accepted by the other parties as an instrument related to the treaty.

3. There shall be taken into account, together with the context:

(a) any subsequent agreement between the parties regarding the interpretation of the treaty or the application of its provisions;

(b) any subsequent practice in the application of the treaty which establishes the agreement of the parties regarding its interpretation;

(c) any relevant rules of international law applicable in the relations between the parties.

4. A special meaning shall be given to a term if it is established that the parties so intended.

Article 32. Supplementary means of interpretation

Recourse may be had to supplementary means of interpretation, including the preparatory work of the treaty and the circumstances of its conclusion, in order to confirm the meaning resulting from the application of article 31, or to determine the meaning when the interpretation according to article 31:

(a) leaves the meaning ambiguous or obscure; or

(b) leads to a result which is manifestly absurd or unreasonable.

Chan v. Korean Air Lines, Ltd.
490 U.S. 122 (1989)

Justice SCALIA delivered the opinion of the Court.

This case presents the question whether international air carriers lose the benefit of the limitation on damages for passenger injury or death provided by the multilateral treaty known as the Warsaw Convention if they fail to provide notice of that limitation in the 10-point type size required by a private accord among carriers, the Montreal Agreement.

I

On September 1, 1983, over the Sea of Japan, a military aircraft of the Soviet Union destroyed a Korean Air Lines, Ltd. (KAL) Boeing 747 en route from Kennedy Airport in New York to Seoul, South Korea. All 269 persons on board the plane perished. Survivors of the victims filed wrongful death actions against KAL. . . . All parties agree that their rights are governed by the Warsaw Convention, a multilateral treaty governing the international carriage of passengers, baggage, and cargo by air. . . .

The present controversy centers on the per passenger damages limitation for personal injury or death. This was fixed at approximately $8,300 by the Convention, but was raised to $75,000 by the Montreal Agreement, an agreement among carriers . . . joined by KAL in 1969. . . . [T]his agreement required carriers to give passengers written notice of the Convention's damage limitations in print size no smaller than 10-point type. The notice of the Convention's liability rules printed on KAL's passenger tickets for the flight in question here appeared in only 8-point type. By motion for partial summary judgment, plaintiffs sought a declaration that this discrepancy deprived KAL of the benefit of the damages limitation.

. . .

[The lower courts ruled against the plaintiffs, who sought Supreme Court review.]

II

Petitioners . . . assert that Article 3 of the Warsaw Convention removes the protection of limited liability if a carrier fails to provide adequate notice of the Convention's liability limitation in its passenger tickets. Second, they contend that the Montreal Agreement's 10-point type requirement supplies the standard of adequate notice under Article 3. Because we reject the first point, we need not reach the second.

Article 3 of the Warsaw Convention provides:

(1) For the transportation of passengers the carriers must deliver a passenger ticket which shall contain the following particulars:
(*a*) The place and date of issue;
(*b*) The place of departure and of destination;
(*c*) The agreed stopping places, provided that the carrier may reserve the right to alter the stopping places in case of necessity, and that, if he exercises that right, the alteration shall not have the effect of depriving the transportation of its international character;
(*d*) The name and address of the carrier or carriers;
(*e*) A statement that the transportation is subject to the rules relating to liability established by this convention.
(2) The absence, irregularity, or loss of the passenger ticket shall not affect the existence or the validity of the contract of transportation, which shall nonetheless be subject to the rules of this convention. Nevertheless, if the carrier accepts a passenger without a passenger ticket having been delivered, he shall not be entitled to avail himself of those provisions of this convention which exclude or limit his liability.

Although Article 3(1)(*e*) specifies that a passenger ticket shall contain "[a] statement that the transportation is subject to the rules relating to liability established by this convention," nothing in Article 3 or elsewhere in the Convention imposes a sanction for failure to provide an "adequate" statement. The only sanction in Article 3 appears in the second clause of Article 3(2), which subjects a carrier to unlimited liability if it "accepts a passenger without a passenger ticket having been delivered." Several courts have equated nondelivery of a ticket, for purposes of this provision, with the delivery of a ticket in a form that fails to provide adequate notice of the Warsaw limitation. . . .

We cannot accept this interpretation. All that the second sentence of Article 3(2) requires in order to avoid its sanction is the "deliver[y]" of "a passenger ticket." Expanding this to mean "a passenger ticket in compliance with the requirements of this Convention" is rendered implausible by the first sentence of Article 3(2), which specifies that "[t]he ... irregularity ... of the passenger ticket shall not affect the existence or the validity of the contract of transportation, which shall nonetheless be subject to the rules of this convention." It is clear from this (1) that an "irregularity" does not prevent a document from being a "passenger ticket"; and (2) that an "irregularity" in a passenger ticket does not eliminate the contractual damages limitation provided for by the Convention. "Irregularity" means the "[q]uality or state of not conforming to rule or law," Webster's Second International Dictionary (1950), and, in the present context, the word must surely refer to the rules established by the Convention, including the notice requirement. Thus, a delivered document does not fail to qualify as a "passenger ticket," and does not cause forfeiture of the damages limitation, merely because it contains a defective notice. When Article 3(2), after making this much clear, continues (in the second sentence) "Nevertheless, if a carrier accepts a passenger without a passenger ticket having been delivered, etc.," it can only be referring to the carrier's failure to deliver any document whatever, or its delivery of a document whose shortcomings are so extensive that it cannot reasonably be described as a "ticket" (for example, a mistakenly delivered blank form, with no data filled in). Quite obviously, the use of 8-point type instead of 10-point type for the liability limitation notice is not a shortcoming of such magnitude; indeed, one might well select that as a polar example of what could not possibly prevent a document from being a ticket.

Besides being incompatible with the language of the Convention, the proposition that, for purposes of Article 3(2), delivering a defective ticket is equivalent to failure to deliver a ticket produces absurd results. It may seem reasonable enough that a carrier "shall not be entitled to avail himself of those provisions of this convention which exclude or limit his liability" when the ticket defect consists precisely of a failure to give the passenger proper notice of those provisions. But there is no textual basis for limiting the "defective-ticket-is-no-ticket" principle to that particular defect. Thus, the liability limitation would also be eliminated if the carrier failed to comply, for example, with the requirement of Article 3(1)(d) that the ticket contain the address of the carrier.

The conclusion that defective compliance with the notice provision does not eliminate the liability limitation is confirmed by comparing Article 3(2) with other provisions of the Convention. Just as Section I . . . (which includes Article 3) specifies what information must be included in passenger tickets, Sections II and III specify what information must be included in, respectively, baggage checks and air waybills for cargo. All three sections require, in identical terms, "[a] statement that the transportation is subject to the rules relating to liability established by this convention." All three sections also provide, again in identical terms, that if the relevant document (ticket, baggage check, or air waybill) has not been delivered (or, in the case of air waybill, "made out"), the carrier "shall not be entitled to avail himself of the provisions of this convention which exclude or limit his liability." But, unlike Section I, Sections II and III also specifically impose the latter sanction for failure to include in the documents certain particulars, including (though not limited to) the notice of liability limitation. Sections II and III thus make doubly clear what the text of Article 3(2) already indicates: that delivery of a defective document is something quite different from failure to deliver a document. And, given the parallel structures of these provisions, it would be a flouting of the text to imply in Section I a sanction not only withheld there but explicitly granted elsewhere. When such an interpretation is allowed, the art of draftsmanship will have become obsolete.

Petitioners and the United States as *amicus curiae* seek to explain the variance between Section I and Sections II and III (as well as the clear text of Article 3) as a drafting error, and lead us through the labyrinth of the Convention's drafting history in an effort to establish this point. It would be absurd, they urge, for defective notice to eliminate liability limits on baggage and air freight, but not on personal injury and death. Perhaps not. It might have been thought, by the representatives from diverse countries who drafted the Convention in 1925 and 1929 (an era when even many States of this country had relatively low limits on wrongful death recovery) that the $8,300 maximum liability established for personal injury or death was a "fair" recovery in any event, so that, even if the defective notice caused the passenger to forgo the purchase of additional insurance, he or his heirs would be treated with rough equity in any event. . . . Another possible explanation for the difference in treatment is that the limitations on liability prescribed for baggage and freight are much more substantial, and thus notice of them is much more important. They include not just a virtually nominal monetary limit, but also total exclusion of liability for "an error in piloting, in the handling of the aircraft, or in navigation." Or perhaps the difference in treatment can be traced to a belief that people were much more likely, if adequate notice was given, to purchase additional insurance on goods than on their own lives. . . .

These estimations of what the drafters might have had in mind are of course speculation, but they suffice to establish that the result the text produces is not necessarily absurd, and hence cannot be dismissed as an obvious drafting error. We must thus be governed by the text — solemnly adopted by the governments of many separate nations — whatever conclusions might be drawn from the intricate drafting history that petitioners and the United States have brought to our attention. The latter may, of course, be consulted to elucidate a text that is ambiguous. But where the text is clear, as it is here, we have no power to insert an amendment. As Justice Story wrote for the Court more than a century and a half ago:

> "[T]o alter, amend, or add to any treaty by inserting any clause, whether small or great, important or trivial, would be on our part an usurpation of power, and not an exercise of judicial functions. It would be to make, and not to construe, a treaty. Neither can this Court supply a *casus omissus* in a treaty, any more than in a law. We are to find out the intention of the parties by just rules of interpretation applied to the subject matter, and, having found that, our duty is to follow it as far as it goes, and to stop where that stops — whatever may be the imperfections or difficulties which it leaves behind."

The Amiable Isabella, 19 U.S. 71 (1821).

For the reasons given above, we agree with the opinion of the Supreme Court of Canada, see *Ludecke v. Canadian Pacific Airlines, Ltd.*, 98 D.L.R.3d 52 (1979), that the Warsaw Convention does not eliminate the limitation on damages for passenger injury or death as a sanction for failure to provide adequate notice of that limitation. Accordingly, we affirm the judgment of the District of Columbia Circuit.

Justice BRENNAN, with whom Justice MARSHALL, Justice BLACKMUN, and Justice STEVENS join, concurring in the judgment.

. . . I agree that the interpretation of the Warsaw Convention advanced by petitioners should be rejected, but I consider it entitled to a more respectful burial than has been accorded. Over the last 25 years, petitioners' argument has been accepted, until the present litigation, by virtually every court in this country that has considered it. . . . It is a view of the Convention that has consistently been adopted by the Executive Branch, and which is pressed on us in this case by the United States as *amicus curiae*. It deserves . . . to be considered without the self-affixed blindfold that prevents the Court from examining anything beyond the treaty language itself.

The Court holds that the sanction of Article 3(2), which consists of the loss of the Convention's limitation on liability under Article 22(1), applies only when no passenger ticket at all is delivered. That is a plausible reading, perhaps even the most plausible reading of the language of the Convention. But it is disingenuous to say that it is the only possible reading. Certainly it is wrong to disregard the wealth of evidence to be found in the Convention's drafting history on the intent of the governments that drafted the document. It is altogether proper that we consider such extrinsic evidence of the treatymakers' intent. The drafters of an international treaty generally are, of course, the instructed representatives of the governments that ultimately ratify the treaty. The record of their negotiations can provide helpful clues to those governments' collective intent, as it took shape during the negotiating process.

There is strong evidence that the drafters of the Warsaw Convention may have meant something other than what the Court thinks that document says. In the first place, the text of the Convention is surely susceptible of an interpretation other than the Court's. Article 3(1) describes as follows what it is the carrier must deliver: "[A] passenger ticket which shall contain the following particulars. . . ." I think it not at all unreasonable to read the term "passenger ticket," when used subsequently in Article 3(2), as shorthand for this longer phrase. . . . The intent of Article 3(2), as a whole, is surely to hold the carrier to the obligations, but to deny it the benefits, of the Convention, if it fails to comply with certain requirements.

Thus, the language of Article 3 does not . . . exclude the interpretation that failure to provide the required notice results in loss of the limitation on liability. On the other hand, the difference between the language of Article 3 and that of Articles 4 and 9 casts some doubt on that reading. Evidence from the drafting history of the Convention is therefore helpful in understanding what the contracting governments intended.

. . .

[I]t is abundantly clear that, throughout the entire drafting process, the delegates intended to apply the same regime of sanctions for failure to comply with the provisions concerning passenger tickets, baggage checks, and air waybills. . . .

The report submitted by Henry de Vos, Reporter of the Second Committee, . . . made crystal clear the parallelism of approach adopted for the three types of transportation documents: "[T]he sanction for transporting passengers without regular tickets is the same as that for the transportation of baggage and of goods." Similarly, the report Monsieur de Vos prepared . . . to accompany its final draft of the Convention contained the following observation "[T]he sanction provided . . . for carriage of passengers without a ticket *or with a ticket not conforming* to the Convention is identical to that provided . . . for carriage of baggage and goods." Second International Conference on Private Aeronautical Law Minutes 247 (R. Horner & D. Legrez trans. 1975) (emphasis added). . . .

. . .

[I]t is absolutely clear that, under [the final draft submitted to the Warsaw Conference], the carrier was to lose the benefit of the liability limitation if it delivered a passenger ticket that did not contain the listed particulars. See Horner & Legrez 258 ("If . . . the carrier accepts the traveler without having drawn up a passenger ticket, *or if the ticket does not contain the particulars indicated hereabove.* . . .") (emphasis added).

[T]he Greek delegation had repeatedly objected to the sanctions clause as too harsh. . . . [A]t [the] Warsaw [Conference], for reasons which do not emerge from the record . . . [t]he preparatory committee accepted [a Greek amendment] to the extent of deleting from Article 3(2) the words, "or if the ticket does not contain the particulars indicated above." The parallel provision in Article 4 was treated somewhat differently. A change was made in which particulars were deemed obligatory, but three — including the liability statement which became particular *(h)* — remained so; thus, the phrase used in the sanctions clause was "or if the baggage check does not contain the particulars set out at *(d)*, *(f)*, and *(h)* above." *Id.* at 156. Articles 8 and 9, concerning the air waybill, were rewritten in a similar fashion.

It is not clear what the reason is for the difference between the final structure of Article 3, on one hand, and Articles 4 and 9, on the other. The Solicitor General views it essentially as a drafting error. . . . It is, to be sure, possible that the drafters intended to create a different regime for the passenger ticket than for the baggage check and the air waybill. . . . But it is puzzling that such a departure from the fundamental principle of applying the same scheme of sanctions to the passenger ticket, the baggage check, and the waybill would have been made without explanation or acknowledgement. . . .

An examination of the Greek proposal that led to the change, as well as what Monsieur de Vos said in presenting it, strengthens the impression that no different treatment of the passenger ticket was intended. The Greek proposal referred to the possibility that the carrier might lose its liability limitation because

> "by simple negligence the carrier has omitted to mention in the passenger ticket the place of issuance, or the point of departure, or his name and address; or even that he keep his former address in the ticket, or finally he does not point out an intermediate stop."

Horner & Legrez 303. The Reporter, in presenting the revision of Article 3 to the plenary session, characterized the Greek concern as follows: "[T]he sanction is too severe when it's a question of a simple omission, of the negligence of an employee of the carrier. . . ." *Id.* at 150. The focus thus appears to have been on clerical errors in filling in the ticket forms. An intent to remove such errors from the list of those that trigger the sanction — as was done also in Article 4 (but not in Article 8) — would not be incompatible with the intent to retain the sanction for failure to include the liability statement, which would hardly result from the same kind of ticket-counter error.

. . .

The Court offers several hypotheses as to why the drafters of the Convention might have determined to treat the notice requirement differently for the passenger ticket and the baggage check. . . . But there is no trace of such a purpose in the Warsaw minutes, as there surely would have been had a decision been made to reverse the relative treatment of the Article 3 and 4 sanctions provisions in the previous draft. It seems much more likely, therefore, that the difference between Articles 3 and 4 on this point was an unintended consequence of other changes that were made at the conference.

Even if we agree [with petitioners], however, that Article 3 of the Warsaw Convention removes the liability limit for failure to provide notice that the transportation is governed by the Convention's liability provisions, that does not end the matter.

Respondent Korean Air Lines undeniably did give petitioners such notice. Petitioners' argument goes beyond this, however, and requires us to determine whether there exists a requirement that the notice given be "adequate," and, if so, whether the notice provided in this case met that standard. . . . If notice is indeed required, it must surely meet some minimal standard of "adequacy." All would agree, no doubt, that notice that literally could be read only with a magnifying glass would be no notice at all. . . . Here, however, the notice given was surely "adequate" under any conventional interpretation of that term. That being so, I cannot agree that we have any license to require that the notice meet some higher standard merely for the sake of a bright line.

. . .

NOTES AND QUESTIONS

1. **U.S. and International Approaches to Treaty Interpretation.** What are the principal differences between the majority's approach and the concurrence's approach in *Chan*? How do they compare to the way one might interpret a statute? What are the principal differences (if any) between the approaches to treaty interpretation taken in *Chan* and the approaches contained in the treaty interpretation provisions of the VCLT excerpted above? As legal texts, should treaties be interpreted in the same manner as other legal texts such as statutes, contracts, or constitutions? Of the principal materials and approaches in the VCLT and *Chan*, which, if any, are not part of ordinary interpretive approaches in other areas?

2.   **Use of Nontextual Materials.** The Justices have frequently differed over the use of a treaty's drafting history and other nontextual evidence of meaning. In *United States v. Stuart*, 489 U.S. 353 (1989), decided the same year as *Chan*, the Court construed provisions of the 1942 Convention Regarding Double Taxation between the United States and Canada, which the respondents claimed prevented the United States from sharing their tax information with Canada. After rejecting the claim on the basis of the treaty's text, the Court, in an opinion by Justice Brennan, also consulted "[n]on-textual sources that often assist us in giving effect to the intent of the Treaty parties," including "the treaty's ratification history and its subsequent operation." Justice Scalia concurred only in the judgment, stating:

> Given that the Treaty's language resolves the issue presented, there is no necessity of looking further to discover "the intent of the Treaty parties," and special reason to avoid the particular materials that the Court unnecessarily consults. . . .
>
> Of course, no one can be opposed to giving effect to "the intent of the Treaty parties." The critical question, however, is whether that is more reliably and predictably achieved by a rule of construction which credits, when it is clear, the contracting sovereigns' carefully framed and solemnly ratified expression of those intentions and expectations, or rather one which sets judges in various jurisdictions at large to ignore that clear expression and discern a "genuine" contrary intent elsewhere. To ask that question is to answer it.
>
> One can readily understand the appeal of making the additional argument that the plain language of a treaty (which is conclusive) does indeed effectuate the genuine intent as shown elsewhere — just as one can understand the appeal, in statutory cases, of pointing out that what the statute provides (which is conclusive) happens to be sound social policy. But using every string to one's bow in this fashion has unfortunate implications. ("It would be wrong; and besides, it wouldn't work.") Here the implication is that, had the extrinsic evidence contradicted the plain language of the Treaty, it would govern. . . .

Justices Kennedy and O'Connor joined the Court's opinion in part but declined to join the sections discussing nontextual evidence. Is the concurrence's position correct? Is it consistent with the VCLT?

In a more recent case, *Monasky v. Taglieri*, 140 S. Ct. 719 (2020), the Supreme Court interpreted a provision of the Hague Convention on the Civil Aspects of International Child Abduction; although it stated that "we begin with the text of the treaty and the context in which the written words are used," the Court went on to consider the Convention's Explanatory Report, the Convention's "drafting and negotiating history," and the conclusions of foreign courts construing the treaty, all of which (the Court found) supported its view. In considering the views of the Convention's signatories, the Court looked to decisions of the Supreme Court of the United Kingdom, the Court of Justice of the European Union, the Supreme Court of Canada, and the High Court of Australia, as well as intermediate appellate courts in Hong Kong and New Zealand, and noted that the petitioner had not identified a single treaty partner whose courts had adopted her position. Justice Thomas concurred, objecting to the use of nontextual evidence, particularly the views of foreign courts. What weight should the opinions of other signatories and their courts have on the textual analysis?

3. ***Travaux Preparatoires.*** A treaty's drafting history is often called the "travaux preparatoires" or just "travaux." *The Restatement (Third) of Foreign Relations Law*, Section 325 note e, states:

> The Vienna Convention [on the Law of Treaties], in Article 32, requires the interpreting body to conclude that the "ordinary meaning" of the text is either obscure or unreasonable before it can look to "supplemental means." . . . Article 32 . . . reflects a reluctance to permit the use of materials constituting the development and negotiation of an agreement (*travaux preparatoires*) as a guide to the interpretation of the agreement. The Convention's inhospitality to *travaux* is not wholly consistent with the attitude of the International Court of Justice and not at all with that of United States courts.

Note that the *Restatement* was written in the 1980s; in more recent times, the U.S. approach — particularly under the influence of Justice Scalia — may reflect more exclusive focus on the text. *But see Zicherman v. Korean Air Lines Co.*, 516 U.S. 217, 226 (1996) (per Justice Scalia) ("[W]e have traditionally considered as aids to [a treaty's] interpretation the negotiating and drafting history (travaux preparatoires) and the post-ratification understanding of the contracting parties."). What do you think is the appropriate role, if any, of *travaux* in treaty interpretation?

4. **Views of the Executive Branch.** A consideration for U.S. courts (though not international courts) is whether to defer to the views of the U.S. executive branch on the meaning of a treaty. *Sumitomo Shoji America, Inc. v. Avagliano*, 457 U.S. 176 (1982), is a standard citation for the proposition that the view of the executive branch in treaty interpretation, "[a]lthough not conclusive, . . . is entitled to great weight." In *El Al Israel Airlines v. Tseng*, 525 U.S. 155 (1999), another Warsaw Convention case, the Court noted somewhat more mildly that "[r]espect is ordinarily due the reasonable views of the Executive Branch concerning the meaning of an international treaty." Note that in *Chan*, the Court disagreed with the executive branch without discussing deference. Should U.S. courts give deference to the executive's treaty interpretations? Or should they make independent decisions about treaty interpretation? Why? In *Abbott v. Abbott*, 560 U.S. 1 (2010), the Court opened its analysis by saying: "'The interpretation of a treaty, like the interpretation of a statute, begins with its text.' *Medellín v. Texas*, 552 U.S. 491, 506 (2008)." After reaching a conclusion based on the treaty language, the majority added:

> This Court's conclusion . . . is supported and informed by the State Department's view on the issue . . . ; see *Sumitomo Shoji America, Inc. v. Avagliano*, 457 U.S. 176, 184-185, n. 10 (1982). . . . There is no reason to doubt that this well-established canon of deference is appropriate here. The Executive is well informed concerning the diplomatic consequences resulting from this Court's interpretation of [the treaty provision at issue].

Justice Stevens, writing for three Justices, dissented. As to the executive's view, he argued:

> The Department of State's position, which supports the Court's conclusion, is newly memorialized, and is possibly inconsistent with the Department's earlier position.
>
> . . . I would not in this case abdicate our responsibility to interpret the Convention's language. This does not seem to be a matter in which deference to the Executive on matters of foreign policy would avoid international conflict; the State Department has made no such argument. Nor is this a case in which the Executive's understanding of the treaty's drafting history is particularly rich or illuminating. Finally, and significantly, the State Department, . . . has failed to disclose to the Court . . . the Executive's postratification conduct, or the conduct of other signatories, to aid us in understanding the accepted meaning of potentially ambiguous terms.
>
> Instead, the Department offers us little more than its own reading of the treaty's text. . . . I see no reason, therefore, to replace our understanding of the Convention's text with that of the Executive Branch.

Are there particular circumstances where deference is more appropriate? Does deference even matter, when (as appears to have been the case in *Abbott*) the Court has already reached a firm conclusion as to the meaning of the treaty? In *Water Splash, Inc. v Menon*, 137 S. Ct. 1504 (2017), the Court, citing *Abbott*, stated that the executive interpretation of the relevant treaty was entitled to "great weight," although in its analysis the Court also concluded that all of the "traditional tools of treaty interpretation" pointed in the same direction. What if the "traditional tools" did not all point in the same direction? Should deference lead a court to reject its view of a treaty's meaning in favor of the executive branch's reading? If not, what is the point of deference? What justifications are there for a U.S. court to second-guess the executive branch's views on foreign relations? In the *Monasky* case discussed in Note 2, the Court did not discuss the views of the executive branch on the treaty interpretation question, although the executive branch had filed a brief expressing its views.

In *BG Group, PLC v. Republic of Argentina*, 572 U.S. 25 (2014), the Court disagreed with the executive branch's reading of a treaty. Justice Breyer, writing for a seven-Justice majority, said only that "while we respect the Government's views about the proper interpretation of treaties" the Court nonetheless reached the opposite conclusion. The majority did not cite *Avagliano* or use the word "deference." Should it matter that the treaty at issue in *BG Group* was a Bilateral Investment Treaty between the United Kingdom and Argentina to which the United States was not a party?

5. **Interpretations of Foreign Courts.** Article 17 of the Warsaw Convention imposes liability on an air carrier for a passenger's death or bodily injury caused by an "accident" that occurred in connection with an international flight. *Olympic Airways v. Husain*, 540 U.S. 644 (2004), turned on the meaning of the word "accident" in Article 17. The question was

whether an asthmatic passenger's death following the airline's refusal to reseat the passenger away from the smoking section constituted an "accident," making the airline liable for the passenger's death. Relying principally on the plain meaning of the term, the Court found that this did constitute an "accident." In dissent, Justice Scalia argued that the Court should have followed the decisions of the courts of several foreign nations, which had used a restrictive definition of "accident" that would not have encompassed the events in *Husain*. In *El Al v. Tseng, supra,* the Court looked to text, drafting history, the views of the executive branch and, at the end of its opinion, noted that "[d]ecisions of other Convention signatories corroborate our understanding . . ." (citing in particular a decision of the British House of Lords, and concluding "[t]he opinions of our sister signatories, we have observed, are entitled to considerable weight"). In *Abbott v. Abbott, supra,* the majority again found that the judgments of foreign courts tended to support the conclusion it had already reached on the basis of the treaty's text, although it conceded that there was some disagreement among foreign jurisdictions. In dissent, Justice Stevens found no international consensus and cited *Husain* for the proposition that "we should not substitute the judgment of other courts for our own." As discussed in Note 2, in *Monasky* the majority relied in part on decisions of foreign courts, to which Justice Thomas objected in a concurrence. Who has the better argument?

6. **Interpretations of International Courts.** In *Sanchez-Llamas v. Oregon,* 548 U.S. 331 (2006), a case under the Vienna Convention on Consular Relations, one question was whether a criminal defendant's rights under the Convention could be lost by failing to raise them at trial. (As discussed earlier, a similar issue was at stake in *Medellín.*) The International Court of Justice (ICJ) had held that procedural default should not apply to Vienna Convention claims, but the petitioners in *Sanchez-Llamas* were not covered directly by that decision (as José Medellín had been). They nonetheless argued that the Supreme Court should follow the ICJ's interpretation of the Convention. The Court observed that the ICJ's interpretation was "entitled only to the 'respectful consideration' due an interpretation of an international agreement by an international court." However, the Court found that the ICJ's "interpretation of Article 36 [as precluding procedural default] is inconsistent with the basic framework of an adversarial system. . . ." *Sanchez-Llamas* is discussed further in Chapter 3.

b. Enforcing Treaties Against the U.S. Government

The preceding discussion illustrates the use of treaties to regulate private behavior. In such situations, the defendant is typically a private litigant. Different considerations may exist when a private litigant attempts to use treaties to control the behavior of the U.S. government. Should treaties be interpreted differently in that context?

United States v. Alvarez-Machain
504 U.S. 655 (1992)

Chief Justice REHNQUIST delivered the opinion of the Court.

. . .

Respondent, Humberto Alvarez-Machain, is a citizen and resident of Mexico. He was indicted for participating in the kidnap and murder of United States Drug Enforcement Administration (DEA) special agent Enrique Camarena-Salazar. . . . The DEA believes that respondent, a medical doctor, participated in the murder by prolonging Agent Camarena's life so that others could further torture and interrogate him. On April 2, 1990, respondent was forcibly kidnapped from his medical office in Guadalajara, Mexico, to be flown by private plane to El Paso, Texas, where he was arrested by DEA officials. The District Court concluded that DEA agents were responsible for respondent's abduction, although they were not personally involved in it. . . .

Apparently, DEA officials had attempted to gain respondent's presence in the United States through informal negotiations with Mexican officials, but were unsuccessful. DEA officials then, through a contact in Mexico, offered to pay a reward and expenses in return for the delivery of respondent to the United States.

Respondent moved to dismiss the indictment, claiming that . . . the District Court lacked jurisdiction to try him because he was abducted in violation of the extradition treaty between the United States and Mexico. [The District Court agreed, and the court of appeals affirmed.] . . .

[The Court reviewed prior precedent, principally *Ker v. Illinois*, 119 U.S. 436 (1886), which indicated that abduction would not bar the prosecution unless it violated the treaty.]

In construing a treaty, as in construing a statute, we first look to its terms to determine its meaning. The Treaty says nothing about the obligations of the United States and Mexico to refrain from forcible abductions of people from the territory of the other nation, or the consequences under the Treaty if such an abduction occurs. . . .

. . . Article 9 of the Treaty . . . provides:

> "1. Neither Contracting Party shall be bound to deliver up its own nationals, but the executive authority of the requested Party shall, if not prevented by the laws of that Party, have the power to deliver them up if, in its discretion, it be deemed proper to do so.
> "2. If extradition is not granted pursuant to paragraph 1 of this Article, the requested Party shall submit the case to its competent authorities for the purpose of prosecution, provided that Party has jurisdiction over the offense."

According to respondent, Article 9 embodies the terms of the bargain which the United States struck: If the United States wishes to prosecute a Mexican national, it may request that individual's extradition. Upon a request from the United States, Mexico may either extradite the individual or submit the case to the proper authorities for prosecution in Mexico. In this way, respondent reasons, each nation preserved its right to choose whether its nationals would be tried in its own courts or by the courts of the other nation. This preservation of rights would be frustrated if either nation were free to abduct nationals of the other nation for the purposes of prosecution. More broadly, respondent reasons, as did the Court of Appeals, that all the processes and restrictions on the obligation to extradite established by the Treaty would make no sense if either nation were free to resort to forcible kidnapping to gain the presence of an individual for prosecution in a manner not contemplated by the Treaty.

We do not read the Treaty in such a fashion. Article 9 does not purport to specify the only way in which one country may gain custody of a national of the other country for the purposes of prosecution. In the absence of an extradition treaty, nations are under no obligation to surrender those in their country to foreign authorities for prosecution. Extradition treaties exist so as to impose mutual obligations to surrender individuals in certain defined sets of circumstances, following established procedures. The Treaty thus provides a mechanism which would not otherwise exist, requiring, under certain circumstances, the United States and Mexico to extradite individuals to the other country, and establishing the procedures to be followed when the Treaty is invoked.

The history of negotiation and practice under the Treaty also fails to show that abductions outside of the Treaty constitute a violation of the Treaty. As the [U.S. executive branch] notes, the Mexican Government was made aware, as early as 1906, of the *Ker* doctrine, and the United States' position that it applied to forcible abductions made outside of the terms of the United States-Mexico Extradition Treaty. Nonetheless, the current version of the Treaty, signed in 1978, does not attempt to establish a rule that would in any way curtail the effect of *Ker*. Moreover, although language which would grant individuals exactly the right sought by respondent had been considered and drafted as early as 1935 by a prominent group of legal scholars sponsored by the faculty of Harvard Law School, no such clause appears in the current Treaty.

Thus, the language of the Treaty, in the context of its history, does not support the proposition that the Treaty prohibits abductions outside of its terms. The remaining question, therefore, is whether the Treaty should be interpreted so as to include an implied term prohibiting prosecution where the defendant's presence is obtained by means other than those established by the Treaty.

Respondent contends that the Treaty must be interpreted against the backdrop of customary international law, and that international abductions are "so clearly prohibited in international law" that there was no reason to include such a clause in the Treaty itself. The international censure of international abductions is further evidenced, according to respondent, by the United Nations Charter and the Charter of the Organization of American States. Respondent does not argue that these sources of international law provide an independent basis for the right respondent asserts not to be tried in the United States, but rather that they should inform the interpretation of the Treaty terms.

. . .

[T]he difficulty with the support respondent garners from international law is that none of it relates to the practice of nations in relation to extradition treaties. . . . [R]espondent would imply terms in the Extradition Treaty from the practice of nations with regards to international law more generally.[8] . . .

. . .

Respondent and his *amici* may be correct that respondent's abduction was "shocking," and that it may be in violation of general international law principles. Mexico has protested the abduction of respondent through diplomatic notes, and the decision of whether respondent should be returned to Mexico, as a matter outside of the Treaty, is a matter for the Executive Branch. We conclude, however, that respondent's abduction was not in violation of the Extradition Treaty between the United States and Mexico, and therefore the rule of *Ker v. Illinois* is fully applicable to this case. The fact of respondent's forcible abduction does not therefore prohibit his trial in a court in the United States for violations of the criminal laws of the United States.

The judgment of the Court of Appeals is therefore reversed, and the case is remanded for further proceedings consistent with this opinion.

. . .

Justice STEVENS, with whom Justice BLACKMUN and Justice O'CONNOR join, dissenting.

. . .

The extradition treaty with Mexico is a comprehensive document containing 23 articles and an appendix listing the extraditable offenses covered by the agreement. . . . From the preamble, through the description of the parties' obligations with respect to offenses committed within as well as beyond the territory of a requesting party, the delineation of the procedures and evidentiary requirements for extradition, the special provisions for political offenses and capital punishment, and other details, the Treaty appears to have been designed to cover the entire subject of extradition. . . .

The Government's claim that the Treaty is not exclusive, but permits forcible governmental kidnapping, would transform these, and other, provisions into little more than verbiage. For example, provisions requiring "sufficient" evidence to grant extradition (Art. 3), withholding extradition for political or military offenses (Art. 5), withholding extradition when the person sought has already been tried (Art. 6), withholding extradition when the statute of limitations for the crime has lapsed (Art. 7), and granting the requested country discretion to refuse to extradite an individual who would face the death penalty in the requesting country (Art. 8), would serve little purpose if the requesting country could simply kidnap the person. . . . In addition, all of these provisions only make sense if they are understood as *requiring* each treaty signatory to comply with those procedures whenever it wishes to obtain jurisdiction over an individual who is located in another treaty nation.

8. Similarly, the Court of Appeals . . . reasoned that international abductions violate the "purpose" of the Treaty, stating that "[t]he requirements extradition treaties impose constitute a means of safeguarding the sovereignty of the signatory nations, as well as ensuring the fair treatment of individuals." The ambitious purpose ascribed to the Treaty by the Court of Appeals, we believe, places a greater burden on its language and history than they can logically bear. . . .

It is true, as the Court notes, that there is no express promise by either party to refrain from forcible abductions in the territory of the other nation. Relying on that omission, the Court, in effect, concludes that the Treaty merely creates an optional method of obtaining jurisdiction over alleged offenders, and that the parties silently reserved the right to resort to self-help whenever they deem force more expeditious than legal process. If the United States, for example, thought it more expedient to torture or simply to execute a person rather than to attempt extradition, these options would be equally available because they, too, were not explicitly prohibited by the Treaty.

That, however, is a highly improbable interpretation of a consensual agreement, which on its face appears to have been intended to set forth comprehensive and exclusive rules concerning the subject of extradition.[14] In my opinion, the manifest scope and object of the treaty itself plainly imply a mutual undertaking to respect the territorial integrity of the other contracting party. . . .[25]

. . .

As the Court observes at the outset of its opinion, there is reason to believe that respondent participated in an especially brutal murder of an American law enforcement agent. That fact, if true, may explain the Executive's intense interest in punishing respondent in our courts. Such an explanation, however, provides no justification for disregarding the Rule of Law that this Court has a duty to uphold. That the Executive may wish to reinterpret the Treaty to allow for an action that the Treaty in no way authorizes should not influence this Court's interpretation. . . .

I respectfully dissent.

NOTES AND QUESTIONS

1. **Using Treaties to Constrain the Executive Branch.** Unlike the cases considered in the prior section, *Alvarez-Machain* involves the attempt by an individual to use a treaty to constrain the behavior of the executive branch. Should this matter for treaty interpretation, in particular for deference to the executive branch? Does it seem to matter to the Court? In terms of interpretation, what seems to matter most to the majority in *Alvarez-Machain*? What seems to matter most to the dissent? What are the problems with not giving deference, especially in cases like *Alvarez-Machain*? What are the advantages?

---

14. In construing a treaty, the Court has the "responsibility to give the specific words of the treaty a meaning consistent with the shared expectations of the contracting parties." *Air France v. Saks*, 470 U.S. 392, 399 (1985). It is difficult to see how an interpretation that encourages unilateral action could foster cooperation and mutual assistance — the stated goals of the Treaty. . . .

25. The United States has offered no evidence from the negotiating record, ratification process, or later communications with Mexico to support the suggestion that a different understanding with Mexico was reached. See Bassiouni, International Extradition: United States Law and Practice, ch. 2, § 4.3, at 82 ("Negotiations, preparatory works, and diplomatic correspondence are an integral part of the] surrounding circumstances, and [are] often relied on by courts in ascertaining the intentions of the parties") [relocated footnote].

2. **The "Objects and Purposes" of a Treaty.** Apart from deference to the executive, what interpretive principles seemed to separate the majority and the dissent in *Alvarez-Machain*? In some cases it is argued that a court should favor the "objects and purposes" of a treaty. Is that what Justice Stevens's dissent in *Alvarez-Machain* reflects? Is this consistent with the Vienna Convention? How should the "objects and purposes" be identified? Does it make sense to refer to objects and purposes that are not reflected in the treaty's text itself? Suppose in negotiating the extradition treaty the United States had proposed a clause expressly stating that suspects could be abducted despite the treaty. What do you think would have happened? What if Mexico had proposed a clause expressly prohibiting abductions?

    In a part of the dissent omitted above, Justice Stevens argued at length that forcible abductions in the territory of another sovereign nation violate customary international law. Should that matter for interpreting the treaty? Does the majority dispute Justice Stevens's view of customary international law?

3. **Interpreting a Treaty Against the Executive Branch.** *Hamdan v. Rumsfeld*, 548 U.S. 557 (2006), is a rare case in which the Court enforced a treaty against the U.S. executive branch contrary to the executive branch's interpretation of the treaty. *Hamdan* concerned the legality of procedures adopted by the executive branch to try suspected terrorists by military commission. The Court first concluded that an Act of Congress, the Uniform Code of Military Justice, allowed military commissions in certain circumstances but required that they comply with international law. The Court next concluded that Article 3 of the Geneva Conventions (to which the United States is a party) applied to the defendant, Hamdan, and that the military commission designed by the President did not comply with Article 3. As the Court explained:

    > Article 3, often referred to as Common Article 3 because ... it appears in all four Geneva Conventions, provides that in a "conflict not of an international character occurring in the territory of one of the High Contracting Parties, each Party to the conflict shall be bound to apply, as a minimum," certain provisions protecting "[p]ersons taking no active part in the hostilities, including members of armed forces who have laid down their arms and those placed *hors de combat* by ... detention." One such provision prohibits "the passing of sentences and the carrying out of executions without previous judgment pronounced by a regularly constituted court affording all the judicial guarantees which are recognized as indispensable by civilized peoples."

    Hamdan, who was accused of involvement with the al-Qaeda terrorist organization but was not the member of the armed forces of any state with which the United States was at war, claimed that the conflict between al-Qaeda and the United States was "not of an international character" and thus Article 3 applied to him. The Court, in a 5-3 opinion by Justice Stevens, agreed:

    > The Court of Appeals thought, and the Government asserts, that Common Article 3 does not apply to Hamdan because the conflict with al Qaeda, being "international in scope," does not qualify as a "conflict not of an international character." That reasoning is erroneous. The term "conflict not of an

international character" is used here in contradistinction to a conflict between nations. . . . Common Article 2 provides that "the present Convention shall apply to all cases of declared war or of any other armed conflict which may arise between two or more of the High Contracting Parties." . . . Common Article 3, by contrast, affords some minimal protection, falling short of full protection under the Conventions, to individuals associated with neither a signatory nor even a nonsignatory "Power" who are involved in a conflict "in the territory of" a signatory. The latter kind of conflict is distinguishable from the conflict described in Common Article 2 chiefly because it does not involve a clash between nations (whether signatories or not). In context, then, the phrase "not of an international character" bears its literal meaning. . . .

Although the official commentaries accompanying Common Article 3 indicate that an important purpose of the provision was to furnish minimal protection to rebels involved in one kind of "conflict not of an international character," *i.e.*, a civil war, the commentaries also make clear "that the scope of the Article must be as wide as possible." . . .

Justice Thomas, joined by Justices Scalia and Alito, argued in dissent:

. . . Hamdan's claim under Common Article 3 of the Geneva Conventions is meritless. Common Article 3 applies to "armed conflict not of an international character occurring in the territory of one of the High Contracting Parties." Pursuant to his authority as Commander in Chief and Chief Executive of the United States, the President has accepted the legal conclusion of the Department of Justice . . . that common Article 3 of Geneva does not apply to . . . al Qaeda . . . detainees, because, among other reasons, the relevant conflicts are international in scope and common Article 3 applies only to "armed conflict not of an international character." Under this Court's precedents, "the meaning attributed to treaty provisions by the Government agencies charged with their negotiation and enforcement is entitled to great weight." *Sumitomo Shoji America, Inc. v. Avagliano*, 457 U.S. 176, 184-185 (1982). . . . Our duty to defer to the President's understanding of the provision at issue here is only heightened by the fact that he is acting pursuant to his constitutional authority as Commander in Chief and by the fact that the subject matter of Common Article 3 calls for a judgment about the nature and character of an armed conflict.

The President's interpretation of Common Article 3 is reasonable and should be sustained. . . . [W]here, as here, an ambiguous treaty provision ("not of an international character") is susceptible of two plausible, and reasonable, interpretations, our precedents require us to defer to the Executive's interpretation.

Should the majority have adopted the executive's interpretation? In cases where, as here, a treaty is being applied against the executive, should deference to the executive's interpretation be absolute? Or should courts, as the branch ordinarily charged with authoritatively determining the law, independently decide how to interpret treaties? Or is a degree of deference somewhere between these positions most appropriate?

4. **Treaties in More than One Language.** In *Sale v. Haitian Centers Council, Inc.*, 509 U.S. 155 (1993), the Court considered a challenge to the executive branch policy of intercepting Haitian refugees at sea before they could

reach the United States and returning them to Haiti. Article 33 of the U.N. Convention on the Status of Refugees provided:

> No Contracting State shall expel or return ("*refouler*") a refugee in any manner whatsoever to the frontiers of territories where his life or freedom would be threatened on account of his race, religion, nationality, membership of a particular social group or political opinion.

In an 8-1 opinion by Justice Stevens, the Court held that this provision did not apply to the U.S. interception and return of refugees on the high seas because the refugees were not in the United States. Relying heavily on the text of the Convention, it found that — although the ordinary English meaning of "return" might include return from the high seas — the French word "refouler" indicated only return from the borders of the returning state. (The Court also relied on the Convention's drafting history, but not on deference to the executive branch's interpretation.) In dissent, Justice Blackmun argued that "return" should be given its ordinary meaning.

5. **The President's Authority to Terminate Treaties.** Rather than "interpret" a treaty if its provisions seem unduly constraining, a President might prefer to terminate or "suspend" the operation of the treaty. For example, in the post-2001 war on terrorism, the Justice Department initially advised the President that he could suspend the Geneva Conventions. Instead, the President interpreted the Conventions not to apply to al-Qaeda prisoners captured in the war on terror (an interpretation the Court rejected in part in *Hamdan*). An earlier case, *Goldwater v. Carter*, involved a challenge to President Carter's decision to terminate a U.S. treaty with Taiwan as part of the President's recognition of the People's Republic of China. The court of appeals, 617 F.2d 697 (D.C. Cir. 1979), found that the President had constitutional power to terminate the treaty; the Supreme Court, in a fractured opinion, 444 U.S. 996 (1979), found the case nonjusticiable. Should the President be able to terminate treaties? Note that the Constitution says nothing specific on the subject. Should it matter whether the termination is in accordance with the treaty's terms or in violation of the treaty's terms?

REVIEW NOTES AND QUESTIONS ON TREATIES

1. Suppose that you are an attorney with a client who wishes to sue to enforce a provision of an international agreement in U.S. court. Can you design a flowchart that shows all the hurdles you will need to surmount? Consider what principal issues you will likely confront at each step. Are there some kinds of treaties that are more or less likely to be enforced?
2. You may get a sense from these materials that courts have a fair amount of discretion in deciding when to enforce or not enforce treaties. If that is so, it may matter whether a court is generally supportive of or skeptical of treaty

enforcement by courts. Why might a court take one or the other view? How would you encourage a court to be less (or more) skeptical of treaty enforcement? How would such skepticism play out in applying particular doctrines of U.S. treaty law?

3. One practical conclusion you should reach is that there are many international agreements in existence, covering a wide range of transnational topics that are at least *potentially* applicable in U.S. court. What does this suggest for a practicing lawyer?

C. Customary International Law in U.S. Courts

After treaties, customary international law is typically understood as the second most important type of international law. Until the early nineteenth century, this form of law was commonly called the "law of nations"; the U.S. Constitution and early court cases use that phrase instead of customary international law.

Unlike treaties, customary international law's place in the U.S. constitutional order is not described in the Constitution's text. The Constitution's only reference to it is in Article I, Section 8, which gives Congress power "To define and punish Piracies and Felonies committed on the high Seas, and Offenses against the Law of Nations." In the United States, many issues involving the modern litigation of customary international law have arisen in cases brought under what is now called the Alien Tort Statute (ATS), a federal law originally passed by the First Congress as part of the Judiciary Act of 1789. The first section below addresses customary international law litigation under the Alien Tort Statute; subsequent sections address other ways that U.S. courts may encounter customary international law.

As with treaties, it is important to remember that customary international law may be applied by different dispute resolution bodies in different ways. To provide a practical dimension to debates over customary international law, this section focuses on the approach of U.S. courts. But other nations' courts have different approaches, as do other dispute resolution bodies such as international courts and arbitral panels.

1. Suing for Customary International Law Violations Under the Alien Tort Statute

28 U.S.C. § 1350 (the Alien Tort Statute) (ATS)

The district courts shall have original jurisdiction of any civil action by an alien, for a tort only, committed in violation of the law of nations or a treaty of the United States.

Filártiga v. Peña-Irala

630 F.2d 876 (2d Cir. 1980)

KAUFMAN, Circuit Judge:

Upon ratification of the Constitution, the thirteen former colonies were fused into a single nation, one which, in its relations with foreign states, is bound both to observe and construe the accepted norms of international law, formerly known as the law of nations. Under the Articles of Confederation, the several states had interpreted and applied this body of doctrine as a part of their common law, but with the founding of the "more perfect Union" of 1789, the law of nations became preeminently a federal concern.

Implementing the constitutional mandate for national control over foreign relations, the First Congress established original district court jurisdiction over "all causes where an alien sues for a tort only (committed) in violation of the law of nations." Judiciary Act of 1789, codified at 28 U.S.C. § 1350. Construing this rarely-invoked provision, we hold that deliberate torture perpetrated under color of official authority violates universally accepted norms of the international law of human rights, regardless of the nationality of the parties. Thus, whenever an alleged torturer is found and served with process by an alien within our borders, § 1350 provides federal jurisdiction. Accordingly, we reverse the judgment of the district court dismissing the complaint for want of federal jurisdiction.

The appellants, plaintiffs below, are citizens of the Republic of Paraguay. Dr. Joel Filártiga, a physician, describes himself as a longstanding opponent of the government of President Alfredo Stroessner, which has held power in Paraguay since 1954. His daughter, Dolly Filártiga, arrived in the United States in 1978 under a visitor's visa, and has since applied for permanent political asylum. The Filártigas brought this action in the Eastern District of New York against Americo Norberto Peña-Irala, also a citizen of Paraguay, for wrongfully causing the death of Dr. Filártiga's seventeen-year-old son, Joelito. Because the district court dismissed the action for want of subject matter jurisdiction, we must accept as true the allegations contained in the Filártigas' complaint and affidavits for purposes of this appeal.

The appellants contend that on March 29, 1976, Joelito Filártiga was kidnapped and tortured to death by Peña, who was then Inspector General of Police in Asuncion, Paraguay. Later that day, the police brought Dolly Filártiga to Peña's home where she was confronted with the body of her brother, which evidenced marks of severe torture. As she fled, horrified, from the house, Peña followed after her shouting, "Here you have what you have been looking for for so long and what you deserve. Now shut up." The Filártigas claim that Joelito was tortured and killed in retaliation for his father's political activities and beliefs.

Shortly thereafter, Dr. Filártiga commenced a criminal action in the Paraguayan courts against Peña and the police for the murder of his son. As a result, Dr. Filártiga's attorney was arrested and brought to police headquarters where, shackled to a wall, Peña threatened him with death. . . .

. . .

In July of 1978, Peña . . . entered the United States under a visitor's visa. He [and a companion] . . . remained in the United States beyond the term of their visas, and were living in Brooklyn, New York, when Dolly Filártiga, who was then living in Washington, D.C., learned of their presence. Acting on information provided by Dolly the Immigration and Naturalization Service arrested Peña and his companion, both of whom were subsequently ordered deported. . . . They had then resided in the United States for more than nine months.

. . . Dolly caused Peña to be served with a summons and civil complaint at the Brooklyn Navy Yard, where he was being held pending deportation. The complaint alleged that Peña had wrongfully caused Joelito's death by torture and sought compensatory and punitive damages of $10,000,000. . . . Jurisdiction is claimed under the general federal question provision, 28 U.S.C. § 1331 and, principally on this appeal, under the Alien Tort Statute, 28 U.S.C. § 1350.

[The district court dismissed the action.] . . . Shortly thereafter, Peña and his companion returned to Paraguay.

Appellants rest their principal argument in support of federal jurisdiction upon the Alien Tort Statute. . . . Since appellants do not contend that their action arises directly under a treaty of the United States, a threshold question on the jurisdictional issue is whether the conduct alleged violates the law of nations. In light of the universal condemnation of torture in numerous international agreements, and the renunciation of torture as an instrument of official policy by virtually all of the nations of the world (in principle if not in practice), we find that an act of torture committed by a state official against one held in detention violates established norms of the international law of human rights, and hence the law of nations.

The Supreme Court has enumerated the appropriate sources of international law. The law of nations "may be ascertained by consulting the works of jurists, writing professedly on public law; or by the general usage and practice of nations; or by judicial decisions recognizing and enforcing that law." *United States v. Smith*, 18 U.S. 153, 160-61 (1820). . . .

The Paquete Habana, 175 U.S. 677 (1900), reaffirmed that

> where there is no treaty, and no controlling executive or legislative act or judicial decision, resort must be had to the customs and usages of civilized nations; and, as evidence of these, to the works of jurists and commentators, who by years of labor, research and experience, have made themselves peculiarly well acquainted with the subjects of which they treat. Such works are resorted to by judicial tribunals, not for the speculations of their authors concerning what the law ought to be, but for trustworthy evidence of what the law really is.

Id. at 700. . . .

Habana is particularly instructive for present purposes, for it held that the traditional prohibition against seizure of an enemy's coastal fishing vessels during wartime, a standard that began as one of comity only, had ripened over the preceding century into "a settled rule of international law" by "the general assent of civilized nations." Thus it is clear that courts must interpret international law not as it was in 1789, but as it has evolved and exists among the nations of the world today.

Definition of Custo 2nd law.

[T]here are few, if any, issues in international law today on which opinion seems to be so united as the limitations on a state's power to torture persons held in its custody. The United Nations Charter (a treaty of the United States) makes it clear that in this modern age a state's treatment of its own citizens is a matter of international concern. It provides:

UNC Art 55.

> With a view to the creation of conditions of stability and well-being which are necessary for peaceful and friendly relations among nations . . . the United Nations shall promote . . . universal respect for, and observance of, human rights and fundamental freedoms for all without distinctions as to race, sex, language or religion.

Id. Art. 55. . . .

While this broad mandate has been held not to be wholly self-executing, this observation alone does not end our inquiry. For although there is no universal agreement as to the precise extent of the "human rights and fundamental freedoms" guaranteed to all by the Charter, there is at present no dissent from the view that the guaranties include, at a bare minimum, the right to be free from torture. This prohibition has become part of customary international law, as evidenced and defined by the Universal Declaration of Human Rights, General Assembly Resolution 217(III)(A) (Dec. 10, 1948) which states, in the plainest of terms, "no one shall be subjected to torture." The General Assembly has declared that the Charter precepts embodied in this Universal Declaration "constitute basic principles of international law." G.A. Res. 2625 (XXV) (Oct. 24, 1970).

UDHR. Authoritative Statement.

Particularly relevant is the Declaration on the Protection of All Persons from Being Subjected to Torture, General Assembly Resolution 3452, 30 U.N. GAOR Supp. (No. 34) 91, U.N. Doc. A/1034 (1975). . . . The Declaration expressly prohibits any state from permitting the dastardly and totally inhuman act of torture. Torture, in turn, is defined as "any act by which severe pain and suffering, whether physical or mental, is intentionally inflicted by or at the instigation of a public official on a person for such purposes as . . . intimidating him or other persons." The Declaration goes on to provide that "(w)here it is proved that an act of torture or other cruel, inhuman or degrading treatment or punishment has been committed by or at the instigation of a public official, the victim shall be afforded redress and compensation, in accordance with national law." This Declaration, like the Declaration of Human Rights before it, was adopted without dissent by the General Assembly.

These U.N. declarations are significant because they specify with great precision the obligations of member nations under the Charter. Since their adoption, "(m)embers can no longer contend that they do not know what human rights they promised in the Charter to promote." Sohn, "A Short History of United Nations Documents on Human Rights," in The United Nations and Human Rights, 18th Report of the Commission (Commission to Study the Organization of Peace ed. 1968). Moreover, a U.N. Declaration is, according to one authoritative definition, "a formal and solemn instrument, suitable for rare occasions when principles of great and lasting importance are being enunciated." 34 U.N. ESCOR, Supp. (No.

8) 15, U.N. Doc. E/cn.4/1/610 (1962) (memorandum of Office of Legal Affairs, U.N. Secretariat).

Accordingly, it has been observed that the Universal Declaration of Human Rights "no longer fits into the dichotomy of 'binding treaty' against 'non-binding pronouncement,' but is rather an authoritative statement of the international community." E. Schwelb, Human Rights and the International Community 70 (1964). Thus, a Declaration creates an expectation of adherence, and "insofar as the expectation is gradually justified by State practice, a declaration may by custom become recognized as laying down rules binding upon the States." 34 U.N. ESCOR, *supra*. Indeed, several commentators have concluded that the Universal Declaration has become, in toto, a part of binding, customary international law.

Turning to the act of torture, we have little difficulty discerning its universal renunciation in the modern usage and practice of nations. The international consensus surrounding torture has found expression in numerous international treaties and accords. *E.g.*, American Convention on Human Rights, Art. 5 ("No one shall be subjected to torture or to cruel, inhuman or degrading punishment or treatment"); International Covenant on Civil and Political Rights; European Convention for the Protection of Human Rights and Fundamental Freedoms, Art. 3. The substance of these international agreements is reflected in modern municipal *i.e.* national law as well. Although torture was once a routine concomitant of criminal interrogations in many nations, during the modern and hopefully more enlightened era it has been universally renounced. According to one survey, torture is prohibited, expressly or implicitly, by the constitutions of over fifty-five nations, including both the United States and Paraguay. Our State Department reports a general recognition of this principle:

> There now exists an international consensus that recognizes basic human rights and obligations owed by all governments to their citizens. . . . There is no doubt that these rights are often violated; but virtually all governments acknowledge their validity.

We have been directed to no assertion by any contemporary state of a right to torture its own or another nation's citizens. Indeed, United States diplomatic contacts confirm the universal abhorrence with which torture is viewed:

> In exchanges between United States embassies and all foreign states with which the United States maintains relations, it has been the Department of State's general experience that no government has asserted a right to torture its own nationals. Where reports of torture elicit some credence, a state usually responds by denial or, less frequently, by asserting that the conduct was unauthorized or constituted rough treatment short of torture.

Having examined the sources from which customary international law is derived, the usage of nations, judicial opinions and the works of jurists, we conclude that official torture is now prohibited by the law of nations. The prohibition is clear and unambiguous, and admits of no distinction between treatment of aliens and citizens. . . . We therefore turn to the question whether the other requirements for jurisdiction are met.

III

Appellee submits that even if the tort alleged is a violation of modern international law, federal jurisdiction may not be exercised consistent with the dictates of Article III of the Constitution. The claim is without merit. Common law courts of general jurisdiction regularly adjudicate transitory tort claims between individuals over whom they exercise personal jurisdiction, wherever the tort occurred. Moreover, as part of an articulated scheme of federal control over external affairs, Congress provided, in the first Judiciary Act, § 9(b), 1 Stat. 73, 77 (1789), for federal jurisdiction over suits by aliens where principles of international law are in issue. The constitutional basis for the Alien Tort Statute is the law of nations, which has always been part of the federal common law.

It is not extraordinary for a court to adjudicate a tort claim arising outside of its territorial jurisdiction. A state or nation has a legitimate interest in the orderly resolution of disputes among those within its borders, and where the *lex loci delicti commissi* is applied, it is an expression of comity to give effect to the laws of the state where the wrong occurred.

. . .

During the eighteenth century, it was taken for granted on both sides of the Atlantic that the law of nations forms a part of the common law. 1 Blackstone, Commentaries 263-64 (1st *ed.* 1765-69); 4 *id.* at 67. Under the Articles of Confederation, the Pennsylvania Court of Oyer and Terminer at Philadelphia, per McKean, Chief Justice, applied the law of nations to the criminal prosecution of the Chevalier de Longchamps for his assault upon the person of the French Consul-General to the United States, noting that "(t)his law, in its full extent, is a part of the law of this state. . . ." *Respublica v. DeLongchamps*, 1 U.S. 113, 119 (1784).

As ratified, [Article III] contained no express reference to cases arising under the law of nations. Indeed, the only express reference to that body of law is contained in Article I, sec. 8, cl. 10, which grants to the Congress the power to "define and punish . . . offenses against the law of nations." Appellees seize upon this circumstance and advance the proposition that the law of nations forms a part of the laws of the United States only to the extent that Congress has acted to define it. This extravagant claim is amply refuted by the numerous decisions applying rules of international law uncodified in any act of Congress. . . .

Thus, it was hardly a radical initiative for Chief Justice Marshall to state in *The Nereide*, 13 U.S. 388, 422 (1815), that in the absence of a congressional enactment, United States courts are "bound by the law of nations, which is a part of the law of the land." These words were echoed in *The Paquete Habana*, "(i)nternational law is part of our law, and must be ascertained and administered by the courts of justice of appropriate jurisdiction, as often as questions of right depending upon it are duly presented for their determination."

. . .

In the twentieth century the international community has come to recognize the common danger posed by the flagrant disregard of basic human rights and particularly the right to be free of torture. Spurred first by the Great War, and then the Second, civilized nations have banded together to prescribe acceptable norms of international behavior. From the ashes of the Second World War arose the United Nations Organization, amid hopes that an era of peace and cooperation had at last begun. Though many of these aspirations have remained elusive goals, that circumstance cannot diminish the true progress that has been made. In the modern age, humanitarian and practical considerations have combined to lead the nations of the world to recognize that respect for fundamental human rights is in their individual and collective interest. Among the rights universally proclaimed by all nations, as we have noted, is the right to be free of physical torture. Indeed, for purposes of civil liability, the torturer has become like the pirate and slave trader before him *hostis humani generis*, an enemy of all mankind. Our holding today, giving effect to a jurisdictional provision enacted by our First Congress, is a small but important step in the fulfillment of the ageless dream to free all people from brutal violence.

[Reversed.]

Sosa v. Alvarez-Machain

542 U.S. 692 (2004)

[The United States suspected Alvarez-Machain, a Mexican citizen living in Mexico, of complicity in crimes committed by drug gangs in Mexico, including the murder of a U.S. agent. U.S. Drug Enforcement Agency (DEA) officials recruited various individuals, including Sosa, a Mexican citizen, to kidnap Alvarez-Machain in Mexico and bring him to the United States for trial. In *United States v. Alvarez-Machain*, excerpted above, the Supreme Court rejected a claim that the kidnapping violated the U.S.-Mexico extradition treaty, and allowed Alvarez-Machain's criminal trial to proceed.]

Justice SOUTER delivered the opinion of the Court.

. . .

The [criminal] case [against Alvarez-Machain] was tried in 1992, and ended at the close of the Government's case, when the District Court granted Alvarez's motion for a judgment of acquittal.

In 1993, after returning to Mexico, Alvarez began the civil action before us here. . . . Alvarez sought damages . . . from Sosa under the ATS, for a violation of the law of nations. . . .

The District Court granted . . . $25,000 in damages to Alvarez on the ATS claim. A three-judge panel of the Ninth Circuit then affirmed the ATS judgment. . . .

A divided en banc court came to the same conclusion. . . . The Circuit . . . relied upon what it called the "clear and universally recognized norm prohibiting arbitrary arrest and detention" to support the conclusion that Alvarez's arrest amounted to a tort in violation of international law. . . . We now reverse. . . .

[The Court first held that Alvarez could not sue the United States due to sovereign immunity under the Federal Tort Claims Act.]

Alvarez has also brought an action under the ATS against petitioner, Sosa, who argues (as does the United States supporting him) that there is no relief under the ATS because the statute does no more than vest federal courts with jurisdiction, neither creating nor authorizing the courts to recognize any particular right of action without further congressional action. Although we agree the statute is in terms only jurisdictional, we think that at the time of enactment the jurisdiction enabled federal courts to hear claims in a very limited category defined by the law of nations and recognized at common law. We do not believe, however, that the limited, implicit sanction to entertain the handful of international law *cum* common law claims understood in 1789 should be taken as authority to recognize the right of action asserted by Alvarez here.

A

. . .

The fact that the ATS was placed in § 9 of the Judiciary Act, a statute otherwise exclusively concerned with federal-court jurisdiction, is itself support for its strictly jurisdictional nature. Nor would the distinction between jurisdiction and cause of action have been elided by the drafters of the Act or those who voted on it. As Fisher Ames put it, "there is a substantial difference between the jurisdiction of courts and rules of decision." 1 Annals of Cong. 807. . . .

But holding the ATS jurisdictional raises a new question, this one about the interaction between the ATS at the time of its enactment and the ambient law of the era. Sosa would have it that the ATS was stillborn because there could be no claim for relief without a further statute expressly authorizing adoption of causes of action. *Amici* professors of federal jurisdiction and legal history take a different tack, that federal courts could entertain claims once the jurisdictional grant was on the books, because torts in violation of the law of nations would have been recognized within the common law of the time. We think history and practice give the edge to this latter position.

1

"When the *United States* declared their independence, they were bound to receive the law of nations, in its modern state of purity and refinement." *Ware v. Hylton*, 3 Dall. 199, 281 (1796) (Wilson, J.). In the years of the early Republic, this law of nations comprised two principal elements, the first covering the general norms governing the behavior of national states with each other: "*the science which teaches the rights subsisting between nations or states, and the obligations correspondent to those rights,*" E. de Vattel, The Law of Nations, Preliminaries § 3. . . . This aspect of the law of nations thus occupied the executive and legislative domains, not the judicial. See 4 W. Blackstone, Commentaries on the Laws of England 68 (1769) ("[O]ffenses against" the law of nations are "principally incident to whole states or nations").

The law of nations included a second, more pedestrian element, however, that did fall within the judicial sphere, as a body of judge-made law regulating the conduct of individuals situated outside domestic boundaries and consequently carrying an international savor. . . . The law merchant emerged from the customary practices of international traders and admiralty required its own transnational regulation. And it was the law of nations in this sense that our precursors spoke about when the Court explained the status of coast fishing vessels in wartime grew from "ancient usage among civilized nations, beginning centuries ago, and gradually ripening into a rule of international law. . . ." *The Paquete Habana*, 175 U.S. 677, 686 (1900).

There was, finally, a sphere in which these rules binding individuals for the benefit of other individuals overlapped with the norms of state relationships. Blackstone referred to it when he mentioned three specific offenses against the law of nations addressed by the criminal law of England: violation of safe conducts, infringement of the rights of ambassadors, and piracy. An assault against an ambassador, for example, impinged upon the sovereignty of the foreign nation and if not adequately redressed could rise to an issue of war. It was this narrow set of violations of the law of nations, admitting of a judicial remedy and at the same time threatening serious consequences in international affairs, that was probably on minds of the men who drafted the ATS with its reference to tort.

2

Before there was any ATS, a distinctly American preoccupation with these hybrid international norms had taken shape owing to the distribution of political power from independence through the period of confederation. The Continental Congress was hamstrung by its inability to "cause infractions of treaties, or of the law of nations to be punished," J. Madison, Journal of the Constitutional Convention 60 (E. Scott ed. 1893). . . .

Appreciation of the Continental Congress's incapacity to deal with this class of cases was intensified by the so-called Marbois incident of May 1784, in which a French adventurer, Longchamps, verbally and physically assaulted the Secretary of the French Legion in Philadelphia. Congress called . . . for state legislation addressing such matters, and concern over the inadequate vindication of the law of nations persisted through the time of the constitutional convention. . . .

The Framers responded by vesting the Supreme Court with original jurisdiction over "all Cases affecting Ambassadors, other public ministers and Consuls." U.S. Const., Art. III, § 2, and the First Congress followed through. The Judiciary Act reinforced this Court's original jurisdiction over suits brought by diplomats, see 1 Stat. 80, ch. 20, § 13, created alienage jurisdiction, § 11 and, of course, included the ATS, § 9. . . .

3

. . . [T]here is every reason to suppose that the First Congress did not pass the ATS as a jurisdictional convenience to be placed on the shelf for use by a future Congress or state legislature that might, some day, authorize the creation of causes of action or itself decide to make some element of the law of nations actionable for the benefit of foreigners. . . .

The second inference to be drawn from the history is that Congress intended the ATS to furnish jurisdiction for a relatively modest set of actions alleging violations of the law of nations. Uppermost in the legislative mind appears to have been offenses against ambassadors; violations of safe conduct were probably understood to be actionable, and individual actions arising out of prize captures and piracy may well have also been contemplated. But the common law appears to have understood only those three of the hybrid variety as definite and actionable, or at any rate, to have assumed only a very limited set of claims. As Blackstone had put it, "offences against this law [of nations] are principally incident to whole states or nations," and not individuals seeking relief in court.

4

. . .

In sum, although the ATS is a jurisdictional statute creating no new causes of action, the reasonable inference from the historical materials is that the statute was intended to have practical effect the moment it became law. The jurisdictional grant is best read as having been enacted on the understanding that the common law would provide a cause of action for the modest number of international law violations with a potential for personal liability at the time.

IV

We think it is correct, then, to assume that the First Congress understood that the district courts would recognize private causes of action for certain torts in violation of the law of nations, though we have found no basis to suspect Congress had any examples in mind beyond those torts corresponding to Blackstone's three primary offenses: violation of safe conducts, infringement of the rights of ambassadors, and piracy. We assume, too, that no development in the two centuries from the enactment of § 1350 to the birth of the modern line of cases beginning with *Filártiga v. Peña-Irala*, has categorically precluded federal courts from recognizing a claim under the law of nations as an element of common law; Congress has not in any relevant way amended § 1350 or limited civil common law power by another statute. Still, there are good reasons for a restrained conception of the discretion a federal court should exercise in considering a new cause of action of this kind. Accordingly, we think courts should require any claim based on the present-day law of nations to rest on a norm of international character accepted by the civilized world and defined with a specificity comparable to the features of the 18th-century paradigms we have recognized. This requirement is fatal to Alvarez's claim.

A

A series of reasons argue for judicial caution when considering the kinds of individual claims that might implement the jurisdiction conferred by the early statute. First, the prevailing conception of the common law has changed since 1789 in a way that counsels restraint in judicially applying internationally generated norms. . . . Now, . . . in most cases where a court is asked to state or formulate a common law principle in a new context, there is a general understanding that the law is not so much found or discovered as it is either made or created. . . . [A] judge deciding in reliance on an international norm will find a substantial element of discretionary judgment in the decision.

Second, along with, and in part driven by, that conceptual development in understanding common law has come an equally significant rethinking of the role of the federal courts in making it. . . . [T]he general practice has been to look for legislative guidance before exercising innovative authority over substantive law. It would be remarkable to take a more aggressive role in exercising a jurisdiction that remained largely in shadow for much of the prior two centuries.

Third, this Court has recently and repeatedly said that a decision to create a private right of action is one better left to legislative judgment in the great majority of cases. *Alexander v. Sandoval*, 532 U.S. 275, 286-287 (2001). . . .

Fourth, the subject of those collateral consequences is itself a reason for a high bar to, for the potential implications for the foreign relations of the United States of recognizing such causes should make courts particularly wary of impinging on the discretion of the Legislative and Executive Branches in managing foreign affairs. It is one thing for American courts to enforce constitutional limits on our own State and Federal Governments' power, but quite another to consider suits under rules that would go so far as to claim a limit on the power of foreign governments over their own citizens, and to hold that a foreign government or its agent has transgressed those limits. Yet modern international law is very much concerned with just such questions, and apt to stimulate calls for vindicating private interests in § 1350 cases. Since many attempts by federal courts to craft remedies for the violation of new norms of international law would raise risks of adverse foreign policy consequences, they should be undertaken, if at all, with great caution.

The fifth reason is particularly important in light of the first four. We have no congressional mandate to seek out and define new and debatable violations of the law of nations, and modern indications of congressional understanding of the judicial role in the field have not affirmatively encouraged greater judicial creativity. . . . Several times, indeed, the Senate has expressly declined to give the federal courts the task of interpreting and applying international human rights law, as when its ratification of the International Covenant on Civil and Political Rights declared that the substantive provisions of the document were not self-executing.

B

These reasons argue for great caution in adapting the law of nations to private rights. . . . [O]ther considerations persuade us that the judicial power should be exercised on the understanding that the door is still ajar subject to vigilant doorkeeping, and thus open to a narrow class of international norms today. . . . For two centuries we have affirmed that the domestic law of the United States recognizes the law of nations. See, *e.g.*, . . . *The Paquete Habana*, 175 U.S., at 700 ("International law is part of our law, and must be ascertained and administered by the courts of justice of appropriate jurisdiction, as often as questions of right depending upon it are duly presented for their determination")[.] It would take some explaining to say now that federal courts must avert their gaze entirely from any international norm intended to protect individuals.

. . . The position we take today has been assumed by some federal courts for 24 years, ever since the Second Circuit decided *Filártiga v. Peña-Irala*. . . . Congress, however, has . . . expressed no disagreement with our view of the proper exercise of the judicial power. . . .

C

We must still, however, derive a standard or set of standards for assessing the particular claim Alvarez raises, and for this case it suffices to look to the historical antecedents. Whatever the ultimate criteria for accepting a cause of action subject to jurisdiction under § 1350, we are persuaded that federal courts should not recognize private claims under federal common law for violations of any international law norm with less definite content and acceptance among civilized nations than the historical paradigms familiar when § 1350 was enacted. *See, e.g., United States v. Smith*, 5 Wheat. 153, 163-180, n. *a* (1820) (illustrating the specificity with which the law of nations defined piracy). This limit upon judicial recognition is generally consistent with the reasoning of many of the courts and judges who faced the issue before it reached this Court. See *Filártiga, supra*, at 890 ("[F]or purposes of civil liability, the torturer has become — like the pirate and slave trader before him — *hostis humani generis*, an enemy of all mankind"); . . . And the determination whether a norm is sufficiently definite to support a cause of action should (and, indeed, inevitably must) involve an element of judgment about the practical consequences of making that cause available to litigants in the federal courts.

Thus, Alvarez's detention claim must be gauged against the current state of international law, looking to those sources we have long, albeit cautiously, recognized. . . .

To begin with, Alvarez cites two well-known international agreements that, despite their moral authority, have little utility under the standard set out in this opinion. He says that his abduction by Sosa was an "arbitrary arrest" within the meaning of the Universal Declaration of Human Rights, G.A. Res. 217A (III) (1948). And he traces the rule against arbitrary arrest not only to the Declaration, but also to article nine of the International Covenant on Civil and Political Rights, to which the United States is a party, and to various other conventions to which it is not. But the Declaration does not of its own force impose obligations as a matter of international law. . . . And, although the Covenant does bind the United States as a matter of international law, the United States ratified the Covenant on the express understanding that it was not self-executing and so did not itself create obligations enforceable in the federal courts. Accordingly, Alvarez cannot say that the Declaration and Covenant themselves establish the relevant and applicable rule of international law. He instead attempts to show that prohibition of arbitrary arrest has attained the status of binding customary international law.

Here, it is useful to examine Alvarez's complaint in greater detail. As he presently argues it, the claim does not rest on the cross-border feature of his abduction. . . . [T]he Court of Appeals rejected that ground of liability for failure to identify a norm of requisite force prohibiting a forcible abduction across a border. Instead, it relied on the conclusion that the law of the United States did not authorize Alvarez's arrest, because the DEA lacked extraterritorial authority . . . and because Federal Rule of Criminal Procedure 4(d)(2) limited the warrant for Alvarez's arrest to "the jurisdiction of the United States." . . .

Alvarez thus invokes a general prohibition of "arbitrary" detention defined as officially sanctioned action exceeding positive authorization to detain under the domestic law of some government, regardless of the circumstances. Whether or not this is an accurate reading of the Covenant, Alvarez cites little authority that a rule so broad has the status of a binding customary norm today. He certainly cites nothing to justify the federal courts in taking his broad rule as the predicate for a federal lawsuit, for its implications would be breathtaking. His rule would support a cause of action in federal court for any arrest, anywhere in the world, unauthorized by the law of the jurisdiction in which it took place. . . .

Alvarez's failure to marshal support for his proposed rule is underscored by the Restatement (Third) of Foreign Relations Law of the United States (1987), which says in its discussion of customary international human rights law that a "state violates international law if, as a matter of state policy, it practices, encourages, or condones . . . prolonged arbitrary detention." *Id.*, § 702. Although the Restatement does not explain its requirements of a "state policy" and of "prolonged" detention, the implication is clear. Any credible invocation of a principle against arbitrary detention that the civilized world accepts as binding customary international law requires a factual basis beyond relatively brief detention in excess of positive authority. Even the Restatement's limits are only the beginning of the enquiry, because although it is easy to say that some policies of prolonged arbitrary detentions are so bad that those who enforce them become enemies of the human race, it may be harder to say which policies cross that line with the certainty afforded by Blackstone's three common law offenses. . . .

Whatever may be said for the broad principle Alvarez advances, in the present, imperfect world, it expresses an aspiration that exceeds any binding customary rule having the specificity we require. Creating a private cause of action to further that aspiration would go beyond any residual common law discretion we think it appropriate to exercise. It is enough to hold that a single illegal detention of less than a day, followed by the transfer of custody to lawful authorities and a prompt arraignment, violates no norm of customary international law so well defined as to support the creation of a federal remedy.

. . .

The judgment of the Court of Appeals is Reversed.

Justice SCALIA, with whom [Chief Justice REHNQUIST] and Justice THOMAS join, concurring in part and concurring in the judgment.

There is not much that I would add to the Court's detailed opinion, and only one thing that I would subtract: its reservation of a discretionary power in the

Federal Judiciary to create causes of action for the enforcement of international-law-based norms. . . .

I

. . .

At the time of its enactment, the ATS provided a federal forum in which aliens could bring suit to recover for torts committed in "violation of the law of nations." The law of nations that would have been applied in this federal forum was at the time part of the so-called general common law.

. . .

This Court's decision in *Erie R. Co. v. Tompkins*, 304 U.S. 64 (1938), signaled the end of federal-court elaboration and application of the general common law. . . . [T]he *Erie* Court extirpated that law with its famous declaration that "[t]here is no federal general common law." . . .

After the death of the old general common law in *Erie* came the birth of a new and different common law pronounced by federal courts. There developed a specifically federal common law (in the sense of judicially pronounced law) for a "few and restricted" areas in which "a federal rule of decision is necessary to protect uniquely federal interests, and those in which Congress has given the courts the power to develop substantive law." . . .

Because post-*Erie* federal common law is made, not discovered, federal courts must possess some federal-common-law-making authority before undertaking to craft it. . . . The general rule . . . is that the vesting of jurisdiction in the federal courts does not in and of itself give rise to authority to formulate federal common law. . . .

The rule against finding a delegation of substantive lawmaking power in a grant of jurisdiction is subject to exceptions, some better established than others. The most firmly entrenched is admiralty law, derived from the grant of admiralty jurisdiction in Article III, § 2, cl. 3, of the Constitution. In the exercise of that jurisdiction federal courts develop and apply a body of general maritime law, the well-known and well-developed venerable law of the sea which arose from the custom among seafaring men. . . .

II

. . .

These conclusions are alone enough to dispose of the present case in favor of petitioner Sosa. None of the exceptions to the general rule against finding substantive lawmaking power in a jurisdictional grant apply. . . . In modern international human rights litigation of the sort that has proliferated since *Filártiga v. Peña-Irala*, a federal court must first *create* the underlying federal command. But "the fact that a rule has been recognized as [customary international law], by itself, is not an adequate basis for viewing that rule as part of federal common law." Meltzer, Customary International Law, Foreign Affairs, and Federal Common Law, 42 Va. J. Int'l L. 513, 519 (2002). . . .

III

. . .

To be sure, today's opinion does not itself precipitate a direct confrontation with Congress by creating a cause of action that Congress has not. But it invites precisely that action by the lower courts, even while recognizing (1) that Congress understood the difference between granting jurisdiction and creating a federal cause of action in 1789, (2) that Congress understands that difference today, and (3) that the ATS itself supplies only jurisdiction. In holding open the possibility that judges may create rights where Congress has not authorized them to do so, the Court countenances judicial occupation of a domain that belongs to the people's representatives. One does not need a crystal ball to predict that this occupation will not be long in coming, since the Court endorses the reasoning of "many of the courts and judges who faced the issue before it reached this Court," including the Second and Ninth Circuits.

. . .

Though it is not necessary to resolution of the present case, one further consideration deserves mention: Despite the avulsive change of *Erie*, the Framers who included reference to "the Law of Nations" in Article I, § 8, cl. 10, of the Constitution would be entirely content with the post-*Erie* system I have described, and quite terrified by the "discretion" endorsed by the Court. That portion of the general common law known as the law of nations was understood to refer to the accepted practices of nations in their dealings with one another (treatment of ambassadors, immunity of foreign sovereigns from suit, etc.) and with actors on the high seas hostile to all nations and beyond all their territorial jurisdictions (pirates). Those accepted practices have for the most part, if not in their entirety, been enacted into United States statutory law, so that insofar as they are concerned the demise of the general common law is inconsequential. The notion that a law of nations, redefined to mean the consensus of states on *any* subject, can be used by a private citizen to control a sovereign's treatment of *its own citizens* within *its own territory* is a 20th-century invention of internationalist law professors and human-rights advocates. See generally Bradley & Goldsmith, Critique of the Modern Position, 110 Harv. L. Rev., at 831-837. The Framers would, I am confident, be appalled by the proposition that, for example, the American peoples' democratic adoption of the death penalty, could be judicially nullified because of the disapproving views of foreigners.

. . .

We Americans have a method for making the laws that are over us. We elect representatives to two Houses of Congress, each of which must enact the new law and present it for the approval of a President, whom we also elect. For over two decades now, unelected federal judges have been usurping this lawmaking power by converting what they regard as norms of international law into American law. Today's opinion approves that process in principle, though urging the lower courts to be more restrained. . . .

American law — the law made by the people's democratically elected representatives — does not recognize a category of activity that is so universally disapproved by other nations that it is automatically unlawful here, and automatically gives rise to a private action for money damages in federal court. That simple principle is what today's decision should have announced.

NOTES AND QUESTIONS

1. **The Rise of ATS Litigation.** Although enacted in 1789, the Alien Tort Statute was rarely invoked prior to the decision in *Filártiga*. After *Filártiga*, many human rights suits were filed against foreign governments and foreign government officials (although suits against governments were generally found to be barred by foreign sovereign immunity). Some courts questioned the basis of these suits. In *Tel-Oren v. Libyan Arab Republic*, 726 F.2d 774 (D.C. Cir. 1984), for example, the court of appeals rejected an ATS claim brought by victims of a terrorist bombing in Israel. Each judge wrote separately. Judge Bork argued that the plaintiffs lacked a cause of action; Judge Robb argued that the case raised a political question; Judge Edwards argued that terrorism was not clearly established as a violation of international law. In general, however, the *Filártiga* approach was accepted and expanded by subsequent courts. *E.g.*, *Kadić v. Karadžić*, 70 F.3d 232 (2d Cir. 1995) (allowing ATS claim by Bosnian Muslims for genocide against a Bosnian Serb leader during Yugoslavian civil war); *In re Estate of Ferdinand Marcos Human Rights Litigation*, 25 F.3d 1467 (9th Cir. 1994) (allowing ATS claim for atrocities committed by former President of the Philippines); *Ababe-Jiro v. Negewo*, 72 F.3d 844 (11th Cir. 1996) (allowing ATS claims against former Ethiopian official).

2. **Practical Implications of ATS Litigation.** What did Filártiga gain by suing under the ATS? Why not bring the claim under Paraguayan law, or U.S. law? Note that Article III of the Constitution does not recognize federal jurisdiction for suits between aliens. Nor does it specifically mention customary international law. Why did Filártiga sue in federal court? Should a U.S. court hear this type of case? Why or why not? What do you think Congress was likely trying to accomplish in passing the ATS, and how does this relate to the *Filártiga* decision?

3. **Finding International Law Under the ATS.** What sources does the court in *Filártiga* use to identify a rule of customary international law? Are they persuasive? Does the Court in *Sosa* have a different approach, or was Alvarez-Machain simply not able to make as strong a showing as Filártiga? According to *Sosa*, what requirements must be satisfied for there to be a rule of customary international law that can be the basis of a suit under the ATS?

4. **ATS Practice After *Sosa*.** Does *Sosa* limit the scope of ATS litigation? The Court in *Sosa* refers favorably to *Filártiga*, but how might *Filártiga* be criticized after *Sosa*? As a plaintiffs' attorney litigating ATS cases after *Sosa*, what parts of the *Sosa* decision would pose challenges that may not have existed before the decision?

5. ***Sosa* and Judicial Caution.** What was the principal difference between Justice Souter's majority opinion in *Sosa* and Justice Scalia's concurrence? What did Souter mean in calling for judicial "caution" in ATS cases? Why did Justice Scalia think this approach did not go far enough in limiting ATS claims? Should ATS claims be limited to the extent called for by Scalia? Are the majority's limits sufficient? Or are the majority's limits excessive?

6. **ATS Policy.** Do cases like *Filártiga* belong in U.S. federal court? What are the potential drawbacks to allowing *Filártiga*-style litigation? What are the potential advantages? Consider *Yousuf v. Samantar*, 699 F.3d 763 (4th Cir. 2012): Samantar, a former prime minister of Somalia under the abusive regime of President Mohamed Siad Barre who became a Virginia resident, was sued in federal court under the ATS by Somali citizens who alleged that he directed torture and other abuse against them in Somalia while he was Prime Minister. Is this a better case for resolution in U.S. court than *Filártiga*? Than *Sosa*?

7. **The Role of International Law.** Is it useful to think of these cases as involving customary international law rather than ordinary domestic law? Consider *Velez v. Sanchez*, 693 F.3d 308 (2d Cir. 2012), in which the plaintiff, Velez, was brought to the United States from Ecuador at age 16 to work in the household of Sanchez, an Ecuadorian living in New York. Velez sued Sanchez under the ATS, among other sources of law, claiming violations of customary international law rules against slavery, forced labor, and involuntary servitude arising from the working conditions to which she was subjected. (She also sued under New York law and the federal Fair Labor Standards Act.) What are the advantages of bringing this claim under international law? What are the disadvantages?

8. **Further Practical Considerations.** Apart from legal doctrines specific to the ATS, what practical difficulties are presented in litigating ATS cases against individual defendants such as Peña-Irala? Why might plaintiffs contemplate suing corporate defendants as well (or instead)? Consider these strategic questions as you read the next case.

Beginning in the 1990s, plaintiffs filed numerous claims under the ATS against multinational corporations alleging complicity in international human rights abuses in a wide range of countries including (among many others) Nigeria, Myanmar, Indonesia, South Africa, Sudan, Papua New Guinea, and Colombia. Some were dismissed on various procedural and evidentiary grounds, some have settled, and none resulted in a final judgment against the defendants; many remained ongoing more than a decade later when the Supreme Court turned its attention to the area.

Kiobel v. Royal Dutch Petroleum Co.

569 U.S. 108 (2013)

Chief Justice ROBERTS delivered the opinion of the Court.

Petitioners, a group of Nigerian nationals residing in the United States, filed suit in federal court against certain Dutch, British, and Nigerian corporations.

Petitioners sued under the Alien Tort Statute, 28 U.S.C. § 1350, alleging that the corporations aided and abetted the Nigerian Government in committing violations of the law of nations in Nigeria. The question presented is whether and under what circumstances courts may recognize a cause of action under the Alien Tort Statute, for violations of the law of nations occurring within the territory of a sovereign other than the United States.

whether/circum recog cause of action (ATS)

I

Petitioners were residents of Ogoniland, an area of 250 square miles located in the Niger delta area of Nigeria and populated by roughly half a million people. When the complaint was filed, respondents Royal Dutch Petroleum Company and Shell Transport and Trading Company, p.l.c., were holding companies incorporated in the Netherlands and England, respectively. Their joint subsidiary, respondent Shell Petroleum Development Company of Nigeria, Ltd. (SPDC), was incorporated in Nigeria, and engaged in oil exploration and production in Ogoniland. According to the complaint, after concerned residents of Ogoniland began protesting the environmental effects of SPDC's practices, respondents enlisted the Nigerian Government to violently suppress the burgeoning demonstrations. Throughout the early 1990's, the complaint alleges, Nigerian military and police forces attacked Ogoni villages, beating, raping, killing, and arresting residents and destroying or looting property. Petitioners further allege that respondents aided and abetted these atrocities by, among other things, providing the Nigerian forces with food, transportation, and compensation, as well as by allowing the Nigerian military to use respondents' property as a staging ground for attacks.

Following the alleged atrocities, petitioners moved to the United States where they have been granted political asylum and now reside as legal residents. They filed suit in the United States District Court for the Southern District of New York, alleging jurisdiction under the Alien Tort Statute [ATS] and requesting relief under customary international law. . . . The [District] [C]ourt denied respondents' motion to dismiss with respect to [several of] the . . . claims, but certified its order for interlocutory appeal pursuant to § 1292(b).

The Second Circuit dismissed the entire complaint, reasoning that the law of nations does not recognize corporate liability. We granted certiorari to consider that question. After oral argument, we directed the parties to file supplemental briefs addressing an additional question: "Whether and under what circumstances the [ATS] allows courts to recognize a cause of action for violations of the law of nations occurring within the territory of a sovereign other than the United States." We heard oral argument again and now affirm the judgment below, based on our answer to the second question.

II

. . .

The question here is . . . whether a claim [under the ATS] may reach conduct occurring in the territory of a foreign sovereign. Respondents contend that claims under the ATS do not, relying primarily on a canon of statutory interpretation known as the presumption against extraterritorial application. That canon provides that "[w]hen a statute gives no clear indication of an extraterritorial application, it has none," *Morrison v. National Australia Bank Ltd.*, and reflects the "presumption that United States law governs domestically but does not rule the world," *Microsoft Corp. v. AT&T Corp.*, 550 U.S. 437, 454 (2007).

This presumption "serves to protect against unintended clashes between our laws and those of other nations which could result in international discord." *EEOC v. Arabian American Oil Co.*, 499 U.S. 244, 248 (1991) (*Aramco*). . . .

. . .

[T]he danger of unwarranted judicial interference in the conduct of foreign policy is magnified in the context of the ATS, because the question is not what Congress has done but instead what courts may do. This Court in *Sosa* [*v. Alvarez-Machain*] repeatedly stressed the need for judicial caution in considering which claims could be brought under the ATS, in light of foreign policy concerns. . . . These concerns, which are implicated in any case arising under the ATS, are all the more pressing when the question is whether a cause of action under the ATS reaches conduct within the territory of another sovereign.

These concerns are not diminished by the fact that *Sosa* limited federal courts to recognizing causes of action only for alleged violations of international law norms that are specific, universal, and obligatory. As demonstrated by Congress's enactment of the Torture Victim Protection Act of 1991, identifying such a norm is only the beginning of defining a cause of action. See *id.*, § 3 (providing detailed definitions for extrajudicial killing and torture); *id.*, § 2 (specifying who may be liable, creating a rule of exhaustion, and establishing a statute of limitations). Each of these decisions carries with it significant foreign policy implications.

The principles underlying the presumption against extraterritoriality thus constrain courts exercising their power under the ATS.

III

Petitioners contend that even if the presumption applies, the text, history, and purposes of the ATS rebut it for causes of action brought under that statute. It is true that Congress, even in a jurisdictional provision, can indicate that it intends federal law to apply to conduct occurring abroad. But to rebut the presumption, the ATS would need to evince a "clear indication of extraterritoriality." *Morrison*. It does not.

To begin, nothing in the text of the statute suggests that Congress intended causes of action recognized under it to have extraterritorial reach. The ATS covers actions by aliens for violations of the law of nations, but that does not imply extraterritorial reach — such violations affecting aliens can occur either within or outside the United States. Nor does the fact that the text reaches "*any* civil action" suggest application to torts committed abroad; it is well established that generic terms like "any" or "every" do not rebut the presumption against extraterritoriality.

Petitioners make much of the fact that the ATS provides jurisdiction over civil actions for "torts" in violation of the law of nations. They claim that in using that word, the First Congress "necessarily meant to provide for jurisdiction over extra-territorial transitory torts that could arise on foreign soil." For support, they cite the common-law doctrine that allowed courts to assume jurisdiction over such "transitory torts," including actions for personal injury, arising abroad.

Under the transitory torts doctrine, however, "the only justification for allowing a party to recover when the cause of action arose in another civilized jurisdiction is a well founded belief that it was a cause of action in that place." *Cuba R. Co. v. Crosby*, 222 U.S. 473, 479 (1912). The question under *Sosa* is not whether a federal court has jurisdiction to entertain a cause of action provided by foreign or even international law. The question is instead whether the court has authority to recognize a cause of action under U.S. law to enforce a norm of international law. The reference to "tort" does not demonstrate that the First Congress "necessarily meant" for those causes of action to reach conduct in the territory of a foreign sovereign. In the end, nothing in the text of the ATS evinces the requisite clear indication of extraterritoriality.

Nor does the historical background against which the ATS was enacted overcome the presumption against application to conduct in the territory of another sovereign. We explained in *Sosa* that when Congress passed the ATS, "three principal offenses against the law of nations" had been identified by Blackstone: violation of safe conducts, infringement of the rights of ambassadors, and piracy. The first two offenses have no necessary extraterritorial application. Indeed, Blackstone — in describing them — did so in terms of conduct occurring within the forum nation.

Two notorious episodes involving violations of the law of nations occurred in the United States shortly before passage of the ATS. Each concerned the rights of ambassadors, and each involved conduct within the Union. In 1784, a French adventurer verbally and physically assaulted Francois Barbe Marbois — the Secretary of the French Legion — in Philadelphia. The assault led the French Minister Plenipotentiary to lodge a formal protest with the Continental Congress and threaten to leave the country unless an adequate remedy were provided. And in 1787, a New York constable entered the Dutch Ambassador's house and arrested one of his domestic servants. . . .

These prominent contemporary examples . . . provide no support for the proposition that Congress expected causes of action to be brought under the statute for violations of the law of nations occurring abroad.

The third example of a violation of the law of nations familiar to the Congress that enacted the ATS was piracy. Piracy typically occurs on the high seas, beyond the territorial jurisdiction of the United States or any other country. This Court has generally treated the high seas the same as foreign soil for purposes of the presumption against extraterritorial application. Petitioners contend that because Congress surely intended the ATS to provide jurisdiction for actions against pirates, it necessarily anticipated the statute would apply to conduct occurring abroad.

Applying U.S. law to pirates, however, does not typically impose the sovereign will of the United States onto conduct occurring within the territorial jurisdiction of another sovereign, and therefore carries less direct foreign policy consequences.

Pirates were fair game wherever found, by any nation, because they generally did not operate within any jurisdiction. We do not think that the existence of a cause of action against them is a sufficient basis for concluding that other causes of action under the ATS reach conduct that does occur within the territory of another sovereign; pirates may well be a category unto themselves.

. . .

Finally, there is no indication that the ATS was passed to make the United States a uniquely hospitable forum for the enforcement of international norms. As Justice Story put it, "No nation has ever yet pretended to be the *custos morum* of the whole world. . . ." *United States v. The La Jeune Eugenie*, 26 F. Cas. 832, 847 (No. 15,551) (CC. Mass. 1822). It is implausible to suppose that the First Congress wanted their fledgling Republic — struggling to receive international recognition — to be the first. Indeed, the parties offer no evidence that any nation, meek or mighty, presumed to do such a thing.

The United States was, however, embarrassed by its potential inability to provide judicial relief to foreign officials injured in the United States. Such offenses against ambassadors violated the law of nations, and if not adequately redressed could rise to an issue of war. The ATS ensured that the United States could provide a forum for adjudicating such incidents. Nothing about this historical context suggests that Congress also intended federal common law under the ATS to provide a cause of action for conduct occurring in the territory of another sovereign.

Indeed, far from avoiding diplomatic strife, providing such a cause of action could have generated it. . . . The presumption against extraterritoriality guards against our courts triggering such serious foreign policy consequences, and instead defers such decisions, quite appropriately, to the political branches.

. . .

IV

On these facts, all the relevant conduct took place outside the United States. And even where the claims touch and concern the territory of the United States, they must do so with sufficient force to displace the presumption against extraterritorial application. Corporations are often present in many countries, and it would reach too far to say that mere corporate presence suffices. If Congress were to determine otherwise, a statute more specific than the ATS would be required.

The judgment of the Court of Appeals is affirmed. . . .

Justice KENNEDY, concurring.

The opinion for the Court is careful to leave open a number of significant questions regarding the reach and interpretation of the Alien Tort Statute. In my view that is a proper disposition. Many serious concerns with respect to human rights abuses committed abroad have been addressed by Congress in statutes such as the Torture Victim Protection Act of 1991 (TVPA), and that class of cases will be determined in the future according to the detailed statutory scheme Congress has enacted. Other cases may arise with allegations of serious violations of international law principles protecting persons, cases covered neither by the TVPA nor by the reasoning and holding of today's case; and in those disputes the proper implementation of the presumption against extraterritorial application may require some further elaboration and explanation.

Justice ALITO, with whom Justice THOMAS joins, concurring.

I concur in the judgment and join the opinion of the Court as far as it goes. Specifically, I agree that when Alien Tort Statute (ATS) "claims touch and concern the territory of the United States, they must do so with sufficient force to displace the presumption against extraterritorial application." This formulation obviously leaves much unanswered, and perhaps there is wisdom in the Court's preference for this narrow approach. I write separately to set out the broader standard that leads me to the conclusion that this case falls within the scope of the presumption.

In *Morrison*, we explained that "the presumption against extraterritorial application would be a craven watchdog indeed if it retreated to its kennel whenever *some* domestic activity is involved in the case." We also reiterated that a cause of action falls outside the scope of the presumption — and thus is not barred by the presumption — only if the event or relationship that was "the focus of congressional concern" under the relevant statute takes place within the United States. . . .

The Court's decision in *Sosa v. Alvarez-Machain* makes clear that when the ATS was enacted, congressional concern was focused on the three principal offenses against the law of nations that had been identified by Blackstone: violation of safe conducts, infringement of the rights of ambassadors, and piracy. The Court therefore held that "federal courts should not recognize private claims under federal common law for violations of any international law norm with less definite content and acceptance among civilized nations than the historical paradigms familiar when [the ATS] was enacted." In other words, only conduct that satisfies *Sosa*'s requirements of definiteness and acceptance among civilized nations can be said to have been the focus of congressional concern" when Congress enacted the ATS. As a result, a putative ATS cause of action will fall within the scope of the presumption against extraterritoriality — and will therefore be barred — unless the domestic conduct is sufficient to violate an international law norm that satisfies *Sosa*'s requirements of definiteness and acceptance among civilized nations.

Justice BREYER, with whom Justice GINSBURG, Justice SOTOMAYOR and Justice KAGAN join, concurring in the judgment.

I agree with the Court's conclusion but not with its reasoning. . . .

Unlike the Court, I would not invoke the presumption against extraterritoriality. Rather, guided in part by principles and practices of foreign relations law, I would find jurisdiction under this statute where (1) the alleged tort occurs on American soil, (2) the defendant is an American national, or (3) the defendant's conduct substantially and adversely affects an important American national interest, and that includes a distinct interest in preventing the United States from becoming a safe harbor (free of civil as well as criminal liability) for a torturer or other common enemy of mankind. . . . In this case, however, the parties and relevant conduct lack sufficient ties to the United States for the ATS to provide jurisdiction.

. . .

Recognizing that Congress enacted the ATS to permit recovery of damages from pirates and others who violated basic international law norms as understood in 1789, *Sosa* essentially leads today's judges to ask: Who are today's pirates?

. . .

In my view the majority's effort to answer the question by referring to the "presumption against extraterritoriality" does not work well. That presumption "rests on the perception that Congress ordinarily legislates with respect to domestic, not foreign matters." [*Morrison.*] The ATS, however, was enacted with "foreign matters" in mind. The statute's text refers explicitly to aliens, treaties, and the law of nations. The statute's purpose was to address "violations of the law of nations, admitting of a judicial remedy and at the same time threatening serious consequences in international affairs." *Sosa*, 542 U.S., at 715. And at least one of the three kinds of activities that we found to fall within the statute's scope, namely piracy, normally takes place abroad.

The majority cannot wish this piracy example away by emphasizing that piracy takes place on the high seas. That is because the robbery and murder that make up piracy do not normally take place in the water; they take place on a ship. And a ship is like land, in that it falls within the jurisdiction of the nation whose flag it flies. . . .

. . .

The majority also writes, "Pirates were fair game wherever found, by any nation, because they generally did not operate within any jurisdiction." I very much agree that pirates were fair game "wherever found." Indeed, that is the point. That is why we asked, in *Sosa*, who are today's pirates? Certainly today's pirates include torturers and perpetrators of genocide. And today, like the pirates of old, they are "fair game" where they are found. Like those pirates, they are "common enemies of all mankind and all nations have an equal interest in their apprehension and punishment." 1 RESTATEMENT § 404 Reporters' Note 1, p. 256. And just as a nation that harbored pirates provoked the concern of other nations in past centuries, so harboring "common enemies of all mankind" provokes similar concerns today.

. . .

In any event, as the Court uses its "presumption against extraterritorial application," it offers only limited help in deciding the question presented, namely under what circumstances the Alien Tort Statute . . . allows courts to recognize a cause of action for violations of the law of nations occurring within the territory of a sovereign other than the United States. The majority . . . makes clear that a statutory claim might sometimes "touch and concern the territory of the United States . . . with sufficient force to displace the presumption." It leaves for another day the determination of just when the presumption against extraterritoriality might be overcome.

II

. . .

I would interpret the statute as providing jurisdiction only where distinct American interests are at issue. Doing so reflects the fact that Congress adopted the present statute at a time when, as Justice Story put it, "No nation ha[d] ever yet pretended to be the *custos morum* of the whole world." *United States v. La Jeune Eugenie*, 26 F. Cas. 832, 847 (No. 15,551) (CC Mass. 1822). That restriction also should help to minimize international friction. . . .

As I have indicated, we should treat this Nation's interest in not becoming a safe harbor for violators of the most fundamental international norms as an important jurisdiction related interest justifying application of the ATS in light of the statute's basic purposes — in particular that of compensating those who have suffered harm at the hands of, *e.g.*, torturers or other modern pirates. . . .

International norms have long included a duty not to permit a nation to become a safe harbor for pirates (or their equivalent). . . .

More recently two lower American courts have, in effect, rested jurisdiction primarily upon that kind of concern. In *Filártiga*, an alien plaintiff brought a lawsuit against an alien defendant for damages suffered through acts of torture that the defendant allegedly inflicted in a foreign nation, Paraguay. Neither plaintiff nor defendant was an American national and the actions underlying the lawsuit took place abroad. The defendant, however, had resided in the United States for more than ninth months before being sued, having overstayed his visitor's visa. Jurisdiction was deemed proper because the defendant's alleged conduct violated a well-established international law norm, and the suit vindicated our Nation's interest in not providing a safe harbor, free of damages claims, for those defendants who commit such conduct.

In *Marcos*, the plaintiffs were nationals of the Philippines, the defendant was a Philippine national, and the alleged wrongful act, death by torture, took place abroad. A month before being sued, the defendant, his family, and others loyal to him fled to Hawaii, where the ATS case was heard. As in *Filártiga*, the court found ATS jurisdiction.

And in *Sosa* we referred to both cases with approval, suggesting that the ATS allowed a claim for relief in such circumstances. Not surprisingly, both before and after *Sosa*, courts have consistently rejected the notion that the ATS is categorically barred from extraterritorial application.

Application of the statute in the way I have suggested is consistent with international law and foreign practice. Nations have long been obliged not to provide safe harbors for their own nationals who commit such serious crimes abroad.

Many countries permit foreign plaintiffs to bring suits against their own nationals based on unlawful conduct that took place abroad. Other countries permit some form of lawsuit brought by a foreign national against a foreign national, based upon conduct taking place abroad and seeking damages. . . .

. . .

Congress, while aware of the award of civil damages under the ATS — including cases such as *Filártiga* with foreign plaintiffs, defendants, and conduct — has not sought to limit the statute's jurisdictional or substantive reach. Rather, Congress has enacted other statutes, and not only criminal statutes, that allow the United States to prosecute (or allow victims to obtain damages from) foreign persons who injure foreign victims by committing abroad torture, genocide, and other heinous acts.

Thus, the jurisdictional approach that I would use is analogous to, and consistent with, the approaches of a number of other nations. It is consistent with the approaches set forth in the Restatement. Its insistence upon the presence of some distinct American interest, . . . all should obviate the majority's concern that our jurisdictional example would lead other nations, also applying the law of nations, to hale our citizens into their courts for alleged violations of the law of nations occurring in the United States, or anywhere else in the world.

. . .

III

Applying these jurisdictional principles to this case, however, I agree with the Court that jurisdiction does not lie. The defendants are two foreign corporations. Their shares, like those of many foreign corporations, are traded on the New York Stock Exchange. Their only presence in the United States consists of an office in New York City (actually owned by a separate but affiliated company) that helps to explain their business to potential investors. The plaintiffs are not United States nationals but nationals of other nations. The conduct at issue took place abroad. And the plaintiffs allege, not that the defendants directly engaged in acts of torture, genocide, or the equivalent, but that they helped others (who are not American nationals) to do so.

Under these circumstances, . . . it would be farfetched to believe, based solely upon the defendants' minimal and indirect American presence, that this legal action helps to vindicate a distinct American interest, such as in not providing a safe harbor for an enemy of all mankind. . . .

I consequently join the Court's judgment but not its opinion.

NOTES AND QUESTIONS

1. **Extraterritorial Application of the ATS.** What is the core of the majority's argument against extraterritorial application of the ATS? Is the argument persuasive? In the majority's view, what is the purpose of the ATS, and why does that purpose not include extraterritorial conduct? Is it clear that the presumption against extraterritoriality should be applied to subject matter jurisdiction statutes like the ATS? Why or why not? Note that Justice Kennedy provided the necessary fifth vote for the majority's opinion. What does his concurrence mean? What uncertainties might he have in mind when he says that uncertainties remain about the application of the presumption against extraterritoriality in ATS cases? What is the point of Justice Alito's concurrence? How does Justice Breyer's approach differ? He reaches the same result as the majority in *Kiobel*; in what types of cases would he reach a different result?
2. **The Future of ATS Litigation.** What remains of ATS litigation after *Kiobel*? What types of claims are clearly not permitted? What types of claims are clearly permitted? What types of claims *might* be permitted? In *Balintulo*

v. Daimler AG, 727 F.3d 174 (2d Cir. 2013), the court indicated that *Kiobel* bars ATS suits for foreign conduct even when the defendant is a U.S. entity. Is that right? Based on the opinions in *Kiobel*, why might it not be right? As to U.S. defendants, might there be ways to rephrase the complaint to claim the conduct occurred in the United States?

In *Al Shimari v. CACI Premier Technology, Inc.*, 758 F.3d 516 (4th Cir. 2014), the court allowed an ATS claim seeking damages against a U.S. corporation for the torture and mistreatment of foreign nationals at the Abu Ghraib prison in Iraq. The court found that the claims "touch and concern" U.S. territory within the meaning of *Kiobel*:

> Here, the plaintiffs' claims allege acts of torture committed by United States citizens who were employed by an American corporation, CACI, which has corporate headquarters located in Fairfax County, Virginia. The alleged torture occurred at a military facility operated by United States government personnel.
>
> In addition, the employees who allegedly participated in the acts of torture were hired by CACI in the United States to fulfill the terms of a contract that CACI executed with the United States Department of the Interior. The contract between CACI and the Department of the Interior was issued by a government office in Arizona, and CACI was authorized to collect payments by mailing invoices to government accounting offices in Colorado. Under the terms of the contract, CACI interrogators were required to obtain security clearances from the United States Department of Defense.
>
> Finally, the allegations are not confined to the assertion that CACI's employees participated directly in acts of torture committed at the Abu Ghraib prison. The plaintiffs also allege that CACI's managers located in the United States were aware of reports of misconduct abroad, attempted to "cover up" the misconduct, and "implicitly, if not expressly, encouraged" it.

Is this sufficient to distinguish *Kiobel*? Would this allow ATS suits against all U.S. corporations? *See also Doe v. Nestlé, S.A.*, 929 F.3d 623 (9th Cir. 2018) (post-*Kiobel*, allowing claims against U.S. entities for complicity in child labor in Africa).

In contrast, in *Cardona v. Chiquita Brands Int'l, Inc.*, 760 F.3d 1185 (11th Cir. 2014), plaintiffs sued Chiquita for allegedly encouraging the Colombian government to commit torture and murder in Colombia. Over a strong dissent, the court of appeals directed a dismissal on the basis of *Kiobel*, distinguishing *Al Shimari*. The dissent argued that *Kiobel* should not apply to U.S corporations and in any event that Chiquita's conduct had occurred at its corporate headquarters in the United States. *See also Adhikari v. Kellogg Brown & Root, Inc.*, 845 F.3d 184 (5th Cir. 2017) (on the basis of *Kiobel*, rejecting ATS claim against U.S. military contractor for actions in Iraq). Can these cases be reconciled? In 2020, the Supreme Court granted certiorari in the *Nestlé* case to address the application of the ATS to U.S. corporations.

3. **Kiobel and Filártiga.** Is *Filártiga* still good law after *Kiobel*? Is there any argument that the *Filártiga* claims "touch[ed] and concern[ed]" the United States? What if the defendant is a U.S. citizen (unlike the defendant in *Filártiga*) and

acted partly from the United States? In *Sexual Minorities Uganda v. Lively*, 254 F. Supp. 3d 262 (D. Mass. 2017), the plaintiff alleged that the U.S. citizen defendant encouraged the Ugandan government's repression of people with same-sex sexual orientation. The defendant acted partly in Uganda and partly from his home in Massachusetts, but the harms all occurred in Uganda; the court dismissed the case on the basis of *Kiobel*. Is that right? Consider the concerns of the *Kiobel* majority. Are they applicable? What would Justice Breyer say? Recall also that a threshold requirement for ATS litigation is a violation of international law. Do discrimination and repression on the basis of sexual orientation violate international law? What sources might you use to answer that question?

4. **Aftermath.** What next for the *Kiobel* plaintiffs? Do they have other options and venues for suing the defendant in the United States or elsewhere? Why did they not pursue those options first? What obstacles might there be to such suits? *See generally* Donald Earl Childress III, *The Alien Tort Statute, Federalism, and the Next Wave of Transnational Litigation*, 100 Geo. L.J. 709 (2012); Seth Davis & Christopher A. Whytock, *State Remedies for Human Rights*, 98 B.U. L. Rev. 397 (2018). In *Kashef v. BNP Paribas S.A.*, 316 F. Supp. 3d 770 (S.D.N.Y. 2018), foreign plaintiffs sued BNP, a French bank with operations in New York, under New York state tort law for aiding and abetting genocide and related atrocities committed by Sudanese forces in Sudan by providing financial services to Sudan through its New York offices in violation of U.S. law. The district court dismissed the claims under the act of state doctrine, a rule discussed in Chapter 12, but the court of appeals reversed. 925 F.3d 53 (2d Cir. 2019). The litigation remains ongoing. Could this be a model for the *Kiobel* plaintiffs?

Jesner v. Arab Bank PLC

138 S. Ct. 1386 (2018)

Justice KENNEDY announced the judgment of the Court and delivered the opinion of the Court with respect to Parts I, II-B-1, and II-C, and an opinion with respect to Parts II-A, II-B-2, II-B-3, and III, in which THE CHIEF JUSTICE and Justice THOMAS join. . . .

I

A

Petitioners are plaintiffs in five [Alien Tort Statute (ATS)] lawsuits filed against Arab Bank in the United States District Court for the Eastern District of New York. . . .

A significant majority of the plaintiffs in these lawsuits — about 6,000 of them — are foreign nationals whose claims arise under the ATS. These foreign nationals are petitioners here. They allege that they or their family members were injured by terrorist attacks in the Middle East over a 10-year period. . . .

Arab Bank is a major Jordanian financial institution with branches throughout the world, including in New York. According to the Kingdom of Jordan, Arab Bank accounts for between one-fifth and one-third of the total market capitalization of the Amman Stock Exchange. Petitioners allege that Arab Bank helped finance attacks by Hamas and other terrorist groups. Among other claims, petitioners allege that Arab Bank maintained bank accounts for terrorists and their front groups and allowed the accounts to be used to pay the families of suicide bombers.

Most of petitioners' allegations involve conduct that occurred in the Middle East. Yet petitioners allege as well that Arab Bank used its New York branch to clear dollar denominated transactions through the Clearing House Interbank Payments System. That elaborate system is commonly referred to as CHIPS. It is alleged that some of these CHIPS transactions benefited terrorists. . . .

During the pendency of this litigation, there was an unrelated case that also implicated the issue whether the ATS is applicable to suits in this country against foreign corporations. *See Kiobel v. Royal Dutch Petroleum Co.*, 621 F.3d 111 (CA2 2010). . . . In *Kiobel*, the Court of Appeals held that the ATS does not extend to suits against corporations. This Court granted certiorari in *Kiobel*.

After additional briefing and reargument in *Kiobel*, this Court held that . . . [d]ismissal of the action was required based on the presumption against extraterritorial application of statutes.

So while this Court in *Kiobel* affirmed the ruling that the action there could not be maintained, it did not address the broader holding of the Court of Appeals that dismissal was required because corporations may not be sued under the ATS. Still, the courts of the Second Circuit deemed that broader holding to be binding precedent. . . . This Court granted certiorari . . . .

II

. . . [T]his Court now must decide whether common-law liability under the ATS extends to a foreign corporate defendant. . . .

Before recognizing a common-law action under the ATS, federal courts must apply the test announced in *Sosa* [*v. Alvarez-Machain*]. An initial, threshold question is whether a plaintiff can demonstrate that the alleged violation is "of a norm that is specific, universal, and obligatory." 542 U.S., at 732. And even assuming that, under international law, there is a specific norm that can be controlling, it must be determined further whether allowing this case to proceed under the ATS is a proper exercise of judicial discretion, or instead whether caution requires the political branches to grant specific authority before corporate liability can be imposed. "[T]he potential implications for the foreign relations of the United States of recognizing such causes should make courts particularly wary of impinging on the discretion of the Legislative and Executive Branches in managing foreign affairs." Id., at 727. . . .

A

. . .

1

In modern times, there is no doubt, of course, that "the international community has come to recognize the common danger posed by the flagrant disregard of basic human rights," leading "the nations of the world to recognize that respect for fundamental human rights is in their individual and collective interest." *Filartiga*, 630 F.2d, at 890. That principle and commitment support the conclusion that human-rights norms must bind the individual men and women responsible for committing humanity's most terrible crimes, not just nation-states in their interactions with one another. "The singular achievement of international law since the Second World War has come in the area of human rights," where international law now imposes duties on individuals as well as nation-states. *Kiobel*, 621 F.3d, at 118.

It does not follow, however, that current principles of international law extend liability — civil or criminal — for human-rights violations to corporations or other artificial entities. This is confirmed by the fact that the charters of respective international criminal tribunals often exclude corporations from their jurisdictional reach.

The Charter for the Nuremberg Tribunal, created by the Allies after World War II, provided that the Tribunal had jurisdiction over natural persons only. . . .

The jurisdictional reach of more recent international tribunals also has been limited to "natural persons." *See* Statute of the International Criminal Tribunal for the Former Yugoslavia, S. C. Res. 827 (May 25, 1993), . . . The Rome Statute of the International Criminal Court, for example, limits that tribunal's jurisdiction to "natural persons." The drafters of the Rome Statute considered, but rejected, a proposal to give the International Criminal Court jurisdiction over corporations.

The international community's conscious decision to limit the authority of these international tribunals to natural persons counsels against a broad holding that there is a specific, universal, and obligatory norm of corporate liability under currently prevailing international law.

2

In light of the sources just discussed, the sources petitioners rely on to support their contention that liability for corporations is well established as a matter of international law lend weak support to their position. . . .

It must be remembered that international law is distinct from domestic law in its domain as well as its objectives. International human-rights norms prohibit acts repugnant to all civilized peoples — crimes like genocide, torture, and slavery, that make their perpetrators "enem[ies] of all mankind." *Sosa*, 542 U.S., at 732. In the American legal system, of course, corporations are often subject to liability for the conduct of their human employees, and so it may seem necessary and natural that corporate entities are liable for violations of international law under the ATS. It is true, furthermore, that the enormity of the offenses that can be committed against persons in violation of international human-rights protections can be cited to show that corporations should be subject to liability for the crimes of their human agents. But the international community has not yet taken that step, at least in the specific, universal, and obligatory manner required by *Sosa*....

There is at least sufficient doubt on the point to turn to *Sosa's* second question — whether the Judiciary must defer to Congress, allowing it to determine in the first instance whether that universal norm has been recognized and, if so, whether it is prudent and necessary to direct its enforcement in suits under the ATS.

B

1

Sosa is consistent with this Court's general reluctance to extend judicially created private rights of action. The Court's recent precedents cast doubt on the authority of courts to extend or create private causes of action even in the realm of domestic law, where this Court has "recently and repeatedly said that a decision to create a private right of action is one better left to legislative judgment in the great majority of cases." 542 U.S., at 727....

This caution extends to the question whether the courts should exercise the judicial authority to mandate a rule that imposes liability upon artificial entities like corporations....

... [T]he separation-of-powers concerns that counsel against courts creating private rights of action apply with particular force in the context of the ATS. The political branches, not the Judiciary, have the responsibility and institutional capacity to weigh foreign-policy concerns. That the ATS implicates foreign relations "is itself a reason for a high bar to new private causes of action for violating international law." *Sosa, supra,* at 727.

In *Sosa*, the Court emphasized that federal courts must exercise "great caution" before recognizing new forms of liability under the ATS.... [A]bsent further action from Congress it would be inappropriate for courts to extend ATS liability to foreign corporations.

2

Even in areas less fraught with foreign-policy consequences, the Court looks to analogous statutes for guidance on the appropriate boundaries of judge-made causes of action. Doing so is even more important in the realm of international law, where "the general practice has been to look for legislative guidance before exercising innovative authority over substantive law." *Sosa, supra,* at 726.

Here, the logical place to look for a statutory analogy to an ATS common-law action is the [Torture Victim Protection Act (TVPA)]*.... Congress took care to delineate the TVPA's boundaries. In doing so, it could weigh the foreign-policy

---

* The TVPA, enacted by Congress in 1992, provides a cause of action for civil damages against foreign officials who commit acts of torture and extrajudicial killing, subject to certain limitations. — EDS.

implications of its rule. Among other things, Congress specified who may be liable, created an exhaustion requirement, and established a limitations period. In *Kiobel*, the Court recognized that "[e]ach of these decisions carries with it significant foreign policy implications." The TVPA reflects Congress' considered judgment of the proper structure for a right of action under the ATS. Absent a compelling justification, courts should not deviate from that model.

The key feature of the TVPA for this case is that it limits liability to "individuals," which, the Court has held, unambiguously limits liability to natural persons. *Mohamad v. Palestinian Authority*, 566 U.S. 449, 453-456 (2012). Congress' decision to exclude liability for corporations in actions brought under the TVPA is all but dispositive of the present case. That decision illustrates that significant foreign-policy implications require the courts to draw a careful balance in defining the scope of actions under the ATS. It would be inconsistent with that balance to create a remedy broader than the one created by Congress. Indeed, it "would be remarkable to take a more aggressive role in exercising a jurisdiction that remained largely in shadow for much of the prior two centuries." *Sosa, supra,* at 726. . . .

Petitioners contend that, instead of the TVPA, the most analogous statute here is the Anti-Terrorism Act. That Act does permit suits against corporate entities. *See* 18 U.S.C. §§ 2331(3), 2333(d)(2). In fact, in these suits some of the foreign plaintiffs joined their claims to those of United States nationals suing Arab Bank under the Anti-Terrorism Act. But the Anti-Terrorism Act provides a cause of action only to "national[s] of the United States," and their "estate, survivors, or heirs." § 2333(a). In contrast, the ATS is available only for claims brought by "an alien." 28 U.S.C. § 1350. A statute that excludes foreign nationals (with the possible exception of foreign survivors or heirs) is an inapt analogy for a common-law cause of action that provides a remedy for foreign nationals only. . . .

3

Other considerations relevant to the exercise of judicial discretion also counsel against allowing liability under the ATS for foreign corporations, absent instructions from Congress to do so. . . .

If . . . the Court were to hold that foreign corporations may be held liable under the ATS, that precedent-setting principle "would imply that other nations, also applying the law of nations, could hale our [corporations] into their courts for alleged violations of the law of nations." *Kiobel*, 569 U.S., at 124. This judicially mandated doctrine, in turn, could subject American corporations to an immediate, constant risk of claims seeking to impose massive liability for the alleged conduct of their employees and subsidiaries around the world, all as determined in foreign courts, thereby "hinder[ing] global investment in developing economies, where it is most needed." Brief for United States as Amicus Curiae . . . .

It is also true, of course, that natural persons can and do use corporations for sinister purposes, including conduct that violates international law. That the corporate form can be an instrument for inflicting grave harm and suffering poses serious and complex questions both for the international community and for Congress. So there are strong arguments for permitting the victims to seek relief from corporations themselves. Yet the urgency and complexity of this problem make it all the more important that Congress determine whether victims of human-rights abuses may sue foreign corporations in federal courts in the United States. Congress, not the Judiciary, is the branch with "the facilities necessary to make fairly such an important policy decision where the possibilities of international discord are so evident and retaliative action so certain." *Kiobel*, 569 U.S., at 116. . . .

C

The ATS was intended to promote harmony in international relations by ensuring foreign plaintiffs a remedy for international-law violations in circumstances where the absence of such a remedy might provoke foreign nations to hold the United States accountable. But here, and in similar cases, the opposite is occurring.

Petitioners are foreign nationals seeking hundreds of millions of dollars in damages from a major Jordanian financial institution for injuries suffered in attacks by foreign terrorists in the Middle East. The only alleged connections to the United States are the CHIPS transactions in Arab Bank's New York branch and a brief allegation regarding a charity in Texas. The Court of Appeals did not address, and the Court need not now decide, whether these allegations are sufficient to "touch and concern" the United States under *Kiobel. See* 569 U.S., at 124-125.

At a minimum, the relatively minor connection between the terrorist attacks at issue in this case and the alleged conduct in the United States well illustrates the perils of extending the scope of ATS liability to foreign multinational corporations like Arab Bank. For 13 years, this litigation has "caused significant diplomatic tensions" with Jordan, a critical ally in one of the world's most sensitive regions. Brief for United States as Amicus Curiae 30. "Jordan is a key counterterrorism partner, especially in the global campaign to defeat the Islamic State in Iraq and Syria." *Id.*, at 31. The United States explains that Arab Bank itself is "a constructive partner with the United States in working to prevent terrorist financing." *Id.*, at 32. Jordan considers the instant litigation to be a "grave affront" to its sovereignty. *See* Brief for Hashemite Kingdom of Jordan as Amicus Curiae 3; *see ibid.* ("By exposing Arab Bank to massive liability, this suit thus threatens to destabilize Jordan's economy and undermine its cooperation with the United States").

This is not the first time, furthermore, that a foreign sovereign has appeared in this Court to note its objections to ATS litigation. *Sosa*, 542 U.S., at 733, n. 21 (noting objections by the European Commission and South Africa); Brief for the Federal Republic of Germany as Amicus Curiae in *Kiobel v. Royal Dutch Petroleum Co.*, O.T. 2012, No. 10-1491, p. 1; Brief for the Government of the United Kingdom of Great Britain and Northern Ireland and the Kingdom of the Netherlands as Amici Curiae in No. 10-1491, p. 3. These are the very foreign-relations tensions the First Congress sought to avoid.

Petitioners insist that whatever the faults of this litigation — for example, its tenuous connections to the United States and the prolonged diplomatic disruptions it has caused — the fact that Arab Bank is a foreign corporate entity, as distinct from a natural person, is not one of them. That misses the point. As demonstrated by this litigation, foreign corporate defendants create unique problems. And courts are not well suited to make the required policy judgments that are implicated by corporate liability in cases like this one.

. . . Accordingly, the Court holds that foreign corporations may not be defendants in suits brought under the ATS. . . .

[A concurring opinion by Justice Thomas is omitted.]

Justice ALITO, concurring in part and concurring in the judgment.

Creating causes of action under the Alien Tort Statute against foreign corporate defendants would precipitate exactly the sort of diplomatic strife that the law was enacted to prevent. As a result, I agree with the Court that we should not take that step, and I join Parts I, II-B-1, and II-C of the opinion of the Court. I write separately to elaborate on why that outcome is compelled not only by "judicial caution," but also by the separation of powers. . . .

The ATS is a jurisdictional statute. . . . By its terms, the ATS does not create any causes of action.

In *Sosa*, however, this Court nevertheless held that federal courts, exercising their authority in limited circumstances to make federal common law, may create causes of action that aliens may assert under the ATS. . . .

For the reasons articulated by Justice Scalia in *Sosa* and by Justice Gorsuch today, I am not certain that *Sosa* was correctly decided. . . . But even taking that decision on its own terms, this Court should not create causes of action under the ATS against foreign corporate defendants. [A] court should decline to create a cause of action as a matter of federal common law where the result would be to further, not avoid, diplomatic strife. Properly applied, that rule easily resolves the question presented by this case. . . .

The ATS was meant to help the United States avoid diplomatic friction. The First Congress enacted the law to provide a forum for adjudicating that "narrow set of violations of the law of nations" that, if left unaddressed, "threaten[ed] serious consequences" for the United States. *Sosa*, 542 U.S., at 715; *see also* Brief for Professors of International Law et al. as Amici Curiae 7-12. Specifically, the First Congress was concerned about offenses like piracy, violation of safe conducts, and infringement of the rights of ambassadors, each of which "if not adequately redressed could rise to an issue of war." *Sosa*, *supra*, at 715. That threat was existentially terrifying for the young Nation. To minimize the danger, the First Congress enacted the ATS, "ensur[ing] that the United States could provide a forum for adjudicating such incidents" and thus helping the Nation avoid further diplomatic imbroglios.

Putting that objective together with the rules governing federal common law generally, the following principle emerges: Federal courts should decline to create federal common law causes of action under *Sosa*'s second step whenever doing so would not materially advance the ATS's objective of avoiding diplomatic strife. And applying that principle here, it is clear that federal courts should not create causes of action under the ATS against foreign corporate defendants. All parties agree that customary international law does not require corporate liability as a general matter. But if customary international law does not require corporate liability, then declining to create it under the ATS cannot give other nations just cause for complaint against the United States.

To the contrary, ATS suits against foreign corporations may provoke — and, indeed, frequently have provoked — exactly the sort of diplomatic strife inimical to the fundamental purpose of the ATS. . . . For example, Jordan considers this suit "a direct affront" to its sovereignty and one that "risks destabilizing Jordan's economy and undercutting one of the most stable and productive alliances the United States has in the Middle East." Brief for Hashemite Kingdom of Jordan as Amicus Curiae 4. Courting these sorts of problems — which seem endemic to ATS litigation — was the opposite of what the First Congress had in mind. . . .

Justice GORSUCH, concurring in part and concurring in the judgment.

I am pleased to join the Court's judgment and Parts I, II-B-1, and II-C of its opinion. Respectfully, though, I believe there are two more fundamental reasons why this lawsuit must be dismissed. A group of foreign plaintiffs wants a federal court to invent a new cause of action so they can sue another foreigner for allegedly breaching international norms. In any other context, a federal judge faced with a request like that would know exactly what to do with it: dismiss it out of hand. Not because the defendant happens to be a corporation instead of a human being. But because the job of creating new causes of action and navigating foreign policy disputes belongs to the political branches. For reasons passing understanding, federal courts have sometimes treated the Alien Tort Statute as a license to overlook these foundational principles. I would end ATS exceptionalism. We should refuse invitations to create new forms of legal liability. . . .

I

. . .

In this case, the plaintiffs . . . want the federal courts to recognize a new cause of action, one that did not exist at the time of the statute's adoption, one that Congress has never authorized. While their request might appear inconsistent with *Sosa*'s explanation of the ATS's modest origin, the plaintiffs say that a caveat later in the opinion saves them. They point to a passage where the Court went on to suggest that the ATS may also afford federal judges "discretion [to] conside[r] [creating] new cause[s] of action" if they "rest on a norm of international character accepted by the civilized world and defined with a specificity comparable to the features of the [three] 18th-century" torts the Court already described. 542 U.S., at 725.

I harbor serious doubts about *Sosa*'s suggestion. In our democracy the people's elected representatives make the laws that govern them. Judges do not. The Constitution's provisions insulating judges from political accountability may promote our ability to render impartial judgments in disputes between the people, but they do nothing to recommend us as policymakers for a large nation. . . .

Nor can I see any reason to make a special exception for the ATS. As *Sosa* initially acknowledged, the ATS was designed as "a jurisdictional statute creating no new causes of action." 542 U.S., at 724. And I would have thought that the end of the matter. A statute that creates no new causes of action . . . creates no new causes of action. To the extent *Sosa* continued on to claim for federal judges the discretionary power to create new forms of liability on their own, it invaded terrain that belongs to the people's representatives and should be promptly returned to them. 542 U.S., at 747 (Scalia, J., concurring in part and concurring in the judgment). . . .

II

Another independent problem lurks here. This is a suit by foreigners against a foreigner over the meaning of international norms. Respectfully, I do not think the original understanding of the ATS or our precedent permits federal courts to hear cases like this. At a minimum, both those considerations and simple common sense about the limits of the judicial function should lead federal courts to require a domestic defendant before agreeing to exercise any *Sosa*-generated discretion to entertain an ATS suit.

. . . Like today's recodified version, the original text of the ATS did not expressly call for a U.S. defendant. But I think it likely would have been understood to contain such a requirement when adopted.

That is because the First Congress passed the Judiciary Act in the shadow of the Constitution. The Act created the federal courts and vested them with statutory authority to entertain claims consistent with the newly ratified terms of Article III. Meanwhile, under Article III, Congress could not have extended to federal courts the power to hear just any suit between two aliens (unless, for example, one was a diplomat). Diversity of citizenship was required. So, because Article III's diversity-of-citizenship clause calls for a U.S. party, and because the ATS clause requires an alien plaintiff, it follows that an American defendant was needed for an ATS suit to proceed.

Precedent confirms this conclusion. In *Mossman v. Higginson*, 4 Dall. 12, 14 (1800), this Court addressed the meaning of a neighboring provision of the Judiciary Act. Section 11 gave the circuit courts power to hear, among other things, civil cases where "an alien is a party." 1 Stat. 78. As with § 9, you might think § 11's language could be read to permit a suit between aliens. Yet this Court held § 11 must instead be construed to refer only to cases "where, indeed, an alien is one party, but a citizen is the other." *Mossman*, 4 Dall., at 14. That was necessary, *Mossman* explained, to give the statute a "constructio[n] consistent" with the diversity jurisdiction clause of Article III. *Ibid.* And as a matter of precedent, I cannot think of a good reason why we would now read § 9 differently than *Mossman* read § 11. . . .

. . . It is one thing for courts to assume the task of creating new causes of action to ensure our citizens abide by the law of nations and avoid reprisals against this country. It is altogether another thing for courts to punish foreign parties for conduct that could not be attributed to the United States and thereby risk reprisals against this country. If a foreign state or citizen violates an "international norm" in a way that offends another foreign state or citizen, the Constitution arms the President and Congress with ample means to address it. Or, if they think best, the political branches may choose to look the other way. But in all events, the decision to impose sanctions in disputes between foreigners over norms is not ours to make. . . .

Justice SOTOMAYOR, with whom Justice GINSBURG, Justice BREYER, and Justice KAGAN join, dissenting.

The Court today holds that the Alien Tort Statute (ATS), 28 U.S.C. § 1350, categorically forecloses foreign corporate liability. In so doing, it absolves corporations from responsibility under the ATS for conscience-shocking behavior. I disagree both with the Court's conclusion and its analytic approach. The text, history, and purpose of the ATS, as well as the long and consistent history of corporate liability in tort, confirm that tort claims for law-of-nations violations may be brought against corporations under the ATS. Nothing about the corporate form in itself raises foreign-policy concerns that require the Court, as a matter of common-law discretion, to immunize all foreign corporations from liability under the ATS, regardless of the specific law-of-nations violations alleged. I respectfully dissent.

I

. . .

A

In *Sosa*, the Court . . . articulated a two-step framework to guide [its] inquiry. First, a court must determine whether the particular international-law norm alleged to have been violated is "accepted by the civilized world and defined with a specificity comparable to the features of the 18th-century paradigms," i.e., "violation of safe conducts, infringement of the rights of ambassadors, and piracy." *Id.*, at 724-725. . . . Second, if that threshold hurdle is satisfied, a court should consider whether allowing a particular case to proceed is an appropriate exercise of judicial discretion.

Sosa's norm-specific first step is inapposite to the categorical question whether corporations may be sued under the ATS as a general matter. International law imposes certain obligations that are intended to govern the behavior of states and private actors. Among those obligations are substantive prohibitions on certain conduct thought to violate human rights, such as genocide, slavery, extrajudicial killing, and torture. Substantive prohibitions like these are the norms at which *Sosa*'s step-one inquiry is aimed and for which *Sosa* requires that there be sufficient international consensus.

Sosa does not, however, demand that there be sufficient international consensus with regard to the mechanisms of enforcing these norms, for enforcement is not a question with which customary international law is concerned. Although international law determines what substantive conduct violates the law of nations, it leaves the specific rules of how to enforce international-law norms and remedy their violation to states, which may act to impose liability collectively through treaties or independently via their domestic legal systems. . . .

B

. . .

The plurality . . . assumes the correctness of its approach because of its view that there exists a distinction in international law between corporations and natural persons. The plurality attempts to substantiate this proposition by pointing to the charters of certain international criminal tribunals and noting that none was given jurisdiction over corporate defendants. That argument, however, confuses the substance of international law with how it has been enforced in particular contexts.

. . .

In fact, careful review of states' collective and individual enforcement efforts makes clear that corporations are subject to certain obligations under international law. For instance, the United States Military Tribunal that prosecuted several corporate executives of IG Farben declared that corporations could violate international law. See 8 Trials of War Criminals Before the Nuernberg Military Tribunals Under Council Control Law No. 10, p. 1132 (1952) ("Where private individuals, including juristic persons, proceed to exploit the military occupancy by acquiring private property against the will and consent of the former owner, such action . . . is in violation of international law"). Similarly, the International Criminal Tribunal for Rwanda found that three nonnatural entities — a private radio station, newspaper, and political party — were responsible for genocide. See *Prosecutor v. Nahimana*, Case No. ICTR-99-52-T, Judgment and Sentence ¶ 953 (Dec. 3, 2003). Most recently, the appeals panel of the Special Tribunal for Lebanon held that corporations may be prosecuted for contempt. See *Prosecutor v. New TV S. A. L.*, Case No. STL-14-05/PT/AP/AR126.1, Decision on Interlocutory Appeal Concerning Personal Jurisdiction in Contempt Proceedings ¶ 74 (Oct. 2, 2014). . . .

Finally, a number of states, acting individually, have imposed criminal and civil liability on corporations for law-of-nations violations through their domestic legal systems. . . .

C

Instead of asking whether there exists a specific, universal, and obligatory norm of corporate liability under international law, the relevant inquiry in response to the question presented here is whether there is any reason — under either international law or our domestic law — to distinguish between a corporation and a natural person who is alleged to have violated the law of nations under the ATS. As explained above, international law provides no such reason. Nor does domestic law. The text, history, and purpose of the ATS plainly support the conclusion that corporations may be held liable.

Beginning with the language of the statute itself, two aspects of the text of the ATS make clear that the statute allows corporate liability. First, the text confers jurisdiction on federal district courts to hear "civil action[s]" for "tort[s]." . . .

Corporations have long been held liable in tort under the federal common law. *See Philadelphia, W., & B. R. Co. v. Quigley*, 21 How. 202, 210 (1859) . . . . This Court "has assumed that, when Congress creates a tort action, it legislates against a legal background of ordinary tort-related . . . rules and consequently intends its legislation to incorporate those rules." *Meyer v. Holley*, 537 U.S. 280, 285 (2003). The presumption, then, is that, in providing for "tort" liability, the ATS provides for corporate liability.

Second, whereas the ATS expressly limits the class of permissible plaintiffs to "alien[s]," § 1350, it does not distinguish among classes of defendants. . . .

. . .

II

At its second step, *Sosa* cautions that courts should consider whether permitting a case to proceed is an appropriate exercise of judicial discretion in light of potential foreign-policy implications. The plurality only assumes without deciding that international law does not impose liability on corporations, so it necessarily proceeds to *Sosa's* second step. Here, too, its analysis is flawed.

A

Nothing about the corporate form in itself justifies categorically foreclosing corporate liability in all ATS actions. Each source of diplomatic friction that respondent Arab Bank and the plurality identify can be addressed with a tool more tailored to the source of the problem than a blanket ban on corporate liability.

Arab Bank contends that foreign citizens should not be able to sue a Jordanian corporation in New York for events taking place in the Middle East. The heart of that qualm was already addressed in *Kiobel*, which held that the presumption against extraterritoriality applies to the ATS. Only where the claims "touch and concern the territory of the United States . . . with sufficient force" can the presumption be displaced. "[M]ere corporate presence" does not suffice. . . .

Arab Bank also bemoans the unfairness of being sued when others — namely, the individuals and organizations that carried out the terrorist attacks — were "the direct cause" of the harm petitioners here suffered. That complaint, though, is a critique of the imposition of liability for financing terrorism, not an argument that ATS suits against corporations generally necessarily cause diplomatic tensions.

Arab Bank further expresses concern that ATS suits are being filed against corporations in an effort to recover for the bad acts of foreign governments or officials. But the Bank's explanation of this problem reveals that the true source of its grievance is the availability of aiding and abetting liability. . . . Yet not all law-of-nations violations asserted against corporations are premised on aiding and abetting liability. . . .

Notably, even the Hashemite Kingdom of Jordan does not argue that there are foreign-policy tensions inherent in suing a corporation generally. Instead, Jordan contends that this particular suit is an affront to its sovereignty because of its extra-territorial character and because of the role that Arab Bank specifically plays in the Jordanian economy.

The majority also cites to instances in which other foreign sovereigns have "appeared in this Court to note [their] objections to ATS litigation," but none of those objections was about the availability of corporate liability as a general matter. . . .

As the United States urged at oral argument, when international friction arises, a court should respond with the doctrine that speaks directly to the friction's source. . . . In addition to the presumption against extraterritoriality, federal courts have at their disposal a number of tools to address any foreign-relations concerns that an ATS case may raise. This Court has held that a federal court may exercise personal jurisdiction over a foreign corporate defendant only if the corporation is incorporated in the United States, has its principal place of business or is oth-erwise at home here, or if the activities giving rise to the lawsuit occurred or had their impact here. *See Daimler AG v. Bauman*, 571 U.S. 117 (2014). Courts also can dismiss ATS suits for a plaintiff's failure to exhaust the remedies available in her domestic forum, on forum non conveniens grounds, for reasons of interna-tional comity, or when asked to do so by the State Department.

. . . Foreclosing foreign corporate liability in all ATS actions, irrespective of circumstance or norm, is simply too broad a response to case-specific concerns that can be addressed via other means.

B

1

The Court urges that "[t]he political branches, not the Judiciary, have the responsibility and institutional capacity to weigh foreign-policy concerns." I agree that the political branches are well poised to assess the foreign-policy concerns attending ATS litigation, which is why I give significant weight to the fact that the Executive Branch, in briefs signed by the Solicitor General and State Department Legal Advisor, has twice urged the Court to reach exactly the opposite conclusion of the one embraced by the majority. . . . Notably, the Government's position that categorically barring corporate liability under the ATS is wrong has been consis-tent across two administrations led by Presidents of different political parties.

Likewise, when Members of Congress have weighed in on the question whether corporations can be proper defendants in an ATS suit, it has been to advise the Court against the rule it now adopts. . . .

2

The plurality instead purports to defer to Congress by relying heavily on the [TVPA] to support its categorical bar. . . . But there is no reason to think that because Congress saw fit to permit suits only against natural persons for two spe-cific law-of-nations violations, Congress meant to foreclose corporate liability for all law-of-nations violations. . . .

Furthermore, Congress repeatedly emphasized in the House and Senate Reports on the TVPA that the statute was meant to supplement the ATS, not replace or cabin it. . . .

. . . To infer from the TVPA that no corporation may ever be held liable under the ATS for any violation of any international-law norm, moreover, ignores that Congress has elsewhere imposed liability on corporations for conduct prohibited by customary international law. For instance, the Antiterrorism Act of 1990 (ATA) created a civil cause of action for U.S. nationals injured by an act of international terrorism and expressly provides for corporate liability. . . .

C

. . . [H]olding corporations accountable for violating the human rights of foreign citizens when those violations touch and concern the United States may well be necessary to avoid the international tension with which the First Congress was concerned. . . . If a corporation owned a fleet of vessels and directed them to seize other ships in U.S. waters, there no doubt would be calls to hold the corporation to account. Finally, take, for example, a corporation posing as a job-placement agency that actually traffics in persons, forcibly transporting foreign nationals to the United States for exploitation and profiting from their abuse. Not only are the individual employees of that business less likely to be able fully to compensate successful ATS plaintiffs, but holding only individual employees liable does not impose accountability for the institution-wide disregard for human rights. Absent a corporate sanction, that harm will persist unremedied. Immunizing the corporation from suit under the ATS merely because it is a corporation, even though the violations stemmed directly from corporate policy and practice, might cause serious diplomatic friction.

Second, the plurality expresses concern that if foreign corporations are subject to liability under the ATS, other nations could hale American corporations into court, . . . a prospect that will deter American corporations from investing in developing economies. The plurality offers no empirical evidence to support these alarmist conjectures, which is especially telling given that plaintiffs have been filing ATS suits against foreign corporations in United States courts for years. . . . Driven by hypothetical worry about besieged American corporations, today's decision needlessly goes much further, encompassing all ATS suits against all foreign corporations, not just those cases with extraterritorial dimensions premised on an aiding and abetting theory.

* * *

In sum, international law establishes what conduct violates the law of nations, and specifies whether, to constitute a law-of-nations violation, the alleged conduct must be undertaken by a particular type of actor. But it is federal common law that determines whether corporations may, as a general matter, be held liable in tort for law-of-nations violations. Applying that framework here, I would hold that the ATS does not categorically foreclose corporate liability. Tort actions against corporations have long been available under federal common law. Whatever the majority might think of the value of modern-day ATS litigation, it has identified nothing to support its conclusion that "foreign corporate defendants create unique problems" that necessitate a categorical rule barring all foreign corporate liability.

. . . I would reverse the decision of the Court of Appeals for the Second Circuit and remand for further proceedings, including whether the allegations here sufficiently touch and concern the United States, *see Kiobel*, 569 U.S., at 124-125, and whether the international law norms alleged to have been violated by Arab Bank — the prohibitions on genocide, crimes against humanity, and financing of terrorism — are of sufficiently definite content and universal acceptance to give rise to a cause of action under the ATS.

NOTES AND QUESTIONS

1. ***Jesner's* Rejection of Foreign Corporation Liability.** What seems to be the central motivating factor of Justice Kennedy's opinion? How does the Court's previous opinion in *Sosa* make his approach possible? Justices Alito and Gorsuch join only a small part of the substance of Justice Kennedy's opinion. What part do they join, and why? What parts do they not join, and why? How do their central concerns differ from Kennedy's, and how are they similar? How are the Alito and Gorsuch opinions similar to or different from each other? What is the consequence of Kennedy obtaining only three votes for parts of his opinion? Why does the dissent not share the concerns of Kennedy, Alito, and Gorsuch?

2. **Jurisdiction and Cause of Action.** All the Justices acknowledge that the ATS provides jurisdiction but does not (in itself) provide a cause of action. What is the difference between jurisdiction and cause of action? Under what circumstances can there be one but not the other? Why does the cause of action issue become important for some Justices but not others?

3. **International Law and Corporate Liability.** The plurality and the dissent debate whether international law recognizes corporate liability, and whether this matters. Should it matter? Suppose it is clear (as the plurality contends) that international criminal tribunals have not held corporations liable for human rights violations. What does that say about the content of international law? What are the implications for ATS law? How do the plurality and dissent differ in answering these questions?

4. **The Torture Victim Protection Act.** As discussed in the *Jesner* opinions, in 1992 Congress passed a somewhat related statute, the Torture Victim Protection Act (TVPA). The TVPA allows suits by both aliens and U.S. citizens against individuals for torture and extrajudicial killing committed under the authority of a foreign nation. In *Mohamad v. Palestinian Authority*, 566 U.S. 449 (2012), the Supreme Court — relying on the statute's plain language — held that the TVPA does not authorize suits against entities (presumably including corporations). Why might this be important to the ATS? Why might it not be?

Some claims are now being brought under the TVPA against individual corporate officers and directors. *See, e.g., Penaloza v. Drummond Co.,* 384 F. Supp. 3d 1328 (N.D. Ala. 2019) (allowing TVPA claims against corporate officers for complicity in human rights violations of Colombian paramilitary group in Colombia); *In re Chiquita Brands International, Inc.,* 190 F. Supp. 3d 1100 (S.D. Fla. 2016) (same); *see also Doe v. Drummond Corp.,* 782 F.3d 576 (11th Cir. 2015) (generally allowing such claims but dismissing for lack of proof in the particular case). Does this represent an end-run of the *Mohamad* decision or admirable creative lawyering? Might this be a solution for the plaintiffs in *Jesner*? What practical difficulties might this approach be likely to encounter?

5. **Views of the Executive Branch.** In a footnote in *Sosa*, the Court suggested that lower courts might take into account the views of the U.S. executive branch in considering whether to allow suits to go forward. Is such an approach appropriate? To the extent that there is deference to the executive, how far should courts go in adopting the executive's position? Why might courts want to defer to the executive branch in such matters? Note that the Court in *Jesner* did not adopt the executive branch's view.

6. **Corporate Liability After *Jesner*.** The defendant in *Jesner* was a foreign corporation. Does *Jesner* bar ATS suits against all foreign corporations? Does it bar ATS suits against U.S. corporations? In *Al Shimari*, an ATS suit against a U.S. corporate defendant discussed above, the district court concluded that *Jesner* only barred suits against foreign corporations. *Al Shimari v. CACI Premier Technology, Inc.,* 320 F. Supp. 3d 781 (E.D. Va. 2018); *accord Doe v. Nestlé, S.A.,* 929 F.3d 623 (9th Cir. 2018); *Estate of Alvarez v. Johns Hopkins University,* 373 F. Supp. 3d 639 (D. Md. 2019) (same, allowing ATS claim against U.S. entity for allegedly tortious medical experimentation). Why should U.S. corporations be treated differently? What arguments could be made that they should not be treated differently? *Compare Doe v. Exxon Mobil Corp.,* 391 F. Supp. 3d 76 (D.D.C. 2019), rejecting ATS liability of U.S. corporations and concluding:

> The Supreme Court's prior precedents counsel against creating a private right of action in this case. International law has not extended the scope of liability to corporations. Accordingly, there is not a specific, universal, and obligatory norm of corporate liability under currently prevailing international law as required by *Sosa* for ATS cases. Also, separation of powers and foreign relations concerns lead the Court to decline to recognize domestic corporate liability under the ATS in circumstances where, as here, the claims have caused significant diplomatic strife.

Is this view compelled by *Jesner*? Is it allowed by *Jesner*?

7. **Aiding and Abetting Liability Under the ATS.** Like *Kiobel* and *Jesner*, many, although not all, corporate ATS cases involve some form of secondary liability based on primary violations by a government. What is the correct standard for aiding and abetting liability, and why is this question important to ATS litigation? Courts of appeal are divided on the question. In *Presbyterian Church*

of Sudan v. Talisman Energy, Inc., 582 F.3d 244 (2d Cir. 2009), plaintiffs sued Talisman, an oil exploration company, for its involvement with the government of Sudan's atrocities during a civil war. The court of appeals upheld the dismissal of the claim on the ground that although Talisman may have known of the atrocities, it did not intend for them to occur. *See also Aziz v. Alcolac, Inc.*, 658 F.3d 388 (4th Cir. 2011) (endorsing the *Talisman* ruling in an ATS claim brought by Iraqi Kurds against a U.S. company that had supplied chemicals used by Saddam Hussein's regime to manufacture mustard gas used against the Kurds in the 1980s). In contrast, in *Doe v. Exxon Mobil Corp.*, 654 F.3d 11 (D.C. Cir. 2011), in which Indonesian citizens claimed government security forces committed abuses while guarding an Exxon gas facility, the court allowed an ATS claim to proceed against the corporation upon proof that the corporation knew or should have known of the violations. Which is the best standard? What considerations would influence this decision? In adopting standards for aiding and abetting liability, should courts apply U.S. law, the local law where the alleged violations occurred, or international law?

2. Direct Application of Customary International Law Outside the Alien Tort Statute

Especially in light of the Supreme Court's decisions in *Kiobel* and *Jesner*, litigants may look for ways to bring customary international law claims other than under the ATS. In reading the following cases, consider what challenges that strategy faces, and whether the law should be more welcoming to such claims.

McKesson Corp. v. Islamic Republic of Iran

672 F.3d 1066 (D.C. Cir. 2012)

[In this long-running litigation, McKesson sued Iran for the taking of McKesson's investment in an Iranian dairy. In a series of prior appeals, the court of appeals held that it had jurisdiction over the claim but that the Treaty of Amity between the United States and Iran, on which McKesson principally based its claim, did not provide a cause of action.]

BROWN, Circuit Judge:

. . .

Having established that this Court has jurisdiction over McKesson's claim [under the commercial activity exception to the Foreign Sovereign Immunities Act (FSIA)],* we must now decide which body of law, if any, provides McKesson with

---

* The FSIA, 28 U.S.C. §§ 1602 et seq., provides federal jurisdiction over suits against foreign governments under certain circumstances. See Chapter 11 below. — EDS.

a private right of action against Iran. We previously held that the Treaty of Amity, as construed under U.S. law, does not provide McKesson with a cause of action, but remanded the case to the district court to determine whether McKesson has a viable cause of action under either customary international law or Iranian law. The district court answered both questions in the affirmative. Although we reverse the court's conclusion with respect to a [customary international law] cause of action, we agree that McKesson's suit may proceed under Iranian law.

. . .

[In a prior decision], the district court noted that customary international law "is a part of the law of the United States, and must be ascertained and enforced by federal courts." Relying heavily on the Restatement (Third) of Foreign Relations Law, the court held that Iran is liable under customary international law because "its actions, aimed at McKesson, a foreign national, were clearly discriminatory" and "Iran neither offered nor provided any compensation to McKesson for its interest in Pak Dairy." [On remand] we asked the district court to consider whether the Supreme Court's intervening decision in *Sosa v. Alvarez-Machain*, 542 U.S. 692 (2004), affected the viability of McKesson's cause of action under customary international law. *Sosa* involved a claim brought under the Alien Tort Statute ("ATS"), 28 U.S.C. § 1350. . . . The Supreme Court held that the ATS, although by its terms purely jurisdictional, can support common law causes of action under customary international law, but only if the norms allegedly violated are sufficiently specific, universal, and obligatory. On remand, the district court found that, like the ATS, the commercial activities exception to the FSIA is "more than a jurisdictional statute," because in enacting it, Congress "demonstrated its intention that courts hear causes of action involving customary international law violations." We disagree.

. . .

The FSIA is purely jurisdictional in nature, and creates no cause of action. . . . The FSIA simply codified the "restrictive theory" of sovereign immunity, under which the immunity of a sovereign is recognized with regard to sovereign or public acts, but not with respect to private acts. The language of § 1605(a)(2) thus refers to commercial activity of foreign governments as a reason why the defense of foreign sovereign immunity is unavailable. It makes no mention, however, of either a private cause of action or customary international law.

[W]e find no evidence — textual or otherwise — suggesting that Congress enacted the commercial activities exception on the understanding that courts would use it to *create* causes of action based on customary international law. Moreover, Congress enacted the FSIA in 1976, just one year after the Supreme Court signaled its reluctance to imply causes of action when faced with statutory silence. *See Cort v. Ash*, 422 U.S. 66, 78-80 (1975). Assuming, as we must, that Congress was aware of all pertinent legal developments when it drafted the FSIA, Congress' decision not to include an express private right of action in any provision of the FSIA reveals that its enactors intended it to be purely jurisdictional.

While the Supreme Court's holding in *Sosa* is not binding here, the Court's extensive and careful scrutiny of the Alien Tort Statute illustrates the unusual circumstances necessary to find that a jurisdictional statute authorizes federal courts to derive new causes of action from customary international law. For example, the Court noted that the particular "anxieties of the preconstitutional period," particularly the Continental Congress's inability to deal with cases involving offenses committed against foreign ambassadors, counseled against interpreting the ATS in a way that would strip it of any practical effect. The Court also explained that, at the time the ATS was passed, a certain small set of actions was universally understood to be within the common law. By contrast, nothing in the legislative history of the FSIA suggests that Congress intended courts to use the commercial activities exception as a vehicle to *create* new causes of action.

Also instructive is the Supreme Court's admonition to the lower courts to use caution when considering customary international law claims. To be sure, the Court did so in the context of the Alien Tort Statute, which it understood to contemplate a "narrow set of violations of the law of nations, admitting of a judicial remedy and at the same time threatening serious consequences in international affairs." *Sosa*. The broader principles the Court expressed, however, are still relevant to this case, in which the Court is also being asked to fashion a federal common law cause of action out of the ambiguous principles of customary international law.

The Court first noted that because common law principles are now regarded as "made" rather than "discovered," a judge deciding on reliance on a perceived international norm "will find a substantial element of discretionary judgment in the decision." The invocation of such judicial discretion — indeed, judicial lawmaking power — would be particularly dangerous in cases such as this one, in which jurisdiction is being asserted over a foreign sovereign.

The Court then noted that the "significant rethinking of the role of federal courts in making [common law]" . . . spawned a general practice of seeking legislative guidance "before exercising innovative authority over substantive law." No such guidance exists here, as the text and legislative history of the FSIA merely establish the conditions in which a court may assert jurisdiction over a foreign sovereign. They do not reveal an intent to encourage — or even allow — courts to infer new common law causes of action.

The Court also emphasized the decision to create a private right of action is better left to legislative judgment — a particularly apt admonition in a case like this one, as creation of a right of action against a foreign government would certainly "raise[] issues beyond the mere consideration whether underlying primary conduct should be allowed or not[.]" Collateral consequences can themselves be a bar, the Court recognized, particularly when the cause of action has "potential implications for the foreign relations of the United States." The Court cautioned that because "many attempts by federal courts to craft remedies for violation of new norms of international law would raise risks of adverse foreign policy consequences, they should be undertaken, if at all, with great caution." In sum, we find that the language and history of the FSIA, particularly when viewed in light of the principles enunciated in *Sosa*, do not support the creation of a private right of action for expropriation based on customary international law [under the commercial activities exception].

. . .

... [A]bsent the compelling and unusual circumstances that animated the Court's analysis in *Sosa*, we decline to imply causes of action in the face of congressional silence. [The court went on to find that McKesson had a cause of action under Iranian law, and affirmed the district court on that basis.]

The Paquete Habana
175 U.S. 677 (1900)

[During the Spanish-American War, the United States imposed a naval blockade on Cuba, then a Spanish possession. The Paquete Habana, a fishing boat based in Havana, Cuba, was at sea when the blockade was imposed, and attempted to return to port. The boat, along with another in similar circumstances, was captured by the U.S. navy and condemned as a prize of war in U.S. district court. The owners appealed.]

Mr. Justice GRAY delivered the opinion of the Court.

...

We are then brought to the consideration of the question whether, upon the facts appearing in these records, the fishing smacks were subject to capture by the armed vessels of the United States during the recent war with Spain.

By an ancient usage among civilized nations, beginning centuries ago and gradually ripening into a rule of international law, coast fishing vessels pursuing their vocation of catching and bringing in fresh fish have been recognized as exempt, with their cargoes and crews, from capture as prize of war. . . .

[The Court exhaustively reviewed the historical treatment of fishing boats during wartime, beginning with Henry IV of England in the fifteenth century, and including practice from Holland, France, and other European nations.]

The doctrine which exempts coast fishermen, with their vessels and cargoes, from capture as prize of war, has been familiar to the United States from the time of the War of Independence. On June 5, 1779, Louis XVI, our ally in that war, addressed a letter to his admiral, informing him that the wish he had always had of alleviating, as far as he could, the hardships of war, had directed his attention to that class of his subjects which devoted itself to the trade of fishing, and had no other means of livelihood; that he had thought that the example which he should give to his enemies, and which could have no other source than the sentiments of humanity which inspired him, would determine them to allow to fishermen the same facilities which he should consent to grant, and that he had therefore given orders to the commanders of all his ships not to disturb English fishermen, nor to arrest their vessels laden with fresh fish, even if not caught by those vessels; provided they had no offensive arms, and were not proved to have made any signals creating a suspicion of intelligence with the enemy, and the admiral was directed to communicate the King's intentions to all officers under his control. . . .

[I]t appears that England, as well as France, during the American Revolutionary War, abstained from interfering with the coast fisheries. . . .

Since the United States became a nation, the only serious interruptions, so far as we are informed, of the general recognition of the exemption of coast fishing vessels from hostile capture, arose out of the mutual suspicions and recriminations of England and France during the wars of the French Revolution. [The Court noted that at that time England, in the words of a leading English admiralty judge, Sir William Scott, took the position that "it has not been usual to make captures of these small fishing vessels; but this rule was a rule of comity only, and not of legal decision; it has prevailed from views of mutual accommodation between neighboring countries, and from tenderness to a poor and industrious order of people." However, the Court went on to find that England by orders in 1806 and 1810 changed its conduct regarding enemy fishing vessels, and after this conflict nations reverted to the practice of exempting fishing boats from hostilities.]

During the wars of the French Empire, as both French and English writers agree, the coast fisheries were left in peace. . . .

In the war with Mexico, in 1846, the United States recognized the exemption of coast fishing boats from capture. . . .

France in the Crimean war in 1854, and in her wars with Italy in 1859 and with Germany in 1870, by general orders, forbade her cruisers to trouble the coast fisheries or to seize any vessel or boat engaged therein unless naval or military operations should make it necessary. . . .

Since the English orders in council of 1806 and 1810 . . . in favor of fishing vessels employed in catching and bringing to market fresh fish, no instance has been found in which the exemption from capture of private coast fishing vessels honestly pursuing their peaceful industry has been denied by England or by any other nation. And the Empire of Japan (the last state admitted into the rank of civilized nations), by an ordinance promulgated at the beginning of its war with China in August, 1894, established prize courts and ordained that "the following enemy's vessels are exempt from detention," including in the exemption "boats engaged in coast fisheries." . . .

International law is part of our law, and must be ascertained and administered by the courts of justice of appropriate jurisdiction as often as questions of right depending upon it are duly presented for their determination. For this purpose, where there is no treaty and no controlling executive or legislative act or judicial decision, resort must be had to the customs and usages of civilized nations, and, as evidence of these, to the works of jurists and commentators who by years of labor, research, and experience have made themselves peculiarly well acquainted with the subjects of which they treat. Such works are resorted to by judicial tribunals not for the speculations of their authors concerning what the law ought to be, but for trustworthy evidence of what the law really is.

[Henry] Wheaton [an American scholar] places among the principal sources international law

"text writers of authority, showing what is the approved usage of nations, or the general opinion respecting their mutual conduct, with the definitions and modifications introduced by general consent."

As to these, he forcibly observes:

> "Without wishing to exaggerate the importance of these writers or to substitute, in any case, their authority for the principles of reason, it may be affirmed that they are generally impartial in their judgment. They are witnesses of the sentiments and usages of civilized nations, and the weight of their testimony increases every time that their authority is invoked by statesmen, and every year that passes without the rules laid down in their works being impugned by the avowal of contrary principles."

Wheaton, International Law (8th ed.), § 15.

[The Court then reviewed leading treatises on international law, including writers from France, Germany, the Netherlands, Spain, Portugal, Austria, and Argentina, most of which argued for a customary rule exempting coastal fishing boats.]

The position taken by the United States during the recent war with Spain was quite in accord with the rule of international law, now generally recognized by civilized nations, in regard to coast fishing vessels.

. . . On April 22, [1898,] the President issued a proclamation declaring that the United States had instituted and would maintain that blockade "in pursuance of the laws of the United States, and the law of nations applicable to such cases." . . .

On April 28, 1898 (after the capture of the two fishing vessels now in question), Admiral Sampson telegraphed to the Secretary of the Navy as follows:

> "I find that a large number of fishing schooners are attempting to get into Havana from their fishing grounds near the Florida reefs and coasts. They are generally manned by excellent seamen, belonging to the maritime inscription of Spain, who have already served in the Spanish navy, and who are liable to further service. As these trained men are naval reserves, most valuable to the Spaniards as artillerymen, either afloat or ashore, I recommend that they should be detained prisoners of war, and that I should be authorized to deliver them to the commanding officer of the army at Key West."

To that communication the Secretary of the Navy, on April 30, 1898, guardedly answered:

> "Spanish fishing vessels attempting to violate blockade are subject, with crew, to capture, and any such vessel or crew considered likely to aid enemy may be detained."

The admiral's dispatch assumed that he was not authorized, without express order, to arrest coast fishermen peaceably pursuing their calling, and the necessary implication and evident intent of the response of the Navy Department were that Spanish coast fishing vessels and their crews should not be interfered with so long as they neither attempted to violate the blockade nor were considered likely to aid the enemy.

The *Paquete Habana*, as the record shows, was a fishing sloop of 25 tons burden, sailing under the Spanish flag, running in and out of Havana, and regularly engaged in fishing on the coast of Cuba. Her crew consisted of but three men. . . .

On her last voyage, she sailed from Havana along the coast of Cuba, about two hundred miles, and fished for twenty-five days off the cape at the west end of the island, within the territorial waters of Spain, and was going back to Havana with her cargo of live fish when she was captured by one of the blockading squadron on April 25, 1898. She had no arms or ammunition on board; she had no knowledge of the blockade, or even of the war, until she was stopped by a blockading vessel; she made no attempt to run the blockade, and no resistance at the time of the capture; nor was there any evidence whatever of likelihood that she or her crew would aid the enemy.

. . .

Upon the facts proved in either case, it is the duty of this Court, sitting as the highest prize court of the United States and administering the law of nations, to declare and adjudge that the capture was unlawful and without probable cause, and it is therefore. . . .

Ordered, that the decree of the district court be reversed, and the proceeds of the sale of the vessel, together with the proceeds of any sale of her cargo, be restored to the claimant, with damages and costs.

Mr. Chief Justice FULLER, with whom concurred Mr. Justice HARLAN and Mr. Justice McKENNA, dissenting:

The district court held these vessels and their cargoes liable because [it was] not "satisfied that, as a matter of law, without any ordinance, treaty, or proclamation, fishing vessels of this class are exempt from seizure."

This Court holds otherwise not because such exemption is to be found in any treaty, legislation, proclamation, or instruction granting it, but on the ground that the vessels were exempt by reason of an established rule of international law applicable to them which it is the duty of the court to enforce.

I am unable to conclude that there is any such established international rule, or that this Court can properly revise action which must be treated as having been taken in the ordinary exercise of discretion in the conduct of war.

. . .

In truth, the exemption of fishing craft is essentially an act of grace, and not a matter of right, and it is extended or denied as the exigency is believed to demand.

It is, said Sir William Scott, "a rule of comity only, and not of legal decision."

The modern view is thus expressed by Mr. Hall [an English international law writer]:

> "England does not seem to have been unwilling to spare fishing vessels so long as they are harmless, and it does not appear that any state has accorded them immunity under circumstances of inconvenience to itself. It is likely that all nations would now refrain from molesting them as a general rule, and would capture them so soon as any danger arose that they or their crews might be of military use to the enemy, and it is also likely that it is impossible to grant them a more distinct exemption."

In the Crimean war, 1854-55, none of the orders in council, in terms, either exempted or included fishing vessels, yet the allied squadrons swept the Sea of Azof of all craft capable of furnishing the means of transportation, and the English admiral in the Gulf of Finland directed the destruction of all Russian coasting vessels not of sufficient value to be detained as prizes except "boats or small craft which may be found empty at anchor, and not trafficking."

It is difficult to conceive of a law of the sea of universal obligation to which Great Britain has not acceded. And I am not aware of adequate foundation for imputing to this country the adoption of any other than the English rule.

. . .

It is needless to review the speculations and repetitions of the writers on international law. [Some] . . . admit that the custom relied on as consecrating the immunity is not so general as to create an absolute international rule; . . . others are to the contrary. Their lucubrations may be persuasive, but not authoritative.

In my judgment, the rule is that exemption from the rigors of war is in the control of the Executive. He is bound by no immutable rule on the subject. It is for him to apply, or to modify, or to deny altogether such immunity as may have been usually extended.

. . .

NOTES AND QUESTIONS

1. **Customary International Law in Admiralty and Maritime Cases.** *The Paquete Habana* is part of a long line of U.S. cases, dating to the eighteenth century, applying customary international law in prize cases and other maritime disputes. INTERNATIONAL LAW IN THE U.S. SUPREME COURT: CONTINUITY AND CHANGE, Chs. 1 & 3 (David L. Sloss, Michael D. Ramsey & William S. Dodge eds., 2011). E.g., *The Lottawanna*, 88 U.S. 558 (1874); *The Scotia*, 81 U.S. 170 (1872); *The Antelope*, 23 U.S. 66 (1825); *Talbot v. Jansen*, 3 U.S. 133 (1795). As in *Paquete Habana*, jurisdiction in these cases arose from a provision in the 1789 Judiciary Act, and successor provisions, giving federal jurisdiction over cases in admiralty, which in turn implemented Article III, Section 2's grant of federal jurisdiction over "all Cases of admiralty and maritime Jurisdiction." What views of customary international law and its relationship to U.S. law are reflected in the *Paquete Habana* majority opinion? Why does the dissent disagree? Is there something unique about admiralty cases that might encourage a unique approach?

2. **Other Direct Applications of Customary International Law.** Prior to 1900, the Supreme Court also sporadically applied customary international law to resolve cases outside of admiralty and maritime jurisdiction. INTERNATIONAL LAW IN THE U.S. SUPREME COURT, *supra*, Chs. 1 & 3. The Court did not appear to think it required special authorization from Congress to do so, as long as it had jurisdiction (although it did not think that the presence of an international law claim in itself conveyed federal jurisdiction). After 1900 and prior to the rise of ATS litigation after *Filártiga*, these cases declined sharply for various reasons unrelated to any theoretical concerns about customary international law. *Id.*, Ch. 7.

3. **Customary International Law and Private Rights of Action.** As reflected in *McKesson*, modern courts typically look for authorization from Congress before recognizing causes of action under customary international law. Should broad grants of federal jurisdiction, such as diversity and federal question jurisdiction, authorize courts to use customary international law as a rule of decision? In *Serra v. Lappin*, 600 F.3d 1191 (9th Cir. 2010), the court of appeals considered a claim by federal prisoners alleging that the low wages they were paid for work performed in prison violated their rights under the Fifth Amendment and various sources of international law. On the international law claim, the court held:

> Plaintiffs assert that "the customs and usages" of the nations of the world . . . form customary international law entitling them to higher wages. This claim fails because customary international law is not a source of judicially enforceable private rights in the absence of a statute conferring jurisdiction over such claims. *See Princz v. Federal Republic of Germany*, 26 F.3d 1166, 1174 n.1 (D.C. Cir. 1994) ("While it is true that 'international law is part of our law,' it is also our law that a federal court is not competent to hear a claim arising under international law absent a statute granting such jurisdiction."); *see also Sosa*, 542 U.S. at 720 ("'[O]ffences against this law of nations are principally incident to whole states or nations,' and not individuals seeking relief in court." (quoting BLACKSTONE, 4 COMMENTARIES 68)). Plaintiffs can point to no statute that brings their claim within our purview.

[handwritten margin note: × private cause of action.]

In a footnote, the court added:

> *See Sosa*, 542 U.S. at 731 n.19 (resisting the implication "that every grant of jurisdiction to a federal court carries with it an opportunity to develop common law" and distinguishing the ATS's unique invitation to entertain "common law claims derived from the law of nations" from the strictures of § 1331 federal-question jurisdiction). If any plaintiff could bring any claim alleging a violation of the law of nations under federal-question jurisdiction, there would be no need for statutes such as the ATS and the Torture Victim Protection Act, which recognize or create limited causes of action for particular classes of plaintiffs (aliens) or particular violations (torture).

Note the implication of *Serra* (and *McKesson*) that if the plaintiff had been an alien instead of a U.S. citizen, a claim might have been available under the ATS. Does that make sense?

4. **The Restatement View.** *The Restatement (Third) of Foreign Relations Law* declares:

> [Section 111(2)] Cases arising under international law or international agreements of the United States are within the Judicial Power of the United States and . . . are within the jurisdiction of the federal courts.
> [Section 111 comment c] The proposition that international law and agreements are law in the United States is addressed largely to the courts. In appropriate cases they apply international law or agreements without the need of enactment by Congress or proclamation by the President.

[Section 111, comment e] Civil actions arising under international law or under a treaty or other international agreement of the United States are within the jurisdiction of the United States district courts. 28 U.S.C. § 1331 [granting federal question jurisdiction]. . . . Customary international law, like other federal law, is part of the "laws . . . of the United States."

How is the *Restatement* different from *McKesson* and *Serra*? What is the significance of the differences in approach?

5. **Other Sources of Private Rights of Action to Enforce Customary International Law.** Some specific jurisdictional statutes might be argued to provide a cause of action to hear international law claims. For example, in addition to the commercial activity exception, another section of the FSIA provides jurisdiction where "rights in property taken in violation of international law are in issue and that property or any property exchanged for such property is present in the United States. . . ." 28 U.S.C. § 1605(a)(3). In a part of the *McKesson* opinion omitted above, the court left open the possibility that this section could provide a cause of action to hear international law claims in some cases; it found it unnecessary to decide the question because the property at issue in *McKesson* was not in the United States.

6. **Customary International Law and State Law.** It is well established in modern law that Congress can override customary international law by statute. *E.g., United States v. Yunis*, 924 F.2d 1086 (D.C. Cir. 1991). What is the appropriate relationship between customary international law and U.S. state law? Unlike treaties, customary international law is not explicitly mentioned in the supremacy clause of Article VI, which gives the Constitution, treaties, and federal statutes supremacy over state law. *See* Michael D. Ramsey, *The Constitution's Text and Customary International Law*, 106 GEO. L.J. 1747 (2018) (arguing on this basis that customary international law is not part of supreme federal law). But in modern practice federal common law is supreme over state law, and to the extent customary international law is encompassed within federal common law, it might also be thought to preempt state law. The *Restatement (Third)* takes this position strongly in Section 111. Perhaps oddly, the issue has infrequently arisen in appellate decisions. Under what circumstances might it arise? How should the issue be resolved? Are state courts interpreting state law free to develop their own views of customary international law? What are the benefits and disadvantages of that approach?

7. **Comparative Perspective.** Courts in other countries are only beginning to grapple with the issue of widespread suits alleging international law violations in foreign countries. In *Nevsun Resources Ltd. v. Araya*, 2020 SCC 5 (2020), Eritrean citizens sued Nevsun (a Canadian corporation) for aiding and abetting human rights violations by the government of Eritrea. Although Canada has no counterpart to the U.S. Alien Tort Statute, a divided Supreme Court of Canada held that the suit could proceed because customary international law is part of the common law of Canada. Should this influence the U.S. approach?

3. Using International Law to Interpret U.S. Law

As the foregoing cases suggest, direct application of customary international law in U.S. courts faces difficulties. An alternative approach is to argue that customary international law can be used to interpret U.S. statutes — and specifically, that U.S. statutes should not be read to violate customary international law. Chapter 1 discusses one important example: the use of customary international law rules of jurisdiction to limit the extraterritorial scope of U.S. law. *E.g.*, *McCulloch v. Sociedad Nacional de Marineros de Honduras*, 372 U.S. 10 (1963). Might customary international law be used elsewhere to limit (or expand) interpretations of U.S. law?

Ma v. Reno

208 F.3d 815 (9th Cir. 2000)

REINHARDT, Circuit Judge:

Kim Ho Ma is an alien who left his native land, Cambodia, as a refugee at the age of two and has resided in the United States as a legal permanent resident since he was six. At the age of seventeen he was involved in a gang-related shooting, and was convicted of manslaughter. After completing his prison sentence some two years later, he was taken into INS custody and ordered removed [to Cambodia] because of that conviction. However, the INS has been unable to remove him, and hundreds of others like him, because Cambodia does not have a repatriation agreement with the United States and therefore will not permit Ma's return.

The question before us is whether, in light of the absence of such an agreement, the Attorney General has the legal authority to hold Ma, who is now twenty two, in detention indefinitely, perhaps for the remainder of his life.

Ma challenged his detention by filing a petition for habeas corpus, under 28 U.S.C. § 2241, in the District Court for the Western District of Washington. That court ruled that Ma's continued detention violates his substantive due process rights under the Fifth Amendment. Respondents, the Immigration and Naturalization Service, Janet Reno (as Attorney General), and Robert Coleman (as INS Acting District Director in Seattle) (hereinafter collectively referred to as "INS") appeal the district court's decision releasing Ma from INS custody. We have jurisdiction and affirm, but on a different basis.

We hold that the INS lacks authority under the immigration laws, and in particular under 8 U.S.C. § 1231(a)(6), to detain [Ma] . . . for more than a reasonable time beyond the normal ninety day statutory period authorized for removal. More specifically, in cases like Ma's, in which there is no reasonable likelihood that the alien will be removed in the reasonably foreseeable future, we hold that it may not detain the alien beyond that statutory removal period. Because we construe the statute as not permitting the indefinite detention of aliens like Ma, we need not decide the substantial constitutional questions raised by the INS's indefinite detention policy.

. . .

Ma's conviction made him removable [from the United States] as an alien convicted of certain crimes under 8 U.S.C. § 1227(a)(2). . . . Although Ma's order of removal became final on October 26, 1998, the INS could not remove him within the ninety day period during which it is authorized to do so because the United States had, and still has, no repatriation agreement with Cambodia. As a result, Ma remained in detention. . . .

In May 1999, . . . the INS conducted the "ninety day" custody review, as provided for in its regulations, to determine if Ma should be released on bond. An INS officer prepared a report after interviewing Ma and reviewing letters and other materials submitted by his family and friends. The officer's report stated that Ma's family was "very supportive," and that if Ma was released he would be able to assist his handicapped 71 year old father in everyday activities. The report also stated that Ma constantly communicates with his younger brother to assure that his brother "does not follow in his footsteps." In addition, the report noted that Ma's older brother runs his own business and would employ Ma if he were released from custody. A deputy district director then reviewed the INS officer's report and issued a decision denying Ma's release. . . .

On September 30, 1999, pursuant to additional internal regulations, the INS again reviewed its decision to continue detaining Ma. . . . Once again, INS officials found that Ma should remain in detention, based on the seriousness of his conviction and also on the ground of his threatened participation in a hunger strike while in custody. The reviewers stated that they were unable to conclude that Ma would "remain non-violent" and abide by the terms of his release. . . . The INS now appeals the district court's decision granting Ma's habeas corpus petition.

In general, after an alien is found removable, the Attorney General is required to remove that alien within ninety days after the removal order becomes administratively final. Many aliens, however, cannot be removed within the ninety day period for various reasons. . . .

Under the statute, aliens [such as Ma, who are removable because of criminal convictions (such as drug offenses, certain crimes of moral turpitude, "aggravated felonies," firearms offenses, and various other crimes] . . . "may be detained beyond the removal period". . . .

INS argues that its authority to "detain beyond the removal period" gives it the authority to detain indefinitely aliens . . . who cannot be removed in the reasonably foreseeable future. Ma argues the opposite — that the INS's authority to detain aliens beyond the removal period does not extend to cases in which removal is not likely in the reasonably foreseeable future. On its face, the statute's text compels neither interpretation: while [the statute] allows for the detention of [aliens such as Ma] "beyond" ninety days, it is silent about how long beyond the ninety day period such detention is authorized. Thus, any construction of the statute must read in some provision concerning the length of time beyond the removal period detention may continue, whether it be "indefinitely," "for a reasonable time," or some other temporal measure.

We . . . construe the statute as providing the INS with authority to detain aliens only for a reasonable time beyond the statutory removal period. In cases in which an alien has already entered the United States and there is no reasonable likelihood that a foreign government will accept the alien's return in the reasonably foreseeable future, we conclude that the statute does not permit the Attorney General to hold the alien beyond the statutory removal period. Rather, the alien must be released subject to the supervisory authority provided in the statute.

We adopt our construction of the statute for several reasons. First, and most important, the result we reach allows us to avoid deciding whether or not INS's indefinite detention policy violates the due process guarantees of the Fifth Amendment. Second, our reading is the most reasonable one — it better comports with the language of the statute and permits us to avoid assuming that Congress intended a result as harsh as indefinite detention in the absence of any clear statement to that effect. Third, reading an implicit "reasonable time" limitation into the statute is consistent with our case law interpreting a similar provision in a prior immigration statute. Finally, the interpretation we adopt is more consonant with international law.

. . .

In interpreting the statute to include a reasonable time limitation, we are . . . influenced by amicus curiae Human Rights Watch's argument that we should apply the well-established *Charming Betsy* rule of statutory construction which requires that we generally construe Congressional legislation to avoid violating international law. . . . *Murray v. The Schooner Charming Betsy*, 6 U.S. 64, 117-118 (1804). We have reaffirmed this rule on several occasions. . . .

We recently recognized that "a clear international prohibition" exists against prolonged and arbitrary detention. *Martinez v. City of Los Angeles*, 141 F.3d 1373, 1384 (9th Cir. 1998). Furthermore, Article 9 of the International Covenant on Civil and Political Rights (ICCPR), which the United States has ratified, . . . provides that "[n]o one shall be subjected to arbitrary arrest and detention." . . .

In the present case, construing the statute to authorize the indefinite detention of removable aliens might violate international law. In *Martinez*, we expressed our approval of a district court decision in this circuit holding that "individuals imprisoned for years without being charged were arbitrarily detained" in violation of international law. . . . Given the strength of the rule of international law, our construction of the statute renders it consistent with the *Charming Betsy* rule.

. . .

We stress that our decision does not leave the government without remedies with respect to aliens who may not be detained permanently while awaiting a removal that may never take place. All aliens ordered released must comply with the stringent supervision requirements set out in [the statute]. Ma will have to appear before an immigration officer periodically, answer certain questions, submit to medical or psychiatric testing as necessary, and accept reasonable restrictions on his conduct and activities, including severe travel limitations. More important, if Ma engages in any criminal activity during this time, including violation of his supervisory release conditions, he can be detained and incarcerated as part of the normal criminal process.

For the foregoing reasons, the district court's decision is
AFFIRMED.*

Serra v. Lappin

600 F.3d 1191 (9th Cir. 2010)

[Plaintiffs were federal prisoners who had worked during their incarceration; they challenged their low wages as violations of international law. In a part of the opinion excerpted above, the court first held that the plaintiffs lacked a cause of action to sue for an international law violation directly. The court then considered plaintiffs' contention that the federal statute authorizing payment of prisoner wages should be construed consistently with international law.]

CLIFTON, Circuit Judge:

. . .

We have allowed ourselves a few sidelong glances at the law of nations in non-ATS cases by applying the canon of statutory construction that "[w]here fairly possible, a United States statute is to be construed as not to conflict with international law or with an international agreement with the U.S." *Munoz v. Ashcroft,* 339 F.3d 950, 958 (9th Cir. 2003) (quoting RESTATEMENT (THIRD) OF FOREIGN RELATIONS LAW § 114 (1987)). The canon is derived from Chief Justice Marshall's statement that

> an act of Congress ought never to be construed to violate the law of nations if any other possible construction remains, and consequently can never be construed to violate neutral rights, or to affect neutral commerce, further than is warranted by the law of nations as understood in this country.

Murray v. The Schooner Charming Betsy, 6 U.S. 64 (1804). The *Charming Betsy* canon is not an inviolable rule of general application, but a principle of interpretation that bears on a limited range of cases. Mindful that "Congress has the power to legislate beyond the limits posed by international law," *Cabrera-Alvarez v. Gonzales,* 423 F.3d 1006, 1009 (9th Cir. 2005), we do not review federal law for adherence to the law of nations with the same rigor that we apply when we must review statutes for adherence to the Constitution. We invoke the *Charming Betsy* canon only where conformity with the law of nations is relevant to considerations of international comity, *see Arc Ecology v. United States Dep't of the Air Force,* 411 F.3d 1092, 1102-03 (9th Cir. 2005), and only "where it is possible to do so

---

* In a parallel case from the Fifth Circuit, the Supreme Court granted review and held that the Fifth Amendment prohibits indefinite detention in Ma's circumstances. *Zadvydas v. Davis,* 533 U.S. 678 (2001). — EDS.

without distorting the statute." *Cabrera-Alvarez*, 423 F.3d at 1010. . . . We decline to determine whether Plaintiffs' rates of pay were in violation of the law of nations because this case meets neither condition for applying the canon.

First, the purpose of the *Charming Betsy* canon is to avoid the negative foreign policy implications of violating the law of nations, and Plaintiffs have offered no reason to believe that their low wages are likely to "embroil[] the nation in a foreign policy dispute." *Arc Ecology*, 411 F.3d at 1102. . . . That the courts should ever invoke the *Charming Betsy* canon in favor of United States citizens is doubtful, because a violation of the law of nations as against a United States citizen is unlikely to bring about the international discord that the canon guards against. In *The Charming Betsy*, the status of the ship's owner as a Danish subject, and thus a neutral in the conflict between the United States and France, was critical to the Court's conclusion that the Non-Intercourse Act of 1800 should not be interpreted to permit the seizure and sale of his ship. We have never employed the *Charming Betsy* canon in a case involving exclusively domestic parties and domestic acts, nor has the Supreme Court. As a general rule, domestic parties must rely on domestic law when they sue each other over domestic injuries in federal court. We need not consider whether the statutory and regulatory regime of federal inmate compensation conflicts with the law of nations because Plaintiffs, as United States citizens and residents, have not demonstrated that their low wages have any possible ramifications for this country's foreign affairs.

Second, the *Charming Betsy* canon comes into play only where Congress's intent is ambiguous, and there is nothing ambiguous about the complete discretion that Congress vested in the Attorney General with regard to inmate pay.[13] Congress is not constrained by international law as it is by the Constitution. . . . As a result, we are bound by a properly enacted statute, provided it be constitutional, even if that statute violates international law. Because the statutes giving the Attorney General discretion over prisoner pay grades are unambiguous, there is no reason for this court to decide whether they accord with the law of nations. Thus, the district court did not err in dismissing Plaintiffs' complaint.

[Affirmed.]

ARC Ecology v. U.S. Department of Air Force

411 F.3d 1092 (9th Cir. 2005)

CALLAHAN, Circuit Judge:

[Plaintiffs, citizens of the Philippines, filed suit under the Comprehensive Environmental Response, Compensation, and Liability Act ("CERCLA"), claiming environmental damage resulting from U.S. government activities at two U.S. military bases located in the Philippines — Clark Air Force Base ("Clark")

---

13. *See* 18 U.S.C. § 4125(d) ("[T]he Attorney General is authorized to provide for the payment to the inmates or their dependents such pecuniary earnings as he may deem proper, under such rules and regulations as he may prescribe."). . . .

and Subic Naval Base ("Subic"). The court first held under the presumption against extraterritoriality that CERCLA did not apply in the Philippines.] . . .

Perhaps recognizing the tenuous nature of their claims under domestic law, the appellants suggest that we should interpret CERCLA to apply extraterritorially so as not to run afoul of international law. The appellants rely on international principles espousing the view that activities within a country's jurisdiction or control should not cause significant injury to the environment of another country. The Restatement of Foreign Relations Law of the United States [§§ 601-602] appears to support this view.[8]

Even if we were to accept the appellants' gloss on international law — that one nation should not injure another nation's environment — it does not follow that denying the appellants a cause of action as of 2002 violates international law. The appellants offer no authority for the proposition that international law recognizes a current claim for a preliminary assessment or cleanup of Philippine territory based on actions taken over a decade ago. Furthermore, assuming that the United States "injured" the Philippines during its operation of Clark and Subic, compensation presumably was or should have been negotiated between the two nations when the United States turned the bases over to the Philippines. Thus, we do not find that the appellants have presented an actual conflict between domestic and international law.

Finally, the appellants' reliance on the *Charming Betsy* canon of statutory construction is misplaced. In *Murray v. Charming Betsy*, 6 U.S. 64 (1804), the Supreme Court had to determine whether a ship could be seized for violating an American embargo against France. The Court interpreted the relevant statute so as to avoid embroiling the nation in a foreign policy dispute unforeseen by either the President or Congress, holding that "an act of Congress ought never to be construed to violate the law of nations if any other possible construction remains."

Charming Betsy is of no comfort to the appellants for at least two reasons. First, as this court has observed, "the Supreme Court has never invoked *Charming Betsy* against the United States in a suit in which it was a party." *United States v. Corey*, 232 F.3d 1166, 1179 (9th Cir. 2000). The concerns that underlie the canon are "obviously much less serious where the interpretation arguably violating international law is urged upon [the court] by the Executive Branch of our government." *Id.* When the Executive Branch is the party advancing a construction of a statute with potential foreign policy implications, we presume that "the President has

---

8. The appellants concede that it is uncertain whether the sources of international law on which they rely provide accurate statements of international law. However respectable the Restatement may be, it "is not a primary source of authority upon which, standing alone, courts may rely for propositions of customary international law." *United States v. Yousef*, 327 F.3d 56, 99 (2d Cir. 2003) (emphasis omitted); *see also C.L. Maddox, Inc. v. Coalfield Servs., Inc.*, 51 F.3d 76, 81 (7th Cir. 1995) ("The Restatement of course is not law."). A court that has had occasion to consider these sources determined that they are unreliable. *Amlon Metals, Inc. v. FMC Corp.*, 775 F. Supp. 668, 671 (S.D.N.Y. 1991). Indeed, the Restatement's own authors admit that "'in a number of particulars the formulations in this Restatement are at variance with positions that have been taken by the United States Government.'" *Yousef*, 327 F.3d at 100. . . .

evaluated the foreign policy consequences of such an exercise of U.S. law and determined that it serves the interests of the United States." *Id.*

For this same reason, the canon plays no role in interpreting the disputed provisions of CERCLA. Moreover, accepting the appellants' broad interpretation of the statute would be the equivalent of forcing the United States to encroach on the territory and affairs of another sovereign. Such an interpretation would make the judiciary the impetus for unintended clashes between our laws and those of other nations which could result in international discord. . . . These are the exact ends that the *Charming Betsy* canon seeks to bypass.

Second, the appellants offer no example of where a court has invoked the *Charming Betsy* canon to extend the effect of domestic legislation into another sovereign's territory. Of course, courts have held just the opposite. "[T]he practice of using international law to limit the extraterritorial reach of statutes is firmly established in our jurisprudence." *Hartford Fire Ins. Co. v. California*, 509 U.S. 764, 818 (Scalia, J., dissenting).

Charming Betsy itself concerned a private dispute, one which the Court resolved by interpreting the relevant statute so as to avoid embroiling our nation in a foreign policy dispute unforeseen by either the President or Congress. Rather than producing harmony with international laws, the appellants' interpretation that CERCLA applies to other countries may result in precisely what *Charming Betsy* seeks to avoid — intrusion on the affairs of foreign sovereigns and international discord. *See United States v. Thomas*, 893 F.2d 1066, 1069 (9th Cir. 1990) (adhering to the *Charming Betsy* canon "out of respect for other nations"). . . . As the Department of Defense recognizes through its own regulations, "[t]reaty obligations and the sovereignty of other nations must be respected, and restraint must be exercised in applying United States laws within foreign nations unless Congress has expressly provided otherwise." Consistent with this perspective, we express no opinion as to what steps, if any, the appellants might take in consulting with their own government to achieve environmental remediation in the region.

. . .

[Affirmed.]

NOTES AND QUESTIONS

1. **The *Charming Betsy* Canon.** On the *Charming Betsy* canon, the origins of the presumption against reading statutes to violate customary international law, and the application of this presumption in extraterritorial jurisdiction cases, see Chapter 1. When is it appropriate to use the *Charming Betsy* canon? Supreme Court decisions involving the *Charming Betsy* canon and customary international law are rare. As indicated in *ARC Ecology*, they have principally been cases involving claims that a U.S. statute exceeded the United States' prescriptive jurisdiction under international law, as discussed

in Chapter 1. Should the canon be limited to these circumstances? Or is it also appropriately applied in other contexts, as in *Ma*? Should U.S. citizens be allowed to invoke the *Charming Betsy* canon? Why do the opinions in *Serra* and *ARC Ecology* conclude that the answer should be no? What reasons might there be to conclude that the answer should at least sometimes be yes? Note that the U.S. Supreme Court decided the *Charming Betsy* case in 1806, long before human rights law became a focus of international law, and that one of the main goals of human rights law is to protect citizens from abuses by their own governments. Does this suggest that the *Charming Betsy* canon should apply in cases like *Serra* because it is a claim by a U.S. citizen against the U.S. government, or that it should not apply because the application of the canon in this context likely was not contemplated by the Supreme Court when *Charming Betsy* was decided?

2. **A Clear Statement Rule or a Way to Resolve Ambiguity?** As with the parallel presumption that ambiguous statutes not be construed to violate treaties, a central question is how clear statutes must be in order to override customary international law (as with treaties, there is no doubt in modern case law that Congress can override customary international law if it wishes). Should the *Charming Betsy* canon be understood as a clear statement rule, a rule for construing statutes that are otherwise utterly ambiguous, or something in between?

3. **Proving a Conflict with International Law.** How clear must the conflict with international law be in order to invoke *Charming Betsy*? In *Ma*, the court said only that "construing the statute to authorize the indefinite detention of removable aliens *might* violate international law" (emphasis added). On the other hand, in *Sosa v. Alvarez-Machain*, excerpted in the ATS reading above, the Supreme Court in a different context cautioned against seeking out new and debatable rules of customary international law; arguably (but not obviously) that caution should also apply in finding rules of customary international law for *Charming Betsy* purposes. Note that in *Sosa* the Court declined to rely on the ICCPR as establishing an enforceable rule against arbitrary detention while the court in *Ma* cited the same provision in support of its reading of the statute. Are these approaches consistent?

4. *Customary International Law and Executive Power*

The application of customary international law in the U.S. legal system raises additional issues when it is used to limit the actions of the U.S. executive branch. As the cases below reflect, such circumstances raise two distinct issues: whether customary international law limits the executive branch directly; and whether statutes authorizing executive branch action should be read not to authorize violations of international law.

Garcia-Mir v. Meese

788 F.2d 1446 (11th Cir. 1986)

[Plaintiffs were Cubans who had come to the United States illegally and were detained pending return to Cuba; because removal was not practical, plaintiffs were detained indefinitely by order of the attorney general. Plaintiffs contended that their detention, among other things, violated customary international law.]

JOHNSON, Circuit Judge:

. . .

The public law of nations was long ago incorporated into the common law of the United States. *The Paquete Habana*, 175 U.S. 677, 700 (1900); *The Nereide*, 13 U.S. 388, 423 (1815); Restatement of the Law of Foreign Relations Law of the United States Sec. 131 comment d. To the extent possible, courts must construe American law so as to avoid violating principles of public international law. *Murray v. The Schooner Charming Betsy*, 6 U.S. 64, 102, 118 (1804). . . . But public international law is controlling only "where there is no treaty and no controlling executive or legislative act or judicial decision. . . ." [*Paquete Habana*], 175 U.S. at 700. Appellees argue that, because general principles of international law forbid prolonged arbitrary detention, we should hold that their current detention is unlawful.

We have previously determined that the general deportation statute, 8 U.S.C.A. Sec. 1227(a) (1985), does not restrict the power of the Attorney General to detain aliens indefinitely. But this does not resolve the question whether there has been an affirmative legislative grant of authority to detain. . . .

The trial court found, correctly, that there has been no affirmative legislative grant to the Justice Department to detain [plaintiffs] without hearings because 8 U.S.C.A. Sec. 1227(c) does not expressly authorize indefinite detention. Thus we must look for a controlling executive act. The trial court found that there was such a controlling act in the Attorney General's termination of the status review plan and in his decision to incarcerate indefinitely pending efforts to deport. The appellees and the amicus challenge this by arguing that a controlling executive act can only come from an act by or expressly sanctioned by the President himself, not one of his subordinates. They rely for that proposition upon *The Paquete Habana* and upon the Restatement of the Law of Foreign Relations Law of the United States. . . .

As to *The Paquete Habana*, that case involved the capture and sale as war prize of several fishing boats during the Spanish-American War. The Supreme Court found this contrary to the dictates of international law. The amicus characterizes the facts of the case such that the Secretary of the Navy authorized the capture and that the Supreme Court held that this did not constitute a controlling executive act because it was not ordered by the President himself. This is a mischaracterization. After the capture of the two vessels at issue, an admiral telegraphed the Secretary for permission to seize fishing ships, to which the Secretary responded that only those vessels "likely to aid enemy may be detained." Seizing fishing boats aiding the enemy would be in obvious accord with international law. But the facts of *The Paquete Habana* showed the boats in question to be innocent of aiding the

Spanish. The Court held that the ships were seized in violation of international law because they were used solely for fishing. It was the admiral who acted in excess of the clearly delimited authority granted by the Secretary, who instructed him to act only consistent with international law. Thus *The Paquete Habana* does not support the proposition that the acts of cabinet officers cannot constitute controlling executive acts. At best it suggests that lower level officials cannot by their acts render international law inapplicable. That is not an issue in this case, where the challenge is to the acts of the Attorney General.

As to the Restatement . . . the most recent version . . . notes that the President, "acting within his constitutional authority, may have the power under the Constitution to act in ways that constitute violations of international law by the United States." The Constitution provides for the creation of executive departments, U.S. Const. art. 2, Sec. 2, and the power of the President to delegate his authority to those departments to act on his behalf is unquestioned. . . . Thus we hold that the executive acts here evident constitute a sufficient basis for affirming the trial court's finding that international law does not control.

. . .

. . . We . . . hold that the appellees have stated no basis for relief under international law because any rights there extant have been extinguished by controlling acts of the executive. . . .

[Affirmed.]

NOTES AND QUESTIONS

1. **Background of *Garcia-Mir*.** The "Mariel boatlift" of 1980, in which over a hundred thousand Cubans — many former prisoners — were expelled from Cuba and sent to the United States illegally, generated numerous cases of Cubans like Garcia-Mir challenging their detention. Most were resolved on similar grounds as *Garcia-Mir*. For example, in *Barrera-Echavarria v. Rison*, 44 F.3d 1441 (9th Cir. 1995), the court held as follows as to the plaintiff's international law claim:

    > Barrera's final claim is that his continued detention violates rules of international law against "prolonged arbitrary detention," which are binding upon the United States. *See The Paquette Habana*, 175 U.S. 677 (1900). The status of international law on this issue and the legality of American policy under that law are not as clear as Barrera and his *amici* would suggest. . . . Even assuming such a rule of international law exists, however, Barrera cannot avail himself of its protections.
    >
    > International law can be binding upon the United States in domestic courts. *The Paquette Habana*, 175 U.S. at 700. It is well-settled, however, that international law controls only "where there is no treaty, and no controlling executive or legislative act or judicial decision." *Id.* . . .
    >
    > [T]he Attorney General has statutory authority to detain Barrera. Given our construction of the statute as consistent with Barrera's detention, along with the Attorney General's decision to detain him and the support of the Supreme

Court's holding in *[Shaughnessy v.] Mezei*, we hold that international law is displaced in this area as well, by a combination of "controlling acts" of the legislative, executive, and judicial branches. *Accord . . . Garcia-Mir v. Meese*, 788 F.2d 1446, 1453-55 (11th Cir.). . . .

In contrast, in *Rodriguez-Fernandez v. Wilkinson*, 505 F. Supp. 787, 798 (D. Kan. 1980), the district court ordered the release of a Cuban refugee from federal prison because his detention violated customary international law. The district court reasoned as follows:

> International law is a part of the laws of the United States which federal courts are bound to ascertain and administer in an appropriate case. . . . *The Paquete Habana*, 175 U.S. 677, (1900); *Filártiga v. Peña-Irala, supra.* Our review of the sources from which customary international law is derived clearly demonstrates that arbitrary detention is prohibited by customary international law. Therefore, even though the indeterminate detention of an excluded alien cannot be said to violate the United States Constitution or our statutory laws, it is judicially remedial as a violation of international law. Petitioner's continued, indeterminate detention on restrictive status in a maximum security prison, without having been convicted of a crime in this country or a determination having been made that he is a risk to security or likely to abscond, is unlawful; and as such amounts to an abuse of discretion on the part of the Attorney General and his delegates.

Can the court's reasoning be reconciled with *Garcia-Mir, Barrera-Echavarria,* and *McKesson*? Is the court's reliance on *The Paquete Habana* and *Filártiga* well placed? Why or why not? The Tenth Circuit affirmed on statutory grounds without reaching the international law issue. 654 F.2d 1382 (10th Cir. 1981). Note that these cases all involved aliens who were not lawfully admitted into the United States, in contrast to the plaintiffs in *Ma v. Reno* and related cases, discussed in earlier reading.

2. **The Meaning of "[C]ontrolling . . . [E]xecutive [A]ction."** *Garcia-Mir* and related cases rely heavily on *The Paquete Habana*'s statement that the Court would look to international law in the absence of a "controlling . . . executive action." What does that mean? After the Supreme Court's initial decision in *The Paquete Habana*, the United States argued that damages for the wrongful capture should be assessed against the officers who seized the boat, not against the United States. The district court rejected that argument and the Supreme Court, in an opinion by Justice Holmes, affirmed. *United States v. The Paquete Habana*, 189 U.S. 453 (1903). Holmes wrote:

> We do not see how it is possible that a decree should be entered against the captors. [The United States] . . . has so far adopted the acts of capture that it would be hard to say that, under the circumstances of these cases, it has not made those acts its own. It is not disputed that the United States might have ordered the vessels to be released. It did not do so. The libels [seeking to condemn the fishing boats] were filed by the United [S]tates on its own behalf, praying a forfeiture to the United States. The statutes in force seemed to contemplate that form of procedure, and such has been the practice under them. The libels alleged a capture pursuant to instructions from the President.

If the capture was "pursuant to instructions from the President," why were those instructions not a "controlling . . . executive action" within the meaning of the first *Paquete Habana* decision? What does the second *Paquete Habana* case suggest, if anything, about *Garcia-Mir*? In any event, what is the proper role of courts in assessing executive branch positions on international law? Does it make sense for the courts to take views contrary to the executive? Or should courts make determinations of international law independently of the executive's views?

3.   **Executive Action and *Charming Betsy*.** As discussed in the prior section, the *Charming Betsy* canon says that statutes should, if possible, be construed not to violate international law. One view of the Mariel boatlift cases is that they were (or should have been) *Charming Betsy* cases. The applicable statutes authorized the Attorney General to enforce immigration laws but (being ambiguous) did not authorize him to violate international law in doing so. This approach is consistent with the later decision in *Ma v. Reno*, excerpted above. Another view is that the *Charming Betsy* canon does not limit executive action, a view consistent with other subsequent cases. A third view is that the Attorney General was acting pursuant to the President's independent constitutional authority to control immigration, which is consistent with at least some of the language in *Garcia-Mir*. Under the latter view, *Charming Betsy* would have no role, and the case would squarely present the question whether the President (through the Attorney General) could violate international law. Which is the best approach?

4.   **The President's Duty to Follow International Law.** Is the President constitutionally bound to follow international law? A possible source of the President's obligation to obey customary international law is Article II, Section 3 of the Constitution: "[The President] . . . shall take Care that the Laws be faithfully executed. . . ." Unlike treaties, however, customary international law is not expressly included in Article VI's "supreme Law of the Land." As indicated in the case excerpts, courts have not directly addressed the source of the President's obligation to customary international law. What are the implications of finding such an obligation?

Al-Bihani v. Obama

590 F.3d 866 (D.C. Cir. 2010)

[The Supreme Court's decision in *Boumediene v. Bush*, 553 U.S. 723 (2008), allowed war-on-terror detainees imprisoned at Guantánamo Bay to file habeas corpus petitions challenging the legality of their detention. Al-Bihani, a Guantánamo detainee, filed such a petition, which the district court denied.]

Brown, Circuit Judge:

Ghaleb Nassar Al-Bihani appeals the denial of his petition for a writ of habeas corpus and seeks reversal or remand. He claims his detention is unauthorized by statute and the procedures of his habeas proceeding were constitutionally infirm. We reject these claims and affirm the denial of his petition.

I

Al-Bihani, a Yemeni citizen, has been held at the U.S. naval base detention facility in Guantanamo Bay, Cuba since 2002. . . . [H]e . . . accompanied and served a paramilitary group allied with the Taliban, known as the 55th Arab Brigade, which included Al Qaeda members within its command structure and which fought on the front lines against the Northern Alliance [in Afghanistan during the U.S. invasion in 2001-02]. He worked as the brigade's cook and carried a brigade-issued weapon, but never fired it in combat. Combat, however — in the form of bombing by the U.S.-led Coalition that invaded Afghanistan in response to the attacks of September 11, 2001 — forced the 55th to retreat from the front lines in October 2001. At the end of this protracted retreat, Al-Bihani and the rest of the brigade surrendered, under orders, to Northern Alliance forces, and they kept him in custody until his handover to U.S. Coalition forces in early 2002. The U.S. military sent Al-Bihani to Guantanamo for detention and interrogation.
. . .

II

Al-Bihani's many arguments present this court with two overarching questions regarding the detainees at the Guantanamo Bay naval base. The first concerns whom the President can lawfully detain pursuant to statutes passed by Congress. The second asks what procedure is due to detainees challenging their detention in habeas corpus proceedings. . . .

A

Al-Bihani challenges the statutory legitimacy of his detention by advancing a number of arguments based upon the international laws of war. He first argues that relying on "support," or even "substantial support" of Al Qaeda or the Taliban as an independent basis for detention violates international law. As a result, such a standard should not be read into the ambiguous provisions of the Authorization for Use of Military Force (AUMF), the Act empowering the President to respond to the attacks of September 11, 2001.* Al-Bihani interprets international law to mean [among other arguments] [that] anyone not belonging to an official state military is a civilian, and civilians, he says, must commit a direct hostile act, such

---

* The AUMF provides that "the President is authorized to use all necessary and appropriate force against those nations, organizations, or persons he determines planned, authorized, committed, or aided the terrorist attacks that occurred on September 11, 2001, or harbored such organizations or persons, in order to prevent any future acts of international terrorism against the United States by such nations, organizations or persons." — EDS.

as firing a weapon in combat, before they can be lawfully detained. Because Al-Bihani did not commit such an act, he reasons his detention is unlawful. . . .

Before considering these arguments in detail, we note that all of them rely heavily on the premise that the war powers granted by the AUMF and other statutes are limited by the international laws of war. This premise is mistaken. There is no indication in the AUMF, [or other related statutes], that Congress intended the international laws of war to act as extra-textual limiting principles for the President's war powers under the AUMF. The international laws of war as a whole have not been implemented domestically by Congress and are therefore not a source of authority for U.S. courts. *See* RESTATEMENT (THIRD) OF FOREIGN RELATIONS LAW OF THE UNITED STATES § 111(3)-(4) (1987). Even assuming Congress had at some earlier point implemented the laws of war as domestic law through appropriate legislation, Congress had the power to authorize the President in the AUMF and other later statutes to exceed those bounds. *See id.* § 115(1)(a).

Further weakening their relevance to this case, the international laws of war are not a fixed code. Their dictates and application to actual events are by nature contestable and fluid. See *id.* § 102 cmts. b & c (stating there is "no precise formula" to identify a practice as custom and that "[i]t is often difficult to determine when [a custom's] transformation into law has taken place"). Therefore, while the international laws of war are helpful to courts when identifying the general set of war powers to which the AUMF speaks, their lack of controlling legal force and firm definition render their use both inapposite and inadvisable when courts seek to determine the limits of the President's war powers.

Therefore, putting aside that we find Al-Bihani's reading of international law to be unpersuasive, we have no occasion here to quibble over the intricate application of. . .amorphous customary principles. The sources we look to for resolution of Al-Bihani's case are the sources courts always look to: the text of relevant statutes and controlling domestic caselaw.

[The court also rejected Al-Bihani's arguments on the merits. Judge Williams concurred in part and concurred in the judgment.]

Al-Bihani v. Obama

619 F.3d 1 (D.C. Cir. 2010)

[Al-Bihani petitioned the court of appeals for rehearing en banc of the decision above, on the ground that it misstated the relationship between U.S. law and international law. The full court denied the petition. Seven judges joined a statement saying that they declined to rehear the issue of the status of international law because it was not necessary to the outcome of the case. Each of the judges of the original panel (Brown, Kavanaugh, and Williams) filed a separate opinion concurring in the denial. The opinions are presented here in a different order to enhance continuity.]

KAVANAUGH, Circuit Judge, concurring in the denial of rehearing en banc:

In the 2001 Authorization for Use of Military Force, Congress authorized the President to wage war against al Qaeda and the Taliban. That war continues. At the President's direction, the U.S. military is detaining Al-Bihani as an enemy belligerent in the ongoing conflict. Al-Bihani has asked this Court to order his release from U.S. military custody. He argues that international-law principles prohibit his continued detention. The premise of Al-Bihani's plea for release is that international-law norms are judicially enforceable limits on the President's war-making authority under the AUMF.

[T]he premise of Al-Bihani's argument is incorrect. International-law norms that have not been incorporated into domestic U.S. law by the political branches are not judicially enforceable limits on the President's authority under the AUMF. This separate opinion explains at great length my reasons for reaching that conclusion.

Al-Bihani's invocation of international law raises two fundamental questions. First, are international-law norms automatically part of domestic U.S. law? Second, even if international-law norms are not automatically part of domestic U.S. law, does the 2001 AUMF incorporate international-law principles as judicially enforceable limits on the President's wartime authority under the AUMF? The answer to both questions is no.

First, international-law norms are not domestic U.S. law in the absence of action by the political branches to codify those norms. Congress and the President can and often do incorporate international-law principles into domestic U.S. law by way of a statute (or executive regulations issued pursuant to statutory authority) or a self-executing treaty. When that happens, the relevant international-law principles become part of the domestic U.S. law that federal courts must enforce, assuming there is a cognizable cause of action and the prerequisites for federal jurisdiction are satisfied. But . . . international-law norms are not enforceable in federal courts unless the political branches have incorporated the norms into domestic U.S. law. . . .

Second, the 2001 AUMF does not expressly or impliedly incorporate judicially enforceable international-law limits on the President's direction of the war against al Qaeda and the Taliban. In authorizing the President to employ force, the AUMF authorizes the President to command the U.S. military to kill, capture, and detain the enemy, as Commanders in Chief traditionally have done in waging wars throughout American history. Congress enacted the AUMF with knowledge that the U.S. Constitution and other federal statutes would limit the President's conduct of the war. But neither the AUMF's text nor contemporaneous statements by Members of Congress suggest that Congress intended to impose judicially enforceable *international-law* limits on the President's authority under the AUMF.

Moreover, . . . the *Charming Betsy* canon does not authorize courts to employ international-law norms when interpreting a statute like the AUMF that broadly authorizes the President to wage war against a foreign enemy. To begin with, . . . the canon does not permit courts to alter their interpretation of federal statutes based on international-law norms that have not been incorporated into domestic

U.S. law. Indeed, . . . [in modern times] the Supreme Court has applied that canon only to support the presumption that a federal statute does not apply extraterritorially. . . . [Second], courts may not invoke the canon against the Executive. . . . [T]he Executive generally has the authority to interpret ambiguous statutes within the bounds of reasonableness and, in so doing, to weigh international-law considerations as much or as little as the Executive sees fit. . . . [Third], [c]ourts have never applied the *Charming Betsy* canon against the Executive to limit the scope of a congressional authorization of war. For good reason: To the extent there is ambiguity in a statutory grant to the President of war-making authority, the President — not an international tribunal or international law — is to resolve the ambiguity in the first instance.

. . .

[T]he limited authority of *the Judiciary* to rely on international law to restrict the American war effort does not imply that *the political branches* should ignore or disregard international-law norms. The principles of the international laws of war (and of international law more generally) deserve the respect of the United States. Violating international-law norms and breaching international obligations may trigger serious consequences, such as subjecting the United States to sanctions, undermining U.S. standing in the world community, or encouraging retaliation against U.S. personnel abroad. Therefore, Congress and the President are often well-advised to take account of international-law principles when considering potential legislation or treaties. And even when international-law norms have not been incorporated into domestic U.S. law, the Executive Branch, to the extent permissible under its constitutional and statutory authority, is often wise to pay close attention to those norms as a matter of sound policy, international obligation, or effective foreign relations. But in our constitutional system of separated powers, it is for Congress and the President — not the courts — to determine in the first instance whether and how the United States will meet its international obligations. When Congress and the President have chosen not to incorporate international-law norms into domestic U.S. law, bedrock principles of judicial restraint and separation of powers counsel that courts respect that decision.

I

Four categories of law are relevant to this case: federal statutes; self-executing treaties . . . ; non-self-executing treaties . . . ; and customary international law.

Those four categories do not share the same status in U.S. law. As I will explain, statutes and self-executing treaties are domestic U.S. law and thus enforceable in U.S. courts. By contrast, non-self-executing treaties and customary international law are not domestic U.S. law. *See Medellín v. Texas*, 552 U.S. 491 (2008); *Sosa v. Alvarez-Machain*, 542 U.S. 692 (2004). Only when international-law principles are incorporated into a statute or a self-executing treaty do they become domestic U.S. law enforceable in U.S. courts.

In this case, none of the purported international-law principles cited by Al-Bihani has been incorporated into a statute or self-executing treaty. Those principles are therefore not part of the domestic law of the United States and, on their own, do not authorize a U.S. court to order Al-Bihani's release from U.S. military detention.

A

In our constitutional system, international-law norms may achieve the status of domestic U.S. law through two mechanisms: incorporation into a statute (or legally binding executive regulation adopted pursuant to a statute) or incorporation into a self-executing treaty.

First, international-law norms may be incorporated into legislation approved by a majority in both Houses of Congress and signed by the President (or enacted over a presidential veto, or by operation of the Constitution's ten-day rule). *See* U.S. Const. art. I, § 7. The important role Congress plays in this sphere is apparent from the text of the Constitution, which specifically authorizes Congress to "define and punish . . . Offences against the Law of Nations." *Id.* art. I, § 8, cl. 10. The delegates to the Constitutional Convention expressly assigned that power to Congress because, as Gouverneur Morris aptly noted at the Convention, international-law principles are "often too vague and deficient to be a rule" without implementing legislation.

Consistent with that constitutionally assigned role, Congress sometimes enacts statutes to codify international-law norms derived from non-self-executing treaties or customary international law, or to fulfill international-law obligations.

. . . When incorporating international-law norms into domestic U.S. law, Congress sometimes simply enacts statutes that refer generically to "international law" (or some variation thereof) without further defining what international law requires. For example, federal piracy statutes permit the capture and forfeiture of vessels used for, and the imprisonment of individuals who commit, acts of "piracy as defined by the law of nations." Similarly, Congress has authorized the President to use military force to detain foreign vessels at American ports when such action is permitted "by the law of nations or the treaties of the United States." It has also empowered the President to impose sanctions on foreign countries that use chemical or biological weapons "in violation of international law." . . .

Second, in addition to being incorporated into a statute (or executive regulation adopted pursuant thereto), international-law principles may become part of domestic U.S. law by means of a self-executing treaty that is made by the President with the concurrence of two-thirds of the Senate. . . .

B

By contrast, international-law principles found in non-self-executing treaties and customary international law, but not incorporated into statutes or self-executing treaties, are not part of domestic U.S. law.

The Supreme Court has squarely held that non-self-executing treaties "are not domestic law." *Medellín*, 552 U.S. at 505 (quotation omitted). . . . The Supreme Court has likewise indicated that customary international law is not automatically part of domestic U.S. law. See *Sosa*, 542 U.S. 692. Customary international law is said to arise from the "general and consistent practice of states followed by them from a sense of legal obligation." Restatement (Third) of Foreign Relations Law of the United States § 102(2) (1987). It is a kind of international common law.

It does not result from any of the mechanisms specified in the U.S. Constitution for the creation of U.S. law. For that reason, although norms of customary international law may obligate the United States internationally, they are not part of domestic U.S. law. Customary-international-law norms become part of domestic U.S. law only if the norms are incorporated into a statute or self-executing treaty.

To be sure, there was a time when U.S. courts stated that customary international law was "part of our law" so that "where there is no treaty, and no controlling executive or legislative act or judicial decision, resort must be had to the customs and usages of civilized nations; and, as evidence of these, to the works of jurists and commentators." *The Paquete Habana*, 175 U.S. 677, 700 (1900). But that oft-quoted statement reflected the notion, common in the early years of the Nation but now discredited, that international law was part of the general common law that federal courts could apply. *See Sosa*, 542 U.S. at 714-15; *Erie R.R. Co. v. Tompkins*, 304 U.S. 64, 79 (1938). . . . But as decided by the Supreme Court in its landmark *Erie* decision in 1938, the view that federal courts may ascertain and enforce international-law norms as part of the general common law is fundamentally inconsistent with a proper understanding of the role of the Federal Judiciary in our constitutional system. In *Erie*, the Supreme Court famously held that there is no general common law enforceable by federal courts. . . .

Erie means that, in our constitutional system of separated powers, federal courts may not enforce law that lacks a domestic sovereign source. *Erie* requires federal courts to identify the sovereign source for every rule of decision, and the appropriate sovereigns under the U.S. Constitution are the federal government and the states. . . .

. . . The Court [in *Sosa*] rejected the notion that all customary-international-law norms are independently enforceable in federal court. The Court decided that, post-*Erie*, federal courts could recognize claims under the Alien Tort Statute for violation of a narrowly defined subset of international-law norms — not on the theory that international law is automatically incorporated into U.S. law, but rather only to give effect to the congressional intent underlying the ATS's grant of jurisdiction in 1789.

Sosa thus confirmed that international-law principles are not automatically part of domestic U.S. law and that those principles can enter into domestic U.S. law only through an affirmative act of the political branches. After all, if customary international law is automatically federal law, then the ATS ought to cover all [customary international law] claims, so long as they also qualify as torts. But *Sosa* rejected this view and instead gave domestic legal force to an extremely limited subset of [customary international law] claims . . . based on its reading of the specific intent of Congress.

C

Al-Bihani cites various international-law norms to challenge his detention. . . .

First, Al-Bihani cites two treaties to which the United States is a party: the Third and Fourth Geneva Conventions of 1949, which were made by President Truman in 1949 and concurred in by the Senate in 1955. . . . Second, Al-Bihani cites a variety of other international-law sources: the 1977 Additional Protocols to the Geneva Conventions (which were signed by the United States under President Carter but never concurred in by the Senate), commentary from the International Committee of the Red Cross, and the writings of various international-law scholars. . . .

Al-Bihani cannot invoke the 1949 Geneva Conventions as a source of domestic U.S. law enforceable in federal court for either of two alternative reasons. To begin with, the 1949 Geneva Conventions are not self-executing treaties and thus are not domestic U.S. law. . . . [In addition,] . . . Congress has since unambiguously repudiated whatever domestic legal effect the Conventions otherwise might have had in this habeas setting. Section 5(a) of the Military Commissions Act of 2006 . . . provides in broad and plain terms: "No person may invoke the Geneva Conventions or any protocols thereto in any habeas corpus or other civil action or proceeding. . . ."

The other international-law sources [al-Bihani] cites — the 1977 Additional Protocols to the Geneva Conventions, Red Cross commentaries, and writings of international-law scholars — may reflect or give rise to principles of customary international law. And those customary-international-law principles may in turn impose obligations on (or raise policy considerations for) the United States in its international relations. The political branches thus may decide to adhere to those international-law norms. But absent incorporation into a statute or a self-executing treaty, such customary-international-law principles are not part of the domestic law of the United States that is enforceable in federal court. . . .

II

. . . Al-Bihani and amici alternatively argue that courts must nonetheless apply international-law principles in resolving cases under the 2001 Authorization for Use of Military Force. In particular, Al-Bihani and amici contend that we should interpret the AUMF as incorporating international-law principles that limit the President's authority under the AUMF to wage war against al Qaeda and the Taliban.

On its face, this is a radical argument. Al-Bihani and amici would have the Federal Judiciary limit the scope of the President's war-making authority — *not* based on the Constitution and *not* based on express language in a statute or self-executing treaty, but rather based on international-law norms that have never been enacted into domestic U.S. law by American lawmakers. For the reasons set forth at length below, the argument advanced by Al-Bihani and amici lacks merit: Congress has broadly authorized the President to wage war against al Qaeda and the Taliban. Neither the AUMF's text nor its legislative history suggests that Congress intended international-law principles to limit the scope of that congressional authorization. Congress often incorporates international-law principles into federal law; it did not do so here. Courts must respect that decision. . . . Moreover, the *Charming Betsy* canon of statutory construction does not authorize courts to read international-law limitations into the authority granted to the President by the AUMF. . . .

A

. . . There is no indication in the text of the AUMF that Congress intended to impose judicially enforceable international-law limits on the President's war-making authority under the AUMF. As explained in Part I of this opinion, Congress has enacted many statutes — including war-related statutes — that expressly refer to international law. But unlike those statutes, the AUMF contains no reference to international law. . . .

B

Even assuming arguendo that the text of the AUMF is ambiguous on this point — which it is not — the statute's legislative history provides no hint that Congress intended to impose judicially enforceable international-law limitations on the President's war-making authority, or on his lesser-included detention authority.

C

. . .

Since passage of the AUMF in 2001, Congress has enacted additional legislation regulating the Executive's conduct of the war. These statutes reveal that Congress has repeatedly responded with new legislation addressing some of the unique issues posed by a war against a non-uniformed enemy. These statutes further demonstrate that Congress knows how to legislate war-related restrictions on the Executive — and does not need or intend for the courts to impose new international-law-based restrictions. For example, as part of the Detainee Treatment Act of 2005, Congress provided in broad terms that "[n]o individual in the custody or under the physical control of the United States Government, regardless of nationality or physical location, shall be subject to cruel, inhuman, or degrading treatment or punishment". . . .

. . . To the extent Congress has not seen the need to regulate every last aspect of the President's waging of war, we can assume that Congress has confidence in the President's ability to exercise his discretion appropriately — and if it loses such confidence, Congress may act anew to further limit that presidential discretion, as it has done on numerous occasions.

D

[T]he default presumption is that international law is not a judicially enforceable limit on a President's wartime authority *unless Congress expressly says it is*. Al-Bihani and amici seek to flip that default presumption by invoking the *Charming Betsy* canon of statutory construction. According to their articulation of that canon, ambiguities in federal statutes must be interpreted in accord with international-law norms that are not themselves domestic U.S. law. *See Murray v. Schooner Charming Betsy*, 6 U.S. 64, 118 (1804); *see also* RESTATEMENT (THIRD)

OF FOREIGN RELATIONS LAW OF THE UNITED STATES § 114 (1987). Al-Bihani and amici thus argue that international law is a judicially enforceable limit on the President's authority under a war-authorizing statute *unless Congress expressly says it is not.* . . .

1

As an initial matter, . . . there is no legitimate basis for courts to alter their interpretation of federal statutes to make those statutes conform with non-self-executing treaties and customary international law, given that those sources lack any status as domestic U.S. law.

With respect to non-self-executing treaties, there is a strong inference that Congress deliberately chose not to incorporate such treaties into domestic U.S. law. . . . As to customary international law, the problems with applying *Charming Betsy* are equally substantial. There was a good argument for interpreting statutes in light of customary international law in the days before *Erie*, when customary international-law principles were considered part of the general common law that all federal courts could enforce. . . . After *Erie* and particularly after *Sosa*, however, it is clear that customary international-law norms, like non-self-executing treaties, are not part of domestic U.S. law. Congress has incorporated customary international law into domestic U.S. law on numerous occasions, including in statutes related to war. Thus, when Congress does not act to incorporate those norms into domestic U.S. law, such non-incorporation presumably reflects a deliberate congressional choice. And it likewise makes sense to conclude that Congress would not want courts to smuggle those norms into domestic U.S. law through the back door by using them to resolve questions of American law. . . .

The Supreme Court's case law since *Erie* is consistent with this limited role for international law as a device for interpreting ambiguous federal statutes. In the seven-plus decades since the Supreme Court's landmark 1938 decision in *Erie*, the Court has invoked *Charming Betsy* only sporadically. It has done so to lend support to a distinct and far narrower canon of statutory construction: the rule that absent a clear statement from Congress, federal statutes do not apply outside the United States. This is often called the presumption against extraterritoriality. . . .

Those extraterritoriality cases constitute a unique category. As the Court has recognized, special concerns counsel against applying domestic U.S. law extraterritorially because doing so can often conflict with the laws of another sovereign. In such situations, the presumption against extraterritoriality serves not just to honor the United States' international-law obligations as a general matter, but to "avoid or resolve conflicts between competing laws" established by two sovereign nations. . . . The Court's citation of *Charming Betsy* in cases applying the presumption against extraterritoriality does not support invocation of the canon outside of that narrow context.

2

[In addition] . . . [t]he *Charming Betsy* canon may not be invoked *against the Executive* to conform statutes to non-self-executing treaties or customary international law. The basic reason is that the Executive — not international law or an international tribunal — possesses the authority in the first instance to interpret ambiguous provisions in statutes and to determine how best to weigh and accommodate international-law principles not clearly incorporated into a statute. . . .

Since *Erie*, the Supreme Court has never invoked the *Charming Betsy* canon to decide a case against the Executive. . . . Importantly, if courts construe an authorizing statute like the AUMF to permit the President to violate international law, those courts would not be placing the United States in violation of international law. Rather, such a violation would occur, if at all, only after the Executive Branch, which is both politically accountable and expert in foreign relations, made an independent judgment to exercise the authority conferred by Congress in a way that violated international law.

3

[Further,] [t]he *Charming Betsy* canon may not be invoked against the Executive *to limit the scope of a congressional authorization of war* — that is, to limit a war-authorizing statute to make it conform with non-self-executing treaties and customary international law. . . .

. . . Applying *Charming Betsy* to a statute like the AUMF would contravene the well-established principle that the Judiciary should not interfere when the President is executing national security and foreign relations authority in a manner consistent with an express congressional authorization. . . .

. . . Many international-law norms are vague, contested, or still evolving. Simply determining the precise content of those norms at any given time entails a considerable exercise of subjective judgment. Applying them to particular factual situations adds another layer of subjectivity. *See Sosa v. Alvarez-Machain*, 542 U.S. 692, 726 (2004) ("a judge deciding in reliance on an international norm will find a substantial element of discretionary judgment in the decision"). . . . And deciding how those international-law norms should apply to a war that differs in fundamental ways from traditional models of armed conflict presents especially thorny questions of policy and prudence. Moreover, judicial assessment of contested international-law norms can take years, but the President often needs to make military decisions immediately or at least quickly — a reality that calls for judicial caution before restraining the President's exercise of war powers.

. . .

To sum up on *Charming Betsy*: The canon exists to the extent it supports applying the presumption against extraterritorial application of federal statutes. Beyond that, after *Erie* and particularly after *Sosa* and *Medellín*, it is not appropriate for courts to use the *Charming Betsy* canon to alter interpretation of federal statutes to conform them to norms found in non-self-executing treaties and customary international law, which Congress has not chosen to incorporate into domestic U.S. law. In the alternative, even if one disagrees with that broader proposition and concludes that use of the *Charming Betsy* canon is appropriate in some such cases, it should not be invoked against the Executive Branch, which has the authority to weigh international-law considerations when interpreting the scope of ambiguous statutes. And even if one also disagrees with that, it is not appropriate for courts to narrow a congressional authorization of war based on international-law norms that are not part of domestic U.S. law.

. . .

F

In this opinion, I have several times reiterated a key point: To the extent permitted by the Constitution and federal statutes, the Executive is free to follow international-law principles as a matter of policy and to conduct its activities in accordance with international law. The Executive is also free to adopt legally binding regulations pursuant to statutory authorization and may, within the bounds permitted by statute, seek to correspond those regulations to international-law principles. A variety of Executive regulations and Army Field Manuals seek to ensure that the military acts consistently with certain international-law norms.

. . .

In exercising his Article II Commander-in-Chief authority, the President is not subject to judicially enforceable *international-law* limitations. Nowhere does the Constitution require the President to comply with foreign or international law. "[U]nder our Constitutional jurisprudence," an "action by the President . . . that is within [his] constitutional authority does not become a violation of the Constitution because the Act places the United States in violation of a treaty provision or of a U.S. obligation under customary law." LOUIS HENKIN, FOREIGN AFFAIRS AND THE UNITED STATES CONSTITUTION 236 (2d ed. 1996). And in its recent decision in *Medellín*, the Supreme Court decisively held that the President's "responsibility to 'take Care that the Laws be faithfully executed'" applies only to "domestic law." 552 U.S. at 532 (quoting U.S. CONST. art. II, § 3). . . .

. . .

In sum, courts enforce constitutionally permissible constraints imposed by Congress on the President's war powers, including those that Congress might derive from international-law principles. Courts likewise enforce judicially manageable constraints imposed by the U.S. Constitution on the President's war powers. In addition, the Executive Branch within its constitutional and statutory bounds may decide, as a matter of international obligation or policy, to follow non-self-executing treaties and customary international-law norms. But all of that is far different from a court on its own invoking international-law principles to restrict the President's direction and management of the war effort. Under our Constitution, it is for the political branches in the first instance to incorporate international-law norms into domestic U.S. law. Congress did not do so when enacting the AUMF. In asking us to nonetheless rely on international-law principles to order Al-Bihani's release from U.S. military custody, the argument of Al-Bihani and amici contravenes bedrock tenets of judicial restraint and separation of powers.

WILLIAMS, Senior Circuit Judge, concurring in the denial of rehearing en banc:
. . . Judge Kavanaugh, I think, fails to adequately distinguish between treatment of international law norms as "judicially enforceable limits" on Presidential

authority, or as "domestic U.S. law," and use of such norms as a "basis for courts to alter their interpretation of federal statutes." By "alter their interpretation," I take Judge Kavanaugh to mean . . . for a court to allow international law to persuade it to adopt a *narrower* interpretation of the President's authority than it would otherwise have chosen. I will assume that Judge Kavanaugh is correct as to the impropriety of the stronger use of international law (treating it as "domestic law"), but I believe him incorrect on the weaker (allowing it to affect a court's statutory interpretation).

. . . Courts use a wide range of information outside the words of a statute to find those words' meaning. This reflects the simple truth that the question of a word's meaning is an empirical one: what have persons in the relevant community actually meant when using the words that appear in a statute? Among the most obvious outside sources to resolve that question are legislative history, usage in other laws and in judicial decisions, and dictionaries. Courts use all three incessantly. Dictionaries, of course, are only scholars' claims as to how people have historically used the words in question. Because military conflict is commonly an international phenomenon, words relating to such conflict are used in international discourse, of which international law is a subset.

. . . It would be an odd member of Congress who supposed that in authorizing the use of military force he was embracing uses equivalent to *all* such uses that have ever occurred: think Nanking 1937-38; Katyn 1940; Lidice 1942; My Lai 1968. More generally, it seems improbable that in authorizing the use of all "necessary and appropriate force" Congress could have contemplated employment of methods clearly and unequivocally condemned by international law.

Judge Kavanaugh agrees with that conclusion, but argues that we infer such limits on Congress's grant of power simply from penalties or prohibitions in *domestic* law. He is surely correct that this is *one* source for finding limits on an authorization of military force, but that does not make it the only legitimate source of such limits. In some circumstances, Judge Kavanaugh's "domestic U.S. law of war," may have relatively little to say on a question that international practice has addressed for centuries. It obviously seemed so to the Supreme Court in *Hamdi v. Rumsfeld*, 542 U.S. 507, 518-21 (2004), where the plurality looked to international norms on the question of whom the President may detain pursuant to the AUMF, and for how long.

Before *Erie R.R. Co. v. Tompkins*, 304 U.S. 64 (1938), U.S. courts undoubtedly used international law to help resolve cases. It appears to have been uncontroversial for international law to serve not only as a species of federal general common law, binding absent contrary domestic law, but also as a source of interpretive guidance regarding statutes passed by Congress . . . . To dispute that commonsensical understanding, after all, requires defending the unlikely view that international law — unlike other known binding laws — offered no useful information whatsoever regarding the meaning of new laws on similar subjects. In Judge Kavanaugh's view, *Erie* effectively proscribed use of international law as "enforceable" U.S. law. But that landmark case left intact the pre-existing alternative role of international law as a store of information regarding the sense of words Congress enacts into laws governing international matters — a role that never depended on international law's being a form of federal general common law (which *Erie* famously banished). *Erie* hardly requires that every last source of information regarding the meaning of words in statutes be an enacted law; if it does, federal courts have been disobeying its command for more than seven decades.

. . .

The plurality's ruling in *Hamdi* uses international law as an interpretive tool in the way I've described. There the petitioner contended that the AUMF simply didn't authorize detention of U.S. citizens. [The Supreme Court rejected this argument]. . . . But the plurality made *explicit* that the detention authority that is a standard tool for states authorized to use force is by no means unlimited: "Certainly, we agree that indefinite detention for the purpose of interrogation is not authorized. Further, we understand Congress' grant of authority for use of 'necessary and appropriate force' to include the authority to detain for the duration of the conflict, and our understanding is based on longstanding law-of-war principles." . . . Thus the plurality answered Hamdi's concern about indefinite duration by saying that the detention authority recognized under the law of war, and thus implicitly conferred by the AUMF, was subject to a *limit* similarly recognized by the law of war.

All of this said, I want to make clear that I agree with Judge Kavanaugh that the President's interpretation of such an authorizing statute is owed "great weight". . . . Thus, when an Article III court is for some reason adjudicating the validity of executive military conduct (an issue to which I return below), and there is uncertainty as to whether the conduct fell within the statutory language, I would expect the court to ask what limits the statute *clearly* set on its grant of authority. In doing so the court would use all the traditional means of statutory interpretation to flesh out the statutory boundaries. These would include historical uses of the terms in relevant contexts, including the discourse of international law. Only conduct beyond the words' clearly established meaning would be off-limits.

Moreover, I should not be taken as saying that courts should take uncertain or disputed propositions of international law and build them into iron constraints on the meaning of congressional grants of authority. Judge Kavanaugh is quite right to quote Gouverneur Morris's observation that international law is "often too vague and deficient to be a rule" without implementing legislation. Courts should approach seemingly authoritative declarations of international law with caution. Even the highest international tribunals appear at times to be influenced in their rulings by the favor in which the disputing nations are held in international circles. Cf. H.R. Res. 713, 108th Cong. (2004) (denouncing the July 9, 2004 decision of the International Court of Justice in the Hague purporting to find Israel's construction of a barrier at the time of the Second Intifada a violation of international law). Thus U.S. courts should not automatically attach weight to rulings of such tribunals, not to mention less authoritative expressions of international law, in the absence of clear reason to believe that they will be consistently and evenhandedly applied, are the product of serious reasoning and are susceptible of practical application.

Finally, Judge Kavanaugh is plainly concerned about the propriety of Article III courts using gauzy notions of international law to rein in the executive's conduct of military operations. I share that concern. But under *Boumediene*, Article III courts evaluate the propriety of the detention of non-U.S. nationals. In doing so they necessarily pass judgment on the admissibility of evidence collected on the battlefield, and thus on the propriety of the methods used for such collection. District courts have been doing so regularly since *Boumediene*. They therefore monitor, and to a degree supervise, the battlefield conduct of the U.S. military. But that is a consequence of *Boumediene*, in which the federal judiciary assumed an entirely new role in the nation's military operations; it is not a product of international law's role in understanding congressional grants of power — a separate matter entirely.

BROWN, Circuit Judge, concurring in the denial of rehearing en banc:

. . .

Judge Williams offers a hazy but ominous hermeneutics. Its animating premise is that *Boumediene v. Bush*, 128 S. Ct. 2229 (2008), used the Suspension Clause to create an opening through which the Judiciary now — as a *constitutional* matter — "monitor[s]" and "supervise[s] the battlefield conduct of the U.S. military." In executing this supervisory role, the Judiciary should survey the spectrum of "international discourse," picking and choosing those propositions that exhibit — by the Judiciary's lights — "serious reasoning," "consistent[] and evenhanded[] appli[cation]," and "practical[ity]" to the point where they are suitable to control the President's conduct of war. Judge Williams states these propositions matter-of-factly, even blithely, as routine matters of statutory interpretation. But that nonchalance is only a mask for what is, at its core, a radical and sweeping claim, one at odds with our Constitution and caselaw. The Constitution entrusts the President — not the Judiciary — with the conduct of war. "The Framers . . . did not make the judiciary the overseer of our government," *Youngstown Sheet & Tube Co. v. Sawyer*, 343 U.S. 579, 594 (1952) (Frankfurter, J., concurring), so *Boumediene* cannot be read — as Judge Williams suggests — to override that basic notion and hand courts authority to deem international norms as binding commands on the Commander-in-Chief. Such a reading would be in tension with the Supreme Court's recognition that courts are "hardly . . . competent" in the realm of foreign affairs, *Banco Nacional de Cuba v. Sabbatino*, 376 U.S. 398, 410 (1964), and with the constitutional principle that prohibits even Congress, let alone the Judiciary, from "interfer[ing] with the [Executive's] command of forces and the conduct of campaigns," *Ex parte Milligan*, 71 U.S. 2, 139 (1866) (Chase, C.J., concurring).

Further, Judge Williams' proposed role for the Judiciary goes far beyond the role the Supreme Court envisioned in *Hamdi v. Rumsfeld* and *Boumediene*. The *Hamdi* plurality forecast a restrained process that "meddles little, if at all, in the strategy or conduct of war, inquiring only into the appropriateness of continuing to detain an individual claimed to have taken up arms against the United States." 542 U.S. 507, 535 (2004). It seems farfetched that "inquiring *only* into the appropriateness" of detention should be freighted with the awesome power of deciding which international constraints to enforce against the President. In a similar vein, the Court in *Boumediene* was circumspect about crafting any substantive rules to control the President's war powers, repeating that it was not addressing the "content of the law that governs petitioners' detention," leaving it to the political branches first to engage in a "debate about how best to preserve Constitutional values while protecting the Nation from terrorism." 128 S. Ct. at 2277.

This sprint into judicial immodesty cannot be redeemed by Judge Williams' argument that international law parallels traditional tools of statutory interpretation, and that by turning to it for substantive meaning courts are only divining the intent of Congress. . . . The varied process by which international law is made — through treaty, tribunal decision, and the constant churn of state practice and *opinio juris* — shares few, if any, of the qualities that give the traditional sources of interpretation their authority. Courts turn to legislative history because it comes from the mouths of legislators and therefore arguably sheds light on their intentions and understandings. Courts examine the usage of terms in other statutes and judicial decisions because our law is a closed and coherent system that strives for internal consistency. And courts consult dictionaries for the same reason most people do: our law, like the rest of our society, is dependent on language's technical meaning among American English speakers. On none of these grounds can the use of international law be justified. . . . [I]nternational discourse, unlike a dictionary, is anything but a source of specific, technical, and shared linguistic meaning. Judge Williams concedes this point, characterizing international law as often "vague and deficient," consisting of "gauzy notions" that are prone to "misuse" by nations for "political purpose[s]," and subject to official criticism by our elected representatives. How can sifting through such an unstable and unreliable trove of meaning be likened to opening a dictionary? How is it advisable or legitimate for courts to take on such a treacherous task, especially when the political branches possess the competency and traditional duty to do the sifting themselves by domestically incorporating international law through statute or rendering treaties self-executing?

. . . The only generally applicable role for international law in statutory interpretation is the modest one afforded by the *Charming Betsy* canon, which counsels courts, where fairly possible, to construe ambiguous statutes so as not to conflict with international law. . . . However, Judge Williams does not appear to confine international law to such a narrow space. By including international discourse among the traditional tools available to courts when interpreting statutes, Judge Williams is not limiting the application of international law to ambiguous statutory text. Generally, a statute's text is only ambiguous if, after "employing traditional tools of statutory construction," a court determines that Congress did not have a precise intention on the question at issue. It is at this point . . . that the *Charming Betsy* canon has had any application in federal courts. . . .

. . . Confronted with a shadowy, non-traditional foe that succeeded in bringing a war to our doorstep by asymmetric means, it was (and still is) unclear how international law applies in all respects to this new context. The prospect is very real that some tradeoffs traditionally struck by the laws of war no longer make sense. That Congress wished the President to retain the discretion to recalibrate the military's strategy and tactics in light of circumstances not contemplated by our international obligations is therefore sensible, and reflects the traditional sovereign prerogative to violate international law or terminate international agreements. *See Garcia-Mir v. Meese*, 788 F.2d 1446, 1455 (11th Cir. 1986) ("[T]he power of the President to disregard international law in service of domestic needs is reaffirmed."). . . .

The only way a court could reach the opposite conclusion is to go beyond the AUMF's text, freeing it — as Judge Williams suggests — to appeal to an international metanarrative, one activated whenever a legal issue touches on matters that strike the judge as transnational in flavor. Judges act prudently when they consciously forego opportunities for policymaking. Therefore, ignoring the text and plain meaning of a statute to privilege a more creative interpretation is the antithesis of prudence. And, in a time of war, it has the inconvenient effect of upending more than a century of our jurisprudence based on an understanding as old as the Republic: that the "conduct of foreign relations of our government is committed by the Constitution to the executive and legislative . . . departments," not to the judiciary. *Oetjen v. Cent. Leather Co.*, 246 U.S. 297, 302 (1918). The only proper judicial role in this case is the truly modest route taken by the panel opinion in *Al-Bihani*. We read "necessary and appropriate" in its traditional sense, taking Congress at its word that the President is to have wide discretion. This is a modest course because the President retains the leeway to implement his authority as broadly or narrowly as he believes appropriate — consistent with international law or not — and the legislature, in turn, may add whatever limits or constraints it deems wise as the war progresses. This ensures that wartime decisions will be informed by the expertise of the political branches, stated in a clear fashion, and that the decisionmakers will be accountable to the electorate.

None of those benefits accrue if the conduct of the military is subject to judicial correction based on norms of international discourse. Such an approach would place ultimate control of the war in the one branch insulated from both the battlefield and the ballot box. That would add further illegitimacy to the unpredictable and ad hoc rules judges would draw from the primordial stew of treaties, state practice, tribunal decisions, scholarly opinion, and foreign law that swirls beyond our borders. It is no comfort to the military to say, as Judge Williams does, that courts will only apply international rules they deem to possess the qualities of serious reason, evenhandedness, and practicality. Those are not judicially manageable standards. Those are buzzwords, the pleasing sound of which nearly lulls the mind into missing the vision of judicial supremacy at the heart of Judge Williams' opinion.

NOTES AND QUESTIONS

1. **Aftermath of *Al-Bihani*.** The U.S. Supreme Court denied Al-Bihani's petition for writ of certiorari without comment. Because opinions on denial of rehearing en banc have no precedential effect, the law of the D.C. Circuit

(where most war-on-terror cases are heard) remains as stated in the *Al-Bihani* panel opinion. Subsequent cases have not directly confronted or resolved the issues.

2. ***Al-Bihani* and *Charming Betsy*.** Note that *Al-Bihani*, like *Garcia-Mir*, can be viewed either as an attempt to use customary international law to constrain the President directly (through limits on the President's executive power) or as an attempt to use customary international law indirectly as an application of the *Charming Betsy* canon to the AUMF (or both).

3. **Broader Arguments for the Use of International Law in U.S. Courts.** The concurring opinions of Judges Kavanaugh, Williams, and Brown in *Al-Bihani* raise a number of issues about U.S. courts using international law. One issue is the amount of deference owed to the executive branch in the interpretation of international law. The executive branch argued in *Al-Bihani* that its interpretations are entitled to "substantial deference." *See* Response to Petition for Rehearing and Rehearing en Banc at 8, n.3 ("Where the laws of war are unclear or analogies to traditional international armed conflicts are inapt, a court should accord substantial deference to the political branches in construing how the laws of war apply to this nontraditional conflict."). Do the concurring opinions agree or disagree with that position?

    Another issue is *how* U.S. courts should use international law. The executive branch argued that interpretation of the AUMF should be informed by the international laws of war:

    > [T]he Government interprets its detention authority under the AUMF to be informed by the laws of war. That interpretation is consistent with longstanding Supreme Court precedent that, generally, statutes should be construed, if possible, as consistent with international law. See, e.g., *Murray v. Schooner Charming Betsy*, 6 U.S. 64 (1804) ("an act of Congress ought never to be construed to violate the law of nations, if any other possible construction remains"). . . . Notably, in *Hamdi*, the plurality applied this approach specifically to the AUMF. . . . Consistent with *Hamdi*, the United States interprets the detention authority granted by the AUMF, as informed by the laws of war.

    Id. at 7-8. Do the concurring opinions agree or disagree with this position? Do you understand the distinction drawn by Judge Williams between this position, based on the *Charming Betsy* canon, and the very different position — advanced by al-Bihani himself but adopted in none of the concurring opinions — that international law can be treated as domestic law that imposes "judicially enforceable limits" on presidential authority? What arguments are there for and against treating international law as a source of judicially enforceable limits on presidential authority? Are Judges Kavanaugh and Brown right that such a position would give too much leeway to judges and unduly constrain the political branches?

REVIEW NOTES AND QUESTIONS ON CUSTOMARY INTERNATIONAL LAW

1. Suppose you have a client who wants to claim an infringement of customary international law in U.S. court. Prepare a checklist of hurdles you will have to overcome in order to get a court to address the merits of the claim. Which ones seem particularly problematic? What additional facts may be important to that assessment?

2. How would you persuade a court that a particular rule helpful to your client is in fact a rule of customary international law? Suppose, for example, you wish to prove the rule suggested in *ARC Ecology* that causing environmental damage in a foreign country violates customary international law. Prepare a research outline listing the possible sources you would investigate. Which ones would be most authoritative in U.S. court? How would your answer differ if you were arguing to a foreign court or an international court?

CHAPTER 3

NONBINDING AND PRIVATE NORMS

Chapters 1 and 2 discussed two different types of law that may apply to a transnational problem: national law (Chapter 1) and international law (Chapter 2). Although national law and international law are different, they share two characteristics. First, they are legally binding. Courts may (or must) apply them as rules of decision. Even if national law and international law are sometimes violated and not always enforced, they are generally recognized as imposing legal obligations. Second, national law and international law are made by nations. National law is made within individual nations through legislation and (depending on the nation) executive, administrative, and judicial bodies. International law is a product of agreement among nations (treaties) or the practice and *opinio juris* of nations (customary international law).

But national law and international law provide an incomplete picture of transnational legal practice. The principles of prescriptive jurisdiction (discussed in Chapter 1) limit the reach of national law, and a large portion of the world's transnational activity remains ungoverned by international law. Thus, even taken together, these two types of law leave considerable gaps in the governance of transnational activity. Non-legally binding and private norms — norms that are not legally binding, not made by nations, or both — help fill these gaps and play an important role in governing transnational activity. For example, as participants in the U.N. General Assembly, nations frequently adopt resolutions. Although made by nations, U.N. General Assembly resolutions generally are not legally binding. Nevertheless, these and other nonbinding norms are often very influential. The International Organization for Standardization (ISO) is a private, nongovernmental organization with members from over 150 nations. The ISO develops voluntary technical standards on matters such as products and services quality management, environmental management, and information security. Although they are nonbinding and not made by nations, ISO standards have been adopted by many businesses around the world and are examples of private norms that play an important role in governing transnational activity.

A . concepts.

B . types of non bidg int'l norms

C . private norms

This chapter introduces nonbinding and private norms. Section A explores the concept of nonbinding norms. Section B discusses several types of nonbinding international norms — norms made by nations, by themselves or through the international courts and other international organizations they create. Nonbinding international norms include, for example, U.N. General Assembly resolutions and declarations of principles. Section C discusses private norms, such as privately made procedural and substantive rules, technical standards, and corporate codes of conduct. As you will learn, private norms generally are nonbinding (and to that extent overlap with the concept of nonbinding norms) — but if incorporated in an enforceable agreement, they may become legally binding on the parties as a matter of contract law.

1 . contexts

2 . why create

3 . influence

As you study the materials in this chapter, keep three questions in mind. *First*, in what contexts are you as a lawyer likely to encounter and use nonbinding norms when you represent your clients? *Second*, why do nations and private actors create nonbinding and private norms in the first place instead of relying on national law and international law? *Third*, what explains the influence that nonbinding and private norms have on transnational activity?

A. The Concept of Nonbinding Norms

As the term "nonbinding norms" suggests, unlike national law and international law, nonbinding norms are not legally binding. However, the distinction between legally binding and nonbinding rules is not self-evident. This section explores some of the issues raised by the effort to distinguish legally binding rules from nonbinding norms.

definition - legally binding

First, what does it mean for a rule to be legally binding? From the perspective of legal philosophy, a rule may be understood as legally binding when it imposes a legal obligation. Legal philosophers have long debated the nature of a legal obligation. As important and interesting as these theoretical debates are, this chapter takes a practice-oriented approach: A rule is legally binding if a court or other adjudicative body will apply it directly as a rule of decision. For example, the California Family Code is legally binding in California in the sense that a California court will apply its provisions as rules of decision. In contrast, if you and your classmates declare the rule that there shall be no law school classes before 10:00 A.M., a court is unlikely to apply it as a rule of decision to prevent your law school from having classes at 8:30 A.M.

Of course, the line between legally binding and nonbinding rules can be very difficult to draw, and ultimately it may be impossible to draw that line objectively. Courts may mistakenly classify a rule as legally binding or nonbinding — or at least there can be disagreement about a court's decision. But even if one cannot scientifically measure whether a rule is legally binding, the issue is one that confronts lawyers routinely in practice. The no-early-morning-classes rule may be obviously non-legally binding, but questions about the constitutionality of a statute, the validity of a treaty, or the very existence of a purported rule of customary international law are much more difficult. This may be less than satisfactory from the perspective of legal theory, but it is part of the reality of legal practice. Not just in transnational practice, and not just when dealing with the issue of legally binding versus nonbinding rules, lawyers are constantly developing, evaluating the strength of, predicting the outcomes of, and striving to persuasively make arguments on issues that do not have clear answers.

Second, even if one accepts (for purposes of this chapter, at least) that a legally binding rule is one that a court or other adjudicative body will directly enforce as a rule of decision, under what conditions is a rule legally binding in this sense? The answer to this question is closely related to the first question — after all, if you don't understand these conditions, it will be very difficult for you to develop and evaluate arguments about whether a particular rule is legally binding and to help a client predict how a judge is likely to decide that issue.

legally binding
— conditions

Legal philosophers have long grappled with these questions, too. One of the great legal philosophers, H.L.A. Hart, called these conditions "rules of recognition" — rules that determine what does and does not count as "law" in a given legal system. *See* H.L.A. HART, THE CONCEPT OF LAW 94-95 (2d ed. 1994) (explaining that a rule of recognition is a "secondary" rule — a "rule about rules" — that identifies valid "primary" legal rules by reference to specific texts or by their characteristics, such as "the fact of their having been enacted by a specific body, or their long customary practice, or their relation to judicial decisions"). One of the basic rules of recognition in the U.S. legal system is that federal legislation is legally binding if it is passed by a majority of both houses of Congress, signed by the President, and does not exceed Congress's constitutional powers or violate constitutionally protected rights. *See, e.g., Norton v. Shelby County*, 118 U.S. 425, 442 (1886) ("An unconstitutional act is not a law; it confers no rights; it imposes no duties; . . . it is, in legal contemplation, as inoperative as though it had never been passed."). And in Chapter 2, you studied some of the basic rules of recognition for binding international law, including the requirements for a treaty to be legally binding and for the creation of binding customary international law.

To make sure you understand the basic idea of rules of recognition, consider this question: Although the no-early-morning-classes rule is clearly not legally binding, *why* — in terms of rules of recognition — isn't it legally binding? And why *is* the California Family Code legally binding? What do your answers to these questions tell you about what it means to impose a legal obligation?

For several reasons these conditions are especially challenging (and interesting) in transnational practice. First, different national legal systems have different rules of recognition. What might count as "law" in one nation might not count as law in another. For instance, different nations have different rules governing the legislative process. Moreover, as discussed in Chapter 2, international law may be legally binding in a pure monist system, but not necessarily in a dualist system like the United States. Second, the rules of recognition in international law are often contested. Although the Vienna Convention on the Law of Treaties adds considerable clarity to the law of treaties, there are, for example, ongoing debates about the extent of *opinio juris* and state practice needed to create legally binding customary international law. Third, as discussed extensively in Chapter 1, the legally binding nature of national law depends largely, but not entirely, on territory. In general, a nation's law is legally binding within its territory. But as Chapter 1 demonstrates, the extent to which a nation's law extends outside its territory is often difficult to determine. Again, this type of ambiguity is not unique to transnational practice. Lawyers in all fields of practice routinely deal with legal uncertainty, and therefore learn to excel at developing, evaluating, and persuasively making legal arguments even in situations where there appears to be no single clear answer.

A third reason why the distinction between legally binding and nonbinding norms is not self-evident is terminological. Some scholars use the term "soft law" to refer to non-legally binding norms. This term signals the importance of nonbinding norms. "Constructivist" scholars point out that principles can shape shared understandings of appropriate behavior, regardless of whether they are legally binding. "Rational institutionalist" scholars emphasize that nations often find it useful to make nonbinding norms and that those norms can influence the behavior of nations (as well as businesses and individuals) just as legal rules can. For example, nonbinding norms may provide focal points for the coordination of cross-border business and the regulation of transnational activity. *See* Gregory Shaffer & Mark A. Pollack, *Hard Law and Soft Law, in* INTERDISCIPLINARY PERSPECTIVES ON INTERNATIONAL LAW AND INTERNATIONAL RELATIONS: THE STATE OF THE ART 198-200 (Jeffrey L. Dunoff & Mark A. Pollack eds., 2013).

Other scholars, without doubting the importance of non-legally binding norms, are critical of the term "soft law." One concern is that the term "soft law" muddies the distinction between legally binding and non-legally binding norms. As one scholar argues, "There is no such thing as 'soft law.' The concept of soft law purports to identify something between binding law and no law. Yet as an analytic or practical matter no meaningful intermediate category exists." Kal Raustiala, *Form and Substance in International Agreements*, 99 AM. J. INT'L L. 581, 586 (2005). There are good reasons to reserve the term "law" for rules that are produced by a recognized lawmaking process — such as those defined in a national constitution or international law's doctrine of sources — and intended to be legally binding in the sense that a court would consider them to be binding rules of decision in adjudication. Legal scholars and social scientists have long sought to understand what is distinctive about law. Normatively, is there a difference between legal obligations and other types of obligations? Behaviorally, do legal rules affect behavior in ways that are systematically different from other types of rules? And how do legal rules affect, and how are they affected by, non-legal rules? These are important questions. But if one conflates legal and non-legal rules into a single concept of law, analyzing these relationships is not possible. Christopher A. Whytock, *The Concept of a Global Legal System, in* THE MANY LIVES OF TRANSNATIONAL LAW: CRITICAL ENGAGEMENTS WITH JESSUP'S BOLD PROPOSAL 72, 81 (Peer Zumbansen ed., 2020).

Without taking a firm position in the terminological debate, we use the term "nonbinding norm" rather than "soft law." We agree that non-legally binding norms are important in transnational practice — hence, this chapter. Nevertheless, the distinction between legally binding and non-legally binding rules remains fundamentally important in legal practice for the simple reason that courts and other legal officials generally apply as rules of decision only rules that they conclude are legally binding.

B. Nonbinding International Norms

To reiterate, nonbinding norms can play an important role in transnational practice even though they are not legally binding. Some of these nonbinding norms are nonbinding international norms — that is, nonbinding norms made by nations or the international courts and other organizations that nations have created. This section discusses three categories of nonbinding international norms: the opinions and decisions of international courts; declarations and the resolutions of international organizations; and international guidelines and codes of conduct. As you study the materials in this section, reflect on two distinct ways that lawyers and judges use nonbinding norms. First, even though nonbinding norms are not themselves binding international law, they can be used as *evidence* suggesting that a particular binding rule of customary international law exists. In what ways might a nonbinding norm be evidence of customary international law? Second, whether or not a given nonbinding norm provides such evidence, it may be persuasive to a court or another party. What factors might influence how persuasive a particular nonbinding norm is likely to be?

1. Decisions of International Courts

Although the diversity of international courts makes it difficult to generalize, international court decisions ordinarily are binding on the parties as to the dispute submitted for adjudication but do not create law or legal precedent that is binding on courts in future cases. For example, as you will recall from Chapter 2, Article 38 of the Statute of the International Court of Justice (ICJ) lists three types [*ICJ Statute 38.*] of international law: treaties, customary international law, and general principles of law. Article 38 also lists "judicial decisions and the teachings of the most highly qualified publicists of the various nations." However, unlike treaties, customary international law, and general principles, Article 38 qualifies the status of judicial decisions and teachings by noting that they are merely "subsidiary means for the determination of rules of law." That is, neither an ICJ decision (nor a scholar!) can "make" binding international law. Article 59 of the ICJ further states that [*X binding except ⇒ parties*] ICJ decisions have "no binding force except between the parties and in respect of that particular case." In other words, it would be a mistake to characterize a decision of the ICJ as creating a legal precedent that is binding in subsequent cases. Why do you think the ICJ Statute does not give judicial decisions binding precedential value?

Nevertheless, judges, lawyers, and scholars routinely refer to international court decisions as evidence of international law's content. As a subsidiary means of determining rules of international law, international court decisions "are extremely important in clarifying the existence of norms, such as whether a customary rule of international law has emerged. The better reasoned the judicial decision . . . and the more prestigious the court . . . , the more persuasive it will [*persuasive*] be as a source." SEAN D. MURPHY, PRINCIPLES OF INTERNATIONAL LAW 114 (3d ed.

2018). The ICJ frequently cites its prior decisions, and lawyers engaged in transnational practice frequently research international court decisions and use them in their arguments, even though those decisions are not legally binding. What is the difference between using these sources as "evidence" of law and using them as binding precedent?

The decisions of international courts can contribute to what two international law scholars have called "international common law." Although these decisions are not binding beyond the parties and the particular case, when they include rulings on the interpretation of a treaty or the content of customary international law, they "shape the meaning of existing legal rules" and they "shape state expectations about what constitutes compliant behavior" with those rules. Andrew T. Guzman & Timothy L. Meyer, *International Soft Law*, 2 J. Legal Analysis 171, 216 (2010). In this way, these decisions can have an important impact on law even if they are not themselves legally binding. As a lawyer making an argument for (or against) a particular interpretation of a treaty, or for (or against) the proposition that a particular rule of customary international law exists, it would be a mistake not to thoroughly research prior court decisions and incorporate them into your argument. On the other hand, it would also be a mistake to characterize those decisions as legally binding precedent or assume that national courts will necessarily follow them.

The following two cases illustrate some of the ways that U.S. courts may treat international court decisions. In the first case, the U.S. Supreme Court considered the effect of an ICJ decision. In the second case, the U.S. Supreme Court referred to decisions of the European Court of Human Rights (ECHR). As you read these cases, ask yourself the following questions: When might a U.S. court find it necessary or useful to refer to international court decisions? Should U.S. courts ever refer to international court decisions? If so, how might they use those decisions? As evidence of international law? As persuasive authority? How much consideration should U.S. courts give to international court decisions when deciding cases? What might happen when U.S. courts decline to follow international court decisions?

Sanchez-Llamas v. Oregon

548 U.S. 331 (2006)

Chief Justice Roberts delivered the opinion of the Court.

Article 36 of the Vienna Convention on Consular Relations addresses communication between an individual and his consular officers when the individual is detained by authorities in a foreign country. These consolidated cases concern the availability of judicial relief for violations of Article 36. . . . We conclude, even assuming the Convention creates judicially enforceable rights, that suppression is not an appropriate remedy for a violation of Article 36, and that a State may apply its regular rules of procedural default to Article 36 claims. We therefore affirm the decisions below.

I

A

[Sanchez-Llamas and another petitioner, Bustillo, were foreign nationals arrested and convicted of crimes in the United States. They were not informed of their right under the Vienna Convention to contact their home country's consulate. Both argued that their convictions should be overturned. The Court assumed without deciding that the Convention created judicially enforceable rights, but rejected Sanchez-Llamas' contention that certain evidence should be suppressed because it was discovered after the failure to notify him of his Convention rights. The Court then turned to Bustillo's claim, which had not been raised at trial and which the lower court had thus treated as procedurally defaulted.]

. . .

C

Petitioner Mario Bustillo, a Honduran national, was with several other men at a restaurant in Springfield, Virginia, on the night of December 10, 1997. That evening, outside the restaurant, James Merry was struck in the head with a baseball bat as he stood smoking a cigarette. He died several days later. Several witnesses at the scene identified Bustillo as the assailant. Police arrested Bustillo the morning after the attack and eventually charged him with murder. Authorities never informed him that he could request to have the Honduran Consulate notified of his detention.

. . . [Bustillo was convicted in Virginia state court.]

After his conviction became final, Bustillo filed a petition for a writ of habeas corpus in state court. There, for the first time, he argued that authorities had violated his right to consular notification under Article 36 of the Vienna Convention. He claimed that if he had been advised of his right to confer with the Honduran Consulate, he "would have done so without delay." Moreover, the Honduran Consulate executed an affidavit stating that "it would have endeavoured to help Mr. Bustillo in his defense" had it learned of his detention prior to trial. . . .

The state habeas court dismissed Bustillo's Vienna Convention claim as "procedurally barred" because he had failed to raise the issue at trial or on appeal. . . .

II

. . .

B

The Virginia courts denied petitioner Bustillo's Article 36 claim on the ground that he failed to raise it at trial or on direct appeal. The general rule in federal habeas cases is that a defendant who fails to raise a claim on direct appeal is barred from raising the claim on collateral review. . . . Bustillo contends, however, that state procedural default rules cannot apply to Article 36 claims. He argues that the Convention requires that Article 36 rights be given "full effect" and that Virginia's procedural default rules "prevented any effect (much less 'full effect') from being given to" those rights.

This is not the first time we have been asked to set aside procedural default rules for a Vienna Convention claim. Respondent Johnson[, the Director of the Virginia Department of Corrections,] and the United States persuasively argue that this question is controlled by our decision in *Breard v. Greene*, 523 U.S. 371 (1998) (*per curiam*). In *Breard*, the petitioner failed to raise an Article 36 claim in state court — at trial or on collateral review — and then sought to have the claim heard in a subsequent federal habeas proceeding. He argued that "the Convention is the 'supreme law of the land' and thus trumps the procedural default doctrine." We rejected this argument as "plainly incorrect," for two reasons. *Ibid.* First, we observed, "it has been recognized in international law that, absent a clear and express statement to the contrary, the procedural rules of the forum State govern the implementation of the treaty in that State." Furthermore, we reasoned that while treaty protections such as Article 36 may constitute supreme federal law, this is "no less true of provisions of the Constitution itself, to which rules of procedural default apply." *Id.*, at 376. In light of *Breard*'s holding, Bustillo faces an uphill task in arguing that the Convention requires States to set aside their procedural default rules for Article 36 claims.

. . .

Bustillo . . . argues that since *Breard*, the ICJ has interpreted the Vienna Convention to preclude the application of procedural default rules to Article 36 claims. The *LaGrand Case (F.R.G. v. U.S.)*, 2001 I.C.J. 466 (Judgment of June 27) (*LaGrand*), and the *Case Concerning Avena and other Mexican Nationals (Mex. v. U.S.)*, 2004 I.C.J. No. 128 (Judgment of Mar. 31) (*Avena*), were brought before the ICJ by the governments of Germany and Mexico, respectively, on behalf of several of their nationals facing death sentences in the United States. The foreign governments claimed that their nationals had not been informed of their right to consular notification. They further argued that application of the procedural default rule to their nationals' Vienna Convention claims failed to give "full effect" to the purposes of the Convention, as required by Article 36. The ICJ agreed, explaining that the defendants had procedurally defaulted their claims "because of the failure of the American authorities to comply with their obligation under Article 36." *LaGrand, supra*, at 497, ¶ 91; see also *Avena, supra*, ¶ 113. Application of the procedural default rule in such circumstances, the ICJ reasoned, "prevented [courts] from attaching any legal significance" to the fact that the violation of Article 36 kept the foreign governments from assisting in their nationals' defense. *LaGrand, supra*, at 497, ¶ 91; see also *Avena, supra*, ¶ 113.

Bustillo argues that *LaGrand* and *Avena* warrant revisiting the procedural default holding of *Breard*. In a similar vein, several *amici* contend that "the United States is *obligated* to comply with the Convention, *as interpreted by the ICJ*." Brief for ICJ Experts 11 (emphases added). We disagree. Although the ICJ's interpretation deserves "respectful consideration," *Breard, supra*, at 375, we conclude that it does not compel us to reconsider our understanding of the Convention in *Breard*.

Under our Constitution, "[t]he judicial Power of the United States" is "vested in one supreme Court, and in such inferior Courts as the Congress may from time to time ordain and establish." Art. III, § 1. That "judicial Power . . . extend[s] to . . . Treaties." *Id.,* § 2. And, as Chief Justice Marshall famously explained, that judicial power includes the duty "to say what the law is." *Marbury v. Madison,* 1 Cranch 137, 177 (1803). If treaties are to be given effect as federal law under our legal system, determining their meaning as a matter of federal law "is emphatically the province and duty of the judicial department," headed by the "one supreme Court" established by the Constitution. *Ibid.*; see also *Williams v. Taylor,* 529 U.S. 362, 378-379 (2000) (opinion of Stevens, J.) ("At the core of [the judicial] power is the federal courts' independent responsibility — independent from its coequal branches in the Federal Government, and independent from the separate authority of the several States — to interpret federal law"). It is against this background that the United States ratified, and the Senate gave its advice and consent to, the various agreements that govern referral of Vienna Convention disputes to the ICJ.

Nothing in the structure or purpose of the ICJ suggests that its interpretations were intended to be conclusive on our courts. The ICJ's decisions have *"no binding force* except between the parties and in respect of that particular case," Statute of the International Court of Justice, Art. 59, 59 Stat. 1062, T.S. No. 993 (1945) (emphasis added). Any interpretation of law the ICJ renders in the course of resolving particular disputes is thus not binding precedent *even as to the ICJ itself*; there is accordingly little reason to think that such interpretations were intended to be controlling on our courts. The ICJ's principal purpose is to arbitrate particular disputes between national governments. *Id.,* at 1055 (ICJ is "the principal judicial organ of the United Nations"); see also Art. 34, *id.,* at 1059 ("Only states [*i.e.,* countries] may be parties in cases before the Court"). While each member of the United Nations has agreed to comply with decisions of the ICJ "in any case to which it is a party," United Nations Charter, Art. 94(1), 59 Stat. 1051, T.S. No. 933 (1945), the Charter's procedure for noncompliance — referral to the Security Council by the aggrieved state — contemplates quintessentially *international* remedies, Art. 94(2), *ibid.* In addition, "[w]hile courts interpret treaties for themselves, the meaning given them by the departments of government particularly charged with their negotiation and enforcement is given great weight." *Kolovrat v. Oregon,* 366 U.S. 187, 194 (1961). Although the United States has agreed to "discharge its international obligations" in having state courts give effect to the decision in *Avena,* it has not taken the view that the ICJ's interpretation of Article 36 is binding on our courts. President Bush, Memorandum for the Attorney General (Feb. 28, 2005), App. to Brief for United States as *Amicus Curiae* in *Medellín v. Dretke,* O.T. 2004, No. 04-5928, p. 9a. Moreover, shortly after *Avena,* the United States withdrew from the Optional Protocol concerning Vienna Convention disputes. Whatever the effect of *Avena* and *LaGrand* before this withdrawal, it is doubtful that our courts should give decisive weight to the interpretation of a tribunal whose jurisdiction in this area is no longer recognized by the United States.

LaGrand and *Avena* are therefore entitled only to the "respectful consideration" due an interpretation of an international agreement by an international court. *Breard,* 523 U.S., at 375. Even according such consideration, the ICJ's interpretation cannot overcome the plain import of Article 36. As we explained in *Breard*, the procedural rules of domestic law generally govern the implementation of an international treaty. *Ibid.* In addition, Article 36 makes clear that the rights it provides "shall be exercised in conformity with the laws and regulations of the receiving State" provided that "full effect . . . be given to the purposes for which the rights accorded under this Article are intended." In the United States, this means that the rule of procedural default — which applies even to claimed violations of our Constitution, see *Engle v. Isaac*, 456 U.S. 107, 129 (1982) — applies also to Vienna Convention claims. Bustillo points to nothing in the drafting history of Article 36 or in the contemporary practice of other signatories that undermines this conclusion.

The ICJ concluded that where a defendant was not notified of his rights under Article 36, application of the procedural default rule failed to give "full effect" to the purposes of Article 36 because it prevented courts from attaching "legal significance" to the Article 36 violation. *LaGrand*, 2001 I.C.J., at 497-498, ¶¶ 90-91. This reasoning overlooks the importance of procedural default rules in an adversary system, which relies chiefly on the *parties* to raise significant issues and present them to the courts in the appropriate manner at the appropriate time for adjudication. See *Castro v. United States*, 540 U.S. 375, 386 (2003) (Scalia, J., concurring in part and concurring in judgment) ("Our adversary system is designed around the premise that the parties know what is best for them, and are responsible for advancing the facts and arguments entitling them to relief"). Procedural default rules are designed to encourage parties to raise their claims promptly and to vindicate "the law's important interest in the finality of judgments." *Massaro*, 538 U.S., at 504. The consequence of failing to raise a claim for adjudication at the proper time is generally forfeiture of that claim. As a result, rules such as procedural default routinely deny "legal significance" — in the *Avena* and *LaGrand* sense — to otherwise viable legal claims.

Procedural default rules generally take on greater importance in an adversary system such as ours than in the sort of magistrate-directed, inquisitorial legal system characteristic of many of the other countries that are signatories to the Vienna Convention. "What makes a system adversarial rather than inquisitorial is . . . the presence of a judge who does not (as an inquisitor does) conduct the factual and legal investigation himself, but instead decides on the basis of facts and arguments pro and con adduced by the parties." *McNeil v. Wisconsin*, 501 U.S. 171, 181, n.2 (1991). In an inquisitorial system, the failure to raise a legal error can in part be attributed to the magistrate, and thus to the state itself. In our system, however, the responsibility for failing to raise an issue generally rests with the parties themselves.

The ICJ's interpretation of Article 36 is inconsistent with the basic framework of an adversary system. Under the ICJ's reading of "full effect," Article 36 claims could trump not only procedural default rules, but any number of other rules requiring parties to present their legal claims at the appropriate time for adjudication. If the State's failure to inform the defendant of his Article 36 rights generally excuses the defendant's failure to comply with relevant procedural rules, then presumably rules such as statutes of limitations and prohibitions against filing successive habeas petitions must also yield in the face of Article 36 claims. This sweeps too broadly, for it reads the "full effect" proviso in a way that leaves little room for Article 36's clear instruction that Article 36 rights "shall be exercised in conformity with the laws and regulations of the receiving State."

. . .

The judgments of the Supreme Court of Oregon and the Supreme Court of Virginia are affirmed.

. . .

[An opinion of Justice Ginsburg concurring in the judgment is omitted.]

Justice BREYER, with whom Justice STEVENS and Justice SOUTER join . . . dissenting.

[Justice Breyer first concluded that the Vienna Convention created judicially enforceable individual rights.]

. . .

III

The more difficult issue, I believe, concerns the nature of the Convention's requirements as to remedy. In particular, Bustillo's case concerns a state procedural default rule. When, if ever, does the Convention require a state court to set aside such a rule in order to hear a criminal defendant's claim that the police did not "inform" him of his "right" to communicate with his "consular post"? The Court says that the answer is "never." In its view, the Convention does not under any circumstances trump a State's ordinary procedural rules requiring a defendant to assert his claims at trial or lose them forever.

In my view, Article 36 of the Convention requires a less absolute answer. Article 36 says that the rights it sets forth "shall be exercised in conformity with the laws and regulations of the receiving State," but it instantly adds, "subject to the proviso . . . that the said laws and regulations must enable *full effect* to be given to the purposes for which the [Article 36] rights are . . . intended." Art. 36(2), 21 U.S.T., at 101 (emphasis added). The proviso means that a State's ordinary procedural default rules apply *unless* (1) the defendant's failure to raise a Convention matter (*e.g.*, that police failed to inform him of his Article 36 rights) can itself be traced to the failure of the police (or other governmental authorities) to inform the defendant of those Convention rights, *and* (2) state law does not provide any other effective way for the defendant to raise that issue (say, through a claim of ineffective assistance of counsel).

Several considerations lead to this conclusion. [Justice Breyer first pointed to the treaty's text and drafting history.]

. . .

Third, the decisions of the ICJ, fairly read, interpret the Convention similarly. In *LaGrand* and *Avena*, the ICJ read the Convention as authorizing an individual foreign national to raise an Article 36 violation at trial or in a postconviction proceeding. *See Avena*, 2004 I.C.J., ¶ 121; *LaGrand*, 2001 I.C.J., at 32-33, ¶ 125. The ICJ added that the Convention requires member states to provide "effective" remedies in their courts for Convention violations. See *Avena, supra,* ¶ 138. And the ICJ made two critical statements in respect to procedural default rules. In *LaGrand,* the court said that in "itself, the [procedural default] rule does *not* violate Article 36 of the Vienna Convention." 2001 I.C.J., at 22, ¶ 90 (emphasis added). Rather, the "problem arises when the procedural default rule does not allow the detained individual to challenge a conviction and sentence by claiming . . . that the competent national authorities failed to comply with their obligation to provide the requisite consular information 'without delay.'" *Ibid.* And the ICJ later specified that the Convention forbids American States to apply a procedural default rule to bar assertion of a Convention violation claim *"where it has been the failure of the United States [or of a State] itself to inform that may have precluded counsel from being in a position to have raised the question of a violation of the Vienna Convention in the initial trial."* *Avena,* 2004 I.C.J., ¶ 113 (emphasis added).

. . .

I will assume that the ICJ's interpretation does not bind this Court in this case. . . . But as the majority points out, the ICJ's decisions on this issue nonetheless warrant our respectful consideration. That "respectful consideration" reflects the understanding that uniformity is an important goal of treaty interpretation. See *Olympic Airways v. Husain,* 540 U.S. 644, 660 (2004) (Scalia, J., dissenting) ("[I]t is reasonable to impute to the parties an intent that their respective courts strive to interpret the treaty consistently"). And the ICJ's position as an international court specifically charged with the duty to interpret numerous international treaties (including the Convention) provides a natural point of reference for national courts seeking that uniformity. See Counter-Memorial of the United States in *Avena,* 2004 I.C.J. No. 128, p. 61, n.128 (Nov. 3, 2003) (even if ICJ decision binds only in particular case, "it is well-settled" that an ICJ decision "may serve as authority beyond a particular case"; citing authorities); Ordonez & Reilly, Effect of the Jurisprudence of the International Court of Justice on National Courts, in International Law Decisions in National Courts 335, 365 (T. Franck & G. Fox eds., 1996) (noting that ICJ cases interpreting treaties "are routinely cited by domestic judges" in many countries "as evidence of international law").

That "respectful consideration" also reflects an understanding of the ICJ's expertise in matters of treaty interpretation, a branch of international law. The ICJ's opinions "are persuasive evidence" of what "[international] law is." 1 Restatement § 103, comment *b,* at 37; see also Morrison, Treaties as a Source of Jurisdiction, Especially in U.S. Practice, in The International Court of Justice at a Crossroads 58, 61 (L. Damrosch ed., 1987); *The Paquete Habana,* 175 U.S. 677, 700 (1900) ("[T]rustworthy evidence of what [international] law really is" can be found in "the works of jurists and commentators, who by years of labor, research and experience have made themselves peculiarly well acquainted with the subjects of which they treat"); L. Henkin, R. Pugh, O. Schachter & H. Smit, International Law: Cases and Materials 120 (3d ed. 1993) ("[T]he decisions of the International Court of Justice are, on the whole, regarded by international lawyers as highly persuasive authority of existing international law").

Thus, this Court has repeatedly looked to the ICJ for guidance in interpreting treaties and in other matters of international law. [Multiple cases from the U.S. Supreme Court and lower courts are cited.]

. . .

Today's decision interprets an international treaty in a manner that conflicts not only with the treaty's language and history, but also with the ICJ's interpretation of the same treaty provision. In creating this last-mentioned conflict, as far as I can tell, the Court's decision is unprecedented.

. . .

Lawrence v. Texas

539 U.S. 558 (2003)

Justice KENNEDY delivered the opinion of the Court.

I

The question before the Court is the validity of a Texas statute making it a crime for two persons of the same sex to engage in certain intimate sexual conduct.

In Houston, Texas, officers of the Harris County Police Department were dispatched to a private residence in response to a reported weapons disturbance. They entered an apartment where one of the petitioners, John Geddes Lawrence, resided. The right of the police to enter does not seem to have been questioned. The officers observed Lawrence and another man, Tyron Garner, engaging in a sexual act. The two petitioners were arrested, held in custody overnight, and charged and convicted before a Justice of the Peace.

The complaints described their crime as "deviate sexual intercourse, namely anal sex, with a member of the same sex (man)." . . . The applicable state law . . . provides: "A person commits an offense if he engages in deviate sexual intercourse with another individual of the same sex." The statute defines "[d]eviate sexual intercourse" as follows:

"(A) any contact between any part of the genitals of one person and the mouth or anus of another person; or
"(B) the penetration of the genitals or the anus of another person with an object."

The petitioners . . . challenged the statute as a violation of the Equal Protection Clause of the Fourteenth Amendment and of a like provision of the Texas Constitution. . . .

The Court of Appeals for the Texas Fourteenth District considered the petitioners' federal constitutional arguments under both the Equal Protection and Due Process Clauses of the Fourteenth Amendment. [The court] rejected the constitutional arguments and affirmed the convictions. . . . The majority opinion indicates that the Court of Appeals considered our decision in *Bowers v. Hardwick,*

[478 U.S. 186 (1986)], to be controlling on the federal due process aspect of the case. *Bowers* then being authoritative, this was proper.

. . .

II

We conclude the case should be resolved by determining whether the petitioners were free as adults to engage in the private conduct in the exercise of their liberty under the Due Process Clause of the Fourteenth Amendment to the Constitution. For this inquiry we deem it necessary to reconsider the Court's holding in *Bowers*.

DPC of the 14th Amendant - right to liberty

. . .

The facts in *Bowers* had some similarities to the instant case. A police officer, whose right to enter seems not to have been in question, observed Hardwick, in his own bedroom, engaging in intimate sexual conduct with another adult male. The conduct was in violation of a Georgia statute making it a criminal offense to engage in sodomy. . . . Hardwick . . . brought an action in federal court to declare the state statute invalid. . . . The Court, in an opinion by Justice White, sustained the Georgia law. Chief Justice Burger and Justice Powell joined the opinion of the Court and filed separate, concurring opinions. Four Justices dissented. . . .

. . .

[T]he *Bowers* Court said: "Proscriptions against that [same-sex sexual activity] have ancient roots." *Id.*, at 192. . . . In academic writings, and in many of the scholarly amicus briefs filed to assist the Court in this case, there are fundamental criticisms of the historical premises relied upon by the majority and concurring opinions in *Bowers*. . . . We need not enter this debate in the attempt to reach a definitive historical judgment, but the following considerations counsel against adopting the definitive conclusions upon which *Bowers* placed such reliance.

At the outset it should be noted that there is no longstanding history in this country of laws directed at homosexual conduct as a distinct matter. . . .

Laws prohibiting sodomy do not seem to have been enforced against consenting adults acting in private. A substantial number of sodomy prosecutions and convictions for which there are surviving records were for predatory acts against those who could not or did not consent, as in the case of a minor or the victim of an assault. . . .

. . .

It was not until the 1970's that any State singled out same-sex relations for criminal prosecution, and only nine States have done so. . . . Post-*Bowers* even some of these States did not adhere to the policy of suppressing homosexual conduct. Over the course of the last decades, States with same-sex prohibitions have moved toward abolishing them. . . .

In summary, the historical grounds relied upon in *Bowers* are more complex than the majority opinion and the concurring opinion by Chief Justice Burger indicate. Their historical premises are not without doubt and, at the very least, are overstated.

It must be acknowledged, of course, that the Court in *Bowers* was making the broader point that for centuries there have been powerful voices to condemn homosexual conduct as immoral. The condemnation has been shaped by religious beliefs, conceptions of right and acceptable behavior, and respect for the traditional family. For many persons these are not trivial concerns but profound and deep convictions accepted as ethical and moral principles to which they aspire and which thus determine the course of their lives. These considerations do not answer the question before us, however. The issue is whether the majority may use the power of the State to enforce these views on the whole society through operation of the criminal law. . . .

Chief Justice Burger joined the opinion for the Court in *Bowers* and further explained his views as follows: "Decisions of individuals relating to homosexual conduct have been subject to state intervention throughout the history of Western civilization. Condemnation of those practices is firmly rooted in Judeo-Christian moral and ethical standards." 478 U.S., at 196. . . . As with Justice White's assumptions about history, scholarship casts some doubt on the sweeping nature of the statement by Chief Justice Burger as it pertains to private homosexual conduct between consenting adults. . . . In all events we think that our laws and traditions in the past half century are of most relevance here. These references show an emerging awareness that liberty gives substantial protection to adult persons in deciding how to conduct their private lives in matters pertaining to sex. . . .

This emerging recognition should have been apparent when *Bowers* was decided. In 1955 the American Law Institute promulgated the Model Penal Code and made clear that it did not recommend or provide for "criminal penalties for consensual sexual relations conducted in private." . . . In 1961 Illinois changed its laws to conform to the Model Penal Code. Other States soon followed. . . .

. . .

The sweeping references by Chief Justice Burger to the history of Western civilization and to Judeo-Christian moral and ethical standards did not take account of other authorities pointing in an opposite direction. A committee advising the British Parliament recommended in 1957 repeal of laws punishing homosexual conduct. . . . Parliament enacted the substance of those recommendations 10 years later.

Of even more importance, almost five years before *Bowers* was decided the European Court of Human Rights* considered a case with parallels to *Bowers* and to today's case. An adult male resident in Northern Ireland alleged he was a practicing homosexual who desired to engage in consensual homosexual conduct. The laws of Northern Ireland forbade him that right. He alleged that he had been questioned, his home had been searched, and he feared criminal prosecution. The court held that the laws proscribing the conduct were invalid under the

---

* The European Court of Human Rights (ECHR) is a regional court (discussed further in Chapter 5) that hears cases involving nations that are members of the Council of Europe (of which the United States is not a member) under the European Convention on Human Rights (to which the United States is not a party). Thus, the ECHR has no jurisdiction over the United States and its decisions can have no binding effect on the United States. — Eds.

European Convention on Human Rights. *Dudgeon v. United Kingdom*, 45 Eur. Ct. H.R. (1981) & ¶ 52. Authoritative in all countries that are members of the Council of Europe (21 nations then, 45 nations now), the decision is at odds with the premise in *Bowers* that the claim put forward was insubstantial in our Western civilization.

In our own constitutional system the deficiencies in *Bowers* became even more apparent in the years following its announcement. The 25 States with laws prohibiting the relevant conduct referenced in the *Bowers* decision are reduced now to 13, of which 4 enforce their laws only against homosexual conduct. In those States where sodomy is still proscribed, whether for same-sex or hetero-sexual conduct, there is a pattern of nonenforcement with respect to consenting adults acting in private. The State of Texas admitted in 1994 that as of that date it had not prosecuted anyone under those circumstances. . . .

. . .

To the extent *Bowers* relied on values we share with a wider civilization, it should be noted that the reasoning and holding in *Bowers* have been rejected else-where. The European Court of Human Rights has followed not *Bowers* but its own decision in *Dudgeon v. United Kingdom*. See *P.G. & J.H. v. United Kingdom*, App. No. 00044787/98, & ¶ 56 (Eur. Ct. H.R., Sept. 25, 2001); *Modinos v. Cyprus*, 259 Eur. Ct. H.R. (1993); *Norris v. Ireland*, 142 Eur. Ct. H.R. (1988). Other nations, too, have taken action consistent with an affirmation of the protected right of homosexual adults to engage in intimate, consensual conduct. See Brief for Mary Robinson et al. as Amici Curiae 11-12. The right the petitioners seek in this case has been accepted as an integral part of human freedom in many other countries. There has been no showing that in this country the governmental interest in cir-cumscribing personal choice is somehow more legitimate or urgent.

The doctrine of stare decisis is essential to the respect accorded to the judg-ments of the Court and to the stability of the law. It is not, however, an inexorable command.

. . .

Bowers was not correct when it was decided, and it is not correct today. It ought not to remain binding precedent. *Bowers v. Hardwick* should be and now is overruled.

The present case does not involve minors. It does not involve persons who might be injured or coerced or who are situated in relationships where consent might not easily be refused. It does not involve public conduct or prostitution. It does not involve whether the government must give formal recognition to any relationship that homosexual persons seek to enter. The case does involve two adults who, with full and mutual consent from each other, engaged in sexual prac-tices common to a homosexual lifestyle. The petitioners are entitled to respect for their private lives. The State cannot demean their existence or control their des-tiny by making their private sexual conduct a crime. Their right to liberty under the Due Process Clause gives them the full right to engage in their conduct with-out intervention of the government.

. . .

The judgment of the Court of Appeals for the Texas Fourteenth District is reversed, and the case is remanded for further proceedings not inconsistent with this opinion.

. . .

Justice Scalia, with whom [Chief Justice Rehnquist] and Justice Thomas join, dissenting.

. . . Constitutional entitlements do not spring into existence because some States choose to lessen or eliminate criminal sanctions on certain behavior. Much less do they spring into existence, as the Court seems to believe, because foreign nations decriminalize conduct. The *Bowers* majority opinion never relied on "values we share with a wider civilization," . . . but rather rejected the claimed right to sodomy on the ground that such a right was not "'deeply rooted in this Nation's history and tradition,'" 478 U.S., at 193-194. . . . *Bowers'* rational-basis holding is likewise devoid of any reliance on the views of a "wider civilization," see *id.*, at 196. . . . The Court's discussion of these foreign views (ignoring, of course, the many countries that have retained criminal prohibitions on sodomy) is therefore meaningless dicta. Dangerous dicta, however, since "this Court . . . should not impose foreign moods, fads, or fashions on Americans." *Foster v. Florida,* 537 U.S. 990 . . . (2002) (Thomas, J., concurring in denial of certiorari).

. . .

I dissent.

NOTES AND QUESTIONS

1. **Practice: ICJ Decisions and International Law.** If the decisions of the ICJ do not create binding legal precedent, in what ways can they matter? More concretely, as a practicing lawyer, how might you use ICJ decisions when representing a client? According to the Court in *Sanchez-Llamas,* the decisions of the ICJ deserve "respectful consideration." What does this mean, and how might this affect your use of international court decisions as a lawyer?

2. **ICJ Decisions and U.S. Law.** Recall the U.S. Supreme Court's decision in *Medellín v. Texas,* discussed in Chapter 2. As review: Why did the Supreme Court in *Medellín* conclude that the ICJ's *Avena* decision was not enforceable in U.S. courts? How is this different from the Supreme Court's refusal to follow the ICJ's *Avena* reasoning in *Sanchez-Llamas*? Is one more justified than the other? In light of these cases, when — if ever — might an ICJ decision be binding on U.S. courts?

3. **International Court Decisions and U.S. Court Decisions.** In *Lawrence v. Texas,* did the U.S. Supreme Court apply the European Court of Human Rights' (ECHR) decision in *Dudgeon v. United Kingdom* as binding legal precedent? If not, how did the Supreme Court use that decision? As evidence

of customary international law? As persuasive authority? In some other way? Why do you think the Supreme Court referred to that decision? Would the Supreme Court's decision have been different if the ECHR had not found a right of adults to engage in consensual same-sex sexual activity?

4. **Practice: The Utility of Considering International Court Decisions.** Why might U.S. judges find it useful to refer to international court decisions, even if they are not legally binding? If you were a judge, would you refer to an international court decision in an opinion? Even if you would not refer to them in your published opinion, would you ever research international court decisions as part of your deliberations? As a lawyer in litigation, should you cite them? As a lawyer counselling a client, should you research them?

5. **The Problems of Using International Court Decisions.** What reasons might there be for U.S. judges to ignore international court decisions? What concerns does Justice Scalia seem to be expressing in his dissenting opinion in *Lawrence*? What concerns does Chief Justice Roberts express in *Sanchez-Llamas*? Is the Court's treatment of international materials in *Sanchez-Llamas* and *Lawrence* consistent? Note that Justice Kennedy was in the majority in both cases — how might he answer? Partly in response to cases like *Lawrence*, some state and federal legislators have proposed that judges should not be allowed to refer to international law, foreign law, or international court decisions. What would your position be on such a proposal?

6. **Foreign Law and International Agreements Not Ratified by the United States.** The Supreme Court has occasionally referred not only to international court decisions, but also to the law of foreign nations and international agreements not ratified by the United States. This has been most notable in the application of the Eighth Amendment's proscription of "cruel and unusual punishments" to the death penalty. For example, in *Roper v. Simmons*, 543 U.S. 551 (2005), the Court found unconstitutional the application of the death penalty to anyone under the age of 18 at the time of the crime. In an opinion by Justice Kennedy, the Court first reviewed a range of U.S. sources and then added:

> Our determination that the death penalty is disproportionate punishment for offenders under 18 finds confirmation in the stark reality that the United States is the only country in the world that continues to give official sanction to the juvenile death penalty. This reality does not become controlling, for the task of interpreting the Eighth Amendment remains our responsibility. Yet . . . the Court has referred to the laws of other countries and to international authorities as instructive for its interpretation of the Eighth Amendment's prohibition of "cruel and unusual punishments." . . .
> . . . Article 37 of the United Nations Convention on the Rights of the Child, which every country in the world has ratified save for the United States and Somalia, contains an express prohibition on capital punishment for crimes committed by juveniles under 18. . . . No ratifying country has entered a reservation to the provision prohibiting the execution of juvenile offenders. Parallel prohibitions are contained in other significant international covenants. See ICCPR, Art. 6(5) (prohibiting capital punishment for anyone under 18 at the

time of offense) (signed and ratified by the United States subject to a reservation regarding Article 6(5)); American Convention on Human Rights: Pact of San José, Costa Rica, Art. 4(5) (same); African Charter on the Rights and Welfare of the Child, Art. 5(3) (entered into force Nov. 29, 1999) (same).

Respondent and his *amici* have submitted, and petitioner does not contest, that only seven countries other than the United States have executed juvenile offenders since 1990: Iran, Pakistan, Saudi Arabia, Yemen, Nigeria, the Democratic Republic of Congo, and China. Since then each of these countries has either abolished capital punishment for juveniles or made public disavowal of the practice. In sum, it is fair to say that the United States now stands alone in a world that has turned its face against the juvenile death penalty.

... The United Kingdom's experience bears particular relevance here in light of the historic ties between our countries and in light of the Eighth Amendment's own origins. The Amendment was modeled on a parallel provision in the English Declaration of Rights of 1689. . . . As of now, the United Kingdom has abolished the death penalty in its entirety; but, decades before it took this step, it recognized the disproportionate nature of the juvenile death penalty; and it abolished that penalty as a separate matter. In . . . 1948, Parliament enacted the Criminal Justice Act, 11 & 12 Geo. 6, ch. 58, prohibiting the execution of any person under 18 at the time of the offense. In the 56 years that have passed since the United Kingdom abolished the juvenile death penalty, the weight of authority against it there, and in the international community, has become well established.

It is proper that we acknowledge the overwhelming weight of international opinion against the juvenile death penalty, resting in large part on the understanding that the instability and emotional imbalance of young people may often be a factor in the crime. The opinion of the world community, while not controlling our outcome, does provide respected and significant confirmation for our own conclusions.

Justice Scalia, joined by Justice Thomas, dissented. As to the use of international sources, the dissent argued:

The Court . . . [notes] that "Article 37 of the United Nations Convention on the Rights of the Child, which every country in the world has ratified *save for the United States* and Somalia, contains an express prohibition on capital punishment for crimes committed by juveniles under 18." (emphasis added). The Court also discusses the International Covenant on Civil and Political Rights (ICCPR), which the Senate ratified only subject to a reservation that ["The United States reserves the right, subject to its Constitutional restraints, to impose capital punishment on any person . . . for crime committed by persons below eighteen years of age."]

Unless the Court has added to its arsenal the power to join and ratify treaties on behalf of the United States, I cannot see how this evidence favors, rather than refutes, its position. That the Senate and the President — those actors our Constitution empowers to enter into treaties, see Art. II, § 2 — have declined to join and ratify treaties prohibiting execution of under-18 offenders can only suggest that *our country* has either not reached a national consensus on the question, or has reached a consensus contrary to what the Court announces. . . .

356 Chapter 3. Nonbinding and Private Norms

More fundamentally, however, the basic premise of the Court's argument — that American law should conform to the laws of the rest of the world — ought to be rejected out of hand. In fact the Court itself does not believe it. In many significant respects the laws of most other countries differ from our law — including not only such explicit provisions of our Constitution as the right to jury trial and grand jury indictment, but even many interpretations of the Constitution prescribed by this Court itself. The Court-pronounced exclusionary rule, for example, is distinctively American. . . . [A] categorical exclusionary rule has been universally rejected by other countries, including those with rules prohibiting illegal searches and police misconduct, despite the fact that none of these countries appears to have any alternative form of discipline for police that is effective in preventing search violations. England, for example, rarely excludes evidence found during an illegal search or seizure and has only recently begun excluding evidence from illegally obtained confessions. Canada rarely excludes evidence and will only do so if admission will bring the administration of justice into disrepute. The European Court of Human Rights has held that introduction of illegally seized evidence does not violate the "fair trial" requirement in Article 6, § 1, of the European Convention on Human Rights.

The Court has been oblivious to the views of other countries when deciding how to interpret our Constitution's requirement that "Congress shall make no law respecting an establishment of religion. . . ." Amdt. 1. Most other countries — including those committed to religious neutrality — do not insist on the degree of separation between church and state that this Court requires. . . .

And let us not forget the Court's abortion jurisprudence, which makes us one of only six countries that allow abortion on demand until the point of viability. . . .

. . . If we took the Court's directive seriously, we would also consider relaxing our double jeopardy prohibition, since the British Law Commission recently published a report that would significantly extend the rights of the prosecution to appeal cases where an acquittal was the result of a judge's ruling that was legally incorrect. We would also curtail our right to jury trial in criminal cases since, despite the jury system's deep roots in our shared common law, England now permits all but the most serious offenders to be tried by magistrates without a jury.

The Court should either profess its willingness to reconsider all these matters in light of the views of foreigners, or else it should cease putting forth foreigners' views as part of the *reasoned basis* of its decisions. To invoke alien law when it agrees with one's own thinking, and ignore it otherwise, is not reasoned decisionmaking, but sophistry. . . .

Although the Supreme Court has referred to foreign law in Eighth Amendment cases, it has been only scattered elsewhere. Nonetheless, the practice has encountered substantial opposition outside the courts, leading to hearings in Congress and even a proposed federal statute that would prohibit the Court from relying on foreign and international sources to interpret the Constitution. Others argue that references to foreign law can be useful and appropriate in constitutional cases. Justice Breyer has been a leading proponent of this view. Are the considerations in using foreign law to interpret the Constitution similar or different from using it to interpret statutes? Is the answer to the challenge posed by Justice Scalia not to use foreign law to interpret the Constitution, or to use it more frequently? Is the dissent in *Roper* correct that the Court's opinion was premised on a view that "American law should conform to the laws of the rest of the world"? If not, then what exactly does the Court mean when it says that its references to international law "confirm" its conclusions? How, if at all, should U.S. courts ever refer to foreign law when interpreting the Constitution? How, if at all, might your answer be different for use of international law and international court decisions?

7. **Comparative Note.** The courts of the United States are just one example of how courts may use nonbinding norms. Consider Australia, for example. The issue before the High Court of Australia in *D'Emden v. Pedder* (1904), 1 CLR 91 (Austl.), was the relationship between the federal government of Australia and the states of Australia. In its opinion, the High Court of Australia consulted the U.S. Constitution and U.S. Supreme Court decisions on questions of federalism. The Court explained that "[s]o far ... as the United States Constitution and the Constitution of the Commonwealth are similar, the construction put upon the former by the Supreme Court of the United States may well be regarded by us in construing the Constitution of the Commonwealth, not as an infallible guide, but as a most welcome aid and assistance." In a much more recent case, *Unions NSW v. New South Wales* [2013] HCA 58 (Austl.), the issue before the High Court of Australia was the constitutionality of a restriction on political campaign donations. The plaintiffs cited a U.S. Supreme Court case, *Citizens United v. Federal Election Commission*, 558 U.S. 310 (2010), which held that political spending is protected speech under the First Amendment of the U.S. Constitution, and that the government may not bar corporations or unions from spending money to support or oppose candidates in elections. The High Court of Australia reasoned that

> [t]he First Amendment to the United States Constitution ... guarantees a right of free speech. It is a personal right to express one's views on any topic, whether that be to participate in the market place of ideas or to pursue the self-realisation involved in the free expression of one's views. In light of the decision in *Citizens United*, it seems that this personal right extends to corporations as well as natural persons. ... The United States decisions shed little direct light on the path to the resolution of the issues of concern here. That is hardly surprising, given that ... the framers of [the Australian Constitution], after carefully examining the United States Constitution, deliberately decided not to transpose its First Amendment, either in whole or in part.

Are the High Court of Australia's approaches to U.S. law in these two cases consistent? Why or why not? How do these approaches compare to the U.S. Supreme Court's references to nonbinding international norms and foreign law in *Lawrence v. Texas* and *Roper v. Simmons*?

2. *Declarations and Resolutions of International Organizations*

Declarations of nations and the resolutions of international organizations are further examples of nonbinding international norms. Declarations are unilateral or joint statements by nations of principles or goals that are not intended to be legally binding. If a declaration is thought indicative of state practice or expressive of *opinio juris*, a declaration may be evidence of a rule of customary international law. Even if it does not provide such evidence, it may be persuasive. However, declarations generally are not legally binding.*

1992 Rio Decla -ration An example of a nonbinding international declaration is the 1992 Rio Declaration on Environment and Development. The Rio Declaration was a result of the 1992 United Nations conference on Environment and Development held in Rio de Janeiro, Brazil, in which 172 nations and thousands of representatives of international and nongovernmental organizations participated. The Rio Declaration declares 27 principles on the global environment and international development. The participating nations negotiated, documented, and published the principles, but they did not follow the treaty-making process. Although it is not legally binding, the Rio Declaration "is often referred to in negotiations or litigation as an authoritative statement of states' political commitments." SEAN D. MURPHY, PRINCIPLES OF INTERNATIONAL LAW 493 (3d ed. 2018). In general, "[s]uch non-legally binding statements are an important means by which the international community pursues a consensus on environmental values, but they are not regarded as themselves altering existing international or national law." *Id.* at 127.

Resolutions of the U.N. General Assembly are another example of nonbinding international norms. The General Assembly is "the main deliberative, policymaking and representative organ of the United Nations. Comprising all 193 Members of the United Nations, it provides a unique forum for multilateral discussion of the full spectrum of international issues covered by the Charter. The Assembly meets in regular session intensively from September to December each year, and thereafter as required." General Assembly of the United Nations, http://www.un.org/en/ga/. General Assembly Resolutions are voted upon formally by U.N. member states. The United Nations maintains records of these votes, as well as the debates leading up to them. For narrowly defined purposes, the General Assembly has authority to adopt binding resolutions (for example, on matters relating to the United Nations' budget), but generally it may only make recommendations. MURPHY, *supra*, at 115.

Like international declarations, General Assembly resolutions may be evidence of customary international law if they constitute relevant state practice or express *opinio juris*. Moreover, like nonbinding international court decisions, they can contribute to the international common law that "shape[s] the meaning of

---

* Sometimes a nation's unilateral declaration may have legal effects. For example, in the *Nuclear Tests* case (*Australia v. France*), the ICJ determined that France was legally bound by its public declaration that it would cease atmospheric testing of nuclear weapons, where the ICJ found that France intended to be bound by the declaration and the declaration was public.

existing legal rules" and "expectations about what constitutes compliant behavior" with those rules. Andrew T. Guzman & Timothy L. Meyer, *International Soft Law*, 2 J. LEGAL ANALYSIS 171, 216 (2010).

The following materials illustrate how lawyers can use — and oppose the use of — international declarations and General Assembly resolutions in litigation in U.S. courts. The materials are from *Flores v. Southern Peru Copper Corp.*, 414 F.3d 233 (2d Cir. 2003). In that case, Peruvian plaintiffs brought personal injury claims against Southern Peru Copper Corporation (SPCC) alleging that pollution from SPCC's copper mining, refining, and smelting operations caused severe lung disease in them and their decedents. One of their arguments was that SPCC's conduct violated customary international law. As you study these materials, keep the following questions in mind: How did the Amici Curiae International Law Scholars in Support of Plaintiffs-Appellants in *Flores v. Southern Peru Copper Corp.*, attempt to advance their argument by using declarations and General Assembly resolutions? Did they use them as evidence of customary international law? Persuasively? In other ways? How did the defendant's lawyers respond? With which side did the court ultimately agree, and why? How does the court's use of nonbinding norms differ from the court's use of them in the *Sanchez-Llamas* and *Lawrence* cases excerpted above?

Brief of Amici Curiae International Law Scholars in Support of Plaintiffs-Appellants and Urging Reversal (Flores v. Southern Peru Copper Corp.)

2002 WL 32496233 (December 4, 2002)

Customary international law protects the rights to life, security of the person, and health. These rights are, without question, universally recognized[8] and obligatory.[9] Moreover, they are universally understood to place obligatory limits on environmental degradation. Judge Weeramantry, then Vice-President of the International Court of Justice, states the customary law view:

> The protection of the environment is . . . a vital part of contemporary human rights doctrine, for it is a sine qua non for numerous human rights such as the right to health and the right to life itself. It is scarcely necessary to elaborate on this, as damage to the environment can impair and undermine all the human rights spoken of in the Universal Declaration and other human rights instruments.

---

8. *E.g.* Life: Universal Declaration of Human Rights, art. 3 (1948); International Covenant on Civil and Political Rights (ICCPR), art. 6 (entered into force, 1976); Security of the person: Universal Declaration, art. 3; ICCPR art. 9; American Declaration on the Rights and Duties of Man, art. I (1948); Health: Universal Declaration, art. 25; International Covenant on Economic, Social and Cultural Rights, art. 12 (in force Jan. 3, 1976) (135 parties); American Declaration, art. XI; Banjul [African] Charter on Human and Peoples' Rights, art. 16 (1982) (50 signatories); Additional Protocol to the American Convention on Human Rights in the Area of Economic Social and Cultural Rights, art. 10 (1988).

9. *E.g.* ICCPR, art. 4, 2, 6; Report on the Situation of Human Rights in Ecuador, ("Ecuador Report"), Inter-American Commission on Human Rights, OEA/Ser.L/V/II.96, Doc. 10 rev. 1, at 91-93, April 24, 1997.

Gabcikovo-Nagymaros Case (Hungary-Slovakia), Judgment of Sept. 25, 1997 (Sep. Op. Vice-President Weeramantry) at 4; see also Convention on Access to Information, Public Participation in Decision-Making and Access to Justice in Environmental Matters ("Aarhus Convention"), Preamble ("adequate protection of the environment is essential to . . . the enjoyment of basic human rights"). Thus, the rights to life, security of the person and health form at least part of the basis of the right to be free from massive and severe environmental harm.

An international consensus supports Judge Weeramantry's conclusion. For example, the 171 states attending the United Nations' World Conference on Human Rights recognized that illicit dumping of toxic waste may seriously threaten the right to life.[10] States have also widely recognized that the right to health encompasses freedom from serious pollution. Article 12 of the International Covenant on Economic, Social and Cultural Rights (ICESCR) specifically requires states to improve "environmental hygiene" in order to protect the right. Similarly, article 24(c) of the Convention on the Rights of the Child (1989), requires states to account for the dangers of pollution in implementing right to health.[11]

. . .

Beginning in 1972, the community of nations has repeatedly recognized that individuals have a right to a minimally adequate environment. In that year, 114 nations, including the United States, declared in the Stockholm Declaration that humankind "has the fundamental right to . . . adequate conditions of life, in an environment of a quality that permits a life of dignity and well-being."[15] The international community reaffirmed its recognition of the right in 1990 when the United Nations General Assembly adopted by consensus a resolution recognizing that "all individuals are entitled to live in an environment adequate for their health and well-being." G.A. Res. 45/94 (1990). Two years later, more than 178 nations including the United States again affirmed the right in the Rio Declaration, which unanimously acclaimed that "[h]uman beings . . . are entitled to a healthy and productive life in harmony with nature." Rio Declaration, Principle 1.

Declarations such as those at Rio and Stockholm are important sources of customary international law. *Filartiga*, 630 F.2d at 883. The recognition in these Declarations that individuals have a right to a minimally adequate environment created "an expectation of adherence." *Id.* Given that Principle 1 of the Rio Declaration has been universally and repeatedly reaffirmed, it is an "authoritative statement of the international community." *See id.*[16]

---

10. Vienna Declaration and Programme of Action, ¶ 11 (1993). The U.N. Human Rights Commission has reiterated that conclusion. Resolution 1995/81, Preamble and art. 1 (1997).

11. On the customary status of the rights codified in the Convention, see *Sadeghi v. INS*, 40 F.3d 1139, 1147 (10th Cir. 1994) (Kane, J. dissenting) (166 nations have ratified Convention and it "has attained the status of customary international law").

15. United Nations conference on the Human Environment, Stockholm Declaration on the Human Environment, Principle 1 (1972).

16. The above quoted language of Principle 1 was reaffirmed verbatim by 179 nations at the 1994 U.N. Conference on Population and Development, Programme of Action, U.N. Doc. A/CONF.171/13 (1994), princ. 2; by 186 nations in the 1995 Copenhagen Declaration, U.N. Doc A/CONF.166/7/Annex (1995) ¶ 8; by 171 nations at the 1996 Second Conference on Human Settlements (Habitat II), Habitat Agenda, ch. I, pmbl. ¶ 2, and by the U.N. Human Rights Commission, Res. 1995/14, ¶ 1 (1995).

Other international and regional agreements also recognize the right to a minimally adequate environment. The Aarhus Convention states that "every person has the right to live in an environment adequate to his or her health and well-being." Preamble; see also art. 1. The Hague Declaration on the Environment recognizes "the right to live in dignity in a viable global environment." In the Americas, Article 11 of the Additional Protocol to the American Convention on Human Rights provides that "[e]veryone shall have the right to live in a healthy environment." Similarly, the Banjul [African] Charter on Human and Peoples' Rights provides that "[a]ll peoples shall have the right to a generally satisfactory environment favorable to their development." Art. 24. The African Commission found this right to be violated by massive oil pollution with serious health effects. SERAC Case. ¶¶ 50, 54.

These documents further demonstrate that the nations of the world universally recognize the right to be free from severe environmental harms.

Brief for Defendant-Appellee Southern Peru Copper Corporation (Flores v. Southern Peru Copper Corp.)

2003 WL 23475680 (January 7, 2003)

Courts must avoid the mistake of analogizing the development of customary international law to the development of common law. "Customary international law results from a general and consistent practice of states followed by them from a sense of legal obligation." RESTATEMENT (THIRD) OF THE FOREIGN RELATIONS LAW OF THE UNITED STATES § 102(2) (1987). Put another way, a rule of customary international law is established by the concurrence of two conditions: (i) the uniform and consistent practice of the generality of nations and (ii) the acceptance by nations that such practice is obligatory. The requirement that a rule achieve general assent through the consistent and obligatory practice of nations before it becomes binding as customary international law is "stringent," *Filartiga*, 630 F.2d at 881. . . .

A rule of customary international law cannot be established by declarations or other pronouncements made at diplomatic conferences — as Plaintiffs pretend — because such pronouncements, by themselves, neither represent state practice nor demonstrate that such practice is treated by nations as obligatory. *See* Anthony D'Amato, *Trashing Customary International Law*, 81 AM. J. INT'L L. 101, 102 (1987) ("[A] customary rule arises out of state practice; it is not necessarily found in UN resolutions and other majoritarian political documents."). Customary international law — as the very name indicates — arises from the consistent practice of nations. *Third Restatement* § 102(2); *Filartiga*, 630 F.2d at 883 (regarding torture, "we have little difficulty discerning its universal renunciation in the modern usage and practice of nations"). Statements in pronouncements such as the Universal Declaration of Human Rights may "create[] an expectation of adherence," but it is only "insofar as the expectation is gradually justified by State practice, [that] a declaration may by custom become recognized as laying down rules binding upon the States" as customary international law. *Filartiga*, 630 F.2d at 883 (internal quotation marks and citation omitted).

Flores v. Southern Peru Copper Corp.

414 F.3d 233 (2d Cir. 2003)

JOSÉ A. CABRANES, Circuit Judge.

. . .

Although customary international law does not protect a right to life or right to health, plaintiffs' complaint may be construed to assert a claim under a more narrowly-defined customary international law rule against intra national pollution.[29] However, the voluminous documents and the affidavits of international law scholars submitted by plaintiffs fail to demonstrate the existence of any such norm of customary international law.

In support of their claims, plaintiffs have submitted the following types of evidence: (i) treaties, conventions, and covenants; (ii) non-binding declarations of the United Nations General Assembly, [and] (iii) other non-binding multinational declarations of principle; (iv) decisions of multinational tribunals. . . .

1. Treaties, Conventions, and Covenants

Plaintiffs rely on numerous treaties, conventions, and covenants in support of their claims. Although these instruments are proper evidence of customary international law to the extent that they create legal obligations among the States parties to them, plaintiffs have not demonstrated that the particular instruments on which they rely establish a legal rule prohibiting intranational pollution.

. . .

2. Non-Binding General Assembly Declarations

Plaintiffs rely on several resolutions of the United Nations General Assembly in support of their assertion that defendant's conduct violated a rule of customary international law. These documents are not proper sources of customary international law because they are merely aspirational and were never intended to be binding on member States of the United Nations.

The General Assembly has been described aptly as "the world's most important political discussion forum," but it is not a law-making body. I *The Charter of the United Nations: A Commentary* 248, 269 (Bruno Simma ed., 2d ed. 2002). General Assembly resolutions and declarations do not have the power to bind member States because the member States specifically denied the General Assembly that power after extensively considering the issue. . . .

The core constitutive principles that emerged from the three major preparatory conferences that led to the adoption of the United Nations Charter were those creating the General Assembly and the Security Council of the United Nations and setting forth their respective purposes and powers. The simplest and clearest

---

29. Because plaintiffs do not allege that defendants' conduct had an effect outside the borders of Peru, we need not consider the customary international law status of transnational pollution. . . .

of these organizing principles was that the General Assembly would provide a forum in which all states, small and large, would enjoy formal juridical equality, with the power to discuss virtually anything; however, as part and parcel of that understanding, it was agreed that, apart from certain internal arrangements such as the Organization's budget and other internal and financial matters not pertinent here, the General Assembly's resolutions would not be binding on States. As one contemporary commentator observed:

> If the Assembly were authorized to take action, to make decisions binding upon the member states, this would mean that it would be the congress or parliament of the world. Had the powers of the Assembly been extended that far, one can be sure that not only the U.S. and Russia, but also France and England, and what are considered the "Middle Powers" (e.g., Brazil and Canada) would have asked for a larger representation. For it is self-evident that they could not have agreed that on vital decisions their powers should be no greater than those, for example, of small states like Nicaragua and Saudi Arabia.

Louis Dolivet, *The United Nations: A Handbook on the New World Organization* 35-36 (1946) (with preface by the first Secretary-General of the United Nations, Trygvie Lie); *see also* Meisler, *United Nations: The First Fifty Years* at 10-14.[37]

The authority to make pronouncements that could be legally binding was reserved to the Security Council, in which each of the identified Great Powers of the post-war era would be permanent members and hold a veto power. . . . Under the Charter of the United Nations, the Security Council was afforded the power (in circumstances where no veto is exercised by a "permanent member") to issue binding resolutions, *United Nations Charter*, ch. VII, whereas the General Assembly was granted the power only to "make recommendations to the Members of the United Nations or to the Security Council or to both," *United Nations Charter*, ch. IV, art. 10.

In sum, as described in The Law of Nations, the classic handbook by Professors Brierly and Waldock of Oxford University: "[A]ll that the General Assembly can do is to discuss and recommend and initiate studies and consider reports from other bodies. It cannot act on behalf of all the members, as the Security Council does, and its decisions are not directions telling the member states what they are or are not to do." J.L. Brierly, *The Law of Nations* 110 (Sir Humphrey Waldock ed.,

---

37. The pre-eminent authority on the law of international institutions, Professor Sir Derek Bowett of Cambridge University, writing in the late 1950s, made precisely the same point:

> The Assembly is a deliberative body, an organ for discussion in the widest sense. It has, of course, power to investigate facts, to make recommendations, but it has no power to bind the members; it cannot take binding decisions as the Security Council can. This means, then, that any analogy with the legislature of a state is very misleading, for the Assembly's functions cannot be legislative in the true sense. The only way in which its recommendations can become binding upon members is for the members to agree in advance to treat those recommendations as binding, but the Assembly's recommendations themselves have no legally binding force.

D.W. Bowett, *The General Assembly, in* The United Nations: The First Ten Years 3, 9-10 (B.A. Wortley ed., 1957). . . .

6th ed. 1963). Because General Assembly documents are at best merely advisory, they do not, on their own and without proof of uniform state practice, evidence an intent by member States to be legally bound by their principles, and thus cannot give rise to rules of customary international law.

Our position is consistent with the recognition in *Filartiga* that the right to be free from torture embodied in the Universal Declaration of Human Rights, has attained the status of customary international law. *Filartiga* cited the Universal Declaration for the proposition that torture is universally condemned, reasoning that "a [United Nations] declaration may by custom become recognized as [a] rule[]" of customary international law. *Filartiga*, 630 F.2d at 883. The Court explained that non-binding United Nations documents such as the Universal Declaration "create[] an expectation of adherence," but they evidence customary international law only "insofar as the expectation is gradually justified by State practice." *Id.*[38]

In considering the Universal Declaration's prohibition against torture, the *Filartiga* Court cited extensive evidence that States, in their domestic and international practices, repudiate official torture. In particular, it recognized that torture is prohibited under law by, inter alia, the constitutions of fifty-five States, *id.* at 884 & n.12, and noted the conclusion expressed by the Executive Branch of our government — the political branch with principal responsibility for conducting the international relations of the United States — that "[t]here now exists an international consensus" against official torture that "virtually all governments acknowledge," *id.* Accordingly, although *Filartiga* did indeed cite the Universal Declaration, this non-binding General Assembly declaration was only relevant to *Filartiga*'s analysis insofar as it accurately described the actual customs and practices of States on the question of torture.

In the instant case, the General Assembly documents relied on by plaintiffs do not describe the actual customs and practices of States. Accordingly, they cannot support plaintiffs' claims.

3. Other Multinational Declarations of Principle

In addition to General Assembly documents, plaintiffs rely on numerous other multinational "declarations" to substantiate their position that defendant's intranational pollution in Peru violated customary international law. A declaration, which may be made by a multinational body, or by one or more States,

---

38. The District of Columbia Circuit has described the Universal Declaration as "merely a non-binding resolution." *Haitian Refugee Ctr. v. Gracey*, 809 F.2d 794, 816 n.17 (D.C. Cir. 1987). Moreover, at the time of its adoption in 1948, it was the explicit position of the United States that the Declaration "is not a treaty . . . [or] an international agreement" and that "[i]t is not and does not purport to be a statement of law or of legal obligation." 19 Dep't State Bull. 751 (1948) (remarks of Eleanor Roosevelt, then a U.S. delegate to the General Assembly). These statements are consistent with *Filartiga*, which recognized that the Universal Declaration constitutes evidence of customary international law only insofar as States have universally abided by its principles out of a sense of legal obligation and mutual concern.

customarily is a "mere general statement of policy [that] is unlikely to give rise to . . . obligation[s] in any strict sense." 1 *Oppenheim's International Law* 1189 (Sir Robert Jennings & Sir Arthur Watts eds., 9th ed. 1996). In undertaking the difficult task of determining the contours of customary international law, a court is not granted a roving commission to pick and choose among declarations of public and private international organizations that have articulated a view on the matter at hand. Such declarations are almost invariably political statements — expressing the sensibilities and the asserted aspirations and demands of some countries or organizations — rather than statements of universally-recognized legal obligations. Accordingly, such declarations are not proper evidence of customary international law.

Occasionally, a document entitled a "declaration" may actually be a binding treaty because the document uses language indicating the parties' intent to be bound and sets forth "definite rules of conduct." *Id.*; *see, e.g., Iran v. United States* (Case A/1), 68 I.L.R. 523, 525 (Iran-U.S. Claims Trib. 1982) (noting that the agreements between the United States and Iran that concluded the hostage crisis were termed "declarations," even though they created legally binding obligations). Only in such rare instances — where the States joining in the self-styled "declaration" intended it to be legally binding — may a party rely on a document entitled a "declaration" as evidence of the customs and practices of the States joining the declaration.

Apart from the General Assembly documents addressed above, plaintiffs principally rely on two multinational declarations in support of their claims. First, they draw our attention to the American Declaration of the Rights and Duties of Man ("American Declaration"), promulgated by the Organization of American States ("OAS"). As one of our sister Circuits has correctly observed, the American Declaration "is an aspirational document which . . . did not on its own create any enforceable obligations on the part of any of the OAS member nations." *Garza v. Lappin*, 253 F.3d 918, 925 (7th Cir. 2001).

Plaintiffs also rely on Principle 1 of the Rio Declaration, which sets forth broad, aspirational principles regarding environmental protection and sustainable development. The Rio Declaration includes no language indicating that the States joining in the Declaration intended to be legally bound by it.

Because neither of these declarations created enforceable legal obligations, they do not provide reliable evidence of customary international law.

NOTES AND QUESTIONS

1. **Practice: Using Nonbinding Norms.** What legal materials do the Amici Curiae International Law Scholars in Support of Plaintiffs-Appellants in *Flores v. Southern Peru Copper Corp.* use to support their argument that international law recognizes environmental rights? What legal materials, if they existed, could have made their argument more convincing? More generally,

why might lawyers use nonbinding international norms as part of their legal advocacy strategies?

2. **Practice: Arguing Against Nonbinding Norms.** What arguments did the defendants in the *Flores* case make to refute the argument that international law imposes legally binding obligations to avoid environmental degradation?

3. **U.S. Courts, Declarations, and U.N. General Assembly Resolutions.** How did the court in the *Flores* case respond to the various legal materials cited by plaintiffs and their amici? Compare the response in *Flores* to that in *Filártiga v. Peña-Irala*, 630 F.2d 876 (2d Cir. 1980) (excerpted in Chapter 2). In *Filártiga* the Second Circuit Court of Appeals held that torture is a violation of international law. It based its conclusion largely on an analysis of various nonbinding international sources, including two U.N. General Assembly resolutions: the Universal Declaration of Human Rights and the Declaration on the Protection of All Persons from Being Subjected to Torture. According to the court, "[t]hese U.N. declarations are significant because they specify with great precision the obligations of member nations under the [U.N.] Charter" and that even if nonbinding, they are among "the sources from which customary international law is derived." *Id.* at 883-84. Which court gave more weight to U.N. General Assembly resolutions and declarations, the *Filártiga* court (in the opinion included in Chapter 2) or the *Flores* court? Can the treatment of those sources of norms by the two courts be reconciled?

4. **Comparing *Flores* and *Lawrence*.** How does the court's use of nonbinding norms in *Flores* differ from the court's use of international court decisions in the *Lawrence* case excerpted above?

5. **Binding Law versus Evidence of Law.** "General Assembly resolutions can serve as evidence of customary international law, but they bind no one." *Institute of Cetacean Research v. Sea Shepherd Conservation Soc.*, 860 F. Supp. 2d 1216, 1236 (W.D. Wash. 2012). Explain how this can be the case. Is this a helpful distinction?

6. **Policy: The Proper Role of Nonbinding Norms.** Should courts be influenced by nonbinding international norms when they decide cases? Why or why not?

7. **Other U.N. Entities.** In addition to the General Assembly, the United Nations has an array of commissions, committees, agencies, and similarly titled bodies devoted to specific topics. For example, the U.N. Human Rights Council is "an inter-governmental body within the United Nations system made up of 47 States responsible for the promotion and protection of all human rights around the globe." *See* http://www.ohchr.org/en/hrbodies/hrc/pages/hrcindex .aspx. Among other things, it commissions and adopts reports on various human rights situations. What legal status, if any, should these reports have? Suppose the Council had found that there is (or is not) a human right to engage in same-sex sexual activity or to be free from environmental pollution? What more, if anything, would you want to know about the Human Rights Council? Other examples of U.N. entities include the World Health Organization (WHO), the U.N. Educational, Scientific and Cultural Organization (UNESCO), and the World Intellectual Property Association (WIPO).

8. **The International Law Commission.** The International Law Commission (ILC) (http://www.un.org/law/ilc/) is a body created in 1948 by the U.N. General Assembly, which provided that the "Commission shall have for its object the promotion of the progressive development of international law and its codification" and that it shall be composed of "persons of recognized competence in international law." The Commission has issued reports regarding many aspects of international law. What legal status, if any, should these have? If you found that the ILC had taken a position favorable to your client in a report, how might you use it in court? In *Republic of Iraq v. ABB AG*, 920 F. Supp. 2d 517, 537 (S.D.N.Y. 2013), the court referred to the ILC's Articles on Responsibility of States for Internationally Wrongful Acts, noting that the Second Circuit's definition of "governmental act" comported with them. Why do you think the court might have found it useful to consider the ILC's work?

9. **Other International Organizations.** In addition to U.N. entities, there are a variety of independent international organizations whose views might be relevant to transnational practice. For example, the International Committee of the Red Cross (ICRC) (http://www.icrc.org/eng/who-we-are/index.jsp) is considered an authoritative commentator on the laws of war. Are the reports of these organizations more or less persuasive authorities than General Assembly Resolutions? Than reports of other U.N. entities?

10. **Comparative Note.** In *Government of the Republic of South Africa v. Grootboom*, 2001 (1) SA 46, the Constitutional Court of South Africa addressed a claim by homeless plaintiffs that their eviction from the land on which they were living violated the South African Constitution. The plaintiffs sought an order directing the government to provide adequate basic temporary shelter or housing for them and their children until they could find permanent housing. They based their claim on Article 26 of the South African Constitution, which is part of the South African Bill of Rights:

    > (1) Everyone has the right to have access to adequate housing. (2) The state must take reasonable legislative and other measures, within its available resources, to achieve the progressive realisation of this right. (3) No one may be evicted from their home, or have their home demolished, without an order of court made after considering all the relevant circumstances. No legislation may permit arbitrary evictions.

    The Court ruled in favor of the plaintiffs. Its reasoning included a discussion of the right to housing under international law. Among other things, the Court discussed the International Covenant on Economic, Social and Cultural Rights and commentary of the U.N. Committee on Economic, Social and Cultural Rights interpreting the Covenant. The Court described the role of international law in its reasoning as follows:

    > [P]ublic international law . . . includ[ing] non-binding as well as binding law . . . may both be used . . . as tools of interpretation. International agreements and customary international law accordingly provide a framework within which [the South African Bill of Rights] can be evaluated and

understood, and for that purpose, decisions of tribunals dealing with comparable instruments, such as the United Nations Committee on Human Rights, the Inter-American Commission on Human Rights, the Inter-American Court of Human Rights, the European Commission on Human Rights, and the European Court of Human Rights, and, in appropriate cases, reports of specialised agencies such as the International Labour Organisation, may provide guidance as to the correct interpretation of particular provisions of [the Bill of Rights]. . . . The relevant international law can be a guide to interpretation but the weight to be attached to any particular principle or rule of international law will vary. However, where the relevant principle of international law binds South Africa, it may be directly applicable.

What are the similarities and differences between this approach to international law and the approach taken by U.S. courts? Which approach is more appropriate? Note that Article 39(1) of the South African Constitution provides that "[w]hen interpreting the Bill of Rights, a court, tribunal or forum — (a) must promote the values that underlie an open and democratic society based on human dignity, equality and freedom; (b) must consider international law; and (c) may consider foreign law." To what extent does this provision explain the differences between the South African and U.S. approach to international law? What is the difference between "considering" international and foreign law, and applying it as binding rules of decision? Why do you think Article 39 uses the term "must" for international law but "may" for foreign law? Why do you think that the framers of the South African Constitution included Article 39 at all?

3. International Codes of Conduct

Another type of nonbinding norm created by nations is focused primarily on influencing the conduct of private actors such as multinational corporations. Among the most prominent of these international codes of conduct are the Guiding Principles on Business and Human Rights, adopted by the U.N. Human Rights Council in 2011. The Guiding Principles were developed by John Ruggie, the Special Representative of the UN Secretary General on Business and Human Rights, with extensive consultation with governmental and nongovernmental actors, including multinational corporations.

The Guiding Principles fall into three categories, corresponding to a three-part "Protect, Respect and Remedy" framework for business and human rights adopted by the UN Human Rights Council in 2008:

- Principles elaborating the duty of nations to protect human rights, including by protecting against human rights abuses by business enterprises.
- Principles elaborating the corporate responsibility to protect human rights, including the duty to avoid violating human rights, the duty to use due diligence to assess actual and potential human rights impacts of their activities,

and the duty to cooperate in the remediation of adverse human rights impacts they have caused or contributed to.

- Principles elaborating the duty of nations to effective remedies for human rights abuses.

The Guiding Principles state that nothing in them "should be read as creating new international law obligations, or as limiting or undermining any legal obligations a State may have undertaken or be subject to under international law with regard to human rights." Instead, the "normative contribution [of the Principles] lies . . . in elaborating the implications of existing standards and practices for States and businesses; integrating them within a single, logically coherent and comprehensive template; and identifying where the current regime falls short and how it should be improved." Although they are not legally binding — or perhaps because they are not legally binding — the three-part framework elaborated by the Guiding Principles has gained widespread acceptance by nations, nongovernmental organizations, and businesses. *See* Special Representative of the United Nations Secretary-General for Business & Human Rights, Applications of the U.N. "Protect, Respect and Remedy" Framework, June 30, 2011 (*available at* http://www.business-humanrights.org/media/documents/applications-of-framework-jun-2011.pdf).

NOTES AND QUESTIONS

1. **The Reasons for Nonbinding Guidelines.** Why do you think the U.N. Human Rights Council adopted nonbinding guidelines on business and human rights instead of proposing a legally binding treaty? Why do you think many nations, nongovernmental organizations, and multinational corporations have been supportive of the Guiding Principles on Business and Human Rights? How might the reaction have been different if it were a legally binding Treaty on Business and Human Rights?

2. **Practice: The Implications of the Guidelines.** As a lawyer advising a multinational business, what advice would you give regarding these guidelines? How important is it that they are described as nonbinding? Is there any harm in refusing to follow the guidelines? In promising to follow them?

3. **International Nonbinding Norms and Treaty Interpretation.** Another type of international nonbinding norms consists of model laws, including model treaties. For example, in the 1960s the Organisation for Economic Co-operation and Development (OECD) drafted and adopted a model bilateral tax convention aimed at avoiding double taxation (Model Convention). The Model Convention is accompanied by extensive commentary prepared by the OECD. The Model Convention is not legally binding; it is simply a model recommended by the OECD that nations can follow when negotiating and concluding tax treaties with other each other. The Model Convention, which has been amended several times, has served as the basis

370 Chapter 3. Nonbinding and Private Norms

for many bilateral tax treaties, including treaties entered by the United States. Although neither the Model Convention nor its commentary is legally binding, U.S. courts have relied on the commentary to interpret legally binding bilateral tax treaties entered by the United States. As one U.S. federal court explains, "Both this court and others have recognized that the [OECD's] 1977 Model Double Taxation Convention on Income and on Capital ('Model Treaty') and the accompanying explanatory Commentary . . . serve as a meaningful guide in interpreting treaties that are based on its provisions." *National Westminster Bank, PLC v. United States*, 58 Fed. Cl. 491, 498 (2003). In that case, a U.S. federal court rejected the U.S. government's interpretation of a provision of the 1975 United States — United Kingdom Convention for the Avoidance of Double Taxation, in part because that interpretation was inconsistent with the commentary on the model treaty. *See also National Westminster Bank, PLC v. United States*, 44 Fed. Cl. 120, 125 (1999) (noting that the commentary is "important and helpful in determining the probable mutual understanding of countries which used the [Model Convention] as the basis for a tax treaty"); *Escobedo v. United States*, 2013 WL 6058485, at *3 (S.D. Cal. 2013) ("Like the U.N., [U.S.] courts too have relied on the commentary of the OECD Model Treaty as the primary source to interpret bilateral income tax treaties.").

4. **International Nonbinding Norms and Statutory Interpretation.** Pursuant to the Dodd-Frank Wall Street Reform and Consumer Protection Act, the U.S. Securities and Exchange Commission (SEC) promulgated a rule imposing certain disclosure requirements for companies that use "conflict minerals" originating in and around the Democratic Republic of the Congo. The National Association of Manufacturers, the Chamber of Commerce, and Business Roundtable challenged the SEC's rule as arbitrary and capricious under the Administrative Procedure Act. The OECD had developed "the only nationally or internationally recognized due diligence framework" on the sourcing of conflict minerals. The OECD due diligence guidelines are not legally binding. However, the SEC expressly based its due diligence rule in part on the OECD framework. The U.S. District Court for the District of Columbia upheld the SEC's rule in part because of the SEC's reliance on the OECD guidelines. *National Ass'n of Mfrs. v. SEC*, 956 F. Supp. 2d 43, 68 n.20 (D.D.C. 2013) (noting the rule's consistency with the OECD guidelines and concluding that the SEC's adherence to the OECD's approach "renders its interpretation all the more reasonable and permissible").

C. Private Norms

Nations and the courts and other organizations they create are not the only makers of nonbinding norms. Private norms also play an important role in transnational practice. As noted above, private norms are norms made by private actors.

If they are incorporated into an enforceable agreement, they may be binding as a matter of contract law. Even if they are not contractually binding, they can — like international nonbinding norms — be persuasive. This section introduces you to four types of private norms that you may encounter in transnational practice: private procedural norms, private substantive norms, corporate codes of conduct, and technical standards. The materials presented in this section are designed to help you understand how lawyers use private norms both when they help their clients plan cross-border business transactions and when they advocate on behalf of their clients in transnational disputes.

1. Private Procedural Norms

The procedural rules governing transnational arbitral proceedings are a leading example of transnational private procedural norms. Arbitration — which is discussed in depth in Chapter 6 — is a dispute resolution method whereby the disputing parties agree to have their dispute resolved by one or more private parties called "arbitrators" as an alternative to litigating the dispute in a court. One of the hallmarks of transnational arbitration is the ability of the disputants themselves to specify the applicable procedural rules. These rules cover matters such as the number and selection of arbitrators, the place and language of the arbitral proceedings, the written submissions and oral arguments that the disputants are allowed to make, the presentation of evidence, and the testimony of witnesses.

In theory, disputants can create their own procedural rules from scratch. In practice, however, they generally specify an existing set of procedural rules, adopting them either in their entirety or with modifications. The world's leading private arbitral institutions have developed various sets of procedural rules. When disputants opt for institutional arbitration, they typically will also opt for the procedural rules of the administering institution. For example, the rules of arbitration developed by the American Arbitration Association's International Centre for Dispute Resolution (ICDR) ordinarily govern arbitrations administered by the ICDR (see www.adr.org), and the rules developed by the International Chamber of Commerce (ICC) ordinarily govern arbitrations administered by the ICC (see https://iccwbo.org/dispute-resolution-services/icc-international-court-arbitration/).

The procedural rules of arbitral institutions apply only if the parties have agreed for them to apply. The following is a model clause suggested by the ICC for parties to use to select arbitration administered by the ICC under the ICC's rules:

> All disputes arising out of or in connection with the present contract shall be finally settled under the Rules of Arbitration of the International Chamber of Commerce by one or more arbitrators appointed in accordance with the said Rules.

However, like all model contract provisions, model arbitration provisions are often customized to meet the parties' specific needs and interests. Among other things, the clauses may be customized to add particular rules or to contractually modify particular provisions of an arbitral institution's rules. This, of course, is typically the job of lawyers. Courts generally will enforce both valid agreements to arbitrate (as discussed in Chapter 6) and arbitral awards made in accordance with valid agreements to arbitrate (as discussed in Chapter 8).

Other private procedural norms have been developed by the International Bar Association. These include Rules on the Taking of Evidence in International Arbitration, Guidelines for Drafting International Arbitration Clauses, and Guidelines on Conflicts of Interest in International Arbitration, which are available at http://www.ibanet.org/Publications/publications_IBA_guides_and_free_materials.aspx.

2. *Private Substantive Norms*

In addition to private procedural norms, there are private substantive norms. Contract provisions are the most pervasive form of private substantive norms — and if they are valid and enforceable under the applicable law of contracts, they are legally binding. Whether they are short and simple or long and complex, contracts provide the basic rules that govern relationships between the contracting parties — including in cross-border relationships. In this sense, contracts are the most common source of private substantive norms governing transnational activity.

But contracts are inevitably incomplete. They cannot cover all issues that may arise between the parties, and often issues of contractual validity and interpretation need to be decided. Choice-of-law principles — such as those discussed in Chapter 1 — are used to determine the applicable law in such situations. Ordinarily, those principles point to the law of a particular nation; and ordinarily, if the parties make a contractual choice of law, a court (or arbitral tribunal) will respect that choice and apply the law selected by the parties.

In some cases, however, the parties may select private substantive norms rather than national law. For example, they may agree to have transnational commercial customs — sometimes called "*lex mercatoria*," "merchant law," or "trade usages" — govern their relationship. Transnational commercial customs are typically unwritten norms based on the customary business practices of firms engaged in cross-border commerce. Parties may also agree to have principles developed by international organizations, such as the UNIDROIT Principles of International Commercial Contracts, govern their contractual relationships. UNIDROIT is the International Institute for the Unification of Private Law, an intergovernmental organization that aims to facilitate global harmonization of commercial law. Working closely with private actors, including lawyers and legal scholars, UNIDROIT drafted the Principles "to establish a balanced set of rules designed for use throughout the world irrespective of the legal traditions and the economic and political conditions of the countries in which they are to be applied." UNIDROIT Principles of International Commercial Contracts xxiii (2010). Among other things, the UNIDROIT Principles cover the formation, validity, interpretation, and performance of contracts. They are not by themselves legally binding, but parties sometimes select them as a source of norms to govern their contracts.

Another source of private norms may be model provisions drafted by private business groups involved in a particular type of commerce. For example, the International Chamber of Commerce provides a set of defined terms, called Incoterms, that parties can use to describe their obligations in international sales contracts. *See* http://www.iccwbo.org/products-and-services/trade-facilitation/incoterms-2010/the-incoterms-rules/. Parties may provide in their contracts that terms in the contract are to be defined as set forth in the Incoterms. The International Chamber of Commerce also publishes the Uniform Customs and Practices for Documentary Credits (UCP) (*see* http://www.iccwbo.org/news/articles/2006/icc%E2%80%99s-new-rules-on-documentary-credits-now-available/), which provide a set of rules for international letters of credit (a common form of financing for international sales transactions). Many international letters of credit specifically provide that they are governed by the UCP. As a lawyer, what do you think the utility is of having such model principles and terms? When advising a client on whether to adopt them, what would you need to know? Should courts or other adjudicative bodies use these sources to fill in gaps, as U.S. courts sometimes use the Restatements?

3. Corporate Codes of Conduct

Corporate codes of conduct are a third form of private norms. These codes are adopted voluntarily by multinational corporations. Sometimes they are drafted by individual corporations for their own use, such as Gap Inc.'s Code of Vendor Conduct (https://www.gapinc.com/content/dam/gapincsite/documents/CodeofVendorConduct_FINAL.pdf) and PepsiCo's Global Code of Conduct (https://www.pepsico.com/about/global-code-of-conduct).

In addition, corporations often adopt model codes of conduct developed by transnational organizations. Consider, for example, the Voluntary Principles on Security and Human Rights, which is "a set of principles that guide companies on providing security for their operations while respecting human rights" (https://www.voluntaryprinciples.org/the-initiative/). The following is an excerpt from the Voluntary Principles:

Voluntary Principles on Security and Human Rights
© 2014 *Voluntary Principles Association*

. . .

In an effort to reduce the risk of [human rights] abuses and to promote respect for human rights generally, we have identified the following voluntary principles to guide relationships between Companies and public security regarding security provided to Companies:

Security Arrangements
Companies should consult regularly with host governments and local communities about the impact of their security arrangements on those communities.

Companies should communicate their policies regarding ethical conduct and human rights to public security providers, and express their desire that security be provided in a manner consistent with those policies by personnel with adequate and effective training.

. . .

Deployment and Conduct

The primary role of public security should be to maintain the rule of law, including safeguarding human rights and deterring acts that threaten Company personnel and facilities. The type and number of public security forces deployed should be competent, appropriate and proportional to the threat.

. . . Companies that provide equipment to public security should take all appropriate and lawful measures to mitigate any foreseeable negative consequences, including human rights abuses and violations of international humanitarian law.

Companies should use their influence to promote the following principles with public security: (a) individuals credibly implicated in human rights abuses should not provide security services for Companies; (b) force should be used only when strictly necessary and to an extent proportional to the threat; and (c) the rights of individuals should not be violated while exercising the right to exercise freedom of association and peaceful assembly, the right to engage in collective bargaining, or other related rights of Company employees as recognized by the Universal Declaration of Human Rights and the ILO Declaration on Fundamental Principles and Rights at Work.

In cases where physical force is used by public security, such incidents should be reported to the appropriate authorities and to the Company. Where force is used, medical aid should be provided to injured persons, including to offenders.

Consultation and Advice

. . .

In their consultations with host governments, Companies should take all appropriate measures to promote observance of applicable international law enforcement principles, particularly those reflected in the UN Code of Conduct for Law Enforcement Officials and the UN Basic Principles on the Use of Force and Firearms.

. . .

Responses to Human Rights Abuses

Companies should record and report any credible allegations of human rights abuses by public security in their areas of operation to appropriate host government authorities. Where appropriate, Companies should urge investigation and that action be taken to prevent any recurrence.

. . .

The full text of the Voluntary Principles is available here: http://www .voluntaryprinciples.org/wp-content/uploads/2019/12/TheVoluntaryPrinciples. pdf. The Voluntary Principles have been adopted by multinational oil companies including BP, Chevron, ConocoPhillips, ExxonMobil, Shell, and Total. Many multinational corporations have also adopted codes governing other fields of their conduct, such as labor and environmental impact. Why do you think multinational corporations would voluntarily come together to adopt such principles? If you were advising a client, would you recommend adopting these principles?

4. Technical Standards

Technical standards are another example of transnational private norms. The leading producer of global technical standards today is the International Organization for Standardization, known as "ISO." The ISO is an independent, nongovernmental organization. Its members are national standards bodies of more than 160 nations. The members meet annually as a General Assembly to decide the ISO's strategic objectives; a Central Secretariat in Geneva, Switzerland, coordinates the ISO's activities; and specialized technical committees lead the development of the ISO's standards. The technical committees are comprised of experts from industry, NGOs, governments, and other stakeholders. As explained on the ISO's website, the ISO "is the world's largest developer of voluntary International Standards. International Standards give state of the art specifications for products, services and good practice, helping to make industry more efficient and effective. Developed through global consensus, they help to break down barriers to international trade. [. . . The ISO was] founded in 1947, and since then [has] published more than 19,500 International Standards covering almost all aspects of technology and business[, f]rom food safety to computers, and agriculture to healthcare. . . ." *See* http://www.iso.org/iso/home/ about.htm.

The ISO 9000 standards, which cover product quality management, are among the ISO's most widely adopted standards. For example, ISO 9001 provides criteria for quality management systems. According to the ISO, over a million businesses in more than 170 countries have adopted this standard. As explained by the ISO, "[t]he standard is based on a number of quality management principles including a strong customer focus, the motivation and implication of top management, the process approach and continual improvement. . . . An organization must perform internal audits to check how its quality management system is working. An organization may decide to invite an independent certification body to verify that it is in conformity to the standard, but there is no requirement for this. Alternatively, it might invite its clients to audit the quality system for themselves." *See* http://www.iso.org/iso/home/standards/management-standards/ iso_9000.htm.

The ISO 14000 standards address environmental management. For example, ISO 14001 provides criteria for environmental management systems. As the

ISO summarizes, this standard "does not state requirements for environmental performance, but maps out a framework that a company or organization can follow to set up an effective environmental management system. It can be used by any organization regardless of its activity or sector. Using ISO 14001[] can provide assurance to company management and employees as well as external stakeholders that environmental impact is being measured and improved." *See* http://www.iso.org/iso/home/standards/management-standards/iso14000.htm. According to one study, ISO 14001 is the world's most widely adopted voluntary environmental standard, with more than 110,000 facilities from 138 countries having received ISO 14001 certification as of 2005. Aseem Prakash & Matthew Potoski, *The International Organization for Standardization as a Global Governor: A Club Theory Perspective, in* WHO GOVERNS THE GLOBE? 72, 75 (Deborah D. Avant et al. eds., 2010).

NOTES AND QUESTIONS

1. **Private Norms and Choice-of-Law Clauses.** It is unsettled whether or when, under choice-of-law principles, national courts will enforce choice-of-law clauses by which the parties generically select noncodified private substantive norms such as *lex mercatoria* or *trade usages*. Should courts enforce such choice-of-law clauses? Why or why not?

2. **Arbitration and Private Norms.** Occasionally, arbitral tribunals will apply transnational private norms. However, it is unclear whether an arbitral tribunal's reliance on such norms will result in a valid and enforceable arbitral award, at least absent the parties' agreement to have those norms apply. Under what circumstances, if any, should arbitral tribunals apply transnational private norms to resolve disputes between the parties? And when, if ever, should U.S. courts — and courts in general — enforce arbitral awards that are based on an arbitrator's application of transnational private norms?

3. **Practice: Advisability of Selecting Private Norms.** Transnational commercial arbitration expert Gary Born argues that *lex mercatoria* "generally fail[s] to provide predictable results, particularly insofar as complex commercial and corporate affairs are concerned. That is confirmed by the great reluctance of commercial parties to agree to choice-of-law clauses selecting nonnational legal systems and the (over-) fertile debate about the content and basic character of such systems. Given this reluctance, and controversy, arbitral tribunals should be extremely hesitant to impose on commercial parties a legal system that they have generally rejected." GARY B. BORN, INTERNATIONAL COMMERCIAL ARBITRATION 2145 (2009). *See also* Christopher A. Whytock, *Private-Public Interaction in Global Governance: The Case of Transnational Commercial Arbitration*, BUS. & POL., Vol. 12, Issue 3, at 14-15 (2010) (summarizing International Chamber of Commerce data from 2003 to 2008

indicating that parties in arbitrations administered by that institution select national law in approximately 80 percent of disputes, and private sources of substantive law in only a very small fraction of cases). Why is it that multinational businesses appear to prefer national law over private norms in their contractual choice-of-law provisions? On the other hand, what might be some of the advantages of selecting private norms in transnational business?

4. **Practice: Avoiding Private Norms.** If your client is entering a contract with another party to govern a cross-border business transaction and, after consultation with your client, you determine that it would be a bad idea to have a court or arbitrator apply transnational private norms to resolve a dispute that might arise out of that transaction, what would you do to minimize the likelihood that such norms would be applied? Suppose there is a set of private rules available for a type of transaction (such as the UCP for letters of credit) but the particular contract in dispute makes no reference to them. How would you argue that the private norm might have relevance to the dispute? How would you argue that it does not?

5. **Practice: Advice Regarding Codes of Conduct.** Why do multinational corporations adopt codes of conduct? If you were advising a multinational corporation, would you recommend that it adopt a code of conduct for its business? What are the advantages and disadvantages of corporate codes of conduct from the perspective of multinational corporations? From the perspective of shareholders? From the perspective of advocates for human rights, fair labor practices, and environmental protection? One unsettled question is the extent to which compliance or noncompliance with corporate codes of conduct may have legal consequences. What do you think? As a lawyer representing a party that has been injured by a corporate act or omission that violated a code of corporate conduct, how might you use the code of conduct in your arguments? How would you expect the corporation's lawyers to respond?

6. **Practice: Helping Clients Draft Codes of Conduct.** Corporations often call on lawyers to help them design and draft codes of global corporate conduct. What considerations would you keep in mind when advising a client on such matters?

7. **Reasons for Technical Standards.** Why do you think corporations adopt technical standards produced by organizations such as the ISO? Once they adopt them, why do they follow them, even though they are not legally binding?

8. **Enforcement and Influence.** Overall, is it plausible to conclude that both nonbinding norms and private norms can influence transnational activity in important ways, even when they are not judicially enforceable? If so, what are the implications of this conclusion for the impact of international law on the behavior of nations and other transnational activity? If nonbinding and private norms affect behavior, does that make us more likely to conclude that international law also affects behavior? Why or why not?

REVIEW NOTES AND QUESTIONS

1. In what contexts are you as a lawyer likely to encounter and use nonbinding norms and private norms when you represent your clients? How would you explain to a client the significance (or lack of significance) of a nonbinding norm applicable to that client's operations or disputes?
2. Why do nations and private actors create nonbinding norms in the first place, and why do private actors develop private norms, contractually enforceable or otherwise, instead of relying on national law and international law?
3. What explains the influence that nonbinding and private norms have on transnational activity?

PART II

HOW CAN TRANSNATIONAL DISPUTES BE RESOLVED?

Part II examines where transnational disputes can be resolved. There are three basic options. First, national courts — the courts of individual sovereign nations — routinely resolve transnational disputes, even those involving parties and events in multiple countries. From a U.S. perspective, these national courts may be either domestic courts (U.S. state or federal courts) or foreign courts (such as the courts of Canada or Mexico). Second, there are international courts and dispute resolution bodies (such as the International Criminal Court or the World Trade Organization) that can resolve some transnational disputes, but they have very limited jurisdiction and cannot hear most claims between private parties. Third, a widely used alternative to litigation in national or international courts for parties seeking to resolve transnational disputes is arbitration or related methods of nonjudicial dispute resolution. Of course, many disputes are not addressed by courts or court-like entities at all, but are resolved among the parties themselves by settlement or other private means. But settlements and other private remedies typically occur in the shadow of the law — that is, against a backdrop of potential judicial or arbitral resolution — because when disputants make settlement decisions, they ordinarily take into account how their dispute would be resolved *if* it went to litigation or arbitration.

Which of these dispute resolution options are available, and which is most appropriate, for a particular transnational dispute? These are some of the most important questions in transnational practice. The process of answering them is sometimes called "forum selection" or (more negatively) "forum shopping." Even in purely domestic U.S. law and practice, forum selection is exceedingly

[handwritten margin notes: 3 options. 1. national courts 2. int'l courts & dr bodies 3. alternatives — other: settlement or other private means — forum selection]

379

important. For example, should the dispute be resolved in state or federal court? The principles of subject matter jurisdiction help determine whether a federal court is an available option. Assuming the federal courts have subject matter jurisdiction, would a federal court be more favorable for your client than a state court, strategically or otherwise? In which states would a state or federal court be authorized to resolve the dispute? The principles of personal jurisdiction help answer that question. Assuming there is personal jurisdiction in multiple states, which state would be most favorable for your client? And what about alternatives to litigation, such as arbitration or mediation? Might one of those methods be more favorable for your client than litigating in state or federal court?

These issues can be even more complex and important in the context of transnational legal problems. The available courts may include not only U.S. state or federal courts, but also foreign courts and international courts. If more than one nation's courts are available, which is likely to be most favorable for your client? For example, in a dispute involving persons, property, or activity with connections to both California and Japan, should your client choose to file the case in California or Japan? Because procedural, legal, cultural, and political differences across nations are often much more significant than across U.S. states, the stakes are often higher than in purely domestic practice. Or, should your client opt for an international court, if one is available with jurisdiction over the dispute? Dispute resolution in international courts operates differently — sometimes very differently — than litigation in national courts. But in some cases, they might be more appropriate for your client than a national court. Or, should the disputants opt for an alternative to litigation, such as negotiation, mediation, or arbitration, to resolve their dispute? The outcomes of disputes often depend on where and how they are resolved. Therefore, these are very important questions in transnational practice.

Importantly, these questions arise both before and after disputes arise. Thus, forum selection is important for both transactional lawyers and litigators. When negotiating an agreement to govern a transnational relationship — say, a business agreement between a U.S. company and a Chinese company — the parties may decide in advance how disputes that arise in the course of the relationship will be resolved, and they indicate their choice in a dispute resolution clause in their agreement. But often disputes arise outside the context of a preexisting dispute resolution agreement. In those cases, it may be difficult for the parties to agree on a forum to resolve their dispute, because one forum may be more favorable to one party and another forum more favorable to the other party.

Part II of this casebook has two goals. The first is to help you understand the different ways that transnational disputes can be resolved, including national courts (such as U.S. state or federal courts or the courts of foreign nations), international courts, and alternative dispute resolution methods like mediation and arbitration. The second is to help you learn the principles that lawyers and judges use to determine which dispute resolution options are available. To pursue these goals, Part II is divided into three chapters. Chapter 4 focuses on national courts' jurisdiction to resolve transnational disputes, with an emphasis on transnational litigation in U.S. courts. Chapter 5 investigates international courts. It focuses on the International Court of Justice (ICJ), but also introduces you to a variety of other international dispute resolution bodies. Chapter 6 introduces you to alternatives to litigation in national or international dispute resolution bodies, with an emphasis on arbitration as a method for resolving transnational disputes.

One might expect litigation in international courts to be the primary forum for transnational disputes. But as this part illustrates, that is not the case. The jurisdiction of international courts is very limited. Most transnational disputes are instead resolved in national courts or through alternative methods of dispute resolution such as negotiation, mediation, or arbitration. Therefore, just as it is important not to be international law–centric, it is essential not to be international court–centric when facing transnational legal problems.

Take note: The issue of *what law* governs transnational activity is separate from the issue of *what forum* can resolve a transnational dispute. Even if a transnational dispute is resolved in a U.S. court, that court may apply a foreign nation's law. However, these two issues can be closely related. For example, as discussed in Chapter 1, a national court generally applies its own choice-of-law principles to determine whether to apply domestic or foreign law. Therefore, when seeking out the jurisdiction that is most likely to apply the law that your client prefers, you must ask not only what that jurisdiction's substantive law is, but also what its choice-of-law principles are. After all, even if a particular jurisdiction's substantive law is most favorable for your client, you won't get the advantage of that law if, based on that jurisdiction's choice-of-law principles, a court there would apply the law of another jurisdiction with less favorable substantive law. Therefore, it is very important to analyze a forum's choice-of-law principles to determine how the choice of that forum may ultimately affect what law would be applied to resolve your client's dispute.

When determining how to resolve a transnational dispute, the stakes are considerable for both client counseling and international relations. In client counseling, often two or more dispute resolution options may be potentially available, one of which may be more favorable to your client than the others — but if you do not understand how these options differ and how to determine which of them are available, you will be unable to give your client sound advice. Beyond client counseling, nations themselves may care about how transnational disputes are resolved. One way that nations regulate transnational activity is by adjudicating disputes arising out of that activity. Therefore, whether a nation's courts are able to adjudicate transnational disputes affects its ability to project regulatory power in the world. When more than one nation's courts attempt to adjudicate a dispute, the result can be international conflict. One way that nations may try to avoid this type of conflict is by creating international law to govern the resolution of transnational disputes. You are encouraged to keep these stakes in mind as you work through the materials that follow.

CHAPTER 4

NATIONAL COURTS

As this is a book on transnational law and practice, your first reaction may be that national courts are unlikely places to resolve disputes involving persons, entities, laws, and events in many different countries. In practice, however, the vast majority of transnational disputes (especially private disputes) that are not resolved through arbitration or other nonjudicial methods are resolved in national courts — whether domestic or foreign.

If national courts are an important forum for resolving transnational disputes, a core question is raised: *which* courts? In the United States, we are familiar with this question of forum selection even in the context of purely domestic disputes. The United States has both U.S. federal courts and a separate system of state courts in each of the 50 U.S. states (plus the courts of the District of Columbia and a number of U.S. territories). Many issues that arise in a basic U.S. course on federal civil procedure relate to this question, especially personal jurisdiction, venue, and federal subject matter jurisdiction. For instance, if a Virginia plaintiff is injured in Virginia by a California corporation, the plaintiff must choose whether to bring suit in state or federal court and whether to bring suit in Virginia or California. Extensive litigation may ensue at the very beginning of a case as the defendant contests the plaintiff's choice of forum.

Transnational litigation presents many similar issues, but the stakes are greatly magnified. In particular cases, the question whether a dispute is resolved in Virginia, New York, or California may matter considerably, but for the most part, regardless of the domestic choice of forum, the parties will face a similar legal system. When the choice is between courts in the United States and courts in other nations, however, the differences may be startling. Some of these differences are discussed in the Introduction to this casebook. For example, there may be procedural differences. U.S. litigants abroad may find that what they assume to be basic ingredients of judicial procedure are unavailable, and foreign litigants in U.S. courts may encounter a litigation process quite unlike anything with which they are familiar. To pick a few examples, jury trials, access to broad party-driven discovery, class actions, and contingency fees are common features of U.S. litigation that may not exist elsewhere. In addition, in the United States, the ordinary rule is that each party pays its own attorneys' fees (known as the "American rule"), whereas in many other nations the losing party is responsible for the other party's attorneys' fees (the "English rule"). There also may be differences in substantive law. For example, strict liability and punitive damages are common in the United States, but less so in many other nations.

The conventional wisdom has been that these differences tend to make the United States a particularly attractive forum for plaintiffs. But there are reasons to question whether this is still the case to the extent it may once have been. As explained in Chapter 1, a court in the United States will not necessarily apply U.S. substantive law because choice-of-law principles may direct the court to apply the substantive law of another nation. This means that filing a suit in the United States is not necessarily an effective way of obtaining U.S. substantive law (although a U.S. court will still apply U.S. procedural law, which may be more favorable to the plaintiff). Moreover, there is evidence that some features of the U.S. legal system are spreading to other nations, such as contingency fees, punitive damages, and class actions. *See* Marcus S. Quintanilla & Christopher A. Whytock, *The New Multipolarity in Transnational Litigation: Foreign Courts, Foreign Judgments, and Foreign Law*, 18 Sw. J. Int'l L. 31 (2011). But the point remains that when making forum selection choices on behalf of a client, it is very important to research and analyze differences in procedural and substantive law between potentially available jurisdictions. Otherwise, you will be unable to provide sound advice about which forum choice will be best for your client.

There are other important forum selection considerations, too. Depending on the nation, foreign legal systems may be much faster or much slower in reaching results. And the practical difficulty of litigating in a foreign nation and in a foreign language amid unfamiliar customs should not be underestimated. As a result, questions that might seem mere technicalities in domestic litigation (such as, should the case be heard in California or Virginia) take on an entirely different significance in transnational disputes, where the question may be: Should the case be heard in California, Virginia, or China? For these reasons, U.S. parties may prefer to litigate in U.S. courts instead of foreign courts, and foreign parties may prefer to litigate in their own nation's courts.

But in order for a party to take advantage of its preferred forum, that forum must be available to resolve the dispute. Many factors affect which nations' courts (if any) are available to hear a case. This chapter focuses on jurisdiction, which must be addressed as a threshold question when determining whether a particular court is available. (Other doctrines that may cause a court to dismiss a transnational case even though it has jurisdiction are discussed in later chapters.) From a transnational perspective, jurisdiction is principally a question of jurisdiction over the parties — what in the United States is called personal jurisdiction, and which may also be called jurisdiction to adjudicate or judicial jurisdiction in other countries. Most developed legal systems have the basic concept that a party having no material connection to the place where the court sits should not be required to litigate there. However, nations have very different views as to what constitutes a sufficient connection to the place.

The conventional belief is that the United States is generally more permissive in establishing personal jurisdiction than many other major legal systems, a circumstance that may give rise to significant tensions and complications in transnational litigation. This belief may also encourage both U.S. and foreign plaintiffs to file cases in the United States in hopes of finding court access there. However, as this chapter shows, recent U.S. Supreme Court cases have narrowed the scope of personal jurisdiction significantly in transnational cases. Moreover, as Chapters 10, 11, and 12 explain, there are a variety of other legal doctrines that U.S. courts can use to dismiss transnational suits even when jurisdiction has been established. These factors — as well as empirical evidence indicating a decline in certain types of transnational litigation in U.S. courts generally — suggest that U.S. courts may no longer be as open to transnational disputes as they once were. *See* Donald Earl Childress III, *Escaping Federal Law in Transnational Cases: The Brave New World of Transnational Litigation*, 93 N.C. L. REV. 995 (2015); Christopher A. Whytock, *The Evolving Forum Shopping System*, 96 CORNELL L. REV. 481 (2011). Nevertheless, U.S. courts continue to resolve a large number of transnational suits each year, and thus their approach to transnational adjudication is worthy of consideration.

This chapter begins by examining personal jurisdiction in U.S. courts with an emphasis on transnational concerns and then gives a comparative perspective. Much of it will reinforce subjects you may have learned in a course on civil procedure, although in other respects it goes far beyond that basic material. Remember to focus on the *transnational* context in what follows. Consider the following overarching question: Why might it be so important to the plaintiff that the case be heard in the United States (and so important to the defendant that it *not* be heard in the United States)? Does this focus give a different perspective on familiar doctrines of personal jurisdiction? How is the potential availability or unavailability of personal jurisdiction in the United States or elsewhere likely to affect the parties' conduct?

This chapter also includes a brief discussion of subject matter jurisdiction in the United States from a transnational perspective. In domestic U.S. litigation, substantial energy and resources are devoted to litigating federal courts' subject matter jurisdiction. U.S. federal courts have limited subject matter jurisdiction, both by federal statute and as a matter of Article III of the U.S. Constitution. Typically, if personal jurisdiction in the United States is established but federal courts lack subject matter jurisdiction, the case can be heard in a U.S. state court. U.S. state courts are courts of general jurisdiction, meaning that they can hear any disputes involving parties over whom they have personal jurisdiction. Thus the question of subject matter jurisdiction in the United States usually involves a choice *within* the U.S. legal system. Nonetheless, there are some difficult and unique issues of subject matter jurisdiction that arise in the transnational context and so are discussed here.

A. Personal Jurisdiction in Transnational Cases

Personal jurisdiction is fundamentally about *where* a defendant can be sued. (A plaintiff typically is understood to consent to the court's jurisdiction by filing the suit.) For the most part, defendants can be sued where they are domiciled (if they are individuals) or where they are incorporated or have their principal place of business (if they are corporations or other entities). There may be other considerations, like convenience, that encourage a court to transfer or dismiss a case brought where the defendant is "at home," but simply as a threshold matter, showing that the defendant's home is where the court is should be sufficient to establish personal jurisdiction, both in the United States and (generally) elsewhere. Once it is established where the defendant is at home, courts in that place have personal jurisdiction to hear all claims against that defendant, even if the claims arose elsewhere and even if the plaintiff is located elsewhere. Thus a corporation incorporated in New York can be sued in New York (either in state or federal court, depending on questions of subject matter jurisdiction and venue), even by, for example, a French plaintiff for events that occurred in Germany. This is called *general jurisdiction* (because the court has jurisdiction generally as to all claims against the defendant).

Another way to establish personal jurisdiction is to show that events on which the claim is based occurred where the court is located and arise out of or are related to a defendant's contacts with the forum. The idea is that if a defendant comes into a place and injures someone, the defendant should not be able to escape the courts of that place simply by going home. Thus, if a French corporation injures a German citizen in New York, the New York courts (state or federal) will usually have personal jurisdiction over the French corporation for a claim that arises out of or relates to that injury even though neither party's home is New York. This is called *specific jurisdiction* (because the court has jurisdiction over the specific claims against the defendant although it does not have personal jurisdiction over the defendant generally).

While the basic ideas of specific and general jurisdiction are widely accepted, there are many difficulties in application that are explored below. In addition, personal jurisdiction may be established in other, more controversial ways. Suppose, for example, a French corporation has no direct presence or operations in the United States, but it has a subsidiary or affiliate that operates in New York. Can the company be sued in New York based on the presence of its subsidiary or affiliate? In transnational business disputes, this question is often of great importance because so many transnational companies operate through subsidiaries. In addition, the United States, unlike most other countries, recognizes so-called tag jurisdiction, by which an individual can be subject to general jurisdiction wherever the individual is found (even temporarily) if the individual can be served with process in that place.

The following subsections take up these and related questions of personal jurisdiction in a transnational context. As you consider them, keep several things in mind. First, notice how intensely territorial this subject is. The question is whether there are enough contacts with the territory of a place — the forum state — to justify the courts of that place taking jurisdiction. Second, nations may have very different ideas of how many contacts and what kinds of contacts are sufficient contacts. Third, remember that the consequences of finding no personal jurisdiction may be not just that the suit must be re-filed in another place, but that the suit must be litigated in an entirely different legal system.

1. *General Jurisdiction*

A plaintiff in a transnational case might prefer to sue a defendant in a forum where there is general jurisdiction (assuming that forum also maximizes the chances of recovery), because the forum court would be able to hear any and all claims against the defendant. When a defendant's "home" (individual or corporate) is in a U.S state, the general jurisdiction inquiry is relatively straightforward. For instance, if a Virginia resident commits a tort anywhere in the world, she is subject to general jurisdiction for any and all claims against her in Virginia. Likewise, if a Virginia corporation commits a tort anywhere in the world, there is general jurisdiction in Virginia. Virginia courts (state or federal) may thus hear all claims against these Virginians, even if those claims involve foreign facts and foreign law, and even if the harm complained of occurred abroad.

The question becomes considerably more complex when the defendant is not domiciled (if an individual) or incorporated and does not have its principal place of business (if a corporation) in the forum state. The U.S. Supreme Court established in *Perkins v. Benguet Mining Co.*, 342 U.S. 437 (1952), that general jurisdiction also exists in a forum where a defendant has "continuous and systematic" contacts. Thus, even if a corporation is incorporated and has its principal place of business in (for example) France, it still may be subject to personal jurisdiction in one of the U.S. states for all claims against it if it has "continuous and systematic" contacts with the forum state. Note the practical importance of general jurisdiction for a foreign defendant: If there is general jurisdiction over the French corporation in one of the U.S. states, then the courts of that state (state or federal) may hear all claims against that defendant, even when those claims involve completely foreign facts and foreign law, and even where the alleged harms occurred abroad (subject to doctrines such as *forum non conveniens*, as discussed in Chapter 10). The cases that follow explore the Supreme Court's current approach to assertions of general jurisdiction based on "continuous and systematic" contacts.

As you read the material below, be sure to note the discussion of specific jurisdiction and how it differs from general jurisdiction, as this will prepare you for more complete treatment of specific jurisdiction in the sections that follow.

Goodyear Dunlop Tires Operations, S.A. v. Brown

564 U.S. 915 (2011)

Justice GINSBURG delivered the opinion of the Court.

This case concerns the jurisdiction of state courts over corporations organized and operating abroad. We address, in particular, this question: Are foreign subsidiaries of a United States parent corporation amenable to suit in state court on claims unrelated to any activity of the subsidiaries in the forum State?

A bus accident outside Paris that took the lives of two 13-year-old boys from North Carolina gave rise to the litigation we here consider. Attributing the accident to a defective tire manufactured in Turkey at the plant of a foreign subsidiary of The Goodyear Tire and Rubber Company (Goodyear USA), the boys' parents commenced an action for damages in a North Carolina state court; they named as defendants Goodyear USA, an Ohio corporation, and three of its subsidiaries, organized and operating, respectively, in Turkey, France, and Luxembourg. Goodyear USA, which had plants in North Carolina and regularly engaged in commercial activity there, did not contest the North Carolina court's jurisdiction over it; Goodyear USA's foreign subsidiaries, however, maintained that North Carolina lacked adjudicatory authority over them.

A state court's assertion of jurisdiction exposes defendants to the State's coercive power, and is therefore subject to review for compatibility with the Fourteenth Amendment's Due Process Clause. *International Shoe Co. v. Washington*, 326 U.S. 310, 316 (1945). Opinions in the wake of the pathmarking *International Shoe* decision have differentiated between general or all-purpose jurisdiction, and specific or case-linked jurisdiction. *Helicopteros Nacionales de Colombia, S.A. v. Hall*, 466 U.S. 408, 414, nn. 8, 9 (1984).

A court may assert general jurisdiction over foreign (sister-state or foreign-country) corporations to hear any and all claims against them when their affiliations with the State are so "continuous and systematic" as to render them essentially at home in the forum State. . . . In contrast to general, all-purpose jurisdiction, specific jurisdiction is confined to adjudication of issues deriving from, or connected with, the very controversy that establishes jurisdiction.

Because the episode-in-suit, the bus accident, occurred in France, and the tire alleged to have caused the accident was manufactured and sold abroad, North Carolina courts lacked specific jurisdiction to adjudicate the controversy. . . . Were the foreign subsidiaries nonetheless amenable to general jurisdiction in North Carolina courts? Confusing or blending general and specific jurisdictional inquiries, the North Carolina courts answered yes. Some of the tires made abroad by Goodyear's foreign subsidiaries, the North Carolina Court of Appeals stressed, had reached North Carolina through "the stream of commerce"; that connection, the Court of Appeals believed, gave North Carolina courts the handle needed for the exercise of general jurisdiction over the foreign corporations.

A connection so limited between the forum and the foreign corporation, we hold, is an inadequate basis for the exercise of general jurisdiction. Such a connection does not establish the "continuous and systematic" affiliation necessary to empower North Carolina courts to entertain claims unrelated to the foreign corporation's contacts with the State.

I

On April 18, 2004, a bus destined for Charles de Gaulle Airport overturned on a road outside Paris, France. Passengers on the bus were young soccer players from North Carolina beginning their journey home. Two 13-year-olds, Julian Brown and Matthew Helms, sustained fatal injuries. The boys' parents, respondents in this Court, filed a suit for wrongful-death damages in the Superior Court of Onslow County, North Carolina, in their capacity as administrators of the boys' estates. Attributing the accident to a tire that failed when its plies separated, the parents alleged negligence in the "design, construction, testing, and inspection" of the tire.

In contrast to the parent company, Goodyear USA, which does not contest the North Carolina courts' personal jurisdiction over it, petitioners [Goodyear Luxembourg Tires, SA (Goodyear Luxembourg), Goodyear Lastikleri T.A.S. (Goodyear Turkey), and Goodyear Dunlop Tires France, SA (Goodyear France)], are not registered to do business in North Carolina. They have no place of business, employees, or bank accounts in North Carolina. They do not design, manufacture, or advertise their products in North Carolina. And they do not solicit business in North Carolina or themselves sell or ship tires to North Carolina customers. Even so, a small percentage of petitioners' tires (tens of thousands out of tens of millions manufactured between 2004 and 2007) were distributed within North Carolina by other Goodyear USA affiliates. These tires were typically custom ordered to equip specialized vehicles such as cement mixers, waste haulers, and boat and horse trailers. Petitioners state, and respondents do not here deny, that the type of tire involved in the accident, a Goodyear Regional RHS tire manufactured by Goodyear Turkey, was never distributed in North Carolina.

Petitioners moved to dismiss the claims against them for want of personal jurisdiction. The trial court denied the motion, and the North Carolina Court of Appeals affirmed. Acknowledging that the claims neither "related to, nor . . . ar[o]se from, [petitioners'] contacts with North Carolina," the Court of Appeals confined its analysis to "general rather than specific jurisdiction," which the court recognized required a "higher threshold" showing: A defendant must have "continuous and systematic contacts" with the forum. That threshold was crossed, the court determined, when petitioners placed their tires "in the stream of interstate commerce without any limitation on the extent to which those tires could be sold in North Carolina."

Nothing in the record, the court observed, indicated that petitioners "took any affirmative action to cause tires which they had manufactured to be shipped into North Carolina." The court found, however, that tires made by petitioners reached North Carolina as a consequence of a "highly-organized distribution process" involving other Goodyear USA subsidiaries. Petitioners, the court noted, made "no attempt to keep these tires from reaching the North Carolina market." Indeed, the very tire involved in the accident, the court observed, conformed to tire standards established by the U.S. Department of Transportation and bore markings required for sale in the United States. As further support, the court invoked North Carolina's "interest in providing a forum in which its citizens are able to seek redress for [their] injuries," and noted the hardship North Carolina plaintiffs would experience "[were they] required to litigate their claims in France," a country to which they have no ties. The North Carolina Supreme Court denied discretionary review.

We granted certiorari to decide whether the general jurisdiction the North Carolina courts asserted over petitioners is consistent with the Due Process Clause of the Fourteenth Amendment.

II

A

The Due Process Clause of the Fourteenth Amendment sets the outer boundaries of a state tribunal's authority to proceed against a defendant. The canonical opinion in this area remains *International Shoe*, 326 U.S. 310, in which we held that a State may authorize its courts to exercise personal jurisdiction over an out-of-state defendant if the defendant has "certain minimum contacts with [the State] such that the maintenance of the suit does not offend traditional notions of fair play and substantial justice." *Id.*, at 316.

. . .

International Shoe distinguished from cases that fit within the "specific jurisdiction" categories, "instances in which the continuous corporate operations within a state [are] so substantial and of such a nature as to justify suit against it on causes of action arising from dealings entirely distinct from those activities." 326 U.S., at 318. Adjudicatory authority so grounded is today called "general jurisdiction." *Helicopteros*, 466 U.S., at 414, n. 9. For an individual, the paradigm forum for the exercise of general jurisdiction is the individual's domicile; for a corporation, it is an equivalent place, one in which the corporation is fairly regarded as at home. See [Brilmayer et al., A General Look at General Jurisdiction, 66 Tex. L. Rev. 721,] 728 (identifying domicile, place of incorporation, and principal place of business as "paradig[m]" bases for the exercise of general jurisdiction).

Since *International Shoe*, this Court's decisions have elaborated primarily on circumstances that warrant the exercise of specific jurisdiction, particularly in cases involving "single or occasional acts" occurring or having their impact within the forum State. As a rule in these cases, this Court has inquired whether there was "some act by which the defendant purposefully avail[ed] itself of the privilege of conducting activities within the forum State, thus invoking the benefits and protections of its laws." *Hanson v. Denckla*, 357 U.S. 235 (1958). . . .

In only two decisions postdating *International Shoe* has this Court considered whether an out-of-state corporate defendant's in-state contacts were sufficiently "continuous and systematic" to justify the exercise of general jurisdiction over claims unrelated to those contacts: *Perkins* and *Helicopteros*.

B

To justify the exercise of general jurisdiction over petitioners, the North Carolina courts relied on the petitioners' placement of their tires in the "stream of commerce." The stream-of-commerce metaphor has been invoked frequently in lower court decisions. . . . Typically, in such cases, a nonresident defendant, acting *outside* the forum, places in the stream of commerce a product that ultimately causes harm *inside* the forum.

. . .

The North Carolina court's stream-of-commerce analysis elided the essential difference between case-specific and all-purpose (general) jurisdiction. Flow of a manufacturer's products into the forum, we have explained, may bolster an affiliation germane to *specific* jurisdiction. But ties serving to bolster the exercise of specific jurisdiction do not warrant a determination that, based on those ties, the forum has *general* jurisdiction over a defendant. . . .

A corporation's "continuous activity of some sorts within a state," *International Shoe* instructed, "is not enough to support the demand that the corporation be amenable to suits unrelated to that activity." 326 U.S., at 318. Our 1952 decision in *Perkins v. Benguet Consol. Mining Co.* remains the textbook case of general jurisdiction appropriately exercised over a foreign corporation that has not consented to suit in the forum.

Sued in Ohio, the defendant in *Perkins* was a Philippine mining corporation that had ceased activities in the Philippines during World War II. To the extent that the company was conducting any business during and immediately after the Japanese occupation of the Philippines, it was doing so in Ohio: the corporation's president maintained his office there, kept the company files in that office, and supervised from the Ohio office "the necessarily limited wartime activities of the company." *Perkins*, 342 U.S., at 447-448. Although the claim-in-suit did not arise in Ohio, this Court ruled that it would not violate due process for Ohio to adjudicate the controversy.

We next addressed the exercise of general jurisdiction over an out-of-state corporation over three decades later, in *Helicopteros*. In that case, survivors of United States citizens who died in a helicopter crash in Peru instituted wrongful-death actions in a Texas state court against the owner and operator of the helicopter, a Colombian corporation. The Colombian corporation had no place of business in Texas and was not licensed to do business there. "Basically, [the company's] contacts with Texas consisted of sending its chief executive officer to Houston for a contract-negotiation session; accepting into its New York bank account checks drawn on a Houston bank; purchasing helicopters, equipment, and training services from [a Texas enterprise] for substantial sums; and sending personnel to [Texas] for training." 466 U.S., at 416. These links to Texas, we determined, did not "constitute the kind of continuous and systematic general business contacts . . . found to exist in *Perkins*," and were insufficient to support the exercise of jurisdiction over a claim that neither "ar[o]se out of . . . no[r] related to" the defendant's activities in Texas. *Id.*, at 415-416.

Helicopteros concluded that "mere purchases [made in the forum State], even if occurring at regular intervals, are not enough to warrant a State's assertion of [general] jurisdiction over a nonresident corporation in a cause of action not related to those purchase transactions." *Id.*, at 418. We see no reason to differentiate from the ties to Texas held insufficient in *Helicopteros*, the sales of petitioners' tires sporadically made in North Carolina through intermediaries. Under the sprawling view of general jurisdiction urged by respondents and embraced by the

North Carolina Court of Appeals, any substantial manufacturer or seller of goods would be amenable to suit, on any claim for relief, wherever its products are distributed.

Measured against *Helicopteros* and *Perkins*, North Carolina is not a forum in which it would be permissible to subject petitioners to general jurisdiction. Unlike the defendant in *Perkins*, whose sole wartime business activity was conducted in Ohio, petitioners are in no sense at home in North Carolina. Their attenuated connections to the State fall far short of the "the continuous and systematic general business contacts" necessary to empower North Carolina to entertain suit against them on claims unrelated to anything that connects them to the State. *Helicopteros*, 466 U.S., at 416.

C

Respondents belatedly assert a "single enterprise" theory, asking us to consolidate petitioners' ties to North Carolina with those of Goodyear USA and other Goodyear entities. Neither below nor in their brief in opposition to the petition for certiorari did respondents urge disregard of petitioners' discrete status as subsidiaries and treatment of all Goodyear entities as a "unitary business," so that jurisdiction over the parent would draw in the subsidiaries as well. Respondents have therefore forfeited this contention, and we do not address it.

For the reasons stated, the judgment of the North Carolina Court of Appeals is Reversed.

NOTES AND QUESTIONS

1. **Practice: Forum Selection.** Why do you think the plaintiff sued in North Carolina rather than in France? Would there likely have been personal jurisdiction in France? A defendant can consent to personal jurisdiction by failing to challenge it in a 12(b) motion. Why do you think the foreign defendants fought against litigation in North Carolina? Why do you think they preferred that the case be heard in a court outside North Carolina and outside the United States? Why didn't Goodyear USA also object to personal jurisdiction in North Carolina? If the *Goodyear* Court's view of general jurisdiction had been articulated before the plaintiffs had filed in North Carolina, would Goodyear USA be subject to general jurisdiction in North Carolina? Why would the North Carolina court be inclined to find general jurisdiction? Do you think other state courts would have found general jurisdiction?

2. **A New Test for General Jurisdiction?** According to the court in *Goodyear*, what is the test for determining whether there is general jurisdiction over a defendant in a particular state? Is there a difference between being "essentially at home" in and having "continuous and systematic contacts" with a forum state? What does it mean for a U.S. corporate defendant to be "at home"? Is

a U.S. company like Wal-Mart subject to jurisdiction in every state? What does it mean for a foreign corporate defendant to be "at home" in the United States? Is there/should there be a difference? Why does the Court include the "at home" language at all? Why do you think the Court didn't simply hold that a corporation is only subject to general jurisdiction in its state of incorporation or principal place of business? Note that in *Daimler AG v. Bauman*, a 2014 decision reprinted below, the Supreme Court clarified that "*Goodyear* did not hold that a corporation may be subject to general jurisdiction only in a forum where it is incorporated or has its principal place of business; it simply typed those places as paradigm all-purpose forums" where a corporation has contacts that are so continuous and systematic as to render it essential at home. Under what circumstances might there be such contacts outside the "paradigm all-purpose forums"?

3. **General versus Specific Jurisdiction.** Note the unique twist of the North Carolina state courts' jurisdictional analysis: It blended the stream of commerce theory (discussed in the next section), which is applicable in the specific jurisdiction context, with general jurisdiction. Is this case only about rejecting that analysis, or does it go beyond mere error correction?

4. **Policy: What Role for General Jurisdiction?** Reading between the lines, it may seem that the current Supreme Court wishes to constrict general jurisdiction. If so, what might be the rationale for this? On the other hand, what reasons might there be to preserve a broad approach to general jurisdiction? What doctrinal and practical reasons can you identify? Why might lower courts be resistant to restricting general jurisdiction?

Daimler AG v. Bauman

571 U.S. 117 (2014)

Justice GINSBURG delivered the opinion of the Court.

This case concerns the authority of a court in the United States to entertain a claim brought by foreign plaintiffs against a foreign defendant based on events occurring entirely outside the United States. The litigation commenced in 2004, when twenty-two Argentinian residents filed a complaint in the United States District Court for the Northern District of California against DaimlerChrysler Aktiengesellschaft (Daimler), a German public stock company, headquartered in Stuttgart, that manufactures Mercedes-Benz vehicles in Germany. The complaint alleged that during Argentina's 1976-1983 "Dirty War," Daimler's Argentinian subsidiary, Mercedes-Benz Argentina (MB Argentina) collaborated with state security forces to kidnap, detain, torture, and kill certain MB Argentina workers, among them, plaintiffs or persons closely related to plaintiffs. Damages for the alleged human-rights violations were sought from Daimler under the laws of the United States, California, and Argentina. Jurisdiction over the lawsuit was predicated on the California contacts of Mercedes-Benz USA, LLC (MBUSA), a subsidiary of

Daimler incorporated in Delaware with its principal place of business in New Jersey. MBUSA distributes Daimler-manufactured vehicles to independent dealerships throughout the United States, including California.

The question presented is whether the Due Process Clause of the Fourteenth Amendment precludes the District Court from exercising jurisdiction over Daimler in this case, given the absence of any California connection to the atrocities, perpetrators, or victims described in the complaint. Plaintiffs invoked the court's general or all-purpose jurisdiction. California, they urge, is a place where Daimler may be sued on any and all claims against it, wherever in the world the claims may arise. For example, as plaintiffs' counsel affirmed, under the proffered jurisdictional theory, if a Daimler-manufactured vehicle overturned in Poland, injuring a Polish driver and passenger, the injured parties could maintain a design defect suit in California. Exercises of personal jurisdiction so exorbitant, we hold, are barred by due process constraints on the assertion of adjudicatory authority.

In *Goodyear Dunlop Tires Operations, S.A. v. Brown*, 131 S. Ct. 2846 (2011), we addressed the distinction between general or all-purpose jurisdiction, and specific or conduct-linked jurisdiction. As to the former, we held that a court may assert jurisdiction over a foreign corporation "to hear any and all claims against [it]" only when the corporation's affiliations with the State in which suit is brought are so constant and pervasive "as to render [it] essentially at home in the forum State." *Id.*, at 2851. Instructed by *Goodyear*, we conclude Daimler is not "at home" in California, and cannot be sued there for injuries plaintiffs attribute to MB Argentina's conduct in Argentina.

I

In 2004, plaintiffs (respondents here) filed suit in the United States District Court for the Northern District of California, alleging that MB Argentina collaborated with Argentinian state security forces to kidnap, detain, torture, and kill plaintiffs and their relatives during the military dictatorship in place there from 1976 through 1983, a period known as Argentina's "Dirty War." Based on those allegations, plaintiffs asserted claims under the Alien Tort Statute, 28 U.S.C. § 1350, and the Torture Victim Protection Act of 1991, 106 Stat. 73, note following 28 U.S.C. § 1350, as well as claims for wrongful death and intentional infliction of emotional distress under the laws of California and Argentina. The incidents recounted in the complaint center on MB Argentina's plant in Gonzalez Catan, Argentina; no part of MB Argentina's alleged collaboration with Argentinian authorities took place in California or anywhere else in the United States.

Plaintiffs' operative complaint names only one corporate defendant: Daimler, the petitioner here. Plaintiffs seek to hold Daimler vicariously liable for MB Argentina's alleged malfeasance. Daimler is a German Aktiengesellschaft (public stock company) that manufactures Mercedes-Benz vehicles in Germany and has its headquarters in Stuttgart. At times relevant to this case, MB Argentina was a subsidiary wholly owned by Daimler's predecessor in interest.

Daimler moved to dismiss the action for want of personal jurisdiction. Opposing the motion, plaintiffs submitted declarations and exhibits purporting to demonstrate the presence of Daimler itself in California. Alternatively, plaintiffs maintained that jurisdiction over Daimler could be founded on the California contacts of MBUSA, a distinct corporate entity that, according to plaintiffs, should be treated as Daimler's agent for jurisdictional purposes.

MBUSA, an indirect subsidiary of Daimler, is a Delaware limited liability corporation. MBUSA serves as Daimler's exclusive importer and distributor in the United States, purchasing Mercedes-Benz automobiles from Daimler in Germany, then importing those vehicles, and ultimately distributing them to independent dealerships located throughout the Nation. Although MBUSA's principal place of business is in New Jersey, MBUSA has multiple California-based facilities, including a regional office in Costa Mesa, a Vehicle Preparation Center in Carson, and a Classic Center in Irvine. According to the record developed below, MBUSA is the largest supplier of luxury vehicles to the California market. In particular, over 10% of all sales of new vehicles in the United States take place in California, and MBUSA's California sales account for 2.4% of Daimler's worldwide sales.

The relationship between Daimler and MBUSA is delineated in a General Distributor Agreement, which sets forth requirements for MBUSA's distribution of Mercedes-Benz vehicles in the United States. That agreement established MBUSA as an "independent contracto[r]" that "buy[s] and sell[s] [vehicles] . . . as an independent business for [its] own account." The agreement "does not make [MBUSA] . . . a general or special agent, partner, joint venturer or employee of DAIMLERCHRYSLER or any DaimlerChrysler Group Company"; MBUSA "ha[s] no authority to make binding obligations for or act on behalf of DAIMLERCHRYSLER or any DaimlerChrysler Group Company."

After allowing jurisdictional discovery on plaintiffs' agency allegations, the District Court granted Daimler's motion to dismiss. Daimler's own affiliations with California, the court first determined, were insufficient to support the exercise of all-purpose jurisdiction over the corporation. Next, the court declined to attribute MBUSA's California contacts to Daimler on an agency theory, concluding that plaintiffs failed to demonstrate that MBUSA acted as Daimler's agent.

The Ninth Circuit at first affirmed the District Court's judgment. Addressing solely the question of agency, the Court of Appeals held that plaintiffs had not shown the existence of an agency relationship of the kind that might warrant attribution of MBUSA's contacts to Daimler. Judge Reinhardt dissented. In his view, the agency test was satisfied and considerations of "reasonableness" did not bar the exercise of jurisdiction. Granting plaintiffs' petition for rehearing, the panel withdrew its initial opinion and replaced it with one authored by Judge Reinhardt, which elaborated on reasoning he initially expressed in dissent.

Daimler petitioned for rehearing and rehearing en banc, urging that the exercise of personal jurisdiction over Daimler could not be reconciled with this Court's decision in *Goodyear Dunlop Tires Operations, S.A. v. Brown*, 131 S. Ct. 2846 (2011). . . .

We granted certiorari to decide whether, consistent with the Due Process Clause of the Fourteenth Amendment, Daimler is amenable to suit in California courts for claims involving only foreign plaintiffs and conduct occurring entirely abroad.

. . .

III

. . .

"The canonical opinion in this area remains *International Shoe*, in which we held that a State may authorize its courts to exercise personal jurisdiction over an out-of-state defendant if the defendant has 'certain minimum contacts with [the State] such that the maintenance of the suit does not offend "traditional notions of fair play and substantial justice."'" *Goodyear*, 131 S. Ct., at 2853 (quoting *International Shoe*, 326 U.S., at 316). . . .

International Shoe's conception of "fair play and substantial justice" presaged the development of two categories of personal jurisdiction. The first category is represented by *International Shoe* itself, a case in which the in-state activities of the corporate defendant "ha[d] not only been continuous and systematic, but also g[a]ve rise to the liabilities sued on." 326 U.S., at 317. *International Shoe* recognized, as well, that "the commission of some single or occasional acts of the corporate agent in a state" may sometimes be enough to subject the corporation to jurisdiction in that State's tribunals with respect to suits relating to that in-state activity. *Id.*, at 318. Adjudicatory authority of this order, in which the suit "aris[es] out of or relate[s] to the defendant's contacts with the forum," *Helicopteros Nacionales de Colombia, S.A. v. Hall*, 466 U.S. 408, 414, n. 8 (1984), is today called "specific jurisdiction."

International Shoe distinguished between, on the one hand, exercises of specific jurisdiction, as just described, and on the other, situations where a foreign corporation's "continuous corporate operations within a state [are] so substantial and of such a nature as to justify suit against it on causes of action arising from dealings entirely distinct from those activities." 326 U.S., at 318. As we have since explained, "[a] court may assert general jurisdiction over foreign (sister-state or foreign-country) corporations to hear any and all claims against them when their affiliations with the State are so 'continuous and systematic' as to render them essentially at home in the forum State." *Goodyear*, 131 S. Ct., at 2851; see *id.* at 2853-2854; . . .

Since *International Shoe*, "specific jurisdiction has become the centerpiece of modern jurisdiction theory, while general jurisdiction [has played] a reduced role." *Goodyear*, 131 S. Ct., at 2854. . . . Our post-*International Shoe* opinions on general jurisdiction, by comparison, are few. "[The Court's] 1952 decision in *Perkins v. Benguet Consol. Mining Co.* remains the textbook case of general jurisdiction appropriately exercised over a foreign corporation that has not consented to suit in the forum." *Goodyear*, 131 S. Ct., at 2856. The defendant in *Perkins*, Benguet, was a company incorporated under the laws of the Philippines, where it operated gold and silver mines. Benguet ceased its mining operations during the Japanese occupation of the Philippines in World War II; its president moved to Ohio, where he kept an office, maintained the company's files, and oversaw the company's activities. *Perkins v. Benguet Consol. Mining Co.*, 342 U.S. 437, 448 (1952). The plaintiff, an Ohio resident, sued Benguet on a claim that neither arose in Ohio nor related to the corporation's activities in that State. We held that the Ohio courts could exercise general jurisdiction over Benguet without offending due process. *Ibid.* That was so, we later noted, because "Ohio was the corporation's principal, if temporary, place of business." *Keeton v. Hustler Magazine, Inc.*, 465 U.S. 770, 780, n. 11 (1984).

Most recently, in *Goodyear*, we answered the question: "Are foreign subsidiaries of a United States parent corporation amenable to suit in state court on claims unrelated to any activity of the subsidiaries in the forum State?" 131 S. Ct., at 2850. That case arose from a bus accident outside Paris that killed two boys from North Carolina. The boys' parents brought a wrongful-death suit in North Carolina state court alleging that the bus's tire was defectively manufactured. The complaint named as defendants not only The Goodyear Tire and Rubber Company (Goodyear), an Ohio corporation, but also Goodyear's Turkish, French, and Luxembourgian subsidiaries. Those foreign subsidiaries, which manufactured tires for sale in Europe and Asia, lacked any affiliation with North Carolina. A small percentage of tires manufactured by the foreign subsidiaries were distributed in North Carolina, however, and on that ground, the North Carolina Court of Appeals held the subsidiaries amenable to the general jurisdiction of North Carolina courts.

We reversed, observing that the North Carolina court's analysis "elided the essential difference between case-specific and all-purpose (general) jurisdiction." *Id.*, at 2855. Although the placement of a product into the stream of commerce "may bolster an affiliation germane to specific jurisdiction," we explained, such contacts "do not warrant a determination that, based on those ties, the forum has general jurisdiction over a defendant." *Id.*, at 2857. As *International Shoe* itself teaches, a corporation's "continuous activity of some sorts within a state is not enough to support the demand that the corporation be amenable to suits unrelated to that activity." 326 U.S., at 318. Because Goodyear's foreign subsidiaries were "in no sense at home in North Carolina," we held, those subsidiaries could not be required to submit to the general jurisdiction of that State's courts. 131 S. Ct., at 2857. See also *J. McIntyre Machinery, Ltd. v. Nicastro*, 131 S. Ct. 2780, 2797-2798 (2011) (Ginsburg, J., dissenting) (noting unanimous agreement that a foreign manufacturer, which engaged an independent U.S.-based distributor to sell its machines throughout the United States, could not be exposed to all-purpose jurisdiction in New Jersey courts based on those contacts).

. . .

IV

With this background, we turn directly to the question whether Daimler's affiliations with California are sufficient to subject it to the general (all-purpose) personal jurisdiction of that State's courts. In the proceedings below, the parties agreed on, or failed to contest, certain points we now take as given. Plaintiffs have never attempted to fit this case into the specific jurisdiction category. Nor did plaintiffs challenge on appeal the District Court's holding that Daimler's own contacts with California were, by themselves, too sporadic to justify the exercise of general jurisdiction. While plaintiffs ultimately persuaded the Ninth Circuit to impute MBUSA's California contacts to Daimler on an agency theory, at no point have they maintained that MBUSA is an alter ego of Daimler.

Daimler, on the other hand, failed to object below to plaintiffs' assertion that the California courts could exercise all-purpose jurisdiction over MBUSA. But see Brief for Petitioner 23, n. 4 (suggestion that in light of *Goodyear*, MBUSA may not be amenable to general jurisdiction in California). We will assume then, for purposes of this decision only, that MBUSA qualifies as at home in California.

A

In sustaining the exercise of general jurisdiction over Daimler, the Ninth Circuit relied on an agency theory, determining that MBUSA acted as Daimler's agent for jurisdictional purposes and then attributing MBUSA's California contacts to Daimler. The Ninth Circuit's agency analysis derived from Circuit precedent considering principally whether the subsidiary "performs services that are sufficiently important to the foreign corporation that if it did not have a representative to perform them, the corporation's own officials would undertake to perform substantially similar services." 644 F.3d, at 920.

This Court has not yet addressed whether a foreign corporation may be subjected to a court's general jurisdiction based on the contacts of its in-state subsidiary. Daimler argues, and several Courts of Appeals have held, that a subsidiary's jurisdictional contacts can be imputed to its parent only when the former is so dominated by the latter as to be its alter ego. The Ninth Circuit adopted a less rigorous test based on what it described as an "agency" relationship. Agencies, we note, come in many sizes and shapes: "One may be an agent for some business purposes and not others so that the fact that one may be an agent for one purpose does not make him or her an agent for every purpose." 2A C.J.S., Agency § 43, p. 367 (2013) (footnote omitted).[13] A subsidiary, for example, might be its parent's agent for claims arising in the place where the subsidiary operates, yet not its agent regarding claims arising elsewhere. The Court of Appeals did not advert to that prospect. But we need not pass judgment on invocation of an agency theory in the context of general jurisdiction, for in no event can the appeals court's analysis be sustained.

---

13. Agency relationships, we have recognized, may be relevant to the existence of specific jurisdiction. "[T]he corporate personality," *International Shoe Co. v. Washington*, 326 U.S. 310, (1945), observed, "is a fiction, although a fiction intended to be acted upon as though it were a fact." *Id.*, at 316. See generally 1 W. Fletcher, Cyclopedia of the Law of Corporations § 30, p. 30 (Supp. 2012-2013) ("A corporation is a distinct legal entity that can act only through its agents."). As such, a corporation can purposefully avail itself of a forum by directing its agents or distributors to take action there. See, *e.g.*, *Asahi*, 480 U.S., at 112, (opinion of O'Connor, J.) (defendant's act of "marketing [a] product through a distributor who has agreed to serve as the sales agent in the forum State" may amount to purposeful availment); *International Shoe*, 326 U.S., at 318, ("the commission of some single or occasional acts of the corporate agent in a state" may sometimes "be deemed sufficient to render the corporation liable to suit" on related claims). See also Brief for Petitioner 24 (acknowledging that "an agency relationship may be sufficient in some circumstances to give rise to specific jurisdiction"). It does not inevitably follow, however, that similar reasoning applies to general jurisdiction. Cf. *Goodyear*, 131 S. Ct., at 2855 (faulting analysis that "elided the essential difference between case-specific and all-purpose (general) jurisdiction").

The Ninth Circuit's agency finding rested primarily on its observation that MBUSA's services were "important" to Daimler, as gauged by Daimler's hypothetical readiness to perform those services itself if MBUSA did not exist. Formulated this way, the inquiry into importance stacks the deck, for it will always yield a pro-jurisdiction answer: "Anything a corporation does through an independent contractor, subsidiary, or distributor is presumably something that the corporation would do 'by other means' if the independent contractor, subsidiary, or distributor did not exist." 676 F.3d, at 777 (O'Scannlain, J., dissenting from denial of rehearing en banc). The Ninth Circuit's agency theory thus appears to subject foreign corporations to general jurisdiction whenever they have an in-state subsidiary or affiliate, an outcome that would sweep beyond even the "sprawling view of general jurisdiction" we rejected in *Goodyear*. 131 S. Ct., at 2856.

B

Even if we were to assume that MBUSA is at home in California, and further to assume MBUSA's contacts are imputable to Daimler, there would still be no basis to subject Daimler to general jurisdiction in California, for Daimler's slim contacts with the State hardly render it at home there.

Goodyear made clear that only a limited set of affiliations with a forum will render a defendant amenable to all-purpose jurisdiction there. "For an individual, the paradigm forum for the exercise of general jurisdiction is the individual's domicile; for a corporation, it is an equivalent place, one in which the corporation is fairly regarded as at home." 131 S. Ct., at 2853-2854. With respect to a corporation, the place of incorporation and principal place of business are "paradig[m] . . . bases for general jurisdiction." *Id.*, at 735. Those affiliations have the virtue of being unique — that is, each ordinarily indicates only one place — as well as easily ascertainable. These bases afford plaintiffs recourse to at least one clear and certain forum in which a corporate defendant may be sued on any and all claims.

Goodyear did not hold that a corporation may be subject to general jurisdiction only in a forum where it is incorporated or has its principal place of business; it simply typed those places paradigm all-purpose forums. Plaintiffs would have us look beyond the exemplar bases *Goodyear* identified, and approve the exercise of general jurisdiction in every State in which a corporation "engages in a substantial, continuous, and systematic course of business." Brief for Respondents 16-17, and nn. 7-8. That formulation, we hold, is unacceptably grasping.

As noted, the words "continuous and systematic" were used in *International Shoe* to describe instances in which the exercise of specific jurisdiction would be appropriate. See 326 U.S., at 317 (jurisdiction can be asserted where a corporation's in-state activities are not only "continuous and systematic, but also give rise to the liabilities sued on"). Turning to all-purpose jurisdiction, in contrast, *International Shoe* speaks of "instances in which the continuous corporate operations within a state [are] so substantial and of such a nature as to justify suit . . . on causes of action arising from dealings entirely distinct from those activities." *Id.*, at 318. Accordingly, the inquiry under *Goodyear* is not whether a foreign corporation's in-forum contacts can be said to be in some sense "continuous and systematic," it is whether that corporation's "affiliations with the State are so 'continuous and systematic' as to render [it] essentially at home in the forum State." 131 S. Ct., at 2851.[19]

Here, neither Daimler nor MBUSA is incorporated in California, nor does either entity have its principal place of business there. If Daimler's California activities sufficed to allow adjudication of this Argentina-rooted case in California, the same global reach would presumably be available in every other State in which MBUSA's sales are sizable. Such exorbitant exercises of all-purpose jurisdiction would scarcely permit out-of-state defendants "to structure their primary conduct with some minimum assurance as to where that conduct will and will not render them liable to suit." *Burger King Corp.*, 471 U.S., at 472.

It was therefore error for the Ninth Circuit to conclude that Daimler, even with MBUSA's contacts attributed to it, was at home in California, and hence subject to suit there on claims by foreign plaintiffs having nothing to do with anything that occurred or had its principal impact in California.[20]

---

19. We do not foreclose the possibility that in an exceptional case, see, *e.g.*, *Perkins*, a corporation's operations in a forum other than its formal place of incorporation or principal place of business may be so substantial and of such a nature as to render the corporation at home in that State. But this case presents no occasion to explore that question, because Daimler's activities in California plainly do not approach that level. It is one thing to hold a corporation answerable for operations in the forum State, quite another to expose it to suit on claims having no connection whatever to the forum State.

20. To clarify in light of Justice Sotomayor's opinion concurring in the judgment, the general jurisdiction inquiry does not "focu[s] solely on the magnitude of the defendant's in-state contacts." General jurisdiction instead calls for an appraisal of a corporation's activities in their entirety, nationwide and worldwide. A corporation that operates in many places can scarcely be deemed at home in all of them. Otherwise, "at home" would be synonymous with "doing business" tests framed before specific jurisdiction evolved in the United States. See von Mehren & Trautman 1142-1144. Nothing in *International Shoe* and its progeny suggests that "a particular quantum of local activity" should give a State authority over a "far larger quantum of . . . activity" having no connection to any in-state activity. Feder, *supra*, at 694.

Justice Sotomayor would reach the same result, but for a different reason. Rather than concluding that Daimler is not at home in California, Justice Sotomayor would hold that the exercise of general jurisdiction over Daimler would be unreasonable "in the unique circumstances of this case." In other words, she favors a resolution fit for this day and case only. True, a multipronged reasonableness check was articulated in *Asahi*, 480 U.S., at 113-114, but not as a free-floating test. Instead, the check was to be essayed when specific jurisdiction is at issue. See also *Burger King Corp. v. Rudzewicz*, 471 U.S. 462, 476-478, (1985). First, a court is to determine whether the connection between the forum and the episode-in-suit could justify the exercise of specific jurisdiction. Then, in a second step, the court is to consider several additional factors to assess the reasonableness of entertaining the case. When a corporation is genuinely at home in the forum State, however, any second-step inquiry would be superfluous.

Justice Sotomayor fears that our holding will "lead to greater unpredictability by radically expanding the scope of jurisdictional discovery." But it is hard to see why much in the way of discovery would be needed to determine where a corporation is at home. Justice Sotomayor's proposal to import *Asahi*'s "reasonableness" check into the general jurisdiction determination, on the other hand, would indeed compound the jurisdictional inquiry. The reasonableness factors identified in *Asahi* include "the burden on the defendant," "the interests of the forum State," "the plaintiff's interest in obtaining relief," "the interstate judicial system's interest in obtaining the most efficient resolution of controversies," "the shared interest of the several States in furthering fundamental substantive social policies," and, in the international context, "the procedural and substantive policies of other nations whose interests are affected by the assertion of jurisdiction." 480 U.S., at 113-115. Imposing such a checklist in cases of general jurisdiction would hardly promote the efficient disposition of an issue that should be resolved expeditiously at the outset of litigation.

C

Finally, the transnational context of this dispute bears attention. The Court of Appeals emphasized, as supportive of the exercise of general jurisdiction, plaintiffs' assertion of claims under the Alien Tort Statute (ATS), 28 U.S.C. § 1350, and the Torture Victim Protection Act of 1991 (TVPA), 106 Stat. 73, note following 28 U.S.C. § 1350. See 644 F.3d, at 927 ("American federal courts, be they in California or any other state, have a strong interest in adjudicating and redressing international human rights abuses."). Recent decisions of this Court, however, have rendered plaintiffs' ATS and TVPA claims infirm. See *Kiobel v. Royal Dutch Petroleum Co.*, 133 S. Ct. 1659, 1669 (2013) (presumption against extraterritorial application controls claims under the ATS); *Mohamad v. Palestinian Authority*, 132 S. Ct. 1702, 1705 (2012) (only natural persons are subject to liability under the TVPA).

The Ninth Circuit, moreover, paid little heed to the risks to international comity its expansive view of general jurisdiction posed. Other nations do not share the uninhibited approach to personal jurisdiction advanced by the Court of Appeals in this case. In the European Union, for example, a corporation may generally be sued in the nation in which it is "domiciled," a term defined to refer only to the location of the corporation's "statutory seat," "central administration," or "principal place of business." European Parliament and Council Reg. 1215/2012, Arts. 4(1), and 63(1), 2012 O.J. (L. 351) 7, 18. See also *id.*, Art. 7(5), 2012 O.J. 7 (as to "a dispute *arising out of the operations of a branch, agency or other establishment*," a corporation may be sued "in the courts for the place where the branch, agency or other establishment is situated" (emphasis added)). The Solicitor General informs us, in this regard, that "foreign governments' objections to some domestic courts' expansive views of general jurisdiction have in the past impeded negotiations of international agreements on the reciprocal recognition and enforcement of judgments." U.S. Brief 2 (citing Juenger, The American Law of General Jurisdiction, 2001 U. Chi. Legal Forum 141, 161-162). See also U.S. Brief 2 (expressing concern that unpredictable applications of general jurisdiction based on activities of U.S.-based subsidiaries could discourage foreign investors); Brief for Respondents 35 (acknowledging that "doing business" basis for general jurisdiction has led to "international friction"). Considerations of international rapport thus reinforce our determination that subjecting Daimler to the general jurisdiction of courts in California would not accord with the "fair play and substantial justice" due process demands. *International Shoe*, 326 U.S., at 316[.]

. . .

Reversed.

Justice SOTOMAYOR, concurring in the judgment.

I agree with the Court's conclusion that the Due Process Clause prohibits the exercise of personal jurisdiction over Daimler in light of the unique circumstances of this case. I concur only in the judgment, however, because I cannot agree with the path the Court takes to arrive at that result.

The Court acknowledges that Mercedes-Benz USA, LLC (MBUSA), Daimler's wholly owned subsidiary, has considerable contacts with California. It has multiple facilities in the State, including a regional headquarters. Each year, it distributes in California tens of thousands of cars, the sale of which generated billions of dollars in the year this suit was brought. And it provides service and sales support to customers throughout the State. Daimler has conceded that California courts may exercise general jurisdiction over MBUSA on the basis of these contacts, and the Court assumes that MBUSA's contacts may be attributed to Daimler for the purpose of deciding whether Daimler is also subject to general jurisdiction.

Are these contacts sufficient to permit the exercise of general jurisdiction over Daimler? The Court holds that they are not, for a reason wholly foreign to our due process jurisprudence. The problem, the Court says, is not that Daimler's contacts with California are too few, but that its contacts with other forums are too many. In other words, the Court does not dispute that the presence of multiple offices, the direct distribution of thousands of products accounting for billions of dollars in sales, and continuous interaction with customers throughout a State would be enough to support the exercise of general jurisdiction over some businesses. Daimler is just not one of those businesses, the Court concludes, because its California contacts must be viewed in the context of its extensive "nationwide and worldwide" operations. In recent years, Americans have grown accustomed to the concept of multinational corporations that are supposedly "too big to fail"; today the Court deems Daimler "too big for general jurisdiction."

The Court's conclusion is wrong. . . . [T]he Court's focus on Daimler's operations outside of California ignores the lodestar of our personal jurisdiction jurisprudence: A State may subject a defendant to the burden of suit if the defendant has sufficiently taken advantage of the State's laws and protections through its contacts in the State; whether the defendant has contacts elsewhere is immaterial.

. . . The Court can and should decide this case on the far simpler ground that, no matter how extensive Daimler's contacts with California, that State's exercise of jurisdiction would be unreasonable given that the case involves foreign plaintiffs suing a foreign defendant based on foreign conduct, and given that a more appropriate forum is available. . . .

I

I begin with the point on which the majority and I agree: The Ninth Circuit's decision should be reversed.

Our personal jurisdiction precedents call for a two-part analysis. The contacts prong asks whether the defendant has sufficient contacts with the forum State to support personal jurisdiction; the reasonableness prong asks whether the exercise of jurisdiction would be unreasonable under the circumstances. *Burger King Corp. v. Rudzewicz*, 471 U.S. 462, 475-478 (1985). As the majority points out, all of the cases in which we have applied the reasonableness prong have involved specific as opposed to general jurisdiction. Whether the reasonableness prong should apply in the general jurisdiction context is therefore a question we have never decided,[1] and it is one on which I can appreciate the arguments on both sides. But it would be imprudent to decide that question in this case given that respondents have failed to argue against the application of the reasonableness prong during the entire 8-year history of this litigation. As a result, I would decide this case under the reasonableness prong without foreclosing future consideration of whether that prong should be limited to the specific jurisdiction context.

We identified the factors that bear on reasonableness in *Asahi Metal Industry Co. v. Superior Court of Cal., Solano Cty.*, 480 U.S. 102 (1987): "the burden on the defendant, the interests of the forum State," "the plaintiff's interest in obtaining relief" in the forum State, and the interests of other sovereigns in resolving the dispute. *Id.*, at 113-114. We held in *Asahi* that it would be "unreasonable and unfair" for a California court to exercise jurisdiction over a claim between a Taiwanese plaintiff and a Japanese defendant that arose out of a transaction in Taiwan, particularly where the Taiwanese plaintiff had not shown that it would be more convenient to litigate in California than in Taiwan or Japan.

The same considerations resolve this case. It involves Argentine plaintiffs suing a German defendant for conduct that took place in Argentina. Like the plaintiffs in *Asahi*, respondents have failed to show that it would be more convenient to litigate in California than in Germany, a sovereign with a far greater interest in resolving the dispute. *Asahi* thus makes clear that it would be unreasonable for a court in California to subject Daimler to its jurisdiction.

. . .

IV

. . .

A

Until today, our precedents had established a straightforward test for general jurisdiction: Does the defendant have "continuous corporate operations within a state" that are "so substantial and of such a nature as to justify suit against it on causes of action arising from dealings entirely distinct from those activities"? *International Shoe Co. v. Washington*, 326 U.S. 310, 318 (1945); see also *Helicopteros Nacionales de Colombia, S. A. v. Hall*, 466 U.S. 408, 416 (1984) (asking whether defendant had "continuous and systematic general business contacts"). In every case where we have applied this test, we have focused solely on the magnitude of the defendant's in-state contacts, not the relative magnitude of those contacts in comparison to the defendant's contacts with other States.

. . .

---

1. The Courts of Appeals have uniformly held that the reasonableness prong does in fact apply in the general jurisdiction context. . . . Without the benefit of a single page of briefing on the issue, the majority casually adds each of these cases to the mounting list of decisions jettisoned as a consequence of today's ruling.

Had the majority applied our settled approach, it would have had little trouble concluding that Daimler's California contacts rise to the requisite level, given the majority's assumption that MBUSA's contacts may be attributed to Daimler and given Daimler's concession that those contacts render MBUSA "at home" in California.

. . .

B

The majority today concludes otherwise. Referring to the "continuous and systematic" contacts inquiry that has been taught to generations of first-year law students as "unacceptably grasping," the majority announces the new rule that in order for a foreign defendant to be subject to general jurisdiction, it must not only possess continuous and systematic contacts with a forum State, but those contacts must also surpass some unspecified level when viewed in comparison to the company's "nationwide and worldwide" activities. Ante, at . . . n. 20.

. . .

C

The majority's concern for the consequences of its decision should have led it the other way, because the rule that it adopts will produce deep injustice in at least four respects.

First, the majority's approach unduly curtails the States' sovereign authority to adjudicate disputes against corporate defendants who have engaged in continuous and substantial business operations within their boundaries. . . .

Second, the proportionality approach will treat small businesses unfairly in comparison to national and multinational conglomerates. Whereas a larger company will often be immunized from general jurisdiction in a State on account of its extensive contacts outside the forum, a small business will not be. For instance, the majority holds today that Daimler is not subject to general jurisdiction in California despite its multiple offices, continuous operations, and billions of dollars' worth of sales there. But imagine a small business that manufactures luxury vehicles principally targeting the California market and that has substantially all of its sales and operations in the State — even though those sales and operations may amount to one-thousandth of Daimler's. Under the majority's rule, that small business will be subject to suit in California on any cause of action involving any of its activities anywhere in the world, while its far more pervasive competitor, Daimler, will not be. That will be so even if the small business incorporates and sets up its headquarters elsewhere (as Daimler does), since the small business' California sales and operations would still predominate when "apprais[ed]" in proportion to its minimal "nationwide and worldwide" operations, ante n. 20.

Third, the majority's approach creates the incongruous result that an individual defendant whose only contact with a forum State is a one-time visit will be subject to general jurisdiction if served with process during that visit, *Burnham v. Superior Court of Cal., County of Marin*, 495 U.S. 604 (1990), but a large corporation that owns property, employs workers, and does billions of dollars' worth of business in the State will not be, simply because the corporation has similar contacts elsewhere (though the visiting individual surely does as well).

Finally, it should be obvious that the ultimate effect of the majority's approach will be to shift the risk of loss from multinational corporations to the individuals harmed by their actions. Under the majority's rule, for example, a parent whose child is maimed due to the negligence of a foreign hotel owned by a multinational conglomerate will be unable to hold the hotel to account in a single U.S. court, even if the hotel company has a massive presence in multiple States. Similarly, a U.S. business that enters into a contract in a foreign country to sell its products to a multinational company there may be unable to seek relief in any U.S. court if the multinational company breaches the contract, even if that company has considerable operations in numerous U.S. forums. Indeed, the majority's approach would preclude the plaintiffs in these examples from seeking recourse anywhere in the United States even if no other judicial system was available to provide relief. I cannot agree with the majority's conclusion that the Due Process Clause requires these results.

. . .

NOTES AND QUESTIONS

1. *Daimler* **and General Jurisdiction.** Recall that the Court held that even if MBUSA's contacts with California were sufficient for general jurisdiction over MBUSA and even if MBUSA's contacts were imputable to Daimler, Daimler still would not be subject to general jurisdiction in California. What was the majority's reasoning behind this holding? Why does Justice Sotomayor disagree in her dissent? Recall from the *Goodyear* case that the Court did not clearly state whether the *only* places where a corporation could be "at home" for general jurisdiction purposes were the corporation's state of incorporation or principal place of business. Did the Court clarify its "at home" language from *Goodyear*? What do you think the Court has in mind in footnote 19 when it refers to an "exceptional case"?

2. **The Post-***Daimler* **Landscape.** In light of *Goodyear* and *Daimler*, consider the following: (a) Suppose you represent a foreign pharmaceutical corporation with 46 employees who sell and market corporate products in Illinois. Is the corporation subject to general jurisdiction in Illinois? *See J.B. ex rel. Benjamin v. Abbot Labs., Inc.*, 2013 WL 452807 (N.D. Ill. 2013) (finding general jurisdiction post-*Goodyear* over a U.S. company in similar circumstances). (b) A South African manufacturer of infant car seats is sued in Texas by the parents of a child injured in Arizona. The foreign manufacturer moves to dismiss for lack of personal jurisdiction. Of the nearly 4 million car seats sold by the manufacturer in the United States, nearly 1 million are distributed by a Texas distributor. For several years, the Texas distributor was the sole

importer and distributer of the product throughout the United States. In that capacity, it represented the manufacturer before retailers, coordinated recalls, and entered into contracts on behalf of the manufacturer. Is there general jurisdiction over the South African manufacturer in Texas? *See Hess v. Bumbo Int'l Trust*, 954 F. Supp. 2d 590 (S.D. Tex. 2013) (finding general jurisdiction). (c) A plaintiff is injured at a resort in Anguilla when she slipped and fell on wet towels on the way to the beach. The plaintiff wishes to sue in Florida. The resort's only connections to Florida are that it has assets managed in Florida and it advertises there. Is there general jurisdiction in Florida? *See Barriere v. Juluca*, 2014 WL 652831 (S.D. Fla. 2014) (finding general jurisdiction and noting that a "contrary result would effectively permit foreign corporations to freely solicit and accept business from Americans in the United States and at the same time be completely shielded from any liability in U.S. courts from any injury that may arise as a result").

Are these cases consistent with *Goodyear* and *Daimler*? In light of these cases, should the Supreme Court in *Goodyear* and *Daimler* have been clearer as to the general jurisdiction analysis? If you were a judge crafting a test, what would it look like? In *BNSF Railway Co. v. Tyrrell*, 137 S. Ct. 1549 (2017), the Court found that a railroad with extensive operations in Montana (but which was incorporated and had its principal place of business elsewhere) was not subject to general jurisdiction in Montana. The Court repeated that finding general jurisdiction outside the "corporation's place of incorporation and its principal place of business" was an "exceptional case." It added (quoting *Daimler*) that "'the general jurisdiction inquiry does not focus solely on the magnitude of the defendant's in-state contacts.' Rather, the inquiry 'calls for an appraisal of a corporation's activities in their entirety'; '[a] corporation that operates in many places can scarcely be deemed at home in all of them.'" Is that helpful?

3. ***Daimler* and Agency and Affiliate Jurisdiction.** Many transnational businesses are structured with multiple tiers of subsidiaries and affiliates that ultimately form part of a corporate "family." What is the effect on personal jurisdiction of operation through subsidiaries and affiliates? Can foreign corporations that only do business abroad but have agents and affiliates in the United States be subject to personal jurisdiction based on the agent's or affiliate's contacts with a forum state? This basis for personal jurisdiction is called agency or affiliate jurisdiction, and can be of great importance in transnational disputes. It poses significant practical and policy concerns. Too narrow a view of agency and affiliate jurisdiction might allow multinational corporations to unjustly shield operations from U.S. jurisdiction; too broad a view might bring into U.S. court disputes with little connection to the United States. But which view did the majority in *Daimler* seem to favor?

4. **Affiliate Jurisdiction After *Daimler*.** How viable is affiliate jurisdiction after *Daimler*? After the Supreme Court's *Daimler* decision, the Ninth Circuit dealt again with agency and affiliate jurisdiction in *Ranza v. Nike, Inc.*, 793 F.3d 1059 (9th Cir. 2015). In this case, plaintiff Ranza, a U.S. citizen who resided in the Netherlands during the events that gave rise to the cause of

action, filed suit against her former employer, Nike European Operations
Netherlands, B.V. (NEON), and NEON's parent company, Nike, Inc., in the
District of Oregon for violations of federal civil rights laws. Ranza alleged that
NEON subjected her to sex and age discrimination. Nike had its headquarters in Oregon and Neon was a wholly owned subsidiary of Nike, organized
as a private limited liability corporation under Netherlands law. The federal
district court held that it lacked personal jurisdiction over NEON and Ranza
appealed.

On appeal, Ranza raised two arguments. First, she argued that NEON
was subject to general jurisdiction in Oregon. Second, she argued in the alternative that Nike's contacts could be attributed to NEON to establish general
jurisdiction. The Ninth Circuit rejected both arguments and explained the
current state of agency and affiliate law as follows.

> Before the Supreme Court's *Daimler* decision, this circuit permitted a plain-
> tiff to pierce the corporate veil for jurisdictional purposes and attribute a local
> entity's contacts to its out-of-state affiliate under one of two separate tests: the
> "agency" test and the "alter ego" test. The agency test required a plaintiff to
> show the subsidiary "perform[ed] services that [were] sufficiently important to
> the foreign corporation that if it did not have a representative to perform them,
> the corporation's own officials would undertake to perform substantially simi-
> lar services." The Supreme Court invalidated this test. It held that focusing on
> whether the subsidiary performs "important" work the parent would have to
> do itself if the subsidiary did not exist "stacks the deck, for it will always yield
> a pro-jurisdiction answer." Such a theory, the Court concluded, sweeps too
> broadly to comport with the requirements of due process. The agency test is
> therefore no longer available to Ranza to establish jurisdiction over NEON.
>
> In contrast to the agency test, the Court left intact this circuit's alter ego
> test for "imputed" general jurisdiction. The alter ego test is designed to deter-
> mine whether the parent and subsidiary are "not really separate entities," such
> that one entity's contacts with the forum state can be fairly attributed to the
> other. The "alter ego . . . relationship is typified by parental control of the sub-
> sidiary's internal affairs or daily operations." We examine Nike's relationship
> with NEON under this alter ego test.

1. Applying the Alter Ego Theory to a Foreign Subsidiary

As an initial matter, NEON argues Ranza is asking us to apply the alter ego
test in an unprecedented fashion. Rather than seeking to impute a subsidiary's
local contacts to a foreign parent, which is the traditional application of the
alter ego test, Ranza seeks to impute a local parent's contacts to a foreign subsidiary. Yet, like the typical application of the alter ego test, Ranza supports
her imputation theory based on the parent Nike's allegedly extensive control
over its subsidiary NEON. Thus, whereas the alter ego test has traditionally
been used to bring a controlling parent into a controlled subsidiary's home
forum, Ranza attempts to use the test to bring a controlled subsidiary into the
controlling parent's home forum.

Ranza offers no binding authority applying the alter ego test in reverse. She
does, however, highlight persuasive reasoning from a district court opinion
addressing this issue in the context of a multidistrict antitrust dispute in which

the plaintiffs sought to establish general jurisdiction over foreign subsidiaries of domestic candy manufacturers . . . .

This is sound reasoning. . . . In fact, exercising general jurisdiction over both entities in the parent's forum is just as defensible (if not more so) under due process principles as haling the parent into the subsidiary's forum. If the two entities are to be treated as a single enterprise, the stronger candidate for the "home" of that enterprise is likely where the controlling parent most closely affiliates. And the enterprise as a whole should reasonably foresee being subject to suit for all of its activities — even those unrelated to the forum — where it most closely affiliates.

We hold the alter ego test may be used to extend personal jurisdiction to a foreign parent *or* subsidiary when, in actuality, the foreign entity is not really separate from its domestic affiliate. We therefore turn to the alter ego inquiry.

2. Alter Ego Application

To satisfy the alter ego test, a plaintiff "must make out a prima facie case '(1) that there is such unity of interest and ownership that the separate personalities [of the two entities] no longer exist and (2) that failure to disregard [their separate identities] would result in fraud or injustice.'" *Unocal*, 248 F.3d at 926. The "unity of interest and ownership" prong of this test requires "a showing that the parent controls the subsidiary to such a degree as to render the latter the mere instrumentality of the former." *Id.* This test envisions pervasive control over the subsidiary, such as when a parent corporation "dictates every facet of the subsidiary's business — from broad policy decisions to routine matters of day-to-day operation." *Id.* (internal quotation marks omitted). Total ownership and shared management personnel are alone insufficient to establish the requisite level of control. . . .

Ranza has presented no evidence Nike and NEON fail to observe their respective corporate formalities. Each entity leases its own facilities, maintains its own accounting books and records, enters into contracts on its own and pays its own taxes. Each has separate boards of directors, and Ranza has been able to identify only one director who served on both company's boards simultaneously. Some employees and management personnel move between the entities, but that does not undermine the entities' formal separation. Ranza has presented no evidence that NEON is undercapitalized, that the two entities fail to keep adequate records or that Nike freely transfers NEON's assets, all of which would be signs of a sham corporate veil.

As in *Unocal*, Ranza has not shown Nike "dictates every facet of [NEON's] business," including "routine matters of day-to-day operation." To be sure, Nike is heavily involved in NEON's operations. Nike exercises control over NEON's overall budget and has approval authority for large purchases; establishes general human resource policies for both entities and is involved in some hiring decisions; operates information tracking systems all of its subsidiaries utilize; ensures the Nike brand is marketed consistently throughout the world; and requires some NEON employees to report to Nike supervisors on a "dotted-line" basis. NEON, however, sets its own prices for its licensed Nike products, takes and fulfills orders for its licensed products using its own inventory, negotiates its own contracts and licenses, makes routine purchasing decisions without Nike's consultation and has its own human resources division that handles day-to-day employment issues, including hiring and firing decisions. . . .

In sum, Nike's involvement in NEON, though substantial, is insufficient to negate the formal separation between the two entities such that they are functionally one single enterprise. Ranza therefore may not attribute Nike's Oregon contacts to NEON for the purpose of personal jurisdiction. And NEON's contacts with Oregon, standing alone, are insufficient to make it amenable to general jurisdiction in that state. We therefore hold the district court properly declined to exercise personal jurisdiction over NEON.

In light of the Ninth Circuit's reasoning, under what circumstances may plaintiffs use agency or affiliate jurisdiction to establish personal jurisdiction? In your view, does the Ninth Circuit adopt the right approach? How would you change the test, or would you discard it altogether?

5. **Policy: Should There Be Affiliate Jurisdiction?** What arguments can you make in favor of and against personal jurisdiction over a corporate defendant based on the contacts of an affiliate of the corporation (such as a corporate subsidiary)? Is agency or affiliate jurisdiction an end-run around *Goodyear* and *Daimler*? Or does it appropriately recognize that legal fictions, such as corporate organization, should not be used to prevent the assertion of personal jurisdiction? If there should be some form of agency or affiliate jurisdiction, what should the limits be?

2. Specific Jurisdiction

This section considers issues arising from claims of specific jurisdiction in transnational cases. As illustrated in the above cases, a court in a particular state may exercise general jurisdiction over a defendant only if the defendant's contacts with that state are so continuous and systematic as to render the defendant at home there — once established, general jurisdiction extends to any claim against the defendant, regardless of whether it is related to those contacts. Fewer contacts are required for specific jurisdiction — but those contacts must be related to the plaintiff's claim and, if established, jurisdiction extends only to claims arising out of and related to those contacts.

To review, there is a two-step process in establishing personal jurisdiction, even in a transnational case. First, does state law (what is usually called a state "long-arm statute") permit jurisdiction? Second, if so, does the Due Process Clause permit jurisdiction? Under the due process standard, for a court to assert personal jurisdiction over a nonresident defendant, including a corporation, the defendant must "have certain minimum contacts with [the forum] such that the maintenance of the suit does not offend traditional notions of fair play and substantial justice." *Int'l Shoe Co. v. Washington*, 326 U.S. 310, 316 (1945). What does this mean? The "defendant's conduct and connection with the forum State" must be "such that [it] should reasonably anticipate being haled into court there." *World-Wide Volkswagen Corp. v. Woodson*, 444 U.S. 286, 297 (1980). For example, when a "corporation purposefully avails itself of the privilege of conducting activities within the forum State, it has clear notice . . . it is subject to suit there." *Id.* There is thus a three-part due process test in specific jurisdiction cases: (1) whether the plaintiff's claims "arise out of or relate to" at least one of the defendant's contacts with the forum; (2) whether the nonresident defendant "purposefully availed" himself of the privilege of conducting activities within the forum state, thus invoking the benefit of the forum state's laws; and (3) whether the exercise of personal jurisdiction comports with "traditional notions of fair play and substantial justice." *Burger King Corp. v. Rudzewicz*, 471 U.S. 462, 472-73 (1985).

We begin by looking at what it means for a defendant to purposefully avail itself of a forum state in the case of tort and contract claims. We then turn to instances where specific personal jurisdiction is premised on a defendant's participation in the "stream of commerce," which generally refers to the movement of goods from manufacturers through distributors to consumers, especially in products liability cases. We then explore the impact of these decisions on the current state of case law in transnational cases.

GT Securities, Inc. v. Klastech GmbH

2014 WL 2928013 (N.D. Cal. 2014)

JOSEPH C. SPERO, United States Magistrate Judge.

I. Introduction

Plaintiff GT Securities, Inc. ("GTK") brings an action for breach of contract against Defendant Klastech GmbH ("Klastech") and an action for interference with contract against Defendant Triangle Venture Capital Group GmbH & Co. KG Nr. IV ("Triangle"). Klastech and Triangle each bring a Motion to Dismiss ("Klastech Motion" and "Triangle Motion," respectively) for lack of personal jurisdiction under Rule 12(b)(2) of the Federal Rules of Civil Procedure. . . . For the reasons stated below, both Motions are DENIED.

II. Background

. . .

GTK is a California corporation with its principal place of business in Los Angeles County, California. Triangle and Klastech are German corporations with their headquarters in Germany. Klastech asserts that it has no operations, offices, or employees in the United States or California. However, GTK argues that Klastech used an independent contractor to sell its products in California prior to its acquisition and that, since its acquisition, its website lists a designated sales representative for the "USA West" with two California phone numbers. Triangle has no offices, employees, directors, managers, agent for service, sales, marketing, or property in California. According to GTK, during the actions that gave rise to this Complaint, Klastech was a wholly owned subsidiary of Triangle. As of January 21, 2013, Klastech has been acquired by PTI, an Arkansas-based corporation.

In September, 2009, Langhans, a principal at Triangle, emailed GTK to inquire about the possibility of engaging its investment management services for Klastech in the exploration of strategic alternatives, including a Transaction. Langhans sent this email from her @triangle-venture.com email account, with a signature block that identified her as an Investment Manager at Triangle Venture Capital Group Management GmbH, to Tabibian [a senior manager] at GTK. It states:

> I received information that you are an expert in transactions in the photonics industries and that you supported the SpectraPhysics-Newport deal in the past.
>
> Triangle has invested in 2006 into a German start-up called KLASTECH which develops and commercializes a new generation of DPSS lasers. We would like to identify potential M & A possibilities and shape the company's future strategy to make i[t] attractive for an exit. Potentially especially the company's patented technology is interesting for its competitors. I would be happy to set up a conference call with my colleague Dr. Geiger to exchange some information about Triangle and Klastech and would like to ask if you are available for a call on Friday.

Langhans and Geiger, another Triangle principal, negotiated the Agreement between GTK and Klastech with the help of sophisticated counsel from Foley & Lardner. . . .

GTK's contractual relationship with Klastech began on July 31, 2010, pursuant to the Agreement negotiated by Triangle. In the Agreement, GTK agreed to share at least bi-weekly written reports of its progress via Tabibian, the individual with "principal senior responsibility for the day to day management." In return for GTK's services under the Agreement, Klastech promised to make three retainer payments of $10,000 each due in July, August, and September of 2010 and to cover GTK's out-of-pocket expenses. In the event of the consummation of a Transaction during GTK's engagement and prior to termination of the Agreement, the Agreement specifies that Klastech pays a minimum "Success Fee" of $400,000, plus an additional amount to be determined based on the ultimate value of the Transaction. Klastech must mention GTK's role as advisor in any press release or public announcement it makes about the Transaction. Klastech is allowed to terminate at any time by giving seven days prior written notice to GTK. In addition, Klastech has no obligation to agree to any other employee of GTK to serve as a suitable replacement of Mr. Tabibian. Under certain circumstances, GTK is still eligible for the "Success Fee" for Transactions consummated after Klastech's termination. The Agreement is governed by New York law.

As contemplated by the Agreement, in August and September 2010, Klastech, Triangle, and GTK exchanged information, developed an Executive Summary presentation for potential acquirors, and communicated several times a week, sometimes daily. In July, August, and September 2010, Klastech made three monthly retainer payments by wire to GTK's California bank account. Between September and December 2010, Tabibian contacted approximately twenty potential acquirors on behalf of GTK, several of which were located in California.

When Tabibian left GTK to work at Citigroup in December 2010, GTK offered Klastech the option to transfer the Agreement to Citigroup or to terminate it. Tabibian informed Triangle of his departure as well and explained to Geiger over the phone that the option to terminate allowed Klastech to keep the engagement open and re-start at GTK without the need for payment of a new retainer. When Tabibian returned to GTK in January 2012 after two years at Citigroup, Klastech executed a subsequent written agreement for additional services.

From January 2012 through July 2012, GTK continued to provide advice, identify potential acquirors, develop approach strategies, and exchange periodic updates with Klastech and Triangle. . . .

On January 28, 2013, Tabibian contacted Madin [the CEO of Klastech] to suggest a meeting in San Francisco, at which point, Madin informed Tabibian that as of January 21, 2013, Klastech had been acquired by PTI pursuant to the Purchase Agreement signed by Klastech, Triangle, and PTI. GTK alleges that Klastech is now wholly owned by and run in close coordination with Arkansas-based PTI. . . .

In accordance with the Agreement, GTK demanded payment of the "Success Fee" from Klastech based upon the Transaction with PTI, which Klastech allegedly refused to pay. GTK alleges that Triangle falsely represented to PTI that Klastech had no obligations to any investment bank or other entity in connection with the Transaction, pointing to the "no broker" provision of the Purchase Agreement, which reads as follows:

> 2.3 *Broker's Fees.* Neither Sellers [Triangle and others] nor Company [Klastech] has liability or any obligation to pay any fees or commissions to any broker, finder, or agent with respect to the transactions contemplated by this Agreement for which Buyer [PTI] or Company could become liable or obligated. Any fees due to brokers engaged by Sellers, or Sellers' consultants and advisors shall be paid by Sellers.
>
> . . .

III. Analysis

A. Personal Jurisdiction

a. Legal Standard

. . .

"For a court to exercise personal jurisdiction over a non-resident defendant, that defendant must have at least 'minimum contacts' with the relevant forum such that the exercise of jurisdiction 'does not offend traditional notions of fair play and substantial justice.'" [*Dole Food Co. v. Watts*, 303 F.3d 1104, 1110-11 (9th Cir. 2002)] (citing *International Shoe Co. v. Washington*, 326 U.S. 310, 316 (1945)). "In judging minimum contacts, a court properly focuses on 'the relationship among the defendant, the forum, and the litigation.'" *Calder v. Jones*, 465 U.S. 781, 788 (1984) (quoting *Shaffer v. Heitner*, 433 U.S. 186, 204 (1977)).

Personal jurisdiction may be either general or specific. *See Bancroft & Masters, Inc. v. Augusta Nat. Inc.*, 223 F.3d 1082, 1086 (9th Cir. 2000). General jurisdiction may be established when a defendant's contacts with a state are "substantial" or "continuous and systematic" such that the defendant "can be haled into court in that state in any action, even if the action is unrelated to those contacts." *Id.* . . .

Nevertheless, "[e]ven if a defendant has not had continuous and systematic contacts with the state sufficient to confer general jurisdiction, a court may exercise specific jurisdiction when the following requirements are met:

> (1) the non-resident defendant must purposefully direct his activities or consummate some transaction with the forum or resident thereof; or perform some act by which he purposefully avails himself of the privileges of conducting activities in the forum, thereby invoking the benefits and protections of its laws;
> (2) the claim must be one which arises out of or relates to the defendant's forum-related activities; and
> (3) the exercise of jurisdiction must comport with fair play and substantial justice, i.e. it must be reasonable.

Dole Food, 303 F.3d at 1111 (internal quotations and citations omitted). . . .

. . . To determine whether the exercise of jurisdiction is reasonable, and therefore, "comports with fair play and substantial justice," courts consider seven factors:

> (1) the extent of the defendants' purposeful injection into the forum state's affairs; (2) the burden on the defendant of defending in the forum; (3) the extent of conflict with the sovereignty of the defendant's state; (4) the forum state's interest in adjudicating the dispute; (5) the most efficient judicial resolution of the controversy; (6) the importance of the forum to the plaintiff's interest in convenient and effective relief; and (7) the existence of an alternative forum.

Dole Food, 303 F.3d at 1114.

. . .

b. Klastech Is Subject to Personal Jurisdiction

While GTK contends that Klastech is subject to both specific and general jurisdiction in California, because the Court finds that there are sufficient contacts with the forum related to the claim to support its exercise of specific jurisdiction, the Court need not decide the question of general jurisdiction over Klastech.

B. Specific Jurisdiction

a. Purposeful Availment

"The purposeful availment requirement ensures that a nonresident defendant will not be haled into court based upon "random, fortuitous or attenuated contacts with the forum state." *Panavision Intern., L.P. v. Toeppen*, 141 F.3d 1316, 1320 (9th Cir. 1998) (quoting *Burger King*, 471 U.S at 475). While a single contract with a resident of the relevant jurisdiction is not necessarily sufficient, the critical issue is whether the contract evidences a substantial relationship with the forum based on prior negotiations, contemplated future consequences, and the terms of the contract. *See Burger King*, 471 U.S. at 475-76. "[W]ith respect to interstate contractual obligations, . . . parties who 'reach out beyond one state and create continuing relationships and obligations with citizens of another state' are subject to regulation and sanction in the other State for the consequences of their activities." *Id.* at 473.

In *Burger King*, despite the defendant's never having been to Florida, his contract with Florida-based plaintiff, Burger King, to establish a franchise in Michigan demonstrated a substantial connection with Florida where defendant "'reach[ed] out beyond' Michigan and negotiated with a Florida corporation for the purchase of a long-term franchise and the manifold benefits that would derive from affiliation with a nationwide organization." *Burger King*, 471 U.S. at 480. The Supreme Court rejected the lower court's determination that, in light of the supervision emanating from Burger King's district office in Michigan, defendant believed that office was the embodiment of Burger King and he had no reason to anticipate a suit outside of Michigan. *Id.* Instead, the Supreme Court pointed to evidence that defendant knew he was "affiliating himself with an enterprise based primarily in Florida" in the form of 1) the contract documents specifying that Burger King operated in Florida and that the agreement was made and enforced there and 2) the parties' course of dealing in which the defendant corresponded with Florida headquarters by mail and phone. *Id.* at 481.

GTK has provided sufficient factual allegations and non-conclusory testimony to establish that Klastech's conduct pursuant to the Agreement gives rise to a "substantial connection" with California by creating "'continuing obligations' between [itself] and [a] resident[ ] of the forum." *See Burger King*, 471 U.S. at 475-76. First, just like the defendant in *Burger King*, Klastech "reached out" to a California corporation to enter into a long-term relationship from which Klastech derived manifold benefits in the form of hundreds of hours of work performed by GTK in California. Pursuant to the Agreement, GTK prepared evaluation materials for a potential Transaction, introduced Klastech to potential acquirors (many of them in California), participated in discussions with potential acquirors, and provided advice to Klastech on its interactions with PTI.

Second, although Klastech claims it believes GTK performed work for it in Germany, there is sufficient evidence to demonstrate that Klastech knew it was "affiliating [itself] with an enterprise based primarily in [California]." *See Burger King*, 471 U.S. at 481. First, the contract documents demonstrate Klastech's affiliation with California, albeit less strongly than in *Burger King* by listing GTK's San Francisco address on every page. Second, the parties' course of dealing provides evidence that Klastech knew it was establishing a long-term relationship that contemplated continuous contact with California. During negotiations, Langhans met with GTK in San Francisco to discuss the business and sales prospects for Klastech. Pursuant to the Agreement, Klastech communicated with GTK regularly (several times a week) via telephone and email, just as the parties in *Burger King* did. Finally, Madin, CEO of Klastech, came to San Francisco to meet with GTK and discuss the status of the work under the Agreement.

Thus, Plaintiff has demonstrated that Klastech knew it was affiliating itself with a California corporation in a manner that would lead to substantial contacts with California. . . .

b. Relatedness of Claim

"The second requirement for specific, personal jurisdiction is that the claim asserted in the litigation arises out of the defendant's forum related activities."

Panavision, 141 F.3d at 1322. The Court must determine if Plaintiff would not have been injured "but for" Defendant's contacts with California. *See id.* . . .

Here, Klastech's refusal to make contractually required payments in California, and to give GTK the contractually required recognition due in California, has caused foreseeable injuries to GTK in California. "But for" Klastech's engagement of GTK to perform services in California and its failure to make contractually required payments in California, GTK would not have suffered financial harm in California. The Court finds that GTK has demonstrated that its claim against Klastech arises out of Klastech's California-related activities.

c. Reasonableness

Next, the Court examines the seven reasonableness factors in turn. First, the Court considers the extent of Klastech's purposeful injection into the forum state. The Court finds that the activities which demonstrate that Klastech purposefully availed itself of the privilege of doing business in California are also sufficient in this case to meet the purposeful injection test. . . . Klastech engaged in repeated communications with GTK manager, Tabibian, in California in furtherance of their contractual relationship, including travelling to California to discuss business with GTK on at least one occasion. Klastech knew GTK had its principal place of business in California and it knew it was affiliating itself with GTK in a manner that would result in substantial contacts with California.

With respect to factor two, burden on the defendant, the fact that Klastech is a German corporation, headquartered in Germany, weighs against jurisdiction. However, Klastech has a designated representative for the USA West with two California telephone numbers, which mitigates Klastech's burden. Klastech's burden is further diminished by the fact that Klastech representatives have traveled to California on several occasions in the past for business, including business directly related to the events that gave rise to this suit. Furthermore, as the Supreme Court explained in *Burger King*, "because 'modern transportation and communications have made it much less burdensome for a party sued to defend himself in a State where he engages in economic activity,' it usually will not be unfair to subject him to the burdens of litigating in another forum for disputes relating to such activity." *Burger King*, 471 U.S. at 474. Therefore, the Court finds that the burden on Klastech of litigating in California only weakly favors Klastech.

The third factor, conflict with the sovereignty of a defendant's state, requires "an examination of the competing sovereign interests in regulating [the defendant's] behavior. *Dole Food*, 303 F.3d at 1115. Because Klastech has submitted as uncontroverted evidence the declaration of Burgess that Klastech is headquartered in Germany, the Court must examine the interests of the United States and Germany in adjudicating this dispute. Klastech currently has an ongoing relationship with the United States because it is a wholly owned and controlled subsidiary of PTI. Klastech also had an ongoing relationship with the United States during the events that gave rise to this claim because its employees travelled to the United States to attend trade shows and in connection with the Agreement. During that time, Klastech used an independent contractor to sell some of its products in California, another connection to the United States. Furthermore, the extent of conflict with Germany's interest in adjudicating this suit is unclear. Although Klastech is headquartered in Germany, GTK has provided affidavits stating that "essentially all of GTK's work pursuant to the Klastech Engagement was performed in California." The Agreement is governed by New York law, not German law. . . . In light of Klastech's past and ongoing U.S.-based relationships, this factor favors GTK.

For factor four, the Court considers the forum state's interest in adjudicating the suit. California has a "'manifest interest' in providing its residents with a convenient forum for redressing injuries inflicted by out-of-state actors." *See Burger King*, 471 U.S. at 473. GTK is a California corporation with its principal place of business in California so this factor favors GTK.

Factor five, concerning efficiency of the forum, examines the location of the witnesses and the evidence, as well as which substantive law governs the dispute. New York law governs the Agreement, but there are no other connections with New York that indicate it would be a more efficient forum than California. . . .

Finally, the Court considers whether an alternative forum is unavailable. There is a split in the Ninth Circuit regarding which party bears the burden on this issue, although the great weight of Ninth Circuit authority favors putting the burden on the plaintiff. Klastech has suggested that Germany or New York would be a valid alternative forum, and GTK has not presented any evidence that it would be precluded from suing Klastech in either jurisdiction. GTK counters that jurisdiction in Germany would be inconvenient and unfair, but this is not the relevant standard. Without any evidence that GTK could not obtain effective relief in Germany, this factor favors Klastech.

. . . Klastech had, and continues to have, ongoing relationships with the U.S., and GTK was the intended audience of all Klastech's communications with California. Of the two factors that favor Klastech, factor two (the burden on the defendant) favors Klastech only weakly, and, with regards to factor seven, the Ninth Circuit has held that "[w]hether another reasonable forum exists becomes an issue only when the forum state is shown to be unreasonable." Thus, the Court finds that in light of the "heavy burden" on Klastech to make a "compelling case," Klastech's ongoing relationship with the U.S. and California, and Klastech's purposeful injection into California, it is not unreasonable for California to exercise personal jurisdiction over Klastech.

Having found that Plaintiff established the first two requirements of personal jurisdiction, and that Klastech failed to present compelling evidence that the exercise of jurisdiction would be unreasonable, the Klastech Motion to Dismiss for lack of personal jurisdiction is DENIED.

C. Triangle Is Subject to Specific Jurisdiction

For the reasons discussed below, the Court finds that GTK has made a prima facie showing that (i) Triangle intentionally committed a "foreign act that is both aimed at and has effect in the forum state," and (ii) GTK's claim arises out of Triangle's forum-related activities. The Court further finds that Triangle has not presented "compelling" evidence that the exercise of jurisdiction is unreasonable. Therefore, the Court will exercise specific, personal jurisdiction over Triangle.

a. Purposeful Direction

The Ninth Circuit often refers to the first element of specific jurisdiction "in shorthand fashion, as the 'purposeful availment' prong." *Yahoo! Inc. v. La Ligue Contre Le Racisme Et L'Antisemitisme*, 433 F.3d 1199, 1206 (9th Cir. 2006) (en banc) (per curiam). Nevertheless, "[d]espite its label, this prong includes both purposeful availment and purposeful direction." *Id.* In tort cases, the relevant inquiry is "whether a defendant *purposefully directs* his activities at the forum state[.]" *Id.* (emphasis added) (internal quotations omitted). "[T]he [Supreme] Court has allowed the exercise of jurisdiction over a defendant whose only 'contact' with the forum state is the 'purposeful direction' of a *foreign* act having *effect* in the forum state." *Haisten v. Grass Valley Medical Reimbursement Fund*, 784 F.2d 1392, 1397 (9th Cir. 1986) (citing *Calder v. Jones*, 465 U.S. 783, 789 (1984)). Under Ninth Circuit precedent, the purposeful direction requirement for tort cases is analyzed under the "effects" test derived from *Calder*.

GTK asserts a claim for tortious interference with contract against Triangle based on its alleged fraudulent representations in the Purchase Agreement and concealment of the existence of the Agreement. Thus, the *Calder* "effects" test applies to determine whether Triangle purposefully directed its conduct at California. Under *Calder*, "the 'effects' test requires that the defendant allegedly have (1) committed an intentional act, (2) expressly aimed at the forum state, (3) causing harm that the defendant knows is likely to be suffered in the forum state." *Dole Food*, 303 F.3d at 1111. . . .

i. Intentional Act

The first prong of purposeful direction is easily satisfied and generally glossed over by the courts. GTK need only allege that Triangle acted intentionally when it represented to PTI that Klastech had no obligations to any investment bank in connection with the Transaction. GTK alleges that despite Triangle's awareness of the Agreement, Triangle knowingly made false representations to PTI, and wrongfully failed to disclose the Agreement, with the intent to induce Klastech to breach the Agreement and to deprive GTK of the payments and other benefits due it under the Agreement. GTK refers to email communications between Tabibian and Langhans, in which Langhans represents herself as reaching out to GTK on behalf of Triangle for its assistance in "identifying potential M & A possibilities" for Klastech and "mak[ing] [Klastech] attractive for an exit." GTK also provides email communications in which Langhans, appearing to represent Triangle, discusses PTI with GTK. GTK has sufficiently alleged that Triangle acted intentionally when it represented in the Purchase Agreement that Klastech had no obligations to any investment bank or other entity in connection with the Transaction.

ii. Express Aiming at Forum State

The "express aiming" requirement "is satisfied when the defendant is alleged to have engaged in wrongful conduct targeted at a plaintiff whom the defendant knows to be a resident of the forum state." *Bancroft & Masters*, 223 F.3d at 1087. However, the Supreme Court recently clarified that the plaintiff cannot be the only link between the defendant and the forum, but rather "the defendant's suit-related conduct must create a substantial connection with the forum State." *Walden v. Fiore*, 134 S. Ct. 1115, 1121-22 (2014) (citing *Helicopteros Nacionales de Colombia, S.A. v. Hall*, 466 U.S. 408, 417 (1984).

In *Walden*, the plaintiffs, who were Nevada residents, sought to establish Nevada's personal jurisdiction over defendant Walden, a Georgia police officer, who seized a large amount of cash from the plaintiffs in Georgia and then allegedly submitted a false probable cause affidavit justifying the seizure. *Id.* at 1117. The Ninth Circuit held that Walden's submission of the false affidavit with the knowledge that it would affect persons with significant Nevada contacts demonstrated sufficient minimum contacts with Nevada related to the claim for Nevada to exercise specific, personal jurisdiction. *Id.* at 1120. The Supreme Court reversed, explaining that the Ninth Circuit improperly shifted the focus of its minimum contacts analysis from defendant's contact with the forum to defendant's contact with the plaintiffs. *Id.* at 1124. Despite the plaintiffs' allegations that they suffered the harm in Nevada, the Court found that no part of the defendant's course of conduct occurred in the forum state, and he formed no jurisdictionally relevant contacts with that forum. *Id.* In sum, the plaintiffs' injury occurred in Nevada simply because that is where plaintiffs chose to be when they desired to use the seized funds, but "none of [the defendant's] challenged conduct had anything to do with Nevada itself." *Id.* at 1125.

. . .

According to the Supreme Court in *Walden*, the key to the exercise of personal jurisdiction in *Calder* was that "the 'effects' caused by defendants' article — *i.e.*, the injury to the plaintiff's reputation in the estimation of the California public — connected the defendants' conduct to *California*, not just to a plaintiff who lived there" because the defendants intentionally circulated the article in California. *Walden*, 134 S. Ct. at 1124.

In determining whether Triangle "expressly aimed" its conduct at California, the Court examines whether Triangle's "suit-related conduct" "connects [it] to the forum in a meaningful way." *See id.* at 1121-22, 25. Relevant contacts include physical presence in the state, as well as conduct demonstrating that Triangle "reached out beyond" its borders to create substantial contact with California. *See id.* at 1112.

The Court finds that Triangle's conduct establishes these necessary contacts with California. First, GTK has presented evidence that Triangle "reached out beyond" Germany to GTK in California, after identifying it through a web search, to negotiate the Agreement for services. Triangle principal, Langhans, then entered California's borders to meet with Tabibian, a decision-maker for GTK, in San Francisco on March 9, 2010 to discuss the business and sale prospects for Klastech. This conduct led to a continuing relationship with GTK in California during which GTK provided advice to Klastech and Triangle on approach strategies for potential acquirors, including several California-based corporations and PTI, the company with which Triangle entered the Purchase Agreement. Also relevant, although not sufficient on its own, is that Triangle's allegedly fraudulent representations in the Purchase Agreement caused GTK economic injury in California, where Triangle knew that GTK was based.

. . . Therefore, the Court finds that Triangle's "intentional, and allegedly tortious, actions were expressly aimed at California." *See Bancroft & Masters*, 223 F.3d at 1087.

iii. Causing Harm in the Forum State

The final element of the *Calder* "effects" test is satisfied if Plaintiff can show that "a jurisdictionally sufficient amount of harm is suffered in the forum state." *Yahoo!*, 433 F.3d at 1207 (en banc). The Ninth Circuit has relied on a corporation's principal place of business in determining the location of its economic injury. *See Dole Food*, 303 F.3d at 1114. "[W]hen a forum in which a plaintiff corporation has its principal place of business is in the same forum toward which defendants expressly aim their acts, the 'effect' test permits that forum to exercise personal jurisdiction." *Id.* Accordingly, in *Dole Food*, the Ninth Circuit held that, where the defendants had expressly aimed their conduct at the same forum where plaintiff had its principal place of business, the plaintiff suffered a jurisdictionally sufficient amount of harm in the forum state. *Id.*

Following *Dole Food*, GTK has suffered a jurisdictionally sufficient amount of harm in California because (i) Triangle's tortious conduct satisfies the "express aiming" requirement and (ii) GTK's principal place of business is in California, which is therefore the location of its economic injury. Specifically, GTK alleges that, as a result of Triangle's harmful conduct, Klastech has refused to pay sums due under the Agreement of not less than $400,000 and to acknowledge publicly GTK's role in the Transaction per the Agreement. As a result, GTK asserts that it has been damaged in California in an amount not less than $400,000 plus the additional costs, including attorneys' fees, it has been forced to incur to enforce its rights.

The Court finds that the foregoing constitutes a "jurisdictionally sufficient" amount of harm that GTK suffered in California and that GTK has established the final element of the *Calder* "effects" test. Accordingly, the Court finds that GTK's allegations demonstrate that Triangle purposefully directed its conduct at California.

2. Relatedness of the Claim

. . .

GTK has sufficiently demonstrated that "but for" Triangle's reaching out to GTK in California, negotiating the Agreement with GTK on behalf of Klastech, continuing to communicate with GTK during the course of its performance of the Agreement, and representing to PTI that Klastech had no obligations to any investment company, GTK would not have suffered harm in California. Accordingly, GTK's allegations and affidavits show that its claim against Triangle arises out of Triangle's forum related contacts.

3. Reasonableness

Next, the Court considers the seven reasonableness factors in turn. For factor one, the Court finds that Triangle's activities, which satisfy the "purposeful direction" prong, demonstrate a sufficient level of purposeful injection into the forum state to support a finding of reasonableness. Triangle principals, Langhans and Geiger, knew GTK had its principal place of business in California, reached out and negotiated the Agreement with GTK on behalf of Klastech, repeatedly communicated with GTK pursuant to the Agreement, and allegedly acted with the intent to deprive GTK of the benefits due it under the Agreement.

Factor two, burden on defendant, weighs more strongly in favor of Triangle than it does for Klastech because Triangle has no ongoing presence in the United States or California. Specifically, Triangle is a German corporation, headquartered in Germany, with no evidence of any connections to California outside of the events that gave rise to this claim. While Langhans traveled to California once in connection with the events that gave rise to this claim, there is no evidence that Triangle employees regularly travel to the United States. Therefore, while not dispositive in light of "modern advances in communications and transportation," this factor favors Triangle.

For factor three, in its "an examination of the competing sovereign interests in regulating [the defendant's] behavior," the Court finds that . . . Triangle's connections to Germany are the same as Klastech's, and therefore, the extent of conflict with Germany's interest in adjudicating this suit is similarly unclear. In sum, the sovereignty factor favors Triangle. . . .

Fourth, California has a "'manifest interest' in providing its residents with a convenient forum for redressing injuries inflicted by out-of-state actors." *See Burger King*, 471 U.S. at 473. Because GTK is a California corporation with its principal place of business in California, this factor favors GTK.

For the fifth factor, it is difficult to determine on the current record whether California would be the most efficient forum for resolution of the dispute. The parties do not offer evidence regarding the location of the witnesses and evidence, but presumably there are some witnesses in Germany (where Triangle is based) and some in California (where GTK is based) so neither forum has a clear efficiency advantage with respect to witnesses. Likewise, the parties do not discuss which substantive law should govern GTK's tort claim. . . . Therefore, at this time, an analysis based on the substantive law does not clearly favor either party. . . . Accordingly, the fact that this Court will exercise personal jurisdiction over Klastech tips this factor in GTK's favor, though only slightly.

Factor six, convenience to plaintiff, favors GTK, which is based in California, but is "is not of paramount importance" in this circuit. *See Dole Food*, 303 F.3d at 1116.

Factor seven, unavailability of an alternative forum, follows a similar analysis for Triangle as it did for Klastech. Triangle has not suggested an alternative forum, but presumably it would prefer to adjudicate this dispute in Germany. As mentioned above, GTK has not presented any evidence that it could not obtain effective relief in Germany. Therefore, without deciding which party bears the burden of proving unavailability of an alternative forum, this factor favors Triangle.

The reasonableness factors weigh slightly in Triangle's favor due to Triangle's lack of ongoing contacts with California or the United States. Nevertheless, Ninth Circuit jurisprudence emphasizes the "heavy burden" of proving a "compelling case" of unreasonableness and has tended to find jurisdiction is reasonable when the factors do not clearly favor either party. *See Dole Food*, 303 F.3d at 1117. Considering all the factors in light of the defendant's burden of presenting a "compelling case," its purposeful injection into California, and its ability to manage travel to and communications with California in the course of the Agreement, the Court concludes that the exercise of jurisdiction over Triangle in California is reasonable.

Having found that GTK established the first two requirements of personal jurisdiction, and that Triangle failed to present compelling evidence that the exercise of jurisdiction would be unreasonable, the Court will assert personal jurisdiction over Triangle. The Triangle Motion to Dismiss for lack of personal jurisdiction is therefore DENIED.

. . .

IV. Conclusion

For the foregoing reasons, Defendants' Motions to Dismiss for Lack of Personal Jurisdiction and Defendant Klastech's Motion to Dismiss for Lack of Subject Matter Jurisdiction are DENIED.

IT IS SO ORDERED.

NOTES AND QUESTIONS

1. **The Framework for Analyzing Specific Jurisdiction in Transnational Cases.** Based on your reading of *Klastech* and the overview of specific jurisdiction in the Supreme Court's unanimous opinion in *Goodyear* (discussed above), what is the basic framework for analyzing the issue of specific jurisdiction? Outline how you would structure an analysis of specific jurisdiction.

2. **Personal Jurisdiction in Tort and Contract Cases.** Note that the personal jurisdiction analysis employed above differed based on whether the claim sounded in contract or tort. What accounts for this difference? Is there really a difference, or is this just semantics? A contract between a plaintiff and a foreign defendant is not sufficient in and of itself to establish personal jurisdiction over the defendant in the forum. *Burger King Corp. v. Rudzewicz*, 471 U.S. 462, 478-79 (1985). This is so because personal jurisdiction does not turn on "mechanical tests or on conceptualistic theories of the place of contracting or of performance." *Id.* at 478. The Supreme Court has instead "emphasized the need for a highly realistic approach that recognizes that a contract is ordinarily but an intermediate step serving to tie up prior business negotiations with future consequences which themselves are the real object of the business transaction. It is these factors — prior negotiations and contemplated future consequences, along with the terms of the contract and the parties' actual course of dealing — that must be evaluated in determining whether the defendant purposefully established minimum contacts within the forum." *Id.*

3. **Personal Jurisdiction and the Internet.** Just as transnational contract and tort cases can be analyzed differently, so too can transnational Internet cases. Although the Supreme Court has not directly addressed the question of what analysis should be employed, most lower courts have embraced the "sliding scale" approach announced in *Zippo Manufacturing Co. v. Zippo Dot Com, Inc.*, 952 F. Supp. 1119 (W.D. Pa. 1997). *See, e.g., ALS Scan, Inc. v. Digital Service Consultants, Inc.*, 293 F.3d 707 (4th Cir. 2002) (citing *Zippo*). In *Zippo*, the court concluded that personal jurisdiction is not proper over a defendant which has merely engaged in passive Internet activity, i.e., the mere posting of information on an Internet website which is accessible to users in foreign jurisdictions. Conversely, *Zippo* recognized that a defendant that enters into contracts with the residents of a foreign jurisdiction that involve the knowing and repeated transmission of computer files over the Internet is engaged in the privilege of conducting commercial activity in the forum. Finally, *Zippo* identified a "middle ground" occupied by interactive websites where a user can exchange information with the host computer; in this category of cases, *Zippo* posits that courts must examine the "level of interactivity and commercial nature of the exchange of information that occurs on the Web site" to determine if sufficient contacts exist to warrant the exercise of jurisdiction. *See Carefirst of Maryland, Inc. v. Carefirst Pregnancy Centers, Inc.*, 334 F.3d 390, 401 (4th Cir. 2003); *Mink v. AAAA Development LLC*, 190 F.3d 333, 336 (5th Cir. 1999); *Cybersell, Inc. v. Cybersell, Inc.*, 130 F.3d 414 (9th Cir. 1997). Under this approach, courts treat interactive websites (such as those that allow you to order products online) and passive websites (such as those that simply post information or advertise) differently. The former will generally subject the defendant to personal jurisdiction, whereas the latter generally require something more to indicate that the defendant purposefully availed itself of the forum state.

4. **What Contacts Matter?** When analyzing contacts for purposes of specific jurisdiction, note that it is the *defendant's* contacts with the forum state that matter. As the Supreme Court explained in *Walden v. Fiore*, 571 U.S. 277, 290 (2014), a "mere injury to a forum resident is not a sufficient connection to the forum" for specific jurisdiction unless the defendant itself (or its product) caused the injury in the forum. Likewise, specific jurisdiction requires an "affiliation between the forum and the underlying controversy," but "the relationship must arise out of contacts that the defendant *himself* creates with the forum state." *Id.* at 283-84 & n.6.

5. **Forum Selection Clauses.** Parties to transnational commercial contracts commonly include a "forum selection" clause designating where disputes arising under the contract may or must be resolved. These clauses generally will be given effect in U.S. courts, and valid forum selection clauses are treated as waiving objections to personal jurisdiction. They are discussed in more detail in Chapter 10. Why do you think parties often agree to such clauses? Why might parties not agree to them? What difficulties might they entail?

In the cases that follow, we take up the question of personal jurisdiction in products liability cases.

Asahi Metal Industry Co., Ltd. v. Superior Court of California, Solano County

480 U.S. 102 (1987)

Justice O'CONNOR announced the judgment of the Court and delivered the unanimous opinion of the Court with respect to Part I, the opinion of the Court with respect to Part II-B, in which THE CHIEF JUSTICE, Justice BRENNAN, Justice WHITE, Justice MARSHALL, Justice BLACKMUN, Justice POWELL, and Justice STEVENS join, and an opinion with respect to Parts II-A and III, in which THE CHIEF JUSTICE, Justice POWELL, and Justice SCALIA join.

This case presents the question whether the mere awareness on the part of a foreign defendant that the components it manufactured, sold, and delivered outside the United States would reach the forum State in the stream of commerce constitutes "minimum contacts" between the defendant and the forum State such that the exercise of jurisdiction "does not offend traditional notions of fair play and substantial justice." *International Shoe Co. v. Washington*, 326 U.S. 310, 316 (1945).

I

On September 23, 1978, on Interstate Highway 80 in Solano County, California, Gary Zurcher lost control of his Honda motorcycle and collided with a tractor. Zurcher was severely injured, and his passenger and wife, Ruth Ann Moreno, was killed. In September 1979, Zurcher filed a product liability action in the Superior Court of the State of California in and for the County of Solano. Zurcher alleged that the 1978 accident was caused by a sudden loss of air and an explosion in the rear tire of the motorcycle, and alleged that the motorcycle tire, tube, and sealant were defective. Zurcher's complaint named, *inter alia*, Cheng Shin Rubber Industrial Co., Ltd. (Cheng Shin), the Taiwanese manufacturer of the tube. Cheng Shin in turn filed a cross-complaint seeking indemnification from its codefendants and from petitioner, Asahi Metal Industry Co., Ltd. (Asahi), the manufacturer of the tube's valve assembly. . . .

California's long-arm statute authorizes the exercise of jurisdiction "on any basis not inconsistent with the Constitution of this state or of the United States." Cal. Civ. Proc. Code Ann. § 410.10. Asahi moved to quash Cheng Shin's service of summons, arguing the State could not exert jurisdiction over it consistent with the Due Process Clause of the Fourteenth Amendment.

In relation to the motion, the following information was submitted by Asahi and Cheng Shin. Asahi is a Japanese corporation. It manufactures tire valve assemblies in Japan and sells the assemblies to Cheng Shin, and to several other tire manufacturers, for use as components in finished tire tubes. Asahi's sales to Cheng Shin took place in Taiwan. The shipments from Asahi to Cheng Shin were sent from Japan to Taiwan. Cheng Shin bought and incorporated into its tire tubes 150,000 Asahi valve assemblies in 1978; 500,000 in 1979; 500,000 in 1980; 100,000 in 1981; and 100,000 in 1982. Sales to Cheng Shin accounted for 1.24 percent of Asahi's income in 1981 and 0.44 percent in 1982. Cheng Shin alleged that approximately 20 percent of its sales in the United States are in California. Cheng Shin purchases valve assemblies from other suppliers as well, and sells finished tubes throughout the world.

In 1983 an attorney for Cheng Shin conducted an informal examination of the valve stems of the tire tubes sold in one cycle store in Solano County. The attorney declared that of the approximately 115 tire tubes in the store, 97 were purportedly manufactured in Japan or Taiwan, and of those 97, 21 valve stems were marked with the circled letter "A", apparently Asahi's trademark. Of the 21 Asahi valve stems, 12 were incorporated into Cheng Shin tire tubes. The store contained 41 other Cheng Shin tubes that incorporated the valve assemblies of other manufacturers. An affidavit of a manager of Cheng Shin whose duties included the purchasing of component parts stated: "In discussions with Asahi regarding the purchase of valve stem assemblies the fact that my Company sells tubes throughout the world and specifically the United States has been discussed. I am informed and believe that Asahi was fully aware that valve stem assemblies sold to my Company and to others would end up throughout the United States and in California." . . .

. . . The Superior Court denied the motion to quash summons, stating: "Asahi obviously does business on an international scale. It is not unreasonable that they defend claims of defect in their product on an international scale."

The Court of Appeal of the State of California issued a peremptory writ of mandate commanding the Superior Court to quash service of summons. The court concluded that "it would be unreasonable to require Asahi to respond in California solely on the basis of ultimately realized foreseeability that the product into which its component was embodied would be sold all over the world including California."

The Supreme Court of the State of California reversed. . . . The court observed: "Asahi has no offices, property or agents in California. It solicits no business in California and has made no direct sales [in California]." Moreover, "Asahi did not design or control the system of distribution that carried its valve assemblies into California." Nevertheless, the court found the exercise of jurisdiction over Asahi to be consistent with the Due Process Clause. It concluded that Asahi knew that some of the valve assemblies sold to Cheng Shin would be incorporated into tire tubes sold in California, and that Asahi benefited indirectly from the sale in California of products incorporating its components. The court considered Asahi's intentional act of placing its components into the stream of commerce — that is, by delivering the components to Cheng Shin in Taiwan — coupled with Asahi's awareness that some of the components would eventually find their way into California, sufficient to form the basis for state court jurisdiction under the Due Process Clause.

We . . . reverse.

II

A

"[T]he constitutional touchstone" of the determination whether an exercise of personal jurisdiction comports with due process "remains whether the defendant purposefully established minimum contacts in the forum State." *Burger King Corp. v. Rudzewicz*, 471 U.S. 462, 474 (1985). . . . [M]inimum contacts must have a basis in "some act by which the defendant purposefully avails itself of the privilege of conducting activities within the forum State, thus invoking the benefits and protections of its laws." *Burger King*, 471 U.S., at 475. "Jurisdiction is proper . . . where the contacts proximately result from actions by the defendant *himself* that create a substantial connection with the forum State." *Ibid.*

Applying the principle that minimum contacts must be based on an act of the defendant, the Court in *World-Wide Volkswagen Corp. v. Woodson*, 444 U.S. 286 (1980), rejected the assertion that a *consumer's* unilateral act of bringing the defendant's product into the forum State was a sufficient constitutional basis for personal jurisdiction over the defendant. It had been argued in *World-Wide Volkswagen* that because an automobile retailer and its wholesale distributor sold a product mobile by design and purpose, they could foresee being haled into court in the distant States into which their customers might drive. The Court rejected this concept of foreseeability as an insufficient basis for jurisdiction under the Due Process Clause. The Court disclaimed, however, the idea that "foreseeability is wholly irrelevant" to personal jurisdiction, concluding that "[t]he forum State does not exceed its powers under the Due Process Clause if it asserts personal jurisdiction over a corporation that delivers its products into the stream of commerce with the expectation that they will be purchased by consumers in the forum State." The Court reasoned:

> "When a corporation purposefully avails itself of the privilege of conducting activities within the forum State, it has clear notice that it is subject to suit there, and can act to alleviate the risk of burdensome litigation by procuring insurance, passing the expected costs on to customers, or, if the risks are too great, severing its connection with the State. Hence if the sale of a product of a manufacturer or distributor . . . is not simply an isolated occurrence, but arises from the efforts of the manufacturer or distributor to serve, directly or indirectly, the market for its product in other States, it is not unreasonable to subject it to suit in one of those States if its allegedly defective merchandise has there been the source of injury to its owners or to others." *Id.*, at 297.

In *World-Wide Volkswagen* itself, the state court sought to base jurisdiction not on any act of the defendant, but on the foreseeable unilateral actions of the consumer. Since *World-Wide Volkswagen*, lower courts have been confronted with cases in which the defendant acted by placing a product in the stream of commerce, and the stream eventually swept defendant's product into the forum State, but the defendant did nothing else to purposefully avail itself of the market in the forum State. Some courts have understood the Due Process Clause, as interpreted in *World-Wide Volkswagen*, to allow an exercise of personal jurisdiction to be based on no more than the defendant's act of placing the product in the stream of commerce. Other courts have understood the Due Process Clause and the above-quoted language in *World-Wide Volkswagen* to require the action of the defendant to be more purposefully directed at the forum State than the mere act of placing a product in the stream of commerce.

. . .

We now find this latter position to be consonant with the requirements of due process. The "substantial connection," *Burger King*, 471 U.S., at 475, between the defendant and the forum State necessary for a finding of minimum contacts must come about by *an action of the defendant purposefully directed toward the forum State. Burger King*, 471 U.S., at 476. The placement of a product into the stream of commerce, without more, is not an act of the defendant purposefully directed toward the forum State. Additional conduct of the defendant may indicate an intent or purpose to serve the market in the forum State, for example, designing the product for the market in the forum State, advertising in the forum State, establishing channels for providing regular advice to customers in the forum State, or marketing the product through a distributor who has agreed to serve as the sales agent in the forum State. But a defendant's awareness that the stream of commerce may or will sweep the product into the forum State does not convert the mere act of placing the product into the stream into an act purposefully directed toward the forum State.

Assuming, *arguendo*, that respondents have established Asahi's awareness that some of the valves sold to Cheng Shin would be incorporated into tire tubes sold in California, respondents have not demonstrated any action by Asahi to purposefully avail itself of the California market. Asahi does not do business in California. It has no office, agents, employees, or property in California. It does not advertise or otherwise solicit business in California. It did not create, control, or employ the distribution system that brought its valves to California. There is no evidence that Asahi designed its product in anticipation of sales in California. On the basis of these facts, the exertion of personal jurisdiction over Asahi by the Superior Court of California exceeds the limits of due process.

B

The strictures of the Due Process Clause forbid a state court to exercise personal jurisdiction over Asahi under circumstances that would offend "traditional notions of fair play and substantial justice." *International Shoe Co. v. Washington*, 326 U.S., at 316.

We have previously explained that the determination of the reasonableness of the exercise of jurisdiction in each case will depend on an evaluation of several factors. A court must consider the burden on the defendant, the interests of the forum State, and the plaintiff's interest in obtaining relief. It must also weigh in its determination "the interstate judicial system's interest in obtaining the most efficient resolution of controversies; and the shared interest of the several States in furthering fundamental substantive social policies." *World-Wide Volkswagen*, 444 U.S., at 292.

A consideration of these factors in the present case clearly reveals the unreasonableness of the assertion of jurisdiction over Asahi, even apart from the question of the placement of goods in the stream of commerce.

Certainly the burden on the defendant in this case is severe. Asahi has been commanded by the Supreme Court of California not only to traverse the distance between Asahi's headquarters in Japan and the Superior Court of California in and for the County of Solano, but also to submit its dispute with Cheng Shin to a foreign nation's judicial system. The unique burdens placed upon one who must defend oneself in a foreign legal system should have significant weight in assessing the reasonableness of stretching the long arm of personal jurisdiction over national borders.

When minimum contacts have been established, often the interests of the plaintiff and the forum in the exercise of jurisdiction will justify even the serious burdens placed on the alien defendant. In the present case, however, the interests of the plaintiff and the forum in California's assertion of jurisdiction over Asahi are slight. All that remains is a claim for indemnification asserted by Cheng Shin, a Taiwanese corporation, against Asahi. The transaction on which the indemnification claim is based took place in Taiwan; Asahi's components were shipped from Japan to Taiwan. Cheng Shin has not demonstrated that it is more convenient for it to litigate its indemnification claim against Asahi in California rather than in Taiwan or Japan.

Because the plaintiff is not a California resident, California's legitimate interests in the dispute have considerably diminished. . . . The dispute between Cheng Shin and Asahi is primarily about indemnification rather than safety standards. Moreover, it is not at all clear at this point that California law should govern the question whether a Japanese corporation should indemnify a Taiwanese corporation on the basis of a sale made in Taiwan and a shipment of goods from Japan to Taiwan. *Phillips Petroleum Co. v. Shutts*, 472 U.S. 797, 821-822 (1985); *Allstate Insurance Co. v. Hague*, 449 U.S. 302, 312-313 (1981). The possibility of being haled into a California court as a result of an accident involving Asahi's components undoubtedly creates an additional deterrent to the manufacture of unsafe components; however, similar pressures will be placed on Asahi by the purchasers of its components as long as those who use Asahi components in their final products, and sell those products in California, are subject to the application of California tort law.

. . . The procedural and substantive interests of other nations in a state court's assertion of jurisdiction over an alien defendant will differ from case to case. In every case, however, those interests, as well as the Federal interest in Government's foreign relations policies, will be best served by a careful inquiry into the reasonableness of the assertion of jurisdiction in the particular case, and an unwillingness to find the serious burdens on an alien defendant outweighed by minimal interests on the part of the plaintiff or the forum State. "Great care and reserve should be exercised when extending our notions of personal jurisdiction into the international field." *United States v. First National City Bank*, 379 U.S. 378, 404 (1965) (Harlan, J., dissenting).

Considering the international context, the heavy burden on the alien defendant, and the slight interests of the plaintiff and the forum State, the exercise of personal jurisdiction by a California court over Asahi in this instance would be unreasonable and unfair.

III

Because the facts of this case do not establish minimum contacts such that the exercise of personal jurisdiction is consistent with fair play and substantial justice, the judgment of the Supreme Court of California is reversed, and the case is remanded for further proceedings not inconsistent with this opinion.

It is so ordered.

Justice BRENNAN, with whom Justice WHITE, Justice MARSHALL, and Justice BLACKMUN join, concurring in part and concurring in the judgment.

I do not agree with the interpretation in Part II-A of the stream-of-commerce theory, nor with the conclusion that Asahi did not "purposely avail itself of the California market." I do agree, however, with the Court's conclusion in Part II-B that the exercise of personal jurisdiction over Asahi in this case would not comport with "fair play and substantial justice," *International Shoe Co. v. Washington*, 326 U.S. 310, 320 (1945). This is one of those rare cases in which "minimum requirements inherent in the concept of 'fair play and substantial justice' . . . defeat the reasonableness of jurisdiction even [though] the defendant has purposefully engaged in forum activities." *Burger King Corp. v. Rudzewicz*, 471 U.S. 462, 477-478 (1985). I therefore join Parts I and II-B of the Court's opinion, and write separately to explain my disagreement with Part II-A.

. . . The stream of commerce refers not to unpredictable currents or eddies, but to the regular and anticipated flow of products from manufacture to distribution to retail sale. As long as a participant in this process is aware that the final product is being marketed in the forum State, the possibility of a lawsuit there cannot come as a surprise. Nor will the litigation present a burden for which there is no corresponding benefit. A defendant who has placed goods in the stream of commerce benefits economically from the retail sale of the final product in the forum State, and indirectly benefits from the State's laws that regulate and facilitate commercial activity. These benefits accrue regardless of whether that participant directly conducts business in the forum State, or engages in additional conduct directed toward that State. Accordingly, most courts and commentators have found that jurisdiction premised on the placement of a product into the stream of commerce is consistent with the Due Process Clause, and have not required a showing of additional conduct.

. . . Part II-A . . . represents a marked retreat from the analysis in *World-Wide Volkswagen v. Woodson*, 444 U.S. 286 (1980). In that case, . . . [t]he Court held that the possibility of an accident in Oklahoma, while to some extent foreseeable in light of the inherent mobility of the automobile, was not enough to establish minimum contacts between the forum State and the retailer or distributor. . . .

[T]he Court contrasted the foreseeability of litigation in a State to which a consumer fortuitously transports a defendant's product (insufficient contacts) with the foreseeability of litigation in a State where the defendant's product was regularly *sold* (sufficient contacts). The Court stated:

> "Hence if the *sale* of a product of a manufacturer or distributor such as Audi or Volkswagen is not simply an isolated occurrence, but arises from the efforts of the manufacturer or distributor to serve, *directly or indirectly*, the market for its product in other States, it is not unreasonable to subject it to suit in one of those States if its allegedly defective merchandise has there been the source of injury to its owner or to others. The forum State does not exceed its powers under the Due Process Clause if it asserts personal jurisdiction over a corporation that delivers its products into the stream of commerce *with the expectation that they will be purchased by consumers* in the forum State." *Id.*, at 297-298 (emphasis added).

. . .

The Court in *World-Wide Volkswagen* thus took great care to distinguish between a case involving goods which reach a distant State through a chain of distribution and a case involving goods which reach the same State because a consumer took them there. The California Supreme Court took note of this distinction, and correctly concluded that our holding in *World-Wide Volkswagen* preserved the stream-of-commerce theory. . . .

In this case, the facts found by the California Supreme Court support its finding of minimum contacts. The court found that "[a]lthough Asahi did not design or control the system of distribution that carried its valve assemblies into California, Asahi was aware of the distribution system's operation, and it knew that it would benefit economically from the sale in California of products incorporating its components." Accordingly, I cannot join the determination in Part II-A that Asahi's regular and extensive sales of component parts to a manufacturer it knew was making regular sales of the final product in California is insufficient to establish minimum contacts with California.

J. McIntyre Machinery, Ltd. v. Nicastro

564 U.S. 873 (2011)

Justice KENNEDY announced the judgment of the Court and delivered an opinion, in which THE CHIEF JUSTICE, Justice SCALIA, and Justice THOMAS join.

Whether a person or entity is subject to the jurisdiction of a state court despite not having been present in the State either at the time of suit or at the time of the alleged injury, and despite not having consented to the exercise of jurisdiction, is a question that arises with great frequency in the routine course of litigation. The rules and standards for determining when a State does or does not have jurisdiction over an absent party have been unclear because of decades-old questions left open in *Asahi Metal Industry Co. v. Superior Court of Cal., Solano Cty.*, 480 U.S. 102 (1987).

Here, the Supreme Court of New Jersey, relying in part on *Asahi*, held that New Jersey's courts can exercise jurisdiction over a foreign manufacturer of a product so long as the manufacturer "knows or reasonably should know that its products are distributed through a nationwide distribution system that might lead to those products being sold in any of the fifty states." *Nicastro v. McIntyre Machinery America, Ltd.*, 201 N.J. 48 (2010). Applying that test, the court concluded that a British manufacturer of scrap metal machines was subject to jurisdiction in New Jersey, even though at no time had it advertised in, sent goods to, or in any relevant sense targeted the State.

That decision cannot be sustained. . . . As a general rule, the exercise of judicial power is not lawful unless the defendant purposefully avails itself of the privilege of conducting activities within the forum State, thus invoking the benefits and protections of its laws. There may be exceptions, say, for instance, in cases involving an intentional tort. But the general rule is applicable in this products-liability case, and the so-called "stream-of-commerce" doctrine cannot displace it.

I

This case arises from a products-liability suit filed in New Jersey state court. Robert Nicastro seriously injured his hand while using a metal-shearing machine manufactured by J. McIntyre Machinery, Ltd. (J. McIntyre). The accident occurred in New Jersey, but the machine was manufactured in England, where J. McIntyre is incorporated and operates. . . .

At oral argument in this Court, Nicastro's counsel stressed three primary facts in defense of New Jersey's assertion of jurisdiction over J. McIntyre.

First, an independent company agreed to sell J. McIntyre's machines in the United States. J. McIntyre itself did not sell its machines to buyers in this country beyond the U.S. distributor, and there is no allegation that the distributor was under J. McIntyre's control.

Second, J. McIntyre officials attended annual conventions for the scrap recycling industry to advertise J. McIntyre's machines alongside the distributor. The conventions took place in various States, but never in New Jersey.

Third, no more than four machines (the record suggests only one), including the machine that caused the injuries that are the basis for this suit, ended up in New Jersey.

In addition to these facts . . . , the New Jersey Supreme Court noted that J. McIntyre held both United States and European patents on its recycling technology. It also noted that the U.S. distributor structured its advertising and sales efforts in accordance with J. McIntyre's direction and guidance whenever possible, and that at least some of the machines were sold on consignment to the distributor.

In light of these facts, the New Jersey Supreme Court concluded that New Jersey courts could exercise jurisdiction over petitioner without contravention of the Due Process Clause. Jurisdiction was proper, in that court's view, because the injury occurred in New Jersey; because petitioner knew or reasonably should have known that its products are distributed through a nationwide distribution system that might lead to those products being sold in any of the fifty states; and because petitioner failed to take some reasonable step to prevent the distribution of its products in this State.

Both the New Jersey Supreme Court's holding and its account of what it called "[t]he stream-of-commerce doctrine of jurisdiction," were incorrect, however. . . .

II

The Due Process Clause protects an individual's right to be deprived of life, liberty, or property only by the exercise of lawful power. This is no less true with respect to the power of a sovereign to resolve disputes through judicial process than with respect to the power of a sovereign to prescribe rules of conduct for those within its sphere. . . .

A court may subject a defendant to judgment only when the defendant has sufficient contacts with the sovereign "such that the maintenance of the suit does not offend traditional notions of fair play and substantial justice." *International Shoe Co. v. Washington*, 326 U.S. 310, 316 (1945). . . . As a general rule, the sovereign's exercise of power requires some act by which the defendant purposefully avails itself of the privilege of conducting activities within the forum State, thus invoking the benefits and protections of its laws, though in some cases, as with an intentional tort, the defendant might well fall within the State's authority by reason of his attempt to obstruct its laws. In products-liability cases like this one, it is the defendant's purposeful availment that makes jurisdiction consistent with traditional notions of fair play and substantial justice.

A person may submit to a State's authority in a number of ways. There is, of course, explicit consent. . . . Citizenship or domicile — or, by analogy, incorporation or principal place of business for corporations — also indicates general submission to a State's powers. *Goodyear Dunlop Tires Operations, S.A. v. Brown.* . . . These examples support exercise of the general jurisdiction of the State's courts and allow the State to resolve both matters that originate within the State and those based on activities and events elsewhere. By contrast, those who live or operate primarily outside a State have a due process right not to be subjected to judgment in its courts as a general matter.

There is also a more limited form of submission to a State's authority for disputes that "arise out of or are connected with the activities within the state." *International Shoe Co.*, at 319. Where a defendant purposefully avails itself of the privilege of conducting activities within the forum State, thus invoking the benefits and protections of its laws, it submits to the judicial power of an otherwise foreign sovereign to the extent that power is exercised in connection with the defendant's activities touching on the State. In other words, submission through contact with and activity directed at a sovereign may justify specific jurisdiction in a suit arising out of or related to the defendant's contacts with the forum.

The imprecision arising from *Asahi*, for the most part, results from its statement of the relation between jurisdiction and the "stream of commerce." The stream of commerce, like other metaphors, has its deficiencies as well as its utility. It refers to the movement of goods from manufacturers through distributors to consumers, yet beyond that descriptive purpose its meaning is far from exact. This Court has stated that a defendant's placing goods into the stream of commerce "with the expectation that they will be purchased by consumers within the forum State" may indicate purposeful availment. *World-Wide Volkswagen Corp. v. Woodson*, 444 U.S. 286, 298 (1980) (finding that expectation lacking). But that statement does not amend the general rule of personal jurisdiction. It merely observes that a defendant may in an appropriate case be subject to jurisdiction without entering the forum — itself an unexceptional proposition — as where manufacturers or distributors seek to serve a given State's market. The principal inquiry in cases of this sort is whether the defendant's activities manifest an intention to submit to the power of a sovereign. . . . Sometimes a defendant does so by sending its goods rather than its agents. The defendant's transmission of goods permits the exercise of jurisdiction only where the defendant can be said to have targeted the forum; as a general rule, it is not enough that the defendant might have predicted that its goods will reach the forum State.

In *Asahi*, an opinion by Justice Brennan for four Justices outlined a different approach. It discarded the central concept of sovereign authority in favor of considerations of fairness and foreseeability. As that concurrence contended, "jurisdiction premised on the placement of a product into the stream of commerce [without more] is consistent with the Due Process Clause," for "[a]s long as a participant in this process is aware that the final product is being marketed in the forum State, the possibility of a lawsuit there cannot come as a surprise." 480 U.S., at 117. It was the premise of the concurring opinion that the defendant's ability to anticipate suit renders the assertion of jurisdiction fair. In this way, the opinion made foreseeability the touchstone of jurisdiction.

The standard set forth in Justice Brennan's concurrence was rejected in an opinion written by Justice O'Connor; but the relevant part of that opinion, too, commanded the assent of only four Justices, not a majority of the Court. . . .

Since *Asahi* was decided, the courts have sought to reconcile the competing opinions. But Justice Brennan's concurrence, advocating a rule based on general notions of fairness and foreseeability, is inconsistent with the premises of lawful judicial power. This Court's precedents make clear that it is the defendant's actions, not his expectations, that empower a State's courts to subject him to judgment.

. . .

[P]ersonal jurisdiction requires a forum-by-forum, or sovereign-by-sovereign, analysis. The question is whether a defendant has followed a course of conduct directed at the society or economy existing within the jurisdiction of a given sovereign, so that the sovereign has the power to subject the defendant to judgment concerning that conduct. Personal jurisdiction, of course, restricts judicial power not as a matter of sovereignty, but as a matter of individual liberty, for due process protects the individual's right to be subject only to lawful power. But whether a judicial judgment is lawful depends on whether the sovereign has authority to render it.

. . .

It must be remembered . . . that although this case and *Asahi* both involve foreign manufacturers, the undesirable consequences of Justice Brennan's approach are no less significant for domestic producers. The owner of a small Florida farm might sell crops to a large nearby distributor, for example, who might then distribute them to grocers across the country. If foreseeability were the controlling criterion, the farmer could be sued in Alaska or any number of other States' courts without ever leaving town. And the issue of foreseeability may itself be contested so that significant expenses are incurred just on the preliminary issue of jurisdiction. Jurisdictional rules should avoid these costs whenever possible.

The conclusion that the authority to subject a defendant to judgment depends on purposeful availment, consistent with Justice O'Connor's opinion in *Asahi*, does not by itself resolve many difficult questions of jurisdiction that will arise in particular cases. The defendant's conduct and the economic realities of the market the defendant seeks to serve will differ across cases, and judicial exposition will, in common-law fashion, clarify the contours of that principle.

III

In this case, petitioner directed marketing and sales efforts at the United States. . . . Here the question concerns the authority of a New Jersey state court to exercise jurisdiction, so it is petitioner's purposeful contacts with New Jersey, not with the United States, that alone are relevant.

Respondent has not established that J. McIntyre engaged in conduct purposefully directed at New Jersey. Recall that respondent's claim of jurisdiction centers on three facts: The distributor agreed to sell J. McIntyre's machines in the United States; J. McIntyre officials attended trade shows in several States but not in New Jersey; and up to four machines ended up in New Jersey. The British manufacturer had no office in New Jersey; it neither paid taxes nor owned property there; and it neither advertised in, nor sent any employees to, the State. Indeed, after discovery the trial court found that the defendant does not have a single contact with New Jersey short of the machine in question ending up in this state. These facts may reveal an intent to serve the U.S. market, but they do not show that J. McIntyre purposefully availed itself of the New Jersey market.

It is notable that the New Jersey Supreme Court appears to agree, for it could "not find that J. McIntyre had a presence or minimum contacts in this State — in any jurisprudential sense — that would justify a New Jersey court to exercise jurisdiction in this case." 201 N.J., at 61. The court nonetheless held that petitioner could be sued in New Jersey based on a stream-of-commerce theory of jurisdiction. As discussed, however, the stream-of-commerce metaphor cannot supersede either the mandate of the Due Process Clause or the limits on judicial authority that Clause ensures. The New Jersey Supreme Court also cited "significant policy reasons" to justify its holding, including the State's "strong interest in protecting its citizens from defective products." *Id.*, at 75. That interest is doubtless strong, but the Constitution commands restraint before discarding liberty in the name of expediency.

*   *   *

Due process protects petitioner's right to be subject only to lawful authority. At no time did petitioner engage in any activities in New Jersey that reveal an intent to invoke or benefit from the protection of its laws. New Jersey is without power to adjudge the rights and liabilities of J. McIntyre, and its exercise of jurisdiction would violate due process. The contrary judgment of the New Jersey Supreme Court is

Reversed.

Justice BREYER, with whom Justice ALITO joins, concurring in the judgment.

The Supreme Court of New Jersey adopted a broad understanding of the scope of personal jurisdiction based on its view that "[t]he increasingly fast-paced globalization of the world economy has removed national borders as barriers to trade." *Nicastro v. McIntyre Machinery America, Ltd.*, 201 N.J. 48, 52 (2010). I do not doubt that there have been many recent changes in commerce and communication, many of which are not anticipated by our precedents. But this case does not present any of those issues. So I think it unwise to announce a rule of broad applicability without full consideration of the modern-day consequences.

In my view, the outcome of this case is determined by our precedents. Based on the facts found by the New Jersey courts, respondent Robert Nicastro failed to meet his burden to demonstrate that it was constitutionally proper to exercise jurisdiction over petitioner J. McIntyre Machinery, Ltd. (British Manufacturer), a British firm that manufactures scrap-metal machines in Great Britain and sells them through an independent distributor in the United States (American Distributor). On that basis, I agree with the plurality that the contrary judgment of the Supreme Court of New Jersey should be reversed.

I

In asserting jurisdiction over the British Manufacturer, the Supreme Court of New Jersey relied most heavily on three primary facts as providing constitutionally sufficient "contacts" with New Jersey, thereby making it fundamentally fair to hale the British Manufacturer before its courts: (1) The American Distributor on one occasion sold and shipped one machine to a New Jersey customer, namely, Mr. Nicastro's employer, Mr. Curcio; (2) the British Manufacturer permitted, indeed wanted, its independent American Distributor to sell its machines to anyone in America willing to buy them; and (3) representatives of the British Manufacturer attended trade shows in such cities as Chicago, Las Vegas, New Orleans, Orlando, San Diego, and San Francisco. . . .

None of our precedents finds that a single isolated sale, even if accompanied by the kind of sales effort indicated here, is sufficient. Rather, this Court's previous holdings suggest the contrary. The Court has held that a single sale to a customer who takes an accident-causing product to a different State (where the accident takes place) is not a sufficient basis for asserting jurisdiction. See *World-Wide Volkswagen Corp. v. Woodson*, 444 U.S. 286 (1980). And the Court, in separate opinions, has strongly suggested that a single sale of a product in a State does not constitute an adequate basis for asserting jurisdiction over an out-of-state defendant, even if that defendant places his goods in the stream of commerce, fully aware (and hoping) that such a sale will take place. See *Asahi Metal Industry Co. v. Superior Court of Cal., Solano Cty.*, 480 U.S. 102, 111, 112 (1987) (opinion of O'Connor, J.) (requiring "something more" than simply placing "a product into the stream of commerce," even if defendant is "awar[e]" that the stream "may or will sweep the product into the forum State"); *id.*, at 117 (Brennan, J., concurring in part and concurring in judgment) (jurisdiction should lie where a sale in a State is part of "the regular and anticipated flow" of commerce into the State, but not where that sale is only an "edd[y]," *i.e.*, an isolated occurrence). . . .

Here, the relevant facts found by the New Jersey Supreme Court show no "regular . . . flow" or "regular course" of sales in New Jersey; and there is no "something more," such as special state-related design, advertising, advice, marketing, or anything else. Mr. Nicastro, who here bears the burden of proving jurisdiction, has shown no specific effort by the British Manufacturer to sell in New Jersey. He has introduced no list of potential New Jersey customers who might, for example, have regularly attended trade shows. And he has not otherwise shown that the British Manufacturer "purposefully avail[ed] itself of the privilege of conducting activities" within New Jersey, or that it delivered its goods in the stream of commerce "with the expectation that they will be purchased" by New Jersey users. *World-Wide Volkswagen*, at 297-298.

There may well have been other facts that Mr. Nicastro could have demonstrated in support of jurisdiction. And the dissent considers some of those facts. . . . But the plaintiff bears the burden of establishing jurisdiction, and here I would take the facts precisely as the New Jersey Supreme Court stated them. . . .

Accordingly, on the record present here, resolving this case requires no more than adhering to our precedents.

II

I would not go further. Because the incident at issue in this case does not implicate modern concerns, and because the factual record leaves many open questions, this is an unsuitable vehicle for making broad pronouncements that refashion basic jurisdictional rules.

A

The plurality seems to state strict rules that limit jurisdiction where a defendant does not "inten[d] to submit to the power of a sovereign" and cannot "be said to have targeted the forum." But what do those standards mean when a company targets the world by selling products from its Web site? And does it matter if, instead of shipping the products directly, a company consigns the products through an intermediary (say, Amazon.com) who then receives and fulfills the orders? And what if the company markets its products through popup advertisements that it knows will be viewed in a forum? Those issues have serious commercial consequences but are totally absent in this case.

B

But though I do not agree with the plurality's seemingly strict no-jurisdiction rule, I am not persuaded by the absolute approach adopted by the New Jersey

Supreme Court and urged by respondent and his *amici*. Under that view, a producer is subject to jurisdiction for a products-liability action so long as it "knows or reasonably should know that its products are distributed through a nationwide distribution system that *might* lead to those products being sold in any of the fifty states." 201 N.J., at 76-77 (emphasis added). In the context of this case, I cannot agree.

For one thing, to adopt this view would abandon the heretofore accepted inquiry of whether, focusing upon the relationship between the defendant, the forum, and the litigation, it is fair, in light of the defendant's contacts with that forum, to subject the defendant to suit there. . . .

For another, I cannot reconcile so automatic a rule with the constitutional demand for minimum contacts and purposeful availment, each of which rest upon a particular notion of defendant-focused fairness. A rule like the New Jersey Supreme Court's would permit every State to assert jurisdiction in a products-liability suit against any domestic manufacturer who sells its products (made anywhere in the United States) to a national distributor, no matter how large or small the manufacturer, no matter how distant the forum, and no matter how few the number of items that end up in the particular forum at issue. What might appear fair in the case of a large manufacturer which specifically seeks, or expects, an equal-sized distributor to sell its product in a distant State might seem unfair in the case of a small manufacturer (say, an Appalachian potter) who sells his product (cups and saucers) exclusively to a large distributor, who resells a single item (a coffee mug) to a buyer from a distant State (Hawaii). I know too little about the range of these or in-between possibilities to abandon in favor of the more absolute rule what has previously been this Court's less absolute approach.

Further, the fact that the defendant is a foreign, rather than a domestic, manufacturer makes the basic fairness of an absolute rule yet more uncertain. I am again less certain than is the New Jersey Supreme Court that the nature of international commerce has changed so significantly as to require a new approach to personal jurisdiction.

It may be that a larger firm can readily "alleviate the risk of burdensome litigation by procuring insurance, passing the expected costs on to customers, or, if the risks are too great, severing its connection with the State." *World-Wide Volkswagen*, at 297. But manufacturers come in many shapes and sizes. It may be fundamentally unfair to require a small Egyptian shirt maker, a Brazilian manufacturing cooperative, or a Kenyan coffee farmer, selling its products through international distributors, to respond to products-liability tort suits in virtually every State in the United States, even those in respect to which the foreign firm has no connection at all but the sale of a single (allegedly defective) good. And a rule like the New Jersey Supreme Court suggests would require every product manufacturer, large or small, selling to American distributors to understand not only the tort law of every State, but also the wide variance in the way courts within different States apply that law.

C

At a minimum, I would not work such a change to the law in the way either the plurality or the New Jersey Supreme Court suggests without a better understanding of the relevant contemporary commercial circumstances. . . .

. . . Accordingly, though I agree with the plurality as to the outcome of this case, I concur only in the judgment of that opinion and not its reasoning.

Justice GINSBURG, with whom Justice SOTOMAYOR and Justice KAGAN join, dissenting.

A foreign industrialist seeks to develop a market in the United States for machines it manufactures. It hopes to derive substantial revenue from sales it makes to United States purchasers. Where in the United States buyers reside does not matter to this manufacturer. Its goal is simply to sell as much as it can, wherever it can. It excludes no region or State from the market it wishes to reach. But, all things considered, it prefers to avoid products liability litigation in the United States. To that end, it engages a U.S. distributor to ship its machines stateside. Has it succeeded in escaping personal jurisdiction in a State where one of its products is sold and causes injury or even death to a local user?

Under this Court's pathmarking precedent in *International Shoe Co. v. Washington*, 326 U.S. 310 (1945), and subsequent decisions, one would expect the answer to be unequivocally, "No." But instead, six Justices of this Court, in divergent opinions, tell us that the manufacturer has avoided the jurisdiction of our state courts, except perhaps in States where its products are sold in sizeable quantities. Inconceivable as it may have seemed yesterday, the splintered majority today "turn[s] the clock back to the days before modern long-arm statutes when a manufacturer, to avoid being haled into court where a user is injured, need only Pilate-like wash its hands of a product by having independent distributors market it." Weintraub, A Map Out of the Personal Jurisdiction Labyrinth, 28 U.C. Davis L. Rev. 531, 555 (1995).

. . .

II

A few points on which there should be no genuine debate bear statement at the outset. First, all agree, McIntyre UK surely is not subject to general (all-purpose) jurisdiction in New Jersey courts, for that foreign-country corporation is hardly "at home" in New Jersey. See *Goodyear Dunlop Tires Operations, S.A. v. Brown*. The question, rather, is one of specific jurisdiction, which turns on an "affiliatio[n] between the forum and the underlying controversy." *Goodyear Dunlop*, at 2851.

Second, no issue of the fair and reasonable allocation of adjudicatory authority among States of the United States is present in this case. New Jersey's exercise of personal jurisdiction over a foreign manufacturer whose dangerous product caused a workplace injury in New Jersey does not tread on the domain, or diminish the sovereignty, of any sister State. Indeed, among States of the United States, the State in which the injury occurred would seem most suitable for litigation of a products liability tort claim. . . .

Third, the constitutional limits on a state court's adjudicatory authority derive from considerations of due process, not state sovereignty. As the Court clarified in *Insurance Corp. of Ireland v. Compagnie des Bauxites de Guinee*, 456 U.S. 694 (1982):

> "The restriction on state sovereign power described in *World-Wide Volkswagen Corp.* . . . must be seen as ultimately a function of the individual liberty interest preserved by the Due Process Clause. That Clause is the only source of the personal jurisdiction requirement and the Clause itself makes no mention of federalism concerns. Furthermore, if the federalism concept operated as an independent restriction on the sovereign power of the court, it would not be possible to waive the personal jurisdiction requirement: Individual actions cannot change the powers of sovereignty, although the individual can subject himself to powers from which he may otherwise be protected." *Id.*, at 703, n. 10.

. . . But see *ante* (plurality opinion) (asserting that "sovereign authority," not "fairness," is the "central concept" in determining personal jurisdiction).

Finally, in *International Shoe* itself, and decisions thereafter, the Court has made plain that legal fictions, notably "presence" and "implied consent," should be discarded, for they conceal the actual bases on which jurisdiction rests. . . .

Whatever the state of academic debate over the role of consent in modern jurisdictional doctrines, the plurality's notion that consent is the animating concept draws no support from controlling decisions of this Court. Quite the contrary, the Court has explained, a forum can exercise jurisdiction when its contacts with the controversy are sufficient; invocation of a fictitious consent, the Court has repeatedly said, is unnecessary and unhelpful. See, *e.g.*, *Burger King Corp. v. Rudzewicz*, 471 U.S. 462, 472 (1985).

III

This case is illustrative of marketing arrangements for sales in the United States common in today's commercial world. A foreign-country manufacturer engages a U.S. company to promote and distribute the manufacturer's products, not in any particular State, but anywhere and everywhere in the United States the distributor can attract purchasers. The product proves defective and injures a user in the State where the user lives or works. Often, as here, the manufacturer will have liability insurance covering personal injuries caused by its products.

When industrial accidents happen, a long-arm statute in the State where the injury occurs generally permits assertion of jurisdiction, upon giving proper notice, over the foreign manufacturer. . . .

The modern approach to jurisdiction over corporations and other legal entities, ushered in by *International Shoe*, gave prime place to reason and fairness. Is it not fair and reasonable, given the mode of trading of which this case is an example, to require the international seller to defend at the place its products cause injury? Do not litigational convenience and choice-of-law considerations point in that direction? On what measure of reason and fairness can it be considered undue to require McIntyre UK to defend in New Jersey as an incident of its efforts to develop a market for its industrial machines anywhere and everywhere in the United States? Is not the burden on McIntyre UK to defend in New Jersey fair, *i.e.*, a reasonable cost of transacting business internationally, in comparison to the burden on Nicastro to go to Nottingham, England to gain recompense for an injury he sustained using McIntyre's product at his workplace in Saddle Brook, New Jersey?

   . . .

In sum, McIntyre UK, by engaging McIntyre America to promote and sell its machines in the United States, "purposefully availed itself" of the United States market nationwide, not a market in a single State or a discrete collection of States. McIntyre UK thereby availed itself of the market of all States in which its products were sold by its exclusive distributor. "Th[e] 'purposeful availment' requirement," this Court has explained, simply "ensures that a defendant will not be haled into a jurisdiction solely as a result of 'random,' 'fortuitous,' or 'attenuated' contacts." *Burger King*, 471 U.S., at 475. Adjudicatory authority is appropriately exercised where actions by the defendant *himself* give rise to the affiliation with the forum. How could McIntyre UK not have intended, by its actions targeting a national market, to sell products in the fourth largest destination for imports among all States of the United States and the largest scrap metal market?

   . . .

B

The Court's judgment also puts United States plaintiffs at a disadvantage in comparison to similarly situated complainants elsewhere in the world. Of particular note, within the European Union, in which the United Kingdom is a participant, the jurisdiction New Jersey would have exercised is not at all exceptional. The European Regulation on Jurisdiction and the Recognition and Enforcement of Judgments provides for the exercise of specific jurisdiction "in matters relating to tort . . . in the courts for the place where the harmful event occurred." Council Reg. 44/2001, Art. 5, 2001 O.J. (L.12) 4. The European Court of Justice has interpreted this prescription to authorize jurisdiction either where the harmful act occurred or at the place of injury. See *Handelskwekerij G.J. Bier B.V. v. Mines de Potasse d'Alsace S.A.*, 1976 E.C.R. 1735, 1748-1749.

   . . .

          *   *   *

For the reasons stated, I would hold McIntyre UK answerable in New Jersey for the harm Nicastro suffered at his workplace in that State using McIntyre UK's shearing machine. While I dissent from the Court's judgment, I take heart that the plurality opinion does not speak for the Court, for that opinion would take a giant step away from the "notions of fair play and substantial justice" underlying *International Shoe*. 326 U.S., at 316.

NOTES AND QUESTIONS

1. **The Framework for Analyzing Specific Jurisdiction in Transnational Products Liability Cases.** Based on your reading of *Asahi* and *Nicastro,* what is the basic framework for analyzing the issue of specific jurisdiction in a transnational case? What two major parts of the framework are apparent in Parts II-A and II-B of the *Asahi* opinion? How would you structure your analysis of each of these two major parts? Outline how you would structure an analysis of specific jurisdiction.

2. **The Stream-of-Commerce Theory.** What is the test for establishing specific jurisdiction based on the entry into the forum state of a product or products through the stream of commerce? As the fractured opinions in *Asahi* and *Nicastro* demonstrate, even if the basic framework for analyzing specific jurisdiction is fairly clear, the Supreme Court has not settled on a majority answer to the stream-of-commerce question. Review the opinions — including the opinions of Justice O'Connor and Justice Brennan in *Asahi* and the opinions of Justice Kennedy, Justice Breyer, and Justice Ginsburg in *Nicastro* — to make sure you understand how they differ regarding the requirements for establishing specific jurisdiction based on a stream-of-commerce theory.

3. **Dealing with Split Opinions.** How, as a lawyer, should you argue cases when the Supreme Court has not adopted a rule by a majority? If you represent a plaintiff trying to establish personal jurisdiction over a defendant, what type of argument might you consider making based on the Court's holding and the facts of the case? What if you represent a defendant, trying to convince a court not to assert personal jurisdiction?

4. **Forum Selection in Transnational Cases:** *Asahi.* Why do you think the plaintiff in *Asahi* sued Cheng Shin in California? Why do you think Cheng Shin pursued its indemnification claim against Asahi in the same court? What other options might the plaintiff and Cheng Shin have had available? If you were Asahi's counsel, why might you want to avoid a U.S. forum? Do you think the case's transnational context affected the Court's decision? Should there be different approaches to specific jurisdiction cases for transnational cases and purely domestic cases?

5. **Forum Selection in Transnational Cases:** *Nicastro.* Why do you think the plaintiff in *Nicastro* sued the defendant in New Jersey? What other options might have been available? Why do you think the defendant opposed personal jurisdiction in New Jersey? What alternative forum might the defendant have preferred, and why?

6. **Stream-of-Commerce Theory: Is Targeting a State or the United States Required?** Why, in Justice Kennedy's plurality opinion in *Nicastro,* isn't targeting the United States generally for business enough to establish personal jurisdiction in New Jersey? Why, in Justice Ginsburg's opinion, did the defendant do more than just target the U.S. market generally? How is this case similar to or different from *World-Wide Volkswagen,* which is discussed by the various opinions?

7. **State of the Law After *Nicastro*.** Lower courts are divided on *Nicastro's* effect. Some courts follow the *Nicastro* plurality, *ESAB Group, Inc. v. Zurich Ins. PLC*, 685 F.3d 376, 392 (4th Cir. 2012), while others read Justice Breyer's concurrence to mean that the law did not change, *Monge v. RG Petro-Mach. (Group) Co.*, 701 F.3d 598, 619-20 (10th Cir. 2012). As such, some courts have continued to apply Justice Brennan's approach. *See In re Chinese Manufactured Drywall Products Liability Litigation*, 742 F.3d 576 (5th Cir. 2014) (describing the split).

8. **Policy: Should Congress Step In?** The *Nicastro* decision was subject to significant criticism in Congress. Specifically, it was argued that on account of the *Nicastro* decision, foreign manufacturers and producers whose products are sold in the United States could escape liability for harms occurring in the United States. A bill was introduced requiring foreign manufacturers to designate agents for service of process. Here is a link to the proposed legislation: https://www.govtrack.us/congress/bills/113/hr1910. Does it fix the problem? Or, does it just create new problems? In light of the materials studies thus far, what, in your view, is the appropriate test for specific jurisdiction in transnational cases?

9. **The Goals of Specific Jurisdiction.** Are the different opinions in *Nicastro* operating under different views of what personal jurisdiction is designed to do? What are these views? What do you think the personal jurisdiction doctrine is designed to accomplish? Why has it been so hard for the Court to reach a majority in these cases?

10. **From Doctrine to Practice.** In light of the above tests for specific jurisdiction, assume you represent a foreign corporation hoping to do business in the United States. Assume also that this company would like to limit its amenability to specific jurisdiction. How would you counsel your client to organize its contacts with the United States?

3. Other Ways to Establish Personal Jurisdiction

a. Tag Jurisdiction and Consent

A U.S. court might also have general personal jurisdiction over a nonresident individual defendant if the plaintiff serves process on the defendant in the forum state. Such jurisdiction, known as "tag jurisdiction" (as in "tag you're it!") or transient jurisdiction, was approved by the Supreme Court in *Burnham v. Superior Court*, 495 U.S. 604 (1990). Burnham, a New Jersey resident, took a business trip to California, during which he visited his children, and he was served with a summons and divorce petition when he returned the children to his wife's California home. He then returned to New Jersey. The Supreme Court held that the California court could assert personal jurisdiction over Burnham based on service on him while voluntarily present in California. While the holding was unanimous, the Justices could not agree on why tag jurisdiction was consistent with the requirements of due process. Justice Scalia, writing for four Justices, reasoned that "[t]he short of the matter is that jurisdiction based on physical presence alone constitutes due process because it is one of the continuing traditions of our legal system that define the due process standard of 'traditional notions of fair play and substantial justice.'" Justice Brennan, also writing for four Justices, criticized Justice Scalia's reliance on tradition and, applying the due process framework adopted in *International Shoe*, concluded that "as a rule the exercise of personal jurisdiction over a defendant based on his voluntary presence in the forum will satisfy the requirements of due process." Justice Stevens, the ninth vote, wrote narrowly to uphold jurisdiction in the case, reasoning that in light of both the traditional acceptance of tag service noted by Scalia and the considerations of fairness emphasized by Brennan that "this is, indeed, a very easy case."

Tag jurisdiction can be important in transnational cases against non-U.S. residents. In *Kadić v. Karadžić*, 70 F.3d 232 (2d Cir. 1995), the court upheld personal jurisdiction over the leader of Bosnian Serb forces who was served with process outside the Russian Embassy in New York while he was visiting the United States to attend peace talks. Importantly, tag jurisdiction gives the forum general jurisdiction over the defendant, which, as you will recall, means that there need not be any relationship between the defendant's contacts with the forum state and the underlying cause of action. For example, the suit in *Kadić* involved allegations of human rights abuses in the Bosnian civil war. Tag jurisdiction is rejected in other major legal systems, including the European Union. Why do you think it is permitted in the United States? Should it be?

A further issue, of great significance to international business, is whether corporations can be "tagged" by service of process on their corporate officers. Lower courts are divided on this question. *E.g., Martinez v. Aero Caribbean*, 764 F.3d 1062 (9th Cir. 2014) (not permitting tag jurisdiction over corporations); *C.S.B. Comoditites, Inc. v. Urban Trends (HK) Ltd.*, 626 F. Supp. 2d 837 (N.D. Ill. 2009) (same); *Northern Light Tech. Inc. v. Northern Lights Club*, 236 F.3d 57 (1st Cir. 2001) (permitting tag jurisdiction over corporations); *Oyuela v. Seacor Marine (Nigeria) Ltd.*, 290 F. Supp. 2d 713 (E.D. La. 2003) (same). Relatedly, a foreign corporation might be amenable to jurisdiction in the United States if it is registered to do business and appoints an agent for service of process in a U.S. state. Such jurisdiction is based on the idea that in registering to do business the corporation consents to the jurisdiction of that state's courts, and its viability remains unresolved. *Compare, e.g., Brown v. Lockheed Martin Corp.*, 814 F.3d 619 (2d Cir. 2016) (holding that Connecticut's business registration statute that required foreign corporations to appoint an in-state agent for service of process did not constitute consent by foreign corporations to the personal jurisdiction of Connecticut's courts) and *King v. Am. Family Mut. Ins. Co.*, 632 F.3d 570 (9th Cir. 2011) (compliance with state registration-appointments statute does not amount to consent to jurisdiction on any claim), *with Knowlton v. Allied Van Lines, Inc.*, 900 F.2d 1196 (8th Cir. 1990) (compliance amounts to consent). As with tag jurisdiction, jurisdiction based on fictional consent is rejected by most other countries. Do you think a foreign corporation should be deemed to consent to jurisdiction by merely registering to do business?

In light of this, a lawyer advising foreign corporations must be careful to point out the possibility that travel to the United States or registration to do business or appointment of agents in the United States may leave the client subject to personal jurisdiction in U.S. courts for any and all claims arising anywhere in the world. However, this does not necessarily mean that a U.S. court will assert jurisdiction in such cases. As discussed in Chapter 10, there are a variety of doctrines (such as *forum non conveniens*) that are frequently invoked by defendants and that may lead a U.S. court to dismiss a transnational suit even if it has personal jurisdiction.

b. Federal Rule of Civil Procedure 4(k)(2)

What if a foreign defendant has multiple contacts with the United States, but they are scattered across many different U.S. states so that no single state can assert general jurisdiction. Might the contacts nonetheless be sufficient for due process purposes in a case in federal court?

Federal Rules of Civil Procedure Rule 4(k)(2) provides:

> *Federal Claim Outside State-Court Jurisdiction.* For a claim that arises under federal law, serving a summons or filing a waiver of service establishes personal jurisdiction over a defendant if:
>
> (A) the defendant is not subject to jurisdiction in any state's courts of general jurisdiction; and
>
> (B) exercising jurisdiction is consistent with the United States Constitution and laws.

Thus, federal courts must follow state rules for personal jurisdiction when sitting in diversity under Rule 4(k)(1)(A). In contrast, when proceeding in federal court under federal law, if a defendant is not subject to jurisdiction in any state, the court can aggregate contacts with the United States as a whole and find jurisdiction. For example, recall in the *Nicastro* case that the defendant, J. McIntyre Machinery, a British corporation, had contacts with various U.S. states but very few contacts with the forum state, New Jersey. If McIntyre had been sued under federal law, therefore, there might have been general personal jurisdiction in federal court under Rule 4(k)(2). As with agency and affiliate jurisdiction, this Rule has the potential to be important in transnational cases in the years to come. The next case explores this possibility.

Johnson v. PPI Technology Services, L.P.

926 F. Supp. 2d 873 (E.D. La. 2013)

CARL J. BARBIER, District Judge.

Before the Court are Defendants Transocean, Ltd. and GlobalSantaFe Offshore Services's Reurged Motion to Dismiss for Lack of Personal Jurisdiction. . . . Having considered the motion and legal memoranda, the record, and the applicable law, the Court finds that Defendants' motion should be GRANTED in part and DENIED in part for the reasons set out more fully below.

Procedural History and Background Facts

This action arises out of claims for maintenance and cure, unseaworthiness, and negligence brought under general maritime law. Plaintiff James Johnson ("Mr. Johnson") filed the instant suit on November 8, 2011, naming as Defendants AFREN, PLC ("AFREN"), PPI Technology, L.P. ("PPI"), PSL, Ltd. ("PSL"), and Transocean, Ltd. ("Transocean"). On March 27, 2012, Plaintiff filed his First Amended Complaint adding GlobalSantaFe Offshore Services ("GSF") as a Defendant. Mr. Johnson's case was consolidated with Robert Croke ("Mr. Croke")'s related case on June 20, 2012. Mr. Croke's case named AFREN, PPI, Transocean, GSF, and Transocean Offshore Deepwater Drilling, Inc. ("TODDI") as Defendants.

Plaintiffs' complaints assert that on November 8, 2010, they were working as seamen on the HIGH ISLAND VII, a mobile rig located approximately twelve miles off the Nigerian coast. Plaintiffs allege that at approximately 12:30 A.M. Nigerian gunmen boarded the rig and took them hostage. Mr. Johnson alleges that while he was being held hostage, the gunmen shot him in his right leg. He contends that after being shot he "remained on the floor in the galley bleeding from the injury to his leg" for approximately three to three-and-a-half hours. He reports that since the alleged incident, he has had to undergo multiple surgeries and continuing therapy on his leg and has been unable to return to work.

Similarly, Mr. Croke alleges that while being held hostage, he was slapped and beaten by the gunmen and, eventually, shot in the foot. Mr. Croke reports that the gunmen took him with them when they left the rig. He asserts that he was held hostage for ten days and tortured. He alleges that after he was rescued, he had two surgeries performed on his foot. He states that he continues to suffer mental and emotional damages as well as physical injury.

Plaintiffs' complaints assert that they have filed suit against the aforementioned Defendants, because (1) PPI and/or PSL employed them; (2) Transocean owned and operated the rig; (3) AFREN had contracted with Transocean to use the rig; and (4) GSF had employees on the rig who were responsible "for maintaining the [rig's] safety, security and protection." Mr. Croke's complaint also independently asserts that TODDI had employees on board who were responsible for ensuring the safety of the rig. Plaintiffs allege that, together, all of these entities knew or should have known that it was extremely likely that Nigerian gunmen would attack the rig, and they failed to properly secure the rig despite that knowledge.

. . .

The Parties' Arguments

. . .

Plaintiffs argue that the Court should apply Rule 4(k)(2) to this case, conferring jurisdiction on GSF because (1) it is not subject to jurisdiction in any particular state's courts, and because (2) exercising jurisdiction would still be consistent with the constitution. Plaintiffs contend that this is appropriate because it is clear that GSF has a relationship with the United States, and GSF has contested jurisdiction in the past in Texas, the most logical state to have personal jurisdiction over GSF since it runs its payroll operations there. Plaintiffs argue that because GSF employs at least 300 Americans, administers its payroll from an office in the United States, and holds itself out as being located in that same office, it has sufficient contacts with the United States to warrant conferring jurisdiction under Rule 4(k)(2). Additionally, Plaintiffs argue that because GSF has objected to jurisdiction in Texas in the past, as a matter of law this Court should find that GSF is not subject to personal jurisdiction in any state and, thus, apply Rule 4(k)(2).

. . .

With regard to Plaintiffs' arguments about Rule 4(k)(2), Defendants assert that numerous corporate changes have taken place since the time in which it contested personal jurisdiction in Texas, thereby implying that Plaintiff has not made out a prima facie case to warrant applying Rule 4(k)(2). Likewise, Defendants argue that even if Plaintiff had made a sufficient case, it has not shown that GSF has sufficient minimum contacts with the United States to satisfy the rule's due process requirement. GSF again asserts that it is a paymaster entity only, and that as such it does not have sufficient minimum contacts with the United States. Thus, GSF argues that conferring jurisdiction through Rule 4(k)(2) would not comport with traditional notions of due process.

Discussion

. . .

As an initial matter, the Court notes that the Plaintiffs have not produced any information or made any argument which supports the proposition that this Court has personal jurisdiction over Transocean. As such, there is no evidence in front of the Court upon which it can make a finding that it does indeed have jurisdiction over Transocean. Therefore, because the Plaintiffs have failed to meet their burden of proof, the Court finds that it does not have personal jurisdiction over Transocean in the instant case; therefore, Transocean will be dismissed from this suit.

Next, the Court addresses the question of whether it has personal jurisdiction over GSF. Plaintiffs have proffered three arguments in support of jurisdiction: (1) that there is general jurisdiction over GSF, (2) that there is jurisdiction over GSF under Rule 4(k)(2), and (3) that GSF and TODDI are a single entity. The Court addresses each of these arguments in turn.

A. General Jurisdiction

In order for a court to exercise general jurisdiction over a defendant, the defendant must have "continuous and systematic general business contacts" with the forum state. *Helicopteros*, 466 U.S. at 415. Contacts between a defendant and the forum state must be extensive to satisfy the systematic and continuous test. The continuous and systematic test for establishing personal jurisdiction is a difficult test to meet. In fact, the Supreme Court has upheld an exercise of personal jurisdiction when the suit was unrelated to the defendant's contacts with a forum only once.

Plaintiffs assert that GSF has the following contacts with Louisiana: (1) it employs forty Louisiana residents to work overseas; (2) it transfers money into Louisiana bank accounts and/or sends Louisiana employees' pay checks and W-2's to Louisiana; and (3) at least one of the Louisiana residents GSF employs attends training in Louisiana, accesses the company intranet in Louisiana, and communicates with his jobsite from Louisiana. The Court finds that these contacts are not sufficient to establish that GSF has "continuous and systematic" contacts with Louisiana. . . .

B. Rule 4(k)(2)

In the alternative, Plaintiff argues that this Court may exercise jurisdiction under Rule 4(k)(2). . . .

In the Fifth Circuit, claims falling under the federal courts' admiralty jurisdiction are considered to be claims arising under federal law for the purposes of Rule 4(k)(2). *World Tanker Carriers Corp. v. M/V Ya Mawlaya*, 99 F.3d 717, 723 (5th Cir. 1996). In order to show that Rule 4(k)(2) applies the plaintiff must demonstrate that (1) the defendant in question is not subject to the general jurisdiction of any other state, and (2) that exercising jurisdiction is consistent with the due process clause of the Fifth Amendment, meaning that the defendant has sufficient minimum contacts with the United States as a whole. *Adams v. Unione Mediterranea Di Sicurta*, 364 F.3d 646, 651 (5th Cir. 2004). The Fifth Circuit has stated "that a piecemeal analysis of the existence *vel non* of jurisdiction in all fifty states is not necessary" to prove part one of the test. *Id.* Rather, the court may confer jurisdiction where the "defendant does not concede to jurisdiction in another state." *Id.*

The Plaintiff must make a prima facie case that the rule applies by showing (1) that the claim asserted arises under federal law, (2) that personal jurisdiction is not available under any situation-specific federal statute, and (3) that the putative defendant's contacts with the nation as a whole suffice to satisfy the applicable constitutional requirements. Additionally, the plaintiff must certify that, based on the information that is readily available to the plaintiff and his counsel, the defendant is not subject to suit in the courts of general jurisdiction of any state. Once plaintiff has made a prima facie case, then the burden shifts to the defendant to produce evidence that demonstrates that it is subject to jurisdiction in another state and/or that it has insufficient contacts with the United States as a whole.

In the instant case, Plaintiffs argue that this case is an admiralty case and, therefore, Rule 4(k)(2) applies. Likewise, in arguing that general jurisdiction does not exist in any other state, Plaintiffs contend that because GSF contested personal jurisdiction in Texas a 2006 case . . . , and because Texas is the state where GSF is most likely to be subject to general jurisdiction as it has an office there, the Court should find that GSF is not subject to the general jurisdiction of any state. . . .

In response, GSF has asserted that while it may have contested jurisdiction in the past, such arguments may not be available to it today, thereby implying that it could be subject to personal jurisdiction in Texas. Nevertheless, in both GSF's reply as well as the additional briefing requested by the Court, the Defendant has refused to concede that it would be subject to personal jurisdiction in Texas or any other state. In fact, in its supplemental memorandum GSF goes so far as to state that, "GSF certainly denies that it is subject to the jurisdiction of this state, but that does not mean that GSF, in order to contest personal jurisdiction here, must stipulate to jurisdiction in some other forum." Unfortunately for GSF, that is exactly what the Fifth Circuit has stated that Rule 4(k)(2) requires it to do. *See Adams*, 364 F.3d at 651 ("If . . . a defendant contends that he cannot be sued in the forum state and refuses to identify any other where suit is possible, the federal court is entitled to use Rule 4(k)(2)."). Moreover, this Court has given Defendants ample opportunity to make such an assertion and, yet, Defendants have refused to do so. . . .

The Court relies on the Fifth Circuit's decision in *Adams* in making this determination. In *Adams*, the court found that the plaintiff had made a prima facie case where: (1) the defendant had contested transfer to New York, a jurisdiction where plaintiff believed personal jurisdiction existed; (2) the defendant generally challenged contacts with the U.S. as a whole; and (3) the defendant had not offered any other venue where personal jurisdiction might be conferred. *Adams*, 364 F.3d at 651. . . . Plaintiffs have shown that GSF has contested jurisdiction in Texas, a jurisdiction where Plaintiffs believe personal jurisdiction should exist. Likewise, throughout Defendants' supplemental memorandum they challenge GSF's contacts with the United States as a whole. Furthermore, despite opportunities in both this and other cases, GSF has not conceded that personal jurisdiction may be conferred in any other U.S. forum. Thus, the Court finds that Plaintiffs' have presented a prima facie case for the application of Rule 4(k)(2).

Accordingly, the Court now examines GSF's contacts with the United States as a whole in order to determine whether it is appropriate to exercise jurisdiction. In understanding GSF's contacts, the Court looks primarily to Mr. McKenzie's 30(b)(6) deposition. In his deposition, Mr. McKenzie explains that GSF's primary purpose is to manage the payroll for TODDI's "ex-pat population." Specifically, GSF issues paychecks, direct deposit, and W-2's to U.S. nationals who work abroad. Mr. McKenzie reiterates throughout his deposition that GSF does not issue payroll for citizens of other countries working abroad, but rather, focuses solely on U.S. citizens — approximately 300. Furthermore, when asked where GSF's W-2's are processed, Mr. McKenzie stated that, "[w]e have a department, a payroll department here in Houston that processes the payroll information for these employees and which is ultimately derived back to the W-2." Likewise, Mr. McKenzie explained that actual review of payroll for GSF happens in Houston, and all of his own work for GSF has occurred in Houston. Moreover, Mr. McKenzie explained that the current controller of the payroll operation, the person who has the authority to sign paychecks or payroll direct deposits for GSF, is currently located in Houston. Thus, Mr. McKenzie's deposition establishes that GSF runs its payroll operations in an office in Houston, that GSF only issues payroll to United States citizens (indeed, it specifically targets U.S. citizens who work abroad), and that

GSF currently issues payroll to 300 U.S. citizens. In addition to Mr. McKenzie's deposition, Plaintiff has also submitted information which demonstrates that on GSF's W-2 forms and pay stubs, the return office address is listed as a 4 Greenway Plaza, Houston, Texas. On whole, the Court finds that this information demonstrates that GSF has general jurisdiction with the United States.

While the Court admits that the question of general jurisdiction is a close call in this case, it finds that GSF cannot have it both ways. GSF cannot effectively run its payroll operations out of Houston, hold itself out to the recipients of its paychecks as having an office in Houston, and only employ United States citizens who work abroad, while at the same time avoiding being brought into court in the United States. In making this determination, the Court looks at the purpose of Rule 4(k)(2) jurisdiction. The Fifth Circuit has explained that Rule 4(k)(2) "was enacted to fill an important gap in the jurisdiction of federal courts in cases arising under federal law." *Adams*, 364 F.3d at 651. "While a defendant may have sufficient contacts with the United States as a whole to satisfy due process concerns, if she had insufficient contacts with any single state, she would not be amenable to service by a federal court sitting in that state. . . ." *Id.* Thus, "Rule 4(k)(2) was adopted in response to this problem of a gap in the courts' jurisdiction. . . ." *Id.* GSF's corporate operations clearly speak to this gap, and this Court finds that this is exactly the type of situation for which the rule was designed. Accordingly, the Court finds that by virtue of Rule 4(k)(2) it has personal jurisdiction over GSF in the instant matter.

Given this conclusion, the Court need not analyze Plaintiffs' assertions that jurisdiction also lies under a single-entity theory. Accordingly,

IT IS HEREBY ORDERED that Defendants' Motion to Dismiss is GRANTED as to Transocean, Ltd. and DENIED as to GlobalSantaFe Offshore Services. . . .

NOTES AND QUESTIONS

1. **The Importance of Rule 4(k)(2).** What is the difference between the basic personal jurisdiction analysis in section A of the court's opinion and the Rule 4(k)(2) analysis in section B? In what types of cases might a plaintiff be able to establish personal jurisdiction based on Rule 4(k)(2) but not based on an ordinary personal jurisdiction analysis?
2. **The Requirements of Rule 4(k)(2).** According to the court in *Johnson*, what requirements must be satisfied for there to be personal jurisdiction based on Rule 4(k)(2)? Why are these obstacles in place?
3. *Nicastro* **Reprise.** In light of the above case, assume that the plaintiff in *Nicastro* pled a federal cause of action. Would personal jurisdiction have been sustained?

4. *A Brief Comparative Look at Adjudicatory Jurisdiction*

Having read the materials thus far, one might be left wondering whether there is a different way to deal with personal jurisdiction — perhaps a way that favors clear rules over the balancing of factors that is part of the Supreme Court's due process analysis. The European Union (EU) has taken such an approach, as reflected in its Regulation 1215/2012 (known as the Brussels I Regulation (Recast)). As you study the EU Regulation, compare it with the U.S. approach to jurisdiction that we have been examining.

Regulation No. 1215/2012 on Jurisdiction and the Recognition and Enforcement of Judgments in Civil and Commercial Matters (Recast)

Chapter II Jurisdiction
Section 1
  General provisions
  Article 4

1. Subject to this Regulation, persons domiciled in a Member State shall, whatever their nationality, be sued in the courts of that Member State.

2. Persons who are not nationals of the Member State in which they are domiciled shall be governed by the rules of jurisdiction applicable to nationals of that Member State.

Article 5

1. Persons domiciled in a Member State may be sued in the courts of another Member State only by virtue of the rules set out in Sections 2 to 7 of this Chapter.

2. In particular, the rules of national jurisdiction of which the Member States are to notify the Commission pursuant to point (a) of Article 76(1) shall not be applicable as against the persons referred to in paragraph 1.

Article 6

1. If the defendant is not domiciled in a Member State, the jurisdiction of the courts of each Member State shall, subject to Article 18(1), Article 21(2) and Articles 24 and 25, be determined by the law of that Member State.

2. As against such a defendant, any person domiciled in a Member State may, whatever his nationality, avail himself in that Member State of the rules of jurisdiction there in force, and in particular those of which the Member States are to notify the Commission pursuant to point (a) of Article 76(1), in the same way as nationals of that Member State.

Section 2
Special jurisdiction
Article 7

A person domiciled in a Member State may be sued in another Member State:

(1) (a) in matters relating to a contract, in the courts for the place of performance of the obligation in question;

(b) for the purpose of this provision and unless otherwise agreed, the place of performance of the obligation in question shall be:

— in the case of the sale of goods, the place in a Member State where, under the contract, the goods were delivered or should have been delivered,

— in the case of the provision of services, the place in a Member State where, under the contract, the services were provided or should have been provided;

(c) if point (b) does not apply then point (a) applies;

(2) in matters relating to tort, delict or quasi-delict, in the courts for the place where the harmful event occurred or may occur;

(3) as regards a civil claim for damages or restitution which is based on an act giving rise to criminal proceedings, in the court seised of those proceedings, to the extent that that court has jurisdiction under its own law to entertain civil proceedings;

(4) as regards a civil claim for the recovery, based on ownership, of a cultural object as defined in point 1 of Article 1 of Directive 93/7/EEC initiated by the person claiming the right to recover such an object, in the courts for the place where the cultural object is situated at the time when the court is seised;

(5) as regards a dispute arising out of the operations of a branch, agency or other establishment, in the courts for the place where the branch, agency or other establishment is situated;

(6) as regards a dispute brought against a settlor, trustee or beneficiary of a trust created by the operation of a statute, or by a written instrument, or created orally and evidenced in writing, in the courts of the Member State in which the trust is domiciled;

(7) as regards a dispute concerning the payment of remuneration claimed in respect of the salvage of a cargo or freight, in the court under the authority of which the cargo or freight in question:

(a) has been arrested to secure such payment; or

(b) could have been so arrested, but bail or other security has been given;

provided that this provision shall apply only if it is claimed that the defendant has an interest in the cargo or freight or had such an interest at the time of salvage.

Article 8

A person domiciled in a Member State may also be sued:

(1) where he is one of a number of defendants, in the courts for the place where any one of them is domiciled, provided the claims are so closely connected that it is expedient to hear and determine them together to avoid the risk of irreconcilable judgments resulting from separate proceedings;

(2) as a third party in an action on a warranty or guarantee or in any other third-party proceedings, in the court seised of the original proceedings, unless these were instituted solely with the object of removing him from the jurisdiction of the court which would be competent in his case;

(3) on a counter-claim arising from the same contract or facts on which the original claim was based, in the court in which the original claim is pending;

(4) in matters relating to a contract, if the action may be combined with an action against the same defendant in matters relating to rights *in rem* in immovable property, in the court of the Member State in which the property is situated.

NOTES AND QUESTIONS

1. **EU/U.S. Comparison.** Compare the bases for jurisdiction under the Brussels I Regulation (Recast) with those permitted under the Due Process Clause. What is the same? What is different? How much do the differences matter?
2. **Applications.** Suppose, in the *Goodyear* case, that the plaintiffs were domiciled in Spain, the bus crash occurred in Italy, and the plaintiffs decided to sue a French subsidiary of Goodyear in the EU. Under the Brussels I Regulation (Recast), where in the EU could the plaintiffs sue the French defendant? Now, let's look at *Nicastro*. Suppose that the injury occurred in Italy. Where in the EU could the plaintiffs sue?
3. **Policy.** Do you think the United States or the EU has the better approach to adjudicatory jurisdiction? What are the benefits of adopting jurisdiction-selecting rules, as has the EU? What are the advantages of the U.S. approach as compared to the EU?

REVIEW NOTES AND QUESTIONS

1. Whether you represent a plaintiff or a defendant, remember to think strategically about forum selection. Which U.S. states (or foreign nations) might provide desirable forums for your client? Consider differences in both procedural

law and substantive law (being sure to take into account the choice-of-law principles a forum will apply to determine which state's or nation's substantive law to apply). Other considerations might include the potential advantages of litigating in your client's home forum, and the potential disadvantages of litigating in the other party's home forum.

2. Once you have identified a strategically desirable forum (if you are representing a plaintiff), or once your client has been sued in a particular forum (if you are representing a defendant), analyze whether the forum is available under the rules of personal jurisdiction. As you do so, keep in mind these basic steps in analyzing personal jurisdiction:

   - First, has the defendant consented to jurisdiction — either by making a general appearance or, in contract cases, by including in the contract a consent-to-jurisdiction clause or forum selection clause specifying the forum (a topic that is discussed in Chapter 10)?
   - Second, is there "tag jurisdiction" over the defendant — that is, was the defendant served in the forum state while voluntarily present there?
   - Third, using the principles of general jurisdiction presented above, analyze whether the defendant's contacts with the forum are sufficiently extensive for there to be general jurisdiction there.
   - Fourth, using the principles of specific jurisdiction presented above, analyze whether the defendant's contacts with the forum are sufficient in quantity and relatedness to the plaintiff's claim for there to be specific jurisdiction there. In cases involving injuries caused by products, can jurisdiction be based on the flow of the product into the forum state through the stream of commerce?
   - Fifth, if a corporate defendant's contacts with the forum are not alone sufficient for general jurisdiction or specific jurisdiction, can an affiliated entity's contacts be imputed to the defendant based on an agency or alter ego theory?
   - Sixth, if the defendant has insufficient contacts with any single U.S. state for there to be personal jurisdiction there, can Rule 4(k)(2) be applied in order to establish personal jurisdiction based on the defendant's nationwide contacts?

3. As we conclude this section, ask yourself the following question: What role does personal jurisdiction serve in transnational litigation? What interests are at stake? Does the U.S. approach to personal jurisdiction strike the right balance? Is there a better approach that could be used?

B. Subject Matter Jurisdiction in Transnational Cases

For a U.S. court to hear a transnational case it must have both personal jurisdiction and subject matter jurisdiction. The issue of subject matter jurisdiction is usually encountered in U.S. federal courts, as U.S. state courts are typically courts of general jurisdiction, which means they can hear any type of case involving any lineup of parties (so long as there is personal jurisdiction). Federal courts, in contrast, are courts of limited jurisdiction, which means that under Article III of the Constitution they may only hear certain types of claims or claims involving certain types of parties. In addition, federal courts' jurisdiction is defined by statute and Congress has not provided federal courts with all the jurisdiction they might possess under Article III. Thus questions of subject matter jurisdiction are both constitutional and statutory.

In representing a client in federal court, the question of subject matter jurisdiction is paramount. Rule 8(a)(1) of the Federal Rules of Civil Procedure requires "a short and plain statement" of the grounds for subject matter jurisdiction, and subject matter jurisdiction must exist at the time of filing. In fact, pleading subject matter jurisdiction without a well-founded basis in the facts and the law could subject you to Rule 11 sanctions.

Because subject matter jurisdiction goes to the core of a federal court's power to hear a case, objections cannot be waived. You do not want to be in the situation where you guess wrong, spend thousands or millions of dollars to litigate a case, win, and then find out on appeal or in enforcement proceedings that subject matter jurisdiction did not exist. But if a federal court has subject matter jurisdiction, a plaintiff may include supplemental claims for which jurisdiction would not otherwise exist. Federal statutes also often allow defendants in cases filed in state court to "remove" the case to federal court where federal jurisdiction exists. In short, unlocking (or preventing) federal subject matter jurisdiction presents many strategic considerations in transnational cases.

Unlike personal jurisdiction, subject matter jurisdiction is largely a question of statutory interpretation. Besides studying the cases, it is beneficial for your practice if you become intimately familiar with the governing statutes, which is why the statutes will be discussed at length below. In what follows, we examine subject matter jurisdiction questions as they arise in transnational cases in three parts. First, we investigate diversity and alienage jurisdiction. Second, we look at federal question or "arising under" jurisdiction. Third, we address related areas such as removal and supplemental jurisdiction.

1. Diversity and Alienage Jurisdiction

In most transnational cases, the primary type of subject matter jurisdiction asserted is diversity jurisdiction. Article III confers judicial power over cases "between a State, or the Citizens thereof, and foreign States, Citizens, or Subjects." Importantly, the focus of this jurisdictional grant is the nature of the *parties* to the suit. The reason for this jurisdictional grant, according to James Madison, was that "foreigners cannot get justice done in [state] courts," especially in cases involving foreign creditors. Madison also explained that such jurisdiction was necessary to "avoid controversies with foreign powers" and to prevent state courts from "drag[ging] the whole community into war." 3 DEBATES IN THE SEVERAL STATE CONVENTIONS ON THE ADOPTION OF THE FEDERAL CONSTITUTION 583 (J. Elliot ed., 1836). Note, however, that Article III does not confer exclusive jurisdiction over such cases. Constitutionally, federal and state courts have *concurrent* jurisdiction to hear claims brought in diversity or alienage. In today's world, does this approach still make sense?

The present statutory provisions dealing with diversity and alienage jurisdiction provide:

28 U.S.C. § 1332

Diversity of Citizenship; amount in controversy; costs

(a) The district courts shall have original jurisdiction of all civil actions where the matter in controversy exceeds the sum or value of $75,000, exclusive of interest and costs, and is between —

(1) citizens of different States;

(2) citizens of a State and citizens or subjects of a foreign state, except that the district courts shall not have original jurisdiction under this subsection of an action between citizens of a State and citizens or subjects of a foreign state who are lawfully admitted for permanent residence in the United States and are domiciled in the same State;

(3) citizens of different States and in which citizens or subjects of a foreign state are additional parties; and

(4) a foreign state, defined in section 1603(a) of this title, as plaintiff and citizens of a State or of different States.

. . .

(c) For the purposes of this section and section 1441 of this title —

(1) a corporation shall be deemed to be a citizen of every State and foreign state by which it has been incorporated and of the State or foreign state where it has its principal place of business. . . .

In reading the statute, did you notice that at least one important type of transnational case is missing? In diversity, the federal judicial power does not extend to alien-versus-alien suits. To bring such a suit in federal court, you would have to show it arises under federal law, which is a topic we will discuss shortly. In light of the concerns with state court justice that prompted alienage jurisdiction, why would the Framers and Congress craft subject matter jurisdiction in this way? In other words, if a federal forum was appropriate generally in transnational cases, why not allow all types of alien suits to be filed in federal court?

As you may have spent substantial time on diversity jurisdiction in civil procedure, we will not dwell on it long. However, to make sure you understand how diversity jurisdiction arises, try your hand at the following lineups. P means plaintiff, D means defendant, and the abbreviations in parentheses refer to the citizenship of the parties (VA = Virginia, CA = California, UK = United Kingdom, FR = France). For each example, be sure to identify which subsection of § 1332 applies. For each, assume that the amount in controversy requirement is met.

Is there subject matter jurisdiction?

1. P(VA) v. D(UK)
2. P(VA) v. D(CA) & D(UK)
3. P(VA) & P(UK) v. D(FR)
4. P(VA) & P(FR) v. D(CA) & D(FR)
5. P(FR) v. D(VA) & D(UK)
6. P(VA) v. D(UK/But Permanent Resident of VA)

Does the diversity statute provide all of the answers? Also, examine 28 U.S.C. § 1332(c)(1). How is the citizenship of a corporation determined for purposes of diversity? For example, what is the citizenship of a corporation that is incorporated in California and has its principal place of business in Virginia? What about a corporation that is incorporated in California and has its principal place of business in France? Note that a corporation can have only one principal place of business. As the Supreme Court has held:

> [A] corporation's principal place of business is the place where a corporation's officers direct, control, and coordinate the corporation's activities. It is the place that Courts of Appeals have called the corporation's "nerve center." And in practice it should normally be the place where the corporation maintains its headquarters — provided that the headquarters is the actual center of direction, control, and coordination, i.e., the "nerve center," and not simply an office where the corporation holds its board meetings (for example, attended by directors and officers who have traveled there for the occasion).

Hertz v. Friend, 559 U.S. 77, 93 (2010). Note further that an unincorporated business, such as a partnership or limited liability company, has the citizenship of all of its partners (in the case of a partnership) or all of its members (in the case of a limited liability company). Moreover, to be a citizen of a U.S. state, an individual must be domiciled in that state and a citizen of the United States. An individual is deemed to be domiciled in the state where he or she resides and intends to remain indefinitely.

2. Federal Question Jurisdiction

Article III, Section 2 of the Constitution grants federal courts jurisdiction in "all Cases, in Law and Equity, arising under this Constitution, the Laws of the United States, and Treaties made . . . under their Authority." Perhaps surprisingly, Congress did not pass legislation giving federal courts general federal question jurisdiction until 1875. Today, 28 U.S.C. § 1331 provides: "The district courts shall have original jurisdiction of all civil actions arising under the Constitution, laws, or treaties of the United States." Unlike diversity jurisdiction, the focus of federal question jurisdiction is on the nature of the *issues* presented in the lawsuit.

Federal law encompasses both statutory law as well as federal common law. Whether a case "arises under" federal law is determined by applying the "well-pleaded complaint" rule. *Louisville & Nashville Railroad Co. v. Mottley*, 211 U.S. 149 (1908). Under this rule, a federal question must appear on the face of the complaint. Federal questions appearing as defenses to state or foreign law claims will not suffice to establish subject matter jurisdiction.

With this background, we now turn to an area of federal subject matter jurisdiction that you likely did not encounter in your civil procedure class that has particular salience in transnational litigation: federal question jurisdiction based on the common law of foreign relations. As you read the cases that follow, ask the following question: How can a case pled under state law be deemed to arise under federal law?

Torres v. Southern Peru Copper Corp.

113 F.3d 540 (5th Cir. 1997)

POLITZ, Chief Judge:

Plaintiffs appeal the district court's orders denying the motion to remand to state court and dismissing the case on the grounds of *forum non conveniens* and comity among nations. For the reasons assigned, we affirm.

Background

Plaintiffs are approximately 700 Peruvian citizens who allege that they have been harmed by sulfur dioxide emissions from Southern Peru Copper Corporation's [SPCC] copper smelting and refining operations in Ilo, Peru. [SPCC is incorporated in Delaware and has its principal place of business in Peru.] Plaintiffs originally sued SPCC and other defendants in Texas state court alleging state-law causes of action such as negligence, intentional tort, and nuisance. Defendants removed the case to federal court; the plaintiffs filed a motion to remand. The district court denied the motion, holding that although diversity jurisdiction was lacking, federal question jurisdiction existed. The district court then dismissed the case on the basis of *forum non conveniens* and comity among nations. Plaintiffs timely appealed.

Analysis

1. Subject Matter Jurisdiction

. . .

A. *Federal Question Jurisdiction*

We analyze a removal action on the basis of federal question jurisdiction under the well-pleaded complaint rule, which requires disclosure of the federal question on the face of the complaint. The complaint must state a cause of action created by federal law or it must assert a state-law cause of action requiring the "resolution of a substantial question of federal law." In making our jurisdictional determination, we examine the entire record for a proper understanding of the true nature of the complaint.

At the outset we reject SPCC's contention that Tex. Civ. Prac. & Rem. Code § 71.031 confers federal question jurisdiction. That provision allows a citizen of a foreign country to bring in the Texas state courts an action for personal injury or death occurring in a foreign nation if, *inter alia*, the country in which the plaintiff is a citizen "has equal treaty rights with the United States on behalf of its citizens." The mere fact that section 71.031 requires a Texas state court to examine treaties to determine whether a plaintiff has standing is insufficient by itself to create federal jurisdiction.

Plaintiffs maintain that because they have asserted only state-law tort claims, the well-pleaded complaint rule precludes us from finding federal question jurisdiction. The state of Peru has protested the lawsuit by filing a letter with the State Department and by submitting an amicus brief to this court. Peru maintains that the litigation implicates some of its most vital interests and, hence, will affect its relations with the United States. SPCC therefore contends that plaintiffs' complaint raises substantial questions of federal law by implicating the federal common law of foreign relations.

That Peru has injected itself into this lawsuit does not, standing alone, create a question of federal law. Its vigorousness in opposing the action, however, has alerted us to the foreign policy issues implicated by this case, which we have confirmed by a close review of the record. The mining industry in Peru, of which SPCC is the largest company, is critical to that country's economy, contributing up to 50% of its export income and 11% of its gross domestic product. Furthermore, the Peruvian government has participated substantially in the activities for which SPCC is being sued. By way of example, the government: (1) owns the land on which SPCC operates; (2) owns the minerals which SPCC extracts; (3) owned the Ilo refinery from 1975 until 1994, during which time pollution from the refinery may have contributed to the injuries complained of by plaintiffs; and (4) grants concessions that allow SPCC to operate in return for an annual fee. Moreover, the government extensively regulates the mining industry.

This action therefore strikes not only at vital economic interests but also at Peru's sovereign interests by seeking damages for activities and policies in which the government actively has been engaged. On the record before us we must conclude that plaintiffs' complaint raises substantial questions of federal common law by implicating important foreign policy concerns. We accordingly affirm the district court's conclusion that it had federal question jurisdiction.

. . .

AFFIRMED.

Patrickson v. Dole Food Company

251 F.3d 795 (9th Cir. 2001)

KOZINSKI, Circuit Judge:

We consider whether the federal courts have jurisdiction over a class action brought by Latin American banana workers against multinational fruit and chemical companies alleged to have exposed the workers to a toxic pesticide.

I

Dibromochloropropane (DBCP) is a powerful pesticide. Tough on pests, it's no friend to humans either. Absorbed by the skin or inhaled, it's alleged to cause sterility, testicular atrophy, miscarriages, liver damage, cancer and other ailments that you wouldn't wish on anyone. Originally manufactured by Dow Chemical and Shell Oil, the pesticide was banned from general use in the United States by the Environmental Protection Agency in 1979. But the chemical companies continued to distribute it to fruit companies in developing nations.

In our case, banana workers from Costa Rica, Ecuador, Guatemala and Panama brought a class action against Dole Food Company, other major fruit companies and chemical companies (hereinafter "Dole") for injuries allegedly sustained from exposure to DBCP in their home countries. This case represents one front in a broad litigation war between these plaintiffs' lawyers and these defendants. . . .

The merits are not before us. Instead, we must decide whether the case is properly in federal court. The workers brought suit in Hawaii state court. Dole responded by impleading two Israeli chemical companies, Dead Sea Bromine Company and Bromine Compounds Limited ("Dead Sea Companies"), which are alleged to have manufactured some of the DBCP used in plaintiffs' home countries. . . . Dole . . . removed based on federal-question jurisdiction, 28 U.S.C. § 1331. The district court denied plaintiffs' remand motion and then dismissed the case for forum non conveniens.

II

Dole was entitled to remove the case to federal court if plaintiffs could have brought it there to begin with. See 28 U.S.C. § 1441(a). We must therefore consider whether plaintiffs could have brought the case in district court under federal-question jurisdiction. . . .[1]

A. Federal-Question Jurisdiction

We are courts of limited jurisdiction. This means we hear only those cases that Congress directs and the Constitution permits us to hear. Under Article III, federal courts may assert jurisdiction over federal questions, extending to all cases "arising under this Constitution, the Laws of the United States, and Treaties made, or which shall be made, under their Authority." U.S. Const. art. III, § 2. Although any federal ingredient may be sufficient to satisfy Article III, the statutory grant of jurisdiction under 28 U.S.C. § 1331 requires more. . . .

Even if the case turns entirely on the validity of a federal defense, federal courts may not assert jurisdiction unless a federal right or immunity is "an element, and an essential one, of the plaintiff's cause of action." *Franchise Tax Bd.*

---

1. Because Dole Food Company is a citizen of the forum state, defendants could not remove based on diversity of citizenship. *See* 28 U.S.C. §1441(b).

v. Construction Laborers Vacation Trust, 463 U.S. 1, 11 (1983). This venerable "well-pleaded complaint" rule keeps us from becoming entangled in state law controversies on the conjecture that federal law may come into play at some point during the litigation; it also ensures that Congress retains control over the size of federal court dockets.

Under conventional principles, the class action here unquestionably arises under state law. Plaintiffs seek relief under the common law of Hawaii for negligence, conspiracy, strict liability, intentional torts and breach of implied warranty. None of the claims has an element premised on a right created by Congress or the Constitution. Dole nonetheless argues that we have federal-question jurisdiction because the case calls for an application of the federal common law of foreign relations.

Although there is no general federal common law, "there are enclaves of federal judge-made law which bind the States." *Banco Nacional de Cuba v. Sabbatino*, 376 U.S. 398, 426 (1964). In *Sabbatino*, the Court held that one of those enclaves concerns the legal principles governing the nation's relationship with other members of the international community. The case considered whether the "act of state doctrine" requires U.S. courts to recognize the validity of the Cuban government's expropriation of private property. A long-standing common law principle, the act of state doctrine precludes courts from questioning the legality of actions that a foreign government has taken within its own borders. *See Underhill v. Hernandez*, 168 U.S. 250, 252 (1897). *Sabbatino* considered whether the doctrine was a matter of state or federal law.

Because the Constitution gives the federal government exclusive authority to manage the nation's foreign affairs, the Court concluded that "rules of international law should not be left to divergent and perhaps parochial state interpretations." *Sabbatino*, 376 U.S. at 425. Whether a foreign state's act is given legal force in the courts of the United States is a "uniquely federal" question directly implicating our nation's foreign affairs. *See id.* at 425-26. Therefore, it was appropriate to fashion a single federal standard to govern such cases, rather than rely on a patchwork of separate state standards. Equally important, the Supreme Court in *Sabbatino* reserved to itself ultimate review of all cases raising the act of state doctrine, rather than leaving them to the various state supreme courts. . . .

Federal-question jurisdiction was not an issue in *Sabbatino*; the district court already had jurisdiction because of diversity of citizenship. The question presented was what substantive law would apply — state law pursuant to *Erie R.R. Co. v. Tompkins*, 304 U.S. 64 (1938), or federal law. *Sabbatino* held that the common law of foreign relations falls outside *Erie*'s general rule and so federal law applies. Federal common law is, of course, federal law; so if a plaintiff's claim arises under the federal common law recognized by *Sabbatino*, the federal courts will have jurisdiction under 28 U.S.C. § 1331.

This is as far as *Sabbatino* goes, and it's not far enough, because nothing in plaintiffs' complaint turns on the validity or invalidity of any act of a foreign state. Plaintiffs seek compensation for injuries sustained from the defendants' manufacture, sale and use of DBCP. Plaintiffs don't claim that any foreign government participated in such activities or that the defendants acted under the color of foreign law. The case — at least as framed by plaintiffs — does not require us to evaluate any act of state or apply any principle of international law. The common law of foreign relations will become an issue only when — and if — it is raised as a defense.

Dole nonetheless argues that we must assert federal-question jurisdiction because the case concerns a vital sector of the economies of foreign countries and so has implications for our nation's relations with those countries. Plaintiffs represent a class of perhaps thousands of foreign nationals who allege that large multinational corporations harmed them in their home countries. Dole argues that, by granting relief, American courts would damage the banana industry — one of the most important sectors of those countries' economies — and cast doubt on the balance those governments have struck between agricultural development and labor safety. Although plaintiffs allege only state law claims, Dole argues, this case implicates the "uniquely federal" interest in foreign relations, and so must be heard in a federal forum. In essence, Dole interprets *Sabbatino* as creating an exception not only to *Erie*, but to the well-pleaded complaint rule as well.

Dole's position is not without support. In *Torres v. Southern Peru Copper Corp.*, 113 F.3d 540, 543 (5th Cir. 1997), the Fifth Circuit asserted federal-question jurisdiction over a state tort action brought by hundreds of Peruvian citizens against an American company because of injuries they had allegedly suffered from exposure to toxic gases during copper smelting and refining operations in Peru. The court concluded that, although the Peruvian government was not a party, it had "participated substantially" in the mining project through ownership of the land and minerals on which the mining operation was located. The court also noted that the mining industry made up a significant part of Peru's gross national product, and the Peruvian government had vigorously protested to our State Department that the case threatened Peru's sovereign interests. As a consequence, the Fifth Circuit held that the "plaintiffs' complaint raises substantial questions of federal common law by implicating important foreign policy concerns." While reaching the opposite result on the facts before it, the Eleventh Circuit seems to have adopted the Fifth Circuit's theory in *Torres*. See *Pacheco de Perez v. AT & T Co.*, 139 F.3d 1368, 1377 (11th Cir. 1998) (noting that, "[w]here a state law action has as a substantial element an issue involving foreign relations or foreign policy matters, federal jurisdiction is present" but concluding that a suit brought by Venezuelan citizens injured in a pipeline explosion did not affect American foreign policy).

Torres and *Pacheco de Perez* relied principally on *Republic of Philippines v. Marcos*, 806 F.2d 344, 353 (2d Cir. 1986), which seems to have been the first case to conclude that "there is federal question jurisdiction over actions having important foreign policy implications." In *Marcos*, the Republic of the Philippines sued its former dictator to enjoin him from disposing of property allegedly looted from the government and claimed as state property under an executive order of the Philippine government. Because the Republic's claims rested on the Philippine executive order, *Marcos* could be read as an act of state case, and the Second Circuit may well have grounded federal jurisdiction entirely on that basis.

However, *Marcos* clearly *said* more, broadly suggesting that federal-question jurisdiction could "probably" be premised on the fact that a case may affect our nation's foreign relations, whether or not federal law is raised by the plaintiff's complaint: "[A]n action brought by a foreign government against its former head of state arises under federal common law because of the necessary implications of such an action for United States foreign relations." *Id.* This reads far too much into *Sabbatino*. As noted, *Sabbatino* was about choice of law, not jurisdiction. The Court left no doubt that the substantive law of foreign relations must be federal, and it stressed the need for national uniformity. But *Sabbatino* does not say that federal courts alone are competent to develop this body of law. To the contrary, *Sabbatino* notes that the law of foreign relations is like other "enclaves of federal judge-made law which bind the States," such as the rules filling the interstices of federal statutes and the laws regulating interstate boundary issues. *Sabbatino*, 376 U.S. at 426. The Court's reference to binding the states makes sense only if one assumes that state courts will be called upon to apply the law of foreign relations. *Sabbatino* says as much: "[T]he act of state doctrine is a principle of decision binding on federal and state courts alike. . . ." *Id.* at 427.

. . .

State courts apply federal law in a wide variety of cases and, by doing so, they necessarily develop it. This does not undermine the nationwide uniformity of federal law much more than having somewhat different applications of federal law in the various federal circuits. Ultimately, the Supreme Court has the final say on any question of federal law, whether it arises in federal or state court, and this is thought sufficient to ensure nationwide uniformity in areas as diverse as criminal procedure, patent law and labor law.

We see no reason to treat the federal common law of foreign relations any differently than other areas of federal law. Certainly, federal courts have preeminence in developing all areas of federal law by virtue of the fact that almost all cases premised on federal law may be brought in or removed to federal court. In addition, Congress has provided federal jurisdiction in certain cases implicating our foreign relations, regardless of the nature of the claim. *See, e.g.,* 28 U.S.C. § 1251(b)(1) (suits where ambassadors or other foreign government officials are parties); *id.* § 1351 (suits against foreign consuls or other diplomatic personnel); *id.* § 1330 (suits against a foreign state); *see also id.* § 1350 (suits brought by an alien for a tort committed in violation of international law). What Congress has not done is to extend federal-question jurisdiction to all suits where the federal common law of foreign relations might arise as an issue. We interpret congressional silence outside these specific grants of jurisdiction as an endorsement of the well-pleaded complaint rule.

We therefore decline to follow *Marcos, Torres* and *Pacheco de Perez* insofar as they stand for the proposition that the federal courts may assert jurisdiction over a case simply because a foreign government has expressed a special interest in its outcome. It may well be that our foreign relations will be implicated by the pendency of a lawsuit on a subject that affects that government's sovereign interests; the courts in *Marcos* and *Torres* certainly believed this to be the case. But we see no logical connection between such an effect and the assertion of federal-question jurisdiction. That the case is litigated in federal court, rather than state court, will not reduce the impact of the case on the foreign government. Federal judges cannot dismiss a case because a foreign government finds it irksome, nor can they tailor their rulings to accommodate a non-party. Federal judges, like state judges, are bound to decide cases before them according to the rule of law. If a foreign government finds the litigation offensive, it may lodge a protest with our government; our political branches can then respond in whatever way they deem appropriate — up to and including passing legislation. Our government may, of course, communicate its own views as to the conduct of the litigation, and the court — whether state or federal — can take those views into account. But it is quite a different matter to suggest that courts — state or federal — will tailor their rulings to accommodate the expressed interests of a foreign nation that is not even a party.

Nor do we understand how a court can go about evaluating the foreign policy implications of another government's expression of interest. Assuming that foreign relations are an appropriate consideration at all, the relevant question is not whether the foreign government is pleased or displeased by the litigation, but how the case affects the interests of the United States. That is an inherently political judgment, one that courts — whether state or federal — are not competent to make. . . . If courts were to take the interests of the foreign government into account, they would be conducting foreign policy by deciding whether it serves our national interests to continue with the litigation, dismiss it on some ground such as forum non conveniens, or deal with it in some other way. *See* Jack L. Goldsmith, *Federal Courts, Foreign Affairs, and Federalism*, 83 Va. L. Rev. 1617, 1667 (1997). Because such political judgments are not within the competence of either state or federal courts, we can see no support for the proposition that federal courts are better equipped than state courts to deal with cases raising such concerns.

As Justice Frankfurter noted in *Romero v. International Terminal Operating Co.*, 358 U.S. 354, 379 (1959), federal courts must be hesitant "to expand the jurisdiction of the federal courts through a broad reading of jurisdictional statutes." If federal courts are so much better suited than state courts for handling cases that might raise foreign policy concerns, Congress will surely pass a statute giving us that jurisdiction. Because we see no evidence that Congress meant for the federal courts to assert jurisdiction over cases simply because foreign governments have an interest in them, we must part company with our sister circuits.

. . .

III

[W]e REVERSE the judgment of the district court and REMAND with instructions that the district court remand the case to Hawaii state court.

NOTES AND QUESTIONS

1. **Removal and Preferences for State or Federal Court.** Note that in both *Torres* and *Patrickson*, the plaintiffs originally filed their claims in state court, and in both cases, the defendants filed notices to remove the actions to federal

court. We will discuss removal in the next section. For now, simply note that removal from state to federal court is allowed only if the federal courts would have subject matter jurisdiction, and ask yourself why the plaintiffs so strongly preferred state court and the defendants so strongly preferred federal court.

2. **Pleading Claims.** Under the well-pleaded complaint rule, mentioned in both *Torres* and *Patrickson*, a federal question must appear on the face of the plaintiff's complaint. Federal law must be the basis for the plaintiff's claim; there is not a federal question merely because federal law is the basis for the defendant's defenses. Based on the well-pleaded complaint rule, what argument against federal subject matter jurisdiction would you make on behalf of the plaintiffs? How might the plaintiffs' preferences for state court proceedings rather than federal court proceedings have influenced the way in which their complaints were drafted and the choice of the law upon which to base their claims?

3. **Finding a Federal Question Based on a Suit's Foreign Relations Implications.** What arguments did the defendants in *Torres* and *Patrickson* make to try to establish federal question jurisdiction notwithstanding the well-pleaded complaint rule? Why did the court in *Torres* accept the defendant's argument, while the court in *Patrickson* rejected the defendant's argument? Can the two cases be reconciled? What facts do you think were especially important for the *Torres* court in deciding to find subject matter jurisdiction? Were similar facts present in *Patrickson*? Or do the two cases reflect fundamentally different views about when the foreign relations implications of a claim can give rise to federal question jurisdiction? What other bases for federal jurisdiction might have been alleged?

4. **Foreign Sovereigns.** In the courts' analyses in the two cases, how important is a foreign nation's involvement with the case? Assume that a foreign country filed a statement noting that it did not oppose the action. Would that change the analysis? Does it seem right that subject matter jurisdiction might be sustained when a foreign nation expresses concern with a case?

5. **Executive Orders.** In one tort case stemming from an airport crash in Khartoum, Sudan, the defendants argued that a court should exercise federal question jurisdiction over plaintiffs' state law claims because Executive Orders issued by the President have the force and effect of federal law and were directly implicated within the four corners of plaintiffs' complaint. In that case, two Executive Orders, 13067 and 13400, pertained to U.S. relations with Sudan. Executive Order 13067 froze Sudanese government property within the United States and prohibited certain business transactions between the United States and Sudan. Executive Order 13400 blocked the transfer of property or interests between the U.S. and Sudanese entities or individuals involved in the Darfur conflict. The defendants argued that plaintiffs based their state law negligent entrustment claim on sanctions created by the Executive Orders, and that the resolution of this claim raises a substantial question of federal law which requires federal court interpretation. The defendants also argued that payment of any monetary damages to plaintiffs would pose a federal question because the Executive Orders prohibit the transfer of property, including the payment of money, to

certain Sudanese individuals or entities. The defendants finally argued that any settlement payment made to plaintiffs must be approved in advance by the federal government to ensure that no individuals or entities involved in the conflict in Darfur receive money in violation of the Executive Order 13400. What should the result be in this case? *See Al Gasim Obied Ibrahim Mohammad v. Airbus, S.A.S.*, 2009 WL 3807090, at *6 (N.D. Ill. 2009).

6. **Circuit Splits.** Has the Ninth Circuit totally closed the door to the argument that state law causes of action touching on foreign affairs may be subject to federal question jurisdiction? Should it? How widely does the Fifth Circuit leave the door open to this argument? Which approach do you think is better?

3. Removal and Supplemental Jurisdiction

You have already seen in the above cases how the federal removal statute might come into play in transnational cases. 28 U.S.C. § 1441 provides in relevant part:

(a) **Generally.** — Except as otherwise expressly provided by Act of Congress, any civil action brought in a State court of which the district courts of the United States have original jurisdiction, may be removed by the defendant or the defendants, to the district court of the United States for the district and division embracing the place where such action is pending.

(b) Removal Based on Diversity of Citizenship. —

(1) In determining whether a civil action is removable on the basis of the jurisdiction under section 1332(a) of this title, the citizenship of defendants sued under fictitious names shall be disregarded.

(2) A civil action otherwise removable solely on the basis of the jurisdiction under section 1332(a) of this title may not be removed if any of the parties in interest properly joined and served as defendants is a citizen of the State in which such action is brought.

(c) Joinder of Federal Law Claims and State Law Claims. —

(1) If a civil action includes —

(A) a claim arising under the Constitution, laws, or treaties of the United States (within the meaning of section 1331 of this title), and

(B) a claim not within the original or supplemental jurisdiction of the district court or a claim that has been made nonremovable by statute, the entire action may be removed if the action would be removable without the inclusion of the claim described in subparagraph (B).

(2) Upon removal of an action described in paragraph (1), the district court shall sever from the action all claims described in paragraph (1)(B) and shall remand the severed claims to the State court from which the action was removed. Only defendants against whom a claim described in paragraph (1)(A) has been asserted are required to join in or consent to the removal under paragraph (1).

. . .

As the statute makes plain, to be removable to federal court an action must be one that would fall within the original jurisdiction of the federal courts. Thus, if you represent a defendant sued in state court, it is important to ascertain whether federal subject matter jurisdiction exists at the beginning of the case. Examining the removal statute carefully, in what sense is the possibility of removal more limited in diversity cases than in other cases? By understanding this, you see why Dole in the *Dole v. Patrickson* case was arguing for federal question jurisdiction. Necessity is the mother of legal invention!

In light of the federal removal statute, can you think of situations where, as a defendant, you would want to remain in state court? Or, do you think it will always be the case that you would want to remove a transnational case?

═══════════════

The removal statute is about federal court access for defendants. Congress has also expanded federal court access for plaintiffs. 28 U.S.C. § 1367 creates "supplemental jurisdiction," which allows federal courts to decide claims against parties that could not be independently brought in federal court:

Supplemental Jurisdiction

(a) Except as provided in subsections (b) and (c) or as expressly provided otherwise by Federal statute, in any civil action of which the district courts have original jurisdiction, the district courts shall have supplemental jurisdiction over all other claims that are so related to claims in the action within such original jurisdiction that they form part of the same case or controversy under Article III of the United States Constitution. Such supplemental jurisdiction shall include claims that involve the joinder or intervention of additional parties.

(b) In any civil action of which the district courts have original jurisdiction founded solely on section 1332 of this title, the district courts shall not have supplemental jurisdiction under subsection (a) over claims by plaintiffs against persons made parties under Rule 14, 19, 20, or 24 of the Federal Rules of Civil Procedure, or over claims by persons proposed to be joined as plaintiffs under Rule 19 of such rules, or seeking to intervene as plaintiffs under Rule 24 of such rules, when exercising supplemental jurisdiction over such claims would be inconsistent with the jurisdictional requirements of section 1332.

(c) The district courts may decline to exercise supplemental jurisdiction over a claim under subsection (a) if —

(1) the claim raises a novel or complex issue of State law,

(2) the claim substantially predominates over the claim or claims over which the district court has original jurisdiction,

(3) the district court has dismissed all claims over which it has original jurisdiction, or

(4) in exceptional circumstances, there are other compelling reasons for declining jurisdiction.

(d) The period of limitations for any claim asserted under subsection (a), and for any other claim in the same action that is voluntarily dismissed at the same time as or after the dismissal of the claim under subsection (a), shall be tolled while the claim is pending and for a period of 30 days after it is dismissed unless State law provides for a longer tolling period.

(e) As used in this section, the term "State" includes the District of Columbia, the Commonwealth of Puerto Rico, and any territory or possession of the United States.

Rundquist v. Vapiano SE

798 F. Supp. 2d 102 (D.D.C. 2011)

Memorandum Opinion

BERYL A. HOWELL, District Judge.

In this case, an international photographer claims that Vapiano restaurants are illegally exploiting her copyrighted works to achieve their chic look. Plaintiff Ewa-Marie Rundquist alleges that Vapiano restaurants in the United States and around the world are unlawfully displaying her copyrighted photographs as a central part of their décor. The plaintiff initiated this case against three corporations she believes to be responsible for this infringement: Vapiano SE, a European company based in Germany, and Vapiano International, LLC and Vapiano Franchise USA, LLC, both of which are incorporated in the United States. Defendant Vapiano SE moves to dismiss all claims against it on grounds that the Court lacks personal jurisdiction and, in the alternative, moves to dismiss all claims relating to infringement occurring in Vapiano restaurants outside the United States for lack of subject matter jurisdiction and on grounds of *forum non conveniens*. The Court concludes that the plaintiff is entitled to a sixty-day period of jurisdictional discovery to ascertain the facts about what Vapiano SE characterizes as the plaintiff's "guesswork" about the company's contacts with this forum. Vapiano SE's motion to dismiss for lack of personal jurisdiction is therefore denied without prejudice. With regard to allegations concerning infringement occurring outside the United States, the Court grants in part and denies in part Vapiano SE's motion to dismiss for lack of subject matter jurisdiction, holding that the Court does not have subject matter jurisdiction over Count I or Count II of the Amended Complaint to the extent that the counts assert Vapiano SE's direct, contributory, or vicarious liability under the Copyright Act for infringement taking place wholly outside the United States, but allowing plaintiff's other claims under the Copyright Act and foreign copyright laws to proceed. Finally, the Court denies Vapiano SE's motion to dismiss claims regarding foreign acts of infringement for *forum non conveniens*.

I. Background

Plaintiff Ewa-Marie Rundquist, a Swedish citizen, is a "highly experienced fashion, lifestyle, and advertising photographer" based in Stockholm, Sweden.

According to the Amended Complaint, her work has appeared in numerous well-known magazines, such as *Vogue, Elle,* and *Glamour,* and has been featured in advertising campaigns for a number of international brands.

In addition to her fashion and advertising work, the plaintiff's pictures have also appeared in several cookbooks, including a cookbook entitled *La Pizza: The True Story from Naples* (hereinafter "*La Pizza*"). *La Pizza* contains a number of the plaintiff's "original and unique" photographs of Italian street scenes and Italians eating and cooking pizza (hereinafter the "Protected Photographs"). Plaintiff states that she owns these photographs and that they "constitute copyrightable subject matter," which is protected under the Copyright Act and by provisions of the Berne Convention for the Protection of Literary and Artistic Works (hereinafter "Berne Convention"), to which the United States is a signatory. Every copy of *La Pizza* contains a notice that the plaintiff is the copyright owner of certain photographs appearing in the book and provides the page numbers on which the plaintiff's Protected Photographs appear.

Plaintiff alleges that her Protected Photographs are being used without permission as a "central décor element" in an upscale Italian restaurant chain named Vapiano, which has restaurants located in the United States and around the world. Specifically, the plaintiff alleges that large mural-sized black and white reproductions of her Protected Photographs appear in all Vapiano restaurants, which have the same décor and a consistent look. Plaintiff also alleges that her Protected Photographs appear on Vapiano websites. In addition to using her photographs without authorization, in no instance is the plaintiff referenced as the photographer or owner of the Protected Photographs.

On November 20, 2009, the plaintiff filed a Complaint in this Court against Vapiano SE; Vapiano International, LLC (hereinafter "Vapiano International"); and Vapiano Franchise USA, LLC (hereinafter "Vapiano USA"). The plaintiff alleges that defendant Vapiano SE, a European public corporation based in Germany, is a franchisor that has established sixty Vapiano restaurants in over sixteen countries around the world, and has more than a hundred new restaurants in development. Vapiano SE is alleged to direct and control the appearance and other operational aspects of all Vapiano restaurants. Additionally, plaintiff claims that Vapiano SE has ownership interests in many, if not all, Vapiano restaurants.

The plaintiff also asserts claims against defendants Vapiano International and Vapiano USA, both of which are Delaware limited liability companies with their [principal] place of business in McLean, Virginia. These companies are alleged to be Vapiano SE's affiliates that are controlled by Vapiano SE and act as Vapiano SE's agents with respect to Vapiano restaurants in the United States.

The plaintiff states that the defendants operate six Vapiano restaurants in the United States, including two in the District of Columbia, and are planning to open eighteen more restaurants in other U.S. cities. The defendants also market, own, operate, license or franchise thirty-five Vapiano restaurants in at least fifteen foreign countries. In all of these restaurants, the plaintiff alleges that the defendants "collectively require and direct . . . prominent[ ] display [of] Plaintiff's Protected Photographs as a central part of those restaurants' décor."

. . .

The plaintiff now asserts the following three causes of action against the defendants for their allegedly infringing copying and display of the Protected Photographs in Vapiano restaurants in the U.S. and abroad and on their websites: (1) direct copyright infringement in violation of the Copyright Act, 17 U.S.C. § 501 *et seq.*; (2) contributory and vicarious copyright infringement in violation of the Copyright Act; and (3) copyright infringement in violation of the copyright laws of fifteen foreign countries (hereinafter "Foreign Copyright Laws"). For these alleged unlawful acts, the plaintiff seeks a permanent injunction to enjoin use of her Protected Photographs in Vapiano restaurants and on the defendants' websites, and a monetary judgment, including actual damages and an accounting of the gains and income derived by the defendants from their use of the plaintiff's protected works.

. . . On September 3, 2010, defendant Vapiano SE moved to dismiss the allegations against it for lack of personal jurisdiction, and also moved to dismiss all claims relating to acts of infringement occurring outside the United States for lack of subject matter jurisdiction and for *forum non conveniens.* . . .

As explained below, Vapiano SE's motion to dismiss for lack of personal jurisdiction is denied because the plaintiff has requested, and is entitled to, a period of discovery regarding Vapiano SE's ties to the District of Columbia prior to the adjudication of this motion. Vapiano SE has also moved to dismiss Counts I and II of the plaintiff's Amended Complaint to the extent that these counts allege infringement in foreign nations, and Count III for lack of subject matter jurisdiction. The Court denies in part and grants in part this motion, dismissing only the allegations contained in Counts I and II of the Amended Complaint that assert Vapiano SE's direct, contributory and vicarious liability under the Copyright Act for the alleged display of Protected Photographs in foreign Vapiano restaurants. The Court maintains jurisdiction to hear such claims against Vapiano International and Vapiano USA. The Court also maintains jurisdiction to hear plaintiff's claims in Count III of the Amended Complaint, which allege that all of the defendants violated the copyright laws of foreign countries.

. . .

III. Vapiano SE's Motion to Dismiss Claims of Infringement Occurring in Foreign Vapiano Restaurants for Lack of Subject Matter Jurisdiction

Vapiano SE has moved to dismiss all claims concerning alleged acts of infringement occurring in Vapiano restaurants located outside the United States, arguing that the Court lacks subject matter jurisdiction to hear such allegations not only against Vapiano SE, but against any defendant. The Court concludes that it has subject matter jurisdiction over allegations in Count I and Count II regarding direct, contributory, or vicarious liability under the Copyright Act for infringement occurring in foreign Vapiano restaurants as to defendants Vapiano International and Vapiano USA, but not against Vapiano SE. The Court also has subject matter jurisdiction over plaintiff's allegations against all three defendants in Count III of the Amended Complaint, which alleges that the defendants violated Foreign Copyright Laws.

A. Standard of Review

Federal courts are fora of limited jurisdiction, only possessing the power authorized by the Constitution and statutes. . . . Therefore, when a defendant brings a motion to dismiss for lack of subject matter jurisdiction pursuant to Federal Rule of Civil Procedure 12(b)(1), the plaintiff bears the burden of establishing by a preponderance of the evidence that the Court possesses jurisdiction. It is well established that in deciding a motion to dismiss for lack of subject matter jurisdiction a court is not limited to the allegations set forth in the complaint, but may also consider material outside of the pleadings in its effort to determine whether the court has jurisdiction in the case. While the complaint is to be construed liberally, the court need not accept factual inferences drawn by plaintiffs if those inferences are not supported by facts alleged in the complaint, nor must the Court accept plaintiffs' legal conclusions.

B. Discussion

The plaintiff asserts three causes of action against the defendants for the alleged infringement of her Protected Photographs. Count I of the plaintiff's Complaint asserts that the defendants are violating Section 501 of the Copyright Act, 17 U.S.C. § 501, by "copying and displaying copies of Plaintiff's Protected Photographs in Vapiano Restaurants in the U.S. and abroad and on Vapiano Websites." Count II of the Complaint alleges that the defendants are liable for contributory and vicarious copyright infringement under the Copyright Act because they "collectively require and direct" the unlawful display of the Protected Photographs in Vapiano Restaurants "as a central part of those restaurants' décor." Count III asserts that the defendants are in violation of Foreign Copyright Laws for infringement of plaintiff's Protected Photographs occurring in Vapiano restaurants outside the United States. Vapiano SE argues that the Court lacks subject matter jurisdiction over any alleged acts of infringement occurring in foreign Vapiano restaurants, under either the Copyright Act, as asserted in Counts I and II of the Amended Complaint, or Foreign Copyright Laws, as asserted in Count III. The Court evaluates the defendant's argument concerning each Count individually.

1. Count I: The Court Does Not Have Subject Matter Jurisdiction over Allegations of Foreign Infringement by Vapiano SE

Vapiano SE seeks dismissal of Count I to the extent that it alleges violations of the Copyright Act for acts of infringement occurring in any Vapiano restaurant located outside the United States. To the extent that this motion would have the Court dismiss from the lawsuit claims relating to all foreign Vapiano restaurants, it sweeps too broadly on the current record. While infringing activity occurring abroad is not actionable under the Copyright Act, the Court does have subject matter jurisdiction over allegations that copyright infringement *inside* the United States is causing further infringement *outside* the United States. The Amended Complaint alleges that defendants Vapiano International and Vapiano USA committed such predicate acts of infringement, but fails to allege with sufficient specificity that Vapiano SE committed any predicate infringing acts inside the United States that resulted in the display of the Protected Photographs in foreign Vapiano restaurants. Accordingly, allegations contained in Count I of the Amended Complaint that Vapiano SE is liable for direct infringement under the Copyright Act for foreign acts of infringement are dismissed.

It is well-established that the Copyright Act does not have extraterritorial effect. *Subafilms, Ltd. v. MGM-Pathe Commc'ns Co.*, 24 F.3d 1088, 1095-96 (9th Cir. 1994) ("The 'undisputed axiom,' that the United States' copyright laws have no application to extraterritorial infringement . . . consistently has been reaffirmed.") . . . Thus, there is no cause of action under the Copyright Act for acts of infringement that occur completely outside the United States. Consequently, a foreign actor who engages in or authorizes infringing activity while abroad, and no part of the infringing activity takes place in the United States, does not thereby violate U.S. copyright law and U.S. courts do not have subject matter jurisdiction over claims arising from that foreign activity.

. . .

2. Count II: The Court Does Not Have Subject Matter Jurisdiction over Allegations of Contributory or Vicarious Liability Under the Copyright Act for Foreign Infringement by Vapiano SE

Count II of the Amended Complaint alleges that the defendants are contributorily and vicariously liable for copyright infringement because they "collectively require and direct" all franchise restaurants to display prominently the plaintiff's Protected Photographs and further facilitate this infringing activity "by providing them with unlawful copies" of the works. Vapiano SE has moved to dismiss Count II to the extent that it asserts contributory and vicarious liability under the Copyright Act for acts of infringement occurring in Vapiano restaurants located abroad. The Court agrees with the defendant that the Court lacks subject matter jurisdiction to hear such claims against Vapiano SE because the plaintiff has failed to allege that Vapiano SE took any predicate act of infringement within the United States.

. . .

3. Count III: The Court Has Subject Matter Jurisdiction over Foreign Copyright Claims

In considering Vapiano SE's argument that liability for foreign acts of infringement contained in Count I and II of the Amended Complaint should be dismissed, the Court discussed the extraterritorial reach of U.S. copyright law. The question now before the Court is whether claims that the defendants violated foreign law, specifically the individual copyright laws of fifteen foreign countries, can be asserted in United States courts. Although Vapiano SE argues that "[c]ourts and commentators have split" on this issue, review of the applicable caselaw reveals that, as the plaintiff explains, "Vapiano has grossly overstated any disagreement" and there is "little to no judicial debate." To the extent that such disagreement does exist, the Court believes that it has the power to adjudicate the claims contained in Count III of the plaintiff's Amended Complaint.

471 F. Supp. 2d

Commentators have maintained that "copyright infringement constitutes a transitory cause of action, and hence, may be adjudicated in the courts of a sovereign other than the one in which the cause of action arose." Melville B. Nimmer, 3 Nimmer on Copyright § 1703. Subscribing to this theory, numerous courts have held that there is no principled reason to bar, in absolute fashion, copyright claims brought under foreign law for lack of subject matter jurisdiction.

The two cases that oppose this view have done so without much discussion. In *ITSI T.V. Prods., Inc. v. California Authority of Racing Fairs*, 785 F. Supp. 854 (E.D. Cal. 1992), the court recognized that while commentators and other courts had concluded that actions for foreign copyright infringement could be brought in U.S. courts, it found "no clear authority" and simply stated that "American courts should be reluctant to enter the bramble bush of ascertaining and applying foreign law without an urgent reason to do so." *Id.* at 866-67. Similarly, in *Music Sales Ltd. v. Charles Dumont & Son, Inc.*, No. 09-cv-1443, 2009 WL 3417446, at *5, 2009 U.S. Dist. LEXIS 97534 (D.N.J. Oct. 19, 2009), the court simply stated that it had "no power to vindicate violations of British law." *Id.* at *5, 2009 U.S. Dist. LEXIS 97534, at *18. These cases seemingly recognize that applying foreign law may be difficult, but they do not provide a principled basis for declining review of these claims as a matter of subject matter jurisdiction.

Aside from arguments that application of foreign law would be burdensome, courts have identified one possible complication to adjudicating claims under foreign copyright law, which deserves comment. In *Vanity Fair Mills v. T. Eaton Co.*, 234 F.2d 633 (2d Cir. 1956), the Second Circuit declined to apply Canadian law in a patent and trademark case because it is not "the province of United States district courts to determine the validity of trademarks which officials of foreign countries have seen fit to grant. To do so would be to welcome conflicts with the administrative and judicial officers of the Dominion of Canada." *Id.* at 647. Citing *Vanity Fair*, the court in *ITSI T.V.* was in part reluctant to adjudicate claims under foreign law because it was unclear "in any given case [whether] the particular foreign law does have administrative formalities which must be satisfied." *ITSI T.V.*, 785 F. Supp. at 866 n. 19. Courts and commentators have noted, however, that "'in adjudicating an infringement action under a foreign copyright law there is . . . no need to pass upon the validity of acts of foreign government officials,' since foreign copyright laws, by and large, do not incorporate administrative formalities which must be satisfied to create or perfect a copyright." *London Film*, 580 F. Supp. at 49 (citing and quoting 3 Nimmer, § 1703). Moreover, administrative formalities "are barred in all nations that adhere to the Berne Convention," *Frink America Inc.*, 961 F. Supp. at 404 (quoting 3 Nimmer, § 1703). In the present case, all of the other countries where Defendants' Vapiano restaurants are located are signatories to the Berne Convention. Thus, the Court will not need to evaluate the propriety of foreign administrative acts. . . .

Having concluded that the Court has the power to adjudicate claims under foreign copyright law, the Court may exert supplemental subject matter jurisdiction over Count III of the plaintiff's Amended Complaint under 28 U.S.C. § 1367(a). Vapiano SE urges the Court to decline supplemental jurisdiction, pursuant to 28 U.S.C. § 1367(c), because the claims of infringement under foreign law "substantially predominate[ ] over any claims over which the Court has original jurisdiction," 28 U.S.C. § 1367(c)(2), and, consequently, this case is a "prime candidate for the 'exceptional circumstances' and 'compelling reason' ground for declining supplemental jurisdiction." The Court does not find these arguments persuasive.

Supplemental jurisdiction "is a doctrine of discretion, not a plaintiff's right." *Shekoyan v. Sibley Int'l*, 409 F.3d 414, 423 (D.C. Cir. 2005). In deciding whether to exercise supplemental jurisdiction, the Court considers matters of judicial economy, convenience and fairness to litigants. It is "a doctrine of flexibility, designed to allow courts to deal with cases involving pendent claims in the manner that most sensibly accommodates a range of concerns and values." *Carnegie-Mellon Univ. v. Cohill*, 484 U.S. 343, 350 (1988).

The Court sees no basis for declining supplemental jurisdiction over Count III of the plaintiff's Amended Complaint. Application of the laws of foreign countries will not overly burden the Court and will promote judicial economy. As the plaintiff states, litigating all of the plaintiff's claims, "which all stem from the same facts[,] . . . in a single forum would significantly reduce litigation costs and simplify discovery." Thus, there is no reason why, as Vapiano SE flippantly suggests, . . . the plaintiff [should] "be sent back across the Atlantic to pursue her European and Asian claims."

Indeed, the case currently before the Court is analogous to *Boosey & Hawkes Music Publishers, Ltd. v. Walt Disney Co.*, 145 F.3d 481 (2d Cir. 1998). In *Boosey & Hawkes*, the Second Circuit reversed the district court's determination that the existence of foreign copyright claims warranted dismissal of the case on *forum non conveniens* grounds, stating "[w]hile reluctance to apply foreign law is a valid factor favoring dismissal . . . standing alone it does not justify dismissal." *Id.* at 492. In that case, as in this one, "[a] trial here promises to begin and end sooner than elsewhere, and would allow the parties to sort out their rights and obligations in a single proceeding" and defendant's efforts to dismiss the case "seeks to split the suit into 18 parts in 18 nations, complicate the suit, delay it, and render it more expensive." *Id.* . . .

In this case, the plaintiff has asserted valid causes of action in an appropriate forum. It is not apparent that plaintiff's claims under foreign law substantially predominate over any of her other claims, and maintaining supplemental jurisdiction over the plaintiff's claims of infringement occurring in foreign nations will certainly expedite resolution of this dispute. Thus, the Court will exercise supplemental jurisdiction over Count III of plaintiff's Amended Complaint.

. . .

NOTES AND QUESTIONS

1. **Arguments for and Against Supplemental Jurisdiction.** What arguments did the plaintiff make in favor of supplemental jurisdiction over Count III? What arguments did the defendant make against supplemental jurisdiction? Why did the court rule in favor of the plaintiff?

2. **Litigation Strategy.** Could plaintiff's foreign law claims have been heard in a U.S. state court? As a strategic matter, why do you think the plaintiff wanted the claims — including Count III — to be heard in federal court instead? And why do you think the plaintiff wanted the foreign claims heard in the United States at all? Why do you think the defendant did not want Count III to be heard in federal court?

3. **What Is the Best Approach?** Do you think the court gets it right? Notice that the supplemental jurisdiction statute gives the district court discretion to refuse jurisdiction when there are novel and complex issues of law. Wouldn't all cases of foreign law raise such issues?

REVIEW NOTES AND QUESTIONS

Carefully review the materials presented in this section. As you do so, keep in mind these basic steps in analyzing subject matter jurisdiction.

- First, do the federal courts have federal question jurisdiction or diversity jurisdiction? If so, the plaintiff can file the case in federal court. If the plaintiff pleads her claim under state law and there is no diversity jurisdiction, can the defendant successfully argue that the suit has implications for foreign relations that create a federal question?

- Second, if the plaintiff files the suit in state court but you, as the lawyer for the defendant, would prefer to have the case heard in federal court, is the case removable?

- Third, in the absence of diversity jurisdiction, can the federal court exercise supplemental jurisdiction over claims that do not arise under federal law?

As we close this chapter, take a step back from the doctrine to see how many strategic choices you face as a lawyer for a plaintiff or a defendant in a transnational case. Which forum will be most advantageous for your client? A national court? If so, a U.S. court or a foreign court? If a U.S. court, a state or federal court? And in which U.S. state? And — separately from the strategic dimension of your analysis — which forums are likely to be available under the law of jurisdiction, including personal jurisdiction and subject matter jurisdiction? The best transnational lawyers identify all the potential forums where a case might be heard and find a way to have their case heard in the forum most favorable for their client.

CHAPTER 5

INTERNATIONAL COURTS

This chapter introduces you to international courts. Unlike national courts, which as described in Chapter 4 are part of individual nations' governments, international courts are created by groups of nations — often as parts of international organizations — and are institutionally separate from national governments. Moreover, while national courts are established by national law (for example, Article III of the U.S. Constitution and Title 28 of the U.S. Code establish the U.S. federal courts), international courts are typically established by treaties — for example, Chapter XIV of the U.N. Charter established the International Court of Justice (ICJ).

Intuitively, you might expect national courts to decide domestic disputes and international courts to decide transnational disputes. In reality there is not such a neat allocation of jurisdiction. As Chapter 4 makes clear, national courts routinely hear transnational cases. Just as it is important not to be "international law–centric" when tackling transnational legal problems, it is important not to be "international court–centric." On the other hand, as you will learn in this chapter, some international courts — such as the European Court of Human Rights (ECHR or ECtHR) and the International Criminal Court (ICC) — have jurisdiction that extends to disputes traditionally understood as domestic. To understand the jurisdiction of international courts, it is necessary to move beyond generalizations about domestic and transnational cases, and instead to perform court-specific jurisdictional analysis, which is the approach we take in this chapter.

The number of international courts[*] has grown rapidly. In 1985, there were only 6 permanent international courts, but by 2011 there were at least 25. Karen J. Alter, *The Evolving International Judiciary*, 7 ANN. REV. L. & SOC. SCI. 387, 388 (2011). However, international courts have limited jurisdiction. As you will learn in this chapter, even the ICJ — which is sometimes inaptly called the "World

---

[*] We use the term "international courts" to refer to any institutional dispute-resolution body created under international law. Some such bodies are officially called "tribunals," "dispute settlement bodies," or similar names.

Court" — has jurisdiction only in narrowly defined circumstances. Nonetheless, international courts form a significant part of the transnational legal system, and transnational practice requires at least basic familiarity with them and how they compare with national courts.

This chapter introduces the principal international courts. Section A addresses the ICJ, which is the international court with the broadest subject matter jurisdiction (for example, it is not limited to resolving disputes of a particular type or under a particular treaty). As Section A illustrates, however, the ICJ's jurisdiction is substantially limited by two basic principles: Only nations may be parties in ICJ proceedings, and nations must consent to the ICJ's jurisdiction.

Section B provides an overview of specialized international courts — those with limited subject matter jurisdiction, such as the ECHR and ICC. It also provides illustrative cases and other materials to allow a more detailed consideration of some leading specialized courts: the Dispute Settlement Mechanism (DSM) of the World Trade Organization (WTO), which has jurisdiction over trade disputes; the International Criminal Court (ICC); the ECHR, a regional human rights court; and the Court of Justice of the European Union (CJEU).

This chapter's goal is to introduce these international courts and their limited and varied jurisdiction. As you study the materials that follow, also keep in mind broader questions: Why have nations created international courts, and why are there a growing number of them? Why have more of them not been established? Should we favor more international courts or international courts with more expansive jurisdiction? What are the benefits and drawbacks of international courts?

A. The International Court of Justice

Created in 1945, the ICJ (http://www.icj-cij.org/) is the principal judicial organ of the United Nations. Chapter XIV of the U.N. Charter contains the provisions establishing the ICJ. The Statute of the International Court of Justice (ICJ Statute) governs the ICJ's organization, jurisdiction, and procedure, and is an integral part of the U.N. Charter. As you analyze the following provisions of the U.N. Charter and the ICJ Statute, consider whether the ICJ's role is as broad as its nickname suggests.

Charter of the United Nations (1945)

Chapter XIV: The International Court of Justice
Article 92

The International Court of Justice shall be the principal judicial organ of the United Nations. It shall function in accordance with the annexed Statute. . . .

Article 93

All Members of the United Nations are ipso facto parties to the Statute of the International Court of Justice.

. . .

Article 94

Each Member of the United Nations undertakes to comply with the decision of the International Court of Justice in any case to which it is a party.

If any party to a case fails to perform the obligations incumbent upon it under a judgment rendered by the Court, the other party may have recourse to the Security Council, which may, if it deems necessary, make recommendations or decide upon measures to be taken to give effect to the judgment.

. . .

Article 96

The General Assembly or the Security Council may request the International Court of Justice to give an advisory opinion on any legal question.

Other organs of the United Nations and specialized agencies, which may at any time be so authorized by the General Assembly, may also request advisory opinions of the Court on legal questions arising within the scope of their activities.

Statute of the International Court of Justice

33 U.N.T.S 993 (June 26, 1945)

Article 1

The International Court of Justice established by the Charter of the United Nations as the principal judicial organ of the United Nations shall be constituted and shall function in accordance with the provisions of the present Statute.

CHAPTER I — ORGANIZATION OF THE COURT
Article 2

The Court shall be composed of a body of independent judges, elected regardless of their nationality from among persons of high moral character, who possess the qualifications required in their respective countries for appointment to the highest judicial offices, or are jurisconsults of recognized competence in international law.

Article 3

1. The Court shall consist of fifteen members, no two of whom may be nationals of the same state.

. . .

Article 4

1. The members of the Court shall be elected by the General Assembly and by the Security Council. . . .

. . .

Article 9

At every election, the electors shall bear in mind not only that the persons to be elected should individually possess the qualifications required, but also that in the body as a whole the representation of the main forms of civilization and of the principal legal systems of the world should be assured.

Article 10

1. Those candidates who obtain an absolute majority of votes in the General Assembly and in the Security Council shall be considered as elected.

2. Any vote of the Security Council . . . for the election of judges . . . shall be taken without any distinction between permanent and non-permanent members of the Security Council.* . . .

Article 31

1. Judges of the nationality of each of the parties shall retain their right to sit in the case before the Court.

2. If the Court includes upon the Bench a judge of the nationality of one of the parties, any other party may choose a person to sit as judge. . . .

3. If the Court includes upon the Bench no judge of the nationality of the parties, each of these parties may proceed to choose a judge as provided in paragraph 2 of this Article.

. . .

CHAPTER II — COMPETENCE OF THE COURT

Article 34

Only states may be parties in cases before the Court. . . .

. . .

---

* The General Assembly and the Security Council are the two main deliberative bodies of the United Nations. All U.N. members are members of the General Assembly and 15 U.N. members are members of the Security Council. Article 23 of the U.N. Charter provides that five of them — China, France, Russia, the United Kingdom, and the United States — shall be permanent members of the Security Council. The General Assembly elects the ten nonpermanent members of the Security Council for two-year terms. Decisions of the Security Council (other than on procedural matters) are made by an affirmative vote of nine members, which must include the concurring votes (or abstentions) of all five permanent members. Thus, the permanent members are said to have a "veto" on the Security Council. — Eds.

Article 36

1. The jurisdiction of the Court comprises all cases which the parties refer to it and all matters specially provided for in the Charter of the United Nations or in treaties and conventions in force.

2. The states parties to the present Statute may at any time declare that they recognize as compulsory ipso facto and without special agreement, in relation to any other state accepting the same obligation, the jurisdiction of the Court in all legal disputes concerning:

   a. the interpretation of a treaty;

   b. any question of international law;

   c. the existence of any fact which, if established, would constitute a breach of an international obligation;

   d. the nature or extent of the reparation to be made for the breach of an international obligation.

3. The declarations referred to above may be made unconditionally or on condition of reciprocity on the part of several or certain states, or for a certain time.

   . . .

6. In the event of a dispute as to whether the Court has jurisdiction, the matter shall be settled by the decision of the Court.

   . . .

Article 38

1. The Court, whose function is to decide in accordance with international law such disputes as are submitted to it, shall apply:

   a. international conventions, whether general or particular, establishing rules expressly recognized by the contesting states;

   b. international custom, as evidence of a general practice accepted as law;

   c. the general principles of law recognized by civilized nations;

   d. . . . judicial decisions and the teachings of the most highly qualified publicists of the various nations, as subsidiary means for the determination of rules of law.

   . . .

CHAPTER III — PROCEDURE
Article 55

1. All questions shall be decided by a majority of the judges present.

2. In the event of an equality of votes, the President or the judge who acts in his place shall have a casting vote.

   . . .

Article 59

The decision of the Court has no binding force except between the parties and in respect of that particular case.

Article 60

The judgment is final and without appeal. In the event of dispute as to the meaning or scope of the judgment, the Court shall construe it upon the request of any party.

. . .

CHAPTER IV — ADVISORY OPINIONS
Article 65

1. The Court may give an advisory opinion on any legal question at the request of whatever body may be authorized by or in accordance with the Charter of the United Nations to make such a request.

. . .

NOTES AND QUESTIONS

1. **The ICJ and the United Nations.** The ICJ is the principal judicial arm of the United Nations. All 193 members of the United Nations (almost every nation in the world) are parties to the ICJ Statute (see U.N. Charter, Article 93). The predecessor to the ICJ was the Permanent Court of International Justice (PCIJ), created under the League of Nations in the early twentieth century. The PCIJ decided a number of cases in the 1920s and 1930s that remain landmarks of international law and continue to be frequently cited by the ICJ, international courts, and national courts as persuasive authority on the content of international law. The PCIJ was dissolved along with the League at the end of the Second World War and replaced by the ICJ.

2. **ICJ Judges.** How many judges are there on the ICJ and how are they elected? Under Article 27 of the U.N. Charter, any of the five permanent members of the United Nations (China, France, Russia, the United Kingdom, and the United States) can "veto" decisions of the U.N. Security Council other than on "procedural matters." Can they veto the election of ICJ judges? Although not required by the ICJ Statute, in practice "[t]he seats are filled in accordance with an informal regional arrangement that ensures that the ICJ represents all the main legal systems of the world." ANTHONY AUST, HANDBOOK OF INTERNATIONAL LAW 414 (2d ed. 2010). Traditionally, permanent members of the Security Council have always been represented on the ICJ. However, in 2017, the United Kingdom's candidate (who was already sitting as a judge on the ICJ and up for re-election) lost the majority vote in the General Assembly. After the United Kingdom withdrew its candidate, India's candidate (also a sitting judge up for re-election) was elected. Some have noted that this emphasizes a change in the power dynamics of the United Nations. How might this impact the legitimacy of the ICJ? Does it merely reflect changing power dynamics in the world more generally?

3. **Ad Hoc Judges.** Consider Article 31 of the ICJ Statute. In effect, Article 31 ensures that a nation that is a party to a dispute may choose a judge of that party's nationality if a judge of that nation is not already sitting on the ICJ. A judge selected under Article 31 is called an *ad hoc judge*. An ad hoc judge serves in addition to the full court, which means that the composition of the ICJ can change from case to case. Why do you think the ICJ Statute allows for parties to a dispute to appoint an ad hoc judge? What are the advantages and disadvantages of allowing ad hoc judges?

4. **ICJ Decisions.** Article 59 of the ICJ Statute provides that "[t]he decision of the Court has no binding force except between the parties and in respect of that particular case." Based on this provision, it is widely recognized that ICJ decisions do not create legal precedent. Why do you think the drafters of the U.N. Charter and the ICJ Statute decided not to give the ICJ authority to create binding legal precedent? Nevertheless, the ICJ and other courts frequently cite ICJ decisions. Why do you think this is the case, and how might you use ICJ decisions as a lawyer even though you know better than to use them as binding legal precedent?

5. **Types of International Law.** According to Article 38(1) of the Statute, which types of law may the ICJ use to resolve disputes? Are there notable omissions or inclusions in this list? How does it compare to the types of law a U.S. court uses?

6. **Contentious Jurisdiction of the ICJ.** The ICJ's jurisdiction to resolve disputes among nations is called its contentious jurisdiction. Contentious jurisdiction requires the consent of the nations that are parties to the dispute. Under the Statute, the requisite consent can be established in three ways: by a *compromis*, by a *compromissory clause*, or by reciprocal *optional clause declarations*.

    a. *Compromis.* Under Article 36(1) of the ICJ Statute, the ICJ's jurisdiction extends to cases that the parties agree to refer to it. Such an agreement is called a "compromis" (which is the French word for an "understanding") or "special agreement." Thus a compromis is an agreement to submit a specific case to the ICJ *after* a dispute has arisen between the parties. For example, Hungary and Slovakia agreed to refer to the ICJ a dispute involving a joint dam project. *Case Concerning Gabcikovo-Nagymaros Project (Hungary/Slovakia)* (Judgment of 25 September 1997). Why might nations agree to make such a submission?

    b. *Compromissory Clause.* A "compromissory clause" is an agreement in a treaty to submit *future* disputes to the ICJ. Under Article 36(1) of the Statute, the ICJ's jurisdiction extends to matters provided for in a compromissory clause. Typically the scope of a compromissory clause is limited to disputes arising out of the treaty containing the clause. Sometimes a compromissory clause is an optional part of a treaty arrangement that only some treaty parties accept (as in the *Avena* case below).

    c. *Optional Clause Declarations.* Under Article 36(2) of the Statute, a nation may declare that it recognizes the ICJ's jurisdiction without any further special agreement in future legal disputes. Such a declaration is known as an "optional clause declaration." Article 36(2) provides that optional clause declarations extend "in relation to any other state accepting the same obligation." Thus, this basis for jurisdiction requires that both parties to a dispute have made optional clause declarations. The ICJ's founders probably envisioned (or at least hoped) that nations would generally adopt this approach. Currently, approximately 70 nations have done so (including major nations such as Germany, India, Mexico, Pakistan, and the United Kingdom). Usually nations include reservations in their optional clause declarations limiting the scope of their consent to the ICJ's jurisdiction. For example, Australia's declaration states:

> The Government of Australia declares that it recognises as compulsory ipso facto and without special agreement, in relation to any other State accepting the same obligation, the jurisdiction of the International Court of Justice in conformity with paragraph 2 of Article 36 of the Statute of the Court, . . .
>
> This declaration does not apply to:
>
> . . . (b) any dispute concerning or relating to the delimitation of maritime zones, including the territorial sea, the exclusive economic zone and the continental shelf, or arising out of, concerning, or relating to the exploitation of any disputed area of or adjacent to any such maritime zone pending its delimitation. . . .

Other major countries, including Russia, China, Brazil, France, Italy, and South Africa, have not made optional clause declarations. As discussed in connection with the *Nicaragua v. United States* case (below), the United States initially made an Article 36(2) declaration but withdrew its consent after the ICJ ruled against it in that case.

7. **Diversity of Optional Clause Declarations.** For a complete list of and links to optional clause declarations, find the "Declarations Recognizing the Jurisdiction of the Court as Compulsory" page of the ICJ's website (http://www.icj-cij.org/jurisdiction/index.php?p1=5&p2=1&p3=3). Visit the page and read some of the optional clause declarations. How do they vary? Which are the broadest, and which are the most restrictive?

8. **Advisory Jurisdiction of ICJ.** In addition to contentious jurisdiction, the ICJ has *advisory jurisdiction* under Article 65. Who can request an advisory opinion from the ICJ?

9. **Example of an Advisory Opinion.** After a series of attacks launched against it from the Palestinian territories, Israel began constructing a "security fence" (in most places a wall) between Israel and the territories (on land within the territories but occupied by Israel). Several nations sought an ICJ advisory opinion on the wall's legality under international law. In December 2003, the General Assembly adopted a resolution requesting such an advisory opinion. In *Legal Consequences of the Construction of a Wall in the Occupied Palestinian Territories* (Opinion of 9 July 2004), the ICJ issued an advisory opinion that construction of the wall was illegal. Because nations are not "parties" to advisory opinion proceedings (although they may have a right to present arguments), this opinion was not legally binding on Israel.

Israel sharply criticized the opinion, principally on the ground that it failed to recognize Israel's need for and right to self-defense, and completed construction of the wall, which remains in place. Given the Charter's limitations on who may request an advisory opinion, how do you think nations went about seeking such an opinion in this case? Why do you think Israel was critical of the opinion, even though it was not legally bound by it? How, if at all, would the result have been different if Israel had been bound? Is the advisory opinion process a useful one? As an advisor to the U.S. government, would you recommend that the United States try to obtain an advisory opinion on a matter of strategic importance, for example the legality of Russia's 2014 annexation of Crimea?

10. **ICJ Workload.** The ICJ's website indicates that approximately 178 cases have been filed with the Court since its inception in 1946, and that 20 were pending in 2019. (By contrast, the U.S. Supreme Court currently hears around 80 cases per year.) Illustrative (though not necessarily typical) cases include:

- *United States Diplomatic and Consular Staff in Tehran (United States v. Iran)* (Judgment of 24 May 1980) (involving Iran's seizure of U.S. embassy staff)
- *Dispute Regarding Navigational and Related Rights (Costa Rica v. Nicaragua)* (Judgment of 13 July 2009) (involving Nicaragua's alleged interference with navigation on a shared river)
- *Pulp Mills on the River Uruguay (Argentina v. Uruguay)* (Judgment of 20 April 2010) (involving environmental damage to a shared river)
- *Jurisdictional Immunities of the State (Germany v. Italy)* (Judgment of 3 February 2012) (involving foreign sovereign immunity in national courts)
- *Territorial and Maritime Dispute (Nicaragua v. Colombia)* (Judgment of 19 November 2012) (territorial boundary dispute)
- *Application of the Convention on the Prevention and Punishment of the Crime of Genocide (Croatia v. Serbia)* (Judgment of 3 February 2015) (involving claims of genocide relating to the persecution of certain persons within the jurisdiction of Serbia)
- *Obligation to Negotiate Access to the Pacific Ocean (Bolivia v. Chile)* (Judgment of 1 October 2018) (involving access to the sea)
- *Jadhav (India v. Pakistan)* (Judgment of 17 July 2019) (involving the Vienna Convention on Consular Relations)

Illustrative cases currently pending at the ICJ include (1) a challenge by Qatar to aspects of a blockade imposed against it by the United Arab Emirates, under the International Convention on the Elimination of All Forms of Racial Discrimination; (2) a challenge by Equatorial Guinea to France's prosecution of Equatorial Guinea's Vice President for corruption, under the diplomatic immunity provisions of the Vienna Convention on Diplomatic Relations; (3) proceedings brought by The Gambia against Myanmar concerning alleged violations of the Convention on the Prevention and Punishment of the Crime of Genocide in Myanmar against members of the Rohingya people; and (4) two challenges by Iran to the United States' responses to Iranian terrorism through denial of sovereign immunity and sanctions (discussed in more detail below).

In 2018, the ICJ ruled that it had authority to order compensatory damages for environmental damage caused by Nicaragua during wrongful occupation of Costa Rican territory. *Certain Activities Carried Out by Nicaragua in the Border Area (Costa Rica v. Nicaragua)*, Feb. 2, 2018. However, it awarded damages of only about $300,000, compared to over $6 million claimed by Costa Rica. Nicaragua paid the money as directed.

Why haven't nations submitted more disputes to the ICJ? How would you advise a government considering a compromis, a compromissory clause, or an optional clause declaration? What more might you want to know about the ICJ or, in the case of a compromis or compromissory clause, about the dispute or treaty in question? Does the ICJ seem best suited to resolve particular types of disputes? Where else might nations go to have their disputes resolved if not the ICJ?

The following cases are examples of the ICJ's contentious jurisdiction. In the first two cases the issue was whether the ICJ had jurisdiction based on optional clause declarations. The third case is an example of a decision on the merits in which jurisdiction was based on a compromissory clause.

Case of Certain Norwegian Loans (France v. Norway)

1957 I.C.J. 9 (July 6, 1957)

[Norway issued bonds to French nationals between 1885 and 1907. The bondholders argued that the bonds "stipulate in gold the amount of [Norway's] obligation [to the bondholders]" and "that [Norway] can only discharge the substance of [its] debt by the payment of the gold value of the [bonds] on the date of payment. . . ." However, in 1931, the Norwegian government decreed that repayment would only be made in Norwegian kroner. The French bondholders requested payment based on gold value, but the negotiations that followed were interrupted by World War II, and ultimately did not result in a settlement of the dispute. After the war, France espoused the claims of the French bondholders and applied to the ICJ for relief.]

. . .

The Application [of France] expressly refers to Article 36, paragraph 2, of the Statute of the Court and to the acceptance of the compulsory jurisdiction of the Court by Norway on November 16th, 1946, and by France on March 1st, 1949. The Norwegian Declaration reads:

"I declare on behalf of the Norwegian Government that Norway recognizes as compulsory ipso facto and without special agreement, in relation to any other State accepting the same obligation, that is to say, on condition of reciprocity, the jurisdiction of the International Court of Justice in conformity with Article

36, paragraph 2, of the Statute of the Court, for a period of ten years as from 3rd October 1946."

The French Declaration reads:

"On behalf of the Government of the French Republic, and subject to ratification, I declare that I recognize as compulsory ipso facto and without special agreement, in relation to any other State accepting the same obligation, that is on condition of reciprocity, the jurisdiction of the International Court of Justice, in conformity with Article 36, paragraph 2, of the Statute of the said Court, for all disputes which may arise in respect of facts or situations subsequent to the ratification of the present declaration, with the exception of those with regard to which the parties may have agreed or may agree to have recourse to another method of peaceful settlement.

This declaration does not apply to differences relating to matters which are essentially within the national jurisdiction as understood by the Government of the French Republic.

The present declaration has been made for five years from the date of the deposit of the instrument of ratification. It shall continue in force thereafter until notice to the contrary is given by the French Government."

On April 20th, 1956, the Norwegian Government filed [various] Preliminary Objections. The first Objection consisted of two parts. In the first part the Norwegian Government maintained that the subject of the dispute was within the exclusive domain of the municipal law of Norway, and that it did not fall within any of the categories of disputes enumerated in Article 36, paragraph 2, of the Statute, by reference to which both Parties had by their Declarations accepted the compulsory jurisdiction of the Court. In the second part of that Objection the Norwegian Government relied upon the reservation in the French Declaration with regard to differences relating to matters which are essentially within the national jurisdiction as understood by the French Government. It challenged the jurisdiction of the Court on both grounds.

. . .

The Court will at the outset direct its attention to the Preliminary Objections of the Norwegian Government. . . .

In the first place, it is contended that the Court, whose function is to decide in accordance with international law such disputes as are submitted to it, can be seised, by means of a unilateral Application, only of legal disputes falling within one of the four categories enumerated in paragraph 2 of Article 36 of the Statute and relating to international law. It is urged that the Application of the French Government asks the Court to interpret loan contracts which, in the view of the Norwegian Government, are governed by municipal law and not by international law.

[Further], . . . the Norwegian Government continues in its Preliminary Objections:

"There can be no possible doubt on this point. If, however, there should still be some doubt, the Norwegian Government would rely upon the reservations made by the French Government in its Declaration of March 1st, 1949. By virtue of the principle of reciprocity, which is embodied in Article 36, paragraph 2, of the Statute of the Court and which has been clearly expressed in the Norwegian Declaration of November 16th, 1946, the Norwegian Government cannot be bound, vis-à-vis the French Government, by undertakings which are either broader or stricter than those given by the latter Government."

It is this second ground of the first Preliminary Objection which the Court will proceed to consider.

It will be recalled that the French Declaration accepting the compulsory jurisdiction of the Court contains the following reservation:

"This declaration does not apply to differences relating to matters which are essentially within the national jurisdiction as understood by the Government of the French Republic."

In the Preliminary Objections filed by the Norwegian Government it is stated:

"The Norwegian Government did not insert any such reservation in its own Declaration. But it has the right to rely upon the restrictions placed by France upon her own undertakings.

Convinced that the dispute which has been brought before the Court by the Application of July 6th, 1955, is within the domestic jurisdiction, the Norwegian Government considers itself fully entitled to rely on this right. Accordingly, it requests the Court to decline, on grounds that it lacks jurisdiction, the function which the French Government would have it assume."

In considering this ground of the Objection the Court notes in the first place that the present case has been brought before it on the basis of Article 36, paragraph 2, of the Statute and of the corresponding Declarations of acceptance of compulsory jurisdiction; that in the present case the jurisdiction of the Court depends upon the Declarations made by the Parties in accordance with Article 36, paragraph 2, of the Statute on condition of reciprocity; and that, since two unilateral declarations are involved, such jurisdiction is conferred upon the Court only to the extent to which the Declarations coincide in conferring it. A comparison between the two Declarations shows that the French Declaration accepts the Court's jurisdiction within narrower limits than the Norwegian Declaration; consequently, the common will of the Parties, which is the basis of the Court's jurisdiction, exists within these narrower limits indicated by the French reservation. . . .

France has limited her acceptance of the compulsory jurisdiction of the Court by excluding beforehand disputes "relating to matters which are essentially within the national jurisdiction as understood by the Government of the French Republic." In accordance with the condition of reciprocity to which acceptance of the compulsory jurisdiction is made subject in both Declarations and which is provided for in Article 36, paragraph 3, of the Statute, Norway, equally with France, is entitled to except from the compulsory jurisdiction of the Court disputes understood by Norway to be essentially within its national jurisdiction.

. . .

The Court considers that the Norwegian Government is entitled, by virtue of the condition of reciprocity, to invoke the reservation contained in the French Declaration of March 1st, 1949; that this reservation excludes from the jurisdiction of the Court the dispute which has been referred to it by the Application of the French Government; that consequently the Court is without jurisdiction to entertain the Application.

   . . .

Case Concerning Military and Paramilitary Activities in and Against Nicaragua (Nicaragua v. United States of America)

1984 I.C.J. 392 (Nov. 26, 1984)

On 9 April 1984 the Ambassador of the Republic of Nicaragua to the Netherlands filed in the Registry of the Court an Application instituting proceedings against the United States of America in respect of a dispute concerning responsibility for military and paramilitary activities in and against Nicaragua.* In order to found the jurisdiction of the Court the Application relied on declarations made by the Parties accepting the compulsory jurisdiction of the Court under Article 36 of its Statute.

   . . .

[Nicaragua also argued the ICJ had jurisdiction under a compromissory clause contained in the Treaty of Friendship, Commerce, and Navigation between Nicaragua and the United States.]

   . . .

The United States made a declaration, pursuant to [Article 36, paragraph 2], on 14 August 1946, containing certain reservations, to be examined below, and expressed to

> "remain in force for a period of five years and thereafter until the expiration of six months after notice may be given to terminate this declaration".

On 6 April 1984 the Government of the United States of America deposited with the Secretary-General of the United Nations a notification, signed by the United States Secretary of State, Mr. George Shultz, referring to the Declaration deposited on 26 August 1946, and stating that:

> "the aforesaid declaration shall not apply to disputes with any Central American State or arising out of or related to events in Central America, any of which disputes shall be settled in such manner as the parties to them may agree.
>
>   Notwithstanding the terms of the aforesaid declaration, this proviso shall take effect immediately and shall remain in force for two years, so as to foster the continuing regional dispute settlement process which seeks a negotiated solution to the interrelated political, economic and security problems of Central America."

This notification will be referred to, for convenience, as the "1984 notification".

   In order to be able to rely upon the United States Declaration of 1946 to found jurisdiction in the present case, Nicaragua has to show that it is a "State

---

* The dispute involved U.S. support for the Contra rebels who were fighting against the Nicaraguan government and U.S. mining of Nicaraguan harbors. — EDS.

accepting the same obligation" within the meaning of Article 36, paragraph 2, of the Statute. For this purpose, Nicaragua relies on a Declaration made by it on 24 September 1929 pursuant to Article 36, paragraph 2, of the Statute of the Permanent Court of International Justice [which is analogous to Article 36 of the ICJ Statute]. . . .

[Nicaragua's optional clause declaration read as follows:

> 24 September 1929
> [Translation from the French]
> On behalf of the Republic of Nicaragua I recognize as compulsory uncondi-tionally the jurisdiction of the Permanent Court of International Justice.
> Geneva, 24 September 1929.
> (Signed) T. F. MEDINA.

The U.S. declaration stated:

> "I, Harry S. Truman, President of the United States of America, declare on behalf of the United States of America, under Article 36, paragraph 2, of the Statute of the International Court of Justice, and in accordance with the Resolution of August 2, 1946, of the Senate of the United States of America (two-thirds of the Senators present concurring therein), that the United States of America recognizes as compulsory ipso facto and without special agreement, in relation to any other state accepting the same obligation, the jurisdiction of the International Court of Justice in all legal disputes hereafter arising concerning
>
> (a) The interpretation of a treaty;
> (b) Any question of international law;
> (c) The existence of any fact which, if established, would constitute a breach of an international obligation;
> (d) The nature or extent of the reparation to be made for the breach of an international obligation;
>
> Provided, that this declaration shall not apply to
>
> (a) Disputes the solution of which the Parties shall entrust to other tribunals by virtue of agreements already in existence or which may be concluded in the future; or
> (b) Disputes with regard to matters which are essentially within the domestic jurisdiction of the United States of America as determined by the United States of America; or
> (c) Disputes arising under a multilateral treaty, unless (1) all parties to the treaty affected by the decision are also parties to the case before the Court, or (2) the United States of America specially agrees to jurisdiction; and
>
> Provided further, that this declaration shall remain in force for a period of five years and thereafter until the expiration of six months after notice may be given to terminate this declaration."].

Nicaragua relies further on paragraph 5 of Article 36 of the Statute of the present Court, which provides that:

> "Declarations made under Article 36 of the Statute of the Permanent Court of International Justice and which are still in force shall be deemed, as between the

parties to the present Statute, to be acceptances of the compulsory jurisdiction of
the International Court of Justice for the period which they still have to run and
in accordance with their terms."

[In a portion of the ICJ's opinion not included here, the ICJ held on the basis
of Article 36(5) of the ICJ Statute that Nicaragua's 1929 optional clause declaration was effective for purposes of determining the jurisdiction of the ICJ in
this case.]

. . .

The acceptance of jurisdiction by the United States which is relied on by
Nicaragua is, as noted above, that dated 14 August 1946. The United States contends however that effect must also be given to the "1984 notification" — the declaration deposited with the Secretary-General of the United Nations on 6 April
1984. It is conceded by Nicaragua that if this declaration is effective as a modification or termination of the Declaration of 14 August 1946, and valid as against
Nicaragua at the date of its filing of the Application instituting the present proceedings (9 April 1984), then the Court is without jurisdiction to entertain those
proceedings, at least under Article 36, paragraphs 2 and 5, of the Statute. It is
however contended by Nicaragua that the 1984 notification is ineffective because
international law provides no basis for unilateral modification of declarations
made under Article 36 of the Statute of the Court, unless a right to do so has been
expressly reserved.

. . .

Declarations of acceptance of the compulsory jurisdiction of the Court are
facultative, unilateral engagements that States are absolutely free to make or not
to make. . . . However, the unilateral nature of declarations does not signify that
the State making the declaration is free to amend the scope and the contents of its
solemn commitments as it pleases.

. . .

The most important question relating to the effect of the 1984 notification is
whether the United States was free to disregard the clause of six months' notice
which, freely and by its own choice, it had appended to its 1946 Declaration. In so
doing the United States entered into an obligation which is binding upon it vis-à-
vis other States parties to the Optional-Clause system. Although the United States
retained the right to modify the contents of the 1946 Declaration or to terminate
it, a power which is inherent in any unilateral act of a State, it has, nevertheless
assumed an inescapable obligation towards other States accepting the Optional
Clause, by stating formally and solemnly that any such change should take effect
only after six months have elapsed as from the date of notice.

The United States has argued that the Nicaraguan 1929 Declaration, being of
undefined duration, is liable to immediate termination, without previous notice,
and that therefore Nicaragua has not accepted "the same obligation" as itself for
the purposes of Article 36, paragraph 2, and consequently may not rely on the six
months' notice proviso against the United States. The Court does not however consider that this argument entitles the United States validly to act in non-application
of the time-limit proviso included in the 1946 Declaration. The notion of reciprocity is concerned with the scope and substance of the commitments entered

into, including reservations, and not with the formal conditions of their creation, duration or extinction.

. . .

Moreover, since the United States purported to act on 6 April 1984 in such a way as to modify its 1946 Declaration with sufficiently immediate effect to bar an Application filed on 9 April 1984, it would be necessary, if reciprocity is to be relied on, for the Nicaraguan Declaration to be terminable with immediate effect. But the right of immediate termination of declarations with indefinite duration is far from established. It appears from the requirements of good faith that they should be treated, by analogy, according to the law of treaties, which requires a reasonable time for withdrawal from or termination of treaties that contain no provision regarding the duration of their validity. Since Nicaragua has in fact not manifested any intention to withdraw its own declaration, the question of what reasonable period of notice would legally be required does not need to be further examined: it need only be observed that from 6 to 9 April would not amount to a "reasonable time".

. . .

In sum, the six months' notice clause forms an important integral part of the United States Declaration and it is a condition that must be complied with in case of either termination or modification. Consequently, the 1984 notification, in the present case, cannot override the obligation of the United States to submit to the compulsory jurisdiction of the Court vis-à-vis Nicaragua, a State accepting the same obligation.

. . .

The question remains to be resolved whether the United States Declaration of 1946, though not suspended in its effects vis-à-vis Nicaragua by the 1984 notification, constitutes the necessary consent of the United States to the jurisdiction of the Court in the present case, taking into account the reservations which were attached to the declaration. Specifically, the United States has invoked proviso (c) to that declaration, which provides that the United States acceptance of the Court's compulsory jurisdiction shall not extend to

> "disputes arising under a multilateral treaty, unless (1) all parties to the treaty affected by the decision are also parties to the case before the Court, or (2) the United States of America specially agrees to jurisdiction".

This reservation will be referred to for convenience as the "multilateral treaty reservation". Of the two remaining provisos to the declaration, it has not been suggested that proviso (a), referring to disputes the solution of which is entrusted to other tribunals, has any relevance to the present case. As for proviso (b), excluding jurisdiction over "disputes with regard to matters which are essentially within the domestic jurisdiction of the United States of America as determined by the United States of America", the United States has informed the Court that it has determined not to invoke this proviso, but "without prejudice to the rights of the United States under that proviso in relation to any subsequent pleadings, proceedings, or cases before this Court".

The United States points out that Nicaragua relies in its Application on four multilateral treaties, namely the Charter of the United Nations, the Charter of the Organization of American States, the Montevideo Convention on Rights and Duties of States of 26 December 1933, and the Havana Convention on the Rights and Duties of States in the Event of Civil Strife of 20 February 1928. In so far as the dispute brought before the Court is thus one "arising under" those multilateral treaties, since the United States has not specially agreed to jurisdiction here, the Court may, it is claimed, exercise jurisdiction only if all treaty parties affected by a prospective decision of the Court are also parties to the case. . . . [T]he United States identifies, as States parties to the four multilateral treaties above mentioned which would be "affected", in a legal and practical sense, by adjudication of the claims submitted to the Court, Nicaragua's three Central American neighbours, Honduras, Costa Rica and El Salvador.

> . . .

It may first be noted that the multilateral treaty reservation could not bar adjudication by the Court of all Nicaragua's claims, because Nicaragua, in its Application, does not confine those claims only to violations of the four multilateral conventions referred to above. On the contrary, Nicaragua invokes a number of principles of customary and general international law that, according to the Application, have been violated by the United States. The Court cannot dismiss the claims of Nicaragua under principles of customary and general international law, simply because such principles have been enshrined in the texts of the conventions relied upon by Nicaragua. The fact that the above-mentioned principles, recognized as such, have been codified or embodied in multilateral conventions does not mean that they cease to exist and to apply as principles of customary law, even as regards countries that are parties to such conventions. Principles such as those of the non-use of force, non-intervention, respect for the independence and territorial integrity of States, and the freedom of navigation, continue to be binding as part of customary international law, despite the operation of provisions of conventional law in which they have been incorporated. Therefore, since the claim before the Court in this case is not confined to violation of the multilateral conventional provisions invoked, it would not in any event be barred by the multilateral treaty reservation in the United States 1946 Declaration.

> . . .

The Court now turns to the question of the admissibility of the Application of Nicaragua. The United States of America contended in its Counter-Memorial that Nicaragua's Application is inadmissible on five separate grounds, each of which, it is said, is sufficient to establish such inadmissibility, whether considered as a legal bar to adjudication or as 'a matter requiring the exercise of prudential discretion in the interest of the integrity of the judicial function'. . . . These grounds will now be examined; but for the sake of clarity it will first be convenient to recall briefly what are the allegations of Nicaragua upon which it bases its claims against the United States.

In its Application instituting proceedings, Nicaragua asserts that: "The United States of America is using military force against Nicaragua and intervening in Nicaragua's internal affairs, in violation of Nicaragua's sovereignty, territorial integrity and political independence and of the most fundamental and universally accepted principles of international law. The United States has created an 'army' of more than 10,000 mercenaries . . . installed them in more than ten base camps in Honduras along the border with Nicaragua, trained them, paid them, supplied them with arms, ammunition, food and medical supplies, and directed their attacks against human and economic targets inside Nicaragua", and that Nicaragua has already suffered and is now suffering grievous consequences as a result of these activities. The purpose of these activities is claimed to be

> "to harass and destabilize the Government of Nicaragua so that ultimately it will be overthrown, or, at a minimum, compelled to change those of its domestic and foreign policies that displease the United States".

The first ground of inadmissibility relied on by the United States is that Nicaragua has failed to bring before the Court parties whose presence and participation is necessary for the rights of those parties to be protected and for the adjudication of the issues raised in the Application. . . .

There is no doubt that in appropriate circumstances the Court will decline, as it did in the case concerning *Monetary Gold Removed from Rome in 1943*, to exercise the jurisdiction conferred upon it where the legal interests of a State not party to the proceedings "would not only be affected by a decision, but would form the very subject-matter of the decision" (I.C.J. Reports 1954, p. 32). Where however claims of a legal nature are made by an Applicant against a Respondent in proceedings before the Court, and made the subject of submissions, the Court has in principle merely to decide upon those submissions, with binding force for the parties only, and no other State, in accordance with Article 59 of the Statute. . . . [O]ther States which consider that they may be affected are free to institute separate proceedings, or to employ the procedure of intervention. There is no trace, either in the Statute or in the practice of international tribunals, of an "indispensable parties" rule of the kind argued for by the United States, which would only be conceivable in parallel to a power, which the Court does not possess, to direct that a third State be made a party to proceedings. The circumstances of the *Monetary Gold* case probably represent the limit of the power of the Court to refuse to exercise its jurisdiction; and none of the States referred to can be regarded as . . . truly indispensable to the pursuance of the proceedings.

Secondly, the United States regards the Application as inadmissible because each of Nicaragua's allegations constitutes no more than a reformulation and restatement of a single fundamental claim, that the United States is engaged in an unlawful use of armed force, or breach of the peace, or acts of aggression against Nicaragua, a matter which is committed by the Charter and by practice to the competence of other organs, in particular the United Nations Security Council. All allegations of this kind are confided to the political organs of the Organization for consideration and determination; the United States quotes Article 24 of the Charter, which confers upon the Security Council "primary responsibility for the maintenance of international peace and security". . . .

It will be convenient to deal with this alleged ground of inadmissibility together with the third ground advanced by the United States namely that the Court should hold the Application of Nicaragua to be inadmissible in view of the subject-matter of the Application and the position of the Court within the United Nations system, including the impact of proceedings before the Court on the ongoing exercise of the "inherent right of individual or collective self-defence" under Article 51 of the Charter. . . .

The United States is thus arguing that the matter was essentially one for the Security Council since it concerned a complaint by Nicaragua involving the use of force. However, . . . the Court is of the view that the fact that a matter is before the Security Council should not prevent it being dealt with by the Court and that both proceedings could be pursued pari passu. . . .

. . . While in Article 12 there is a provision for a clear demarcation of functions between the General Assembly and the Security Council, in respect of any dispute or situation, that the former should not make any recommendation with regard to that dispute or situation unless the Security Council so requires, there is no similar provision anywhere in the Charter with respect to the Security Council and the Court. The Council has functions of a political nature assigned to it, whereas the Court exercises purely judicial functions. Both organs can therefore perform their separate but complementary functions with respect to the same events.

. . .

The fourth ground of inadmissibility put forward by the United States is that the Application should be held inadmissible in consideration of the inability of the judicial function to deal with situations involving ongoing conflict. The allegation, attributed by the United States to Nicaragua, of an ongoing conflict involving the use of armed force contrary to the Charter is said to be central to, and inseparable from, the Application as a whole, and is one with which a court cannot deal effectively without overstepping proper judicial bounds. The resort to force during ongoing armed conflict lacks the attributes necessary for the application of the judicial process, namely a pattern of legally relevant facts discernible by the means available to the adjudicating tribunal, establishable in conformity with applicable norms of evidence and proof, and not subject to further material evolution during the course of, or subsequent to, the judicial proceedings. It is for reasons of this nature that ongoing armed conflict must be entrusted to resolution by political processes. . . .

. . .

The Court is bound to observe that any judgment on the merits in the present case will be limited to upholding such submissions of the Parties as have been supported by sufficient proof of relevant facts, and are regarded by the Court as sound in law. A situation of armed conflict is not the only one in which evidence of fact may be difficult to come by, and the Court has in the past recognized and made allowance for this. . . . As to the possibility of implementation of the judgment, the Court will have to assess this question also on the basis of each specific submission, and in the light of the facts as then established; it cannot at this stage rule out a priori any judicial contribution to the settlement of the dispute by declaring the Application inadmissible. It should be observed however that the Court neither can nor should contemplate the contingency of the judgment not being complied with. Both the Parties have undertaken to comply with the decisions of the Court, under Article 94 of the Charter; and [o]nce the Court has found that a State has entered into a commitment concerning its future conduct it is not the Court's function to contemplate that it will not comply with it.

The fifth and final contention of the United States under this head is that the Application should be held inadmissible because Nicaragua has failed to exhaust the established processes for the resolution of the conflicts occurring in Central America. In the contention of the United States, the Contadora process, to which Nicaragua is party, is recognized both by the political organs of the United Nations and by the Organization of American States, as the appropriate method for the resolution of the issues of Central America. . . .

With regard to the contention of the United States of America that the matter raised in the Nicaraguan Application was part of the Contadora Process, the Court considers that even the existence of active negotiations in which both parties might be involved should not prevent both the Security Council and the Court from exercising their separate functions under the Charter and the Statute of the Court. . . .

. . .

In the light of the foregoing, the Court is unable to accept either that there is any requirement of prior exhaustion of regional negotiating processes as a precondition to seising the Court; or that the existence of the Contadora process constitutes in this case an obstacle to the examination by the Court of the Nicaraguan Application and judicial determination in due course of the submissions of the Parties in the case. The Court is therefore unable to declare the Application inadmissible, as requested by the United States, on any of the grounds it has advanced as requiring such a finding.

. . .

Consequently, the Court finds that the Nicaraguan Declaration of 24 September 1929 is valid, and that Nicaragua accordingly was, for the purposes of Article 36, paragraph 2, of the Statute of the Court, a "State accepting the same obligation" as the United States of America at the date of filing of the Application, so as to be able to rely on the United States Declaration of 26 August 1946. The Court also finds that despite the United States notification of 6 April 1984, the present Application is not excluded from the scope of the acceptance by the United States of America of the compulsory jurisdiction of the Court. Accordingly the Court finds that the two Declarations do afford a basis for the jurisdiction of the Court.

[The Court also found that the compromissory clause in the Treaty of Friendship, Commerce, and Navigation provided an independent basis for jurisdiction.]

NOTES AND QUESTIONS

1. **The Reciprocity Principle.** The *Norwegian Loans* case illustrates the reciprocity principle that applies to optional clause declarations. As Article 36(2) states, optional clause declarations provide jurisdiction "in relation to any other state accepting the *same obligation*" (emphasis added). As one

commentator summarizes, this means that "a State can rely not only on its own reservations, *but also on any made by the other State.* So, if two States have a dispute that arose in, say, 1990, and the declaration of one of them excludes disputes arising before 1995, the ICJ will not have jurisdiction. In essence, therefore, jurisdiction amounts to the lowest common denominator of two reservations." ANTHONY AUST, HANDBOOK OF INTERNATIONAL LAW 417 (2d ed. 2010). Norway's declaration, like many other optional clause declarations, itself contains language imposing a reciprocity condition ("Norway recognizes as compulsory ipso facto and without special agreement, in relation to any other State accepting the same obligation, that is to say, on condition of reciprocity. . . ."); but because Article 36(2) itself expresses the reciprocity principle, the outcome of the *Norwegian Loans* case likely would have been the same even without the reciprocity language in Norway's declaration. THOMAS BUERGENTHAL & SEAN D. MURPHY, PUBLIC INTERNATIONAL LAW 97 (5th ed. 2013).

2. **Self-Judging Clauses.** Consider the reservation in France's optional clause declaration in the *Norwegian Loans* case, which provides as follows: "This declaration does not apply to differences relating to matters which are essentially within the national jurisdiction *as understood by the Government of the French Republic."* A similar reservation was included in the U.S. optional clause declaration in the *Nicaragua* case: "[T]his declaration shall not apply to [d]isputes with regard to matters which are essentially within the domestic jurisdiction of the United States of America *as determined by the United States of America. . . ."* This kind of reservation is sometimes called a "self-judging clause" because (as the italicized words indicate) they allow the nation making the reservation to decide itself whether a matter is "domestic" and thus excluded from ICJ's jurisdiction under the optional clause. Why would a nation include a self-judging clause? What are the disadvantages of a self-judging clause — for the nation including one in its optional clause declaration and for the ICJ system overall? Why didn't the United States argue that the self-judging clause in its optional clause declaration precluded jurisdiction in the *Nicaragua* case? Think about this from the perspective of a lawyer deciding which arguments to make and which not to make. What might have happened if the United States did make the argument?

3. **The Timing of the 1984 Notification.** Nicaragua decided in January 1984 that it would sue the United States in the ICJ. On April 6, 1984 the United States issued the so-called 1984 notification, which narrowed the scope of the U.S. optional clause declaration to exclude disputes with any Central American nation. On April 9, 1984 Nicaragua filed its application against the United States in the ICJ. What might explain this interesting timing? How might the United States have learned of the impending suit? Why might it not have learned earlier? How else might have the United States reacted?

4. **The Arguments in *Nicaragua v. United States.*** What arguments did Nicaragua assert for the ICJ's jurisdiction? What counter-arguments did the United States make? Why did the ICJ ultimately rule in favor of Nicaragua on the question of jurisdiction?

5. **Admissibility.** Even if the ICJ has jurisdiction in a particular case, it may apply various "admissibility doctrines" to decline to assert its jurisdiction. As one commentator explains: "[T]he [ICJ] has developed a number of prudential grounds for finding a case *inadmissible*, and thus declining to decide it. These grounds are analogous to the prudential reasons that U.S. federal courts often refuse to hear cases, even though jurisdiction is otherwise proper. [Consider, for example, the doctrines of standing and ripeness, the political question doctrine, and the *forum non conveniens* doctrine. — EDS.] For example, the Court will dismiss a case if its subject-matter has become moot. . . . Somewhat more controversially, the Court will dismiss a case because of failure to exhaust local remedies. . . ." DAVID J. BEDERMAN, INTERNATIONAL LAW FRAMEWORKS 262 (3d ed. 2010). What arguments did the United States make on admissibility, and how did the ICJ respond?

6. **The U.S. Reaction.** The U.S. government was highly critical of the ICJ's decision. On January 18, 1985, it submitted the following letter to the ICJ:

> The United States has given the deepest and most careful consideration to the [ICJ's] judgment, to the findings reached by the Court, and to the reasons given by the Court in support of those findings. On the basis of that examination, the United States is constrained to conclude that the judgment of the Court was clearly and manifestly erroneous as to both fact and law. The United States remains firmly of the view, for the reasons given in its written and oral pleadings that the Court is without jurisdiction to entertain the dispute, and that the Nicaraguan application . . . is inadmissible.
>
> Accordingly, it is my duty to inform you that the United States intends not to participate in any further proceedings in connection with this case, and reserves its rights in respect of any decision by the Court regarding Nicaragua's claims.

Moreover, on October 7, 1985, the United States gave notice of the termination of its optional clause declaration. The ICJ proceedings continued without U.S. participation, and the ICJ subsequently decided the merits of Nicaragua's application, holding that the United States violated international law by, among other things, "training, arming, equipping, financing and supplying the contra forces or otherwise encouraging, supporting and aiding military and paramilitary activities in and against Nicaragua" and "by laying mines in the internal or territorial waters of the Republic of Nicaragua." The ICJ rejected the argument that the United States was acting in collective self-defense, as allowed under international law, with Nicaragua's neighbors El Salvador and Honduras, whose governments Nicaragua had allegedly tried to destabilize by supporting rebel groups.

The United States refused to abide by the judgment and used its veto at the U.N. Security Council to block proposed resolutions that would have called on the United States to comply. In Nicaragua's 1990 presidential election, the U.S.-supported opposition candidate Violeta Barrios de Chamorro defeated the incumbent President Daniel Ortega. Relations between Nicaragua and the United States improved, and on September 30, 1991, Nicaragua formally discontinued its proceedings before the ICJ. The United States has not reinstated its optional clause declaration.

Case Concerning Avena and Other Mexican Nationals
(Mexico v. United States of America)

2004 I.C.J. 12 (March 31, 2004)

. . .

On 9 January 2003 the United Mexican States (hereinafter referred to as "Mexico") filed in the Registry of the Court an Application instituting proceedings against the United States of America (hereinafter referred to as the "United States") for "violations of the Vienna Convention on Consular Relations" of 24 April 1963 (hereinafter referred to as the "Vienna Convention") allegedly committed by the United States.

In its Application, Mexico based the jurisdiction of the Court on Article 36, paragraph 1, of the Statute of the Court and on Article I of the Optional Protocol concerning the Compulsory Settlement of Disputes, which accompanies the Vienna Convention (hereinafter referred to as the "Optional Protocol").*

. . .

The present proceedings have been brought by Mexico against the United States on the basis of the Vienna Convention, and of the Optional Protocol providing for the jurisdiction of the Court over "disputes arising out of the interpretation or application" of the Convention. Mexico and the United States are, and were at all relevant times, parties to the Vienna Convention and to the Optional Protocol. Mexico claims that the United States has committed breaches of the Vienna Convention in relation to the treatment of a number of Mexican nationals who have been tried, convicted and sentenced to death in criminal proceedings in the United States. . . . These criminal proceedings have been taking place in nine different States of the United States . . . between 1979 and the present.

. . .

The provisions of the Vienna Convention of which Mexico alleges violations are contained in Article 36. . . . Paragraph 1(*b*) of that Article provides that if a national of that State "is arrested or committed to prison or to custody pending trial or is detained in any other manner", and he so requests, the local consular post of the sending State is to be notified. The Article goes on to provide that the "competent authorities of the receiving State" shall "inform the person concerned without delay of his rights" in this respect. Mexico claims that in the present case these provisions were not complied with by the United States authorities

---

* The Optional Protocol provides:

The States Parties to the present Protocol and to the Vienna Convention on Consular Relations, hereinafter referred to as "the Convention", . . .
    Have agreed as follows:

Article I

    Disputes arising out of the interpretation or application of the Convention shall lie within the compulsory jurisdiction of the International Court of Justice and may accordingly be brought before the Court by an application made by any party to the dispute being a Party to the present Protocol.

— Eds.

in respect of the 52 Mexican nationals the subject of its claims. As a result, the United States has according to Mexico committed breaches of paragraph 1(*b*). . . .

The underlying facts alleged by Mexico may be briefly described as follows: some are conceded by the United States, and some disputed. Mexico states that all the individuals the subject of its claims were Mexican nationals at the time of their arrest. It further contends that the United States authorities that arrested and interrogated these individuals had sufficient information at their disposal to be aware of the foreign nationality of those individuals. According to Mexico's account, in 50 of the specified cases, Mexican nationals were never informed by the competent United States authorities of their rights under Article 36, paragraph 1(*b*), of the Vienna Convention and, in the two remaining cases, such information was not provided "without delay", as required by that provision. Mexico has indicated that in 29 of the 52 cases its consular authorities learned of the detention of the Mexican nationals only after death sentences had been handed down. In the 23 remaining cases, Mexico contends that it learned of the cases through means other than notification to the consular post by the competent United States authorities under Article 36, paragraph 1(*b*). It explains that in five cases this was too late to affect the trials, that in 15 cases the defendants had already made incriminating statements, and that it became aware of the other three cases only after considerable delay.

. . . Of the 52 cases referred to in Mexico's final submissions, 49 are currently at different stages of the proceedings before United States judicial authorities at state or federal level. . . . The Court has been informed of the variety of types of proceedings and forms of relief available in the criminal justice systems of the United States, which can differ from state to state. In very general terms, and according to the description offered by both Parties in their pleadings, it appears that the 52 cases may be classified into three categories: 24 cases which are currently in direct appeal; 25 cases in which means of direct appeal have been exhausted, but post-conviction relief (*habeas corpus*), either at State or at federal level, is still available; and three cases in which no judicial remedies remain. The Court also notes that, in at least 33 cases, the alleged breach of the Vienna Convention was raised by the defendant either during pre-trial, at trial, on appeal or in *habeas corpus* proceedings, and that some of these claims were dismissed on procedural or substantive grounds and others are still pending.

. . .

[The Court first reviewed the facts of each particular case and in most instances found that the requisite notification had not been made by the arresting authorities.]

On this aspect of the case, the Court thus concludes:

(1) that the United States committed breaches of the obligation incumbent upon it under Article 36, paragraph 1(*b*), of the Vienna Convention to inform detained Mexican nationals of their rights under that paragraph . . . ;

(2) that the United States committed breaches of the obligation incumbent upon it under Article 36, paragraph 1(*b*) to notify the Mexican consular post of the detention of the Mexican nationals . . . ;

(3) that by virtue of its breaches of Article 36, paragraph 1(*b*), as described in subparagraph (2) above, the United States also violated the obligation incumbent upon it under Article 36, paragraph 1(*a*), of the Vienna Convention to enable Mexican consular officers to communicate with and have access to their nationals, as well as its obligation under paragraph 1(*c*) of that Article regarding the right of consular officers to visit their detained nationals; [and]

(4) that the United States, by virtue of these breaches of Article 36, paragraph 1(*b*), also violated the obligation incumbent upon it under paragraph 1(*c*) of that Article to enable Mexican consular officers to arrange for legal representation of their nationals. . . .

Mexico asks the Court to adjudge and declare that "the United States violated its obligations under Article 36(2) of the Vienna Convention by failing to provide meaningful and effective review and reconsideration of convictions and sentences impaired by a violation of Article 36(1)".

. . . Article 36, paragraph 2, provides:

> "The rights referred to in paragraph 1 of this article shall be exercised in conformity with the laws and regulations of the receiving State, subject to the proviso, however, that the said laws and regulations must enable full effect to be given to the purposes for which the rights accorded under this article are intended."

In this connection, Mexico has argued that the United States "By applying provisions of its municipal law to defeat or foreclose remedies for the violation of rights conferred by Article 36 — thus failing to provide meaningful review and reconsideration of severe sentences imposed in proceedings that violated Article 36 . . . has violated, and continues to violate, the Vienna Convention."

More specifically, Mexico contends that:

> "The United States uses several municipal legal doctrines to prevent finding any legal effect from the violations of Article 36. U.S. courts, at both the state and federal level, continue to invoke default doctrines to bar any review of Article 36 violations . . . even when the national had been unaware of his rights to consular notification and communication and thus his ability to raise their violation as an issue at trial, due to the competent authorities' failure to comply with Article 36."

Against this contention by Mexico, the United States argues that:

> "the criminal justice systems of the United States address all errors in process through both judicial and executive clemency proceedings, relying upon the latter when rules of default have closed out the possibility of the former. That is, the 'laws and regulations' of the United States provide for the correction of mistakes that may be relevant to a criminal defendant to occur through a combination of judicial review and clemency. These processes together, working with other competent authorities, give full effect to the purposes for which Article 36(1) is intended, in conformity with Article 36(2). And, insofar as a breach of Article 36(1) has occurred, these procedures satisfy the remedial function of Article 36(2) by allowing the United States to provide review and reconsideration of convictions and sentences. . . ."

The "procedural default" rule in United States law [generally provides] . . . that a defendant who could have raised, but fails to raise, a legal issue at trial will generally not be permitted to raise it in future proceedings, on appeal or in a petition for a writ of *habeas corpus*. The rule requires exhaustion of remedies, *inter alia*, at the state level and before a *habeas corpus* motion can be filed with federal courts. . . .

In itself, the rule does not violate Article 36 of the Vienna Convention. The problem arises when the procedural default rule does not allow the detained individual to challenge a conviction and sentence by claiming, in reliance on Article 36, paragraph 1, of the Convention, that the competent national authorities failed to comply with their obligation to provide the requisite consular information 'without delay', thus preventing the person from seeking and obtaining consular assistance from the sending State. . . . [Thus], the procedural default rule may . . . prevent courts from attaching legal significance to the fact, *inter alia*, that the violation of the rights set forth in Article 36, paragraph 1, prevented Mexico, in a timely fashion, from retaining private counsel for certain nationals and otherwise assisting in their defence. In such cases, application of the procedural default rule would have the effect of preventing "full effect [from being] given to the purposes for which the rights accorded under this article are intended", and thus violate paragraph 2 of Article 36. The Court notes moreover that in several of the cases cited in Mexico's final submissions the procedural default rule has already been applied, and that in others it could be applied at subsequent stages in the proceedings. However, in none of the cases, . . . have the criminal proceedings against the Mexican national concerned already reached a stage at which there is no further possibility of judicial re-examination of those cases; that is to say, all possibility is not yet excluded of "review and reconsideration" of conviction and sentence. . . .

Legal Consequences of the Breach

Having concluded that in most of the cases brought before the Court by Mexico in the 52 instances, there has been a failure to observe the obligations prescribed by Article 36, paragraph 1(*b*), of the Vienna Convention, the Court now proceeds to the examination of the legal consequences of such a breach and of what legal remedies should be considered for the breach.

Mexico . . . asks the Court to adjudge and declare:

> ". . . that pursuant to the injuries suffered by Mexico in its own right and in the exercise of diplomatic protection of its nationals, Mexico is entitled to full reparation for these injuries in the form of *restitutio in integrum*;
>
> . . . that this restitution consists of the obligation to restore the *status quo ante* by annulling or otherwise depriving of full force or effect the conviction and sentences of all 52 Mexican nationals; [and]
>
> . . . that this restitution also includes the obligation to take all measures necessary to ensure that a prior violation of Article 36 shall not affect the subsequent proceedings."

In support . . . , Mexico argues that "It is well-established that the primary form of reparation available to a State injured by an internationally wrongful act is *restitutio in integrum*", and that "The United States is therefore obliged to take the necessary action to restore the *status quo ante* in respect of Mexico's nationals detained, tried, convicted and sentenced in violation of their internationally recognized rights". To restore the *status quo ante*, Mexico contends that "restitution here must take the form of annulment of the convictions and sentences that resulted from the proceedings tainted by the Article 36 violations", and that "It follows from the very nature of *restitutio* that, when a violation of an international obligation is manifested in a judicial act, that act must be annulled and thereby deprived of any force or effect in the national legal system". Mexico therefore asks in its submissions that the convictions and sentences of the 52 Mexican nationals be annulled, and that, in any future criminal proceedings against these 52 Mexican nationals, evidence obtained in breach of Article 36 of the Vienna Convention be excluded.

. . .

The general principle on the legal consequences of the commission of an internationally wrongful act was stated by the Permanent Court of International Justice in the *Factory at Chorzów* case as follows: "It is a principle of international law that the breach of an engagement involves an obligation to make reparation in an adequate form." (*Factory at Chorzów, Jurisdiction, 1927, P.C.I.J., Series A, No. 9,* p. 21.) What constitutes "reparation in an adequate form" clearly varies depending upon the concrete circumstances surrounding each case and the precise nature and scope of the injury, since the question has to be examined from the viewpoint of what is the "reparation in an adequate form" that corresponds to the injury. In a subsequent phase of the same case, the Permanent Court went on to elaborate on this point as follows:

> "The essential principle contained in the actual notion of an illegal act — a principle which seems to be established by international practice and in particular by the decisions of arbitral tribunals — is that reparation must, as far as possible, wipe out all the consequences of the illegal act and reestablish the situation which would, in all probability, have existed if that act had not been committed."
> (*Factory at Chorzów, Merits, 1928, P.C.I.J., Series A, No. 17,* p. 47.)

. . .

Similarly, in the present case the Court's task is to determine what would be adequate reparation for the violations of Article 36. It should be clear from what has been observed above that the internationally wrongful acts committed by the United States were the failure of its competent authorities to inform the Mexican nationals concerned, to notify Mexican consular posts and to enable Mexico to provide consular assistance. It follows that the remedy to make good these violations should consist in an obligation on the United States to permit review and reconsideration of these nationals' cases by the United States courts, . . . with a view to ascertaining whether in each case the violation of Article 36 committed by the competent authorities caused actual prejudice to the defendant in the process of administration of criminal justice.

The Court reaffirms that the case before it concerns Article 36 of the Vienna Convention and not the correctness as such of any conviction or sentencing. The question of whether the violations of Article 36, paragraph 1, are to be regarded as having, in the causal sequence of events, ultimately led to convictions and severe penalties is an integral part of criminal proceedings before the courts of the United States and is for them to determine in the process of review and reconsideration. In so doing, it is for the courts of the United States to examine the facts, and in particular the prejudice and its causes, taking account of the violation of the rights set forth in the Convention.

It is not to be presumed, as Mexico asserts, that partial or total annulment of conviction or sentence provides the necessary and sole remedy. In this regard, Mexico cites the recent Judgment of this Court in the case concerning the *Arrest Warrant of 11 April 2000 (Democratic Republic of the Congo v. Belgium)*, in which the Court ordered the cancellation of an arrest warrant issued by a Belgian judicial official in violation of the international immunity of the Congo Minister for Foreign Affairs. However, the present case has clearly to be distinguished from the *Arrest Warrant* case. In that case, the question of the legality under international law of the act of issuing the arrest warrant against the Congolese Minister for Foreign Affairs by the Belgian judicial authorities was itself the subject-matter of the dispute. Since the Court found that act to be in violation of international law relating to immunity, the proper legal consequence was for the Court to order the cancellation of the arrest warrant in question (*I.C.J. Reports 2002*, p. 33). By contrast, in the present case it is not the convictions and sentences of the Mexican nationals which are to be regarded as a violation of international law, but solely certain breaches of treaty obligations which preceded them.

Mexico has further contended that the right to consular notification and consular communication under the Vienna Convention is a fundamental human right that constitutes part of due process in criminal proceedings and should be guaranteed in the territory of each of the Contracting Parties to the Vienna Convention; according to Mexico, this right, as such, is so fundamental that its infringement will *ipso facto* produce the effect of vitiating the entire process of the criminal proceedings conducted in violation of this fundamental right. Whether or not the Vienna Convention rights are human rights is not a matter that this Court need decide. The Court would, however, observe that neither the text nor the object and purpose of the Convention, nor any indication in the *travaux préparatoires*, support the conclusion that Mexico draws from its contention in that regard.

For these reasons, Mexico's . . . submissions cannot be upheld. . . .

While the Court has rejected the . . . submissions of Mexico relating to the remedies for the breaches by the United States of its international obligations under Article 36 of the Vienna Convention, the fact remains that such breaches have been committed, as the Court has found, and it is thus incumbent upon the Court to specify what remedies are required in order to redress the injury done to Mexico and to its nationals by the United States through non-compliance with those international obligations. . . .

In this regard, Mexico . . . also asks the Court to adjudge and declare:

"That to the extent that any of the 52 convictions or sentences are not annulled, the United States shall provide, by means of its own choosing, meaningful and effective review and reconsideration of the convictions and sentences of the

52 nationals, and that this obligation cannot be satisfied by means of clemency proceedings or if any municipal law rule or doctrine [that fails to attach legal significance to an Article 36(1) violation] is applied."

On this question of "review and reconsideration", the United States takes the position that it has indeed conformed its conduct to [this standard]. . . . In a further elaboration of this point, the United States argues that choice of means for allowing the review and reconsideration . . . must be left to the United States, but that Mexico would not leave this choice to the United States but have the Court undertake the review instead and decide at once that the breach requires the conviction and sentence to be set aside in each case".

. . . It should be underlined, however, that this freedom in the choice of means for such review and reconsideration is not without qualification: . . . such review and reconsideration has to be carried out by taking account of the violation of the rights set forth in the Convention, including, in particular, the question of the legal consequences of the violation upon the criminal proceedings that have followed the violation.

. . .

However, the Court wishes to point out that the current situation in the United States criminal procedure, as explained by the Agent at the hearings, is that "If the defendant alleged at trial that *a failure of consular information resulted in harm to a particular right essential to a fair trial*, an appeals court can *review how the lower court handled that claim of prejudice*", but that "*If the foreign national did not raise his Article 36 claim at trial, he may face procedural constraints* [i.e., the application of the procedural default rule] on raising that particular claim in direct or collateral judicial appeals" (emphasis added). As a result, a claim based on the violation of Article 36, paragraph 1, of the Vienna Convention, however meritorious in itself, could be barred in the courts of the United States by the operation of the procedural default rule. . . .

It is not sufficient for the United States to argue that "[w]hatever label [the Mexican defendant] places on his claim, his right . . . must and will be vindicated if it is raised *in some form* at trial" (emphasis added), and that "In that way, even though a failure to label the complaint as a breach of the Vienna Convention may mean that he has technically speaking forfeited his right to raise this issue as a Vienna Convention claim, on appeal that failure would not bar him from independently asserting *a claim that he was prejudiced because he lacked this critical protection needed for a fair trial*."

The crucial point in this situation is that, by the operation of the procedural default rule as it is applied at present, the defendant is effectively barred from raising the issue of the violation of his rights under Article 36 of the Vienna Convention and is limited to seeking the vindication of his rights under the United States Constitution.

The rights guaranteed under the Vienna Convention are treaty rights which the United States has undertaken to comply with in relation to the individual concerned, irrespective of the due process rights under United States constitutional law. In this regard, the Court would point out that what is crucial in the review and reconsideration process is the existence of a procedure which guarantees that full weight is given to the violation of the rights set forth in the Vienna Convention, whatever may be the actual outcome of such review and reconsideration.

[T]he Court is of the view that, in cases where the breach of the individual rights of Mexican nationals under Article 36, paragraph 1(*b*), of the Convention has resulted, in the sequence of judicial proceedings that has followed, in the individuals concerned being subjected to prolonged detention or convicted and sentenced to severe penalties, the legal consequences of this breach have to be examined and taken into account in the course of review and reconsideration. The Court considers that it is the judicial process that is suited to this task.

For these reasons,

THE COURT,

. . .

By fourteen votes to one, *Finds* that, by not informing, without delay upon their detention, the 51 Mexican nationals referred to . . . above of their rights under Article 36, paragraph 1(*b*), of the Vienna Convention on Consular Relations of 24 April 1963, the United States of America breached the obligations incumbent upon it under that subparagraph; . . .

By fourteen votes to one, *Finds* that the appropriate reparation in this case consists in the obligation of the United States of America to provide, by means of its own choosing, review and reconsideration of the convictions and sentences of the Mexican nationals . . . ;

. . . Unanimously, *Takes note* of the commitment undertaken by the United States of America to ensure implementation of the specific measures adopted in performance of its obligations under Article 36, paragraph 1(*b*), of the Vienna Convention; and *finds* that this commitment must be regarded as meeting the request by the United Mexican States for guarantees and assurances of non-repetition;

. . . Unanimously, *Finds* that, should Mexican nationals nonetheless be sentenced to severe penalties, without their rights under Article 36, paragraph 1(*b*), of the Convention having been respected, the United States of America shall provide, by means of its own choosing, review and reconsideration of the conviction and sentence, so as to allow full weight to be given to the violation of the rights set forth in the Convention. . . .

NOTES AND QUESTIONS

1. **The Result in *Avena*.** What is the holding of the *Avena* decision? Is that a victory for the Mexican nationals such as Avena? What happens next? *See Medellín v. Texas*, 552 U.S. 491 (2008), excerpted in Chapter 2.
2. **Espousal of Individual Claims.** *Avena* is somewhat unusual in that it involves the rights of particular private individuals. Recall that Article 34 of the ICJ

Statute provides that "[o]nly states may be parties in cases before the Court." Therefore, the affected Mexican nationals could not themselves be parties to the case. Instead, they depended on their government to "espouse" their claims and pursue those claims on their behalf. Under what circumstances might a government be most (and least) likely to espouse a claim of one of its nationals? If you are a lawyer and your client's government declines to espouse her claim, what are your options?

3. **Enforcement of ICJ Rulings.** According to Article 94 of the U.N. Charter, all members of the United Nations undertake to abide by ICJ rulings in cases in which they are parties. What happens if they do not? Article 94 also directs that a failure to abide by an ICJ ruling may be referred to the Security Council. Is that likely to be effective? Why might nations abide by ICJ rulings even if there is not a legally effective enforcement mechanism? In what sort of cases is the ICJ likely to play the most effective role?

4. **Jurisdiction Based on a Compromissory Clause.** As noted in *Avena*, the Vienna Convention on Consular Relations has an Optional Protocol containing a compromissory clause that allows the ICJ to resolve "[d]isputes arising out of the interpretation or application of the Convention." Many nations are not parties to the Optional Protocol even though they are parties to the Convention. After the decision in *Avena*, the United States withdrew from the Optional Protocol, although it remained a party to the Convention. Why would it decide to do so? What are the costs to the United States of withdrawing?

   In some cases, there is a potentially applicable compromissory clause, but the parties dispute its scope. For example, in *Application of the International Convention on the Elimination of All Forms of Racial Discrimination (Georgia v. Russian Federation)*, Georgia brought an application against Russia alleging that Russia "sponsored and supported racial discrimination through attacks against, and mass-expulsion of, ethnic Georgians, as well as other ethnic groups, in the South Ossetia and Abkhazia regions of the Republic of Georgia," in violation of the 1965 International Convention on the Elimination of All Forms of Racial Discrimination (CERD). Georgia relied on Article 22 of the CERD. Under Article 22, "[a]ny dispute between two or more States Parties with respect to the interpretation or application of this Convention, which is not settled by negotiation or by the procedures expressly provided for in this Convention, shall, at the request of any of the parties to the dispute, be referred to the International Court of Justice for decision, unless the disputants agree to another mode of settlement." Russia argued, among other things, that the phrase "which is not settled by negotiation" means that negotiations are a precondition for ICJ jurisdiction under Article 22; that Georgia had failed to negotiate to settle the dispute; and that the ICJ therefore lacked jurisdiction. The ICJ agreed, and in its Preliminary Objections Judgment of April 1, 2011 it found that it lacked jurisdiction. *Application of the Convention on Elimination of All Forms of Racial Discrimination (Georgia v. Russian Federation)*, http://www.icj-cij.org/docket/index.php?p1=3&k=4d&case=140&code=GR&p3=4.

In 2016, Iran filed a case against the United States at the ICJ based on the United States' alleged failure to protect Iran's assets from seizure to pay judgments obtained in U.S. courts by terrorism victims. *See* ICJ Press Release, *Iran institutes proceedings against the United States with regard to a dispute concerning alleged violations of the 1955 Treaty of Amity*, June 15, 2016, *available at* https://www.icj-cij.org/files/case-related/164/19032.pdf. As discussed in Chapter 11, international law generally recognizes the immunity of governments and their assets in foreign jurisdictions, subject to exceptions, and the United States implements that principle by statute. However, one of the U.S. statutory exceptions, which is arguably not recognized by international law, is for "state sponsors of terrorism." The U.S. executive branch has designated Iran as a state sponsor of terrorism, thus denying Iran immunity for certain terrorism claims. In particular, a U.S. statute directs that certain assets of Iran's central bank, Bank Markazi, be used to satisfy judgments in favor of terrorism victims. The U.S. Supreme Court upheld the statute in *Bank Markazi v. Peterson*, 136 S. Ct. 1310 (2016), after which Iran filed its case with the ICJ. Iran alleged ICJ jurisdiction under the 1955 U.S.-Iran Treaty of Amity, Economic Relations, and Consular Rights, in which the parties consented to ICJ jurisdiction to resolve disputes under the treaty. The litigation remains ongoing.

Is the United States likely to comply with an adverse decision on the merits, if there is one? Why or why not? If not, why would Iran file the claim?

In 2018, Iran filed a second case against the United States requesting provisional measures, alleging that actions taken by the United States in imposing economic sanctions violated the U.S.-Iran Treaty of Amity. The ICJ heard arguments in August 2018 on Iran's request. In October 2018, the ICJ unanimously indicated the following provisional measures: (1) The United States "shall remove, by means of its choosing, any impediments arising from the measures announced on 8 May 2018 to the free exportation to the territory of the Islamic Republic of Iran of" medicines and medical devices; foodstuffs and agricultural commodities; and spare parts, equipment, and associated services necessary for the safety of civil aviation; (2) the United States "shall ensure that licenses and necessary authorizations are granted and that payments and other transfers of funds are not subject to any restriction in so far as they relate to the goods and services referred to in point (1)"; and (3) both parties "shall refrain from any action which might aggravate or extend the dispute before the Court or make it more difficult to resolve." The litigation remains ongoing.

Also in October 2018, immediately after the ICJ's order on provisional measures, the United States announced its withdrawal from the Treaty of Amity. *See* Edward Wong & David Sanger, *U.S. Withdraws from 1955 Treaty Normalizing Relations with Iran*, N.Y. Times, Oct. 3, 2018.

In September 2018, Palestine instituted proceedings against the United States with respect to a dispute concerning alleged violations of the Vienna Convention on Diplomatic Relations of 1961 flowing from the relocation of the U.S. Embassy in Israel to Jerusalem. In November 2018, the Registrar of the Court invited the parties to a meeting with the President of the Court to ascertain the views of the parties as to procedure. Shortly before that meeting was to occur, the United States submitted a letter to the Court questioning the ICJ's jurisdiction, as the United States did not consider itself to be in a treaty relationship with Palestine. The United States also informed the Court that due to this lack of jurisdiction it would not participate in the proposed meeting of the parties. Representatives of Palestine met with the President, and the Court ordered the parties to file a memorial and counter-memorial limited to jurisdiction. The case is still pending.

In response to this filing, the United States in October 2018 withdrew from the Optional Protocol on Compulsory Jurisdiction to the Vienna Convention on Diplomatic Relations. What might be the consequences of these withdrawals for U.S. engagement with international courts? *See* Scott R. Anderson, *Walking Away from the World Court*, Lawfare, Oct. 5, 2018, *available at* https://www.lawfareblog.com/walking-away-world-court.

B. Specialized International Courts

Unlike the ICJ, other international courts are specialized in the sense that their subject matter jurisdiction is limited to specific types of cases. Generally, the jurisdiction of specialized courts is further limited to nations that are parties to a particular treaty or members of a particular regional organization. This section introduces you to some of the world's principal specialized international courts. In reading about each court, consider: (a) Why are the decisions being made at the international rather than the national level? (b) What difficulties might arise from making the decision at the international level? (c) What sources of law will the court use, and how will it determine the content of that law? and (d) How are decisions likely to be enforced?

1. *The Dispute Settlement Mechanism of the World Trade Organization*

The World Trade Organization (WTO) (http://www.wto.org/) was established in 1995 by the Agreement Establishing the World Trade Organization (WTO Agreement). It built upon the General Agreement on Tariffs and Trade (GATT), an agreement made among leading trading nations shortly after the Second World War. The WTO currently has over 160 members — most, although not all, of the world's nations. According to Article III of the WTO Agreement, the WTO shall, among other things, "facilitate the implementation, administration and operation, and further the objectives," of a wide range of multilateral trade agreements, and "provide the forum for negotiations" among members on multilateral trade relations. As summarized on the WTO's website, http://www.wto.org/english/thewto_e/whatis_e/tif_e/agrm1_e.htm, these multilateral trade agreements:

> cover goods, services and intellectual property. They spell out the principles of liberalization, and the permitted exceptions. They include individual countries'

commitments to lower customs tariffs and other trade barriers, and to open and keep open services markets. They set procedures for settling disputes. They prescribe special treatment for developing countries. They require governments to make their trade policies transparent by notifying the WTO about laws in force and measures adopted, and through regular reports by the secretariat on countries' trade policies.

Prior to the creation of the WTO, nations had difficulty resolving trade disputes that arose under its predecessor, the GATT. A leading innovation of the WTO was its Dispute Settlement Understanding (DSU), which is a part of the WTO Agreement. The procedures established by the DSU are commonly referred to as the WTO Dispute Settlement Mechanism (DSM). The DSM is administered by the Dispute Settlement Body (DSB), which consists of all of the WTO's members.

The DSM has four basic steps. First, a member complaining of another member's violation of one of the WTO agreements may request consultations with that member. Second, if those consultations fail to produce a settlement, the complaining member may ask the DSB to appoint a "panel" (composed of experts in trade law) to determine whether the other member has violated the agreement. The panel presents its determination in a report. A member may, as a third step, appeal the panel's report to the Appellate Body. The Appellate Body is a standing body composed of seven persons appointed by the DSB for four-year terms, and three of whom serve on any one case. The Appellate Body may review legal but not factual questions concerning the dispute, and it may uphold, modify, or reverse the panel report. Fourth, the DSB adopts the Appellate Body report (or the panel report, if it is not appealed) by "reverse consensus" — that is, the report is adopted unless the DSB unanimously rejects it.

The WTO has no ability to force member nations to change their laws or trade practices. Instead, the DSB issues a recommendation to the losing party that it bring its trade practices into compliance with WTO rules. If the losing party fails to follow the DSB recommendation, the DSB may authorize the prevailing party to retaliate by suspending trade concessions with the losing party (typically, by raising tariffs or imposing import restrictions on the losing party's products). In effect, this means that the individual members decide whether to change their trade practices in accordance with a DSB recommendation or to incur the costs of the other member's retaliation.

Depending on how cases are counted, as of 2020 the WTO dispute settlement process had heard around 595 disputes since its inception in 1995 and had issued over 350 rulings. Many of these cases involved challenges to tariffs (duties charged on imported products) or to regulations regarding what sort of products may be imported. Others involved subsidies to exports or import-competing products; unfair pricing of exported products; intellectual property; and some investment disputes. Many have been fairly mundane or technical, but others encompassed significant issues of social policy. For example, in a dispute in which the United States was a defendant, various shrimp exporting countries challenged U.S. rules that required shrimp harvesters to take measures to assure that sea turtles were not harmed in the shrimp harvesting process; the U.S. rules prevented the sale in the United States of shrimp not harvested in compliance with the U.S. rules. The WTO Appellate Body held that the U.S. approach violated the WTO agreements, although in a cautious decision it left considerable room for the United States to modify its regulations to continue to give some protection to sea turtles. *United States — Import prohibition of certain shrimp and shrimp products* (WTO Report of the Appellate Body, Nov. 6, 1998, *see* http://www.wto.org/english/tratop_e/envir_ e/edis08_e.htm). Even technical cases can have substantial implications: For example, in a long-running dispute, the United States and the European Union have accused each other of violating the WTO agreements by giving subsidies to their leading aircraft manufacturers, Boeing and Airbus, respectively. *See* http:// www.wto.org/english/tratop_e/dispu_e/cases_e/ds316_e.htm and http://www.wto .org/english/tratop_e/dispu_e/cases_e/ds353_e.htm (summarizing the disputes). Another very contentious case, involving the EU's ban on importing meat from cows treated with growth hormones, is excerpted below.

Although the WTO is often associated with trade in goods, its agreements also cover trade in services, intellectual property, and trade-related investment.

NOTES AND QUESTIONS

1. **Trade-Related Dispute Settlement.** Many people regard the WTO dispute settlement mechanism as a success. How would you measure success in this context? Broad compliance with WTO rulings? A small number of retaliatory actions? What factors might contribute to the WTO's success, especially as compared to other international courts? Is it the dispute settlement process itself, which encourages negotiation and allows for appellate review? Is it something unique to resolving trade disputes?

2. **Enforcement and the DSM.** Does the WTO have an effective enforcement mechanism? Like ICJ decisions, WTO decisions are not self-executing (automatically part of domestic law) in the United States (or in most other countries). Even after a favorable decision, an exporter's remedy will depend on the importing country changing its trade laws and practices (e.g., lowering its tariffs or easing its import barriers). Is that likely to happen? What remedy is there if it does not? Does this make sense as an enforcement mechanism? What are its limitations? What alternatives might there be?

3. **Practice: The WTO and Private Parties.** As with the ICJ, only nations can be parties to the WTO dispute settlement procedures. Thus, if you represent a U.S. exporter who feels that import restrictions in the EU violate the WTO Agreement, your only course is to ask the U.S. government to bring a complaint. What considerations are likely to affect the government's decision? Why do you think the WTO process does not permit individuals to bring suit directly?

4. Policy. In an escalating dispute, since 2011 the United States has blocked appointments to fill vacancies on the WTO appellate body. As a result, beginning in 2019 the appellate body no longer had the minimum three members needed to hear new appeals. Why might the United States pursue such a policy? What does it suggest about the structure of the WTO dispute resolution system? What alternative structures, if any, might be feasible?

EC Measures Concerning Meat and Meat Products (Hormones)

World Trade Organization, Report of the Appellate Body (16 January 1998)

The European Communities [EC]* . . . appeal from certain issues of law and legal interpretations in the Panel Reports, *EC Measures Concerning Meat and Meat Products (Hormones)*. . . .

The Panel dealt with a complaint against the European Communities relating to an EC prohibition of imports of meat and meat products derived from cattle to which [certain hormones] . . . had been administered for growth promotion purposes. . . .

[The United States and Canada, in separate complaints, challenged the EC ban as a violation of the Agreement on the Application of Sanitary and Phytosanitary Measures (SPS Agreement), one of the agreements that form part of the WTO.]

The Panel . . . [found that] [t]he European Communities, by maintaining sanitary measures which are not based on a risk assessment, has acted inconsistently with the requirements contained in Article 5.1 of the [SPS Agreement]. . . . [The EC appealed the Panel decision to the Appellate Body.]

The European Communities submits that the Panel erred in considering that the precautionary principle** was [irrelevant to the analysis]. The precautionary principle is already, in the view of the European Communities, a general customary rule of international law or at least a general principle of law, the essence of which is that it applies not only in the management of a risk, but also in the assessment thereof. It is claimed that the Panel therefore erred in stating that the application of the precautionary principle "would not override the explicit wording in Article 5.1 and 5.2 [of the SPS Agreement]", and in suggesting that the principles might be in conflict with those Articles. The European Communities asserts that Article 5.1 and 5.2 . . . of the SPS Agreement do not prescribe a particular type of risk assessment, but rather simply identify factors that need to be taken into account. Thus, these provisions do not prevent Members from being cautious when setting health standards in the face of conflicting scientific information and uncertainty.

. . .

---

* Predecessor of the European Union (EU). — Eds.
** Although there are many formulations, the general implication of the precautionary principle is that where there is a plausible threat of harm, absence of complete scientific conclusions or consensus should not be a barrier to taking action to prevent the threat. — Eds.

In the view of the United States, the claim of the European Communities that there is a generally-accepted principle of international law which may be referred to as the "precautionary principle" is erroneous as a matter of international law. The United States does not consider that the "precautionary principle represents a principle of customary international law"; rather, it may be characterized as an "approach". . . . The European Communities does not [the United States argues] explain how "the precautionary principle" affects the requirements in the SPS Agreement that a measure be "based on" scientific principles and a risk assessment, and not maintained without sufficient scientific evidence. The EC's invocation of a "precautionary principle" cannot create a risk assessment where there is none, nor can a "principle" create "sufficient scientific evidence" where there is none.

. . .

The Panel was correct, according to the United States, in finding that in order that a measure may be "based on" a risk assessment, the scientific principles underlying the measure must reflect the scientific conclusions reached by the scientists conducting the risk assessment. The United States submits that the European Communities did not, at any time during the panel proceeding, produce a risk assessment identifying any risk.

. . .

We are asked by the European Communities to reverse the finding of the Panel relating to the precautionary principle. . . .

The status of the precautionary principles in international law continues to be the subject of debate among academics, law practitioners, regulators and judges. The precautionary principle is regarded by some as having crystallized in to a general principle of customary international *environmental law*. Whether it has been widely accepted by Members as a principle of *general* or *customary* international law appears less than clear. We consider, however, that it is unnecessary, and probably imprudent, for the Appellate Body in this appeal to take a position on this important, but abstract, question. . . .

It appears to us important, nevertheless, to note some aspects of the relationship of the precautionary principles to the SPS Agreement. First, the principle has not been written into the SPS Agreement as a ground for justifying SPS measures that are otherwise inconsistent with the obligations of Members set out in particular provisions of that Agreement. . . . [A] panel . . . may, of course, and should, bear in mind that responsible, representative governments commonly act from perspectives of prudence and precaution where risks of irreversible, e.g., life-terminating, damage to human health are concerned. . . . [H]owever, the precautionary principle does not, by itself, and without a clear textual directive to that effect, relieve a panel from the duty of applying normal (i.e. customary international law) principles of treaty interpretation in reading the provisions of the SPS Agreement.

We accordingly agree with the finding of the Panel that the precautionary principle does not override the provisions of Articles 5.1. and 5.2 of the SPS Agreement.

. . .

[A] Member may decide to promulgate an SPS measure that conforms to an international standard. Such a measure would embody the international standard completely.... Such a measure enjoys the benefit of a presumption (albeit a rebuttable one) that it is consistent with the relevant provisions of the SPS Agreement....

[A] Member may decide to set for itself a level of protection different from that implicit in the international standard, and to implement or embody that level of protection in a measure not "based on" the international standard. The Member's appropriate level of protection may be higher than that implied in the international standard. The right of a Member to determine its own appropriate level of sanitary protection is an important right.

The right of a Member to define its appropriate level of protection is not, however, an absolute or unqualified right. Article 3.3 . . . makes this clear:

> Members may introduce or maintain sanitary or phytosanitary measures which result in a higher level of sanitary or phytosanitary protection than would be achieved by measures based on the relevant international standards, guidelines or recommendations, if there is a scientific justification, or as a consequence of the level of sanitary or phytosantitary protection a Member determines to be appropriate in accordance with the relevant provisions of . . . Article 5. Notwithstanding the above, all measures which result in a level of sanitary or phytosanitary protection different from that which would be achieved by measures based on international standards, guidelines or recommendations shall not be inconsistent with any other provision of this Agreement.

> . . .

Article 3.3 is evidently not a model of clarity in drafting and communication.... On balance, we agree with the Panel's finding that although the European Communities has established for itself a level of protection higher, or more exacting, that the level of protection implied in the relevant [international] standards, guidelines or recommendations, the European Communities was bound to comply with the requirements established in Article 5.1....

In generalized terms, the object and purpose of Article 3 is to promote the harmonization of the SPS measures of Members on as wide a basis as possible, while recognizing and safeguarding, at the same time, the right and duty of Members to protect the life and health of their people. The ultimate goal of the harmonization of SPS measures is to prevent the use of such measures for arbitrary or unjustifiable discrimination between Members or as a disguised restriction on international trade, without preventing Members from adopting or enforcing measures which are both "necessary to protect" human life or health and based on scientific principles, and without requiring them to change their appropriate level of protection. The requirements of a risk assessment under Article 5.1, as well as of "sufficient scientific evidence" under Article 2.2, are essential for the maintenance of the delicate and carefully negotiated balance in the SPS Agreement between the shared, but sometimes competing, interests of promoting international trade and protecting the life and health of human beings. We conclude that the Panel's finding that the European Communities is required by Article 3.3 to comply with the requirements of Article 5.1 is correct....

We turn to the appeal of the European Communities for the Panel's conclusion that, by maintaining SPS measures which are not based on a risk assessment, the European Communities acted inconsistently with the requirements contained in Article 5.1 of the SPS Agreement.

Article 5.1 of the SPS Agreement provides:

> Members shall ensure that their sanitary or phytosantiary measures are based on an assessment . . . of the risks to human . . . life or health, taking into account risk assessment techniques developed by the relevant international organizations.

[T]he Panel considered that Article 5.1 may be viewed as a specific application of the basic obligations contained in Article 2.2 of the SPS Agreement, which reads as follows:

> Members shall ensure that any sanitary or phytosanitrary measure is applied only to the extent necessary to protect human, animal or plant life or health, is based on scientific principles and is not maintained without sufficient scientific evidence. . . .

We agree with this general conclusion and would also stress that Article 2.2 and 5.1 should constantly be read together. . . .

. . .

We believe that Article 5.1, when contextually read as it should be, in conjunction with and as informed by Article 2.2 of the SPS Agreement, requires that the results of the risk assessment must sufficiently warrant — that is to say, reasonably support — the SPS measure at stake. The requirement that an SPS measure be "based on" a risk assessment is a substantive requirement that there be a rational relationship between the measure and the risk assessment.

We do not believe that a risk assessment has to come to a monolithic conclusion that coincides with the scientific conclusion or view implicit in the SPS measure. The risk assessment could set out both the prevailing view representing the "mainstream" of scientific opinion, as well as opinions of scientists taking a divergent view. . . . In most cases, responsible and representative governments tend to base their legislative and administrative measures on "mainstream" scientific opinion. In other cases, equally responsible and representative governments may act in good faith on the basis of what, at the given time, may be a divergent opinion coming from qualified and respected sources. By itself, this does not necessarily signal the absence of a reasonable relationship between the SPS measure and the risk assessment, especially where the risk involved is life-threatening in character and is perceived to constitute a clear and imminent threat to public health and safety. Determination of presence or absence of that relationship can only be done on a case-to-case basis. . . .

We turn now to the application by the Panel of the substantive requirements of Article 5.1 to the EC measures at stake in the present case. . . . [The Appellate Body set forth six sets of scientific material relied upon by the EC.]

[W]e agree [with the Panel] that the scientific reports listed above do not rationally support the EC import prohibition.

. . .

Most, if not all, of the scientific studies referred to by the European Communities, in respect of the five hormones involved here, concluded that their use for growth purposes is "safe" if the hormones are administered in accordance with the requirements of good veterinary practice. Where the condition of observance of good veterinary practice . . . is not followed, the logical inference is that the use of such hormones for growth purposes may or may not be "safe". . . .

The question that arises, therefore, is whether the European Communities did, in fact, submit a risk assessment demonstrating and evaluating the existence and level of risk arising in the present case from abusive use of hormones and the difficulties of control of the administration of hormones for growth promotion purposes. . . . The record of the panel proceeding shows that the risk arising from abusive use of hormones for growth promotion combined with control problems for the hormones at issue, may have been examined on two occasions in a scientific manner. . . . However, none of the original studies and evidence [from the first occasion] was submitted to the Panel. . . . [As to the second occasion,] the study presented a theoretical framework for the systematic analysis of such problems, but did not itself investigate and evaluate the actual problems that have arisen. . . .

In the absence of any other relevant documentation, we find that the European Communities did not actually proceed to an assessment, within the meaning of Article[] 5.1 . . . , of the risks arising from the failure of observance of good veterinary practices combined with problems of control of the use of hormones for growth promotion purposes. The absence of such a risk assessment, when considered in conjunction with the conclusion actually reached by most, if not all, of the scientific studies relating to the other aspects of risk noted earlier, leads us to the conclusion that no risk assessment that reasonably supports or warrants the import prohibition embodied in the EC Directive was furnished to the Panel. We affirm, therefore, the ultimate conclusion of the Panel that the EC import prohibition is not based on a risk assessment within the meaning of Article[] 5.1 . . . of the SPS Agreement and is, therefore, inconsistent with the requirements of Article 5.1.

Since we have concluded above that an SPS measure, to be consistent with Article 3.3, has to comply with, inter alia, the requirements contained in Article 5.1, it follows that the EC measures at issue, by failing to comply with Article 5.1, are also inconsistent with Article 3.3 of the SPS Agreement.

. . .

The Appellate Body recommends that the Dispute Settlement Body request the European Communities to bring the SPS measures found in this report and the Panel Reports, as modified by this Report, to be inconsistent with the SPS Agreement into conformity with the obligations of the European Communities under that Agreement.

NOTES AND QUESTIONS

1. **The Beef Hormone Case as a Trade Case.** In what sense was the beef hormone case about trade? Is it significant that growth hormones are widely used in Canada and the United States but not in Europe? The EC did

not allow hormone-treated beef to be sold at all, whether imported or not. Why might this still be unfair to other nations? Suppose U.S. and Canadian beef producers are much more efficient than European beef producers. What might you expect Europeans to do to restrict U.S. and Canadian imports (assuming the WTO Agreement clearly prevents them from simply banning or limiting imports from the United States and Canada)?

2. **The Legitimacy of the Precautionary Principle.** What is the role of the precautionary principle in the beef hormone dispute? What did the EC argue, and what did the WTO appellate body decide? Is that right? Why shouldn't the level of risk be determined at the national level rather than at the international level? Does the result show (as some people argued) that the WTO has too much power over local policymaking?

3. **The Caseload of the WTO Panels.** The beef hormone case represents one type of case heard by the panels — a challenge to a regulatory standard for products sold in a member nation's market. Other types of WTO cases include, for example:

> — Challenges to tariffs, *e.g., China — Anti-dumping and countervailing duties on certain automobiles from the United States,* WTO panel report of May 23, 2014, *see* http://www.wto.org/english/tratop_e/dispu_e/440r_e.pdf (finding that China's tariffs on U.S. car imports violated the WTO agreements)
>
> — Challenges to limits or quotas on imports and exports of particular products, *e.g., China — Measures related to the Exportation of Rare Earths, Tungsten, and Molybdenum,* WTO panel report of March 26, 2014, *see* http://www.wto.org/english/tratop_e/dispu_e/cases_e/ds431_e.htm (finding that China's limits on exports of "rare earths" violated the WTO agreements)
>
> — Challenges to subsidies given by member governments to companies that compete with foreign producers, *e.g., United States — Measures Affecting Trade in Large Civil Aircraft,* Appellate Body Report of Mar. 12, 2012, *see* http://www.wto.org/english/tratop_e/dispu_e/cases_e/ds353_e.htm (finding that the United States improperly gave subsidies to Boeing, Inc., a U.S. aircraft manufacturer).

4. **Enforcement.** As noted above, the WTO has no ability to force member nations to change their laws or practices. Instead, the WTO may authorize retaliatory action on the part of nations injured by a wrongful trade practice. In the beef hormone case, the European Communities refused to withdraw the import ban. The WTO therefore authorized the United States and Canada to increase tariffs on EC products, which they did. Does this make sense as an enforcement mechanism? Why do you think the Europeans refused to comply? Should other measures be taken to assure compliance? Are there advantages to not insisting on compliance?

2. Human Rights Courts

There currently is no global human rights court. (As review, ask yourself: Why can't the ICJ play this role?) However, there are a variety of regional human rights courts, including the influential European Court of Human Rights, established by a treaty to which essentially all European nations are parties. Consider why no global court has been established. Should one be established?

The European Court of Human Rights (ECHR or ECtHR).   The ECHR (http://www.echr.coe.int/Pages/home.aspx?p=home&c=) is currently the world's most active human rights court. The ECHR was established in 1959 to hear cases arising under the European Convention on Human Rights, which enshrines a wide range of civil and political rights and freedoms. Currently, 47 European nations are parties to the Convention and subject to the jurisdiction of the ECHR.

Article 32 of the European Convention provides that "[t]he jurisdiction of the Court shall extend to all matters concerning the interpretation and application of the Convention and the Protocols thereto which are referred to it" in accordance with the terms of the Convention. Under Article 33, "Any High Contracting Party may refer to the Court any alleged breach of the provisions of the Convention and the Protocols thereto by another High Contracting Party." In addition, under Article 34, "The Court may receive applications from any person, non-governmental organisation or group of individuals claiming to be the victim of a violation by one of the High Contracting Parties of the rights set forth in the Convention or the Protocols thereto." However, Article 35 requires the ECHR to reject applications that do not meet various admissibility requirements, including exhaustion of local remedies. After a judgment has been delivered by a panel of seven judges (called a "chamber"), the parties may request referral of the case to a Grand Chamber composed of 17 judges for further review.

The ECHR sits in Strasbourg, France. Thousands of applications are filed with the ECHR each year, but many of them are declared inadmissible and do not result in a judgment on the merits. Since its establishment, the ECHR has delivered more than 16,000 judgments on the merits. According to a study covering the period from 1959 to 2012, almost half of them have concerned five members: Turkey (2,870), Italy (2,229), the Russian Federation (1,346), Poland (1,019), and Romania (938). Of the total number of judgments it has delivered since 1959, the Court has found at least one violation of the Convention by the respondent nation in 83 percent of cases. *European Court of Human Rights, Overview 1959-2012 (available at* http://www.echr.coe.int/Documents/Overview_19592012_ENG.pdf). Some of these decisions have been quite sweeping and controversial, and unlike many other international courts the ECHR has some significant ability to enforce its judgments by directing monetary compensation.

The Inter-American Court of Human Rights (IACHR).   The IACHR (http://www.corteidh.or.cr/) was established in 1979 pursuant to the American Convention on Human Rights, which was adopted by the Organization of American States (OAS) in 1969 and entered into force in 1978. Like the European

Convention, the American Convention protects a wide range of civil and political rights. Twenty-three of the 35 members of the OAS are parties to the American Convention. The United States is a member of the OAS but is not a party to the American Convention. The American Convention also established the Inter-American Commission on Human Rights.

Article 61 of the American Convention provides that "[o]nly the States Parties and the Commission shall have the right to submit a case to the Court." According to Article 62(3), "[t]he jurisdiction of the Court shall comprise all cases concerning the interpretation and application of the provisions of this Convention that are submitted to it, provided that the States Parties to the case recognize or have recognized such jurisdiction. . . ." Such recognition may be by special agreement or pursuant to Article 62(1) by which "[a] State Party may . . . declare that it recognizes as binding, ipso facto, and not requiring special agreement, the jurisdiction of the Court on all matters relating to the interpretation or application of this Convention." Over 20 nations have filed Article 62(1) declarations. Individuals may not file applications before the IACHR, but under Article 44 they may lodge petitions with the Inter-American Commission (subject to various admissibility requirements), which may in turn submit the matter to the IACHR.

The IACHR sits in San José, Costa Rica. It has typically issued between 10 and 25 judgments per year. In a prominent case, *Atala Riffo and Daughters v. Chile* (IACHR, Feb. 24, 2012), the court ruled in favor of a lesbian mother in a child custody dispute. The Chilean courts had awarded custody to the father on the grounds that the mother's sexual orientation posed a risk to the well-being of the children. The IACHR found, among other things, that the decisions of the Chilean courts violated the right to equality and nondiscrimination in Article 24 of the American Convention. *See* http://corteidh.or.cr/docs/casos/articulos/seriec_239_ing.pdf.

The African Court on Human and Peoples' Rights (ACHPR).   The ACHPR (http://www.african-court.org/en/) was established by a protocol to the African Charter on Human and Peoples' Rights that entered into force in 2005. The African Charter was adopted by the Organization for African Unity (the predecessor of the African Union [AU]) in 1981, and entered into force in 1986. Under the African Charter, parties recognize the rights, duties, and freedoms enshrined in the Charter and undertake to adopt legislative or other measures to give effect to them. The rights and freedoms include, among many others, the right to freedom from discrimination, freedom of assembly, and the right to education, and the duties include the duty to exercise rights "with due regard to the rights of others, collective security, morality and common interest."

Article 3 of the protocol provides that "[t]he jurisdiction of the Court shall extend to all cases and disputes submitted to it concerning the interpretation and application of the Charter, this Protocol and any other relevant Human Rights instrument ratified by the States concerned." The ACHPR may provide advisory opinions at the request of AU members or AU organs. In addition, cases may be submitted to the ACHPR by (1) the African Commission on Human and Peoples' Rights; (2) a State Party that has lodged a complaint at the Commission; (3) a

State Party against which a complaint has been lodged at the Commission; (4) a State Party whose citizen is a victim of a human rights violation; and (5) African intergovernmental organizations. In addition, a member state may make a declaration allowing the ACHPR to accept cases against it instituted by nongovernmental organizations with observer status before the commission or by individuals.

The ACHPR sits in Banjul, The Gambia. It issued its first judgment in 2009.

Hirst v. United Kingdom

[2005] ECHR 681 (European Court of Human Rights, 6 October 2005) (Grand Chamber)

. . .

On 11 February 1980 the applicant [Hirst] pleaded guilty to manslaughter [in British court] on the ground of diminished responsibility. His guilty plea was accepted on the basis of medical evidence that he was a man with a severe personality disorder to such a degree that he was amoral. He was sentenced to a term of discretionary life imprisonment. . . . [Subsequently his parole was denied,] the Parole Board considering that he continued to present a risk of serious harm to the public.

The applicant, who is barred by section 3 of the Representation of the People Act 1983 [a British statute] from voting in parliamentary or local elections, issued proceedings in the High Court [of Great Britain] under section 4 of the Human Rights Act 1998, seeking a declaration that this provision was incompatible with the European Convention on Human Rights. . . .

In the Divisional Court judgment dated 4 April 2001, Lord Justice Kennedy noted that section 3 had a long history and cited the Secretary of State's reasons, given in the proceedings, for maintaining the current policy:

> "By committing offences which by themselves or taken with any aggravating circumstances including the offender's character and previous criminal record require a custodial sentence, such prisoners have forfeited the right to have a say in the way the country is governed for that period. There is more than one element to punishment than forcible detention. Removal from society means removal from the privileges of society, amongst which is the right to vote for one's representative."

. . . The applicant's claims were accordingly dismissed. . . .

[Hirst then brought an application to the European Court of Human Rights.] . . . He relied on Article 3 of Protocol No. 1 [to the European Convention on Human Rights] which provides:

> "The High Contracting Parties undertake to hold free elections at reasonable intervals by secret ballot, under conditions which will ensure the free expression of the opinion of the people in the choice of the legislature."

The Chamber [of the European Court of Human Rights, composed of seven judges] found that the exclusion from voting imposed on convicted prisoners in detention was disproportionate. It had regard to the fact that it stripped a large group of people of the vote; that it applied automatically irrespective of the length of the sentence or the gravity of the offence; and that the results were arbitrary and anomalous, depending on the timing of elections. [The U.K. government then appealed to the Grand Chamber, that is, an expanded court of 17 judges.]

. . .

The Court has had frequent occasion to highlight the importance of democratic principles underlying the interpretation and application of the Convention, and it would take this opportunity to emphasise that the rights guaranteed under Article 3 of Protocol No. 1 are crucial to establishing and maintaining the foundations of an effective and meaningful democracy governed by the rule of law. . . .

As pointed out by the applicant, the right to vote is not a privilege. In the twenty-first century, the presumption in a democratic State must be in favour of inclusion, as may be illustrated, for example, by the parliamentary history of the United Kingdom and other countries where the franchise was gradually extended over the centuries from select individuals, elite groupings or sections of the population approved of by those in power. Universal suffrage has become the basic principle. . . .

Nonetheless, the rights bestowed by Article 3 of Protocol No. 1 are not absolute. There is room for implied limitations and Contracting States must be allowed a margin of appreciation in this sphere.

There has been much discussion of the breadth of this margin in the present case. The Court reaffirms that the margin in this area is wide. . . . There are numerous ways of organising and running electoral systems and a wealth of differences, inter alia, in historical development, cultural diversity and political thought within Europe which it is for each Contracting State to mould into their own democratic vision.

It is, however, for the Court to determine in the last resort whether the requirements of Article 3 of Protocol No. 1 have been complied with; it has to satisfy itself that the conditions do not curtail the rights in question to such an extent as to impair their very essence and deprive them of their effectiveness; that they are imposed in pursuit of a legitimate aim; and that the means employed are not disproportionate. In particular, any conditions imposed must not thwart the free expression of the people in the choice of the legislature — in other words, they must reflect, or not run counter to, the concern to maintain the integrity and effectiveness of an electoral procedure aimed at identifying the will of the people through universal suffrage. For example, the imposition of a minimum age may be envisaged with a view to ensuring the maturity of those participating in the electoral process or, in some circumstances, eligibility may be geared to criteria, such as residence, to identify those with sufficiently continuous or close links to, or a stake in, the country concerned. Any departure from the principle of universal suffrage risks undermining the democratic validity of the legislature thus elected and the laws it promulgates. Exclusion of any groups or categories of the general population must accordingly be reconcilable with the underlying purposes of Article 3 of Protocol No. 1. The present case highlights the status of the right to vote of convicted prisoners who are detained.

The case-law of the Convention organs has, in the past, accepted various restrictions on certain convicted persons.

. . .

This is, however, the first time that the Court has had occasion to consider a general and automatic disenfranchisement of convicted prisoners. . . .

In this case, the Court would begin by underlining that prisoners in general continue to enjoy all the fundamental rights and freedoms guaranteed under the Convention save for the right to liberty, where lawfully imposed detention expressly falls within the scope of Article 5 of the Convention. . . . Any restrictions on these other rights must be justified, although such justification may well be found in the considerations of security, in particular the prevention of crime and disorder, which inevitably flow from the circumstances of imprisonment. . . .

There is no question, therefore, that a prisoner forfeits his Convention rights merely because of his status as a person detained following conviction. Nor is there any place under the Convention system, where tolerance and broadmindedness are the acknowledged hallmarks of democratic society, for automatic disenfranchisement based purely on what might offend public opinion.

This standard of tolerance does not prevent a democratic society from taking steps to protect itself against activities intended to destroy the rights or freedoms set forth in the Convention. Article 3 of Protocol No. 1, which enshrines the individual's capacity to influence the composition of the law-making power, does not therefore exclude that restrictions on electoral rights could be imposed on an individual who has, for example, seriously abused a public position or whose conduct threatened to undermine the rule of law or democratic foundations. The severe measure of disenfranchisement must not, however, be resorted to lightly and the principle of proportionality requires a discernible and sufficient link between the sanction and the conduct and circumstances of the individual concerned. . . .

. . .

The Court will therefore determine whether the measure in question pursued a legitimate aim in a proportionate manner having regard to the principles identified above.

(a) Legitimate Aim

The Court points out that Article 3 of Protocol No. 1 does not, like other provisions of the Convention, specify or limit the aims which a restriction must pursue. A wide range of purposes may therefore be compatible with Article 3. The Government have submitted that the measure pursues the aim of preventing crime by sanctioning the conduct of convicted prisoners and also of enhancing civic responsibility and respect for the rule of law. The Court notes that, at the time of the passage of the latest legislation, the Government stated that the aim of the bar on convicted prisoners was to confer an additional punishment. This was also the position espoused by the Secretary of State in the domestic proceedings brought by the applicant. While the primary emphasis at the domestic level may have been the idea of punishment, it may nevertheless be considered as implied in the references to the forfeiting of rights that the measure is meant to act as an incentive for citizen-like conduct.

Although rejecting the notion that imprisonment after conviction involves the forfeiture of rights beyond the right to liberty, and especially the assertion that voting is a privilege not a right, the Court accepts that section 3 may be regarded as pursuing the aims identified by the Government. . . .

(b) Proportionality

. . .

The breadth of the margin of appreciation has been emphasised by the Government who argued that, where the legislature and domestic courts have considered the matter and there is no clear consensus among Contracting States, it must be within the range of possible approaches to remove the right to vote from any person whose conduct was so serious as to merit imprisonment.

As to the weight to be attached to the position adopted by the legislature and judiciary in the United Kingdom, there is no evidence that Parliament has ever sought to weigh the competing interests or to assess the proportionality of a blanket ban on the right of a convicted prisoner to vote. It is true that the question was considered by the multi-party Speaker's Conference on Electoral Law in 1968 which unanimously recommended that a convicted prisoner should not be entitled to vote. It is also true that the working party which recommended the amendment to the law to allow unconvicted prisoners to vote recorded that successive governments had taken the view that convicted prisoners had lost the moral authority to vote and did not therefore argue for a change in the legislation. It may be said that, by voting the way they did to exempt unconvicted prisoners from the restriction on voting, Parliament implicitly affirmed the need for continued restrictions on the voting rights of convicted prisoners. Nonetheless, it cannot be said that there was any substantive debate by members of the legislature on the continued justification in light of modern-day penal policy and of current human rights standards for maintaining such a general restriction on the right of prisoners to vote.

It is also evident from the judgment of the Divisional Court that the nature of the restrictions, if any, to be imposed on the right of a convicted prisoner to vote was generally seen as a matter for Parliament and not for the national courts. The court did not, therefore, undertake any assessment of proportionality of the measure itself. It may also be noted that the court found support in the decision of the Federal Court of Appeal [of Canada], which was later overturned by the Canadian Supreme Court.

As regards the existence or not of any consensus among Contracting States, the Court notes that, although there is some disagreement about the legal position in certain States, it is undisputed that the United Kingdom is not alone among Convention countries in depriving all convicted prisoners of the right to vote. It may also be said that the law in the United Kingdom is less far-reaching than in certain other States. Not only are exceptions made for persons committed to prison for contempt of court or for default in paying fines, but unlike the position in some countries, the legal incapacity to vote is removed as soon as the person ceases to be detained. However, the fact remains that it is a minority of Contracting States in which a blanket restriction on the right of convicted prisoners to vote is imposed or in which there is no provision allowing prisoners to vote. Even according to the Government's own figures, the number of such States does not exceed thirteen. Moreover, and even if no common European approach to the problem can be discerned, this cannot in itself be determinative of the issue.

Therefore, while the Court reiterates that the margin of appreciation is wide, it is not all-embracing. Further, although the situation was somewhat improved by the 2000 Act which for the first time granted the vote to persons detained on remand, section 3 of the 1983 Act remains a blunt instrument. It strips of their Convention right to vote a significant category of persons and it does so in a way which is indiscriminate. The provision imposes a blanket restriction on all convicted prisoners in prison. It applies automatically to such prisoners, irrespective of the length of their sentence and irrespective of the nature or gravity of their offence and their individual circumstances. Such a general, automatic and indiscriminate restriction on a vitally important Convention right must be seen as falling outside any acceptable margin of appreciation, however wide that margin might be, and as being incompatible with Article 3 of Protocol No. 1.

. . .

FOR THESE REASONS, THE COURT
1. Holds by twelve votes to five that there has been a violation of Article 3 of Protocol No. 1; . . .
4. Holds unanimously that the finding of a violation constitutes in itself sufficient just satisfaction for any non-pecuniary damage sustained by the applicant;
5. Holds by twelve votes to five . . . that the respondent State is to pay the applicant, within three months, . . . EUR 23,000 (twenty three thousand euros) in respect of costs and expenses incurred by the applicant's legal representatives in the Strasbourg proceedings. . . .

Joint Dissenting Opinion of Judges WILDHABER, COSTA, LORENZEN, KOVLER and JEBENS
We are not able to agree with the conclusion of the majority that there has been a violation of Article 3 of Protocol No. 1 because convicted prisoners, under the legislation of the United Kingdom, are prevented from voting while serving their sentence. . . .

In accordance with Article 3 of Protocol No. 1, the Contracting States are obliged "to hold free elections at reasonable intervals by secret ballot, under conditions which will ensure the free expression of the opinion of the people in the choice of the legislature". The wording of this Article is different from nearly all other substantive clauses in the Convention and its Protocols in that it does not directly grant individual rights and contains no other conditions for the elections, including in relation to the scope of a right to vote, than the requirement that "the free expression of the opinion of the people" must be ensured. This indicates that the guarantee of a proper functioning of the democratic process was considered to be of primary importance. . . .

As stated above, the Court has consistently held in its case-law that the Contracting States have a wide margin of appreciation in this sphere. The Court has furthermore accepted that the relevant criteria may vary according to historical and political factors peculiar to each State.

In the light of such considerations, Article 3 of Protocol No. 1 cannot be considered to preclude restrictions on the right to vote that are of a general character, provided that they are not arbitrary and do not affect "the free expression of the opinion of the people", examples being conditions concerning age, nationality, or residence. . . .

The majority have reaffirmed that the margin of appreciation in this area is wide, and have rightly paid attention to the numerous ways of organising and running electoral systems and the wealth of differences in this field in terms of, inter alia, historical development, cultural diversity and political thought within Europe. Nonetheless, the majority have concluded that a general restriction on voting for persons serving a prison sentence "must be seen as falling outside any acceptable margin of appreciation, however wide that margin might be". In our opinion, this categorical finding is difficult to reconcile with the declared intention to adhere to the Court's consistent case-law to the effect that Article 3 of Protocol No. 1 leaves a wide margin of appreciation to the Contracting States in determining their electoral system. In any event, the lack of precision in the wording of that Article and the sensitive political assessments involved call for caution. Unless restrictions impair the very essence of the right to vote or are arbitrary, national legislation on voting rights should be declared incompatible with Article 3 only if weighty reasons justify such a finding. We are unable to agree that such reasons have been adduced.

It has been part of the Court's reasoning in some cases in recent years to emphasise its role in developing human rights and the necessity to maintain a dynamic and evolutive approach in its interpretation of the Convention and its Protocols in order to make reforms or improvements possible. The majority have not made reference to this case-law, but that does not in our opinion change the reality of the situation that their conclusion is in fact based on a "dynamic and evolutive" interpretation of Article 3 of Protocol No 1.

We do not dispute that it is an important task for the Court to ensure that the rights guaranteed by the Convention system comply with "present-day conditions", and that accordingly a "dynamic and evolutive" approach may in certain situations be justified. However, it is essential to bear in mind that the Court is not a legislator and should be careful not to assume legislative functions. An "evolutive" or "dynamic" interpretation should have a sufficient basis in changing conditions in the societies of the Contracting States, including an emerging consensus as to the standards to be achieved. We fail to see that this is so in the present case.

. . .

According to the information available to the Court, some eighteen countries out of the forty-five Contracting States have no restrictions on prisoners' right to vote (see paragraph 33 of the judgment). On the other hand, in some thirteen

States prisoners are not able to vote either because of a ban in their legislation or de facto because appropriate arrangements have not been made. It is essential to note that in at least four of those States the disenfranchisement has its basis in a recently adopted Constitution (Russia, Armenia, Hungary and Georgia). In at least thirteen other countries more or less far-reaching restrictions on prisoners' right to vote are prescribed in domestic legislation, and in four of those States the restrictions have a constitutional basis (Luxembourg, Austria, Turkey and Malta). The finding of the majority will create legislative problems not only for States with a general ban such as exists in the United Kingdom. . . . [T]he judgment in the present case implies that all States with such restrictions will face difficult assessments as to whether their legislation complies with the requirements of the Convention.

Our conclusion is that the legislation in Europe shows that there is little consensus about whether or not prisoners should have the right to vote. In fact, the majority of member States know such restrictions, although some have blanket and some limited restrictions. Thus, the legislation in the United Kingdom cannot be claimed to be in disharmony with a common European standard.

Furthermore, the majority attach importance to an alleged lack of evidence that the Parliament of the United Kingdom "has ever sought to weigh the competing interests or to assess the proportionality of a blanket ban on the right of a convicted prisoner to vote". . . . We disagree with this objection as it is not for the Court to prescribe the way in which national legislatures carry out their legislative functions. It must be assumed that section 3 of the Representation of the People Act 2000 reflects political, social and cultural values in the United Kingdom.

Regarding in particular the requirement that any restrictions must not be disproportionate, we consider it essential to underline that the severity of the punishment not only reflects the seriousness of the crime committed, but also the relevance and weight of the aims relied on by the respondent Government when limiting voting rights for convicted persons. We do not rule out the possibility that restrictions may be disproportionate in respect of minor offences and/or very short sentences. However, there is no need to enter into this question in the circumstances of the present case. The Court has consistently held in its case-law that its task is not normally to review the relevant law and practice in abstracto, but to determine whether the manner in which they were applied to, or affected, the applicant gave rise to a violation of the Convention. It is, in our opinion, difficult to see in what circumstances restrictions on voting rights would be acceptable, if not in the case of persons sentenced to life imprisonment. Generally speaking, the Court's judgment concentrates above all on finding the British legislation incompatible with the Convention in abstracto. We regret that despite this focus it gives the States little or no guidance as to what would be Convention-compatible solutions. Since restrictions on the right to vote continue to be compatible, it would seem obvious that the deprivation of the right to vote for the most serious offences such as murder or manslaughter, is not excluded in the future. . . .

Our own opinion whether persons serving a prison sentence should be allowed to vote in general or other elections matters little. Taking into account the sensitive political character of this issue, the diversity of the legal systems within the Contracting States and the lack of a sufficiently clear basis for such a right in Article 3 of Protocol No. 1, we are not able to accept that it is for the Court to impose on national legal systems an obligation either to abolish disenfranchisement for prisoners or to allow it only to a very limited extent.

NOTES AND QUESTIONS

1. **Regional Human Rights Courts.** Why have human rights courts, to the extent they exist, developed at the regional level? What factors might make the European Court of Human Rights particularly successful? How would you measure its success?

2. **Human Rights Law in the ECHR.** What is the source of law used by the ECHR? How does the Court's majority determine the content of that law in *Hirst*? How does the dissent criticize the majority's approach? Should it have mattered in *Hirst* that in the United States (and in a number of other democracies) prisoners do not have a right to vote? Should it matter that nothing in the Convention says anything one way or the other specifically about prisoners voting, and that for many years after the Convention's adoption, member nations generally restricted prisoner voting?

3. **The Role of the ECHR.** Is the ECHR decision in *Hirst* too intrusive on national sovereignty? Many people in Britain thought it was. In response, Britain did not alter its voting rules, leading to additional rounds of litigation as well as various proposals in the U.K. Parliament for new legislation. In general, the ECHR's principal method of direct enforcement is to award costs and damages against a state found to be in violation. In addition, most member states have national legislation (akin to Britain's Human Rights Act) that requires national law to conform to the Convention as expounded by the ECHR, and thus looks to national courts to enforce it. As the British experience with felon voting illustrates, however, full implementation of ECHR rulings often depends on the will of the political branches of the particular countries affected. The standoff between the United Kingdom and the ECHR persisted for 12 years, as the United Kingdom refused to implement the decision. In November 2017, the U.K. government proposed extending the franchise to a very small number of prisoners (principally, those on temporary release). The Council of Europe, the diplomatic organization that oversees implementation of the European Convention on Human Rights, indicated that this would be an acceptable implementation of *Hirst*, and the U.K. government plans to go forward with that limited reform. *See* House of Commons Library, *Prisoners' voting rights: developments since May 2015*, https://researchbriefings .parliament.uk/ResearchBriefing/Summary/CBP-7461.

    Britain's withdrawal from the EU (discussed below) does not affect its status under the European Convention on Human Rights, which is a distinct undertaking. There have also been calls for Britain to withdraw from the Convention, including in reaction to the *Hirst* decision.

4. **Proportionality and the Margin of Appreciation.** Note the *Hirst* court's reference to the principles of proportionality and the margin of appreciation. What do these terms mean? They are concepts developed by the ECHR when considering whether a member state has breached the Convention. They encourage the court to take into account cultural, historical, and other factors that might make a particular nation's action reasonable. As a result, the ECHR might rule differently when similar challenges are brought from different nations. Why do you think the ECHR would adopt these principles as part of its jurisprudence? Were they properly applied in *Hirst*?

5. **Implications of ECHR Rulings.** The ECHR applies a particular treaty, the European Convention on Human Rights, which has its own distinct wording. Nonetheless, its decisions are sometimes thought persuasive as to the scope of human rights more broadly. What is the significance of ECHR decisions for countries such as the United States, which is not a party to the Convention establishing the Court? Note that the U.S. Supreme Court previously held that the U.S. Constitution does not entitle prisoners to vote. Should U.S. courts reconsider that decision in light of *Hirst*? Why should lawyers in private practice in the United States care about decisions of the ECHR?

6. **ECHR Caseload.** The ECHR has an enormous caseload (so much so that there is a substantial backlog of cases). Some of them are extremely consequential for national policy. For example, in 2010 France passed a law making it illegal to conceal one's face in public; the ECHR subsequently rejected a human rights challenge brought by a Muslim woman who wished to wear a burqa, the traditional Islamic garment that covers a woman's face and body. *S.A.S. v. France* (ECHR, July 1, 2014). As noted in Chapter 3, the ECHR ruled in *Dudgeon v. United Kingdom* that the Convention protected same-sex sexual activity. However, in *Hämäläinen v. Finland* (judgement of July 16, 2014), the Court confirmed earlier rulings that the Convention did not require recognition of same-sex marriage. Many ECHR cases involve rights similar to those set forth in the U.S. Constitution, including for example free speech, fairness of criminal procedures, nondiscrimination, and privacy (although, as in *Hirst*, the Court frequently reaches results that differ from the likely result in the United States). In addition, the Court has found that at least some of the provisions of the Convention create "positive" rights (that is, rights obliging the government to act to protect individuals) as well as the "negative rights" familiar in the United States (that is, rights protecting individuals from government action). Note also that, unlike the international courts and tribunals mentioned above, individuals have the ability to bring cases to the ECHR.

3. International Criminal Courts

Ad Hoc International Criminal Courts. After World War II, the victorious Allies established military tribunals at Nuremberg, Germany, and Tokyo, Japan, to try German and Japanese leaders for war crimes, crimes against humanity, and crimes against peace (aggression). Many defendants were convicted (although some were acquitted), and they were given punishments including the death penalty. This approach to international criminal punishment was not repeated until the 1990s. Then, in the aftermath of the brutal conflict accompanying the break-up of Yugoslavia, the U.N. Security Council established the International Criminal Tribunal for the former Yugoslavia (ICTY) (http://www.icty.org/), "for the sole purpose of prosecuting persons responsible for serious violations of international humanitarian law committed in the territory of the former Yugoslavia." U.N. Sec. Council Res. 827 (1993). The ICTY conducted numerous trials of Serbian, Bosnian, and Croatian leaders and combatants, many of whom were convicted and are serving (or have served) jail time. In 1995, the U.N. Security Council created a similar tribunal, the International Criminal Tribunal for Rwanda (ICTR) (http://www.unictr.org/), to try participants in the 1994 genocide in Rwanda. Like the ICTY, the ICTR conducted numerous trials and imposed punishments on numerous individuals. In 2010, the U.N. Security Council established the International Residual Mechanism for Criminal Tribunals (https://www.irmct.org/en). The Mechanism now performs essential functions previously carried out by the ICTY (which closed in 2017) and the ICTR (which closed in 2015).

Other criminal courts with international components are hybrid or "mixed" courts that are essentially national in structure but have international support and participation. These include the Special Panels of the Dili District Court (also called the East Timor Tribunal) established in 2000, the Special Court for Sierra Leone established in 2002 (http://www.sc-sl.org/), the Extraordinary Chambers in the Courts of Cambodia established in 2003 (http://www.eccc.gov.kh/en), and the Special Tribunal for Lebanon established in 2007 (http://www.stl-tsl.org/).

The International Criminal Court (ICC). The ICC (http://www.icc-cpi.int/en_menus/icc/Pages/default.aspx) was established as a permanent international criminal court pursuant to the 1998 Rome Statute (http://www.icc-cpi.int), which entered into force in 2002. Currently, over 123 countries are parties to the Rome Statute, including 33 from Africa, 19 from Asia-Pacific, 18 from Eastern Europe, 28 from Latin America and the Caribbean, and 25 from Western European and North America. The United States is not a party to the Rome Statute; although it signed the Rome Statute, it later declared that it did not intend to ratify and sought to withdraw its signature. Other major nonparty countries include Russia, China, Israel, Iran, India, Pakistan, and Indonesia.

The ICC's jurisdiction has five important limitations. First, the ICC only has jurisdiction over "the most serious crimes of concern to the international community as a whole" that are specified in Article 5 of the Rome Statute: the crime of genocide, crimes against humanity, war crimes, and the crime of aggression — each as defined in detail in Articles 6, 7, 8, and 8 *bis* of the Rome Statute.

Second, the ICC has jurisdiction only with respect to crimes committed after the Rome Statute's entry into force on July 1, 2002 (or, for nations that become parties to the Rome Statute after its entry into force, crimes committed after the Rome Statute's entry into force for that nation, unless that nation otherwise declares).

Third, the ICC may only exercise jurisdiction over a situation that is brought before it in one of the three ways permitted by Article 13: (a) a party to the Rome Statute refers a situation to the ICC's Prosecutor; (b) the U.N. Security Council refers a situation to the Prosecutor; or (c) the Prosecutor initiates an investigation *proprio muto* — that is, on her own initiative — subject to the authorization of a pretrial chamber of the ICC.

Fourth, except in cases referred by the U.N. Security Council, under Article 12, the ICC may only exercise jurisdiction if the nation where the alleged criminal act occurred or the nation of which the accused is a national is a party to the Rome Statute. The Security Council may refer situations to the Prosecutor even when the alleged crimes occurred in a nonparty nation and the accused are nationals of a nonparty nation. For example, based on Security Council referrals the ICC asserted jurisdiction over situations involving the conduct of Libyan nationals in Libya and Sudanese nationals in Sudan, even though neither Libya nor Sudan is a party to the Rome Statute.

Fifth, even if the ICC would otherwise have jurisdiction, a case may be inadmissible based on the principle of complementarity, according to which the ICC jurisdiction "shall be complementary to national criminal jurisdictions" (Rome Statute, Article 1). In general, this means that the ICC will not accept a case if a nation with jurisdiction over it has investigated the matter and prosecuted or decided not to prosecute the persons concerned, or is currently investigating or prosecuting the matter. This exception does not apply if the relevant nation is unwilling or unable to carry out the investigation or prosecution, or the investigation or prosecution was for the purpose of shielding the person concerned from the ICC or otherwise was not conducted independently or impartially in accordance with the norms of due process recognized by international law.

The ICC sits in The Hague, Netherlands. There have been 27 cases before the Court, with some cases involving more than one suspect. The Court has issued 34 arrest warrants, and 16 people have been detained in the ICC detention center and have appeared before the Court.

NOTES AND QUESTIONS

1. **The Emergence of International Criminal Courts.** What factors likely contributed to the creation of the ad hoc criminal tribunals in 1993-1994? What might have prevented such tribunals from developing earlier? What are their strengths and limitations? Why do you think there are not more ad hoc tribunals today?

2. **The Scope of the International Criminal Court.** When can the ICC act, and what are the limits on its jurisdiction? What are the steps for bringing a prosecution in the ICC? Is this a broad or a narrow grant of power? What are the practical limits on the ICC's effectiveness? Is the ICC a worthwhile project? What are the arguments in favor of having such an institution (as opposed to prosecuting international crimes in national courts or in ad hoc tribunals)? What problems might it create?

3. **ICC Membership.** As noted, although many nations are parties to the ICC (including almost all European and Latin American countries, and many from sub-Saharan Africa), many important nations are not. The United States declined to join. (President Clinton signed the Rome Statute but did not submit it to the Senate for consent to ratification, and subsequently President George W. Bush withdrew the U.S. signature; President Obama did not seek to have the United States join.) A considerable debate in the United States and elsewhere surrounded the U.S. refusal to ratify. One of the reasons for U.S. refusal is concern that U.S. soldiers or other U.S. nationals could be subjected to the ICC's jurisdiction without U.S. consent. To review your understanding of the ICC's jurisdiction, under what circumstances could this occur? Can it occur even though the United States is not a party? Why do you think other nations refused to join the ICC?

4. **ICC Cases.** Unlike some of the ad hoc tribunals such as the ICTY and ICTR, the ICC has not been very successful so far in developing a caseload. Since its inception, the court has, as of 2020, reached a judgment in only 12 cases — 8 convictions and 4 acquittals, with appeals still pending. Except as noted below, the court as of this writing has 13 situations under investigation (Congo, Uganda, Sudan, Central African Republic, Kenya, Libya, Ivory Coast, Mali, Georgia, Burundi, Bangladesh/Myanmar, and Afghanistan). Due to the disproportionate focus of the ICC's caseload on Africa, some have argued that the ICC is a tool of the "West" because it investigates small, poor states and ignores crimes potentially committed by rich and powerful Western states. Although several of the court's African investigations were "self-referrals," others were not. Kenya in particular has protested the court's indictment of several of its leaders, including Uhuru Kenyatta, who was later elected president. In December 2014, the prosecutor withdrew the charges against Uhuru Kenyatta. Several African countries, most prominently South Africa, have threatened or actually announced plans to withdraw from the ICC. In 2017, South Africa's withdrawal was blocked by a South African court on the ground that withdrawal required approval of South Africa's parliament, and it is unclear whether the South African government will continue to press for withdrawal. Also in 2017, the African Union, an association of African nations, adopted a nonbinding resolution calling upon members to withdraw from the ICC, in part on the ground that the court focuses too much on situations in Africa and neglects situations in other parts of the world. Burundi withdrew in 2017, shortly after the prosecutor opened an investigation into events in Burundi. In 2018, with the prosecutor considering an investigation into events in the Philippines, the President of the Philippines announced

that his country would begin the process of withdrawal. The Philippines withdrew in 2019.

In 2016, the ICC opened an investigation into alleged war crimes committed during the 2008 conflict between Russia and Georgia. *See* https://www.icc-cpi.int/georgia. This is the ICC's first full-scale investigation of a situation outside of Africa. Note that although Russia is not a party to the ICC statute, Georgia is, and the alleged war crimes occurred in Georgia. What obstacles is this investigation likely to encounter? What would be the basis for the ICC's jurisdiction?

Also in 2016, the Court reached several additional verdicts, including a guilty verdict against Ahmad al Faqi al Mahdi, who was convicted of the war crime of destroying historic and religious buildings in Timbuktu, Mali, as part of an al Qaeda-affiliated group. As of 2019, the court had indicted 42 defendants, some of whom remain at large (the ICC does not try defendants *in abstenia*). Five persons have been convicted, and approximately 20 proceedings are ongoing.

In 2020, the Appeals Chamber of the ICC found that the ICC Prosecutor is authorized to investigate crimes alleged to have been committed on the territory of Afghanistan since May 1, 2003, as well as other alleged crimes that have a nexus to the armed conflict in Afghanistan, are sufficiently linked to the situation in Afghanistan, and were committed on the territory of other State Parties to the ICC statute. The Prosecutor will be seeking to investigate crimes against humanity and war crimes by the Taliban and other forces operating in Afghanistan. The Prosecutor will also probe alleged war crimes by U.S. military personnel in Afghanistan and by members of the CIA in detention facilities in Afghanistan and on the territory of other State Parties to the ICC statute. The United States is not a party to the ICC and has refused to cooperate with the ICC.

5. **Referral by the Security Council.** In addition to developing its own cases, the ICC can hear cases referred to it by the U.N. Security Council. A key point is that the Security Council may refer situations to the Prosecutor even when the alleged crimes occurred in a nonparty country and the accused are nationals of a nonparty nation. As noted, the Council has referred cases against the leaders of the existing regime in Sudan for crimes in the Darfur region, and against the leaders of the former regime in Libya for crimes during the Libyan uprising of 2011. Neither Sudan nor Libya is party to the Rome Statute, and neither is currently cooperating with the ICC in pursuing the prosecutions. During the negotiations leading to the creation of the ICC, the United States wanted Security Council referral to be the only way a case could reach the ICC. Recall how decisions are made at the Security Council. What are the advantages and disadvantages of this approach? Why did the United States likely favor it? Why did other countries likely oppose it?

6. **Enforcement.** The ICTY and other criminal courts have been able to enforce their judgments because the defendants were in their custody and because the courts themselves have the power to order persons to be imprisoned. However, they have the initial difficulty of getting accused persons into

custody so that a trial can be held, a project that typically requires cooperation from national law enforcement personnel. The ICTY was fortunate that it received substantial cooperation from local law enforcement. When is this sort of cooperation likely, and when not?

4. Courts of Regional Economic and Political Organizations

Some specialized international courts serve as the judicial branch of regional economic and political organizations. The leading example is the Court of Justice of the European Union (CJEU), which is the judicial body of the European Union (EU) (http://curia.europa.eu), a political and economic association of 27 European nations. The CJEU consists of two principal courts, the Court of Justice (sometimes still called by its prior name, the European Court of Justice, or ECJ) and the General Court, both of which sit in Luxembourg. In general, these courts hear cases involving interpretations of EU law (established by various treaties among the EU members and by EU institutions acting pursuant to those treaties) and claims that EU members have failed to fulfill their obligations under EU law. The CJEU has an enormous workload, amounting to hundreds of cases per year. It also has considerably more ability to enforce its judgments than many other international courts, chiefly because its judgments are generally given direct effect in the judicial systems of EU members. Although many of its decisions involve matters relating to the EU's common market in goods and services, they may have implications beyond simple trade disputes; moreover, as the case below indicates, the CJEU also applies the Charter of Fundamental Rights of the European Union, giving it a significant role as a human rights court. In a 2016 referendum in the United Kingdom, voters chose to leave the EU, with the withdrawal formally accomplished in 2020, subject to a transition period. The United Kingdom remains within the jurisdiction of the CJEU until the end of the transition period.

In addition to the CJEU, there are other courts of regional economic and political organizations. These include the Court of Justice of the Benelux Economic Union (http://www.courbeneluxhof.be/fr/index.asp), the Court of Justice of the Andean Community (http://www.tribunalandino.org.ec/sitetjca/index.php), and the Community Court of Justice of the Economic Community of West African States (ECOWAS) (http://www.courtecowas.org/).

Google Spain SL, and Google Inc. v. Agencia Española de Protección de Datos (AEPD), and Mario Costeja González
Court of Justice of the European Union, May 13, 2014

This request for a preliminary ruling concerns the interpretation of . . . Directive 95/46/EC of the European Parliament and of the Council of 24 October 1995 on the protection of individuals with regard to the processing of personal data and on the free movement of such data and of Article 8 of the Charter of Fundamental Rights of the European Union ("the Charter").

The request has been made in proceedings between, on the one hand, Google Spain SL ("Google Spain") and Google Inc. and, on the other, the Agencia Española de Protección de Datos (Spanish Data Protection Agency; "the AEPD") and Mr Costeja González concerning a decision by the AEPD upholding the complaint lodged by Mr Costeja González against those two companies and ordering Google Inc. to adopt the measures necessary to withdraw personal data relating to Mr Costeja González from its index and to prevent access to the data in the future.

. . .

On 5 March 2010, Mr Costeja González, a Spanish national resident in Spain, lodged with the AEPD a complaint against . . . Google Spain and Google Inc. The complaint was based on the fact that, when an internet user entered Mr Costeja González's name in the search engine of the Google group ("Google Search"), he would obtain links to two pages of La Vanguardia's newspaper, of 19 January and 9 March 1998 respectively, on which an announcement mentioning Mr Costeja González's name appeared for a real-estate auction connected with attachment proceedings for the recovery of social security debts.

By that complaint, Mr Costeja González . . . requested that Google Spain or Google Inc. be required to remove or conceal the personal data relating to him so that they ceased to be included in the search results and no longer appeared in the links to La Vanguardia. Mr Costeja González stated in this context that the attachment proceedings concerning him had been fully resolved for a number of years and that reference to them was now entirely irrelevant.

By decision of 30 July 2010, the AEPD . . . [upheld] the complaint . . . against Google Spain and Google Inc. . . . .

Google Spain and Google Inc. brought separate actions against that decision before the Audiencia Nacional (National High Court [of Spain]). . . . .

[T]he Audiencia Nacional decided to stay the proceedings and to refer [various] . . . questions to the Court for a preliminary ruling. . . . .

[The CJEU first considered whether Directive 95/46 applied to operators of search engines, which involved the question whether the search engine was "processing personal data" and whether the operator was a "controller" of the search engine as defined in the Directive.]

. . .

Article 2(b) of Directive 95/46 defines "processing of personal data" as "any operation or set of operations which is performed upon personal data, whether or not by automatic means, such as collection, recording, organisation, storage, adaptation or alteration, retrieval, consultation, use, disclosure by transmission, dissemination or otherwise making available, alignment or combination, blocking, erasure or destruction".

As regards in particular the internet, the Court has already had occasion to state that the operation of loading personal data on an internet page must be considered to be such "processing" within the meaning of Article 2(b) of Directive 95/46 (see Case C-101/01 *Lindqvist* EU:C:2003:596, paragraph 25).

So far as concerns the activity at issue in the main proceedings, it is not contested that the data found, indexed and stored by search engines and made available to their users include information relating to identified or identifiable natural persons and thus "personal data" within the meaning of Article 2(a) of that directive.

Therefore, it must be found that, in exploring the internet automatically, constantly and systematically in search of the information which is published there, the operator of a search engine "collects" such data which it subsequently "retrieves", "records" and "organises" within the framework of its indexing programmes, "stores" on its servers and, as the case may be, "discloses" and "makes available" to its users in the form of lists of search results. As those operations are referred to expressly and unconditionally in Article 2(b) of Directive 95/46, they must be classified as "processing" within the meaning of that provision, regardless of the fact that the operator of the search engine also carries out the same operations in respect of other types of information and does not distinguish between the latter and the personal data.

. . .

As to the question whether the operator of a search engine must be regarded as the "controller" in respect of the processing of personal data that is carried out by that engine in the context of an activity such as that at issue in the main proceedings, it should be recalled that Article 2(d) of Directive 95/46 defines "controller" as "the natural or legal person, public authority, agency or any other body which alone or jointly with others determines the purposes and means of the processing of personal data".

It is the search engine operator which determines the purposes and means of that activity and thus of the processing of personal data that it itself carries out within the framework of that activity and which must, consequently, be regarded as the "controller" in respect of that processing pursuant to Article 2(d).

. . .

It follows . . . that Article 2(b) and (d) of Directive 95/46 are to be interpreted as meaning that, first, the activity of a search engine consisting in finding information published or placed on the internet by third parties, indexing it automatically, storing it temporarily and, finally, making it available to internet users according to a particular order of preference must be classified as 'processing of personal data' within the meaning of Article 2(b) when that information contains personal data and, second, the operator of the search engine must be regarded as the "controller" in respect of that processing, within the meaning of Article 2(d).

. . .

[The CJEU next considered whether the Directive applied to the activities of Google, a U.S. company, as a result of its operations in Spain through its Spanish subsidiary. This question turned on whether Google had an "establishment" in the EU and whether the processing of the personal data was "carried out in the context of the activities" of the establishment, as required by the Directive.]

. . .

It is not disputed that Google Spain engages in the effective and real exercise of activity through stable arrangements in Spain. As it moreover has separate legal personality, it constitutes a subsidiary of Google Inc. on Spanish territory and, therefore, an "establishment" within the meaning of Article 4(1)(a) of Directive 95/46.

In order to satisfy the criterion laid down in that provision, it is also necessary that the processing of personal data by the controller be "carried out in the context of the activities" of an establishment of the controller on the territory of a Member State.

Google Spain and Google Inc. dispute that this is the case since the processing of personal data at issue in the main proceedings is carried out exclusively by Google Inc., which operates Google Search without any intervention on the part of Google Spain; the latter's activity is limited to providing support to the Google group's advertising activity which is separate from its search engine service.

Nevertheless, . . . Article 4(1)(a) of Directive 95/46 does not require the processing of personal data in question to be carried out "by" the establishment concerned itself, but only that it be carried out "in the context of the activities" of the establishment.

Furthermore, in the light of the objective of Directive 95/46 of ensuring effective and complete protection of the fundamental rights and freedoms of natural persons, and in particular their right to privacy, with respect to the processing of personal data, those words cannot be interpreted restrictively . . . .

It is to be noted in this context that it is clear in particular from recitals 18 to 20 in the preamble to Directive 95/46 and Article 4 thereof that the European Union legislature sought to prevent individuals from being deprived of the protection guaranteed by the directive and that protection from being circumvented, by prescribing a particularly broad territorial scope.

In the light of that objective of Directive 95/46 and of the wording of Article 4(1)(a), it must be held that the processing of personal data for the purposes of the service of a search engine such as Google Search, which is operated by an undertaking that has its seat in a third State but has an establishment in a Member State, is carried out "in the context of the activities" of that establishment if the latter is intended to promote and sell, in that Member State, advertising space offered by the search engine which serves to make the service offered by that engine profitable.

. . .

[Having concluded that the Directive applied to Google, the CJEU next considered whether the Directive required Google to comply with Costeja González's request.]

The Court has already held that the provisions of Directive 95/46, in so far as they govern the processing of personal data liable to infringe fundamental freedoms, in particular the right to privacy, must necessarily be interpreted in the light of fundamental rights, which, according to settled case-law, form an integral part of the general principles of law whose observance the Court ensures and which are now set out in the Charter (see, in particular, Case C-274/99 P *Connolly* v *Commission* EU:C:2001:127, paragraph 37, and *Österreichischer Rundfunk and Others* EU:C:2003:294, paragraph 68).

Article 7 of the Charter guarantees the right to respect for private life, whilst Article 8 of the Charter expressly proclaims the right to the protection of personal data. Article 8(2) and (3) specify that such data must be processed fairly for specified purposes and on the basis of the consent of the person concerned or some other legitimate basis laid down by law, that everyone has the right of access to data which have been collected concerning him or her and the right to have the data rectified, and that compliance with these rules is to be subject to control by an independent authority. Those requirements are implemented inter alia by Articles 6, 7, 12, 14 and 28 of Directive 95/46.

Article 12(b) of Directive 95/46 provides that Member States are to guarantee every data subject the right to obtain from the controller, as appropriate, the rectification, erasure or blocking of data the processing of which does not comply with the provisions of Directive 95/46, in particular because of the incomplete or inaccurate nature of the data. . . .

It is in the light of those considerations that it is necessary to interpret and apply the provisions of Directive 95/46 governing the data subject's rights when he lodges with the supervisory authority or judicial authority a request such as that at issue in the main proceedings.

It must be pointed out at the outset that, as has been found in paragraphs 36 to 38 of the present judgment, processing of personal data, such as that at issue in the main proceedings, carried out by the operator of a search engine is liable to affect significantly the fundamental rights to privacy and to the protection of personal data when the search by means of that engine is carried out on the basis of an individual's name, since that processing enables any internet user to obtain through the list of results a structured overview of the information relating to that individual that can be found on the internet — information which potentially concerns a vast number of aspects of his private life and which, without the search engine, could not have been interconnected or could have been only with great difficulty — and thereby to establish a more or less detailed profile of him. Furthermore, the effect of the interference with those rights of the data subject is heightened on account of the important role played by the internet and search engines in modern society, which render the information contained in such a list of results ubiquitous. . . .

In the light of the potential seriousness of that interference, it is clear that it cannot be justified by merely the economic interest which the operator of such an engine has in that processing. However, inasmuch as the removal of links from the list of results could, depending on the information at issue, have effects upon the legitimate interest of internet users potentially interested in having access to that information, in situations such as that at issue in the main proceedings a fair balance should be sought in particular between that interest and the data subject's fundamental rights under Articles 7 and 8 of the Charter. Whilst it is true that the data subject's rights protected by those articles also override, as a general rule, that interest of internet users, that balance may however depend, in specific cases, on the nature of the information in question and its sensitivity for the data subject's private life and on the interest of the public in having that information, an interest which may vary, in particular, according to the role played by the data subject in public life.

. . .

As regards Article 12(b) of Directive 95/46, . . . incompatibility [with the Directive] may result not only from the fact that such data are inaccurate but, in particular, also from the fact that they are inadequate, irrelevant or excessive in relation to the purposes of the processing, that they are not kept up to date, or that they are kept for longer than is necessary unless they are required to be kept for historical, statistical or scientific purposes.

It follows from those requirements, laid down in Article 6(1)(c) to (e) of Directive 95/46, that even initially lawful processing of accurate data may, in the course of time, become incompatible with the directive where those data are no longer necessary in the light of the purposes for which they were collected or processed. That is so in particular where they appear to be inadequate, irrelevant or no longer relevant, or excessive in relation to those purposes and in the light of the time that has elapsed.

Therefore, if it is found, following a request by the data subject pursuant to Article 12(b) of Directive 95/46, that the inclusion in the list of results displayed following a search made on the basis of his name of the links to web pages published lawfully by third parties and containing true information relating to him personally is, at this point in time, incompatible with Article 6(1)(c) to (e) of the directive because that information appears, having regard to all the circumstances of the case, to be inadequate, irrelevant or no longer relevant, or excessive in relation to the purposes of the processing at issue carried out by the operator of the search engine, the information and links concerned in the list of results must be erased.

. . .

As the data subject may, in the light of his fundamental rights under Articles 7 and 8 of the Charter, request that the information in question no longer be made available to the general public by its inclusion in such a list of results, it should be held . . . that those rights override, as a rule, not only the economic interest of the operator of the search engine but also the interest of the general public in finding that information upon a search relating to the data subject's name. However, that would not be the case if it appeared, for particular reasons, such as the role played by the data subject in public life, that the interference with his fundamental rights is justified by the preponderant interest of the general public in having, on account of inclusion in the list of results, access to the information in question.

As regards a situation such as that at issue in the main proceedings, which concerns the display, in the list of results that the internet user obtains by making a search by means of Google Search on the basis of the data subject's name, of links to pages of the on-line archives of a daily newspaper that contain announcements mentioning the data subject's name and relating to a real-estate auction connected with attachment proceedings for the recovery of social security debts, it should be held that, having regard to the sensitivity for the data subject's private life of the information contained in those announcements and to the fact that its initial publication had taken place 16 years earlier, the data subject establishes a right that that information should no longer be linked to his name by means of such a list. Accordingly, since in the case in point there do not appear to be particular reasons substantiating a preponderant interest of the public in having, in the context of such a search, access to that information, a matter which is, how-ever, for the referring court to establish, the data subject may, by virtue of Article 12(b) and subparagraph (a) of the first paragraph of Article 14 of Directive 95/46, require those links to be removed from the list of results.

. . .

NOTES AND QUESTIONS

1. **The European Court of Human Rights and the European Court of Justice.** Note that Europe has two principal regional courts. The European Court of Human Rights (ECHR), discussed above, sits in Strasbourg, France, and hears claims brought under the European Convention on Human Rights. The Court of Justice of the European Union (CJEU), which sits in Luxembourg, hears claims brought under the treaties constituting the European Union (EU) and under regulations and directives promulgated by EU entities. A number of European nations, such as Russia and Turkey, are within the jurisdiction of the ECHR but are not members of the EU and thus are not within the jurisdiction of the CJEU.

2. **Subject Matter of CJEU Cases.** Much of the CJEU's workload is princi-pally concerned with economic regulations related to the EU's objective of establishing a single European market. For example, in a well-known early case, *Commission v. Federal Republic of Germany* (Court of Justice of the European Communities 1988), the court's predecessor held that Germany's beer purity law (requiring beer to contain only specified ingredients) imper-missibly blocked imports from other countries such as The Netherlands where beer was brewed under different standards. In a more recent case, *Åklagaren v. Percy Mickelsson and Joakim Roos* (Court of Justice of the European Union, June 4, 2009), the court considered whether Sweden's regulations sharply limiting the places in which jet skis could be operated interfered with the sin-gle market by discouraging sales in Sweden of jet skis manufactured in other EU countries. In the *Mickelsson* case, the court observed:

> Even if the national regulations at issue do not have the aim or effect of treating goods coming from other Member States less favourably . . . the restriction which they impose on the use of a product in the territory of a Member State may, depending on its scope, have a considerable influence on the behaviour of consumers, which may, in turn, affect the access of that product to the market of that Member State.
>
> Consumers, knowing that the use permitted by such regulations is very limited, have only a limited interest in buying that product.
>
> In that regard, where the national regulations for the designation of nav-igable waters and waterways have the effect of preventing users of personal watercraft from using them for the specific and inherent purposes for which they were intended or of greatly restricting their use . . . such regulations

have the effect of hindering the access to the domestic market in question for those goods. . . .

The court concluded:

> It is not open to dispute that a restriction or a prohibition on the use of personal watercraft are appropriate means for the purpose of ensuring that the environment is protected. However, for the national regulations to be capable of being regarded as justified, it is also incumbent on the national authorities to show that their restrictive effects on the free movement of goods do not go beyond what is necessary to achieve that aim.

As the *Google Spain* case illustrates, however, EU law also encompasses protection for individual rights, such as the right to protection of personal data. As a result, there may be overlap between the subject matter of CJEU cases and ECHR cases.

3. **Bringing a Case to the CJEU.** Most CJEU cases reach the court either as references for preliminary rulings requested by national courts, or as direct actions brought (typically) by the European Commission, an EU entity. How did the *Google Spain* case reach the CJEU? Why did the CJEU have jurisdiction? What law was it applying?

4. **Extraterritorial Scope of EU Regulations.** Note that in the *Google Spain* case, the court applied the EU Directive to the search activities of Google outside the EU. How was this justified? Is that a sufficient justification? What are the limits of the EU's regulation of Google? What are the implications of this case for U.S. businesses considering operations in Europe?

5. **The Right to Be Forgotten.** The *Google Spain* case has been described as recognizing a "right to be forgotten," and has been controversial on that ground. *E.g.*, Lorena Jaume-Palasi, *"Google Spain case": Court decision privatises the public sphere*, INTERNET POL'Y REV., May 27, 2014, *available at* http://policyreview.info/articles/news/google-spain-case-court-decision-privatises-public-sphere/291. Should it matter that the "personal data" at issue in the case was a matter of public record? What limits does the court place on the right to be forgotten? Are they sufficient? Where do they come from? If the decision is incorrect (as many people have argued), where did the Court err? For a useful short summary and critique of the Google Spain case, see *International Decisions: Google Spain SL v. Agencia Espanola de Proteccion de Datos*, 108 AM. J. INT'L L. 502 (2014).

5. *The International Tribunal for the Law of the Sea*

The International Tribunal for the Law of the Sea (ITLOS) (www.itlos.org) was established by the 1982 United Nations Convention on the Law of the Sea, which entered into force in November 1994. The first case (*St. Vincent and the Grenadines v. Guinea*) was submitted to the Tribunal in 1997. Currently, 168 nations are parties to the Convention; the United States is not a party because the

Senate has not consented to ratification of the Law of the Sea Convention. Under Part XV of the Convention, ITLOS is one of four alternative dispute settlement methods, along with the ICJ and two types of arbitral tribunals. A party to the Convention may choose one or more of those methods by declaration. If the parties to a dispute have not accepted the same method, then ITLOS may not hear the dispute unless the parties otherwise agree.

ITLOS has jurisdiction over disputes concerning the interpretation or application of the Convention and over disputes submitted to it pursuant to the provisions of any other agreement conferring jurisdiction on ITLOS. ITLOS also has jurisdiction over applications for the prompt release of a detained vessel or its crew. In addition, under certain circumstances, ITLOS may give advisory opinions.

The ITLOS sits in Hamburg, Germany. Like many international courts, only nations may be parties before the ITLOS, and the ITLOS does not have any direct methods of enforcing its judgments. To date, 22 cases have been submitted to ITLOS. As an example, in the ARA "Libertad" Case (*Argentina v. Ghana*) (order of 15 December 2012), the Court directed Ghana to release the Argentine warship *Fragata Libertad*, which Ghana had seized in Ghana's territorial waters in connection with the execution of a private party's judgment against Argentina. Ghana complied with the order.

REVIEW NOTES AND QUESTIONS

1. **The ICJ and Other International Courts.** What are the similarities and differences between the ICJ on one hand and the various "specialized" international courts on the other? How would you explain to a client the strengths and weaknesses of the ICJ as a dispute resolution body? How is your assessment going to change depending on whether the client is a government or a nongovernmental person or entity?

2. **Jurisdiction of Specialized Courts.** As noted in the introduction to this chapter, to understand the jurisdiction of international courts it is necessary to move beyond generalizations about domestic and transnational cases and instead to perform careful court-specific jurisdictional analysis. Which of the specialized courts discussed above, if any, would have jurisdiction over the following disputes, and under what circumstances?

    a. A dispute between a car manufacturer in one nation and a purchaser of one of its cars in another nation.

    b. A claim by an individual that a European nation has violated his human rights.

    c. A claim by an individual that a nation that is a party to the American Convention on Human Rights has violated her human rights.

    d. A claim by one nation that a national of another nation has committed a crime.

    e. A claim by a business from one nation that another nation has violated international trade law.

3. **Proliferation of Specialized International Courts.** Some experts have expressed concerns about the proliferation of specialized international courts. For example, some have argued that the spread of these courts may lead to the fragmentation of international law and to conflicts between the jurisprudence of different courts. Should this be a concern? Is there anything that can be done about it?

4. **Importance of International Court Decisions.** What significance do international courts have for lawyers in private practice in the United States? Because most international courts have limited jurisdiction and/or hear claims only from governments, it is unlikely that many U.S. lawyers will ever litigate a case in an international court. Are there still reasons for U.S. lawyers to care about the structure and decisions of international courts?

5. **Alternatives.** For disputes where no international court has jurisdiction, what alternatives might be considered for resolving the dispute?

CHAPTER 6

ALTERNATIVE DISPUTE RESOLUTION

What if you want to avoid courts in transnational cases, and what if you would like more flexibility to choose the procedures that would govern your dispute? Indeed, what if you wanted to choose the decisionmaker? Under those circumstances, you should consider alternatives to litigation, such as negotiation, mediation, and arbitration. Together, these and other nonlitigation dispute resolution methods are often called *alternative dispute resolution* or **ADR**. These methods are widely used in both domestic and transnational practice.

This chapter introduces you to ADR in transnational practice. Section A provides an overview of ADR by distinguishing negotiation, mediation, and arbitration from litigation, and discussing factors to consider when advising a client whether to choose litigation or an alternative to litigation. Section B examines some of the most common issues surrounding arbitration as a method for resolving transnational disputes, with a focus on one type of transnational arbitration — transnational *commercial* arbitration. Section C and Section D provide brief introductions to investor-state arbitration and state-state arbitration.

A. Alternatives to Litigation in Transnational Practice

A starting point for understanding the differences between litigation and various ADR methods is to compare their basic characteristics. Does the method require the parties' consent? Does it involve a third party? If so, what is the third party's role? What kind of outcome might the method produce? And how flexible is the method? These differences are summarized in **Table 1** and are discussed in detail below.

Litigation is nonconsensual. If a plaintiff sues a defendant where the defendant is subject to personal and subject matter jurisdiction and the defendant has been properly served, the defendant is required to participate in the lawsuit whether or not the defendant has consented to litigation. Failure to participate may result in a default judgment. Litigation involves a third-party decision maker — a judge and

Table 1

Basic Differences Between Different Dispute Resolution Methods

	Consensual?	Third Party?	Third Party's Role?	Outcome?	Flexibility
Litigation	No	Yes (judge, jury)	Decide	Judgment (legally binding)	Low
Negotiation	Yes	No	N/A	Possible settlement agreement (may be legally binding)	High
Mediation	Yes	Yes (mediator)	Facilitate	Possible settlement agreement (may be legally binding)	High
Arbitration	Yes	Yes (arbitrator)	Decide	Award (legally binding)	High

sometimes (in the United States, at least) a jury. Judges and juries are provided by the government, so parties don't have to pay for them (unless you count taxes), but you also don't get to pick your decision maker. Most judges (and all juries) are generalists, so it cannot be assured that the decision maker will be an expert on the law or subject matter of the case. Moreover, in many (if not most) nations, including the United States, courts are very busy and simultaneously handle a large number of cases. As a result, the litigation process often moves slowly and only limited attention may be given to your case. Appeals and other procedural matters may further delay resolution. Once the case is finally resolved, the court will issue a judgment that is legally binding on the parties. But this may not assure complete resolution in a transnational case. As discussed further in Chapter 7, sometimes one nation's courts will recognize or enforce a judgment of a court in another nation, but in the absence of a treaty requiring enforcement there is no general rule of international law that requires this. As a result, cross-border enforcement of court judgments is often very difficult and sometimes not possible. Further, litigation follows detailed rules established by the government, leaving little room for flexibility by parties wanting to customize the dispute resolution process to suit the needs of their specific case. For example, the general rule in the United States is that lawsuits (including papers filed, hearings, and trial) are open to the public, even if the parties would like the proceedings to be private.

Negotiation is the process of direct bargaining between two disputants. It is consensual — a party cannot legally be forced to negotiate without its consent (but if the disputants have entered into a valid and enforceable contract that includes an agreement to negotiate in good faith, they would have a contractual obligation to do so). Negotiation does not involve a third party. Often, lawyers negotiate on behalf of disputants — their role is not to decide the dispute, but rather to advise and represent their respective clients in the negotiation process (just as lawyers represent clients in litigation). Typically, the goal of negotiation as a dispute resolution method is to reach a settlement agreement. There is no requirement or guarantee that a settlement will be reached, but if the parties enter a settlement agreement that is a valid contract, it may be legally enforceable. Negotiation is very flexible. The parties have complete control over the time, place, and procedures for negotiation. For example, if they desire to keep their negotiations private, they may agree to do so.

There are often significant barriers to negotiation. Disputants may find it difficult to communicate with each other effectively for emotional reasons or due to differences of language or culture. They may also find it difficult to think beyond their own bargaining positions, making an agreement difficult to reach.

Mediation — which, like negotiation, is a consensual dispute resolution method — can sometimes help disputants (and their lawyers) overcome these barriers. Like litigation (and arbitration, discussed below), mediation involves a third party — a mediator. However, unlike litigation and arbitration, a mediator's role is not to decide the dispute or otherwise to determine the outcome. Instead, the mediator facilitates negotiation by helping the disputants communicate effectively, focus on their respective interests instead of their bargaining positions, and think creatively about potential settlement arrangements. Like negotiation, the outcome of mediation may be a negotiated settlement agreement that constitutes an enforceable contract. Also like negotiation, mediation is highly flexible. The parties can select their own mediator (for whom they also need to pay, typically by the hour), and the time, place, and procedures for the mediation are up to the parties.

Arbitration is similar to litigation, but differs in important ways. Unlike litigation, arbitration requires the consent of the parties. Absent a valid agreement to arbitrate, a party cannot be forced to arbitrate. In the agreement to arbitrate, the parties may agree for the arbitration to be confidential. Like litigation, arbitration involves a third-party decision maker — an arbitrator. But unlike a judge or jury, the arbitrator is not provided by a government (although often arbitrators are former judges). The disputants (typically called claimant and respondent) choose the number of arbitrators they wish to have (often one or three), they select the arbitrator or arbitrators, and they pay for the arbitrator(s). Like a judge in litigation (but unlike a mediator in mediation), the role of the arbitrator is to decide the dispute. The arbitrator's decision is called an award (not a judgment), and like a court judgment an award is legally binding on the parties. Many nations are parties to the Convention on the Recognition and Enforcement of Foreign Arbitral Awards (the "New York Convention"), which is discussed in this chapter below and in greater detail in Chapter 8. However, there is no equivalent global treaty covering foreign court judgments. As a result, cross-border enforcement of arbitral awards is generally more reliable than the cross-border enforcement of court judgments. Unlike a court judgment, there ordinarily is no right to appeal an arbitral award to either a court or to other arbitrators. Fairly narrow grounds are available for challenging the validity or the enforcement of an arbitral award (as discussed in Chapter 8), but otherwise arbitral awards are generally final once issued. Unlike litigation, but like negotiation and mediation, arbitration is a very flexible dispute resolution method. In addition to choosing their arbitrators, the disputants may select the time, place, and procedures for the arbitration.

NOTES AND QUESTIONS

1. **Advantages and Disadvantages of Litigation.** A basic premise of ADR is that litigation is not always the most appropriate method for resolving a dispute. What are some of the potential disadvantages of litigation — in general or in particular types of disputes — that might support this premise? In what kinds of situations might litigation be advantageous as a method of dispute resolution?
2. **Alternatives to Litigation.** What are some of the potential advantages and disadvantages of negotiation and mediation as methods of transnational dispute resolution? What are some of the potential advantages and disadvantages of arbitration as a method of transnational dispute resolution? Do these alternatives respond to the perceived disadvantages of litigation?
3. **Public versus Private Proceedings.** What reasons might a party have for wanting a dispute resolution process to be private and confidential? What reasons might a party have for wanting a dispute resolution process to be public? Try to think of some specific types of disputes to give as examples. Of course, privacy ultimately depends on nondisclosure by the parties. What steps might you recommend to the parties to decrease the likelihood of disclosure by either or both parties?
4. **When to Use Mediation.** One group of experienced transnational practitioners has offered this overview of factors to consider when determining whether mediation is likely to be an appropriate dispute resolution method:

    Cases Not Suited for Mediation
        A relatively narrow set of circumstances make a case clearly ill suited for [mediation]. These can be sketched as follows:

    - Where a legal, commercial, or other precedent needs to be set;
    - Where summary disposition is available quickly and efficiently;
    - Where one of the parties requires emergency injunctive or other protective relief;
    - Where a party actively seeks public attention to the dispute; or
    - Where there is no real interest in settlement for other apparent reasons.

    Cases Clearly Suited for Mediation
        Another set of circumstances can make mediation a clearly attractive avenue of resolving a dispute. These may be summarized as follows:

- As an alternative to international arbitration, or cases in which court litigation is expected to impose significant costs on the parties, which may or may not be justified by the reasonable value of the claim;
- Points of disagreement may have been exaggerated and sharpened by differences in culture, language, and the parties' legal regimes;
- The parties are deadlocked in settlement negotiations;
- Complexities of law, fact, or relations are likely to protract proceedings and make any judgment particularly susceptible to appeal;
- There are multiple actions involving common parties; or
- The issues involved are sensitive or require the disclosure of sensitive information, or the parties otherwise wish to avoid public attention.

Other Cases

Many cases, of course, will fall into a gray area where careful consideration of the circumstances may be required to determine whether mediation is appropriate.

Michael McIlwrath, Elpidio Villarreal & Amy Crafts, *Finishing Before You Start: International Mediation, in* INTERNATIONAL LITIGATION STRATEGIES AND PRACTICE 41, 43-44 (Barton Legum ed., 2005).

5. **Types of Transnational Arbitration.** There are three basic types of transnational arbitration, classified by the types of parties involved.

- **Transnational commercial arbitration** is the arbitration of disputes arising from transnational relationships of a commercial nature. There is no universally accepted definition of the term "commercial." Ordinarily, it is broadly defined. For example, a footnote to Article 1 of the U.N. Commission on International Trade Law (UNCITRAL) Model Law on International Commercial Arbitration emphasizes that "[t]he term 'commercial' should be given a wide interpretation so as to cover matters arising from all relationships of a commercial nature, whether contractual or not. Relationships of a commercial nature include, but are not limited to, the following transactions: any trade transaction for the supply or exchange of goods or services; distribution agreement; commercial representation or agency; factoring; leasing; construction of works; consulting; engineering; licensing; investment; financing; banking; insurance; exploitation agreement or concession; joint venture and other forms of industrial or business cooperation; carriage of goods or passengers by air, sea, rail or road." Ordinarily, the parties to transnational commercial relationships are businesses. However, businesses sometimes enter into commercial relationships with government entities, and when disputes arise out of those relationships, they are sometimes resolved through transnational commercial arbitration. Transnational commercial arbitration is the most common type of transnational arbitration. It is the focus of Section B below.
- **Investor-state arbitration** is the arbitration of disputes between an investor from one nation (a "foreign investor") and the government of another nation in which the investment is made (a "host nation"). Like other

BIT

types of arbitration, investor-state arbitration is consensual: Both the foreign investor and the host nation must give their consent. Usually the host nation's consent is found in a bilateral investment treaty (BIT) or similar agreement between that nation and the foreign investor's home nation. A typical BIT provides that each nation consents to arbitration of investment disputes with investors from the other nation. The foreign investor's consent ordinarily takes the form of an election to arbitrate the dispute. The international law of foreign investment is well beyond the scope of this chapter. However, you will understand investor-state arbitration more easily if you take note of one of the basic principles of foreign investor protection: the principle of fair and equitable treatment of foreign investors by the host nation. Many claims submitted by foreign investors to investor-state arbitration are claims that the host nation denied them fair and equitable treatment. Investor-state arbitration is an important and growing area of transnational practice. It is discussed in Section C below.

- **State-state arbitration** is the arbitration of disputes between two nations. It is sometimes referred to as "international arbitration." State-state arbitration is very briefly discussed in Section D below.

There also is a distinction between **institutional arbitration** and **ad hoc arbitration**. Institutional arbitration is administered by a preexisting arbitral institution. Institutional arbitration requires agreement by the parties to have arbitration administered by an arbitral institution and payment of a fee for the institution's services. The world's leading arbitral institutions include the American Arbitration Association's International Centre for Dispute Resolution (http://www.icdr.org/), the International Chamber of Commerce (http://www.iccwbo.org/products-and-services/arbitration-and-adr/arbitration/), and the London Court of International Arbitration (http://www.lcia.org/). Arbitral institutions have lists of arbitrators from which the parties can choose; they can administer and oversee the arbitration; and they have rules of arbitral procedure that the parties may elect to use.

In ad hoc arbitration, the parties make their own arrangements for administration of the arbitration instead of paying an arbitral institution for its services. Even with ad hoc arbitration, however, the parties need not create procedural rules from scratch. They may agree to have their arbitration governed by rules designed for ad hoc arbitration, such as the UNCITRAL Arbitration Rules (http://www.uncitral.org/uncitral/en/uncitral_texts/arbitration/2010Arbitration_ rules.html). Alternatively, the parties may agree to have their arbitration governed by the rules of an arbitral institution without having that institution administer the arbitration.

What do you see as the major advantages and disadvantages of institutional arbitration? What do you see as the major advantages and disadvantages of ad hoc arbitration?

6. **Comparing Arbitration Services.** Visit the websites of a few institutions that offer transnational arbitration services. Search for information about the International Centre for Dispute Resolution, the International Chamber of

Commerce, and the London Court of International Arbitration — but also try to find other ones. What services do these institutions offer, and what, according to them, is the value of their services? Are they materially different? Which one would you advise a client to use?

B. Transnational Commercial Arbitration

Just as parties can consent to various obligations through contract, parties can contractually select the substantive law that will govern their relationship and the court that will hear disputes arising between them (see Chapters 1 and 10). With arbitration, the parties can go further, and contractually specify the time, place, and procedures for dispute resolution, and select their own third-party decision makers. Today, arbitration is a widely used method for resolving transnational commercial, financial, and investment disputes. This section provides a closer look at arbitration as a method for transnational dispute resolution, with a focus on transnational commercial arbitration. Specifically, it discusses arbitration agreements, including factors to consider when deciding whether to agree to arbitration, and it introduces you to some of the more common legal issues surrounding transnational arbitration, including the enforcement of arbitration agreements.

1. Why Choose Arbitration?

Let's begin with a hypothetical. Imagine that you are a lawyer practicing in New York and your client, a New York corporation, enters into a contract with a Chinese corporation to import nuts and bolts for industrial manufacturing. You are about to begin negotiating the part of the contract that governs how disputes between the parties will be resolved. First, you consider litigation as a dispute resolution method. But litigation in which nation's courts? The "home forum" — in this case, a New York court — won't always be the best strategic choice for your client, but several factors will often point toward that choice. First, New York will presumably be the most convenient place for you and your client to litigate. Second, you are probably most familiar with the judges, procedures, and legal culture of your home jurisdiction. Third, you might think that your client will get a fairer hearing — or maybe even a distinct advantage — in your client's home court compared to another nation's court. But a similar set of considerations may lead the lawyers representing the Chinese corporation to conclude that a Chinese court would be their client's best choice. In addition to the convenience of litigating at home, the Chinese lawyers are presumably more familiar with the Chinese legal system than the U.S. legal system, and they may believe their client would be more favored by Chinese judges than a U.S. judge or jury. So even if the parties can agree on litigation, they may be unable to agree on which nation's courts to litigate in. Of course, the parties could agree on a disinterested forum — say

England or Japan. But, if suit is filed in one of those places, you would have to face an unfamiliar legal system (as well as travel), and you may find it even more difficult to assess the probability of outcomes. Furthermore, even if the English or Japanese court enters a judgment in your client's favor, there is no assurance that you would be able to enforce the judgment in either China or the United States.

Enter transnational commercial arbitration. Rather than opt for litigation, the companies could agree that an arbitrator (or more likely three arbitrators, with one chosen by one party, another chosen by the other party, and the third arbitrator selected by the two party-selected arbitrators) will hear the dispute in a mutually agreeable location, say Singapore or Washington, D.C. If the dispute is a technical one, the parties could choose arbitrators with the relevant technical expertise. This is a real benefit considering that you cannot choose the judge you will get in a court system (and you have no advance notice of her expertise) even if you choose a particular forum to hear the dispute. The parties can also contract as to what law the arbitrators will apply, including Chinese or New York or some other substantive law, or even nonstate norms such as religious law or trade customs (sometimes called *lex mercatoria*). The parties can also specify the procedures that will be employed. For instance, there could be limited discovery. This might mean a substantial cost savings for the parties (although it would also limit the parties' ability to obtain relevant information from each other). They could also select the way the arbitration will be conducted in terms of witnesses and testimony. In so doing, the process could be less formal and more flexible than litigation generally. The parties could also agree to keep the proceedings confidential. As legal proceedings are generally public proceedings, the confidentiality available in arbitration might be very desirable if information presented in the proceedings is likely to be damaging to the reputation or business of either or both of the parties. Confidential arbitration might also help a party keep business or trade secrets from open view. Arbitration can also facilitate the resolution of all of the parties' disputes in one forum, as opposed to the potential for parallel proceedings in multiple countries. Finally, depending on the circumstances, arbitration may be faster and cheaper than litigation.

Flexibility is often an important advantage of transnational commercial arbitration over litigation in transnational cases. But perhaps the greatest advantage is that, thanks to the New York Convention, arbitral awards are generally final and enforceable in most nations subject to limited defenses. As you will learn later in Chapter 8, which is devoted to enforcing arbitral awards, enforcement considerations strongly favor arbitration over litigation in many transnational cases.

Remember that as a consensual dispute resolution method, arbitration depends on the consent of both parties. Unless there is an agreement to arbitrate, there can be no arbitration. There are two main problems surrounding agreements to arbitrate. First, *when* should a party agree to arbitrate — that is, when is arbitration the most appropriate dispute resolution method, one that is preferable to litigation? Second, once you conclude that arbitration is the preferred dispute resolution method, *how* do you agree to arbitrate?

Let's start with the first problem. It is sometimes said that arbitration is *the* preferred method of transnational dispute resolution. But it is important not to generalize. As discussed above, arbitration has both advantages and disadvantages, and in practice deciding whether to arbitrate is a very case-specific decision that depends on the consideration of various factors.

Two expert transnational practitioners suggest the following:

Considerations in Favour of Choosing . . . Arbitration

The following factors should influence a decision to choose . . . arbitration over the courts, provided that the courts being considered are available to the parties and have a reputation for fairness (independence), efficiency and competence. If the available courts do not have a reputation for fairness, efficiency or competence or, worse, if they are known to be corrupt, then we would not recommend that they be considered as a viable option. An affirmative answer to any of the following questions suggests that international arbitration should at least be considered as the method of dispute resolution for the contract in question.

    . . .

- *Neutrality*: Does a party wish to avoid the home courts of the other?
- *Enforcement*: Is it likely there will be a need to enforce a right of payment against assets of a party located outside the country where the court decision would be rendered?
- *Efficiency*: Is the time from the start of the litigation to obtaining an enforceable judgment in the available court likely to be excessive when compared with . . . arbitration?
- *Cost*: Will the cost of litigating in the courts significantly exceed the cost of . . . arbitration?
- *Flexibility*: Is it important for the parties to be able to design their own bespoke dispute resolution process for this contract?
- *Competence*: Is it likely that complex or technical issues will be involved that may challenge the capabilities of the court?
- *Convenience*: Is the dispute likely to require witnesses and documents located in different countries and involve languages that are not the same as that or those of the available court?
- *Confidentiality*: Is it important for the parties to keep their disputes out of the public eye?
- *Moderation*: Is it desirable to avoid the risk of potentially extreme or unusual decisions by a court?

    . . .

Considerations in Favour of Choosing Court Litigation

The following considerations could lead a party to prefer litigation in an available court. Once again, however, the underlying premise is that the court has a reputation for fairness, efficiency and competence. An affirmative answer to any of the following questions would suggest that the parties should at least consider dispute resolution in the available court.

    . . .

- *Appeals*: Is it desirable to preserve the right of appeal of an adverse decision?
- *Multiple parties*: Is it desirable to preserve the right to join third parties in the litigation?
- *Cost*: Is litigating in court cheaper than . . . arbitration?

- *Speed:* Is the time taken until receiving an enforceable judgment reasonable compared to . . . arbitration?
- *Clear resolution:* Is it desirable to obtain a determination of a contractual provision that is a clear-cut victory for one side rather than a middle ground?
- *Settlement promotion:* Does the party favour or desire the inclination of courts to nudge parties towards settlement, often by providing an early indication of the likely outcome, before all the evidence is in?

MICHAEL MCILWRATH & JOHN SAVAGE, INTERNATIONAL ARBITRATION AND MEDIATION: A PRACTICAL GUIDE 97-101 (2010).

Another factor to consider is whether one of the parties to a contract is a foreign government. As discussed in Chapter 11, foreign sovereign immunity and related doctrines can bar litigation against a nation in another nation's courts, and many nations limit their exposure to suits in their own courts. To circumvent this barrier to suit, a private party from one nation entering a contract with a foreign nation could seek the foreign nation's consent to litigation in the private party's courts. The foreign nation may be reluctant to consent to litigation in another nation's courts and the private party may be reluctant to consent to litigation in the foreign nation's courts, but to avoid this choice the parties may agree to arbitrate disputes arising out of the contract. Moreover, as discussed in Chapter 11, if a foreign nation makes a valid agreement to arbitrate, exceptions to immunity may allow judicial enforcement of that agreement and a resulting arbitral award against the foreign nation. For these reasons, arbitration is often perceived as advantageous in transnational contracts between private parties and governments.

If you conclude that arbitration is the most appropriate dispute resolution method, the next problem is *how* to agree to arbitrate. There are two basic types of agreements to arbitrate: ex ante or "pre-dispute" arbitration agreements and ex post or "post-dispute" arbitration agreements. In transnational commercial arbitration, pre-dispute arbitration agreements typically take the form of arbitration clauses in contracts. As discussed in more detail below, in investor-state arbitration, the basis for arbitration is typically a bilateral investment treaty between the investor's nation and the nation in which the investment is made. And in the case of state-state arbitration, the basis for arbitration is typically found in a treaty provision (akin to a compromissory clause submitting treaty disputes to the International Court of Justice (ICJ)). Post-dispute arbitration agreements, as the name indicates, are agreements to arbitrate a dispute that are entered by the disputants *after* the dispute arises. Post-dispute arbitration agreements are less common than pre-dispute arbitration agreements. But they are possible, and in some cases may be sensible for both of the disputants based on factors such as those listed above. For example, two states may agree to state-state arbitration pursuant to a special post-dispute agreement (akin to a compromis between states submitting a dispute to the ICJ).

NOTES AND QUESTIONS

1. **Pre-Dispute Arbitration Clauses.** Imagine that in your first job after law school, your supervising attorney asks you to draft an arbitration clause for a client's contract. What should be included in the arbitration clause? As a new lawyer, where would you look for ideas about how to draft an arbitration clause? Consider the model arbitration clauses suggested by the International Centre for Dispute Resolution (ICDR) (https://www.adr.org/sites/default/files/document_repository/Drafting%20Dispute%20Resolution%20Clauses%20A%20Practical%20Guide.pdf) and the International Chamber of Commerce (ICC) (http://www.iccwbo.org/products-and-services/arbitration-and-adr/arbitration/standard-icc-arbitration-clauses/). How would an arbitration clause differ if you selected ad hoc rather than institutional arbitration?

2. **Post-Dispute Arbitration Clauses.** Parties sometimes agree to arbitrate disputes after they arise. However, this is not common. Why do you think this is the case?

3. **Initiating Arbitration.** Assuming that there is an arbitration agreement, what steps do you need to take to initiate arbitration? The answer depends on the rules contained in or specified by the arbitration agreement. Look at the ICC rules (http://www.iccwbo.org/products-and-services/arbitration-and-adr/arbitration/icc-rules-of-arbitration/). What needs to be done? Is it complicated?

2. Enforcing Arbitration Agreements

Let's return again to our hypothetical New York corporation. Assume that it has paid and placed an order for some number of nuts and bolts with the Chinese corporation. For whatever reason, the Chinese corporation keeps the payment but does not ship the goods. After attempting to resolve the dispute amicably, the New York corporation decides to invoke the arbitration agreement in the contract. Hopefully, the New York corporation hired good lawyers who drafted a sound arbitration clause that precisely identified whether this would be an institutional or ad hoc arbitration.

Let's take a look at procedure. Your first step as the lawyer for the New York corporation would be to file a request for arbitration. This is similar to a complaint filed in court that you should be familiar with from civil procedure. At this point, the Chinese corporation has several options. First, it can answer the request and submit to the arbitration. In so doing, it can also file its own claims against the New York corporation and have those claims resolved as part of the arbitration. Second, it can refuse to participate in the arbitration. This is a perilous path, as it might lead to an ex parte award (similar to a default judgment), and might foreclose options for challenging the arbitral award in enforcement proceedings (discussed in detail in Chapter 8). Third, it can challenge jurisdiction before the arbitral tribunal. We will discuss shortly the ability of arbitrators to determine their jurisdiction. Fourth, it can go to a national court and seek a declaration that the arbitration clause is invalid or unenforceable and request an injunction restraining the arbitral tribunal from proceeding. Most of the cases that follow will be concerned with the latter strategy. Relatedly, it could take the offensive by filing suit against the other party and seeking a stay of the arbitration proceedings. As you can see, there are many opportunities for overlap and interplay between national courts and arbitral tribunals.

If your client is a party to a contract with an arbitration clause, and a dispute arises out of the contract, what can you do if the other party files a lawsuit in a court instead of initiating arbitration? As a first step toward understanding your options, it is important to understand the legal framework for the enforcement of arbitration agreements. The applicable rules are a combination of international law and national law. The principal international legal instrument is the Convention on the Recognition and Enforcement of Foreign Arbitral Awards, commonly known as the New York Convention. In the United States, the Federal Arbitration Act (FAA) is the principal source of domestic arbitral law, and in many countries (and in several U.S. states) legislation based on the UNCITRAL Model Law on International Commercial Arbitration (the "UNCITRAL Model Law") provides another important source of domestic law governing the enforcement of arbitration agreements. As you review these materials, identify the methods available to enforce arbitration agreements and identify potential arguments for and against enforcement of arbitration agreements. Note: In 2019, the American Law Institute approved the *Restatement of the Law, The U.S. Law of International Commercial and Investor-State Arbitration*. Chapter 2 of this new *Restatement* focuses on enforcement of arbitration agreements, and clarifies the relationship between the applicable rules of national law and international law that govern arbitration agreements.

Convention on the Recognition and Enforcement of Foreign Arbitral Awards (The "New York Convention")

330 U.N.T.S. 38 (June 10, 1958)

Article I

1. This Convention shall apply to the recognition and enforcement of arbitral awards made in the territory of a State other than the State where the recognition and enforcement of such awards are sought, and arising out of differences between persons, whether physical or legal. It shall also apply to arbitral awards not considered as domestic awards in the State where their recognition and enforcement are sought.

. . .

Article II

1. Each Contracting State shall recognize an agreement in writing under which the parties undertake to submit to arbitration all or any differences which have arisen or which may arise between them in respect of a defined legal relationship, whether contractual or not, concerning a subject matter capable of settlement by arbitration.

2. The term "agreement in writing" shall include an arbitral clause in a contract or an arbitration agreement, signed by the parties or contained in an exchange of letters or telegrams.

3. The court of a Contracting State, when seized of an action in a matter in respect of which the parties have made an agreement within the meaning of this article, shall, at the request of one of the parties, refer the parties to arbitration, unless it finds that the said agreement is null and void, inoperative or incapable of being performed.

Federal Arbitration Act

Title 9, United States Code

Chapter 1. General Provisions
§ 1 — "Maritime transactions" and "commerce" defined; exceptions to operation of title

"Maritime transactions", as herein defined, means charter parties, bills of lading of water carriers, agreements relating to wharfage, supplies furnished vessels or repairs to vessels, collisions, or any other matters in foreign commerce which, if the subject of controversy, would be embraced within admiralty jurisdiction; "commerce", as herein defined, means commerce among the several States or with foreign nations, or in any Territory of the United States or in the District of Columbia, or between any such Territory and another, or between any such Territory and any State or foreign nation, or between the District of Columbia and any State or Territory or foreign nation, but nothing herein contained shall apply to contracts of employment of seamen, railroad employees, or any other class of workers engaged in foreign or interstate commerce.

§ 2 — Validity, irrevocability, and enforcement of agreements to arbitrate

A written provision in any maritime transaction or a contract evidencing a transaction involving commerce to settle by arbitration a controversy thereafter arising out of such contract or transaction, or the refusal to perform the whole or any part thereof, or an agreement in writing to submit to arbitration an existing controversy arising out of such a contract, transaction, or refusal, shall be valid, irrevocable, and enforceable, save upon such grounds as exist at law or in equity for the revocation of any contract.

. . .

§ 4 — Failure to arbitrate under agreement; petition to United States court having jurisdiction for order to compel arbitration; notice and service thereof; hearing and determination

A party aggrieved by the alleged failure, neglect, or refusal of another to arbitrate under a written agreement for arbitration may petition any United States district court which, save for such agreement, would have jurisdiction under title 28, in a civil action or in admiralty of the subject matter of a suit arising out of the controversy between the parties, for an order directing that such arbitration proceed in the manner provided for in such agreement. Five days' notice in writing of such application shall be served upon the party in default. Service thereof shall be made in the manner provided by the Federal Rules of Civil Procedure. The court shall hear the parties, and upon being satisfied that the making of the agreement for arbitration or the failure to comply therewith is not in issue, the court shall make an order directing the parties to proceed to arbitration in accordance with the terms of the agreement. The hearing and proceedings, under such agreement, shall be within the district in which the petition for an order directing such arbitration is filed. If the making of the arbitration agreement or the failure, neglect, or refusal to perform the same be in issue, the court shall proceed summarily to the trial thereof. If no jury trial be demanded by the party alleged to be in default, or if the matter in dispute is within admiralty jurisdiction, the court shall hear and determine such issue. Where such an issue is raised, the party alleged to be in default may, except in cases of admiralty, on or before the return day of the notice of application, demand a jury trial of such issue, and upon such demand the court shall make an order referring the issue or issues to a jury in the manner provided by the Federal Rules of Civil Procedure, or may specially call a jury for that purpose. If the jury finds that no agreement in writing for arbitration was made or that there is no default in proceeding thereunder, the proceeding shall be dismissed. If the jury finds that an agreement for arbitration was made in writing and that there is a default in proceeding thereunder, the court shall make an order summarily directing the parties to proceed with the arbitration in accordance with the terms thereof.

. . .

Chapter 2. Convention on the Recognition and Enforcement of Foreign Arbitral Awards

§ 201 — Enforcement of Convention

The Convention on the Recognition and Enforcement of Foreign Arbitral Awards of June 10, 1958, shall be enforced in United States courts in accordance with this chapter.

§ 202 — Agreement or award falling under the Convention

An arbitration agreement or arbitral award arising out of a legal relationship, whether contractual or not, which is considered as commercial, including a transaction, contract, or agreement described in section 2 of this title, falls under the Convention. An agreement or award arising out of such a relationship which is entirely between citizens of the United States shall be deemed not to fall under the Convention unless that relationship involves property located abroad, envisages performance or enforcement abroad, or has some other reasonable relation with one or more foreign states. For the purpose of this section a corporation is a citizen of the United States if it is incorporated or has its principal place of business in the United States.

§ 203 — *Jurisdiction; amount in controversy*

An action or proceeding falling under the Convention shall be deemed to arise under the laws and treaties of the United States. The district courts of the United States (including the courts enumerated in section 460 of title 28) shall have original jurisdiction over such an action or proceeding, regardless of the amount in controversy.

§ 204 — *Venue*

An action or proceeding over which the district courts have jurisdiction pursuant to section 203 of this title may be brought in any such court in which save for the arbitration agreement an action or proceeding with respect to the controversy between the parties could be brought, or in such court for the district and division which embraces the place designated in the agreement as the place of arbitration if such place is within the United States.

§ 205 — *Removal of cases from State courts*

Where the subject matter of an action or proceeding pending in a State court relates to an arbitration agreement or award falling under the Convention, the defendant or the defendants may, at any time before the trial thereof, remove such action or proceeding to the district court of the United States for the district and division embracing the place where the action or proceeding is pending. The procedure for removal of causes otherwise provided by law shall apply, except that the ground for removal provided in this section need not appear on the face of the complaint but may be shown in the petition for removal. For the purposes of Chapter 1 of this title any action or proceeding removed under this section shall be deemed to have been brought in the district court to which it is removed.

§ 206 — *Order to compel arbitration; appointment of arbitrators*

A court having jurisdiction under this chapter may direct that arbitration be held in accordance with the agreement at any place therein provided for, whether that place is within or without the United States. Such court may also appoint arbitrators in accordance with the provisions of the agreement.

§ 208 — *Chapter 1; residual application*

Chapter 1 applies to actions and proceedings brought under this chapter to the extent that chapter is not in conflict with this chapter or the Convention as ratified by the United States.

UNCITRAL Model Law on International Commercial Arbitration

CHAPTER I. GENERAL PROVISIONS
Article 1. Scope of application

(1) This Law applies to international commercial[2] arbitration, subject to any agreement in force between this State and any other State or States.

(2) The provisions of this Law, except articles 8, 9, 17 H, 17 I, 17 J, 35 and 36, apply only if the place of arbitration is in the territory of this State.

(3) An arbitration is international if:

(a) the parties to an arbitration agreement have, at the time of the conclusion of that agreement, their places of business in different States; or

(b) one of the following places is situated outside the State in which the parties have their places of business:

(i) the place of arbitration if determined in, or pursuant to, the arbitration agreement;

(ii) any place where a substantial part of the obligations of the commercial relationship is to be performed or the place with which the subject-matter of the dispute is most closely connected; or

(c) the parties have expressly agreed that the subject matter of the arbitration agreement relates to more than one country.

(4) For the purposes of paragraph (3) of this article:

(a) if a party has more than one place of business, the place of business is that which has the closest relationship to the arbitration agreement;

(b) if a party does not have a place of business, reference is to be made to his habitual residence.

. . .

CHAPTER II. ARBITRATION AGREEMENT
Option I

Article 7. Definition and form of arbitration agreement

(1) "Arbitration agreement" is an agreement by the parties to submit to arbitration all or certain disputes which have arisen or which may arise between them in respect of a defined legal relationship, whether contractual or not. An arbitration agreement may be in the form of an arbitration clause in a contract or in the form of a separate agreement.

(2) The arbitration agreement shall be in writing.

(3) An arbitration agreement is in writing if its content is recorded in any form, whether or not the arbitration agreement or contract has been concluded orally, by conduct, or by other means.

---

2. The term "commercial" should be given a wide interpretation so as to cover matters arising from all relationships of a commercial nature, whether contractual or not. Relationships of a commercial nature include, but are not limited to, the following transactions: any trade transaction for the supply or exchange of goods or services; distribution agreement; commercial representation or agency; factoring; leasing; construction of works; consulting; engineering; licensing; investment; financing; banking; insurance; exploitation agreement or concession; joint venture and other forms of industrial or business cooperation; carriage of goods or passengers by air, sea, rail or road.

(4) The requirement that an arbitration agreement be in writing is met by an electronic communication if the information contained therein is accessible so as to be useable for subsequent reference; "electronic communication" means any communication that the parties make by means of data messages; "data message" means information generated, sent, received or stored by electronic, magnetic, optical or similar means, including, but not limited to, electronic data interchange (EDI), electronic mail, telegram, telex or telecopy.

(5) Furthermore, an arbitration agreement is in writing if it is contained in an exchange of statements of claim and defence in which the existence of an agreement is alleged by one party and not denied by the other.

(6) The reference in a contract to any document containing an arbitration clause constitutes an arbitration agreement in writing, provided that the reference is such as to make that clause part of the contract.

Option II

Article 7. Definition of arbitration agreement

"Arbitration agreement" is an agreement by the parties to submit to arbitration all or certain disputes which have arisen or which may arise between them in respect of a defined legal relationship, whether contractual or not.

Article 8. Arbitration agreement and substantive claim before court

(1) A court before which an action is brought in a matter which is the subject of an arbitration agreement shall, if a party so requests not later than when submitting his first statement on the substance of the dispute, refer the parties to arbitration unless it finds that the agreement is null and void, inoperative or incapable of being performed.

(2) Where an action referred to in paragraph (1) of this article has been brought, arbitral proceedings may nevertheless be commenced or continued, and an award may be made, while the issue is pending before the court.

. . .

The following case illustrates how courts resolve issues involving the enforcement of arbitration agreements under the FAA and the New York Convention. Pay close attention to how the court deals with the question of whether there is a valid and enforceable arbitration agreement.

Prokopeva v. Carnival Corp.
2008 WL 4276975 (S.D. Tex. 2008)

ORDER COMPELLING ARBITRATION

JANIS GRAHAM JACK, District Judge.

On this day came on to be considered the motion of Defendant Carnival Corporation d/b/a Carnival Cruise Lines (hereinafter, "Carnival") to compel arbitration of the above-styled action, and to stay the action pending conclusion of the arbitration proceedings. For the reasons set forth below, the Court hereby GRANTS Carnival's motion to compel. The Court ORDERS that the above-styled action be submitted to arbitration in accordance with Paragraph No. 7 of the "Seafarer's Agreement" signed by Plaintiff and Carnival Cruise Lines, and that this case be stayed pending the outcome of that arbitration.

I. *Jurisdiction*

The Court has jurisdiction over this action pursuant to 9 U.S.C. § 203, which states that "[a]n action or proceeding falling under the [New York] Convention shall be deemed to arise under the laws and treaties of the United States. The district courts of the United States . . . shall have original jurisdiction over such an action or proceeding, regardless of the amount in controversy." As set forth below, this action falls under the Convention and the corresponding enabling legislation, the "Convention Act," 9 U.S.C. §§ 201-208, and therefore the Court has jurisdiction under 9 U.S.C. § 203.

II. *Background*

Plaintiff Yana Prokopeva, a citizen of Russia, was a "seafarer" working as an Assistant Stateroom Stewardess aboard the M/V Conquest, a Carnival vessel. Plaintiff claims that in July, 2007, sometime after the Conquest had "embarked on its journey from Galveston, Texas," Plaintiff was injured and "suffered severely painful and disabling injuries to her back and body generally." Plaintiff alleges that these injuries have "render[ed] her incapacitated from work" and "result[ed] in permanent physical impairment." Plaintiff claims that she was injured "in the course and scope of her employment for Defendants." Plaintiff claims that she suffered her various injuries through the "negligence of the Defendants, their agents, servants, employees, or representatives, and/or the unseaworthiness of the vessel."

Plaintiff filed her Complaint against Defendants Carnival Corp., d/b/a Carnival Cruise Lines, Inc. and the Cruise Ship Conquest (together, "Defendants") on July 1, 2008. Plaintiff brings the following claims against the Defendants: (1) a negligence claim under the "Jones Act," 46 U.S.C. § 30104; (2) a claim for "maintenance and cure"; and (3) a claim that the Conquest was "unseaworthy" because of a lack of sufficient and appropriate personnel, defective operational policies and procedures, and improper equipment. Plaintiff seeks "maintenance and cure" damages, actual/compensatory damages, costs, expenses, pre- and post-judgment interest, and attorney's fees.

Defendant Carnival filed its answer to Plaintiff's Original Complaint on July 27, 2008. In its Answer, Carnival raises defenses pursuant to Federal Rules of Civil Procedure 12(b)(3) and 12(b)(6), and claims that "[t]his action is governed by mandatory arbitration and should be dismissed."

On August 22, 2008, Defendant Carnival filed an opposed motion to compel arbitration of Plaintiff's claims, pursuant to an arbitration clause in the "Seafarer's Agreement" employment contract signed by Carnival and Plaintiff. . . .

III. Discussion

A. Seafarer's Agreement

Plaintiff and Carnival Cruise Lines entered into a "Seafarer's Agreement," which was in effect at all times relevant to this litigation. Per the Seafarer's Agreement, Plaintiff was to work as a "Hotel Stewardess" for Carnival, on Crew No. 406454. The Seafarer's Agreement became effective upon Plaintiff reporting to work on her assigned vessel, and per the Agreement, the employment relations between Plaintiff and Carnival were "governed by the terms of [the] Agreement."

The Seafarer's Agreement contains the following Paragraph [Paragraph 7] re: arbitration:

> *Arbitration.* **Except for a wage dispute governed by CCL's [Carnival Cruise Lines'] Wage Grievance Policy and Procedure, any and all disputes arising out of or in connection with this Agreement, including any question regarding its existence, validity, or termination, or Seafarer's service on the vessel, shall be referred to and finally resolved by arbitration under the American Arbitration Association/International Centre for Dispute Resolution International Rules, which Rules are deemed to be incorporated by reference into this clause.** The number of arbitrators shall be one. The place of arbitration shall be London, England, Monaco, Panama City, Panama or Manila, Philippines, whichever is closer to Seafarer's home country. The Seafarer and CGL must arbitrate in the designated jurisdiction, to the exclusion of all other jurisdictions. The language of the arbitral proceedings shall be English. Each party shall bear its own attorney's fees, but CCL [Carnival Cruise Lines] shall pay for the costs of arbitration as assessed by the AAA. Seafarer agrees to appear for medical examinations by doctors designated by CCL [Carnival Cruise Lines] in specialties relevant to any claims Seafarer asserts, and otherwise the parties agree to waive any and all rights to compel information from each other. (emphasis in original).

The Seafarer's Agreement also states as follows in Paragraph No. 6: "*Commercial Legal Relationship.* Seafarer and Cruise Line acknowledge and agree that Seafarer's employment with CCL [Carnival Cruise Lines] constitutes a commercial legal relationship between the parties." (emphasis in original). [Paragraph 8 of the Seafarer's Agreement is a choice-of-law clause providing that "[t]his Agreement shall be governed by, and all disputes arising under or in connection with this Agreement or Seafarer's service on the vessel shall be resolved in accordance with, the laws of the flag of the vessel on which Seafarer is assigned at the time the cause of action accrues, without regard to principles of conflicts of laws thereunder."]

Finally, the Seafarer's Agreement provides that "[i]n consideration for the offer of employment made herein, Seafarer accepts each and every term and condition of this Agreement, ***including but not limited to . . . the arbitration/choice of law provisions in paragraphs 7 and 8.*** Seafarer acknowledges that CCL [Carnival Cruise Lines] would not have entered into this Seafarer's Agreement or otherwise employed Seafarer if Seafarer had not agreed to all such terms and conditions."

(emphasis added). Plaintiff Yana Prokopeva signed the Seafarer's Agreement, as did a representative of Carnival Cruise Lines.

B. *Convention on the Recognition and Enforcement of Foreign Arbitral Awards*

1. *The Convention/Convention Act*

In 1970, Congress enacted the enabling legislation for the Convention on the Recognition and Enforcement of Foreign Arbitral Awards [the New York Convention], 9 U.S.C. §§ 201-208. (The enabling legislation is generally referred to as the "Convention Act", 9 U.S.C. §§ 201-208). *See Scherk v. Alberto-Culver Co.*, 417 U.S. 506, 520 n. 15 (1974) ("On June 10, 1958, a special conference of the United Nations Economic and Social Council adopted the Convention on the Recognition and Enforcement of Foreign Arbitral Awards. In 1970 the United States acceded to the treaty, (1970) 3 U.S.T. 2517, T.I.A.S. No. 6997, and Congress passed Chapter 2 of the United States Arbitration Act, 9 U.S.C. § 201 *et seq.*, in order to implement the Convention."). "The goal of the Convention, and the principal purpose underlying American adoption and implementation of it, was to encourage the recognition and enforcement of commercial arbitration agreements in international contracts and to unify the standards by which agreements to arbitrate are observed and arbitral awards are enforced in the signatory countries." *Id.*

Section 201 of the Convention Act, 9 U.S.C. § 201, states that "[t]he Convention on the Recognition and Enforcement of Foreign Arbitral Awards of June 10, 1958, shall be enforced in United States courts in accordance with this chapter." Section 206 of the Convention Act, 9 U.S.C. § 206, states that "[a] court having jurisdiction under [the Convention] *may direct that arbitration be held in accordance with the agreement at any place therein provided for, whether that place is within or without the United States.* Such court may also appoint arbitrators in accordance with the provisions of the agreement." 9 U.S.C. § 206 (emphasis added). Section 207 of the Convention Act provides that "[w]ithin three years after an arbitral award falling under the Convention is made, any party to the arbitration may apply to any court having jurisdiction under this chapter for an order confirming the award as against any other party to the arbitration. The court shall confirm the award unless it finds one of the grounds for refusal or deferral of recognition or enforcement of the award specified in the said Convention."

2. *Requirements for Application of the Convention*

"If an international arbitration clause falls under the Convention Act, the Convention requires district courts to order arbitration." *Lim v. Offshore Specialty Fabricators, Inc.*, 404 F.3d 898, 903 (5th Cir. 2005); *see also* 9 U.S.C. § 201 ("The Convention . . . shall be enforced in United States courts. . . ."). "In determining whether the Convention requires compelling arbitration in a given case, courts conduct only a very limited inquiry." *Freudensprung v. Offshore Tech. Servs., Inc.*, 379 F.3d 327, 339 (5th Cir. 2004). . . . Per that limited inquiry, "[t]he Convention applies to international arbitration clauses when" the following four criteria are met:

(1) there is an agreement in writing to arbitrate the dispute;
(2) the written agreement provides for arbitration in the territory of a Convention signatory;
(3) the agreement arises out of a commercial legal relationship; and
(4) a party to the agreement is not an American citizen.

Lim, 404 F.3d at 903; "If these [four] requirements are met, the Convention requires district courts to order arbitration." Francisco v. Stolt Achievement MT, 293 F.3d 270, 273 (5th Cir. 2002) (emphasis added).

C. Application of Convention to Seamen's Employment Contracts

The Fifth Circuit has specifically held that "the Convention applies to seamen's contracts" Lim, 404 F.3d at 898. In Francisco, the Fifth Circuit affirmed the district court's order compelling arbitration in a case where "[plaintiff] Francisco, a Philippine national, signed a written employment contract stating that claims and disputes arising from his employment, including personal injury claims, were subject to arbitration in the Philippines." Francisco, 293 F.3d at 274. The plaintiff in the case argued that the Convention should not apply to seamen contracts of employment, because such contracts are specifically excluded from coverage under the Federal Arbitration Act. The Fifth Circuit considered and rejected all of the plaintiff's arguments against application of the Convention. . . .

D. The Court Must Grant Carnival's Motion to Compel Arbitration

In this case, as set forth above, the Court is to conduct a "limited inquiry" into whether to compel arbitration of Plaintiff's claims, in accordance with Paragraph No. 7 of the Seafarer's Agreement. Freudensprung, 397 F.3d at 339. That limited inquiry is to address whether the case satisfies the four criteria set forth above. . . . This case does satisfy the four criteria, and per the Convention and the Convention Act, the Court must compel the case to arbitration in accordance with the Seafarer's Agreement, in London, Monaco, Panama or the Philippines, whichever is closest to Plaintiff's home country.

4 criteria

1. Requirement No. 1: Written Agreement to Arbitrate

First, there is an "agreement in writing to arbitrate the dispute". Specifically, Plaintiff and Carnival entered into the Seafarer's Agreement, and Paragraph No. 7 of the Agreement specifically states that all disputes (except for wage disputes governed by Carnival's wage grievance policy) "arising out of or in connection with" the Seafarer's Agreement, including any dispute regarding the Seafarer's "service on the vessel," shall be resolved by arbitration. This dispute definitively arises out the Seafarer's Agreement, specifically with regard to Plaintiff's service on the vessel, as Plaintiff claims that she was hurt "[w]hile aboard the vessel and in the course and scope of her employment," after the vessel had "embarked on its journey from Galveston, Texas."

2. Requirement No. 2: [Agreement to Arbitrate in Territory of Convention Signatory]

The written Seafarer's Agreement in this case does provide for "arbitration in the territory of a Convention signatory". *Francisco*, 293 F.3d at 273. Specifically, the Seafarer's Agreement provides for arbitration in London, England, Monaco, Panama City, Panama, or Manila, Philippines, whichever location is closest to the Seafarer's home country. The United Kingdom, Monaco, Panama and the Philippines are all signatories to the Convention. . . .

3. Requirement No. 3: Agreement Must Arise out of a Commercial Legal Relationship

The Seafarer's Agreement in this case does arise out of a commercial legal relationship. First, the Fifth Circuit has specifically held that an employment agreement is a "commercial" agreement that would be covered by the Convention. *Francisco*, 293 F.3d at 274. Second, the Seafarer's Agreement itself states very clearly that the agreement arises out of a commercial legal relationship:

> *Commercial Legal Relationship.* Seafarer and Cruise Line acknowledge and agree that Seafarer's employment with CCL [Carnival Cruise Lines] constitutes a commercial legal relationship between the parties.

(Seafarer's Agreement, ¶ 6) (emphasis in original). . . .

4. Requirement No. 4: Non U.S. Citizen

The fourth and final requirement for Convention coverage is that a party to the agreement must not be an American citizen. As Plaintiff states in her Original Complaint, Plaintiff is a Russian citizen. . . .

5. The Court Compels Plaintiff's Case to Arbitration

As set forth above, the four criteria set forth by the Fifth Circuit have been satisfied, and *the Court must accordingly compel this case to arbitration*. The Court therefore GRANTS Carnival's motion to compel arbitration in accordance with Paragraph No. 7 of the Seafarer's Agreement between Plaintiff and Carnival. Per Paragraph no. 7 of the Seafarer's Agreement, the arbitration is to take place in London, England, Monaco, Panama City, Panama, or Manila, Philippines, whichever is closer to Plaintiff's home country. The arbitration is to take place under the rules of the American Arbitration Association/International Centre for Dispute Resolution, and comport in all other respects with Paragraph No. 7 of the Seafarer's Agreement between Plaintiff and Carnival. The Court hereby STAYS this case pending the outcome of the arbitration proceedings, and the parties are charged with the duty of providing the Court with timely notice of the conclusion of the arbitration.

IV. Conclusion

For the reasons set forth above, the Court hereby GRANTS Carnival's motion to compel arbitration, STAYS the above-styled action pending conclusion of the arbitration proceedings, and ORDERS the parties to provide the Court with timely notice of the conclusion of the arbitration.

1. **Arbitration Agreements.** Why do you think Carnival included an arbitration clause in its Seafarer's Agreement? Why do you think Prokopeva accepted this clause as part of the agreement? Why do you think Prokopeva filed a lawsuit instead of arbitrating the dispute?

2. **Compelling Arbitration.** Why did the district court compel arbitration? Why did it matter whether the relationship between the disputants in this case was commercial? Why did the court conclude that the relationship *was* commercial? What role did Paragraph 6 of the Seafarer's Agreement play in the court's analysis? What role *should* a provision in an agreement like Paragraph 6 play in a court's determination of whether a relationship is commercial? Recall the definition of "commercial" set forth above. What argument, if any, could you make in good faith on behalf of Prokopeva that the relationship was *not* commercial? You may wish to refer to the footnote to Article 1 of the UNCITRAL Model Law on International Commercial Arbitration referred to above to answer this question.

3. **Procedural Issues.** Take note of the procedural posture in this case. The plaintiff sued the defendant in a U.S. federal district court. The defendant then moved to compel arbitration. The question before the district court in resolving the motion was not a merits question but merely one of whether the case could be heard in the first instance in court or whether it must go before an arbitral tribunal. What would have happened if Carnival did not move to compel arbitration? What is the basis for the district court's subject matter jurisdiction over this case?

4. **From Doctrine to Practice.** Reread the arbitration clause in the Seafarer's Agreement, and consider the following notes and questions:

   - Does the arbitration clause call for ad hoc or institutional arbitration? How do you know? An important part of any arbitration clause is a clear agreement on whether the arbitration will be ad hoc or institutional and, if institutional, what the administering institution will be. If the arbitration will be ad hoc, the arbitration clause should include procedures for various matters typically addressed by the procedural rules of arbitral institutions, such as the procedures for initiating arbitration and selecting the arbitrators.

   - What procedural rules will govern the arbitration? Another important part of any arbitration clause is a clear indication of the procedural rules.

   - How many arbitrators will there be? What reasons might favor this choice? What reasons might favor a different number of arbitrators? A statement of the number of arbitrators is yet another important part of an arbitration clause.

   - Note that the agreement also identifies the place of arbitration, which is sometimes called the "arbitral seat." The arbitral seat can be a significant choice because, as discussed in Chapter 8, it is the jurisdiction that has the authority, in accordance with its law, to vacate or set aside an arbitral award.

- Why do you think that in addition to designating the place of arbitration, the arbitration clause also states that the parties "must arbitrate in the designated jurisdiction, to the exclusion of all other jurisdictions"?
- Why do you think the arbitration clause in the Seafarer's Agreement bars most opportunities for the parties to compel each other to produce information? Such limitations on discovery are not uncommon. What are the advantages of such limitations? What are the disadvantages? In the arbitration clause in the Seafarer's Agreement, what discovery *is* allowed? Why do you think the clause contains this exception to the limitation on discovery? Which party is most likely to benefit from this exception? If you were a lawyer representing a seafarer like Prokopeva, what exceptions to the limitation on discovery might you seek on her behalf? Do you think Carnival would have agreed to those further exceptions? Why or why not? In the real world, how often (if ever) would you expect a party in Prokopeva's situation to have a lawyer representing her when deciding whether to work on a cruise ship?
- Note that the arbitration clause in the Seafarer's Agreement also contains other important provisions that you should always consider when drafting an arbitration clause in transnational practice, such as (1) the designation of the language to be used in the arbitration, (2) the allocation of attorneys' fees (remember that lawyers ordinarily represent the parties in arbitration, just as they do in litigation), and (3) the payment for the arbitration itself (which includes both the fees of the administering arbitral institution, if there is one, and the fees of the arbitrator or arbitrators). All of these notes and questions highlight the importance of a basic practice pointer: Always focus on the precise terms of arbitration clauses when negotiating, drafting, and interpreting them, just as you should focus on the precise terms of any contract.

5. **Court Review of Arbitration Clauses.** According to the opinion in this case, how extensively should a district court review an arbitration agreement? What is the ultimate source of this conclusion? When might an agreement not be enforced? *See, e.g., Norcast, S.àr.l. v. Castle Harlan, Inc.,* 2014 WL 43492 (S.D.N.Y. 2014) (denying a motion to compel arbitration where Norcast did not sign the agreement); *Apple & Eve, LLC v. Yantai North Andre Juice Co., Ltd,* 610 F. Supp. 2d 226 (E.D.N.Y. 2009) (denying a motion to compel where the moving party had not arbitrated the action in China for over two years, and thus waived the right to arbitrate); *AGP Indus. SA (PERU) v. JPS Elastromerics Corp.,* 511 F. Supp. 2d 212 (D. Mass. 2007) (holding that preprinted arbitration clauses on the back of invoices were not agreements in writing and thus the motion to compel arbitration was denied). Can you imagine any hypothetical facts that would allow Prokopeva or someone in a similar position to resist enforcement of the agreement to arbitrate?

6. **The Severability Presumption.** In order to compel arbitration, there must be a valid arbitration agreement between the parties. Note that the existence, validity, or legality of the contract itself does not necessarily affect the arbitration agreement. The doctrine of severability provides that an arbitration agreement, even though included in an underlying contract, is an autonomous agreement. In other words, an arbitration agreement is a separate contract from the underlying contract. Put a different way, the arbitration clause is a contract within a contract. As such, defects in the formation of the contract subject to arbitration do not necessarily prevent the arbitration clause itself from being valid and enforceable. Why do you think this presumption exists?

7. **Commonly Raised Questions.** The following questions tend to arise with great frequency when courts are asked to compel arbitration.

    - Did the parties agree to arbitrate? This is sometimes described as a question of formation and validity.
    - If the parties did agree, what is the scope of the agreement? Are the issues in dispute covered by the agreement?
    - Can the agreement be enforced by or against nonsignatories? *See GE Energy Power Conversion France SAS v. Outokumpu Stainless USA LLC*, 140 S. Ct. 1637 (2020) (holding that doctrine of equitable estoppel may allow enforcement of arbitration agreement by nonsignatory).
    - Has the party seeking arbitration waived their right to arbitrate by, for instance, engaging in litigation as to the subject matter in dispute?
    - Might the issues subject to the arbitration agreement be nonarbitrable? The question of nonarbitrability will be discussed in the next section.

8. **Other Procedural Options.** Besides filing a motion to compel arbitration, U.S. courts may be asked to resolve other issues at an early stage in the arbitral proceedings. For instance, a party may file a motion to stay litigation. Such a motion is common when only some claims or parties in a contract are subject to arbitration. Another option is a motion for an anti-suit injunction, which enjoins a party from instituting or continuing proceedings in a foreign nation. A party might also file a motion for provisional measures, which asks a U.S. court to freeze assets, protect property, or order other forms of preliminary injunctive relief.

9. **Other Applicable Law.** The legal instruments presented above are not the only parts of the legal framework governing the enforcement of transnational arbitration agreements. For example, Article 1 of the Inter-American Convention on International Commercial Arbitration provides that "[a]n agreement in which the parties undertake to submit to arbitral decision any differences that may arise or have arisen between them with respect to a commercial transaction is valid." The Inter-American Convention has 19 parties, including the United States and most major Latin American countries. It is directly enforceable in U.S. courts (*see* 9 U.S.C. § 301), and U.S. courts are authorized to compel arbitration in accordance with an agreement covered by the Inter-American Convention (*see* 9 U.S.C. § 303). What happens if both the New York Convention and the

Inter-American Convention would apply to the same arbitral award? Section 305 of the FAA provides as follows: "When the requirements for application of both the Inter-American Convention and the [New York Convention] are met, determination as to which Convention applies shall, unless otherwise expressly agreed, be made as follows: (1) If a majority of the parties to the arbitration agreement are citizens of a State or States that have ratified or acceded to the Inter-American Convention and are member States of the Organization of American States, the Inter-American Convention shall apply. (2) In all other cases the [New York Convention] shall apply."

3. Arbitrability

Another important question is whether the type of dispute involved is arbitrable — that is, whether it is a type of dispute that may be resolved by arbitration or whether, as a matter of public policy, it must be litigated in a court. The following cases explore this question.

Scherk v. Alberto-Culver Co.

417 U.S. 506 (1974)

Mr. Justice STEWART delivered the opinion of the Court.

Alberto-Culver Co., the respondent, is an American company incorporated in Delaware with its principal office in Illinois. It manufactures and distributes toiletries and hair products in this country and abroad. During the 1960's Alberto-Culver decided to expand its overseas operations, and as part of this program it approached the petitioner Fritz Scherk, a German citizen residing at the time of trial in Switzerland. Scherk was the owner of three interrelated business entities, organized under the laws of Germany and Liechtenstein, that were engaged in the manufacture of toiletries and the licensing of trademarks for such toiletries. An initial contact with Scherk was made by a representative of Alberto-Culver in Germany in June 1967, and negotiations followed at further meetings in both Europe and the United States during 1967 and 1968. In February 1969 a contract was signed in Vienna, Austria, which provided for the transfer of the ownership of Scherk's enterprises to Alberto-Culver, along with all rights held by these enterprises to trademarks in cosmetic goods. The contract contained a number of express warranties whereby Scherk guaranteed the sole and unencumbered ownership of these trademarks. In addition, the contract contained an arbitration clause providing that "any controversy or claim (that) shall arise out of this agreement or the breach thereof" would be referred to arbitration before the International Chamber of Commerce in Paris, France, and that "(t)he laws of the State of Illinois, U.S.A. shall apply to and govern this agreement, its interpretation and performance."

The closing of the transaction took place in Geneva, Switzerland, in June 1969. Nearly one year later Alberto-Culver allegedly discovered that the trademark rights purchased under the contract were subject to substantial encumbrances that threatened to give others superior rights to the trademarks and to restrict or preclude Alberto-Culver's use of them. Alberto-Culver thereupon tendered back to Scherk the property that had been transferred to it and offered to rescind the contract. Upon Scherk's refusal, Alberto-Culver commenced this action for damages and other relief in a Federal District Court in Illinois, contending that Scherk's fraudulent representations concerning the status of the trademark rights constituted violations of § 10(b) of the Securities Exchange Act of 1934, and Rule 10b-5 promulgated thereunder. . . .

In response, Scherk filed a motion . . . to stay the action pending arbitration in Paris pursuant to the agreement of the parties. Alberto-Culver, in turn, opposed this motion and sought a preliminary injunction restraining the prosecution of arbitration proceedings. . . . [T]he District Court denied Scherk's motion . . . and . . . granted a preliminary order enjoining Scherk from proceeding with arbitration. In taking these actions the court relied entirely on this Court's decision in *Wilko v. Swan*, 346 U.S. 427, which held that an agreement to arbitrate could not preclude a buyer of a security from seeking a judicial remedy under the Securities Act of 1933, in view of the language of § 14 of that Act, barring "(a)ny condition, stipulation, or provision binding any person acquiring any security to waive compliance with any provision of this subchapter. . . ." The Court of Appeals for the Seventh Circuit, with one judge dissenting, affirmed, upon what it considered the controlling authority of the *Wilko* decision. Because of the importance of the question presented we granted Scherk's petition for a writ of certiorari.

I

The United States Arbitration Act, now 9 U.S.C. § 1 et seq., reversing centuries of judicial hostility to arbitration agreements, was designed to allow parties to avoid "the costliness and delays of litigation," and to place arbitration agreements "upon the same footing as other contracts. . . ." H.R. Rep. No. 96, 68th Cong., 1st Sess., 1, 2 (1924). Accordingly the Act provides that an arbitration agreement such as is here involved "shall be valid, irrevocable, and enforceable, save upon such grounds as exist at law or in equity for the revocation of any contract." 9 U.S.C. § 2. The Act also provides in § 3 for a stay of proceedings in a case where a court is satisfied that the issue before it is arbitrable under the agreement, and § 4 of the Act directs a federal court to order parties to proceed to arbitration if there has been a "failure, neglect, or refusal" of any party to honor an agreement to arbitrate.

In *Wilko v. Swan*, this Court acknowledged that the Act reflects a legislative recognition of the "desirability of arbitration as an alternative to the complications of litigation," 346 U.S., at 431, but nonetheless declined to apply the Act's provisions. That case involved an agreement between Anthony Wilko and Hayden, Stone & Co., a large brokerage firm, under which Wilko agreed to purchase on margin a number of shares of a corporation's common stock. Wilko alleged that his purchase of the stock was induced by false representations on the part of the defendant concerning the value of the shares, and he brought suit for damages under § 12(2) of the Securities Act of 1933. The defendant responded that Wilko had agreed to submit all controversies arising out of the purchase to arbitration, and that this agreement, contained in a written margin contract between the parties, should be given full effect under the Arbitration Act.

The Court found that "(t)wo policies, not easily reconcilable, are involved in this case." 346 U.S., at 438. On the one hand, the Arbitration Act stressed "the need for avoiding the delay and expense of litigation," *id.*, at 431, and directed that such agreements be "valid, irrevocable, and enforceable" in federal courts. On the other hand, the Securities Act of 1933 was "(d)esigned to protect investors" and to require "issuers, underwriters, and dealers to make full and fair disclosure of the character of securities sold in interstate and foreign commerce and to prevent fraud in their sale," by creating "a special right to recover for misrepresentation. . . ." 346 U.S., at 431. In particular, the Court noted that § 14 of the Securities Act, 15 U.S.C. § 77n, provides:

> "Any condition, stipulation, or provision binding any person acquiring any security to waive compliance with any provision of this subchapter or of the rules and regulations of the Commission shall be void."

The Court ruled that an agreement to arbitrate "is a 'stipulation,' and (that) the right to select the judicial forum is the kind of 'provision' that cannot be waived under § 14 of the Securities Act." 346 U.S., at 434-435. Thus, Wilko's advance agreement to arbitrate any disputes subsequently arising out of his contract to purchase the securities was unenforceable under the terms of § 14 of the Securities Act of 1933.

Alberto-Culver, relying on this precedent, contends that the District Court and Court of Appeals were correct in holding that its agreement to arbitrate disputes arising under the contract with Scherk is similarly unenforceable in view of its contentions that Scherk's conduct constituted violations of the Securities Exchange Act of 1934 and rules promulgated thereunder. For the reasons that follow, we reject this contention and hold that the provisions of the Arbitration Act cannot be ignored in this case.

. . .

Accepting the premise . . . that the operative portions of the language of the 1933 Act relied upon in *Wilko* are contained in the Securities Exchange Act of 1934, the respondent's reliance on *Wilko* in this case ignores the significant and, we find, crucial differences between the agreement involved in *Wilko* and the one signed by the parties here. Alberto-Culver's contract to purchase the business entities belonging to Scherk was a truly international agreement. Alberto-Culver is an American corporation with its principal place of business and the vast bulk of its activity in this country, while Scherk is a citizen of Germany whose companies were organized under the laws of Germany and Liechtenstein. The negotiations leading to the signing of the contract in Austria and to the closing in Switzerland took place in the United States, England, and Germany, and involved consultations with legal and trademark experts from each of those countries and from Liechtenstein. Finally, and most significantly, the subject matter of the contract concerned the sale of business enterprises organized under the laws of and primarily situated in European countries, whose activities were largely, if not entirely, directed to European markets.

Such a contract involves considerations and policies significantly different from those found controlling in *Wilko*. In *Wilko*, quite apart from the arbitration provision, there was no question but that the laws of the United States generally, and the federal securities laws in particular, would govern disputes arising out of the stock-purchase agreement. The parties, the negotiations, and the subject matter of the contract were all situated in this country, and no credible claim could have been entertained that any international conflict-of-laws problems would arise. In this case, by contrast, in the absence of the arbitration provision considerable uncertainty existed at the time of the agreement, and still exists, concerning the law applicable to the resolution of disputes arising out of the contract.

Such uncertainty will almost inevitably exist with respect to any contract touching two or more countries, each with its own substantive laws and conflict-of-laws rules. A contractual provision specifying in advance the forum in which disputes shall be litigated and the law to be applied is, therefore, an almost indispensable precondition to achievement of the orderliness and predictability essential to any international business transaction. Furthermore, such a provision obviates the danger that a dispute under the agreement might be submitted to a forum hostile to the interests of one of the parties or unfamiliar with the problem area involved.

A parochial refusal by the courts of one country to enforce an international arbitration agreement would not only frustrate these purposes, but would invite unseemly and mutually destructive jockeying by the parties to secure tactical litigation advantages. In the present case, for example, it is not inconceivable that if Scherk had anticipated that Alberto-Culver would be able in this country to enjoin resort to arbitration he might have sought an order in France or some other country enjoining Alberto-Culver from proceeding with its litigation in the United States. Whatever recognition the courts of this country might ultimately have granted to the order of the foreign court, the dicey atmosphere of such a legal no-man's-land would surely damage the fabric of international commerce and trade, and imperil the willingness and ability of businessmen to enter into international commercial agreements.

The exception to the clear provisions of the Arbitration Act carved out by *Wilko* is simply inapposite to a case such as the one before us. In *Wilko* the Court reasoned that "(w)hen the security buyer, prior to any violation of the Securities Act, waives his right to sue in courts, he gives up more than would a participant in other business transactions. The security buyer has a wider choice of courts and venue. He thus surrenders one of the advantages the Act gives him. . . ." 346 U.S., at 435. In the context of an international contract, however, these advantages become chimerical since, as indicated above, an opposing party may by speedy resort to a foreign court block or hinder access to the American court of the purchaser's choice.

Two Terms ago in *The Bremen v. Zapata Off-Shore Co.*, 407 U.S. 1, we rejected the doctrine that a forum-selection clause of a contract, although voluntarily adopted by the parties, will not be respected in a suit brought in the United States "unless the selected state would provide a more convenient forum than the state in which suit is brought." Rather, we concluded that a "forum clause should control absent a strong showing that it should be set aside." We noted that "much uncertainty and possibly great inconvenience to both parties could arise if a suit could be maintained in any jurisdiction in which an accident might occur or if jurisdiction were left to any place (where personal or in rem jurisdiction might be established). The elimination of all such uncertainties by agreeing in advance on a forum acceptable to both parties is an indispensable element in international trade, commerce, and contracting."

An agreement to arbitrate before a specified tribunal is, in effect, a specialized kind of forum-selection clause that posits not only the situs of suit but also the procedure to be used in resolving the dispute. The invalidation of such an agreement in the case before us would not only allow the respondent to repudiate its solemn promise but would, as well, reflect a "parochial concept that all disputes must be resolved under our laws and in our courts. . . . We cannot have trade and commerce in world markets and international waters exclusively on our terms, governed by our laws, and resolved in our courts." *Id.*, at 9.

For all these reasons we hold that the agreement of the parties in this case to arbitrate any dispute arising out of their international commercial transaction is to be respected and enforced by the federal courts in accord with the explicit provisions of the Arbitration Act.

Accordingly, the judgment of the Court of Appeals is reversed and the case is remanded to that court with directions to remand to the District Court for further proceedings consistent with this opinion.

It is so ordered.

Reversed and remanded.

[A dissent by Justice Douglas, joined by Justices Brennan, White, and Marshall, is omitted.]

NOTES AND QUESTIONS

1. **The Arbitration Agreement.** What is Alberto-Culver's argument that the arbitration clause is unenforceable? Should it matter that Alberto-Culver originally agreed to the arbitration clause? Why do you think Alberto-Culver did not want to arbitrate?

2. **Public Policy.** Look at the language of the federal securities laws. They seem to clearly forbid agreements to waive access to federal courts. How does the Court come to a different conclusion? Isn't Congress's intent clear that cases such as this should proceed in federal court? The Court makes much of the fact that this is an international agreement that is important for international

trade and commerce. Should such agreements be treated differently than domestic agreements? Why or why not?

3. **Forum Selection Clauses.** The Court analogizes the arbitration clause to a forum selection clause. It states that such clauses should, in general, not be set aside. Does such a rationale apply in cases of public law where public rights are sought to be vindicated? Why or why not? Based on the Court's discussion, are arbitration clauses similar to or different from forum selection clauses? (Forum selection clauses are discussed further in Chapter 10.)

[handwritten margin note: NY convention & other statutes]

Mitsubishi Motors Corp. v. Soler Chrysler-Plymouth, Inc.

473 U.S. 614 (1985)

Justice BLACKMUN delivered the opinion of the Court.

The principal question presented by these cases is the arbitrability, pursuant to the Federal Arbitration Act and the Convention on the Recognition and Enforcement of Foreign Arbitral Awards (Convention), of claims arising under the Sherman Act, 15 U.S.C. § 1 *et seq.*, and encompassed within a valid arbitration clause in an agreement embodying an international commercial transaction.

I

Petitioner-cross-respondent Mitsubishi Motors Corporation (Mitsubishi) is a Japanese corporation which manufactures automobiles and has its principal place of business in Tokyo, Japan. Mitsubishi is the product of a joint venture between, on the one hand, Chrysler International, S.A. (CISA), a Swiss corporation registered in Geneva and wholly owned by Chrysler Corporation, and, on the other, Mitsubishi Heavy Industries, Inc., a Japanese corporation. The aim of the joint venture was the distribution through Chrysler dealers outside the continental United States of vehicles manufactured by Mitsubishi and bearing Chrysler and Mitsubishi trademarks. Respondent-cross-petitioner Soler Chrysler-Plymouth, Inc. (Soler), is a Puerto Rico corporation with its principal place of business in Pueblo Viejo, Guaynabo, Puerto Rico.

On October 31, 1979, Soler entered into a Distributor Agreement with CISA which provided for the sale by Soler of Mitsubishi-manufactured vehicles within a designated area, including metropolitan San Juan. On the same date, CISA, Soler, and Mitsubishi entered into a Sales Procedure Agreement (Sales Agreement) which, referring to the Distributor Agreement, provided for the direct sale of Mitsubishi products to Soler and governed the terms and conditions of such sales. Paragraph VI of the Sales Agreement, labeled "Arbitration of Certain Matters," provides:

> "All disputes, controversies or differences which may arise between [Mitsubishi] and [Soler] out of or in relation to Articles I-B through V of this Agreement or for the breach thereof, shall be finally settled by arbitration in Japan in accordance with the rules and regulations of the Japan Commercial Arbitration Association."

Initially, Soler did a brisk business in Mitsubishi-manufactured vehicles. As a result of its strong performance, its minimum sales volume, specified by Mitsubishi and CISA, and agreed to by Soler, for the 1981 model year was substantially increased. In early 1981, however, the new-car market slackened. Soler ran into serious difficulties in meeting the expected sales volume, and by the spring of 1981 it felt itself compelled to request that Mitsubishi delay or cancel shipment of several orders. About the same time, Soler attempted to arrange for the transshipment of a quantity of its vehicles for sale in the continental United States and Latin America. Mitsubishi and CISA, however, refused permission for any such diversion, citing a variety of reasons, and no vehicles were transshipped. Attempts to work out these difficulties failed. Mitsubishi eventually withheld shipment of 966 vehicles, apparently representing orders placed for May, June, and July 1981 production, responsibility for which Soler disclaimed in February 1982.

The following month, Mitsubishi brought an action against Soler in the United States District Court for the District of Puerto Rico under the Federal Arbitration Act and the Convention. Mitsubishi sought an order, pursuant to 9 U.S.C. §§ 4 and 201, to compel arbitration in accord with the Sales Agreement. Shortly after filing the complaint, Mitsubishi filed a request for arbitration before the Japan Commercial Arbitration Association. *Id.*

Soler denied the allegations and counterclaimed against both Mitsubishi and CISA. It alleged numerous breaches by Mitsubishi of the Sales Agreement, raised a pair of defamation claims, and asserted causes of action under the Sherman Act, 15 U.S.C. § 1 *et seq.*; the federal Automobile Dealers' Day in Court Act, 70 Stat. 1125, 15 U.S.C. § 1221 *et seq.*; the Puerto Rico competition statute, P.R. Laws Ann., Tit. 10, § 257 *et seq.* (1976); and the Puerto Rico Dealers' Contracts Act, P.R. Laws Ann., Tit. 10, § 278 *et seq.* (1978 and Supp. 1983). In the counterclaim premised on the Sherman Act, Soler alleged that Mitsubishi and CISA had conspired to divide markets in restraint of trade. To effectuate the plan, according to Soler, Mitsubishi had refused to permit Soler to resell to buyers in North, Central, or South America vehicles it had obligated itself to purchase from Mitsubishi; had refused to ship ordered vehicles or the parts, such as heaters and defoggers, that would be necessary to permit Soler to make its vehicles suitable for resale outside Puerto Rico; and had coercively attempted to replace Soler and its other Puerto Rico distributors with a wholly owned subsidiary which would serve as the exclusive Mitsubishi distributor in Puerto Rico.

After a hearing, the District Court ordered Mitsubishi and Soler to arbitrate each of the issues raised in the complaint and in all the counterclaims save two and a portion of a third. With regard to the federal antitrust issues, it recognized that the Courts of Appeals . . . uniformly had held that the rights conferred by the antitrust laws were of a character inappropriate for enforcement by arbitration. . . . The District Court held, however, that the international character of the Mitsubishi-Soler undertaking required enforcement of the agreement to arbitrate even as to the antitrust claims. It relied on *Scherk v. Alberto-Culver Co.*, 417 U.S. 506, 515-520 (1974), in which this Court ordered arbitration, pursuant to a provision embodied in an international agreement, of a claim arising under the Securities Exchange Act of 1934. . . .

The United States Court of Appeals for the First Circuit affirmed in part and reversed in part. . . .

Finally, after endorsing the doctrine . . . precluding arbitration of antitrust claims, the Court of Appeals concluded that neither this Court's decision in *Scherk* nor the Convention required abandonment of that doctrine in the face of an international transaction. 723 F.2d, at 164-168. Accordingly, it reversed the judgment of the District Court insofar as it had ordered submission of "Soler's antitrust claims" to arbitration. Affirming the remainder of the judgment, the court directed the District Court to consider in the first instance how the parallel judicial and arbitral proceedings should go forward.

We granted certiorari primarily to consider whether an American court should enforce an agreement to resolve antitrust claims by arbitration when that agreement arises from an international transaction.

II

At the outset, we address the contention raised in Soler's cross-petition that the arbitration clause at issue may not be read to encompass the statutory counterclaims stated in its answer to the complaint. In making this argument, Soler does not question the Court of Appeals' application of ¶ VI of the Sales Agreement to the disputes involved here as a matter of standard contract interpretation. Instead, it argues that as a matter of law a court may not construe an arbitration agreement to encompass claims arising out of statutes designed to protect a class to which the party resisting arbitration belongs "unless [that party] has expressly agreed" to arbitrate those claims, by which Soler presumably means that the arbitration clause must specifically mention the statute giving rise to the claims that a party to the clause seeks to arbitrate. Soler reasons that, because it falls within the class for whose benefit the federal and local antitrust laws and dealers' Acts were passed, but the arbitration clause at issue does not mention these statutes or statutes in general, the clause cannot be read to contemplate arbitration of these statutory claims.

Soler does suggest that, because the title of the clause referred only to "certain matters," and the clause itself specifically referred only to "Articles I-B through V," *ibid.*, it should be read narrowly to exclude the statutory claims. Soler ignores the inclusion within those "certain matters" of "[a]ll disputes, controversies or differences which may arise between [Mitsubishi] and [Soler] out of or in relation to [the specified provisions] or for the breach thereof." Contrary to Soler's suggestion, the exclusion of some areas of possible dispute from the scope of an arbitration clause does not serve to restrict the reach of an otherwise broad clause in the areas in which it was intended to operate. Thus, insofar as the allegations underlying the statutory claims touch matters covered by the enumerated articles, the Court of Appeals properly resolved any doubts in favor of arbitrability.

We . . . find no warrant in the Arbitration Act for implying in every contract within its ken a presumption against arbitration of statutory claims. The Act's centerpiece provision makes a written agreement to arbitrate "in any maritime transaction or a contract evidencing a transaction involving commerce . . . valid, irrevocable, and enforceable, save upon such grounds as exist at law or in equity for the revocation of any contract." 9 U.S.C. § 2. The "liberal federal policy favoring arbitration agreements," *Moses H. Cone Memorial Hospital v. Mercury Construction Corp.*, 460 U.S. 1, 24 (1983), manifested by this provision and the Act as a whole, is at bottom a policy guaranteeing the enforcement of private contractual arrangements: the Act simply "creates a body of federal substantive law establishing and regulating the duty to honor an agreement to arbitrate." *Id.*, at 25, n. 32. As this Court recently observed, "[t]he preeminent concern of Congress in passing the Act was to enforce private agreements into which parties had entered," a concern which "requires that we rigorously enforce agreements to arbitrate." *Dean Witter Reynolds Inc. v. Byrd*, 470 U.S. 213, 221 (1985).

Accordingly, the first task of a court asked to compel arbitration of a dispute is to determine whether the parties agreed to arbitrate that dispute. The court is to make this determination by applying the "federal substantive law of arbitrability, applicable to any arbitration agreement within the coverage of the Act." *Moses H. Cone Memorial Hospital*, 460 U.S., at 24. And that body of law counsels

> "that questions of arbitrability must be addressed with a healthy regard for the federal policy favoring arbitration. . . . The Arbitration Act establishes that, as a matter of federal law, any doubts concerning the scope of arbitrable issues should be resolved in favor of arbitration, whether the problem at hand is the construction of the contract language itself or an allegation of waiver, delay, or a like defense to arbitrability." *Moses H. Cone Memorial Hospital*, 460 U.S., at 24-25.

Thus, as with any other contract, the parties' intentions control, but those intentions are generously construed as to issues of arbitrability.

There is no reason to depart from these guidelines where a party bound by an arbitration agreement raises claims founded on statutory rights. Some time ago this Court expressed "hope for [the Act's] usefulness both in controversies based on statutes or on standards otherwise created," *Wilko v. Swan*, 346 U.S. 427, 432 (1953) (footnote omitted); and we are well past the time when judicial suspicion of the desirability of arbitration and of the competence of arbitral tribunals inhibited the development of arbitration as an alternative means of dispute resolution. Just last Term in *Southland Corp., supra*, where we held that § 2 of the Act declared a national policy applicable equally in state as well as federal courts, we construed an arbitration clause to encompass the disputes at issue without pausing at the source in a state statute of the rights asserted by the parties resisting arbitration. 465 U.S., at 15, and n. 7. Of course, courts should remain attuned to well-supported claims that the agreement to arbitrate resulted from the sort of fraud or overwhelming economic power that would provide grounds "for the revocation of any contract." 9 U.S.C. § 2. But, absent such compelling considerations, the Act itself provides no basis for disfavoring agreements to arbitrate statutory claims by skewing the otherwise hospitable inquiry into arbitrability.

That is not to say that all controversies implicating statutory rights are suitable for arbitration. There is no reason to distort the process of contract interpretation, however, in order to ferret out the inappropriate. Just as it is the congressional policy manifested in the Federal Arbitration Act that requires courts liberally to construe the scope of arbitration agreements covered by that Act, it is the congressional intention expressed in some other statute on which the courts must rely to identify any category of claims as to which agreements to arbitrate will be held unenforceable. For that reason, Soler's concern for statutorily protected classes provides no reason to color the lens through which the arbitration clause is read. By agreeing to arbitrate a statutory claim, a party does not forgo the substantive rights afforded by the statute; it only submits to their resolution in an arbitral, rather than a judicial, forum. It trades the procedures and opportunity for review of the courtroom for the simplicity, informality, and expedition of arbitration. We must assume that if Congress intended the substantive protection afforded by a given statute to include protection against waiver of the right to a judicial forum, that intention will be deducible from text or legislative history. Having made the bargain to arbitrate, the party should be held to it unless Congress itself has evinced an intention to preclude a waiver of judicial remedies for the statutory rights at issue. Nothing, in the meantime, prevents a party from excluding statutory claims from the scope of an agreement to arbitrate.

In sum, the Court of Appeals correctly conducted a two-step inquiry, first determining whether the parties' agreement to arbitrate reached the statutory issues, and then, upon finding it did, considering whether legal constraints external to the parties' agreement foreclosed the arbitration of those claims. We endorse its rejection of Soler's proposed rule of arbitration-clause construction.

III

We now turn to consider whether Soler's antitrust claims are nonarbitrable even though it has agreed to arbitrate them. In holding that they are not, the Court of Appeals followed the decision of the Second Circuit in *American Safety Equipment Corp. v. J.P. Maguire & Co.*, 391 F.2d 821 (1968). Notwithstanding the absence of any explicit support for such an exception in either the Sherman Act or the Federal Arbitration Act, the Second Circuit there reasoned that "the pervasive public interest in enforcement of the antitrust laws, and the nature of the claims that arise in such cases, combine to make . . . antitrust claims . . . inappropriate for arbitration." *Id.*, at 827-828. We find it unnecessary to assess the legitimacy of the *American Safety* doctrine as applied to agreements to arbitrate arising from domestic transactions. As in *Scherk v. Alberto-Culver Co.*, 417 U.S. 506 (1974), we conclude that concerns of international comity, respect for the capacities of foreign and transnational tribunals, and sensitivity to the need of the international commercial system for predictability in the resolution of disputes require that we enforce the parties' agreement, even assuming that a contrary result would be forthcoming in a domestic context.

Even before *Scherk*, this Court had recognized the utility of forum-selection clauses in international transactions. In *The Bremen*, an American oil company, seeking to evade a contractual choice of an English forum and, by implication, English law, filed a suit in admiralty in a United States District Court against the German corporation which had contracted to tow its rig to a location in the Adriatic Sea. Notwithstanding the possibility that the English court would enforce provisions in the towage contract exculpating the German party which an American court would refuse to enforce, this Court gave effect to the choice-of-forum clause. It observed:

> "The expansion of American business and industry will hardly be encouraged if, notwithstanding solemn contracts, we insist on a parochial concept that all disputes must be resolved under our laws and in our courts. . . . We cannot have trade and commerce in world markets and international waters exclusively on our terms, governed by our laws, and resolved in our courts." 407 U.S., at 9.

Recognizing that "agreeing in advance on a forum acceptable to both parties is an indispensable element in international trade, commerce, and contracting," *id.*, at 13-14, the decision in *The Bremen* clearly eschewed a provincial solicitude for the jurisdiction of domestic forums.

Identical considerations governed the Court's decision in *Scherk*, which categorized "[a]n agreement to arbitrate before a specified tribunal [as], in effect, a specialized kind of forum-selection clause that posits not only the situs of suit but also the procedure to be used in resolving the dispute." 417 U.S., at 519. . . .

The Bremen and *Scherk* establish a strong presumption in favor of enforcement of freely negotiated contractual choice-of-forum provisions. Here, as in *Scherk*, that presumption is reinforced by the emphatic federal policy in favor of arbitral dispute resolution. And at least since this Nation's accession in 1970 to the Convention and the implementation of the Convention in the same year by amendment of the Federal Arbitration Act, that federal policy applies with special force in the field of international commerce. Thus, we must weigh the concerns of *American Safety* against a strong belief in the efficacy of arbitral procedures for the resolution of international commercial disputes and an equal commitment to the enforcement of freely negotiated choice-of-forum clauses.

At the outset, we confess to some skepticism of certain aspects of the *American Safety* doctrine. As distilled by the First Circuit, 723 F.2d, at 162, the doctrine comprises four ingredients. First, private parties play a pivotal role in aiding governmental enforcement of the antitrust laws by means of the private action for treble damages. Second, "the strong possibility that contracts which generate antitrust disputes may be contracts of adhesion militates against automatic forum determination by contract." Third, antitrust issues, prone to complication, require sophisticated legal and economic analysis, and thus are "ill-adapted to strengths of the arbitral process, *i.e.*, expedition, minimal requirements of written rationale, simplicity, resort to basic concepts of common sense and simple equity." Finally, just as "issues of war and peace are too important to be vested in the generals, . . . decisions as to antitrust regulation of business are too important to be lodged in arbitrators chosen from the business community — particularly those from a foreign community that has had no experience with or exposure to our law and values." See *American Safety*, 391 F.2d, at 826-827.

Initially, we find the second concern unjustified. The mere appearance of an antitrust dispute does not alone warrant invalidation of the selected forum on the undemonstrated assumption that the arbitration clause is tainted. A party resisting arbitration of course may attack directly the validity of the agreement to arbitrate.

Moreover, the party may attempt to make a showing that would warrant setting aside the forum-selection clause-that the agreement was "[a]ffected by fraud, undue influence, or overweening bargaining power"; that "enforcement would be unreasonable and unjust"; or that proceedings "in the contractual forum will be so gravely difficult and inconvenient that [the resisting party] will for all practical purposes be deprived of his day in court." *The Bremen*, 407 U.S., at 12, 15, 18. But absent such a showing — and none was attempted here — there is no basis for assuming the forum inadequate or its selection unfair.

Next, potential complexity should not suffice to ward off arbitration. We might well have some doubt that even the courts following *American Safety* subscribe fully to the view that antitrust matters are inherently insusceptible to resolution by arbitration, as these same courts have agreed that an undertaking to arbitrate antitrust claims entered into *after* the dispute arises is acceptable. And the vertical restraints which most frequently give birth to antitrust claims covered by an arbitration agreement will not often occasion the monstrous proceedings that have given antitrust litigation an image of intractability. In any event, adaptability and access to expertise are hallmarks of arbitration. The anticipated subject matter of the dispute may be taken into account when the arbitrators are appointed, and arbitral rules typically provide for the participation of experts either employed by the parties or appointed by the tribunal. Moreover, it is often a judgment that streamlined proceedings and expeditious results will best serve their needs that causes parties to agree to arbitrate their disputes; it is typically a desire to keep the effort and expense required to resolve a dispute within manageable bounds that prompts them mutually to forgo access to judicial remedies. In sum, the factor of potential complexity alone does not persuade us that an arbitral tribunal could not properly handle an antitrust matter.

For similar reasons, we also reject the proposition that an arbitration panel will pose too great a danger of innate hostility to the constraints on business conduct that antitrust law imposes. International arbitrators frequently are drawn from the legal as well as the business community; where the dispute has an important legal component, the parties and the arbitral body with whose assistance they have agreed to settle their dispute can be expected to select arbitrators accordingly. We decline to indulge the presumption that the parties and arbitral body conducting a proceeding will be unable or unwilling to retain competent, conscientious, and impartial arbitrators.

We are advised by Mitsubishi and *amicus* International Chamber of Commerce, without contradiction by Soler, that the arbitration panel selected to hear the parties' claims here is composed of three Japanese lawyers, one a former law school dean, another a former judge, and the third a practicing attorney with American legal training who has written on Japanese antitrust law.

The Court of Appeals was concerned that international arbitrators would lack "experience with or exposure to our law and values." 723 F.2d, at 162. The obstacles confronted by the arbitration panel in this case, however, should be no greater than those confronted by any judicial or arbitral tribunal required to determine foreign law. Moreover, while our attachment to the antitrust laws may be stronger than most, many other countries, including Japan, have similar bodies of competition law.

We are left, then, with the core of the *American Safety* doctrine — the fundamental importance to American democratic capitalism of the regime of the antitrust laws. Without doubt, the private cause of action plays a central role in enforcing this regime. As the Court of Appeals pointed out:

> "'A claim under the antitrust laws is not merely a private matter. The Sherman Act is designed to promote the national interest in a competitive economy; thus, the plaintiff asserting his rights under the Act has been likened to a private attorney-general who protects the public's interest.'" 723 F.2d, at 168, quoting *American Safety*, 391 F.2d, at 826.

The treble-damages provision wielded by the private litigant is a chief tool in the antitrust enforcement scheme, posing a crucial deterrent to potential violators.

The importance of the private damages remedy, however, does not compel the conclusion that it may not be sought outside an American court. Notwithstanding its important incidental policing function, the treble-damages cause of action conferred on private parties by § 4 of the Clayton Act, 15 U.S.C. § 15, and pursued by Soler here by way of its third counterclaim, seeks primarily to enable an injured competitor to gain compensation for that injury.

. . .

There is no reason to assume at the outset of the dispute that international arbitration will not provide an adequate mechanism. To be sure, the international arbitral tribunal owes no prior allegiance to the legal norms of particular states; hence, it has no direct obligation to vindicate their statutory dictates. The tribunal, however, is bound to effectuate the intentions of the parties. Where the parties have agreed that the arbitral body is to decide a defined set of claims which includes, as in these cases, those arising from the application of American antitrust law, the tribunal therefore should be bound to decide that dispute in accord with the national law giving rise to the claim. And so long as the prospective litigant effectively may vindicate its statutory cause of action in the arbitral forum, the statute will continue to serve both its remedial and deterrent function.

We therefore have no occasion to speculate on this matter at this stage in the proceedings, when Mitsubishi seeks to enforce the agreement to arbitrate, not to enforce an award. Nor need we consider now the effect of an arbitral tribunal's failure to take cognizance of the statutory cause of action on the claimant's capacity to reinitiate suit in federal court. We merely note that in the event the choice-of-forum and choice-of-law clauses operated in tandem as a prospective waiver of a party's right to pursue statutory remedies for antitrust violations, we would have little hesitation in condemning the agreement as against public policy.

Having permitted the arbitration to go forward, the national courts of the United States will have the opportunity at the award-enforcement stage to ensure that the legitimate interest in the enforcement of the antitrust laws has been addressed. The Convention reserves to each signatory country the right to refuse enforcement of an award where the "recognition or enforcement of the award would be contrary to the public policy of that country." Art. V(2)(b), 21 U.S.T., at 2520. While the efficacy of the arbitral process requires that substantive review at the award-enforcement stage remain minimal, it would not require intrusive inquiry to ascertain that the tribunal took cognizance of the antitrust claims and actually decided them.

Needless to say, we intimate no views on the merits of Soler's antitrust claims.

As international trade has expanded in recent decades, so too has the use of international arbitration to resolve disputes arising in the course of that trade. The controversies that international arbitral institutions are called upon to resolve have increased in diversity as well as in complexity. Yet the potential of these tribunals for efficient disposition of legal disagreements arising from commercial relations has not yet been tested. If they are to take a central place in the international legal order, national courts will need to "shake off the old judicial hostility to arbitration," *Kulukundis Shipping Co. v. Amtorg Trading Corp.*, 126 F.2d 978, 985 (CA2 1942), and also their customary and understandable unwillingness to cede jurisdiction of a claim arising under domestic law to a foreign or transnational tribunal. To this extent, at least, it will be necessary for national courts to subordinate domestic notions of arbitrability to the international policy favoring commercial arbitration.

In acceding to the Convention the Senate restricted its applicability to commercial matters, in accord with Art. I(3). Yet in implementing the Convention by amendment to the Federal Arbitration Act, Congress did not specify any matters it intended to exclude from its scope. . . . The utility of the Convention in promoting the process of international commercial arbitration depends upon the willingness of national courts to let go of matters they normally would think of as their own. Doubtless, Congress may specify categories of claims it wishes to reserve for decision by our own courts without contravening this Nation's obligations under the Convention. But we decline to subvert the spirit of the United States' accession to the Convention by recognizing subject-matter exceptions where Congress has not expressly directed the courts to do so.

Accordingly, we "require this representative of the American business community to honor its bargain," *Alberto-Culver Co. v. Scherk*, 484 F.2d 611, 620 (CA7 1973) (Stevens, J., dissenting), by holding this agreement to arbitrate "enforce[able] . . . in accord with the explicit provisions of the Arbitration Act." *Scherk*, 417 U.S., at 520.

The judgment of the Court of Appeals is affirmed in part and reversed in part, and the cases are remanded for further proceedings consistent with this opinion.

It is so ordered.

[A dissent by Justice Stevens, joined by Justice Brennan and by Justice Marshall in part, is omitted.]

NOTES AND QUESTIONS

1. **The Non-Arbitrability Doctrine.** Note the Court's statement that "we conclude that concerns of international comity, respect for the capacities of foreign and transnational tribunals, and sensitivity to the need of the international

commercial system for predictability in the resolution of disputes require that we enforce the parties' agreement, even assuming that a contrary result would be forthcoming in a domestic context." As such, U.S. federal courts must take into account the strong federal policy in favor of arbitration when considering motions to compel arbitration, which means that arbitration will be compelled in most cases. Is the U.S. approach in favor of arbitration appropriate? In light of the above cases, what would Congress need to do to place limits on arbitrability?

2. **Transnational Context.** Notice again, as in *Scherk*, the importance placed by the Court on the transnational nature of this case. In light of this reasoning, what limits, if any, are there to submitting transnational claims to arbitration? In light of these and other more recent cases, one arbitration scholar has noted that the "category of 'inarbitrable disputes'" in the United States is a "null set." Alan Scott Rau, *The Culture of American Arbitration and the Lessons of ADR*, 40 Tex. Int'l L.J. 449, 452 (2005). Is this the right approach?

3. **Public Policy.** Is it a good idea as a matter of policy to allow arbitration of public law claims — e.g., claims involving public regulatory interests? The fact that these are public law claims illustrates the importance of the public interest in learning about and being involved in the dispute. Yet, arbitration is about a private contract, and is often conducted outside of public view. Does the Court appropriately balance these concerns? Note the idea that U.S. federal courts are able to take a "second look" at the dispute after the arbitration is complete when it is asked to enforce an arbitral award. According to the Court in *Mitsubishi*, "[h]aving permitted the arbitration to go forward, the national courts of the United States will have the opportunity at the award-enforcement stage to ensure that the legitimate interest in the enforcement of the antitrust laws has been addressed." Is affording such a look enough of a protection for the public interests involved? Is it appropriate for all claims to be subject to arbitration if agreed to by the parties? What limits are there to such an approach?

4. Who Decides Arbitrability?

Finally, in answering the questions above there is an important antecedent question: Who should decide issues related to the interpretation, validity, and enforceability of arbitration agreements: arbitrators or national courts? The next case explores this topic. Take note: This case involves a different type of transnational arbitration — investor-state arbitration — and a different procedural posture — it arises not as a motion to compel arbitration but on a motion to confirm an arbitral award under the New York Convention (a topic that will be explored in full detail in Chapter 8). We will discuss investor-state arbitration shortly. To prepare for that discussion, notice how the Court compares transnational commercial arbitration and investor-state arbitration in reaching its decision.

BG Group, PLC v. Republic of Argentina

572 U.S. 25 (2014)

Justice BREYER delivered the opinion of the Court.

Article 8 of an investment treaty between the United Kingdom and Argentina contains a dispute-resolution provision, applicable to disputes between one of those nations and an investor from the other. See Agreement for the Promotion and Protection of Investments, Art. 8(2), Dec. 11, 1990 (hereinafter Treaty). The provision authorizes either party to submit a dispute "to the decision of the competent tribunal of the Contracting Party in whose territory the investment was made," *i.e.*, a local court. Art. 8(1). And it provides for arbitration

> "(i) where, after a period of eighteen months has elapsed from the moment when the dispute was submitted to the competent tribunal . . . , the said tribunal has not given its final decision; [or]
> "(ii) where the final decision of the aforementioned tribunal has been made but the Parties are still in dispute." Art. 8(2)(a).

The Treaty also entitles the parties to agree to proceed directly to arbitration. Art. 8(2)(b).

This case concerns the Treaty's arbitration clause, and specifically the local court litigation requirement set forth in Article 8(2)(a). The question before us is whether a court of the United States, in reviewing an arbitration award made under the Treaty, should interpret and apply the local litigation requirement *de novo*, or with the deference that courts ordinarily owe arbitration decisions. That is to say, who — court or arbitrator — bears primary responsibility for interpreting and applying the local litigation requirement to an underlying controversy? In our view, the matter is for the arbitrators, and courts must review their determinations with deference.

I

A

In the early 1990's, the petitioner, BG Group plc, a British firm, belonged to a consortium that bought a majority interest in an Argentine entity called MetroGAS. MetroGAS was a gas distribution company created by Argentine law in 1992, as a result of the government's privatization of its state-owned gas utility. Argentina distributed the utility's assets to new, private companies, one of which was MetroGAS. It awarded MetroGAS a 35-year exclusive license to distribute natural gas in Buenos Aires, and it submitted a controlling interest in the company to international public tender. BG Group's consortium was the successful bidder.

At about the same time, Argentina enacted statutes providing that its regulators would calculate gas "tariffs" in U.S. dollars, and that those tariffs would be set at levels sufficient to assure gas distribution firms, such as MetroGAS, a reasonable return.

In 2001 and 2002, Argentina, faced with an economic crisis, enacted new laws. Those laws changed the basis for calculating gas tariffs from dollars to pesos, at a rate of one peso per dollar. The exchange rate at the time was roughly three pesos to the dollar. The result was that MetroGAS' profits were quickly transformed into losses. BG Group believed that these changes (and several others) violated the Treaty; Argentina believed the contrary.

B

In 2003, BG Group, invoking Article 8 of the Treaty, sought arbitration. The parties appointed arbitrators; they agreed to site the arbitration in Washington, D.C.; and between 2004 and 2006, the arbitrators decided motions, received evidence, and conducted hearings. BG Group essentially claimed that Argentina's new laws and regulatory practices violated provisions in the Treaty forbidding the "expropriation" of investments and requiring that each nation give "fair and equitable treatment" to investors from the other. Argentina denied these claims, while also arguing that the arbitration tribunal lacked "jurisdiction" to hear the dispute. According to Argentina, the arbitrators lacked jurisdiction because: (1) BG Group was not a Treaty-protected "investor"; (2) BG Group's interest in MetroGAS was not a Treaty-protected "investment"; and (3) BG Group initiated arbitration without first litigating its claims in Argentina's courts, despite Article 8's requirement. In Argentina's view, "failure by BG to bring its grievance to Argentine courts for 18 months renders its claims in this arbitration inadmissible."

In late December 2007, the arbitration panel reached a final decision. It began by determining that it had "jurisdiction" to consider the merits of the dispute. In support of that determination, the tribunal concluded that BG Group was an "investor," that its interest in MetroGAS amounted to a Treaty-protected "investment," and that Argentina's own conduct had waived, or excused, BG Group's failure to comply with Article 8's local litigation requirement. The panel pointed out that in 2002, the President of Argentina had issued a decree staying for 180 days the execution of its courts' final judgments (and injunctions) in suits claiming harm as a result of the new economic measures. In addition, Argentina had established a "renegotiation process" for public service contracts, such as its contract with MetroGAS, to alleviate the negative impact of the new economic measures. But Argentina had simultaneously barred from participation in that "process" firms that were litigating against Argentina in court or in arbitration. These measures, while not making litigation in Argentina's courts literally impossible, nonetheless "hindered" recourse "to the domestic judiciary" to the point where the Treaty implicitly excused compliance with the local litigation requirement. Requiring a private party in such circumstances to seek relief in Argentina's courts for 18 months, the panel concluded, would lead to "absurd and unreasonable result[s]."

On the merits, the arbitration panel agreed with Argentina that it had not "expropriate[d]" BG Group's investment, but also found that Argentina had denied BG Group "fair and equitable treatment." It awarded BG Group $185 million in damages.

C

In March 2008, both sides filed petitions for review in the District Court for the District of Columbia. BG Group sought to confirm the award under the

New York Convention and the Federal Arbitration Act. Argentina sought to vacate the award in part on the ground that the arbitrators lacked jurisdiction.

The District Court denied Argentina's claims and confirmed the award. But the Court of Appeals for the District of Columbia Circuit reversed. In the appeals court's view, the interpretation and application of Article 8's local litigation requirement was a matter for courts to decide *de novo*, *i.e.*, without deference to the views of the arbitrators. The Court of Appeals then went on to hold that the circumstances did not excuse BG Group's failure to comply with the requirement. Rather, BG Group must "commence a lawsuit in Argentina's courts and wait eighteen months before filing for arbitration." Because BG Group had not done so, the arbitrators lacked authority to decide the dispute. And the appeals court ordered the award vacated.

BG Group filed a petition for certiorari. Given the importance of the matter for international commercial arbitration, we granted the petition.

II

As we have said, the question before us is who — court or arbitrator — bears primary responsibility for interpreting and applying Article 8's local court litigation provision. Put in terms of standards of judicial review, should a United States court review the arbitrators' interpretation and application of the provision *de novo*, or with the deference that courts ordinarily show arbitral decisions on matters the parties have committed to arbitration?

. . .

III

Where ordinary contracts are at issue, it is up to the parties to determine whether a particular matter is primarily for arbitrators or for courts to decide. If the contract is silent on the matter of who primarily is to decide "threshold" questions about arbitration, courts determine the parties' intent with the help of presumptions.

On the one hand, courts presume that the parties intend courts, not arbitrators, to decide what we have called disputes about "arbitrability." These include questions such as "whether the parties are bound by a given arbitration clause," or "whether an arbitration clause in a concededly binding contract applies to a particular type of controversy." *Howsam v. Dean Witter Reynolds, Inc.*, 537 U.S. 79, 84 (2002); accord, *Granite Rock Co. v. Teamsters*, 561 U.S. 287, 299-300 (2010) (disputes over "formation of the parties' arbitration agreement" and "its enforceability or applicability to the dispute" at issue are "matters . . . the court must resolve" (internal quotation marks omitted)).

On the other hand, courts presume that the parties intend arbitrators, not courts, to decide disputes about the meaning and application of particular procedural preconditions for the use of arbitration. See *Howsam, supra,* at 86 (courts assume parties "normally expect a forum-based decisionmaker to decide forum-specific *procedural* gateway matters" (emphasis added)). These procedural matters include claims of "waiver, delay, or a like defense to arbitrability." *Moses H. Cone Memorial Hospital v. Mercury Constr. Corp.*, 460 U.S. 1, 25 (1983). And they include the satisfaction of "prerequisites such as time limits, notice, laches, estoppel, and other conditions precedent to an obligation to arbitrate." *Howsam, supra,* at 85.

The provision before us is of the latter, procedural, variety. The text and structure of the provision make clear that it operates as a procedural condition precedent to arbitration. It says that a dispute "shall be submitted to international arbitration" if "one of the Parties so requests," as long as "a period of eighteen months has elapsed" since the dispute was "submitted" to a local tribunal and the tribunal "has not given its final decision." Art. 8(2). It determines *when* the contractual duty to arbitrate arises, not *whether* there is a contractual duty to arbitrate at all. Neither does this language or other language in Article 8 give substantive weight to the local court's determinations on the matters at issue between the parties. To the contrary, Article 8 provides that *only* the "arbitration decision shall be final and binding on both Parties." Art. 8(4). The litigation provision is consequently a purely procedural requirement — a claims-processing rule that governs when the arbitration may begin, but not whether it may occur or what its substantive outcome will be on the issues in dispute.

Moreover, the local litigation requirement is highly analogous to procedural provisions that both this Court and others have found are for arbitrators, not courts, primarily to interpret and to apply. See *Howsam, supra,* at 85 (whether a party filed a notice of arbitration within the time limit provided by the rules of the chosen arbitral forum "is a matter presumptively for the arbitrator, not for the judge").

Finally, as we later discuss in more detail, we can find nothing in Article 8 or elsewhere in the Treaty that might overcome the ordinary assumption. It nowhere demonstrates a contrary intent as to the delegation of decisional authority between judges and arbitrators. Thus, . . . arbitrators [should] primarily . . . interpret and to apply the local litigation provision.

> . . .

V

Argentina correctly argues that it is nonetheless entitled to court review of the arbitrators' decision to excuse BG Group's noncompliance with the litigation requirement, and to take jurisdiction over the dispute. It asks us to provide that review, and it argues that even if the proper standard is "a [h]ighly [d]eferential" one, it should still prevail. Having the relevant materials before us, we shall provide that review. But we cannot agree with Argentina that the arbitrators "exceeded their powers" in concluding they had jurisdiction.

The arbitration panel made three relevant determinations:

> (1) "As a matter of treaty interpretation," the local litigation provision "cannot be construed as an absolute impediment to arbitration,"
> (2) Argentina enacted laws that "hindered" "recourse to the domestic judiciary" by those "whose rights were allegedly affected by the emergency measures"; that sought "to prevent any judicial interference with the emergency legislation";

and that "excluded from the renegotiation process" for public service contracts "any licensee seeking judicial redress";

(3) under these circumstances, it would be "absurd and unreasonable" to read Article 8 as requiring an investor to bring its grievance to a domestic court before arbitrating.

The first determination lies well within the arbitrators' interpretive authority. Construing the local litigation provision as an "absolute" requirement would mean Argentina could avoid arbitration by, say, passing a law that closed down its court system indefinitely or that prohibited investors from using its courts. Such an interpretation runs contrary to a basic objective of the investment treaty. Nor does Argentina argue for an absolute interpretation.

As to the second determination, Argentina does not argue that the facts set forth by the arbitrators are incorrect. Thus, we accept them as valid.

The third determination is more controversial. Argentina argues that neither the 180-day suspension of courts' issuances of final judgments nor its refusal to allow litigants (and those in arbitration) to use its contract renegotiation process, taken separately or together, warrants suspending or waiving the local litigation requirement. We would not necessarily characterize these actions as rendering a domestic court-exhaustion requirement "absurd and unreasonable," but at the same time we cannot say that the arbitrators' conclusions are barred by the Treaty. The arbitrators did not "'stra[y] from interpretation and application of the agreement'" or otherwise "'effectively dispens[e]'" their "'own brand of . . . justice.'" *Stolt-Nielsen S.A. v. AnimalFeeds Int'l Corp.*, 559 U.S. 662, 671 (2010) (providing that it is only when an arbitrator engages in such activity that "'his decision may be unenforceable'" (quoting *Major League Baseball Players Assn. v. Garvey*, 532 U.S. 504, 509 (2001) (*per curiam*))).

Consequently, we conclude that the arbitrators' jurisdictional determinations are lawful. The judgment of the Court of Appeals to the contrary is reversed.

It is so ordered.

[A concurring opinion of Justice Sotomayor is omitted.]

Chief Justice ROBERTS, with whom Justice KENNEDY joins, dissenting.

The Court begins by deciding a different case, "initially treat[ing] the document before us as if it were an ordinary contract between private parties." The "document before us," of course, is nothing of the sort. It is instead a treaty between two sovereign nations: the United Kingdom and Argentina. No investor is a party to the agreement. . . . It should come as no surprise that, after starting down the wrong road, the majority ends up at the wrong place.

I would start with the document that *is* before us and take it on its own terms. That document is a bilateral investment treaty between the United Kingdom and Argentina, in which Argentina agreed to take steps to encourage U.K. investors to invest within its borders (and the United Kingdom agreed to do the same with respect to Argentine investors). The Treaty does indeed contain a completed agreement for arbitration — between the signatory countries. Art. 9. The Treaty also includes, in Article 8, certain provisions for resolving any disputes that might arise between a signatory country and an investor, who is not a party to the agreement.

One such provision — completely ignored by the Court in its analysis — specifies that disputes may be resolved by arbitration when the host country and an investor "have so agreed." Art. 8(2)(b). No one doubts that, as is the normal rule, whether there was such an agreement is for a court, not an arbitrator, to decide.

When there is no express agreement between the host country and an investor, they must form an agreement in another way, before an obligation to arbitrate arises. The Treaty by itself cannot constitute an agreement to arbitrate with an investor. How could it? No investor is a party to that Treaty. Something else must happen to *create* an agreement where there was none before. Article 8(2)(a) makes clear what that something is: An investor must submit his dispute to the courts of the host country. After 18 months, or an unsatisfactory decision, the investor may then request arbitration.

Submitting the dispute to the courts is thus a condition to the formation of an agreement, not simply a matter of performing an existing agreement. Article 8(2)(a) constitutes in effect a unilateral *offer* to arbitrate, which an investor may accept by complying with its terms. To be sure, the local litigation requirement might not be absolute. In particular, an investor might argue that it was an implicit aspect of the unilateral offer that he be afforded a reasonable opportunity to submit his dispute to the local courts. Even then, however, the question would remain whether the investor has managed to form an arbitration agreement with the host country pursuant to Article 8(2)(a). That question under Article 8(2)(a) is — like the same question under Article 8(2)(b) — for a court, not an arbitrator, to decide. I respectfully dissent from the Court's contrary conclusion.

. . .

NOTES AND QUESTIONS

1. **Who Decides What?** According to the Court, what matters are for courts to decide and what matters are for arbitrators? How much deference should a court give to arbitration decisions? What presumptions does the Court say courts should apply to determine how much deference to give? How do those presumptions differ depending on the type of questions that are at issue? Which presumption does the Court apply in this case? And why does Chief Justice Roberts disagree?

2. **Implications for Drafting Arbitration Agreements.** As a lawyer for a client entering an arbitration agreement, how might you draft the agreement to help ensure that arbitrators and not a court (or vice versa) have the final word on an issue?

3. **Who Should Decide?** What is the appropriate allocation of power between arbitrators and courts in deciding disputes concerning arbitration agreements? Is a court or the arbitrators in a better position to determine whether the arbitration clause's terms have been met?

4. **Impact.** Why does this allocation of authority matter? What is the harm in allowing courts as opposed to arbitral tribunals to resolve jurisdictional

questions? As you think through this question, consider the following: In *Prima Paint Corp. v. Flood & Conklin Mfg. Co.*, 388 U.S. 395 (1967), the Supreme Court held that a defense of fraud in the inducement of a contract is to be decided by the arbitrator, but in *First Options of Chicago, Inc. v. Kaplan*, 514 U.S. 938 (1995), the Court held that whether a party has agreed to arbitrate can be decided by a court. What accounts for this distinction?

BG Group involved arbitration between a foreign investor and a host nation — that is, investor-state arbitration. This is the focus of the next section.

C. Investor-State Arbitration

So far, this chapter has focused primarily on transnational commercial arbitration, except for the case above. This section briefly describes another common type of transnational arbitration: investor-state arbitration (also called investor-state dispute settlement or ISDS). Investor-state arbitration is the arbitration of investment disputes between an investor from one nation (a "foreign investor") and another nation in which the investment is made (a "host nation").

Like other types of arbitration, investor-state arbitration is consensual: both the foreign investor and the host nation must give their consent. Usually the host nation's consent is found in a bilateral investment treaty (BIT) or a free trade agreement (FTA) between the host nation and the foreign investor's home nation. A typical treaty provides that each nation that is a party to the treaty consents to arbitration of investment disputes with investors from the other party. The idea behind allowing for this type of arbitration is that it encourages foreign investors to invest in host nations by providing their investments with protection through arbitration. For instance, a company might be unwilling to acquire a foreign business or form a foreign subsidiary in a host nation without such protection, for fear that any disputes arising out of that investment would not be resolved fairly and favorably in the host nation's courts. Typically, protected rights in BITs and FTAs include fair and equitable treatment, full protection and security by a host nation's police forces, guarantees that investors will be able to transfer assets freely in and out of the host nation, and protections against state expropriations of assets. As *BG Group* illustrates, the typical investor-state arbitration claim is based on alleged unfair treatment of the foreign investor by the host nation.

For example, the United States-Argentina BIT (formally called the Treaty between the United States of America and the Argentine Republic concerning the Encouragement and Reciprocal Protection of Investment) provides as follows:

Article VII

1. For purposes of this Article, an investment dispute is a dispute between a Party and a national or company of the other Party arising out of or relating to (a) an investment agreement between that Party and such national or company; (b) an investment authorization granted by that Party's foreign

investment authority to such national or company; or (c) an alleged breach of any right conferred or created by this Treaty with respect to an investment.

2. In the event of an investment dispute, the parties to the dispute should initially seek a resolution through consultation and negotiation. If the dispute cannot be settled amicably, the national or company concerned may choose to submit the dispute, under one of the following alternatives, for resolution: (a) to the courts or administrative tribunals of the Party that is a party to the dispute; or (b) in accordance with any applicable, previously agreed dispute-settlement procedures; or (c) in accordance with the terms of paragraph 3.

3. (a) Provided that the national or company concerned has not submitted the dispute for resolution under paragraph 2 (a) or (b) and that six months have elapsed from the [date] on which the dispute arose, the national or company concerned may choose to consent in writing to the submission of the dispute for settlement by binding arbitration:

> (i) to the International Centre for the Settlement of Investment Disputes ("Centre") established by the Convention on the Settlement of Investment Disputes between States and Nationals of other States, done at Washington, March 18, 1965 ("ICSID convention"), provided that the Party is a party to such Convention; or

> (ii) to the Additional Facility of the Centre, if the Centre is not available; or

> (iii) in accordance with the Arbitration Rules of the United Nations Commission on International Trade Law (UNCITRAL); or

> (iv) to any other arbitration institution, or in accordance with any other arbitration rules, as may be mutually agreed between the parties to the dispute.

(b) once the national or company concerned has so consented, either party to the dispute may initiate arbitration in accordance with the choice so specified in the consent.

4. Each Party hereby consents to the submission of any investment dispute for settlement by binding arbitration in accordance with the choice specified in the written consent of the national or company under paragraph 3. Such consent, together with the written consent of the national or company when given under paragraph 3 shall satisfy the requirement for:

> (a) written consent of the parties to the dispute for Purposes of Chapter II of the ICSID Convention (Jurisdiction of the Centre) and for purposes of the Additional Facility Rules; and

> (b) an "agreement in writing" for purposes of Article II of the United Nations Convention on the Recognition and Enforcement of Foreign Arbitral Awards, done at New York, June 10, 1958 ("New York Convention").

As the foregoing provisions illustrate, in investor-state arbitration pursuant to a BIT, the foreign investor's consent is the consent it may give to arbitration of investment disputes (in this case, pursuant to paragraph 3(a)) and the host nation's consent is the consent granted in the BIT itself (in this case, in paragraph 4).

The international law of investor protection is well beyond the scope of this casebook. However, to understand the sorts of investor-state claims that are typically submitted to arbitration, it is helpful to understand some of the basic principles of investor protection. Like the consent to arbitration, substantive principles of investor protection are ordinarily contained in a BIT. For example, the United States-Argentina BIT provides as follows:

Article II

1. Each Party shall permit and treat investment, and activities associated therewith, on a basis no less favorable than that accorded in like situations to investment or associated activities of its own nationals or companies, or of nationals or companies of any third country, whichever is the most favorable, subject to the right of each Party to make or maintain [certain] exceptions. . . .

. . .

3. (a) Investment shall at all times be accorded fair and equitable treatment, shall enjoy full protection and security and shall in no case be accorded treatment less than that required by international law.

(b) Neither Party shall in any way impair by arbitrary or discriminatory measures the management, operation, maintenance, use, enjoyment, acquisition, expansion, or disposal of investments. . . .

. . .

Article IV

1. Investments shall not be expropriated or nationalized either directly or indirectly through measures tantamount to expropriation or nationalization ("expropriation") except: for a public purpose; in a nondiscriminatory manner; upon payment of prompt, adequate and effective compensation; and in accordance with due process of law and the general principles of treatment provided for in Article II (3).

. . .

If the host nation violates investor protections guaranteed by a BIT, the foreign investor may submit its claim to arbitration pursuant to the BIT. In a specialized book or course on investor protection or investor-state arbitration, you can learn more about the important field of international investor protection law.

NOTES AND QUESTIONS

1. **Public Policy.** Why would investors want to have investor-state arbitration available as an option for resolving investment disputes? Why would nations want investor-state arbitration available as an option for resolving investment disputes? When thinking about this, be sure to keep in mind what dispute resolution options would be available if arbitration were not an option.

2. **Deciding Disputes.** The International Centre for Settlement of Investment Disputes (ICSID) is the leading institution for the resolution of international investment disputes. It was established under the auspices of the World Bank by the Convention on the Settlement of Investment Disputes between States and Nationals of Other States (ICSID Convention), which is a multilateral international treaty. The ICSID Convention entered into force on October 14, 1966. Currently over 154 contracting states have ratified the Convention. Under Article 25(1) of the ICSID Convention, the jurisdiction of ICSID "shall extend to any legal dispute arising directly out of an investment, between a Contracting State (or any constituent subdivision or agency of a Contracting State designated to the Centre by that State) and a national of another Contracting State, which the parties to the dispute consent in writing to submit to [ICSID]." Many BITs — like the United States-Argentina BIT excerpted above — provide for ICSID arbitration of foreign investment disputes. ICSID administers and provides rules for investor-state arbitration, but like other arbitral institutions, the designated arbitrators resolve disputes, not ICSID itself. As one group of experts puts it:

> Today, any company considering a new investment in a developing country and any financing entity playing a role in the investment must be aware of ICSID. At the project negotiation and documentation stage, counsel for investors, financiers and government entities must be attuned to possible rights and responsibilities under the ICSID Convention and under available BITs. In sum, advisers to all sides must be at least familiar with the ICSID arbitration regime long before actual disputes might begin to develop.
>
> Similarly, when a dispute arises in connection with an existing foreign investment, counsel for the investor must consider all of the potentially applicable BITs to identify the substantive rights and arbitral mechanisms that may be envisaged under them. This must be done promptly and effectively, because parties that commence litigation or pursue other arbitration remedies may unknowingly waive the essential right of access to ICSID.

LUCY REED, JAN PAULSSON & NIGEL BLACKABY, GUIDE TO ICSID ARBITRATION vii-viii (2004).

3. **Importance of Investor-State Arbitration.** Investor-state arbitration is a growing field of transnational legal practice. According to a 2019 study of the U.N. Conference on Trade and Development (UNCTAD), the annual number of publicly known investor-state arbitrations was under 10 in the 1980s and almost all of the 1990s, but the number increased dramatically in the 2000s. At least 71 treaty-based investor-state arbitrations were initiated in 2018 (50 of which were filed with ICSID). The total number of known treaty-based investor-state arbitrations reached 942 by the end of 2018. However, given that arbitrations can be kept confidential, the actual number is likely higher. *See* Fact Sheet on Investor-State Dispute Settlement Cases in 2018 (May 2019), *available at* https://unctad.org/en/PublicationsLibrary/diaepcbinf2019d4_en.pdf.

4. **Parties in Investor-State Arbitration.** The UNCTAD study also found that most investor-state arbitrations involve claims brought by investors from

developed nations against the governments of developing nations. Among the findings:

- Of the 71 new cases in 2018, most were filed by investors from developed nations against developing countries and transition economies.
- Overall, at least 117 governments have responded to one or more investment treaty arbitrations. Argentina continues to be the most frequent respondent (60 cases) followed by Spain (49), Venezuela (37), Czechia (38), Egypt (33), Mexico (30), Poland (30), Canada (28), India (24), the Russian Federation (24), Ecuador (23), and Ukraine (23).
- Investor-state arbitrations have been initiated most frequently by claimants from the United States (174 cases, or 11.5 percent of all known disputes), the Netherlands (108 cases), the United Kingdom (78), Germany (62), Spain (50), Canada (49), and France (49).

Does this raise policy concerns? Why or why not? On the one hand, it could be perceived as raising policy concerns insofar as the system operates in a one-sided manner that either redistributes resources toward developed countries or reinforces status quo resource imbalances. On the other hand, the availability of investor-state arbitration may be precisely what gives developed nation investors the security they want before transferring resources to developing countries. What might explain the growing number of investor-state arbitrations?

As investor-state arbitrations have grown, they have become more controversial. Some nations and commentators feel that they intrude on the sovereignty of the host nation to make necessary regulations of foreign investment and assign arbitrators too great a role in second-guessing such regulations. A number of countries have begun to back away from the system of investor-state arbitration, either by withdrawing from ICSID, declining to sign additional BITs, or limiting arbitration remedies in new investor-protection agreements. Notably, while the original North American Free Trade Agreement (NAFTA) had investment protections with investor-state arbitration as a dispute settlement procedure, the agreement replacing NAFTA, the U.S.-Mexico-Canada Agreement (USMCA), limits investor-state arbitration substantially: Canada declined to join its investor-state arbitration provisions, and between the United States and Mexico the scope of arbitration is sharply reduced (including elimination of arbitration for alleged denials of fair and equitable treatment).

5. **The Public/Private Distinction.** An interesting aspect of investor-state arbitration is that it blurs the boundaries between private parties and international law and between domestic law and international law. Consent to transnational commercial arbitration takes the form of an agreement between the two disputants; in contrast, a host nation's consent to BIT-based investor-state arbitration is in a BIT with another nation, not in an agreement directly with the foreign investor. In other words, the BIT gives a private foreign investor the right to elect arbitration even though it is not a party to the BIT. Moreover, through investor-state arbitration, international law can be applied to review the host nation's regulations (e.g., labor and environmental regulations) and their impact on foreign investors and performance of the host nation's

domestic legal institutions, and if they fail to comport with international principles of investor protection, international law may offer the foreign investor a remedy against the host nation.

For an example of what's often at stake in investor-state arbitration, consider the following case. Bear Creek Mining Corp., a Canadian corporation, sought to develop a silver mine in Peru. Peru's government initially supported the project and issued the necessary approvals to begin exploration. However, the project encountered substantial opposition from local indigenous communities on environmental and cultural grounds, and protests escalated into violence. After a new government was elected in Peru, the government revoked its approval, contending that Bear Creek had not properly consulted with local interests nor filed adequate environmental studies. Bear Creek filed for ICSID arbitration under the Canada-Peru FTA, and the arbitrators issued a substantial award in its favor; among other things, they concluded that Peru's initial approval of the project had created a "reasonable expectation" that Bear Creek would be able to proceed with the project. *Bear Creek Mining Corp. v. Peru*, ICSID Case No. ARB/14/21 (2017). Does this represent appropriate protection for investment against arbitrary action by the host nation, or undue interference with the host nation's ability to protect environmental and cultural resources?

6. **Take Note.** In 2019, the American Law Institute approved the *Restatement of the Law, The U.S. Law of International Commercial and Investor-State Arbitration*. Chapter 5 of the new *Restatement* covers the role of U.S. courts in the investor-state arbitration process.

D. State-State Arbitration

Another type of transnational arbitration is state-state arbitration (sometimes referred to as international or interstate arbitration). Just as two commercial parties may file claims against one another in transnational commercial arbitration and an investor may bring claims against a state under a Bilateral Investment Treaty (BIT), states may avail themselves of the arbitration process to resolve disputes among themselves. In the modern period, state-state arbitration is said to begin with the Jay Treaty of 1794. In 1899, the Permanent Court of Arbitration (PCA) was established in the Peace Palace in The Hague (it is presently housed in the same building as the ICJ) to resolve disputes between states in an amicable fashion and avoid the use of force. There are presently 122 contracting parties to the founding conventions of the PCA.

The PCA is the registry for three state-state arbitrations at present. *See* https://pca-cpa.org/en/cases/. How do states agree to arbitrate? The predominant way is through treaties. For instance, the 1982 U.N. Convention on the Law of the Sea (UNCLOS) contains rules for the resolution of disputes between state parties

arising out of the interpretation or application of UNCLOS. *See* http://www
.pca-cpa.org/showpage.asp?pag_id=1288. Since the 1982 Convention came into
force in 1994, the PCA has served as registry for 13 UNCLOS cases. Besides maritime
disputes between nations, the PCA also hears territorial disputes between nations.

Nations may also consent to state-state arbitration through compromissory
clauses in other treaties, such as BITs. For instance, Article VIII of the United
States-Argentina BIT provides that "[a]ny dispute between the Parties concerning the interpretation or application of the Treaty which is not resolved through
consultations or other diplomatic channels, shall be submitted, upon the request
of either Party, to an arbitral tribunal for binding decision in accordance with the
applicable rules of international law."

NOTES AND QUESTIONS

1. **Why Would a Nation Choose Arbitration?** Throughout this chapter, we
   have discussed the many factors a private party might consider to elect arbitration over litigation in national or international courts (or vice versa). Are the
   same factors relevant to nations in the context of state-state arbitration? Are
   there different reasons that a nation would opt to bring suit before an arbitral
   panel as opposed to (for example) the ICJ?
2. **Public Policy.** Putting aside the procedural advantages of state-state arbitration, are there public policy reasons that these cases should be decided by
   courts rather than by arbitrators? Or vice versa?
3. **Enforcement.** In 2016, the Permanent Court of Arbitration issued an award
   resolving a dispute under UNCLOS instituted by the Republic of Philippines
   against the People's Republic of China regarding whether China was permitted to build on various islands in the South China Sea. China claims almost
   the entire South China Sea, through which more than $5 trillion in trade
   moves annually. Brunei, Malaysia, the Philippines, Taiwan, and Vietnam also
   have claims in the sea, which is thought to be rich in energy deposits. The
   Tribunal found in favor of the Philippines. For a press release issued by the
   PCA as well as the complete award, see https://pca-cpa.org/en/news/pca-press-
   release-the-south-china-sea-arbitration-the-republic-of-the-philippines-v-the-
   peoples-republic-of-china/. After the Tribunal's decision, China rejected the
   ruling. Many countries, including the United States, Japan, Australia, and
   New Zealand, have called the award legally binding and have urged both parties, especially China, to comply with it. Other countries, including Russia,
   have expressed concern about the award.

   What might account for these diverging views on the legitimacy and
   enforceability of this state-state arbitration award?

REVIEW NOTES AND QUESTIONS

1. As you review this chapter's materials, focus on the following overarching questions:

   - What are the distinguishing features of litigation and the ADR methods discussed in this chapter — negotiation, mediation, and arbitration?
   - What are the comparative advantages and disadvantages of litigation and arbitration? In what types of situations might you advise a client to choose litigation rather than arbitration? In what types of situations might you advise a client to choose arbitration rather than litigation?
   - If you are drafting an arbitration agreement for a client, what key provisions would you include in the agreement?
   - If your client has an arbitration agreement, and the other party files a lawsuit in a court or simply refuses to arbitrate, what steps would you consider taking on behalf of your client to enforce the arbitration agreement?

2. In light of all the cases we have considered, what is your view of transnational arbitration? Does it resolve the issues highlighted in the introduction? Does it enable party autonomy? Is it an end-run around state authority? Should there be a more significant role for national courts in determining what types of disputes may be arbitrated rather than litigated?

HOW CAN DISPUTE RESOLUTION OUTCOMES BE ENFORCED?

Sometimes a party will fail to abide by a dispute resolution outcome—such as a court judgment after litigation, a settlement agreement reached through negotiation or mediation, or an arbitral award produced by arbitration. In those situations, what can the other party do to encourage—or compel—the noncomplying party to abide by the judgment, settlement agreement, or arbitral award?

There are various possibilities, including negotiation with the noncomplying party, adverse publicity, or other forms of pressure to encourage compliance. In the case of a settlement agreement, the beneficiary of a dispute resolution outcome may file a lawsuit against the noncomplying party to enforce the agreement. In the case of litigation or arbitration, the beneficiary may file a court action to enforce the resulting court judgment or arbitral award. Or the beneficiary may conclude that the costs of seeking compliance (which may include attorneys' fees and other costs of litigation) are likely to exceed the expected benefits, in which case it may do nothing.

Part III of the casebook introduces you to one important method for enforcing transnational dispute resolution outcomes: judicial enforcement. The primary focus is on judicial enforcement in U.S. courts of transnational dispute resolution outcomes. Chapter 7 focuses on enforcement of court judgments. Chapter 8 focuses on the enforcement of arbitral awards.

judicial enforce-ment of dispute resolution outcome

court judgements / arbitral awards

COURT JUDGMENTS

Recall the *Chevron-Ecuador* case discussed at the end of the Introduction to this casebook. In 1993, residents of the Lago Agrio region of the Amazon rainforest in the Republic of Ecuador sued Texaco, Inc., a U.S. corporation, in the U.S. District Court for the Southern District of New York. The complaint alleged extensive environmental damage and personal injuries caused by Texaco's oil extraction operations in Ecuador, as part of a joint venture with Ecuador's national oil company, Petroecuador. At Texaco's request, the U.S. court dismissed the suit, concluding that it had "everything to do with Ecuador, and nothing to do with the United States," and therefore should be brought in Ecuadorian courts. *Aguinda v. Texaco, Inc.*, 142 F. Supp. 2d 534, 537 (S.D.N.Y. 2001). The U.S. Court of Appeals for the Second Circuit affirmed. *Aguinda v. Texaco, Inc.*, 303 F.3d 470 (2d Cir. 2002). Meanwhile, Chevron Corp., also a U.S. corporation, acquired Texaco in 2001; it thereafter terminated its operations in Ecuador and no longer has a business presence there.

After the court dismissed the U.S. lawsuit, the Lago Agrio plaintiffs sued Chevron in Ecuador. Chevron argued that Texaco had entered an agreement with Ecuador and Petroecuador whereby Texaco agreed to take certain environmental remediation measures; that Ecuador and Petroecuador agreed to release Texaco from liability upon completion of those measures; and that Texaco fulfilled all of its obligations under the agreement and was therefore released from liability. The Ecuadorian court disagreed, finding Chevron liable for personal injury and environmental damage as Texaco's successor, and entered a $17.2 billion judgment against Chevron. Ecuadorian courts of appeal later affirmed the judgment (but reduced its amount to $8.6 billion).

Chevron — which no longer had significant assets in Ecuador — refused to pay. It argued that the Ecuadorian judgment was invalid because the Ecuadorian legal system did not provide due process and the proceedings leading to the judgment were tainted by fraud and other improper conduct, including by the plaintiffs' lawyers. The plaintiffs disagreed, and argued that any purported defects in the trial court proceedings had been adequately addressed on appeal in Ecuador.

What, if anything, could the plaintiffs do to compel Chevron to pay the judgment? What steps could have been taken in Ecuador? In the United States? In other nations? And what about Chevron? What could it do to avoid being forced to pay a judgment that it deems invalid? Who should decide whether Chevron's allegations of fraud and misconduct are true? The Ecuadorian appellate courts? A U.S. court? Some other court?

This chapter focuses on these and related issues, with an emphasis on judicial enforcement of court judgments in transnational disputes. If a court enters a judgment and the losing party does not voluntarily abide by it, the prevailing party may seek to enforce the judgment by enlisting judicial assistance. As background, this chapter first explores methods for enforcing U.S. court judgments in the United States. It then explores methods for enforcing the judgments of foreign nations' courts in U.S. courts, with an emphasis on foreign country money judgments — the most common type of foreign judgment. It also briefly considers the question of enforcement of judgments of international courts. Finally, this chapter considers enforcement of judgments in non-U.S. courts, especially enforcement of U.S. court judgments.

Throughout this chapter, you should keep in mind the distinction between *recognition* and *enforcement* of a foreign judgment. Recognition means a court's decision to treat another court's judgment as conclusive, such as for purposes of issue preclusion (traditionally called collateral estoppel) or claim preclusion (traditionally called res judicata). Enforcement is a court's decision to authorize the application of the coercive power of the government (such as the seizure of property by a sheriff) to compel a party to comply with a judgment. Recognition generally is understood as a necessary first step before enforcement of a foreign judgment, but courts often make enforcement decisions without explicitly analyzing recognition as a distinct issue.

A further essential perspective is how issues of enforcement affect other aspects of transnational practice. Consider how what you learn about enforcement would influence how you might advise clients in earlier phases of transnational practice, including negotiating deals and planning dispute resolution strategy.

A. Enforcing U.S. State and Federal Court Judgments Within the United States

How can a party enforce a judgment entered by a U.S. court after the adjudication of a transnational dispute? For example, a plaintiff may obtain a judgment against a defendant ordering the defendant to pay the plaintiff a sum of money (for example, damages in a tort or contract claim). This type of judgment is called a *money judgment*. The party owed the money is called the *judgment creditor* and the party obligated to pay the money is called the *judgment debtor*.

If the judgment debtor refuses to pay the judgment creditor the amount ordered by the money judgment — that is, if the defendant fails to *satisfy* the judgment voluntarily — then the plaintiff can attempt to enforce the judgment through a process called *execution*. Although the detailed steps vary from state to state, the process typically begins when, at the judgment creditor's request, the court issues an order called a ***writ of execution*** authorizing a sheriff or other government official to seize or otherwise assert control over property of the judgment debtor. The seized property will be sold at a public auction, with the proceeds being paid to the judgment creditor to satisfy the judgment and any additional proceeds being returned to the judgment debtor. Property subject to execution may include property in possession of the judgment debtor or property of the judgment debtor held by a third party, such as funds in bank accounts of the judgment debtor or wages or other income owed to the judgment debtor. Such a third party is called a ***garnishee*** and the process of transferring such property to satisfy a judgment is called ***garnishment***. There are limits to the types of property that may be used for execution, including limits designed to ensure that the judgment debtor will have sufficient resources to provide for basic necessities. These exemptions, like other aspects of enforcement, vary from state to state. In federal court, the law governing the execution of judgments ordinarily is state law. FED. R. CIV. P. 69. For a detailed discussion of execution, see JACK H. FRIEDENTHAL, MARY KAY KANE & ARTHUR R. MILLER, CIVIL PROCEDURE § 15.7 (5th ed. 2015).

A court has no authority to issue a writ of execution against property located outside its territorial jurisdiction. Therefore, if the judgment debtor has no property in the state where the judgment was entered, the judgment creditor may be unable to enforce the judgment there. However, if the judgment creditor is able to locate assets of the judgment debtor in another U.S. state, the judgment creditor may attempt to enforce the judgment in that other state. Note that in federal court, Rule 69 of the Federal Rules of Civil Procedure allows a prevailing party to seek judge-ordered discovery of a judgment debtor's assets to aid enforcement of a judgment. Under the Full Faith and Credit Clause of the U.S. Constitution and its implementing statute,* U.S. states generally must give full faith and credit to the judgments of the courts of other U.S. states (***sister states***) — including through enforcement. In other words, a U.S. state ordinarily must treat a judgment of another U.S. state as if the judgment were a judgment of one of its own courts. In addition, U.S. state and federal courts generally must give full faith and credit to federal court judgments, and U.S. federal courts generally must give full faith and credit to state court judgments. The exceptions to the full-faith-and-credit requirement are very narrow. The only well-established exceptions are lack of personal jurisdiction, lack of subject matter jurisdiction, and fraud. For a more detailed discussion of the recognition and enforcement of U.S. state and federal court judgments in the United States, see WILLIAM M. RICHMAN, WILLIAM L. REYNOLDS & CHRISTOPHER A. WHYTOCK, UNDERSTANDING CONFLICT OF LAWS §§ 109-117 (4th ed. 2013).

---

* Under Article IV, Section 1 of the U.S. Constitution, "Full Faith and Credit shall be given in each State to the Public Acts, Records, and judicial Proceedings of every other State. And the Congress may by general Laws prescribe the Manner in which such Acts, Records, and Proceedings shall be proved, and the Effect thereof." According to 28 U.S.C. § 1738, the judicial proceedings of any court of any state, territory, or possession of the United States "shall have the same full faith and credit in every court within the United States and its Territories and Possessions as they have by law or usage in the courts of such State, Territory or Possession from which they are taken."

Streamlined registration procedures are available for enforcing a judgment of one federal court in another federal court,* and such procedures are also available in many states for enforcing federal and sister-state judgments, including states that have adopted legislation based on the 1964 Revised Uniform Enforcement of Foreign Judgments Act (note that the term "foreign" in the title of this uniform act is generally understood as referring to judgments of U.S. federal or sister-state courts, not judgments of courts of foreign nations). In other states, the judgment creditor must file a separate action to enforce the judgment.

Judgments ordering injunctive relief rather than the payment of money may be enforced by holding the noncomplying party in contempt of court. The court may impose a fine against and, in some circumstances, order incarceration of, a person in contempt of court. Declaratory judgments are not subject to enforcement as such, as they only declare the legal rights and obligations of the parties without ordering a further remedy. But under full faith and credit, a court in one U.S. state generally must recognize the declaratory judgments of sister U.S. states, including by granting them issue or claim preclusive effect.

B. Enforcing Foreign Judgments in U.S. Courts

1. Foundations

The full-faith-and-credit obligations of U.S. states do not extend to foreign nations. What, then, is the basis for the recognition and enforcement of *foreign judgments* — that is, the judgments of the courts of foreign nations — in the United States? Customary international law does not require nations to recognize or enforce other nations' court judgments. As we will see, there are treaties governing recognition and enforcement — but the United States is not currently a party to any of them. However, U.S. courts recognize and enforce foreign judgments based on the doctrine of "comity."

What is comity? The U.S. Supreme Court explained the concept in *Hilton v. Guyot*, which is widely understood to be the seminal statement of U.S. law governing the enforcement of foreign judgments:

> No law has any effect, of its own force, beyond the limits of the sovereignty from which its authority is derived. The extent to which the law of one nation, as put in force within its territory, whether by executive order, by legislative act, or by judicial decree, shall be allowed to operate within the dominion of another nation, depends upon what our greatest jurists have been content to call "the comity of nations." Although the phrase has been often criticised, no satisfactory substitute has been suggested.
>
> "Comity," in the legal sense, is neither a matter of absolute obligation, on the one hand, nor of mere courtesy and good will, upon the other. But it is the recognition which one nation allows within its territory to the legislative, executive or judicial acts of another nation, having due regard both to international duty

---

* 28 U.S.C. § 1963.

and convenience, and to the rights of its own citizens, or of other persons who are under the protection of its laws.

Hilton v. Guyot, 159 U.S. 113, 163-64 (1895). The *Hilton* case continues to be widely cited, both for the proposition that comity is the theoretical basis for recognition and enforcement of foreign judgments, and as authority for the circumstances in which comity will be extended to recognize or enforce a foreign judgment:

> [W]here there has been opportunity for a full and fair trial abroad before a court of competent jurisdiction, conducting the trial upon regular proceedings, after due citation or voluntary appearance of the defendant, and under a system of jurisprudence likely to secure an impartial administration of justice between the citizens of its own country and those of other countries, and there is nothing to show either prejudice in the court, or in the system of laws under which it was sitting, or fraud in procuring the judgment, or any other special reason why the comity of this nation should not allow it full effect, the merits of the case should not, in an action brought in this country upon the judgment, be tried afresh, as on a new trial or an appeal, upon the mere assertion of the party that the judgment was erroneous in law or in fact. The defendants, therefore, cannot be permitted, upon that general ground, to contest the validity or the effect of the judgment sued on.

Id. at 202-03.

Today, there are two primary sources of law governing the recognition and enforcement of foreign judgments in U.S. courts: (1) state legislation and (2) common law. Most states have adopted legislation based on one of two model acts drafted by the Uniform Law Commission: the Uniform Foreign Money-Judgments Recognition Act of 1962 (the "1962 Uniform Act") or the Uniform Foreign-Country Money Judgments Recognition Act of 2005 (the "2005 Uniform Act").* Currently, 11 states plus the U.S. Virgin Islands have legislation based on the 1962 Uniform Act, and 26 states have legislation based on the 2005 Uniform Act.

A second source of law governing the recognition and enforcement of foreign judgments in U.S. courts is common law. State courts in states without applicable legislation apply state common law rules. As an implication of the *Erie* doctrine, federal courts sitting in diversity apply state law to govern the recognition and enforcement of foreign country judgments. In non-diversity cases, federal courts apply federal common law. As noted above, *Hilton v. Guyot* continues to be widely cited as common law authority. A comprehensive restatement of the common law governing the recognition and enforcement of foreign judgments is contained in the *Restatement (Fourth) of the Foreign Relations Law of the United States,* Chapter 8.

---

* In addition, the American Law Institute drafted a proposed federal statute to govern the enforcement of foreign judgments. AMERICAN LAW INSTITUTE, RECOGNITION AND ENFORCEMENT OF FOREIGN JUDGMENTS ACT: ANALYSIS AND PROPOSED FEDERAL STATUTE (2006). However, Congress has not adopted the proposal.

As a first step toward learning the law of foreign judgments, review the following excerpts from the 2005 Uniform Act and the *Restatement (Fourth)*.

Uniform Foreign-Country Money Judgments Recognition Act of 2005

SECTION 3. APPLICABILITY.

(a) Except as otherwise provided in subsection (b), this [act] applies to a foreign-country judgment to the extent that the judgment:

(1) grants or denies recovery of a sum of money; and

(2) under the law of the foreign country where rendered, is final, conclusive, and enforceable.

(b) This [act] does not apply to a foreign-country judgment, even if the judgment grants or denies recovery of a sum of money, to the extent that the judgment is:

(1) a judgment for taxes;

(2) a fine or other penalty; or

(3) a judgment for divorce, support, or maintenance, or other judgment rendered in connection with domestic relations.

(c) A party seeking recognition of a foreign-country judgment has the burden of establishing that this [act] applies to the foreign-country judgment.

SECTION 4. STANDARDS FOR RECOGNITION OF FOREIGN-COUNTRY JUDGMENT.

(a) Except as otherwise provided in subsections (b) and (c), a court of this state shall recognize a foreign-country judgment to which this [act] applies.

(b) A court of this state may not recognize a foreign-country judgment if:

(1) the judgment was rendered under a judicial system that does not provide impartial tribunals or procedures compatible with the requirements of due process of law;

(2) the foreign court did not have personal jurisdiction over the defendant; or

(3) the foreign court did not have jurisdiction over the subject matter.

(c) A court of this state need not recognize a foreign-country judgment if:

(1) the defendant in the proceeding in the foreign court did not receive notice of the proceeding in sufficient time to enable the defendant to defend;

(2) the judgment was obtained by fraud that deprived the losing party of an adequate opportunity to present its case;

(3) the judgment or the . . . cause of action . . . on which the judgment is based is repugnant to the public policy of this state or of the United States;

(4) the judgment conflicts with another final and conclusive judgment;

(5) the proceeding in the foreign court was contrary to an agreement between the parties under which the dispute in question was to be determined otherwise than by proceedings in that foreign court;

(6) in the case of jurisdiction based only on personal service, the foreign court was a seriously inconvenient forum for the trial of the action;

(7) the judgment was rendered in circumstances that raise substantial doubt about the integrity of the rendering court with respect to the judgment; or

(8) the specific proceeding in the foreign court leading to the judgment was not compatible with the requirements of due process of law.

(d) A party resisting recognition of a foreign-country judgment has the burden of establishing that a ground for nonrecognition stated in subsection (b) or (c) exists.

. . .

SECTION 7. EFFECT OF RECOGNITION OF FOREIGN-COUNTRY JUDGMENT.

If the [U.S.] court . . . finds that the foreign-country judgment is entitled to recognition under this [act] then, to the extent that the foreign-country judgment grants or denies recovery of a sum of money, the foreign-country judgment is:

(1) conclusive between the parties to the same extent as the judgment of a sister state entitled to full faith and credit in this state would be conclusive; and

(2) enforceable in the same manner and to the same extent as a judgment rendered in this state.

SECTION 8. STAY OF PROCEEDINGS PENDING APPEAL OF FOREIGN-COUNTRY JUDGMENT.

If a party establishes that an appeal from a foreign-country judgment is pending or will be taken, the court may stay any proceedings with regard to the foreign-country judgment until the appeal is concluded, the time for appeal expires, or the appellant has had sufficient time to prosecute the appeal and has failed to do so.

. . .

Restatement (Fourth) of the Foreign Relations Law of the United States (2018)

§ 481 Recognition of Foreign Judgments

Except as provided in §§ 483-484 and § 489, a final, conclusive, and enforceable judgment of a court of a foreign state granting or denying recovery of a sum of money, or determining a legal controversy, is entitled to recognition by courts in the United States.

§ 482 Procedure to Obtain Recognition
A person seeking recognition of a foreign judgment must either initiate a civil proceeding for that purpose in a court of competent jurisdiction or properly raise the issue in an existing proceeding.

§ 483 Mandatory Grounds for Nonrecognition
A court in the United States will not recognize a judgment of a court of a foreign state if:

(a) the judgment was rendered under a judicial system that does not provide impartial tribunals or procedures compatible with fundamental principles of fairness;

(b) the court that rendered the judgment did not have personal or subject-matter jurisdiction; or

(c) the judgment rested on a claim of defamation and the SPEECH Act forbids its recognition or enforcement.

§ 484 Discretionary Grounds for Nonrecognition
To the extent provided by applicable law, a court in the United States need not recognize a judgment of a court of a foreign state if:

(a) the party resisting recognition did not receive adequate notice of the proceeding in the foreign court in sufficient time to enable it to defend;

(b) the judgment was obtained by fraud that deprived the party resisting recognition of an adequate opportunity to present its case;

(c) the judgment or the claim on which the judgment is based is repugnant to the public policy of the State in which recognition is sought or of the United States;

(d) the judgment conflicts with another final and conclusive judgment;

(e) the proceeding in the foreign court was contrary to an agreement between the parties to commit resolution of the dispute in question exclusively to another forum;

(f) in cases in which the foreign court's jurisdiction rested only on personal service, the foreign court was a seriously inconvenient forum for resolution of the dispute;

(g) the judgment was rendered in circumstances that raise substantial doubt about the integrity of the rendering court with respect to the judgment;

(h) the specific proceeding in the foreign court leading to the judgment was not compatible with fundamental principles of fairness; or

(i) the courts of the state of origin would not recognize a comparable U.S. judgment.

§ 485 Burdens of Proof
(1) A party seeking recognition of a foreign judgment has the burden of proving: (a) that the foreign judgment is final, conclusive, and enforceable under the law of the country in which it was rendered; and (b) that the foreign judgment is not for taxes, fines, or other penalties.

(2) A party seeking to rely on the preclusive effect of a foreign judgment has the burden of proving that the claim or issue is precluded.

(3) A party resisting recognition of a final, conclusive, and enforceable foreign judgment has the burden of proving that one or more of the grounds stated in §§ 483 and 484 exist.

§ 486 Enforcement of Foreign Judgments

A foreign money judgment entitled to recognition under § 481 is enforceable in the same manner and to the same extent as a judgment rendered in the State in which enforcement is sought.

. . .

§ 488 Foreign Injunctions

Except as provided in §§ 483-484 and § 489, a final and conclusive judgment of a court of a foreign state in an action seeking an injunction or a comparable nonmonetary remedy is entitled to recognition by courts in the United States. However, the question of what remedies to grant as a result of recognition of the foreign judgment, including whether to provide injunctive relief, does not depend on the remedies provided by the rendering court.

§ 489 Tax and Penal Judgments

Courts in the United States do not recognize or enforce judgments rendered by the courts of foreign states to the extent such judgments are for taxes, fines, or other penalties, unless authorized by a statute or an international agreement.

NOTES AND QUESTIONS

1. **Policy: Why Enforce?** Why should a U.S. court ever recognize or enforce a foreign judgment? Why shouldn't a U.S. court always recognize and enforce foreign judgments?

2. *Hilton* **versus the** *Restatement.* Compare the Supreme Court's principles of foreign judgment enforcement in the excerpt from *Hilton v. Guyot* with the American Law Institute's restatement of those principles. How are they similar? How are they different?

3. **The** *Restatement* **versus the 2005 Uniform Act.** Now compare the American Law Institute's restatement of the principles of foreign judgment enforcement with the Uniform Law Commission's 2005 Uniform Act. How are they similar? How are they different?

4. **Coverage of the 2005 Uniform Act.** To which kinds of foreign judgments does the 2005 Uniform Act apply? To which kinds does it not apply? Why do you think the 2005 Uniform Act excludes certain types of judgments from its coverage? With the usual exception of foreign "public law" judgments such as tax judgments or fines and penalties, U.S. courts may recognize or enforce foreign judgments not covered by the 2005 Uniform Act based on common law principles. See the excerpts from the *Restatement.*

5. **Mandatory and Discretionary Exceptions.** Note the distinction in the 2005 Uniform Act and the *Restatement (Fourth)* between mandatory grounds for refusing recognition of a foreign judgment (a court "may not recognize . . .") and discretionary grounds for refusing recognition (a court "need not recognize . . ."). Using different language, the 1962 Uniform Act makes the same distinction. Why do you think there are both mandatory and discretionary grounds? Is it a good idea to prohibit a U.S. court from recognizing or enforcing certain types of foreign judgments? Is it a good idea to give courts discretion to decide whether to recognize or enforce other types of foreign judgments?

6. **Burdens of Proof in Enforcement Actions.** Review the excerpts from the 2005 Uniform Act and the *Restatement (Fourth)* again. How do they allocate the burdens of judgment creditors and judgment debtors to establish the grounds for enforcing or refusing to recognize or enforce a foreign judgment?

7. **Intrinsic versus Extrinsic Fraud.** There is a widely (if not universally) accepted distinction between **intrinsic fraud** and **extrinsic fraud**. As the drafters' comments to the 2005 Uniform Act explain:

> Subsection 4(c)(2) [the fraud exception] limits the type of fraud that will serve as a ground for denying recognition to extrinsic fraud. This provision is consistent with the interpretation of the comparable provision in subsection 4(b)(2) of the 1962 Uniform Act by the courts, which have found that only extrinsic fraud — conduct of the prevailing party that deprived the losing party of an adequate opportunity to present its case — is sufficient under the 1962 Uniform Act. Examples of extrinsic fraud would be when the plaintiff deliberately had the initiating process served on the defendant at the wrong address, deliberately gave the defendant wrong information as to the time and place of the hearing, or obtained a default judgment against the defendant based on a forged confession of judgment. When this type of fraudulent action by the plaintiff deprives the defendant of an adequate opportunity to present its case, then it provides grounds for denying recognition of the foreign-country judgment. Extrinsic fraud should be distinguished from intrinsic fraud, such as false testimony of a witness or admission of a forged document into evidence during the foreign proceeding. Intrinsic fraud does not provide a basis for denying recognition under subsection 4(c)(2), as the assertion that intrinsic fraud has occurred should be raised and dealt with in the rendering court.

Section 4, Comment 7. *See also Restatement (Fourth)* § 484, cmt. d, which does not use the terms "extrinsic" and "intrinsic" but adopts the same distinction:

> A court in the United States will not recognize a foreign judgment obtained by fraud if the effect of the fraud was to deprive the losing party of an adequate opportunity to present its case and there was no adequate opportunity for correction of the fraud in the foreign proceeding, including a timely appeal. False testimony or forged evidence does not by itself provide a basis for nonrecognition because it should have been raised and dealt with in the foreign proceeding. Evidence that the plaintiff deliberately served the plaintiff at the wrong address, deliberately misled the defendant about the time or place of a

hearing, or obtained a default judgment based on a forged confession of judgment could be grounds for nonrecognition if the defendant was deprived of an adequate opportunity to present its case. Evidence that the party who benefited from the foreign judgment materially deceived the court as to significant and relevant issues also may justify nonrecognition, if the party opposing recognition has an adequate explanation for its failure to detect the fraud during the course of the foreign proceeding and if the rendering court offered no means for addressing the fraud after it was discovered.

What is the reason for this distinction? Should fraud, no matter what kind, be a basis for nonrecognition? Why or why not?

8. **Reciprocity.** Section 484(i) of the Restatement includes a discretionary ground for refusing recognition and enforcement that is not included in the 2005 Uniform Act: "To the extent provided by applicable law, a court in the United States need not recognize a judgment of a court of a foreign state if . . . the courts of the state of origin would not recognize a comparable U.S. judgment. However, as the *Restatement* explains, neither federal common law nor the law of most states has this exception:

> Most U.S. States today will recognize a foreign judgment even if the issuing forum would not accord the same treatment to a similar U.S. judgment, but a few States make reciprocity a mandatory or discretionary ground for recognition. The rule of unilateral recognition represents an evolution of U.S. law from *Hilton v. Guyot*, 159 U.S. 113 (1895), which imposed a reciprocity requirement as a matter of general common law. In listing reciprocity as a ground for denying recognition, this Section indicates only that the minority of States that follow *Hilton* on this point are free to do so. Neither international nor federal law requires reciprocity, but it also is true that neither forbids reciprocity.

Id., cmt. k. What might be the purpose of a reciprocity requirement? What might be some of the disadvantages of a reciprocity requirement? In practice, who is most likely to bear the costs of a reciprocity requirement? The judgment creditor or the judgment debtor? Is the reciprocity requirement fair to the parties?

9. **The 2005 Uniform Act versus the 1962 Uniform Act.** There are various significant differences between the 1962 Uniform Act and the 2005 Uniform Act, the most important of which is that the 1962 Uniform Act does not include two discretionary exceptions: § 4(c)(7) ("the judgment was rendered in circumstances that raise substantial doubt about the integrity of the rendering court with respect to the judgment") and § 4(c)(8) ("the specific proceeding in the foreign court leading to the judgment was not compatible with the requirements of due process of law"). Why do you think these additional exceptions were added? What are some of the possible advantages and disadvantages of adding these exceptions?

10. **Adoption of the Uniform Acts.** As noted above, currently 37 states plus the District of Columbia and the U.S. Virgin Islands have adopted legislation based on the 1962 Uniform Act or the 2005 Uniform Act. As a result, there

is some degree of uniformity of foreign judgment enforcement law within the United States. However, it is extremely important to read a state's recognition and enforcement legislation carefully, because even legislation based on a uniform act may not follow the act exactly.

11.   **Federal Law and the Enforcement of Foreign Judgments.** In 2010, Congress passed the SPEECH Act, which prohibits U.S. state and federal courts from enforcing foreign defamation judgments that would violate the U.S. Constitution's protections of freedom of speech and press. 28 U.S.C. § 4102. However, Congress has yet to adopt general legislation on the recognition and enforcement of foreign judgments (such as the American Law Institute's proposed Recognition and Enforcement of Foreign Judgments Act). Should there be uniform federal law to govern the recognition and enforcement of foreign judgments? What would be the advantages and disadvantages of federalizing this area of law?

12.   **The Hague Convention on Choice of Court Agreements.** In 2005, the Hague Conference on Private International Law concluded the Convention on Choice of Court Agreements. The Convention entered into force in 2015 and currently has 32 parties. The United States has signed but not ratified the Convention. The Convention applies (subject to exceptions) in transnational cases involving civil or commercial matters where the parties have entered an exclusive choice of court agreement. The general rule is that "[a] judgment given by a court of a Contracting State designated in an exclusive choice of court agreement shall be recognized and enforced in other Contracting States" without review of the merits or the rendering court's findings of fact. *Id.*, art. 8. Exceptions allow a court to refuse recognition or enforcement based on lack of capacity to conclude the choice of court agreement, inadequate notice of the proceedings in the rendering court, fraud in connection with a matter of procedure, manifest incompatibility with public policy, and inconsistency with another judgment. *Id.*, art. 9 Although modest in scope, the Convention promises to enhance the ability of commercial parties to rely upon choice of court agreements in transnational business. Choice of court agreements (commonly called forum selection clauses) are discussed in Chapter 10.

13.   **The Hague Convention on Enforcement of Foreign Judgments.** In 2019, the Hague Conference concluded the Convention on the Recognition and Enforcement of Foreign Judgments in Civil or Commercial Matters. At present only two nations have signed the Convention, and it has not yet entered into force. The scope of this Convention is broader than that of the Convention on Choice of Court Agreements. Article 1 defines the scope of the Convention:

> 1. This Convention shall apply to the recognition and enforcement of judgments in civil or commercial matters. It shall not extend in particular to revenue, customs or administrative matters.
>
> 2. This Convention shall apply to the recognition and enforcement in one Contracting State of a judgment given by a court of another Contracting State.

Article 2 lists matters that are excluded from the Convention's scope (such as family law and intellectual property matters). Article 4(1), the Convention's central provision, provides: "A judgment given by a court of a Contracting State (State of origin) shall be recognised and enforced in another Contracting State (requested State) in accordance with the provisions of this Chapter. Recognition or enforcement may be refused only on the grounds specified in this Convention." Article 5 enumerates different grounds for a court's jurisdiction over a defendant that make a judgment from that court eligible for recognition and enforcement under the Convention. Article 7(1) contains a list of exceptions to Article 4(1)'s general rule favoring recognition and enforcement:

> Recognition or enforcement may be refused if—
>   (a) the document which instituted the proceedings or an equivalent document, including a statement of the essential elements of the claim—
>   (i) was not notified to the defendant in sufficient time and in such a way as to enable them to arrange for their defence, unless the defendant entered an appearance and presented their case without contesting notification in the court of origin, provided that the law of the State of origin permitted notification to be contested; or
>   (ii) was notified to the defendant in the requested State in a manner that is incompatible with fundamental principles of the requested State concerning service of documents;
>   (b) the judgment was obtained by fraud;
>   (c) recognition or enforcement would be manifestly incompatible with the public policy of the requested State, including situations where the specific proceedings leading to the judgment were incompatible with fundamental principles of procedural fairness of that State and situations involving infringements of security or sovereignty of that State;
>   (d) the proceedings in the court of origin were contrary to an agreement, or a designation in a trust instrument, under which the dispute in question was to be determined in a court of a State other than the State of origin;
>   (e) the judgment is inconsistent with a judgment given by a court of the requested State in a dispute between the same parties; or
>   (f) the judgment is inconsistent with an earlier judgment given by a court of another State between the same parties on the same subject matter, provided that the earlier judgment fulfils the conditions necessary for its recognition in the requested State.

Compare these exceptions to those in the 2005 Uniform Act and the *Restatement*. What are the most significant differences? Should the United States ratify the Convention? What would it gain and what would it be giving up in doing so?

2. *Enforcing Foreign Money Judgments in U.S. Courts*

There are different types of foreign judgments. A plaintiff may obtain a judgment from a foreign court ordering a defendant to pay the plaintiff a sum of money (for example, damages in a tort or contract claim). This type of foreign country judgment is called a *foreign money judgment*. As with domestic money judgments, the party owed the money is called the judgment creditor and the party obligated to pay the money is called the judgment debtor. But there are also foreign declaratory judgments and foreign judgments ordering injunctive relief. The 1962 Uniform Act and 2005 Uniform Act apply only to foreign money judgments. U.S. courts may nevertheless recognize or enforce other types of foreign judgments under the more general principles stated in *Hilton v. Guyot* and the *Restatement*. Moreover, special rules apply to the recognition and enforcement of foreign judgments in family matters, such as foreign support or child custody orders.

Foreign money judgments are the type of foreign judgments that most lawyers are most likely to encounter in practice. Therefore, this section provides an in-depth examination of the recognition and enforcement of foreign money judgments in U.S. courts. For a discussion of the recognition and enforcement of foreign judgments other than money judgments, see VED P. NANDA, DAVID K. PANSIUS, DAVID K. PANSIUS & BRYAN NEIHART, LITIGATION OF INTERNATIONAL DISPUTES IN U.S. COURTS § 20:20 (2019). For a discussion of the recognition and enforcement of foreign judgments in family matters specifically, see WILLIAM M. RICHMAN, WILLIAM L. REYNOLDS & CHRISTOPHER A. WHYTOCK, UNDERSTANDING CONFLICT OF LAWS §§ 128, 131 (4th ed. 2013).

Both the 1962 Uniform Act and the 2005 Uniform Act create a general rule in favor of the recognition and enforcement of foreign money judgments. Look at the excerpt from the 2005 Uniform Act above. Where is this general rule found in the 2005 Uniform Act? As discussed above, however, the two Acts also contain mandatory and discretionary exceptions to the general rule. In the materials that follow, we focus on two types of exceptions: procedural fairness exceptions and the public policy exception.

a. Procedural Fairness Exceptions

Some exceptions to the enforcement of foreign judgments help protect the procedural rights of judgment debtors. Which of the 2005 Uniform Act's exceptions might serve this purpose? The next two cases examine these exceptions. In one case, the court held that the judgment should be enforced. In the other, the court held that the judgment should not be enforced. As you study these cases, identify the reasons given for the different outcomes. Are they persuasive? Are there reasons the courts might not have mentioned? In addition, consider the different types of evidence that each court relied on to reach its holding.

Midbrook Flowerbulbs Holland B.V. v. Holland America Bulb Farms, Inc.

874 F.3d 604 (9th Cir. 2017)

BEA, Circuit Judge:

After the collapse of the Dutch Tulip Bubble of 1637, we've heard little about that flower's market. But it hasn't gone away.

This action grows out of a family business dispute: The Dutch shipper of tulip bulbs to his brother in America claims his brother shorted him. The dispute was litigated at three court levels in Holland. The shipper won. Now he comes to Seattle to enforce his judgment. Enforce it the district court did. The American importer-buyer appeals that judgment. He will lose.

I. Background

A. Factual Background

Holland America Bulb Farms, Inc. ("Holland America") is a Washington corporation that grows and sells tulips and other varieties of cut flowers. Its sole owners, Benno and Klazina Dobbe, founded Holland America together after immigrating to the United States from the Netherlands in 1980.

In 1994, Holland America began purchasing flower bulbs from Midbrook Flowerbulbs Holland, B.V. ("Midbrook"), a Dutch corporation in which Arie Dobbe, Benno's brother, was a manager and part owner. Midbrook purchased flower bulbs from farms in the Netherlands and elsewhere, packaged them for shipment, and exported them to Holland America's farm in Washington. Though Holland America and Midbrook never entered into a written agreement regarding payment, Benno and Arie orally agreed that Holland America would pay Midbrook its "actual costs on a one to one basis plus a commission."

For each shipment, Midbrook sent Holland America an invoice in Dutch guilders.[1] Instead of paying these invoices directly to Midbrook in guilders, Holland America deposited a lump sum of dollars into a Dutch bank account in Midbrook's name (the "dollar account"). At "fixed intervals," Midbrook withdrew dollars from the dollar account, exchanged them into guilders, and then deposited them into a second Dutch bank account (the "guilder account"), which was also in its name. Then, when the invoices became due, Midbrook paid itself the invoiced amount of guilders from the guilder account. Midbrook regularly sent Holland America statements for the two accounts, and Holland America was responsible for ensuring that there were enough dollars in the dollar account to cover the periodic transfers to the guilder account.

Sometime in 1997, Benno Dobbe noticed that Midbrook's costs "appeared to be higher than the bulb import costs that [his] competitors were obtaining from other Dutch suppliers." Benno became suspicious that Midbrook was overcharging Holland America, and he asked Arie to provide documentation substantiating Midbrook's costs. Arie assured Benno that Midbrook's invoices were correct, but he refused to provide the requested documentation. In June 1999, the parties agreed that they would "terminate their relationship" the following year, but that Midbrook would "still handle the export of the flower bulb harvest [in the fall] of 1999." Between January 11 and May 22, 2000, Midbrook sent Holland America invoices for the 1999 harvest which totaled 3,211,568

---

1. The Netherlands did not adopt the Euro as its currency until 2002.

guilders. Holland America never deposited dollars into the dollar account sufficient to cover these invoices, and Midbrook overdrew the dollar account to pay itself for them.

B. Procedural Background

1. Proceedings in the Alkmaar District Court

In 2002, Midbrook filed a lawsuit against Holland America in the Alkmaar District Court in the Netherlands, seeking payment for the 1999 harvest shipments. Holland America did not deny that it had not paid Midbrook for the 1999 harvest; rather, it argued that Midbrook had "invoiced [Holland America] for too high an amount for years," and that Holland America had "[over]paid more in total during the period from 1994 to August 2000 . . . than Midbrook had invoiced [for the 1999 harvest]." Though Holland America "provisionally estimated" the amount of the overcharge to be $4,434,387 (roughly 9 million guilders), it asked the court to "order Midbrook to provide its bookkeeping records for the years 1984 up to and including December 2000" so that Holland America could "more particularly specif[y]" its damages.

In a series of "judgments" . . . the Alkmaar District Court rejected Holland America's counterclaim and entered judgment in Midbrook's favor. . . . [T]he court made several rulings. [I]t noted that Midbrook claimed in its briefing "that it [had] agreed with [Holland America] on October 22, 1999 that [Holland America], after receiving a credit note in the amount of . . . 100,000 [guilders], would have no more right to compensation for damages from improper invoicing in the past." The court ruled that Midbrook would be given "the opportunity [ ] to provide evidence for [this] agreement."

. . .

The district court . . . [heard] from witnesses from both parties regarding the settlement agreement, which allegedly took place at a meeting between Benno and Arie Dobbe in October 1999 at Midbrook's offices in the Netherlands. Midbrook's witnesses were Johannes Elling, Midbrook's tax advisor; and Elisabeth Dobbe-Ruygrok, Arie Dobbe's wife and a secretary at Midbrook. Elling and Dobbe-Ruygrok both testified that they were present at the meeting when Benno and Arie agreed to settle Holland America's claims for 100,000 guilders. Holland America's two witnesses, Benno Dobbe and Hugo Dobbe (another of Benno's brothers), testified that no such agreement was reached at the meeting, and that they had come to the Netherlands only because Arie had promised them that they could examine Midbrook's records, which Arie ultimately did not allow them to do. The district court found that Midbrook's witnesses were not credible and therefore determined that no settlement agreement had been reached.

Having disposed of the settlement issue, the court proceeded to address the parties' claims regarding the invoices for the harvests of 1994-99. It directed Holland America to "specify the [ ] invoices [to which it objected] concretely, submitting them . . . and indicat[ing] which amounts Midbrook invoiced unjustifiably to [Holland America] and why." Then, the court explained, Midbrook would "be given the opportunity to respond" by "provid[ing] insight into the structure of the invoices" identified by Holland America with "documented evidence."

. . .

. . . The court then summarized Holland America's objections to 1999 harvest invoices, and stated that Midbrook would be given "the opportunity to respond to [these objections] with documentation."

. . . [T]he district court addressed each of Holland America's objections to the 1999 harvest invoices in detail, rejecting some but granting others. In total, the district court concluded that Midbrook had wrongly charged Holland America 40,403 guilders for the 1999 harvest.

The court then explained how it would calculate Midbrook's damages. Because Midbrook had paid itself for the 1999 harvest by overdrawing the dollar account, Midbrook's damages were equal to "the overdraft position of the dollar account" in March 2004 (when Midbrook closed that account and converted the deficit into euros), less the amount that Midbrook had "wrongfully charged" to Holland America. In October 2006, after receiving some additional information from Midbrook regarding its bank statements, the district court . . . awarded Midbrook €1,033,291 (at the time, the equivalent of $1,250,592), plus any interest that had accrued since Midbrook converted the dollar account balance into euros in March 2004.

2. Proceedings in the Amsterdam Court of Appeal

Holland America then appealed the Alkmaar District Court's judgment to the Amsterdam Court of Appeal. . . . Midbrook cross-appealed, arguing that the Alkmaar District Court had erroneously rejected its contention that the parties had settled Holland America's claims for the harvests of 1994-1998.

[T]he Amsterdam Court of Appeal reversed the district court's determination that Holland America had not agreed to settle its claims for the harvests of 1994-1998. The court noted that "[i]t is an established fact that a credit was issued by Midbrook for an amount of [ ] 100,000 [guilders]," and that "[c]onsidering the relationship between the parties . . . , it is unlikely that Midbrook would not have demanded [ ] consideration 'in exchange' for this credit." Thus, "[unlike] the District Court," the court of appeal "consider[ed] [it] proven that the parties concluded [a] [settlement] agreement." In light of this finding, the court denied Holland America's requests for documentation substantiating the invoices for the harvests of 1994-1998.

The court of appeal also denied Holland America's discovery requests with respect to the 1999 harvest. The court explained that Holland America had been given a chance to "identify in concrete terms the specific costs that it had been invoiced against which its objections were [ ] directed"; that Midbrook had then "complied with its obligation to provide insights into the costs that it had [ ] charged"; and that Holland America's "objections [were] discussed one by one by the District Court." Thus, the court concluded, Holland America had already been given an opportunity to contest the correctness of the invoices for the 1999 harvest, and it was entitled to no further discovery on the issue.

As to the bank statements for the dollar and guilder accounts, the Amsterdam Court of Appeal agreed with Holland America that "in principle," it was "entitled to the full details of the dollar account and the [guilder] account relationship." Though the court noted that there was some evidence that Holland America had "regularly requested a 'dollar and guilder balance sheet' [from Midbrook]" and that Holland America therefore likely possessed these documents already, it nonetheless ordered Midbrook to produce the statements for two accounts for the period running from January 1994 to January 2000.

. . .

. . . [A]fter Midbrook submitted corrected versions of the two bank account statements[,] [t]he court found that, as a result of the corrections, the surplus in the guilder account on January 1, 2000 was 460,862 guilders — not 312,642 guilders as the district court had found — and it adjusted the amount of damages calculated by the district court to €959,324 plus interest and costs on appeal.

Finally, the court of appeal again addressed Holland America's requests for discovery. . . . Because Holland America "fail[ed] to specify which items in the current account . . . should be substantiated with supporting evidence," . . . the court concluded that its discovery request was "too general and must be denied."

3. Proceedings in the Supreme Court of the Netherlands

Holland America appealed the Amsterdam Court of Appeal's decision to the Supreme Court of the Netherlands. In December 2012, the supreme court summarily dismissed the appeal. . . .

4. Proceedings in the U.S. District Court for the Western District of Washington

In May 2014, Midbrook filed a diversity action against Holland America in the U.S. District Court for the Western District of Washington, seeking recognition of the Amsterdam Court of Appeal's October 2006 judgment (the "Dutch judgment") under Washington's Uniform Foreign-Country Money Judgments Recognition Act ("UFCMJRA"). *See* Wash. Rev. Code §§ 6.40A.010-6.40A.902. . . .

Midbrook . . . moved for summary judgment.

Holland America opposed the motion, arguing that under section 4(c)(8) of the UFCMJRA, the district court "need not" recognize the Dutch judgment, because "[t]he specific proceeding in the [Dutch] court leading to the judgment was not compatible with the requirements of due process of law."

The district court granted Midbrook's motion for summary judgment. . . . Holland America then filed a motion for reconsideration, which the district court denied. In December 2014, the district court entered a final judgment in Midbrook's favor for €2,200,513 (the amount of the Dutch judgment plus interest for the period leading up to December 2014). Holland America then timely filed this appeal.

II. Standard of Review

We review *de novo* a district court's determination that a foreign-court money judgment does not qualify for nonrecognition under one of the UFCMJRA's discretionary exceptions. *See Naoko Ohno v. Yuko Yasuma*, 723 F.3d 984, 1001-02 (9th Cir. 2013). . . .

III. Discussion

A. The District Court Did Not Err by Granting Midbrook's Motion for Summary Judgment

In 1962, the National Conference of Commissioners on Uniform State Laws ("NCCUSL") promulgated the Uniform Foreign Money-Judgment Recognition Act ("UFMJRA") to codify the states' rules regarding the recognition of foreign money judgments. *See* UFMJRA, Prefatory Note. The aim of this codification was to "make it more likely that judgments rendered in [the] state[s] [will] be recognized abroad." *Id.* In 2005, NCCUSL promulgated the Uniform Foreign-Court Money Judgments Recognition Act ("UFCMJRA") to update the 1962 act. *See* UFCMJRA, Prefatory Note. Washington adopted the updated UFCMJRA in 2009. *See* Wash. Rev. Code §§ 6.40A.010-6.40A.902.

Under section 4(a) of the UFCMJRA, when a party files an action seeking recognition[9] of a "foreign-country judgment," the court "*shall* recognize" that judgment if it "[g]rants or denies recovery of a sum of money; and . . . under the law of the foreign country where rendered, is final, conclusive, and enforceable." *See* Wash. Rev. Code §§ 6.40A.010-.030 (emphasis added). Once the party seeking recognition demonstrates that the foreign-country judgment satisfies these *prima facie* requirements, *see id.* § 6.40A.020(3), the burden shifts to the party resisting recognition to prove that a ground for nonrecognition applies. *See id.* § 6.40A.030(4).

Sections 4(b) and (c) of the UFCMJRA provide eleven grounds — three mandatory and eight discretionary — for a court to refuse to recognize a foreign-country judgment. *See* Rev. Code Wash. §§ 6.40A.030(2)-(3). Two of these grounds are relevant to this appeal: Section 4(b)(1) provides that "[a] court . . . *may not* recognize a foreign-country judgment if . . . the judgment was rendered *under a judicial system* that does not provide impartial tribunals or procedures compatible with the requirements of due process of law." *See* Wash. Rev. Code § 6.40A.030(2)(a) (emphasis added). Section 4(c)(8), by contrast, provides that "a court *need not* recognize a foreign-country judgment if . . . [t]he *specific proceeding* in the foreign court leading to the judgment was not compatible with the requirements of due process of law." *See id.* § 6.40A.030(3)(h).

On appeal, Holland America does not argue that Midbrook has failed to make its *prima facie* showing that the Dutch judgment "[g]rants or denies recovery of a sum of money" and "is final, conclusive, and enforceable" under Dutch law. Nor

---

9. "Recognition of a judgment means that the forum court accepts the determination of legal rights and obligations made by the rendering court in the foreign country. Recognition of a foreign-country judgment must be distinguished from enforcement of that judgment. Enforcement of the foreign-country judgment involves the application of the legal procedures of the state to ensure that the judgment debtor obeys the foreign-country judgment." UFCMJRA § 4 cmt. 2.

does Holland America argue that the Dutch judicial system as a whole "does not provide . . . procedures compatible with the requirements of due process of law." Rather, it argues only that the "specific proceeding[s]" in the Dutch courts which led to the Dutch judgment were "not compatible with the requirements of due process of law" under section 4(c)(8). This is so, Holland America argues, for two reasons: first, the Alkmaar District Court and the Amsterdam Court of Appeal "denied [Holland America] access to a majority of Midbrook's cost records and therefore deprived it of the opportunity to provide any defense in the contract action"; and second, the Amsterdam Court of Appeal "arbitrarily and without basis overturned the Alkmaar District Court's credibility rulings regarding whether the parties had reached a settlement."

1. Legal Standard

As an initial matter, we must identify the legal standard that governs whether specific proceedings in a foreign court were "compatible with the requirements of due process of law" under section 4(c)(8). Holland America urges us to apply "American due process principles" — that is, to interpret the phrase "due process of law" as incorporating by reference the requirements of the Due Process Clauses of the Fifth and Fourteenth Amendments. Midbrook, by contrast, argues for a more permissive, "international" standard of due process.[10] Because the parties ask us to interpret a provision of a Washington statute, we begin by looking to the decisions of the Washington courts. If those decisions are unavailing and the question is one of first impression, we must identify the result we think the Washington Supreme Court would reach if it were presented with the same question. . . .

Washington's UFCMJRA does not define the phrase "due process of law," *see* Rev. Code Wash. § 6.40A.010 (defining certain terms used in the statute), and the Washington courts have not yet addressed the meaning of the phrase as used in section 4(c)(8). Nor has any state supreme court or any federal court of appeals addressed the phrase's meaning in section 4(c)(8) of any other state's version of the UFCMJRA. *See* Rev. Code Wash. § 6.40A.900 ("In applying and construing this uniform act, consideration must be given to the need to promote uniformity of the law with respect to its subject matter among states that enact it.").

In the absence of any binding authority on point, the commentary to section 4 of the UFCMJRA is instructive:

> Subsection 4(c)(8) . . . allows the forum court to deny recognition to the foreign-country judgment if the court finds that the specific proceeding in the foreign court was not compatible with the requirements of *fundamental fairness.* . . . [I]t

---

10. To be clear, Midbrook does not claim that any primary source of international law — such as a treaty or rule of customary international law — governs the process to which Holland America was entitled in the Dutch courts. Rather, Midbrook urges us to apply the "international concept of due process" formulated by the Seventh Circuit in interpreting the phrase "due process of law" in a similar provision of Illinois's UFMJRA. *See Society of Lloyd's v. Ashenden*, 233 F.3d 473, 477 (7th Cir. 2000). Though we find the reasoning of that case persuasive, we adopt the phrase "fundamental fairness" because that phrase — unlike the phrase "international due process" — appears in the commentary to the UFCMJRA.

can be contrasted with subsection 4(b)(1), which requires the forum court to deny recognition to the foreign-country judgment if the forum court finds that the entire judicial system in the foreign country where the foreign-country judgment was rendered does not provide procedures compatible with the requirements of fundamental fairness. *While the focus of subsection 4(b)(1) is on the foreign country's judicial system as a whole, the focus of subsection 4(c)(8) is on the particular proceeding that resulted in the specific foreign-country judgment under consideration.* Thus, the difference is that between showing, for example, that there has been such a breakdown of law and order in the particular foreign country that judgments are rendered on the basis of political decisions rather than the rule of law throughout the judicial system versus a showing that for political reasons the particular party against whom the foreign-country judgment was entered was denied *fundamental fairness* in the particular proceedings leading to the foreign-country judgment.

UFCMJRA § 4 cmt. 12 (emphasis added). This comment states that section 4(c)(8) allows for nonrecognition of a foreign money judgment if "the specific proceeding in the foreign court was not compatible with the requirements of fundamental fairness." As an example, it gives a foreign proceeding in which judgment was entered against a "particular party" for "political reasons"; elsewhere, the comment states that "evidence of corruption" may also render a proceeding fundamentally unfair. *See id.* Nowhere does the comment cite our Constitution's Due Process Clauses or otherwise intimate that the phrase "due process of law" was intended literally to incorporate their requirements.

Moreover, by contrasting section 4(c)(8) with section 4(b)(1), the comment suggests that the phrase "compatible with the requirements of due process of law" has the same meaning in both provisions.[11] And as another comment to section 4 states, section 4(b)(1) uses the standard "stated authoritatively by the Supreme Court . . . in *Hilton v. Guyot,* 159 U.S. 113, 205, 16 S. Ct. 139, 40 L. Ed. 95 (1895)":

> As indicated in [*Hilton*], a mere difference in the procedural system is not a sufficient basis for nonrecognition. . . . The focus of inquiry is not whether the procedure in the rendering country is similar to U.S. procedure, but rather on the basic fairness of the foreign-country procedure. Procedural differences, such as absence of jury trial or different evidentiary rules are not sufficient to justify denying recognition under subsection (b)(1), so long as the essential elements of impartial administration and basic procedural fairness have been provided in the foreign proceeding.

UFCMJRA § 4 cmt. 5 (citations and internal quotation marks omitted); *see also Tonga Air Services, Ltd. v. Fowler,* 118 Wash. 2d 718, 826 P.2d 204, 209 (1992) (finding that "due process of law" was satisfied under the predecessor to section 4(b)(1) of Washington's UFCMJRA where, *inter alia,* foreign law "impose[d]

---

11. Indeed, this reading is consistent with the presumption of consistent usage, a fundamental canon of statutory construction. *See, e.g., Util. Air Reg. Group v. E.P.A.,* 134 S. Ct. 2427, 2441 (2014) ("One ordinarily assumes that identical words used in different parts of the same act are intended to have the same meaning." (citations and internal quotation marks omitted)). . . .

more onerous standards for the introduction of documentary evidence on foreigners" and there was no verbatim transcript of the foreign proceedings). Taken together, these two comments demonstrate that section 4(c)(8) — like section 4(b)(1) — requires only "basic" or "fundamental" fairness for a specific foreign proceeding to be "compatible with the requirements of due process of law."

Our conclusion that section 4(c)(8) requires only "fundamental fairness" is buttressed by the prefatory note to the UFCMJRA, which states that the act's purpose is to "make it more likely that money judgments rendered in that state would be recognized in other countries." Certainly, it would undermine this purpose to enforce only those foreign judgments which resulted from proceedings that conformed to our own notions of constitutional due process. *See Ashenden*, 233 F.3d at 476 (rejecting the argument that foreign courts should have to follow "the latest twist and turn of our courts regarding, for example, the circumstances under which due process requires an opportunity for a hearing in advance of the deprivation of a substantive right rather than afterwards"). Such a high bar would encourage foreign powers to condition the enforcement of *our* judgments on the satisfaction of *their* procedural requirements, which could be just as onerous as our own.

. . .

In sum, both the commentary and prefatory note to the UFCMJRA demonstrate that under section 4(c)(8), courts ask only whether the party resisting judgment "was denied fundamental fairness in the particular proceedings leading to the foreign-country judgment," not whether the foreign proceedings literally conformed to the requirements of due process under our own Constitution. UFCMJRA § 4 cmt. 12. To demonstrate a lack of "fundamental fairness," the party resisting the judgment must point to more than mere "procedural differences" — like a lack of trial by jury or "different evidentiary rules" — between the process that the party received in the foreign proceeding and the process to which it would have been entitled here. UFCMJRA § 4 cmt. 5. Rather, the party must establish a deprivation of "basic procedural fairness" by, for example, proffering evidence of "corruption" or that the foreign judgment was entered for "political reasons." *See* UFCMJRA § 4 cmt. 12. We proceed to consider whether Holland America has satisfied this standard with respect to the Dutch proceedings. Thus, it is not necessary for us to decide whether process accorded to Midbrook also passed muster under American standards of due process.[13]

2. Holland America's Discovery Requests

First, Holland America argues that it was denied due process in the Dutch proceedings because the Alkmaar District Court and the Amsterdam Court of Appeal "denied [Holland America] access to a majority of Midbrook's cost records." Holland America cites no authority for the proposition that "fundamental fairness" requires that a litigant be afforded an opportunity for pretrial discovery, and

---

13. The "cardinal principle of judicial restraint" is that "if it is not necessary to decide more, it is necessary not to decide more." *PDK Labs. Inc. v. U.S. D.E.A.*, 362 F.3d 786, 799 (D.C. Cir. 2004) (Roberts, J., concurring in part and concurring in judgment).

we are aware of none. *See, e.g., Ashenden,* 233 F.3d at 479-80 ("[T]he right to pretrial discovery is not a part of the U.S. concept of due process, let alone of international due process.") (internal citations omitted).

In any case, we need not decide whether it would violate fundamental fairness to deny a party the opportunity to take *any* pretrial discovery, because here, Holland America was afforded *some* pretrial discovery. Instead of ordering Midbrook to produce all of its cost and banking records, as one of our federal district courts might have done, the Dutch courts ordered Holland America to identify specific records that it wished to discover and to explain why it needed them. Then, in each case where Holland America complied, the Dutch courts ordered Midbrook to produce documentation.

For example, although the Dutch courts repeatedly denied Holland America's requests for documentation substantiating *all* of the costs underlying Midbrook's invoices, the Alkmaar District Court afforded Holland America the opportunity to identify and explain "[the] amounts [that] Midbrook invoiced unjustifiably to [Holland America] and why." The court then ordered Midbrook to respond to Holland America's arguments with supporting documentation, and, after it received Midbrook's responses, it addressed Holland America's objections one by one.

Likewise, although the Dutch courts did not grant Holland America access to *all* of Midbrook's records related to the dollar and guilder accounts, the Amsterdam Court of Appeal *did* order Midbrook to produce the statements of those accounts. Then, it gave Holland America an opportunity to challenge the accuracy of those statements, addressed Holland America's objections one by one, granted several of them, and adjusted Midbrook's damages award accordingly. Far from comparing to "corruption" or the entry of judgment against Holland America for "political reasons," UFCMJRA § 4 cmt. 12, the Dutch courts' treatment of Holland America's discovery requests was a mere "procedural difference" that is insufficient to establish that the Dutch proceedings were fundamentally unfair.

Our conclusion is buttressed by the fact that not even constitutional due process — a standard which our sister circuits have recognized as being more demanding than "fundamental fairness"[14] — requires full pretrial discovery. . . . Thus, given that Holland America would not have been entitled to full pretrial discovery even under our own constitutional standards, we have no difficulty holding that Holland America was not denied fundamental fairness in the Dutch proceedings.

---

14. In applying the "fundamental fairness" standard to evaluate foreign *judicial systems* under section 4(b)(1), our sister circuits have consistently recognized that constitutional due-process standards are more demanding. *See Society of Lloyd's v. Ashenden,* 233 F.3d 473, 477 (7th Cir. 2000) (interpreting the predecessor to section 4(b)(1) of Illinois's UFCMJRA as employing an "international concept of due process" that was "less demanding" than "the complex concept that has emerged from American case law"); *DeJoria v. Maghreb Petroleum Expl., S.A.,* 804 F.3d 373, 380 (5th Cir. 2015) (recognizing that under the predecessor to section 4(b)(1) of Texas's UFCMJRA, "the foreign judicial system must only be fundamentally fair" and "need not comply with the traditional rigors of American due process" (citations, alterations, and internal quotation marks omitted)); *Society of Lloyd's v. Reinhart,* 402 F.3d 982, 994-95 (10th Cir. 2005) (similar, regarding the predecessor to section 4(b)(1) of New Mexico's UFCMJRA).

3. Reversal of the Alkmaar District Court's Factual Finding and Credibility Determination

Next, Holland America argues that it was denied due process when the Amsterdam Court of Appeal overturned the Alkmaar District Court's factual finding denying the existence of the parties' alleged October 1999 settlement agreement without deferring to the district court's determination that the testimony of two of Midbrook's witnesses was not credible and thus vitiated any such settlement agreement.

Again, the authorities cited by Holland America fall far short of establishing that "fundamental fairness" requires a foreign appellate court to defer to a foreign trial court's factual findings. . . .

In any case, we are convinced that Holland America was afforded fundamental fairness here, because the Amsterdam Court of Appeal gave a good reason for overturning the Alkmaar District Court's finding that the parties had reached no settlement agreement in October 1999. As the court of appeal explained:

> It is an established fact that a credit was issued by Midbrook for an amount of [ ] 100,000 [guilders]. [Holland America] does not declare in any way what consideration on its part stood against this credit. Considering the relationship between the parties . . . it is unlikely that Midbrook would not have demanded a certain consideration "in exchange" for this credit. On the other hand, it is plausible that the parties would have wanted to clear up the past before working together for one final year.

Thus, the court of appeal's reversal of the district court's factual finding was based not only on its own evaluation of the credibility of Midbrook's witnesses, but also on the unexplained 100,000 guilder payment, which the court of appeal interpreted as a settlement of past accounts between the parties. Especially in light of this additional ground for reversal, the court of appeal's reversal reflects at most a mere "procedural difference" between U.S. and Dutch law, UFCMJRA § 4 cmt. 5, and was therefore fundamentally fair.

We are further persuaded of this conclusion because again, Holland America has failed to establish that even the more exacting standards of constitutional due process would have required a United States appellate court to defer to a trial court's factual determination under like circumstances. . . . Thus, Holland America could claim no constitutional violation had an American appellate court taken the same action as the Amsterdam Court of Appeal, and this too suggests that the Dutch proceedings were fundamentally fair.

. . .

IV. Conclusion

We AFFIRM the district court's order granting summary judgment for Midbrook. . . .

DeJoria v. Maghreb Petroleum Exploration, S.A.

2018 WL 1057029 (W.D. Tex. 2018)

REPORT AND RECOMMENDATION OF THE UNITED STATES MAGISTRATE JUDGE

ANDREW W. AUSTIN, United States Magistrate Judge

. . .

I. Factual Background

As summarized by the Court of Appeals for the Fifth Circuit, the factual background of this case is as follows:

> John Paul DeJoria [the co-founder of the Paul Mitchell line of hair products] ("DeJoria") was a major investor in an American company called Skidmore Energy, Inc. ("Skidmore"), which was engaged in oil exploration and technology projects in Morocco. In pursuit of its goals, Skidmore formed and capitalized a Moroccan corporation, Lone Star Energy Corporation ("Lone Star") (now Maghreb Petroleum Exploration, S.A., or "MPE"). Corporations established under Moroccan law are required to have a "local" shareholder. For Lone Star, that local shareholder was Mediholding, S.A., owned by Prince Moulay Abdallah Alaoui, a first cousin of the Moroccan King, King Mohammed VI.

In March 2000, Lone Star entered into an "Investment Agreement" obligating it to invest in hydrocarbon exploration in Morocco. King Mohammed assured DeJoria that he would line up additional investors for the project to ensure adequate funding. Armadillo Holdings ("Armadillo") (now Mideast Fund for Morocco, or "MFM"), a Liechtenstein-based company, agreed to make significant investments in Lone Star. In the negotiations leading up to this agreement, Skidmore represented to Armadillo that Skidmore previously invested $27.5 million in Lone Star and that Lone Star's market value was roughly $175.75 million.

On August 20, 2000, King Mohammed gave a nationally televised speech to announce the discovery of "copious and high-quality oil" in Morocco. Three days later, then–Moroccan Minister of Energy Youssef Tahiri, accompanied by DeJoria and DeJoria's business partner Michael Gustin, traveled to the site and held a press conference claiming that the discovered oil reserves would fulfill Morocco's energy needs for decades. Moroccans celebrated this significant news, as the King's announcement was the only stimulus likely to revive Morocco's sluggish economy. The Moroccan stock market soared.

There was one major problem: the oil reserves were not as plentiful as announced. The "rosy picture" of Moroccan energy independence did not materialize, damaging both the Moroccan government's credibility and Lone Star's viability. As a result, the business relationship between MFM and Skidmore/DeJoria suffered. Lone Star replaced DeJoria and Gustin on Lone Star's Board of Directors. DeJoria has not been to Morocco since 2000 and claims that his life would have been endangered had he returned.

Unhappy with the return on its initial investment in Lone Star, MFM sued Skidmore, DeJoria, Gustin, and a number of other Skidmore officers in their individual capacities in Moroccan court. MFM asserted that Skidmore fraudulently induced its investment by misrepresenting Skidmore's actual investment in Lone Star. MPE later joined as a plaintiff in the suit and claimed that Skidmore's fraudulent misrepresentations deprived Lone Star of necessary capital. In response, Skidmore filed two quickly-dismissed lawsuits against MPE, MFM, and other parties in the United States.

After nearly seven years of considering MPE and MFM's suit, the Moroccan court ruled against DeJoria and Gustin but absolved five of their co-defendants — including Skidmore — of liability. The court entered judgment in favor of MPE and MFM for approximately $122.9 million.

. . .

II. Procedural Background

A. Original District Court Proceedings

After the Moroccan court entered the $122.9 million judgment against DeJoria, he sued MPE and MFM in Texas state court, challenging recognition of the judgment under the previous version of Texas's Uniform Foreign Country Money-Judgment Recognition Act (hereinafter the "1981 Texas Recognition Act") [which was based on the 1962 Uniform Act]. MPE/MFM removed the action to federal district court based on diversity of citizenship and the case was assigned to United States District Judge James R. Nowlin. DeJoria then filed a "Motion for Nonrecognition of Foreign Judgment" in the District Court arguing that the Moroccan judgment should not be recognized under the 1981 Texas Recognition Act because: (1) the judgment was rendered under a system that does not provide impartial tribunals or procedures compatible with the requirements of due process of law; (2) the Moroccan court lacked personal jurisdiction over DeJoria; (3) the cause of action on which the judgment is based is repugnant to the public policy of Texas; (4) the court rendering the judgment is a seriously inconvenient forum for the trial of the action; (5) Moroccan courts do not recognize Texas judgments; (6) the judgment was not final and conclusive; and (7) the judgment was not authenticated.

The District Court began and ended its analysis with DeJoria's first argument, finding that the Moroccan Judgment should not be recognized under § 36.005(a)(1) of the 1981 Texas Recognition Act ("the judgment was rendered under a system that does not provide impartial tribunals or procedures compatible with the requirements of due process of law"). . . . The District Court found that Moroccan judges are not independent and are susceptible to being pressured by members of the Moroccan royal family, finding that

> the Moroccan royal family's commitment to the sort of independent judiciary
> necessary to uphold the rule of law has and continues to be lacking in ways that

raise serious questions about whether any party that finds itself involved in a legal dispute in which the royal family has an apparent interest — be it economic or political — in the outcome of the case could ever receive a fair trial.

Based on the evidence before it, the District Court held that "DeJoria or some similarly situated party" could not have received adequately fair procedures to warrant enforcement of the Moroccan judgment. The District Court concluded, "[a]bsent an act of tremendous bravery by the judge, there is no conceivable set of facts or circumstances in which DeJoria could have prevailed in the underlying case. Such a proceeding is not, was not, and can never be 'fundamentally fair.'"

B. The Fifth Circuit's Opinion

MPE/MFM appealed the District Court's ruling to the Court of Appeals for the Fifth Circuit, arguing that the judgment should be reversed because DeJoria had failed to meet his burden to prove that the entire Moroccan judicial system does not meet due process standards as required under § 36.005(a)(1) of the 1981 Texas Recognition Act. The Fifth Circuit agreed and held that DeJoria had failed to meet his heavy burden under § 36.005(a)(1) to demonstrate that the Moroccan judicial system "as a whole is so lacking in impartial tribunals or procedures compatible with due process so as to justify routine non-recognition of the foreign judgments." The Court found that "[t]he Moroccan judicial system does not present an exceptional case of 'serious injustice' that renders the entire system fundamentally unfair and incompatible with due process." The Fifth Circuit also rejected DeJoria's alternative arguments that the Moroccan court lacked personal jurisdiction over him, and that Moroccan courts do not recognize Texas judgments. The Court did not address DeJoria's public policy and inconvenient forum claims, however, stating in a footnote that those "arguments were not raised on appeal and are thus waived." The Fifth Circuit concluded its Opinion with the boilerplate directive: "For the foregoing reasons the judgment of the district court is REVERSED and this matter is REMANDED for further proceedings consistent with this opinion." On June 20, 2016, the Supreme Court denied the petition for writ of certiorari.

C. Proceedings After Remand

. . .

On April 23, 2017, the undersigned ordered the Parties to file briefing on DeJoria's Motion for Non-Recognition by July 31, 2017. However, on June 1, 2017, the Texas Legislature repealed the 1981 Texas Recognition Act and enacted an updated version of the Act. *See* Uniform Foreign-Country Money Judgments Recognition Act, Act of May 22, 2017, 85th Leg., R.S., ch. 390 (codified at Tex. Civ. Prac. & Rem. Code § 36A.001, et seq.). Because the statute had a direct impact on issues before the Court and the legislature made the statute retroactive to pending cases, the Court extended the Parties' briefing deadlines in the case.

DeJoria argues in his Motion for Non–Recognition that the Moroccan judgment should not be recognized because: (1) the Moroccan judgment falls squarely

624   Chapter 7. Court Judgments

within the Amended Act's provisions allowing non-recognition where the particular foreign proceedings lacked due process or where there is substantial doubt about the integrity of the rendering court with respect to the judgment; (2) the Due Process Clause of the United States Constitution prohibits enforcing the Moroccan judgment; and (3) the Moroccan judgment is repugnant to Texas public policy.

III. Analysis

As noted, after the remand of this case by the Fifth Circuit, the Texas Legislature repealed the 1981 Texas Recognition Act and replaced it with the updated model statute produced by the National Conference of Commissioners on Uniform State Laws. The bill's sponsor stated that the bill "updates the Act based on the 2005 Uniform Foreign-Country Money Judgments Recognition Act, ensuring that Texans enjoy due process protection when defending against foreign country judgments in Texas courts." Bill Analysis, S.B. 944, 85th Leg., R.S. (March 21, 2017). The Amended Act retained the prior statute's grounds for non-recognition, including the mandatory due process requirement, but adds the following case-specific bases for non-recognition:

> (7) the judgment was rendered in circumstances that raise substantial doubt about the integrity of the rendering court with respect to the judgment;
> (8) the specific proceeding in the foreign court leading to the judgment was not compatible with the requirements of due process of law.

Id. at §§ 36A.004(c)(7) & (8). In addition, the Amended Act now permits non-recognition when "the judgment or the cause of action on which the judgment is based is repugnant to the public policy of this state or the United States." *Id.* at § 36A.004(c)(3). Each of these new grounds for non-recognition are discretionary grounds. The new amendments apply to all pending lawsuits, such as the instant case, without regard to whether the suit was commenced before or after the effective date of the Act (June 1, 2017). Tex. Civ. Prac. & Rem. Code § 36A.004 historical note (West 2017 Supp.) [Act of May 22, 2017, 85th Leg., § 3 (S.B. 944)].

As was the case under the previous version, the party resisting recognition of the foreign judgment — here DeJoria — has the burden of establishing a ground for nonrecognition exists. Amended Act at § 36A.004(d); *Diamond Offshore (Bermuda), Ltd. v. Haaksman*, 355 S.W.3d 842, 845 (Tex. App.–Houston [14th Dist.] 2011, pet. denied) ("Unless the judgment debtor satisfies its burden of proof by establishing one or more of the specific grounds for nonrecognition, the court is required to recognize the foreign judgment.").

A. Does the Amended Act's Retroactivity Clause Violate the Texas Constitution?

Section 3 of the Amended Act provides: "This Act applies to a pending suit in which the issue of recognition of a foreign-country money judgment is or has been raised without regard to whether the suit was commenced before, on, or after the effective date [June 1, 2017] of this Act." Amended Act § 36A.004 historical note (West 2017 Supp.) [Act of May 22, 2017, 85th Leg., § 3 (S.B. 944)]. MPE/MFM argue that this section of the Amended Act violates the Texas Constitution's prohibition on retroactive laws.

The Texas Constitution provides that: "No bill of attainder, ex post facto law, retroactive law, or any law impairing the obligation of contracts, shall be made." Tex. Const. Art. I, § 16. . . . While there is "[n]o bright-line test" for determining whether a statute is unconstitutionally retroactive, the Texas Supreme Court has directed courts to look at three factors: (1) the nature and strength of the public interest served by the statute as evidenced by the Legislature's factual findings; (2) the nature of the prior right impaired by the statute; and (3) the extent of the impairment. [*Robinson v. Crown Cork & Seal Col., Inc.*, 335 S.W.3d 126, 145 (Tex. 2010).]

a. Public Interest Served by the Statute

In *Robinson*, the Texas Supreme Court stated that "[t]here must be a compelling public interest to overcome the heavy presumption against retroactive laws." *Robinson*, 335 S.W.3d at 146. The legislative record in this case indicates that the Legislature enacted the Amended Act after the Fifth Circuit's decision in this case in order to protect the due process protections for Texas citizens involved in international business. The bill's sponsor in the Texas Senate explained the intent of the legislation:

> A recent federal court decision called into question whether the Texas Act protects Texans' individual due process rights by foreign court systems. S.B. 944 updates the Act based on the 2005 Uniform Foreign-Country Money Judgments Recognition Act, ensuring that Texans enjoy due process protection when defending against foreign country judgments in Texas courts.
>
> According to the Uniform Law Commission, the increase in international trade in the United States has also meant more litigation in foreign judicial systems. This means more judgments to be enforced from country to country. There is strong need for uniformity between states with respect to the law governing foreign country money-judgments. There is also a strong public policy need to make sure basic individual protections and rights are recognized in any foreign court system that attempts to use our Texas courts to enforce their judgments on our citizens and businesses.
>
> Unfortunately, not all foreign court systems honor basic individual and system due process protections recognized by U.S. state courts (such as the Texas state court system). The provisions of S.B. 944 ensure that Texans' individual due process rights continue to be recognized by foreign judicial systems before those foreign judgments are enforced by Texas courts.

Bill Analysis, S.B. 944, 85th Leg., R.S. (March 21, 2017). The stated purpose of the Amended Act is thus to greater protect the due process rights of Texas citizens. Obviously, protecting the due process rights of its citizens is a *compelling* public interest. . . .

While MPE/MFM cannot dispute that the Amended Act serves a compelling public interest, they argue that as was the case in *Robinson*, the Amended Act was enacted only to benefit DeJoria and no one else and thus it was not in the public interest. [In *Robinson*, the Texas statute in question absolved an asbestos manufacturer of liability in pending litigation brought by plaintiffs' claiming they contracted mesothelioma due to exposure to the defendant's products. The Texas Supreme Court found that "the legislative record is fairly clear" that the statute was enacted "to help only [defendant] and no one else. The Texas Supreme Court further held that] "[t]he only public benefit achieved by the statute was the reduction of [defendant's] liability due to asbestos litigation — a benefit we decline[ ] to find sufficiently compelling to overcome the presumption that retroactive laws are unconstitutional."

In contrast to *Robinson*, the Legislature's stated purpose for adopting the Amended Act (as explained above) was to better protect Texans' due process rights with regard to the enforcement of foreign judgments. Unlike the case in *Robinson*, the Legislature did not enact the legislation to abrogate a plaintiff's common law cause of action in order to benefit one corporate party. In addition, the fact that DeJoria lobbied for the passage of the Amended Act and may have directly benefitted from that legislation does not mean that the Amended Act is not in the public interest. By the express terms of the statute, its application is not limited just to DeJoria and instead provides due process protection to all similarly situated parties.

b. Nature of the Rights and Extent of Their Impairment by the Statute

Even if MPE/MFM could demonstrate that the Amended Act was not in the public interest, the other two *Robinson* factors clearly demonstrate that the Amended Act does not violate the Texas Constitution. The second and third prongs of the *Robinson* test consider "the nature of the prior right impaired by the statute," and "the extent of the impairment." *Robinson*, 335 S.W.3d at 145.

MPE/MFM have failed to identify what prior right was impaired by the Amended Act. Instead, MPE/MFM argue that the "new Act changed the controlling law and provided DeJoria with two new non-recognition grounds in §§ (c)(7) and (c)(8) and altered the § (c)(3) policy ground." Dkt. No. 129 at 50. Unlike the case in *Robinson* where the statute entirely extinguished the plaintiff's common law causes of action against the corporate defendant, the Amended Act does not eliminate any of MPE/MFM's grounds for recognition of the foreign judgment in this case. Instead, it simply provides additional grounds for non-recognition. Statutes "that do not deprive the parties of a substantive right . . . may be applied to cases pending at the time of enactment." MPE/MFM have failed to demonstrate that the Amended Act impaired any of their rights whatsoever.

Accordingly, the Court rejects MPE/MFM's contention that the Amended Act cannot be applied retroactively to this case.

B. Amended Act

DeJoria devotes the majority of his briefing to argue that the Court should not recognize the Moroccan judgment based on § 36A.004(c)(8) of the Amended Act, and the Court will do the same. That section is a discretionary provision which provides that a court is not required to recognize a foreign judgment if "the specific proceeding in the foreign court leading to the judgment was not compatible with the requirements of due process of law." Amended Act at § 36A.004(c)(8). The Amended Act does not define "due process of law." However, the Comments to the 2005 Uniform Act, which the Amended Act was modeled on, explain that this subsection "allows the forum court to deny recognition to the foreign-country judgment if the court finds that the specific proceeding in the foreign court was not compatible with the requirements of *fundamental fairness.*" Unif. Foreign-Country Money Judgments Recognition Act § 4 at comment 12 (emphasis added).[5] In looking at the meaning of due process of law as used in § 36.005(a)(1) of the 1981 Texas Recognition Act, the Fifth Circuit stated "the statute requires only the use of procedures compatible with the requirements of due process" and that "the foreign proceedings need not comply with the traditional rigors of American due process to meet the requirements of enforceability under the statute." "That is, the foreign judicial system must only be 'fundamentally fair' and 'not offend against basic fairness.'" *Id.* The United States Supreme Court has repeatedly held that "[a] fair trial in a fair tribunal is a basic requirement of due process.". . .

DeJoria contends that, under the new statute, the facts found by Judge Nowlin in the original proceedings make it a foregone conclusion that DeJoria has demonstrated the requirements of non-recognition under § 36A.004(c)(8) of the Amended Act. . . .

. . .

Judge Nowlin made the following findings relevant to whether DeJoria received due process in the Moroccan proceedings specific to him, and the Court adopts these findings here:

> [T]he Moroccan royal family's commitment to the sort of independent judiciary necessary to uphold the rule of law has and continues to be lacking in ways that raise serious questions about whether any party that finds itself involved in a legal dispute in which the royal family has an apparent interest — be it economic or political — in the outcome of the case could ever receive a fair trial.

*   *   *

> Together, the USAID report and the foreign minister's comments paint a picture of a judicial system in which judges feel tremendous pressure to render judgments that comply with the wishes of the royal family and those closely affiliated with it.

*   *   *

---

5. As the comments to the 2005 Uniform Act explain: "While the focus of subsection 4(b)(1) is on the foreign country's judicial system as a whole, the focus of subsection 4(c)(8) is on the particular proceeding that resulted in the specific foreign-country judgment under consideration. Thus, the difference is that between showing, for example, that there has been such a breakdown of law and order in the particular foreign country that judgments are rendered on the basis of political decisions rather than the rule of law throughout the judicial system versus a showing that for political reasons the particular party against whom the foreign-country judgment was entered was denied fundamental fairness in the particular proceedings leading to the foreign-country judgment." Unif. Foreign-Country Money Judgments Recognition Act § 4 at comment 12.

As a general matter, MPE/MFM's suggestion that the circumstances surrounding the case do not warrant real concerns that the King or royal family corrupted the judicial proceedings is simply not credible.

* * *

As for MPE/MFM's suggestion that there is no evidence that the King particularly cared about DeJoria or his role in the Talsint oil project, the evidence plainly suggests otherwise. On Monday, January 27, 2007, "Le Journal," a Moroccan daily newspaper, ran a feature story under the headline "The Talsint Oil Lie." Citing a letter sent by Skidmore Chairman (and DeJoria partner) Michael Gustin to the King and other top officials, the article "accused the King and some officials of bribery and disinformation" in regards to Skidmore's exploration and attempted production of oil in south eastern Morocco in 2000. Neither the story nor the paper would survive for very long. The next day, Le Journal suddenly retracted the story, stating (without any meaningful explanation) that everything they had published was untrue. The paper also announced — again without any explanation — that it would voluntarily go out of circulation for an undisclosed period of time. Two days later, a sister publication reported that the author of the "offensive" Le Journal article (who also served as Le Journal's editor-in-chief) and Le Journal's publisher were both compelled to appear at the Justice Center so that they could be interrogated by criminal prosecutors about their involvement with the story.

* * *

Given the narrative power that [a] verdict [against them] would undoubtedly have, MPE/MFM's suggestion that a man who cared enough about maintaining his image to intimidate and prosecute a whole paper into submission had no interest in the outcome of a case which could either re-enforce his favored image or, alternatively, make him appear foolish if not downright dishonest for having promised so much oil during his now infamous speech simply does not add up. These facts would have been readily apparent to any judge presiding over this case. Given the King's history of retaliation, not only against judges who displease him but against anyone who threatens his narrative relating to his involvement in Talsint, the Court cannot conceive of any set of circumstances in which the presiding judge in the underlying case would not have felt tremendous pressure to side with MPE/MFM.

* * *

The King's behavior suggests a strong preference that DeJoria be portrayed as a fraudster who misled the King (since, if DeJoria did not, the King appears dishonest, incompetent, or both in retrospect). Whether or not the King, Prince, or some other official picked up the phone and ordered the judge to find against DeJoria is, in some sense, beside the point. Even if no such phone call was ever made, the Court nevertheless cannot, in good conscience, conclude that Morocco provided Mr. DeJoria with adequate due process to warrant enforcement in this country.

* * *

[T]he likelihood that DeJoria could have or did receive a fair hearing in which the outcome was not pre-ordained is too minimal to permit the Court to overlook the serious issues with both the system and the application present in this case.

* * *

Here, there is extensive evidence suggesting that Morocco's judiciary is dominated by the royal family (through no fault of the judiciary, which would prefer to be left alone to do its job). Additionally, the evidence plainly shows that members of the royal family had a political and economic interest in the outcome of the underlying case. This is a deadly combination, for the confluence of circumstances makes it highly likely that the royal family impacted the judicial oversight of a proceeding in which they themselves had an interest.

* * *

"[A] common sense reading of the evidence" in this case unequivocally supports the conclusion that John Paul DeJoria could not have expected to obtain a fair hearing in Morocco had he attempted to fight the charges against him. While the evidence plainly suggests that Morocco's judges wish to obtain the freedom from pressure necessary to impartially conduct the business of the court system, the evidence also reveals that any judge presiding over DeJoria's case would have had to ignore either an explicit or implicit threat to his career — if not to his safety and well-being — in order to find against MPE/MFM. Absent an act of tremendous bravery by the judge, there is no conceivable set of facts or circumstances in which DeJoria could have prevailed in the underlying case. Such a proceeding is not, was not, and can never be "fundamentally fair."

In addition to Judge Nowlin's factual findings, the record in this case contains the following evidence showing that DeJoria was denied due process in this case.

a. DeJoria's Ability to Attend the Proceedings

DeJoria contends that he was unable to personally appear at any of the court proceedings, as he had a legitimate fear that either his safety or liberty would be at risk had he traveled to Morocco once the dispute leading to the lawsuit arose. . . . The only record evidence that MPE/MFM offer to controvert DeJoria's claim comes from their retained expert's affidavit, dated in 2013 — a dozen years after the relevant events — in which he brushes off Gustin and DeJoria's fear as a simple "poor understanding of Morocco." But it is clear that DeJoria was not basing his fear on some sort of misunderstanding, but instead on a specific death threat delivered to his business partner. As Mr. Gustin explained:

> On May 22, 2001, after having received a death threat in connection with Lone Star's activities in Morocco, at a meeting of Lone Star's Board of Directors, I resigned as Lone Star's President/CEO and Chairman as a result of the death threat. I cannot reveal details of this threat without compromising the safety of innocent people still in Morocco. . . . I left the Board meeting in progress in Rabat, Morocco for the reason that I no longer felt secure as to my personal safety if I remained in Morocco and/or in my two executive positions with Lone Star. I left Morocco on May 23, 2001, and I have never been back to Morocco since that time.

He further explained that "I told Mr. DeJoria that I understood the threat to be directed at Mr. DeJoria, as well as at me, and that I believed it was unsafe for either me or Mr. DeJoria to return to Morocco." DeJoria testified that immediately following the board meeting, Gustin informed him of the threat, "and on many occasions thereafter, he related to me the facts of the death threat and his concern for our personal safety should either of us ever return to Morocco." DeJoria's own understanding, from this information, was that it would not be safe for him to attend the court proceedings in Morocco. *Id.*

And though MPE/MFM's paid expert belittled these fears, third party attorneys who practiced or resided in Morocco, and who addressed these issues during the relevant time frame, found the fears credible. . . .

Weighing all of this evidence, the Court concludes that DeJoria's fear of traveling to Morocco was credible, and that the fear arose not from a general danger of traveling in Morocco, but rather from this specific litigation, and the political and other interests of the Moroccan royal family in the litigation. . . . Thus, the Court finds that in the circumstances of this particular case, DeJoria was unable to personally appear to defend himself and offer testimony to rebut the claims made against him in the Moroccan lawsuit.

b. DeJoria's Ability to Retain Counsel

The parties hotly contest whether the political nature of DeJoria's case, and the King's political interest in the underlying oil exploration project and in the case itself, prevented DeJoria from being able to obtain legal counsel in the Moroccan proceedings. . . .

A review of the record leads the Court to conclude that DeJoria was in fact unable to retain counsel to represent him, and again, this was due to the fact that he was a defendant in a case that was of great political interest to the King of Morocco, and his interests were adverse to the King's. First, the only testimony MPE/MFM offer to directly address this point . . . does not identify any Moroccan attorney that actually was willing to represent DeJoria in the case. [Their retained expert] only makes conclusory statements such as "it is not at all uncommon for Moroccan attorneys to represent unpopular figures in Moroccan courts." And though he claims that "there are many attorneys in Morocco who would have been willing to represent DeJoria," he notably fails to identify a single one, nor does he even indicate that *he* would have represented DeJoria had he been approached. DeJoria's evidence was more specific. DeJoria explained that Gustin contacted Bernard Dessaix, a French attorney licensed to practice in Morocco, about representing their interests in the case. After "multiple phone conferences and letters" Dessaix declined representation, and explained the risks an attorney would face if he or she represented Skidmore, DeJoria or the other defendants in the case:

> Clearly it is not only unsafe for Mr GUSTIN and Mr DEJORJA to go to Morocco in a case involving his Highness Prince Moulay Abdellah Alaoui, a first cousin of his Majesty King Mohammed VI, King of Morocco, and his partners, but it is also unsafe and unwise for any lawyer/barrister from any country to go there and plead against his Highness Prince Moulay Abdallah Alaoui and his partners to argue that anyone descending from the Prophet Mohammed did not keep his word. The potential risks to one's welfare are unacceptable.

> . . .

[W]eighing all the evidence before it, the Court concludes that DeJoria was in fact unable to retain counsel to represent him during the time the Moroccan case was active, and again, this was due to the fact that he was a defendant in a case that was of great political interest to the King of Morocco, and his interests were adverse to the King's. In reaching this conclusion, the Court has taken into account not only that which is set out above, but also that numerous Moroccan attorneys warned DeJoria or his partners of the personal risks they faced if they returned to Morocco, and that an attorney could face if he represented them, that DeJoria had substantial resources with which to hire an attorney and yet nevertheless no attorney made an appearance for him, and finally, that direct evidence of the King's feelings with regard to those who took up DeJoria's side of things was demonstrated in his shutting down a newspaper that dared to suggest that perhaps MPE/MFM's narrative of the events with Skidmore, et al. was incorrect (as Judge Nowlin detailed in his findings).[14]

c. The Independence of the Experts

Lastly, the evidence in the record shows that the Moroccan court was determined to award damages against DeJoria, even when the very experts the court retained advised otherwise. Specifically, the Moroccan court record indicates that over the seven years that the case remained pending, the court retained five experts to advise the court on whether any damages had been suffered as a result of the defendants' allegedly wrongful acts. After reciting in detail that experts were engaged to "determine the value of the damages and losses that may have been incurred by the Claimants as a result of the Defendants' actions," the judgment notes that reports were submitted by three experts — Saleh Al-Ghazouli, Al-Saadiya Fatthi, and Mohamed Al-Karimi. These three experts, according to the judgment "concluded that they could not provide any firm opinion on the matter." *Id.* at 13. So, rather than entering judgment that the claimants take nothing, the court "ordered a new assessment and assigned the task to expert Saad Al-Omani." *Id.* And what was this expert's assessment? We do not know, because the judgment states, without explanation, that he was too was replaced, this time by Ahmed A-Khardal, the fifth expert to be engaged by the court. Khardal submitted his report on January 22, 2009, and was the first of the experts to conclude that there were damages incurred. This time, there was no dismissal of the expert, and by the end of 2009, the Moroccan court entered judgment against Gustin and DeJoria for 98% of the damages Khardal recommended. *Id.*

. . .

[T]he number of experts engaged, and the length of time the case was pending appears to be evidence of the difficulty the commercial court judges had in coming up with a colorable basis on which to impose liability on Gustin and DeJoria, and the struggle they had finding an expert to support an award of damages.

---

14. MPE/MFM argue that even if the underlying proceedings suffered from all of these defects, DeJoria waived any complaint he might have because he did not file an appeal, which would have led to a de novo review of the case. The problem with this argument is that it assumes DeJoria could have retained an attorney to file the appeal, and participate in the de novo review. As already found, that was not the case. So this is not like the cases MPE/MFM cite, where the party who was contesting recognition of a judgment was not prevented from participating in their appeal, but instead simply chose to stop fighting in the foreign country, and to bring their fight back to the U.S. Here, DeJoria was denied the ability to fight the case in Morocco at trial or on appeal.

5. *Conclusions*

Based upon the findings made by Judge Nowlin, and those made herein, the Court finds that DeJoria has presented sufficient evidence to demonstrate that "the specific proceeding in the foreign court leading to the judgment was not compatible with the requirements of due process of law." Amended Act § 36A.004(c)(8). The facts demonstrate that DeJoria was denied an impartial tribunal because the royal family had a clear political interest in the outcome of the underlying case which "was not compatible with the requirements of due process of law." The Comments to the 2005 Uniform Act provide that non-recognition will be satisfied by "a showing that *for political reasons* the particular party against whom the foreign-country judgment was entered was denied fundamental fairness in the particular proceedings leading to the foreign-country judgment." § 4 cmt. ¶ 12 (emphasis added.) This is the situation in the case at bar. The failed oil exploration project was a significant political embarrassment for the King. This in turn led to a death threat being lodged against DeJoria and him having to remain outside of Morocco, to him being unable to find an attorney willing to represent him in the dispute, and thus to MPE/MFM being completely unopposed in their suit. Despite the lack of opposition, the court struggled to find an expert who would certify the award of any damages, but the Court doggedly persisted until such an expert was located, and once located, awarded 98% of what he recommended. The ability to appear, either in person or through counsel, is a fundamental requirement of due process, as is a fair tribunal that acts independently of political influence. All of that was lacking here. Section (c)(8) presents a discretionary ground for non-recognition, and, as Judge Nowlin found in the initial proceedings, the Court once again believes that the proper exercise of its discretion in this case is to grant the motion for non-recognition.[15]

IV. Recommendation

The undersigned RECOMMENDS that the District Court GRANT John Paul DeJoria's Motion For Non-Recognition under § 36A.004(c)(8) of the Texas Uniform Foreign-Country Money Judgments Recognition Act.

[The district court accepted and adopted the Report and Recommendation of the Magistrate Judge and granted DeJoria's Motion for Non-Recognition. *DeJoria v. Maghreb Petroleum Exploration, S.A.*, 2018 WL 1830789 (W.D. Tex. 2018). The court of appeals affirmed. *DeJoria v. Maghreb Petroleum Exploration, S.A.*, 935 F.3d 381 (5th Cir. 2019).]

---

15. DeJoria also requests non-recognition based on § 36A.004(c)(7) of the Amended Act, which applies to cases that "raise substantial doubt about the integrity of the rendering court with respect to the judgment." Given the findings regarding the pressures on Moroccan judges in cases involving political issues impacting the King, as well as the findings on there being musical chair experts, there may be sufficient evidence to support a (c)(7) finding. But because the finding under (c)(8) is stronger, and sufficient in its own right to support this outcome, the Court will not reach that issue. Likewise, for the same reason, the Court need not reach the public policy argument under (c)(3), nor decide whether there is an independent Due Process right to non-recognition, and if that argument is subsumed within the terms of subsection (c)(8) of the Amended Act.

1. **Practice: Litigation Strategy.** Why do you think the judgment creditor in *Midbrook* filed its action to enforce the Dutch judgment in Washington rather than in the Netherlands? Why do you think the judgment debtor in *DeJoria* filed his action to challenge the Moroccan judgment in Texas rather than in Morocco? Why were these actions in U.S. federal court? Why did the federal courts use state law to determine enforceability?

2. **Practice: Locating Assets.** How do you think the judgment creditors in *Midbrook* knew that the judgment debtor had assets in Washington against which the judgment might be enforced? How, in general, would you attempt to locate assets of a judgment debtor when representing a judgment creditor?

3. **Reconciling the Cases.** In *Midbrook*, the court held that the Dutch judgment was enforceable. What arguments did the judgment debtor in *Midbrook* make against enforcement, and why did the court reject them? In *DeJoria*, the court held that the Moroccan judgment was not enforceable. What arguments did the judgment debtor make against enforcement, and why did the court accept them? On what factual grounds can the *Midbrook* and *DeJoria* cases be reconciled?

4. **The Due Process Standard.** What standard of due process did the courts use in *Midbrook* and *DeJoria*? Why didn't the court instead apply ordinary U.S. due process standards to assess the foreign legal proceedings? What are the advantages and disadvantages of the standard applied in these cases? Sometimes this standard is called the "international due process" standard. *See* footnote 10 of the *Midbrook* opinion. Which is stricter, ordinary U.S. due process standards or the standard applied by the courts in *Midbrook* and *DeJoria*?

5. **The Due Process Exception: Systemic versus Case-Specific.** Both the 1962 Uniform Act and the 2005 Uniform Act include a systemic due process exception to the recognition and enforcement of foreign judgments. *See* 1962 Uniform Act § 4(a)(1) ("A foreign judgment is not conclusive if . . . the judgment was rendered under a system which does not provide impartial tribunals or procedures compatible with the requirements of due process of law . . .) and 2005 Uniform Act § 4(b)(1) ("A court of this state may not recognize a foreign-country judgment if . . . the judgment was rendered under a judicial system that does not provide impartial tribunals or procedures compatible with the requirements of due process of law . . ."). The 2005 Uniform Act, however, added an exception not contained in the 1962 Uniform Act: a case-specific due process exception. *See* 2005 Uniform Act § 4(c)(8): "A court of this state need not recognize a foreign-country judgment if . . . the specific proceeding in the foreign court leading to the judgment was not compatible with the requirements of due process of law." How are these two exceptions different? How are they similar? Are they both necessary? What are the advantages and disadvantages of having both grounds for refusing recognition and enforcement of a foreign judgment?

6. **Litigating the Systemic and Case-Specific Exceptions.** As explained in the *DeJoria* case, at the time DeJoria filed his action in Texas, Texas's foreign judgment recognition statute was based on the 1962 Uniform Act and thus lacked a case-specific due process exception. Therefore, in an earlier stage of the litigation, DeJoria argued that the systemic due process exception applied and that the court was not permitted to recognize or enforce the Moroccan judgment. The district court agreed, but the court of appeals rejected the argument, holding that "DeJoria . . . failed to meet his burden to prove that the entire Moroccan judicial system does not meet due process standards." Later, DeJoria argued that the case-specific due process exception applied and that the court could therefore refuse to recognize and enforce the Moroccan judgment. The district court agreed and the court of appeals affirmed. What change occurred that allowed DeJoria to make that new argument? Based on what facts could the court of appeals conclude that the systemic due process exception did not apply but the case-specific due process exception did apply?

What showing should be required to meet the 1962 Act's systemic exception? In finding that the systemic exception did not apply, the court of appeals in *DeJoria* distinguished prior cases that had refused enforcement:

> For example, in *Bank Melli Iran v. Pahlavi*, the Ninth Circuit refused to enforce an Iranian judgment and concluded that the Iranian judicial system did not comport with due process standards. 58 F.3d 1406, 1411-13 (9th Cir. 1995). The court relied on official reports advising Americans against traveling to Iran during the relevant time period and identifying Iran as an official state sponsor of terror. Further, the court noted that Iranian trials were private, politicized proceedings, and recognized that the Iranian government itself did not "believe in the independence of the judiciary." Judges were subject to continuing scrutiny and potential sanction and could not be expected to be impartial to American citizens. Further, "revolutionary courts" had the power to usurp and overrule decisions of the Iranian civil courts. Attorneys were also warned against "representing politically undesirable interests." Based on this evidence, the court concluded that the Iranian judicial system simply could not produce fair proceedings.
>
> Similarly, in *Bridgeway Corp. v. Citibank*, the Second Circuit declined to recognize a Liberian judgment rendered during the Liberian Civil War. 201 F.3d 134, 144 (2d Cir. 2000). There, the court observed that, during the relevant time period, "Liberia's judicial system was in a state of disarray and the provisions of the Constitution concerning the judiciary were no longer followed." Further, official State Department Country Reports noted that the Liberian judicial system — already marred by "corruption and incompetent handling of cases" — completely "collapsed" following the outbreak of fighting. Because the court concluded that there was "sufficiently powerful and uncontradicted documentary evidence describing the chaos within the Liberian judicial system during the period of interest," it refused to enforce the Liberian judgment.
>
> *Pahlavi* and *Bridgeway* thus exemplify how a foreign judicial system can be so fundamentally flawed as to offend basic notions of fairness. Unlike the Iranian system in *Pahlavi*, there is simply no indication that it would be

impossible for an American to receive due process or impartial tribunals in Morocco. . . . Because Morocco's judicial system is not in such a dire situation, it does not present the unusual case of a foreign judicial system that offends against basic fairness.

Is it appropriate for a U.S. court to call into question the judicial system of another country in an enforcement proceeding? Might U.S. courts be reluctant to do so? What might be the foreign relations implications if a U.S. court holds that a foreign country's judicial system "does not provide impartial tribunals or procedures compatible with the requirements of due process of law"? Are the implications different if a court instead holds that "the specific proceeding in the foreign court leading to the judgment was not compatible with the requirements of due process of law"?

7. **Relationship Between Litigation Strategies and Legislative Strategies.** The court of appeals provided additional background and commentary on the process that led to the amendment of the Texas Recognition Act during the *DeJoria* litigation:

> While the sound and fury continued apace in the trial court, a second front in this dispute opened, this time in the Texas legislature. With the testimonial aid of one of DeJoria's lawyers, the 2017 legislative session was considering updating the Recognition Act to the 2005 uniform act. Among other changes, the new law would add two discretionary grounds for nonrecognition: a court would be able to deny recognition if "the judgment was rendered in circumstances that raise substantial doubt about the integrity of the rendering court with respect to the judgment" or, more importantly in this case, if "the specific proceeding in the foreign court leading to the judgment was not compatible with the requirements of due process of law." 2005 Unif. Act § 4(c)(7)-(8).
>
> These substantive differences between the old and new law were not the focus of hearings on the bill. Instead, a change not found in the new Uniform Law nor in the versions of that law passed by other states drew the most attention. The drafters had made the law retroactive to pending cases. The only pending case the legislators were told about was this one. Despite the concern of at least one legislator that the law was going to change the outcome of this case midstream, the law was adopted with the retroactivity provision.
>
> With his legislative victory in hand, DeJoria returned to the district court to inform it of the change in Texas law. . . .
>
> We are mindful that the whiff of home cooking also pervades the Texas side of this case. There is a deep irony in allowing DeJoria to contend he was denied due process in Morocco when it was his lobbying efforts that changed the rules of the game midway through the proceedings in the United States.

DeJoria v. Maghreb Petroleum Exploration, S.A., 935 F.3d 381, 387-89 (5th Cir. 2019). What do you think of this combination of litigation strategies and legislative strategies? Is it a good example of lawyers using litigation and lobbying skills to zealously represent their client? Or is it an improper blending of law and politics?

8. **Practice: Judgment Creditor Strategies.** If you are a lawyer for a judgment creditor trying to compel the judgment debtor to pay the amount owed under

a foreign judgment, what enforcement strategies would you consider? What facts would you investigate and what arguments would you consider if you were seeking enforcement in the United States? What enforcement strategies might you consider outside the United States, and what factual and legal questions would you need to answer to evaluate those strategies?

9. **Practice: Judgment Debtor Strategies.** If you are a lawyer for a judgment debtor trying to avoid enforcement of a foreign judgment in a U.S. court, what facts would you investigate and what arguments would you consider?

Review the summary of the *Chevron-Ecuador* case in the introduction to this chapter. The judgment creditors in that case did not try to enforce the Ecuadorian judgment against Chevron Corp. in the United States. They did, however, seek enforcement in several other nations, including Argentina, Brazil, and Canada. If you were a lawyer for a judgment debtor in Chevron's situation, what factual and legal research would you need to do to develop arguments against enforcement in foreign nations?

What other strategies might you consider on behalf of your client? One strategy attempted by Chevron Corp. was to ask a U.S. court to issue an injunction prohibiting the judgment creditors from seeking enforcement anywhere in the world. The district court granted the injunction, but the court of appeals reversed, finding that Chevron could not seek such an order unless the Ecuadorian plaintiffs attempted to enforce their judgment in the United States and that a U.S. court does not have the authority to determine whether another nation's courts may enforce a judgment. *Chevron Corp. v. Naranjo*, 667 F.3d 232, 234 (2d Cir. 2012). Should a U.S. court be able to enjoin foreign judgment creditors from trying to enforce a foreign judgment in foreign nations? If so, under what circumstances might this be appropriate? Could this sort of extraterritorial application of a U.S. court's authority be reconciled with the presumption against extraterritoriality that is applied to U.S. statutes, discussed in Chapter 1?

Later, in a related action, the district court issued an injunction prohibiting action to enforce the judgment against Chevron in the United States only. This time, the court of appeals affirmed. It reasoned that "the geographic scope of the *Naranjo* injunction and scope of the injunction granted in the District Court Judgment [in the present action] are different. The *Naranjo* injunction was essentially global, prohibiting actions toward enforcement of the Judgment anywhere outside of Ecuador. The geographic scope of the present District Court Judgment anti-enforcement injunction . . . is limited to the United States: [It enjoins] taking actions toward enforcement in courts of the United States; but 'nothing [ ]in [the District Court Judgment] enjoins, restrains or otherwise prohibits . . . filing or prosecuting any action for recognition or enforcement of the Judgment . . . in courts outside the United States. . . .'" *Chevron Corporation v. Donziger*, 833 F.3d 74, 144 (2d Cir. 2016). What is the legal significance of this difference in geographic scope? Why did this difference lead the court of appeals to reach different outcomes? Do you agree with the distinction? Why or why not?

As another strategy, Chevron initiated arbitration proceedings against Ecuador in 2009 pursuant to the Ecuador-U.S. Bilateral Investment Treaty. Bilateral investment treaties (BITs) are treaties between two nations that give each other's investors certain protections. BITs also give investors the right to submit investment disputes to arbitration instead of the courts of the nation where they have invested. As discussed in more detail in Chapter 6, arbitration is a dispute resolution method whereby the disputants agree to have private third parties called "arbitrators" resolve the dispute. Typically, each party selects an arbitrator of its choice, and the two arbitrators so selected then select a third arbitrator. In the arbitral proceedings, Chevron sought an award* releasing Chevron from liability and finding that Ecuador or Petroecuador "exclusively liable for any judgment that may be issued in the Lago Agrio Litigation." Claimant's Notice of Arbitration, *Chevron Corp. and Texaco Petrol. Co. v. Republic of Ecuador*, PCA Case No. 2009-23 (Sept. 23, 2009), *available at* http://www.chevron.com/documents/pdf/EcuadorBITEn.pdf. The arbitral tribunal issued interim awards ordering Ecuador "to take all measures to suspend or cause to be suspended the enforcement and recognition within and without Ecuador" of the Lago Agrio judgment until the panel issues a decision on the merits. Fourth Interim Award on Interim Measures, *Chevron Corp. and Texaco Petrol. Co. v. Republic of Ecuador*, PCA Case No. 2009-23, at 25-26 (Feb. 7, 2013). Should arbitrators be able to review the decisions of national courts and issue orders preventing enforcement of those decisions? Why or why not? Note that Chevron (the foreign investor/judgment debtor) and Ecuador (the host nation) were the parties to the arbitral proceedings, but the Ecuadorian plaintiffs (the judgment creditors) were not. How, if at all, does this affect your answers to these questions? Should judgment creditors be required parties in this type of arbitration? Why or why not?

b. The Public Policy Exception

In addition to procedural considerations, another ground for nonenforcement is that enforcement would be repugnant to public policy. The following case examines this exception. As you read it, consider the following questions: Should the public policy exception be easy or difficult to invoke successfully? What are the difficulties in administering it? Also note that the issue in this case is recognition of a foreign judgment, not enforcement of a foreign judgment. What is the difference, and why is recognition important in this case?

Southwest Livestock and Trucking Company, Inc. v. Ramón
169 F.3d 317 (5th Cir. 1999)

EMILIO M. GARZA, Circuit Judge:
Defendant-Appellant, Reginaldo Ramón, appeals the district court's grant of summary judgment in favor of Plaintiffs-Appellees, Southwest Livestock & Trucking Co., Inc., Darrel Hargrove and Mary Jane Hargrove. Ramón contends

---

* The dispute resolution outcome in arbitration is called an "award" rather than a "judgment."

that the district court erred by not recognizing a Mexican judgment, that if recognized would preclude summary judgment against him. We vacate the district court's summary judgment and remand.

I

Darrel and Mary Jane Hargrove (the "Hargroves") are citizens of the United States and officers of Southwest Livestock & Trucking Co., Inc. ("Southwest Livestock"), a Texas corporation involved in the buying and selling of livestock. In 1990, Southwest Livestock entered into a loan arrangement with Reginaldo Ramón ("Ramón"), a citizen of the Republic of Mexico. Southwest Livestock borrowed $400,000 from Ramón. To accomplish the loan, Southwest Livestock executed a "pagaré" — a Mexican promissory note — payable to Ramón with interest within thirty days. Each month, Southwest Livestock executed a new pagaré to cover the outstanding principal and paid the accrued interest. Over a period of four years, Southwest Livestock made payments towards the principal, but also borrowed additional money from Ramón. In October of 1994, Southwest Livestock defaulted on the loan. With the exception of the last pagaré executed by Southwest Livestock, none of the pagarés contained a stated interest rate. Ramón, however, charged Southwest Livestock interest at a rate of approximately fifty-two percent. The last pagaré stated an interest rate of forty-eight percent, and under its terms, interest continues to accrue until Southwest Livestock pays the outstanding balance in full.

After Southwest Livestock defaulted, Ramón filed a lawsuit in Mexico to collect on the last pagaré. The Mexican court granted judgment in favor of Ramón, and ordered Southwest Livestock to satisfy its debt and to pay interest at forty-eight percent. . . . The Mexican appellate court . . . affirmed the judgment. . . .

After Ramón filed suit in Mexico, but prior to the entry of the Mexican judgment, Southwest Livestock brought suit in United States District Court, alleging that the loan arrangement violated Texas usury laws. Southwest Livestock then filed a motion for partial summary judgment, claiming that the undisputed facts established that Ramón charged, received and collected usurious interest in violation of Texas law. Ramón also filed a motion for summary judgment. By then the Mexican court had entered its judgment, and Ramón sought recognition of that judgment. He claimed that, under principles of collateral estoppel and res judicata, the Mexican judgment barred Southwest Livestock's suit. The district court judge referred both motions to a magistrate judge.

The magistrate judge recommended that the district court grant Southwest Livestock's motion for summary judgment as to liability under Texas usury law, and recommended that it hold a trial to determine damages. In reaching her decision, the magistrate judge first addressed whether the Texas Uniform Foreign Country Money-Judgment Recognition Act (the "Texas Recognition Act") required the district court to recognize the Mexican judgment. See Tex. Civ. Prac. & Rem. Code Ann. § 36.001 et seq. (West 1998). As the magistrate judge observed, a judgment "that is not refused recognition . . . is conclusive between the parties to the extent that it grants or denies recovery of a sum of money." Tex. Civ. Prac. & Rem.

Code Ann. § 36.004 (West 1998). The magistrate judge concluded that, contrary to Southwest Livestock's position, the Mexican court properly acquired personal jurisdiction over Southwest Livestock, and therefore, lack of jurisdiction could not constitute a basis for nonrecognition. Nonetheless, according to the magistrate judge, "the district court would be well within its discretion in not recognizing the Mexican judgment on the grounds that it violates the public policy of the state of Texas." Thus, the magistrate judge decided that the Mexican judgment did not bar Southwest Livestock's suit. The magistrate judge then addressed whether the district court should apply Texas or Mexican law to its resolution of Southwest Livestock's usury claim. The magistrate judge concluded that, under Texas choice of law rules, the district court should apply Texas law. Under Texas law, Ramón undisputably charged usurious interest.

The district court adopted the magistrate judge's recommendation, granting Southwest Livestock's motion for summary judgment as to liability under Texas usury law, and denying Ramón's motion for summary judgment. The district court agreed that the Mexican judgment violated Texas public policy, and that Texas law applied. The district court then heard evidence on the question of damages and granted $5,766,356.93 to Southwest Livestock. The district court also ordered that amount to "increase by $1,677.00 for every day after November 17, 1997, until the date this Judgment is signed," and awarded Southwest Livestock post-judgment interest and attorneys' fees. Ramón appealed.

Ramón asks us to reverse the district court's grant of summary judgment in favor of Southwest Livestock. He contends that the district court erred by failing to recognize the Mexican judgment. He also argues that the district court erred by applying Texas law. According to Ramón, the district court should have applied Mexican law because the pagarés executed by Southwest Livestock designated Mexico as the place of payment, and Mexico has the most significant relationship to the loan transaction. Ramón also objects to the district court's continuing charge for usury. . . .

Southwest Livestock . . . contends that the district court properly withheld recognition of the Mexican judgment and properly applied Texas law. Additionally, as an alternative ground for upholding the district court's decision not to recognize the Mexican judgment, Southwest Livestock argues that Ramón failed to serve it with proper service of process, and therefore, the Mexican court lacked personal jurisdiction.

II

We must determine first whether the district court properly refused to recognize the Mexican judgment. Our jurisdiction is based on diversity of citizenship. Hence, we must apply Texas law regarding the recognition of foreign country money-judgments. *See Erie R.R. Co. v. Tompkins*, 304 U.S. 64, 58 (1938). . . .

Under the Texas Recognition Act, a court must recognize a foreign country judgment assessing money damages unless the judgment debtor establishes one of ten specific grounds for nonrecognition. *See* Tex. Civ. Prac. & Rem. Code Ann. § 36.005 (West 1998); *Dart v. Balaam*, 953 S.W.2d 478, 480 (Tex. App. — Fort

Worth 1997, no writ) (noting that "[t]he party seeking to avoid recognition has the burden of proving a ground for nonrecognition"). Southwest Livestock contends that it established a ground for nonrecognition. It notes that the Texas Constitution places a six percent interest rate limit on contracts that do not contain a stated interest rate. *See* Tex. Const. art. XVI, § 11. It also points to a Texas statute that states that usury is against Texas public policy. *See* Vernon's Tex. Civ. Stat., art. 5069-1C.001 ("All contracts for usury are contrary to public policy"). Thus, according to Southwest Livestock, the Mexican judgment violates Texas public policy, and the district court properly withheld recognition of the judgment.

We review the district court's grant of summary judgment de novo. . . . In reviewing the district court's decision, we note that the level of contravention of Texas law has "to be high before recognition [can] be denied on public policy grounds." . . . The narrowness of the public policy exception reflects a compromise between two axioms — res judicata and fairness to litigants — that underlie our law of recognition of foreign country judgments. . . .

To decide whether the district court erred in refusing to recognize the Mexican judgment on public policy grounds, we consider the plain language of the Texas Recognition Act. . . . Section 36.005(b)(3) of the Texas Recognition Act permits the district court not to recognize a foreign country judgment if "*the cause of action* on which the judgment is based is repugnant to the public policy" of Texas. Tex. Civ. Prac. & Rem. Code Ann. § 36.005(b)(3) (West 1998) (emphasis added). This subsection of the Texas Recognition Act does not refer to the judgment itself, but specifically to the "cause of action on which the judgment is based." Thus, the fact that a judgment offends Texas public policy does not, in and of itself, permit the district court to refuse recognition of that judgment. *See Norkan Lodge Co. Ltd. v. Gillum*, 587 F. Supp. 1457, 1461 (N.D. Tex. 1984) (noting that a "judgment may only be attacked in the event that 'the cause of action [on] which the judgment is based is repugnant to the public policy of this state,' not the judgment itself").

In this case, the Mexican judgment was based on an action for collection of a promissory note. This cause of action is not repugnant to Texas public policy. *See, e.g., Akin v. Dahl*, 661 S.W.2d 914 (Tex. 1983) (enforcing a suit for the collection of a promissory note). Under the Texas Recognition Act, it is irrelevant that the Mexican judgment itself contravened Texas's public policy against usury. Thus, the plain language of the Texas Recognition Act suggests that the district court erred in refusing to recognize the Mexican judgment.

Southwest Livestock, however, argues that we should not interpret the Texas Recognition Act according to its plain language. Southwest Livestock contends that Texas courts will not enforce rights existing under laws of other jurisdictions when to do so would violate Texas public policy. . . . It believes that the reasoning of the Texas Supreme Court in *DeSantis v. Wackenhut Corp.*, 793 S.W.2d 670 (Tex. 1990), requires us to affirm the district court's decision not to recognize the Mexican judgment. In *DeSantis*, the Court refused to apply Florida law to enforce a noncompetition agreement, even though the agreement contained an express choice of Florida law provision, and Florida had a substantial interest in the transaction. The Court concluded that "the law governing enforcement of noncompetition agreements is fundamental policy in Texas, and that to apply the law of another state to determine the enforceability of such an agreement in the circumstances of a case like this would be contrary to that policy." *Id.* at 681. Southwest Livestock argues similarly that the law governing usury constitutes a fundamental policy in Texas, and that to recognize the Mexican judgment would transgress that policy.

We find that, contrary to Southwest Livestock's argument, *DeSantis* does not support the district court's grant of summary judgment. First, in *DeSantis* the Court refused to enforce an agreement violative of Texas public policy; it did not refuse to recognize a foreign judgment. Recognition and enforcement of a judgment involve separate and distinct inquiries. *See Guinness v. Ward*, 955 F.2d 875, 889 (4th Cir. 1992) (noting the difference between recognizing and enforcing a foreign judgment); *see also* Restatement (Third) of Foreign Relations Law § 481 cmt. b (1986) (distinguishing between the recognition and enforcement of judgments). Second, unlike in *DeSantis*, where the plaintiff sought to use foreign law offensively to enforce the noncompetition agreement, in this case, Ramón seeks recognition of the Mexican judgment as an affirmative defense to Southwest Livestock's usury claim. Different considerations apply when a party seeks recognition of a foreign judgment for defensive purposes. As Justice Brandeis once stated:

> [T]he company is in a position different from that of a plaintiff who seeks to enforce a cause of action conferred by the laws of another state. The right which it claims should be given effect is set up by way of defense to an asserted liability; and to a defense different considerations apply. A state may, on occasion, decline to enforce a foreign cause of action. In so doing, it merely denies a remedy leaving unimpaired the plaintiff's substantive right, so that he is free to enforce it elsewhere. But to refuse to give effect to a substantive defense under the applicable law of another state, as under the circumstances here presented, subjects the defendant to irremediable liability. This may not be done.

Bradford Elec. Light Co. v. Clapper, 286 U.S. 145, 160 (1932). . . . Third, *DeSantis* involved a noncompetition agreement, and as we have explained elsewhere, "noncompetition agreements implicate an arguably stronger Texas public policy than usurious contracts." *Admiral Ins. Co. v. Brinkcraft Dev.*, 921 F.2d 591, 594 (5th Cir.1991).

We find our decision in *Woods-Tucker Leasing Corp. v. Hutcheson-Ingram Development Co.*, 642 F.2d 744 (5th Cir.1981), more helpful than *DeSantis*.[4] In *Woods-Tucker*, we considered "whether a bankruptcy court sitting in Texas should honor a party contractual choice of Mississippi law in determining whether to apply the Texas or Mississippi usury statute to a transaction . . . between a Texas partnership and a Mississippi-headquartered corporate subsidiary of a Georgia corporation."

---

4. We acknowledge that *Woods-Tucker* involves a sister state judgment, which distinguishes it from this case. *See Reading & Bates Constr. Co. v. Baker Energy Resources Corp.*, 976 S.W.2d 702, 714 (Tex. App. — Houston [1st Dist.] 1998, writ denied) ("Giving full faith and credit to the judgment of a sister state is vastly different than according it to a foreign country judgment."). Nevertheless, we find the decision in *Woods-Tucker* informative.

Id. at 745. In deciding to honor the parties' choice of Mississippi law, we noted that applying Mississippi law did not offend any Texas fundamental public policy:

> To be sure, it is the underlying policy of each state's usury laws to protect necessitous borrowers within its borders. Yet, as we have noted, we have found no Texas cases that have invalidated a party choice of law on grounds that the application of a foreign usury statute would violate public policy.

Id. at 753 n. 13. We also relied on the Supreme Court's decision in *Seeman v. Philadelphia Warehouse Co.*, 274 U.S. 403. In *Seeman*, the Supreme Court emphasized its policy of "upholding contractual obligations assumed in good faith." It stated that, although parties may not willfully evade otherwise applicable usury laws by "entering into [a] contract . . . [that] has no normal relation to the transaction," if the rate of interest "allowed by the laws of the place of performance is higher than that permitted at the place of the contract," the parties may contract for a higher rate of interest without incurring the penalties of usury. *Id.* at 407-08. . . . *Woods-Tucker*, and its reliance on *Seeman*, indicates that, although Texas has a strong public policy against usury, this policy is not inviolable.

We are especially reluctant to conclude that recognizing the Mexican judgment offends Texas public policy under the circumstances of this case. The purpose behind Texas usury laws is to protect unsophisticated borrowers from unscrupulous lenders. This case, however, does not involve the victimizing of a naive consumer. Southwest Livestock is managed by sophisticated and knowledgeable people with experience in business. Additionally, the evidence in the record does not suggest that Ramón misled or deceived Southwest Livestock. Southwest Livestock and Ramón negotiated the loan in good faith and at arm's length. In short, both parties fully appreciated the nature of the loan transaction and their respective contractual obligations.

Accordingly, in light of the plain language of the Texas Recognition Act, and after consideration of our decision in *Woods-Tucker* and the purpose behind Texas public policy against usury, we hold that Texas's public policy does not justify withholding recognition of the Mexican judgment. The district court erred in deciding otherwise.

III

For the foregoing reasons, we VACATE the district court's summary judgment, and REMAND for further proceedings.

NOTES AND QUESTIONS

1. **Recognition versus Enforcement.** The issue in *Southwest Livestock* was not whether to enforce a foreign judgment, but instead whether to recognize a foreign judgment. What is the difference? If Ramón was not asking the U.S. court to enforce the Mexican judgment, what, precisely, was he asking the court to do with that judgment?

2. **Practice: What's at Stake?** What was at stake for the litigants in *Southwest Livestock*? What was the consequence of the U.S. court recognizing the Mexican judgment? What would have happened in the U.S. court proceeding if the court had instead refused to recognize the Mexican judgment?

3. **The Applicable Law in Recognition and Enforcement Actions.** What law did the court apply to the issue of whether to recognize the Mexican judgment in *Southwest Livestock*, and why?

4. **The Public Policy Exception.** As *Southwest Livestock* illustrates, the public policy exception to the recognition and enforcement of foreign country money judgments is narrow. Mere differences in law or policy between the forum state and a foreign state are insufficient to trigger the exception. How did Southwest Livestock argue that the public policy exception prevented recognition in this case? Why did the court disagree? Note that there are some subtle but important differences between various approaches to the public policy exception. The public policy exception in the 1962 Uniform Act provides that "[a] foreign judgment need not be recognized if . . . the cause of action on which the judgment is based is repugnant to the public policy of this state. . . ." § 4(b)(3). In contrast, § 4(c)(3) of the 2005 Uniform Act, the relevant public policy may include not only state public policy, but also the public policy of the United States. Moreover, under the 1962 Uniform Act, a judgment need not be recognized if the *cause of action* is repugnant to public policy. In contrast, under the 2005 Uniform Act and according to the *Restatement*, a judgment need not be recognized if either the cause of action *or the judgment itself* is repugnant to public policy. These may seem to be minor differences. But as *Southwest Livestock* illustrates, they can have important, even outcome-determinative, consequences. As you saw, the case was decided under the 1962 Act. Would the case have come out differently under the 2005 Uniform Act?

5. **Public Policy and the Constitution.** Although the public policy exception is a narrow one, courts have used it to avoid enforcement when constitutional rights are at stake. Consider *Telnikoff v. Matusevitch*, 347 Md. 561 (1997). Telnikoff (an English citizen) sued Matusevitch (a Maryland resident) in an English court, alleging that he was libeled by a letter published by Matusevitch in a London newspaper. The English court entered a libel judgment against Matusevitch, and Telnikoff then filed an action in a Maryland court to enforce the judgment. The Court of Appeals of Maryland declined to enforce the judgment based on the public policy exception in its version of the 1962 Uniform Act, finding that the "English libel judgment is based upon principles which are so contrary to Maryland's public policy concerning freedom of the press and defamation actions that recognition of the judgment should be denied." *Id.* at 575. What makes this case different from *Southwest Livestock*? What does the *Telnikoff* case suggest about the relationship between the U.S. Constitution and U.S. state constitutions on the one hand, and the public policy exception on the other hand? As noted above, the SPEECH Act now prohibits U.S. state and federal courts from enforcing foreign defamation judgments that would violate the U.S. Constitution's protections of

freedom of speech and press. 28 U.S.C. § 4102. Also consider *Osorio v. Dole Food Co.*, 665 F. Supp. 2d 130 (S.D. Fla. 2009), which involved a $97 million Nicaraguan judgment obtained against Dole Food Co. by Nicaraguan citizens who alleged that they suffered harm, including sterility, due to exposure to dibromochloropropane (DBCP), an agricultural pesticide used by Dole on its banana farms in Nicaragua. The judgment was based in part on a special Nicaraguan law — Special Law 364 — passed specifically to deal with DBCP litigation. The law provided that "plaintiffs who prove that (1) they were exposed to DBCP and (2) are now sterile, are entitled to an irrefutable presumption that DBCP exposure caused their sterility." *Id.* at 1314. The plaintiffs sought to enforce the judgment against Dole in U.S. district court in Florida. The court refused to enforce the judgment because, among other things, the special law's irrefutable presumption of causation, which the Nicaraguan trial court applied in the case, violated clearly established Florida public policy. *Id.* at 1345. Citing *Southwest Livestock* for the proposition that the public policy exception is narrow, the court found that the public policy exception nevertheless barred enforcement in this case:

> Defendants argue that the irrefutable presumption of causation relied upon in the Judgment is repugnant to Florida public policy because it deprived them of their basic right to defend themselves. The Court agrees. For a presumption to comport with due process under Florida law (1) "there must be a rational connection between the fact proved and the ultimate fact presumed" and (2) "there must be a right to rebut [the presumption] in a fair manner." *Straughn v. K & K Land Mgmt., Inc.*, 326 So. 2d 421, 424 (Fla. 1976). As the Court has explained, the presumption of causation in Special Law 364 contradicts known scientific fact and affords no opportunity for rebuttal. It creates liability by legislative fiat and mandates large damage awards without determining whether the defendants actually injured the plaintiffs. Special Law 364's presumption of causation would, therefore, be unconstitutional in Florida.

Id. at 1346. What do the *Telnikoff* and *Dole* cases suggest about the types of arguments judgment debtors should explore when considering a defense against enforcement of a foreign judgment on public policy grounds?

6. **Practice: Ethics and Professional Responsibility.** If you were the lawyer for Southwest Livestock in the *Southwest Livestock* case, would you have advised your client to file an action in a Texas court to argue against recognition of the Mexican judgment on the basis of usury? Reflect upon this not only in terms of law and strategy, but also ethics.

7. **Applying the Public Policy Exception.** Was *Southwest Livestock* correctly decided? Why should a Texas court enforce a judgment based on a contract that Texas would regard as unfair and illegal if made in Texas? Should a Texas court enforce a judgment based on a gambling contract (if gambling is illegal in Texas) or a contract to purchase a product that is illegal in Texas? What about a contract containing provisions that are racially discriminatory?

How can a court (or a lawyer advising a client) determine where this line is drawn?

8. **Practice: A Look at the Briefing.** The briefs of the parties in *Southwest Livestock*, including an amicus curiae brief filed by the government of Mexico, can be found here: 1998 WL 34114646 Brief of Appellant (Jan. 1, 1998); 1998 WL 34114648 Appellees' Brief (Sept. 8, 1998); 1998 WL 34114645 Reply Brief of Appellant (Sept. 18, 1998); and 1998 WL 34114647 Amicus Curiae Brief of the Government of the United Mexican States in Support of the Defendant-Appellant (Aug. 6, 1998).

9. **Comparative Note.** Pursuant to Regulation (EU) No. 1215/2012 of the European Parliament and of the Council of 12 December 2012 on Jurisdiction and the Recognition and Enforcement of Judgments in Civil and Commercial Matters (Recast) (known as the "Brussels I Regulation"), nations that are members of the European Union (EU) are generally required to recognize and enforce the judgments of the courts of other EU member nations. The Regulation recognizes, however, five grounds for refusing recognition and enforcement:

    *   recognition is "manifestly contrary to public policy" in the Member State addressed;
    *   the judgment is a default judgment and the defendant was not served "in sufficient time and in such a way as to enable him to arrange for his defence, unless the defendant failed to commence proceedings to challenge the judgment when it was possible for him to do so";
    *   the judgment is irreconcilable with a judgment given between the same parties in the Member State addressed;
    *   the judgment is irreconcilable with an earlier judgment given in another Member State or in a third State involving the same cause of action and between the same parties, and the earlier judgment fulfills the conditions necessary for its recognition in the Member State addressed; or
    *   the judgment conflicts with the special jurisdictional provisions of the Brussels I Regulation applicable to insurance matters, consumer contracts, and individual employment contracts (which are intended to protect parties assumed to be relatively weak), or provisions applicable to situations in which courts of a particular Member State have exclusive jurisdiction; provided that the court in which enforcement is sought is bound by the findings of fact on which the court of origin based its jurisdiction.

    How is the Brussels I Regulation similar to and different from the U.S. approach to foreign judgments? How is it similar to and different from the U.S. approach to U.S. sister-state judgments? Under what circumstances might you as a U.S. lawyer find it necessary to seek recognition or enforcement of a judgment under the Brussels I Regulation?

3. Enforcing International Court Judgments

So far, this chapter has focused solely on the recognition and enforcement of the judgments of national courts. What about the judgments of international courts? Valid international court judgments may be legally binding on the United States, but they are not necessarily enforceable in U.S. courts. For example, *Medellín v. Texas* (discussed in Chapter 2) involved the judgment of the International Court of Justice (ICJ) against the United States in the *Case Concerning Avena and Other Mexican Nationals (Mexico v. United States)*, providing that Medellín and other Mexican nationals were entitled to review and reconsideration of state-court convictions and sentences due to U.S. violations of the Vienna Convention on Consular Relations. Medellín filed an application for a writ of habeas corpus in a Texas state court relying on the ICJ's judgment.

The issue before the U.S. Supreme Court in the *Medellín* case was whether the ICJ's judgment in *Avena* was directly enforceable as domestic law in a U.S. court. As the Supreme Court explained: "No one disputes that the *Avena* decision — a decision that flows from the treaties through which the United States submitted to ICJ jurisdiction with respect to Vienna Convention disputes — constitutes an international law obligation on the part of the United States. But not all international law obligations automatically constitute binding federal law enforceable in United States courts. The question we confront here is whether the *Avena* judgment has automatic domestic legal effect such that the judgment of its own force applies in state and federal courts." 552 U.S. 491, 504 (2008).

The Supreme Court held that the *Avena* judgment was not directly enforceable in U.S. courts. The Optional Protocol to the Vienna Convention subjected the United States to the compulsory jurisdiction of the ICJ for disputes arising out of the Convention. But the Supreme Court held that this amounted to "a bare grant of jurisdiction" and did not render ICJ judgments in such disputes domestically enforceable. *Id.* at 508. Article 94(1) of the U.N. Charter provides that "[e]ach Member of the United Nations undertakes to comply with the decision of the [ICJ] in any case to which it is a party." But the Supreme Court held that this provision was neither self-executing nor implemented by Congress, and that it therefore did not render ICJ judgments automatically enforceable in U.S. courts. Instead, it agreed with the executive branch's contention that "the phrase 'undertakes to comply' is not 'an acknowledgement that an ICJ decision will have immediate legal effect in the courts of U.N. members,' but rather 'a commitment on the part of U.N. Members to take future action through their political branches to comply with an ICJ decision.'" *Id.* at 508.

The law regarding the domestic enforceability of international court judgments is not well developed. However, based on the *Medellín* decision, it is unlikely that a U.S. court would conclude that it is required to enforce an international court decision without domestic legislation or a self-executing treaty requiring it to do so. Nevertheless, in some cases U.S. courts may give effect to international court judgments voluntarily. For example, courts in at least two states — Nevada and Oklahoma — provided postconviction relief to Mexican nationals in accordance with the ICJ's *Avena* judgment. *See Gutierrez v. State of Nevada*, 2012

WL 4355518 (Nev. 2012); *Torres v. Oklahoma,* 2004 WL 3711623 (Okla. Crim. App. 2004). As the Nevada Supreme Court explained, "without an implementing mandate from Congress, state procedural default rules do not have to yield to *Avena,* [but] they may yield, if actual prejudice can be shown." *Gutierrez,* 2012 WL 4355518, at *1. As a matter of policy, should U.S. courts enforce the judgments of international courts? Why shouldn't international court judgments be treated similarly to foreign court judgments?

In theory, at least, international court judgments may be enforced internationally. For example, Article 94(2) of the U.N. Charter provides that "[i]f any party to a case fails to perform the obligations incumbent upon it under a judgment rendered by the [ICJ], the other party may have recourse to the Security Council, which may, if it deems necessary, make recommendations or decide upon measures to be taken to give effect to the judgment." However, Article 94(2) has only rarely been invoked and has yet to result in the adoption of enforcement measures by the Security Council.

Compliance with international court judgments is more likely to be the result of processes that are less formal and coercive, and more decentralized, than enforcement. For example, the beneficiaries of an international court judgment and other interested parties may lobby government officials, and other nations may apply diplomatic pressure, to encourage compliance. Moreover, a party contemplating noncompliance with an international court judgment may decide to comply voluntarily because of concerns about the negative impact noncompliance may have on its reputation or on the benefits of reciprocal compliance from other nations.

Despite the limits of domestic court enforcement and centralized international enforcement, the record of compliance with ICJ decisions is generally "good, though not perfect." Colter Paulson, *Compliance with Final Judgments of the International Court of Justice Since 1987,* 98 AM. J. INT'L L. 434, 460 (2004). Lawyers representing parties in matters involving international court judgments should remember that political, diplomatic, and other nonlegal factors such as those discussed above are as likely to play an important role in determining outcomes as formal legal processes.

C. Enforcing U.S. Judgments in Foreign Courts

So far, we've been considering recognition and enforcement of "foreign" (non-U.S.) judgments in U.S. courts. But lawyers in the United States often confront the problem from the opposite perspective: How can a U.S. judgment be recognized or enforced abroad?

A challenge is that different nations have different rules governing the recognition and enforcement of foreign judgments — rules with which you may not be familiar at all. Some nations may have rules similar to those reflected in the 1962 Uniform Act, the 2005 Uniform Act, and the *Restatement,* but others may have very different rules. Some nations generally refuse to recognize or enforce foreign judgments unless they have a treaty with the foreign nation providing for recognition and enforcement. Some nations require reciprocity. While some nations have an approach that may superficially resemble the basic U.S. approach — that is, a general rule in favor of enforcement, subject to exceptions — the exceptions can vary and, even when they appear similar to a U.S. exception, they may be applied differently. Thus, as one expert on this topic summarizes: "[T]here are jurisdictions that liberally recognize and enforce U.S. judgments coming their way, at least as a general matter," but "[a]t the other end of the spectrum, there are a number of countries where U.S. judgments are for the most part given no effect." Samuel P. Baumgartner, *Understanding the Obstacles to the Recognition and Enforcement of U.S. Judgments Abroad*, 45 N.Y.U. J. Int'l L. & Pol. 965, 967 (2013).

Some of the barriers to enforcement of U.S. money judgments abroad stem from more general differences between U.S. law and the law of other nations. For example, U.S. money judgments that include punitive damages often raise special problems. Many legal systems outside the United States do not have the equivalent of U.S. punitive damages. These systems tend to limit civil judgments to compensation and restitution, and view punishment and deterrence — the common U.S. rationale for punitive damages — as being the exclusive province of criminal law. From this perspective, the imposition of punitive damages is sometimes understood as an imposition of a criminal sanction in civil litigation — something that raises serious concerns of public policy and, potentially, constitutional rights. For this reason, some foreign nations refuse on public policy grounds to enforce money judgments that include punitive damages and some may enforce only the portion of the judgment that provides compensation. Similarly, U.S. money judgments entered in actions where jurisdiction over the defendant was based solely on service of the defendant in the forum state ("transient" or "tag" jurisdiction) or based solely on business activities of the defendant in the forum state unrelated to the plaintiff's claim ("doing business jurisdiction") may face barriers to recognition and enforcement in nations that do not accept these bases for personal jurisdiction. Baumgartner, *supra*.

The Hague Convention on Choice of Court Agreements and the Hague Convention on the Recognition and Enforcement of Foreign Judgments in Civil or Commercial Matters (both discussed above) could greatly facilitate enforcement of U.S. judgments abroad. So far, however, the United States has not become a party to the Convention on Choice of Court Agreements (which entered into force in 2015) and has not signed the Convention on the Recognition and Enforcement of Foreign Judgments in Civil or Commercial Matters. Why do you think this is the case? Consider again whether the United States should join these conventions. What would be the advantages and disadvantages of doing so?

NOTES AND QUESTIONS

1. **Representing a Defendant with a Favorable U.S. Judgment.** Imagine that plaintiff sues defendant in a U.S. court, and defendant prevails. Plaintiff then files the same lawsuit against defendant in a German court. If you represent

the defendant, what argument might you make on behalf of your client in the German court?

2. **Representing a Plaintiff with a Favorable U.S. Judgment.** Imagine instead that the plaintiff prevails and obtains a money judgment in its favor, but the defendant refuses to comply with the judgment. If you represent the plaintiff (now judgment creditor), under what circumstances might you find it important to consider enforcement of the judgment in Germany? What type of factual investigation and legal research would you need to undertake to decide whether it would be worthwhile to pursue enforcement there?

3. **Assisting Clients in a Foreign Nation.** If you are representing a client that is seeking (or opposing) recognition or enforcement of a U.S. judgment in another nation, what practical challenges are you likely to face as a U.S. lawyer? For example, how would you attempt to adequately learn the other nation's law governing foreign judgments? What if the law is in a language that you do not read? How comfortable would you feel navigating another nation's legal system? And how would you determine whether the other nation's law governing the practice of law would allow you to represent a client in proceedings there? What practical steps might you consider taking to solve these problems?

NOTES ON SPECIAL ISSUES IN THE ENFORCEMENT OF COURT JUDGMENTS

1. **Practice: Finding the Judgment Debtor's Assets.** If you were a lawyer representing a judgment creditor, what steps would you take to locate assets of the judgment debtor against which a judgment might be enforced? Note that once a judgment creditor seeks enforcement of a foreign judgment, discovery may be available to facilitate identification of assets. Consider, for example, Rule 69(a)(2) of the Federal Rules of Civil Procedure, which provides that "[i]n aid of the judgment or execution, the judgment creditor . . . may obtain discovery from any person — including the judgment debtor — as provided in these rules or by the procedure of the state where the court is located." *Cagan v. Gadman*, 2012 WL 5422270 (E.D.N.Y. 2012) (noting availability of discovery to locate assets for enforcement of a U.K. court judgment in New York enforcement proceedings). In addition, 28 U.S.C. § 1782(a) authorizes U.S. courts to provide discovery in support of foreign enforcement proceedings. It provides that "[t]he district court of the district in which a person resides or is found may order him to give his testimony or statement or to produce a document or other thing for use in a proceeding in a foreign or international tribunal. . . ." *In re Clerici*, 481 F.3d 1324 (11th Cir. 2007) (holding that discovery under 28 U.S.C. § 1782 was available from U.S. federal court in Florida to assist proceedings in Panama to enforce a Panamanian judgment). Aside from discovery, what methods might you consider using to locate a judgment debtor's assets?

2. **Personal Jurisdiction.** Must a U.S. court have personal jurisdiction over the award debtor in proceedings to enforce foreign court judgments? The *Restatement (Fourth)* Section 482, Comment b, provides the following answer:

> To recognize a foreign judgment, a court must also have personal jurisdiction. Normally jurisdiction will exist only if the persons whom the decision recognizing the foreign judgment will bind have sufficient contacts with the forum to satisfy due process as well as the forum's rules for personal jurisdiction. In the case of a proceeding to enforce a foreign judgment, however, the presence of assets belonging to any person against whom enforcement is sought will satisfy due process.

3. *Forum Non Conveniens.* The *forum non conveniens* doctrine — discussed in Chapter 10 — allows a U.S. court to dismiss an action if a foreign court is an adequate and more appropriate alternative forum, based on consideration of various private and public interest factors. A court may dismiss an action based on the *forum non conveniens* doctrine even if it has personal jurisdiction and subject matter jurisdiction. Should the *forum non conveniens* doctrine allow a U.S. court to dismiss proceedings to enforce foreign court judgments? There is little case law on this question. However, at least one court has strongly suggested that the doctrine may not be used to dismiss enforcement actions. In *Abu Dhabi Commercial Bank PJSC v. Saad Trading, Contracting and Financial Services Co.*, 986 N.Y.S.2d 454 (2014), the Appellate Division of the New York Supreme Court affirmed the lower court's denial of the judgment debtor's motion to dismiss an action to enforce an English judgment on *forum non conveniens* grounds. (Be sure to distinguish the argument that the enforcing court is inconvenient, which is the argument here, from the argument that the foreign court that rendered the judgment was inconvenient, which is a possible ground for nonenforcement under § 4(c)(6) of the 2005 Uniform Act.) According to the court, inconvenience of the enforcing court is not one of the grounds for nonenforcement specified in New York's enforcement statute and, in any event, "defendant bears no hardship, since there is nothing to defend. The merits were decided in England, and plaintiff seeks no new relief. There are no witnesses to be inconvenienced or necessary evidence beyond the court's jurisdiction." *Id.* at 459. *See also Shipcraft v. Arms Corp. of the Philippines, Inc.*, 2013 WL 649415 (N.Y. Sup. 2013) (rejecting judgment debtor's argument that the court should dismiss enforcement action on *forum non conveniens* grounds because the doctrine "applies to active litigation, not to ministerial recognition of already-issued judgments"). Do you find this reasoning convincing? Why or why not?

REVIEW NOTES AND QUESTIONS

1. What is the difference between recognition and enforcement? As a practical matter, under what circumstances would you pursue recognition on behalf of a client? Under what circumstances would you pursue enforcement on behalf of a client?

2. What steps can be taken to enforce U.S. court judgments in the United States? What law governs the recognition and enforcement of U.S. sister-state judgments?

3. What steps can be taken to enforce foreign judgments in the United States? As a lawyer, how would you go about answering the following key questions regarding the enforcement of foreign money judgments?

   - Where does the judgment debtor have assets?
   - What law will the court apply to determine whether to recognize and enforce the judgment? When will state law apply and when will federal law apply? What are some of the ways that the law of foreign judgments varies from one U.S. state to another?
   - Under the applicable law, what are the requirements for recognition and enforcement? Are those requirements satisfied in your case?
   - Under the applicable law, what are the available grounds for refusing recognition and enforcement? Do any of those grounds apply in your case?

4. What methods would you consider using to attempt to influence a nation to comply with an international court judgment?

5. What steps would you take to enforce a U.S. judgment in a foreign court? What do you need to investigate? *When* should you investigate? What sources of assistance might you consider? How might the Hague Convention on Choice of Court Agreements affect the recognition and enforcement of U.S. judgments abroad if the United States were to become a party?

6. Consider the *Chevron-Ecuador* case described at the beginning of this chapter. If you were a lawyer representing the plaintiffs (judgment creditors), what steps might you consider taking to enforce the Ecuadorian judgment against Chevron? What factual and legal questions would you need answers to before deciding upon a course of action? What steps other than judicial enforcement might you consider? If you were a lawyer representing Chevron, what arguments might you consider making against enforcement of the Ecuadorian judgment in the United States? What factual and legal research would you need to do to assess arguments against enforcement of the Ecuadorian judgment in other nations?

7. How do the rules governing enforcement affect legal strategy for U.S.-based lawyers? (a) Imagine that you are representing a U.S. client that is entering

a business agreement with a non-U.S. party, and that you are negotiating the agreement's dispute resolution provisions. What provisions would you consider seeking in order to increase the likelihood that your client would be able to enforce a dispute resolution outcome? What factual and legal questions would you need to answer before deciding on these provisions? (b) Now imagine that your U.S. client is involved in a dispute with a non-U.S. party, that there is no agreement regarding dispute resolution, and your client is contemplating litigation. What factual and legal questions would you need to answer before making a sound decision about where to file your client's lawsuit? From a judgment enforcement perspective, under what circumstances might you find it inadvisable to sue in a U.S. court? What if the only basis for jurisdiction in a U.S. court was "tag" jurisdiction? What if the primary reason for suing in a U.S. court is to obtain punitive damages? Under what circumstances might you find it inadvisable to sue in another nation's courts?

CHAPTER 8

ARBITRAL AWARDS

As discussed in Chapter 6, arbitration is a widely used alternative to litigation as a method of transnational dispute resolution. Instead of litigation in national courts, private parties (and sometimes a private party and a nation) may use **transnational commercial arbitration** to resolve disputes arising out of transnational commercial activity. A nation and a foreign investor in that nation may use **investor-state arbitration** to resolve disputes arising out of the investment. And rather than referring a dispute to an international court such as the International Court of Justice, two nations may use **state-state arbitration** to resolve disputes between them.

There is a fundamental distinction between enforcing an arbitration agreement, which is the agreement of two or more parties to arbitrate a dispute, and enforcing an **arbitral award**, which is the decision of an arbitrator or a panel of arbitrators produced by the agreed upon arbitral proceedings. As discussed in Chapter 6, if one party to an arbitration agreement refuses to arbitrate a dispute covered by that agreement, the other party may file legal proceedings to enforce the agreement. This chapter focuses on a different type of enforcement: enforcement of arbitral awards. Like court judgments, valid arbitral awards are legally binding. But just as a judgment debtor might not satisfy a court judgment voluntarily, a party against whom an arbitral award is made — an **award debtor** — might refuse to satisfy an arbitral award voluntarily. In that case, the beneficiary of the arbitral award — the **award creditor** — may seek the assistance of a court to enforce the award against the award debtor.

This chapter introduces you to the basic rules governing the enforcement of arbitral awards in transnational arbitration. It focuses on enforcement issues involving awards in transnational *commercial* arbitration because these are the ones that lawyers most often encounter in practice. Section A presents the legal framework for the enforcement of arbitral awards in transnational commercial arbitration. Section B discusses measures to confirm or vacate an arbitral award in the nation in which the award was made — the so-called **arbitral seat**. Section C discusses proceedings to recognize or enforce an arbitral award in nations other than the arbitral seat. The chapter concludes with notes and questions on special problems in the enforcement of arbitral awards in transnational commercial arbitration and on enforcement in the context of investor-state and state-state arbitration.

A. Legal Framework

Chapter 6 presented the legal framework for the enforcement of transnational commercial arbitration agreements. As that chapter explained, the rules are contained in a combination of international law and national law. The principal international legal instrument is the Convention on the Recognition and Enforcement of Foreign Arbitral Awards, commonly known as the New York Convention. In the United States, the Federal Arbitration Act (FAA) is the principal source of domestic arbitral law, and in many nations (and in several U.S. states), legislation based on the UNCITRAL Model Law on International Commercial Arbitration (the "UNCITRAL Model Law") provides another important source of domestic law governing the enforcement of arbitration agreements.* These international and domestic legal instruments also contain rules governing awards in transnational commercial arbitration. In addition, in 2019, the American Law Institute approved the *Restatement of the Law, The U.S. Law of International Commercial and Investor-State Arbitration*. Chapter 4 of that *Restatement* covers the role of U.S. courts in the enforcement of transnational commercial arbitration awards. As discussed in Chapter 6, one of the frequently touted advantages of arbitration over litigation as a method of transnational dispute resolution is that it is generally easier to enforce a foreign arbitral award than it is to enforce a foreign court judgment.

Some of the key provisions of the New York Convention, the FAA, and the UNCITRAL Model Law are provided below. As you study them, consider what it is about the legal framework for the enforcement of awards in transnational commercial arbitration that creates the enforcement advantage that arbitration is said to have over litigation as a transnational dispute resolution method.

Convention on the Recognition and Enforcement of Foreign Arbitral Awards (the "New York Convention")

330 U.N.T.S 38 (June 10, 1958)

Article I

1. This Convention shall apply to the recognition and enforcement of arbitral awards made in the territory of a State other than the State where the recognition and enforcement of such awards are sought, and arising out

---

* The UNCITRAL Model Law was adopted by the U.N. Commission on International Trade Law (UNCITRAL) in 1985 and was amended in 2006. For the text of the UNCITRAL Model Law, see http://www.uncitral.org/uncitral/en/uncitral_texts/arbitration/1985Model_arbitration.html.

of differences between persons, whether physical or legal. It shall also apply to arbitral awards not considered as domestic awards in the State where their recognition and enforcement are sought.

. . .

Article III

Each Contracting State shall recognize arbitral awards as binding and enforce them in accordance with the rules of procedure of the territory where the award is relied upon, under the conditions laid down in the following articles. There shall not be imposed substantially more onerous conditions or higher fees or charges on the recognition or enforcement of arbitral awards to which this Convention applies than are imposed on the recognition or enforcement of domestic arbitral awards.

Article IV

1. To obtain the recognition and enforcement mentioned in the preceding article, the party applying for recognition and enforcement shall, at the time of the application, supply:

(a) The duly authenticated original award or a duly certified copy thereof;

(b) The original agreement referred to in article II [that is, the arbitration agreement] or a duly certified copy thereof.

2. If the said award or agreement is not made in an official language of the country in which the award is relied upon, the party applying for recognition and enforcement of the award shall produce a translation of these documents into such language. The translation shall be certified by an official or sworn translator or by a diplomatic or consular agent.

Article V

1. Recognition and enforcement of the award may be refused, at the request of the party against whom it is invoked, only if that party furnishes to the competent authority where the recognition and enforcement is sought, proof that:

(a) The parties to the agreement referred to in article II [that is, the arbitration agreement] were, under the law applicable to them, under some incapacity, or the said agreement is not valid under the law to which the parties have subjected it or, failing any indication thereon, under the law of the country where the award was made; or

(b) The party against whom the award is invoked was not given proper notice of the appointment of the arbitrator or of the arbitration proceedings or was otherwise unable to present his case; or

(c) The award deals with a difference not contemplated by or not falling within the terms of the submission to arbitration, or it contains decisions on matters beyond the scope of the submission to arbitration, provided that, if the decisions on matters submitted to arbitration can be separated from those not so submitted, that part of the award which contains decisions on matters submitted to arbitration may be recognized and enforced; or

(d) The composition of the arbitral authority or the arbitral procedure was not in accordance with the agreement of the parties, or, failing such agreement, was not in accordance with the law of the country where the arbitration took place; or

(e) The award has not yet become binding on the parties, or has been set aside or suspended by a competent authority of the country in which, or under the law of which, that award was made.

2. Recognition and enforcement of an arbitral award may also be refused if the competent authority in the country where recognition and enforcement is sought finds that:

(a) The subject matter of the difference is not capable of settlement by arbitration under the law of that country; or

(b) The recognition or enforcement of the award would be contrary to the public policy of that country.

Article VI

If an application for the setting aside or suspension of the award has been made to a competent authority referred to in article V(1)(e), the authority before which the award is sought to be relied upon may, if it considers it proper, adjourn the decision on the enforcement of the award and may also, on the application of the party claiming enforcement of the award, order the other party to give suitable security.

Article VII

1. The provisions of the present Convention shall not ... deprive any interested party of any right he may have to avail himself of an arbitral award in the manner and to the extent allowed by the law or the treaties of the country where such award is sought to be relied upon.

. . .

Federal Arbitration Act

Title 9, United States Code

Chapter 1. General Provisions

. . .

§ 9. *Award of arbitrators; confirmation; jurisdiction; procedure*

If the parties in their agreement have agreed that a judgment of the court shall be entered upon the award made pursuant to the arbitration, and shall specify the court, then at any time within one year after the award is made any party to the arbitration may apply to the court so specified for an order confirming the award, and thereupon the court must grant such an order unless the award is vacated, modified, or corrected as prescribed in section[ ] 10 ... of this title. . . .

§ 10. *Same; vacation; grounds; rehearing*

(a) In any of the following cases the United States court in and for the district wherein the award was made may make an order vacating the award upon the application of any party to the arbitration — (1) where the award was procured by corruption, fraud, or undue means; (2) where there was evident partiality or corruption in the arbitrators, or either of them; (3) where the arbitrators were guilty of misconduct in refusing to postpone the hearing, upon sufficient cause shown, or in refusing to hear evidence pertinent and material to the controversy; or of any other misbehavior by which the rights of any party have been prejudiced; or (4) where the arbitrators exceeded their powers, or so imperfectly executed them that a mutual, final, and definite award upon the subject matter submitted was not made.

(b) If an award is vacated and the time within which the agreement required the award to be made has not expired, the court may, in its discretion, direct a rehearing by the arbitrators.

. . .

Chapter 2. Convention on the Recognition and Enforcement of Foreign Arbitral Awards

§ 201. Enforcement of Convention

The Convention on the Recognition and Enforcement of Foreign Arbitral Awards of June 10, 1958 [i.e., the New York Convention], shall be enforced in United States courts in accordance with this chapter.

§ 202. Agreement or award falling under the Convention

An arbitration agreement or arbitral award arising out of a legal relationship, whether contractual or not, which is considered as commercial . . . , falls under the Convention. An agreement or award arising out of such a relationship which is entirely between citizens of the United States shall be deemed not to fall under the Convention unless that relationship involves property located abroad, envisages performance or enforcement abroad, or has some other reasonable relation with one or more foreign states. For the purpose of this section a corporation is a citizen of the United States if it is incorporated or has its principal place of business in the United States.

§ 203. Jurisdiction; amount in controversy

An action or proceeding falling under the Convention shall be deemed to arise under the laws and treaties of the United States. The district courts of the United States (including the courts enumerated in section 460 of title 28) shall have original jurisdiction over such an action or proceeding, regardless of the amount in controversy.

. . .

§ 207. Award of arbitrators; confirmation; jurisdiction; proceeding

Within three years after an arbitral award falling under the Convention is made, any party to the arbitration may apply to any court having jurisdiction under this chapter for an order confirming the award as against any other party to the arbitration. The court shall confirm the award unless it finds one of the grounds for refusal or deferral of recognition or enforcement of the award specified in the said Convention.

§ 208. *Chapter 1; residual application*

Chapter 1 applies to actions and proceedings brought under this chapter to the extent that chapter is not in conflict with this chapter or the Convention as ratified by the United States.

UNCITRAL Model Law on International Commercial Arbitration

Article 34. Application for Setting Aside as Exclusive Recourse Against Arbitral Award

. . .

(2) An arbitral award may be set aside by the court specified [herein as the court of this State competent to hear matters arising under this Model Law] only if:

    (a) the party making the application furnishes proof that:

        (i) a party to the arbitration agreement [. . .] was under some incapacity; or the said agreement is not valid under the law to which the parties have subjected it or, failing any indication thereon, under the law of this State; or

        (ii) the party making the application was not given proper notice of the appointment of an arbitrator or of the arbitral proceedings or was otherwise unable to present his case; or

        (iii) the award deals with a dispute not contemplated by or not falling within the terms of the submission to arbitration, or contains decisions on matters beyond the scope of the submission to arbitration, provided that, if the decisions on matters submitted to arbitration can be separated from those not so submitted, only that part of the award which contains decisions on matters not submitted to arbitration may be set aside; or

        (iv) the composition of the arbitral tribunal or the arbitral procedure was not in accordance with the agreement of the parties, unless such agreement was in conflict with a provision of this Law from which the parties cannot derogate, or, failing such agreement, was not in accordance with this Law; or

    (b) the court finds that:

        (i) the subject-matter of the dispute is not capable of settlement by arbitration under the law of this State; or

        (ii) the award is in conflict with the public policy of this State.

. . .

Article 36. Grounds for Refusing Recognition or Enforcement

(1) Recognition or enforcement of an arbitral award, irrespective of the country in which it was made, may be refused only:

(a) at the request of the party against whom it is invoked, if that party furnishes to the competent court where recognition or enforcement is sought proof that:

(i) a party to the arbitration agreement [as defined in the Model Law] was under some incapacity; or the said agreement is not valid under the law to which the parties have subjected it or, failing any indication thereon, under the law of the country where the award was made; or

(ii) the party against whom the award is invoked was not given proper notice of the appointment of an arbitrator or of the arbitral proceedings or was otherwise unable to present his case; or

(iii) the award deals with a dispute not contemplated by or not falling within the terms of the submission to arbitration, or it contains decisions on matters beyond the scope of the submission to arbitration, provided that, if the decisions on matters submitted to arbitration can be separated from those not so submitted, that part of the award which contains decisions on matters submitted to arbitration may be recognized and enforced; or

(iv) the composition of the arbitral tribunal or the arbitral procedure was not in accordance with the agreement of the parties or, failing such agreement, was not in accordance with the law of the country where the arbitration took place; or

(v) the award has not yet become binding on the parties or has been set aside or suspended by a court of the country in which, or under the law of which, that award was made; or

(b) if the court finds that:

(i) the subject-matter of the dispute is not capable of settlement by arbitration under the law of this State; or

(ii) the recognition or enforcement of the award would be contrary to the public policy of this State.

(2) If an application for setting aside or suspension of an award has been made to a court referred to in paragraph (1)(a)(v) of this article, the court where recognition or enforcement is sought may, if it considers it proper, adjourn its decision and may also, on the application of the party claiming recognition or enforcement of the award, order the other party to provide appropriate security.

NOTES AND QUESTIONS

1. **The New York Convention.** The New York Convention currently has more than 160 parties, including the United States.* The New York Convention is a treaty. Recall that treaties are one of the principal types of international law, but that even a treaty to which the United States is a party is not necessarily

---

* *See* Status, 1958 — Convention on the Recognition and Enforcement of Foreign Arbitral Awards, https://uncitral.un.org/en/texts/arbitration/conventions/foreign_arbitral_awards/status2.

enforceable in U.S. courts (see Chapter 2). Is the New York Convention enforceable in U.S. courts? Why or why not?

2. **Foreign Awards versus Nondomestic Awards.** Note that under Article I, the New York Convention applies to two types of awards: *foreign awards*, meaning "arbitral awards made in the territory of a State other than the State where the recognition and enforcement of such awards are sought," and *nondomestic awards*, meaning "arbitral awards not considered as domestic awards in the State where their recognition and enforcement are sought." Based on your analysis of the legal materials presented above, what types of awards would be considered nondomestic in the United States? To be more concrete: In an enforcement proceeding in a U.S. court, to which of the following awards would the New York Convention apply: (a) an arbitral award made in Turkey between a U.S. party and a Turkish party; (b) an arbitral award made in Turkey between two U.S. parties; (c) an arbitral award made in Turkey between two Turkish parties; (d) an arbitral award made in the United States between a U.S. party and a Turkish party; (e) an arbitral award made in the United States between two U.S. parties involving property located in Turkey; and (f) an arbitral award made in the United States between two U.S. parties relating solely to a contract between the parties to provide services in the United States? Of those awards to which the New York Convention would apply, which are "foreign" and which are "nondomestic" awards?

3. **The New York Convention's Pro-Enforcement Policy.** The New York Convention's general rule is that Contracting States shall recognize and enforce foreign arbitral awards (see Article III). Thus, the New York Convention is sometimes said to embody a "pro-enforcement bias." But this general rule is subject to exceptions that are set forth as a series of grounds for refusing enforcement (see Article V). In proceedings to enforce a foreign arbitral award in a U.S. court, if the award debtor provides proof that one of the specified grounds for nonenforcement exists, is the judge required to refuse enforcement? Why or why not?

4. **Burdens of Proof Under the New York Convention.** Which party — the award debtor or the award creditor — has the burden to prove whether or not a ground for refusing enforcement exists? What burden, if any, does the other party bear? Note the difference between Article V(1) and Article V(2). What do you think might be the reason for that difference?

5. **Domestic Law of Transnational Arbitration.** Many nations have domestic legislation governing arbitration, including the enforcement of arbitral awards. More than 80 nations have legislation based on the UNCITRAL Model Law.* It is important to note that the UNCITRAL Model Law, like

---

* *See* Status, 1985 — UNCITRAL Model Law on International Commercial Arbitration, with amendments as adopted in 2006, https://uncitral.un.org/en/texts/arbitration/modellaw/commercial_arbitration/status. In addition, various political subdivisions of several countries, including several states of the United States, have adopted legislation based on the UNCITRAL Model Law.

all model laws, is merely a text suggested for legislators to consider; actual legislative enactments may vary significantly from the model law. When researching the law of a particular jurisdiction, it is very important to refer to that jurisdiction's actual legislation, not to the text of a model law. In the United States, the principal federal statute governing arbitration is the FAA.

6. **Other Sources of Law Governing the Enforcement of Arbitral Awards.** The legal instruments presented above are not the only parts of the legal framework governing the enforcement of awards in transnational commercial arbitration. For example, there are other relevant international agreements. Articles 4, 5, and 6 of the Inter-American Convention on International Commercial Arbitration (the "Panama Convention") have provisions governing the enforcement of foreign arbitral awards that are substantially similar to Articles III, V, and VI of the New York Convention. Like the New York Convention, the Inter-American Convention is directly enforceable in U.S. courts pursuant to the Federal Arbitration Act. *See* FAA § 301. Parties to the Inter-American Convention include the United States and many Latin American nations. What happens if both the New York Convention and the Inter-American Convention would apply to the same arbitral award? Section 305 of the FAA provides:

> When the requirements for application of both the Inter-American Convention and the [New York Convention] are met, determination as to which Convention applies shall, unless otherwise expressly agreed, be made as follows: (1) If a majority of the parties to the arbitration agreement are citizens of a State or States that have ratified or acceded to the Inter-American Convention and are member States of the Organization of American States, the Inter-American Convention shall apply. (2) In all other cases the [New York Convention] shall apply.

If an arbitral award is made in a nation that is not a party to the New York Convention or the Inter-American Convention, a U.S. court may enforce it in accordance with the FAA's general provisions.

7. **Transnational Arbitration's Enforcement Advantage.** As Chapter 6 discusses, a frequently touted advantage of arbitration over litigation as a method of transnational dispute resolution is that it is generally easier to enforce foreign arbitral awards than it is to enforce foreign court judgments. What is it about the legal framework for the enforcement of awards in transnational commercial arbitration that creates this advantage?

The following case introduces several of the Convention's grounds for non-enforcement. Pay close attention to the court's approach to interpretation of the New York Convention and to the relationship between the Convention (which is international law) and the FAA (which is national law).

Parsons & Whittemore Overseas Co., Inc. v. Societe Generale de L'Industrie du Papier (RAKTA)

508 F.2d 969 (2d Cir. 1974)

J. JOSEPH SMITH, Circuit Judge:

Parsons & Whittemore Overseas Co., Inc. (Overseas), an American corporation, appeals from the entry of summary judgment . . . by . . . the Southern District of New York on the counter-claim by Societe Generale de L'Industrie du Papier (RAKTA), an Egyptian corporation, to confirm a foreign arbitral award[*] holding Overseas liable to RAKTA for breach of contract. . . . Jurisdiction is based on 9 U.S.C. 203, which empowers federal district courts to hear cases to recognize and enforce foreign arbitral awards, and 9 U.S.C. 205, which authorizes the removal of such cases from state courts, as was accomplished in this instance.[2] We affirm the district court's confirmation of the foreign award. . . .

In November 1962, Overseas consented by written agreement with RAKTA to construct, start up and, for one year, manage and supervise a paperboard mill in Alexandria, Egypt. The Agency for International Development (AID), a branch of the United States State Department, would finance the project by supplying RAKTA with funds with which to purchase letters of credit in Overseas' favor. Among the contract's terms was an arbitration clause, which provided a means to settle differences arising in the course of performance, and a "force majeure" clause, which excused delay in performance due to causes beyond Overseas' reasonable capacity to control.

Work proceeded as planned until May, 1967. Then, with the Arab-Israeli Six Day War on the horizon, recurrent expressions of Egyptian hostility to Americans — nationals of the principal ally of the Israeli enemy — caused the majority of the Overseas work crew to leave Egypt. On June 6, the Egyptian government broke diplomatic ties with the United States and ordered all Americans expelled from Egypt except those who would apply and qualify for a special visa.

Having abandoned the project for the present with the construction phase near completion, Overseas notified RAKTA that it regarded this postponement as excused by the force majeure clause. RAKTA disagreed and sought damages for breach of contract. Overseas refused to settle and RAKTA, already at work on completing the performance promised by Overseas, invoked the arbitration clause. Overseas responded by calling into play the clause's option to bring a dispute directly to a three-man arbitral board governed by the rules of the International Chamber of Commerce. After several sessions in 1970, the tribunal issued a preliminary award, which recognized Overseas' force majeure defense as good only during the period from May 28 to June 30, 1967. In so limiting Overseas' defense, the arbitration court emphasized that Overseas had made no more than a perfunctory effort to secure special visas and that AID's notification that it was withdrawing financial backing did not justify Overseas' unilateral decision to abandon the

---

[*] The court notes that the award is a foreign award but does not specify the foreign nation in which the award was made. — EDS.

2. Overseas initiated suit in New York Supreme Court and the case was removed to federal court on RAKTA's petition.

project.[3] After further hearings in 1972, the tribunal made its final award in March, 1973: Overseas was held liable to RAKTA for $312,507.45 in damages for breach of contract and $30,000 for RAKTA's costs; additionally, the arbitrators' compensation was set at $49,000, with Overseas responsible for three-fourths of the sum.

Subsequent to the final award, Overseas in the action here under review sought a declaratory judgment to prevent RAKTA from collecting the award out of a letter of credit issued in RAKTA's favor by Bank of America at Overseas' request. The letter was drawn to satisfy any "penalties" which an arbitral tribunal might assess against Overseas in the future for breach of contract. RAKTA contended that the arbitral award for damages met the letter's requirement of "penalties" and counter-claimed to confirm and enter judgment upon the foreign arbitral award. Overseas' defenses to this counterclaim, all rejected by the district court, form the principal issues for review on this appeal. Four of these defenses are derived from the express language of the applicable United Nations Convention on the Recognition and Enforcement of Foreign Arbitral Awards (Convention), and a fifth is arguably implicit in the Convention. These include: enforcement of the award would violate the public policy of the United States, the award represents an arbitration of matters not appropriately decided by arbitration; the tribunal denied Overseas an adequate opportunity to present its case; the award is predicated upon a resolution of issues outside the scope of contractual agreement to submit to arbitration; and the award is in manifest disregard of law. . . .

I. Overseas' Defenses Against Enforcement

In 1958 the Convention was adopted by 26 of the 45 states participating in the United Nations Conference on Commercial Arbitration held in New York. For the signatory state, the New York Convention superseded the Geneva Convention of 1927. The 1958 Convention's basic thrust was to liberalize procedures for enforcing foreign arbitral awards: While the Geneva Convention placed the burden of proof on the party seeking enforcement of a foreign arbitral award and did not circumscribe the range of available defenses to those enumerated in the convention, the 1958 Convention clearly shifted the burden of proof to the party defending against enforcement and limited his defenses to seven set forth in Article V. Not a signatory to any prior multilateral agreement on enforcement of arbitral awards, the United States declined to sign the 1958 Convention at the outset. The United States ultimately acceded to the Convention, however, in 1970 . . . and implemented its accession with 9 U.S.C. 201-208. Under 9 U.S.C. 208, the existing Federal Arbitration Act, 9 U.S.C. 1-14, applies to the enforcement of foreign awards except to the extent to which the latter may conflict with the Convention. . . .

---

3. RAKTA represented to the tribunal that it was prepared to finance the project without AID's assistance.

A. Public Policy

Article V(2)(b) of the Convention allows the court in which enforcement of a foreign arbitral award is sought to refuse enforcement, on the defendant's motion or sua sponte, if "enforcement of the award would be contrary to the public policy of (the forum) country." The legislative history of the provision offers no certain guidelines to its construction. Its precursors in the Geneva Convention and the 1958 Convention's ad hoc committee draft extended the public policy exception to, respectively, awards contrary to "principles of the law" and awards violative of "fundamental principles of the law." [On the one hand], the Convention's failure to include similar language signifies a narrowing of the defense. On the other hand, [perhaps] this omission [i]s indicative of an intention to broaden the defense.

Perhaps more probative, however, are the inferences to be drawn from the history of the Convention as a whole. The general pro-enforcement bias informing the Convention and explaining its supersession of the Geneva Convention points toward a narrow reading of the public policy defense. An expansive construction of this defense would vitiate the Convention's basic effort to remove preexisting obstacles to enforcement. . . . Additionally, considerations of reciprocity — considerations given express recognition in the Convention itself[4] — counsel courts to invoke the public policy defense with caution lest foreign courts frequently accept it as a defense to enforcement of arbitral awards rendered in the United States.

We conclude, therefore, that the Convention's public policy defense should be construed narrowly. Enforcement of foreign arbitral awards may be denied on this basis only where enforcement would violate the forum state's most basic notions of morality and justice.

Under this view of the public policy provision in the Convention, Overseas' public policy defense may easily be dismissed. Overseas argues that various actions by United States officials subsequent to the severance of American-Egyptian relations — most particularly, AID's withdrawal of financial support for the Overseas-RAKTA contract — required Overseas, as a loyal American citizen, to abandon the project. Enforcement of an award predicated on the feasibility of Overseas' returning to work in defiance of these expressions of national policy would therefore allegedly contravene United States public policy. In equating "national" policy with United States "public" policy, the appellant quite plainly misses the mark. To read the public policy defense as a parochial device protective of national political interests would seriously undermine the Convention's utility. This provision was not meant to enshrine the vagaries of international politics under the rubric of "public policy." Rather, a circumscribed public policy doctrine was contemplated by the Convention's framers and every indication is that the United States, in acceding to the Convention, meant to subscribe to this supranational emphasis. Cf. *Scherk v. Alberto-Culver Co.*, 417 U.S. 506 (1974).

---

4. "A Contracting State shall not be entitled to avail itself of the present Convention against other Contracting States except to the extent that it is itself bound to apply the Convention." New York Convention, Article XIV.

To deny enforcement of this award largely because of the United States' falling out with Egypt in recent years would mean converting a defense intended to be of narrow scope into a major loophole in the Convention's mechanism for enforcement. We have little hesitation, therefore, in disallowing Overseas' proposed public policy defense.

B. Non-Arbitrability

Article V(2)(a) authorizes a court to deny enforcement, on a defendant's or its own motion, of a foreign arbitral award when "the subject matter of the difference is not capable of settlement by arbitration under the law of that (the forum) country." Under this provision, a court sitting in the United States might, for example, be expected to decline enforcement of an award involving arbitration of an antitrust claim in view of domestic arbitration cases which have held that antitrust matters are entrusted to the exclusive competence of the judiciary. On the other hand, it may well be that the special considerations and policies underlying a "truly international agreement," *Scherk v. Alberto-Culver Co.*, *supra*, 417 U.S. 506 at 515, call for a narrower view of non-arbitrability in the international than the domestic context. *Compare id.* with *Wilko v. Swan*, 346 U.S. 427 (1953) (enforcement of international but not domestic, agreement to arbitrate claim based on alleged Securities Act violations).*

Resolution of Overseas' non-arbitrability argument, however, does not require us to reach such difficult distinctions between domestic and foreign awards. For Overseas' argument, that "United States foreign policy issues can hardly be placed at the mercy of foreign arbitrators who are charged with the execution of no public trust and whose loyalties are to foreign interests," Brief for Appellant at 23, plainly fails to raise so substantial an issue of arbitrability. The mere fact that an issue of national interest may incidentally figure into the resolution of a breach of contract claim does not make the dispute not arbitrable. Rather, certain categories of claims may be non-arbitrable because of the special national interest vested in their resolution. Furthermore, even were the test for non-arbitrability of an ad hoc nature, Overseas' situation would almost certainly not meet the standard, for Overseas grossly exaggerates the magnitude of the national interest involved in the resolution of its particular claim. Simply because acts of the United States are somehow implicated in a case one cannot conclude that the United States is vitally interested in its outcome. Finally, the Supreme Court's decision in favor of arbitrability in a case far more prominently displaying public features than the instant one, *Scherk v. Alberto-Culver Co.*, *supra*, compels by analogy the conclusion that the foreign award against Overseas dealt with a subject arbitrable under United States law.

---

* In *Mitsubishi Motors Corp. v. Soler Chrysler-Plymouth, Inc.*, 473 U.S. 614 (1985), decided after the *Parsons & Whittemore* case and discussed in Chapter 6, the U.S. Supreme Court held that U.S. antitrust claims could be arbitrated. — EDS.

The court below was correct in denying relief to Overseas under the Convention's non-arbitrability defense to enforcement of foreign arbitral awards. There is no special national interest in judicial, rather than arbitral, resolution of the breach of contract claim underlying the award in this case.

C. Inadequate Opportunity to Present Defense

Under Article V(1)(b) of the Convention, enforcement of a foreign arbitral award may be denied if the defendant can prove that he was "not given proper notice . . . or was otherwise unable to present his case." This provision essentially sanctions the application of the forum state's standards of due process. . . .

Overseas seeks relief under this provision for the arbitration court's refusal to delay proceedings in order to accommodate the speaking schedule of one of Overseas' witnesses, David Nes, the United States Chargé d'Affaires in Egypt at the time of the Six Day War. This attempt to state a due process claim fails for several reasons. First, inability to produce one's witnesses before an arbitral tribunal is a risk inherent in an agreement to submit to arbitration. By agreeing to submit disputes to arbitration, a party relinquishes his courtroom rights — including that to subpoena witnesses — in favor of arbitration "with all of its well known advantages and drawbacks." *Washington-Baltimore Newspaper Guild, Local 35 v. The Washington Post Co.*, 442 F.2d 1234, 1238 (D.C. Cir. 1971). Secondly, the logistical problems of scheduling hearing dates convenient to parties, counsel and arbitrators scattered about the globe argues against deviating from an initially mutually agreeable time plan unless a scheduling change is truly unavoidable. In this instance, Overseas' allegedly key witness was kept from attending the hearing due to a prior commitment to lecture at an American university — hardly the type of obstacle to his presence which would require the arbitral tribunal to postpone the hearing as a matter of fundamental fairness to Overseas. Finally, Overseas cannot complain that the tribunal decided the case without considering evidence critical to its defense and within only Mr. Nes' ability to produce. In fact, the tribunal did have before it an affidavit by Mr. Nes in which he furnished, by his own account, "a good deal of the information to which I would have testified." Moreover, had Mr. Nes wished to furnish all the information to which he would have testified, there is every reason to believe that the arbitration tribunal would have considered that as well.

The arbitration tribunal acted within its discretion in declining to reschedule a hearing for the convenience of an Overseas witness. Overseas' due process rights under American law, rights entitled to full force under the Convention as a defense to enforcement, were in no way infringed by the tribunal's decision.

D. Arbitration in Excess of Jurisdiction

Under Article V(1)(c), one defending against enforcement of an arbitral award may prevail by proving that:

> The award deals with a difference not contemplated by or not falling within the terms of the submission to arbitration, or it contains decisions on matters beyond the scope of the submission to arbitration. . . .

This provision tracks in more detailed form 10(d) of the Federal Arbitration Act, 9 U.S.C. 10(d), which authorizes vacating an award "where the arbitrators exceeded their powers." Both provisions basically allow a party to attack an award predicated upon arbitration of a subject matter not within the agreement to submit to arbitration. This defense to enforcement of a foreign award, like the others already discussed, should be construed narrowly. Once again a narrow construction would comport with the enforcement-facilitating thrust of the Convention. In addition, the case law under the similar provision of the Federal Arbitration Act strongly supports a strict reading. *See, e.g., United Steelworkers of America v. Enterprise Wheel & Car Corp.*, 363 U.S. 593 (1960).

In making this defense as to three components of the award, Overseas must therefore overcome a powerful presumption that the arbitral body acted within its powers. Overseas principally directs its challenge at the $185,000 awarded for loss of production. Its jurisdictional claim focuses on the provision of the contract reciting that "neither party shall have any liability for loss of production." The tribunal cannot properly be charged, however, with simply ignoring this alleged limitation on the subject matter over which its decision-making powers extended. Rather, the arbitration court interpreted the provision not to preclude jurisdiction on this matter. As in *United Steelworkers of America v. Enterprise Wheel & Car Corp., supra,* the court may be satisfied that the arbitrator premised the award on a construction of the contract and that it is "not apparent," 363 U.S. 593 at 598, that the scope of the submission to arbitration has been exceeded.

The appellant's attack on the $60,000 awarded for start-up expenses and $30,000 in costs cannot withstand the most cursory scrutiny. In characterizing the $60,000 as "consequential damages" (and thus proscribed by the arbitration agreement), Overseas is again attempting to secure a reconstruction in this court of the contract — an activity wholly inconsistent with the deference due arbitral decisions on law and fact. The $30,000 in costs is equally unassailable, for the appellant's contention that this portion of the award is inconsistent with guidelines set by the International Chamber of Commerce is twice removed from reality. First of all, contrary to Overseas' representations, these guidelines (contained in the Guide to ICC Arbitration. . . .) do not require, as a pre-condition to an award of expenses, express authority for such an award in the arbitration clause. The arbitration agreement's silence on this matter, therefore, is not determinative in the case under review. Secondly, since the parties in fact complied with the Guide's advice to reach agreement on this matter prior to arbitration — i.e., the request by each for such an award for expenses amounts to tacit agreement on this point — any claim of fatal deviation from the Guide is disingenuous to say the least.

Although the Convention recognizes that an award may not be enforced where predicated on a subject matter outside the arbitrator's jurisdiction, it does not sanction second-guessing the arbitrator's construction of the parties' agreement. The appellant's attempt to invoke this defense, however, calls upon the court to ignore this limitation on its decision-making powers and usurp the arbitrator's role. The district court took a proper view of its own jurisdiction in refusing to grant relief on this ground.

E. Award in "Manifest Disregard" of Law

Both the legislative history of Article V, see *supra*, and the statute enacted to implement the United States' accession to the Convention[6] are strong authority for treating as exclusive the bases set forth in the Convention for vacating an award. On the other hand, the Federal Arbitration Act, specifically 9 U.S.C. 10, has been read to include an implied defense to enforcement where the award is in "manifest disregard" of the law. *Wilko v. Swan*, 346 U.S. 427, 436 (1953); *Saxis Steamship Co. v. Multifacs International Traders, Inc.*, 375 F.2d 577, 582 (2d Cir. 1967).

This case does not require us to decide, however, whether this defense stemming from dictum in *Wilko*, *supra*, obtains in the international arbitration context.[*] For even assuming that the "manifest disregard" defense applies under the Convention, we would have no difficulty rejecting the appellant's contention that such "manifest disregard" is in evidence here. Overseas in effect asks this court to read this defense as a license to review the record of arbitral proceedings for errors of fact or law — a role which we have emphatically declined to assume in the past and reject once again. "Extensive judicial review frustrates the basic purpose of arbitration, which is to dispose of disputes quickly and avoid the expense and delay of extended court proceedings." *Saxis Steamship Co., supra*, 375 F.2d 577 at 582.

Insofar as this defense to enforcement of awards in "manifest disregard" of law may be cognizable under the Convention, it, like the other defenses raised by the appellant, fails to provide a sound basis for vacating the foreign arbitral award. We therefore affirm the district court's confirmation of award.

. . .

Affirmed.

NOTES AND QUESTIONS

1. **Practice: Litigation Strategy.** Why do you think RAKTA sought enforcement of the arbitral award against Overseas in the United States rather than in Egypt?
2. **Consent to Arbitration.** As discussed in Chapter 6, arbitration requires the consent of the parties to arbitrate. What was the source of consent in this case?
3. **Grounds for Refusal.** What were Overseas' arguments against enforcement of the arbitral award? Why did the court reject each of these arguments? In light of the court's decision, which grounds do you think are hardest to prove?

---

6. ". . . The court shall confirm the award unless it finds one of the grounds for refusal or deferral of recognition or enforcement specified in the said Convention." 9 U.S.C. 207.

* This issue has been partially resolved in later cases that appear below. — EDS.

4. **Public Policy.** Why does the court adopt a narrow interpretation of the public policy exception in Article V(2)(B) of the New York Convention? According to one court, the public policy defense is available "only in those circumstances 'where enforcement would violate our most basic notions of morality and justice.'" *Telenor Mobile Commc'ns A.S. v. Storm LLC*, 584 F.3d 396, 411 (2d Cir. 2009). What do you think the court means by "basic notions of morality and justice"? How should courts identify such notions? As a lawyer, what sources might you use to make arguments about whether such notions are implicated in a given case?

5. **Nonarbitrability.** According to the court in *Parsons & Whittemore Overseas*, to be nonarbitrable under Article V(2)(a) the claims must reflect a "special national interest vested in their resolution." The Supreme Court subsequently held that it would not "recogniz[e] subject-matter exceptions where Congress has not expressly directed the courts to do so." *Mitsubishi Motors Corp. v. Soler Chrysler-Plymouth, Inc.*, 473 U.S. 614, 639 (1985). In light of *Mitsubishi*, what do you need to plead to show nonarbitrability?

6. **Inadequate Opportunity to Present a Defense.** In the view of one leading commentator, "Article V(1)(b) is best viewed as providing the basis for uniform international standards of procedural fairness." GARY B. BORN, INTERNATIONAL COMMERCIAL ARBITRATION 2738 (2009). Can you think of examples of procedures that might violate such international standards?

7. **Excess of Jurisdiction.** In light of the court's discussion of Article V(1)(c) of the New York Convention in *Parsons & Whittemore Overseas*, in what circumstances does an arbitral tribunal exceed its jurisdiction? Does an arbitral tribunal act within its jurisdiction when its conclusions of law or fact are clearly erroneous?

8. **Manifest Disregard of Law.** The status of manifest disregard of law as a ground for refusing enforcement of arbitral awards is addressed in the cases that follow. However, as the court in *Parsons & Whittemore Overseas* points out, even if it applies, its scope is very narrow. *See also Telenor*, 584 F.3d at 407 ("examples of manifest disregard . . . tend to be extreme, such as explicitly reject[ing] controlling precedent or otherwise reaching a decision that strains credulity or lacks even a barely colorable justification"). In light of this, what role can this doctrine play in policing arbitral awards?

9. **Interpretation and the Convention's "Pro-Enforcement Bias."** According to the court, the New York Convention has a "general pro-enforcement bias" that "points toward a narrow reading" of defenses against enforcement. What might be the reasons for a pro-enforcement bias? Are there reasons why this bias might be undesirable? What are the implications of a pro-enforcement bias for award creditors, award debtors, and dispute resolution planning?

10. **The Relationship Between International Law and National Law.** Consider two ways in which the New York Convention and the FAA interact in the court's opinion. First, the court notes that the FAA "implemented" the New York Convention. What does the court mean, and why is this important? Second, the court discusses § 10 of the FAA to determine whether enforcement should be refused on the basis of manifest disregard of law. Why is

there a question about whether this ground for refusal should be considered at all in this case? How is the court able to decide the case without definitely resolving this particular question?

11. **Practice: Alternatives to Judicial Enforcement of Arbitral Awards.** This case, and the other materials in this chapter, deal with court proceedings to compel an award debtor to comply with an arbitral award. But like all litigation, enforcement proceedings can be very costly. In some cases, the anticipated costs of enforcement proceedings may exceed the amount of the arbitral award. In all cases, the real value of an arbitral award is, in effect, reduced by the costs the award creditor must incur to enforce it, should enforcement prove necessary. As a lawyer representing an award creditor, what nonjudicial measures might you consider to help your client avoid the costs of formal enforcement proceedings while increasing the likelihood that the award debtor will satisfy the award voluntarily?

NOTES ON THE DIFFERENCE BETWEEN PROCEEDINGS INSIDE AND OUTSIDE THE ARBITRAL SEAT

In the materials presented above, you may have noticed a distinction between two fundamental arbitration concepts. The first is the concept of *vacating* an arbitral award (*see* FAA § 10), which is sometimes referred to as "setting aside" (*see* New York Convention art. V(1)(e) and UNCITRAL Model Law art. 34) or "annulling" an award. This is also known as *vacatur*. Only a court in the *arbitral seat* — that is, in the nation where the arbitral award was made — may vacate an arbitral award. *See* New York Convention art. V(1)(e) (referring to "the country in which . . . that award was made"); UNCITRAL Model Law art. 1 (provisions for setting aside awards "apply only if the place of arbitration is in the territory of this State").* Thus, "[t]he only time that a U.S. court may hear a motion to vacate an arbitral award is when the underlying arbitration is seated in the United States, since an award may only be set aside . . . in the place of arbitration. . . ." S.I. STRONG, INTERNATIONAL COMMERCIAL ARBITRATION: A GUIDE FOR U.S. JUDGES 64 (2012). If a court in the arbitral seat vacates an arbitral award, the award has no legal effect in the arbitral seat. Whether the award has legal effect outside the arbitral seat is, as we will see, a more complicated matter.

The second concept is *recognition and enforcement*. In contrast to vacating an arbitral award, recognition and enforcement may occur in a court in a nation other than the arbitral seat. From the perspective of such a court, the arbitral award is "foreign," since the award was made in a different nation — hence the reference to the recognition and enforcement of "foreign" arbitral awards.

---

* The parties may designate as the "arbitral seat" a nation other than the nation where the arbitration takes place.

As one expert explains, "When a court 'recognizes' an award, it acknowledges that the award is valid and binding, and thereby gives it an effect similar to that of a court judgment," including preclusive effect in related arbitration or litigation. Margaret L. Moses, The Principles and Practice of International Commercial Arbitration 203 (2008). Enforcement, on the other hand, is the application of the state's coercive power to compel compliance with an arbitral award, typically by attaching and selling assets of the award debtor and paying the proceeds to the award creditor in satisfaction of the award. Thus, whereas a court outside the arbitral seat may not vacate an award, it may hear a request to recognize and enforce it. From a U.S. perspective, if the arbitration is seated outside the United States, a U.S. court would only have the authority to decide whether to recognize or enforce the award, not whether to vacate it.

You may have also discovered that there is a relationship between vacating an award and recognizing and enforcing an award. Specifically, under Article V(1)(e) of the New York Convention, a court in a nation other than the arbitral seat may refuse recognition and enforcement of a foreign arbitral award if it has been vacated by a court "of the country in which . . . that award was made," and under Article VI, a court may stay proceedings to recognize or enforce a foreign arbitral award "[i]f an application for the setting aside or suspension of the award has been made" to a court in the nation in which the award was made. In fact, the grounds for vacating an arbitral award set forth in Article 34 of the UNCITRAL Model Law are virtually the same as the grounds for refusing recognition and enforcement of a foreign arbitral award set forth in the New York Convention and Article 36 of the UNCITRAL Model Law. According to one expert, "the predominant tendency of contemporary arbitration legislation (including the UNCITRAL Model Law) is to limit the grounds on which an award can be annulled to ones paralleling those permitted, for non-recognition of an award, under Article V of the New York Convention." Born, *supra*, at 2553.

Finally, you may have noticed that the FAA and some U.S. courts use the terms "confirmation" and "enforcement" interchangeably. This usage is confusing. Technically, *confirmation* (like vacatur) occurs only in the arbitral seat, when a court there transforms the arbitral award into a judgment. Therefore, U.S. courts may confirm awards only in arbitrations seated in the United States. In terms of strategy, if the award debtor has assets in the arbitral seat, then the award creditor might seek confirmation as a step toward enforcement there. For foreign arbitral awards, the proper term is not "confirmation," but rather "recognition and enforcement." Thus, proceedings to vacate or to confirm an arbitral award can only take place in the arbitral seat, while in courts outside the arbitral seat there may only be recognition and enforcement proceedings. For this reason, the FAA's reference to "confirmation" is misleading. Importantly, however, an award may be recognized and enforced even if it has not first been confirmed in the arbitral seat. Therefore, if the award debtor has no assets in the arbitral seat, the award creditor may decide to proceed directly to enforcement in another nation where the award debtor does have assets, without first seeking confirmation in the arbitral seat.

In summary, the parties to transnational commercial arbitration may bring some types of proceedings regarding an award only in courts in the arbitral seat, and others only in courts outside the arbitral seat. Section B focuses on the former, including proceedings to confirm or vacate arbitral awards.* Section C focuses on the latter, including proceedings to recognize or enforce foreign arbitral awards.

B. Measures in the Arbitral Seat: Proceedings to Confirm and Vacate Arbitral Awards

The following case involves a confirmation proceeding in a U.S. court. Pay close attention to the reasons why this is a confirmation rather than a recognition and enforcement proceeding, and consider the implications of this distinction for the grounds potentially available for vacating the award.

Yusuf Ahmed Alghanim & Sons v. Toys "R" Us, Inc.

126 F.3d 15 (2d Cir. 1997)

MINER, Circuit Judge.

Appeal from a judgment entered in the United States District Court for the Southern District of New York (McKenna, J.) denying respondents' cross-motion to vacate or modify an arbitration award and granting the petition to confirm the award. The court found that while the petition for confirmation was brought under the Convention on the Recognition and Enforcement of Foreign Arbitral Awards, respondents' cross-motion to vacate or modify the award was properly brought under the Federal Arbitration Act, and thus those claims were governed by the Federal Arbitration Act's implied grounds for vacatur. Nonetheless, the court granted the petition to confirm the award, finding that respondents' allegations of error in the arbitral award were without merit.

For the reasons that follow, we affirm.

Background

In November of 1982, respondent-appellant Toys "R" Us, Inc. (collectively with respondent-appellant TRU (HK) Limited, "Toys 'R' Us") and petitioner-appellee Yusuf Ahmed Alghanim & Sons, W.L.L. ("Alghanim"), a privately owned Kuwaiti business, entered into a License and Technical Assistance Agreement (the "agreement") and a Supply Agreement. Through the agreement, Toys "R" Us granted Alghanim a limited right to open Toys "R" Us stores and use its trademarks

License & Tech Ass + Supply

---

* We do not discuss two other types of proceedings that may be pursued in the arbitral seat: proceedings to correct or interpret arbitral awards. For an in-depth discussion, see BORN, *supra*, ch. 23.

in Kuwait and 13 other countries located in and around the Middle East (the "territory"). Toys "R" Us further agreed to supply Alghanim with its technology, expertise and assistance in the toy business.

From 1982 to the December 1993 commencement of the arbitration giving rise to this appeal, Alghanim opened four toy stores, all in Kuwait. According to Toys "R" Us, the first such store, opened in 1983, resembled a Toys "R" Us store in the United States, but the other three, two of which were opened in 1985 and one in 1988, were small storefronts with only limited merchandise. It is uncontested that Alghanim's stores lost some $6.65 million over the 11-year period from 1982 to 1993, and turned a profit only in one year of this period.

lost $6.65 - 11ys

Following the Gulf War, both Alghanim and Toys "R" Us apparently concluded that their relationship needed to be altered. Representatives of Alghanim and Toys "R" Us's International Division met in September of 1991 and February of 1992. Alghanim expressed a desire for Toys "R" Us to contribute capital toward Alghanim's expansion into other countries. Alghanim advised that it would be willing to proceed in the business only under a new joint venture agreement that would shift a substantial portion of responsibility for capital expenditures to Toys "R" Us. Toys "R" Us was unwilling to take on a greater portion of this responsibility.

On July 20, 1992, Toys "R" Us purported to exercise its right to terminate the agreement, sending Alghanim a notice of non-renewal stating that the agreement would terminate on January 31, 1993. Alghanim responded on July 30, 1992, stating that because its most recently opened toy store had opened on January 16, 1988, the initial term of the agreement ended on January 16, 1993. Alghanim asserted that Toys "R" Us's notice of non-renewal was four days late in providing notice six months before the end of the initial period. According to Alghanim, under the termination provision of the agreement, Toys "R" Us's failure to provide notice more than six months before the fifth year after the opening of the most recent store automatically extended the term of the agreement for an additional two years, until January 16, 1995.

On September 2, 1992, Toys "R" Us sent a second letter. Toys "R" Us explained that, on further inspection of the agreement, it had determined that the initial term of the agreement expired on December 31, 1993, and it again gave notice of non-renewal. In this letter, Toys "R" Us also directed Alghanim not to open any new toy stores and warned that failure to comply with that direction could constitute a breach of the agreement.

Through the balance of 1992 and 1993, the parties unsuccessfully attempted to renegotiate the agreement or devise a new arrangement. In September of 1993, the parties discussed Alghanim's willingness to relinquish its rights under the agreement. In one discussion, Amin Kadrie, Alghanim's chief operating officer and the head of its toy business, offered to "release the business right now" if Toys "R" Us would "give us $2 million for the losses we've incurred [in] trying to develop this business." Toys "R" Us declined, offering instead to buy Alghanim's inventory at Alghanim's cost. The parties could not agree upon a reconciliation.

At the end of 1993, Toys "R" Us contracted with Al-Futtaim Sons Co., LLC ("Al-Futtaim") for the post-Alghanim rights to open Toys "R" Us stores in five of the countries under the agreement, including Kuwait, and with ATA Development

Co. ("ATA") for the post-Alghanim rights to open Toys "R" Us stores in Saudi Arabia. These two companies initially offered $30 million for the rights, and eventually paid a total of $22.5 million.

On December 20, 1993, Toys "R" Us invoked the dispute-resolution mechanism in the agreement, initiating an arbitration before the American Arbitration Association. Toys "R" Us sought a declaration that the agreement was terminated on December 31, 1993. Alghanim responded by counterclaiming for breach of contract.

On May 4, 1994, the arbitrator denied Toys "R" Us's request for declaratory judgment. The arbitrator found that, under the termination provisions of the agreement, Alghanim had the absolute right to open toy stores, even after being given notice of termination, as long as the last toy store was opened within five years. The parties then engaged in substantial document and expert discovery, motion practice, and a 29-day evidentiary hearing on Alghanim's counterclaims.

On July 11, 1996, the arbitrator awarded Alghanim $46.44 million for lost profits under the agreement, plus 9 percent interest to accrue from December 31, 1994. The arbitrator's findings and legal conclusions were set forth in a 47-page opinion.

Alghanim petitioned the district court to confirm the award under the Convention on the Recognition and Enforcement of Foreign Arbitral Awards of June 10, 1958 ("Convention"). . . . Toys "R" Us cross-moved to vacate or modify the award under the Federal Arbitration Act ("FAA"), 9 U.S.C. § 1 et seq., arguing that the award was clearly irrational, in manifest disregard of the law, and in manifest disregard of the terms of the agreement. The district court concluded that "[t]he Convention and the FAA afford overlapping coverage, and the fact that a petition to confirm is brought under the Convention does not foreclose a cross-motion to vacate under the FAA, and the Court will consider [Toys "R" Us's] cross-motion under the standards of the FAA." By judgment entered December 20, 1996, the district court confirmed the award, finding Toys "R" Us's objections to the award to be without merit. This appeal followed.

Discussion

I. Availability of the FAA's Grounds for Relief in Confirmation Under the Convention

Toys "R" Us argues that the district court correctly determined that the provisions of the FAA apply to its cross-motion to vacate or modify the arbitral award. In particular, Toys "R" Us contends that the FAA and the Convention have overlapping coverage. Thus, Toys "R" Us argues, even though the petition to confirm the arbitral award was brought under the Convention, the FAA's implied grounds for vacatur should apply to Toys "R" Us's cross-motion to vacate or modify because the cross-motion was brought under the FAA. We agree that the FAA governs Toys "R" Us's cross-motion.

A. Applicability of the Convention

Neither party seriously disputes the applicability of the Convention to this case and it is clear to us that the Convention does apply. The Convention provides that it will

> apply to the recognition and enforcement of arbitral awards made in the territory of a State other than the State where the recognition and enforcement of such awards are sought, and arising out of differences between persons, whether physical or legal. It shall also apply to arbitral awards *not considered as domestic awards* in the State where their recognition and enforcement are sought.

Convention art. I(1) (emphasis added). The Convention does not define non-domestic awards. *See Bergesen v. Joseph Muller Corp.*, 710 F.2d 928, 932 (2d Cir. 1983). However, 9 U.S.C. § 202, one of the provisions implementing the Convention, provides that

> [a]n agreement or award arising out of such a relationship which is entirely between citizens of the United States shall be deemed not to fall under the Convention unless that relationship involves property located abroad, envisages performance or enforcement abroad, or has some other reasonable relation with one or more foreign states.

In *Bergesen*, we held "that awards 'not considered as domestic' denotes awards which are subject to the Convention not because made abroad, but because made within the legal framework of another country, e.g., pronounced in accordance with foreign law or involving parties domiciled or having their principal place of business outside the enforcing jurisdiction." 710 F.2d at 932. The Seventh Circuit similarly has interpreted § 202 to mean that "any commercial arbitral agreement, unless it is between two United States citizens, involves property located in the United States, and has no reasonable relationship with one or more foreign states, falls under the Convention." *Jain v. de Méré*, 51 F.3d 686, 689 (7th Cir. [1995]).

The Convention's applicability in this case is clear. The dispute giving rise to this appeal involved two nondomestic parties and one United States corporation, and principally involved conduct and contract performance in the Middle East. Thus, we consider the arbitral award leading to this action a non-domestic award and thus within the scope of the Convention.

B. Authority Under the Convention to Set Aside an Award Under Domestic Arbitral Law

Toys "R" Us argues that the district court properly found that it had the authority under the Convention to apply the FAA's implied grounds for setting aside the award. We agree.

Under the Convention, the district court's role in reviewing a foreign arbitral award is strictly limited: "The court shall confirm the award unless it finds one of the grounds for refusal or deferral of recognition or enforcement of the award specified in the said Convention." 9 U.S.C. § 207. Under Article V of the Convention, the grounds for refusing to recognize or enforce an arbitral award are:

> (a) The parties to the agreement . . . were . . . under some incapacity, or the said agreement is not valid under the law . . . ; or
> (b) The party against whom the award is invoked was not given proper notice of the appointment of the arbitrator or of the arbitration proceedings . . . ; or
> (c) The award deals with a difference not contemplated by or not falling within the terms of the submission to arbitration, or it contains decisions on matters beyond the scope of the submission to arbitration . . . ; or
> (d) The composition of the arbitral authority or the arbitral procedure was not in accordance with the agreement of the parties . . . ; or
> (e) The award has not yet become binding on the parties, or has been set aside or suspended by a competent authority of the country in which, or under the law of which, that award was made.

Convention art. V(1). Enforcement may also be refused if "[t]he subject matter of the difference is not capable of settlement by arbitration," or if "recognition or enforcement of the award would be contrary to the public policy" of the country in which enforcement or recognition is sought. *Id*. art. V(2). These seven grounds are the only grounds explicitly provided under the Convention.

In determining the availability of the FAA's implied grounds for setting aside, the text of the Convention leaves us with two questions: (1) whether, in addition to the Convention's express grounds for refusal, other grounds can be read into the Convention by implication, much as American courts have read implied grounds for relief into the FAA, and (2) whether, under Article V(1)(e), the courts of the United States are authorized to apply United States procedural arbitral law, i.e., the FAA, to nondomestic awards rendered in the United States. We answer the first question in the negative and the second in the affirmative.

1. Availability Under the Convention of Implied Grounds for Refusal

We have held that the FAA and the Convention have "overlapping coverage" to the extent that they do not conflict. *Bergesen*, 710 F.2d at 934; *see* 9 U.S.C. § 208 (FAA may apply to actions brought under the Convention "to the extent that [the FAA] is not in conflict with [9 U.S.C. §§ 201-208] or the Convention as ratified by the United States"). However, by that same token, to the extent that the Convention prescribes the exclusive grounds for relief from an award under the Convention, that application of the FAA's implied grounds would be in conflict, and is thus precluded. *See, e.g., M & C Corp. v. Erwin Behr GmbH & Co., KG*, 87 F.3d 844, 851 (6th Cir. 1996).

In *Parsons & Whittemore Overseas Co. v. Societe Generale de L'Industrie du Papier (Rakta)*, 508 F.2d 969 (2d Cir. 1974), we declined to decide whether the implied defense of "manifest disregard" applies under the Convention, having decided that even if it did, appellant's claim would fail. Nonetheless, we noted that "[b]oth the legislative history of Article V and the statute enacted to implement the United States' accession to the Convention are strong authority for treating as exclusive the bases set forth in the Convention for vacating an award." *Id*.

There is now considerable caselaw holding that, in an action to confirm an award rendered in, or under the law of, a foreign jurisdiction, the grounds for relief enumerated in Article V of the Convention are the only grounds available for setting aside an arbitral award. *See, e.g., M & C,* 87 F.3d at 851 (concluding that the Convention's exclusive grounds for relief "do not include miscalculations of fact or manifest disregard of the law"); *International Standard Elec. Corp. v. Bridas Sociedad Anonima Petrolera, Industrial y Comercial,* 745 F. Supp. 172, 181-82 (S.D.N.Y. 1990) (refusing to apply a "manifest disregard of law" standard on a motion to vacate a foreign arbitral award); *Brandeis Intsel Ltd. v. Calabrian Chems. Corp.,* 656 F. Supp. 160, 167 (S.D.N.Y. 1987) ("In my view, the 'manifest disregard' defense is not available under Article V of the Convention or otherwise to a party . . . seeking to vacate an award of foreign arbitrators based upon foreign law."). . . . This conclusion is consistent with the Convention's pro-enforcement bias. *See, e.g., Scherk v. Alberto-Culver Co.,* 417 U.S. 506, 519-20 & n. 15 (1974); *Parsons,* 508 F.2d at 973. We join these courts in declining to read into the Convention the FAA's implied defenses to confirmation of an arbitral award.

2. Nondomestic Award Rendered in the United States

Although Article V provides the exclusive grounds for refusing confirmation under the Convention, one of those exclusive grounds is where "[t]he award . . . has been set aside or suspended by a competent authority of the country in which, or under the law of which, that award was made." Convention art. V(1)(e). Those courts holding that implied defenses were inapplicable under the Convention did so in the context of petitions to confirm awards rendered abroad. These courts were not presented with the question whether Article V(1)(e) authorizes an action to set aside an arbitral award under the domestic law of the state in which, or under which, the award was rendered. We, however, are faced head-on with that question in the case before us, because the arbitral award in this case was rendered in the United States, and both confirmation and vacatur were then sought in the United States.

We read Article V(1)(e) of the Convention to allow a court in the country under whose law the arbitration was conducted to apply domestic arbitral law, in this case the FAA, to a motion to set aside or vacate that arbitral award. The district court in *Spector v. Torenberg,* 852 F. Supp. 201 (S.D.N.Y. 1994), reached the same conclusion as we do now, reasoning that, because the Convention allows the district court to refuse to enforce an award that has been vacated by a competent authority in the country where the award was rendered, the court may apply FAA standards to a motion to vacate a nondomestic award rendered in the United States.

The Seventh Circuit has agreed, albeit in passing, that the Convention "contemplates the possibility of the award's being set aside in a proceeding under local law." *Lander,* 107 F.3d at 478 (citing Article V(1)(e)). Likewise, the United States District Court for the District of Columbia has found that, in an arbitration conducted in Egypt and under Egyptian law, nullification of the award by the Egyptian courts falls within Article V(1)(e). *See Chromalloy Aeroservices v. Arab Republic of Egypt,* 939 F. Supp. 907, 909 (D.D.C. 1996).

Our conclusion also is consistent with the reasoning of courts that have refused to apply non-Convention grounds for relief where awards were rendered outside the United States. For example, the Sixth Circuit in *M & C* concluded that it should not apply the FAA's implied grounds for vacatur, because the United States did not provide the law of the arbitration for the purposes of Article V(1)(e) of the Convention. 87 F.3d at 849. Similarly, in *International Standard*, the district court decided that only the state under whose procedural law the arbitration was conducted has jurisdiction under Article V(1)(e) to vacate the award, whereas on a petition for confirmation made in any other state, only the defenses to confirmation listed in Article V of the Convention are available. 745 F. Supp. at 178.

This interpretation of Article V(1)(e) also finds support in the scholarly work of commentators on the Convention and in the judicial decisions of our sister signatories to the Convention. There appears to be no dispute among these authorities that an action to set aside an international arbitral award, as contemplated by Article V(1)(e), is controlled by the domestic law of the rendering state.[3]

. . .

There is no indication in the Convention of any intention to deprive the rendering state of its supervisory authority over an arbitral award, including its authority to set aside that award under domestic law.

. . .

[U]nder the Convention, the power and authority of the local courts of the rendering state remain of paramount importance.

. . .

From the plain language and history of the Convention, it is thus apparent that a party may seek to vacate or set aside an award in the state in which, or under the law of which, the award is rendered. Moreover, the language and history of the Convention make it clear that such a motion is to be governed by domestic law of the rendering state, despite the fact that the award is nondomestic within the meaning of the Convention as we have interpreted it in *Bergesen*, 710 F.2d at 932.

In sum, we conclude that the Convention mandates very different regimes for the review of arbitral awards (1) in the state in which, or under the law of which, the award was made, and (2) in other states where recognition and enforcement are sought. The Convention specifically contemplates that the state in which, or under the law of which, the award is made, will be free to set aside or modify an award in accordance with its domestic arbitral law and its full panoply of express and implied grounds for relief. *See* Convention art. V(1)(e). However, the Convention is equally clear that when an action for enforcement is brought

---

3. Although most courts and commentators assume that Article V(1)(e) is applicable to the state in which the award is rendered, we note that Article V(1)(e) specifically contemplates the possibility that an award could be rendered in one state, but under the arbitral law of another state. *See* Convention art. V(1)(e) ("or has been set aside or suspended by a competent authority of the country in which, *or under the law of which*, that award was made" (emphasis added)). In the rare instance where that is the case, Article V(1)(e) would apply to the state that supplied the arbitral law under which the award was made. This situation may be so rare as to be a "dead letter."

in a foreign state, the state may refuse to enforce the award only on the grounds explicitly set forth in Article V of the Convention.

II. Application of FAA Grounds for Relief

Having determined that the FAA does govern Toys "R" Us's cross-motion to vacate, our application of the FAA's implied grounds for vacatur is swift. The Supreme Court has stated "that courts of appeals should apply ordinary, not special, standards when reviewing district court decisions upholding arbitration awards." *First Options of Chicago, Inc. v. Kaplan*, 514 U.S. 938, 948 (1995). We review the district court's findings of fact for clear error and its conclusions of law de novo. *See id.*

"[T]he confirmation of an arbitration award is a summary proceeding that merely makes what is already a final arbitration award a judgment of the court." *Florasynth, Inc. v. Pickholz*, 750 F.2d 171, 176 (2d Cir. 1984). The review of arbitration awards is "very limited . . . in order to avoid undermining the twin goals of arbitration, namely, settling disputes efficiently and avoiding long and expensive litigation." *Folkways Music Publishers, Inc. v. Weiss*, 989 F.2d 108, 111 (2d Cir. 1993). Accordingly, "the showing required to avoid summary confirmance is high." *Ottley v. Schwartzberg*, 819 F.2d 373, 376 (2d Cir. 1987).

More particularly, "[t]his court has generally refused to second guess an arbitrator's resolution of a contract dispute." *John T. Brady & Co. v. Form-Eze Sys., Inc.*, 623 F.2d 261, 264 (2d Cir. 1980). As we have explained: "An arbitrator's decision is entitled to substantial deference, and the arbitrator need only explicate his reasoning under the contract in terms that offer even a barely colorable justification for the outcome reached in order to withstand judicial scrutiny." *In re Marine Pollution Serv., Inc.*, 857 F.2d 91, 94 (2d Cir. 1988).

However, awards may be vacated, see 9 U.S.C. § 10, or modified, *see id.* § 11, in the limited circumstances where the arbitrator's award . . . is in "manifest disregard of the law," *Fahnestock & Co. v. Waltman*, 935 F.2d 512, 515-16 (2d Cir. 1991). We find that [this implied ground is not] met in the present case.

A. *Manifest Disregard of the Law*

Toys "R" Us argues that the arbitrator manifestly disregarded New York law on lost profits awards for breach of contract by returning a speculative award. This contention is without merit. "[M]ere error in the law or failure on the part of the arbitrator[ ] to understand or apply the law" is not sufficient to establish manifest disregard of the law. *Fahnestock*, 935 F.2d at 516. For an award to be in "manifest disregard of the law,"

> [t]he error must have been obvious and capable of being readily and instantly perceived by the average person qualified to serve as an arbitrator. Moreover, the term "disregard" implies that the arbitrator appreciates the existence of a clearly governing legal principle but decides to ignore or pay no attention to it.

Merrill Lynch, 808 F.2d at 933.

In the instant case, the arbitrator was well aware of and carefully applied New York's law on lost profits.[4] The arbitrator specifically addressed *Kenford Co. v. County of Erie*, 67 N.Y.2d 257 (1986), which contains New York's law on the subject and upon which Toys "R" Us relied in its arguments, and concluded:

> I do not think the *Kenford* case rules out damages in this case. *Kenford* disallowed damages based on future profits from concessions in a domed stadium that was never built. . . . In this case [*Alghanim*], which is forced into the estimating posture because of [Toys "R" Us's] breach, bases its damages not on its own experience but on [Toys "R" Us's]. [Toys "R" Us] has hundreds of toy stores worldwide. Since it has been found that the Agreements require [Toys "R" Us] to provide a wide variety of services, similar to what it provides its own toy stores, I find that [Alghanim's] method of estimating damages is reasonable and believable, and provides a sound basis on which to fashion the award.

We find no manifest disregard of the law in this analysis.

Toys "R" Us also argues that the arbitrator manifestly disregarded the law of lost profits by ignoring the facts that (1) Alghanim's toy business had lost a total of $6.65 million over the course of its existence under the agreement, and (2) Alghanim itself offered to relinquish its rights for $2 million. Toys "R" Us further contends that the calculation of lost profits was irrational. We reject these contentions as well.

The fact that Alghanim lost $6.65 million over ten years does not make the arbitrator's award of future lost profits of $46 million "completely irrational." Past losses do not necessarily negate any expectation of future profits. *See, e.g., Lamborn v. Dittmer*, 873 F.2d 522, 533 (2d Cir. 1989) ("[W]e reject outright the suggestion in Dittmer's papers that a business with no history of profits is necessarily valueless.").

As to the purported $2 million buyout offer, no witness has testified that the $2 million figure was an estimate of the value of Alghanim's toy business. Kadrie, the primary Alghanim officer involved with the toy business, testified that, in his understanding, settlement with Toys "R" Us would serve to provide Alghanim "some relief on the cost of liquidating [its] inventory." Accordingly, Alghanim argues that $2 million was the value Alghanim placed on its inventory at the time. Furthermore, according to a Toys "R" Us executive, Kadrie, in making this offer, expressly stated that the $2 million was to recoup losses Alghanim had incurred in trying to develop the business. Therefore, there is no proof that this figure was Alghanim's, or anyone else's, estimation of the value of the business. Thus, the arbitrator did not manifestly disregard lost profits law in refusing to treat the $2 million figure as a buyout offer.

We also reject Toys "R" Us's contention that the arbitrator's calculation of lost profits was in manifest disregard of the law. Toys "R" Us contends that the actual operating results of the Toys "R" Us stores in the territory since the breach of the agreement have been lower than the arbitrator's valuation would suggest. The arbitrator explicitly addressed this issue, reasoning that

---

4. There is no dispute that New York law controls.

[Alghanim's] damages are to be calculated as of September 2, 1992 and are based on what its rights were worth at that time. More importantly, since the start of this case in late 1993 it has been clear that large stakes are involved and that [Toys "R" Us's] actual results of operations in the Middle East could have a bearing on this case. The record does not provide a sufficient basis to disentangle [Toys "R" Us's] actual results . . . from what might have been the business results of [Toys "R" Us's] Mid-East venture if this case had never existed.

There is no manifest disregard in the arbitrator's refusal to credit actual operating results for the period following the breach in calculating the value of the business at the time of the breach.

Toys "R" Us also argues that the arbitrator was wholly irrational in calculating the value of the Saudi Arabian rights as the $15 million ATA initially offered for those rights, when ultimately ATA only paid $7.5 million. However, the fact that a disinterested third party valued the Saudi Arabian rights at $15 million near the time of the breach provides a rational basis for accepting that valuation. Therefore, we see no manifest disregard in the arbitrator's use in his calculations of the bid price, rather than the actual closing price, for the sale to ATA. Thus, we see no merit in Toys "R" Us's contentions of manifest disregard of the law.

. . .

We have carefully considered Toys "R" Us's remaining contentions and find them all to be without merit.

Conclusion

For the foregoing reasons, the judgment of the district court is affirmed.

NOTES AND QUESTIONS

1. **Practice: What Are the Stakes?** What is at stake for the parties in this case? What would have been the award creditor's options if the U.S. court vacated rather than confirmed the award? What does the award creditor gain from confirmation?
2. **Practice: Litigation Strategy.** Why do you think the award creditor sought confirmation in a U.S. court rather than recognition and enforcement in another nation?
3. **Evaluating the Arguments.** What was Toys "R" Us's primary argument in favor of vacating the award? Why did the court reject it and instead decide to enforce the award?
4. **Confirmation, Enforcement, and the New York Convention.** Why does the New York Convention apply in this case? Is the award in this case a foreign arbitral award or another type of award? What is a "nondomestic" award? Why is this a confirmation rather than a recognition and enforcement proceeding? Explain why this distinction matters for the grounds available to resist confirmation.

5. **The "Two Regime" Theory and Manifest Disregard of the Law.** The court concludes that there are two "very different regimes" for the review of arbitral awards. What are these "regimes" and how does the difference matter for the outcome of this case? The "two regime" theory is widely, but not universally, accepted. According to one leading expert, "[m]ost national courts and commentators have . . . concluded," like the *Toys "R" Us* court, "that the New York Convention imposes no limits on the grounds which may be relied upon to annul an award in the arbitral seat." GARY B. BORN, INTERNATIONAL COMMERCIAL ARBITRATION 2554 (2009). Based on this understanding, a court in the arbitral seat may vacate an award on grounds recognized by its own national law, even if those grounds are not recognized by the New York Convention.

However, some U.S. courts have instead concluded that actions to vacate arbitral awards must be limited to the New York Convention's grounds for refusing recognition and enforcement. *Id.* at 2557. *See, e.g., Industrial Risk Insurers v. M.A.N. Gutehoffnungshutte GmbH*, 141 F.3d 1434, 1441 (11th Cir. 1998) (holding that arbitral award made in Florida "must be confirmed unless [award debtors] can successfully assert one of the seven defenses against enforcement of the award enumerated in Article V of the New York Convention"). According to this view, the New York Convention's grounds are exclusive and a court in the arbitral seat may not apply national law grounds to vacate an award covered by the New York Convention. In your opinion, which is the better view? The essential practical point is that you should be sure to do careful district- and circuit-specific legal research if you represent an award creditor or award debtor in a proceeding to confirm or vacate a nondomestic arbitral award in a U.S. court. Globally, the practical significance of the two-regime theory may be decreasing, since "most developed national arbitration regimes have adopted broadly similar approaches to the available grounds for annulment of international arbitral awards — generally, but not always, limiting such review to bases paralleling those applicable to non-recognition of awards in Article V of the New York Convention." BORN, *supra*, at 2552.

The *Restatement* takes the position that the two regimes are exclusive of each other. On the one hand, the exclusive grounds for vacating or denying confirmation of a nondomestic award covered by the New York Convention or the Panama Convention are those contained in FAA § 10. On the other hand, the exclusive grounds for denying recognition or enforcement of a foreign award covered by one of those conventions are the grounds contained in that convention. *See* RESTATEMENT OF THE LAW, THE U.S. LAW OF INTERNATIONAL COMMERCIAL AND INVESTOR-STATE ARBITRATION § 4.9, cmt. c ("Exclusive grounds for post-award relief. A court may not vacate or deny confirmation of a U.S. Convention award or deny recognition or enforcement of a non-Convention award on a ground other than those specified in FAA § 10. Likewise, a court may not deny recognition or enforcement of a foreign Convention award on a ground other than those specified in the New York or Panama Convention.").

The *Restatement* also takes the position that the exclusive nature of FAA § 10 means that the implied ground of manifest disregard of the law is not available even for nondomestic awards — that is, it is not a ground for vacating or denying confirmation of a nondomestic award nor is it a ground for denying recognition or enforcement of a foreign award. *See id.*, § 4.9, cmt. c ("[U]nder the FAA and the Conventions, courts do not review the merits of an arbitral award. Neither mistake of law nor mistake of fact, even if egregious, or manifest disregard of the law, is a ground for vacating or denying confirmation, recognition, or enforcement of an international arbitral award."); § 4.20(c) ("A court does not vacate or deny confirmation of a U.S. Convention award or deny recognition or enforcement of a non-Convention award for manifest disregard of the law."). What do you think of this position? What if it is obvious that an arbitral panel has ignored a clearly applicable law?

6. **Agreements for Enhanced Judicial Review.** In *Hall Street Associates, L.L.C. v. Mattel, Inc.*, 552 U.S. 576, 579 (2008), the U.S. Supreme Court held (regarding a domestic arbitration) that the parties to an arbitration agreement may not contractually enhance the degree of judicial review of an arbitral award beyond the review available under the FAA. In that case, the parties had agreed as follows: "The United States District Court for the District of Oregon may enter judgment upon any award, either by confirming the award or by vacating, modifying or correcting the award. The Court shall vacate, modify or correct any award: (i) where the arbitrator's findings of facts are not supported by substantial evidence, or (ii) where the arbitrator's conclusions of law are erroneous." The Supreme Court found the agreement unenforceable. Why shouldn't parties be able to choose their preferred dispute resolution approach, including enhanced judicial review of an arbitral award? Does the outcome in *Hall Street* suggest what the Supreme Court might think of the disputed "manifest disregard of the law" exception discussed in Note 5?

7. **Practice: Planning for Enforcement.** Assume that your client is entering an agreement with a Turkish business, and the two parties have agreed to include an arbitration clause in the agreement. The parties wish to ensure that manifest disregard of the law and other grounds specified in the FAA will not be available to a potential future award debtor as a defense against enforcement. What advice might you give them?

8. **Review of Arbitration Terminology.** Was the arbitration in the *Toys "R" Us* case an ad hoc or institutional arbitration? How do you know?

9. **Practice: A Look at the Briefs.** Some of the parties' briefs in this case are available here: 1997 WL 33484150 (Appellate Brief) Reply Brief for Respondents-Appellants (Apr. 17, 1997); 1997 WL 33633312 (Appellate Brief) Reply Brief for Respondents-Appellants (Apr. 17, 1997); 1997 WL 33484149 (Appellate Brief) Brief for Petitioner-Appellee (Mar. 24, 1997); 1997 WL 33633311 (Appellate Brief) Brief for Petitioner-Appellee (Mar. 24, 1997); 1997 WL 33484148 (Appellate Brief) Brief for Respondents-Appellants (Feb. 21, 1997); and 1997 WL 33633310 (Appellate Brief) Brief for Respondents-Appellants (Feb. 21, 1997).

C. Measures Outside the Arbitral Seat: Proceedings to Enforce Foreign Arbitral Awards

Whereas the court in the *Toys "R" Us* case decided whether to confirm or vacate a nondomestic arbitral award, this section deals with decisions whether to recognize or enforce foreign arbitral awards — that is, awards made in nations other than the United States. As the last section indicated, there is some debate about whether the New York Convention's grounds for refusal are exclusive in proceedings to vacate a nondomestic award in a court in the arbitral seat. The situation is clearer for foreign awards: Based on Articles III and V of the New York Convention and § 207 of the FAA, it is well established that the New York Convention's grounds for refusing recognition or enforcement of a foreign arbitral award are exclusive. Nevertheless, there are still some unresolved issues regarding enforcement of foreign arbitral awards under the New York Convention. The materials in this section focus on one of these issues: Should a court enforce a foreign arbitral award that has been vacated by a court in the arbitral seat? The following case discusses the different ways that courts have answered this question. Before reading it, review Article V of the New York Convention. What does it have to say about this issue?

Thai-Lao Lignite (Thailand) Co., Ltd. v. Government of the Lao People's Democratic Republic

997 F. Supp. 2d 214 (S.D.N.Y. 2014)

KIMBA M. WOOD, District Judge.

On August 5, 2011, this Court entered a judgment against the Government of the Lao People's Democratic Republic ("Respondent") enforcing a $57 million arbitral award in favor of Thai-Lao Lignite (Thailand) Co., Ltd. ("TLL") and Hongsa Lignite (Lao PDR), Co. Ltd. ("HLL") (collectively, "Petitioners"). On December 27, 2012, the Malaysian High Court vacated the arbitral award underlying the Court's judgment. In light of that ruling, Respondent moves to vacate the Court's judgment enforcing the arbitral award pursuant to Federal Rule of Civil Procedure 60(b)(5)* and Article (V)(1)(e) of the United Nations Convention on the Recognition and Enforcement of Foreign Arbitral Awards (the "New York Convention"), as implemented by the Federal Arbitration Act, 9 U.S.C. § 201 et seq. . . . For the reasons that follow, Respondent's motion is GRANTED. . . .

---

* Rule 60(b)(5) provides that "[o]n motion and just terms, the court may relieve a party or its legal representative from a final judgment, order, or proceeding [if] . . . the judgment has been satisfied, released, or discharged; it is based on an earlier judgment that has been reversed or vacated; or applying it prospectively is no longer equitable." — EDS.

I. Relevant Background

1. The Project Development Agreement and Arbitration

This case concerns a dispute between TLL, HLL, and Respondent arising out of a Project Development Agreement ("PDA") that TLL and Respondent entered into on July 22, 1994. In the PDA, TLL and Respondent agreed to submit any dispute arising out of the PDA to arbitration in Kuala Lumpur, Malaysia. The PDA further provided that

> Any award or determination of the arbitral panel shall be final, nonappealable, binding, and conclusive upon the parties, and judgment may be entered in any court of competent jurisdiction. The parties waive to the extent permitted by law any rights to appeal or any review of such award by any court or tribunal of competent jurisdiction.

Respondent affirmatively waived sovereign immunity "from jurisdiction, attachment (both before and after judgment), and execution to which it might otherwise be entitled in any action or proceeding relating in any way to this Agreement."

On October 5, 2006, Respondent sent Petitioners a Notice of Termination of the PDA; on July 26, 2007, Petitioners initiated arbitration. Petitioners contended that Respondent violated the PDA by improperly seeking to terminate it without cause, and without following the procedures for termination outlined in the agreement. . . .

The panel . . . concluded that Respondent had breached the PDA by improperly terminating it, and . . . awarded Petitioners $57,210,000 in damages, which included the total investment cost, a premium, interest, and attorneys' fees. Subsequently, Petitioners initiated proceedings seeking to enforce the arbitral award against Respondent.

2. Enforcement Proceedings in New York

In New York, Petitioners initially filed their petition to confirm the award in the Supreme Court of the State of New York, New York County, Commercial Division, on June 8, 2010. On July 9, 2010, Respondent removed the case to this Court. . . . On August 3, 2011, this Court denied Respondent's motion to dismiss and granted Petitioners' petition to confirm the arbitral award. . . .

3. Malaysian Litigation

On October 19, 2010, Respondent initiated proceedings to set aside the arbitral award in the High Court of Malaya at Kuala Lumpur. . . .

. . .

[T]he Malaysian High Court set aside the arbitral award. The High Court agreed with Respondent that the arbitrators had exceeded their jurisdiction and thereby violated § 37(1)(a)(iv) and (v) of Malaysia's Arbitration Act of 2005. Under

§ 37(1)(a)(iv), an arbitral award may be set aside if the award deals with a dispute not contemplated by, or not falling within, the terms of the arbitral agreement; under § 37(1)(a)(v), an award may be set aside if the award contains decisions on matters beyond the scope of the arbitral agreement. The High Court found that the arbitrators had exceeded the jurisdiction granted to them by the PDA by (1) assuming jurisdiction over disputes concerning two contracts the parties had entered into before the PDA was created, and (2) admitting and adjudicating claims by non-parties to the PDA. The High Court ordered re-arbitration of the dispute before a new panel of arbitrators. Petitioners appealed the High Court's decision. The Malaysian Court of Appeal agreed with the High Court that the arbitrators had exceeded the jurisdiction granted to them by the PDA and affirmed the High Court's decision.

II. Discussion

In light of the Malaysian High Court's ruling setting aside the arbitral award, Respondent moves, pursuant to Federal Rule of Civil Procedure 60(b)(5) and Article (V)(1)(e) of the New York Convention, for an order vacating this Court's August 5, 2011, judgment. Respondent argues that the New York Convention calls for vacatur under the circumstances of this case, and that under *Baker Marine (Nig.) Ltd. v. Chevron (Nig.) Ltd.*, 191 F.3d 194 (2d Cir. 1999), vacatur is required absent extraordinary circumstances not present here. Petitioners urge the Court to deny Respondent's motion, arguing that . . . neither the New York Convention nor Second Circuit case law requires vacatur; and . . . [that] there are adequate reasons for this Court not to defer to the Malaysian judgment.

1. Background Law and Precedent

. . . "Under the [New York] Convention, 'the country in which, or under the [arbitration] law of which, [an] award was made' is said to have primary jurisdiction over the arbitration award. All other signatory States are secondary jurisdictions. . . ." *Karaha Bodas Co., L.L.C. v. Perusahaan Pertambangan Minyak Dan Gas Bumi Negara*, 335 F.3d 357, 364 (5th Cir. 2003).

Article V(1)(e) of the New York Convention provides that recognition and enforcement of an arbitral award by a court with secondary jurisdiction over an arbitral award "may be refused, at the request of the party against whom it is invoked" if the award "has been set aside or suspended by a competent authority of the country in which, or under the law of which, that award was made." "Pursuant to this provision of the Convention, a secondary Contracting State normally may not enforce an arbitration award that has been lawfully set aside by a 'competent authority' in the primary Contracting State." *TermoRio S.A. E.S.P. v. Electranta S.P.*, 487 F.3d 928, 935 (D.C. Cir. 2007). Petitioners do not contest that the Malaysian High Court is a "competent authority" as defined by Article V(1)(e); rather, Petitioners argue that this Court has the discretion not to defer to the Malaysian court's decision.

. . .

There are few decisions defining the scope of the discretion a court with secondary jurisdiction has to enforce an arbitral award that has been vacated by a court with primary jurisdiction over the award. Only two Circuit Courts of Appeal have addressed the issue, the Second Circuit Court of Appeals in *Baker Marine (Nig.) Ltd. v. Chevron (Nig.) Ltd.*, 191 F.3d 194 (2d Cir. 1999) and the D.C. Circuit Court of Appeals in *TermoRio S.A. E.S.P. v. Electranta S.P.*, 487 F.3d 928 (D.C. Cir. 2007).

In *Baker Marine*, the Second Circuit Court of Appeals held that where a court with primary jurisdiction over an arbitral award issues a decision setting aside the award, U.S. courts will honor that decision in the absence of an "adequate reason" not to do so. In *Baker Marine*, three companies agreed to arbitrate any of their business disputes in Nigeria, under the laws of Nigeria. Arbitration ensued and resulted in two awards to Baker Marine of a total of $2.98 million. Baker Marine sought enforcement of the arbitral awards in Nigeria, but the Nigerian courts set aside the awards. . . . Baker Marine then brought an action in the Northern District of New York seeking confirmation of the awards. The district court denied Baker Marine's petition, concluding that under the Convention and principles of comity, it would not be proper to enforce a foreign arbitral award . . . when such an award has been set aside by the Nigerian Courts. The Second Circuit affirmed.

Baker Marine made two principal arguments on appeal. First, Baker Marine argued that "the awards were set aside by the Nigerian courts for reasons that would not be recognized under U.S. law as valid grounds for vacating an arbitration award, and that under Article VII [of the New York Convention], it may invoke this country's national arbitration law, notwithstanding the action of the Nigerian court." The Second Circuit rejected Baker Marine's first argument, holding that

> It is sufficient answer that the parties contracted in Nigeria that their disputes would be arbitrated under the laws of Nigeria. . . . Nothing suggests that the parties intended United States domestic arbitral law to govern their disputes. . . .

Second, Baker Marine argued that the Article (V)(1)(e)'s use of the term "may," rather than a mandatory term implies that the court might have enforced the awards, notwithstanding the Nigerian judgments vacating them. The Second Circuit also rejected this argument, stating that, "It is sufficient answer that Baker Marine has shown no adequate reason for refusing to recognize the judgments of the Nigerian court."

In a footnote, the Second Circuit distinguished the facts in *Baker Marine* from the facts in *In re Chromalloy Aeroservices*, 939 F. Supp. 907 (D.D.C. 1996) [hereinafter *Chromalloy*]. In *Chromalloy*, Egypt and a U.S. company (CAS) had entered into an agreement providing that disputes would be submitted to arbitration in Egypt and that the arbitral panel's decision "shall be final and binding and cannot be made subject to any appeal or other recourse." The arbitral panel ordered Egypt to pay CAS monetary damages. CAS subsequently filed a petition in the District Court for the District of Columbia ("D.C. District Court") seeking enforcement of the arbitral award. Shortly thereafter, Egypt filed an appeal with the Egyptian Court of Appeal seeking to set aside the award. The Egyptian Court of Appeal suspended the award, and Egypt filed a motion in the D.C. District Court to dismiss CAS's petition to enforce the award. The district court held that the arbitration award was valid and enforceable, because Egypt's appeal to the Egyptian Court of Appeal abrogated Egypt's contractual promise not to appeal the award, and recognizing the result of the appeal would violate the "U.S. public policy in favor of final and binding arbitration of commercial disputes." The Second Circuit distinguished *Chromalloy* on its facts, emphasizing that, (1) unlike the petitioner in *Chromalloy*, Baker Marine was not a U.S. citizen and did not initially seek confirmation of the award in the U.S.; and (2) unlike Egypt, the companies in *Baker Marine* did not violate a promise in appealing the arbitral award.

The only other Circuit Court of Appeals that has considered the issue of enforcing a vacated, foreign arbitration award is the D.C. Circuit Court of Appeals in *TermoRio S.A. E.S.P. v. Electranta S.P.*, 487 F.3d 928 (D.C. Cir. 2007) [hereinafter *TermoRio*]. In *TermoRio*, the D.C. Circuit Court of Appeals held that normally a court sitting in secondary jurisdiction should not enforce an arbitral award vacated by a court with primary jurisdiction over the award, but that there are certain circumstances in which doing so may be appropriate. In that case, TermoRio S.A. E.S.P. ("TermoRio") and Electrificadora del Atlantico S.A. E.S.P. ("Electranta"), a Colombian public utility company, entered into a contract that provided for any dispute between the parties to be resolved by binding arbitration in Colombia. An arbitral panel ordered Electranta to pay TermoRio damages, but subsequently Colombia's highest administrative court set aside the arbitration award on the ground that the arbitration clause in the parties' contract violated Colombian law. TermoRio then filed suit in the District Court for the District of Columbia seeking enforcement of the arbitral award. The district court dismissed the action for failure to state a claim upon which relief could be granted and, in the alternative, on the ground of forum non conveniens. The D.C. Circuit affirmed.

Like Baker Marine, TermoRio argued that the "may" in Article V(1)(e) of the New York Convention gave U.S. courts the discretion to enforce an award, notwithstanding that it had been vacated in another country. Specifically, TermoRio contended that "a state is not required to give effect to foreign judicial proceedings grounded on policies which do violence to its own fundamental interests." TermoRio argued that the district court should have exercised this discretion because "the [Colombian court's] decision was contrary to both domestic Colombian and international law; recognition of that decision would frustrate clearly expressed international and United States policy; and the process leading to the nullification decision demonstrated the Colombian government's determination to deny Plaintiffs fair process." The D.C. Circuit Court of Appeals rejected TermoRio's arguments, stating that

> Accepting that there is a narrow public policy gloss on Article V(1)(e) of the Convention and that a foreign judgment is unenforceable as against public policy to the extent that it is repugnant to fundamental notions of what is decent and just in the United States, [TermoRio's] claims still fail. [TermoRio] [has] neither alleged nor provided any evidence to suggest that the parties' proceedings before [the Colombian court] or the judgment of that court violated any basic notions of justice to which we subscribe.

In affirming the district court's decision, the D.C. Circuit generally sub-scribe[d] to the reasoning of the Second Circuit in *Baker Marine*, which it found consistent with the view that, "[w]hen a competent foreign court has nullified a foreign arbitration award, United States courts should not go behind that decision absent extraordinary circumstances not present in this case." The Court found that, "Because there is nothing in the record . . . indicating that the proceedings before the [Colombian court] were tainted or that the judgment of that court is other than authentic, the District Court was, as it held, obliged to respect it." Enforcing the award "would seriously undermine a principal precept of the New York Convention an arbitration award does not exist to be enforced in other Contracting States if it has been lawfully set aside by a competent authority in the State in which the award was made."

The most recent decision concerning the enforcement of a vacated arbitral award was issued by Judge Hellerstein of this Court. In *Corporación Mexicana de Mantenimiento Integral, S. de R.L. de C.V.* ("COMMISA") v. *PEMEX-Exploración y Producción* ("PEP"), 962 F. Supp. 2d 642 (S.D.N.Y. 2013) [here-inafter *PEMEX*], COMMISA and PEP, an instrumentality of Mexico, entered into two contracts that provided that disputes would be arbitrated. Each party accused the other of breaching contractual obligations; after conciliation efforts failed, COMMISA initiated arbitration. Two weeks later, PEP issued an adminis-trative rescission of the contracts. While the arbitration was under way, two new statutes were passed in Mexico. The first statute gave the Tax and Administrative Court jurisdiction over any case challenging an administrative rescission (so long as the challenge was filed within 45 days of the purported rescission). The second statute stated that challenges to administrative rescissions could no longer be arbi-trated. The arbitral panel issued an award in favor of COMMISA. COMMISA subsequently sought and obtained an order from Judge Hellerstein confirming the award. PEP . . . filed proceedings in the Mexican courts to nullify the award. . . . The Eleventh Collegiate Court [of Mexico] held that the award was invalid, rely-ing in part on the second new statute. . . .

In light of the Eleventh Collegiate Court's decision, the Second Circuit Court of Appeals remanded the case to Judge Hellerstein to address what effect the nullification should have on the arbitral award and his decision confirming the award. Article V of the Panama Convention, like Article V of the New York Convention, states that "recognition and execution of [the arbitral award] may be refused" if the award has been nullified by a "competent authority" of the state in which, or according to the law of which, the arbitration award was conducted. Judge Hellerstein found that the use of the word "may" gave him some discre-tion, but noted that due to the Second Circuit's opinion in *Baker Marine* and the D.C. Circuit's opinion in *TermoRio*, that discretion was narrow. He noted that *Baker Marine* did not define the scope of a court's discretion, but that *TermoRio* did so as follows[:] if the judgment of nullification "is repugnant to fundamen-tal notions of what is decent and just in the United States" or, if the judgment "violated any basic notions of justice in which we subscribe," then it need not be followed. Applying the *TermoRio* standard, Judge Hellerstein declined to defer to the Eleventh Collegiate Court's decision, and again confirmed the arbitral award, finding that the Eleventh Collegiate Court's decision violated basic notions of justice in that it applied a law that was not in existence at the time the parties' contract was formed and left COMMISA without an apparent ability to litigate its claims.

2. Application

The use of the permissive "may" in Article (V)(1)(e) of the New York Convention gives this Court discretion to enforce a foreign arbitral award where the award has been nullified by a court in the state with primary jurisdiction over the award. That discretion, however, is narrowly confined. Its scope is stated explicitly in *TermoRio*. That discretion may be exercised only when the foreign judgment setting aside the award is "repugnant to fundamental notions of what is decent and just in the State where enforcement is sought" or violates "basic notions of justice." This standard is high and infrequently met and should be found [o]nly in clearcut cases.

Petitioners fail to demonstrate that the circumstances of this case meet the "extraordinary circumstances" envisioned by TermoRio and found to exist by Judge Hellerstein in *PEMEX*. As described below, the alleged errors Petitioners point out in the proceedings before the Malaysian courts and in the judgments of those courts do not rise to the level of violating basic notions of justice such that the Court here should ignore comity considerations and disregard the Malaysian judgments.

. . .

The Court will not disregard comity considerations and refuse to recognize the Malaysian courts' judgments unless Petitioners can demonstrate that the process before the Malaysian courts "violated basic notions of justice." . . .

. . .

Petitioners . . . argue that that the High Court's decision setting aside the arbitral award does not deserve deference. However, Petitioners' criticisms of the Malaysian High Court's decision at best show weaknesses in the Malaysian court's legal reasoning, and ultimately fail to demonstrate that the judgment violates basic notions of justice.

Petitioners first complain that Respondent allegedly waived its jurisdictional objection when it stated that "the Tribunal is an appropriate forum to hear disputes arising out of the Prior Contracts" in a submission to the tribunal and the High Court committed error by failing to quote this alleged waiver. Petitioners' argument fails because although the High Court did not explicitly quote the Respondent's alleged waiver, the High Court did conduct an extensive analysis into (1) whether Respondent properly objected to the arbitral tribunal's jurisdiction, and (2) whether Respondent waived its jurisdictional objection. Ultimately, the High Court held that, as a matter of Malaysian law, the Respondent (1) had properly objected to the arbitral tribunal's jurisdiction, and (2) had not waived its jurisdictional objection. Because Petitioners do not allege that the High Court's determination was contrary to Malaysian law or otherwise critique the determination, the Court finds that no violation of "basic notions of justice occurred."

Second, Petitioners take issue with the fact that the High Court failed to give preclusive effect to the rulings of this Court and the Second Circuit Court of

Appeals on arbitral jurisdiction. This argument is unpersuasive, in that it fails to account for the fact that the Malaysian High Court was evaluating de novo whether the arbitrators had exceeded their jurisdiction, whereas this Court and the Second Circuit's decisions applied a deferential standard of review to this same issue.

Last, Petitioners fault the High Court for not according any res judicata effect to the opinions upholding the award by this Court or the Second Circuit Court of Appeals. However, the Malaysian High Court had no obligation to grant res judicata effect to the decisions enforcing the arbitral award by courts of secondary jurisdiction. A decision by a court of secondary jurisdiction confirming an arbitral award "is not truly a decision on the merits; rather, it is an order to enforce an award resulting from litigation elsewhere, which is not necessarily given res judicata effect in foreign jurisdictions." *Karaha Bodas Co., L.L.C. v. Perusahaan Pertambangan Minyak Dan Gas Bumi Negara*, 335 F.3d 357, 372 (5th Cir. 2003).

. . .

The facts of this case simply do not amount to the extraordinary circumstances contemplated by *TermoRio*. This is not a case in which the Respondent is an entity of Malaysia's government, which might raise a suspicion of the Malaysian courts' partiality; rather, Malaysia is a neutral, third country that the parties mutually chose as the seat of the arbitration. This case is therefore distinguishable from both *PEMEX* and *Chromalloy*. In *PEMEX*, Judge Hellerstein found that the Mexican court's judgment violated basic notions of justice because (1) the court retroactively applied a law not in existence at the time the parties entered into their contract; and (2) the private party was left without a remedy to litigate the dispute that the arbitrators had decided in its favor, because by the time the court issued its opinion, the short limitations period in the correct forum had already ended. Judge Hellerstein found the lack of remedy "particularly unjust" because the private party was therefore liable to the government instrumentality for damages "even though there [had] been no full hearing on the merits outside the arbitration."

In contrast, the Malaysian High Court here set aside the arbitral award on a universally-recognized ground — that the arbitrators exceeded their jurisdiction. Furthermore the decision did not leave Petitioners here without a remedy. The High Court merely ordered re-arbitration before a different panel of arbitrators. Petitioners also pursued their right to appeal the High Court's decision and received a decision from the Malaysian Court of Appeal affirming the High Court's decision.

. . .

Because the Court finds that the process before the Malaysian courts and the judgments of those courts did not violate basic notions of justice, the Court GRANTS Respondent's motion to vacate.*

. . .

---

* The court of appeals affirmed the district court's decision. *Thai-Lao Lignite (Thailand) Co., Ltd. v. Government of the Lao People's Democratic Republic*, 864 F.3d 172 (2d Cir. 2017). –EDS.

NOTES AND QUESTIONS

1. **Practice: What's at Stake?** Why do you think the award creditor sought enforcement in a U.S. court instead of in Malaysia, the arbitral seat? Why in the United States instead of another nation outside the arbitral seat?

2. **Practice: Transaction Planning and Selection of the Arbitral Seat.** On what grounds did the Malaysian court in *Thai-Lao* decide to vacate the arbitral award? Are they grounds for vacating an award under the FAA? Under the UNCITRAL Model Law? If you represent a client that is negotiating a business agreement that includes an arbitration clause, and assuming that you would like to minimize the likelihood that an arbitral award will be vacated by the arbitral seat, what research might you consider doing before selecting the arbitral seat?

3. **Foreign Arbitral Awards Vacated in the Arbitral Seat.** According to the court in the *Thai-Lao* case, when, if ever, may a U.S. court enforce a foreign arbitral award that has been vacated in the arbitral seat? What does the New York Convention say about the enforcement of awards vacated in the arbitral seat? Is the court's view required by the New York Convention? Why or why not? What reasons outside the New York Convention might support this view?

4. **The *Baker Marine* and *TermoRio* Cases.** As the court in *Thai-Lao* discusses, the Second Circuit in *Baker Marine* and the D.C. Circuit in *TermoRio* also declined to enforce foreign arbitral awards that had been vacated by a court in the arbitral seat. According to the Second Circuit, may such awards ever be enforced by a U.S. court? If so, under what circumstances? According to the D.C. Circuit, may foreign awards vacated in the arbitral seat ever be enforced by a U.S. court? If so, under what circumstances? What arguments did the award creditors in these two cases make in favor of enforcement, and why did those arguments fail?

5. **The *Chromalloy* and *PEMEX* Cases.** The courts in the *Chromalloy* and *PEMEX* cases, also discussed in the *Thai-Lao* opinion, did enforce arbitral awards that had been vacated by a court in the arbitral seat. Can these decisions be reconciled with *Thai-Lao*, *Baker Marine*, and *TermoRio*? Why or why not?

   The Second Circuit affirmed the *PEMEX* decision. The court of appeals emphasized that the Mexican court in annulling the arbitral award applied a statute that retroactively prohibited arbitration of the subject matter of the contract (as described in the *Thai-Lao Lignite* case above):

   > [The] discretion of a district court to enforce an arbitral award annulled in the awarding jurisdiction . . . is constrained by the prudential concern of international comity, which remains vital notwithstanding that it is not expressly codified in the Panama Convention.
   >
   > Accordingly, "a final judgment obtained through sound procedures in a foreign country is generally conclusive . . . unless . . . enforcement of the judgment would offend the public policy of the state in which enforcement is sought." . . .

Precedent is sparse; but the few cases that are factually analogous have endorsed this approach. See *Baker Marine (Nig.) Ltd. v. Chevron (Nig.) Ltd.*, 191 F.3d 194, 197 n.3 (2d Cir. 1999) ("Recognition of the Nigerian [annulment of the arbitral award] in this case does not conflict with United States public policy."); see also *TermoRio S.A. E.S.P. v. Electranta S.P.*, 487 F.3d 928, 938 (D.C. Cir. 2007) ("*Baker Marine* is consistent with the view that when a competent foreign court has nullified a foreign arbitration award, United States courts should not go behind that decision absent extraordinary circumstances not present in this case" . . .).

Consequently, although [the court has] discretion in enforcing a foreign arbitral award that has been annulled in the awarding jurisdiction, . . . the exercise of that discretion here is appropriate only to vindicate "fundamental notions of what is decent and just" in the United States.

Applying this standard, we conclude that the Southern District did not abuse its discretion in confirming the arbitral award notwithstanding invalidation of the award in the Mexican courts. The high hurdle of the public policy exception is surmounted here by four powerful considerations[, including] the repugnancy of retroactive legislation. . . .

Any court should act with trepidation and reluctance in enforcing an arbitral award that has been declared a nullity by the courts having jurisdiction over the forum in which the award was rendered. However, we do not think that the Southern District second-guessed the Eleventh Collegiate Court, which appears only to have been implementing the law of Mexico. Rather, the Southern District exercised discretion, as allowed by treaty, to assess whether the nullification of the award offends basic standards of justice in the United States. We hold that in the rare circumstances of this case, the Southern District did not abuse its discretion by confirming the arbitral award at issue because to do otherwise would undermine public confidence in laws and diminish rights of personal liberty and property. Taken together, these circumstances validate the exercise of discretion and justify affirmance.

Corporación Mexicana de Mantenimiento Integral, S. de R.L. de C.V. v. PEMEX-Exploración y Producción, 832 F.3d 92, 105-10 (2d Cir. 2016). What is the relationship between the rules governing the enforcement of foreign country court judgments (discussed in Chapter 7) and the enforcement of foreign arbitral awards that have been annulled in the arbitral seat?

6. **Comparative Note.** Globally, there is a split between jurisdictions that will and those that will not enforce awards that have been vacated in the arbitral seat. As one pair of experts summarize: "[M]ost jurisdictions around the world are likely to refuse enforcement of an award that has been set aside in another country. However, this is not the universal position: courts in certain countries have been receptive in the past to enforcing awards set aside elsewhere based on local annulment standards, and this trend may grow as international arbitration around the world becomes more transnational in character and less deferential towards the place of arbitration." MICHAEL MCILWRATH & JOHN SAVAGE, INTERNATIONAL ARBITRATION AND MEDIATION: A PRACTICAL GUIDE 357 (2010). In general, what do you think the best position is?

7. **Foreign Arbitral Awards and Foreign Judgments.** This case — like other recognition and enforcement cases where a court in the arbitral seat vacated the award — can be understood as not only a foreign arbitral award case, but also a foreign judgment case. As the materials in Chapter 7 show, U.S. courts generally recognize and enforce foreign judgments, subject to a variety of exceptions. In *Thai-Lao*, what was the foreign judgment that was at issue? Under the rules governing the enforcement of foreign judgments, would that judgment be enforceable? Why or why not?

8. **Parallel Litigation.** Cases like *Thai-Lao*, *Baker Marine*, and *TermoRio* are examples of "parallel litigation," which is a challenging transnational legal problem. Proceedings arising out of the arbitration were taking place simultaneously in two jurisdictions — proceedings to vacate the award in the arbitral seat, and proceedings to enforce the award in the United States. Further issues relating to parallel litigation are discussed in Chapter 10 below.

NOTES ON SPECIAL ISSUES IN THE ENFORCEMENT OF ARBITRAL AWARDS

1. **Practice: Finding the Award Debtor's Assets.** Often in transnational commercial arbitration, the parties agree to a neutral arbitral seat — one to which neither of them has a substantial relationship. But neither party is likely to have assets there. This means that enforcement of a resulting arbitral award in the arbitral seat often will not be a meaningful option. A leading reason for attempting to enforce arbitral awards outside the arbitral seat is to enforce awards where the award debtor has assets that can be attached to satisfy the award. With this in mind, why do you think the award debtors in *Thai-Lao* and the cases discussed therein sought enforcement in the United States instead of in the arbitral seat? As a lawyer for an award creditor, what methods might you consider using to locate assets of an award debtor?

2. **Personal Jurisdiction.** Must a U.S. court have personal jurisdiction over the award debtor in proceedings to enforce foreign arbitral awards? It is fairly well accepted that the answer is "yes." *See, e.g., Frontera Resources Azerbaijan Co. v. State Oil Co. of the Azerbaijan Republic*, 582 F.3d 393 (2d Cir. 2009); *Glencore Grain Rotterdam B.V. v. Shivnath Rai Harnarain Co.*, 284 F.3d 1114 (9th Cir. 2002). However, there is some variation across circuits about what contacts are sufficient to satisfy due process in enforcement proceedings. For example, some circuits suggest that the presence of any assets of the award debtor in the forum state suffices for enforcement there against those assets. *See, e.g., Glencore, supra*, at 1127 (noting that "[c]onsiderable authority" supporting the position that the presence of property of the award debtor in the enforcement forum is sufficient for personal jurisdiction "even if that property has no relationship to the underlying controversy between the parties"). Another view is that the property upon which personal jurisdiction is based must be related to

the award creditor's claim. *See, e.g., Base Metal Trading, Ltd. v. OJSC,* 283 F.3d 208 (4th Cir. 2002); *Frontera Resources, supra.* Therefore, careful forum-specific research is necessary when analyzing personal jurisdiction in proceedings to enforce arbitral awards in U.S. courts. Section 4.25 of the *Restatement* provides the following guidance:

Personal Jurisdiction in Post-Award Action

(a) The adequacy of jurisdiction over the defendant in a post-award action is determined by the generally applicable statutory and constitutional standards governing the exercise of such jurisdiction.

(b) Unless forum law provides otherwise, jurisdiction over the defendant in a post-award action may be based on the presence of the defendant's property within the court's jurisdiction, whether or not the property bears any relationship to the underlying dispute. Whether this exercise of jurisdiction requires the attachment of such property is determined by the forum's rules governing quasi-in-rem jurisdiction. If jurisdiction over the defendant is based solely on the presence of property within the court's jurisdiction, the resulting judgment may be entered only up to the value of that property, or any bond posted in substitution thereof.

3. *Forum Non Conveniens.* The *forum non conveniens* doctrine — discussed in Chapter 10 — allows a U.S. court to dismiss an action if a foreign court is an adequate and more appropriate alternative forum, based on consideration of various private and public interest factors. A court may dismiss an action based on the *forum non conveniens* doctrine even if it has personal jurisdiction and subject matter jurisdiction. Does the *forum non conveniens* doctrine allow a U.S. court to dismiss proceedings to enforce foreign arbitral awards? Commentators suggest that the better answer is "no." *See, e.g.,* MARGARET L. MOSES, THE PRINCIPLES AND PRACTICE OF INTERNATIONAL COMMERCIAL ARBITRATION 207 (2008). However, in *Monegasque De Reassurances S.A.M. v. Nak Naftogaz of Ukraine,* 311 F.3d 488 (2d Cir. 2002), the court of appeals upheld a *forum non conveniens* dismissal of proceedings to enforce an arbitral award. As with personal jurisdiction, forum-specific research is required to determine the availability of the *forum non conveniens* doctrine in arbitral award enforcement proceedings. Section 4.27 of the *Restatement* takes the following position:

Forum Non Conveniens in Post-Award Action

(a) An action to confirm or vacate a U.S. Convention award or enforce a foreign Convention award is not subject to a stay or dismissal in favor of a foreign court on forum non conveniens grounds.

(b) A court may, in accordance with the standards generally applicable to forum non conveniens motions, stay or dismiss an action to enforce a non Convention award in favor of a foreign court that also has authority to enforce the award.

4. **Foreign Sovereign Immunity and Planning Business Transactions.** What if you represent an award creditor seeking enforcement of an arbitral award against an award debtor that is a foreign nation (or an agency or instrumentality of a foreign nation)? Under the customary international law doctrine of

foreign sovereign immunity, one nation is generally immune from suit in the courts of another nation. The United States codified the doctrine in the Foreign Sovereign Immunities Act of 1976 (FSIA). Under a broad rule of immunity, an award debtor that is a foreign nation (or an agency or instrumentality of a foreign nation) — like the Lao People's Democratic Republic in the *Thai-Lao* case — might be immune from suit in a U.S. court. However, there are exceptions to immunity, some of which may apply in proceedings to enforce arbitral awards. Why did the court in *Thai-Lao* conclude that foreign sovereign immunity was not a barrier to the award creditor's enforcement action in that case? If you are representing a client that is entering a business agreement with a foreign nation, and the agreement has an arbitration clause, what else might you advise your client to include in the agreement to reduce the likelihood that foreign sovereign immunity would be a barrier to enforcement? Chapter 11 discusses foreign sovereign immunity in detail, including exceptions that can facilitate enforcement of arbitral awards against foreign sovereigns.

NOTES ON ENFORCEMENT OF INVESTOR-STATE AND STATE-STATE ARBITRAL AWARDS

1. **Annulment of Investor-State Arbitral Awards.** Transnational commercial arbitration is the most common form of arbitration in transnational practice, but a growing number of lawyers deal with investor-state arbitration, which is introduced in Chapter 6. As with transnational commercial arbitration, enforcement issues may arise regarding awards resulting from investor-state arbitration, especially issues related to enforcement against foreign nations and foreign governmental entities (discussed in Chapter 11 on foreign sovereign immunity). However, the rules and procedures governing enforcement are different. As Chapter 6 explained, a leading mechanism for arbitrating investor-state disputes is the International Centre for the Settlement of Investment Disputes (ICSID), which is governed by the ICSID Convention. Under Article 52 of the ICSID Convention, a party may request annulment of an ICSID award on one of five grounds: (a) that the arbitral tribunal was not properly constituted; (b) that the tribunal has manifestly exceeded its powers; (c) that there was corruption on the part of a member of the tribunal; (d) that there has been a serious departure from a fundamental rule of procedure; or (e) that the award has failed to state the reasons on which it is based. An ad hoc committee of three ICSID arbitrators then determines whether to grant the request. None of the committee members "shall have been a member of the tribunal which rendered the award, shall be of the same nationality as any such member, shall be a national of the State party to the dispute or of the State whose national is a party to the dispute, shall have been designated to the Panel of Arbitrators by either of those States, or shall have acted as a conciliator in the same dispute." *Id.*

2. Recognition and Enforcement of Investor-State Arbitral Awards. If the award is not annulled pursuant to Article 52, then it is subject to recognition and enforcement in accordance with Section 6 of the ICSID Convention, which provides as follows:

Section 6. Recognition and Enforcement of the Award

Article 53

(1) The award shall be binding on the parties and shall not be subject to any appeal or to any other remedy except those provided for in this Convention. Each party shall abide by and comply with the terms of the award except to the extent that enforcement shall have been stayed pursuant to the relevant provisions of this Convention.

(2) For the purposes of this Section, "award" shall include any decision interpreting, revising or annulling such award pursuant to Articles 50, 51 or 52.

Article 54

(1) Each Contracting State shall recognize an award rendered pursuant to this Convention as binding and enforce the pecuniary obligations imposed by that award within its territories as if it were a final judgment of a court in that State. A Contracting State with a federal constitution may enforce such an award in or through its federal courts and may provide that such courts shall treat the award as if it were a final judgment of the courts of a constituent state.

(2) A party seeking recognition or enforcement in the territories of a Contracting State shall furnish to a competent court or other authority which such State shall have designated for this purpose a copy of the award certified by the Secretary-General. Each Contracting State shall notify the Secretary-General of the designation of the competent court or other authority for this purpose and of any subsequent change in such designation.

(3) Execution of the award shall be governed by the laws concerning the execution of judgments in force in the State in whose territories such execution is sought.

Article 55

Nothing in Article 54 shall be construed as derogating from the law in force in any Contracting State relating to immunity of that State or of any foreign State from execution.

In actions to enforce ICSID awards against foreign sovereigns in U.S. courts, must award creditors establish personal jurisdiction over the foreign sovereign? *See Mobil Cerro Negro, Limited v. Bolivarian Republic of Venezuela,* 863 F.3d 96, 112 (2d Cir. 2017) ("The [Foreign Sovereign Immunities Act (FSIA)] controls actions to enforce ICSID awards. We conclude that the FSIA provides the sole source of jurisdiction — subject matter and personal — for federal courts over actions brought to enforce ICSID awards against foreign sovereigns; [and] that the FSIA's service and venue requirements must be satisfied before federal district courts may enter judgment on such awards. . . . Although the FSIA provides subject matter jurisdiction over this proceeding, the FSIA's service and venue requirements have not been satisfied here. Accordingly, the District Court lacked personal jurisdiction over Venezuela" and the award creditor's ex parte enforcement action must be dismissed.).

Chapter 5 of the *Restatement* covers the role of U.S. courts in the investor-state arbitration process, including the role of U.S. courts in providing post-award relief in investor-state arbitration.

3. **New York Convention versus ICSID Convention.** Compare the enforcement provisions of the New York Convention with those of the ICSID Convention. From the perspective of an award creditor, what are some of the advantages and disadvantages of the two treaties' enforcement provisions?

4. **Recognition and Enforcement of State-State Arbitral Awards.** State-state arbitration, also introduced in Chapter 6, is relatively uncommon compared to transnational commercial arbitration. But in this context, too, enforcement issues can arise. Like arbitral awards in transnational commercial arbitration and investor-state arbitration, arbitral awards in state-state arbitration are legally binding. Also like arbitral awards in these other contexts, an unsuccessful party will not necessarily comply with the award voluntarily. However, as one expert puts it, whereas parties to transnational commercial arbitration can rely upon international agreements and domestic courts for enforcement, "States . . . find it much more difficult either to challenge an inter-state award or to enforce it, because in international law, although rules relating to validity and implementation exist, there is a lack of compulsory procedures to make them effective." J.G. MERRILLS, INTERNATIONAL DISPUTE SETTLEMENT 107 (5th ed. 2011). But "[t]his does not mean that arbitral awards [in state-state arbitration] are widely disregarded." *Id.* Why might this be the case? What steps can be taken in state-state arbitration agreements or after the issuance of a state-state arbitral award to maximize the likelihood that an unsuccessful state party will abide by the terms of the award?

REVIEW NOTES AND QUESTIONS

1. As you review this chapter's materials, keep in mind two overarching questions: Which proceedings relating to awards in transnational commercial arbitration are available in courts in the arbitral seat and which are available in courts outside the arbitral seat? And which defenses against arbitral awards are available in these two contexts?

2. As two experts summarize: "[O]ne of the chief attractions of international arbitration is that the resulting awards are better currency abroad than judgments of state courts, thanks in large part to the New York Convention, with its broad membership and limited grounds for refusal of enforcement. However, the ease of enforcement of international arbitral awards is relative — being easier to enforce than court judgments does not necessarily mean being easy to enforce." MICHAEL MCILWRATH & JOHN SAVAGE, INTERNATIONAL ARBITRATION

AND MEDIATION: A PRACTICAL GUIDE 361 (2010). As you review this chapter's materials, pay close attention both to those aspects of the legal framework for enforcing arbitral awards that are likely to facilitate enforcement, and those that may pose barriers.

3. As you have seen, there is a general presumption that courts will enforce arbitral awards and there is "an almost sacrosanct principle" that they will do so without reviewing the merits of the arbitrators' decisions. GARY B. BORN, INTERNATIONAL COMMERCIAL ARBITRATION 2865 (2009). What are the advantages and disadvantages of a method of dispute resolution that combines this strong presumption in favor of enforcement with little or no opportunity for review of the dispute resolution outcome? What are the implications for the types of disputes you would advise a client to submit to arbitration and those you would instead advise a client to submit to litigation? If you are advising a client on submitting a dispute to arbitration, would you want courts to be able to review the resulting award (for example, for "manifest disregard of the law") or not?

4. Suppose you represent a client who is a party to a contract with an arbitration clause and a dispute has arisen under that contract. Your client is considering initiating arbitration, but wants to know, if the arbitration yields an award in the client's favor, what will happen next and how likely it is that the award will be paid. Can you briefly explain what steps you would consider taking on behalf of your client to obtain payment of the award from the award debtor? What additional information would you want to have in order to think through those steps?

PART IV

ADVANCED TOPICS IN TRANSNATIONAL LITIGATION

The first three parts of this casebook introduced you to the fundamentals of transnational law and practice. Part I of this casebook reviewed the different types of law that may apply to transnational legal problems. Part II explained the different methods that may be available to resolve disputes arising out of transnational legal problems. Part III introduced you to methods for enforcing transnational dispute resolution outcomes: enforcement of judgments and arbitral awards.

This part of the casebook moves beyond the fundamentals and explores advanced topics in transnational litigation with a focus on U.S. practice. Chapter 9 examines how one serves a defendant with process in a transnational case. Chapter 10 reviews issues related to the fact that in many transnational cases more than one forum may have jurisdiction over the dispute. Chapter 11 examines the doctrine of foreign sovereign immunity that arises when suit is brought against a foreign government or its agencies, instrumentalities, and officials. Chapter 12 looks at various doctrines that may limit the ability to bring transnational cases that affect U.S. foreign policy. Finally, Chapter 13 takes a look at how one conducts discovery in transnational cases.

CHAPTER 9

TRANSNATIONAL SERVICE OF PROCESS

It is important to remember that identifying the governing law and appropriate forum is but one step, albeit an important one, in actually litigating a transnational case. To start the process in motion, the plaintiff (or the plaintiff's lawyer) has to draft a complaint, file it with a court, and serve it (along with a summons) on the defendant. As you may recall from Civil Procedure, service of process is the name for the formal delivery of documents that provide a defendant with notice of a suit. In the United States, constitutional protections of due process require that the notice provided be reasonably calculated to alert a defendant of the action and afford her an opportunity to defend. *Mullane v. Central Hanover Bank & Trust Co.*, 339 U.S. 306, 314 (1950).

A. Overview: Service of Process Under U.S. Law and the Hague Service Convention

In the United States, service of process is governed by the rules of the court in which the action is filed (subject to the requirements of due process). That is, in state court, process is served according to the rules of the particular state, while in federal court, process is served according to the Federal Rules of Civil Procedure. Rule 4 of the Federal Rules describes the acceptable means of effective service of process in U.S. District Court. The requirements vary depending on whether service is on an individual, a corporation, or a government entity, and on whether service is effected within or outside the United States.

Let's begin with a quick review of domestic service under the Federal Rules. Under Rule 4, once the complaint has been drafted and filed with the court, it must be served with a summons on the defendant or defendants. The Federal Rules provide specific guidelines as to these requirements in Rule 4(a)-(j). A plaintiff may request, by notice sent by first class mail, that the defendant waive service of process. Under Rule 4(d)(3), waiving service expands the defendant's time to answer the complaint to 60 days after the request was sent (for defendants in the United States) and 90 days (for defendants outside the United States), instead of the standard 21 days). Under Rule 4(d)(2), a domestic defendant who fails to waive service without good cause may be liable for the plaintiff's costs of effecting service.

If a party does not waive service, the general approach for service on individuals is governed by Rule 4(e) and for corporations by Rule 4(h):

Federal Rules of Civil Procedure

Rule 4(e) SERVING AN INDIVIDUAL WITHIN A JUDICIAL DISTRICT OF THE UNITED STATES. Unless federal law provides otherwise, an individual — other than a minor, an incompetent person, or a person whose waiver has been filed — may be served in a judicial district of the United States by:

(1) following state law for serving a summons in an action brought in courts of general jurisdiction in the state where the district court is located or where service is made; or

(2) doing any of the following:

(A) delivering a copy of the summons and of the complaint to the individual personally;

(B) leaving a copy of each at the individual's dwelling or usual place of abode with someone of suitable age and discretion who resides there; or

(C) delivering a copy of each to an agent authorized by appointment or by law to receive service of process.

Rule 4(h) SERVING A CORPORATION, PARTNERSHIP, OR ASSOCIATION. Unless federal law provides otherwise or the defendant's waiver has been filed, a domestic or foreign corporation, or a partnership or other unincorporated association that is subject to suit under a common name, must be served:

(1) in a judicial district of the United States:

(A) in the manner prescribed by Rule 4(e)(1) for serving an individual; or

(B) by delivering a copy of the summons and of the complaint to an officer, a managing or general agent, or any other agent authorized by appointment or by law to receive service of process and — if the agent is one authorized by statute and the statute so requires — by also mailing a copy of each to the defendant. . . .

Note that Rules 4(e) and 4(h)(1) address service "in a judicial district of the United States" regardless of whether the defendant is a foreign citizen or resident. In contrast, service on individuals, corporations, and partnerships made "at a place not within any judicial district of the United States" is governed by Rule 4(f) and 4(h)(2):

Federal Rules of Civil Procedure

Rule 4(f) SERVING AN INDIVIDUAL IN A FOREIGN COUNTRY. Unless federal law provides otherwise, an individual — other than a minor, an incompetent person, or a person whose waiver has been filed — may be served at a place not within any judicial district of the United States:

(1) by any internationally agreed means of service that is reasonably calculated to give notice, such as those authorized by the Hague Convention on the Service Abroad of Judicial and Extrajudicial Documents;

(2) if there is no internationally agreed means, or if an international agreement allows but does not specify other means, by a method that is reasonably calculated to give notice:

(A) as prescribed by the foreign country's law for service in that country in an action in its courts of general jurisdiction;

(B) as the foreign authority directs in response to a letter rogatory or letter of request; or

(C) unless prohibited by the foreign country's law, by:

(i) delivering a copy of the summons and of the complaint to the individual personally; or

(ii) using any form of mail that the clerk addresses and sends to the individual and that requires a signed receipt; or

(3) by other means not prohibited by international agreement, as the court orders.

Rule 4(h) SERVING A CORPORATION, PARTNERSHIP, OR ASSOCIATION. Unless federal law provides otherwise or the defendant's waiver has been filed, a domestic or foreign corporation, or a partnership or other unincorporated association that is subject to suit under a common name, must be served:

. . .

(2) at a place not within any judicial district of the United States, in any manner prescribed by Rule 4(f) for serving an individual, except personal delivery under (f)(2)(C)(i).

As explained by Rule 4(f), service can be made pursuant to an international treaty, such as the Hague Convention on the Service Abroad of Judicial and Extrajudicial Documents (the Hague Service Convention). In the absence of an international agreement, service can be made within the foreign nation (1) in the manner defendants are ordinarily served within that nation; (2) as directed by that nation in response to a letter rogatory, which is a request from a U.S. court to a court in another nation to perform a judicial act; or (3) unless prohibited by foreign law, for individual defendants, through personal service or mail with signed receipt. Finally, service can be made by other means not prohibited by international agreements as the U.S. court may order. In light of this brief overview, how, if at all, are corporations treated differently?

Before examining cases regarding transnational service of process, it is useful to provide a brief overview of the Hague Service Convention, which will be discussed in the cases that follow.

The Convention is the most commonly used method for serving parties in civil and commercial matters outside the United States. It is an international treaty that seeks to codify procedures for service of process among the parties to the Convention and eliminate the need for service through consular or diplomatic channels. Currently over 75 nations are parties to the Convention, although not all of them have agreed to all of its methods of service. For more information on the Convention, see https://www.hcch.net/en/instruments/conventions/full-text/?cid=17. Another important internationally agreed means of service is the Inter-American Convention on Letters Rogatory, which is modeled on the Hague Service Convention. For more information on that Convention, see https://www.oas.org/juridico/english/treaties/b-36.html.

The Hague Service Convention requires each member nation to establish a Central Authority to receive requests for service of documents from other parties to the Convention. Art. 2. The Central Authority must, upon receiving the request, serve the documents under applicable local law or by another means requested by the applicant, so long as that way is compatible with local law. Art. 5. Once service is effected, the Central Authority must return a certificate of service to the requesting party, which may then be filed in the U.S. court. If the document cannot be served, the Central Authority must provide a certificate setting out the reasons preventing service. The Convention also allows service by international registered mail or direct service through an agent in the destination state, although many parties to the Convention have opted out of these provisions.

So long as the request for service complies with the terms of the Hague Service Convention, the nation addressed may not refuse to effect service unless it deems that compliance with the request would infringe on its sovereignty or security. The Convention specifically provides that the nation addressed may *not* refuse to comply based solely on the ground that it claims exclusive jurisdiction over the subject matter of the action or that its internal law would not permit the action on which the application is based. The Convention only applies in civil or commercial proceedings.

When contemplating service under the Hague Service Convention, it is important to note that the procedures for different countries vary widely and, when faced with a defendant who can be found in multiple countries, it is critical to consider these differences when deciding where to serve the defendant. Some countries, such as Israel and Germany, take a much more formalistic approach to service under the Hague Convention than others, such as France. These formal distinctions can make a significant difference. For example, Article 10(a) of the Hague Convention specifically permits sending judicial documents by mail unless the signatory nation has objected to such service. It may be possible to effect service in a nonobjecting nation such as France by a letter sent via registered mail, whereas service in neighboring Germany (which has objected) would require service through the Central Authority.

Practice Tip: The Hague Service Convention is intended to provide uniformity of practice among most of its signatories, but some countries have made specific reservations and declarations regarding particular methods of service. Practitioners must be aware of them and their impact on service in a nation that has ratified the Convention subject to them. A list of member nations and their declarations and reservations is maintained in the "status table" available at the Convention's website, https://www.hcch.net/en/instruments/conventions/status-table/?cid=17.

Let's now examine some common issues related to transnational service of process: (1) Are you effecting transnational service? (Section B); (2) How do you effect service under the Hague Service Convention? (Section C); and (3) How do you effect transnational service outside the Convention framework? (Section D).

B. Domestic versus Transnational Service of Process

A threshold question for service in a transnational case is whether you need to effect transnational service at all. Recall that the Federal Rules (and the rules of most U.S. states) turn on the *place* where service is made, not the residence or citizenship of the person or entity being served. As to a foreign individual, for example, U.S. rules of "tag" service allow service if the individual visits the United States and is presented with the documents while present in the United States (look at Rule 4(e) above to see why this is true). State and federal law also provide other ways to serve transnational defendants within the United States.

In contrast, a different set of rules likely applies when service is made outside the United States. (Look at Rule 4(f) above to see why this is true in federal court.) In addition to Rule 4(f), as set forth in the next case, the Hague Service Convention provides in Article 1 that it "shall apply in all cases, in civil or commercial matters, where there is occasion to transmit a judicial or extrajudicial document for service abroad." While it may often be clear where service is being made, that is not always true, as the next case illustrates.

Volkswagenwerk Aktiengesellschaft v. Schlunk

486 U.S. 694 (1988)

Justice O'CONNOR delivered the opinion of the Court.

This case involves an attempt to serve process on a foreign corporation by serving its domestic subsidiary which, under state law, is the foreign corporation's involuntary agent for service of process. We must decide whether such service is compatible with the Convention on Service Abroad of Judicial and Extrajudicial Documents in Civil and Commercial Matters, Nov. 15, 1965 (Hague Service Convention), [1969] 20 U.S.T. 361, T.I.A.S. No. 6638.

I

The parents of respondent Herwig Schlunk were killed in an automobile accident in 1983. Schlunk filed a wrongful death action on their behalf in the Circuit Court of Cook County, Illinois. Schlunk alleged that Volkswagen of America,

Inc. (VWoA), had designed and sold the automobile that his parents were driving, and that defects in the automobile caused or contributed to their deaths. . . . Schlunk successfully served his complaint on VWoA, and VWoA filed an answer denying that it had designed or assembled the automobile in question. Schlunk then amended the complaint to add as a defendant Volkswagen Aktiengesellschaft (VWAG), which is the petitioner here. VWAG, a corporation established under the laws of the Federal Republic of Germany, has its place of business in that country. VWoA is a wholly owned subsidiary of VWAG. Schlunk attempted to serve his amended complaint on VWAG by serving VWoA as VWAG's agent.

VWAG filed a special and limited appearance for the purpose of quashing service. VWAG asserted that it could be served only in accordance with the Hague Service Convention, and that Schlunk had not complied with the Convention's requirements. The Circuit Court denied VWAG's motion. It first observed that VWoA is registered to do business in Illinois and has a registered agent for receipt of process in Illinois. The court then reasoned that VWoA and VWAG are so closely related that VWoA is VWAG's agent for service of process as a matter of law, notwithstanding VWAG's failure or refusal to appoint VWoA formally as an agent. The court relied on the facts that VWoA is a wholly owned subsidiary of VWAG, that a majority of the members of the board of directors of VWoA are members of the board of VWAG, and that VWoA is by contract the exclusive importer and distributor of VWAG products sold in the United States. The court concluded that, because service was accomplished within the United States, the Hague Service Convention did not apply.

. . . For reasons similar to those given by the Circuit Court, the Appellate Court determined that VWoA is VWAG's agent for service of process under Illinois law, and that the service of process in this case did not violate the Hague Service Convention. After the Supreme Court of Illinois denied VWAG leave to appeal, VWAG petitioned this Court for a writ of certiorari to review the Appellate Court's interpretation of the Hague Service Convention. We granted certiorari to address this issue. . . .

II

The Hague Service Convention is a multilateral treaty that was formulated in 1964 by the Tenth Session of the Hague Conference of Private International Law. . . . [It] was intended to provide a simpler way to serve process abroad, to assure that defendants sued in foreign jurisdictions would receive actual and timely notice of suit, and to facilitate proof of service abroad. . . .

The primary innovation of the Convention is that it requires each state to establish a central authority to receive requests for service of documents from other countries. 20 U.S.T. 362, T.I.A.S. 6638, Art. 2. Once a central authority receives a request in the proper form, it must serve the documents by a method prescribed by the internal law of the receiving state or by a method designated by the requester and compatible with that law. Art. 5. The central authority must then provide a certificate of service that conforms to a specified model. Art. 6. A state also may consent to methods of service within its boundaries other than a request to its central authority. Arts. 8-11, 19. The remaining provisions of the Convention that are relevant here limit the circumstances in which a default judgment may be entered against a defendant who had to be served abroad and did not appear, and provide some means for relief from such a judgment. Arts. 15, 16.

Article 1 defines the scope of the Convention, which is the subject of controversy in this case. It says: "The present Convention shall apply in all cases, in civil or commercial matters, where there is occasion to transmit a judicial or extra-judicial document for service abroad." 20 U.S.T., at 362. The equally authentic French version says, "La présente Convention est applicable, en matière civile ou commerciale, dans tous les cas où un acte judiciaire ou extrajudiciaire doit être transmis à l'étranger pour y être signifié ou notifié." *Ibid.* . . . This language is mandatory. . . . By virtue of the Supremacy Clause, U.S. Const., Art. VI, the Convention pre-empts inconsistent methods of service prescribed by state law in all cases to which it applies. Schlunk does not purport to have served his complaint on VWAG in accordance with the Convention. Therefore, if service of process in this case falls within Article 1 of the Convention, the trial court should have granted VWAG's motion to quash.

When interpreting a treaty, we begin with the text of the treaty and the context in which the written words are used. Other general rules of construction may be brought to bear on difficult or ambiguous passages. Treaties are construed more liberally than private agreements, and to ascertain their meaning we may look beyond the written words to the history of the treaty, the negotiations, and the practical construction adopted by the parties.

The Convention does not specify the circumstances in which there is "occasion to transmit" a complaint "for service abroad." But at least the term "service of process" has a well-established technical meaning. Service of process refers to a formal delivery of documents that is legally sufficient to charge the defendant with notice of a pending action. The legal sufficiency of a formal delivery of documents must be measured against some standard. The Convention does not prescribe a standard, so we almost necessarily must refer to the internal law of the forum state. If the internal law of the forum state defines the applicable method of serving process as requiring the transmittal of documents abroad, then the Hague Service Convention applies.

. . .

[We are not persuaded] that the general purposes of the Convention require a different conclusion. One important objective of the Convention is to provide means to facilitate service of process abroad. Thus the first stated purpose of the Convention is "to create" appropriate means for service abroad, and the second stated purpose is "to improve the organization of mutual judicial assistance for that purpose by simplifying and expediting the procedure." 20 U.S.T., at 362. By requiring each state to establish a central authority to assist in the service of process, the Convention implements this enabling function. Nothing in our decision today interferes with this requirement.

VWAG correctly maintains that the Convention also aims to ensure that there will be adequate notice in cases in which there is occasion to serve process abroad. Thus compliance with the Convention is mandatory in all cases to which it applies, and Articles 15 and 16 provide an indirect sanction against those who ignore it. Our interpretation of the Convention does not necessarily advance this particular objective, inasmuch as it makes recourse to the Convention's means of service dependent on the forum's internal law. But we do not think that this country, or any other country, will draft its internal laws deliberately so as to circumvent the Convention in cases in which it would be appropriate to transmit judicial documents for service abroad. For example, there has been no question in this country of excepting foreign nationals from the protection of our Due Process Clause. Under that Clause, foreign nationals are assured of either personal service, which typically will require service abroad and trigger the Convention, or substituted service that provides "notice reasonably calculated, under all the circumstances, to apprise interested parties of the pendency of the action and afford them an opportunity to present their objections." *Mullane v. Central Hanover Bank & Trust Co.*, 339 U.S. 306, 314 (1950).

Furthermore, nothing that we say today prevents compliance with the Convention even when the internal law of the forum does not so require. The Convention provides simple and certain means by which to serve process on a foreign national. Those who eschew its procedures risk discovering that the forum's internal law required transmittal of documents for service abroad, and that the Convention therefore provided the exclusive means of valid service. In addition, parties that comply with the Convention ultimately may find it easier to enforce their judgments abroad. For these reasons, we anticipate that parties may resort to the Convention voluntarily, even in cases that fall outside the scope of its mandatory application.

III

In this case, the Illinois long-arm statute authorized Schlunk to serve VWAG by substituted service on VWoA, without sending documents to Germany. See Ill. Rev. Stat., ch. 110, ¶ 2-209(a)(1) (1985). VWAG has not petitioned for review of the Illinois Appellate Court's holding that service was proper as a matter of Illinois law. VWAG contends, however, that service on VWAG was not complete until VWoA transmitted the complaint to VWAG in Germany. According to VWAG, this transmission constituted service abroad under the Hague Service Convention.

VWAG explains that, as a practical matter, VWoA was certain to transmit the complaint to Germany to notify VWAG of the litigation. Indeed, as a legal matter, the Due Process Clause requires every method of service to provide "notice reasonably calculated, under all the circumstances, to apprise interested parties of the pendency of the action and afford them an opportunity to present their objections." *Mullane v. Central Hanover Bank & Trust Co., supra*, at 314. VWAG argues that, because of this notice requirement, every case involving service on a foreign national will present an "occasion to transmit a judicial . . . document for service abroad" within the meaning of Article 1. VWAG emphasizes that in this case, the Appellate Court upheld service only after determining that "the relationship between VWAG and VWoA is so close that it is certain that VWAG was fully apprised of the pendency of the action by delivery of the summons to VWoA." 145 Ill. App. 3d, at 606.

We reject this argument. Where service on a domestic agent is valid and complete under both state law and the Due Process Clause, our inquiry ends and the Convention has no further implications. Whatever internal, private communications take place between the agent and a foreign principal are beyond the concerns of this case. The only transmittal to which the Convention applies is a transmittal abroad that is required as a necessary part of service. And, contrary to VWAG's assertion, the Due Process Clause does not require an official transmittal of documents abroad every time there is service on a foreign national. Applying this analysis, we conclude that this case does not present an occasion to transmit a judicial document for service abroad within the meaning of Article 1. Therefore the Hague Service Convention does not apply, and service was proper. The judgment of the Appellate Court is
   Affirmed.

[A concurring opinion of Justice Brennan, with whom Justices Marshall and Blackmun joined, is omitted.]

NOTES AND QUESTIONS

1. **The Hague Service Convention and State Law.** Note that the claim in *Schlunk* was filed in Illinois state court. Assuming the Illinois service rules do not refer to the Hague Service Convention, why would the Convention govern service in Illinois courts? *When* will it govern service in Illinois courts?
2. **Domestic Service on Transnational Defendants.** According to the Court, why doesn't the Hague Service Convention apply in *Schlunk*? Is the Court's reasoning persuasive? Or does its reasoning provide too many opportunities for an end-run around the Convention? Are there any limits on what state law can authorize for service of process in transnational cases?
3. **Application of the Convention to Transnational Defendants.** In light of *Schlunk*, when does the Hague Service Convention apply to service on transnational defendants? What would have been the result if Illinois law did not provide for "substituted service" on VWoA in the United States? What would have been the result if the *Schlunk* litigation had been filed in federal court? (To answer this question, review the excerpts from the Federal Rules of Civil Procedure in the prior section.)
4. **From Doctrine to Practice.** Why would the plaintiff prefer to serve process under the state rules instead of the Hague Service Convention? What are the advantages and disadvantages of each approach?
5. **What If the Convention Applies, But It Is Not Followed?** Failure to follow the Hague Service Convention may lead to the defendant filing a motion to dismiss for improper service under Rule 12(b)(5) or its equivalent under state law. Courts have taken different approaches to resolving such motions. Some courts have dismissed the case, even if another form of notice was given. Other courts have held that so long as some form of adequate notice is received then

the case should not be dismissed. In light of this, why would it be important to follow the Convention? As Chapter 7 discusses, inadequate service is also a grounds for nonenforcement of a judgment in some jurisdictions. How does that relate to the importance of following the Convention?

C. Service Under the Hague Service Convention

When the Convention applies, how does it operate? To answer this question, let's begin by looking at the Convention.

Convention on the Service Abroad of Judicial and Extrajudicial Documents in Civil or Commercial Matters

658 U.N.T.S. 163 (Nov. 15, 1965)

The States signatory to the present Convention,

Desiring to create appropriate means to ensure that judicial and extrajudicial documents to be served abroad shall be brought to the notice of the addressee in sufficient time,

Desiring to improve the organisation of mutual judicial assistance for that purpose by simplifying and expediting the procedure,

Have resolved to conclude a Convention to this effect and have agreed upon the following provisions:

Article 1

The present Convention shall apply in all cases, in civil or commercial matters, where there is occasion to transmit a judicial or extrajudicial document for service abroad.

This Convention shall not apply where the address of the person to be served with the document is not known.

Chapter I — Judicial Documents

Article 2

Each Contracting State shall designate a Central Authority which will undertake to receive requests for service coming from other Contracting States and to proceed in conformity with the provisions of Articles 3 to 6.

Each State shall organise the Central Authority in conformity with its own law.

Article 3

The authority or judicial officer competent under the law of the State in which the documents originate shall forward to the Central Authority of the State addressed a request conforming to the model annexed to the present Convention, without any requirement of legalisation or other equivalent formality.

The document to be served or a copy thereof shall be annexed to the request. The request and the document shall both be furnished in duplicate.

Article 4

If the Central Authority considers that the request does not comply with the provisions of the present Convention it shall promptly inform the applicant and specify its objections to the request.

Article 5

The Central Authority of the State addressed shall itself serve the document or shall arrange to have it served by an appropriate agency, either —

a. by a method prescribed by its internal law for the service of documents in domestic actions upon persons who are within its territory, or
b. by a particular method requested by the applicant, unless such a method is incompatible with the law of the State addressed.

Subject to sub-paragraph (b) of the first paragraph of this Article, the document may always be served by delivery to an addressee who accepts it voluntarily.

If the document is to be served under the first paragraph above, the Central Authority may require the document to be written in, or translated into, the official language or one of the official languages of the State addressed.

That part of the request, in the form attached to the present Convention, which contains a summary of the document to be served, shall be served with the document.

Article 6

The Central Authority of the State addressed or any authority which it may have designated for that purpose, shall complete a certificate in the form of the model annexed to the present Convention.

The certificate shall state that the document has been served and shall include the method, the place and the date of service and the person to whom the document was delivered. If the document has not been served, the certificate shall set out the reasons which have prevented service.

The applicant may require that a certificate not completed by a Central Authority or by a judicial authority shall be countersigned by one of these authorities.

The certificate shall be forwarded directly to the applicant.

. . .

Article 8

Each Contracting State shall be free to effect service of judicial documents upon persons abroad, without application of any compulsion, directly through its diplomatic or consular agents.

Any State may declare that it is opposed to such service within its territory, unless the document is to be served upon a national of the State in which the documents originate.

Article 9

Each Contracting State shall be free, in addition, to use consular channels to forward documents, for the purpose of service, to those authorities of another Contracting State which are designated by the latter for this purpose.

Each Contracting State may, if exceptional circumstances so require, use diplomatic channels for the same purpose.

Article 10

Provided the State of destination does not object, the present Convention shall not interfere with —

a. the freedom to send judicial documents, by postal channels, directly to persons abroad,
b. the freedom of judicial officers, officials or other competent persons of the State of origin to effect service of judicial documents directly through the judicial officers, officials or other competent persons of the State of destination,
c. the freedom of any person interested in a judicial proceeding to effect service of judicial documents directly through the judicial officers, officials or other competent persons of the State of destination.

Article 11

The present Convention shall not prevent two or more Contracting States from agreeing to permit, for the purpose of service of judicial documents, channels of transmission other than those provided for in the preceding Articles and, in particular, direct communication between their respective authorities.

. . .

Article 13

Where a request for service complies with the terms of the present Convention, the State addressed may refuse to comply therewith only if it deems that compliance would infringe its sovereignty or security.

It may not refuse to comply solely on the ground that, under its internal law, it claims exclusive jurisdiction over the subject-matter of the action or that its internal law would not permit the action upon which the application is based.

The Central Authority shall, in case of refusal, promptly inform the applicant and state the reasons for the refusal.

Article 14

Difficulties which may arise in connection with the transmission of judicial documents for service shall be settled through diplomatic channels.

. . .

NOTES AND QUESTIONS

1. **Practice: The Convention's Procedures.** As an attorney for a U.S. plaintiff, how and when would you use the Hague Service Convention to serve a defendant in a foreign nation? Make a flowchart of its approach to service of process. What threshold questions must you ask? How confident are you in the Convention's use of a "central authority" for service in each nation? What remedy do you have if the central authority does not act as the Convention envisions? Why might a plaintiff want to avoid the Convention's regime for service?

2. **Practice: Alternatives to the Central Authority.** What alternatives to the central authority mechanism does the Hague Service Convention allow? When are they allowed? Suppose you are serving process on a defendant in Germany. What do you need to investigate? *See* https://www.hcch.net/en/instruments/conventions/status-table/?cid=17 (listing the parties to the Convention and the reservations they have made to its procedures).

3. **Practice: Alternatives to the Convention.** What if a nation consistently fails to allow service through the Hague Service Convention? In 2003, Russia "unilaterally suspended all judicial cooperation with the United States in civil and commercial matters." *Nuance Communications, Inc. v. Abbyy Software House*, 626 F.3d 1222, 1238 (Fed. Cir. 2010). In light of this, a number of courts approved alternative service methods, even without a prior (and most likely pointless) attempt to serve through the Convention. *E.g.*, *id.* at 1239; *In re Potash Antitrust Litig.*, 667 F. Supp. 2d 907, 931 (N.D. Ill. 2009); *Arista Records LLC v. Media Servs. LLC*, 69 Fed. R. Serv. 3d 1623 (S.D.N.Y. 2008). What provision of the Federal Rules allows this? As a plaintiff's attorney, how would you proceed?

4. **Policy.** What is the policy behind the Hague Service Convention? Is it achieved by the framework adopted?

Another common question is how the Hague Service Convention and the Federal Rules of Civil Procedure work together. The next case considers this question.

Brockmeyer v. May

383 F.3d 798 (9th Cir. 2004)

WILLIAM A. FLETCHER, Circuit Judge:

Plaintiffs in this case attempted to serve process on an English defendant by using ordinary first class mail to send a summons and complaint from the United States to England. We join the Second Circuit in concluding that the Convention on the Service Abroad of Judicial and Extrajudicial Documents ("Hague Convention," or the "Convention") does not prohibit — or, in the words of the Convention, does not "interfere with" — service of process by international mail. But this conclusion tells us only that the Hague Convention does not prohibit such service. For service by international mail to be effective in federal court, it must also be affirmatively authorized by some provision in federal law.

Federal Rule of Civil Procedure 4 governs service of process in federal district court. In this case, after determining that the Hague Convention does not prohibit service by international mail, the necessary next step is to analyze Rule 4(f) to determine whether it affirmatively authorizes such service. The plaintiffs' attempted service fails because they failed to follow the requirements of that rule. We therefore reverse and remand to the district court with instructions to vacate the judgment.

I. Background: Plaintiffs' Attempts to Serve Process

Ronald B. Brockmeyer is the owner of [a] trademark, under which he publishes and distributes adult entertainment media and novelties. On August 3, 1998, Brockmeyer and his company, Eromedia, filed suit against Marquis Publications, Ltd. ("Marquis") and several other defendants in federal district court in the Southern District of New York, alleging trademark infringement and various state-law causes of action. Marquis is a company registered under British law. Plaintiffs' counsel made two attempts to serve on Marquis.

Plaintiffs' counsel made his first attempt on October 7, 1998. He sent the summons and complaint, together with a request for waiver of service, by ordinary first class mail to a post office box in England. Marquis did not respond.

. . .

Plaintiffs' counsel made his second attempt at service . . . on October 21, 1999. This time, instead of sending the summons and complaint together with a request for waiver of service, he sent only the summons and complaint. He sent them by first class mail to the same post office box in England to which he had previously sent the request for waiver. Marquis still did not respond.

Default was entered by the court clerk against several defendants (not including Marquis) on November 24, 1999. Default was entered against Marquis a year later, on November 8, 2000. On February 22, 2002, the district court entered a default judgment of $410,806.12, plus attorneys' fees and costs, against Marquis and two German defendants.

The German defendants moved to set aside the default judgment against them. On June 6, 2002, the district court granted the motion on the ground that they had not been properly served under the Hague Convention and German law. The court ordered plaintiffs to serve the German defendants properly within 90 days or face dismissal. The district court subsequently gave plaintiffs a two-month extension until November 4, 2002. Seven days before the expiration of the extended deadline, plaintiffs' counsel finally submitted documents to the German Central Authority for service. The Central Authority rejected the documents the same day for failure to comply with German law. Almost two months later, plaintiffs' counsel resubmitted documents to the German Central Authority. Nothing in the record indicates whether these resubmitted documents complied with German law. On January 2, 2003, the district court dismissed the suit against the German defendants for failure to serve process within the time allowed under the extended deadline. Plaintiffs have not appealed that dismissal.

Marquis moved independently to set aside the default judgment against it. Among other things, Marquis contended that international mail service must be made by certified or registered mail. On June 26, 2002, the district court denied Marquis's motion, holding that plaintiffs' second attempt at service had been successful. It ruled that mail service is not forbidden by the Hague Convention, and that service on an English defendant by ordinary international first class mail is proper.

Marquis appeals the district court's denial of its motion to set aside plaintiffs' default judgment. . . . Once service is challenged, plaintiffs bear the burden of establishing that service was valid under Rule 4.

II. Discussion

A. The Hague Convention

The resolution of this appeal depends on whether Marquis was properly served. Because service of process was attempted abroad, the validity of that service is controlled by the Hague Convention, to the extent that the Convention applies. *Volkswagenwerk Aktiengesellschaft v. Schlunk*, 486 U.S. 694, 705 (1988) ("[C]ompliance with the Convention is mandatory in all cases to which it applies.").

The Hague Convention, ratified by the United States in 1965, regularized and liberalized service of process in international civil suits. The primary means by which service is accomplished under the Convention is through a receiving country's "Central Authority." The Convention affirmatively requires each member country to designate a Central Authority to receive documents from another member country. *See* Hague Convention, art. 2. The receiving country can impose certain requirements with respect to those documents (for example, that they be translated into the language of that country). *See id.*, art. 5. If the documents comply with applicable requirements, the Convention affirmatively requires the Central Authority to effect service in its country. *See id.*, arts. 4 & 5.

The Convention also provides that it does not "interfere with" other methods of serving documents. Article 10(a) of the Convention recites: "Provided the State of destination does not object, the present Convention shall *not interfere with* — (a) the freedom to *send* judicial documents, by postal channels, directly to persons abroad." (Emphasis added.) American courts have disagreed about whether the phrase "the freedom to *send* judicial documents" in Article 10(a) includes within its meaning the freedom to *serve* judicial documents.

. . .

Today we join the Second Circuit in holding that the meaning of "send" in Article 10(a) includes "serve." *See Ackermann* [*v. Levine*], 788 F.2d [830] at 838 [(2d Cir. 1986)]. In so doing, we also join the essentially unanimous view of other member countries of the Hague Convention. . . .

We agree with the Second Circuit that this holding is consistent with the purpose of the Convention to facilitate international service of judicial documents. . . .

. . .

The United States government, through the State Department, has specifically disapproved [of decisions to the contrary]. . . .

State Department circulars also indicate that service by mail is permitted in international civil litigation. *See, e.g.,* U.S. Dep't of State, *Circular: Service of Process Abroad, in Selected Materials in Int'l Litig. and Arbitration,* 688 PLI/Lit. 777, 1021 (2003). The State Department circular tailored to the United Kingdom specifies that mail service by international registered mail is allowed.

The purpose and history of the Hague Convention, as well as the position of the U.S. State Department, convince us that "send" in Article 10(a) includes "serve." We therefore hold that the Convention permits — or, in the words of the Convention, does not "interfere with" — service of process by international mail, so long as the receiving country does not object.

B. Rule 4(f): "Service Upon Individuals in a Foreign Country"

Article 10(a) does not itself affirmatively authorize international mail service. It merely provides that the Convention "shall not interfere with" the "freedom" to use postal channels if the "State of destination" does not object to their use. As the Rapporteur for the Convention wrote in explaining Article 10(a), "It should be stressed that in permitting the utilization of postal channels, . . . the draft convention did not intend to pass on the validity of this mode of transmission under the law of the forum state: *in order for the postal channel to be utilized, it is necessary that it be authorized by the law of the forum state.*" 1 Ristau § 4-3-5, at 205 (emphasis added) (quoting Service Convention Negotiating Document); *see also id.* at 162 ("Even though a contracting state may not object to methods of service of foreign judicial documents in its territory in a manner other than as provided for in the Convention . . . it is still necessary that the law of the state where the action is pending authorize the particular method of service employed.") (emphasis added).

In other words, we must look outside the Hague Convention for affirmative authorization of the international mail service that is merely not forbidden by

Article 10(a). Any affirmative authorization of service by international mail, and any requirements as to how that service is to be accomplished, must come from the law of the forum in which the suit is filed.

Federal Rule of Civil Procedure 4(h)(2) directs that service on a foreign corporation, if done outside of the United States, shall be effected "in any manner prescribed for individuals by subdivision [4](f) except personal delivery as provided in paragraph (2)(C)(i) thereof," unless a waiver of service has been obtained and filed. No waiver of service under Rule 4(d) was obtained in this case. To determine whether service of process was proper, we therefore look to Federal Rule of Civil Procedure 4(f). As will be seen, no part of Rule 4(f) authorizes service by ordinary international first class mail.

1. Rule 4(f)(1)

Rule 4(f)(1) authorizes service by those methods of service authorized by international agreements, including the Hague Convention. . . .

The Hague Convention affirmatively authorizes service of process through the Central Authority of a receiving state. Rule 4(f)(1), by incorporating the Convention, in turn affirmatively authorizes use of a Central Authority. However, Rule 4(f)(1) does not go beyond means of service affirmatively authorized by international agreements. It is undisputed that Brockmeyer did not use either the Central Authority under the Hague Convention or any other internationally agreed means for accomplishing service. Rule 4(f)(1), therefore, does not provide a basis for service in this case.

2. Rule 4(f)(2)(C)(ii)

Explicit, affirmative authorization for service by international mail is found only in Rule 4(f)(2)(C)(ii) (previously Rule 4(i)(1)(D)). This rule authorizes service abroad by mail for which a signed receipt is required, when such mail is addressed and mailed by the clerk of the federal district court in which the suit is filed. . . .

It is undisputed that the plaintiffs in this case did not comply with the requirements of Rule 4(f)(2)(C)(ii), as notice was not sent by the clerk of the district court, nor by a form of mail requiring a signed receipt. Rule 4(f)(2)(C)(ii) therefore does not provide a basis for service in this case.

3. Rule 4(f)(3)

Rule 4(f)(3) (previously Rule 4(i)(1)(E)) affirmatively authorizes the federal district court to direct any form of service that is not prohibited by an international agreement. . . .

. . .

Courts have authorized a variety of alternative methods of service abroad under current Rule 4(f)(3) and former Rule 4(i)(1)(E), including not only ordinary mail and e-mail but also publication and telex. However, . . . plaintiffs are required to take a step that the plaintiffs in this case failed to take: They must obtain prior court approval for the alternative method of serving process. Rule 4(f)(3) thus is of no use to plaintiffs in this case.

4. Rule 4(f)(2)(A)

Because it is undisputed in this case that the plaintiffs neither effected service under the Hague Convention or other international agreement in accordance with Rule 4(f)(1), nor effected service by registered mail by the clerk of the court in accordance with the requirements of Rule 4(f)(2)(C)(ii), nor obtained a court order in accordance with Rule 4(f)(3), the only remaining section on which plaintiffs can conceivably rely is Rule 4(f)(2)(A). Rule 4(f)(2)(A) (previously Rule 4(i)(1)(A)) affirmatively authorizes service by means used in the receiving country for service in an action in its courts of general jurisdiction. As we read Rule 4(f)(2)(A), such means do not include service by international mail.

. . .

The district court held that service was proper because the United Kingdom allows service for domestic suits in that country by both ordinary and registered post. A number of factors counsel against reading Rule 4(f)(2)(A) to authorize service by international mail, however.

First, the common understanding of Rule 4(f)(2)(A) is that it is limited to personal service. A well-known example of service under Rule 4(f)(2)(A) is "substituted service in Italy by delivery to the concierge of the building where the person to be served lives, as long as the method of service is likely to give the actual notice required by United States due process concepts." Gary N. Horlick, *A Practical Guide to Service of United States Process Abroad*, 14 Int'l Law. 637, 640 (1980) (interpreting previous Rule 4(i)(1)(A) (1963)). Consistent with this example, courts have applied Rule 4(f)(2)(A) to approve personal service carried out in accordance with foreign law.

Another reason to read Rule 4(f)(2)(A) not to authorize service by international mail is the explicit mention of international registered mail in Rule 4(f)(2)(C)(ii), considered above, and the absence of any such mention in Rule 4(f)(2)(A). Indeed, the Advisory Committee Note to Rule 4(i)(1)(D), Rule 4(f)(2)(C)(ii)'s nearly identical predecessor, stated that "service by mail is proper *only* when it is addressed to the party to be served and a form of mail requiring a signed receipt is used." (emphasis added).

A further reason to read Rule 4(f)(2)(A) not to authorize service on foreign defendants by international mail to England — and, in particular, by ordinary international first class mail — is found in an exchange between the British government and the United States Department of State in 1991, in which the British objected to a then-proposed revision to Federal Rule of Civil Procedure 4. As amended, this proposal eventually became what is now Rule 4(d), authorizing a plaintiff to request a waiver of service.

Current Rule 4(d) allows a plaintiff to send a summons and complaint by ordinary first class mail, with a request for waiver of service. If the defendant agrees to waive service, the defendant's waiver has the same effect as actual service. Waiver of service under Rule 4(d) is valid for both domestic and foreign defendants. As originally proposed in 1989, Rule 4(d) would have assessed costs incurred in effecting service against all defendants who failed to waive service, including defendants outside the United States. The British government strongly objected to assessment of costs against non-waiving defendants living in the United Kingdom. *See*

Letter from Edwin D. Williamson, Legal Adviser, U.S. Dep't of State, to Chief Justice Rehnquist (April 19, 1991) ("Williamson letter"). The British Embassy transmitted to the State Department a diplomatic note expressing its objection, which the State Department in turn forwarded to Chief Justice Rehnquist.

The diplomatic note stated, in relevant part: "The proposed new paragraph (d)(2) of Rule 4 would impose on a defendant who has received notice of the commencement of the action a duty to waive service of the summons. Inasmuch as this procedure, which would coerce a waiver of service of the summons, would be equally applicable to United Kingdom citizens resident in the United Kingdom, the British Government would object to it. The waiver system would conflict with the Hague Service Convention, and it would be oppressive, since agreement would be elicited under the threat of the proposed sanction in costs. . . ." [T]he British Government would object to the proposed waiver system for commencing proceedings against those resident in the United Kingdom. The proposed system would, moreover, run contrary to the public policy of the United Kingdom, which is that litigation affecting persons resident in the United Kingdom and commenced in foreign jurisdictions should be properly documented in public form.

The Supreme Court returned the proposal to the Civil Rules Advisory Committee for further study "in the light of various comments that had been received, most notably from the British Embassy." 146 F.R.D. 515 (1992) (Excerpt from the Report of the Judicial Conference Committee on Rules of Practice and Procedure). In response, the Advisory Committee revised the proposed rule to eliminate the provision assessing costs of service against foreign defendants that decline to waive service. The Committee specifically explained that its revision addressed concerns raised by the British government.

The objection of the British government to the proposed rule makes sense only if the British government understood Rule 4(f) not to permit service by ordinary, international first class mail against a defendant in England. This is so because if Rule 4(f)(2)(A) had authorized service by international first class mail, a plaintiff would never need to send a request for waiver of service by international first class mail. The plaintiff would simply *effect service* by international first class mail.

The purpose of Rule 4(f)(2)(A) supports our interpretation of the exchange between the British Embassy and the State Department and our conclusion that the rule does not authorize ordinary international mail service to England. According to the 1963 Committee Notes accompanying Rule 4(i)(1)(A), the predecessor to Rule 4(f)(2)(A), the purpose of the Rule is to provide an alternative method of service "that is likely to create least objection in the place of service." From the exchange, it is clear that an interpretation of Rule 4(f)(2)(A) permitting service of process on an English defendant by ordinary first class mail sent from the United States is not "likely to create least objection in the place of service." Rather, this exchange shows us that such an interpretation is likely to create a substantial objection.

Finally, we have found no cases upholding service of process by international mail under Rule 4(f)(2)(A). Rather, there are a number of cases *rejecting* service of process by international mail under that rule. *See, e.g., Prewitt Enters. v. OPEC*, 353 F.3d 916, 925 (11th Cir. 2003) (rejecting plaintiff's argument that

Rule 4(f)(2)(A) authorized service of process on OPEC by international registered mail sent to Austria); *Res. Ventures, Inc. v. Res. Mgmt. Int'l*, 42 F. Supp. 2d 423, 430 (D. Del. 1999) (holding that service of process by international registered mail to Indonesia was not an appropriate method of service under Rule 4(f)(2)(A)); *Dee-K Enters. v. Heveafil Sdn. Bhd.*, 174 F.R.D. 376, 378-79 (E.D. Va. 1997) (holding that rule 4(f)(2)(A) was inapplicable to authorize service of process by international mail to Indonesia or Malaysia).

We therefore conclude, along with the other courts that have considered the question, that Rule 4(f)(2)(A) does not authorize service of process by ordinary first class international mail.

Conclusion

Today we join the Second Circuit in holding that the Hague Convention allows service of process by international mail. At the same time, we hold that any service by mail in this case was required to be performed in accordance with the requirements of Rule 4(f). Service by international mail is affirmatively authorized by Rule 4(f)(2)(C)(ii), which requires that service be sent by the clerk of the court, using a form of mail requiring a signed receipt. Service by international mail is also affirmatively authorized by Rule 4(f)(3), which requires that the mailing procedure have been specifically directed by the district court. Service by international mail is not otherwise affirmatively authorized by Rule 4(f). Plaintiffs neither followed the procedure prescribed in Rule 4(f)(2)(C)(ii) nor sought the approval of the district court under Rule 4(f)(3). They simply dropped the complaint and summons in a mailbox in Los Angeles, to be delivered by ordinary, international first class mail. There is no affirmative authorization for such service in Rule 4(f). The attempted service was therefore ineffective, and the default judgment against Marquis cannot stand.

REVERSED and REMANDED, with instructions to VACATE the judgment.

NOTES AND QUESTIONS

1. **The Hague Service Convention and the Federal Rules.** The Hague Service Convention is said to be the exclusive means of service of process in cases to which it applies. Does *Brockmeyer* provide an end-run around that approach? Assuming Article 10(a) does not prohibit service of process by postal channels, what more is required, in the court's view?

2. **The Supreme Court's Resolution.** In *Water Splash, Inc. v. Menon*, 137 S. Ct. 1504 (2017), the Supreme Court resolved the circuit split mentioned in *Brockmeyer* regarding whether service by mail constitutes effective service on a party abroad. The Court unanimously held that Article 10(a) of the Hague Service Convention does not prohibit service of process by mail. But according to the Court, "just because traditional tools of treaty interpretation

unmistakably demonstrate" that service by mail is permitted, "this does not mean that the Convention affirmatively authorizes service by mail. Article 10(a) simply provides that, as long as the receiving state does not object, the Convention does not 'interfere with . . . the freedom' to serve documents through postal channels. In other words, in cases governed by the Hague Service Convention, service by mail is permissible if two conditions are met: first, the receiving state has not objected to service by mail; and second, service by mail is authorized under otherwise-applicable law." *Id.* at 1513. Does this confirm the decision in *Brockmeyer?* On remand, the Texas Court of Appeals held that Texas rules did not permit service by mail to be sent by plaintiff's counsel. *Menon v. Water Splash, Inc.*, 2018 WL 344040 (Tex. App. 2018). Is that consistent with the Supreme Court's holding? Is it consistent with *Brockmeyer?*

3. **The Importance of Declarations and Reservations.** Recall from earlier in this chapter that the Hague Service Convention allows countries to make declarations and reservations to particular provisions. Why is this significant in light of *Brockmeyer* and *Water Splash?* Look again at the "status table," https://www.hcch.net/en/instruments/conventions/status-table/?cid=17. Can you identify countries making declarations or reservations to Article 10? Why does this matter? Did the foreign country in *Brockmeyer* or *Water Splash* have such a declaration or reservation? How do you know?

4. **From Doctrine to Practice: Email Service.** What legal and factual questions would you need to answer to determine whether a particular method of service would be effective? Combining the Federal Rules and the Convention, what does your flowchart look like? What if you wanted to serve a foreign defendant by email or social media — is that allowed by the Convention? Does the Convention apply to service by email? Does sending an email to a defendant in a foreign nation attaching a copy of a summons and the complaint qualify as "service abroad"? (Recall why that matters.) Does the Convention forbid service of process by email? What provision of the Convention might be read to allow service by email? Is that a plausible reading? What else would you need to know? District courts are divided on this point. *E.g., Anova Applied Electronics, Inc. v. Hong King Group, Ltd.*, 2020 WL 419518 (D. Mass. 2020) (Convention does not permit service by email on company located in China); *Lexmark Int'l Inc. v. Ink Technologies Printer Supplies, LLC*, 291 F.R.D. 172 (S.D. Ohio 2013) (Convention allows service by email on company located in China). Which is the better view?

5. **Service on Foreign Sovereigns.** The Foreign Sovereign Immunities Act (FSIA), covered in Chapter 11, provides special rules for serving process on foreign governments and other sovereign entities. These rules are distinct from the Federal Rules and the Hague Convention, and they must be followed precisely. As discussed in Chapter 11, in 2019 the Supreme Court overturned a multi-billion-dollar judgment against the Republic of Sudan on the ground that Sudan was not properly served under the FSIA.

D. International Service Outside of the Convention

How do you effect service abroad when there is no applicable international agreement? (To review: When would there not be an applicable international agreement?) Look again at Federal Rule 4(f) (assuming you are in federal court). In some situations, the course is straightforward. Rule 4(f)(2)(A) allows service "as prescribed by the foreign country's law for service in that country in an action in its courts of general jurisdiction" and Rule 4(f)(2)(C) allows service "unless prohibited by the foreign country's law" by personal delivery or by return-receipt mail. Thus, if the nation in which service is to be made has permissive service rules, in the ordinary case there should not be material difficulties. For example, if the nation, like the United States, generally allows service by personal delivery and by return-receipt mail, these methods can be used.

However, it is important to understand that many nations (especially those with civil law legal systems) have more restrictive or formalistic service requirements. In such situations there may not be any easy way to serve, and resort may have to be made to Rule 4(f)(2)(B), which provides for service "as the foreign authority directs in response to a letter rogatory or letter of request." Letters rogatory are requests from the court of one nation to a court in another nation to perform an act, such as service. Letters rogatory are customarily transmitted by diplomatic channels involving the U.S. State Department, which may entail considerable delays. *See* https://travel.state.gov/content/travel/en/legal/travel-legal-considerations/internl-judicial-asst/Service-of-Process.html (describing letters rogatory as "a time consuming cumbersome process" that "may take a year or more"). There is also no assurance that the foreign authorities will act upon a letter rogatory. As noted above, one purpose of the Hague Service Convention was to limit the need to rely on letters rogatory for service within nations that are parties to it.

Rule 4(f)(3) of the Federal Rules provides an additional avenue for service outside the Hague Service Convention. The next case explores this area.

Rio Properties, Inc. v. Rio International Interlink

284 F.3d 1007 (9th Cir. 2002)

TROTT, Circuit Judge.

Las Vegas hotel and casino operator Rio Properties, Inc. ("RIO") sued Rio International Interlink ("RII"), a foreign Internet business entity, asserting various statutory and common law trademark infringement claims. The district court entered default judgment against RII for failing to comply with the court's discovery orders. RII now appeals the sufficiency of the service of process, effected via email and regular mail pursuant to Federal Rule of Civil Procedure 4(f)(3), the district court's exercise of personal jurisdiction, and ultimately, the entry of default judgment and the award of attorneys' fees and costs. We . . . affirm the district court's decision.

Background

RIO owns the RIO All Suite Casino Resort, the "Best Hotel Value in the World" according to *Travel and Leisure Magazine,* not to mention the "Best Overall Hotel in Las Vegas," according to the *Zagat Survey of Resorts, Hotels and Spas.* In addition to its elegant hotel, RIO's gambling empire consists of the Rio Race & Sports Book, which allows customers to wager on professional sports. To protect its exclusive rights in the "RIO" name, RIO registered numerous trademarks with the United States Patent and Trademark Office. When RIO sought to expand its presence onto the Internet, it registered the domain name, *www.play-rio.com.* At that address, RIO operates a website that informs prospective customers about its hotel and allows those enticed by Lady Luck to make reservations.

RII is a Costa Rican entity that participates in an Internet sports gambling operation, doing business variously as Rio International Sportsbook, Rio Online Sportsbook, or Rio International Sports. RII enables its customers to wager on sporting events online or via a 1-800 telephone number. Far from a penny ante operation, RII grosses an estimated $3 million annually.

RIO became aware of RII's existence by virtue of RII's advertisement in the *Football Betting Guide '98 Preview.* RIO later discovered, in the Nevada edition of the *Daily Racing Form,* another RII advertisement which invited customers to visit RII's website, *www.riosports.com.* RII also ran radio spots in Las Vegas as part of its comprehensive marketing strategy.

Upon learning of RII, RIO fired off an epistle demanding that RII cease and desist from operating the *www.riosports.com* website. Although RII did not formally respond, it promptly disabled the objectionable website. Apparently not ready to cash in its chips, RII soon activated the URL *http://www.betrio.com* to host an identical sports gambling operation. Perturbed, RIO filed the present action alleging various trademark infringement claims and seeking to enjoin RII from the continued use of the name "RIO."

To initiate suit, RIO attempted to locate RII in the United States for service of process. RIO discovered that RII claimed an address in Miami, Florida when it registered the allegedly infringing domain names. As it turned out, however, that address housed only RII's international courier, IEC, which was not authorized to accept service on RII's behalf. Nevertheless, IEC agreed to forward the summons and complaint to RII's Costa Rican courier.

After sending a copy of the summons and complaint through IEC, RIO received a telephone call from Los Angeles attorney John Carpenter ("Carpenter") inquiring about the lawsuit. Apparently, RII received the summons and complaint from IEC and subsequently consulted Carpenter about how to respond. Carpenter indicated that RII provided him with a partially illegible copy of the complaint and asked RIO to send him a complete copy. RIO agreed to resend the complaint and, in addition, asked Carpenter to accept service for RII; Carpenter politely declined. Carpenter did, however, request that RIO notify him upon successful completion of service of process on RII.

Thus thwarted in its attempt to serve RII in the United States, RIO investigated the possibility of serving RII in Costa Rica. Toward this end, RIO searched international directory databases looking for RII's address in Costa Rica. These efforts proved fruitless however; the investigator learned only that RII preferred communication through its email address, *email@betrio.com*, and received snail mail, including payment for its services, at the IEC address in Florida.

Unable to serve RII by conventional means, RIO filed an emergency motion for alternate service of process. RII opted not to respond to RIO's motion. The district court granted RIO's motion, and pursuant to Federal Rules of Civil Procedure 4(h)(2) and 4(f)(3), ordered service of process on RII through the mail to Carpenter and IEC and via RII's email address, *email@betrio.com*.

Court order in hand, RIO served RII by these court-sanctioned methods. RII filed a motion to dismiss for insufficient service of process and lack of personal jurisdiction. The parties fully briefed the issues, and the district court denied RII's motion without a hearing. RII then filed its answer, denying RIO's allegations and asserting twenty-two affirmative defenses.

As the case proceeded, RIO propounded discovery requests and interrogatories on RII. RIO granted RII two informal extensions of time in which to respond. Nonetheless, RII's eventual responses were almost entirely useless, consisting largely of the answer "N/A," ostensibly meaning "Not Applicable." After additional futile attempts to elicit good faith responses from RII, RIO brought a motion to compel discovery. In granting RIO's motion, the district court warned that in the event RII failed to comply, monetary sanctions would be an insufficient remedy and that "preclusive sanctions" would be awarded. When RII failed to comply with the district court's discovery order, RIO moved for terminating sanctions. Although RII belatedly complied, in part, with RIO's discovery request, the district court granted RIO's motion for sanctions and entered default judgment against RII. Citing RII's reprehensible conduct and bad faith, the district court additionally directed RII to pay reasonable attorneys' fees and costs to RIO in the amount of $88,761.50 and $7,859.52 respectively.

RII now appeals the sufficiency of the court-ordered service of process, the district court's exercise of personal jurisdiction as well as the propriety of the default judgment, and the award of attorneys' fees and costs.

Discussion

I. Alternative Service of Process

A. *Applicability of Rule 4(f)(3)*

We review for an abuse of discretion the district court's decision regarding the sufficiency of service of process. Federal Rule of Civil Procedure 4(h)(2) authorizes service of process on a foreign business entity in the manner prescribed by Rule 4(f) for individuals. The subsection of Rule 4(f) relevant to our decision, Rule 4(f)(3), permits service in a place not within any judicial district of the United States "by . . . means not prohibited by international agreement as may be directed by the court."

As obvious from its plain language, service under Rule 4(f)(3) must be (1) directed by the court; and (2) not prohibited by international agreement. No other limitations are evident from the text. In fact, as long as court-directed and not prohibited by an international agreement, service of process ordered under Rule 4(f)(3) may be accomplished in contravention of the laws of the foreign country. *See Mayoral-Amy v. BHI Corp.*, 180 F.R.D. 456, 459 n.4 (S.D. Fla. 1998). *But see* Fed. R. Civ. P. 4(f)(2) advisory committee notes (stating that under Rule 4(f)(2), "[s]ervice by methods that would violate foreign law is not generally authorized").

RII argues that Rule 4(f) should be read to create a hierarchy of preferred methods of service of process. RII's interpretation would require that a party attempt service of process by those methods enumerated in Rule 4(f)(2), including by diplomatic channels and letters rogatory, before petitioning the court for alternative relief under Rule 4(f)(3). We find no support for RII's position. No such requirement is found in the Rule's text, implied by its structure, or even hinted at in the advisory committee notes.

By all indications, court-directed service under Rule 4(f)(3) is as favored as service available under Rule 4(f)(1)[4] or Rule 4(f)(2). Indeed, Rule 4(f)(3) is one of three separately numbered subsections in Rule 4(f), and each subsection is separated from the one previous merely by the simple conjunction "or." Rule 4(f)(3) is not subsumed within or in any way dominated by Rule 4(f)'s other subsections; it stands independently, on equal footing. Moreover, no language in Rules 4(f)(1) or 4(f)(2) indicates their primacy, and certainly Rule 4(f)(3) includes no qualifiers or limitations which indicate its availability only after attempting service of process by other means.

The advisory committee notes ("advisory notes") bolster our analysis. Beyond stating that service ordered under Rule 4(f)(3) must comport with constitutional notions of due process and must not be prohibited by international agreement, the advisory notes indicate the availability of alternate service of process under Rule 4(f)(3) without first attempting service by other means. Specifically, the advisory notes suggest that in cases of "urgency," Rule 4(f)(3) may allow the district court to order a "special method of service," even if other methods of service remain incomplete or unattempted.

Thus, examining the language and structure of Rule 4(f) and the accompanying advisory committee notes, we are left with the inevitable conclusion that service of process under Rule 4(f)(3) is neither a last resort nor extraordinary relief. It is merely one means among several which enables service of process on an international defendant.

. . .

Applying this proper construction of Rule 4(f)(3) and its predecessor, trial courts have authorized a wide variety of alternative methods of service including publication, ordinary mail, mail to the defendant's last known address, delivery to the defendant's attorney, telex, and most recently, email. *See SEC v. Tome*, 833 F.2d 1086, 1094 (2d Cir. 1987) (condoning service of process by publication in the *Int'l Herald Tribune*); *Smith v. Islamic Emirate*, Nos. 01 Civ. 10132, 01 Civ. 10144, 2001

---

4. A federal court would be prohibited from issuing a Rule 4(f)(3) order in contravention of an international agreement, including the Hague Convention referenced in Rule 4(f)(1). The parties agree, however, that the Hague Convention does not apply in this case because Costa Rica is not a signatory.

WL 1658211, at *2-*3, 2001 U.S. Dist. LEXIS 21712, at *5-*13 (S.D.N.Y. Dec. 26, 2001) (authorizing service of process on terrorism impresario Osama bin Laden and al-Qaeda by publication); *Levin v. Ruby Trading Corp.*, 248 F. Supp. 537, 541-44 (S.D.N.Y. 1965) (employing service by ordinary mail); *Int'l Controls Corp. v. Vesco*, 593 F.2d 166, 176-78 (2d Cir. 1979) (approving service by mail to last known address); *Forum Fin. Group*, 199 F.R.D. at 23-24 (authorizing service to defendant's attorney); *New Eng. Merchs. Nat'l Bank v. Iran Power Generation & Transmission Co.*, 495 F. Supp. 73, 80 (S.D.N.Y. 1980) (allowing service by telex for Iranian defendants); *Broadfoot v. Diaz (In re Int'l Telemedia Assoc.)*, 245 B.R. 713, 719-20 (Bankr. N.D. Ga. 2000) (authorizing service via email).

In this case, RIO attempted to serve RII by conventional means in the United States. Although RII claimed an address in Florida, that address housed only IEC, RII's international courier, which refused to accept service of process on RII's behalf. RII's attorney, Carpenter, who was specifically consulted in this matter, also declined to accept service of process. RIO's private investigator subsequently failed to discover RII's whereabouts in Costa Rica. Thus unable to serve RII, RIO brought an emergency motion to effectuate alternative service of process.

Contrary to RII's assertions, RIO need not have attempted every permissible means of service of process before petitioning the court for alternative relief. Instead, RIO needed only to demonstrate that the facts and circumstances of the present case necessitated the district court's intervention. Thus, when RIO presented the district court with its inability to serve an elusive international defendant, striving to evade service of process, the district court properly exercised its discretionary powers to craft alternate means of service. We expressly agree with the district court's handling of this case and its use of Rule 4(f)(3) to ensure the smooth functioning of our courts of law.

B. Reasonableness of the Court Ordered Methods of Service

Even if facially permitted by Rule 4(f)(3), a method of service of process must also comport with constitutional notions of due process. To meet this requirement, the method of service crafted by the district court must be "reasonably calculated, under all the circumstances, to apprise interested parties of the pendency of the action and afford them an opportunity to present their objections." *Mullane v. Cent. Hanover Bank & Trust Co.*, 339 U.S. 306, 314, (1950).

Without hesitation, we conclude that each alternative method of service of process ordered by the district court was constitutionally acceptable. In our view, each method of service was reasonably calculated, under these circumstances, to apprise RII of the pendency of the action and afford it an opportunity to respond.

In particular, service through IEC was appropriate because RII listed IEC's address as its own when registering the allegedly infringing domain name. The record also reflects that RII directed its customers to remit payment to IEC's address. Moreover, when RIO sent a copy of the summons and complaint to RII through IEC, RII received it. All told, this evidence indicates that RII relied heavily upon IEC to operate its business in the United States and that IEC could effectively pass information to RII in Costa Rica.

Service upon Carpenter was also appropriate because he had been specifically consulted by RII regarding this lawsuit. He knew of RII's legal positions, and it seems clear that he was in contact with RII in Costa Rica. Accordingly, service to Carpenter was also reasonably calculated in these circumstances to apprise RII of the pendency of the present action.

Finally, we turn to the district court's order authorizing service of process on RII by email at *email@betrio.com*. We acknowledge that we tread upon untrodden ground. The parties cite no authority condoning service of process over the Internet or via email, and our own investigation has unearthed no decisions by the United States Courts of Appeals dealing with service of process by email and only one case anywhere in the federal courts. Despite this dearth of authority, however, we do not labor long in reaching our decision. Considering the facts presented by this case, we conclude not only that service of process by email was proper — that is, reasonably calculated to apprise RII of the pendency of the action and afford it an opportunity to respond — but in this case, it was the method of service most likely to reach RII.

To be sure, the Constitution does not require any particular means of service of process, only that the method selected be reasonably calculated to provide notice and an opportunity to respond. In proper circumstances, this broad constitutional principle unshackles the federal courts from anachronistic methods of service and permits them entry into the technological renaissance. As noted by the court in *New England Merchants*, in granting permission to effect service of process via telex on Iranian defendants:

> Courts . . . cannot be blind to changes and advances in technology. No longer do we live in a world where communications are conducted solely by mail carried by fast sailing clipper . . . ships. Electronic communication via satellite can and does provide instantaneous transmission of notice and information. No longer must process be mailed to a defendant's door when he can receive complete notice at an electronic terminal inside his very office, even when the door is steel and bolted shut.

495 F. Supp. at 81. We agree wholeheartedly.

Although communication via email and over the Internet is comparatively new, such communication has been zealously embraced within the business community. RII particularly has embraced the modern e-business model and profited immensely from it. In fact, RII structured its business such that it could be contacted *only* via its email address. RII listed no easily discoverable street address in the United States or in Costa Rica. Rather, on its website and print media, RII designated its email address as its preferred contact information.

Unlike the Iranian officials in *New England Merchants*, RII had neither an office nor a door; it had only a computer terminal. If any method of communication is reasonably calculated to provide RII with notice, surely it is email — the method of communication which RII utilizes and prefers. In addition, email was the only court-ordered method of service aimed directly and instantly at RII, as opposed to methods of service effected through intermediaries like IEC and Carpenter. Indeed, when faced with an international e-business scofflaw, playing hide-and-seek with the federal court, email may be the only means of effecting service of process. Certainly in this case, it was a means reasonably calculated to apprise RII of the pendency of the lawsuit, and the Constitution requires nothing more.

. . .

[Affirmed.]

NOTES AND QUESTIONS

1. **Rule 4.** In light of the *Rio* court's analysis, are there any prerequisites to the availability of a Rule 4(f)(3) order?
2. **Avoiding Service of Process.** Note that the defendant in *Rio* was avoiding service. This is precisely the situation the Federal Rules seek to avoid through the waiver provisions. Assume the defendant had been a U.S. domiciliary. Would the result have been different?
3. **The Internet.** Note that at the time *Rio* was decided, Costa Rica was not a party to the Hague Service Convention. Why does that matter? Does it matter for other innovative methods of service such as social media? Could U.S. courts permit service of legal documents via Facebook? If so, under what circumstances? *See FTC v. Pecon Software, Ltd.*, 2013 WL 4016272 (S.D.N.Y. 2013) (permitting service on defendants in India via Facebook messaging and email accounts).
4. **Foreign Law.** Is service in violation of foreign law authorized in light of the *Rio* court's analysis? Does it matter whether the defendant is located in a country that is a party to the Hague Service Convention?

REVIEW NOTES AND QUESTIONS

1. As an attorney bringing a transnational suit, what factual and legal questions do you need to answer to plan your approach to service of process? What do you need to know about the defendant? What do you need to know about the defendant's home nation? What do you need to know about the Hague Service Convention?
2. How aggressive or cautious should you be in serving process? For example, suppose you are in a situation in which the Hague Service Convention indicates service through a nation's central authority. Will you proceed in that way or seek alternatives? What alternatives might there be? What are the risks of seeking alternatives? What are the risks of attempting to serve through the central authority?
3. Suppose you are attempting to serve process in a nation that is not a party to the Hague Service Convention. In what respects is your task more difficult than if the nation was a party to the Convention? Are there any respects in which it might be easier?

CHAPTER 10

ALTERNATIVE FORUMS

It frequently happens in a transnational dispute that more than one forum has jurisdiction over the parties and the controversy. Which forum should be the one to resolve it? That is often a question of great consequence to the parties, because (as discussed in Chapter 4) the procedures, the remedies, and even the applicable law may depend on which forum hears the dispute. This chapter considers three important issues that may arise in the face of multiple potential forums, principally from the perspective of litigation in U.S. courts.

First, a defendant may argue that the forum chosen by the plaintiff, though permissible (in the sense of having jurisdiction) is inconvenient, because the dispute is more closely connected to a different forum. This is typically called *forum non conveniens* (literally, "inconvenient forum").

Second, the claims (or closely related claims) may be filed in more than one forum. This situation is called "parallel proceedings." Here the parties may take several approaches. A party (typically the defendant) may ask one forum to dismiss or stay the proceedings so that the case can go forward in the other forum. This request is often called *lis alibi pendens* (literally, "proceedings pending elsewhere" — or just *lis pendens*) or international abstention. Alternatively, a party (typically the plaintiff) might ask a forum to enjoin the other party from proceeding in the other forum. This request is usually called a motion for an anti-suit injunction.

A third issue arises when the parties appear to have agreed upon a forum that is different from the one in which the suit is filed. This situation usually involves a contract with a forum selection clause — that is, a provision in the contract in which the parties agree to resolve disputes in a specified forum. The question then becomes whether this clause can be enforced by causing the nonselected forum to dismiss the claim in favor of the selected one.

A. *Forum Non Conveniens*

The first case below is the Supreme Court's leading decision on the *forum non conveniens* doctrine. As you read it and the case that follows it, keep litigation strategy in mind. Ask yourself why the plaintiffs filed their lawsuits in the United States, why the defendants preferred to resolve the dispute in a foreign country (and what procedural maneuvers it took to get there), and why the parties cared so much about this transnational forum selection issue.

Piper Aircraft Co. v. Reyno
454 U.S. 235 (1981)

Justice MARSHALL delivered the opinion of the Court.

These cases arise out of an air crash that took place in Scotland. Respondent, acting as representative of the estates of several Scottish citizens killed in the accident, brought wrongful death actions against petitioners that were ultimately transferred to the United States District Court for the Middle District of Pennsylvania. Petitioners moved to dismiss on the ground of *forum non conveniens*. After noting that an alternative forum existed in Scotland, the District Court granted their motions. The United States Court of Appeals for the Third Circuit reversed. The Court of Appeals based its decision, at least in part, on the ground that dismissal is automatically barred where the law of the alternative forum is less favorable to the plaintiff than the law of the forum chosen by the plaintiff. Because we conclude that the possibility of an unfavorable change in law should not, by itself, bar dismissal, and because we conclude that the District Court did not otherwise abuse its discretion, we reverse.

I

A

In July, 1976, a small commercial aircraft crashed in the Scottish highlands during the course of a charter flight from Blackpool to Perth. The pilot and five passengers were killed instantly. The decedents were all Scottish subjects and residents, as are their heirs and next of kin. There were no eyewitnesses to the accident. At the time of the crash, the plane was subject to Scottish air traffic control.

The aircraft, a twin-engine Piper Aztec, was manufactured in Pennsylvania by petitioner Piper Aircraft Co. (Piper). The propellers were manufactured in Ohio by petitioner Hartzell Propeller, Inc. (Hartzell). At the time of the crash, the aircraft was registered in Great Britain and was owned and maintained by Air Navigation and Trading Co., Ltd. (Air Navigation). It was operated by McDonald Aviation, Ltd. (McDonald), a Scottish air taxi service. Both Air Navigation and McDonald were organized in the United Kingdom. The wreckage of the plane is now in a hangar in Farnsborough, England.

The British Department of Trade investigated the accident shortly after it occurred. A preliminary report found that the plane crashed after developing a spin, and suggested that mechanical failure in the plane or the propeller was responsible. At Hartzell's request, this report was reviewed by a three-member Review Board, which held a 9-day adversary hearing attended by all interested parties. The Review Board found no evidence of defective equipment and indicated that pilot error may have contributed to the accident. The pilot, who had obtained his commercial pilot's license only three months earlier, was flying over high ground at an altitude considerably lower than the minimum height required by his company's operations manual.

In July, 1977, a California probate court appointed respondent Gaynell Reyno administratrix of the estates of the five passengers. Reyno is not related to and does not know any of the decedents or their survivors; she was a legal secretary to the attorney who filed this lawsuit. Several days after her appointment, Reyno commenced separate wrongful death actions against Piper and Hartzell in the Superior Court of California, claiming negligence and strict liability. Air Navigation, McDonald, and the estate of the pilot are not parties to this litigation. The survivors of the five passengers whose estates are represented by Reyno filed a separate action in the United Kingdom against Air Navigation, McDonald, and the pilot's estate. Reyno candidly admits that the action against Piper and Hartzell was filed in the United States because its laws regarding liability, capacity to sue, and damages are more favorable to her position than are those of Scotland. Scottish law does not recognize strict liability in tort. Moreover, it permits wrongful death actions only when brought by a decedent's relatives. The relatives may sue only for "loss of support and society."

On petitioners' motion, the suit was removed to the United States District Court for the Central District of California. Piper then [successfully] moved for transfer to the United States District Court for the Middle District of Pennsylvania, pursuant to 28 U.S.C. § 1404(a).[4]

. . .

B

In May, 1978, after the suit had been transferred, both Hartzell and Piper moved to dismiss the action on the ground of *forum non conveniens*. The District Court granted these motions in October, 1979. It relied on the balancing test set forth by this Court in *Gulf Oil Corp. v. Gilbert*, 330 U.S. 501 (1947), and its companion case, *Koster v. Lumbermens Mut. Cas. Co.*, 330 U.S. 518 (1947). In those decisions, the Court stated that a plaintiff's choice of forum should rarely be disturbed. However, when an alternative forum has jurisdiction to hear the case, and when trial in the chosen forum would "establish . . . oppressiveness and vexation to a defendant . . . out of all proportion to plaintiff's convenience," or when the "chosen forum [is] inappropriate because of considerations affecting

---

4. Section 1404(a) provides:

"For the convenience of parties and witnesses, in the interest of justice, a district court may transfer any civil action to any other district or division where it might have been brought."

the court's own administrative and legal problems," the court may, in the exercise of its sound discretion, dismiss the case. *Koster, supra,* at 330 U.S. 524. To guide trial court discretion, the Court provided a list of "private interest factors" affecting the convenience of the litigants, and a list of "public interest factors" affecting the convenience of the forum. *Gilbert, supra,* at 330 U.S. 508-509.[6]

After describing our decisions in *Gilbert* and *Koster,* the District Court . . . began by observing that an alternative forum existed in Scotland; Piper and Hartzell had agreed to submit to the jurisdiction of the Scottish courts and to waive any statute of limitations defense that might be available. It then stated that plaintiff's choice of forum was entitled to little weight. The court recognized that a plaintiff's choice ordinarily deserves substantial deference. It noted, however, that Reyno

> "is a representative of foreign citizens and residents seeking a forum in the United States because of the more liberal rules concerning products liability law,"

and that

> "the courts have been less solicitous when the plaintiff is not an American citizen or resident, and particularly when the foreign citizens seek to benefit from the more liberal tort rules provided for the protection of citizens and residents of the United States."

The District Court next examined several factors relating to the private interests of the litigants, and determined that these factors strongly pointed towards Scotland as the appropriate forum. Although evidence concerning the design, manufacture, and testing of the plane and propeller is located in the United States, the connections with Scotland are otherwise "overwhelming." The real parties in interest are citizens of Scotland, as were all the decedents. Witnesses who could testify regarding the maintenance of the aircraft, the training of the pilot, and the investigation of the accident — all essential to the defense — are in Great Britain. Moreover, all witnesses to damages are located in Scotland. Trial would be aided by familiarity with Scottish topography, and by easy access to the wreckage.

The District Court reasoned that, because crucial witnesses and evidence were beyond the reach of compulsory process, and because the defendants would not be able to implead potential Scottish third-party defendants, it would be "unfair to make Piper and Hartzell proceed to trial in this forum." The survivors had brought separate actions in Scotland against the pilot, McDonald, and Air

---

6. The factors pertaining to the private interests of the litigants included the "relative ease of access to sources of proof; availability of compulsory process for attendance of unwilling, and the cost of obtaining attendance of willing, witnesses; possibility of view of premises, if view would be appropriate to the action; and all other practical problems that make trial of a case easy, expeditious and inexpensive." *Gilbert,* 330 U.S. at 508. The public factors bearing on the question included the administrative difficulties flowing from court congestion; the "local interest in having localized controversies decided at home"; the interest in having the trial of a diversity case in a forum that is at home with the law that must govern the action; the avoidance of unnecessary problems in conflict of laws, or in the application of foreign law; and the unfairness of burdening citizens in an unrelated forum with jury duty. *Id.* at 509.

Navigation. "[I]t would be fairer to all parties and less costly if the entire case was presented to one jury with available testimony from all relevant witnesses."[7] . . .

The District Court concluded that the relevant public interests also pointed strongly towards dismissal. The court determined that Pennsylvania law would apply to Piper and Scottish law to Hartzell if the case were tried in the Middle District of Pennsylvania.[8] As a result, [the court found that] "trial in this forum would be hopelessly complex and confusing for a jury." In addition, the court noted that it was unfamiliar with Scottish law and thus would have to rely upon experts from that country. The court also found that the trial would be enormously costly and time-consuming; that it would be unfair to burden citizens with jury duty when the Middle District of Pennsylvania has little connection with the controversy; and that Scotland has a substantial interest in the outcome of the litigation.

In opposing the motions to dismiss, respondent contended that dismissal would be unfair because Scottish law was less favorable. The District Court explicitly rejected this claim. It reasoned that the possibility that dismissal might lead to an unfavorable change in the law did not deserve significant weight; any deficiency in the foreign law was a "matter to be dealt with in the foreign forum."

C

On appeal, the United States Court of Appeals for the Third Circuit reversed and remanded for trial. The decision to reverse appears to be based on two alternative grounds. First, the Court held that the District Court abused its discretion in conducting the *Gilbert* analysis. Second, the Court held that dismissal is never appropriate where the law of the alternative forum is less favorable to the plaintiff.

We granted certiorari in these cases to consider the questions they raise concerning the proper application of the doctrine of *forum non conveniens*.

II

The Court of Appeals erred in holding that plaintiffs may defeat a motion to dismiss on the ground of *forum non conveniens* merely by showing that the

---

7. The District Court explained that inconsistent verdicts might result if petitioners were held liable on the basis of strict liability here, and then required to prove negligence in an indemnity action in Scotland. Moreover, even if the same standard of liability applied, there was a danger that different juries would find different facts and produce inconsistent results.

8. Under *Klaxon v. Stentor Electric Mfg. Co.*, 313 U.S. 487 (1941), a court ordinarily must apply the choice of law rules of the State in which it sits. However, where a case is transferred pursuant to 28 U.S.C. § 1404(a), it must apply the choice of law rules of the State from which the case was transferred. *Van Dusen v. Barrack*, 376 U.S. 612 (1946). Relying on these two cases, the District Court concluded that California choice of law rules would apply to Piper, and Pennsylvania choice of law rules would apply to Hartzell. It further concluded that California applied a "governmental interests" analysis in resolving choice of law problems, and that Pennsylvania employed a "significant contacts" analysis. The court used the "governmental interests" analysis to determine that Pennsylvania liability rules would apply to Piper, and the "significant contacts" analysis to determine that Scottish liability rules would apply to Hartzell.

substantive law that would be applied in the alternative forum is less favorable to the plaintiffs than that of the present forum. The possibility of a change in substantive law should ordinarily not be given conclusive or even substantial weight in the *forum non conveniens* inquiry.

. . .

[B]y holding that the central focus of the *forum non conveniens* inquiry is convenience, *Gilbert* implicitly recognized that dismissal may not be barred solely because of the possibility of an unfavorable change in law. Under *Gilbert*, dismissal will ordinarily be appropriate where trial in the plaintiff's chosen forum imposes a heavy burden on the defendant or the court, and where the plaintiff is unable to offer any specific reasons of convenience supporting his choice.[15] If substantial weight were given to the possibility of an unfavorable change in law, however, dismissal might be barred even where trial in the chosen forum was plainly inconvenient.

The Court of Appeals' decision is inconsistent with this Court's earlier *forum non conveniens* decisions in another respect. Those decisions have repeatedly emphasized the need to retain flexibility. In *Gilbert*, the Court refused to identify specific circumstances "which will justify or require either grant or denial of remedy." Similarly, in *Koster*, the Court rejected the contention that, where a trial would involve inquiry into the internal affairs of a foreign corporation, dismissal was always appropriate. . . . And in *Williams v. Green Bay & Western R. Co.*, 326 U.S. 549 (1946), we stated that we would not lay down a rigid rule to govern discretion, and that "[e]ach case turns on its facts." If central emphasis were placed on any one factor, the *forum non conveniens* doctrine would lose much of the very flexibility that makes it so valuable.

In fact, if conclusive or substantial weight were given to the possibility of a change in law, the *forum non conveniens* doctrine would become virtually useless. Jurisdiction and venue requirements are often easily satisfied. As a result, many plaintiffs are able to choose from among several forums. Ordinarily, these plaintiffs will select that forum whose choice of law rules are most advantageous. Thus, if the possibility of an unfavorable change in substantive law is given substantial weight in the *forum non conveniens* inquiry, dismissal would rarely be proper.

. . .

The Court of Appeals' approach . . . also poses substantial practical problems. If the possibility of a change in law were given substantial weight, deciding motions to dismiss on the ground of *forum non conveniens* would become quite difficult. Choice of law analysis would become extremely important, and the courts would frequently be required to interpret the law of foreign jurisdictions. First, the trial court would have to determine what law would apply if the case were tried in the chosen forum, and what law would apply if the case were tried in the alternative forum. It would then have to compare the rights, remedies, and procedures available under the law that would be applied in each forum. Dismissal would

---

15. In other words, *Gilbert* held that dismissal may be warranted where a plaintiff chooses a particular forum not because it is convenient, but solely in order to harass the defendant or take advantage of favorable law. This is precisely the situation in which the Court of Appeals' rule would bar dismissal.

be appropriate only if the court concluded that the law applied by the alternative forum is as favorable to the plaintiff as that of the chosen forum. The doctrine of *forum non conveniens*, however, is designed in part to help courts avoid conducting complex exercises in comparative law. As we stated in *Gilbert*, the public interest factors point towards dismissal where the court would be required to "untangle problems in conflict of laws, and in law foreign to itself." 330 U.S. at 509.

Upholding the decision of the Court of Appeals would result in other practical problems. At least where the foreign plaintiff named an American manufacturer as defendant, a court could not dismiss the case on grounds of *forum non conveniens* where dismissal might lead to an unfavorable change in law. The American courts, which are already extremely attractive to foreign plaintiffs,[18] would become even more attractive. The flow of litigation into the United States would increase and further congest already crowded courts.

. . .

We do not hold that the possibility of an unfavorable change in law should *never* be a relevant consideration in a *forum non conveniens* inquiry. Of course, if the remedy provided by the alternative forum is so clearly inadequate or unsatisfactory that it is no remedy at all, the unfavorable change in law may be given substantial weight; the district court may conclude that dismissal would not be in the interests of justice.[22] In these cases, however, the remedies that would be provided by the Scottish courts do not fall within this category. Although the relatives of the decedents may not be able to rely on a strict liability theory, and although their potential damages award may be smaller, there is no danger that they will be deprived of any remedy or treated unfairly.

III

The Court of Appeals also erred in rejecting the District Court's *Gilbert* analysis. The Court of Appeals stated that more weight should have been given to

---

18. First, all but 6 of the 50 American States . . . offer strict liability. Rules roughly equivalent to American strict liability are effective in France, Belgium, and Luxembourg. West Germany and Japan have a strict liability statute for pharmaceuticals. However, strict liability remains primarily an American innovation. Second, the tort plaintiff may choose, at least potentially, from among 50 jurisdictions if he decides to file suit in the United States. Each of these jurisdictions applies its own set of malleable choice of law rules. Third, jury trials are almost always available in the United States, while they are never provided in civil law jurisdictions. Even in the United Kingdom, most civil actions are not tried before a jury. Fourth, unlike most foreign jurisdictions, American courts allow contingent attorney's fees, and do not tax losing parties with their opponents' attorney's fees. Fifth, discovery is more extensive in American than in foreign courts.

22. At the outset of any *forum non conveniens* inquiry, the court must determine whether there exists an alternative forum. Ordinarily, this requirement will be satisfied when the defendant is "amenable to process" in the other jurisdiction. *Gilbert*, 330 U.S. at 506-507. In rare circumstances, however, where the remedy offered by the other forum is clearly unsatisfactory, the other forum may not be an adequate alternative, and the initial requirement may not be satisfied. Thus, for example, dismissal would not be appropriate where the alternative forum does not permit litigation of the subject matter of the dispute. Cf. *Phoenix Canada Oil Co., Ltd. v. Texaco, Inc.*, 78 F.R.D. 445 (Del. 1978) (court refuses to dismiss, where alternative forum is Ecuador, it is unclear whether Ecuadorean tribunal will hear the case, and there is no generally codified Ecuadorean legal remedy for the unjust enrichment and tort claims asserted).

the plaintiff's choice of forum, and criticized the District Court's analysis of the private and public interests. However, the District Court's decision regarding the deference due plaintiff's choice of forum was appropriate. Furthermore, we do not believe that the District Court abused its discretion in weighing the private and public interests.

A

The District Court acknowledged that there is ordinarily a strong presumption in favor of the plaintiff's choice of forum, which may be overcome only when the private and public interest factors clearly point towards trial in the alternative forum. It held, however, that the presumption applies with less force when the plaintiff or real parties in interest are foreign.

The District Court's distinction between resident or citizen plaintiffs and foreign plaintiffs is fully justified. . . . When the home forum has been chosen, it is reasonable to assume that this choice is convenient. When the plaintiff is foreign, however, this assumption is much less reasonable. Because the central purpose of any *forum non conveniens* inquiry is to ensure that the trial is convenient, a foreign plaintiff's choice deserves less deference.

The *forum non conveniens* determination is committed to the sound discretion of the trial court. It may be reversed only when there has been a clear abuse of discretion; where the court has considered all relevant public and private interest factors, and where its balancing of these factors is reasonable, its decision deserves substantial deference. Here, the Court of Appeals expressly acknowledged that the standard of review was one of abuse of discretion. In examining the District Court's analysis of the public and private interests, however, the Court of Appeals seems to have lost sight of this rule, and substituted its own judgment for that of the District Court.

(1)

In analyzing the private interest factors, the District Court stated that the connections with Scotland are "overwhelming." This characterization may be somewhat exaggerated. Particularly with respect to the question of relative ease of access to sources of proof, the private interests point in both directions. As respondent emphasizes, records concerning the design, manufacture, and testing of the propeller and plane are located in the United States. She would have greater access to sources of proof relevant to her strict liability and negligence theories if trial were held here. However, the District Court did not act unreasonably in concluding that fewer evidentiary problems would be posed if the trial were held in Scotland. A large proportion of the relevant evidence is located in Great Britain.

The Court of Appeals found that the problems of proof could not be given any weight because Piper and Hartzell failed to describe with specificity the evidence they would not be able to obtain if trial were held in the United States. It suggested that defendants seeking *forum non conveniens* dismissal must submit affidavits identifying the witnesses they would call and the testimony these witnesses would provide if the trial were held in the alternative forum. Such detail is not necessary. Piper and Hartzell have moved for dismissal precisely because many crucial witnesses are located beyond the reach of compulsory process, and thus are difficult to identify or interview. Requiring extensive investigation would defeat the purpose of their motion. Of course, defendants must provide enough information to enable the District Court to balance the parties' interests. Our examination of the record convinces us that sufficient information was provided here. Both Piper and Hartzell submitted affidavits describing the evidentiary problems they would face if the trial were held in the United States.

The District Court correctly concluded that the problems posed by the inability to implead potential third-party defendants clearly supported holding the trial in Scotland. Joinder of the pilot's estate, Air Navigation, and McDonald is crucial to the presentation of petitioners' defense. If Piper and Hartzell can show that the accident was caused not by a design defect, but rather by the negligence of the pilot, the plane's owners, or the charter company, they will be relieved of all liability. It is true, of course, that, if Hartzell and Piper were found liable after a trial in the United States, they could institute an action for indemnity or contribution against these parties in Scotland. It would be far more convenient, however, to resolve all claims in one trial. The Court of Appeals rejected this argument. Forcing petitioners to rely on actions for indemnity or contributions would be "burdensome," but not "unfair." Finding that trial in the plaintiff's chosen forum would be burdensome, however, is sufficient to support dismissal on grounds of *forum non conveniens*.

(2)

The District Court's review of the factors relating to the public interest was also reasonable. On the basis of its choice of law analysis, it concluded that, if the case were tried in the Middle District of Pennsylvania, Pennsylvania law would apply to Piper and Scottish law to Hartzell. It stated that a trial involving two sets of laws would be confusing to the jury. It also noted its own lack of familiarity with Scottish law. Consideration of these problems was clearly appropriate under *Gilbert*; in that case, we explicitly held that the need to apply foreign law pointed towards dismissal.

. . .

Scotland has a very strong interest in this litigation. The accident occurred in its airspace. All of the decedents were Scottish. Apart from Piper and Hartzell, all potential plaintiffs and defendants are either Scottish or English. As we stated in *Gilbert*, there is "a local interest in having localized controversies decided at home." 330 U.S. at 509. Respondent argues that American citizens have an interest in ensuring that American manufacturers are deterred from producing defective products, and that additional deterrence might be obtained if Piper and Hartzell were tried in the United States, where they could be sued on the basis of both negligence and strict liability. However, the incremental deterrence that would be gained if this trial were held in an American court is likely to be insignificant. The American interest in this accident is simply not sufficient to justify the enormous commitment of judicial time and resources that would inevitably be required if the case were to be tried here.

IV

The Court of Appeals erred in holding that the possibility of an unfavorable change in law bars dismissal on the ground of *forum non conveniens*. It also erred in rejecting the District Court's *Gilbert* analysis. The District Court properly decided that the presumption in favor of the respondent's forum choice applied with less than maximum force because the real parties in interest are foreign. It did not act unreasonably in deciding that the private interests pointed towards trial in Scotland. Nor did it act unreasonably in deciding that the public interests favored trial in Scotland. Thus, the judgment of the Court of Appeals is
Reversed.

[Justice White joined only Parts I and II of the opinion. A partial dissent by Justice Stevens, joined by Justice Brennan, is omitted. Justices Powell and O'Connor did not participate.]

Loya v. Starwood Hotels & Resorts Worldwide, Inc.

583 F.3d 656 (9th Cir. 2009)

RYMER, Circuit Judge:
This appeal involves applicability of the doctrine of *forum non conveniens* to claims arising out of the death of a Washington resident while scuba diving off the coast of Mexico on an expedition arranged by the resort at which he was staying in Cabo San Lucas. . . . We agree [with the district court] that the doctrine of *forum non conveniens* may be invoked in this case, and conclude that the district court did not clearly abuse its discretion in applying it. Accordingly, we affirm.

I

Gillian Loya's husband, Ricardo, died in a scuba diving accident off the Mexican coast where he was vacationing at the Westin Resort & Spa Los Cabos (a Starwood Hotel and Resorts Worldwide hotel) in San Jose del Cabo, Baja California Sur. . . . Allegedly, the guide was underage by PADI standards (PADI certifies dive centers), abandoned Ricardo, and failed to rescue him. Loya, a Washington resident, filed an action against these entities and others in Washington state court for dereliction of duty that resulted in her husband's wrongful death. The complaint also asserted claims under the Washington Consumer Protection Act (WCPA) and the Washington Timeshare Act (WTA) for falsely advertising that the Westin Resort provided safe scuba diving activities. Starwood removed on the basis of diversity and admiralty jurisdiction. . . .

When Loya sought partial summary judgment on her state law claims, Starwood cross-moved for dismissal on the ground of *forum non conveniens*. The district court denied Loya's motion but granted Starwood's. In doing so, the court rejected Loya's argument that the doctrine of *forum non conveniens* is inapplicable because [the federal Death on the High Seas Act (DOHSA)] provides the exclusive remedy for American beneficiaries and mandates venue in a United States district court. Instead, . . . the court held that . . . whether or not DOHSA applies to this action, the Act does not preclude *forum non conveniens* dismissal. The court then ruled that an adequate alternative forum was available. After considering private and public interest factors, it concluded that dismissal was appropriate for the main reasons that Baja California Sur, Mexico is a more convenient forum, and the nucleus of Loya's case is the place where the accident occurred.

. . .

II

[The court of appeals first held that the DOHSA did not preclude application of *forum non conveniens*.]

III

Given our conclusion that the district court *could* dismiss on grounds of *forum non conveniens*, the remaining question is whether it clearly abused its discretion in doing so. . . .

A party moving to dismiss on grounds of forum non conveniens must show two things: (1) the existence of an adequate alternative forum, and (2) that the balance of private and public interest factors favors dismissal. This showing must overcome the great deference due plaintiffs because a showing of convenience by a party who has sued in his home forum will usually outweigh the inconvenience the defendant may have shown. Private interest factors include (1) relative ease of access to sources of proof; (2) the availability of compulsory process for attendance of hostile witnesses, and cost of obtaining attendance of willing witnesses; (3) possibility of viewing subject premises; (4) all other factors that render trial of the case expeditious and inexpensive. Public interest factors include (1) administrative difficulties flowing from court congestion; (2) imposition of jury duty on the people of a community that has no relation to the litigation; (3) local interest in having localized controversies decided at home; (4) the interest in having a diversity case tried in a forum familiar with the law that governs the action; (5) the avoidance of unnecessary problems in conflicts of law.

The district court found that Baja California Sur, Mexico provides an adequate forum because all defendants agreed to accept service, submit to the jurisdiction, and waive any statute of limitations defenses; Loya could bring a tort-based suit there; and Mexican courts would afford some remedy, even though less than available in this country. (Loya's expert, a Mexican lawyer experienced in advising foreign litigants about the Mexican legal system, declared that any wrongful death recovery would be capped, in accordance with a formula driven by the highest daily minimum wage in the region, at $12,000-13,000, with little likelihood for recovery of moral damages or at least none in excess of $4,000. He also indicated that Mexican attorneys do not work on a contingency basis and his firm would charge about $50,000 to litigate this case.)

Addressing the private interest factors, the court found that the relative ease of access to sources of proof and obtaining witnesses favor Starwood, as does the fact that a Mexican judgment would be enforceable in the United States. It noted that, although Loya has sued American defendants rather than the Mexican subsidiaries of Starwood and Raintree, Ricardo Loya's death and the activities leading up to the accident occurred in Mexico and that, other than Gillian Loya (who was not on the dive), Ricardo Loya's diving partner (who lives in California and will not willingly go to Cabo), and the friends with whom the Loyas went on the trip, potential liability witnesses and relevant documentation are located in Mexico. In the trial court's view, other factors did not favor either side.

With respect to public interest factors, the court found that court congestion in Baja California Sur weighs in favor of Loya. While Washington has an interest in preventing misrepresentations to its residents about the safety of a Mexican vacation, the court held that Mexico's substantial interest in holding businesses operating in Mexico accountable and insuring that foreign tourists are treated fairly favors Starwood given that the gravamen of Loya's complaint is that Starwood, operating in Mexico, caused Ricardo Loya's death. In evaluating the public interest in having trial in a forum familiar with the governing law, the court looked to the test Washington applies to determine choice of law (if laws conflict, then the laws of the forum with the "most significant relationship" govern). It concluded that Mexican law may apply to some issues, particularly the applicable standard of care and interpretation of any liability release signed by Ricardo Loya. In the court's view, the need to apply foreign law strongly favors dismissal based on *forum non conveniens*. Finally, the court found no cause to burden Washington jurors with this litigation given that most of the allegedly wrongful conduct took place in Mexico and among non-Washington defendants.

Considering all these factors, the district court found that dismissal was appropriate for two important reasons: Baja California Sur is an adequate alternative forum, and the nucleus of Loya's case is where Ricardo Loya's accident occurred. On balance, the court believed that the public and private factors weigh in favor of Starwood. Thus, it concluded that Baja California Sur is the more convenient, therefore appropriate, forum.

Loya emphasizes the heightened deference owed to American citizens suing American defendants in their home forum. We afford greater deference to a plaintiff's choice of home forum because it is reasonable and convenient. However, the deference due is far from absolute. A district court has discretion to decide that a foreign forum is more convenient. Here, Baja California Sur is where the scuba diving trip was arranged, documented, outfitted, undertaken, and investigated. We cannot say that the court acted unreasonably in deciding that these circumstances made Baja California Sur a more convenient, and appropriate, forum.

Loya also focuses on the considerable difference in potential recovery, as well as in the cost of pursuing this action, in Mexico. The remedy afforded may not be so clearly inadequate or unsatisfactory that it is no remedy at all. However, that the law, or the remedy afforded, is less favorable in the foreign forum is not determinative. *Piper Aircraft [v. Reyno]*, 454 U.S. at 247 (stating that "[t]he possibility of a change in substantive law should ordinarily not be given conclusive or even substantial weight in the *forum non conveniens* inquiry.". A foreign forum must only provide the plaintiff with some remedy in order for the alternative forum to be adequate. . . . Unquestionably, Mexico provides a remedy for breach of contract and for wrongful death. Having taken all of these considerations into account, the district court's conclusion that Baja California Sur was nevertheless a more convenient forum is not unreasonable. *See Piper Aircraft*, 454 U.S. at 249 (observing that convenience is the central focus of the *forum non conveniens* inquiry, and rejecting the notion that the possibility of an unfavorable change in law should be given substantial weight so as to bar dismissal even where trial in the chosen forum is plainly inconvenient).

. . .

In sum, the trial court considered all the relevant factors and balanced the interests reasonably. Given this, we owe its decision substantial deference.

. . .

AFFIRMED.

KLEINFELD, Circuit Judge, dissenting:

I respectfully dissent. The district court treated *forum non conveniens* as less than the exceptional tool to be employed sparingly that it is, and applied it overly aggressively.

. . .

Though the death giving rise to this case occurred in Mexico's waters, the American connections with the case are very substantial indeed. Loya was American, as are his wife — who is personal representative of his estate — and his children. Loya died, as we understand the facts, while scuba diving at the Westin resort in Cabo San Lucas, a death that might have been prevented had the resort used someone competent and properly certified to manage his oxygen tank, and had the potential rescue vessel not passed by without performing a rescue. The Loyas' lawsuit focuses on the American timeshare and resort companies that they claim ought to have assured higher safety standards to Americans vacationing in their resort in Mexico.

By contrast, in *Piper Aircraft Co. v. Reyno*, the Supreme Court decision laying out the *forum non conveniens* law we must apply, a U.K. air taxi crashed a U.K.-owned plane in the Scottish highlands, killing the pilot and passengers, all of whom, along with their heirs and next of kin, were Scottish. . . .

I have not found precedent for so aggressive an exclusion of an American plaintiff from American courts under the doctrine in any other case, and I think it is mistaken here.

The Supreme Court decision in *Piper Aircraft Co. v. Reyno* gives us the necessary guidance. That Scottish air crash, described above, was properly dismissed for *forum non conveniens*, and the Court rejected the Third Circuit view that more favorable law, alone, in the plaintiff's choice of forum was sufficient reason to deny *forum non conveniens* dismissal. The decision reaffirmed, though, that the "plaintiff's choice of forum should rarely be disturbed." The rule in *Piper* is that *forum non conveniens* dismissal is appropriate only "when trial in the chosen forum would establish . . . oppressiveness and vexation to a defendant . . . out of

744   Chapter 10. Alternative Forums

all proportion to plaintiff's convenience, or when the chosen forum[is] inappropriate because of considerations affecting the court's own administrative and legal problems." That stringent rule has not been applied in this case.

. . .

Piper carefully qualified its rule that law more favorable to the plaintiff is not a good ground automatically to deny *forum non conveniens* dismissal. "[I]f the remedy provided by the alternative forum is so clearly inadequate or unsatisfactory that it is no remedy at all, the unfavorable change in law may be given substantial weight; the district court may conclude that dismissal would not be in the interests of justice." That is the case here. The Loya family has no practical Mexican remedy. The papers set out that their remedy in Mexico would be limited to damages of about $17,000, and that they would be required to spend over $50,000 to secure that remedy.

In addition to the impracticality of any remedy in Mexico, the Loyas face an insuperable obstacle in proving their case there. The decedent's diving partner is unwilling to go to Mexico again. That is plausible, considering the horrible experience, and the deterrent of knowing that Mexican law does not provide compensation if he dies there.

Our disagreement is limited to application of law to facts, but that matters. *Piper* holds that there is no "rigid rule" governing discretion, just a multi-factor set of considerations, and "each case turns on its facts." The Loyas ought to be able to sue in Washington — their and the decedent's home — from where they arranged their Mexican vacation with an American company and the Mexican companies it partnered with.

NOTES AND QUESTIONS

1. **Litigation Strategy.** Why do you think the plaintiffs in *Piper* and *Loya* filed their lawsuits in the United States? Why do you think the defendants preferred not to have the lawsuits heard in the United States? More generally, what factors should you consider when there appear to be two or more potentially available forums and you need to make a forum selection decision on behalf of your client? Why is the *forum non conveniens* doctrine strategically useful when a defendant is sued in a U.S. court but concludes that a foreign court would be more favorable?

2. **The Adequate Alternative Forum Requirement.** A court may not dismiss a suit on *forum non conveniens* grounds unless there is an adequate alternative forum. Thus, an essential step in the analysis is to determine whether the defendant's proposed foreign court is an adequate alternative. According to the Supreme Court in *Piper*, how is the adequate alternative forum requirement ordinarily satisfied? When, according to the Court, might the requirement not be satisfied? In practice, how much of a barrier do you think the adequate alternative forum requirement is likely to be to defendants seeking

forum non conveniens dismissals? If you were representing a defendant on a *forum non conveniens* motion, how might you try to improve the likelihood that the judge would find that this requirement is satisfied? The *Restatement (Fourth) of the Foreign Relations Law of the United States*, Section 424, Comment d, observes:

> A federal court will not dismiss on grounds of forum non conveniens unless there exists an available and adequate alternative forum. An alternative forum is generally considered available if all parties are amenable to process and come within the foreign forum's jurisdiction. An alternative forum is general considered adequate if the parties will not be deprived of all remedies or treated unfairly.

3. **The Presumption in Favor of the Plaintiff's Choice of a U.S. Forum.** Another step in *forum non conveniens* analysis is to determine the strength of the presumption in favor of the plaintiff's choice of a U.S. forum. In *Piper*, the Court said that the defendant has a "heavy burden" in establishing a *forum non conveniens* dismissal and that "there is ordinarily a strong presumption in favor of the plaintiff's choice of forum." Did the court in *Loya* apply this strong presumption? An empirical analysis of *forum non conveniens* decisions found that U.S. district court judges grant motions to dismiss on *forum non conveniens* grounds at an estimated rate of 47 percent in their published decisions. Christopher A. Whytock, *The Evolving Forum Shopping System*, 96 Cornell L. Rev. 481, 502-03 (2011); *see also* Donald Earl Childress III, *Erie's International Effect: A Reply*, 108 Nw. U. L. Rev. Colloquy 1, 11 (2013) (indicating that since 2007 district courts may be dismissing at much higher rates). Does this suggest that there is a "strong presumption" in practice? Do you think the presumption was more convincingly overcome in *Loya* or *Piper*? In considering *forum non conveniens* dismissal, what fact(s) were especially harmful to the plaintiff in *Piper*? If *Loya* was correctly decided, what cases involving an injury abroad could be brought in U.S. courts?

Although *Piper* stated that there is a strong presumption in favor of the plaintiff's choice of a U.S. forum, it also held that "the presumption applies with less force when the plaintiff [is] foreign" rather than a U.S. citizen. What is the Court's rationale for having a weaker presumption for foreign plaintiffs? Do you think this rationale is convincing? One empirical study suggests that the *forum non conveniens* doctrine's distinction between U.S. and foreign plaintiffs makes an important difference in practice: "[O]ther things being equal, U.S. district court judges are approximately 25% more likely to dismiss on forum non conveniens grounds when the plaintiff is foreign than when the plaintiff is a U.S. citizen." Whytock, *supra*, at 527; *see also* Childress, *supra*, at 11 (noting that the dismissal rate could be as high as 70 percent). However, as the court in *Loya* points out, this does not mean that suits filed in U.S. court by U.S. citizens cannot be dismissed on *forum non conveniens* grounds. Should judges use the *forum non conveniens* doctrine to dismiss cases filed in U.S. courts by U.S. citizens, as happened in *Loya*? Several other courts in cases relating to American citizens' injuries in foreign hotels have rejected *forum non conveniens* motions. *DiFederico v. Marriott, Inc.*, 714 F.3d 796 (4th Cir. 2013), involved the terrorist bombing of a hotel in Pakistan in which the plaintiff's husband was killed. The court found that Pakistan was not an adequate alternative forum, principally based on the security situation in that country. *Guidi v. Inter-Continental Hotels, Corp.*, 224 F.3d 142 (2d Cir. 2000), involved a shooting in a hotel in Egypt. The district court granted a motion for *forum non conveniens* but the court of appeals reversed, principally on two grounds. First, it found that the district court had not given sufficient weight to the plaintiffs' choice of their home forum, and that where a plaintiff sues in her home forum that choice "should not be disturbed if the forum is not so oppressive and vexatious to [the defendant] as to overwhelm the convenience to Plaintiffs of suing in their home forum." Second, it found that

> the substantial and unusual emotional burden on Plaintiffs if they were required to travel to Egypt provided additional support for keeping the case in their chosen forum. . . . Plaintiffs are atypical in that they are either the widows or the victim of a murderous act directed specifically against foreigners. Understandably, they are strongly adverse to litigating in a country where foreigners have been the targets of hostile attacks. . . .

Are these cases distinguishable from *Loya*?

In *Shi v. New Mighty U.S. Trust*, 918 F.3d 944 (D.C. Cir. 2019), the district court granted a *forum non conveniens* motion where a Taiwanese citizen sued defendant entities located in the District of Columbia, alleging that the defendants participated in a scheme to deny her inheritance of her husband's estate. The court of appeals reversed, finding that the district court had misapplied the public and private factors. The court of appeals emphasized that defendants seeking such dismissal bear a "heavy burden" and that the motion should be granted only in "exceptional circumstances." Among other things, the court found that the presumption for the plaintiff's choice of forum should generally exist even for a non-U.S. plaintiff, and that difficulties of travel and translation were overstated by the district court in light of modern technology. A key consideration appeared to be that the defendants were located in the chosen forum. Why should that matter?

4. **The Private and Public Interest Factors.** Another step in *forum non conveniens* analysis is to apply the private and public interest factors and to determine in a given case whether these factors point strongly enough toward the defendant's proposed alternative foreign court to overcome the presumption in favor of the plaintiff's choice of a U.S. court. The Supreme Court's list of private and public interest factors in *Piper* comes from one of its seminal cases on the *forum non conveniens* doctrine, *Gilbert v. Gulf Oil Co*, 330 U.S. 501 (1947). Are these the right set of factors? Should some be less important than others, especially in light of changes in technology or other circumstances since 1947? Which seem most important to the Court in *Piper*? In *Loya*? In *Gilbert*, the Court included in its list of private interest factors "questions as to the enforceability of a judgment if one is obtained." *Id*. at 508. What questions do you think the Court had in mind? Why do you think these questions

might be important in the context of a *forum non conveniens* motion? Should this factor have been considered in *Piper* and *Loya*? In *Carijano v. Occidental Petroleum Corp.*, 643 F.3d 1216 (9th Cir. 2011), the court reversed the district court's decision to grant defendant's *forum non conveniens* motion because, among other things, the lower court failed to consider the enforceability factor.

5. **Changes in Law and *Forum Non Conveniens* Dismissals.** Note the consequences of the *forum non conveniens* dismissal for the plaintiff in *Loya*. Does it make sense that a *forum non conveniens* dismissal should change the applicable law? Does Washington's law apply to Loya's claim? If so, what is the justification for not applying it? Is it fair to make Loya subject to the damages limitation in Mexican law? Is it fair to Starwood to *not* make Loya subject to the damages limitation? What if the law at issue was a federal statutory claim (such as antitrust) — should a court dismiss in favor of a forum that would not apply U.S. law?

6. **Subsequent Treatment of *Forum Non Conveniens* in the Supreme Court.** In *Sinochem International Co. Ltd. v. Malaysia International Shipping Co.*, 549 U.S. 422 (2007), the Supreme Court held that a district court may grant a motion for *forum non conveniens* dismissal without first resolving whether it has jurisdiction. The Court concluded: "[W]here subject-matter or personal jurisdiction is difficult to determine, and *forum non conveniens* considerations weigh heavily in favor of dismissal, the court properly takes the less burdensome course." Does that make sense as a legal matter? Why does this sequencing matter in practice? In its opinion, the Court remarked in passing that "[a] defendant invoking *forum non conveniens* ordinarily bears a heavy burden in opposing the plaintiff's chosen forum. When the plaintiff's choice is not its home forum, however, the presumption in the plaintiff's favor applies with less force, for the assumption that the chosen forum is appropriate is in such cases less reasonable." (citing *Piper*). Is that what *Piper* said? The Supreme Court described the facts in *Sinochem* as "a textbook case for immediate *forum non conveniens* dismissal." The facts, as the Court described them, were as follows:

> The underlying controversy concerns alleged misrepresentations by a Chinese corporation to a Chinese admiralty court resulting in the arrest of a Malaysian vessel in China. In 2003, petitioner [Sinochem] . . . , a Chinese state-owned importer, contracted with Triorient Trading, Inc. (Triorient), a domestic corporation that is not a party to this suit, to purchase steel coils. Pursuant to the agreement, Triorient would receive payment under a letter of credit by producing a valid bill of lading certifying that the coils had been loaded for shipment to China on or before April 30, 2003.
>
> Triorient subchartered a vessel owned by respondent Malaysia International Shipping Corporation (Malaysia International), a Malaysian company, to transport the coils to China. Triorient then hired a stevedoring company to load the steel coils at the Port of Philadelphia. A bill of lading, dated April 30, 2003, triggered payment under the letter of credit.
>
> . . . Sinochem petitioned the Guangzhou Admiralty Court in China for . . . arrest of the vessel that carried the steel coils to China. In support of

its petition, Sinochem alleged that the Malaysian company had falsely back-dated the bill of lading. The Chinese tribunal ordered the ship arrested the same day.

Thereafter, . . . Sinochem timely filed a complaint against Malaysia International and others in the Guangzhou Admiralty Court. Sinochem's complaint repeated the allegation that the bill of lading had been falsified resulting in unwarranted payment. Malaysia International contested the jurisdiction of the Chinese tribunal. The admiralty court rejected Malaysia International's jurisdictional objection, and that ruling was affirmed on appeal by the Guangdong Higher People's Court.

[S]hortly after the Chinese court ordered the vessel's arrest, Malaysia International filed the instant action against Sinochem in the United States District Court for the Eastern District of Pennsylvania. Malaysia International asserted in its federal court pleading that Sinochem's preservation petition to the Guangzhou court negligently misrepresented the "vessel's fitness and suitability to load its cargo." As relief, Malaysia International sought compensation for the loss it sustained due to the delay caused by the ship's arrest.

Is it obvious that Malaysia International's claim should be dismissed for *forum non conveniens*? What should Malaysia International argue?

7. **Conditional Dismissals.** A district court may condition *forum non conveniens* dismissal on the defendant agreeing to various matters to facilitate the foreign litigation. *In re Union Carbide Corp. Gas Plant Disaster in Bhopal, India*, 809 F.2d 195 (2d Cir. 1987), involved a massive explosion in India that killed numerous persons. The Indian victims sued Union Carbide Corp., the American owner, in U.S. court, and Union Carbide sought a *forum non conveniens* dismissal in favor of Indian courts. The district court granted the motion subject to several conditions.

On appeal, the Second Circuit first affirmed the dismissal, remarking that "it might reasonably be concluded that it would have been an abuse of discretion to deny a *forum non conveniens* dismissal." What factors likely influenced the court in reaching this decision? Should it have mattered that the Indian government opposed dismissal on the grounds that Indian courts were incapable of handling a mass tort litigation of this magnitude?

The court of appeals then addressed the conditions to which the defense objected on appeal. It approved conditions that the defendant consent to personal jurisdiction in India and waive the statute of limitations. But it rejected two other conditions: first, that the defendant consent to enforceability of any Indian judgment against it, and second, that it consent to broad U.S.-style discovery. What were the Indian plaintiffs concerned about in seeking these conditions? Were the conditions the district court imposed on Union Carbide unreasonable?

8. **Suit in the Alternative Forum.** A *forum non conveniens* dismissal is not a transfer of venue — U.S. courts have no authority to transfer cases to another nation's legal system. Thus, a *forum non conveniens* dismissal is just that — a dismissal. The case will not proceed in foreign court unless the plaintiff re-files the suit there and the foreign court accepts jurisdiction. This does not always,

or even usually, happen. According to one well-known study conducted in the mid-1980s, plaintiffs rarely re-filed their cases abroad after a *forum non conveniens* dismissal. David W. Robertson, *Forum Non Conveniens in America and England: "A Rather Fantastic Fiction,"* 103 L.Q. REV. 398, 418-20 (1987) (finding that only 14.5 percent of personal injury plaintiffs and 16.6 percent of commercial plaintiffs re-filed cases abroad after *forum non conveniens* dismissals). Why do you think this would be the case? Why would a plaintiff find it worthwhile to pursue a claim in the United States, but not to pursue the same claim abroad? How might plaintiffs' tendency not to re-file abroad make the *forum non conveniens* doctrine an especially attractive strategic option for defendants? What do you think happened to the lawsuits in *Piper* and *Loya* after they were dismissed on *forum non conveniens* grounds?

9. **Litigation Strategy for Defendants.** Should a defendant always move for *forum non conveniens* dismissal if it is a plausible argument? Consider *Aguinda v. Texaco, Inc.*, 303 F.3d 470 (2d Cir. 2002), and its aftermath. A large group of Ecuadorian plaintiffs sued Texaco in U.S. court, alleging environmental damage from Texaco's oil extraction operations in Ecuador. Texaco successfully moved for *forum non conveniens* dismissal after agreeing to submit to jurisdiction in Ecuador, and the court of appeals affirmed. After first rejecting the plaintiffs' argument that Ecuador was not an adequate alternative forum, the court found that the balance of relevant factors favored dismissal:

> Private interests include "the relative ease of access to sources of proof; availability of compulsory process for attendance of unwilling, and the cost of obtaining attendance of willing, witnesses; possibility of view of the premises, if view would be appropriate to the action; and all other practical problems that make trial of a case easy, expeditious and inexpensive." *Gulf Oil Corp. v. Gilbert*, 330 U.S. 501, 508 (1947). We find no abuse of discretion in the district court's conclusion that these interests "weigh heavily" in favor of an Ecuadorian forum. The relative ease of access to sources of proof favors proceeding in Ecuador. All plaintiffs, as well as members of their putative classes, live in Ecuador or Peru. Plaintiffs sustained their injuries in Ecuador and Peru, and their relevant medical and property records are located there. Also located in Ecuador are the records of decisions taken by the Consortium, along with evidence of Texaco's defenses implicating the roles of PetroEcuador and the Republic. By contrast, plaintiffs have failed to establish that the parent Texaco made decisions regarding oil operations in Ecuador or that evidence of any such decisions is located in the U.S.
>
> If these cases proceeded to trial, it would be onerous for a New York court to manage the translation difficulties arising from cases with 55,000 putative class members of different indigenous groups speaking various dialects. In addition, it would be far more feasible for an Ecuadorian court to view the polluted areas in question than for a New York court to do so. We also find significant that the Republic and PetroEcuador, neither of which are parties to the current suits, could be joined if the cases were resumed in Ecuador. *See Piper Aircraft*, 454 U.S. at 259 (noting that "inability to implead potential third-party defendants" supports holding trial in Scotland). . . .

To the extent that evidence exists within the U.S., plaintiffs' concerns are partially addressed by Texaco's stipulation to allow use of the discovery already obtained. Furthermore, Texaco's counsel agreed at oral argument that Texaco would not oppose further discovery in Ecuador that would otherwise be available in the U.S.

. . .

Public interest considerations include administrative difficulties associated with court congestion; the unfairness of imposing jury duty on a community with no relation to the litigation; the interest in having localized controversies decided at home; and avoiding difficult problems in conflict of laws and the application of foreign law. *Gilbert*, 330 U.S. at 508-09. The district court was within its discretion in concluding that the public interest factors tilt in favor of dismissal.

After the dismissal in the United States, the plaintiffs re-filed the case in Ecuador (against Chevron Corp., which purchased Texaco in 2001 and which plaintiffs sued for successor liability under Ecaudorian law). As a later case recounted:

After seven years of litigation, on February 14, 2011, the trial court issued its decision, finding Chevron liable for $8.6 billion of damages, with an $8.6 billion punitive damages award to be added unless Chevron apologized within fourteen days of the opinion's issuance. Chevron did not apologize; the pending judgment is thus for $17.2 billion.

Chevron Corp. v. Naranjo, 667 F.3d 232, 236 (2d Cir. 2012). Chevron then brought suit in the United States to block enforcement of the Ecuadorian judgment on the ground that "[plaintiffs] and their lawyers pursued that litigation by a variety of unethical, corrupt, and illegal means" and thus that "the Ecuadorian judgment [wa]s fundamentally tainted by fraud." *Id.* at 236-37. Chevron further "argue[d] that the Ecuadorian judiciary is so captured by political interests as to be incapable of producing a judgment that the New York courts can enforce." Chevron raised its objections with the court in Ecuador, which nonetheless issued judgment against Chevron. U.S. courts ultimately blocked enforcement of the judgment in the United States (and a number of other countries also refused enforcement), but enforcement efforts remain ongoing. In retrospect, was the *forum non conveniens* motion in *Aguinda* a mistake? Should a defendant who argued at the *forum non conveniens* stage that its preferred foreign court was an "adequate alternative forum" be able to argue at the enforcement stage that the same foreign court suffered from inadequacies that should preclude enforcement of the judgment against it?

10. **Appellate Review of *Forum Non Conveniens* Motions.** In *Piper*, the U.S. Supreme Court noted that a district court's *forum non conveniens* decision may be reversed "only when there has been a clear abuse of discretion." In *Van Cauwenberghe v. Baird*, 486 U.S. 517 (1988), the Supreme Court held that a district court's denial of a *forum non conveniens* motion is not an immediately appealable order. What are the implications of these decisions for plaintiffs and defendants in transnational cases?

11. **Comparative Perspectives.** Generally speaking, the *forum non conveniens* doctrine exists in common law jurisdictions such as the United Kingdom, Canada, and Australia, unless modified by statute or treaty, and is rare in civil law jurisdictions. The European Court of Justice (ECJ) expressly rejected *forum non conveniens*, at least for defendants located in the European Union. In *Owusu v. Jackson*, Case C-281/02 (ECJ 2005), a case similar on its facts to *Loya*, a U.K. citizen sued in U.K. court for injuries suffered while vacationing in Jamaica. The defendants (an individual U.K. citizen and various Jamaican companies) sought a *forum non conveniens* dismissal in favor of Jamaican courts, as would be potentially available under U.K. domestic law. The U.K. court referred the question to the ECJ, which decided that such dismissals were not allowed under the Convention and related regulations (the U.K. at the time was a member of the EU). According to the ECJ:

> Respect for the principles of legal certainty, which is one of the objectives of the Brussels Convention, would not be fully guaranteed if the court having jurisdiction under the Convention had to be allowed to apply the forum non conveniens doctrine. . . .
>
> The defendants in the main proceedings emphasize the negative consequences which would result in practice from the obligation the English courts would then be under to try this case, inter alia as regards the expense of the proceedings, . . . the logistical difficulties resulting from geographic distance, the need to assess the merits of the case according to Jamaican standards, the enforceability in Jamaica of a default judgment and the impossibility of enforcing cross-claims against other defendants. . . .
>
> In that regard, genuine as those difficulties may be, suffice it to observe that such consequences, which are precisely those which may be taken into account when forum non conveniens is considered, are not such as to call into question the mandatory nature of the fundamental rule of jurisdiction contained in Article 2 of the Brussels Convention. . . .

Is that a better rule? What are the costs of *forum non conveniens*? What are the advantages?

12. **International Comity.** Should it matter to U.S. courts that a case is likely to upset a foreign government or affect U.S. foreign relations? Why or why not? Some courts have described a separate doctrine of "international comity" that might suggest dismissal in such circumstances. In *Bigio v. Coca-Cola Co.*, 448 F.3d 176 (2d Cir. 2006), for example, the plaintiffs were Canadian citizens who claimed that their family property in Egypt had been wrongfully seized by the Egyptian government and then operated by Coca-Cola (as a bottling plant). The district court dismissed the claim under the doctrines of international comity or in the alternative *forum non conveniens*. The court of appeals reversed. As to international comity, the court of appeals said:

> [T]he only issue of international comity properly raised here is whether adjudication of this case by a United States court would offend amicable working relationships with Egypt. . . .
>
> Throughout the long pendency of this lawsuit, the Government of Egypt has never raised the slightest objection to adjudication of the instant

controversy by United States courts. Moreover, this Court has already determined that resolution of this case by United States courts will "not likely impact on international relations" with Egypt. In its present posture, this is a common law suit for damages primarily between Canadian citizens and a United States company, which may likely focus on what Coca-Cola knew about the Bigios' ownership rights before it acquired its present interest in the Egyptian bottling plant. While adjudication of plaintiffs' common law claims may also require some modest application of Egyptian law, the courts of this Circuit are regularly called upon to interpret foreign law without thereby offending principles of international comity.

In a separate discussion, the court also reversed the dismissal on *forum non conveniens* grounds, emphasizing the substantial deference owed to a plaintiff's choice of forum. Should the result be different if the Egyptian government (or the U.S. State Department) objected? Does it make sense to think of comity as a separate doctrine from *forum non conveniens*?

In *Mujica v. AirScan, Inc.*, 771 F.3d 580 (9th Cir. 2014), the court considered a claim by Colombian citizens that two U.S. companies were complicit in the Colombian air force's bombing of a Colombian village in 1998. After first rejecting plaintiffs' federal claims under the Alien Tort Statute (ATS) and the Torture Victim Protection Act (TVPA) (see Chapter 2), the court considered claims under California state law and rejected them on basis of international comity. It first held that international comity was a doctrine of federal common law that could overcome state law claims, and then applied the following test:

> [A] court "evaluate[s] several factors, including [1] the strength of the United States' interest in using a foreign forum, [2] the strength of the foreign governments' interests, and [3] the adequacy of the alternative forum" [quoting *Ungaro-Benages v. Dresdner Bank AG*, 379 F.3d 1227 (11th Cir. 2004)].

As to U.S. interests, the court observed:

> The (nonexclusive) factors we should consider when assessing U.S. interests include (1) the location of the conduct in question, (2) the nationality of the parties, (3) the character of the conduct in question, (4) the foreign policy interests of the United States, and (5) any public policy interests. When some or all of a plaintiff's claims arise under state law, the state's interests, if any, should be considered as well.

Applying these factors, the court found the analysis to favor dismissal on grounds of comity. As to the U.S. interest, the court found it "mixed" due to the presence of California-based corporations as defendants, but the court was influenced by a U.S. State Department Statement of Interest (SOI) filed with the district court, saying that U.S. diplomatic interests favored resolution of the case in Colombia. As to Colombian interests, the court found them strong based on the location of the incident and a statement of the Colombian government that it preferred resolution in Colombia. The court then found the Colombian forum adequate and available, as the Colombian government supported the litigation and had allowed civil claims against the government and criminal charges against the individuals involved. It therefore directed dismissal of the claims.

How is this approach different (if at all) from *forum non conveniens*? Does it leave too much room for dismissal of claims that ought to be heard in the United States? Consider the following perspective:

> The Supreme Court has repeatedly said that federal courts have a "virtually unflagging obligation" to exercise jurisdiction. *Colorado River Water Conservation District v. United States*, 424 U.S. 800, 817 (1976). . . . The [Supreme] Court has described the doctrine of forum non conveniens as an exception to this obligation, which applies "in certain narrow circumstances." [*Quackenbush v. Allstate Ins. Co.*, 517 U.S. 706, 721 (1996).] . . . The extension of [the doctrine of comity] to permit abstention in the absence of a parallel foreign proceeding appears questionable in light of the federal courts' "virtually unflagging obligation" to exercise jurisdiction.

RESTATEMENT (FOURTH) OF THE FOREIGN RELATIONS LAW OF THE UNITED STATES § 424, Reporters' Note 9. *But see Cooper v. Tokyo Electric Power Co. Holdings Inc.*, 960 F.3d 549 (9th Cir. 2020) (affirming dismissal on grounds of international comity of personal injury claims arising from tsunami-related damage to the Fukushima nuclear power plant in Japan).

13. ***Forum Non Conveniens* in State Court.** As the foregoing cases reflect, federal courts apply a federal common law doctrine of *forum non conveniens* without regard to state law, even if the basis of federal jurisdiction is diversity. Can you explain how this is consistent with the *Erie* doctrine?

Would it be a problem if state and federal *forum non conveniens* doctrines substantially diverged? This was the case for a while in Texas, where the doctrine was abolished under state law. *Dow Chemical Co. v. Castro Alfaro*, 786 S.W.2d 674 (Tex. 1990) (concluding that Texas law precluded *forum non conveniens* dismissals for personal injury); Tex. Civ. Proc. & Rem. Code § 71.051(i) (overturning *Castro Alfaro* and reestablishing the doctrine). As a practical matter this may be a limited concern because most state courts have an almost equivalent version of *forum non conveniens* doctrine that they apply in state proceedings. However, some outliers exist. *See* Donald Earl Childress III, *Rethinking Legal Globalization: The Case of Transnational Personal Jurisdiction*, 54 WM. & MARY L. REV. 1489, 1539 (2013) (noting that "Delaware courts apply an 'overwhelming hardship' test, which is more stringent than the federal standard [and] Montana courts reject the doctrine outright in most cases").

B. Parallel Proceedings

Forum non conveniens issues arise when a plaintiff files a lawsuit in a U.S. court and the defendant seeks dismissal of the suit in favor of a foreign court. But this is not the only context in which challenges can be posed by the existence of multiple potential forums. Sometimes similar claims are filed in two different nations at the same time. This is the problem of parallel proceedings. For example, a party that expects to have a claim filed against it by another party in the United States may preemptively file an action for a declaratory judgment (or its equivalent) in its favor on the same claim in its preferred foreign court; if the other party then files its claim in a U.S. court, essentially the same action will be pending in two different jurisdictions. This section explores two methods that can be used to deal with this type of problem: *lis alibi pendens* stays and anti-suit injunctions.

1. Lis Alibi Pendens/*Abstention*

The following cases introduce the rules governing a motion for *lis alibi pendens*, which is a request that a court in one nation stay or dismiss its proceedings in favor of similar proceedings in another nation's court.

Finova Capital Corp. v. Ryan Helicopters USA, Inc.

180 F.3d 896 (7th Cir. 1999)

CUDAHY, Circuit Judge.

This diversity action involves a dispute over the ownership of two helicopters located on the Island of St. Lucia in the British West Indies. The helicopters were leased by Ryan Helicopters USA from Rotorcraft Partnership Ltd. and operated on St. Lucia by Ryan's subsidiary, St. Lucia Helicopters Ltd. When the deal turned sour, Ryan and St. Lucia Helicopters sued Rotorcraft in the High Court of St. Lucia. Some months later, Finova Corporation, a financing company that had succeeded to the rights of Rotorcraft, filed this action in the district court [in Illinois] naming Ryan and St. Lucia Helicopters as defendants.[1] The district court denied Ryan's motion to dismiss the action but agreed to stay the proceedings pending the completion of the St. Lucia suit. Finova now appeals the stay and we affirm.

Ryan's and Finova's rival bids for ownership of the helicopters are based on the lease agreement concluded between Ryan and Rotorcraft on September 28, 1992. The agreement provided that Ryan would lease the two helicopters for a period of 60 months. It also gave Ryan an option to purchase the helicopters for

---

1. Ryan Helicopters is a Florida corporation and St. Lucia Helicopters a St. Lucia corporation. . . . Rotorcraft is incorporated in Maryland but conducts business in Illinois. Rotorcraft's president, James Panoff, is an Illinois citizen. Finova is a Delaware corporation with its principal place of business in Phoenix, Arizona. For ease of discussion, we use "Ryan" throughout to refer to Ryan and St. Lucia Helicopters collectively.

$157,622 at the conclusion of the lease term, provided that no payments were due and owing. . . . On August 29, 1996, Ryan and Rotorcraft entered into a supplemental agreement directed toward the remaining payments due under the lease. The supplemental agreement designated either St. Lucia or Illinois as a forum for the resolution of disputes and, similarly, either the laws of St. Lucia or of Illinois as the applicable law. Around this time, Rotorcraft assigned all of its rights and interests under the lease to Finova.

On October 15, 1997, the date the lease expired, Ryan sued Rotorcraft and its president, James Panoff, in the High Court of St. Lucia seeking a declaration that it was entitled to ownership of the helicopters on the payment of certain outstanding sums. The following February, Finova applied to intervene in the St. Lucia proceeding. In an order dated April 7, 1998, the St. Lucia court granted Finova's application and Ryan subsequently amended its pleadings to include Finova as a party. Also on April 7, 1998, the St. Lucia court entered a default judgment against Rotorcraft and Panoff. Meanwhile, Finova had made moves of its own to assert its rights under the lease. Prior to the expiration of the lease, and again shortly thereafter, Finova wrote to Ryan demanding the return of the helicopters. On February 6, 1998 — a few weeks before it intervened in the St. Lucia proceedings — Finova filed suit in Illinois seeking a declaration of ownership under the lease and the return of the helicopters. Ryan moved to dismiss the suit on the basis of the pending St. Lucia action. The district court denied the motion to dismiss but granted Ryan's alternative motion to stay the proceedings pending the completion of the litigation in St. Lucia. The district court reasoned that the parties had not designated Illinois as the exclusive forum for the resolution of disputes under the lease and supplemental agreement and that exceptional circumstances existed that militated in favor of abstention. Finova challenges this decision, which we review for abuse of discretion.

Although federal courts have a "virtually unflagging obligation" to exercise the jurisdiction conferred on them by Congress, in exceptional cases, a federal court should stay a suit and await the outcome of parallel proceedings as a matter of "wise judicial administration, giving regard to the conservation of judicial resources and comprehensive disposition of litigation." *Colorado River Water Conservation Dist. v. United States*, 424 U.S. 800, 817 (1976). . . . Courts usually grapple with the issue of abstention in the context of parallel state court proceedings. The situation is somewhat different where, as here, "the alternate forum is not the tribunal of a state of the federal union to which, under our Constitution, we owe a special obligation of comity." *Ingersoll Milling Mach. Co. v. Granger*, 833 F.2d 680, 685 (7th Cir. 1987). Nevertheless, in the interests of international comity, we apply the same general principles with respect to parallel proceedings in a foreign court.

In assessing the propriety of abstention, our first task is to determine whether the federal and foreign proceedings are in fact parallel. Suits are parallel if substantially the same parties are litigating substantially the same issues simultaneously in two fora. We have little difficulty in concluding that these conditions are satisfied in the present case. Indeed, counsel for Finova conceded as much at oral argument. The parties to the proceedings in the district court and in St. Lucia are substantially the same. Ryan and Finova are the parties in interest. (The absence of Rotorcraft and Panoff in the federal action is immaterial given that Finova has assumed Rotorcraft's rights under the lease.) In addition, the respective courts have been asked to resolve the same central issue, namely, who owns the helicopters under the terms of the lease. Since the principal matter of contention is identical, the granting of relief in one forum would dispose of the claims raised in the other. Thus, we agree with the district court that the proceedings are parallel.

Our next task is to balance the considerations that weigh in favor of, and against, abstention, bearing in mind the exceptional nature of the measure. Relying on the guidance of the Supreme Court, we have previously considered a long list of factors: (1) the identity of the court that first assumed jurisdiction over the property; (2) the relative inconvenience of the federal forum; (3) the need to avoid piecemeal litigation; (4) the order in which the respective proceedings were filed; (5) whether federal or foreign law provides the rule of decision; (6) whether the foreign action protects the federal plaintiff's rights; (7) the relative progress of the federal and foreign proceedings; and (8) the vexatious or contrived nature of the federal claim. Reviewing the decision below in light of *Colorado River* and its progeny, we conclude that the district court did not abuse its discretion in entering the stay.

It is clear that the High Court of St. Lucia was the first to exercise jurisdiction over the subject matter of the dispute: Ryan filed suit in St. Lucia on October 15, 1997 whereas Finova instituted proceedings in the district court on February 6, 1998. Finova protests that the St. Lucia proceedings did not become operative until April 7, 1998, when the St. Lucia court allowed it to intervene. But since Rotorcraft and Panoff — Finova's predecessors in interest — were named in the St. Lucia suit from the outset, the omission of Finova was a mere technicality for present purposes. Finova does not suggest that it was unaware of the St. Lucia litigation at the time it filed the present action and it concedes that the St. Lucia court had jurisdiction over substantially the same issue that it raised in the district court. Thus, we endorse the district court's determination that the St. Lucia court was the first to act.

The parties argue at length about the relative inconvenience of St. Lucia or Illinois as a location for the conduct of the litigation. Finova keenly disputes Ryan's contention that the majority of witnesses and documents are in St. Lucia and points out that *its* chief witness (James Panoff) is an Illinois citizen. The district court sided with Ryan on this score. We believe that the issue is more finely balanced and that the underlying dispute is closely connected to both locations. Recall that one of the parties to the original lease (Rotorcraft) is based in Illinois, the other (Ryan) in Florida and its subsidiary (Ryan Helicopters) in St. Lucia. We are mindful that the predominance of activity under the lease — notably the operation of the helicopters — took place in St. Lucia. But the parties acknowledged ties to both locations by including alternatives in the choice of forum clause in their supplemental agreement. Since St. Lucia and Illinois were expressly selected as acceptable fora for the resolution of disputes, neither side can credibly claim that it is being forced to litigate in an inconvenient forum. In these circumstances, we are reluctant to place much importance on convenience as a factor.

We do think it significant that the helicopters — the subject matter of the dispute — are located on the Island of St. Lucia. Finova attempts to play this down by emphasizing that the underlying dispute between the parties is contractual and not *in rem*. But there is more at issue here than the nature of the action. As long as the helicopters remain in St. Lucia, they fall within the exclusive jurisdiction of the High Court of St. Lucia for all practical purposes. If the district court were to grant the relief Finova seeks — a declaration of ownership and the return of the helicopters — the enforcement of the order would lie in the hands of the St. Lucia court. Moreover, since both proceedings turn on the same core issue, this is a case where one can predict with some confidence that the foreign court litigation will probably eliminate the need for any further proceedings in federal court. Thus, considerations of judicial economy — notably the need to avoid protracted, piece-meal litigation — favored staying the district court proceedings.

One of the principal reasons why federal courts exercise jurisdiction in the face of parallel proceedings is the need to protect the rights of the federal plaintiff. The fact that this is a diversity suit prompted the district court to conclude that there is no strong federal interest in this case. We have previously recognized that the presumption in favor of jurisdiction applies with equal vigor to diversity suits. *See Evans Transp. Co. v. Scullin Steel Co.*, 693 F.2d 715, 717 (7th Cir. 1982). . . . But while it is one thing to say that a diversity case requires the same showing of exceptional circumstances to justify abstention, it is quite another to suggest — as Finova does — that this contractual dispute raises particular concerns over the ability of the foreign court to protect Finova's substantive rights. This is not a case involving the application of legal rights or principles unique to, or specially protected by, federal law; the federal interest in the adjudication of a contractual dispute — even one governed by Illinois (as opposed to St. Lucia) law — is far from overwhelming. It was not unreasonable for the district court to conclude that St. Lucia had a substantial interest in the case and that its courts are equipped to resolve it.[4] The parties had conceded as much in their supplemental agreement (providing that a dispute could be resolved by an Illinois or a St. Lucia court apply-ing the laws of either place). Thus, considerations of international comity were furthered by the entry of the stay.

Notwithstanding all of the above, we recognize that the case for abstention here is not watertight; indeed, we think it a closer call than the district court suggests. As noted above, we are less impressed with the importance of conve-nience as a factor in this case. In addition, the St. Lucia case was filed only four months before the federal action and was still in its preliminary stages. Finova correctly notes that the relative infancy of the St. Lucia proceedings distinguishes the present case from cases . . . where we endorsed abstention in the face of par-allel proceedings that were a good deal further down the road to completion. But

---

4. We have previously observed that a district court cannot be faulted for rejecting "the paro-chial concept that all disputes must be resolved under our laws and in our courts." *Ingersoll*, 833 F.2d at 685. Finova suggests that the High Court of St. Lucia is not equipped to handle this case. But St. Lucia was selected by Rotorcraft — Finova's predecessor in interest — as an acceptable forum for the resolution of disputes. Contrary to Finova's contentions, we have no reason to doubt that the St. Lucia court will adjudicate the claim effectively.

while we may part company with the district court on these discrete issues, it is not our task simply to substitute our own perspective. Finova seems to believe that the existence of these factors — indeed of *any* factor favoring district court jurisdiction — is enough in itself to preclude abstention. We disagree. The decision to abstain is based on an assessment of the totality of the circumstances, and the Supreme Court has cautioned against placing too much weight on any specific factor. *See Colorado River*, 424 U.S. at 818-19. We believe that the district court's decision was the product of a careful weighing of the factors pertinent to the case at hand and we cannot fault the overall finding that exceptional circumstances favored abstention. We are mindful also that, rather than dismissing the action, the district court took the more measured step of staying the proceedings. *See Ingersoll*, 833 F.2d at 686 ("This approach protects the substantial rights of the parties while permitting the district court to manage its time effectively. . . . Such a common sense approach is clearly within the sound discretion of the trial court."). . . . In the circumstances, we conclude that the district court acted within its discretion in entering the stay.

AFFIRMED.

Seguros del Estado, S.A. v. Scientific Games, Inc.

262 F.3d 1164 (11th Cir. 2001)

Appellant Scientific Games, Inc., appeals the district court's denial of its motion to dismiss, wherein Appellant asserted . . . the doctrine of *lis alibi pendens* applied. Appellant also appeals the district court's grant of summary judgment to Appellee Seguros del Estado, S.A.

This case involves three agreements: (1) a contract between Appellant and Empresa Colombiana de Recursos Para la Salud, S.A. (Ecosalud), a Colombian governmental entity, under which Appellant created and managed a national instant lottery in Colombia (Lottery Contract); (2) a bond which was required under the Lottery Contract, taken out by Appellant and payable by Appellee to Ecosalud (Bond); and (3) an indemnification agreement which required Appellant to reimburse Appellee for sums paid to Ecosalud and for any interest paid on such sums (Indemnification Agreement). On appeal, Appellant . . . [argues that] in light of pending litigation in Colombia, this case should be dismissed under principles of international comity and the *lis alibi pendens* doctrine. . . .

We affirm. . . .

Background

On March 12, 1992, Ecosalud entered the Lottery Contract with (1) Appellant, (2) PKI Associates, Inc., a New York corporation, and (3) Daibutsu, Inc., a Panamanian corporation (collectively, Contractors). The Contractors formed a Colombian operating company, Wintech de Colombia, S.A. (Wintech), to run the lottery and thereafter assigned the Lottery Contract to Wintech. Clause 41 of the Lottery Contract required the Contractors to obtain a bond from a

Colombian insurance company in the amount of $4 million or its equivalent in Colombian pesos. This bond was to guarantee the Contractors' performance of their obligations under the Lottery Contract, including the payment of any penalties. Appellee issued to Appellant the Bond, whose initial term was from March 12, 1992, to March 12, 1993. As partial consideration for the Bond, Appellant executed the Indemnification Agreement with Appellee. This Agreement required Appellant to "immediately reimburse" Appellee for any sums paid to Ecosalud under the terms of the Bond and to pay interest to Appellee on these sums "at the current banking interest rate in effect in Colombia." An amendment to the Bond, dated May 15, 1992, provided for the automatic renewal of the policy at the end of each period until one year after the expiration of the Lottery Contract. Another amendment, dated March 2, 1993, extended the Bond's term of effectiveness through March 12, 1994.

On July 1, 1993, Ecosalud issued a Declaration of Caducity, Administrative Resolution No. 246 (the Declaration). In this Declaration, Ecosalud terminated the Lottery Contract based on a determination that the Contractors breached the Contract. Furthermore, Ecosalud found the Contractors and Wintech jointly and severally liable and proclaimed Ecosalud was owed in excess of $4 million under the terms of the Lottery Contract. Finally, Ecosalud stated in the Declaration that Appellee was jointly and severally liable for $4 million pursuant to the Bond. The Bond provides that "[a] casualty shall be deemed to have occurred[,] . . . in the event of breach of the contract, when the Administrative Resolution that declared the caducity of the contract or the breach thereof for reasons attributable to the contractor is final and binding. . . ." The Bond obligates Appellee, under these circumstances, to pay Ecosalud within a month following a request for payment. Appellee received notice of the Declaration on July 7, 1993, and provided Appellant with written notice on July 12, 1993.

Pursuant to the request of Appellant and Appellee that it reconsider the Declaration, Ecosalud confirmed the Declaration by issuing Administrative Resolution No. 493 on October 15, 1993. On March 15, 1994, Appellant challenged the Declaration and Resolution No. 493 in a Colombian administrative court and sought temporary suspension of the Declaration during the appeal. In May 1994, the administrative court denied the request for temporary suspension. The appeal remains pending.

Following negotiations, Appellee reached a settlement with Ecosalud on September 29, 1994. The settlement obligated Appellee to pay Ecosalud $2.4 million, in lieu of the contractually mandated sum of $4 million. On November 1, 1994, Appellee paid Ecosalud $2.4 million. The next day, Appellee notified Appellant of this payment and demanded reimbursement pursuant to the Indemnification Agreement. Appellant failed to reimburse Appellee, thereby giving rise to this litigation.

On April 2, 1998, Appellee filed suit in United States District Court, Northern District of Georgia, seeking to recover from Appellant for breach of contract and unjust enrichment. On May 7, 1998, Appellee filed a motion for summary judgment based on its breach of contract claim. Appellee sought a $2.4 million reimbursement plus pre-judgment interest on that amount at the rate specified in the

Indemnification Agreement. On May 12, 1998, Appellant filed a motion to dismiss . . . based on the legal doctrine[] of *lis alibi pendens*. . . .

In its order dated September 28, 1999, the district court denied Appellant's motion to dismiss, . . . concluding that *lis alibi pendens* was inapplicable. The district court proceeded to grant Appellee's motion for summary judgment. In so doing, the court concluded as follows: the Bond and Indemnification Agreement were in effect when the Declaration was issued; Resolution No. 493 rendered the Declaration "final and binding;" Appellee properly notified Appellant; Appellee's settlement with Ecosalud was reasonable; and Appellant is liable to Appellee for reimbursement of the principal amount, plus interest. . . . This appeal followed.

II. Discussion

Motion to Dismiss

Appellant asserts its motion to dismiss should have been granted since . . . the doctrine of *lis alibi pendens* applies due to related, ongoing litigation in Colombia. . . .

. . .

We review the district court's decision declining to apply the principle of *lis alibi pendens* for abuse of discretion. *Lis alibi pendens* is a doctrine rooted in international comity which permits a court to refuse to exercise jurisdiction in the face of parallel litigation that is ongoing in another country.

Appellant argues the district court should have stayed this case in the face of the suit challenging the Declaration which is pending before a Colombian administrative court. Specifically, Appellant argues the invalidation of the Declaration by the Colombian court would render Appellee's indemnification claim baseless, as Appellee would have no obligation to pay on the Bond. According to Appellant, the central issue in both this case and the Colombian case is the validity of the Declaration, and Appellee and Appellant are parties to both suits and are bound by the result of both suits. Deciding this case, therefore, would effectively decide the pending Colombian case and violate principles of international comity. Appellant also argues that, if this Court affirms the district court's judgment and the Colombian court subsequently invalidates the Declaration, staying this case would avoid "a meaningless cycle of round-robin litigation" in which Appellant would have to sue Ecosalud for recovery of its reimbursement to Appellee. Finally, Appellant maintains this Court should invoke *lis alibi pendens* here as we did in a related case. *See Empresa Colombiana de Recursos Para La Salud, S.A. v. Scientific Games, Inc.*, 136 F.3d 142 (11th Cir. 1998).

The issue here is whether the district court abused its discretion in declining to invoke the doctrine of *lis alibi pendens*. We conclude it did not.

The application of *lis alibi pendens* turns on whether a court should exercise its jurisdiction where *parallel* proceedings are ongoing in a foreign nation. . . . The threshold question, therefore, is whether this case is parallel to the ongoing case in Colombia. *See Finova Capital Corp. v. Ryan Helicopters U.S.A., Inc.*, 180 F.3d 896, 898 (7th Cir. 1999). We conclude the two cases are not parallel since they involve materially different issues, documents, and parties.

At issue in the Colombian case is the validity of the Declaration and, therefore, whether Appellant breached the Lottery Contract and whether Ecosalud properly invoked Clauses 42 and 43 of the Lottery Contract. These clauses provide the bases for which Ecosalud may declare caducity and demand payment of the penalty. By contrast, at issue in this case is whether Appellee is entitled to reimbursement from Appellant under the terms of the Indemnification Agreement and, by reference, the terms of the Bond. Thus, while this case has been *precipitated by* Ecosalud's issuance of the Declaration, it does not directly *involve* the validity of the Declaration or the Lottery Contract.

Furthermore, the outcome of this case will not affect the outcome of the Colombian case, as Appellant claims. This case will determine only whether the penalty sum will be outlaid by Appellant rather than by Appellee. In other words, if Appellee prevails, the risk of the overall transaction would be transferred from Appellee to Appellant. A decision in this case would not, therefore, effectively decide the outcome of the litigation currently pending in Colombia.

Next, the parties are not the same. . . . [T]he attorney who submitted a filing for Appellee in the Colombian litigation, Dr. German Espinosa-Restrepo, testified in a deposition that Appellee was not a party in the Colombian case. Rather, Dr. Espinosa testified that Appellee, as a third party with a relationship to the subject matter in litigation, was summoned into the action to state its position in the suit. Dr. Espinosa testified that Appellee, in its filing with the Colombian court, stated that "it has no relationship whatsoever with this action because its rights that arose in the payment of the obligation will be pursued against [Appellant] both based in the subrogation action [permitted under Colombian law] or based on the indemnity agreement like in this case in the United States." The text of the filing bears out this characterization: "By virtue of the insurer's right of subrogation established by Article 1098 of the Colombian Commercial Code, and the utilization of the counterguarantee [*i.e.*, Indemnification Agreement] issued by [Appellant], [Appellee] is attempting to collect at said company's domicile (Alpharetta — Atlanta, Georgia, USA)." Another expert for Appellee, Dr. Jorge Mora Sanchez, similarly declared that Appellee is not a party to any litigation between Appellant and Ecosalud in Colombia. Upon reviewing the expert legal testimony on both sides, we conclude Appellee is not an integral party in the pending Colombian litigation.

Finally, we draw a contrast between this case, where *lis alibi pendens* is not applicable, and two cases cited by Appellant where the doctrine was applicable. First, *Empresa Colombiana de Recursos Para La Salud, S.A. v. Scientific Games, Inc.* and a pending Colombian case dealt with the same issue — whether Ecosalud has the right to enforce the Executable Document, required under Clause 27(3) of the Lottery Contract. These cases also directly involved the same parties — Appellant and Ecosalud. Similarly, *Posner v. Essex Ins. Co.*, 178 F.3d 1209 (11th Cir. 1999), and an ongoing suit in Bermuda involved the same issue — the validity and therefore the effect of homeowner insurance policies — and the same parties — a homeowner and an insurance company. This case and the pending Colombian case directly involve neither the same issues nor the same parties.

For the reasons stated above, we conclude the district court did not abuse its discretion in declining to stay this case based on the doctrine of *lis alibi pendens*.

NOTES AND QUESTIONS

1. **Parallel Proceedings in Domestic Cases.** The problem of parallel proceedings is not unique to transnational litigation, although it may have greater significance in transnational cases for reasons discussed in other forum-selection contexts. In domestic litigation, there may be parallel suits filed in two state courts, in state and federal court, or in two federal courts. In *Colorado River Water Conservation Dist. v. United States*, 424 U.S. 800 (1976), the Supreme Court addressed a federal court's ability to abstain in the face of parallel state proceedings; it noted that abstention is rarely applicable, but it listed an array of relevant factors to consider and found abstention proper in the particular case. *Colorado River* is frequently cited in international abstention cases. Should the test for abstention be more or less demanding in transnational cases?

2. ***Lis Alibi Pendens* and Litigation Strategy.** Parallel proceedings often arise because a defendant in an action in one nation files a related claim in the courts of another nation. Why would a defendant do that? In *Ryan*, why do you think Finova filed a claim against Ryan in the United States after Ryan had already filed a claim against Finova's predecessor (Rotocraft) in St. Lucia? In *Seguros del Estado*, why do you think Seguros filed a claim against Scientific Games in the United States after Scientific Games had already initiated administrative court proceedings in Colombia? Why do you think Ryan and Scientific Games did not want the U.S. actions to proceed? On each side, are there legitimate reasons (as opposed to illegitimate reasons)? How can a court tell the difference?

3. **The Standard for *Lis Alibi Pendens*.** What is the standard used by the courts to determine whether to grant a *lis alibi pendens* stay or dismissal? Although the courts sometimes say that stay or dismissal under *lis alibi pendens* is exceptional, is that true? In what respect were the facts in *Ryan* exceptional? In *Posner v. Essex Ins. Co. Ltd.*, 178 F.3d 1209 (11th Cir. 1999), cited in *Seguros del Estado*, the court of appeals directed a stay of U.S. proceedings in favor of proceedings in Bermuda, based on three factors: "(1) a proper level of respect for the acts of our fellow sovereign nations — a rather vague concept referred to in American jurisprudence as international comity; (2) fairness to litigants; and (3) efficient use of scarce judicial resources." It concluded:

> The district court here properly evaluated these issues in making its decision, concluding that they weighed in favor of abstaining. With respect to the first factor, international comity, the district court found no evidence that the Bermuda court was not competent to hear the claims or would not use fair and just proceedings in deciding the case. The district court also noted that the insurance "policies are governed by Bermuda law, and their underwriter,

Essex, is a Bermuda corporation," in determining that "[i]nternational comity . . . weighs in favor of abstention." Plaintiffs have not challenged these conclusions. As the district court recognized, the second and third . . . factors — fairness and judicial resources — also counsel in favor of abstention. With respect to fairness, the facts that Essex filed the Bermuda action nearly a year before the commencement of this case, and allowing both actions to proceed risks inconsistent judgments, outweigh any convenience that the parties might enjoy in the Florida forum. Finally, although this case and the Bermuda action are not identical, they do involve significantly common issues and parties. The district court correctly concluded, therefore, that "[s]carce judicial resources . . . would be used most efficiently if the Bermuda action were to proceed to conclusion before this Court entertained Posner's insurance policy related claim."

What if anything is exceptional about these facts? In *Royal and Sun Alliance Ins. Co. of Canada v. Century Int'l Arms, Inc.*, 466 F.3d 88 (2d Cir. 2006), in contrast, the court of appeals reversed a *lis alibi pendens* dismissal, emphasizing the need for exceptional circumstances:

> In the context of parallel proceedings in a foreign court, a district court should be guided by the principles upon which international comity is based: the proper respect for litigation in and the courts of a sovereign nation, fairness to litigants, and judicial efficiency. . . . Proper consideration of these principles will no doubt require an evaluation of various factors, such as the similarity of the parties, the similarity of the issues, the order in which the actions were filed, the adequacy of the alternate forum, the potential prejudice to either party, the convenience of the parties, the connection between the litigation and the United States, and the connection between the litigation and the foreign jurisdiction. *See, e.g., Finova Capital Corp.*, 180 F.3d at 898-99. . . . This list is not exhaustive, and a district court should examine the "totality of the circumstances," *Finova Capital Corp.*, 180 F.3d at 900, to determine whether the specific facts before it are sufficiently exceptional to justify abstention.
>
> In the present case, the district court did not identify any exceptional circumstances that would support abstention, and therefore the dismissal of the action was an abuse of discretion. The district court's decision to dismiss the action was based on four factors: the existence of the Canadian action against Century Canada, Century America's consent to jurisdiction in Canada, the affiliation between Century America and Century Canada, and the adequacy of Canadian judicial procedures. These factors led the district court to conclude that the action in Canada was a parallel action that provided an adequate forum for RSA's claims, and that therefore a dismissal of the case was warranted.
>
> The existence of a parallel action in an adequate foreign jurisdiction must be the beginning, not the end, of a district court's determination of whether abstention is appropriate. As we explained above, circumstances that routinely exist in connection with parallel litigation cannot reasonably be considered exceptional circumstances, and therefore the mere existence of an adequate parallel action, by itself, does not justify the dismissal of a case on grounds of international comity abstention. Rather, additional circumstances

must be present — such as a foreign nation's interest in uniform bankruptcy proceedings — that outweigh the district court's general obligation to exercise its jurisdiction. The district court did not identify any such special circumstances.

Royal Sun involved a dispute over insurance payments between Royal Sun (an insurer) and two affiliated firearms manufacturers, Century America and Century Canada. Royal Sun initially sued the Canadian affiliate in Canada and then sued the U.S. affiliate in New York. What exceptional circumstances, if any, might exist? How (if at all) is this different from *Posner*? Does it make sense to have the two suits proceed in parallel (as the court of appeals directed)? What happens if they reach inconsistent verdicts? What happens if one is decided while the other is still pending?

As you think through these questions, recall the list of factors identified by the *Finova* court. How are these factors similar to or different than the factors employed in evaluating *forum non conveniens* motions? What other factors might a court consider when a stay is requested?

4. **International Comity.** What role does international comity play in *lis alibi pendens* dismissals? What do courts mean by international comity in this context? Is it the same as in the *forum non conveniens* context?

5. **Comparative Perspective.** The European Union addresses the problem of parallel proceedings with a "first-in-time rule." According to Article 29(1) of EU Regulation No. 1215/2012 on Jurisdiction and the Recognition and Enforcement of Judgments in Civil and Commercial Matters (Recast), the general rule is that "where proceedings involving the same cause of action and between the same parties are brought in the courts of different Member States, any court other than the court first seised shall of its own motion stay its proceedings. . . ." In effect this rule provides a bright-line first-filed rule for *lis alibi pendens* situations involving the courts of two Member States. If it applied, how would this rule resolve the cases excerpted above? Would that produce better outcomes in those cases? If parties know that this is the rule, what behavior might it encourage? Note that the EU's general first-in-time rule is subject to a notable exception: "[W]here a court of a Member State on which [a valid forum selection agreement] confers exclusive jurisdiction is seised, any court of another Member State shall stay the proceedings until such time as the court seised on the basis of the agreement declares that it has no jurisdiction under the agreement." *Id.*, Article 31. Forum selection agreements are discussed below in Section C.

2. *International Anti-Suit Injunctions*

A second method for addressing parallel proceedings is the anti-suit injunction, whereby a court in one nation enjoins a party before it from pursuing similar proceedings in a foreign nation's court. As you read the cases that follow, pay close attention not only to the rules governing anti-suit injunctions, but also to the difference between anti-suit injunctions and *lis pendens* stays.

China Trade & Development Corp. v. M.V. Choong Yong

837 F.2d 33 (2d Cir. 1987)

GEORGE C. PRATT, Circuit Judge.

[T]he United States District Court for the Southern District of New York . . . permanently enjoined Ssangyong Shipping Co., Ltd. ("Ssangyong") from proceeding in the courts of Korea with its action against China Trade & Development Corp., Chung Hua Trade & Development Corp. and Soybean Importers Joint Committee of the Republic of China (collectively, "China Trade").

The district court had granted the injunction because it found that (1) the parties in the Korean action are the same as the parties in this action; (2) the issue of liability raised by Ssangyong in the Korean court is the same as the issue of liability raised here; (3) the Korean litigation would be vexatious to the plaintiffs in the United States action, which was commenced first; and (4) allowing the Korean litigation to proceed would result in a race to judgment.

Because no important policy of the forum would be frustrated by allowing the Korean action to proceed, and because the Korean action poses no threat to the jurisdiction of the district court, we conclude that the interests of comity are not overbalanced by equitable factors favoring an injunction, and we hold that the district court abused its discretion when it enjoined Ssangyong, a Korean corporation, from proceeding in the courts of Korea. We therefore reverse.

Background

In 1984 China Trade sought to import 25,000 metric tons of soybeans into the Republic of China from the United States. Ssangyong, a Republic of Korea corporation, agreed to transport the soybeans on its ship the M.V. CHOONG YONG. The vessel ran aground, however, and as China Trade contends, the soybeans, contaminated by seawater, became virtually valueless.

The litigation leading to this appeal began in 1985 when attorneys for China Trade attached the M.V. BOO YONG, another vessel owned by Ssangyong, which was then located in the Central District of California. To release the vessel, the parties agreed that China Trade would lift the attachment and discontinue the California action and, in exchange, Ssangyong would provide security in the amount of $1,800,000, the approximate value of the attached vessel, and would appear in an action to be commenced by China Trade in the Southern District of New York and waive any right to dismissal of the new action on the ground of forum non conveniens.

China Trade then commenced this action in the southern district seeking $7,500,000 in damages from Ssangyong for failure to deliver the soybeans. Both parties proceeded to prepare the case for trial through extensive discovery that has included both depositions and document production that required trips to Korea and to the Republic of China. Trial was scheduled to begin in September 1987.

On April 22, 1987, while discovery was still progressing, Ssangyong's Korean attorneys filed a pleading in the District Court of Pusan, commencing an action, similar to our declaratory judgment action, which seeks confirmation that Ssangyong is not liable for China Trade's loss. Nearly two months later Ssangyong's New York counsel forwarded a copy of this pleading to counsel for China Trade. Immediately, and before taking any action in the district court of Pusan, China Trade moved by order to show cause in this action for an injunction against further prosecution of the Korean action.

To determine whether to enjoin the foreign litigation, the district court . . . articulated two threshold requirements for such an injunction: (1) the parties must be the same in both matters, and (2) resolution of the case before the enjoining court must be dispositive of the action to be enjoined.

When these threshold requirements are met, five factors are suggested in determining whether the foregoing action should be enjoined: (1) frustration of a policy in the enjoining forum; (2) the foreign action would be vexatious; (3) a threat to the issuing court's in rem or quasi in rem jurisdiction; (4) the proceedings in the other forum prejudice other equitable considerations; or (5) adjudication of the same issues in separate actions would result in delay, inconvenience, expense, inconsistency, or a race to judgment.

Judge Motley found after a hearing that the two threshold requirements were met, since in both actions the parties and the issues of liability are the same. She then considered the additional five factors and found that the Korean litigation in this case would (1) be vexatious to the plaintiffs and (2) result in expense and a race to judgment. Considering these findings sufficient, the district court permanently enjoined Ssangyong's prosecution of the Korean action. This appeal followed.

Discussion

. . .

The power of federal courts to enjoin foreign suits by persons subject to their jurisdiction is well-established. The fact that the injunction operates only against the parties, and not directly against the foreign court, does not eliminate the need for due regard to principles of international comity, because such an order effectively restricts the jurisdiction of the court of a foreign sovereign. Therefore, an anti-foreign-suit injunction should be used sparingly, and should be granted only with care and great restraint.

Concurrent jurisdiction in two courts does not necessarily result in a conflict. When two sovereigns have concurrent in personam jurisdiction one court will ordinarily not interfere with or try to restrain proceedings before the other. "[P]arallel proceedings on the same in personam claim should ordinarily be allowed to proceed simultaneously, at least until a judgment is reached in one which can be pled as res judicata in the other," [*Laker Airways, Ltd. v. Sabena Belgian World Airlines*, 731 F.2d 909, 926-27 (D.C. Cir. 1984)].

Since parallel proceedings are ordinarily tolerable, the initiation before a foreign court of a suit concerning the same parties and issues as a suit already pending in a United States court does not, without more, justify enjoining a party from proceeding in the foreign forum.

In general we agree with the approach taken by Judge Motley. She began by inquiring (1) whether the parties to both suits are the same and (2) whether resolution of the case before the enjoining court would be dispositive of the enjoined action. She apparently found that both of these prerequisites were met here. While there is some question as to whether the Korean courts would recognize a judgment of the southern district, it is not necessary to determine that question of Korean law because the injunction is deficient for another reason. Judge Motley found the necessary additional justification for this injunction in two [factors] . . . : "vexatiousness" of the parallel proceeding to China Trade and a "race to judgment" causing additional expense. However, since these factors are likely to be present whenever parallel actions are proceeding concurrently, an anti-suit injunction grounded on these additional factors alone would tend to undermine the policy that allows parallel proceedings to continue and disfavors anti-suit injunctions. Having due regard to the interests of comity, we think that in the circumstances of this case two . . . other factors . . . take on much greater significance in determining whether Ssangyong should be enjoined from proceeding in its Korean action: (A) whether the foreign action threatens the jurisdiction of the enjoining forum, and (B) whether strong public policies of the enjoining forum are threatened by the foreign action. *See Laker v. Sabena*, 731 F.2d at 927, 937.

A. Protecting Jurisdiction

. . . [I]f a foreign court is not merely proceeding in parallel but is attempting to carve out exclusive jurisdiction over the action, an injunction may . . . be necessary to protect the enjoining court's jurisdiction. In the *Laker* litigation, for example, when the English Court of Appeal enjoined Laker's litigation of its claims against British defendants in a United States court under United States law, the United States district court, in order to protect its own jurisdiction, enjoined other defendants in the Laker action from seeking similar injunctions from the English Court of Appeal. *Laker v. Sabena*, 731 F.2d at 917-21.

In the present case, however, there does not appear to be any threat to the district court's jurisdiction. While the Korean court may determine the same liability issue as that before the southern district, the Korean court has not attempted to enjoin the proceedings in New York. Neither the Korean court nor Ssangyong has sought to prevent the southern district from exercising its jurisdiction over this case.

B. Important Public Policies

An anti-suit injunction may also be appropriate when a party seeks to evade important policies of the forum by litigating before a foreign court. While an injunction may be appropriate when a party attempts to evade compliance with a statute of the forum that effectuates important public policies, an injunction is not appropriate merely to prevent a party from seeking slight advantages in the substantive or procedural law to be applied in a foreign court.

The possibility that a United States judgment might be unenforceable in Korea is no more than speculation about the race to judgment that may ensue whenever courts have concurrent jurisdiction. Moreover, we cannot determine at this point whether a judgment of the United States court in an amount exceeding the 1.8 million dollar bond would be enforceable in Korea even if the Korean action were now enjoined. Should plaintiffs prevail, enforcement of any excess amount against Ssangyong in Korea may well require relitigation in the Korean courts of the issue of liability. In these circumstances, we are not persuaded that Ssangyong, the party seeking to litigate in the foreign tribunal, is attempting to evade any important policy of this forum.

Conclusion

The equitable factors relied upon by the district court in granting the anti-suit injunction are not sufficient to overcome the restraint and caution required by international comity. Because the Korean litigation poses no threat to the jurisdiction of the district court or to any important public policy of this forum, we conclude that the district court abused its discretion by issuing the injunction. Reversed.

BRIGHT, Senior Circuit Judge, dissenting:

. . .

In its analysis of whether equitable considerations justified the issuance of an injunction, the [district] court found the crucial facts relating to injunctive relief as follows:

. . .

> Discovery for the case proceeded and was completed. Trial was scheduled by this court, without objection, for September 21, 1987. Ssangyong, however, some 2 1/2 years after [the accident and 1 1/2 years after] this action was begun, then proceeded to file a suit in Pusan Court of the Republic of Korea, naming the same parties to the action, as well as the same issues. Plaintiffs herein move to enjoin the defendant from proceeding with that action.
>
> The court finds as facts that the parties to the two actions are the same and that resolution of the action before this court would be dispositive of the Korean action.
>
> The court also finds that the Korean action would be vexatious to plaintiffs, and that the Korean action could potentially frustrate the proceedings before this court.

Id. at 2-3. Those facts receive ample support from the record, and I accept them as true for the purposes of this appeal.

In addressing its power, as well as the discretionary factors in the issuance of an injunction barring a litigant from pursuing a simultaneous remedy in a foreign forum, the district judge stated:

> The first question that this court must address is whether it should grant an injunction enjoining the defendants from proceeding with their lawsuit in Korea. It is

recognized that courts have the power to enjoin litigants from pursuing simultaneous contests in a foreign forum. However, comity militates against granting such relief, since the issuance of an injunction can deprive the other country in which the suit is instituted of its sovereignty to some extent. Defendants rely heavily on *Laker*, which suggests that "The fundamental corollary to concurrent jurisdiction must ordinarily be respected: parallel proceedings in the same in personam claim should ordinarily be allowed to proceed simultaneously, at least until a judgment is reached in one which can be pled as res judicata in the other." *Laker*, however, also emphasizes that if a substantial amount of time has elapsed between the commencement of the two actions, equitable principles make it more appropriate to enjoin the second action. In the instant case, almost 2 1/2 years elapsed before the defendants brought suit in Korea, making this an appropriate case to issue an injunction even under the strict standard required by *Laker*.

. . . Clearly the action in Korea would be vexatious to the plaintiffs, considering that defendants waited 2 1/2 years to commence the action in that forum and had never made a motion, mention or pled *forum non conveniens* with regard to the proceeding in the United States. Moreover, it appears that defendants would like to get what would amount to a declaratory judgment from the Korean court stating that they are not liable for the damages incurred by plaintiff, thus rendering a judgment by this court in favor of plaintiff unenforceable in that locale. Such a result could frustrate the outcome of the proceeding in the United States. It seems as if a race to judgment between the two forums would necessarily result if defendants were allowed to pursue the lawsuit in Korea. Furthermore, the second action in Korea will force plaintiffs to pursue a course of action half way around the world, forcing plaintiffs to incur great expense. Thus, there is a strong argument for this court to issue an injunction against the defendants.

Id. at 3-6. I approve of this analysis and would affirm the grant of the injunction in this case.

In examining the record, I also note several additional factors which would justify restricting Ssangyong Shipping from seeking to affect the New York litigation by proceeding with a declaratory judgment action in Korea.

1. Ssangyong has agreed to litigating the damage action in the Southern District of New York. That litigation will resolve the liability issues under provisions of the United States Carriage of Goods by Sea Act of 1936, 46 U.S.C. Sec. 1300, et seq. (1982). The same Act will underlie the liability determination in Korea.

2. The Korean action may serve only as a harassment to plaintiff and will multiply legal proceedings. Should the Korean courts absolve Ssangyong of responsibility for the cargo loss, that judgment, for want of personal jurisdiction over the ship or the parties or for other reasons, may not affect the action of the Southern District of New York in its proceeding. Should the courts of Korea find liability, the plaintiffs may, nevertheless, be required to proceed with a full trial in New York, or the case in the Southern District of New York may already have been concluded.

It seems to me that in this day of exceedingly high costs of litigation, where no comity principles between nations are at stake in resolving a piece of commercial litigation, courts have an affirmative duty to prevent a litigant from hopping halfway around the world to a foreign court as a means of confusing, obfuscating and complicating litigation already pending for trial in a court in this country. This is especially true when that court has been processing the case for almost two years and has acquired personal jurisdiction over the parties and subject matter jurisdiction over the claim. I perceive no abuse of a trial judge's discretion in the ruling of Judge Motley. I would affirm the grant of the injunction in this case.

Quaak v. Klynveld Peat Marwick Goerderler Bedrijfsrevisoren

361 F.3d 11 (1st Cir. 2004)

SELYA, Circuit Judge.

. . .

The genesis of the problem in this case lies with an auditing engagement accepted by Klynveld Peat Marwick Goerdeler Bedrijfsrevisoren (KPMG-B), a Belgian firm that served as the auditor for a publicly-traded company, Lernout & Hauspie Speech Products, N.V. (L & H). L & H's collapse precipitated a flood of actions against KPMG-B and others in the courts of this country, alleging massive securities fraud. KPMG-B refused to produce relevant auditing records and associated work papers, asserting that to do so would violate Belgian law. A magistrate judge rejected this assertion and ordered production.

In response, KPMG-B repaired to a Belgian court requesting that substantial penalties be imposed on those who might "take any step of a procedural or other nature in order to proceed with the discovery-procedure." The plaintiffs in the pending American litigation (who had obtained the turnover order in the first instance) implored the district court to enjoin KPMG-B from pursuing the Belgian action. The district court obliged. KPMG-B immediately appealed. . . . We now affirm the district court's order.

I. Background

As said, this appeal arises out of a welter of cases having a common theme: the allegation that KPMG-B and others perpetrated large-scale securities fraud leading to L & H's collapse. Those cases include several class actions. . . . The district court has consolidated all the cases. . . .

KPMG-B is a target of an ongoing criminal investigation in Belgium, which arises out of the L & H fiasco. It is also a principal defendant in the aforedescribed securities fraud litigation. KPMG-B has not disputed the district court's in personam jurisdiction. It did seek to secure dismissal of the securities fraud litigation on *forum non conveniens* grounds, but failed in that effort. . . .

. . . In September of 2002, [plaintiffs] served document requests for KPMG-B's work papers. *See* Fed. R. Civ. P. 34. The plaintiffs did not get very far; KPMG-B refused to comply with the requests, asseverating that Belgian law prohibited it from divulging the information sought. While this game of cat and mouse was taking place, the plaintiffs, acting on KPMG-B's advice, became civil coprosecutors in the ongoing Belgian criminal investigation. Through this participation, they were able to examine all the documents that were not deemed confidential by the

Belgian prosecutor, but they were not permitted to copy documents for use in the securities fraud litigation.

Tantalized by their glimpse of the work papers, the securities fraud plaintiffs moved to compel their production. A [U.S.] magistrate judge took briefing and heard argument on the applicability of and exceptions to the Belgian secrecy law. On November 13, 2003, he rejected KPMG-B's arguments and ordered production of the work papers on or before the close of business on December 1, 2003.

On November 27, 2003 — Thanksgiving day — KPMG-B filed an ex parte petition with a court in Brussels, seeking to enjoin the securities fraud plaintiffs from "taking any step" to proceed with the requested discovery. To ensure compliance, they asked the Belgian court to impose a fine of one million Euros for each violation of the proposed injunction. The Belgian court refused to act ex parte; instead, it directed that notice be provided to the securities fraud plaintiffs and scheduled a hearing for December 16, 2003. On December 1, KPMG-B gave notice of the institution of the Belgian action to the securities fraud plaintiffs . . . [and] moved to stay the turnover order.

Faced with the threat of extravagant fines, the securities fraud plaintiffs sought the district court's protection. On December 9, the magistrate judge issued a report and recommendation urging the entry of an order enjoining KPMG-B from proceeding with its Belgian action. The district judge held a hearing two days later and issued an antisuit injunction. . . . We granted a limited stay of the injunction, permitting KPMG-B to appear at the December 16 hearing in Brussels for the sole purpose of requesting a continuance. The Belgian court has been fully cooperative, and the foreign action has been continued periodically during the pendency of this expedited appeal. There has been no further action with regard to the turnover order itself.

. . .

III. Analysis

Determining the appropriateness of an international antisuit injunction is a highly nuanced exercise. An inquiring court must find a way to accommodate conflicting, mutually inconsistent national policies without unduly interfering with the judicial processes of a foreign sovereign. *See Laker Airways Ltd. v. Sabena, Belgian World Airlines*, 731 F.2d 909, 916 (D.C. Cir. 1984). This task is particularly formidable given the absence of guidance from the Supreme Court. . . .

A. Articulating the Standards

It is common ground that federal courts have the power to enjoin those subject to their personal jurisdiction from pursuing litigation before foreign tribunals. *See, e.g., Kaepa, Inc. v. Achilles Corp.*, 76 F.3d 624, 626 (5th Cir. 1996); *China Trade & Dev. Corp. v. M.V. Choong Yong*, 837 F.2d 33, 35 (2d Cir. 1987). The exercise of that power must be tempered, however, by the accepted proposition that parallel proceedings on the same in personam claim generally should be allowed to proceed simultaneously. *Laker Airways*, 731 F.2d at 926. The decisional calculus must take account of this presumption in favor of concurrent jurisdiction. It also must take account of considerations of international comity. After all, even though an international antisuit injunction operates only against the parties, it effectively restricts the jurisdiction of a foreign sovereign's courts. *See, e.g., China Trade,* 837 F.2d at 35-36.

Federal courts have been consentient in endorsing these principles. Beyond that point, however, the waters grow murky. The courts of appeals have differed as to the legal standards to be employed in determining whether the power to enjoin an international proceeding should be exercised. Two basic views have emerged. For ease in reference, we shall call the more permissive of these views the liberal approach and the more restrictive of them the conservative approach.

The liberal approach has been championed by two courts of appeals: the Fifth Circuit, *Kaepa,* 76 F.3d at 627, and the Ninth Circuit, *Seattle Totems Hockey Club, Inc. v. Nat'l Hockey League,* 652 F.2d 852, 855-56 (9th Cir. 1981). . . . Under this approach, an international antisuit injunction is appropriate whenever there is a duplication of parties and issues and the court determines that the prosecution of simultaneous proceedings would frustrate the speedy and efficient determination of the case. We do not mean to suggest that courts employing the liberal approach do not give weight to considerations of international comity. For the most part, they do — but they tend to define that interest in a relatively narrow manner and to assign it only modest weight. *See, e.g., Kaepa,* 76 F.3d at 627 (noting that an international antisuit injunction does not "actually threaten relations" between the two involved nations).

Four courts of appeals have espoused the conservative approach for gauging the propriety of international antisuit injunctions. *See Stonington Partners, Inc. v. Lernout & Hauspie Speech Prods.,* 310 F.3d 118, 126 (3d Cir. 2002); *Gau Shan Co. v. Bankers Trust Co.,* 956 F.2d 1349, 1355 (6th Cir. 1992); *China Trade,* 837 F.2d at 36 (2d Cir.); *Laker Airways,* 731 F.2d at 927 (D.C. Cir.). Under this approach, the critical questions . . . are whether the foreign action either imperils the jurisdiction of the forum court or threatens some strong national policy. . . .

We reject the liberal approach. We deem international comity an important integer in the decisional calculus — and the liberal approach assigns too low a priority to that interest. In the bargain, it undermines the age-old presumption in favor of concurrent parallel proceedings — a value judgment that leaves us uneasy — and presumes that public policy always favors allowing a suit pending in an American court to go forward without any substantial impediment. To cinch matters, this approach gives far too easy passage to international antisuit injunctions. We understand that the judicial process is a cornerstone of the American way of life — but in an area that raises significant separation of powers concerns and implicates international relations, we believe that the law calls for a more cautious and measured approach.

The conservative approach has more to commend it. First, it recognizes the rebuttable presumption against issuing international antisuit injunctions (and, thus, honors the presumption favoring the maintenance of parallel proceedings). Second, it is more respectful of principles of international comity. Third, it compels an inquiring court to balance competing policy considerations. Last — but far from least — it fits snugly with the logic of *Canadian Filters*, in which we said that issuing an international antisuit injunction is a step that should "be taken only with care and great restraint" and with the recognition that international comity is a fundamental principle deserving of substantial deference. 412 F.2d at 578.

We stop short, however, of an uncritical acceptance of the conservative approach. The recent expositions of that approach have come to regard the two main rationales upon which international antisuit injunctions may be grounded — preservation of jurisdiction and protection of important national policies — as exclusive. We are uncomfortable with this gloss, for it evinces a certain woodenness. In our view, the sensitive and fact-specific nature of the inquiry counsels against the use of inflexible rules.

We therefore reject this reworking of the conservative approach and instead endorse its traditional version. That version is not only more flexible but also more consistent with *Laker Airways* — which we regard as the seminal opinion in this field of law. The *Laker Airways* court did not suggest that its two stated rationales were the only ones that could justify issuing an international antisuit injunction. Rather, the court indicated that it was prudent to use a wider-angled lens, making clear that the equitable considerations surrounding each request for an injunction should be examined carefully.

In order to provide guidance for the district courts, we spell out the manner in which our preferred approach operates. The gatekeeping inquiry is, of course, whether parallel suits involve the same parties and issues. Unless that condition is met, a court ordinarily should go no further and refuse the issuance of an international antisuit injunction. If — and only if — this threshold condition is satisfied should the court proceed to consider all the facts and circumstances in order to decide whether an injunction is proper. In this analysis, considerations of international comity must be given substantial weight — and those considerations ordinarily establish a rebuttable presumption against the issuance of an order that has the effect of halting foreign judicial proceedings.

We acknowledge that the task of determining when a litigant has overcome this presumption is a difficult one. That is partly because comity is an elusive concept. The Supreme Court has defined it as "the recognition which one nation allows within its territory to the legislative, executive or judicial acts of another nation, having due regard both to international duty and convenience, and to the rights of its own citizens or of other persons who are under the protection of its laws." *Hilton v. Guyot*, 159 U.S. 113, 164 (1895). Judge Aldrich trenchantly described it as "a blend of courtesy and expedience." *Canadian Filters*, 412 F.2d at 578. Whatever definition is employed, it is pellucid that comity is not a matter of rigid obligation, but, rather, a protean concept of jurisdictional respect. And to complicate matters, comity, like beauty, sometimes is in the eye of the beholder.

We hasten to add that although the definition of comity may be tenebrous, its importance could not be more clear. In an increasingly global economy, commercial transactions involving participants from many lands have become common fare. This world economic interdependence has highlighted the importance of comity, as international commerce depends to a large extent on "the ability of merchants to predict the likely consequences of their conduct in overseas markets." *Gau Shan*, 956 F.2d at 1355. This predictability, in turn, depends on cooperation, reciprocity, and respect among nations. That helps to explain the enduring need for a presumption — albeit a rebuttable one — against the issuance of international antisuit injunctions.

In the final analysis, rebutting this presumption involves a continual give and take. In the course of that give and take, the presumption may be counterbalanced by other facts and factors particular to a specific case. These include (but are by no means limited to) such things as: the nature of the two actions (i.e., whether they are merely parallel or whether the foreign action is more properly classified as interdictory); the posture of the proceedings in the two countries; the conduct of the parties (including their good faith or lack thereof); the importance of the policies at stake in the litigation; and, finally, the extent to which the foreign action has the potential to undermine the forum court's ability to reach a just and speedy result.

Seen in this light, we agree that either the preservation of jurisdiction or the safeguarding of important national policies may afford a sufficient basis for the issuance of an international antisuit injunction. We do not, however, attach talismanic significance to concepts such as jurisdiction-stripping and insults to public policy. Instead, we hold that in every case a district court should examine the totality of the circumstances in deciding whether a particular case warrants the issuance of an international antisuit injunction. *See Laker Airways*, 731 F.2d at 927 ("There are no precise rules governing the appropriateness of antisuit injunctions."). If, after giving due regard to the circumstances (including the salient interest in international comity), a court supportably finds that equitable considerations preponderate in favor of relief, it may issue an international antisuit injunction.

B. Applying the Standards

Against this backdrop, we ponder whether the district court acted within the realm of its discretion when it enjoined KPMG-B from pursuing the Belgian litigation. We conclude that it did.

. . .

. . . The parties and issues are substantially similar, thus satisfying the gatekeeping inquiry. The district judge acknowledged the importance of comity concerns in her published opinion. A reading of the hearing transcript leaves no doubt that she was fully aware of the potential ramifications with respect to international comity and that she gave heavy weight to those concerns. However, she placed on the opposite pan of the scale the character of the foreign action, the public policy favoring the safeguarding of investors from securities fraud, the need to protect the court's own processes, and the balance of the equities. In the end, the court determined that those factors counterbalanced comity concerns in the peculiar circumstances of this case. Having conducted an independent review, we find that determination fully supportable.

The essential character of the Belgian action is easily discerned. In it, KPMG-B seeks to impose huge financial penalties on the securities fraud plaintiffs should they take any steps to enforce the district court's turnover order. This attempt to chill legitimate discovery by in terrorem tactics can scarcely be viewed as anything but an effort to "quash the practical power of the United States courts." *Laker Airways*, 731 F.2d at 938; *see United States v. Davis*, 767 F.2d 1025, 1029 (2d Cir. 1985) (upholding injunction of foreign proceeding where the "sole purpose" of instituting that proceeding "was to block compliance with a legitimate trial sub-poena"). Thus, the foreign action is plainly interdictory in nature.

Where, as here, a party institutes a foreign action in a blatant attempt to evade the rightful authority of the forum court, the need for an antisuit injunction crests. *See Laker Airways*, 731 F.2d at 929-30. Fairly read, KPMG-B's petition to the Belgian tribunal seeks to arrest the progress of the securities fraud action by thwarting the very discovery that the district court, which is intimately familiar with the exigencies of the underlying case, has deemed essential to the continued prosecution of the action against *any* of the defendants. In technical terms, this may not constitute a frontal assault on the district court's jurisdiction, but the practical effect is the same. That is a matter of considerable import: a court has a right — indeed, a duty — to preserve its ability to do justice between the parties in cases that are legitimately before it.

The equities also counsel in favor of affirming the district court's order. This is not a case in which a trial court is enabling a fishing expedition. The securities fraud plaintiffs have . . . actually seen the documents that they seek. Consequently, they know that they are not fishing in an empty stream.

In weighing the equities, we also think it noteworthy that KPMG-B, not the securities fraud plaintiffs or the district court, set the stage for a crisis of comity. If KPMG-B had not filed a foreign petition calculated to generate interference with an ongoing American case, the district court would have had no need to issue a defensive injunction that sought only to preserve the court's ability to adjudicate the claims before it according to the law of the United States. And, finally, KPMG-B's actions are harder to accept because it had available to it other options for seeking resolution of its client confidentiality concerns. The most obvious choice was to pursue and exhaust its position in the federal judicial system before attempting to sidetrack that system. Alternatively, it could have sought clarification from the Belgian courts without raising the stakes to a level that necessarily precipitated a direct conflict with the pending securities fraud action. It eschewed these options. Having called the tune, it hardly seems inequitable that KPMG-B must now pay the piper.

. . .

IV. Conclusion

We do not mean to minimize the potential difficulty of the situation that KPMG-B faces. To some extent, however, that situation is the natural consequence of its decision to ply its wares in the lucrative American marketplace. Having elected to establish a major presence in the United States, KPMG-B must have anticipated that it would be subject to suit in this country (and, thus, subject to pretrial discovery rules that are pandemic to the American justice system). *See* Restatement (Third) of Foreign Relations Law § 442, reporters' note 1 (1987) (noting "that persons who do business in the United States . . . are subject to the burdens as well as the benefits of United States law, including the laws on discovery"). While courts should take care to demonstrate due respect for any special problem confronted by a foreign litigant on account of its nationality, a foreign national that chooses to engage in business in the United States likewise must demonstrate due respect for the operation of the American judicial system.

. . . [A]n international antisuit injunction, like any other injunction, is an equitable remedy designed to bring the scales into balance. In this case, the district court acted defensively to protect its own authority from an interdictory strike and we are confident that, in doing so, the court kept the balance steady and true.

[Affirmed.]

NOTES AND QUESTIONS

1. **Litigating Strategies in *China Trade*.** How did the parties' litigating strategies develop in *China Trade*? What doctrines underlie those developments? Why is the case in the United States in the first place? From China Trade's perspective, what are the problems with the action in Korea? Are those problems sufficient to justify an anti-suit injunction? What substantial mistake did China Trade make in the early phases of the litigation? Why do you think Ssangyong filed the Korean action while the U.S. action was pending?

   Parallel proceedings typically arise (as in *China Trade*) where a defendant in a case in one jurisdiction files a parallel suit as the plaintiff in another jurisdiction. In *1st Source Bank v. Neto*, 861 F.3d 607 (7th Cir. 2017), the plaintiff bank initially filed suit in Indiana (its home jurisdiction) and then filed a parallel suit in Brazil, the home jurisdiction of the defendant. The claim was to enforce a guaranty of a debt owed to the bank. The U.S. court upheld the district court's refusal to issue an anti-suit injunction against the Brazilian suit after finding that it was not "vexatious or oppressive." Is that the right standard? Under that standard, is that the right result? Why might the bank choose to file as plaintiff in both Indiana and Brazil?

2. **The "Conservative" Approach to Anti-Suit Injunctions.** The court in *Quaak* claims to (mostly) be following the "conservative" approach to anti-suit injunctions exemplified by *China Trade*, and yet it upholds an injunction. In what respect is *Quaak* a better case for an injunction? What should the defendant emphasize in that case?

3. **The "Liberal" Approach to Anti-Suit Injunctions.** As an example of the "liberal" approach to anti-suit injunctions, the court in *Quaak* cites *Kaepa, Inc. v. Achilles Corp.*, 76 F.3d 624 (5th Cir. 1996), which upheld an anti-suit injunction issued by the district court. In that case, the court described the facts as follows:

   > This case arises out of a contractual dispute between two sophisticated, private corporations: Kaepa, an American company which manufactures athletic shoes; and Achilles, a Japanese business enterprise with annual sales that

approximate one billion dollars. In April 1993, the two companies entered into a distributorship agreement whereby Achilles obtained exclusive rights to market Kaepa's footwear in Japan. The distributorship agreement expressly provided that Texas law and the English language would govern its interpretation, that it would be enforceable in San Antonio, Texas, and that Achilles consented to the jurisdiction of the Texas courts.

Kaepa grew increasingly dissatisfied with Achilles's performance under the contract. Accordingly, in July of 1994, Kaepa filed suit in Texas state court, alleging (1) fraud and negligent misrepresentation by Achilles to induce Kaepa to enter into the distributorship agreement, and (2) breach of contract by Achilles. Thereafter, Achilles removed the action to federal district court, and the parties began a laborious discovery process which to date has resulted in the production of tens of thousands of documents. In February 1995, after appearing in the Texas action, removing the case to federal court, and engaging in comprehensive discovery, Achilles brought its own action in Japan, alleging mirror-image claims: (1) fraud by Kaepa to induce Achilles to enter into the distributorship agreement, and (2) breach of contract by Kaepa.

Back in Texas, Kaepa promptly filed a motion asking the district court to enjoin Achilles from prosecuting its suit in Japan (motion for an antisuit injunction). Achilles in turn moved to dismiss the federal court action on the ground of forum non conveniens. The district court denied Achilles's motion to dismiss and granted Kaepa's motion to enjoin, ordering Achilles to refrain from litigating the Japanese action and to file all of its counterclaims with the district court. . . .

What arguments would you expect the parties to make in support of and in opposition to an anti-suit injunction? Should it be upheld under the analysis of *Quaak* and *China Trade*? Should it be upheld as a policy matter?

4. **Anti-Suit Injunctions and "Comity."** What do the courts mean by "comity" in considering anti-suit injunctions? What are the policy concerns against issuing such injunctions? Note that an anti-suit injunction is directed at the party (over whom the court has jurisdiction), not at a foreign court. Does that make them less problematic from a comity perspective?

5. **Anti-Suit Injunctions and Arbitration.** Anti-suit injunctions may be issued to protect arbitration proceedings and awards. *Karaha Bodas Co., L.L.C. v. Perusahaan Pertambangan Minyak Dan Gas*, 500 F.3d 111 (2d Cir. 2007), for example, involved a long-running dispute between a private Cayman Islands company (KBC) and the Indonesian state oil company (Pertamina) regarding a geothermal power plant in Indonesia. KBC had obtained an arbitral award in Switzerland and enforced it against Pertamina's assets in New York. Pertamina subsequently brought suit against KBC in the Cayman Islands claiming the award was based on fraud, and sought damages equal to the amount paid to KBC as a result of the award. Applying *China Trade*, the Second Circuit upheld an anti-suit injunction against the Cayman Islands suit, which it held was designed to "vitiate" the payment ordered by the New York court. Similarly, in *Paramedics Electromedicina Comercial, Ltda v. GE Medical Systems Information Technologies, Inc.*, 369 F.3d 645 (2d Cir.

2004), the court upheld an anti-suit injunction against litigation in Brazil to protect the U.S. court's order to arbitrate the dispute according to the parties' contractual agreements.

6. **Comparative Perspectives.** As with previous doctrines studied in this chapter, there are substantial differences between common law jurisdictions (most of which have some form of anti-suit injunction) and civil law jurisdictions (where anti-suit injunctions are rarely thought appropriate). In *Turner v. Grovit and Others* (ECJ 2004), the European Court of Justice (ECU) ruled that the 1968 Brussels Convention on Jurisdiction and the Enforcement of Judgments in Civil and Commercial Matters (the predecessor to the Brussels I Regulation discussed above) barred "the grant of an injunction whereby a court of a Contracting State prohibits a party to proceedings pending before it from commencing or continuing legal proceedings before a court of another Contracting State, even where that party is acting in bad faith with a view to frustrating the existing proceedings. . . ." Turner, a U.K. citizen, had been employed in Spain. After resigning his position, he brought suit in the United Kingdom against his former employer, claiming "that he had been the victim of efforts to implicate him in illegal conduct, which, in his opinion, were tantamount to unfair dismissal." The U.K. Employment Tribunal gave judgment to Turner. At the same time, the employer sued Turner in Spain, claiming "compensation for losses allegedly resulting from Mr. Turner's professional conduct." Turner requested an anti-suit injunction from the U.K. courts. The U.K. Court of Appeals issued the injunction, finding that "the proceedings in Spain had been brought in bad faith in order to vex Mr. Turner in the pursuit of his application before the Employment Tribunal." The U.K. House of Lords, on appeal, referred the question to the ECJ, which found the injunction improper. According to the ECJ, "[i]n so far as the conduct of which the defendant [the employer] is criticized consists in recourse to the jurisdiction of the court of another Member State, the judgment made as to the abusive nature of that conduct implies an assessment of the appropriateness of bringing proceedings before a court of another Member State. Such an assessment runs counter to the principle of mutual trust which . . . underpins the Convention and prohibits a court . . . from reviewing the jurisdiction of the court of another Member State." Keeping in mind that the Brussels Convention (and, after the Convention, the Brussels I Regulation, and now the Brussels I Regulation (Recast)) contains jurisdictional rules specifying when a court of an EU member nation may and may not hear a case and when it must stay its proceedings, what type of "mutual trust" do you think the ECJ had in mind? And based on this mutual trust, what do you think the ECJ might have expected the Spanish court to do in this case?

Would Turner be entitled to an anti-suit injunction in U.S. courts on these facts, if Turner had been a U.S. citizen and brought his case in the United States? Are there advantages to a strict rule against anti-suit injunctions, as the ECJ appears to impose?

C. Forum Selection Clauses

Given the uncertainty about where transnational claims can be heard, parties may prefer to specify in advance, by contract, a court to resolve their disputes. Forum selection clauses (also called "choice of court" clauses) typically state that disputes arising in a contractual relationship will be (or may be) resolved in the national courts of a particular country.* (Alternatively, contracting parties might include a clause agreeing to resolve disputes through arbitration or other alternative dispute resolution method, an approach addressed in Chapter 6.) Forum selection clauses are common in transnational business contracts. Consider, however, under what circumstances a contract might not include one, even where lawyers might consider it standard practice to do so.

But including a forum selection clause may only substitute one uncertainty for another. Are forum selection clauses enforceable as a general matter? When, if ever, should courts refuse to enforce them? Can they apply to noncontractual as well as contractual claims? Can they be enforced by persons or entities that are not parties to the contract? This section considers those and related questions.

1. Enforcing Forum Selection Clauses

The Bremen v. Zapata Off-Shore Co.

407 U.S. 1 (1972)

Mr. Chief Justice BURGER delivered the opinion of the Court.

We granted certiorari to review a judgment of the United States Court of Appeals for the Fifth Circuit declining to enforce a forum selection clause governing disputes arising under an international towage contract between petitioners and respondent. . . . For the reasons stated hereafter, we vacate the judgment of the Court of Appeals.

In November, 1967, respondent Zapata, a Houston-based American corporation, contracted with petitioner Unterweser, a German corporation, to tow Zapata's ocean-going, self-elevating drilling rig *Chaparral* from Louisiana to a point off Ravenna, Italy, in the Adriatic Sea, where Zapata had agreed to drill certain wells.

. . . The contract submitted by Unterweser contained the following provision, which is at issue in this case:

"Any dispute arising must be treated before the London Court of Justice."

In addition, the contract contained two clauses purporting to exculpate Unterweser from liability for damages to the towed barge.

After reviewing the contract and making several changes, but without any alteration in the forum selection or exculpatory clauses, a Zapata vice-president executed

---

* Thus these clauses are typically agreed upon prior to a dispute arising. Note that parties may also in effect agree to a forum by failing to raise issues of personal jurisdiction, *forum non conveniens*, etc., once a suit is filed.

the contract and forwarded it to Unterweser in Germany, where Unterweser accepted the changes, and the contract became effective.

On January 5, 1968, Unterweser's deep sea tug *Bremen* departed Venice, Louisiana, with the *Chaparral* in tow bound for Italy. On January 9, while the flotilla was in international waters in the middle of the Gulf of Mexico, a severe storm arose. The sharp roll of the *Chaparral* in Gulf waters caused its elevator legs, which had been raised for the voyage, to break off and fall into the sea, seriously damaging the *Chaparral*. In this emergency situation, Zapata instructed the *Bremen* to tow its damaged rig to Tampa, Florida, the nearest port of refuge.

On January 12, Zapata, ignoring its contract promise to litigate "any dispute arising" in the English courts, commenced a suit in admiralty in the United States District Court at Tampa, seeking $3,500,000 damages against Unterweser *in personam* and the *Bremen in rem*, alleging negligent towage and breach of contract. Unterweser responded by invoking the forum clause of the towage contract, . . . or, in the alternative, to stay the action pending submission of the dispute to the "London Court of Justice." Shortly thereafter, . . . Unterweser commenced an action against Zapata seeking damages for breach of the towage contract in the High Court of Justice in London, as the contract provided; Zapata appeared in that court to contest jurisdiction, but its challenge was rejected, the English courts holding that the contractual forum provision conferred jurisdiction.[4]

[The district court denied Unterweser's motions.] . . .

. . . On appeal, a divided panel of the Court of Appeals affirmed, and, on rehearing *en banc*, the panel opinion was adopted, with six of the 14 *en banc* judges dissenting. . . .

We hold, with the six dissenting members of the Court of Appeals, that far too little weight and effect were given to the forum clause in resolving this controversy. For at least two decades, we have witnessed an expansion of overseas

---

4. Zapata appeared specially and moved to set aside service of process outside the country. Justice Karminski of the High Court of Justice denied the motion on the ground the contractual choice of forum provision conferred jurisdiction, and would be enforced absent a factual showing it would not be "fair and right" to do so. He did not believe Zapata had made such a showing, and held that it should be required to "stick to [its] bargain." The Court of Appeal dismissed an appeal on the ground that Justice Karminski had properly applied the English rule. Lord Justice Willmer stated that rule as follows:

> "The law on the subject, I think, is not open to doubt. . . . It is always open to parties to stipulate . . . that a particular Court shall have jurisdiction over any dispute arising out of their contract. Here, the parties chose to stipulate that disputes were to be referred to the 'London Court,' which I take as meaning the High Court in this country. *Prima facie*, it is the policy of the Court to hold parties to the bargain into which they have entered. . . . But that is not an inflexible rule, as was shown, for instance, by the case of *The Fehmarn*, [1957] 1 Lloyd's Rep. 511; (C.A.) [1957] 2 Lloyd's Rep. 551. . . .
>
> "I approach the matter, therefore, in this way, that the Court has a discretion, but it is a discretion which, in the ordinary way and in the absence of strong reason to the contrary, will be exercised in favour of holding parties to their bargain. The question is whether sufficient circumstances have been shown to exist in this case to make it desirable, on the grounds of balance of convenience, that proceedings should not take place in this country. . . ."

[1968] 2 Lloyd's Rep. 158, 162-163.

commercial activities by business enterprises based in the United States. The barrier of distance that once tended to confine a business concern to a modest territory no longer does so. Here we see an American company with special expertise contracting with a foreign company to tow a complex machine thousands of miles across seas and oceans. The expansion of American business and industry will hardly be encouraged if, notwithstanding solemn contracts, we insist on a parochial concept that all disputes must be resolved under our laws and in our courts. Absent a contract forum, the considerations relied on by the Court of Appeals would be persuasive reasons for holding an American forum convenient in the traditional sense, but in an era of expanding world trade and commerce, the absolute aspects of the doctrine of the [court of appeals] have little place, and would be a heavy hand indeed on the future development of international commercial dealings by Americans. We cannot have trade and commerce in world markets and international waters exclusively on our terms, governed by our laws, and resolved in our courts.

Forum selection clauses have historically not been favored by American courts. Many courts, federal and state, have declined to enforce such clauses on the ground that they were "contrary to public policy," or that their effect was to "oust the jurisdiction" of the court. Although this view apparently still has considerable acceptance, other courts are tending to adopt a more hospitable attitude toward forum selection clauses. This view, advanced in the well reasoned dissenting opinion in the instant case, is that such clauses are *prima facie* valid, and should be enforced unless enforcement is shown by the resisting party to be "unreasonable" under the circumstances. We believe this is the correct doctrine to be followed by federal district courts sitting in admiralty. . . . This approach is substantially that followed in other common law countries, including England. It is the view advanced by noted scholars, and that adopted by the Restatement of the Conflict of Laws. It accords with ancient concepts of freedom of contract, and reflects an appreciation of the expanding horizons of American contractors who seek business in all parts of the world. Not surprisingly, foreign businessmen prefer, as do we, to have disputes resolved in their own courts, but, if that choice is not available, then in a neutral forum with expertise in the subject matter. Plainly, the courts of England meet the standards of neutrality and long experience in admiralty litigation. The choice of that forum was made in an arm's length negotiation by experienced and sophisticated businessmen, and, absent some compelling and countervailing reason, it should be honored by the parties and enforced by the courts.

The argument that such clauses are improper because they tend to "oust" a court of jurisdiction is hardly more than a vestigial legal fiction. It appears to rest at core on historical judicial resistance to any attempt to reduce the power and business of a particular court, and has little place in an era when all courts are overloaded and when businesses, once essentially local, now operate in world markets. It reflects something of a provincial attitude regarding the fairness of other tribunals. No one seriously contends in this case that the forum selection clause "ousted" the District Court of jurisdiction over Zapata's action. The threshold question is whether that court should have exercised its jurisdiction to do more than give effect to the legitimate expectations of the parties, manifested in their freely negotiated agreement, by specifically enforcing the forum clause.

There are compelling reasons why a freely negotiated private international agreement, unaffected by fraud, undue influence, or overweening bargaining power, such as that involved here, should be given full effect. In this case, for example, we are concerned with a far from routine transaction between companies of two different nations contemplating the tow of an extremely costly piece of equipment from Louisiana across the Gulf of Mexico and the Atlantic Ocean, through the Mediterranean Sea to its final destination in the Adriatic Sea. In the course of its voyage, it was to traverse the waters of many jurisdictions. The *Chaparral* could have been damaged at any point along the route, and there were countless possible ports of refuge. That the accident occurred in the Gulf of Mexico and the barge was towed to Tampa in an emergency were mere fortuities. It cannot be doubted for a moment that the parties sought to provide for a neutral forum for the resolution of any disputes arising during the tow. Manifestly, much uncertainty and possibly great inconvenience to both parties could arise if a suit could be maintained in any jurisdiction in which an accident might occur or if jurisdiction were left to any place where the *Bremen* or Unterweser might happen to be found. The elimination of all such uncertainties by agreeing in advance on a forum acceptable to both parties is an indispensable element in international trade, commerce, and contracting. There is strong evidence that the forum clause was a vital part of the agreement, and it would be unrealistic to think that the parties did not conduct their negotiations, including fixing the monetary terms, with the consequences of the forum clause figuring prominently in their calculations. Under these circumstances, as Justice Karminski reasoned in sustaining jurisdiction over Zapata in the High Court of Justice, "[t]he force of an agreement for litigation in this country, freely entered into between two competent parties, seems to me to be very powerful."

Thus, in the light of present-day commercial realities and expanding international trade, we conclude that the forum clause should control absent a strong showing that it should be set aside. Although their opinions are not altogether explicit, it seems reasonably clear that the District Court and the Court of Appeals placed the burden on Unterweser to show that London would be a more convenient forum than Tampa, although the contract expressly resolved that issue. The correct approach would have been to enforce the forum clause specifically unless Zapata could clearly show that enforcement would be unreasonable and unjust, or that the clause was invalid for such reasons as fraud or overreaching. Accordingly, the case must be remanded for reconsideration.

We note, however, that there is nothing in the record presently before us that would support a refusal to enforce the forum clause. The Court of Appeals suggested that enforcement would be contrary to the public policy of the forum . . . , because of the prospect that the English courts would enforce the clauses of the towage contract purporting to exculpate Unterweser from liability for damages to the *Chaparral*. A contractual choice of forum clause should be held unenforceable if enforcement would contravene a strong public policy of the forum in which suit is brought, whether declared by statute or by judicial decision. It is clear, however, that [any policy against exculpatory clauses in the domestic setting] does not reach this case. . . . [C]onsiderations with respect to the towage business strictly in American waters . . . are not controlling in an international commercial agreement. . . .

Courts have also suggested that a forum clause, even though it is freely bargained for and contravenes no important public policy of the forum, may nevertheless be "unreasonable" and unenforceable if the chosen forum is seriously inconvenient for the trial of the action. Of course, where it can be said with reasonable assurance that, at the time they entered the contract, the parties to a freely negotiated private international commercial agreement contemplated the claimed inconvenience, it is difficult to see why any such claim of inconvenience should be heard to render the forum clause unenforceable.

We are not here dealing with an agreement between two Americans to resolve their essentially local disputes in a remote alien forum. In such a case, the serious inconvenience of the contractual forum to one or both of the parties might carry greater weight in determining the reasonableness of the forum clause. The remoteness of the forum might suggest that the agreement was an adhesive one, or that the parties did not have the particular controversy in mind when they made their agreement; yet even there, the party claiming should bear a heavy burden of proof. Similarly, selection of a remote forum to apply differing foreign law to an essentially American controversy might contravene an important public policy of the forum. . . .

This case, however, involves a freely negotiated international commercial transaction between a German and an American corporation for towage of a vessel from the Gulf of Mexico to the Adriatic Sea. As noted, selection of a London forum was clearly a reasonable effort to bring vital certainty to this international transaction, and to provide a neutral forum experienced and capable in the resolution of admiralty litigation. Whatever "inconvenience" Zapata would suffer by being forced to litigate in the contractual forum as it agreed to do was clearly foreseeable at the time of contracting. In such circumstances, it should be incumbent on the party seeking to escape his contract to show that trial in the contractual forum will be so gravely difficult and inconvenient that he will, for all practical purposes, be deprived of his day in court. Absent that, there is no basis for concluding that it would be unfair, unjust, or unreasonable to hold that party to his bargain.

. . . Nevertheless, to allow Zapata opportunity to carry its heavy burden of showing not only that the balance of convenience is strongly in favor of trial in Tampa (that is, that it will be far more inconvenient for Zapata to litigate in London than it will be for Unterweser to litigate in Tampa), but also that a London trial will be so manifestly and gravely inconvenient to Zapata that it will be effectively deprived of a meaningful day in court, we remand for further proceedings.

. . .

The judgment of the Court of Appeals is vacated, and the case is remanded for further proceedings consistent with this opinion.

Vacated and remanded.

[A concurring opinion of Justice White is omitted.]

Mr. Justice DOUGLAS, dissenting.

. . . [A] contract which exempts the tower from liability for its own negligence is not enforceable [in the United States], though there is evidence in the present record that it is enforceable in England. . . .

It is said that, because these parties specifically agreed to litigate their disputes before the London Court of Justice, the District Court, absent "unreasonable" circumstances, should have honored that choice by declining to exercise its jurisdiction. The forum selection clause, however, is part and parcel of the exculpatory provision in the towing agreement which, as mentioned . . . , is not enforceable in American courts.

Judges in this country have traditionally been hostile to attempts to circumvent the public policy against exculpatory agreements. For example, clauses specifying that the law of a foreign place (which favors such releases) should control have regularly been ignored. . . .

The instant stratagem of specifying a foreign forum is essentially the same as invoking a foreign law of construction, except that the present circumvention also requires the American party to travel across an ocean to seek relief. . . . [W]e should not countenance devices designed solely for the purpose of evading [the U.S. rule]. . . .

NOTES AND QUESTIONS

1. **Contracting and Litigation Strategy.** Why would Unterweser, a German company, prefer to litigate in London rather than Tampa? Is that a reason for the U.S. court to enforce the forum selection clause, or to refuse to enforce it? Why do you think the contract didn't call for litigation in Germany? Is Zapata a sympathetic party? What should it have done to protect itself? Why do you think it didn't? Should that matter?

2. **Enforceability of Forum Selection Clauses.** After *The Bremen*, when would a forum selection clause not be enforced? What characteristics specific to the Zapata/Unterweser contract does the Court mention in support of its decision? What if these were not present? In *Carnival Cruise Lines, Inc. v. Shute*, 499 U.S. 585 (1991), a passenger (Shute) suffered injuries from a fall aboard a cruise ship in international waters. Shute sued Carnival, the cruise operator, in federal court in her home state of Washington, and Carnival sought to enforce a clause selecting Florida courts, which appeared on the back of

Shute's ticket. The court of appeals, applying *The Bremen*, refused to enforce the clause because it was not freely bargained for and because the court found Shute physically and financially incapable of litigating in Florida. The Supreme Court, in a 7-2 decision by Justice Blackmun, reversed, rejecting both grounds. The Court added:

> It bears emphasis that forum selection clauses contained in form passage contracts are subject to judicial scrutiny for fundamental fairness. In this case, there is no indication that [Carnival] set Florida as the forum in which disputes were to be resolved as a means of discouraging cruise passengers from pursuing legitimate claims. Any suggestion of such a bad faith motive is belied by two facts: [Carnival] has its principal place of business in Florida, and many of its cruises depart from and return to Florida ports. Similarly, there is no evidence that [Carnival] obtained respondents' accession to the forum clause by fraud or overreaching. Finally, respondents have conceded that they were given notice of the forum provision and, therefore, presumably retained the option of rejecting the contract with impunity. In the case before us, therefore, we conclude that the Court of Appeals erred in refusing to enforce the forum selection clause.

In dissent, Justice Stevens noted that Shute did not receive her ticket (containing the forum selection clause) until she had already paid for the cruise and for travel from her home in Washington. Should that matter? After *Shute*, are there any circumstances under which a forum selection clause would be unenforceable?

3. **Forum Selection Clauses in Other Contexts.** Both *The Bremen* and *Shute* involve federal admiralty law. U.S. federal courts applying state law in diversity actions have often, though not universally, concluded that forum selection is a procedural issue governed by federal common law, not by state law, under the *Erie* doctrine. *E.g., Wong v. PartyGaming Ltd.*, 589 F.3d 821 (6th Cir. 2009). *But see Rafael Rodriguez Barril, Inc. v. Conbraco Industries, Inc.*, 619 F.3d 90 (1st Cir. 2010) (noting that this remains an open issue). Potentially, state courts applying state law might take a less favorable view of forum selection clauses. What difficulties might that create? In practice, though, most states have similarly embraced forum selection clauses. *See Barril, supra* (declining to resolve the state/federal choice-of-law question because both federal law and applicable state law would enforce the clause). What central policies support enforcing forum selection clauses that would account for this broad acceptance? What might such policies suggest about the circumstances under which forum selection clauses should not be enforced?

4. **Comparative Perspective.** As always, one should not assume that U.S. law is typical. Although forum selection clauses in international business contracts are commonly enforced worldwide, other jurisdictions may not share the U.S. inclination to enforce them in consumer contracts. For example, in *Douez v. Facebook, Inc.*, 2017 S.C.C. 33, the Canadian Supreme Court refused to enforce a forum selection clause in a contract between the plaintiff

and Facebook in a suit arising from the plaintiff's Facebook account. The three-Justice plurality reasoned:

> Forum selection clauses serve a valuable purpose and are commonly used and regularly enforced. However, forum selection clauses divert public adjudication of matters out of the provinces, and court adjudication in each province is a public good. Because forum selection clauses encroach on the public sphere of adjudication, Canadian courts do not simply enforce them like any other clause. Where no legislation overrides the forum selection clause, [a two-step approach] . . . applies to determine whether to enforce a forum selection clause and stay an action brought contrary to it. At the first step, the party seeking a stay must establish that the clause is valid, clear and enforceable and that it applies to the cause of action before the court. If this party succeeds, the onus shifts to the plaintiff who must show strong cause why the court should not enforce the forum selection clause and stay the action. At this second step of the test, a court must consider all the circumstances, including the convenience of the parties, fairness between the parties and the interests of justice. Public policy may also be a relevant factor at this step. The strong cause factors have been interpreted and applied restrictively in the commercial context, but commercial and consumer relationships are very different. Irrespective of the formal validity of the contract, the consumer context may provide strong reasons not to enforce forum selection clauses. . . . When considering whether it is reasonable and just to enforce an otherwise binding forum selection clause in a consumer contract, courts should take account of all the circumstances of the particular case, including public policy considerations relating to the gross inequality of bargaining power between the parties and the nature of the rights at stake.
>
> With respect to the first step . . . , the forum selection clause contained in Facebook's terms of use is enforceable. At the second step of the test, however, [plaintiff] has met her burden of establishing that there is strong cause not to enforce the forum selection clause. A number of different factors, when considered cumulatively, support a finding of strong cause. Most importantly, the claim involves a consumer contract of adhesion between an individual consumer and a large corporation and a statutory cause of action implicating the quasi-constitutional privacy rights of British Columbians. It is clear from the evidence that there was gross inequality of bargaining power between the parties. Individual consumers in this context are faced with little choice but to accept Facebook's terms of use. Additionally, Canadian courts have a greater interest in adjudicating cases impinging on constitutional and quasi-constitutional rights because these rights play an essential role in a free and democratic society and embody key Canadian values. This matter requires an interpretation of a statutory privacy tort and only a local court's interpretation of privacy rights under the *Privacy Act* will provide clarity and certainty about the scope of the rights to others in the province. Overall, these public policy concerns weigh heavily in favour of strong cause.
>
> Two other secondary factors also suggest that the forum selection clause should not be enforced. First, even assuming that a California court could or would apply the *Privacy Act*, the interests of justice support having the action adjudicated by the British Columbia Supreme Court. The lack of evidence concerning whether a California court would hear [plaintiff's] claim

is not determinative. The British Columbia Supreme Court, as compared to a California one, is better placed to assess the purpose and intent of the legislation and to decide whether public policy or legislative intent prevents parties from opting out of rights created by the *Privacy Act* through a choice of law clause in favour of a foreign jurisdiction. Second, the expense and inconvenience of requiring British Columbian individuals to litigate in California, compared to the comparative expense and inconvenience to Facebook, further supports a finding of strong cause. The chambers judge found it would be more convenient to have Facebook's books and records made available for inspection in British Columbia than requiring [plaintiff] to travel to California to advance her claim. There is no reason to disturb this finding.

One Justice concurred in the judgment on the grounds that the clause was unconscionable and hence unenforceable at the first step. Three dissenting Justices would have enforced the clause.

Does this decision suggest that forum selection clauses in consumer contracts are generally unenforceable in Canada, as some alarmed commentators contended after it was announced? Contrast *Douez* with *Feggestad v. Kerzner International Bahamas Limited*, 843 F.3d 915 (11th Cir. 2016), which upheld a forum selection clause choosing courts of the Bahamas in a tort dispute between a hotel in the Bahamas and a U.S.-resident hotel guest who was injured on the hotel property. The court noted that the clause had not been negotiated and had only been communicated to the plaintiff in terms and conditions contained in a hyperlink in an email confirmation of the plaintiff's reservation, which the plaintiff had not read. The court nonetheless found no unfairness because the plaintiff had an opportunity to read the terms in the hyperlink. What relevant differences might there be between the situation in *Douez* and the situation in *Feggestad*? How would you argue that a *Feggestad*-type clause should be enforced in Canada after *Douez*?

Petersen v. Boeing Co.

715 F.3d 276 (9th Cir. 2013)

Before: HARRY PREGERSON, STEPHEN REINHARDT, and WILLIAM A. FLETCHER, Circuit Judges.

PER CURIAM:

I

Plaintiff Robin P. Petersen . . . is a former Navy pilot with the rank of Commander who was recruited to work in Saudi Arabia as a flight instructor for Boeing International Support Services ("BISS"), a wholly-owned subsidiary of The Boeing Corporation ("Boeing"). Except as otherwise indicated, the following account describes the facts as alleged in the Complaint.

Prior to departing for Saudi Arabia, Petersen was required to sign a preliminary employment agreement. That agreement did not contain a forum selection clause. On arrival in Saudi Arabia, however, he was forced to sign a second employment agreement — which he was not given time to read and which he was told he must sign or else return immediately to the United States at his own expense. This agreement contained a forum selection clause requiring any contractual disputes to be resolved in the Labor Courts of Saudi Arabia. Petersen signed the second agreement without reading it, as he was instructed to do by his employer.

Petersen's passport was then confiscated; he was effectively imprisoned in his housing compound under miserable living conditions; and his work environment was marked by rampant safety and ethics violations. When he attempted to resign and return to the United States, his employer refused to return his passport for a period of nearly three months. During his time in Saudi Arabia, Petersen contracted an upper respiratory infection as a result of his living conditions and was permanently maimed as a result of receiving inadequate surgical treatment for an Achilles tendon tear, which he would have had treated in the United States had he been permitted to leave Saudi Arabia.

When he finally returned to the United States (after the intervention of the United States Consulate in Jeddah), Petersen brought suit against Boeing and BISS alleging breach of contract as well as several statutory and common law claims. In addition to his Complaint, his submissions to the district court included a sworn affidavit claiming that (1) he was not financially capable of traveling to Saudi Arabia in order to institute proceedings against his employer; (2) he would be subjected to harsh conditions and internal travel restrictions if he were somehow able to return to Saudi Arabia; and (3) the forum selection clause was foisted on him through fraud and undue pressure. He also submitted a report from the United States Department of State tending to demonstrate that (1) he would not be *legally* permitted to travel to Saudi Arabia; (2) he would not in any event be able to obtain a fair trial in Saudi Arabia; and (3) his employer could detain him in Saudi Arabia for the entire duration of any legal proceedings. The district court nonetheless dismissed the entire lawsuit without a hearing under Federal Rule of Civil Procedure 12(b)(3) for improper venue, holding that the forum selection clause was enforceable, relying largely on our opinion in *Spradlin v. Lear Siegler Mgmt. Servs. Co.*, 926 F.2d 865 (9th Cir. 1991). . . .

II

We review a district court's decision to enforce a forum selection clause under Rule 12(b)(3) for abuse of discretion. In doing so, however, we "must draw all reasonable inferences in favor of the non-moving party and resolve all factual conflicts in favor of the nonmoving party." The non-moving party's pleadings need not be accepted as true, however, and we may consider facts outside the pleadings.

. . .

III

The enforceability of forum selection clauses is governed by federal law. The applicable federal law was first announced in *M/S Bremen v. Zapata Off-Shore Co.*, 407 U.S. 1 (1972), and later refined in *Carnival Cruise Lines, Inc. v. Shute*, 499 U.S. 585 (1991). Under *Bremen*, there are three reasons a forum selection clause may be unenforceable: (1) if the inclusion of the clause in the agreement was the product of fraud or overreaching; (2) if the party wishing to repudiate the clause would effectively be deprived of his day in court were the clause enforced; and (3) if enforcement would contravene a strong public policy of the forum in which suit is brought. Both the second and first *Bremen* exceptions are at issue here, and we address them in that order.

A

In *Spradlin*, we indicated that we were "troubled" by an employer's "standard inclusion of a Saudi Arabian forum selection clause in employment contracts when it is highly foreseeable that terminated American employees will be required to return to the United States and will thus face considerable obstacles in bringing wrongful termination actions." 926 F.2d at 869. Nonetheless, we reluctantly enforced the forum selection clause in *Spradlin* in light of the plaintiff's failure "to come forward . . . with *anything* beyond the most general and conclusory allegations of fraud and inconvenience." *Id.* at 868 (emphasis added). In particular, we noted that Spradlin had not "brought to the district court's attention" *any* facts "that would have militated against enforcing the forum selection clause," in particular where relevant witnesses were located, whether Spradlin was unable to return to Saudi Arabia, and any facts about the costs of litigating in Saudi Arabia, the availability of counsel there, and his financial ability to bear the costs of Saudi litigation. We therefore were "compelled to affirm" the enforcement of the Saudi forum selection clause.

. . .

Here, Petersen did precisely what we held that the employee in *Spradlin* needed to have done . . . : he provided specific evidence sufficient to demonstrate that he would be wholly foreclosed from litigating his claims against Boeing and BISS in a Saudi forum. His sworn affidavit states that he lacked the resources to litigate in Saudi Arabia and that he was concerned about returning to Saudi Arabia (even if possible) in light of having been held as a "virtual prisoner" there. Evidence submitted by Petersen corroborated his concerns: the United States Department of State's *2009 Human Rights Report* on Saudi Arabia states that "[i]n practice, the judiciary was not independent" and that "the judiciary was subject to influence" by powerful individuals within the executive or legislative branch. Furthermore, "judges may discount the testimony of . . . persons of other [non-Muslim] religions." Most important, employers "involved in a commercial or labor dispute with foreign employees may ask authorities to prohibit the employees from departing the country until the dispute is resolved," often with the intent to "force the employee to accept a disadvantageous settlement or risk deportation without any settlement." . . .

Petersen's proposed First Amended Complaint alleged . . . that he would need to travel to Saudi Arabia to litigate his claim, but that he would be unable to do so because he would not be eligible for a visa. This allegation is confirmed by the State Department's public travel advisory regarding travel to Saudi Arabia, of which we take judicial notice. The advisory states that visas are available for Americans to visit Saudi Arabia only for "business and work, to visit close relatives, and for transit and religious visits by Muslims" and "all visas require a sponsor. . . ." Even assuming that Petersen could somehow *enter* Saudi Arabia, the same report confirms his fears that he would be trapped there again: "Persons involved in legal cases are not permitted to leave the Kingdom until the case has been resolved or abandoned," which "generally takes several months." Also, unlike Spradlin, Petersen plausibly alleged that the majority of his witnesses would be American. He named at least 16 such witnesses, including other Boeing/BISS employees who experienced similar conditions during their time in Saudi Arabia and United States–based recruiters working for Boeing/BISS. Finally, Petersen plausibly alleged that he was warned by Boeing/BISS managers — presumably the same individuals responsible for detaining him in Saudi Arabia against his will — that Boeing, which provides training to the Saudi air force under the program in which Petersen was participating, enjoys a "very close relationship" with the Saudi government.

. . . [E]ven without the additional allegations, we hold that the district court erred by not — at the very least — conducting an evidentiary hearing to determine whether enforcement of the forum selection clause at issue here would effectively preclude Petersen's day in court, based on the admissible evidence Petersen presented.[4]

B

In addition, Petersen argues that the forum selection clause should not be enforced under the first *Bremen* exception because he was induced to agree to the clause only through fraud or overreaching. To establish the invalidity of a forum selection clause on the basis of fraud or overreaching, the party resisting enforcement must show that the *inclusion of that clause in the contract* was the product of fraud or coercion.

Petersen has done just that. His sworn affidavit states that the initial employment contract he signed in the United States made no mention of a Saudi forum selection clause, but that he was required to sign a new employment contract containing such a clause upon his arrival in Saudi Arabia. His new supervisor, however, did not permit him time to read the agreement and told him that failure to sign it would result in his being forced to return immediately to the United States at his own expense. These specific facts, contained in an admissible affidavit, are sufficient, if true, to demonstrate that the forum selection clause's inclusion in the

---

4. . . . We also note that here, unlike the passengers in *Carnival Cruise Lines*, Petersen introduced evidence and allegations that he lacked notice of the forum selection clause, that the clause would further Boeing/BISS's bad-faith motive of discouraging Petersen from pursuing legitimate claims, and that Petersen did not have the option of rejecting the contract with impunity.

employment agreement was obtained via fraud or overreaching by taking undue advantage of Petersen's vulnerable position as a newly-arrived employee in Saudi Arabia. . . . Therefore, the district court abused its discretion by dismissing on the basis of the forum selection clause without at the very least holding an evidentiary hearing as to whether Petersen was induced to assent to the forum selection clause through fraud or overreaching.[5]

Conclusion

We hold that the evidence submitted and the allegations made by Petersen were more than sufficient to create a triable issue of fact as to whether the forum selection clause at issue here is enforceable under *Bremen*. The district court therefore abused its discretion by granting BISS's motion to dismiss without convening an evidentiary hearing. . . .

[Reversed and remanded.]

NOTES AND QUESTIONS

1. **The Standard for Enforcing Forum Selection Clauses.** Is *Petersen* consistent with *The Bremen*? With *Carnival Cruise*? Does it lead to substantial doubt about the enforceability of forum selection clauses? How would you advise Boeing with respect to future contractual arrangements?
2. **Litigation Strategy.** What is likely to happen on remand in *Petersen*? What would you expect Boeing to argue?
3. **Factors Influencing Enforceability.** Courts applying *The Bremen* and *Carnival Cruise* have identified a four-part test for deciding whether a forum selection clause is enforceable. As one court described its analysis:

> [F]orum-selection and choice-of-law clauses are presumptively valid where the underlying transaction is fundamentally international in character. The party seeking to avoid the forum-selection clause bears "a heavy burden of proof." *M/S Bremen v. Zapata Off-Shore Co.*, 407 U.S. 1 (1972). Nevertheless, this presumption of validity may be overcome by a clear showing that the clauses are unreasonable under the circumstances." As such, forum-selection clauses are unenforceable as "unreasonable under the circumstances" only where:
>
> > (1) their formation was induced by fraud or overreaching; (2) the plaintiff effectively would be deprived of its day in court because of the inconvenience or unfairness of the chosen forum; (3) the fundamental

5. . . . Boeing and BISS take the position that Petersen was presented with a full copy of the employment agreement he signed in Saudi Arabia prior to arriving there. We recognize that some evidence in the record might be consistent with this account. Because Petersen's sworn testimony is to the contrary, however, he created a triable issue of fact as to any potential fraud. The question cannot, therefore, be resolved against him absent an evidentiary hearing.

unfairness of the chosen law would deprive the plaintiff of a remedy; or (4) enforcement of such provisions would contravene a strong public policy.

Liles v. Ginn-La West End, Ltd., 631 F.3d 1242 (11th Cir. 2011). Is that a fair characterization of *The Bremen* and *Carnival Cruise*? Are the factors helpful? Are there other factors that should be included?

4. **Choice of Forum and *Forum Non Conveniens*.** Can a party to a contract containing a forum selection clause later object to that forum on grounds of *forum non conveniens* (discussed in Section A of this chapter)? In *AAR Int'l, Inc. v. Nimelias Enterprises S.A.*, 250 F.3d 510 (7th Cir. 2001), the court of appeals (citing authority from other circuits) held that a *forum non conveniens* motion could not be brought unless the forum selection clause was invalid under *The Bremen* and related cases. Is that consistent with the policies of *forum non conveniens*? Would a contrary rule be consistent with the policies underlying *The Bremen*? Some forum selection clauses also include a provision expressly waiving *forum non conveniens* objections.

5. **Choice of Forum and Choice of Law.** In the excerpt in Note 3 above, forum selection clauses are treated together with choice-of-law clauses (discussed above, Chapter 1) in terms of enforceability. In what respects are they similar and different? What can be the impact of a forum selection clause on the parties and on the outcome of a case? What can be the impact of a choice-of-law clause on the parties and on the outcome of a case? Should the analyses of the two be similar? How can a forum selection clause affect what law will be applied to decide a case? How can you determine whether a contractually selected court will apply its own nation's law or the law of another nation? As a practical matter, it is extremely common for contracts that contain a forum selection clause to also contain (often in the same section of the contract) a choice-of-law clause. Sometimes, a forum in one nation and the law of another nation is selected. Why might parties find that agreeable?

6. **Comparative Perspective.** Under the European Union's regulations, choice-of-law clauses are generally valid (with exceptions for certain kinds of contracts). Article 25 of European Union Regulation No. 1215/2012 on Jurisdiction and the Recognition and Enforcement of Judgments in Civil and Commercial Matters (Recast) provides:

> If the parties, regardless of their domicile, have agreed that a court or the courts of a Member State are to have jurisdiction to settle any disputes which have arisen or which may arise in connection with a particular legal relationship, that court or those courts shall have jurisdiction, unless the agreement is null and void as to its substantive validity under the law of that Member State. Such jurisdiction shall be exclusive unless the parties have agreed otherwise. The agreement conferring jurisdiction shall be either:
>
> (a) in writing or evidenced in writing;
> (b) in a form which accords with practices which the parties have established between themselves; or
> (c) in international trade or commerce, in a form which accords with a usage of which the parties are or ought to have been aware and

which in such trade or commerce is widely known to, and regularly observed by, parties to contracts of the type involved in the particular trade or commerce concerned.

Is the EU approach similar to the U.S. approach? How would a case like *Petersen* be argued under the EU rules if the contract chose the courts of an EU member? What if, as in *Petersen*, the contract chose the courts of a nonmember?

7. **Hague Convention on Choice of Court Agreements.** In June 2005, the Hague Conference on Private International Law adopted a Convention on Choice of Court Agreements (*see* http://www.hcch.net/index_en.php?act=conventions.text&cid=98). Under Article 5 of the Convention, "[t]he court or courts of a Contracting State designated in an exclusive choice of court agreement shall have jurisdiction to decide a dispute to which the agreement applies, unless the agreement is null and void under the law of that State" and "shall not decline to exercise jurisdiction on the ground that the dispute should be decided in a court of another State." Under Article 6, subject to narrow exceptions, "[a] court of a Contracting State other than that of the chosen court shall suspend or dismiss proceedings to which an exclusive choice of court agreement applies. . . ." Article 8 provides that "[a] judgment given by a court of a Contracting State designated in an exclusive choice of court agreement shall be recognised and enforced in other Contracting States," subject only to the limited grounds for refusal contained in the Convention. (The enforcement of judgments is discussed in detail in Chapter 7.) The Convention entered into force in 2015 and has been ratified by Mexico, Singapore, the United Kingdom, and the European Union; the United States has signed but not ratified it.

2. *Scope of Forum Selection Clauses*

Adams v. Raintree Vacation Exchange, LLC

702 F.3d 436 (7th Cir. 2012)

POSNER, Circuit Judge.

This appeal requires us to consider the enforceability of a forum selection clause by entities not named as parties to the contract in which the clause appears.

The plaintiffs are 250 purchasers of timeshare interests in villas at a resort known as Club Regina . . . in San José del Cabo, a resort area on the Pacific Coast in Baja California (which despite its name is part of Mexico). The plaintiffs bought these interests between 2004 and 2006 from a Mexican company named Desarrollos Turísticos Regina, S. de R.L. de C.V., which the parties call DTR. DTR is not a party to the appeal and indeed no longer exists, having become a Raintree affiliate named CR Resorts Holding, S. de R.L. de C.V., through a series of mergers in 2007 and 2009.

Each contract between a timeshare purchaser and DTR stated that "in case of controversy on the interpretation and compliance with the rights and obligations of this Agreement, the parties hereby agree to submit themselves to the applicable laws and competent courts of the City of Mexico, Federal District, expressly waiving any other forum that may correspond to them by reason of their present or future domiciles." (Not very good English, but DTR is, as we said, a Mexican company.)

. . .

The plaintiffs allege that defendant Raintree Vacation Exchange, LLC, in cahoots with defendant Starwood Vacation Ownership, Inc. . . . defrauded them by "pretend[ing] to have a Mexican subsidiary (DTR) take in money for [building the villas that the plaintiffs thought they were buying interests in] that would never be built." Raintree and Starwood are in the vacation resort business. Raintree operates a "vacation club" that consists of multiple timeshare resorts, while Starwood owns and operates a number of hotels and resorts including the Westin hotel chain.

The plaintiffs filed their suit in an Illinois state court. The defendants removed it to the federal district court in Chicago . . . [and then] moved to dismiss it on the basis of the forum selection clause quoted above. The judge granted the motion after an evidentiary hearing and so dismissed the suit for improper venue, precipitating this appeal.

. . .

Rather than Raintree and Starwood being parties to the sale contracts that contain the forum selection clause, DTR was the only party on the selling side (the plaintiffs being the buyers). But (to simplify a tangled corporate structure slightly) a Raintree affiliate owns a Spanish holding company that owns CR Resorts Holding, which as we noted is DTR's successor. Raintree argues that this ownership chain creates a "sufficient relationship" between it and CR Resorts Holding to authorize Raintree to enforce the forum selection clause.

A number of cases say that the test for whether a nonparty to a contract containing such a clause can nonetheless enforce it (and whether the nonparty will be bound by the clause if, instead of suing, it is sued) is whether the nonparty is "closely related" to the suit. This is a vague standard, but it can be decomposed into two reasonably precise principles, which we'll call "affiliation" and "mutuality," the first being applicable to Raintree and the second to Starwood.

A forum selection clause is sometimes enforced by or against a company that is under common ownership (for example as parent and subsidiary) with — that is, an affiliate of — a party to a contract containing the clause. . . .

Still, there has to be a reason, rather than the mere fact of affiliation, for a nonparty to a contract to be able to invoke, or to be bound by, a clause in it. There *is* a reason when a subsidiary is a party to a contract that contains a forum selection clause and the other party to the contract sues the parent under the contract. The parent should be allowed to invoke the clause and thus insist that the suit be litigated in the same court in which, pursuant to the clause, its subsidiary is being sued.

So courts have ruled in the parallel situation of an arbitration clause. Having agreed to arbitrate certain issues, a company shouldn't be allowed, by the facile device of suing an affiliate of the other signatory of the arbitration agreement, to litigate them instead.

A flat rule against enforcing forum selection clauses against affiliates of the parties to contracts containing such clauses would conduce to similar abuses. . . .

Were it not for judicial willingness in appropriate circumstances to enforce forum selection clauses against affiliates of signatories, such clauses often could easily be evaded. For example, a signatory of a contract containing such a clause might shift the business to which the contract pertained to a corporate affiliate — perhaps one created for the very purpose of providing a new home for the business — thereby nullifying the clause. Conversely, a signatory who wanted to enforce the clause might be inhibited from shifting his business to a corporate affiliate even though the shift made good business sense.

A literal approach to interpreting forum selection clauses — an approach that always ignored affiliates of the signatories — could also undermine the contribution that such clauses have been praised for making to certainty in commercial transactions, *see, e.g., Carnival Cruise Lines, Inc. v. Shute*, 499 U.S. 585, 593-94 (1991); *The Bremen v. Zapata Off-Shore Co.*, 407 U.S. 1, 13 and n.5 (1972), particularly international transactions, as in this case. The literal approach provides certainty as to which parties can invoke the clause (only the signatories), but creates uncertainty as to the forum itself, because a party may be able to avoid the designated forum by manipulating affiliate relationships. On balance it seems better to let the parties decide in the contract whether to limit the forum selection clause to the named entities than for the law to impose such a limit as a default provision to govern in the absence of specification of other entities to be bound. The latter approach would greatly complicate the negotiation of such clauses because the parties would have to strain to close all the loopholes that would open if only entities named in the contract could *ever* invoke or be made subject to such a clause.

The application of the affiliation doctrine to Raintree is straightforward. Raintree is the parent of DTR's successor, CR Resorts Holding, and can therefore enforce the forum selection clause in DTR's contracts with the plaintiffs since the effect is merely to substitute one party for another (that is, for DTR) *bound by the forum selection clause to which the plaintiffs had agreed*. Raintree is not trying by substituting itself for DTR to change the forum agreed on in the clause. . . . The plaintiffs by signing the contracts containing the forum selection clause agreed to litigate in Mexico and Raintree is not trying to alter that agreement. Why should it matter that DTR can no longer sue or be sued in its own name, because of its corporate metamorphosis?

The plaintiffs at times claim not to believe that Raintree is the parent (more likely the great-grandparent, given the intermediate subsidiaries) of DTR, and at other times claim that both Raintree and Starwood controlled DTR from the outset, and they complain that the district judge didn't allow them to conduct discovery that would have confirmed their dark though contradictory suspicions. She allowed limited discovery, which neither confirmed any of those suspicions nor provided grounds for still further discovery — especially since the plaintiffs' counsel inexplicably failed to depose the witnesses for Raintree who had given declarations concerning the ownership chain linking Raintree to DTR. Anyway how can the plaintiffs complain about the substitution of Raintree for a party they agreed to litigate with (if there were a dispute) in Mexico, when that party can no longer be sued because it has been merged into Raintree?

So much for Raintree; what of Starwood? It is not in the ownership chain that includes CR Resorts Holding, though it bought a significant part of the assets of the resort property that DTR had planned to develop. But it can invoke the forum selection clause on a different ground from that of affiliation: mutuality. The gist of the plaintiffs' complaint is that Raintree owed Starwood $10 million and that the two firms caused DTR to use the money it raised from the sales of the time-shares to pay off Raintree's debt instead of building the villas. The plaintiffs are thus alleging a conspiracy between Raintree and Starwood to defraud them, and the question is whether an alleged conspirator can invoke the forum selection clause contained in a contract, signed by his alleged co-conspirator, that created or advanced the conspiracy. The answer is yes — maybe not in every case, but in this one, where the suit accuses Raintree and Starwood of being secret principals of DTR, their agent in dealing with the timeshare buyers and thus in executing the fraud.

A contract that the agent of secret principals makes with a third party can be enforced, at the third party's option of course . . . against the secret principals. So the plaintiffs, because they alleged that Starwood (together with Raintree, by virtue of the conspiracy) controlled DTR, could have held Starwood to the forum selection clause had they wanted to sue in Mexico — and from this it follows that Starwood can hold the plaintiffs to the clause in the opposite situation and thus defend the suit in Mexico. Were it not for this principle of mutuality, the plaintiffs would have a choice of forums, and Starwood would not; and that could not have been the intention behind a clause that makes Mexico the exclusive forum irrespective of the parties' domiciles. All Starwood is doing in invoking the forum selection clause to which it is not a party is accepting one of the premises of the plaintiff's suit — that DTR is indeed simply a cat's paw of Starwood — and pointing out that the implication is that the timeshare contracts, including the forum selection clause, are really between the plaintiffs and Starwood. Because Raintree is alleged to be a secret principal along with Starwood, it can enforce the forum selection clause on the same ground as Starwood, as well as on the affiliation ground that we discussed earlier.

From a practical standpoint it is evident that the case should be litigated as one case in one court in one country, and not as two cases in two courts in two countries. Suppose the plaintiffs wanted to sue both Raintree and Starwood in Mexico. We said they would be entitled to sue Raintree there regardless of mutuality — could Starwood insist that *it* be sued in the United States? That wouldn't make sense.

The plaintiffs have another string to their bow, however, though one that makes only a faintly audible twang: they argue that a forum selection clause does not apply to a fraud suit. Wrong. Obviously if the clause were itself a product of fraud it would be unenforceable. But even if the contracts of sale to the plaintiffs that contain the clause are fraudulent, it doesn't follow that the clause is. The clause is not unclear, in illegible print, in Sanskrit or hieroglyphics, or otherwise suggestive of fraudulent intent. And there is no evidence that the defendants tried to mislead the plaintiffs concerning the meaning of the clause, or selected a foreign forum to make it difficult for the plaintiffs to enforce their rights under the contracts — Mexico after all was where the contracts were to be performed. *See Carnival Cruise Lines, Inc. v. Shute*, 499 U.S. at 595. . . . And as the clause applies to any "controversy on the interpretation and compliance with the rights and obligations of" the contracts of sale, it is broad enough to encompass tort suits that arise out of the contract.

The dismissal of the suit is

Affirmed.

NOTES AND QUESTIONS

1. **Law and Policy of Enforcing Forum Selection Clauses by Nonsignatories.** On what theory does the court allow Raintree to enforce the forum selection clause? On what theory does the court allow Starwood to enforce the forum selection clause? What is the difference between these two theories? What if plaintiffs had sued a corporate officer of DTR for fraud — would the clause apply to this claim as well?

2. **Practical Aspects of Forum Selection Clauses.** Who is the more sympathetic party in *Adams*? What could the plaintiffs have done to protect themselves? What could Raintree and Starwood have done to protect themselves?

3. **Enforceability in *Adams*.** Is it clear that the forum selection clause in *Adams* was enforceable (at least as to claims against the contracting party) under *The Bremen* and *Carnival Cruise*?

4. **Roadmapping Forum Selection Clauses.** As *Adams* suggests, there are at least three distinct issues regarding the scope of a forum selection clause:

   a. *Is the Clause Mandatory or Permissive?* That is, does the clause require the use of the specified court, or merely allow the use of the specified court? What would be an example of a clause that does the former, a clause that does the latter, and a clause that is ambiguous? Is a consent-to-jurisdiction clause — a clause whereby the parties agree to submit to the jurisdiction of a particular court — mandatory or permissive?

   b. *What Claims Are Covered by the Clause?* In *Adams*, the plaintiffs sued for fraud (a tort), not for breach of contract. Why? Why should that be covered by a *contractual* forum selection? How might the way the clause is drafted affect the question of whether noncontractual claims are included?

   c. *What Parties Are Covered by the Clause?* This is the core question in *Adams*. Why shouldn't the answer be that a contractual clause covers only the parties to the contract (and their successors)? As the court in *Adams* indicates, courts have routinely applied forum selection clauses to claims against parties who did not sign the applicable contract. How far should this practice extend? In *Magi XXI, Inc. v. Stato della Citta del Vaticano*, 714 F.3d 714 (2d Cir. 2013), the plaintiff, Magi, contracted with a private company called Second Renaissance for the right to make candles, chocolates, and other gift items bearing images of artwork owned by the Vatican. Second Renaissance in turn had a contract with the Vatican Office of Publications, a governmental entity of Vatican City (a sovereign nation, albeit a very small one), giving it such a right. Each of the contracts had a clause exclusively selecting the courts of Vatican City for dispute resolution. Magi subsequently claimed that it had not been given access to all of the artwork contemplated by its contract with Second Renaissance, and among other things sued Vatican City (which was not party to the contract with Magi). The court of appeals nonetheless held that the forum selection clause in the Magi–Second Renaissance contract required Magi to bring its claims against Vatican City in Vatican courts because Vatican City was "closely related" to the Magi–Second Renaissance contract. Is that right? Does it matter what claims Magi was asserting against Vatican City?

REVIEW NOTES AND QUESTIONS

1. It is obviously important for potential litigants to think about the issues in this chapter before litigation begins. Suppose you represent a European company facing a potential claim by a U.S. resident. Assume there are no issues of personal jurisdiction. What strategic considerations should you have in mind? How does the doctrine of *forum non conveniens* affect your assessment? How does the doctrine of *lis alibi pendens* affect your assessment? How does the prospect of an anti-suit injunction affect your assessment? How do these all relate to each other? How confident are you that you can predict what a U.S. court (or a European court) will hold? Now consider the same issues from the perspective of the U.S. party.

2. Do your answers in Question 1 suggest the advisability of a forum selection clause in future contractual relationships? Would such a clause actually bring more certainty to forum selection? How would you draft and negotiate the clause to help assure it is enforced in the manner intended by your client? Specifically, what pitfalls should you consider in drafting a forum selection clause?

CHAPTER 11

FOREIGN SOVEREIGN IMMUNITY

Suits against foreign governments and related persons and entities involve special considerations. One reason is the foreign sovereign immunity doctrine, which (subject to exceptions) makes foreign governments generally immune from suit in another nation's courts. Foreign sovereign immunity is typically justified on either the formal ground that, because nations are equal and independent sovereigns under international law, the courts of one nation do not have authority to sit in judgment of another nation absent that nation's consent, or on the functional ground that the doctrine promotes amicable relations among sovereigns. Note that foreign sovereign immunity is a defense; it does not bar nations from bringing suits as plaintiffs in the courts of other nations.

Although foreign sovereign immunity is a doctrine of customary international law, it substantially depends on implementation at the national level because it is a doctrine of immunity from suit in national courts. Nations implement the doctrine through national courts and, in some nations, national legislation. Nations violate customary international law if they fail to grant foreign sovereign immunity in their courts when customary international law would require it. For example, in a case discussed below, the International Court of Justice (ICJ) held that Italy violated the customary international law of foreign sovereign immunity by allowing a suit to proceed in its courts against Germany. *Jurisdictional Immunities of the State (Germany v. Italy)*, ICJ Judgment of 3 Feb. 2012.

As this chapter explains, the law of foreign sovereign immunity contains substantial exceptions and uncertainties. For example, what constitutes a sovereign entity entitled to claim foreign sovereign immunity? What if the foreign sovereign consents to suit, or otherwise acts in the manner of a private party subject to suit? What if one national government directs its courts to hear certain types of cases against foreign sovereigns without regard to immunity?

Each national court system has its own way of implementing foreign sovereign immunity. Litigation against foreign governments and their agencies and instrumentalities in U.S. courts heavily depends on a single federal statute, the Foreign Sovereign Immunities Act (FSIA), passed in 1976, as amended. Prior to 1976, foreign sovereign immunity in the United States was a common law rule. Between the mid-1940s and 1976, the U.S. State Department took the lead on deciding whether foreign nations would be immune in suits in U.S. courts, and the Supreme Court held that courts were bound to defer to State Department determinations. *Ex parte Republic of Peru*, 318 U.S. 578, 588 (1943); *Republic of Mexico v. Hoffman*, 324 U.S. 30 (1945). Congress enacted the FSIA to codify and standardize U.S. practice, and to alleviate diplomatic pressure on the executive branch by transferring immunity decisions to the courts. *See* 28 U.S.C. § 1602 ("Claims of foreign states to immunity should henceforth be decided by courts of the United States and of the States. . . ."). As described below, the FSIA covers many, but not all, questions of foreign sovereign immunity in U.S. courts (state and federal).

The FSIA's structure is intricate but, in general, relatively straightforward. Section 1603 is the definitions section, which among other things is vital in determining which entities are and are not covered by the FSIA. Section 1604 sets forth the general rule that a "foreign state" — defined in § 1603 to include an "agency or instrumentality of a foreign state" — is immune from suit in U.S. state and federal courts. Sections 1605 to 1607 describe a series of exceptions to immunity (with § 1605(a) containing the most important ones); if one of these exceptions applies, the FSIA provides for nonexclusive federal jurisdiction (both subject matter and personal jurisdiction) over the suit against the foreign sovereign, and § 1606 provides that (except for punitive damages), "the foreign state shall be liable in the same manner and to the same extent as a private individual under like circumstances."

The remaining provisions cover related matters such as enforcement of judgments and service of process involving foreign governments, which often entail special rules and limitations. Status as a "foreign state" under the FSIA also has various procedural consequences, some of which are explored below. Some defendants — particularly foreign state officials — may be able to claim immunity under U.S. common law even though they are not covered by the FSIA.

This chapter examines the U.S. law of foreign sovereign immunity. Section A focuses on what counts as a "foreign state" for purposes of FSIA immunity. Section B discusses the FSIA's various exceptions to the general principle of foreign sovereign immunity. Section C shifts to immunities that may exist under common law, including the immunity of foreign government officials. The remainder of the chapter discusses special rules under the FSIA governing the enforcement of judgments against foreign sovereigns (Section D) and service of process on foreign sovereigns (Section E).

A. The Scope of the FSIA: What Is a Foreign State?

The FSIA provides immunity only for foreign states. Therefore, FSIA practice requires close attention to how the FSIA defines "foreign state."

Foreign Sovereign Immunities Act, 28 U.S.C. § 1603

For purposes of this chapter —

(a) A "foreign state", except as used in section 1608 of this title, includes a political subdivision of a foreign state or an agency or instrumentality of a foreign state as defined in subsection (b).

(b) An "agency or instrumentality of a foreign state" means any entity —

(1) which is a separate legal person, corporate or otherwise, and

(2) which is an organ of a foreign state or political subdivision thereof, or a majority of whose shares or other ownership interest is owned by a foreign state or political subdivision thereof, and

(3) which is neither a citizen of a State of the United States as defined in section 1332 (c) and (e) of this title, nor created under the laws of any third country.

Foreign Sovereign Immunities Act, 28 U.S.C. § 1604

Subject to existing international agreements to which the United States is a party at the time of enactment of this Act a foreign state shall be immune from the jurisdiction of the courts of the United States and of the States except as provided in sections 1605 to 1607 of this chapter.

28 U.S.C. § 1330

(a) The district courts shall have original jurisdiction without regard to amount in controversy of any nonjury civil action against a foreign state as defined in section 1603(a) of this title as to any claim for relief in personam with respect to which the foreign state is not entitled to immunity either under sections 1605-1607 of this title or under any applicable international agreement.

(b) Personal jurisdiction over a foreign state shall exist as to every claim for relief over which the district courts have jurisdiction under subsection (a) where service has been made under section 1608 of this title.

Dole Food Co. v. Patrickson

538 U.S. 468 (2003)

Justice KENNEDY delivered the opinion of the Court.

Foreign states may invoke certain rights and immunities in litigation under the Foreign Sovereign Immunities Act of 1976. Some of the Act's provisions also may be invoked by a corporate entity that is an "instrumentality" of a foreign state as defined by the Act. The corporate entities in this action claim instrumentality status to invoke the Act's provisions allowing removal of state-court actions to federal court. As the action comes to us, it presents two questions. The first is whether a corporate subsidiary can claim instrumentality status where the foreign state does not own a majority of its shares but does own a majority of the shares of a corporate parent one or more tiers above the subsidiary. The second question is whether a corporation's instrumentality status is defined as of the time an alleged tort or other actionable wrong occurred or, on the other hand, at the time suit is filed. . . .

I

The underlying action was filed in a state court in Hawaii in 1997 against Dole Food Company and other companies. . . . Plaintiffs in the action were a group of farm workers from Costa Rica, Ecuador, Guatemala, and Panama who alleged injury from exposure to dibromochloropropane, a chemical used as an agricultural pesticide in their home countries. The Dole petitioners impleaded petitioners Dead Sea Bromine Co., Ltd., and Bromine Compounds, Ltd. (collectively, the Dead Sea Companies). The merits of the suit are not before us.

. . . The Dead Sea Companies removed [the action to the U.S. District Court for the District of Hawaii]. They claimed to be instrumentalities of a foreign state as defined by the FSIA, entitling them to removal under [28 U.S.C.] § 1441(d). The District Court held that the Dead Sea Companies are not instrumentalities of a foreign state for purposes of the FSIA and are not entitled to removal on that basis. [The Dead Sea Companies appealed.]

. . . The Court of Appeals [held] . . . that the Dead Sea Companies . . . did not meet the Act's definition of instrumentality.

In order to prevail here, the Dead Sea Companies must show both that instrumentality status is determined as of the time the alleged tort occurred and that they can claim instrumentality status even though they were but subsidiaries of a parent owned by the State of Israel. . . . [W]e now affirm.

II

A

Title 28 U.S.C. § 1441(d) governs removal of actions against foreign states. It provides that "[a]ny civil action brought in a State court against a foreign state as defined in [28 U.S.C. § 1603(a)] may be removed by the foreign state to the district court of the United States for the district and division embracing the place where such action is pending." . . .

B

The Court of Appeals resolved the question of the FSIA's applicability by holding that a subsidiary of an instrumentality is not itself entitled to instrumentality status. Its holding was correct.

The State of Israel did not have direct ownership of shares in either of the Dead Sea Companies at any time pertinent to this suit. Rather, these companies were, at various times, separated from the State of Israel by one or more intermediate corporate tiers. For example, from 1984-1985, Israel wholly owned a company called Israeli Chemicals, Ltd.; which owned a majority of shares in another company called Dead Sea Works, Ltd.; which owned a majority of shares in Dead Sea Bromine Co., Ltd.; which owned a majority of shares in Bromine Compounds, Ltd.

The Dead Sea Companies, as indirect subsidiaries of the State of Israel, were not instrumentalities of Israel under the FSIA at any time. Those companies cannot come within the statutory language which grants status as an instrumentality of a foreign state to an entity a "majority of whose shares or other ownership interest is owned by a foreign state or political subdivision thereof." § 1603(b)(2). We hold that only direct ownership of a majority of shares by the foreign state satisfies the statutory requirement.

Section 1603(b)(2) speaks of ownership. The Dead Sea Companies urge us to ignore corporate formalities and use the colloquial sense of that term. They ask whether, in common parlance, Israel would be said to own the Dead Sea Companies. We reject this analysis. In issues of corporate law structure often matters. It is evident from the Act's text that Congress was aware of settled principles of corporate law and legislated within that context. The language of § 1603(b)(2) refers to ownership of "shares," showing that Congress intended statutory coverage to turn on formal corporate ownership. Likewise, § 1603(b)(1), another component of the definition of instrumentality, refers to a "separate legal person, corporate or otherwise." In light of these indicia that Congress had corporate formalities in mind, we assess whether Israel owned shares in the Dead Sea Companies as a matter of corporate law, irrespective of whether Israel could be said to have owned the Dead Sea Companies in everyday parlance.

A basic tenet of American corporate law is that the corporation and its shareholders are distinct entities. . . . A corporate parent which owns the shares of a subsidiary does not, for that reason alone, own or have legal title to the assets of the subsidiary; and, it follows with even greater force, the parent does not own or have legal title to the subsidiaries of the subsidiary. . . .

Applying these principles, it follows that Israel did not own a majority of shares in the Dead Sea Companies. The State of Israel owned a majority of shares, at various times, in companies one or more corporate tiers above the Dead Sea Companies, but at no time did Israel own a majority of shares in the Dead Sea Companies. Those companies were subsidiaries of other corporations.

The veil separating corporations and their shareholders may be pierced in some circumstances, and the Dead Sea Companies essentially urge us to interpret the FSIA as piercing the veil in all cases. The doctrine of piercing the corporate veil, however, is the rare exception, applied in the case of fraud or certain other exceptional circumstances, and usually determined on a case-by-case basis. . . . The text of the FSIA gives no indication that Congress intended us to depart from the general rules regarding corporate formalities.

Where Congress intends to refer to ownership in other than the formal sense, it knows how to do so. Various federal statutes refer to "direct and indirect ownership." . . . The absence of this language in 28 U.S.C. § 1603(b) instructs us that Congress did not intend to disregard structural ownership rules.

The FSIA's definition of instrumentality refers to a foreign state's majority ownership of "shares or other ownership interest." § 1603(b)(2). The Dead Sea Companies would have us read "other ownership interest" to include a state's "interest" in its instrumentality's subsidiary. The better reading of the text, in our view, does not support this argument. The words "other ownership interest," when following the word "shares," should be interpreted to refer to a type of interest other than ownership of stock. The statute had to be written for the contingency of ownership forms in other countries, or even in this country, that depart from conventional corporate structures. The statutory phrase "other ownership interest" is best understood to accomplish this objective. Reading the term to refer to a state's interest in entities lower on the corporate ladder would make the specific reference to "shares" redundant. Absent a statutory text or structure that requires us to depart from normal rules of construction, we should not construe the statute in a manner that is strained and, at the same time, would render a statutory term superfluous.

The Dead Sea Companies say that the State of Israel exercised considerable control over their operations, notwithstanding Israel's indirect relationship to those companies. They appear to think that, in determining instrumentality status under the Act, control may be substituted for an ownership interest. Control and ownership, however, are distinct concepts. . . . The terms of § 1603(b)(2) are explicit and straightforward. Majority ownership by a foreign state, not control, is the benchmark of instrumentality status. We need not delve into Israeli law or examine the extent of Israel's involvement in the Dead Sea Companies' operations. Even if Israel exerted the control the Dead Sea Companies describe, that would not give Israel a "majority of [the companies'] shares or other ownership interest." The statutory language will not support a control test that mandates inquiry in every case into the past details of a foreign nation's relation to a corporate entity in which it does not own a majority of the shares.

The better rule is the one supported by the statutory text and elementary principles of corporate law. A corporation is an instrumentality of a foreign state under the FSIA only if the foreign state itself owns a majority of the corporation's shares.

We now turn to the second question before us, which provides an alternative reason for affirming the Court of Appeals.

C

To be entitled to removal under § 1441(d), the Dead Sea Companies must show that they are entities "a majority of whose shares or other ownership interest is owned by a foreign state." § 1603(b)(2). We think the plain text of this provision, because it is expressed in the present tense, requires that instrumentality status be determined at the time suit is filed.

Construing § 1603(b) so that the present tense has real significance is consistent with the longstanding principle that the jurisdiction of the Court depends upon the state of things at the time of the action brought. It is well settled, for example, that federal-diversity jurisdiction depends on the citizenship of the parties at the time suit is filed. The Dead Sea Companies do not dispute that the time suit is filed is determinative under § 1332(a)(4), which provides for suits between "a foreign state, defined in section 1603(a) . . . , as plaintiff and citizens of a State or of different States." It would be anomalous to read § 1441(d)'s words, "foreign state as defined in section 1603(a)," differently.

The Dead Sea Companies urge us to administer the FSIA like other status-based immunities, such as the qualified immunity accorded a state actor, that are based on the status of an officer at the time of the conduct giving rise to the suit. We think its comparison is inapt. Our cases applying those immunities do not involve the interpretation of a statute.

The reason for the official immunities in those cases does not apply here. The immunities for government officers prevent the threat of suit from crippling the proper and effective administration of public affairs. Foreign sovereign immunity, by contrast, is not meant to avoid chilling foreign states or their instrumentalities in the conduct of their business but to give foreign states and their instrumentalities some protection from the inconvenience of suit as a gesture of comity between the United States and other sovereigns.

Any relationship recognized under the FSIA between the Dead Sea Companies and Israel had been severed before suit was commenced. As a result, the Dead Sea Companies would not be entitled to instrumentality status even if their theory that instrumentality status could be conferred on a subsidiary were accepted.

. . .

For these reasons, we hold first that a foreign state must itself own a majority of the shares of a corporation if the corporation is to be deemed an instrumentality of the state under the provisions of the FSIA; and we hold second that instrumentality status is determined at the time of the filing of the complaint.

Justice BREYER, with whom Justice O'CONNOR joins, concurring in part and dissenting in part.

. . . Unlike the majority, I believe that the statutory phrase "other ownership interest . . . owned by a foreign state," 28 U.S.C. § 1603(b)(2), covers a Foreign Nation's legal interest in a Corporate Subsidiary, where that interest consists of the Foreign Nation's ownership of a Corporate Parent that owns the shares of the Subsidiary.

. . . The corporate defendants here, subsidiaries of a foreign parent corporation, fall within [the] definition [of an instrumentality of a foreign state] if "a majority of [their] shares or *other ownership interest is owned by*" a foreign nation. § 1603(b)(2) (emphasis added). The relevant foreign nation does not *directly* own a majority of the corporate subsidiaries' shares. But (simplifying the facts) it does own a corporate parent, which, in turn, owns the corporate subsidiaries' shares.

Does this type of majority-ownership interest count as an example of what the statute calls an "other ownership interest"? . . .

The statute's language, standing alone, cannot answer the question. That is because the words "own" and "ownership" — neither of which is defined in the

806   Chapter 11. Foreign Sovereign Immunity

FSIA — are not technical terms or terms of art but common terms, the precise legal meaning of which depends upon the statutory context in which they appear.

Thus, this Court has held that "*shipowne[r]*" can include a corporate shareholder even though, technically speaking, the corporation, not the shareholder, owns the ship. *Flink v. Paladini*, 279 U.S. 59, 62-63 (1929) (emphasis added). Moreover, this Court has held that a trademark can be "*owned by*" a parent corporation even though, technically speaking, a subsidiary corporation, not the parent, registered and thus owned the mark. *K mart Corp. v. Cartier, Inc.*, 486 U.S. 281, 292 (1988). . . . Similarly, here the words "other ownership interest" might, or might not, refer to the kind of majority-ownership interest that arises when one owns the shares of a parent that, in turn, owns a subsidiary. If a shareholder in Company A is an "owner" of Company N's ship, as in *Flink*, then why should the shareholder not be an "owner" of Company N's subsidiary? If Company N's trademark can be said to be "owned by" its shareholder, as in *K mart*, then why should Company N's subsidiary not be said to be "owned by" its shareholder? And, at the very least, can we not say that the shareholder has an "ownership interest" in the subsidiary? . . .

Judges are free to consider statutory language in light of a statute's basic purposes. And here, as in *Flink, supra*, and *K mart, supra*, an examination of those purposes sheds considerable light. The statute itself makes clear that it seeks: (1) to provide a foreign-state defendant in a legal action the right to have its claim of a sovereign immunity bar decided by the "courts of the United States," *i.e.*, the federal courts, 28 U.S.C. § 1604; see § 1441(d); and (2) to make certain that the merits of unbarred claims against foreign states, say, states engaging in commercial activities, see § 1605(a)(2), will be decided "in the same manner" as similar claims against "a private individual," § 1606; but (3) to guarantee a foreign state defending an unbarred claim certain protections, including a prohibition of punitive damages, the right to removal to federal court, a trial before a judge, and other procedural rights (related to service of process, venue, attachment, and execution of judgments). §§ 1330, 1391(f), 1441(d), 1606, 1608-1611.

Most important for present purposes, the statute seeks to guarantee these protections to the foreign nation not only when it acts directly in its own name but also when it acts through separate legal entities, including corporations and other "organ[s]." 28 U.S.C. § 1603(b). Given these purposes, what might lead Congress to grant protection to a Foreign Nation acting through a Corporate Parent but deny the same protection to the Foreign Nation acting through, for example, a wholly owned Corporate Subsidiary? The answer to this question is: In terms of the statute's purposes, *nothing at all* would lead Congress to make such a distinction.

As far as this statute is concerned, decisions about how to incorporate, how to structure corporate entities, or whether to act through a single corporate layer or through several corporate layers are matters purely of form, not of substance. The need for federal-court determination of a sovereign immunity claim is no less important where subsidiaries are involved. The need for procedural protections is no less compelling. The risk of adverse foreign policy consequences is no less great.

That is why I doubt the majority's claim that its reading of the text of the FSIA is "[t]he better reading," leading to "[t]he better rule[.]" The majority's rule is not better for a foreign nation, say, Mexico or Honduras, which may use a tiered corporate structure to manage and control important areas of national interest, such as natural resources, and, as a result, will find its ability to use the federal courts to adjudicate matters of national importance and potential sensitivity restricted. Congress is most unlikely to characterize as "better" a rule tied to legal formalities that undercuts its basic jurisdictional objectives. And working lawyers will now have to factor into complex corporate restructuring equations (determining, say, whether to use an intermediate holding company when merging or disaggregating even wholly owned government corporations) a risk that the government might lose its previously available access to federal court. . . .

NOTES AND QUESTIONS

1. **Practice: What Was at Stake?** In *Dole*, why did it matter whether the Dead Sea Companies were covered by the FSIA? What probably happened after the Supreme Court decision? What would have happened if the Dead Sea Companies had prevailed in the Supreme Court? How does the FSIA definitional section, at issue in *Dole*, relate to the rest of the FSIA?
2. **Statutory Analysis in *Dole*.** Note how the Court in *Dole* purports to derive its result from a close reading of the statutory language. Is it persuasive? Is that the right approach? What other factors should perhaps be considered? As a lawyer for the Dead Sea Companies, what else might you want to investigate?
3. **Subject Matter Jurisdiction and Personal Jurisdiction over Foreign Sovereigns.** 28 U.S.C. § 1330, excerpted above, conveys personal jurisdiction as well as subject matter jurisdiction if an FSIA exception to immunity exists. Is that constitutional? For example, in *Dole* the Dead Sea Companies were not U.S. entities and the alleged injuries occurred in other countries. If the Due Process Clause applied, what would the plaintiffs have to show to gain jurisdiction over the Dead Sea Companies? Why might the Due Process Clause not apply? *See Price v. Socialist People's Libyan Arab Jamahiriya*, 294 F.3d 82 (D.C. Cir. 2002) (concluding that a foreign state is not a "person" for constitutional purposes). If a foreign state is not a "person," what about a foreign-state-owned corporation? *See Frontera Resources Azerbaijan Co. v. State Oil Co. of the Azerbaijan Republic*, 582 F.3d 393 (2d Cir. 2009) (suggesting without deciding that the analysis might be different for state-owned corporations unless they were alter egos of the foreign state).
4. **Organs of a Foreign State.** Even if the Dead Sea Companies were not majority owned by Israel for purposes of the FSIA, is there another way they might be an "agency or instrumentality" that would enjoy the FSIA's protections? Look closely at the FSIA's definition of "agency or instrumentality." In *California Department of Water Resources v. Powerex Corp.*, 533 F.3d 1087 (9th Cir. 2008), defendant Powerex was a subsidiary of BC Hydro, which was owned by the government of the Province of British Columbia, Canada. The court of appeals, without considering whether Powerex was majority-owned by a foreign state, found that it was an "organ" of British Columbia and thus covered

by the FSIA's definition of "agency or instrumentality." The court in *Powerex* explained that

> an entity is an organ of a foreign state . . . if it engages in a public activity on behalf of the foreign government. To determine whether an entity satisfies this definitional test, courts examine the circumstances surrounding the entity's creation, the purpose of its activities, its independence from the government, the level of government financial support, its employment policies, and its obligations and privileges under state law. An entity may be an organ of a foreign state even if it has some autonomy from the foreign government. Consistent with Congress's intent, this court defines "organ" broadly, mindful that "agency or instrumentality of a foreign state" could assume a variety of forms, including a state trading corporation, a mining enterprise, a transport organization such as a shipping line or airline, a steel company, a central bank, an export association, a government procurement agency or a department or ministry which acts and is suable in its own name.

Id. at 1098. Under the text of the statute, can an indirect subsidiary of a foreign state nonetheless be an "organ"? In a part of the *Dole* case that the Supreme Court did not review, the court of appeals also held that the Dead Sea Companies were not "organs" of Israel. *Patrickson v. Dole Food Co.*, 251 F.3d 795 (9th Cir. 2001). Considering the *Powerex* criteria, what facts if true might support this conclusion?

5. **Piercing the Corporate Veil.** Can a U.S. court apply "veil piercing" rules to look behind a foreign corporate structure? Should it? What source of law should it use? Under somewhat different circumstances, in *First National City Bank v. Banco Para el Comercio Exterior de Cuba*, 462 U.S. 611 (1983), the Supreme Court found that a Cuban bank was actually a part of the Cuban government, even though it purported to be a separate corporate entity. The Court said it was using a combination of federal common law and international law to reach its result. Does that make sense?

6. **Individuals and Foreign Sovereign Immunity.** Are foreign state officials covered by the FSIA? For many years, many courts held that they were, on the authority of *Chuidian v. Philippine National Bank*, 912 F.2d 1095 (9th Cir. 1990). However, in *Samantar v. Yousuf*, 560 U.S. 305 (2010), the Supreme Court unanimously held that the immunity of individuals is not governed by the FSIA, principally by applying the text of the Act. What are arguments for and against this position? Look carefully at the FSIA, especially its definitions section. Individual immunity after *Samantar* is discussed in Section C below.

7. **Retroactivity and the FSIA.** In *Republic of Austria v. Altmann*, 541 U.S. 677 (2004), the Supreme Court considered whether the FSIA applied to conduct that occurred before the FSIA was adopted. Altmann claimed that various paintings in the possession of the Republic of Austria had been seized from her family during the Nazi era, and she sued for their return. Austria claimed that it was entitled to sovereign immunity under the common law rules in place at the time the alleged seizure occurred. The Court (over Justice Kennedy's dissent) held that courts should "appl[y] the FSIA to all

pending cases regardless of when the underlying conduct occurred." Is that consistent with *Dole*?

8. **No Alternate Sources of Jurisdiction over Foreign Sovereigns.** In *Argentine Republic v. Amerada Hess Shipping Corp.*, 488 U.S. 428 (1989), the Supreme Court held that "the FSIA [is] the sole basis for obtaining jurisdiction over a foreign state in our courts." The plaintiff, Amerada Hess, a Liberian corporation, sued Argentina for allegedly bombing one of its ships in violation of international law during Argentina's war with the United Kingdom over ownership of the Falkland Islands. Amerada Hess argued that U.S. courts should recognize jurisdiction over foreign states for violations of international law pursuant to the Alien Tort Statute (ATS), which provides jurisdiction when an alien sues for a tort in violation of the law of nations or a treaty of the United States (see Chapter 2). The court of appeals agreed, holding that the ATS (which predated the FSIA) provided an alternate basis of jurisdiction over foreign states. The Supreme Court rejected that argument and found immunity because the FSIA contained no applicable exception. Is that the right answer? What factors would you consider in answering that question? What factors does *Dole* suggest you should consider?

9. **Suit Against Foreign States by Foreign Citizens.** In *Verlinden BV v. Central Bank of Nigeria*, 461 U.S. 480 (1983), the Supreme Court held that the FSIA gives subject matter jurisdiction in federal court over all claims against foreign states, even if no other source of federal jurisdiction exists. The case involved a breach of contract claim against Nigeria, with no U.S. citizen plaintiffs and no federal law apart from the FSIA. Is that the right result? Should this sort of case be in federal court? What would happen if it wasn't in federal court? Note that (in most cases) the FSIA does not purport to create a cause of action, only to grant jurisdiction.

10. **Practice: Invoking the FSIA.** As a plaintiff's litigation counsel, would you want the defendant to be a foreign state or not? On what might that depend, apart from the question of immunity?

11. **Practice: Transactional Implications of the FSIA.** As counsel for a private corporation in a transaction in which the other party is privately owned, do you need to be concerned about the FSIA? If so, how might you evaluate and address these concerns? As you reflect on this, consider the exceptions to immunity discussed below.

B. FSIA Exceptions to Immunity

If an entity is covered by the FSIA's definition of "foreign state," suit can be brought in U.S. courts against that entity only if there is an applicable exception to immunity in the FSIA. Section 1605(a) of the FSIA contains the principal exceptions to immunity.

1. *Waiver*

Foreign Sovereign Immunities Act, 28 U.S.C. § 1605

(a) A foreign state shall not be immune from the jurisdiction of courts of the United States or of the States in any case —

(1) in which the foreign state has waived its immunity either explicitly or by implication, notwithstanding any withdrawal of the waiver which the foreign state may purport to effect except in accordance with the terms of the waiver. . . .

Capital Ventures International v. Republic of Argentina

552 F.3d 289 (2d Cir. 2009)

KATZMANN, Circuit Judge.

This case calls upon us . . . to determine whether the Republic of Argentina explicitly waived its sovereign immunity from suit in the United States as to claims relating to bonds issued by Argentina under German law.

Plaintiff-appellant Capital Ventures International ("CVI") appeals from a judgment of the United States District Court for the Southern District of New York . . . dismissing, for lack of subject matter jurisdiction, those of CVI's claims that relate to bonds issued by defendant-appellee Republic of Argentina ("Argentina" or "the Republic") under German law. . . . We find that there is subject matter jurisdiction over the claims relating to the German bonds because Argentina explicitly waived its sovereign immunity to suit in United States courts on those claims. . . .

CVI is the beneficial owner of certain bonds issued by the Republic of Argentina. One group of the bonds owned by CVI is governed by German law, and these bonds are denominated in Deutsche Marks and Euros ("the German bonds"). Each German bond was issued pursuant to its own offering circular. Section 13 of the offering circulars provides in part:

> (3) The Republic hereby irrevocably submits to the non-exclusive jurisdiction of the District Court (Landgericht) in Frankfurt am Main and any federal court sitting in the City of Buenos Aires as well as any appellate court of any thereof, in any suit, action or proceeding against it arising out of or relating to these Bonds. The Republic hereby irrevocably waives — to the fullest extent it may effectively do so — the defense of an inconvenient forum to the maintenance of such suit or action or such proceeding and any present or future objection to such suit, action or proceeding whether on the grounds of venue, residence or domicile. The Republic agrees that a final judgment in any such suit, action or proceeding in the courts mentioned above shall be conclusive and may be enforced in other jurisdictions by suit on the judgment or any other method provided by law.
>
> (4) To the extent that the Republic has or hereafter may acquire any immunity (sovereign or otherwise) from jurisdiction of any court or from any legal process (whether through service or notice, attachment prior to judgment, attachment

in aid of execution, execution or otherwise), with respect to itself or its revenues, assets or properties, the Republic hereby irrevocably waives such immunity in respect of its obligations under the Bonds to the extent it is permitted to do so under applicable law. . . .

In December 2001, Argentina declared a moratorium on the payment of principal and interest on its foreign debt and stopped paying principal and interest on the bonds at issue here. In response to the default, on various dates in 2005 and 2006, CVI accelerated the bonds it owned, making the principal immediately due.

The instant lawsuit was filed in the Southern District on April 25, 2005. . . . [T]he district court ruled that it lacked subject matter jurisdiction over the claims relating to CVI's German bonds because Argentina was entitled to sovereign immunity with respect to those claims; the district court accordingly dismissed the German bond claims. Construing section 13(3) and (4) of the offering circulars, the district court concluded that Argentina had not explicitly waived its sovereign immunity in U.S. courts in section 13. Instead, it held that subsection 3 was a limited submission to the jurisdiction of courts in Frankfurt and Buenos Aires. The district court reasoned that "whatever [subsection 4] means it should not be read as reading out of this instrument the reference to Frankfurt and the city of Buenos Aires." Accordingly, while acknowledging that the language of subsection 4 was "very broad," the district court ultimately held that "where there is an expressed grant of jurisdiction in specific places . . . a general waiver of sovereign immunity [as in subsection 4] does not mean that . . . suit can be brought any place in the world." . . .

The Foreign Sovereign Immunities Act ("FSIA") is the sole source for subject matter jurisdiction over any action against a foreign state. The FSIA provides that foreign sovereigns are immune from suit unless a specific exception to sovereign immunity applies. One such exception is that a foreign state is not immune from suit "in any case . . . in which the foreign state has waived its immunity either explicitly or by implication." [FSIA] § 1605(a)(1). The term "explicit," in this context, takes its normal meaning of "clear and unambiguous." . . .

In the offering circulars, Argentina explicitly waived its sovereign immunity to suit in U.S. courts on claims related to the German bonds. Section 13(4) of the offering circulars provides that, "[t]o the extent that the Republic has or hereafter may acquire any immunity (sovereign or otherwise) from jurisdiction of any court or from any legal process . . . , the Republic hereby irrevocably waives such immunity in respect of its obligations under the Bonds to the extent it is permitted to do so under applicable law." This provision clearly and unambiguously waives Argentina's "immunity (sovereign or otherwise)" in "*any*" court." This clear language satisfies the FSIA's requirement of an "explicit" waiver.

Argentina advances the argument that section 13(4), read in conjunction with section 13(3), merely allows for judgments obtained pursuant to section 13(3) to be enforced in other courts. However, the language of subsection 4 is not so limited. Subsection 4 refers to "any legal process (whether through service or notice, attachment prior to judgment, attachment in aid of execution, execution or otherwise)," language that contemplates actions other than those to enforce judgments. Further, subsection 3 ends with the provision that "a final judgment in any such suit . . . in the courts mentioned above . . . may be enforced in other jurisdictions by suit on the judgment or any other method provided by law." If the Republic's interpretation of subsection 4 were adopted, this last sentence in subsection 3 would render subsection 4 superfluous, a result that should be avoided. Further, if subsection 4 were intended to discuss enforcement in other jurisdictions, we would expect that the same terms in the last sentence of subsection 3 would be repeated in subsection 4 — but they are not. Accordingly, we do not read section 13(4) as applying only to the enforcement of judgments.

Argentina also argues that reading section 13(4) as a waiver of sovereign immunity in any court renders subsection 3 superfluous, a result which, as just discussed, is disfavored. According to Argentina, under such a reading Argentina has "agree[d] to jurisdiction in Germany and Argentina" in subsection 3 and also "agree[d] to jurisdiction everywhere" in subsection 4. Of course, such an interpretation of section 13(4) would render subsection 3 superfluous — but that is not what subsection 4 says. Subsection 4 is a waiver of Argentina's "immunity (sovereign or otherwise)," but it does not waive other objections to suit that Argentina might have, such as objections based on lack of personal jurisdiction, improper venue, or forum non conveniens. Section 13(3), on the other hand, provides that Argentina "submits to the non-exclusive jurisdiction" of the courts in Frankfurt and Buenos Aires as well as "waives . . . the defense of an inconvenient forum . . . and any . . . objection . . . on the grounds of venue, residence or domicile." It is thus clear that reading subsection 4 as a waiver of sovereign immunity in any court does not render subsection 3 superfluous.

Argentina also presses the argument that the case law reveals a requirement that, to be explicit, a waiver must contain a reference to the United States or a specific jurisdiction within the United States. We do not find such a requirement in the cases. Of course, a specific reference to the United States can be helpful in determining that a waiver meets the FSIA's requirement of explicitness, . . . but the statutory requirement is only that the waiver be "explicit." There can be explicit waivers without a reference to the United States, as the waiver of immunity in "any court" in this case illustrates. *See also Walker Int'l Holdings Ltd. v. Republic of Congo*, 395 F.3d 229, 234 (5th Cir. 2004) (finding an explicit waiver under the FSIA where a contract read "[t]he Congo hereby irrevocably renounces to claim any immunity during any procedure relating to any arbitration decision handed down by an Arbitration Court"); *World Wide Minerals, Ltd. v. Republic of Kazakstan*, 296 F.3d 1154, 1162 & n.13 (D.C. Cir. 2002) (finding an "express waiver[] of sovereign immunity" where the waiver said "[i]n respect of any arbitration or legal action or proceedings arising out of or in connection with this Agreement, . . . [the Kazakhstan State Committee] hereby irrevocably agrees not to claim and hereby irrevocably waives . . . immunity for itself and the assets of the Republic of Kazakstan to the full extent permitted by the laws of such jurisdiction"). Any other result would stray from the plain meaning of the statutory language.

Despite Argentina's argument, *Argentine Republic v. Amerada Hess Shipping Corp.*, 488 U.S. 428 (1989), does not require a contrary result. In *Amerada Hess*, the Supreme Court stated that it did not "see how a foreign state can waive its immunity under § 1605(a)(1) by signing an international agreement that contains no mention of a waiver of immunity to suit in United States courts or even the availability of a cause of action in the United States." *Id.* at 442-43. Argentina would have us read this language as a requirement that, for a waiver to satisfy the FSIA's explicitness requirement, it must mention the United States in some way. That is not the holding of *Amerada Hess.* The international agreements at issue in *Amerada Hess* were the Geneva Convention on the High Seas, Apr. 29, 1958, 13 U.S.T. 2312, and the Pan American Maritime Neutrality Convention, Feb. 20, 1928, 47 Stat. 1989 — neither of which mentions waiving sovereign immunity at all, let alone in the United States. The offering circulars at issue here, which are contracts between Argentina and the bondholders, are far removed from multi-party international agreements and do discuss waiver of sovereign immunity to suit in *any* court, thereby indicating waiver of immunity to suit in United States courts. Accordingly, *Amerada Hess* does not control the outcome here.

There is likewise no support in our cases for Argentina's suggestion that the mention of specific, non-United States jurisdictions in subsection 3 of the offering circulars precludes a finding that Argentina waived its sovereign immunity to suit in the United States. Of course it is true that there will be cases in which, when a document mentions a non-U.S. jurisdiction, there will be no explicit waiver for FSIA purposes because it will be clear that there is no intent to waive sovereign immunity in United States courts. *See, e.g., Eaglet Corp. v. Banco Cent. De Nicar.,* 839 F. Supp. 232, 234 (S.D.N.Y. 1993) (finding no explicit waiver where jurisdictional clause stated "[t]his Agreement is governed by English law and therefore BCN submits to the nonexclusive jurisdiction of the English High Court of Justice"); *Atl. Tele-Network Inc. v. Inter-Am. Dev. Bank,* 251 F. Supp. 2d 126, 133 (D.D.C. 2003) (finding that a broad, non-geographically limited waiver of immunity, when "juxtapos[ed] immediately below a choice-of-law selection clause (specifying the law of Guyana) and above a forum-selection clause (specifying the courts of Guyana)," does not waive immunity in the United States). It is not true, however, that the mere mention of a non-U.S. jurisdiction will preclude a finding of waiver, because the statute requires only that the waiver be "explicit." As the waiver at issue here demonstrates, a waiver of sovereign immunity can be explicit even when other provisions of the document are applicable only to specific, non-United States jurisdictions.

Accordingly, because we find that Argentina explicitly waived its sovereign immunity to suits in the United States relating to the German bonds, we reverse the district court's dismissal of CVI's German bond claims. . . .

Sampson v. Federal Republic of Germany

250 F.3d 1145 (7th Cir. 2001)

MANION, Circuit Judge.

Jacob Sampson, pro se, sued Germany for his imprisonment in Nazi concentration camps, and sued Germany . . . for reparations from funds created for Holocaust survivors. The district court dismissed the complaint concluding that Germany was immune from suit. . . . Sampson appeals. We affirm.

I.

Sampson's complaint alleges horrors which are beyond belief, and the evils he describes cannot be condemned in strong enough terms. In 1939, Sampson was imprisoned in the Lodz ghetto in Poland. He was subsequently transported by cattle car to the Auschwitz concentration camp, where he was forced to perform slave labor. At Auschwitz, the Gestapo killed all sixty members of his family. Sampson somehow survived, and he is now a United States citizen and resident of Chicago. . . .

Subsequently, Sampson filed suit in federal district court against Germany . . . seeking $10 million plus costs. Sampson sought compensation from Germany based on his enslavement during World War II. . . .

The district court dismissed the claims against Germany, concluding Germany was immune from suit under the Foreign Sovereign Immunities Act ("FSIA"). . . .

Sampson appealed the dismissals to this court. On appeal, this court appointed Dean Howard Eisenberg and Professor Joseph Kearney of Marquette University Law School as amicus curiae ("Amicus") to argue on Sampson's behalf. . . . The United States government filed a brief as amicus curiae in support of Germany's argument that it had sovereign immunity for its acts during World War II.

II.

. . .

Sampson and Amicus argue that this court has jurisdiction under Section 1605(a)(1) of the FSIA, which provides an exception to sovereign immunity where a "foreign state has waived its immunity . . . by implication." Specifically, Sampson and Amicus argue that a violation of a nonderogable *jus cogens* norm of customary international law constitutes an implied waiver of a foreign state's sovereign immunity.

To understand this argument some additional background is necessary. Customary international law is the "general and consistent practice of states followed by them from a sense of obligation." *See* Restatement (Third), The Foreign Relations Law of the United States § 102(2) (1987). Courts determine the content of customary international law by "consulting the works of jurists, writing professedly on public law; or by the general usage and practice of nations; or by judicial decisions recognizing and enforcing that law." *United States v. Smith*, 18 U.S. 153, 160-61 (1820).

A *jus cogens* norm is a special type of customary international law. A *jus cogens* norm "'is a norm accepted and recognized by the international community of states as a whole as a norm from which no derogation is permitted and which can be modified only be a subsequent norm of general international law having the same character.'" *See Siderman de Blake v. Republic of Argentina*, 965 F.2d 699, 714 (9th Cir. 1992) (quoting Vienna Convention on the Law of Treaties, art. 53, May 23, 1969, 1155 U.N.T.S. 332, 8 I.L.M. 679). Most famously, *jus cogens* norms supported the prosecutions in the Nuremberg trials. *See Siderman*, 965 F.2d at 715 ("The universal and fundamental rights of human beings identified by Nuremberg — rights against genocide, enslavement, and other inhumane acts . . . — are the direct ancestors of the universal and fundamental norms recognized as *jus cogens*.").

. . . While *jus cogens* and customary international law are related, they differ in one important respect. Customary international law, like international law defined by treaties and other international agreements, rests on the consent of states. In contrast, a state is bound by *jus cogens* norms even if it does not consent to their application.

[Sampson and Amicus argue that] [i]nternational law does not recognize an act that violates *jus cogens* as a sovereign act. Thus, a violation of *jus cogens* norms would not be entitled to the immunity afforded by international law. . . . In addition, they note that the House Report when the FSIA was enacted stated that "the central premise of the bill [is] [t]hat decisions on claims by foreign states to sovereign immunity are best made by the judiciary on the basis of a statutory regime which incorporates standards recognized under international law." Accordingly, they urge us to hold that the FSIA's implied waiver exception to sovereign immunity extends to violations of *jus cogens* norms.

Initially, we note that we have held in other contexts that the implied waiver provision of the FSIA is to be narrowly construed. *See Frolova v. Union of Soviet Socialist Republics*, 761 F.2d 370, 377 (7th Cir. 1985). In fact, "courts rarely find that a nation has waived its sovereign immunity, particularly with respect to suits brought by third parties, without strong evidence that this is what the foreign state intended." *Id.* Thus, an implied waiver depends upon the foreign government's having at some point indicated its amenability to suit.

In this case, there is no evidence that Germany indicated, either expressly or implicitly, that it was willing to be sued in the United States based on actions during World War II. Sampson responds that the following constitutes evidence that Germany waived its sovereign immunity: a letter from the German government stating that the German people is responsible for the past; a letter from the Claims Conference [on Holocaust claims] stating that Sampson was eligible to receive compensation payments; and a holding by the German Supreme Constitutional Court regarding *jus cogens* norms. But these statements do not indicate an intent by the state of Germany to be subject to suit in United States courts; they merely demonstrate that Germany recognizes that its actions during World War II constituted violations of *jus cogens* norms. Nor is there any other evidence in the record, much less the strong evidence sufficient to demonstrate Germany's intent to waive its immunity. . . .

Amicus argues in response that while an implied waiver under Section 1605(a)(1) must generally demonstrate a clear intent by the state to waive its sovereign immunity, that principle does not apply to cases involving violations of *jus cogens* norms of international law. [It is argued that] [*j*]*us cogens* norms are by definition nonderogable, and thus when a state thumbs its nose at such a norm, in effect overriding the collective will of the entire international community, the state cannot be performing a sovereign act entitled to immunity.

Amicus further points to Chief Justice Marshall's famous statement that "an act of Congress ought never to be construed to violate the law of nations if any other possible construction remains," *see Murray v. The Schooner Charming Betsy*, 6 U.S. 64, 118 (1804), arguing that because under international law violations of *jus cogens* norms constitute a waiver of immunity, we should interpret them as a waiver under the FSIA also. The principle on which Amicus relies in making this argument is known as the "*Charming Betsy* canon," and it has traditionally justified a narrow interpretation of ambiguous legislation to avoid violations of international law.

While the *Charming Betsy* canon directs courts to construe ambiguous statutes to avoid conflicts with international law, international law itself does not mandate Article III jurisdiction over foreign sovereigns. In other words, although *jus cogens* norms may address sovereign immunity in contexts where the question is whether international law itself provides immunity, *e.g.*, the Nuremberg proceedings, *jus cogens* norms do not require Congress (or any government) to create jurisdiction. Because international law is silent on the grant of federal court jurisdiction at issue, we interpret the FSIA without reference to the *Charming Betsy* canon.

Nevertheless, Amicus argues that the *Charming Betsy* canon requires us to construe the terms of an ambiguous statute so that it is consistent with the content of international law. Even assuming the FSIA is ambiguous, Amicus's reading of *Charming Betsy* would require us to apply the canon even where it is unnecessary to avoid a violation of international law. As Judge Ginsburg noted in *Princz* [*v. Federal Republic of Germany*, 26 F.3d 1166 (D.C. Cir. 1994)]:

> We think that something more nearly express [than the FSIA-implied waiver provision] is wanted before we impute to the Congress an intention that the federal courts assume jurisdiction over the countless human rights cases that might well be brought by the victims of all the ruthless military juntas, presidents-for-life, and murderous dictators of the world, from Idi Amin to Mao Zedong. Such an expansive reading of § 1605(a)(1) would likely place an enormous strain not only upon our courts but, more to the immediate point, upon our country's diplomatic relations with any number of foreign nations. In many if not most cases the outlaw regime would no longer even be in power and our Government could have normal relations with the government of the day — unless disrupted by our courts, that is.

Moreover, although international law is "part of our law," it does not follow that federal statutes must be read to reflect the norms of international law. *Cf. United States v. Yunis*, 924 F.2d 1086, 1091 (D.C. Cir. 1991) ("Our duty is to enforce the Constitution, laws and treaties of the United States, not to conform the law of the land to norms of customary international law."). Since customary international law in the modern era is often based on the contents of multi-lateral treaties to which the United States attaches reservations (or refuses to join at all), there is also little reason to indulge in a presumption that Congress intends courts to mold ambiguous statutes into consistency with customary international law. Use of the canon so as to effectively incorporate customary international law into federal statutes when the political branches of our government may have rejected the international law at issue seems dubious at best.

. . .

There is even less justification for an expansive reading of *Charming Betsy* in light of the chameleon qualities of international law. If courts were to interpret statutes according to their view of what best fits the changing nuances of customary international law, they would frequently make decisions that run up against the foreign policy of the other two branches of our government. And rather than encouraging peaceful relations with other nations, such an expansive reading of the *Charming Betsy* canon would predictably create tensions in cases like this one, which involve jurisdiction over foreign sovereigns.

Amicus argues that the phrase "waive[r] . . . by implication" in section 1605(a)(1), in conjunction with a legislative history that references common law examples of waiver, indicates a congressional intent that courts develop a common law to determine when an implied waiver occurs. That would mean a decision whether an implied waiver exists would be based on the evolving recognition of *jus cogens* norms in United States courts. If anything, the legislative history of section 1605(a)(1) cuts against Amicus's argument by providing very specific examples of implied waiver: "(1) a foreign state has agreed to arbitration in another country; (2) a foreign state has agreed that a contract is governed by the law of a particular country; and (3) a foreign state has filed a responsive pleading in a case without raising the defense of sovereign immunity." *Frolova*, 761 F.2d at 377. These are all narrow examples which have a nexus with legal proceedings in the United States, and do not suggest a congressional intent that the list of potential waivers be extended. Courts have been reluctant to stretch claims of implied waiver beyond these examples. . . .

Moreover, Amicus's common law argument would be ground-breaking. Amicus encourages this court to engage in an evolving understanding of waiver, an understanding which is necessarily subject to the vagaries of customary international law. Customary international law can evolve unpredictably without reference to the understandings of courts or Congress. While it is true that Congress intended the FSIA to be "a statutory regime which incorporates standards recognized under international law," H.R. Rep. No. 1487, *reprinted in* 1976 U.S.C.C.A.N., at 6613, Amicus's suggestion would entail a truly novel and possibly unrestrained form of jurisdiction. Congress's general desire to follow standards recognized under international law does not provide the foundation needed to support that proposed reading of an implied waiver. As this court has noted, "[n]o legislation pursues its purposes at all costs. Deciding what competing values will or will not be sacrificed to the achievement of a particular objective is the very essence of legislative choice — and it frustrates rather than effectuates legislative intent simplistically to assume that whatever furthers the statute's primary objective must be the law." *Continental Can Co. v. Chicago Truck Drivers, Helpers and Warehouse Workers Union (Independent) Pension Fund*, 916 F.2d 1154, 1159 (7th Cir. 1990) (Easterbrook, J.). Congress could not have intended to confer a jurisdiction so malleable on Article III courts without a clear statement to that effect.

Also, *jus cogens* norms are even now an uncertain means to determine whether a foreign sovereign has waived jurisdiction, and missteps in this area would have profound effect. A leading treatise on international law has stated that *jus cogens* is "a comparatively recent development and there is no general agreement as to which rules have this character." *See* Oppenheim's International Law 7 (9th ed. 1992). The absence of agreement among international law scholars is so striking that one commentator expressed the status of *jus cogens* in the following terms: "no one knows where *jus cogens* comes from, no one knows whether or how or why it is part of international law, no one knows its content, no one knows how to modify it once it is articulated, and indeed no one knows whether it even exists." *See* Anthony D'Amato, *Human Rights as Part of Customary International Law: A Plea for Change of Paradigms*, 25 Ga. J. Int'l & Comp. L. 47, 57 (1995-1996). We do not question that the allegations in Sampson's complaint rise to the level of *jus cogens* violations — they are a paradigm case — but that does not mean that Congress intended an implicit waiver provision to encompass this expanding legal doctrine. . . .

In interpreting the FSIA, we are mindful that "judicial resolution of cases bearing significantly on sensitive foreign policy matters, like the case before us, might have serious foreign policy implications which courts are ill-equipped to anticipate or handle." *Frolova*, 761 F.2d at 375. The potential scope of a customary international law exception to foreign sovereign immunity, even in the *jus cogens* context, would allow for a major, open-ended expansion of our jurisdiction into an area with substantial impact on the United States' foreign relations. As noted by the Supreme Court in *Oetjen v. Central Leather Co.*, 246 U.S. 297, 302 (1918), "[t]he conduct of the foreign relations of our government is committed by the constitution to the Executive and Legislative — 'the political' — Departments of the Government." Deference to the foreign policy of the political branches of our government requires us to exercise caution before inferring that Congress intended the implied waiver provision to cover cases like this one. We again determine, as we did in *Frolova*, that our jurisdiction under the FSIA should be construed narrowly, and conclude that Congress did not create an exception to foreign sovereign immunity under the FSIA for violations of *jus cogens* norms. . . .

Affirmed.

NOTES AND QUESTIONS

1. **Practice: Drafting Express Waivers.** Although in principle it is possible for a foreign state to expressly agree to litigate a dispute in U.S. courts after the dispute arises, in practice this is rare. Most express waivers occur, as in *Capital Ventures*, in contracts signed as part of a business transaction. Is the contractual waiver in *Capital Ventures* unambiguous? Could anything be done to make it less ambiguous? What about the other contractual waivers to which the court refers in its discussion: Do you agree that the court characterizes them correctly?

2. **Implied Waivers.** In ordinary cases, what constitutes an implied waiver? Consider the three examples from the FSIA's legislative history, discussed in *Sampson*:

> With respect to implicit waivers, the courts have found such waivers in cases where a foreign state has agreed to arbitration in another country or where a foreign state has agreed that the law of a particular country should govern a

contract. An implicit waiver would also include a situation where a foreign state has filed a responsive pleading in an action without raising the defense of sovereign immunity.

H.R. Rep. No. 1487, 94th Cong., 2d Sess. 18 (1976), *reprinted in* 1976 U.S.C.C.A.N. 6604, 6617. Are these good examples? Can you think of other noncontractual situations in which a court might find an implied waiver?

In *Siderman de Blake v. Republic of Argentina*, 965 F.2d 699 (9th Cir. 1992), the court concluded that Argentina's use of U.S. courts to harass the plaintiff constituted an implied waiver with respect to certain of the plaintiff's claims against it, although the court expressly cautioned:

> We do not suggest that because Argentina may have implicitly waived its immunity in this suit, any foreign sovereign which takes actions against a private party in our courts necessarily opens the way to all manner of suit by that party. To support a finding of implied waiver, there must exist a direct connection between the sovereign's activities in our courts and the plaintiff's claims for relief. Only because the Sidermans have presented evidence indicating that Argentina's invocation of United States judicial authority was part and parcel of its efforts to torture and persecute Jose Siderman have they advanced a sufficient basis for invoking that same authority with respect to their causes of action for torture.

In *Joseph v. Office of Consulate General of Nigeria*, 830 F.2d 1018, 1022 (9th Cir. 1987), the court concluded that the foreign state waived immunity by signing a lease regarding real property in San Francisco, California, because the lease included a provision awarding attorneys' fees to the prevailing party in litigation. But in *Barapind v. Government of the Republic of India*, 844 F.3d 824 (9th Cir. 2016), the court rejected a claim of implied waiver where the Indian government, in an exchange of diplomatic notes, promised the United States that Barapind would not be tortured if extradited from the United States to India. Barapind alleged that he was tortured after extradition, but the court found no implied waiver because nothing suggested India "contemplated the involvement of the courts of the United States" or "intended . . . to avail itself of the privileges or protections of the courts of the United States," expressly distinguishing *Joseph* and *Siderman*. Does that seem correct?

3. **Implied Waiver and Human Rights Violations.** In *Sampson*, what is the plaintiff's argument that Germany's conduct creates an implied waiver? Why does the court reject it? In *Princz v. Federal Republic of Germany*, discussed in *Sampson*, the court similarly rejected a claim that a *jus cogens* violation constituted a waiver of immunity. Judge Wald dissented, writing in part:

> The international consensus endorsing the existence and force of *jus cogens* norms solidified in the aftermath of World War II. The universal and fundamental rights of human beings identified by Nuremberg — rights against genocide, enslavement, and other inhumane acts — are the direct ancestors of the universal and fundamental norms recognized as *jus cogens*. . . .
>
> Because the Nuremberg Charter's definition of "crimes against humanity" includes what are now termed *jus cogens* norms, a state is never entitled to immunity for any act that contravenes a *jus cogens* norm, regardless of where

or against whom that act was perpetrated. The rise of *jus cogens* norms limits state sovereignty in the sense that the general will of the international community of states, and other actors, will take precedence over the individual wills of states to order their relations. *Jus cogens* norms are by definition nonderogable, and thus when a state thumbs its nose at such a norm, in effect overriding the collective will of the entire international community, the state cannot be performing a sovereign act entitled to immunity. When the Nazis tore off Princz's clothes, exchanged them for a prison uniform and a tattoo, shoved him behind the spiked barbed wire fences of Auschwitz and Dachau, and sold him to the German armament industry as fodder for their wartime labor operation, Germany rescinded any claim under international law to immunity from this court's jurisdiction.

The exercise of jurisdiction over the Nazi officials at Nuremberg was by no means a single aberration in international law. Under the principle of universal jurisdiction, for certain offenses (including, but not limited to, *jus cogens* violations) a state can exercise jurisdiction over an offender in custody even if that state has neither a territorial link to the offense nor any connection to the nationality of the victim or offender. . . . The most recent example of a prescription of jurisdiction by the international community over *jus cogens* violations carried out within the confines of a state's own territory is the United Nations' Statute of the International War Crimes Tribunal for the former Yugoslavia ("Statute"). . . . The Statute contains absolutely no indication that foreign sovereign immunity could provide a valid defense to the exercise of the tribunal's jurisdiction. Thus the clear import of international law is to disavow a foreign sovereign's claims to immunity where that sovereign is accused of violating universally accepted norms of conduct essential to the preservation of the international order. In other words, under international law, a state waives its right to sovereign immunity when it transgresses a *jus cogens* norm. . . .

Should the question of implied waiver for *jus cogens* violations be decided as a matter of statutory interpretation or customary international law? What if customary international law held that there is no immunity for *jus cogens* violations? Although the Supreme Court declined to review *Princz*, *Sampson*, and related cases, the question of immunity for *jus cogens* violations has recently resurfaced in connection with immunity claimed by foreign officials. See Section C below.

4. **Customary International Law and Immunity.** Regarding the customary international law of foreign sovereign immunity, consider the ICJ's 2012 decision in *Jurisdictional Immunities of the State* (*Germany v. Italy*). In that case, Italy allowed a suit in its courts against Germany for Nazi-era war crimes, notwithstanding Germany's assertion of foreign sovereign immunity. Germany sued Italy in the ICJ, arguing that by allowing the suit, Italy violated the customary international law of foreign sovereign immunity. Among other things, Italy argued that international law does not provide immunity for violations of *jus cogens* norms, such as the war crimes in the Italian court case. The ICJ rejected Italy's argument, finding that customary international law recognized no such exception and that Italy therefore violated that law by allowing the suit against Germany. What are the implications of this decision for the plaintiffs? What would be the implications for the doctrine of foreign sovereign immunity if,

contrary to the ICJ's decisions, each nation were able to define the scope of immunity in its own way? What should be the implications, if any, of the ICJ decision on the U.S. law of foreign sovereign immunity?

The U.N. Convention on Jurisdictional Immunities of States and Their Property, adopted in 2004, attempts to codify the customary international law of foreign sovereign immunity but has not yet entered into force because it has not received the required 30 ratifications. The Convention was prepared by the U.N. International Law Commission (ILC), which was established in 1948. According to Article 1 of the Statute of the ILC, it "shall have for its object the promotion of the progressive development of international law and its codification." One way the ILC pursues this mandate is by codifying principles of customary international law in "draft articles" that may eventually be adopted by nations in the form of treaties. Its draft articles, including those that led to the Convention, are often considered to be important evidence of customary international law. Is the U.N. Convention relevant to defining the scope of foreign sovereign immunity in the United States? How would you argue that it should be? How would you argue that it should not be?

5. **Policy: Holding Foreign Sovereigns to Their Waivers.** Is the FSIA correct to recognize contractual waiver of foreign sovereign immunity? What if the waiver was made by a prior and possibly illegitimate government, or if it violated the law of the foreign state? What if the waiver involves matters fundamental to the security and sovereignty of the nation (as was arguably true for Argentina in *Capital Ventures*)?

2. Commercial Activity

Foreign Sovereign Immunities Act, 28 U.S.C. § 1605

(a) A foreign state shall not be immune from the jurisdiction of courts of the United States or of the States in any case —

. . .

(2) in which the action is based upon a commercial activity carried on in the United States by the foreign state; or upon an act performed in the United States in connection with a commercial activity of the foreign state elsewhere; or upon an act outside the territory of the United States in connection with a commercial activity of the foreign state elsewhere and that act causes a direct effect in the United States[.]

Foreign Sovereign Immunities Act, 28 U.S.C. § 1603

For purposes of this chapter —

. . .

(d) A "commercial activity" means either a regular course of commercial conduct or a particular commercial transaction or act. The commercial character of an activity shall be determined by reference to the nature of the course of conduct or particular transaction or act, rather than by reference to its purpose.

(e) A "commercial activity carried on in the United States by a foreign state" means commercial activity carried on by such state and having substantial contact with the United States.

Republic of Argentina v. Weltover, Inc.

504 U.S. 607 (1992)

Justice SCALIA delivered the opinion of the Court.

This case requires us to decide whether the Republic of Argentina's default on certain bonds issued as part of a plan to stabilize its currency was an act taken "in connection with a commercial activity" that had a "direct effect in the United States" so as to subject Argentina to suit in an American court under the Foreign Sovereign Immunities Act of 1976, 28 U.S.C. § 1602 et seq.

I

[Argentina issued government bonds to private creditors to raise money to repay certain international currency obligations.] These bonds, called "Bonods," provide for payment of interest and principal in United States dollars; payment may be made through transfer on the London, Frankfurt, Zurich, or New York market, at the election of the creditor. . . .

When the Bonods began to mature in May 1986, Argentina concluded that it lacked sufficient foreign exchange to retire them. Pursuant to a Presidential Decree, Argentina unilaterally extended the time for payment and offered bondholders substitute instruments as a means of rescheduling the debts. Respondents, two Panamanian corporations and a Swiss bank who hold, collectively, $1.3 million of Bonods, refused to accept the rescheduling and insisted on full payment, specifying New York as the place where payment should be made. Argentina did not pay, and respondents then brought this breach-of-contract action in the United States District Court for the Southern District of New York, relying on the Foreign Sovereign Immunities Act of 1976 as the basis for jurisdiction. Petitioners moved to dismiss for lack of subject-matter jurisdiction. . . . The District Court denied these motions, and the Court of Appeals affirmed. . . .

II

. . . Under the [FSIA], a "foreign state *shall* be immune from the jurisdiction of the courts of the United States and of the States" unless one of several statutorily defined exceptions applies. § 1604 (emphasis added). The FSIA thus provides the "sole basis" for obtaining jurisdiction over a foreign sovereign in the United States. See *Argentine Republic v. Amerada Hess Shipping Corp.*, 488 U.S. 428,

434-439 (1989). The most significant of the FSIA's exceptions — and the one at issue in this case — is the "commercial" exception of § 1605(a)(2). . . .

In the proceedings below, respondents relied only on the third clause of § 1605(a)(2) to establish jurisdiction, and our analysis is therefore limited to considering whether this lawsuit is (1) "based . . . upon an act outside the territory of the United States"; (2) that was taken "in connection with a commercial activity" of Argentina outside this country; and (3) that "cause[d] a direct effect in the United States." The complaint in this case alleges only one cause of action on behalf of each of the respondents, viz., a breach-of-contract claim based on Argentina's attempt to refinance the Bonods rather than to pay them according to their terms. The fact that the cause of action is in compliance with the first of the three requirements — that it is "based upon an act outside the territory of the States" (presumably Argentina's unilateral extension) — is uncontested. The dispute pertains to whether the unilateral refinancing of the Bonods was taken "in connection with a commercial activity" of Argentina, and whether it had a "direct effect in the United States." We address these issues in turn.

A

. . . [The FSIA's definition of "commercial activity" in § 1603(d)] leaves the critical term "commercial" largely undefined. . . . Fortunately, however, the FSIA was not written on a clean slate. . . . [T]he Act (and the commercial exception in particular) largely codifies the so-called "restrictive" theory of foreign sovereign immunity first endorsed by the State Department in 1952.* The meaning of "commercial" is the meaning generally attached to that term under the restrictive theory at the time the statute was enacted.

[W]e conclude that when a foreign government acts, not as regulator of a market, but in the manner of a private player within it, the foreign sovereign's actions are "commercial" within the meaning of the FSIA. Moreover, because the Act provides that the commercial character of an act is to be determined by reference to its "nature" rather than its "purpose," 28 U.S.C. § 1603(d), the question is not whether the foreign government is acting with a profit motive or instead with the aim of fulfilling uniquely sovereign objectives. Rather, the issue is whether the particular actions that the foreign state performs (whatever the motive behind them) are the *type* of actions by which a private party engages in trade and traffic or commerce. . . . Thus, a foreign government's issuance of regulations limiting foreign currency exchange is a sovereign activity, because such authoritative control of commerce cannot be exercised by a private party; whereas a contract to buy army boots or even bullets is a "commercial" activity, because private companies can similarly use sales contracts to acquire goods, see, *e.g., Stato di Rumania*

---

* The "restrictive" theory of sovereign immunity holds that foreign states are not immune in respect of their commercial activities; in contrast the "absolute" theory holds the foreign sovereigns are generally immune for all acts. The former gradually replaced the latter in international law in the twentieth century. — EDS.

v. Trutta, [1926] Foro It. I 584, 585-586, 589 (Corte di Casso del Regno, Italy), translated and reprinted in part in 26 Am. J. Int'l L. 626-629 (Supp. 1932).

The commercial character of the Bonods is confirmed by the fact that they are in almost all respects garden-variety debt instruments: They may be held by private parties; they are negotiable and may be traded on the international market (except in Argentina); and they promise a future stream of cash income. We recognize that, prior to the enactment of the FSIA, there was authority suggesting that the issuance of public debt instruments did not constitute a commercial activity. There is, however, nothing distinctive about the state's assumption of debt (other than perhaps its purpose) that would cause it always to be classified as [sovereign rather than commercial]. . . . Because the FSIA has now clearly established that the "nature" governs, we perceive no basis for concluding that the issuance of debt should be treated as categorically different from other activities of foreign states.

Argentina contends that, although the FSIA bars consideration of "purpose," a court must nonetheless fully consider the *context* of a transaction in order to determine whether it is "commercial." Accordingly, Argentina claims that the Court of Appeals erred by defining the relevant conduct in what Argentina considers an overly generalized, acontextual manner and by essentially adopting a *per se* rule that all "issuance of debt instruments" is "commercial." We have no occasion to consider such a *per se* rule, because it seems to us that even in full context, there is nothing about the issuance of these Bonods (except perhaps its purpose) that is not analogous to a private commercial transaction.

Argentina points to the fact that the transactions in which the Bonods were issued did not have the ordinary commercial consequence of raising capital or financing acquisitions. Assuming for the sake of argument that this is not an example of judging the commerciality of a transaction by its purpose, the ready answer is that private parties regularly issue bonds, not just to raise capital or to finance purchases, but also to refinance debt. That is what Argentina did here. . . .

Argentina argues that the Bonods differ from ordinary debt instruments in that they "were created by the Argentine Government to fulfill its obligations under a foreign exchange program designed to address a domestic credit crisis, and as a component of a program designed to control that nation's critical shortage of foreign exchange." In this regard, Argentina relies heavily on *De Sanchez v. Banco Central de Nicaragua*, 770 F.2d 1385 (1985), in which the Fifth Circuit took the view that "[o]ften, the essence of an act is defined by its purpose"; that unless "we can inquire into the purposes of such acts, we cannot determine their nature"; and that, in light of its purpose to control its reserves of foreign currency, Nicaragua's refusal to honor a check it had issued to cover a private bank debt was a sovereign act entitled to immunity. Indeed, Argentina asserts that the line between "nature" and "purpose" rests upon a "formalistic distinction [that] simply is neither useful nor warranted." We think this line of argument is squarely foreclosed by the language of the FSIA. However difficult it may be in some cases to separate "purpose" (*i.e.*, the *reason* why the foreign state engages in the activity) from "nature" (*i.e.*, the outward form of the conduct that the foreign state performs or agrees to perform), the statute unmistakably commands that to be done, 28 U.S.C. § 1603(d). We agree with the Court of Appeals that it is irrelevant *why* Argentina participated in the bond market in the manner of a private actor; it matters only that it did so. We conclude that Argentina's issuance of the Bonods was a "commercial activity" under the FSIA.

B

The remaining question is whether Argentina's unilateral rescheduling of the Bonods had a "direct effect" in the United States, 28 U.S.C. § 1605(a)(2).

We . . . have little difficulty concluding that Argentina's unilateral rescheduling of the maturity dates on the Bonods had a "direct effect" in the United States. Respondents had designated their accounts in New York as the place of payment, and Argentina made some interest payments into those accounts before announcing that it was rescheduling the payments. Because New York was thus the place of performance for Argentina's ultimate contractual obligations, the rescheduling of those obligations necessarily had a "direct effect" in the United States: Money that was supposed to have been delivered to a New York bank for deposit was not forthcoming. We reject Argentina's suggestion that the "direct effect" requirement cannot be satisfied where the plaintiffs are all foreign corporations with no other connections to the United States.

. . .

We conclude that Argentina's issuance of the Bonods was a "commercial activity" under the FSIA; that its rescheduling of the maturity dates on those instruments was taken in connection with that commercial activity and had a "direct effect" in the United States; and that the District Court therefore properly asserted jurisdiction, under the FSIA, over the breach-of-contract claim based on that rescheduling. Accordingly, the judgment of the Court of Appeals is

Affirmed.

NOTES AND QUESTIONS

1. **The Structure of the Commercial Activity Exception.** Is the statutory language coherent? What three categories of nonimmune commercial activity does it establish? Can you think of examples of each? Can you give examples of commercial activity that is clearly immune from suit under the FSIA and of commercial activity that clearly is not immune from suit under the FSIA?
2. **Direct Effects in the United States.** What is sufficient to establish a direct effect in the United States? What would be the result in *Weltover* if the Bonods had not called for payment in the United States, but in some other country? What recourse, if any, might be available to the bondholders in that situation? Does that make sense? Does it seem likely that in agreeing to pay in New York, Argentina understood that it was agreeing to suit in U.S. courts? Does it matter? Other than failure to pay at a designated place of payment in the United States, as in *Weltover*, what facts would tend to show a direct effect in the United States? Should financial losses felt in the United States (for example, by a U.S. citizen or entity) be sufficient?

EIG Energy Fund XIV, L.P. v. Petroleo Brasileiro, S.A., 894 F.3d 339 (D.C. Cir. 2018), involved a U.S. fund's investment in the Brazilian energy sector that allegedly lost value due to fraud and misrepresentations of Petroleo Brasileiro (Petrobras), the Brazilian state oil company. The court found a direct effect in the United States for purposes of the commercial activity exception because Petrobras specifically targeted U.S. investors and Petrobras' fraud caused economic loss to those investors. Why should it matter that Petrobras targeted U.S. investors? Wouldn't the effect in the United States (the economic loss) be the same if Petrobras had not known the identity of the investors? Should it matter (as the D.C. Circuit found) that some of Petrobras' misrepresentations occurred during discussions with EIG in the United States? What if all the discussions had been in Brazil?

Similarly, *Atlantica Holdings v. Sovereign Wealth Fund Samruk-Kazyna JSC*, 813 F.3d 98 (2d Cir. 2016), found a direct effect in the United States where plaintiffs invested in debt instruments issued by an instrumentality of the Kazakhstan government; after the investment lost value, plaintiffs sued the sovereign instrumentality for fraud. The alleged fraud (misrepresentation in the sale) occurred outside the United States, but the plaintiffs were U.S. residents. The court concluded:

> A tort's locus — also known as the *locus delicti*, or "place of wrong" — is the place where the last event necessary to make an actor liable for an alleged tort takes place. And, since a tort action traditionally has not been viewed as complete until the plaintiff suffers injury or loss, the cause of action has generally been considered to arise at the place where this damage was sustained [citing, inter alia, Christopher A. Whytock, *Myth of Mess? International Choice of Law in Action*, 84 N.Y.U. L. Rev. 719, 724-25 (2009)]. Thus, a determination that a tort's locus is the United States is, in effect, often a determination that the plaintiff has been injured in this country by the defendant's tortious actions — meaning that those actions caused a "direct effect" (the plaintiff's injury) in this country. As a result, such a determination will ordinarily be sufficient, if not invariably necessary, to confer FSIA jurisdiction under our precedents.

Does *Atlantica* mean that essentially any financial loss by a U.S. resident would provide an exception to immunity? If so, is that problematic from a legal or policy perspective?

In *Frank v. Commonwealth of Antigua and Barbuda*, 842 F.3d 362 (5th Cir. 2015), plaintiff invested in a Ponzi scheme operated by Allen Stanford; Antigua allegedly facilitated the Ponzi scheme. When the Ponzi scheme collapsed, plaintiff, a U.S. citizen, suffered financial losses and sued Antigua. The court found no direct effect: "Defining 'direct effect' to permit jurisdiction when a foreign state's actions precipitate reactions by third parties, which reactions then have an impact on a plaintiff, would foster uncertainty in both foreign states and private counter-parties . . . . While Antigua may have helped facilitate Stanford's sale of the fraudulent [certificates of deposit], Stanford's criminal activity served as an intervening act interrupting the causal chain between Antigua's actions and any effect on investors." Is that holding consistent with *EIG Energy* and *Atlantica*? Should it matter that the harm involved actions of a third party?

3. **Activity in the United States.** In *Sachs v. Republic of Austria*, 695 F.3d 1021 (9th Cir. 2012), plaintiff, a U.S. citizen and resident, was injured in a railway accident in Innsbruck, Austria, and sued the Austrian government and the Austrian state railroad. She had purchased her ticket in the United States through an agency owned by various European railways, including the Austrian railroad. A panel of the court of appeals found that the commercial activity exception did not apply, but was unable to agree on a rationale. One judge argued that the Austrian railroad itself had not conducted any business in the United States and the actions of the ticket agency could not be attributed to the railroad. A second judge concurred on the ground that even if the agency's actions could be attributed to the railway, the plaintiff's claim was not based on the ticket sales (rather, it was based on negligence occurring entirely within Austria). A third judge dissented on the grounds that the actions of the ticket agent constituted commercial activity by Austria in the United States. Can you see how the statute potentially allows each of these results? On rehearing en banc, the court of appeals, by an 8-3 vote, found that the commercial activity exception to immunity applied, substantially for the reasons set forth in the previous dissent. 737 F.3d 584 (9th Cir. 2013) (en banc). What is the right result? Is this the sort of case that should be heard in the United States? Would it belong in the United States if the defendant was not a foreign sovereign?

    The U.S. Supreme Court unanimously reversed the en banc Ninth Circuit in *OBB Personenverkehr AG v. Sachs*, 136 S. Ct. 390 (2015), holding (like the concurring judge in the original panel decision) that Sachs's claim was "based on" an act outside the United States, namely the operation of the train that injured her. Look again at the cases in Note 2 above: Could Sachs argue that the accident outside the United States had a "direct effect" in the United States because she was a U.S. resident?

4. **What Counts as Commercial Activity: Sovereign Contracts.** In *Weltover*, Justice Scalia refers to an Italian case that found no immunity for a foreign government that breached a contract to purchase army boots. Is that the right result under the FSIA? What if the government had contracted to purchase fighter aircraft? Apart from the reference to the Italian case, the Court makes no mention of foreign or international cases. Is there anything wrong with that approach? In *MOL, Inc. v. People's Republic of Bangladesh*, 736 F.2d 1326 (9th Cir. 1984), MOL sued Bangladesh for breach of a licensing agreement that allowed MOL to export monkeys from Bangladesh in return for payments to Bangladesh and various other obligations. Is this suit based on a commercial activity within the meaning of the FSIA? The court held it was not, because "the granting and revocation of a license to export a natural resource are sovereign acts." Is that consistent with *Weltover*? What should MOL have done (but presumably did not do) in drafting the contract?

    In *Guevara v. Republic of Peru*, 468 F.3d 1289 (11th Cir. 2012), Peru offered a reward for information leading to the arrest of a fugitive; Guevara provided the information but Peru refused to pay the reward. The court held this to be a commercial activity because Peru was merely seeking to buy information, as a private party might. Is this consistent with *MOL?* With *Weltover?* Even if it was commercial, should immunity be found?

5. **What Counts as Commercial Activity: Business Operations.** In an early decision in the long-running litigation between McKesson Corp. and Iran (see Chapter 2), the court of appeals found that Iran lacked immunity under the commercial activity exception. Although the facts were complex and disputed, the court (pre-*Weltover*) appeared to conclude that Iran had used its control over the board of directors of Pak Dairy, an Iranian company, to block payment of dividends due to McKesson as a minority shareholder in Pak, and to interfere with McKesson's ability to participate in the management of the dairy. *Foremost-McKesson, Inc. v. Islamic Republic of Iran*, 905 F.2d 438 (D.C. Cir. 1990) (affirming district court ruling that "the nature of the actions complained of by [McKesson] sound in the nature of a dispute between majority and minority shareholders"). Is that a commercial activity within the meaning of *Weltover?*

6. **What Counts as Commercial Activity: Torts.** In *Saudi Arabia v. Nelson*, 507 U.S. 349 (1992), Nelson, a U.S. citizen, was recruited in the United States to work in a government hospital in Saudi Arabia. He claimed that while working at the hospital he attempted to report unsafe working conditions and in retaliation Saudi police wrongfully imprisoned and tortured him. Is this claim "based upon" a commercial activity within the meaning of the FSIA? The Supreme Court (in an opinion by Justice Souter, joined in full by four other Justices) held that it was not, relying heavily on the Court's prior decision in *Weltover*:

> [In *Weltover*], [i]n the course of holding the refinancing to be a commercial activity for purposes of the Act, we observed that the statute "largely codifies the so-called 'restrictive' theory of foreign sovereign immunity first endorsed by the State Department in 1952." We accordingly held that the meaning of "commercial" for purposes of the Act must be the meaning Congress understood the restrictive theory to require at the time it passed the statute.
>
> Under the restrictive, as opposed to the "absolute," theory of foreign sovereign immunity, a state is immune from the jurisdiction of foreign courts as to its sovereign or public acts (*jure imperii*), but not as to those that are private or commercial in character (*jure gestionis*). We explained in *Weltover* . . . that a state engages in commercial activity under the restrictive theory where it exercises "only those powers that can also be exercised by private citizens," as distinct from those "powers peculiar to sovereigns." Put differently, a foreign state engages in commercial activity for purposes of the restrictive theory only where it acts "in the manner of a private player within" the market. 504 U.S., at 614; *see* Restatement (Third) of the Foreign Relations Law of the United States § 451 (1987) ("Under international law, a state or state instrumentality is immune from the jurisdiction of the courts of another state, except with respect to claims arising out of activities of the kind that may be carried on by private persons"). . . .
>
> Unlike Argentina's activities that we considered in *Weltover*, the intentional conduct alleged here (the Saudi Government's wrongful arrest, imprisonment, and torture of Nelson) could not qualify as commercial under the restrictive theory. The conduct boils down to abuse of the power of its police by the Saudi

Government, and however monstrous such abuse undoubtedly may be, a foreign state's exercise of the power of its police has long been understood for purposes of the restrictive theory as peculiarly sovereign in nature.

Justice White concurred in the judgment, finding that the injury claims were commercial because they were based upon Nelson's employment by the hospital. However, he found that the injury did not "have a sufficient nexus with the United States" to invoke the commercial activity exception (presumably meaning it had no "direct effect"). In addition to direct claims of physical injury, Nelson claimed that Saudi Arabia and the hospital had negligently failed to warn him of the dangers of working in Saudi Arabia when he was hired. Justice Kennedy, dissenting in part, argued that this claim was (a) based upon a commercial activity; and (b) occurred in the United States. Justice Stevens dissented as to all of Nelson's claims, for which he would have found no immunity.

7. **Commercial Activity by Affiliates**. In *Arch Trading Co. v. Republic of Ecuador*, 839 F.3d 193 (2d Cir. 2016), plaintiffs, non-U.S. entities, alleged that Ecuador had seized their property in Ecuador in violation of international law and that the property was held by instrumentalities of Ecuador with commercial ties to the United States. The court concluded:

> Plaintiffs do not contend that either CFN or the Trust [the entities holding the allegedly expropriated property] is *itself* engaged in commercial activity in the United States. Rather, they argue primarily that we should impute to each the United States activities of several other entities. . . . But CFN and the Trust are entities distinct from the subsidiaries and other Ecuadorean entities to which plaintiffs point. The presumption of legal separateness established by the Supreme Court in *First National City Bank v. Banco Para el Comercio Exterior de Cuba*, 462 U.S. 611 (1983) ("*Bancec*"), and respect for international comity compel us to treat these legally separate entities as just that, unless plaintiffs can demonstrate that CFN and the Trust exercise significant and repeated control over the [entities'] day-to-day operations. Plaintiffs have failed to clear this substantial bar and therefore have not satisfied the requirements of Section 1605(a)(3).

Why was it important to plaintiffs to establish commercial activity in the United States? Specifically, on what part of the FSIA were they relying?

3. Expropriation

Foreign Sovereign Immunities Act, 28 U.S.C. § 1605

(a) A foreign state shall not be immune from the jurisdiction of courts of the United States or of the States in any case —

. . .

(3) in which rights in property taken in violation of international law are in issue and that property or any property exchanged for such property

is present in the United States in connection with a commercial activity carried on in the United States by the foreign state; or that property or any property exchanged for such property is owned or operated by an agency or instrumentality of the foreign state and that agency or instrumentality is engaged in a commercial activity in the United States[.]

Cassirer v. Kingdom of Spain

616 F.3d 1019 (9th Cir. 2010) (en banc)

RYMER, Circuit Judge:

Claude Cassirer is an American citizen whose grandmother's Pissarro painting was allegedly confiscated in 1939 by an agent of the Nazi government in Germany because she was a Jew. He filed suit in federal district court to recover the painting, or damages, from the Kingdom of Spain and the Thyssen-Bornemisza Collection Foundation, an instrumentality of Spain, which now claims to own the painting. Spain and the Foundation moved to dismiss, asserting, among other things, sovereign immunity pursuant to the Foreign Sovereign Immunities Act (FSIA), 28 U.S.C. § 1602, *et seq.* . . .

Cassirer relies on the "international takings" or "expropriation" exception in the FSIA that confers subject matter jurisdiction over a foreign state when "rights in property taken in violation of international law" are at issue; the property is owned "by an agency or instrumentality of the foreign state"; and the instrumentality "is engaged in a commercial activity in the United States." 28 U.S.C. § 1605(a)(3). Spain and the Foundation maintain that this exception is not applicable because the painting was taken in violation of international law by Germany, not by either of them, and because the Foundation is not engaged in commercial activity in the United States sufficient to trigger the exception. . . .

Our review is constrained because this is an appeal before final judgment has been entered. Generally, we may review only final decisions of a district court, but our jurisdiction also extends to a small category of collateral orders that are separate from the merits and can't effectively be reviewed on appeal from a final judgment. A ruling that denies sovereign immunity is such an order. . . .

On the issue of sovereign immunity, we conclude that § 1605(a)(3) does not require the foreign state against whom the claim is made to be the one that took the property. We are satisfied that the record supports the district court's finding of a sufficient commercial activity in the United States by the Foundation. . . .

I

The property at issue is an oil painting by the French impressionist master Camille Pissarro, *Rue Saint-Honoré, après-midi, effet de pluie*. It was completed in 1897 and sold in 1898 to Cassirer's great-grandfather, Julius Cassirer, who lived in Germany. The painting remained in the family for some forty years, eventually passing to Lilly Cassirer, Cassirer's grandmother, upon her husband's death. . . .

In 1939 Lilly decided she had no choice but to leave Germany. By that time . . . German Jews had been deprived of their civil rights, including their German citizenship; their property was being "Aryanized"; and the Kristallnacht pogroms had taken place throughout the country. Permission was required both to leave and to take belongings. The Nazi government appointed Munich art dealer Jakob Scheidwimmer as the official appraiser to evaluate the works of art, including the Pissarro painting, that Lilly wished to take with her. Scheidwimmer refused to allow her to take the painting out of Germany and demanded that she hand it over to him for approximately $360. Fearing she would not otherwise be allowed to go, and knowing she would not actually get the money because the funds would be paid into a blocked account, Lilly complied.

Scheidwimmer traded the painting to another art dealer, who was also persecuted and fled Germany for Holland. After Germany invaded Holland, the Gestapo confiscated the painting and returned it to Germany, where it was sold at auction to an anonymous purchaser in 1943. It turned up at a New York gallery in 1952 and was sold to a St. Louis collector; it was sold again in 1976 to a New York art dealer who, in turn, sold it to Baron Hans-Heinrich Thyssen-Bornemisza. Bornemisza lived in Switzerland and was a preeminent private collector.

In 1988, Spain paid the Baron $50 million to lease his collection for ten years. Five years into the lease, Spain paid the Foundation $327 million to purchase the entire collection, including the Pissarro painting. As part of the agreement, Spain provided the Villahermosa Palace in Madrid to the Foundation, free of charge, for use as the Thyssen-Bornemisza Museum.

Claude Cassirer, Lilly's heir, discovered in 2000 that the painting was on display at the Thyssen-Bornemisza Museum in Madrid. He asked Spain's Minister for Education, Culture and Sports, who was chair of the Foundation's board, to return it. The request was refused. In 2003, five members of Congress wrote the Minister requesting return of the painting; this request, too, was rejected. Cassirer did not try to obtain the painting through judicial proceedings in Spain, or to pursue other remedies in Spain or Germany, before bringing suit in the United States.

He filed this action against the Foundation and Spain in the Central District of California on May 10, 2005. The complaint avers that Germany confiscated the painting based on Lilly's status as a Jew and as part of its genocide against Jews; hence the taking was in violation of international law. It alleges that the Foundation is engaged in numerous commercial activities in the United States that include borrowing art works from American museums; encouraging United States residents to visit the museum and accepting entrance fees from them; selling various items to United States citizens including images of the painting; and maintaining a web site where United States citizens may buy admission tickets using United States credit cards and view the paintings on display, including *Rue Saint-Honoré, après-midi, effect de pluie*. The complaint seeks imposition of a constructive trust and return of the painting or, alternatively, recovery of damages for conversion.

The Foundation filed a motion to dismiss based on lack of subject matter and personal jurisdiction, and improper venue. Spain followed with its own motion to dismiss. The district court allowed Cassirer to conduct jurisdictional discovery into the Foundation's commercial activity in the United States. Both motions were then denied. . . . [A panel of the Ninth Circuit affirmed as to the sovereign immunity issue, and the Circuit agreed to rehear the case en banc.]

II

. . . It is well settled that sovereign immunity is within [a] small category of cases from which an immediate appeal will lie. The point of immunity is to protect a foreign state that is entitled to it from being subjected to the jurisdiction of courts in this country, protection which would be meaningless were the foreign state forced to wait until the action is resolved on the merits to vindicate its right not to be in court at all. Thus, we have jurisdiction to review the district court's order denying sovereign immunity. . . . [W]e have no appellate jurisdiction to review the district court's denial of motions to dismiss for lack of personal jurisdiction and a case or controversy.

III

Under the statutory scheme, a district court has subject matter jurisdiction over claims against a foreign state with respect to which the foreign state is not entitled to immunity. 28 U.S.C. § 1330(a). A foreign state is immune except as specified in the FSIA. 28 U.S.C. § 1604. The FSIA has a number of exceptions, but Cassirer invokes only the "expropriation" exception in § 1605(a)(3). . . .

So far as the first condition is concerned, a taking offends international law when it does not serve a public purpose, when it discriminates against those who are not nationals of the country, or when it is not accomplished with payment of just compensation. . . . On appeal, neither Spain nor the Foundation contends that Germany's actions with respect to the painting were not a taking in violation of international law.

So far as the commercial activity prong is concerned, just the second clause is pertinent here as there is no dispute the painting is not "present in the United States." Thus, there is jurisdiction under § 1605(a)(3) if the Foundation, which admittedly owns the painting and concedes it is an instrumentality of Spain for purposes of the statute, "is engaged in a commercial activity in the United States." . . .

A

. . .

We agree with the district court that the plain language of the statute does not require that the foreign state against whom the claim is made be the entity which took the property in violation of international law. Section 1605(a)(3) simply excepts from immunity "a foreign state" in any case "in which rights in *property taken in violation of international law* are in issue." (emphasis added). The text is written in the passive voice, which focuses on an event that occurs without respect to a specific actor. . . . It would have to be rewritten in order to carry the meaning the Foundation ascribes to it. That is, the statute would need to say that a foreign state is not immune in a case "in which rights in property taken *by the foreign state in violation of international law are in issue.*"

In the normal event our task is over when a statute is clear on its face. Thus, we take the plain meaning of the text to be the meaning that Congress intended. As the words and grammatical construct in § 1605(a)(3) are clear, we understand that Congress meant for jurisdiction to exist over claims against a foreign state whenever property that its instrumentality ends up claiming to own had been taken in violation of international law, so long as the instrumentality engages in a commercial activity in the United States. . . .

Our reading of the text is buttressed by the articulated purpose of the FSIA to immunize foreign states for their public, but not for their commercial, acts. As Congress declared: "Under international law, states are not immune from the jurisdiction of foreign courts insofar as their commercial activities are concerned." 28 U.S.C. § 1602 (Findings and Declaration of Purpose). Consistent with this purpose, § 1605(a)(3) restricts jurisdiction over an entity of a foreign state that owns property taken in violation of international law to those engaged in commercial activity in the United States. . . .

[T]he Foundation posits that bizarre consequences unintended by Congress will occur if § 1605(a)(3) is interpreted as granting jurisdiction against foreign entities regardless of who did the expropriating or when, and regardless of whether the defendant was a good faith purchaser. We cannot say whether floodgates might open, but in any event, jurisdictional boundaries are for Congress to set, not for courts to write around. This said, restraints are in place that deflect the risk. The FSIA is purely jurisdictional; it doesn't speak to the merits or to possible defenses that may be raised to cut off stale claims or curtail liability. In addition, the statute constrains its own reach by restricting jurisdiction to rights in property, taken in violation of international law, that is now in the hands of a foreign state or its instrumentality, when that instrumentality is engaged in a commercial activity in the United States. And decisional law further limits the universe of potential claimants, for instance, by excluding nationals of the expropriating country from the scope of § 1605(a)(3).

In sum, the statute states that the property at issue must have been "taken in violation of international law." It does not state "taken in violation of international law by the foreign state being sued." The legislative history does not clearly indicate that Congress meant something other than what it said. Indeed, the text would have to be redrafted to say what the Foundation wishes it said. For these reasons, we conclude that § 1605(a)(3) does not require that the foreign state against whom suit is brought be the foreign state that took the property at issue in violation of international law.

B

The Foundation maintains that its activities in the United States are *de minimis*, and lack the requisite connection to the property in question. It submits that the district court incorrectly held that the activity need not be "commercial" in the ordinary sense, or be related to the expropriated property, or be substantial.

It is clear that activity need not be motivated by profit to be commercial for purposes of the FSIA. As § 1603(d) provides, the commercial character of an activity depends on its nature rather than its purpose. Thus, it does not matter that the Foundation's activities are undertaken on behalf of a non-profit museum to further its cultural mission.

After allowing jurisdictional discovery on the issue, the district court found that the Foundation engages in commercial activities in the United States that include: buying books, posters, and post cards; purchasing books about Nazi expropriation of works of art; selling posters and books, and licensing reproductions of images; paying United States citizens to write for exhibit catalogs; shipping gift shop items to purchasers in the United States, including a poster of the Pissarro painting; recruiting writers and speakers to provide services at the museum; permitting a program to be filmed at the museum that included the Pissarro painting and was shown on Iberia Airlines flights between Spain and the United States; placing advertisements in magazines distributed in the United States, and sending press releases, brochures, and general information to Spain's tourism offices in the United States, at least one of which mentions the Pissarro by name; distributing the museum bulletin, "Perspectives," to individuals in the United States; borrowing and loaning artworks, though not the painting; and maintaining a website through which United States citizens sign up for newsletters, view the collection — including the Pissarro painting — and purchase advance admission tickets through links to third-party vendors. These findings are supported in the record and are not clearly erroneous.

The Foundation faults the district court for having failed to require a nexus between the activity and the lawsuit, as well as a quantum of activity that has a substantial connection with the United States. It suggests that Congress meant to meld traditional concepts of personal jurisdiction with subject matter jurisdiction under the FSIA. However, the second clause of § 1605(a)(3) contains no requirement that a lawsuit arise out of specific activity having to do with the property in the United States, that is, there is no express analogue to the traditional doctrine of specific jurisdiction, nor does it explicitly require any particular level of activity or conduct commensurate to that normally contemplated for general jurisdiction. In this, § 1605(a)(3) differs from the "commercial activity" exception in § 1605(a)(2), which does provide that a foreign state is not immune from jurisdiction where "the action is based upon a commercial activity carried on in the United States by the foreign state" or upon an act committed elsewhere that "causes a direct effect in the United States." The difference between the two exceptions shows that Congress knew how to draw upon traditional notions of personal jurisdiction when it wanted to, and did. Beyond this, the statute says nothing particularly helpful about what constitutes "a" commercial activity that is either a "regular course of commercial conduct" or a "particular commercial transaction or act." Instead, Congress left it to the courts to flesh out on a case-by-case basis. . . .

Here, the Foundation has had many contacts with the United States, including some that encourage Americans to visit the museum where the Pissarro is featured, and some that relate to the painting itself. . . . [W]e cannot say its endeavors fall short of being a commercial activity for jurisdictional purposes under the second prong of § 1605(a)(3). . . .

Accordingly, we affirm the district court's order denying motions by Spain and the Foundation to dismiss for lack of subject matter jurisdiction.

GOULD, Circuit Judge, with whom KOZINSKI, Chief Judge, joins, dissenting:

I would reverse and remand with instructions for the district court to dismiss, on the theory that the Foreign Sovereign Immunities Act ("FSIA"), under 28 U.S.C. § 1605(a)(3), has not waived the sovereign immunity of Spain or its instrumentality the Foundation. . . .

The statute does not expressly say that the property must be taken "by the foreign state" (as Spain and the Foundation contend). But neither does the statute expressly say the property must be taken "by any foreign state" (as Cassirer contends). This lack of clarity is sufficient to conclude that the statute is ambiguous and subject to review of the legislative history for evidence of congressional intent. . . .

[The *Restatement (Third) of Foreign Relations Law of the United States,* Section 455, Comment c (1987) says]:

> [T]he FSIA provides that if the property was *taken by the foreign state* in violation of international law, and if the property is . . . owned or operated by an instrumentality *of the foreign state* that is engaged in commercial activity in the United States, there is a sufficient basis for jurisdiction to adjudicate claims to the property. [Emphasis added.] . . .

Congress intended the FSIA to be consistent with international law. The central premise of the FSIA is that "decisions on claims by foreign states to sovereign immunity are best made by the judiciary on the basis of a statutory regime which incorporates standards recognized under international law." H.R. Rep. No. 94-1487, at 14 (1976), *reprinted in* 1976 U.S.C.C.A.N. 6604, 6613. Section 1605(a)(3) is based upon the general presumption that states abide by international law and, hence, violations of international law are not sovereign acts. When customary international law concludes that an act by a foreign state, that is, the taking of property in violation of international law, is no longer a sovereign act, the foreign state is no longer entitled to sovereign immunity. International law therefore supports the exercise of jurisdiction over foreign states that have themselves taken property in violation of international law; it does not support the exercise of jurisdiction over sovereign entities that have legitimately acquired property that was at some other time and by some other foreign state taken in violation of international law. . . .

The productive inquiry here is to ask what Congress intended by § 1605(a)(3), or, some might say, what Congress would have intended if the case presented had been expressly considered. Because I do not believe that Congress would have intended Spain to suffer loss of its sovereign immunity by this provision if it had no complicity in the unlawful taking, I do not join the position of the majority.

Also, the majority takes no heed of the fact that there may be important diplomatic implications of its decision. Rather than asking the United States

Department of Justice and United States Department of State to weigh in on the question whether the majority's statutory interpretation has diplomatic implications for the United States, the majority rushes head-long to give a procedural remedy to Cassirer.

. . .

[I]t has long been understood that statutes should not be construed to violate the law of nations if any other interpretation is possible. *See Murray v. The Schooner Charming Betsy*, 6 U.S. 64 (1804). . . .

[S]aying a taking by Nazi Germany in violation of international law waives the sovereign immunity of some innocent nation that comes upon the property later through legitimate means is a position that would not be accepted under international law. *See* . . . *Restatement (Third) of Foreign Relations Law of the United States* § 207 ("A state is responsible for any violation of *its* obligations under international law. . . ." (emphasis added)); *id.* § 712 ("A state is responsible under international law for injury resulting from . . . a taking *by the state* of the property of a national of another state. . . ." (emphasis added)). . . .

The principle of comity tells us the same thing. "Comity is the recognition which one nation allows within its territory to the legislative, executive or judicial acts of another nation." *Dependable Highway Express, Inc. v. Navigators Ins. Co.*, 498 F.3d 1059, 1067 (9th Cir. 2007). Thus it seems to me that because Spain is a sovereign with immunity from suit, we should respect that unless we have better reason than merely a deserving victim of Nazi aggression. Equally important, and I think a part of comity, is the common sense notion of the golden rule. We should not do to other nations what we would not want other nations to do to us. I am concerned that by indulging now the sympathetic claim of Cassirer as a Jewish heir with entitlement to priceless art stolen by Nazi Germany, but doing so at the cost of fairness to Spain and disrespect of its sovereignty, we will likely sow the seeds of maltreatment of the United States and its officials in foreign courts.

Hence, I respectfully dissent.

NOTES AND QUESTIONS

1. **The Structure of the Expropriation Exception.** What categories of nonimmune expropriation activity does the statute establish? Why should there be more than one category? Can you think of examples of each in which immunity is clearly denied?

2. **The Outcome in *Cassirer*.** Why is *Cassirer* a difficult case? Note that the court finds that the museum engaged in commercial activity. Why was *Cassirer* not argued under the commercial activity exception? Note also that the court affirms the district court's denial of sovereign immunity as to both Spain and the museum. Is that correct as a statutory matter? What is the dissent's principal argument? On what authority does it rely? Should it matter that, as the dissent points out, the *Restatement (Third) of Foreign Relations Law* expressly rejects the majority's view? Why might it not matter?

3. **Practice: Interlocutory Appeal of Denials of Sovereign Immunity.** *Cassirer* is an appeal of a denial of sovereign immunity. In the broader context of civil litigation, why is that an unusual procedural posture? Why should appeals of sovereign immunity denials be treated differently?

4. **Takings versus Other Violations of International Law.** Note that § 1605(a)(3) provides an exception for certain takings of property in violation of international law, while the effect of decisions such as *Sampson* and *Princz*, discussed above, is that immunity remains for other violations of international law such as torture and genocide. Can this difference in treatment be justified?

5. **Other Cases Involving Stolen Property.** In a somewhat similar case, *Agudas Chasidei Chabad of U.S. v. Russian Federation*, 528 F.3d 934 (D.C. Cir. 2008), the court of appeals found an exception to immunity under § 1605(a)(3) in a suit involving religious books and manuscripts allegedly owned by a Jewish organization and seized by the Soviet Union during World War II. The materials were held by the Russian State Library and the Russian State Military Archive, both of which the court found to conduct commercial activities in the United States by, among other things, entering into contracts with U.S. publishers to publish materials held by the Library and the Archive. If you were a lawyer advising a foreign museum, would you recommend taking measures to avoid exposure to such suits? Which measures?

6. **Takings of Property of a Government's Own Citizens.** In *Simon v. Republic of Hungary*, 812 F.3d 127 (D.C. Cir. 2016), the court allowed some claims to proceed against the Hungarian state railway company for seizures of property of Jews during the Holocaust. Although the property itself was not present in the United States, the defendant railway was alleged to own some of the property (or property exchanged for that property), and it engaged in commercial activity in the United States. The court found this sufficient to defeat immunity (at least at a preliminary stage) against the Hungarian railway, but not against the Hungarian government itself. Is that consistent with the statute's text?

The international law of takings generally applies only to the taking of foreigners' property, not to the government's taking of its own citizens' property. In *Simon*, the plaintiffs (who were Hungarian citizens or heirs of Hungarian citizens) successfully argued that the taking had been in the context of genocide, and therefore there had been a violation of international law even though the government took the property of its own citizens. In 2020, the Supreme Court granted certiorari in a related case to review this claim.

Helmerich & Payne Int'l Drilling Co. v. Venezuela, 784 F.3d 804 (D.C. Cir. 2015), similarly involved the Venezuelan government's taking of the property of a Venezuelan corporation, which Venezuela argued could not violate international law. However, the Venezuelan company was a subsidiary of a U.S. company; the plaintiffs contended that the government had seized the property because it was ultimately owned by U.S. citizens, and that this discriminatory action violated international law. The D.C. Circuit found this "nonfrivolous" argument for FSIA jurisdiction sufficient to defeat Venezuela's motion to dismiss.

The U.S. Supreme Court reversed, holding that the plaintiffs must actually prove, as a threshold jurisdictional matter, that the Venezuelan action violated international law, not merely make a "nonfrivolous" argument that it did. *Bolivarian Republic of Venezuela v. Helmerich & Payne Int'l Drilling Co.*, 137 S. Ct. 1312 (2017). But presumably the plaintiff would in any event eventually have to prove that Venezuela's conduct violated international law to recover on the merits. Why would the seemingly technical issue of the pleading standard matter to the litigants, so much that they pursued the issue to the U.S. Supreme Court? What policy of the FSIA supports the Supreme Court's decision?

On remand, the D.C. Circuit held that taking the subsidiary's property did not violate international law. However, it went on to hold that Venezuela, by interfering with the parent's control of the subsidiary, had also taken the parent's property, and that this taking violated international law. *Helmerich & Payne Int'l Drilling Co. v. Bolivarian Republic of Venezuela*, 743 Fed. Appx. 442 (D.C. Cir. 2018). Is that enough to defeat immunity? What else will the plaintiffs need to show?

7. **Exhaustion of Remedies.** Should a plaintiff claiming expropriation be required first to exhaust remedies in the defendant nation before bringing suit in the United States? Under what circumstances? In *Abelesz v. Magyar Nemzeti Bank*, 692 F.3d 691 (7th Cir. 2012), the court imposed an exhaustion requirement on plaintiffs seeking to recover for Holocaust-era takings by the Hungarian state bank and railroad. The court found that "claimants in these plaintiffs' situations [must] either . . . pursue and exhaust domestic remedies in Hungary or . . . show convincingly that such remedies are clearly a sham or inadequate or that their application is unreasonably prolonged." The court continued:

> As we consider this exhaustion issue, we cannot overlook the comity and reciprocity between sovereign nations that dominate international law. The plaintiffs suing the railway seek a judgment from a U.S. court ordering the national railway to pay plaintiffs as much as $1.25 billion. The plaintiffs suing the bank seek as much as $75 billion. The sum of damages sought by plaintiffs would amount to nearly 40 percent of Hungary's annual gross domestic product in 2011. Divided among Hungary's current population of 10 million people, that is more than $7500 per person. We should consider how the United States would react if a foreign court ordered the U.S. Treasury or the Federal Reserve Bank to pay a group of plaintiffs 40 percent of U.S. annual gross domestic product, which would be roughly $6 trillion, or $20,000 for every resident in the United States. And consider further the reaction if such an order were based on events that happened generations ago in the United States itself, without any effort to secure just compensation through U.S. courts. If U.S. courts are ready to exercise jurisdiction to right wrongs all over the world, including those of past generations, we should not complain if other countries' courts decide to do the same.
>
> Hungary, a modern republic and member of the European Union, deserves a chance to address these claims. That is not to say that U.S. courts have no place in this sort of case. If plaintiffs choose to pursue their claims in Hungary but find the way barred by inaction or hostility, the U.S. courts may be available to consider their claims. But Hungary should first have the opportunity

to address these alleged takings, by its own means and under its own legal system . . . .

In contrast, *Philipp v. Federal Republic of Germany*, 894 F.3d 406 (D.C. Cir. 2018), expressly disagreed with the decision in *Abelesz*, finding no exhaustion requirement for claimants to an art collection suing a German government-owned museum. The court principally relied on the fact that the FSIA conveys jurisdiction without providing for an exhaustion requirement. Should that be conclusive? Should it matter whether international law requires or doesn't require exhaustion? In 2020, the Supreme Court agreed to review this question.

4. Noncommercial Torts and Terrorism

Foreign Sovereign Immunities Act, 28 U.S.C. § 1605

(a) A foreign state shall not be immune from the jurisdiction of courts of the United States or of the States in any case —

. . .

(5) not otherwise encompassed in paragraph (2) above, in which money damages are sought against a foreign state for personal injury or death, or damage to or loss of property, occurring in the United States and caused by the tortious act or omission of that foreign state or of any official or employee of that foreign state while acting within the scope of his office or employment; except this paragraph shall not apply to —

(A) any claim based upon the exercise or performance or the failure to exercise or perform a discretionary function regardless of whether the discretion be abused, or

(B) any claim arising out of malicious prosecution, abuse of process, libel, slander, misrepresentation, deceit, or interference with contract rights. . . .

Foreign Sovereign Immunities Act, 28 U.S.C. § 1605A

(a) In General. —

(1) No immunity. — A foreign state shall not be immune from the jurisdiction of courts of the United States or of the States in any case not otherwise covered by this chapter in which money damages are sought against a foreign state for personal injury or death that was caused by an act of torture, extrajudicial killing, aircraft sabotage, hostage taking, or the provision of material support or resources for such an act if such act or provision of material support or resources is engaged in by an official, employee, or agent of such foreign state while acting within the scope of his or her office, employment, or agency.

(2) Claim heard. — The court shall hear a claim under this section if — (A)(i) (I) the foreign state was designated as a state sponsor of terrorism at the time the act described in paragraph (1) occurred, or was so designated as a result of such act, and . . . either remains so designated when the claim is filed under this section or was so designated within the 6-month period before the claim is filed under this section; . . . [and]

(ii) the claimant or the victim was, at the time the act described in paragraph (1) occurred — (I) a national of the United States; (II) a member of the armed forces; or (III) otherwise an employee of the Government of the United States, or of an individual performing a contract awarded by the United States Government, acting within the scope of the employee's employment. . . .

USAA Casualty Insurance Co. v. Permanent Mission of the Republic of Namibia

681 F.3d 103 (2d Cir. 2011)

JOSE A. CABRANES, Circuit Judge:

. . .

At some point before the events that gave rise to this action, the Republic of Namibia made the decision to house the chancery, or base of operations, of its Permanent Mission to the United Nations in a Manhattan townhouse located at 135 E. 36th Street (the "Building"). The Mission commissioned extensive interior construction in order to render the Building suitable for a diplomatic mission. To perform the proposed construction, the Mission hired an independent general contractor, Federation Development Corporation ("Federation"), which in turn hired a subcontractor, Ryback Development, Inc. ("Ryback") (together with Federation, the "Contractors").

The townhouse adjoining the Building, 133 E. 36th Street, was then owned by Robert Adelman and insured by USAA Casualty Insurance Co. ("USAA"). The Building was separated from the Adelman townhouse by a brick and mortar party wall, upon which the support beams of the Adelman townhouse rested. In early December 2008, Ryback employees began pouring a reinforced concrete wall in the interior of the Building, alongside the existing party wall. On December 15, as the concrete wall was being poured, the party wall collapsed, causing substantial damage to Adelman's property. Adelman filed an insurance claim with USAA, which paid Adelman $397,730 for his damages.

. . . USAA brought suit as Adelman's subrogee against the Contractors and the Mission (jointly, the "defendants") in New York State Supreme Court. . . . [T]he Mission removed the suit to federal court. . . .

In alleging that the Mission had committed a tort against Adelman, USAA relied primarily upon Section 3309.8 of the New York City Building Code. . . . USAA alleged that the Mission had violated that section of the Building Code by, among other things, "failing to shore up the common wall." [The District Court denied immunity and the Mission appealed.]

. . . A foreign state's permanent mission to the United Nations is indisputably the "embodiment" of that state. Accordingly, as USAA concedes, the Mission is entitled to rely on the defense of sovereign immunity unless an exception to the FSIA applies.

USAA argues that three exceptions to the FSIA bestow subject matter jurisdiction over the Mission in this case: (1) the "tortious activity" exception, (2) the "commercial activity" exception, and (3) the "immovable property" exception. Because we agree with the District Court that the tortious activity exception applies, we likewise do not address the applicability of the other two exceptions. . . .

The tortious activity exception to the FSIA permits courts to exercise jurisdiction over foreign sovereigns where the plaintiff seeks money damages for . . . damage to or loss of property, occurring in the United States and caused by the tortious act or omission of [the] foreign state. . . . In determining whether an alleged action is a tort within the meaning of this federal statute, we have applied the law of the state in which the locus of injury occurred — in this case, New York. Accordingly, we first identify the act or omission complained of, and then address whether that act or omission is in fact tortious under the law of the State of New York.

[In an extended discussion of New York law, the court found that "the Mission was under a nondelegable duty, pursuant to regulation, to ensure that the structural integrity of the party wall was maintained during construction."]

. . .

Having decided that the Mission's alleged failure to shore up the party wall was a tort, we now turn to the "exception to the exception" that allows a foreign state to retain its immunity when the allegedly tortious activity took place during the exercise of a "discretionary function." The discretionary function exception preserves the immunity of a sovereign nation when it would otherwise be abrogated by the tortious activity exception if two conditions are met: (1) the acts alleged to be negligent must be discretionary, in that they involve an element of judgment or choice and are not compelled by statute or regulation, and (2) the judgment or choice in question must be grounded in considerations of public policy or susceptible to policy analysis.

Cases construing the discretionary function exception in the FSIA draw heavily on case law interpreting a similar exception in the [Federal Tort Claims Act (FTCA)]. . . . [T]he discretionary function rule is designed to prevent judicial second-guessing of decisions grounded in social, economic, and political policy of a foreign state through the medium of an action in tort. Therefore, if the act or omission deemed to be tortious is based upon the exercise or performance or the failure to exercise or perform a discretionary function regardless of whether the discretion be abused, the foreign sovereign nation retains its immunity from suit under the FSIA.

[I]f an action is "compelled by statute or regulation," it is not discretionary for purpose of the discretionary function exception. In *United States v. Gaubert*, the Supreme Court explained that

> [t]he requirement of judgment or choice is not satisfied if a federal statute, regulation or policy specifically prescribes a course of action for the [Government] to follow. . . . [I]f a regulation mandates particular conduct, and the [Government]

obeys the direction, the Government will be protected because the action will be deemed in furtherance of the policies which led to the promulgation of the regulation. If the [Government] violates the mandatory regulation, there will be no shelter from liability because there is no room for choice and the action will be contrary to policy. On the other hand, if a regulation allows the [Government] discretion, the very existence of the regulation creates a strong presumption that a discretionary act authorized by the regulation involves consideration of the same policies which led to the promulgation of the regulations.

We have already held that the Mission's compliance with its duty to ensure the protection of the party wall was specifically compelled by regulation and was non-delegable. Our holding above controls our analysis of the discretionary function exception as well. The Mission's alleged failure to ensure the integrity of the wall constituted a "violat[ion of] the mandatory regulation," and the Mission can therefore find "no shelter from liability" within the discretionary tort exception to the FSIA.

. . .

The Mission argues that the construction, including the failure to shore up the wall, was an activity undertaken to implement its discretionary policy decision to locate its chancery at the Building. In other words, the Mission argues that it is immunized from suit by the FSIA because the accident occurred in the course of construction that implemented this policy decision.

It is true, of course, that the discretionary function exception generally protects not only the initiation of discretionary activities but also the decisions made about how to implement those activities. Nevertheless, the fact that certain implementing actions may be insulated from FSIA liability does not mean that *any* action implementing or executing a discretionary policy will be shielded from liability. Rather, implementing acts must themselves involve the exercise of policy judgment.

Although in some instances, the determination of whether an act or omission involved the exercise of policy judgment may be fraught with difficulty, it is clear to us that the failure to protect a wall during a construction project is not a matter of policy analysis. . . . Although the Mission was not under an obligation to construct the chancery at any particular location (or, for that matter, to construct a chancery at all), once it decided to do so it could not disregard the nondelegable duty of care imposed upon it by the New York City Building Code. Accordingly, we hold that the obligation to protect the party wall was not discretionary, and that the Mission cannot avail itself of the protection of the FSIA's discretionary function exception. . . .

Doe v. Bin Laden

663 F.3d 64 (2d Cir. 2011)

Before: KEARSE, CALABRESI, and WESLEY, Circuit Judges.
PER CURIAM.

Defendant-Appellant Afghanistan appeals from an order of the United States District Court for the District of Columbia denying without prejudice its motion to vacate entry of default and to dismiss the complaint. For the reasons explained below, we agree with the district court that Plaintiff-Appellee John Doe's suit is properly considered under the noncommercial tort exception to foreign sovereign immunity provided by 28 U.S.C. § 1605(a)(5). . . .

In January 2002, Plaintiff-Appellee John Doe filed suit in the United States District Court for the District of Columbia, in his role as executor of the estate and personal representative of his wife Jane Doe, who perished in the terrorist attacks of September 11, 2001, as well as in his individual capacity. His complaint brought claims, arising from the events of that infamous day, of assault and battery, false imprisonment, intentional infliction of emotional distress, conspiracy, wrongful death and violation of the Anti-Terrorism Act, 18 U.S.C. § 2333.

On the conspiracy and wrongful death counts, Doe named among the defendants the nation of Afghanistan. He asserted subject matter jurisdiction under the Foreign Sovereign Immunities Act ("FSIA"), 28 U.S.C. §§ 1330, 1602 et seq., which provides subject matter jurisdiction for lawsuits against foreign governments only when one of several enumerated exceptions applies. Doe rested his complaint against Afghanistan on § 1605(a)(5), known as the noncommercial tort exception.

. . . Afghanistan . . . argued that claims like Doe's, predicated on terrorist acts, can only be brought under the terrorism exception, § 1605A. That exception is not available against Afghanistan, all agree, because the State Department has not designated Afghanistan as a state sponsor of terrorism.

In September 2008, the district court denied without prejudice the motion to vacate and dismiss, concluding that Doe's suit was properly cognizable under the noncommercial tort exception rather than the terrorism exception. The court concluded, however, that a definitive ruling on the existence of subject matter jurisdiction could not yet be made because two factual disputes remained: (a) whether the Taliban acted as the nation of Afghanistan when it allegedly entered the conspiracy alleged in the complaint and (b) whether any such action was "discretionary" within the meaning of § 1605(a)(5)(A). . . .

But rather than proceed with discovery, Afghanistan appealed the denial of its motion to the Court of Appeals for the District of Columbia Circuit. In November 2009, that court transferred the appeal and all pending motions to this Court. . . .

As with any question of statutory interpretation, we start with the text. The text of the noncommercial tort exception of the FSIA provides jurisdiction for cases that (1) are noncommercial, (2) seek "money damages," (3) for "personal injury or death, or damage to or loss of property," (4) that "occur[ed] in the United States," and (5) that was "caused by the tortious act," (6) "of [a defendant] foreign state or [its] employee . . . acting within the scope of his . . . employment," unless (7) the claim is based on a discretionary act or (8) it is for "malicious prosecution, abuse of process, libel, slander, misrepresentation, deceit, or interference with contract rights." 28 U.S.C. § 1605(a)(5). There is no question that the first five requirements are present and that the last exclusion does not apply. Specifically, there is no doubt that the terrorist acts giving rise to the harms at issue — aircraft sabotage, extrajudicial killing, and conspiracy to support the same — are all torts. Additionally, the complaint alleged nondiscretionary acts by employees of the foreign state within the scope of their employment. Therefore, at the pleading stage, the claim appears to fit within the noncommercial tort exception.

Afghanistan, however, urges us to shun this "plain language" reading. It argues for a narrow reading of the noncommercial tort exception under which the later-added "terrorism exception" acts not as an *additional* basis of jurisdiction but as an implicit *limitation* on the already-existing jurisdiction conferred by the noncommercial tort exception. Allowing the noncommercial tort exception to govern would, the argument goes, let the plaintiffs shoehorn a claim properly brought under one exception into another, which would violate the longstanding judicial tradition in FSIA cases.

But this conclusion can only be reached if one concludes that these claims "properly" belong under the terrorism exception and no other. And that conclusion, in turn, relies on the belief that to hold otherwise would leave the terrorism exception impotent because then no case would exist that is both (a) within the ambit of the terrorism exception and (b) not "otherwise covered by [the FSIA]." 28 U.S.C. § 1605A. That is, Afghanistan's argument for the narrow reading of the noncommercial tort exception rests on the factual premise that there exists no set of cases covered by the terrorism exception that fall outside the noncommercial tort exception. This premise is, however, demonstrably false.

To begin with, the very language of the statute undercuts the premise. The noncommercial tort exception applies only to injuries or damages "occurring *in the United States*." 28 U.S.C. § 1605(a)(5) (emphasis added). Accordingly, the noncommercial tort exception does not cover a wrongful death suit brought against a foreign state as the result of a bombing abroad. *E.g., Smith v. Socialist People's Libyan Arab Jamahiriya*, 101 F.3d 239, 246 (2d Cir. 1996) (affirming dismissal of a case against Libya for the bombing of Pan Am flight 103 for lack of subject matter jurisdiction, in part, because the bombing did not occur in the United States but over Scotland and hence could not be subject to the noncommercial tort exception). . . . [*Smith*] is precisely the type of wrong the terrorism exception encompasses: under that exception, no geographic limitation applies so long as the victim is a U.S. national, member of the U.S. armed forces, or U.S. government employee. 28 U.S.C. § 1605A(a)(2)(A)(ii). A bombing abroad killing U.S. nationals is not only a paradigmatic example of terrorism, it is the precise — and only — example Congress cited when it originally added the terrorism exception to the FSIA. The report from the House Committee on the Judiciary describes Section 804 of the Comprehensive Antiterrorism Act of 1995 — what would become the terrorism exception to the FSIA — as "*responding* to the tragedy of the Pan Am 103 bombing." H.R. Rep. No. 104-383, at 62 (1995) (emphasis added). Clearly, the bombing of Pan Am 103 over Lockerbie, Scotland by terrorists affiliated with the Libyan government was not actionable under the noncommercial tort exception because neither the bombing nor the injuries occurred in the United States. But it did kill U.S. nationals. And, as such, it seemed to Congress to be a wrong demanding a remedy.

The history of the Pan Am 103 litigation in this very Court illustrates the work that can be done only by the terrorism exception even accepting a literal reading of the noncommercial tort exception. Applying the pre-amendment version of the FSIA, this Court correctly dismissed a suit brought by the estates of Pan Am 103 victims because the noncommercial tort exception failed to encompass the explosion occurring in Scottish airspace. But after the addition of the terrorism exception — and in the first circuit court case to apply the new exception — a different panel allowed the refiled suit to go forward. It found that the terrorism exception supplied a new, sufficient, and constitutional source of jurisdiction over plaintiffs' wrongful death claims based on aircraft sabotage. *Rein v. Socialist People's Libyan Arab Jamahiriya*, 162 F.3d 748, 762-63 (2d Cir. 1998).

All this is to say, Afghanistan's proposed narrow reading of the noncommercial tort exception would not so much be a reading of the statute as it would be a decision that the terrorism exception amounts to a partial repeal by implication of the noncommercial tort exception. Prior to the terrorism exception's enactment, several courts had allowed suits against foreign governments under the noncommercial tort exception for tortious — and arguably "terrorist" — acts occurring in the United States. For example, in *Liu v. Republic of China*, 892 F.2d 1419, 1425 (9th Cir. 1989), the Ninth Circuit allowed the widow of a man killed by Taiwanese intelligence forces in California to maintain a wrongful death action against the Taiwanese government. Similarly, in *Letelier v. Republic of Chile*, 488 F. Supp. 665, 674 (D.D.C. 1980), the district court permitted a wrongful death suit against the Chilean government for its alleged role in a car bombing in the District of Columbia. Under the narrow reading of the noncommercial tort exception urged by Afghanistan, both these cases would now be barred (unless Taiwan and Chile were designated state sponsors of terrorism) because the alleged acts constitute extrajudicial killings, i.e., acts specifically listed in the terrorism exception. Were the narrow reading correct, the enactment of the terrorism exception would therefore have constituted a repudiation of the then-prevailing interpretation of the noncommercial tort exception.

But such an implicit repudiation runs against all canons of interpretation. Congress is presumed to be aware of a judicial interpretation of a statutory section and partial amendment of a statute without touching the previously interpreted section constitutes an implicit adoption of the prior interpretation, absent a clear indication to the contrary.

In the debate surrounding the adoption of the terrorism exception, these prior cases were explicitly discussed, so Congress was actually, and not just presumptively, aware of their existence, yet no one even suggested — let alone argued — either that they were incorrectly decided or that the proposed amendment would overturn their reasoning. *See Foreign Sovereign Immunities Act: Hearing on S.825 Before the Subcomm. on Courts and Admin. Practice of the S. Comm. on the Judiciary* ("Senate Hearing"), 103d Cong. 82 (1994) (discussing these cases).

In this same vein, were Afghanistan's proposed narrow reading correct, the enactment of the terrorism exception would represent a contraction rather than an expansion of jurisdiction over foreign states. The legislative history of the terrorism exception, however, suggests just the opposite. When the basic structure of the terrorism exception was first debated in Congress in 1992 and again in

1994, the House Committee Report explained that the provision was "necessary to clarify and *expand* the circumstances in which an American . . . can bring suit in U.S. courts against a foreign government under the FSIA." H.R. Rep. No. 103-702, at 3 (1994) (emphasis added); *accord* H.R. Rep. No. 102-900, at 3-4 (1992). Similarly, the report on the provision that would go on to become the terrorism exception twice explained that it would amend the FSIA to "grant" jurisdiction. H.R.Rep. No. 104-383, at 41, 62 (1995). Both supporters and opponents of the bill thought it would "expand the [then-]present jurisdiction of [the] courts" to cover claims arising outside the United States. Senate Hearing at 2 (statement of Sen. Heflin, supporting the bill); *see also id.* at 86-87 (statement of Sen. Thurmond, opposing the bill).

Additionally, and even apart from the noncommercial tort exception's plain text and this legislative history, application of the familiar canon of construction *expressio unius est exclusio alterius* to the noncommercial tort exception supports the broad reading. The noncommercial tort exception excludes from its scope "any claim arising out of malicious prosecution, abuse of process, libel, slander, misrepresentation, deceit, or interference with contract rights." 28 U.S.C. § 1605(a)(5)(B). Noticeably absent from this list are the torts listed in the terrorism exception — "an act of torture, extrajudicial killing, aircraft sabotage, hostage taking, or the provision of material support or resources for such an act." 28 U.S.C. § 1605A(a)(1). But, Afghanistan would have us, in effect, narrow the noncommercial tort exception precisely by adding these additional torts to the § 1605(a)(5)(B) list of excluded torts. Had Congress wished the § 1605(a)(5)(B) list to include those torts, it could easily have added them to that list itself.

The text, history, and purpose of the statute make clear that the statute does not counsel a narrow reading. . . . But are there not also cases that seemingly are covered by both exceptions, and does not their existence lend some support to the narrow reading? . . .

There are, of course, just such overlaps. But, Congress has expressly provided in the statute for how to determine which exception dominates. It did so by *limiting* the terrorism exception to "any case not otherwise covered by [the FSIA]." 28 U.S.C. § 1605A(a)(1). In other words, Congress expressly stated that the terrorism exception should only apply when the preexisting exceptions failed to cover a case. . . . Accordingly, we hold that the statutory text does not support Afghanistan's proposed narrow reading of the noncommercial tort exception, and that the terrorism exception, rather than limiting the jurisdiction conferred by the noncommercial tort exception, provides an additional basis for jurisdiction.

. . .

Let us be clear: we make no judgment as to whether the allegations in the complaint are sufficient to state a claim or even to provide jurisdiction. Indeed, the district court had ordered further discovery to provide for fact finding with regard to whether the alleged acts were attributable to Afghanistan and whether they were discretionary. . . . What we decide today is simply that limited discovery to determine whether jurisdiction exists should proceed. . . .

1. **Torts and the Discretionary Function Exception.** In light of *USAA Casualty*, what would constitute a "discretionary function"? What is the effect of finding a "discretionary function"? Is the (alleged) decision to support terrorism, as claimed in the *Bin Laden* case, a discretionary function? Should it matter if the duty in *USAA Casualty* arose from common law rather than a regulation? Should it matter if Namibia (a developing country) directed its contractors to save money on the project by using an inferior approach to reinforcing the wall?

2. **Torts Occurring in the United States.** When does a tort occur "in the United States" for purposes of the FSIA tort exception? In a subsequent appeal of some of the claims in the September 11, 2001 cases, the court of appeals held that the "entire tort" must occur in the United States, and dismissed claims against certain Saudi entities on the grounds that the alleged conduct (giving support to al-Qaeda) occurred outside the United States. *In re Terrorist Attacks on September 11, 2001*, 714 F.3d 109 (2d Cir. 2013). Plaintiffs argued unsuccessfully that because the injuries occurred in the United States that the exception was appropriate. Can that holding be reconciled with the language of the FSIA? The court of appeals relied on the Supreme Court's decision in *Argentine Republic v. Amerada Hess Shipping Corp.*, 488 U.S. 428 (1989), where, the court of appeals explained,

> the Supreme Court considered whether courts in the United States had jurisdiction over a suit brought by two Liberian corporations against the Argentine Republic to recover damages stemming from a tort allegedly committed by Argentina's armed forces on the high seas in violation of international law. The Court held that the action was barred by the FSIA, holding that the noncommercial tort exception "covers only torts occurring within the territorial jurisdiction of the United States."

Can *Amerada Hess* be distinguished? Even if it can, can the court of appeals' decision be justified by reference to the international system? After *In re Terrorist Attacks*, what about an act that is planned abroad but carried out in the United States? In the context of a more conventional tort, what about an oil spill that occurs outside the United States but causes damage in the United States? *See In re Sedco, Inc.*, 543 F. Supp. 561 (S.D. Tex. 1982) (finding no tort exception under such circumstances).

In 2016, Congress passed the Justice Against Sponsors of Terrorism Act (JASTA), which amended the FSIA to add § 1605B, creating an exception to immunity for nations that played a role in terrorist attacks on U.S. territory, even if their acts occurred outside the United States. (President Obama vetoed the bill, but Congress overrode the veto.) As a result, claims against Saudi Arabia for allegedly facilitating the September 11 attacks, which had been dismissed on sovereign immunity grounds, were partially reinstated. *In re Terrorist Attacks on September 11, 2001*, 298 F. Supp. 3d 631 (S.D.N.Y. 2018). Compare § 1605B to § 1605A and § 1605(a)(5) (the non-commercial tort exception). Why is § 1605B a significant change? Why did President Obama likely oppose it?

3. **Tort Exception versus Commercial Activity Exception.** Consider *Saudi Arabia v. Nelson*, discussed earlier in connection with the commercial activity exception. Why was *Nelson* not a tort exception case? Why was *USAA Casualty* a tort exception case rather than a commercial activity case?

4. **Tort Exception versus Terrorism Exception.** In a case involving Saudi defendants, the Second Circuit had previously held that claims for acts of terrorism could only proceed under the FSIA's terrorism exception, 28 U.S.C. § 1605A. *In re Terrorist Attacks on September 11, 2001*, 538 F.3d 71 (2d Cir. 2008). The court argued:

> Congress enacted the first iteration of the Terrorism Exception in 1996 in order to "give American citizens an important economic and financial weapon against . . . outlaw states" that sponsor terrorism by providing "safe havens, funding, training, supplying weaponry, medical assistance, false travel documentation, and the like." H.R. Rep. No. 104-383, at 62 (1995). An FSIA exception for terrorist acts "had long been sought by victims' groups," but it "had been consistently resisted by the executive branch," which feared that such an amendment to the FSIA "might cause other nations to respond in kind, thus potentially subjecting the American government to suits in foreign countries for actions taken in the United States."
>
> The State Department has never designated [Saudi Arabia] a state sponsor of terrorism. As a consequence, the Terrorism Exception is inapplicable here. No plaintiff argues otherwise. But to apply the Torts Exception where the conduct alleged amounts to terrorism within the meaning of the Terrorism Exception would evade and frustrate that key limitation on the Terrorism Exception.
>
> By definition, the acts listed in the Terrorism Exception are torts. If the Torts Exception covered terrorist acts and thus encompassed the conduct set forth in the Terrorism Exception, there would be no need for plaintiffs ever to rely on the Terrorism Exception when filing suit. An important procedural safeguard — that the foreign state be designated a state sponsor of terrorism — would in effect be vitiated. We decline to read the statute in a way that would deprive the Terrorism Exception (or its limitations) of meaning. To assure that the FSIA serves its purpose, its exceptions must be separately administered.

Second Circuit rules allow a subsequent panel to overrule a prior one, so long as no member of the court objects. No member of the court objected to the ruling in *Bin Laden*, even though the judges from the prior opinion remained on the court. Which case has the better argument?

5. **Ongoing Terrorism Litigation.** Since the enactment of § 1605A, numerous cases have been brought against designated state sponsors of terrorism (principally Iran). *E.g.*, *Leibovitch v. Islamic Republic of Iran*, 697 F.3d 561 (7th Cir. 2011) (finding exception to immunity in a case based on a terrorist attack on U.S. and Israeli citizens by a Palestinian group in Israel). In *Leibovitch*, the court also observed:

> We pause to note that there are significant questions regarding the wisdom of combating international terrorism through private civil suits. Because terrorism

involves a broad range of foreign policy considerations, many commentators have argued that the political branches must address the matter as opposed to a broad range of courts and judges adjudicating competing cases and controversies. *See Iran Terrorism Litig.*, 659 F. Supp. 2d at 38 (D.D.C. 2009) ("If the decade-long history of these FSIA terrorism actions has revealed anything, it is that the Judiciary cannot resolve the intractable political dilemmas that frustrate these lawsuits; only Congress and the President can. Today, at the start of a new presidential administration — one that has sought engagement with Iran on a host of critical issues — it may be time for our political leaders here in Washington to seek a fresh approach."); *see also, e.g.*, Anne-Marie Slaughter & David Bosco, *Plaintiff's Diplomacy*, Foreign Aff. 102 (Sept./Oct. 2000); Daveed Gartenstein-Ross, A Critique of the Terrorism Exception to the Foreign Sovereign Immunities Act, 34 N.Y.U. J. Int'l L. & Pol. 887 (2002). Whatever the merits of this debate, we are obliged to focus on statutory text and congressional intent and we do not find evidence to support the conclusion that Congress intended to foreclose claims by noncitizen family members when it enacted § 1605A(c).

Is the terrorism exception a useful addition to the FSIA, either from the perspective of victims or from the perspective of U.S. diplomacy? As a practical matter, these cases have not generally produced much recovery because Iran and other sponsors of terrorism tend not to have assets in the United States. However, in 2008 plaintiffs in terrorism suits against Iran identified $1.75 billion in assets in a previously unknown bank account in New York held by Clearstream Banking LLC, a financial intermediary, on behalf of Bank Markazi, the Iranian Central Bank. After protracted litigation and statutory intervention by Congress, the Supreme Court affirmed an order directing turnover of the funds to plaintiffs to partially satisfy their judgment. *Bank Markazi v. Peterson*, 136 S. Ct. 1310 (2016). (As discussed in Chapter 5, Iran filed a claim against the United States at the ICJ contending that U.S. failure to accord sovereign immunity protection to Iran's assets in the United States violated international law.) The Court later found that Iranian-owned artifacts in possession of the University of Chicago could not be seized to satisfy a terrorism judgment. *Rubin v. Islamic Republic of Iran*, 138 S. Ct. 816 (2018). Enforcement of judgments against foreign sovereigns is discussed in Section D below.

Successful plaintiffs in terrorism cases have also sought to enforce their judgments against foreign sovereign assets in third countries (especially in Europe), but so far European courts have been unwilling to enforce the U.S. judgments. Why might these courts refuse enforcement? Enforcement of U.S. judgments in foreign courts is discussed in Chapter 7.

5. *Other FSIA Exceptions*

The FSIA contains several other exceptions to immunity that are infrequently invoked. For example, FSIA § 1605(a)(4) provides an exception for claims involving rights in fixed property located in the United States. (Arguably the claim in

USAA Casualty could have come within this exception.) FSIA § 1605(b) provides an exception for certain maritime claims.

In addition, FSIA § 1607 provides an exception to immunity for certain counterclaims. In *First National City Bank v. Banco Para el Comercio Exterior de Cuba*, 462 U.S. 611 (1987), a Cuban government-owned bank, referred to as "Bancec," sued City Bank in U.S. court to recover amounts City Bank owed it. City Bank counterclaimed for the Cuban government's expropriation of City Bank's assets in Cuba. The Supreme Court allowed the counterclaim under § 1607 even though Cuba would likely otherwise have been immune from City Bank's suit. As noted above, the Court held that Bancec was not a separate legal entity from Cuba; therefore City Bank's claim was properly brought as a counterclaim in Bancec's suit. What implications does this section have for advising clients in international practice?

Finally, in an important exception for international business, FSIA § 1605(a)(6) provides an exception to immunity for suits to compel arbitration or to confirm an arbitration award. Why is this exception important? What implications does it have for transnational transactional practice? Arbitration and enforcement of arbitration awards are discussed in Chapters 6 and 8. Note, however, that execution against foreign sovereign assets to satisfy an arbitration award remains limited by a separate part of the FSIA, as discussed below.

C. Common Law Immunities

Prior to 1976, foreign sovereign immunity in the United States was a matter of common law (from the mid-twentieth century, decisively influenced by the U.S. State Department's understanding of the customary international law of foreign sovereign immunity). As discussed above, in 1976 Congress enacted the FSIA, largely (but not entirely) codifying U.S. rules of foreign sovereign immunity. But the FSIA was not comprehensive; among other things, the Supreme Court held in *Samantar v. Yousuf*, 560 U.S. 305 (2010), that it did not cover the immunities of individual foreign officials. In the following case, on remand from the Supreme Court's *Samantar* decision, the court considered whether such individuals had common law immunity even though they were not covered by the FSIA.

Yousuf v. Samantar

699 F.3d 763 (4th Cir. 2012)

TRAXLER, Chief Judge:

For the second time in this case, we are presented with the question of whether Appellant Mohamed Ali Samantar enjoys immunity from suit under the Torture Victim Protection Act of 1991 ("TVPA"), 28 U.S.C. § 1350 note, and the Alien Tort Statute ("ATS"), *see* 28 U.S.C. § 1350. In the previous appeal, we rejected Samantar's claim to statutory immunity under the Foreign Sovereign Immunities Act ("FSIA") . . . but held open the possibility that Samantar could successfully invoke an immunity doctrine arising under pre-FSIA common law. The Supreme Court affirmed our reading of the FSIA and likewise suggested Samantar would have the opportunity to assert common law immunity on remand. . . .

On remand to the district court, Samantar sought dismissal of the claims against him based on common law immunities afforded to heads of state and also to other foreign officials for acts performed in their official capacity. The district court rejected his claims for immunity and denied the motion to dismiss. For the reasons that follow, we agree with the district court and affirm its decision.

I.

. . . Samantar was a highranking government official in Somalia while the military regime of General Mohamed Barre held power from about 1969 to 1991. Plaintiffs are natives of Somalia and members of the prosperous and well-educated Isaaq clan, which the [Barre] government viewed as a threat. Plaintiffs allege that they, or members of their families, were subjected to torture, arbitrary detention and extrajudicial killing by government agents under the command and control of Samantar, who served as Minister of Defense from January 1980 to December 1986, and as Prime Minister from January 1987 to September 1990.

Following the collapse of the Barre regime in January 1991, Samantar fled Somalia for the United States. He now resides in Virginia as a permanent legal resident. Two of the plaintiffs also reside in the United States, having become naturalized citizens.

Plaintiffs brought a civil action against Samantar under the TVPA and the ATS. . . . It is now clear after [the Supreme Court ruling in] *Samantar* that the common law, not the FSIA, governs the claims to immunity of individual foreign officials. . . .

On remand [after the Supreme Court decision], Samantar renewed his motion to dismiss based on two common law immunity doctrines. First, Samantar alleged he was entitled to head-of-state immunity because at least some of the alleged wrongdoing occurred while Samantar was Prime Minister. Second, Samantar sought foreign official immunity on the basis that any actions for which the plaintiffs sought to hold him responsible were taken in the course and scope of his official duties.

The district court renewed its request to the State Department for a response to Samantar's immunity claims. Despite having remained silent during Samantar's first appeal, the State Department here took a position expressly opposing immunity for Samantar. The United States submitted to the district court a Statement of Interest (SOI) announcing that the Department of State, having considered "the potential impact of such a[n] [immunity] decision on the foreign relations interests of the United States," had determined that Samantar was not entitled to immunity from plaintiffs' lawsuit. The SOI indicated that two factors were particularly important to the State Department's determination that Samantar should not enjoy immunity. First, the State Department concluded that Samantar's claim for immunity was undermined by the fact that he "is a former official of a state with no currently recognized government to request immunity on his behalf," or to take a position as to "whether the acts in question were taken in an official capacity." Noting that "[t]he immunity protecting foreign officials for their official acts ultimately belongs to the sovereign rather than the official," the government reasoned that Samantar should not be afforded immunity "[i]n the absence of a recognized government . . . to assert or waive [Samantar's] immunity[.]" Second, Samantar's status as a permanent legal resident was particularly relevant to the State Department's immunity determination. According to the SOI, "U.S. residents like Samantar who enjoy the protections of U.S. law ordinarily should be subject to the jurisdiction of our courts, particularly when sued by U.S. residents" or naturalized citizens such as two of the plaintiffs.

The district court denied Samantar's motion to dismiss . . . .

Samantar . . . contends that the order denying him immunity cannot stand because the district court improperly deferred to the Department of State and abdicated its duty to independently assess his immunity claim. . . . Second, Samantar argues that under the common law, he is entitled to immunity for all actions taken within the scope of his duties and in his capacity as a foreign government official, and that he is immune to any claims alleging wrongdoing while he was the Somali Prime Minister. . . .

II.

Before proceeding further, we must decide the appropriate level of deference courts should give the Executive Branch's view on case-specific questions of individual foreign sovereign immunity. The FSIA displaced the common law regime for resolving questions of foreign *state* immunity and shifted the Executive's role as primary decision maker to the courts. After [the Supreme Court's decision in] *Samantar*, it is clear that the FSIA did no such thing with respect to the immunity of *individual* foreign officials; the common law, not the FSIA, continues to govern foreign official immunity. . . . The extent of the State Department's role, however, depends in large part on what kind of immunity has been asserted. . . .

In this case, Samantar claims two forms of immunity: (1) head-of-state immunity and (2) "foreign official" or "official acts" immunity. Head-of-state immunity is a doctrine of customary international law pursuant to which an incumbent head of state is immune from the jurisdiction of a foreign state's courts. Like the related doctrine of sovereign state immunity, the rationale of head-of-state immunity is to promote comity among nations by ensuring that leaders can perform their duties without being subject to detention, arrest or embarrassment in a foreign country's legal system. A head-of-state recognized by the United States government is absolutely immune from personal jurisdiction in United States courts unless that immunity has been waived by statute or by the foreign government recognized by the United States. Although all forms of individual immunity derive from the State, head-of-state immunity is tied closely to the sovereign immunity of foreign states. Indeed, head-of-state immunity is premised on the concept that a state and its ruler are one for purposes of immunity.

Samantar also seeks immunity on the separate ground that all of the actions for which plaintiffs seek to hold him liable occurred during the course of his official duties within the Somali government. *See Restatement (Second) of Foreign Relations Law* § 66(f) (stating that "[t]he immunity of a foreign state . . . extends to . . . any . . . public minister, official, or agent of the state with respect to acts performed in his official capacity if the effect of exercising jurisdiction would be to enforce a rule of law against the state"); *Matar v. Dichter*, 563 F.3d 9, 14 (2d Cir. 2009) ("At the time the FSIA was enacted, the common law of foreign sovereign immunity recognized an individual official's entitlement to immunity for acts performed in his official capacity.") . . . This is a conduct-based immunity that applies to current and former foreign officials. . . .

The United States, participating as *amicus curiae*, takes the position that federal courts owe absolute deference to the State Department's view of whether a foreign official is entitled to sovereign immunity on either ground. According to the government, under long-established Supreme Court precedent, the State Department's opinion on any foreign immunity issue is binding upon the courts. . . .

We begin by observing that, although the doctrine of foreign sovereign immunity has well-established roots in American jurisprudence, the Executive Branch's assumption of the role of primary decision-maker on various foreign sovereign immunity matters is of a more recent vintage. Foreign sovereign immunity, insofar as American courts are concerned, has its doctrinal roots in *The Schooner Exchange v. McFaddon*, 11 U.S. 116 (1812), which ushered in nearly a century of "absolute" or "classical" immunity, under which a sovereign could not, without his consent, be made a respondent in the courts of another sovereign. . . . [D]uring the lengthy period of absolute immunity, courts did not necessarily consider themselves obliged to follow executive pronouncements regarding immunity. In *The Schooner Exchange* itself, for example, the Court received and considered the view of the Executive Branch on the immunity claim but conducted its own independent review of the relevant international law doctrines. As late as the 1920s, the Court still did not necessarily view questions of foreign sovereign immunity as matters solely for the Executive Branch. For example, the Court in *Berizzi Bros. Co. v. Steamship Pesaro*, 271 U.S. 562, 576 (1926), concluded that a steamship owned by a foreign sovereign was entitled to immunity despite the fact that the Secretary of State had expressed the opposite view earlier in the litigation.

It was not until the late 1930s — in the context of in rem actions against foreign ships — that judicial deference to executive foreign immunity determinations emerged as standard practice. *See Compania Espanola de Navegacion Maritima, S.A. v. The Navemar*, 303 U.S. 68, 74 (1938) . . . ; *Ex parte Republic of Peru*, 318 U.S. 578, 587-89 (1943); *Republic of Mexico v. Hoffman*, 324 U.S. 30, 34-36 (1945). . . .

Thus, at the time that Congress enacted the FSIA, the clearly established practice of judicial deference to executive immunity determinations had been expressed largely in admiralty cases. In this pre-FSIA era, decisions involving claims of *individual* foreign sovereign immunity were scarce. But, to the extent such individual claims arose, they generally involved status-based immunities such as head-of-state immunity, *see, e.g., Ye v. Zemin*, 383 F.3d 620, 624-25 (7th Cir. 2004), or diplomatic immunity arising under international treaties. . . . The rare cases involving immunity asserted by lower-level foreign officials provided inconsistent results. . . .

The Constitution assigns the power to "receive Ambassadors and other public Ministers" to the Executive Branch, U.S. Const. art. II, § 3, which includes, by implication, the power to accredit diplomats and recognize foreign heads of state. Courts have generally treated executive "suggestions of immunity" for heads of state as a function of the Executive's constitutional power and, therefore, as controlling on the judiciary. Like diplomatic immunity, head-of-state immunity involves "a formal act of recognition," that is "a quintessentially executive function" for which absolute deference is proper.

Accordingly, consistent with the Executive's constitutionally delegated powers and the historical practice of the courts, we conclude that the State Department's pronouncement as to head-of-state immunity is entitled to absolute deference. The State Department has never recognized Samantar as the head of state for Somalia; indeed, the State Department does not recognize the Transitional Federal Government or any other entity as the official government of Somalia, from which immunity would derive in the first place. The district court properly deferred to the State Department's position that Samantar be denied head-of-state immunity.

Unlike head-of-state immunity and other status-based immunities, there is no equivalent constitutional basis suggesting that the views of the Executive Branch control questions of foreign official immunity. Such cases do not involve any act of recognition for which the Executive Branch is constitutionally empowered; rather, they simply involve matters about the scope of defendant's official duties.

This is not to say, however, that the Executive Branch has no role to play in such suits. These immunity decisions turn upon principles of customary international law and foreign policy, areas in which the courts respect, but do not automatically follow, the views of the Executive Branch. With respect to foreign official immunity, the Executive Branch still informs the court about the diplomatic effect of the court's exercising jurisdiction over claims against an official of a foreign state, and the Executive Branch may urge the court to grant or deny official act immunity based on such considerations. That function, however, concerns the general assessment of a case's impact on the foreign relations of the United States, rather than a controlling determination of whether an individual is entitled to conduct-based immunity.

In sum, we give absolute deference to the State Department's position on status-based immunity doctrines such as head-of-state immunity. The State Department's determination regarding conduct-based immunity, by contrast, is not controlling, but it carries substantial weight in our analysis of the issue.

III.

. . .

We turn to the remaining question of whether Samantar is entitled to foreign official immunity under the common law. In considering the contours of foreign official immunity, we must draw from the relevant principles found in both international and domestic immunity law, as well as the experience and judgment of the State Department, to which we give considerable, but not controlling, weight.

From the earliest Supreme Court decisions, international law has shaped the development of the common law of foreign sovereign immunity. *See The Schooner Exchange*, 11 U.S. at 136, 145-46 (noting that "a principle of public law" derived from "common usage" and "common opinion" that "national ships of war, entering the port of a friendly power open for their reception, are to be considered as exempted by the consent of that power from its jurisdiction"); *Restatement (Third) of the Foreign Relations Law* part IV, ch. 5, subch. A intro. note ("The immunity of a state from the jurisdiction of the courts of another state is an undisputed principle of customary international law."). Indeed, an important purpose of the FSIA was the codification of international law at the time of the FSIA's enactment. . . . Even after the FSIA was enacted, international law continued to be relevant to questions of foreign sovereign immunity as the Court interpreted the FSIA in light of international law.

As previously noted, customary international law has long distinguished between status-based immunity afforded to sitting heads-of-state and conduct-based immunity available to other foreign officials, including former heads-of-state. With respect to conduct-based immunity, foreign officials are immune from "claims arising out of their official acts while in office." *Restatement (Third) of Foreign Relations Law* § 464, reprt. note 14; *Matar*, 563 F.3d at 14 ("An immunity based on acts — rather than status — does not depend on tenure in office."). This type of immunity stands on the foreign official's actions, not his or her status, and therefore applies whether the individual is currently a government official or not. This conduct-based immunity for a foreign official derives from the immunity of the State: "The doctrine of the imputability of the acts of the individual to the State . . . in classical law . . . imputes the act solely to the state, who alone is responsible for its consequence. In consequence any act performed by the individual as an act of the State enjoys the immunity which the State enjoys." Hazel Fox, *The Law of State Immunity* at 455 (2d ed. 2008).

. . . By the time the FSIA was enacted, numerous domestic courts had embraced the notion, stemming from international law, that "[t]he immunity of a foreign state . . . extends to . . . any . . . public minister, official, or agent of the state with respect to acts performed in his official capacity if the effect of exercising jurisdiction would be to enforce a rule of law against the state." *Restatement (Second) of Foreign Relations Law* § 66(f). . . .

These cases sketch out the general contours of official-act immunity: a foreign official may assert immunity for official acts performed within the scope of his duty, but not for private acts where the officer purports to act as an individual and not as an official, such that a suit directed against that action is not a suit against the sovereign. A foreign official or former head-of-state will therefore not be able to assert this immunity for private acts that are not arguably attributable to the state, such as drug possession or fraud. . . .

In response, plaintiffs contend that Samantar cannot raise this immunity as a shield against atrocities such as torture, genocide, indiscriminate executions and prolonged arbitrary imprisonment or any other act that would violate a *jus cogens* norm of international law. A *jus cogens* norm, also known as a "peremptory norm of general international law," can be defined as "a norm accepted and recognized by the international community of States as a whole as a norm from which no derogation is permitted and which can be modified only by a subsequent norm of general international law having the same character." *Vienna Convention on the Law of Treaties* art. 53, May 23, 1969, 1155 U.N.T.S. 331. . . . Prohibitions against the acts involved in this case — torture, summary execution and prolonged arbitrary imprisonment — are among these universally agreed-upon norms. Unlike private acts that do not come within the scope of foreign official immunity, *jus cogens* violations may well be committed under color of law and, in that sense, constitute acts performed in the course of the foreign official's employment by the Sovereign.

However, as a matter of international and domestic law, *jus cogens* violations are, by definition, acts that are not officially authorized by the Sovereign. There has been an increasing trend in international law to abrogate foreign official immunity for individuals who commit acts, otherwise attributable to the State, that violate *jus cogens* norms — *i.e.*, they commit international crimes or human rights violations. . . . A number of decisions from foreign national courts have reflected a willingness to deny official-act immunity in the criminal context for alleged *jus cogens* violations, most notably the British House of Lords' *Pinochet* decision denying official-acts immunity to a former Chilean head of state accused of directing widespread torture. *See Regina v. Bartle, ex parte Pinochet*, 38 I.L.M. 581, 593-95 (H.L. 1999) (concluding that official-acts immunity is unavailable to shield foreign officials from prosecution for international crimes because acts of torture do not constitute officially-approved acts).[6]

. . . Some foreign national courts have pierced the veil of official-acts immunity to hear civil claims alleging *jus cogens* violations, but the *jus cogens* exception appears to be less settled in the civil context. *Compare Ferrini v. Germany*, Oxford Rep Int'l in Dom Cts 19 (Italian Ct. of Cassation 2004) (denying "the functional immunity of foreign state organs" for *jus cogens* violations in criminal context), *with Jones v. Saudi Arabia*, 129 I.L.R. 713, at ¶24 (H.L. 2006) (rejecting *jus cogens* exception to foreign official immunity in civil context). American courts have generally followed the foregoing trend, concluding that *jus cogens* violations are not legitimate official acts and therefore do not merit foreign official immunity but still recognizing that head-of-state immunity, based on status, is of an absolute nature and applies even against *jus cogens* claims. . . . We conclude that, under international and domestic law, officials from other countries are not entitled to foreign official immunity for *jus cogens* violations, even if the acts were performed in the defendant's official capacity.

---

6. In spite of this, allegations of *jus cogens* violations do not overcome head-of-state or any other status-based immunity. *See, e.g., Case Concerning the Arrest Warrant of 11 April 2000 (Democratic Republic of Congo v. Belgium) (2002)* ICJ 3 (concluding that the sitting foreign minister of the Democratic Republic of Congo was entitled to status-based immunity against alleged *jus cogens* violations).

Moreover, we find Congress's enactment of the TVPA, and the policies it reflects, to be both instructive and consistent with our view of the common law regarding these aspects of *jus cogens*. Plaintiffs asserted claims against Samantar under the TVPA which authorizes a civil cause of action against "[a]n individual who, under actual or apparent authority, or color of law, of any foreign nation...subjects an individual to torture" or "extrajudicial killing." Pub. L. 102-256, § 2(a), 28 U.S.C. 1350 note. . . . Thus, in enacting the TVPA, Congress essentially created an express private right of action for individuals victimized by torture and extrajudicial killing that constitute violations of *jus cogens* norms. *See* S. Rep. No. 102-249, at 8 (1991) ("[B]ecause no state officially condones torture or extrajudicial killings, few such acts, if any, would fall under the rubric of 'official actions' taken in the course of an official's duties."). . . .

In its SOI, the State Department submitted a suggestion of non-immunity . . . [which] add[s] substantial weight in favor of denying immunity. Because the State Department has not officially recognized a Somali government, the court does not face the usual risk of offending a foreign nation by exercising jurisdiction over the plaintiffs' claims. Likewise, as a permanent legal resident, Samantar has a binding tie to the United States and its court system.

Because this case involves acts that violated *jus cogens* norms, including torture, extrajudicial killings and prolonged arbitrary imprisonment of politically and ethnically disfavored groups, we conclude that Samantar is not entitled to conduct based official immunity under the common law, which in this area incorporates international law. Moreover, the SOI has supplied us with additional reasons to support this conclusion. Thus, we affirm the district court's denial of Samantar's motion to dismiss based on foreign official immunity. . . .

NOTES AND QUESTIONS

1. **Head of State Immunity and Foreign Official Immunity.** Note that Samantar claimed two kinds of common law immunity. What are the differences? From a defendant's perspective, what are the advantages and disadvantages of each? Why did the court think Samantar was not entitled to either? Is it puzzling that Samantar claimed head-of-state immunity?

2. **Policy: Justifying Official Immunities.** What justifies head-of-state immunity? Consider *Ye v. Zemin*, 383 F.3d 620 (7th Cir. 2004), mentioned in *Samantar*, in which plaintiffs sued the President of China for his alleged actions in suppressing adherents of Falun Gong, described as "a spiritual movement of Chinese origin." Why should U.S. courts hesitate to hear such as case? Would the answer be different if the suit involved an ordinary traffic accident alleging President Zemin's negligent driving? Is it relevant that the FSIA does not grant immunity to individuals? What if the claims were made against ordinary Chinese officials rather than against President Zemin — how would this change the applicable law? Should it change the applicable law?

3. **Comparative Perspective.** In *Jones v. Ministry of Interior of the Kingdom of Saudi Arabia*, [2006] UKHL 26, mentioned in *Samantar*, the U.K. House of Lords (acting as its highest court) found immunity for a foreign state and its agents in a claim alleging torture. The claimants argued that "the grant of immunity to the Kingdom [of Saudi Arabia] on behalf of itself or its servants would be inconsistent with a peremptory norm of international law, a jus cogens applicable erga omnes and superior in effect to other rules of international law, which requires that the practice of torture should be suppressed and the victims of torture compensated." Lord Hoffmann, in an opinion with which the other Lords indicated approval, stated in part:

> A peremptory norm or jus cogens is defined in article 53 of the Vienna Convention of the Law of Treaties of 23 May 1969 (which provides that a treaty is void if, at the time of its conclusion, it conflicts with such a norm) as: "a norm accepted and recognised by the international community of states as a whole as a norm from which no derogation is permitted" . . . . [T]here is no doubt that the prohibition on torture is such a norm: for its recognition as such in this country, see *R v Bow Street Metropolitan Stipendiary Magistrate, Ex p Pinochet Ugarte (No 3)* [2000] 1 AC 147. Torture cannot be justified by any rule of domestic or international law. But the question is whether such a norm conflicts with a rule which accords state immunity.
>
> The jus cogens is the prohibition on torture. But the United Kingdom, in according state immunity to the Kingdom [of Saudi Arabia], is not proposing to torture anyone. Nor is the Kingdom, in claiming immunity, justifying the use of torture. It is objecting . . . to the jurisdiction of the English court to decide whether it used torture or not. As Hazel Fox has said (*The Law of State Immunity* (2002), 525):
>
> > "State immunity is a procedural rule going to the jurisdiction of a national court. It does not go to substantive law; it does not contradict a prohibition contained in a jus cogens norm but merely diverts any breach of it to a different method of settlement. Arguably, then, there is no substantive content in the procedural plea of state immunity upon which a jus cogens mandate can bite."
>
> To produce a conflict with state immunity, it is therefore necessary to show that the prohibition on torture has generated an ancillary procedural rule which, by way of exception to state immunity, entitles or perhaps requires states to assume civil jurisdiction over other states in cases in which torture is alleged. Such a rule may be desirable and, since international law changes, may have developed. But, . . . it is not *entailed* by the prohibition of torture.
>
> Whether such an exception is now recognised by international law must be ascertained in the normal way from treaties, judicial decisions and the writings of reputed publicists.

Lord Hoffman found little evidence of state practice supporting a denial of immunity and added:

> The notion that acts contrary to jus cogens cannot be official acts has not been well received by eminent writers on international law. Professor Antonio Cassese, who presided over the Appeals Chamber of the International Criminal

> Tribunal for the Former Yugoslavia, described it as "unsound and even prepos-
> terous": see "When May Senior State Officials be Tried for International
> Crimes? Some Comments on the *Congo v Belgium* Case" (2002) 13 EJIL 853-
> 875 . . . at p 869, while Professor Andrea Gattini gave it short shrift in a foot-
> note: see "War Crimes and State Immunity in the *Ferrrini* Decision" (2005)
> Journal of International Criminal Justice 224-242, at p 234 n 41 ("an argument
> which can be easily discarded"). More moderately, in a comment on the pres-
> ent case, Hazel Fox said that it was "directly contrary to current international
> law": (2005) 121 LQR 353-359, at p 355.

Lord Hoffmann distinguished the prior case involving General Pinochet because it was a criminal rather than a civil proceeding. He also dismissed the differing U.S. cases with the observation that they are "contrary to custom-ary international law." Is this persuasive? Should it cause the United States to reconsider the *Samantar* decision? How would the Fourth Circuit respond?

4. **Determining the International Law Rule of Official Immunity.** Assuming that the customary international law of immunity is relevant to the question of foreign official immunity in the United States, how should it be determined? Is the right question whether states have recognized an exception to immunity for *jus cogens* violations or whether states have recognized immunity for *jus cogens* violations? Might these questions yield different answers? The U.N. International Law Commission (ILC), discussed earlier in this chapter, is currently working on Draft Articles on the Immunity of State Officials from Foreign Criminal Jurisdiction. Once completed, should the draft articles pro-vide another resource that U.S. courts can use to determine customary inter-national law's rules of foreign official immunity?

5. *Jus Cogens* **and Foreign Sovereign Immunity.** Note that in the United States, under *Amerada Hess* a foreign state would be entitled to immunity against most *jus cogens* claims, since (a) the FSIA is the sole method of obtaining jurisdic-tion over a foreign state; (b) there is no express FSIA exception for *jus cogens* violations; and (c) it is unlikely that the statutory exceptions would apply to most such claims. Recall that in *Sampson*, *Princz*, and related cases, plaintiffs attempted unsuccessfully to use the waiver exception to create an exception for *jus cogens* violations. Does it make sense to have one rule for foreign state immunity and another rule for foreign official immunity? Does it make sense to say that *jus cogens* violations cannot be official acts of the state? Does that mean that the genocidal acts of Nazi Germany were not "official" acts?

6. **The Significance of the TVPA.** Is it significant that Yousuf sued Samantar under the TVPA, a statute whose central purpose is to provide a cause of action for victims of official torture? Can the TVPA be reconciled with a broad version of foreign official immunity as described in *Jones*? Can it be reconciled with foreign official immunity under the direction of the U.S. executive branch, as argued (unsuccessfully) by the U.S. government in *Samantar*?

   In *Lewis v. Mutond*, 918 F.3d 142 (D.C. Cir. 2019), the court considered a TVPA suit by a U.S. citizen allegedly detained and tortured by police in the Democratic Republic of the Congo (DRC); the defendants were individ-ual police officers and other DRC officials. After the U.S. State Department declined to issue a statement of interest in support of immunity, the court's majority applied the common law of foreign official immunity, reflected (it said) in Section 66 of the *Restatement (Second) of Foreign Relations of the United States.* It found no immunity principally because the effect of exercising jurisdiction would not be to enforce a rule against the foreign state. In particular, the majority found that the plaintiff did not "seek[ ] to draw on the DRC's treasury or force the state to take specific action." Concurring, Judge Randolph sharply disputed that the *Restatement* reflected common law or that it was applicable; in his view, the TVPA categorically displaced common law conduct-based immunity. How are these approaches consistent with or different from the Fourth Circuit in *Samantar*?

In contrast, in *Dogan v. Barak*, 932 F.3d 888 (9th Cir. 2019), the court found common law immunity in a TVPA action against former Israeli defense minister Ehud Barak. The plaintiffs' son was killed when Israeli forces, in an operation allegedly planned and directed by Barak, seized a ship attempting to pass through an Israeli naval blockade of the Gaza territory.

7. **Foreign Relations Implications.** Is the holding in *Samantar* problematic for U.S. foreign relations with respect to suits brought in the United States? Is it problematic in terms of suits that might be brought abroad?

8. **Statutory and Treaty-Based Immunities.** Immunities may be conveyed on foreign persons and entities by treaties or other statutes. Diplomatic and consular property and personnel, for example, have treaty-based immunities, as do some international organizations such as the United Nations. *E.g., Broidy Capital Management LLC v. Benomer*, 944 F.3d 436 (2d Cir. 2019) (finding diplomatic immunity under the Vienna Convention on Diplomatic Relations for a Moroccan diplomat alleged to have stolen files from plaintiffs' computer and rejecting application of the Convention's commercial activity exception); *Brzak v. United Nations*, 597 F.3d 107 (2d Cir. 2010) (finding treaty-based immunity for the United Nations). Other international organizations have statutory immunity under the International Organizations Immunities Act (IOIA), 22 U.S.C. § 288a(b). Enacted in 1945, the IOIA provides that specified international organizations shall have "the same immunity" as foreign sovereigns. In *Jam v. International Finance Corporation*, 139 S. Ct. 759 (2019), the Supreme Court concluded that this language meant that international organizations have the same immunity that foreign sovereigns would have under the FSIA at the time the suit is commenced, not the same immunity that foreign sovereigns had at the time the IOIA was enacted. Can you see why this distinction matters? Recall the history of foreign sovereign immunity since 1945.

D. Enforcing Judgments Against Foreign Governments

In addition to the immunity rules discussed above, the FSIA has special rules for enforcing judgments against foreign governments and their agencies and instrumentalities. Somewhat confusingly, these do not track the immunity and exceptions set out in FSIA §§ 1604-1605. As a result, even if a foreign sovereign is not immune from suit, most or all of its assets in the United States might be immune from execution. Consider: What course of action should a plaintiff pursue in such situations?

Foreign Sovereign Immunities Act, 28 U.S.C. § 1609

Subject to existing international agreements to which the United States is a party at the time of enactment of this Act the property in the United States of a foreign state shall be immune from attachment arrest and execution except as provided in sections 1610 and 1611 of this chapter.

Foreign Sovereign Immunities Act, 28 U.S.C. § 1610

(a) The property in the United States of a foreign state, as defined in section 1603(a) of this chapter, used for a commercial activity in the United States, shall not be immune from attachment in aid of execution, or from execution, upon a judgment entered by a court of the United States or of a State after the effective date of this Act, if —

(1) the foreign state has waived its immunity from attachment in aid of execution or from execution either explicitly or by implication, notwithstanding any withdrawal of the waiver the foreign state may purport to effect except in accordance with the terms of the waiver, or

(2) the property is or was used for the commercial activity upon which the claim is based, or

(3) the execution relates to a judgment establishing rights in property which has been taken in violation of international law or which has been exchanged for property taken in violation of international law, or . . .

(6) the judgment is based on an order confirming an arbitral award rendered against the foreign state, provided that attachment in aid of execution, or execution, would not be inconsistent with any provision in the arbitral agreement, . . .

(b) In addition to subsection (a), any property in the United States of an agency or instrumentality of a foreign state engaged in commercial activity in the United States shall not be immune from attachment in aid of execution, or from execution, upon a judgment entered by a court of the United States or of a State after the effective date of this Act, if —

(1) the agency or instrumentality has waived its immunity from attachment in aid of execution or from execution either explicitly or implicitly, . . . or

(2) the judgment relates to a claim for which the agency or instrumentality is not immune by virtue of section 1605(a)(2), (3), or (5) or 1605(b) of this chapter . . . , or

(3) the judgment relates to a claim for which the agency or instrumentality is not immune by virtue of section 1605A of this chapter. . . ."*

Republic of Argentina v. NML Capital, Ltd.

573 U.S. 134 (2014)

Justice Scalia delivered the opinion of the Court.

We must decide whether the Foreign Sovereign Immunities Act of 1976 (FSIA or Act) limits the scope of discovery available to a judgment creditor in a federal postjudgment execution proceeding against a foreign sovereign.

I. Background

In 2001, petitioner, Republic of Argentina, defaulted on its external debt. In 2005 and 2010, it restructured most of that debt by offering creditors new securities (with less favorable terms) to swap out for the defaulted ones. Most bondholders went along. Respondent, NML Capital, Ltd. (NML), among others, did not.

NML brought 11 actions against Argentina in the Southern District of New York to collect on its debt, and prevailed in every one.[1] It is owed around $2.5 billion, which Argentina has not paid. Having been unable to collect on its judgments from Argentina, NML has attempted to execute them against Argentina's property. That postjudgment litigation "has involved lengthy attachment proceedings before the district court and multiple appeals." *EM Ltd. v. Republic of Argentina*, 695 F.3d 201, 203, and n. 2 (CA2 2012). . . .

Since 2003, NML has pursued discovery of Argentina's property. In 2010, "[i]n order to locate Argentina's assets and accounts, learn how Argentina moves its assets through New York and around the world, and accurately identify the places and times when those assets might be subject to attachment and execution (whether under [United States law] or the law of foreign jurisdictions)," *id.*, at 203, NML served subpoenas on two nonparty banks, Bank of America (BOA) and Banco de la Nación Argentina (BNA), an Argentinian bank with a branch in New York City. For the most part, the two subpoenas target the same kinds of information: documents relating to accounts maintained by or on behalf of Argentina, documents identifying the opening and closing dates of Argentina's accounts,

---

* Section 1611 of the FSIA contains various exceptions-to-the-exceptions of § 1610, including that the § 1610 exceptions do not apply to funds held by foreign central banks and assets intended for military activity. — Eds.

1. The District Court's jurisdiction rested on Argentina's broad waiver of sovereign immunity memorialized in its bond indenture agreement, which states: "To the extent that [Argentina] or any of its revenues, assets or properties shall be entitled . . . to any immunity from suit . . . from attachment prior to judgment . . . from execution of a judgment or from any other legal or judicial process or remedy, . . . [Argentina] has irrevocably agreed not to claim and has irrevocably waived such immunity to the fullest extent permitted by the laws of such jurisdiction (and consents generally for the purposes of the [FSIA] to the giving of any relief or the issue of any process in connection with any Related Proceeding or Related Judgment). . . ."

current balances, transaction histories, records of electronic fund transfers, debts owed by the bank to Argentina, transfers in and out of Argentina's accounts, and information about transferors and transferees. . . .

Argentina, joined by BOA, moved to quash the BOA subpoena. NML moved to compel compliance. . . .

The District Court denied the motion to quash and granted the motions to compel. . . .

. . . Argentina appealed, arguing that the court's order transgressed the [FSIA] because it permitted discovery of Argentina's extraterritorial assets. The Second Circuit affirmed, holding that "because the Discovery Order involves discovery, not attachment of sovereign property, and because it is directed at third-party banks, not at Argentina itself, Argentina's sovereign immunity is not infringed."

We granted certiorari.

II. Analysis

A

The rules governing discovery in postjudgment execution proceedings are quite permissive. Federal Rule of Civil Procedure 69(a)(2) states that, "[i]n aid of the judgment or execution, the judgment creditor . . . may obtain discovery from any person — including the judgment debtor — as provided in the rules or by the procedure of the state where the court is located." . . . The general rule in the federal system is that, subject to the district court's discretion, "[p]arties may obtain discovery regarding any nonprivileged matter that is relevant to any party's claim or defense." Fed. Rule Civ. Proc. 26(b)(1).

. . . We . . . assume without deciding that . . . as the Second Circuit concluded below, "in a run-of-the-mill execution proceeding . . . the district court would have been within its discretion to order the discovery from third-party banks about the judgment debtor's assets located outside the United States." 695 F.3d, at 208. The single, narrow question before us is whether the [FSIA] specifies a different rule when the judgment debtor is a foreign state.

B

To understand the effect of the Act, one must know something about the regime it replaced. Foreign sovereign immunity is, and always has been, "a matter of grace and comity on the part of the United States, and not a restriction imposed by the Constitution." *Verlinden B.V. v. Central Bank of Nigeria,* 461 U.S. 480, 486 (1983). Accordingly, this Court's practice has been to "defe[r] to the decisions of the political branches" about whether and when to exercise judicial power over foreign states. *Ibid.* For the better part of the last two centuries, the political branch making the determination was the Executive, which typically requested immunity in all suits against friendly foreign states. *Id.,* at 486-487. But then, in 1952, the State Department embraced (in the so-called Tate Letter) the "restrictive" theory of sovereign immunity, which holds that immunity shields only a foreign sovereign's public, noncommercial acts. The Tate Letter "thr[ew] immunity determinations into some disarray," since "political considerations sometimes led the Department to file suggestions of immunity in cases where immunity would not have been available under the restrictive theory." *Republic of Austria v. Altmann*, 541 U.S. 677, 690 (2004). Further muddling matters, when in particular cases the State Department did *not* suggest immunity, courts made immunity determinations generally by reference to prior State Department decisions. Hence it was that sovereign immunity decisions were being made in two different branches, subject to a variety of factors, sometimes including diplomatic considerations. Not surprisingly, the governing standards were neither clear nor uniformly applied.

Congress abated the bedlam in 1976, replacing the old executive-driven, factor-intensive, loosely common-law-based immunity regime with the [FSIA's] comprehensive set of legal standards governing claims of immunity in every civil action against a foreign state. The key word there — which goes a long way toward deciding this case — is *comprehensive*. We have used that term often and advisedly to describe the Act's sweep. . . . This means that "[a]fter the enactment of the FSIA, the Act — and not the pre-existing common law — indisputably governs the determination of whether a foreign state is entitled to sovereign immunity." *Samantar v. Yousuf*, 560 U.S. 305, 313 (2010). As the Act itself instructs, "[c]laims of foreign states to immunity should henceforth be decided by courts . . . in conformity with the principles *set forth in this [Act]*." 28 U.S.C. § 1602 (emphasis added). Thus, any sort of immunity defense made by a foreign sovereign in an American court must stand on the Act's text. Or it must fall.

The text of the Act confers on foreign states two kinds of immunity. First and most significant, "a foreign state shall be immune from the jurisdiction of the courts of the United States . . . except as provided in sections 1605 to 1607." § 1604. That provision is of no help to Argentina here: A foreign state may waive jurisdictional immunity, § 1605(a)(1), and in this case Argentina did so. Consequently, the Act makes Argentina "liable in the same manner and to the same extent as a private individual under like circumstances." § 1606.

The Act's second immunity-conferring provision states that "the property in the United States of a foreign state shall be immune from attachment[,] arrest[,] and execution except as provided in sections 1610 and 1611 of this chapter." § 1609. The exceptions to this immunity defense (we will call it "execution immunity") are narrower. "The property in the United States of a foreign state" is subject to attachment, arrest, or execution if (1) it is "used for a commercial activity in the United States," § 1610(a), *and* (2) some other enumerated exception to immunity applies, such as the one allowing for waiver. The Act goes on to confer a more robust execution immunity on designated international-organization property, § 1611(a), property of a foreign central bank, § 1611(b)(1), and "property of a foreign state . . . [that] is, or is intended to be, used in connection with a military activity" . . . § 1611(b)(2).

That is the last of the Act's immunity-granting sections. There is no third provision forbidding or limiting discovery in aid of execution of a foreign-sovereign judgment debtor's assets. Argentina concedes that no part of the Act "expressly address[es] [postjudgment] discovery." Quite right. The Act speaks of discovery only once, in a subsection requiring courts to stay discovery requests directed to the United States that would interfere with criminal or national-security matters, § 1605(g)(1). And that section explicitly suspends certain Federal Rules of Civil Procedure when such a stay is entered, see § 1605(g)(4). . . . Far from containing the "plain statement" necessary to preclude application of federal discovery rules, the Act says not a word on the subject.

Argentina would have us draw meaning from this silence. . . . Because the Act gives "no indication that it was authorizing courts to inquire into state property beyond the court's limited enforcement authority," Argentina contends, discovery of assets that do not fall within an exception to execution immunity . . . is forbidden.

. . . Argentina maintains that, if a judgment creditor could not ultimately execute a judgment against certain property, then it has no business pursuing discovery of information pertaining to that property. But the reason for these subpoenas is that NML *does not yet know* what property Argentina has and where it is, let alone whether it is executable under the relevant jurisdiction's law. . . . [T]he subpoenas . . . ask for information about Argentina's worldwide assets generally, so that NML can identify where Argentina may be holding property that *is* subject to execution. To be sure, that request is bound to turn up information about property that Argentina regards as immune. But NML may think the same property *not* immune. In which case, Argentina's self-serving legal assertion will not automatically prevail; the District Court will have to settle the matter.

. . .

Today's decision leaves open what Argentina thinks is a gap in the statute. Could the 1976 Congress really have meant not to protect foreign states from postjudgment discovery "clearinghouses"? The riddle is not ours to solve (if it can be solved at all). It is of course possible that, had Congress anticipated the rather unusual circumstances of this case (foreign sovereign waives immunity; foreign sovereign owes money under valid judgments; foreign sovereign does not pay and apparently has no executable assets in the United States), it would have added to the Act a sentence conferring categorical discovery-in-aid-of-execution immunity on a foreign state's extraterritorial assets. Or, just as possible, it would have done no such thing. Either way, "[t]he question . . . is not what Congress 'would have wanted' but what Congress enacted in the FSIA." *Republic of Argentina v. Weltover, Inc.*, 504 U.S. 607, 618 (1992).

Nonetheless, Argentina and the United States urge us to consider the worrisome international-relations consequences of siding with the lower court. Discovery orders as sweeping as this one, the Government warns, will cause "a substantial invasion of [foreign states'] sovereignty," and will "[u]ndermin[e] international comity." Worse, such orders might provoke "reciprocal adverse treatment of the United States in foreign courts," and will "threaten harm to the United States' foreign relations more generally[.]" These apprehensions are better directed to that branch of government with authority to amend the Act — which,

866   Chapter 11. Foreign Sovereign Immunity

as it happens, is the same branch that forced our retirement from the immunity-by-factor-balancing business nearly 40 years ago.

The judgment of the Court of Appeals is affirmed.

. . .

[A dissenting opinion of Justice Ginsburg is omitted. Justice Sotomayor did not participate in the decision of the case.]

<hr>

NOTES AND QUESTIONS

1. **Practice: FSIA Limits on Execution.** Under what circumstances might a foreign state not be immune from suit under the FSIA but still have immunity from execution? Is this a problem for plaintiffs contemplating suit against foreign sovereigns? What litigation planning steps does it suggest?

2. **Practice: What Was at Stake in NML?** Why did NML want the discovery order it sought in this case? Why did Argentina resist it, given that the order would not require it to actually give up any assets? What alternative discovery order did Argentina want?

3. **The Structure of the Statute.** Why could Argentina claim (some) immunity from execution in *NML* even though it could not claim immunity from suit? What is the key difference in the two parts of the statute? Does this difference make sense from a policy perspective? Note that in the bond contract Argentina waived immunity from execution. Why did it still have some immunity against execution? Why didn't Argentina's immunity from execution matter to the Supreme Court?

4. **Enforcement of Arbitration Awards.** Note that FSIA § 1610(a)(6) allows attachment and execution on commercial property to enforce judgments confirming arbitration awards, irrespective of waiver. Why should arbitration awards be treated differently from court judgments? What limitations are there on enforcing arbitration awards against foreign sovereigns in the United States? Do these limits undermine FSIA § 1605(a)(6), which rejects immunity for suits to confirm arbitration awards?

5. **Discovery and the FSIA.** In *NML*, Justice Scalia concludes that because the FSIA makes no mention of discovery orders (other than in an unrelated provision), it provides foreign sovereigns no protection from them. Is this persuasive? Is there a way to argue that § 1609 does implicate discovery orders? Is there another way Argentina might argue that U.S. law protected it?

6. **Execution in Other Countries.** NML argued, in support of its discovery order, that it needed information about assets in other countries to decide whether it could execute on those assets. Why should that be a concern of the United States? Note that enforcement of U.S. judgments in foreign jurisdictions would be a matter of foreign law (and perhaps international law). In an earlier effort at enforcement, Argentine bondholders attempted to seize an Argentine navy ship docked at a port in the Republic of Ghana. Authorities in Ghana initially

approved attachment of the ship. Argentina then successfully sought an order for release from the International Tribunal for the Law of the Sea (ITLOS) pursuant to the Law of the Sea Convention — to which both Argentina and Ghana (but not the United States) were parties — on the ground that warships have immunity under the Convention. *The "ARA Libertad" Case (Argentina v. Ghana),* order of 15 December 2013. Ghana released the ship after the ITLOS order.

7. **Other Postjudgment Remedies.** In *NML,* the Court notes that Argentina had refinanced most of its defaulted bonds, although NML had refused to agree to the refinancing. In another part of the *NML* litigation, the district court concluded that Argentina was violating the original bond agreement by paying interest on the refinanced bonds and not repaying the bonds held by NML. At NML's request, the district judge enjoined Argentina from making any further payments on the refinanced bonds until it paid NML. Argentina appealed, arguing that the injunction violated the FSIA because it interfered with Argentina's use of immune assets. The court of appeals affirmed, *NML Capital, Ltd. v. Republic of Argentina,* 727 F.3d 230 (2d Cir. 2013), and the Supreme Court, on the same day that it decided the discovery order case, denied Argentina's petition for a writ of certiorari. Is it appropriate for U.S. courts to enjoin foreign sovereigns from taking certain actions? Does the decision in the discovery order case indicate why Argentina's argument in the injunction case was unavailing? As a practical matter, why do you think NML wanted the injunction? After the Supreme Court denied certiorari, Argentina defaulted on the refinanced bond debt. Eventually, after a new government was elected in Argentina, Argentina settled the dispute with NML.

E. Serving Process on Foreign Sovereigns

The FSIA also has special rules for serving process on foreign sovereigns and their agencies and instrumentalities. (Service of process on ordinary transnational defendants is covered in Chapter 9.) Federal Rule of Civil Procedure 4(j)(1) provides that a "foreign state or its political subdivision, agency, or instrumentality must be served in accordance with" the FSIA.

Foreign Sovereign Immunities Act, 28 U.S.C. § 1608

(a) Service in the courts of the United States and of the States shall be made upon a foreign state or political subdivision of a foreign state:

(1) by delivery of a copy of the summons and complaint in accordance with any special arrangement for service between the plaintiff and the foreign state or political subdivision; or

(2) if no special arrangement exists, by delivery of a copy of the summons and complaint in accordance with an applicable international convention on service of judicial documents; or

(3) if service cannot be made under paragraphs (1) or (2), by sending a copy of the summons and complaint and a notice of suit, together with a translation of each into the official language of the foreign state, by any form of mail requiring a signed receipt, to be addressed and dispatched by the clerk of the court to the head of the ministry of foreign affairs of the foreign state concerned, or

(4) if service cannot be made within 30 days under paragraph (3), by sending two copies of the summons and complaint and a notice of suit, together with a translation of each into the official language of the foreign state, by any form of mail requiring a signed receipt, to be addressed and dispatched by the clerk of the court to the Secretary of State in Washington, District of Columbia, to the attention of the Director of Special Consular Services — and the Secretary shall transmit one copy of the papers through diplomatic channels to the foreign state and shall send to the clerk of the court a certified copy of the diplomatic note indicating when the papers were transmitted.

. . .

(b) Service in the courts of the United States and of the States shall be made upon an agency or instrumentality of a foreign state:

(1) by delivery of a copy of the summons and complaint in accordance with any special arrangement for service between the plaintiff and the agency or instrumentality; or

(2) if no special arrangement exists, by delivery of a copy of the summons and complaint either to an officer, a managing or general agent, or to any other agent authorized by appointment or by law to receive service of process in the United States; or in accordance with an applicable international convention on service of judicial documents; or

(3) if service cannot be made under paragraphs (1) or (2), and if reasonably calculated to give actual notice, by delivery of a copy of the summons and complaint, together with a translation of each into the official language of the foreign state —

(A) as directed by an authority of the foreign state or political subdivision in response to a letter rogatory or request or

(B) by any form of mail requiring a signed receipt, to be addressed and dispatched by the clerk of the court to the agency or instrumentality to be served, or

(C) as directed by order of the court consistent with the law of the place where service is to be made.

NOTES AND QUESTIONS

1. **Serving a Sovereign versus Serving an Agency or Instrumentality.** Note that § 1608 provides different rules for serving "a foreign state or political subdivision of a foreign state" (§ 1608(a)) and for serving "an agency or instrumentality

of a foreign state (§ 1608(b)). What are the differences? Which one seems easier? Why are the two treated differently?

2. **Is the Defendant a Sovereign or an Agency or Instrumentality of a Foreign Sovereign?** For most purposes, the FSIA treats foreign sovereigns and their agencies or instrumentalities the same. Because § 1608 treats them differently, courts and litigants must find a way to tell the difference. In *Transaero, Inc. v. La Fuerza Aerea Boliviana*, 30 F.3d 148 (D.C. Cir. 1994), for example, the plaintiff served the defendant — the Bolivian Air Force — by registered mail in accordance with § 1608(b). When the Air Force failed to respond, the plaintiff obtained a default judgment; the claim was a breach of a contract to supply aviation parts, and the district court found jurisdiction under the FSIA's commercial activity exception. The Air Force then entered an appearance and moved to quash service, on the ground that it was part of the sovereign, and therefore service had to be made under § 1608(a). How would you answer this question? If you represented a plaintiff suing the Bolivian Air Force, which method of service would you chose?

   In *Transaero*, a divided court of appeals found the service defective. The majority adopted what it called a "categorical rule" that "depends on whether the defendant is the type of entity that is an integral part of a foreign state's political structure, or rather an entity whose structure and function is predominantly commercial." Applying this rule, it found the Air Force to be part of the sovereign (even though in the particular case it was acting in a commercial manner). The dissent thought the question should be decided on an entity-by-entity basis, based on a "factual investigation into the question whether the particular entity had been treated as a separate legal person." What would that entail? Which is the better reading of the statute? Which is the better rule for litigants?

3. **Strict Compliance.** In the *Transaero* case discussed in Note 2, the plaintiff further argued that its failure to strictly comply with § 1608(a) should be excused because it acted in good faith and the Bolivian Air Force received actual notice of the suit. The court of appeals rejected that argument:

> The authorities generally hold that section 1608(b) may be satisfied by technically faulty service that gives adequate notice to the foreign state. . . .
>
> Leniency in this case would disorder the statutory scheme. The Committee Report states that section 1608(a) "sets forth the exclusive procedures for service on a foreign state," but contains no such admonition for section 1608(b). *See* H.R. Rep. No. 1487 at 24, *reprinted in* 1976 U.S.C.C.A.N. at 6623. Section 1608(b)(3) allows simple delivery "if reasonably calculated to give actual notice," showing that Congress was there concerned with substance rather than form; but the analogous subsection of section 1608(a) says nothing about actual notice. The distinction is neatly tailored to the differences between "foreign states" and "agencies or instrumentalities." The latter, typically international commercial enterprises, often possess a sophisticated knowledge of the United States legal system that other organs of foreign governments may lack. *Cf. Practical Concepts, Inc. v. Republic of Bolivia*, 811 F.2d 1543, 1546 (D.C. Cir. 1987) (in suit against foreign state, the rule that objections to personal

jurisdiction are waived by an appearance should be sparingly applied because of foreign unfamiliarity with legal process). Thus section 1608(a) mandates service of the Ministry of Foreign Affairs, the department most likely to understand American procedure. We hold that strict adherence to the terms of 1608(a) is required. As Transaero failed to do so, the Bolivian Air Force was not properly served.

Is that the right result? What policy interest does it protect?

4. **Substantial Compliance.** In *Magness v. Russian Federation*, 247 F.3d 609 (5th Cir. 2001), the plaintiffs sued the Russian government and the State Diamond Fund (an agency of the Russian government) for expropriation of property. After a default judgment, the defendants objected to the methods of service. As to the Russian government, the court of appeals followed *Transaero* and held that strict compliance with § 1608(a) was required. As to the agency, the court held that "substantial compliance" was sufficient under § 1608(b) so long as the defendant had actual notice of the suit. However, the court went on to hold on the facts that the plaintiffs had the burden of showing actual notice, and that they had not met that burden. Is that the right approach? As a plaintiff, how might you be able to show actual notice to a sovereign defendant?

5. **The Proper Place for Service.** In *Republic of Sudan v. Harrison*, 139 S. Ct. 1048 (2019), a case arising from the attack on the Navy ship U.S.S. Cole in Yemen, plaintiffs purported to serve process on the Republic of Sudan by delivering process to the Sudanese Embassy in Washington, D.C., addressed to the Minister of Foreign Affairs. After plaintiffs obtained a default judgment and attempted to enforce it against Sudanese assets in New York banks, Sudan entered a limited appearance contesting the validity of the service. The court of appeals held that plaintiffs had satisfied the statutory requirement that service be made on the Minister of Foreign Affairs, but the U.S. Supreme Court reversed. Justice Alito wrote for an eight-Justice majority, concluding:

> The most natural reading of [FSIA § 1608(a)(3)] is that service must be mailed directly to the foreign minister's office in the foreign state . . . .
>
> A key term in § 1608(a)(3) is the past participle "addressed." A letter or package is "addressed" to an intended recipient when his or her name and "address" is placed on the outside of the item to be sent. And the noun "address," in the sense relevant here, means "the designation of a place (as a residence or place of business) where a person or organization may be found or communicated with." Webster's Third New International Dictionary 25 (1971) . . . . Since a foreign nation's embassy in the United States is neither the residence nor the usual place of business of that nation's foreign minister and is not a place where the minister can customarily be found, the most common understanding of the minister's "address" is inconsistent with the interpretation of § 1608(a)(3) adopted by the court below and advanced by respondents.

The Court also observed:

> Finally, respondents contend that it would be "the height of unfairness to throw out [their] judgment" based on the highly technical argument belatedly raised by petitioner. We understand respondents' exasperation and recognize

that enforcing compliance with § 1608(a)(3) may seem like an empty formality in this particular case, which involves highly publicized litigation of which the Government of Sudan may have been aware prior to entry of default judgment. But there are circumstances in which the rule of law demands adherence to strict requirements even when the equities of a particular case may seem to point in the opposite direction. . . .

Justice Thomas dissented, arguing that "the FSIA neither specifies nor precludes the use of any particular address. Instead, the statute requires only that the packet be sent to a particular person — 'the head of the ministry of foreign affairs.'"

REVIEW NOTES AND QUESTIONS

1. As a lawyer considering suit against a defendant connected with a foreign government, how would you approach the key questions of immunity? Consider: How do you determine whether the defendant is a "foreign state"? If it is a foreign state, what are the most likely exceptions to immunity? What if the defendant is not a foreign state? How might that affect your options to pursue your suit? If the defendant is a foreign state and no exception applies, what options, if any, might you have other than suit in U.S. court? How would you assess those options compared to a suit in a U.S. court?

2. As a lawyer representing a client contemplating a business transaction with a foreign sovereign, what does the law of foreign sovereign immunity suggest about how to structure the deal? What contractual options will you suggest your client pursue? How will you advise your client regarding the likelihood of adequate legal remedies? Remember that, in the event the sovereign breaches the contract, you will need to think not just about how to obtain a judgment but also about how to enforce the judgment. Can you think of a structural solution that might avoid foreign sovereign immunity altogether?

3. As a lawyer representing a client who wishes to sue an individual who is or was an official in a foreign government, how would you outline the immunity issues you will confront? What do you need to know about the claim? What do you need to know about the official? What else might be determinative of the outcome?

4. What do you think are the most persuasive policy justifications underlying foreign sovereign immunity? Does the doctrine as developed in the FSIA and the caselaw respond to those policy justifications? What trade-offs does foreign sovereign immunity entail? Are its justifications adequate in light of the trade-offs? What modifications, if any, might be appropriate?

CHAPTER 12

FOREIGN AFFAIRS LIMITS ON TRANSNATIONAL CASES

Many transnational cases are ordinary tort or contract disputes whose parties happen to be located in different nations; individually, these cases often have few implications beyond the immediate parties. But other cross-border controversies involve wider disputes that may raise significant issues of national foreign policy. In these cases, there may be questions about whether domestic courts, rather than the political branches of national governments that control foreign policy, should be involved in their resolution.

As discussed in Chapter 11, these concerns may arise when a foreign nation, its agencies or instrumentalities, or its officials are defendants in U.S. courts. Even in the absence of a foreign sovereign defendant, however, wide-ranging transnational disputes can take on aspects of foreign policy. As a result, U.S. courts have developed various judicial doctrines that may allow them to avoid making decisions in transnational litigation that has potential foreign policy implications.

This chapter examines three of these doctrines. First, the act of state doctrine declares (subject to various limitations and exceptions) that courts in the United States will not adjudicate the validity of the acts of foreign nations done in their own territory. As illustrated below, this doctrine is distinct from foreign sovereign immunity and may apply in cases where the foreign nation is not itself a defendant. Second, the political question doctrine holds that courts will dismiss cases that properly should be resolved by the "political branches" (that is, the executive and legislative branches). This doctrine exists in domestic cases as well, but it is sometimes thought to have particular force in transnational cases because of the political branches' role in conducting foreign policy. Third, state courts and state law may be precluded from reaching some transnational disputes by the constitutional doctrine of federal foreign affairs preemption, which holds that power over foreign affairs belongs (at least to some extent) to the national government rather than to state governments.

As you study the materials in this chapter, keep in mind the following questions: Why do the political branches — the executive and Congress — play the leading role in foreign policy? To which branches does the Constitution allocate different foreign affairs powers? Which branches are most (and least) competent institutionally to make foreign policy decisions? Should courts dismiss potentially valid legal claims merely because they implicate foreign policy? How else might parties vindicate their legal rights if their claims are dismissed based on these doctrines? By using these doctrines to dismiss claims, do courts abdicate their responsibility to decide legal issues?

A. The Act of State Doctrine

As discussed in Chapter 11, foreign sovereign immunity bars some claims challenging acts of foreign governments. But immunity is not always available when sovereign acts are at issue, for example because the foreign sovereign is the plaintiff rather than the defendant or is not party to the suit, or because the applicable law provides an exception to immunity. In these circumstances, though, judging the wrongfulness of the foreign act may still offend foreign sovereigns and raise substantial foreign policy issues. Should courts be concerned about this danger? The act of state doctrine, considered in this subsection, is a common law doctrine allowing U.S. courts to avoid making some such judgments. As you read the following cases, consider not only how the doctrine is structured, but also whether it is well designed to accomplish its objectives.

1. Basic Elements

Banco Nacional de Cuba v. Sabbatino

376 U.S. 398 (1964)

Mr. Justice HARLAN delivered the opinion of the Court.

The question which brought this case here, and is now found to be the dispositive issue, is whether the so-called act of state doctrine serves to sustain petitioner's claims in this litigation. Such claims are ultimately founded on a decree of the Government of Cuba expropriating certain property, the right to the proceeds of which is here in controversy. The act of state doctrine in its traditional formulation precludes the courts of this country from inquiring into the validity of the public acts a recognized foreign sovereign power committed within its own territory.

I

In February and July of 1960, respondent Farr, Whitlock & Co., an American commodity broker, contracted to purchase Cuban sugar . . . from a wholly owned subsidiary of Compania Azucarera Vertientes-Camaguey de Cuba (C.A.V.), a corporation organized under Cuban law whose capital stock was owned principally by United States residents. Farr, Whitlock agreed to pay for the sugar in New York upon presentation of the shipping documents and a sight draft.

On July 6, 1960, the Congress of the United States amended the Sugar Act of 1948 to permit a presidentially directed reduction of the sugar quota for Cuba. On the same day, President Eisenhower exercised the granted power. The day of the congressional enactment, the Cuban Council of Ministers adopted "Law No. 851," which characterized this reduction in the Cuban sugar quota as an act of "aggression, for political purposes" on the part of the United States, justifying the taking of countermeasures by Cuba. The law gave the Cuban President and Prime Minister discretionary power to nationalize by forced expropriation property or enterprises in which American nationals had an interest. Although a system of compensation was formally provided, the possibility of payment under it may well be deemed illusory. Our State Department has described the Cuban law as "manifestly in violation of those principles of international law which have long been accepted by the free countries of the West. It is in its essence discriminatory, arbitrary and confiscatory."

Between August 6 and August 9, 1960, the sugar covered by the contract between Farr, Whitlock and C.A.V. was loaded, destined for Morocco, onto the S.S. Hornfels, which was standing offshore at the Cuban port of Jucaro (Santa Maria). On the day loading commenced, the Cuban President and Prime Minister, acting pursuant to Law No. 851, issued Executive Power Resolution No. 1. It provided for the compulsory expropriation of all property and enterprises, and of rights and interests arising therefrom, of certain listed companies, including C.A.V., wholly or principally owned by American nationals. The preamble reiterated the alleged injustice of the American reduction of the Cuban sugar quota and emphasized the importance of Cuba's serving as an example for other countries to follow "in their struggle to free themselves from the brutal claws of Imperialism." In consequence of the resolution, the consent of the Cuban Government was necessary before a ship carrying sugar of a named company could leave Cuban waters. In order to obtain this consent, Farr, Whitlock, on August 11, entered into contracts, identical to those it had made with C.A.V., with the Banco Para el Comercio Exterior de Cuba, an instrumentality of the Cuban Government. The S.S. Hornfels sailed for Morocco on August 12.

Banco Exterior assigned the bills of lading to petitioner, also an instrumentality of the Cuban Government, which instructed its agent in New York, Societe Generale, to deliver the bills and a sight draft in the sum of $175,250.69 to Farr, Whitlock in return for payment. Societe Generale's initial tender of the documents was refused by Farr, Whitlock, which on the same day was notified of C.A.V.'s claim that, as rightful owner of the sugar, it was entitled to the proceeds. In return for a promise not to turn the funds over to petitioner or its agent, C.A.V. agreed to indemnify Farr, Whitlock for any loss. Farr, Whitlock subsequently accepted the shipping documents, negotiated the bills of lading to its customer, and received payment for the sugar. It refused, however, to hand over the proceeds to Societe Generale. Shortly thereafter, Farr, Whitlock was served with an order of the New York Supreme Court, which had appointed [Peter] Sabbatino [a New York resident] as Temporary Receiver of C.A.V.'s New York assets, enjoining it from taking any action in regard to the money claimed by C.A.V. that might result in its removal from the State. Following this, Farr, Whitlock, pursuant to court order, transferred the funds to Sabbatino, to abide the event of a judicial determination as to their ownership.

Petitioner [Banco Nacional] then instituted this action in the Federal District Court for the Southern District of New York. Alleging conversion of the bills of lading[,] it sought to recover the proceeds thereof from Farr, Whitlock and to enjoin [Sabbatino] from exercising any dominion over such proceeds. Upon motions to dismiss and for summary judgment, the District Court . . . [addressed] the question of Cuba's title to the sugar, on which rested petitioner's claim of conversion. While acknowledging the continuing vitality of the act of state doctrine, the court believed it inapplicable when the questioned foreign act is in violation of international law. Proceeding on the basis that a taking invalid under international law does not convey good title, the District Court found the Cuban expropriation decree to violate such law in three separate respects: it was motivated by a retaliatory, and not a public, purpose; it discriminated against American nationals; and it failed to provide adequate compensation. Summary judgment against petitioner was accordingly granted.

The Court of Appeals, affirming the decision on similar grounds, relied on two letters (not before the District Court) written by State Department officers which it took as evidence that the Executive Branch had no objection to a judicial testing of the Cuban decree's validity. The court was unwilling to declare that any one of the infirmities found by the District Court rendered the taking invalid under international law, but was satisfied that, in combination, they had that effect. We granted certiorari because the issues involved bear importantly on the conduct of the country's foreign relations and, more particularly, on the proper role of the Judicial Branch in this sensitive area. For reasons to follow, we decide that the judgment below must be reversed.

. . .

IV

The classic American statement of the act of state doctrine, which appears to have taken root in England as early as 1674, *Blad v. Bamfield*, 36 Eng. Rep. 992, and began to emerge in the jurisprudence of this country in the late eighteenth and early nineteenth centuries, is found in *Underhill v. Hernandez*, 168 U.S. 250 [1897], where Chief Justice Fuller said for a unanimous Court:

> "Every sovereign state is bound to respect the independence of every other sovereign state, and the courts of one country will not sit in judgment on the acts of the government of another, done within its own territory. Redress of grievances by reason of such acts must be obtained through the means open to be availed of by sovereign powers as between themselves."

Following this precept, the Court in that case refused to inquire into acts of Hernandez, a revolutionary Venezuelan military commander whose government had been later recognized by the United States, which were made the basis of a damage action in this country by Underhill, an American citizen, who claimed that he had had unlawfully assaulted, coerced, and detained in Venezuela by Hernandez.

None of this Court's subsequent cases in which the act of state doctrine was directly or peripherally involved manifest any retreat from *Underhill*. . . . On the contrary, in two of these cases, *Oetjen* [*v. Central Leather Co.*] and *Ricaud* [*v. American Metals Co.*], the doctrine as announced in *Underhill* was reaffirmed in unequivocal terms.

. . .

The outcome of this case, therefore, turns upon whether any of the contentions urged by respondents against the application of the act of state doctrine in the premises is acceptable: (1) that the doctrine does not apply to acts of state which violate international law, as is claimed to be the case here; (2) that the doctrine is inapplicable unless the Executive specifically interposes it in a particular case; and (3) that, in any event, the doctrine may not be invoked by a foreign government plaintiff in our courts.

V

Preliminarily, we discuss the foundations on which we deem the act of state doctrine to rest, and more particularly the question of whether state or federal law governs its application in a federal diversity case.

We do not believe that this doctrine is compelled either by the inherent nature of sovereign authority, as some of the earlier decision seem to imply, or by some principle of international law. If a transaction takes place in one jurisdiction and the forum is in another, the forum does not, by dismissing an action or by applying its own law, purport to divest the first jurisdiction of its territorial sovereignty; it merely declines to adjudicate, or makes applicable its own law to parties or property before it. The refusal of one country to enforce the penal laws of another is a typical example of an instance when a court will not entertain a cause of action arising in another jurisdiction. While historic notions of sovereign authority do bear upon the wisdom of employing the act of state doctrine, they do not dictate its existence.

That international law does not require application of the doctrine is evidenced by the practice of nations. Most of the countries rendering decisions on the subject [fail] to follow the rule rigidly. No international arbitral or judicial decision discovered suggests that international law prescribes recognition of sovereign acts of foreign governments, and apparently no claim has ever been raised before an international tribunal that failure to apply the act of state doctrine constitutes a breach of international obligation. If international law does not prescribe use of the doctrine, neither does it forbid application of the rule even if it is claimed that the act of state in question violated international law. The traditional view of international law is that it establishes substantive principles for determining whether one country has wronged another. Because of its peculiar "nation to nation" character, the usual method for an individual to seek relief is to exhaust local remedies and then repair to the executive authorities of his own state to persuade them to champion his claim in diplomacy or before an international tribunal. Although it is, of course, true that United States courts apply international law as a part of our own in appropriate circumstances, the public law of nations can hardly dictate to a country which is, in theory, wronged how to treat that wrong within its domestic borders.

Despite the broad statement in *Oetjen* that "The conduct of the foreign relations of our government is committed by the Constitution to the Executive and Legislative . . . departments," it cannot, of course, be thought that every case or controversy which touches foreign relations lies beyond judicial cognizance. The text of the Constitution does not require the act of state doctrine; it does not irrevocably remove from the judiciary the capacity to review the validity of foreign acts of state.

The act of state doctrine does, however, have "constitutional" underpinnings. It arises out of the basic relationships between branches of government in a system of separation of powers. It concerns the competency of dissimilar institutions to make and implement particular kinds of decisions in the area of international relations. The doctrine, as formulated in past decisions, expresses the strong sense of the Judicial Branch that its engagement in the task of passing on the validity of foreign acts of state may hinder, rather than further, this country's pursuit of goals both for itself and for the community of nations as a whole in the international sphere. . . .

We could, perhaps, in this diversity action, avoid the question of deciding whether federal or state law is applicable to this aspect of the litigation. New York has enunciated the act of state doctrine in terms that echo those of federal decisions . . . .

However, we are constrained to make it clear that an issue concerned with a basic choice regarding the competence and function of the Judiciary and the National Executive in ordering our relationships with other members of the international community must be treated exclusively as an aspect of federal law. It seems fair to assume that the Court did not have rules like the act of state doctrine in mind when it decided *Erie R. Co. v. Tompkins*. Soon thereafter, Professor Philip C. Jessup, now a judge of the International Court of Justice, recognized the potential dangers were *Erie* extended to legal problems affecting international relations. He cautioned that rules of international law should not be left to divergent and perhaps parochial state interpretations. His basic rationale is equally applicable to the act of state doctrine.

. . .

We conclude that the scope of the act of state doctrine must be determined according to federal law.

VI

If the act of state doctrine is a principle of decision binding on federal and state courts alike, but compelled by neither international law nor the Constitution, its continuing vitality depends on its capacity to reflect the proper distribution of functions between the judicial and political branches of the Government on matters bearing upon foreign affairs. It should be apparent that the greater the degree of codification or consensus concerning a particular area of international law, the more appropriate it is for the judiciary to render decisions regarding it, since the courts can then focus on the application of an agreed principle to circumstances of fact, rather than on the sensitive task of establishing a principle not inconsistent with the national interest or with international justice. It is also evident that some aspects of international law touch much more sharply on national nerves than do others; the less important the implications of an issue are for our foreign relations, the weaker the justification for exclusivity in the political branches. The balance of relevant considerations may also be shifted if the government which perpetrated the challenged act of state is no longer in existence, . . . for the political interest of this country may, as a result, be measurably altered. Therefore, rather than laying down or reaffirming an inflexible and all-encompassing rule in this case, we decide only that the Judicial Branch will not examine the validity of a taking of property within its own territory by a foreign sovereign government, extant and recognized by this country at the time of suit, in the absence of a treaty or other unambiguous agreement regarding controlling legal principles, even if the complaint alleges that the taking violates customary international law.

There are few if any issues in international law today on which opinion seems to be so divided as the limitations on a state's power to expropriate the property of aliens. There is, of course, authority, in international judicial and arbitral decisions, in the expressions of national governments, and among commentators for the view that a taking is improper under international law if it is not for a public purpose, is discriminatory, or is without provision for prompt, adequate, and effective compensation. However, Communist countries, although they have in fact provided a degree of compensation after diplomatic efforts, commonly recognize no obligation on the part of the taking country. Certain representatives of the newly independent and underdeveloped countries have questioned whether rules of state responsibility toward aliens can bind nations that have not consented to them, and it is argued that the traditionally articulated standards governing expropriation of property reflect "imperialist" interests, and are inappropriate to the circumstances of emergent states.

The disagreement as to relevant international law standards reflects an even more basic divergence between the national interests of capital importing and capital exporting nations, and between the social ideologies of those countries that favor state control of a considerable portion of the means of production and those that adhere to a free enterprise system. It is difficult to imagine the courts of this country embarking on adjudication in an area which touches more sensitively the practical and ideological goals of the various members of the community of nations.

When we consider the prospect of the courts' characterizing foreign expropriations, however justifiably, as invalid under international law and ineffective to pass title, the wisdom of the precedents is confirmed. . . .

The possible adverse consequences of a conclusion to the contrary of that implicit in these cases in highlighted by contrasting the practices of the political branch with the limitations of the judicial process in matters of this kind. Following an expropriation of any significance, the Executive engages in diplomacy aimed to assure that United States citizens who are harmed are compensated fairly. Representing all claimants of this country, it will often be able, either by bilateral or multilateral talks, by submission to the United Nations, or by the employment of economic and political sanctions, to achieve some degree of general redress. Judicial determinations of invalidity of title can, on the other hand, have only an occasional impact, since they depend on the fortuitous circumstance of the property in question being brought into this country. Such decisions would, if the acts involved were declared invalid, often be likely to give offense to the expropriating country; since the concept of territorial sovereignty is so deep-seated, any state may resent the refusal of the courts of another sovereign to accord validity to acts within its territorial borders. Piecemeal dispositions of this sort involving the probability of affront to another state could seriously interfere with negotiations being carried on by the Executive Branch, and might prevent or render less favorable the terms of an agreement that could otherwise be reached. Relations with third countries which have engaged in similar expropriations would not be immune from effect.

The dangers of such adjudication are present regardless of whether the State Department has, as it did in this case, asserted that the relevant act violated international law. If the Executive Branch has undertaken negotiations with an expropriating country, but has refrained from claims of violation of the law of nations, a determination to that effect by a court might be regarded as a serious insult, while a finding of compliance with international law would greatly strengthen the bargaining hand of the other state with consequent detriment to American interests.

Even if the State Department has proclaimed the impropriety of the expropriation, the stamp of approval of its view by a judicial tribunal, however, impartial, might increase any affront, and the judicial decision might occur at a time, almost always well after the taking, when such an impact would be contrary to our national interest. Considerably more serious and far-reaching consequences would flow from a judicial finding that international law standards had been met if that determination flew in the face of a State Department proclamation to the contrary. When articulating principles of international law in its relations with other states, the Executive Branch speaks not only as an interpreter of generally accepted and traditional rules, as would the courts, but also as an advocate of standards it believes desirable for the community of nations and protective of national concerns. In short, whatever way the matter is cut, the possibility of conflict between the Judicial and Executive Branches could hardly be avoided.

. . .

Another serious consequence of the exception pressed by respondents would be to render uncertain titles in foreign commerce, with the possible consequence of altering the flow of international trade. If the attitude of the United States courts were unclear, one buying expropriated goods would not know if he could safely import them into this country. Even were takings known to be invalid, one would have difficulty determining, after goods had changed hands several times, whether the particular articles in question were the product of an ineffective state act.

Against the force of such considerations, we find respondents' countervailing arguments quite unpersuasive. Their basic contention is that United States courts could make a significant contribution to the growth of international law, a contribution whose importance, it is said, would be magnified by the relative paucity of decisional law by international bodies. But, given the fluidity of present world conditions, the effectiveness of such a patchwork approach toward the formulation of an acceptable body of law concerning state responsibility for expropriations is, to say the least, highly conjectural. Moreover, it rests upon the sanguine presupposition that the decisions of the courts of the world's major capital exporting country and principal exponent of the free enterprise system would be accepted as disinterested expressions of sound legal principle by those adhering to widely different ideologies.

It is contended that . . . it is the function of the courts to justly decide individual disputes before them. Perhaps the most typical act of state case involves the original owner or his assignee suing one not in association with the expropriating state who has had "title" transferred to him. But it is difficult to regard the claim of the original owner, who otherwise may be recompensed through diplomatic channels, as more demanding of judicial cognizance than the claim of title by the innocent third party purchaser, who, if the property is taken from him, is without any remedy.

Respondents claim that the economic pressure resulting from the proposed exception to the act of state doctrine will materially add to the protection of United States investors. We are not convinced, even assuming the relevance of this contention.

Expropriations take place for a variety of reasons, political and ideological, as well as economic. When one considers the variety of means possessed by this country to make secure foreign investment, the persuasive or coercive effect of judicial invalidation of acts of expropriation dwindles in comparison. The newly independent states are in need of continuing foreign investment; the creation of a climate unfavorable to such investment by wholesale confiscations may well work to their long-run economic disadvantage. Foreign aid given to many of these countries provides a powerful lever in the hands of the political branches to ensure fair treatment of United States nationals. Ultimately, the sanctions of economic embargo and the freezing of assets in this country may be employed. Any country willing to brave any or all of these consequences is unlikely to be deterred by sporadic judicial decisions directly affecting only property brought to our shores. If the political branches are unwilling to exercise their ample powers to effect compensation, this reflects a judgment of the national interest which the judiciary would be ill advised to undermine indirectly.

. . .

However offensive to the public policy of this country and its constituent States an expropriation of this kind may be, we conclude that both the national interest and progress toward the goal of establishing the rule of law among nations are best served by maintaining intact the act of state doctrine in this realm of its application.

. . .

The judgment of the Court of Appeals is reversed, and the case is remanded to the District Court for proceedings consistent with this opinion. . . .

Mr. Justice WHITE, dissenting.

I am dismayed that the Court has, with one broad stroke, declared the ascertainment and application of international law beyond the competence of the courts of the United States in a large and important category of cases. I am also disappointed in the Court's declaration that the acts of a sovereign state with regard to the property of aliens within its borders are beyond the reach of international law in the courts of this country. However clearly established that law may be, a sovereign may violate it with impunity, except insofar as the political branches of the government may provide a remedy. This backward-looking doctrine, never before declared in this Court, is carried a disconcerting step further: not only are the courts powerless to question acts of state proscribed by international law, but they are likewise powerless to refuse to adjudicate the claim founded upon a foreign law; they must render judgment, and thereby validate the lawless act. Since the Court expressly extends its ruling to all acts of state expropriating property, however clearly inconsistent with the international community, all discriminatory expropriations of the property of aliens, as for example the taking of properties of persons belonging to certain races, religions or nationalities, are entitled to automatic validation in the courts of the United States. No other civilized country has found such a rigid rule necessary for the survival of the Executive Branch of its government; the Executive of no other government seems to require such insulation from international law adjudications in its courts; and no other judiciary is apparently so incompetent to ascertain and apply international law.

. . .

Alfred Dunhill of London, Inc. v. Republic of Cuba

425 U.S. 682 (1976)

Mr. Justice WHITE delivered the opinion of the Court.

[The underlying facts arose out of Cuba's nationalization of its cigar industry. Somewhat oversimplified, they were as follows. After the nationalization (called an "intervention"), the Cuban government appointed its own personnel (called the "interventors") to continue to operate the cigar industry, including for export. Dunhill, a British cigar importer, purchased cigars before and after the intervention. After the intervention, Dunhill mistakenly paid the interventors for cigars purchased before the intervention. Dunhill sought return of the payments, which the interventors refused.]

The District Court and the Court of Appeals held that, for purposes of this litigation interventors were not entitled to the pre-intervention accounts receivable by virtue of the 1960 confiscation and that, despite other arguments to the contrary, nothing based on their claim to those accounts entitled interventors to retain monies mistakenly paid on those accounts by importers. We do not disturb these conclusions. The Court of Appeals nevertheless observed that interventors had "ignored" demands for the return of the monies and had "fail[ed] to honor the importers' demand (which was confirmed by the Cuban government's counsel at trial)." This conduct was considered to be "the Cuban government's repudiation of its obligation to return the funds" and to constitute an act of state not subject to question in our courts.

. . . Concededly, [the interventors] declined to pay over the funds; but refusal to repay does not necessarily . . . demonstrate that, in addition to authority to operate commercial businesses, to pay their bills and to collect their accounts receivable, interventors had been invested with sovereign authority to repudiate all or any part of the debts incurred by those businesses. Indeed, it is difficult to believe that they had the power selectively to refuse payment of legitimate debts arising from the operation of those commercial enterprises.

In *The Gul Djemal*, 264 U.S. 90 (1924), a supplier libeled and caused the arrest of the *Gul Djemal*, a steamship owned and operated for commercial purposes by the Turkish Government, in an effort to recover for supplies and services sold to and performed for the ship. The ship's master, a duly commissioned officer of the Turkish Navy, appeared in court and asserted sovereign immunity, claiming that such an assertion defeated the court's jurisdiction. A direct appeal was taken to this Court, where it was held that the master's assertion of sovereign immunity was insufficient because his mere representation of his government as master of a commercial ship furnished no basis for assuming he was entitled to represent the sovereign in other capacities. Here there is no more reason to suppose that the interventors possess governmental, as opposed to commercial, authority than there was to suppose that the master of the *Gul Djemal* possessed such authority. The master of the *Gul Djemal* claimed the authority to assert sovereign immunity while the interventors claim that they had the authority to commit an act of state, but the difference is unimportant. In both cases, a party claimed to have had the authority to exercise sovereign power. In both, the only authority shown is commercial authority.

We thus disagree with the Court of Appeals that the mere refusal of the interventors to repay funds followed by a failure to prove that interventors "were not acting within the scope of their authority as agents of the Cuban government" satisfied respondents' burden of establishing their act of state defense. Nor do we consider *Underhill v. Hernandez*, 168 U.S. 25 (1897), heavily relied upon by the Court of Appeals, to require a contrary conclusion. In that case, and in *Oetjen v. Central Leather Co.*, 246 U.S. 297 (1918), and *Ricaud v. American Metal Co.*, 246 U.S. 304 (1918), it was apparently concluded that the facts were sufficient to demonstrate that the conduct in question was the public act of those with authority to exercise sovereign powers and was entitled to respect in our courts. We draw no such conclusion from the facts of the case before us now. As the District Court found, the only evidence of an act of state other than the act of nonpayment by interventors was "a statement by counsel for the interventors, during trial, that the Cuban Government and the interventors denied liability and had refused to make repayment." But this merely restated respondents' original legal position and adds little, if anything, to the proof of an act of state. No statute, decree, order, or resolution of the Cuban Government itself was offered in evidence indicating that Cuba had repudiated its obligations in general or any class thereof or that it had, as a sovereign matter, determined to confiscate the amounts due three foreign importers.

. . .

Mr. Justice MARSHALL, with whom Mr. Justice BRENNAN, Mr. Justice STEWART, and Mr. Justice BLACKMUN join, dissenting.

The act of state doctrine commits the courts of this country not to sit in judgment on the acts of a foreign government performed within its own territory. Under any realistic view of the facts of this case, the interventors' retention of and refusal to return funds paid to them by Dunhill constitute an act of state, and no affirmative recovery by Dunhill can rest on the invalidity of that conduct. The Court of Appeals so concluded, and I would affirm its judgment.

. . .

The interventors have not taken any discrete, overt action for which to claim the status of an act of state. Rather, they have received and long retained the money paid to them for pre-intervention shipments, and they have ignored Dunhill's demands for its return. The Court declines to view this course of conduct as reflecting an exercise of sovereign power to retain the funds at issue after they arrived in Cuba . . . .

I do not understand the Court to suggest, however, that the act of state doctrine can be triggered only by a "statute, decree, order, or resolution" of a foreign government, or that the presence of an act of state can only be demonstrated by some affirmative action by the foreign sovereign. While it is true that an act of state generally takes the form of an executive or legislative step formalized in a decree or measure, that is only because duly constituted governments generally act through formal means. When they do not, their acts are no less the acts of a state, and the doctrine, being a practical one, is no less applicable. Thus, in *Underhill v. Hernandez*, 168 U.S. 250 (1897), where the plaintiff sought recovery for his detention in Venezuela by reason of the then revolutionary forces' refusal to grant him a passport out of Ciudad Bolivar, the Court held that the act of state doctrine "must necessarily extend to the agents of governments ruling by paramount force as [a] matter of fact." The cases of *Oetjen v. Central Leather Co.*, 246 U.S. 297 (1918), and *Ricaud v. American Metal Co.*, 246 U.S. 304 (1918), are further illustrations of the practical approach the Court has always taken in determining whether an act of state is present. In each case, the plaintiff claimed title to goods purchased from Mexican sellers but confiscated by generals of the Constitutionalist Carranza forces before delivery to the plaintiffs. The Generals, Villa and Pereyra respectively, had sold the goods to intermediate purchasers for the furtherance of the revolution, and the goods thereafter came into the United States in the possession of the defendant assignees. The Court held that the seizures in question must be viewed as the action, in time of civil war, of a duly commissioned agent of the prevailing Mexican Government, and could not be subjected to the scrutiny of another sovereign's courts.

These cases demonstrate not only that an act of state need not be formalized in any particular manner, but also that it need not take the form of active, rather than passive, conduct. Had General Villa come accidentally into possession of the hides sought to be replevied in *Oetjen*, instead of seizing them, and then simply refused the plaintiff's demand for possession, the result could not have been any different. Indeed, so far as the report of the *Underhill* case reveals, the plaintiff, in seeking recovery for his detention, challenged no more than General Hernandez' refusal to do anything when he demanded his passport.

That a foreign sovereign has issued no formal decree and performed no "affirmative" act is not fatal, then, to an act of state claim. If the foreign state has exercised a sovereign power either to act or to refrain from acting, there is an act of state. . . .

The Court, I take it, does not dispute that a refusal to act constitutes an act of state when shown to reflect the exercise of sovereign power. Rather, the Court finds no exercise of sovereign power to retain the funds at issue after they arrived in Cuba. . . .

[However,] [c]ounsel for the interventors and the Republic of Cuba stated at trial, in his brief to this Court, and again in his oral argument in this Court:

> "[U]nder the act of state doctrine the Cuban government, in accepting, expropriating, seizing, nationalizing, whatever other words you want, to take this money, has done so pursuant to a regulation, a law, a decree of the government of Cuba, and therefore the courts of this state will not look into the matter nor will the federal court."
>
> "Now, I am not talking about the extraterritorial effect of an act of state. I am talking about a territorial effect, namely, the seizure or the acceptance or the appropriation of this money when it got down to Cuba. . . . And at that time, the Cuban government took this money and, under the act of state doctrine, it belongs to the Cuban government."

. . .

The above-quoted statements of counsel are not themselves acts of state. But as authoritative representations of the position of counsel's clients, the interventors and the Republic of Cuba, with respect to the monies in their possession, these statements do serve to confirm that the continued retention of those monies has been undertaken as an exercise of sovereign power.

W.S. Kirkpatrick & Co., Inc. v. Environmental Tectonics Corp., International

493 U.S. 400 (1990)

Justice SCALIA delivered the opinion of the Court.

. . .

In this case, we must decide whether the act of state doctrine bars a court in the United States from entertaining a cause of action that does not rest upon the asserted invalidity of an official act of a foreign sovereign, but that does require imputing to foreign officials an unlawful motivation (the obtaining of bribes) in the performance of such an official act.

I

The facts as alleged in respondent's complaint are as follows: In 1981, Harry Carpenter, who was then Chairman of the Board and Chief Executive Officer of petitioner W.S. Kirkpatrick & Co., Inc. (Kirkpatrick), learned that the Republic of Nigeria was interested in contracting for the construction and equipment of an aeromedical center at Kaduna Air Force Base in Nigeria. He made arrangements with Benson "Tunde" Akindele, a Nigerian citizen, whereby Akindele would endeavor to secure the contract for Kirkpatrick. It was agreed that, in the event the contract was awarded to Kirkpatrick, Kirkpatrick would pay to two Panamanian entities controlled by Akindele a "commission" equal to 20% of the contract price, which would in turn be given as a bribe to officials of the Nigerian Government. In accordance with this plan, the contract was awarded to petitioner W.S. Kirkpatrick & Co., International (Kirkpatrick International), a wholly owned subsidiary of Kirkpatrick; Kirkpatrick paid the promised "commission" to the appointed Panamanian entities; and those funds were disbursed as bribes. All parties agree that Nigerian law prohibits both the payment and the receipt of bribes in connection with the award of a government contract.

Respondent Environmental Tectonics Corporation, International, an unsuccessful bidder for the Kaduna contract, learned of the 20% "commission" and brought the matter to the attention of the Nigerian Air Force and the United States Embassy in Lagos. Following an investigation by the Federal Bureau of Investigation, the United States Attorney for the District of New Jersey brought charges against both Kirkpatrick and Carpenter for violations of the Foreign Corrupt Practices Act of 1977, and both pleaded guilty.

Respondent then brought this civil action in the United States District Court for the District of New Jersey against Carpenter, Akindele, petitioners, and others, seeking damages under the Racketeer Influenced and Corrupt Organizations Act, the Robinson-Patman Act, and the New Jersey Anti-Racketeering Act. The defendants moved to dismiss the complaint under Rule 12(b)(6) of the Federal Rules of Civil Procedure on the ground that the action was barred by the act of state doctrine.

The District Court, having requested and received a letter expressing the views of the legal advisor to the United States Department of State as to the applicability of the act of state doctrine, treated the motion as one for summary judgment under Rule 56 of the Federal Rules of Civil Procedure, and granted the motion. . . . [T]the court held that respondent's suit had to be dismissed because, in order to prevail, respondents would have to show that

> "the defendants or certain of them intended to wrongfully influence the decision to award the Nigerian Contract by payment of a bribe, that the Government of Nigeria, its officials, or other representatives knew of the offered consideration for awarding the Nigerian Contract to Kirkpatrick, that the bribe was actually received or anticipated and that, 'but for' the payment or anticipation of the payment of the bribe, ETC would have been awarded the Nigerian Contract."

The Court of Appeals for the Third Circuit reversed. . . .

II

This Court's description of the jurisprudential foundation for the act of state doctrine has undergone some evolution over the years. We once viewed the doctrine as an expression of international law, resting upon "the highest considerations of international comity and expediency," *Oetjen v. Central Leather Co.*, 246 U.S.

297 (1918). We have more recently described it, however, as a consequence of domestic separation of powers, reflecting "the strong sense of the Judicial Branch that its engagement in the task of passing on the validity of foreign acts of state may hinder" the conduct of foreign affairs, *Banco Nacional de Cuba v. Sabbatino*, 376 U.S. 398 (1964). Some Justices have suggested possible exceptions to application of the doctrine, where one or both of the foregoing policies would seemingly not be served: an exception, for example, for acts of state that consist of commercial transactions, since neither modern international comity nor the current position of our Executive Branch accorded sovereign immunity to such acts, see *Alfred Dunhill of London, Inc. v. Republic of Cuba*, 425 U.S. 682 (1976) (opinion of White, J.); or an exception for cases in which the Executive Branch has represented that it has no objection to denying validity to the foreign sovereign act, since then the courts would be impeding no foreign policy goals. . . .

We find . . . [that] the predicate for application of the act of state doctrine does not exist. Nothing in the present suit requires the court to declare invalid, and thus ineffective as "a rule of decision for the courts of this country," *Ricaud v. American Metal Co.*, 246 U.S. 304 (1918), the official act of a foreign sovereign.

In every case in which we have held the act of state doctrine applicable, the relief sought or the defense interposed would have required a court in the United States to declare invalid the official act of a foreign sovereign performed within its own territory. In *Underhill v. Hernandez*, 168 U.S. 250 (1897), holding the defendant's detention of the plaintiff to be tortious would have required denying legal effect to "acts of a military commander representing the authority of the revolutionary party as government, which afterwards succeeded and was recognized by the United States." In *Oetjen v. Central Leather Co.* and in *Ricaud v. American Metal Co.* denying title to the party who claimed through purchase from Mexico would have required declaring that government's prior seizure of the property, within its own territory, legally ineffective. In *Sabbatino*, upholding the defendant's claim to the funds would have required a holding that Cuba's expropriation of goods located in Havana was null and void. In the present case, by contrast, neither the claim nor any asserted defense requires a determination that Nigeria's contract with Kirkpatrick International was, or was not, effective.

Petitioners point out, however, that the facts necessary to establish respondent's claim will also establish that the contract was unlawful. Specifically, they note that, in order to prevail, respondent must prove that petitioner Kirkpatrick made, and Nigerian officials received, payments that violate Nigerian law, which would, they assert, support a finding that the contract is invalid under Nigerian law. Assuming that to be true, it still does not suffice. The act of state doctrine is not some vague doctrine of abstention, but a *"principle of decision* binding on federal and state courts alike." *Sabbatino, supra*, 376 U.S. at 427 (emphasis added). As we said in *Ricaud*, "the act within its own boundaries of one sovereign State . . . becomes . . . a rule of decision for the courts of this country." 246 U.S. at 310. Act of state issues only arise when a court *must decide* — that is, when the outcome of the case turns upon — the effect of official action by a foreign sovereign. When that question is not in the case, neither is the act of state doctrine. That is the situation here. Regardless of what the court's factual findings may suggest as to the legality of the Nigerian contract, its legality is simply not a question to be decided in the present suit, and there is thus no occasion to apply the rule of decision that the act of state doctrine requires.

. . .

Petitioners insist, however, that the policies underlying our act of state cases — international comity, respect for the sovereignty of foreign nations on their own territory, and the avoidance of embarrassment to the Executive Branch in its conduct of foreign relations — are implicated in the present case because, as the District Court found, a determination that Nigerian officials demanded and accepted a bribe would impugn or question the nobility of a foreign nation's motivations, and would result in embarrassment to the sovereign or constitute interference in the conduct of foreign policy of the United States. The United States, as *amicus curiae*, favors the same approach to the act of state doctrine, though disagreeing with petitioners as to the outcome it produces in the present case. We should not, the United States urges, "attach dispositive significance to the fact that this suit involves only the 'motivation' for, rather than the 'validity' of, a foreign sovereign act," and should eschew "any rigid formula for the resolution of act of state cases generally." In some future case, perhaps, "litigation . . . based on alleged corruption in the award of contracts or other commercially oriented activities of foreign governments could sufficiently touch on national nerves that the act of state doctrine or related principles of abstention would appropriately be found to bar the suit," and we should therefore resolve this case on the narrowest possible ground, *viz.*, that the letter from the legal advisor to the District Court gives sufficient indication that, "in the setting of this case," the act of state doctrine poses no bar to adjudication.

These urgings are deceptively similar to what we said in *Sabbatino*, where we observed that sometimes, even though the validity of the act of a foreign sovereign within its own territory is called into question, the policies underlying the act of state doctrine may not justify its application. We suggested that a sort of balancing approach could be applied — the balance shifting against application of the doctrine, for example, if the government that committed the challenged act of state is no longer in existence. But what is appropriate in order to avoid unquestioning judicial acceptance of the acts of foreign sovereigns is not similarly appropriate for the quite opposite purpose of expanding judicial incapacities where such acts are not directly (or even indirectly) involved. It is one thing to suggest, as we have, that the policies underlying the act of state doctrine should be considered in deciding whether, despite the doctrine's technical availability, it should nonetheless not be invoked; it is something quite different to suggest that those underlying policies are a doctrine unto themselves, justifying expansion of the act of state doctrine (or, as the United States puts it, unspecified "related principles of abstention") into new and uncharted fields.

The short of the matter is this: Courts in the United States have the power, and ordinarily the obligation, to decide cases and controversies properly presented to them. The act of state doctrine does not establish an exception for cases and controversies that may embarrass foreign governments, but merely requires that, in the process of deciding, the acts of foreign sovereigns taken within their own jurisdictions shall be deemed valid. That doctrine has no application to the present case, because the validity of no foreign sovereign act is at issue.

The judgment of the Court of Appeals for the Third Circuit is affirmed.

. . .

NOTES AND QUESTIONS

1. **Understanding the *Sabbatino* Case.** The facts of *Sabbatino* are complex, and it may help to diagram the underlying transaction. Whose interest did Sabbatino represent? What was the nature of the plaintiff's claim? Was the act of state doctrine invoked by the plaintiff or the defendant? What was the doctrine's effect on the outcome of the litigation? What would have happened if the doctrine had not applied? What is the basis — including the constitutional basis — for the act of state doctrine?

2. **The Act of State Doctrine and Foreign Sovereign Immunity.** Note that the act of state doctrine is distinct from foreign sovereign immunity, which was covered in Chapter 11. Why was foreign sovereign immunity not an issue in *Sabbatino*? In many act of state cases there is no sovereign party. For example, *Oetjen v. Central Leather Co.*, 246 U.S. 297 (1918), and *Ricaud v. American Metal Co.*, 246 U.S. 304 (1918) — two classic act of state cases discussed in *Sabbatino* and *Dunhill* — were disputes between wholly private parties. In a part of the *Sabbatino* case omitted above, the Court described the cases as follows:

> *Oetjen* involved a seizure of hides from a Mexican citizen as a military levy by General Villa, acting for the forces of General Carranza, whose government was recognized by this country subsequent to the trial but prior to decision by this Court. The hides were sold to a Texas corporation which shipped them to the United States and assigned them to defendant. As assignee of the original owner, plaintiff replevied the hides, claiming that they had been seized in violation of the Hague Conventions.
>
> In *Ricaud*, the facts were similar — another general of the Carranza forces seized lead bullion as a military levy — except that the property taken belonged to an American citizen. The . . . opinion stated that the rule:

>> does not deprive the courts of jurisdiction once acquired over a case. It requires only that when it is made to appear that the foreign government has acted in a given way on the subject matter of the litigation, the details of such action or the merit of the result cannot be questioned, but must be accepted by our courts as a rule for their decision. To accept a ruling authority and to decide accordingly is not a surrender or abandonment of jurisdiction, but is an exercise of it. It results that the title to the property in this case must be determined by the result of the action taken by the military authorities of Mexico. . . .

Why did the act of state doctrine come into play in those cases, and what was its effect? What does it mean to say the foreign act "must be accepted . . . as a rule of decision"? For a modern application of the act of state doctrine to resolve property claims between two private parties, see *Von Saher v. Norton Simon Museum*, 897 F.3d 1141 (9th Cir. 2018) (court could not reexamine acts of Netherlands government giving title to person from whom museum obtained a disputed painting).

In addition, as in *Dunhill*, a foreign sovereign defendant may invoke the act of state doctrine even in the absence of foreign sovereign immunity. (Note that because foreign sovereign immunity is jurisdictional, it is typically decided first.) Why might there not have been immunity in *Dunhill*? Does that suggest that there should not have been an act of state concern also?

3. **Purposes of the Act of State Doctrine.** According to the Court in *Sabbatino*, the act of state doctrine is motivated by concerns over the conduct of foreign affairs. Is that an adequate explanation? Why would a decision on the merits in *Sabbatino* have been a problem? Are act of state cases particularly problematic for foreign affairs? What does the doctrine assume about federal/state relations in the area of foreign affairs and about the role of the executive branch in making determinations about the content of international law?

4. **Elements of the Act of State Doctrine.** It may be useful to think of the act of state doctrine as requiring the presence of certain basic elements, subject to several potential exceptions discussed in the next subsection. What are these basic elements? The Court in *Sabbatino* quoted the "classic" statement of the doctrine from *Underhill v. Hernandez*, 168 U.S. 250 (1897): "[T]he courts of one country will not sit in judgment on the acts of the government of another, done within its own territory." Is that helpful? What elements does it suggest? Why did this formulation require application of the act of state doctrine in *Underhill*, in which a U.S. citizen sued a Venezuelan general for wrongfully detaining him in Venezuela?

5. **Acts Within Foreign Sovereign Territory.** The *Underhill* statement quoted above implies that sovereign acts done *outside* sovereign territory are not covered by the doctrine. In *Agudas Chasidei Chabad of U.S. v. Russian Federation*, 528 F.3d 934 (D.C. Cir. 2008), also discussed in Chapter 11, plaintiff sought the return of religious books and documents allegedly seized by the Soviet government (immunity was defeated by the takings exception to the Foreign Sovereign Immunities Act (FSIA)). After rejecting immunity, the court considered the act of state doctrine. It held that the doctrine did not apply to at least some of the books and documents, because they had been seized by the Soviet army in Poland. On the other hand, the court found that the doctrine might bar claims with respect to documents seized by the Soviet army in Russia. Does that make sense? Are the foreign policy considerations different?

6. **Sovereign Acts.** Why did the majority in *Dunhill* think the act of state doctrine did not apply? Does it make sense to say that the acts of a government agent are not acts of the government? In the long-running dispute between McKesson Corporation and Iran, encountered elsewhere in this book (Chapters 2 and 11), Iran claimed among other things that the suit was barred by the act of state doctrine. *McKesson Corp. v. Islamic Republic of Iran*, 672 F.3d 1066 (D.C. Cir. 2012). Iran had allegedly used its influence over the board of directors of

Pak Dairy to deprive McKesson of its rights as a minority shareholder in Pak. The court of appeals refused to apply the act of state doctrine, holding in part:

> Although the Supreme Court has not defined the contours of the "official action" requirement of the act of state doctrine, the courts of appeals have understood the concept as referring to conduct that is by nature distinctly sovereign, i.e., conduct that cannot be undertaken by a private individual or entity. For example, this Court held that the denial of an official license permitting the removal of uranium from Kazakhstan was a sovereign act, as was a transfer of corporate shares to a state entity. *World Wide Minerals, Ltd. v. Republic of Kazakhstan*, 296 F.3d 1154, 1165-66 (D.C. Cir. 2002). In direct contrast to the facts in this case, the Court emphasized that the "transfer and alleged conversion were accomplished pursuant to an official decree of the Republic of Kazakhstan." Similarly, this Court applied the act of state doctrine where a foreign government's finance minister officially ordered payment of a tax to the foreign government through a "private letter ruling, which under Brazilian law binds the parties." *Riggs Nat. Corp. v. Comm'r of Internal Revenue Serv.*, 163 F.3d 1363, 1366-68 (D.C. Cir. 1999). *See also Society of Lloyd's v. Siemon-Netto*, 457 F.3d 94, 102-03 (D.C. Cir. 2006) (applying the act of state doctrine to preclude a challenge to the validity of a foreign statute). In each of these cases, the Court applied the act of state doctrine to preclude challenges to actions that, by their nature, could only be undertaken by a sovereign power.
>
> The facts of this case differ dramatically from prior cases in which the act of state doctrine applied. Although McKesson has characterized its claim as one for "expropriation," this is not a typical expropriation case in which a foreign government acts in its sovereign capacity to take private property for a public purpose. Rather, this case turns on claims that agents of the Iranian government — acting as representatives of various agencies and companies — took over Pak's board of directors, froze out McKesson's board members, and stopped paying McKesson's dividends. The facts allege a pattern of conduct by Iran's agents that cannot fairly be characterized as public or official acts of a sovereign government. Iran did not pass a law, issue an edict or decree, or engage in formal governmental action explicitly taking McKesson's property for the benefit of the Iranian public. Instead, it allegedly took control of Pak's board of directors and abused its position as majority shareholder, making McKesson's claims akin to a corporate dispute between majority and minority shareholders. This is not the type of "public act[] [of] a foreign sovereign power" to which the act of state doctrine applies. *Sabbatino*, 376 U.S. at 401. . . .

Does it make sense in this context to distinguish between "public" and "private" acts? Might commercial acts also have substantial foreign policy implications?

7. **Sitting in Judgment on Sovereign Acts.** Why did the Court not apply the act of state doctrine in *Kirkpatrick*? What does it mean for a U.S. court to "sit in judgment" on a foreign act, or (as *Kirkpatrick* put it) to "declare invalid" a sovereign act? Why was that not the case in *Kirkpatrick*, where the premise of the suit was that Kirkpatrick had bribed a Nigerian official and had been wrongly awarded the contract?

8. **The Act of State Doctrine in Human Rights Litigation.** In *Kashef v. BNP Paribas S.A.*, 925 F.3d 53 (2d Cir. 2019), plaintiffs sued BNP, a French bank

with operations in New York, under New York state tort law for aiding and abetting genocide and related atrocities committed by Sudanese forces in Sudan; plaintiffs alleged that BNP had facilitated the genocide by providing financial services to Sudan through its New York offices in violation of U.S. law. On appeal, the court reversed the district court's application of the act of state doctrine to bar the suit. According to the court of appeals, (1) under *Kirkpatrick*, the doctrine did not apply because the suit did not require the court to determine the validity of an act of Sudan; (2) under *Dunhill*, there was no evidence that the alleged wrongful acts were the official policy of Sudan (indeed, they were illegal under Sudanese law); and (3) in any event, the alleged wrongful acts violated *jus cogens* norms of international law and therefore were not shielded by the act of state doctrine. Are these correct applications of *Kirkpatrick* and *Dunhill*, respectively? How would you argue otherwise? Why should it be the case that the act of state doctrine cannot apply to *jus cogens* norms?

9. **Review.** Can you state the basic elements of the act of state doctrine? Which one was not present in *Dunhill*? Which one was not present in *Kirkpatrick*? Were the others present in those cases? Can you explain why all of the basic elements were present in *Sabbatino, Oetjen,* and *Underhill*? For a recent application of the act of state doctrine, see *Sea Breeze Salt, Inc. v. Mitsubishi Corporation*, 899 F.3d 1064 (9th Cir. 2018) (barring antitrust claim by U.S. sea salt buyer contending that Mitsubishi conspired with the Mexican state salt-producing corporation to monopolize sea salt production and sales in Mexico). Can you see why all of the act of state doctrine's basic elements likely were present?

2. Exceptions to the Act of State Doctrine

Kalamazoo Spice Extraction Co. v. The Provisional Military Government of Socialist Ethiopia

729 F.2d 422 (6th Cir. 1984)

KEITH, Circuit Judge.

This is an appeal from a district court judgment, which . . . held that the act of state doctrine as interpreted by the Supreme Court in *Banco Nacional De Cuba v. Sabbatino*, 376 U.S. 398 (1964), precluded judicial inquiry into the validity of an expropriation by the Ethiopian government of shares in an Ethiopian business entity held by an American corporation.

Appellant, Kalamazoo Spice Extraction Company (Kal-Spice)[,] is an American corporation which, in a joint venture with Ethiopian citizens, established the Ethiopian Spice Extraction Company (ESESCO) in 1966, an Ethiopian based corporation. . . .

The Provisional Military Government of Socialist Ethiopia (PMGSE) came to power in 1974. As part of its program to assure that Ethiopian industries would "be operated according to the philosophy of Ethiopian socialism", the PMGSE announced the seizure of "control of supervision and a majority shareholding" of a number of corporations, including ESESCO, in February 1975. As a result of the expropriation, Kal-Spice's ownership interest in ESESCO was reduced from 80% to approximately 39%.

In December 1975, the PMGSE established a Compensation Commission. The Commission's purpose was to compensate those claimants whose property had been expropriated. Kal-Spice claimed it was entitled to compensation of $11,000,000. In October 1981, the PMGSE offered Kal-Spice the equivalent of $450,000 in Ethiopian currency. Kal-Spice, however, has rejected the PMGSE's offer. [Kal-Spice brought suit in U.S. court, but the district court dismissed the claim.]

. . .

We . . . reverse and remand for the reasons set forth below.

The act of state doctrine is an exception to the general rule that a court of the United States, where appropriate jurisdictional standards are met, will decide cases before it by choosing the rules appropriate for decision from among various sources of law, including international law.

. . .

[A]ppellant Kal-Spice, as well as the United States Departments of State, Treasury, Justice, and the American Bar Association, as amici curiae, request that this Court recognize a "treaty exception" to the act of state doctrine. According to appellant and amici, the following language in *Sabbatino* provides the basis for a treaty exception:

> [T]he Judicial Branch will not examine the validity of a taking of property within its own territory by a foreign sovereign government, extant and recognized by this country at the time of suit, in the absence of a treaty or other unambiguous agreement regarding controlling legal principles, even if the complaint alleges that the taking violates customary international law.

This language and the existence of a treaty between the United States and Ethiopia[,] assert[] appellant and amici, requires a "treaty" exception to the rule that a United States court will not exercise jurisdiction over a foreign sovereign for an act done by that sovereign within its borders. The treaty in existence between the United States and Ethiopia is the 1953 Treaty of Amity and Economic Relations (Treaty of Amity). Article VIII, paragraph two of that treaty provides:

> Property of nationals and companies of either High Contracting Party, including interests in property, shall receive the most constant protection and security within the territories of the other High contracting party. *Such property shall not be taken except for a public purpose, nor shall it be taken without prompt payment of just and effective compensation* (emphasis added).

Kal-Spice unsuccessfully argued before the district court that this treaty provision was the type referred to by the Supreme Court in *Sabbatino*, which would allow a United States court to exercise jurisdiction over a claim of expropriation of property by a foreign sovereign. Specifically, Kal-Spice alleged that the "prompt payment of just and effective compensation" provision of the Treaty of Amity set forth controlling legal principles which was referred to by the Supreme Court in *Sabbatino*.

The district court, however, . . . agreed with the PMGSE's position that this provision of the treaty calling for the "prompt payment of just and effective compensation" was ambiguous. It found that this provision was "so inherently general, doubtful and susceptible to multiple interpretation that in the absence of an established body of law to clarify their meaning a court cannot reasonably be asked to apply them to a particular set of facts." The failure of the treaty to provide a controlling legal standard provided a possibility of conflict with the Executive Branch. It is this potential conflict, concluded the district court, that underlies the act of state doctrine.

We do not agree with the district court's decision that the provision of the treaty requiring payment of prompt, just and effective compensation fails to provide a controlling legal standard. To the contrary, we find that this is a controlling legal standard in the area of international law. As the appellant and amici correctly point out, the term "prompt, just and effective compensation" and similar terms are found in many treaties where the United States and other nations are parties.

The 1953 United States-Ethiopia Treaty of Amity and Economic Relations is one of a series of treaties, also known as the FCN Treaties, between the United States and foreign nations negotiated after World War II. As the legislative history of these treaties indicates, they were adopted to protect American citizens and their interests abroad. Almost all of these treaties contain sections which provide for "prompt, adequate, and effective compensation", "just compensation", or similar language regarding compensation for expropriated property.

. . .

Banco Nacional de Cuba v. Chase Manhattan Bank, 658 F.2d 875 (2d Cir. 1981), provides an example of the utility of the "prompt, just and effective compensation" standard that is employed in many treaties. In *Chase Manhattan Bank*, the Second Circuit was faced with the task of determining the value of Cuban branches of Chase Manhattan which had been expropriated by the Cuban revolutionary government. After examining several theories regarding the appropriate standard for the compensation of expropriated property, the court concluded Chase Manhattan Bank was entitled to the net asset value of the branches that were expropriated by the Cuban government.

We do not suggest, however, by our citation of *Chase Manhattan Bank*, that the district court in the present case is bound to use the same method employed in *Chase Manhattan Bank* for determining compensation, if any, to which Kal-Spice will be entitled. There are sufficient factual differences in the present case and *Chase Manhattan Bank*, e.g., nature of the property expropriated, status of the expropriated property, the facts surrounding the expropriation, etc., which may call for a different compensation standard. The citation to *Chase Manhattan Bank* is only for the purpose of illustrating the point that the standard of compensation provided for in the Treaty of Amity between Ethiopia and the United States can provide a basis for determining the extent of compensation to which Kal-Spice may be entitled.

Moreover, the Supreme Court's decision in *Sabbatino* . . . requires a reversal of the district court decision that the 1953 Treaty of Amity was too ambiguous to be susceptible to judicial interpretation. As the Supreme Court stated in *Sabbatino*:

It should be apparent that the greater the degree of codification or consensus concerning a particular area of international law, the more appropriate it is for the judiciary to render decisions regarding it, since the courts can then focus on the application of an agreed principle to circumstances of fact rather than on the sensitive task of establishing a principle not inconsistent with the national interest or with international justice.

Numerous treaties employ the standard of compensation used in the 1953 Treaty of Amity between Ethiopia and the United States. Undoubtedly, the widespread use of this compensation standard is evidence that it is an agreed upon principle in international law.

Nor will adjudication in this matter interfere with any efforts by the Executive branch to resolve this matter. In fact, the Executive branch has also intervened in this matter through the Departments of State, Treasury, and Justice who have filed a joint amicus brief urging that the 1953 Treaty of Amity makes the act of state doctrine inapplicable. Obviously, the Executive branch feels that an adjudication in this matter is appropriate. Thus, the Supreme Court's concern in *Sabbatino* for judicial interference with foreign policy activity by the Executive branch is not a consideration in this case.

Additionally, there is a great national interest to be served in this case, i.e., the recognition and execution of treaties that we enter into with foreign nations. Article VI of the Constitution provides that treaties made under the authority of the United States shall be the supreme law of the land. Accordingly, the Supreme Court has recognized that treaties, in certain circumstances, have the force and effect of a legislative enactment. The failure of this court to recognize a properly executed treaty would indeed be an egregious error because of the position that treaties occupy in our body of laws.

. . .

Our decision that the 1953 Treaty of Amity makes the act of state doctrine inapplicable only begins this controversy. The district court must determine what rights, if any, the treaty confers upon Kal-Spice. We recognize that further proceedings will be an arduous task for all parties involved. However, proper briefing of this issue before the court should lead to the resolution of this dispute.

[Reversed.]

NOTES AND QUESTIONS

1. **Treaty Exception.** The *Kalamazoo* case expressly creates a "treaty exception" to the act of state doctrine, allowing U.S. court adjudication even though the basic elements of the act of state doctrine are present. (As a review, why are those elements present in *Kalamazoo*?) Does this exception follow from *Sabbatino*, as the court argues? Is it clear what standards will be used to resolve the merits of the case? Is it clear that there will not be material foreign policy implications from a judicial decision on the merits of Kal-Spice's claim?

2. **Executive Branch Statements and the "Bernstein Exception."** The *Kalamazoo* court also seems highly influenced by the participation of the U.S. executive branch supporting Kal-Spice. Why should that matter to the application of the act of state doctrine? Are there difficulties in relying on it? Recall the history of foreign sovereign immunity, where similar statements were employed and there were worries of politicization that led Congress to enact the FSIA. Should this case come out differently if the executive branch had a different position, or no position? In a series of early act of state cases, the Second Circuit gave a decisive role to the executive branch. As described in *Sabbatino*, 376 U.S. at 419:

> In *Bernstein v. Van Heyghen Freres Societe Anonyme*, 163 F.2d 246 [1947], suit was brought to recover from an assignee property allegedly taken, in effect, by the Nazi Government because plaintiff was Jewish. Recognizing the odious nature of this act of state, the court, through Judge Learned Hand, nonetheless refused to consider it invalid on that ground. Rather, it looked to see if the Executive had acted in any manner that would indicate that United States Courts should refuse to give effect to such a foreign decree. Finding no such evidence, the court sustained dismissal of the complaint. In a later case involving similar facts, the same court again assumed examination of the German acts improper, *Bernstein v. N.V. Nederlandsche-Amerikaansche Stoomvaart-Maatschappij*, 173 F.2d 71 [1949], but, quite evidently following the implications of Judge Hand's opinion in the earlier case, amended its mandate to permit evidence of alleged invalidity, 210 F.2d 375 [1954], subsequent to receipt by plaintiff's attorney of a letter from the Acting Legal Adviser to the State Department written for the purpose of relieving the court from any constraint upon the exercise of its jurisdiction to pass on that question.

   The Court in *Sabbatino* declined to "pass upon" this so-called Bernstein exception. In *First National City Bank v. Banco Nacional de Cuba*, 406 U.S. 759 (1972), the U.S. State Department expressly stated that the act of state doctrine should not bar examination of the foreign governmental acts challenged in that case. A three-Justice plurality would have found this communication (called a "Bernstein letter") decisive under the *Bernstein* cases, but six Justices rejected that view (four of those Justices dissented, while the other two concurred in rejecting the act of state doctrine on other grounds). What do these events suggest about deference to the executive branch in modern act of state cases? What if the executive branch submits a "reverse Bernstein" letter calling for the court to impose the act of state doctrine?

3. **Other Exceptions: Governments No Longer in Existence.** A number of courts have held or suggested that the act of state doctrine should not protect the acts of foreign governments that no longer exist. Why might that be the case? The exception was discussed in *Konowaloff v. Metropolitan Museum of Art*, 702 F.3d 140 (2d Cir. 2012), in which the court of appeals applied the act of state doctrine to bar a claim to recover a confiscated painting from the museum. Konowaloff was the heir of a Russian art collector whose property had been seized by the Soviet government in Russia in 1918. Through a series of transactions, the museum ended up ostensibly owning a painting from the

collection, which Konowaloff sought to recover. The court found that the Soviet confiscation had transferred title and that under *Sabbatino* its validity could not be challenged by Konowaloff. Among other holdings, it rejected Konowaloff's argument that the fall of the Soviet Union and its replacement by a successor government of Russia put the case within an exception to the act of state doctrine, distinguishing earlier cases where the successor regime had disavowed the acts of the prior regime and the act of state doctrine had not applied. *E.g., Bigio v. Coca-Cola Co.*, 239 F.3d 440, 453 (2d Cir. 2001) (act of state doctrine did not apply to seizures of property by former government of Egypt where new government ordered the return of the seized property); *Republic of Philippines v. Marcos*, 806 F.2d 344, 359 (2d Cir. 1986) (act of state doctrine did not apply where successor government of the Philippines itself initiated claim in U.S. courts against former dictator for seized property).

4. **Other Exceptions: Commercial Activity.** The *Dunhill* case, discussed in the prior subsection, involved the refusal of a state-owned cigar business to pay a debt. Justice White, joined by three other Justices, argued that even if the refusal was an act of state, it should not be protected from challenge because it was a commercial act (recall that foreign sovereign immunity has a commercial act exception). Although not a holding (five Justices declined to join it), lower courts have sometimes treated Justice White's opinion as indicating a commercial activity exception (although many courts have rejected the exception, *e.g., Honduras Aircraft Registry, Ltd. v. Government of Honduras*, 129 F.3d 543, 550 (11th Cir. 1997)). Is the proposed commercial activity exception consistent with the rationale for the doctrine set out in *Sabbatino*? When would it apply? In *Spectrum Stores, Inc. v. Citgo Petroleum Corp.*, 632 F.3d 938 (5th Cir. 2011), the court considered an antitrust claim against foreign state-owned oil companies for price fixing at the direction of their governments. Should the act of state doctrine apply?

5. **Other Exceptions: *Jus Cogens*.** Does the rationale for the treaty exception suggest a similar exception for well-established rules of customary international law? *Doe v. Unocal Co.*, 395 F.3d 932 (9th Cir. 2002), was an Alien Tort Statute case brought by victims of alleged slavery, torture, and extrajudicial killing committed by the government of Myanmar (Burma). The court held that the act of state doctrine did not bar a claim against Unocal for aiding the government, in significant part because *jus cogens* norms of international law, such as those involved in the case, reflect a high degree of international consensus. *Id.* at 958-60 (compare the *Kashef* case, discussed in Note 8 of the prior section, excluding *jus cogens* claims from the act of state doctrine on a different theory). Does a *jus cogens* exception follow from the rationale of *Sabbatino*? Should it matter if the executive branch opposed or endorsed the suit? Should it matter that (as the court also held) the government of Myanmar could not be sued directly because of sovereign immunity?

    In *Belhaj v. Straw*, [2017] UKSC 3, the U.K. Supreme Court reached a similar conclusion on somewhat different grounds. The case involved suits against U.K. officials for assisting wrongful acts by various foreign governments including the United States in the course of the war on terrorism. Rejecting an act of state defense, the court concluded that a public policy exception should apply "at least [to] the allegations of complicity in torture, unlawful detention, enforced rendition and disappearance." The Canadian Supreme Court, also in the context of human rights litigation, flatly stated that the act of state doctrine is not part of Canadian law. *Nevsun Resources Ltd. v. Araya*, 2020 SCC 5 (2020).

6. **Other Exceptions: The Hickenlooper Amendment.** In response to the *Sabbatino* decision, Congress passed a statutory provision (called the "Second Hickenlooper Amendment" after its sponsor, Senator Hickenlooper) directing that

> no court in the United States shall decline on the ground of the federal act of state doctrine to make a determination on the merits giving effect to the principles of international law in a case in which a claim of title or other right to property is asserted by any party . . . based upon (or traced through) a confiscation or other taking . . . in violation of the principles of international law . . . .

Does this overturn *Sabbatino*? Does it undermine the act of state doctrine generally? According to the *Restatement (Fourth) of Foreign Relations Law of the United States*, Section 444, Comment h, "[c]ourts . . . have largely confined [the Amendment] to disputes over tangible property when either the property in question or proceeds from the property in question are within U.S. territory at the time of the suit." *See also id.*, Reporters' Note 11 (listing cases and noting some contrary holdings); *Compania de Gas de Nuevo Laredo, S.A. v. Entex, Inc.*, 686 F.2d 322, 327 (5th Cir. 1982) (finding the Amendment unavailable, and the act of state doctrine applicable, to a dispute over property located in Mexico). What might be the basis of this limit on the Amendment?

B. The Political Question Doctrine

As described in the next case, another judge-created doctrine, the political question doctrine, directs that some matters are suitable only for resolution by the "political" branches (that is, the President and Congress), not by the judiciary. Although the political question doctrine applies to some domestic matters as well, it is often thought to have particular force in foreign affairs. As a result, it may pose a barrier to judicial resolution of some transnational claims. In reading the next case, consider how this doctrine is similar to and different from the act of state doctrine.

Jaber v. United States

861 F.3d 241 (D.C. Cir. 2017)

BROWN, Circuit Judge:

Following the terrorist attacks of September 11, 2001, Congress authorized the President "to use all necessary and appropriate force" against al-Qaeda, the

Taliban, and associated forces. *See* Authorization for Use of Military Force, Pub. L. No. 107-40 § 2(a), 115 Stat. 224 (2001). Since then, the Executive has increasingly relied upon unmanned aerial vehicles, or "drones," to target and kill enemies in the War on Terror. This case concerns an alleged drone misfire — a bombing that resulted in unnecessary loss of civilian life.

Plaintiffs . . . seek a declaratory judgment stating their family members were killed in the course of a U.S. drone attack in violation of international law governing the use of force, the Torture Victim Protection Act ("TVPA"), and the Alien Tort Statute ("ATS"). The district court dismissed their claims primarily on political question grounds, and Plaintiffs appeal. At this stage of proceedings, we must accept all factual allegations asserted in the Complaint as true.

I.

In late-August 2012, the bin Ali Jaber family gathered in Khashamir, Yemen for a week-long wedding celebration. On August 24th, Ahmed Salem bin Ali Jaber ("Salem"), an imam in the port town of Mukalla, was asked to give a guest sermon at a local Khashamir mosque. His sermon, a direct challenge to al Qaeda to justify its attacks on civilians, apparently did not go overlooked by local extremists. On August 29th, three young men arrived at Salem's father's house and asked to speak with Salem.

. . . Fearful of the men, Salem asked Waleed bin Ali Jaber ("Waleed"), one of the town's two policemen, to accompany him to meet them. . . .

Shortly thereafter, members of the bin Ali Jaber family heard the buzzing of the drone, and then heard and saw the orange and yellow flash of a tremendous explosion. According to witnesses, the first two strikes directly hit Salem, Waleed, and two of the three strangers. The third missile seemed to have been aimed at where the third visitor was located. . . . The fourth strike hit the men's car. Plaintiffs now contend a U.S.-operated drone deployed the four Hellfire missiles that killed the five men.

. . .

Plaintiffs allege Salem and Waleed were collateral damage in a "signature strike," an attack where the U.S. targets an unidentified person (here, the three men) based on a pattern of suspicious behavior as identified through metadata. Plaintiffs further claim "the drone operator(s) waited until Salem and Waleed joined the three [men] to strike," in violation of international law, since there was ample opportunity to strike when the men were (1) alone in the Yemeni countryside where they could be targeted without fear of civilian casualties or (2) in locations where Yemeni officials could easily take them into custody.

Shortly after this lawsuit was filed, . . . the government moved to dismiss this action for lack of subject matter jurisdiction and failure to state a claim upon which relief may be granted. The district court granted the motion . . . [and] held . . . [that] Plaintiffs' claims were . . . barred on political question grounds. . . . Plaintiffs timely appealed.

II.

. . .

"The nonjusticiability of a political question" as articulated by the Supreme Court "is primarily a function of the separation of powers." *Baker v. Carr*, 369 U.S. 186, 210 (1962). The doctrine "excludes from judicial review," however sympathetic the allegations, "those controversies which revolve around policy choices and value determinations constitutionally committed for resolution to the halls of Congress or the confines of the Executive Branch." *Japan Whaling Ass'n v. Am. Cetacean Soc'y*, 478 U.S. 221, 230 (1986). The framework laid out by the Supreme Court in *Baker v. Carr* articulates the contours of the doctrine:

> Prominent on the surface of any case held to involve a political question is found [1] a textually demonstrable constitutional commitment of the issue to a coordinate political department; or [2] a lack of judicially discoverable and manageable standards for resolving it; or [3] the impossibility of deciding without an initial policy determination of a kind clearly for nonjudicial discretion; or [4] the impossibility of a court's undertaking independent resolution without expressing lack of the respect due coordinate branches of government; or [5] an unusual need for unquestioning adherence to a political decision already made; or [6] the potentiality of embarrassment from multifarious pronouncements by various departments on one question.

369 U.S. at 217. . . .

A.

Plaintiffs seek a declaration stating the drone strike that killed their relatives violated domestic and international law, an issue they claim courts are constitutionally required to decide. The government responds with this Court's *en banc* decision in *El-Shifa Pharmaceutical Industries Co. v. United States*, 607 F.3d 836 (D.C. Cir. 2010). There, this Court held "[t]he political question doctrine bars our review of claims that, regardless of how they are styled, call into question the prudence of the political branches in matters of foreign policy or national security constitutionally committed to their discretion." *Id.* at 842. Here, *El-Shifa* controls; even "a statute providing for judicial review does not override Article III's requirement that federal courts refrain from deciding political questions." *Id.* at 843.

In *El-Shifa*, the Court addressed a U.S. retaliatory strike against a factory in Sudan believed to be associated with the bin Ladin terrorist network and involved in the production of materials for chemical weapons. The owners of the El-Shifa factory sued, alleging they were producing medicine for the Sudanese people, not chemical weapons, and arguing the strike was a mistake. They sought compensation for the destruction of their plant under the Federal Tort Claims Act ("FTCA") and the law of nations; they further asserted a cause of action in defamation based on U.S. government statements asserting the El-Shifa plant had ties to bin Ladin and functioned as part of his terror network.

The [*El-Shifa*] Court adopted a functional approach to the political question doctrine, distinguishing between nonjusticiable "claims requiring [courts] to decide whether taking military action was wise — a policy choice and value determination constitutionally committed for resolution to the halls of Congress or the confines of the Executive Branch" — and fully justiciable "claims presenting purely legal issues such as whether the government had legal authority to act." *Id.* at 842. Since the allegations in *El-Shifa*, set forth as purely statutory claims, ultimately required the Court "to decide whether the United States' attack on the plant was mistaken and not justified" and "to determine the factual validity of the government's stated reasons for the strike," the Court held the case presented a nonjusticiable political question. *Id.* at 844. "If the political question doctrine means anything in the arena of national security and foreign relations, it means the courts cannot assess the merits of the President's decision to launch an attack on a foreign target, and the plaintiffs ask us to do just that." *Id.* . . .

It would be difficult to imagine precedent more directly adverse to Plaintiffs' position. While Plaintiffs clearly assert claims under the TVPA and ATS, the precise grounds they raise in their Complaint call for a court to pass judgment on the wisdom of Executive's decision to commence military action — mistaken or not — against a foreign target. For example, the Complaint alleges:

- "[n]o urgent military purpose or other emergency justified" the drone strike;
- killing the alleged targets was not "strictly unavoidable" to defend against an "imminent threat of death" to the "United States or its allies"; and
- the risk to nearby civilians was excessive in comparison to the military objective since "there [was] no evidence" the three men were "legitimate military targets," and "there were no U.S. or Yemeni forces or military objectives in the vicinity that were in need of protection against three young Yemeni men."

To resolve Plaintiffs' claims, a reviewing court *must* determine whether the U.S. drone strike in Khashamir was mistaken and not justified. As *El-Shifa* warns, these questions are the province of the political branches, regardless of the statutes under which Plaintiffs may seek to sue. . . .

Plaintiffs will no doubt find this result unjust, but it stems from constitutional and pragmatic constraints on the Judiciary. In matters of political and military strategy, courts lack the competence necessary to determine whether the use of force was justified.

. . . Put simply, it is not the role of the Judiciary to second-guess the determination of the Executive, in coordination with the Legislature, that the interests of the U.S. call for a particular military action in the ongoing War on Terror. To be sure, courts have reviewed claims brought by individuals incarcerated at Guantanamo Bay on charges of terrorism and other war crimes. *See* . . . *Al Bahlul v. United States*, 840 F.3d 757 (D.C. Cir. 2016) (en banc). But while "the political question doctrine does not preclude judicial review of prolonged Executive detention predicated on an enemy combatant determination," that is "because the Constitution specifically contemplates a judicial role in this area." *El-Shifa*, 607 F.3d at 848. There is, in contrast, "no comparable constitutional commitment to the courts for review of a military decision to launch a missile at a foreign target." *Id.* at 849.

B.

Plaintiffs argue their reading of *El-Shifa* gains support from the Supreme Court's opinion in *Zivotofsky v. Clinton*, 566 U.S. 189 (2012), which held the political question did not bar judicial review of a claim attacking the constitutionality of a statute allegedly regulating the Executive. Again, Plaintiffs' claim fails.

In *Zivotofsky*, the Court considered a statute directing the Secretary of State, upon request, to issue a registration of birth or passport to a U.S. citizen born in Jerusalem that identified the individual's place of birth as "Jerusalem, Israel." . . . [T]he U.S. Embassy later refused Zivotofsky's request to list his place of birth as Jerusalem, Israel and issued a passport and registration of birth listing only "Jerusalem." . . . [T]he question before the Court concerned whether the statute was constitutional. Accordingly, the Court held the question justiciable, reasoning Zivotofsky did not "ask the courts to determine whether Jerusalem is the capital of Israel" but sought only to vindicate his statutory right to have Israel designated as his place of birth on his passport.

Zivotofsky confirms no *per se* rule renders a claim nonjusticiable solely because it implicates foreign relations. Rather, it recognizes that, in foreign policy cases, courts must first ascertain if "[t]he federal courts are . . . being asked to supplant a foreign policy decision of the political branches with the courts' own unmoored determination" or, instead, merely tasked with, for instance, the "familiar judicial exercise" of determining how a statute should be interpreted or whether it is constitutional. In the latter case, the claim is justiciable.

Therefore, if the court is called upon to serve as a forum for reconsidering the wisdom of discretionary decisions made by the political branches in the realm of foreign policy or national security," then the political question doctrine is implicated, and the court cannot proceed. Zivotofsky sought only to enforce a statute alleged to directly regulate the Executive, and the reviewing court needed to determine only "if Zivotofsky's interpretation of the statute [was] correct, and whether the statute [was] constitutional." *Zivotofsky*, 566 U.S. at 196. The Court was not called upon to impose its own foreign policy judgment on the political branches, only to say whether the congressional statute encroached on the Executive's constitutional authority. This is the wheelhouse of the Judiciary, and accordingly, it does not constitute a nonjusticiable political question. Here, however, Plaintiffs assert claims under the TVPA and ATS that would require the Court to second-guess the wisdom of the Executive's decision to employ lethal force against a national security target — to determine, among other things, whether an "urgent military purpose or other emergency justified" a particular drone strike. Indeed, Plaintiffs' request is more analogous to an action challenging the Secretary of State's independent refusal to recognize Israel as the rightful sovereign of the city of Jerusalem, a decision clearly committed to executive discretion.

C.

Plaintiffs note the Executive has made a number of public statements and issued several memoranda setting forth its legal analysis justifying drone strikes and, presumably, defining the outer limits of when those strikes are appropriate. These

Executive statements, however, do not constitute an invitation to the Judiciary to intrude upon the traditional executive role.

The George W. Bush and Barack Obama Administrations may have laid out the legal rules they understood to govern their conduct, but they did not concede authority to the Judiciary to enforce those rules. Nor could they. While an Executive may self-regulate during his term in office, it is the courts, and not executive branch attorneys, that possess the power to "say what the law is." *Marbury v. Madison*, 5 U.S. 137, 177 (1803). And it is the Executive, and not a panel of the D.C. Circuit, who commands our armed forces and determines our nation's foreign policy. As explained at length above, courts are not constitutionally permitted to encroach upon Executive powers, even when doing so may be logistically, if not constitutionally, manageable.

For example, when reviewing the Secretary of State's designation of a group as a "foreign terrorist organization" under the Antiterrorism and Effective Death Penalty Act, the D.C. Circuit held it may constitutionally decide whether the government has followed the proper procedures, whether the organization is foreign, and whether it has engaged in terrorist activity, *but not* whether "the terrorist activity of the organization threatens the security of United States nationals or the national security of the United States." *People's Mojahedin Org. of Iran v. U.S. Dep't of State (PMOI)*, 182 F.3d 17, 21-24 (D.C. Cir. 1999) (quoting 8 U.S.C. § 1189(a)(1)(C)). The Court held the last criterion — however straightforwardly articulated — presented a nonjusticiable political question because the Secretary's determination of whether the terrorist activities at issue constituted threats to the U.S. "are political judgments, decisions of a kind for which the Judiciary has neither aptitude, facilities nor responsibility and have long been held to belong in the domain of political power not subject to judicial intrusion or inquiry." *Id.* at 23.

III.

In short, *El-Shifa* controls the Court's analysis here and compels dismissal of Plaintiffs' claims. . . .

[Affirmed.]

NOTES AND QUESTIONS

1. **The Political Question Doctrine.** What is a "political question"? According to *Baker v. Carr*, discussed in *Jaber*, what factors should a court consider when deciding whether to dismiss a claim on political question grounds? What is the rationale for the political question doctrine? Is it based on constitutional foundations? On prudential concerns about institutional competence? Both? Should a party's legal claim be dismissed because it raises a political question? What are the implications for the ability of parties to vindicate their legal rights? What are the implications for judicial review of executive action? Some argue

that courts abdicate their responsibility to hear legal claims when they dismiss them based on the political question doctrine. *E.g.*, THOMAS FRANCK, POLITICAL QUESTIONS, JUDICIAL ANSWERS (1992). When, if ever, might this be the case?

2. **The Political Question Doctrine in *Jaber*.** What factors caused the court in *Jaber* to find that the claims presented a political question? Does the court adequately distinguish cases such as *Al Bahlul*, in which the court reviewed the executive's decision to detain at Guantánamo Bay persons the executive determined to be terrorists? Does it make sense that courts can review decisions to detain but not decisions to kill? Suppose Congress passes a law providing that the President can use drone strikes only in cases of "great military necessity"; would a case with *Jaber*'s facts still be a political question?

In *Al Shimari v. CACI Premier Technology Inc.*, 840 F.3d 147 (4th Cir. 2016), the court found no political question in a suit against a U.S. military contractor for alleged torture at the Abu Ghraib prison in Iraq. How might that outcome be distinguished from *Jaber*? In *Wu v. United States*, 777 F.3d 175 (4th Cir. 2015), the court applied the political question doctrine in a case involving the U.S. Navy's capture of a Taiwanese fishing boat that had been seized by Somali pirates. During the capture, the boat's captain, who was being held prisoner by the pirates, was accidentally killed by U.S. naval gunfire, and after the seizure the U.S. Navy sank the boat rather than tow it to shore. In a subsequent suit by the captain's widow, the court found her tort and property claims against the U.S. Navy barred by the political question doctrine. Is that consistent with *Al Shimari*? With *Jaber*?

3. **The *Zivotofsky* Decision.** In *Zivotofsky v. Clinton*, 566 U.S. 189 (2012), discussed in *Jaber*, the Supreme Court arguably cut back on the *Baker v. Carr* formulation of the political question doctrine. As the *Jaber* court describes, *Zivotofsky* involved the constitutionality of a statute that allowed U.S. citizens born in Jerusalem to direct the U.S. State Department to indicate, on a U.S. passport, birth in "Jerusalem, Israel" rather than just "Jerusalem." The State Department preferred the latter in light of the unsettled sovereignty of Jerusalem. Zivotofsky's parents sued to compel the State Department to issue the passport required by the statute (Zivotofsky having been born in Jerusalem). The U.S. executive branch responded that the statute was unconstitutional as an infringement on the President's executive power. The court of appeals dismissed the suit as a political question and the Supreme Court reversed. In its opinion, the Court considered only two of the *Baker* factors (textual commitment and manageable standards), and did not refer to the six-factor test. In a strongly worded opinion, the Court held that the case involved assessing the constitutionality of a statute, which was the core of the judicial power under *Marbury*:

> At least since *Marbury v. Madison*, 1 Cranch 137 (1803), we have recognized that when an Act of Congress is alleged to conflict with the Constitution, "[i]t is emphatically the province and duty of the judicial department to say what the law is." *Id.*, at 177. That duty will sometimes involve the "[r]esolution of litigation challenging the constitutional authority of one of the three branches," but courts cannot avoid their responsibility merely "because the issues have political implications." *INS v. Chadha*, 462 U.S. 919, 943 (1983).

In this case, determining the constitutionality of § 214(d) involves deciding whether the statute impermissibly intrudes upon Presidential powers under the Constitution. If so, the law must be invalidated and Zivotofsky's case should be dismissed for failure to state a claim. If, on the other hand, the statute does not trench on the President's powers, then the Secretary must be ordered to issue Zivotofsky a passport that complies with § 214(d). Either way, the political question doctrine is not implicated. "No policy underlying the political question doctrine suggests that Congress or the Executive . . . can decide the constitutionality of a statute; that is a decision for the courts." *Id.*, at 941-942.

The Secretary contends that "there is 'a textually demonstrable constitutional commitment'" to the President of the sole power to recognize foreign sovereigns and, as a corollary, to determine whether an American born in Jerusalem may choose to have Israel listed as his place of birth on his passport. Perhaps. But there is, of course, no exclusive commitment to the Executive of the power to determine the constitutionality of a statute. The Judicial Branch appropriately exercises that authority, including in a case such as this, where the question is whether Congress or the Executive is aggrandizing its power at the expense of another branch.

Does the court in *Jaber* adequately distinguish *Zivotofsky*? How is *Jaber* different?

4. **Other Applications of the Political Question Doctrine: Treaty Termination.** In *Goldwater v. Carter*, 444 U.S. 996 (1979), President Carter gave notice of termination of the U.S.-Taiwan mutual defense treaty as part of the restoration of diplomatic relations with mainland China; Senator Goldwater sued to block the President's action on the ground that the Constitution required the Senate to consent to termination of a treaty. The Court did not reach the merits of the claim; Justice Rehnquist, writing for a four-Justice plurality, argued that the case presented a political question. Is that consistent with the Court's later decision in *Zivotofsky* (which did not cite *Goldwater*)? Should it matter if the President acted consistent with or in violation of the treaty? In a separate opinion, Justice Brennan objected that "the suggestion that this case presents a political question is incompatible with this Court's willingness on previous occasions to decide whether one branch of our Government has impinged upon the power of another." Was the claim in *Goldwater* somehow different than other separation-of-powers disputes?

5. **Other Applications of the Political Question Doctrine: Human Rights Claims.** In *Alperin v. Vatican Bank*, 410 F.3d 532 (9th Cir. 2005), the plaintiffs claimed conversion, unjust enrichment, restitution, the right to an accounting, and human rights violations and violations of international law arising out of the Vatican Bank's alleged involvement with the Nazi-backed Ustasha regime in Yugoslavia during World War II. The district court dismissed the claims under the political question doctrine and the court of appeals reversed in part. The court of appeals observed:

We conclude that the claims for conversion, unjust enrichment, restitution, and an accounting with respect to lost and looted property are not committed to the political branches. Recovery for lost and looted property, however, stands in stark contrast to the broad allegations tied to the Vatican Bank's alleged

906   Chapter 12. Foreign Affairs Limits on Transnational Cases

assistance to the war objectives of the Ustasha, including the slave labor claims, which essentially call on us to make a retroactive political judgment as to the conduct of war. Such judgment calls are, by nature, political questions.

As to the property claims, the court concluded that they "ultimately boil down to whether the Vatican Bank is wrongfully holding assets. Deciding this sort of controversy is exactly what courts do. The presence of a foreign defendant with some relationship to a foreign government and claims stemming from World War II atrocities tinge this case with political overtones, but the underlying property issues are not 'political questions' that are constitutionally committed to the political branches." In contrast, as to the broader claims that the Bank assisted the Ustasha regime in committing war crimes such as genocide and slave labor, and in escaping accountability after the war, the court concluded:

> It is axiomatic that the Constitution vests the power to wage war in the President as Commander in Chief, U.S. Const. art. II, § 2, cl. 1, and the ability to seize and subject to disciplinary measures those enemies who in their attempt to thwart or impede our military effort have violated the law of war is an important incident to this power. . . .
>
> Following World War II, the Executive Branch exercised its authority in a number of ways, including through the Nuremberg Trials, which included prosecution for "murder, extermination, enslavement, [and] deportation" among other crimes against humanity, war crimes, and crimes against peace. Charter of the International Military Tribunal, Aug. 8, 1945, 59 Stat. 1546, 1547, 82 U.N.T.S. 279. Simply because the Nuremberg Charter does not expressly preclude national courts from trying war criminals, does not mean that it is our place to step in a half-century later and condemn the Vatican Bank and related parties for "participat[ing] in the activities of the Ustasha Regime in furtherance of the commission of war crimes, crimes against humanity, [and] crimes against peace." We are not a war crimes tribunal. To act as such would require us to intrude unduly on certain policy choices and value judgments that are constitutionally committed to the political branches, for we do not and cannot know why the Allies made the policy choice not to prosecute the Ustasha and the Vatican Bank.

One judge dissented, arguing that all the claims were political questions:

> [T]he record compels us to take our lead from Chief Justice Marshall who said that "[q]uestions, in their nature political, or which are, by the Constitution and laws, submitted to the executive, can *never* be made in this court." *Marbury v. Madison*, 5 U.S. 137 (1803) (emphasis added). The *Baker* court repeated this "clearly settled" principle, which emanates from our Constitution's careful allocation and separation of powers between our three branches, and in so doing identified "foreign relations" as one of the areas in which nonjusticiable political questions routinely arise . . . .
>
> [U]nlike the majority, I read this principle to include *all* matters that fall by their constitutional DNA into this sphere, whether the political branches have done anything about them or not. . . .
>
> Notwithstanding appellants' lawyers' ability to cast this dispute in "garden-variety" legal terms, i.e., conversion, unjust enrichment, restitution, etc., the

ineffable fact remains that this functionally is a lawsuit against (1) the Vatican itself, (2) the Vatican Bank, which is an instrumentality of the sovereign state of the Vatican, and (3) untold others — including probably the Pope — seeking relief for World War II wrongs against foreigners committed by the Nazis and their allies in Europe almost sixty years ago. . . . Stripped to its essentials, this is a derivative lawsuit against a sovereign seeking "reparations" for injuries and losses suffered during wartime at the hands of the Nazis and their alleged accomplices. As acknowledged by the majority, the Vatican has filed a note of protest and asked our State Department to intervene. This set of facts and circumstances involving a foreign sovereign strikes me as demanding a "single-voiced statement" of our government's views, not a series of judgments by our courts. I conclude, therefore, that the foreign policy quintessence of this case renders it as a subject matter beyond the power of the judiciary to intrude or to inquire.

In *Kadić v. Karadžić*, 70 F.3d 232 (2d Cir. 1995), the court of appeals rejected a political question objection to a suit against Karadžić, a leader of Serbian forces in Bosnia, for war crimes committed during the Yugoslavian civil war of the early 1990s. The court in *Alperin* acknowledged that *Kadić* was factually similar but distinguished it. What facts might be important to finding the claims in *Kadić* distinct (for political question purposes) from the claims that the *Alperin* court found non-justiciable?

In *Al-Tamimi v. Adelson*, 916 F.3d 1 (D.C. Cir. 2019), the court held that the status of disputed territory in the West Bank was a political question but whether Israeli soliders were committing genocide was not. The case involved a claim against multiple individual, corporate, and governmental entities alleging a conspiracy to expel non-Jews from the West Bank. Is that result consistent with *Alperin*? With *Jaber*?

6. **Other Applications of the Political Question Doctrine: Economic Relations.** In *Spectrum Stores, Inc. v. Citgo Petroleum Corp.*, 632 F.3d 938 (5th Cir. 2011), plaintiffs sued the state-owned oil companies of various oil-producing nations for price fixing under the U.S. antitrust laws. As the court described the arguments:

> Appellants contend that this litigation does not involve a textual commitment to another branch, as the complaints merely require the court to interpret domestic antitrust law and apply it to conduct within the United States having only tangential effects on foreign affairs. In contrast, Appellees characterize the pleadings as seeking to condemn the actions of foreign sovereigns and interfere with the longstanding foreign policy of the political branches.

The court of appeals dismissed the claim as a political question (as well as under the act of state doctrine), concluding:

> By adjudicating this case, the panel would be reexamining critical foreign policy decisions, including the Executive Branch's longstanding approach of managing relations with foreign oil-producing states through diplomacy rather than private litigation, as discussed in the government's amicus brief and in several official statements of administration policy. In accordance with this policy, the Department of Justice has, upon thorough consideration, declined to bring a

Sherman Act case on behalf of the United States. Any merits ruling in this case, whether it vindicates or condemns the acts of [foreign states], would reflect a value judgment on their decisions and actions — a diplomatic determination textually committed to the political branches.

Is that consistent with *Alperin*? With *Zivotofsky*? Should it matter to a court whether a claim might interfere with U.S. diplomacy? Can courts determine the potential for interference, apart from deferring to the executive branch?

7. **Other Candidates for Political Question Dismissal.** Consider cases examined previously in this book in the context of distinct issues, including the Alien Tort Statute, personal jurisdiction, *forum non conveniens*, and foreign sovereign immunity. Are many of these cases possible candidates for political question dismissal? Is that a better ground for deciding them?

C. Foreign Affairs Preemption of State Law

The act of state doctrine and the political question doctrine, discussed in the prior subsections, relate to the relative competence of the judiciary and the political branches (especially the executive) of the federal government to address sensitive transnational disputes. In U.S. constitutional terms, they are doctrines animated by separation of powers. A distinct constitutional concern in transnational cases may be one of federalism. To what extent should federal interests in managing U.S. foreign policy displace state laws from resolving transnational disputes?

American Insurance Association v. Garamendi
539 U.S. 396 (2003)

Justice SOUTER delivered the opinion of the Court.

California's Holocaust Victim Insurance Relief Act of 1999 (HVIRA or Act), Cal. Ins. Code Ann. §§ 13800-13807, requires any insurer doing business in that State to disclose information about all policies sold in Europe between 1920 and 1945 by the company itself or anyone "related" to it. The issue here is whether HVIRA interferes with the National Government's conduct of foreign relations. We hold that it does, with the consequence that the state statute is preempted.

I

A

The Nazi Government of Germany engaged not only in genocide and enslavement but theft of Jewish assets, including the value of insurance policies, and in particular policies of life insurance, a form of savings held by many Jews in Europe before the Second World War. . . . After the war, even a policy that had escaped confiscation was likely to be dishonored, whether because insurers denied its existence or claimed it had lapsed from unpaid premiums during the persecution, or because the government would not provide heirs with documentation of the policyholder's death. Responsibility as between the government and insurance companies is disputed, but at the end of the day, the fact is that the value or proceeds of many insurance policies issued to Jews before and during the war were paid to the Reich or never paid at all.

These confiscations and frustrations of claims fell within the subject of reparations, which became a principal object of Allied diplomacy soon after the war. . . .

[A]ttention to reparations intentionally [was] deferred[] when the western Allies moved to end their occupation and reestablish a sovereign Germany as a buffer against Soviet expansion. They worried that continued reparations would cripple the new Federal Republic of Germany economically, and so decided in the London Debt Agreement to put off consideration of claims arising out of the second World War by countries which were at war with or were occupied during that war, and by nationals of such countries, against the Reich and agencies of the Reich until the final settlement of the problem of reparation. These terms were construed by German courts as postponing resolution of foreign claims against both the German Government and German industry, to await the terms of an ultimate postwar treaty.

. . . West Germany enacted its own restitution laws in 1953 and 1956, and signed agreements with 16 countries for the compensation of their nationals, including the Luxembourg Agreement with Israel. . . . Despite a payout of more than 100 billion deutsch marks as of 2000 these measures left out many claimants and certain types of claims, and when the agreement reunifying East and West Germany was read by the German courts as lifting the London Debt Agreement's moratorium on Holocaust claims by foreign nationals, class action lawsuits for restitution poured into United States courts against companies doing business in Germany during the Nazi era.

These suits generated much protest by the defendant companies and their governments, to the point that the Government of the United States took action to try to resolve [them]. From the beginning, the Government's position, represented principally by Under Secretary of State (later Deputy Treasury Secretary) Stuart Eizenstat, stressed mediated settlement "as an alternative to endless litigation" promising little relief to aging Holocaust survivors. Ensuing negotiations at the national level produced the German Foundation Agreement, signed by President Clinton and German Chancellor Schroder in July 2000, in which Germany agreed to enact legislation establishing a foundation funded with 10 billion deutsch marks contributed equally by the German Government and German companies, to be used to compensate all those "who suffered at the hands of German companies during the National Socialist era."

The willingness of the Germans to create a voluntary compensation fund was conditioned on some expectation of security from lawsuits in United States courts, and after extended dickering President Clinton put his weight behind two specific measures toward that end. First, the Government agreed that whenever a German company was sued on a Holocaust era claim in an American court, the Government of the United States would submit a statement that "it would be in the foreign policy interests of the United States for the Foundation to be the exclusive forum and remedy for the resolution of all asserted claims against German companies arising from their involvement in the National Socialist era and World War II." Though unwilling to guarantee that its foreign policy interests would "in themselves provide an independent legal basis for dismissal," that being an issue for the courts, the Government agreed to tell courts "that U.S. policy interests favor dismissal on any valid legal ground." On top of that undertaking, the Government promised to use its "best efforts, in a manner it considers appropriate," to get state and local governments to respect the foundation as the exclusive mechanism.

As for insurance claims specifically, both countries agreed that the German Foundation would work with the International Commission on Holocaust Era Insurance Claims (ICHEIC), a voluntary organization formed in 1998 by several European insurance companies, the State of Israel, Jewish and Holocaust survivor associations, and the National Association of Insurance Commissioners, the organization of American state insurance commissioners. The job of the ICHEIC, chaired by former Secretary of State Eagleburger, includes negotiation with European insurers to provide information about unpaid insurance policies issued to Holocaust victims and settlement of claims brought under them. It has thus set up procedures for handling demands against participating insurers, including "a reasonable review . . . of the participating companies' files" for production of unpaid policies, "an investigatory process to determine the current status" of insurance policies for which claims are filed, and a "claims and valuation process to settle and pay individual claims," employing "relaxed standards of proof."

. . .

The German Foundation pact has served as a model for similar agreements with Austria and France, and the United States Government continues to pursue comparable agreements with other countries.

B

While these international efforts were underway, California's Department of Insurance began its own enquiry into the issue of unpaid claims under Nazi-era insurance policies, prompting state legislation designed to force payment by defaulting insurers. . . .

State legislative efforts culminated . . . with passage of Assembly Bill No. 600, 1999 Cal. Stats. ch. 827, the first section of which amended the State's Code of Civil Procedure to allow state residents to sue in state court on insurance claims based on acts perpetrated in the Holocaust and extended the governing statute of limitations to December 31, 2010. The section of the bill codified as HVIRA, at issue here, requires "[a]ny insurer currently doing business in the state" to disclose the details of "life, property, liability, health, annuities, dowry, educational, or casualty insurance policies" issued "to persons in Europe, which were in effect between 1920 and 1945." The duty is to make disclosure not only about policies the particular insurer sold, but also about those sold by any "related company," including "any parent, subsidiary, reinsurer, successor in interest, managing general agent, or affiliate company of the insurer," whether or not the companies were related during the time when the policies subject to disclosure were sold. Nor is the obligation restricted to policies sold to "Holocaust victims" as defined in the Act; it covers policies sold to anyone during that time. The insurer must report the current status of each policy, the city of origin, domicile, or address of each policyholder, and the names of the beneficiaries, all of which is to be put in a central registry open to the public. The mandatory penalty for default is suspension of the company's license to do business in the State....

II

[P]etitioners here, several American and European insurance companies and the American Insurance Association (a national trade association), filed suit for injunctive relief against respondent insurance commissioner of California, challenging the constitutionality of HVIRA. [The court of appeals held that the HVIRA did not exceed the state's constitutional authority.] We ... reverse.

III

The principal argument for preemption made by petitioners and the United States as *amicus curiae* is that HVIRA interferes with foreign policy of the Executive Branch, as expressed principally in the executive agreements with Germany, Austria, and France. The major premises of the argument, at least, are beyond dispute. There is, of course, no question that at some point an exercise of state power that touches on foreign relations must yield to the National Government's policy, given the "concern for uniformity in this country's dealings with foreign nations" that animated the Constitution's allocation of the foreign relations power to the National Government in the first place. *Banco Nacional de Cuba v. Sabbatino*, 376 U.S. 398, 427, n.25 (1964); see *Crosby v. National Foreign Trade Council*, 530 U.S. 363, 381-382, n. 16 (2000) ("'[T]he peace of the WHOLE ought not to be left at the disposal of a PART'" (quoting The Federalist No. 80, pp. 535-536 (J. Cooke ed. 1961) (A. Hamilton))); *Id.*, No. 44, at 299 (J. Madison) (emphasizing "the advantage of uniformity in all points which relate to foreign powers"); *Id.*, No. 42, at 279 (J. Madison) ("If we are to be one nation in any respect, it clearly ought to be in respect to other nations")....

Nor is there any question generally that there is executive authority to decide what that policy should be. Although the source of the President's power to act in foreign affairs does not enjoy any textual detail, the historical gloss on the "executive Power" vested in Article II of the Constitution has recognized the President's "vast share of responsibility for the conduct of our foreign relations." *Youngstown Sheet & Tube Co. v. Sawyer*, 343 U.S. 579, 610-611 (1952) (Frankfurter, J., concurring). While Congress holds express authority to regulate public and private dealings with other nations in its war and foreign commerce powers, in foreign affairs the President has a degree of independent authority to act....

At a more specific level, our cases have recognized that the President has authority to make "executive agreements" with other countries, requiring no ratification by the Senate or approval by Congress, this power having been exercised since the early years of the Republic. See *Dames & Moore v. Regan*, 453 U.S. 654, 679, 682-683 (1981); *United States v. Pink*, 315 U.S. 203, 223, 230 (1942); *United States v. Belmont*, 301 U.S. 324, 330-331 (1937). . . .

The executive agreements at issue here do differ in one respect from those just mentioned insofar as they address claims associated with formerly belligerent states, but against corporations, not the foreign governments. But the distinction does not matter. Historically, wartime claims against even nominally private entities have become issues in international diplomacy, and three of the postwar settlements dealing with reparations implicating private parties were made by the Executive alone. Acceptance of this historical practice is supported by a good pragmatic reason for depending on executive agreements to settle claims against foreign corporations associated with wartime experience. As shown by the history of insurance confiscation mentioned earlier, untangling government policy from private initiative during wartime is often so hard that diplomatic action settling claims against private parties may well be just as essential in the aftermath of hostilities as diplomacy to settle claims against foreign governments. While a sharp line between public and private acts works for many purposes in the domestic law, insisting on the same line in defining the legitimate scope of the Executive's international negotiations would hamstring the President in settling international controversies.

Generally, then, valid executive agreements are fit to preempt state law, just as treaties are, and if the agreements here had expressly preempted laws like HVIRA, the issue would be straightforward. See *Belmont, supra*, at 327, 331; *Pink, supra*, at 223, 230-231. But petitioners and the United States as *amicus curiae* both have to acknowledge that the agreements include no preemption clause, and so leave their claim of preemption to rest on asserted interference with the foreign policy those agreements embody. Reliance is placed on our decision in *Zschernig v. Miller*, 389 U.S. 429 (1968).

Zschernig dealt with an Oregon probate statute prohibiting inheritance by a nonresident alien, absent showings that the foreign heir would take the property "without confiscation" by his home country and that American citizens would enjoy reciprocal rights of inheritance there. . . . [B]y the time Zschernig (an East German resident) brought his challenge, it was clear that the Oregon law in practice had invited "minute inquiries concerning the actual administration of foreign law," and so was providing occasions for state judges to disparage certain foreign regimes, employing the language of the anti-Communism prevalent here at the height of the Cold War. Although the Solicitor General, speaking for the State Department, denied that the state statute unduly interfered with the United States' conduct of foreign relations, the Court was not deterred from exercising its own judgment to invalidate the law as an "intrusion by the State into the field of foreign affairs which the Constitution entrusts to the President and the Congress," *id.*, at 432.

The *Zschernig* majority relied on statements in a number of previous cases open to the reading that state action with more than incidental effect on foreign affairs is preempted, even absent any affirmative federal activity in the subject area of the state law, and hence without any showing of conflict. The Court cited the pronouncement in *Hines v. Davidowitz*, 312 U.S. 52, 63 (1941), that "[o]ur system of government is such that the interest of the cities, counties and states, no less than the interest of the people of the whole nation, imperatively requires that federal power in the field affecting foreign relations be left entirely free from local interference." . . .

Justice Harlan, joined substantially by Justice White, disagreed with the *Zschernig* majority on this point, arguing that its implication of preemption of the entire field of foreign affairs was at odds with some other cases suggesting that in the absence of positive federal action "the States may legislate in areas of their traditional competence even though their statutes may have an incidental effect on foreign relations." 389 U.S., at 459 (opinion concurring in result) (citing cases).[10] Thus, for Justice Harlan it was crucial that the challenge to the Oregon statute presented no evidence of a "specific interest of the Federal Government which might be interfered with" by the law. He would, however, have found preemption in a case of "conflicting federal policy," and on this point the majority and Justices Harlan and White basically agreed: state laws "must give way if they impair the effective exercise of the Nation's foreign policy," *id.*, at 440 (opinion of the Court).

It is a fair question whether respect for the executive foreign relations power requires a categorical choice between the contrasting theories of field and conflict preemption evident in the *Zschernig* opinions,[11] but the question requires no answer here. For even on Justice Harlan's view, the likelihood that state legislation will produce something more than incidental effect in conflict with express foreign policy of the National Government would require preemption of the state law. And since on his view it is legislation within "areas of . . . traditional competence" that gives a State any claim to prevail, it would be reasonable to consider the strength of the state interest, judged by standards of traditional practice, when deciding how serious a conflict must be shown before declaring the state law preempted. Judged by these standards, we think petitioners and the Government have demonstrated a sufficiently clear conflict to require finding preemption here.

IV

A

To begin with, resolving Holocaust-era insurance claims that may be held by residents of this country is a matter well within the Executive's responsibility

---

10. Justice Harlan concurred in the majority's result because he would have found the Oregon statute preempted by a 1923 treaty with Germany. . . .

11. The two positions can be seen as complementary. If a State were simply to take a position on a matter of foreign policy with no serious claim to be addressing a traditional state responsibility, field preemption might be the appropriate doctrine, whether the National Government had acted and, if it had, without reference to the degree of any conflict, the principle having been established that the Constitution entrusts foreign policy exclusively to the National Government. Where, however, a State has acted within what Justice Harlan called its "traditional competence," but in a way that affects foreign relations, it might make good sense to require a conflict, of a clarity or substantiality that would vary with the strength or the traditional importance of the state concern asserted. . . .

for foreign affairs. Since claims remaining in the aftermath of hostilities may be sources of friction acting as an impediment to resumption of friendly relations between the countries involved, there is a longstanding practice of the national Executive to settle them in discharging its responsibility to maintain the Nation's relationships with other countries. The issue of restitution for Nazi crimes has in fact been addressed in Executive Branch diplomacy and formalized in treaties and executive agreements over the last half century, and although resolution of private claims was postponed by the Cold War, securing private interests is an express object of diplomacy today, just as it was addressed in agreements soon after the Second World War. Vindicating victims injured by acts and omissions of enemy corporations in wartime is thus within the traditional subject matter of foreign policy in which national, not state, interests are overriding, and which the National Government has addressed.

The exercise of the federal executive authority means that state law must give way where, as here, there is evidence of clear conflict between the policies adopted by the two. The foregoing account of negotiations toward the three settlement agreements is enough to illustrate that the consistent Presidential foreign policy has been to encourage European governments and companies to volunteer settlement funds in preference to litigation or coercive sanctions. . . . As for insurance claims in particular, the national position, expressed unmistakably in the executive agreements signed by the President with Germany and Austria, has been to encourage European insurers to work with the ICHEIC to develop acceptable claim procedures, including procedures governing disclosure of policy information. This position, of which the agreements are exemplars, has also been consistently supported in the high levels of the Executive Branch, as mentioned already. The approach taken serves to resolve the several competing matters of national concern apparent in the German Foundation Agreement: the national interest in maintaining amicable relationships with current European allies; survivors' interests in a "fair and prompt" but nonadversarial resolution of their claims so as to "bring some measure of justice . . . in their lifetimes"; and the companies' interest in securing "legal peace" when they settle claims in this fashion. . . .

California has taken a different tack of providing regulatory sanctions to compel disclosure and payment, supplemented by a new cause of action for Holocaust survivors if the other sanctions should fail. The situation created by the California legislation calls to mind the impact of the Massachusetts Burma law on the effective exercise of the President's power, as recounted in the statutory preemption case, *Crosby v. National Foreign Trade Council*, 530 U.S. 363 (2000). HVIRA's economic compulsion to make public disclosure, of far more information about far more policies than ICHEIC rules require, employs "a different, state system of economic pressure," and in doing so undercuts the President's diplomatic discretion and the choice he has made exercising it. Whereas the President's authority to provide for settling claims in winding up international hostilities requires flexibility in wielding "the coercive power of the national economy" as a tool of diplomacy, HVIRA denies this, by making exclusion from a large sector of the American insurance market the automatic sanction for noncompliance with the State's own policies on disclosure. Quite simply, if the California law is enforceable the President has less to offer and less economic and diplomatic leverage as a consequence. The law thus "compromise[s] the very capacity of the President to speak for the Nation with one voice in dealing with other governments" to resolve claims against European companies arising out of World War II. [*Crosby*,] 530 U.S., at 381.[14]

B

The express federal policy and the clear conflict raised by the state statute are alone enough to require state law to yield. If any doubt about the clarity of the conflict remained, however, it would have to be resolved in the National Government's favor, given the weakness of the State's interest, against the backdrop of traditional state legislative subject matter, in regulating disclosure of European Holocaust-era insurance policies in the manner of HVIRA.

The commissioner would justify HVIRA's ambitious disclosure requirement as protecting "legitimate consumer protection interests" in knowing which insurers have failed to pay insurance claims. But, quite unlike [generally applicable consumer protection laws], HVIRA effectively singles out only policies issued by European companies, in Europe, to European residents, at least 55 years ago. Limiting the public disclosure requirement to these policies raises great doubt that the purpose of the California law is an evaluation of corporate reliability in contemporary insuring in the State.

Indeed, there is no serious doubt that the state interest actually underlying HVIRA is concern for the several thousand Holocaust survivors said to be living in the State. But this fact does not displace general standards for evaluating a State's claim to apply its forum law to a particular controversy or transaction, under which the State's claim is not a strong one. "Even if a plaintiff evidences his desire for forum law by moving to the forum, we have generally accorded such a move little or no significance." *Phillips Petroleum Co. v. Shutts*, 472 U.S. 797, 820 (1985); see *Allstate Ins. Co. v. Hague*, 449 U.S. 302, 311 (1981) ("[A] postoccurrence change of residence to the forum State — standing alone — [is] insufficient to justify application of forum law").

But should the general standard not be displaced, and the State's interest recognized as a powerful one, by virtue of the fact that California seeks to vindicate the claims of Holocaust survivors? The answer lies in recalling that the very same objective dignifies the interest of the National Government in devising its chosen mechanism for voluntary settlements, there being about 100,000 survivors in the country, only a small fraction of them in California. As against the responsibility of the United States of America, the humanity underlying the state statute could

---

14. It is true that the President in this case is acting without express congressional authority, and thus does not have the "plenitude of Executive authority" that "controll[ed] the issue of preemption" in *Crosby v. National Foreign Trade Council*, 530 U.S. 363, 376 (2000). But in *Crosby* we were careful to note that the President possesses considerable independent constitutional authority to act on behalf of the United States on international issues, and conflict with the exercise of that authority is a comparably good reason to find preemption of state law.

not give the State the benefit of any doubt in resolving the conflict with national policy.

C

The basic fact is that California seeks to use an iron fist where the President has consistently chosen kid gloves. We have heard powerful arguments that the iron fist would work better, and it may be that if the matter of compensation were considered in isolation from all other issues involving the European Allies, the iron fist would be the preferable policy. But our thoughts on the efficacy of the one approach versus the other are beside the point, since our business is not to judge the wisdom of the National Government's policy; dissatisfaction should be addressed to the President or, perhaps, Congress. The question relevant to pre-emption in this case is conflict, and the evidence here is "more than sufficient to demonstrate that the state Act stands in the way of [the President's] diplomatic objectives." *Crosby, supra*, at 386. . . .

[The Court also rejected arguments that Congress had approved the state statute.]

The judgment of the Court of Appeals for the Ninth Circuit is reversed. . . .

Justice GINSBURG, with whom Justice STEVENS, Justice SCALIA, and Justice THOMAS join, dissenting.

Responding to Holocaust victims' and their descendents' long-frustrated efforts to collect unpaid insurance proceeds, California's Holocaust Victim Insurance Relief Act of 1999 (HVIRA), Cal. Ins. Code Ann. § 13800 *et seq.*, requires insurance companies operating in the State to disclose certain information about insurance policies they or their affiliates wrote in Europe between 1920 and 1945. In recent years, the Executive Branch of the Federal Government has become more visible in this area, undertaking foreign policy initiatives aimed at resolving Holocaust era insurance claims. Although the federal approach differs from California's, no executive agreement or other formal expression of foreign policy disapproves state disclosure laws like the HVIRA. Absent a clear statement aimed at disclosure requirements by the "one voice" to which courts properly defer in matters of foreign affairs, I would leave intact California's enactment.

I

As the Court observes, the Nazi regimentation of inhumanity we characterize as the Holocaust, marked most horrifically by genocide and enslavement, also entailed widespread destruction, confiscation, and theft of property belonging to Jews. For insurance policies issued in Germany and other countries under Nazi control, historical evidence bears out, the combined forces of the German Government and the insurance industry engaged in larcenous takings of gigantic proportions. . . .

The Court depicts Allied diplomacy after World War II as aimed in part at settling confiscated and unpaid insurance claims. But the multilateral negotiations that produced the Potsdam, Yalta, and like accords failed to achieve any global resolution of such claims. European insurers, encountering no official compulsion, were themselves scarcely inclined to settle claims; turning claimants away, they relied on the absence of formal documentation and other technical infirmities that legions of Holocaust survivors were in no position to remedy. For over five decades, untold Holocaust-era insurance claims went unpaid.

In the late 1990's, litigation in American courts provided a spur to action. Holocaust survivors and their descendents initiated class-action suits against German and other European firms seeking compensation for, *inter alia*, the confiscation of Jewish bank assets, the use of Jewish slave labor, and the failure to pay Jewish insurance claims.

In the insurance industry, the litigation propelled a number of European companies to agree on a framework for resolving unpaid claims outside the courts. This concord prompted the 1998 creation of the International Commission on Holocaust Era Insurance Claims (ICHEIC). . . .

At least until very recently, however, ICHEIC's progress has been slow and insecure. . . .

Moreover, ICHEIC has thus far settled only a tiny proportion of the claims it has received. Evidence submitted in a series of class actions filed against Italian insurer Generali indicated that by November 2001, ICHEIC had resolved only 797 of 77,000 claims. . . .

Finally, although ICHEIC has directed its members to publish lists of unpaid Holocaust-era policies, that nonbinding directive had not yielded significant compliance at the time this case reached the Court. . . . For a prime example, Generali — which may have sold more life insurance and annuity policies in Eastern Europe during the Holocaust than any other company — reportedly maintains a 340,000-name list of persons to whom it sold insurance between 1918 and 1945, but has refused to disclose the bulk of the information on the list.

II

A

California's disclosure law, the HVIRA, was enacted a year after ICHEIC's formation. Observing that at least 5,600 documented Holocaust survivors reside in California, Cal. Ins. Code Ann. § 13801(d), the HVIRA declares that "[i]nsurance companies doing business in the State of California have a responsibility to ensure that any involvement they or their related companies may have had with insurance policies of Holocaust victims [is] disclosed to the state". The HVIRA accordingly requires insurance companies doing business in California to disclose information concerning insurance policies they or their affiliates sold in Europe between 1920 and 1945, and directs California's Insurance Commissioner to store the information in a publicly accessible "Holocaust Era Insurance Registry." The Commissioner is further directed to suspend the license of any insurer that fails to comply with the HVIRA's reporting requirements.

These measures, the HVIRA declares, are "necessary to protect the claims and interests of California residents, as well as to encourage the development of a resolution to these issues through the international process or through direct action by the State of California, as necessary." Information published in the HVIRA's registry could, for example, reveal to a Holocaust survivor residing in California the existence of a viable claim, which she could then present to ICHEIC for resolution.

. . . The HVIRA imposes no duty to pay any claim, nor does it authorize litigation on any claim. It mandates only information *disclosure*, and our assessment of the HVIRA is properly confined to that requirement alone.

B

The Federal Government, after prolonged inaction, has responded to the Holocaust-era insurance issue by diplomatic means. Executive agreements with Germany, Austria, and France, the Court observes, are the principal expressions of the federal approach. Signed in July 2000, the German Foundation Agreement establishes a voluntary foundation, funded by public and private sources, to address Holocaust-era claims. . . .

The German Foundation Agreement commits the Federal Government to certain conduct. It provides, for example, that when a German company is sued in a United States court on a Holocaust-era claim, the Federal Government will file with the court a statement that "the President of the United States has concluded that it would be in the foreign policy interests of the United States for the [German] Foundation to be the exclusive forum and remedy for the resolution of all asserted claims against German companies arising from their involvement in the National Socialist era and World War II." The agreement also provides that "[t]he United States will recommend dismissal on any valid legal ground (which, under the U.S. system of jurisprudence, will be for the U.S. courts to determine)." The agreement makes clear, however, that "[t]he United States does not suggest that its policy interests concerning the Foundation in themselves provide an independent legal basis for dismissal."

III

A

The President's primacy in foreign affairs, I agree with the Court, empowers him to conclude executive agreements with other countries. Our cases do not catalog the subject matter [meant] for executive agreement, but we have repeatedly acknowledged the President's authority to make such agreements to settle international claims. And in settling such claims, we have recognized, an executive agreement may preempt otherwise permissible state laws or litigation. The executive agreements to which we have accorded preemptive effect, however, warrant closer inspection than the Court today endeavors.

In *United States v. Belmont*, 301 U.S. 324 (1937), the Court addressed the Litvinov Assignment, an executive agreement incidental to the United States' recognition of the Soviet Union. . . . The Litvinov Assignment clearly assigned to the United States the claims in issue; the enforceability of that assignment, the Court stressed, "is not and cannot be subject to any curtailment or interference on the part of the several states."

United States v. Pink, 315 U.S. 203 (1942), again addressed state-imposed obstacles to the Litvinov Assignment. . . .

Four decades later, in *Dames & Moore v. Regan*, 453 U.S. 654 (1981), the Court gave effect to an executive agreement arising out of the Iran hostage crisis. One of the agreement's announced "purpose[s]" was "to terminate all litigation as between the Government of each party and the nationals of the other, and to bring about the settlement and termination of all such claims through binding arbitration." *Id.*, at 665 (quoting the agreement). The agreement called for the formation of an Iran-United States Claims Tribunal to arbitrate claims not settled within six months. In addition, under the agreement the United States undertook

> "to terminate all legal proceedings in United States courts involving claims of United States persons and institutions against Iran and its state enterprises, to nullify all attachments and judgments obtained therein, to prohibit all further litigation based on such claims, and to bring about the termination of such claims through binding arbitration."

In line with these firm commitments, the Court held that the agreement and the executive order implementing it validly "suspended" litigation in United States courts against Iranian interests.

Notably, the Court in *Dames & Moore* was emphatic about the "narrowness" of its decision. *Id.*, at 688. "We do not decide," the Court cautioned, "that the President possesses plenary power to settle claims, even as against foreign governmental entities." *Ibid.* Before sustaining the President's action, the Court determined: (1) Congress "had implicitly approved" the practice of claim settlement by executive agreement; (2) the alternative forum created under the executive agreement was "capable of providing meaningful relief"; (3) Congress had not in any way disapproved or resisted the President's action; and (4) the settlement of claims was "a necessary incident to the resolution of a major foreign policy dispute between our country and another".

Together, *Belmont*, *Pink*, and *Dames & Moore* confirm that executive agreements directed at claims settlement may sometimes preempt state law. The Court states that if the executive "agreements here had expressly preempted laws like HVIRA, the issue would be straightforward." One can safely demur to that statement, for, as the Court acknowledges, no executive agreement before us expressly preempts the HVIRA. Indeed, no agreement so much as mentions the HVIRA's sole concern: public disclosure.

B

Despite the absence of express preemption, the Court holds that the HVIRA interferes with foreign policy objectives implicit in the executive agreements. I would not venture down that path.

The Court's analysis draws substantially on *Zschernig v. Miller*, 389 U.S. 429 (1968). In that case, the Oregon courts had applied an Oregon escheat statute to deny an inheritance to a resident of a Communist bloc country. The Oregon courts so ruled because the claimant failed to satisfy them that his country's laws would allow U.S. nationals to inherit estates, nor had the claimant shown he would actually receive payments from the Oregon estate with no confiscation by his home government. Applying Oregon's statutory conditions, the Court concluded, required Oregon courts to "launc[h] inquiries into the type of governments that obtain in particular foreign nations," rendering "unavoidable judicial criticism of nations established on a more authoritarian basis than our own". Such criticism had a "direct impact upon foreign relations," the Court said, and threatened to "impair the effective exercise of the Nation's foreign policy". The Court therefore held the statute unconstitutional as applied in that case.

We have not relied on *Zschernig* since it was decided, and I would not resurrect that decision here. The notion of "dormant foreign affairs preemption" with which *Zschernig* is associated resonates most audibly when a state action "reflect[s] a state policy critical of foreign governments and involve[s] 'sitting in judgment' on them." L. Henkin, Foreign Affairs and the United States Constitution 164 (2d ed. 1996). . . . The HVIRA entails no such state action or policy. It takes no position on any contemporary foreign government and requires no assessment of any existing foreign regime. It is directed solely at private insurers doing business in California, and it requires them solely to disclose information in their or their affiliates' possession or control. I would not extend *Zschernig* into this dissimilar domain.[4]

Neither would I stretch *Belmont, Pink,* or *Dames & Moore* to support implied preemption by executive agreement. . . . Here . . . none of the executive agreements extinguish any underlying claim for relief. The United States has agreed to file precatory statements advising courts that dismissing Holocaust-era claims accords with American foreign policy, but the German Foundation Agreement confirms that such statements have no legally binding effect. It remains uncertain, therefore, whether even *litigation* on Holocaust-era insurance claims must be abated in deference to the German Foundation Agreement or the parallel agreements with Austria and France. Indeed, ambiguity on this point appears to have been the studied aim of the American negotiating team.

If it is uncertain whether insurance *litigation* may continue given the executive agreements on which the Court relies, it should be abundantly clear that those agreements leave *disclosure* laws like the HVIRA untouched. The contrast with the Litvinov Assignment at issue in *Belmont* and *Pink* is marked. That agreement spoke directly to claim assignment in no uncertain terms; *Belmont* and *Pink*

---

4. The Court also places considerable weight on *Crosby v. National Foreign Trade Council,* 530 U.S. 363 (2000). As the Court acknowledges, however, *Crosby* was a statutory preemption case. The state law there at issue posed "an obstacle to the accomplishment of Congress's full objectives under the [relevant] federal Act." 530 U.S., at 373. That statutory decision provides little support for preempting a state law by inferring preclusive foreign policy objectives from precatory language in executive agreements.

confirmed that state law could not invalidate the very assignments accomplished by the agreement. Here, the Court invalidates a state disclosure law on grounds of conflict with foreign policy "embod[ied]" in certain executive agreements although those agreements do not refer to state disclosure laws specifically, or even to information disclosure generally. It therefore is surely an exaggeration to assert that the "HVIRA threatens to frustrate the operation of the particular mechanism the President has chosen" to resolve Holocaust-era claims. If that were so, one might expect to find some reference to laws like the HVIRA in the later-in-time executive agreements. There is none.

To fill the agreements' silences, the Court points to statements by individual members of the Executive Branch. But we have never premised foreign affairs preemption on statements of that order. We should not do so here lest we place the considerable power of foreign affairs preemption in the hands of individual sub-Cabinet members of the Executive Branch. Executive officials of any rank may of course be expected faithfully to represent the President's chosen policy, but no authoritative text accords such officials the power to invalidate state law simply by conveying the Executive's views on matters of federal policy. The displacement of state law by preemption properly requires a considerably more formal and binding federal instrument.

Sustaining the HVIRA would not compromise the President's ability to speak with one voice for the Nation. To the contrary, by declining to invalidate the HVIRA in this case, we would reserve foreign affairs preemption for circumstances where the President, acting under statutory or constitutional authority, has spoken clearly to the issue at hand. . . . As I see it, courts step out of their proper role when they rely on no legislative or even executive text, but only on inference and implication, to preempt state laws on foreign affairs grounds.

In sum, assuming, *arguendo*, that an executive agreement or similarly formal foreign policy statement targeting disclosure could override the HVIRA, there is no such declaration here. Accordingly, I would leave California's enactment in place, and affirm the judgment of the Court of Appeals.

Movsesian v. Victoria Versicherung AG

670 F.3d 1067 (9th Cir. 2012) (en banc)

GRABER, Circuit Judge:
Section 354.4 of the California Code of Civil Procedure vests California courts with jurisdiction over certain insurance claims brought by "Armenian Genocide victim[s]" and extends the statute of limitations for such claims. Under that statute, individual Plaintiffs, including Vazken Movsesian, filed this class action against various insurers. One of the defendant insurance companies filed a Federal Rule of Civil Procedure 12(b)(6) motion to dismiss the claims, arguing, among other things, that section 354.4 is preempted under the foreign affairs doctrine. . . . We hold that section 354.4 is preempted and, accordingly, reverse the district court's contrary ruling.

Factual and Procedural History

In 2000, the California legislature enacted section 354.4, which provides that California courts may entertain various insurance claims brought by "Armenian Genocide victim[s]" arising out of policies issued or in effect between 1875 and 1923. The law also extends the statute of limitations for such claims. Section 354.4 reads in relevant part:

(a) The following definitions govern the construction of this section:
  (1) "Armenian Genocide victim" means any person of Armenian or other ancestry living in the Ottoman Empire during the period of 1915 to 1923, inclusive, who died, was deported, or escaped to avoid persecution during that period.
  (2) "Insurer" means an insurance provider doing business in the state, or whose contacts in the state satisfy the constitutional requirements for jurisdiction, that sold life, property, liability, health, annuities, dowry, educational, casualty, or any other insurance covering persons or property to persons in Europe or Asia at any time between 1875 and 1923.

(b) Notwithstanding any other provision of law, any Armenian Genocide victim, or heir or beneficiary of an Armenian Genocide victim, who resides in this state and has a claim arising out of an insurance policy or policies purchased or in effect in Europe or Asia between 1875 and 1923 from an insurer described in paragraph (2) of subdivision (a), may bring a legal action or may continue a pending legal action to recover on that claim in any court of competent jurisdiction in this state, which court shall be deemed the proper forum for that action until its completion or resolution.

(c) Any action, including any pending action brought by an Armenian Genocide victim or the heir or beneficiary of an Armenian Genocide victim, whether a resident or nonresident of this state, seeking benefits under the insurance policies issued or in effect between 1875 and 1923 shall not be dismissed for failure to comply with the applicable statute of limitation, provided the action is filed on or before December 31, 2010.

In 2003, Movsesian and several other individuals filed this class action against [various German insurance companies]. . . . The class consists of persons of Armenian descent who claim benefits under Defendants' life insurance policies issued or in effect in the Ottoman Empire between 1875 and 1923.

Plaintiffs seek damages from Defendants on theories of breach of contract, breach of the covenant of good faith and fair dealing, unjust enrichment, and constructive trust. Plaintiffs rely on section 354.4 in order to bring their claims now. . . .

The district court held that section 354.4 is not preempted under the foreign affairs doctrine. . . .

Discussion

A. The Foreign Affairs Doctrine and Field Preemption

The Constitution gives the federal government the exclusive authority to administer foreign affairs. *See, e.g., United States v. Pink*, 315 U.S. 203, 233 (1942) ("Power over external affairs is not shared by the States; it is vested in the national government exclusively."); *Hines v. Davidowitz*, 312 U.S. 52, 63 (1941) ("The Federal Government, representing as it does the collective interests of the forty-eight states, is entrusted with full and exclusive responsibility for the conduct of affairs with foreign sovereignties. . . . Our system of government is such that the interest of the cities, counties and states, no less than the interest of the people of the whole nation, imperatively requires that federal power in the field affecting foreign relations be left entirely free from local interference.").

Under the foreign affairs doctrine, state laws that intrude on this exclusively federal power are preempted. Foreign affairs preemption encompasses two related, but distinct, doctrines: conflict preemption and field preemption. *Am. Ins. Ass'n v. Garamendi*, 539 U.S. 396, 418-20 (2003). Under conflict preemption, a state law must yield when it conflicts with an express federal foreign policy.

But the Supreme Court has made clear that, even in the absence of any express federal policy, a state law still may be preempted under the foreign affairs doctrine if it intrudes on the field of foreign affairs without addressing a traditional state responsibility. This concept is known as field preemption or "dormant foreign affairs preemption."

In *Pink*, 315 U.S. at 233, and *Hines*, 312 U.S. at 63, the Supreme Court recognized that the Constitution implicitly grants to the federal government a broad foreign affairs power. *See also Deutsch*, 324 F.3d at 709 ("Because the Constitution mentions no general foreign affairs power, and because only a few specified powers related to foreign affairs are expressly denied the states, one might assume that, with certain exceptions, states are free to pursue their own foreign policies. This is not, however, the case. To the contrary, the Supreme Court has long viewed the foreign affairs powers specified in the text of the Constitution as reflections of a generally applicable constitutional principle that power over foreign affairs is reserved to the federal government."). The existence of this general foreign affairs power implies that, even when the federal government has taken no action on a particular foreign policy issue, the state generally is not free to make its own foreign policy on that subject.

For example, in *Zschernig v. Miller*, 389 U.S. 429, 440-41 (1968), the Supreme Court recognized that, even in the absence of any treaty, federal statute, or executive order, a state law may be unconstitutional if it "disturb[s] foreign relations" or "establish[es] its own foreign policy." There, the Court considered the constitutionality of an Oregon probate law that imposed conditions under which aliens could receive Oregon property by succession or testamentary disposition. The state statute provided for escheat unless the nonresident alien could demonstrate that the foreign country from which the alien came granted various reciprocal rights to United States citizens.

The Oregon statute conflicted with no express policy of the federal government. Indeed, the federal government's amicus curiae brief stated: "The government does not contend that the application of the Oregon escheat statute in the circumstances of this case unduly interferes with the United States' conduct of foreign relations."

But the absence of a conflict did not settle the question of preemption. Instead, the Court analyzed the purpose and operation of the Oregon statute to determine whether it constituted an "intrusion by the State into the field of foreign affairs which the Constitution entrusts to the President and the Congress." *Id.* at 432. In order for field preemption to apply, the Oregon law had to have "more than some incidental or indirect effect in foreign countries." *Id.* at 434.

The Court concluded that application of the Oregon law invited courts to conduct detailed inquiries into the political systems and conduct of foreign nations. In applying the statute,

> the probate courts of various States have launched inquiries into the type of governments that obtain in particular foreign nations — whether aliens under their law have enforceable rights, whether the so-called "rights" are merely dispensations turning upon the whim or caprice of government officials, whether the representation of consuls, ambassadors, and other representatives of foreign nations is credible or made in good faith, whether there is in the actual administration in the particular foreign system of law any element of confiscation.

Id. at 433-34. The application of the law therefore required value-laden judgments about the actions and policies of foreign nations and the credibility of foreign representatives. "As one reads the Oregon decisions, it seems that foreign policy attitudes, the freezing or thawing of the 'cold war,' and the like are the real desiderata. Yet they of course are matters for the Federal Government, not for local probate courts." *Id.* at 437-38. The Court also noted that "[s]uch attitudes are not confined to the Oregon courts," citing a number of decisions from other states expressing a desire to keep United States money out of the grasp of communist or authoritarian nations.

Although the Oregon probate statute conflicted with no federal law and appeared, at first blush, simply to regulate property — a traditional area of state responsibility — the Supreme Court held that the law was preempted under the foreign affairs doctrine. *Id.* at 440-41. "The statute as construed seems to make unavoidable judicial criticism of nations established on a more authoritarian basis than our own. It seems inescapable that the type of probate law that Oregon enforces affects international relations in a persistent and subtle way." *Id.* at 440.

More than three decades later, in *Garamendi*, the Supreme Court clarified when the application of the field preemption doctrine might be appropriate. There, the Court addressed the constitutionality of California's Holocaust Victim Insurance Relief Act of 1999 ("HVIRA"), which required any insurer doing business in California to disclose information about all policies it sold in Europe between 1920 and 1945. *Garamendi*, 539 U.S. at 401. Although the Court ultimately concluded that HVIRA was preempted because of a direct conflict with express federal policy, the Court also provided valuable insight into the doctrine of field preemption. The Court explained:

> The two positions [conflict preemption and field preemption] can be seen as complementary. If a State were simply to take a position on a matter of foreign policy with no serious claim to be addressing a traditional state responsibility, field preemption might be the appropriate doctrine, whether the National Government had acted and, if it had, without reference to the degree of any conflict, the principle having been established that the Constitution entrusts foreign policy exclusively to the National Government. Where, however, a State

has acted within what Justice Harlan called its "traditional competence," but in a way that affects foreign relations, it might make good sense to require a conflict, of a clarity or substantiality that would vary with the strength or the traditional importance of the state concern asserted.

Id. at 419 n. 11. With respect to HVIRA, the Court rejected the contention that the statute concerned a traditional state responsibility merely because it involved insurance. Noting the narrow scope of the statute and the nature of the legislative findings accompanying it, the Court observed that "there is no serious doubt that the state interest actually underlying HVIRA is concern for the several thousand Holocaust survivors said to be living in the State." *Id.* at 426. Thus, *Garamendi* suggests that, under a field preemption analysis, when a state law (1) has no serious claim to be addressing a traditional state responsibility and (2) intrudes on the federal government's foreign affairs power, the Supremacy Clause prevents the state statute from taking effect.

In *Von Saher* [*v. Norton Simon Museum*, 592 F.3d 954 (9th Cir. 2010)], we applied those principles to a California statute that extended the statute of limitations for civil actions to recover looted Holocaust-era artwork. After concluding that the statute, Cal. Civ. Proc. Code § 354.3, did not conflict directly with any express federal foreign policy, we conducted a thorough field preemption analysis and held the statute unconstitutional.

First, we addressed the question whether section 354.3 concerned an area of traditional state responsibility. We acknowledged that the general subject area of the statute, the regulation of stolen property, is traditionally an area of state responsibility. But we did not stop there. Instead, we inquired into the "real purpose" of the statute to determine whether it concerned an area of traditional state responsibility:

> Property, of course, is traditionally regulated by the state. But § 354.3 cannot be fairly categorized as a garden variety property regulation. Section 354.3 does not apply to all claims of stolen art, or even all claims of art looted in war. The statute addresses only the claims of Holocaust victims and their heirs.
>
> Courts have consistently struck down state laws which purport to regulate an area of traditional state competence, but in fact, affect foreign affairs. *See, e.g.,* *Garamendi*, 539 U.S. at 425-26 (rejecting purported state interest in regulating insurance business and blue sky laws); *Crosby* [*v. Nat'l Foreign Trade Council*], 530 U.S. [363,] 367, 373 n. 7 [(2000)] (rejecting purported state interest in taxing and spending); *Zschernig v. Miller*, 389 U.S. 429, 437-38 (1968) (rejecting purported state interest in regulating descent of property); *Deutsch*, 324 F.3d at 707 (rejecting purported state interest in procedural rules).
>
> The *Garamendi* Court in dicta rejected the "traditional state interests" advanced by California in support of HVIRA, finding instead that the real purpose of the state law was the "concern for the several thousand Holocaust survivors said to be living in the state." Though § 354.3 purports to regulate property, an area traditionally left to the states, like HVIRA, § 354.3's real purpose is to provide relief to Holocaust victims and their heirs.

Von Saher, 592 F.3d at 964. We concluded that, although the statute's goal of providing relief to Holocaust victims was laudable, "[i]n so doing, California can make 'no serious claim to be addressing a traditional state responsibility.'" *Id.* at 965 (quoting *Garamendi*, 539 U.S. at 419 n. 11).

We then turned to the question whether section 354.3 intruded on a power expressly or impliedly reserved by the Constitution to the federal government. *Id.* at 965-68. Section 354.3 attempted to provide redress for wartime wrongs, and "[t]he legislative findings accompanying the statute repeatedly reference the 'Nazi regime,' 'Nazi persecution,' and 'the many atrocities' the Nazis committed." The application of the statute would often entail inquiry into the reparation efforts of foreign nations, which itself would involve an examination of underlying allegations of Nazi transgressions. We ultimately concluded that section 354.3 intruded on the federal government's power to make and resolve war, holding that the federal government's failure to act did not "justify California's intrusion into a field occupied exclusively by the federal government."

Field preemption is a rarely invoked doctrine. Supreme Court jurisprudence makes clear, however, that field preemption may be appropriate when a state intrudes on a matter of foreign policy with no real claim to be addressing an area of traditional state responsibility. We followed that guidance in *Von Saher*, and we must follow it here.

B. The Constitutionality of Section 354.4

Keeping in mind the principles that we have just articulated, we now address the constitutionality of section 354.4.

1. Section 354.4 Does Not Concern an Area of Traditional State Responsibility.

Plaintiffs argue that section 354.4 concerns an area of traditional state responsibility because it regulates insurance. But, as we noted in *Von Saher*, the required inquiry cannot begin and end, as Plaintiffs suggest, with the area of law that the state statute addresses. On the contrary, we must look further to determine the "real purpose of the state law." *Id.* at 964; *see also Garamendi*, 539 U.S. at 425-26 (rejecting purported state interest in regulating insurance business and blue sky laws, and concluding that the real purpose of the statute was to provide redress for Holocaust victims); *Von Saher*, 592 F.3d at 964 ("Though § 354.3 purports to regulate property, an area traditionally left to the states, like HVIRA, § 354.3's real purpose is to provide relief to Holocaust victims and their heirs."); *cf. Zschernig*, 389 U.S. at 440 ("The several States, of course, have traditionally regulated the descent and distribution of estates. But those regulations must give way if they impair the effective exercise of the Nation's foreign policy.").

Here, the text and legislative history of section 354.4 leave no doubt that the law "cannot be fairly categorized as a garden variety" insurance regulation. *Von Saher*, 592 F.3d at 964. Section 354.4 is *not* a neutral law of general application. It applies only to a certain class of insurance policies (those issued or in effect in Europe and Asia between 1875 and 1923) and specifies a certain class of people ("Armenian Genocide" victims and their heirs) as its intended beneficiaries. . . . And, just as in *Garamendi*, the legislative findings accompanying the statute plainly reveal its true purpose. *See* S. 1915 § 1(c), 1999-2000 Reg. Sess. (Cal. 2000) ("It is the specific intent of the Legislature to ensure that Armenian Genocide victims and their heirs be permitted to have an expeditious, inexpensive, and fair forum in which to resolve their claims. . . ."). . . .

Thus, it is clear that the real purpose of section 354.4 is to provide potential monetary relief and a friendly forum for those who suffered from certain foreign events. This is precisely the same purpose underlying HVIRA, the statute held unconstitutional in *Garamendi*, and section 354.3, the state law held preempted in *Von Saher*. As *Garamendi* and *Von Saher* make clear, that goal, however laudable it may be, "is not an area of 'traditional state responsibility,' and the statute is therefore subject to a field preemption analysis." *Von Saher*, 592 F.3d at 965; *see also Garamendi*, 539 U.S. at 425-26 (noting the weakness of the state's interest in vindicating the insurance claims of Holocaust survivors). In sum, section 354.4 does not concern an area of traditional state responsibility.

2. *Section 354.4 Intrudes on the Federal Government's Foreign Affairs Power.*

We turn, finally, to the question whether section 354.4 intrudes on a power expressly or impliedly reserved to the federal government. We conclude that section 354.4 intrudes on the federal government's exclusive power to conduct and regulate foreign affairs.

Section 354.4 has "more than some incidental or indirect effect" on foreign affairs. *Zschernig*, 389 U.S. at 434. The statute expresses a distinct political point of view on a specific matter of foreign policy. It imposes the politically charged label of "genocide" on the actions of the Ottoman Empire (and, consequently, present-day Turkey) and expresses sympathy for "Armenian Genocide victim[s]." Cal. Civ. Proc. Code § 354.4. The law establishes a particular foreign policy for California — one that decries the actions of the Ottoman Empire and seeks to provide redress for "Armenian Genocide victim[s]" by subjecting foreign insurance companies to lawsuits in California. *See id.; Zschernig*, 389 U.S. at 441 (holding that, even in the absence of a conflicting federal policy, a state may violate the constitution by "establish[ing] its own foreign policy").

Furthermore, the statute's jurisdictional grant is predicated on a determination that the claim is brought by an "Armenian Genocide victim, or heir or beneficiary of an Armenian Genocide victim." Cal. Civ. Proc. Code § 354.4(b). " 'Armenian Genocide victim' means any person of Armenian or other ancestry living in the Ottoman Empire during the period of 1915 to 1923, inclusive, who died, was deported, or escaped to avoid persecution during that period." *Id.* § 354.4(a)(1). Courts applying this provision may therefore have to decide whether the policyholder "escaped to avoid persecution," *id.*, which in turn would require a highly politicized inquiry into the conduct of a foreign nation. . . .

The passage of nearly a century since the events in question has not extinguished the potential effect of section 354.4 on foreign affairs. On the contrary, Turkey expresses great concern over the issue, which continues to be a hotly contested matter of foreign policy around the world. *See, e.g., Turkey retaliates over French 'genocide' bill*, BBC, Dec. 22, 2011 (reporting that the Turkish prime minister announced measures against France after the French National Assembly passed a bill criminalizing denial of the "Armenian Genocide"); Peter Baker, *Obama Marks Genocide Without Saying the Word*, N.Y. Times, Apr. 25, 2010, at A10 (noting that President Obama was careful to avoid using the word "genocide" during a commemorative speech in an attempt to "avoid alienating Turkey, a NATO ally, which adamantly rejects the genocide label").

In conclusion, section 354.4 expresses a distinct point of view on a specific matter of foreign policy. Its effect on foreign affairs is not incidental; rather, section 354.4 is, at its heart, intended to send a political message on an issue of foreign affairs by providing relief and a friendly forum to a perceived class of foreign victims. Nor is the statute merely expressive. Instead, the law imposes a concrete policy of redress for "Armenian Genocide victim[s]," subjecting foreign insurance companies to suit in California by overriding forum-selection provisions and greatly extending the statute of limitations for a narrowly defined class of claims. Thus, section 354.4 "has a direct impact upon foreign relations and may well adversely affect the power of the central government to deal with those problems." *Zschernig*, 389 U.S. at 441. Section 354.4 therefore intrudes on the federal government's exclusive power to conduct and regulate foreign affairs.

Conclusion

Because California Code of Civil Procedure section 354.4 does not concern an area of traditional state responsibility and intrudes on the field of foreign affairs entrusted exclusively to the federal government, we hold that section 354.4 is preempted. We remand the case to the district court with instructions to dismiss all claims revived by that statute.

REVERSED and REMANDED with instructions.

NOTES AND QUESTIONS

1. **Statutory and Treaty Preemption in Foreign Affairs Related Cases.** Statutory preemption — the rule that federal statutes override conflicting state statutes — is frequently litigated in both domestic and transnational cases. *Crosby v. Nat'l Foreign Trade Council*, 530 U.S. 363 (2000), discussed in *Garamendi* and *Movsesian*, is an example: The Court held that a state statute restricting companies from doing business in Myanmar was preempted by a similar but less extensive and more flexible federal statute. In *Crosby*, the Court declined to say whether preemption might be easier to establish in foreign affairs related cases due to the greater federal interest. *Hines v. Davidowitz*, another case mentioned in the excerpts, was also a statutory preemption case. Similarly, as discussed in Chapter 2, self-executing treaties preempt inconsistent state statutes. These results arise from the supremacy clause of Article VI of the Constitution, which states: "This Constitution, and the Laws of the United States which shall be made in Pursuance thereof; and all Treaties made, or

which shall be made, under the Authority of the United States shall be the supreme Law of the Land. . . ."

2. **Non–Article VI Preemption.** In *Garamendi* and related cases, there was no obvious source of Article VI law to displace the state law: No treaty or statute applied. However, the state laws nonetheless were displaced. What explains this result? Notice the majority and dissent in *Garamendi* arguing in footnotes about whether *Crosby* is a useful precedent. Are there advantages to allowing some room for state activity here? Would unacceptable consequences result if *Garamendi* and *Movsesian* had come out the other way?

3. **The Scope of Executive Preemption.** Did the preemption in *Garamendi* arise from conflict with the executive agreements (which function to some extent like treaties, as established in cases such as *United States v. Belmont*, discussed in Chapter 2), or did it arise from conflict with the President's foreign policy more broadly? How did the HVIRA conflict with the German Foundation Agreement? In the subsequent case *Medellín v. Texas*, 552 U.S. 491 (2008), discussed in Chapter 2, the President argued on the basis of *Garamendi* that presidential policy of complying with decisions of the International Court of Justice should displace an inconsistent state law. In a part of the decision omitted from Chapter 2, the Court rejected the President's contention, describing *Garamendi* as a case about executive agreements:

> The United States relies on a series of cases in which this Court has upheld the authority of the President to settle foreign claims pursuant to an executive agreement. *See Garamendi*, 539 U.S., at 415; *Dames & Moore*, 453 U.S., at 679-680; *United States v. Pink*, 315 U.S. 203, 229 (1942); *United States v. Belmont*, 301 U.S. 324, 330 (1937). . . .
>
> The claims-settlement cases involve a narrow set of circumstances: the making of executive agreements to settle civil claims between American citizens and foreign governments or foreign nationals. They are based on the view that "a systematic, unbroken, executive practice, long pursued to the knowledge of the Congress and never before questioned," can "raise a presumption that the [action] had been [taken] in pursuance of its consent." *Dames & Moore, supra*, at 686. As this Court explained in *Garamendi*,
>
>> Making executive agreements to settle claims of American nationals against foreign governments is a particularly longstanding practice. . . . Given the fact that the practice goes back over 200 years, and has received congressional acquiescence throughout its history, the conclusion that the President's control of foreign relations includes the settlement of claims is indisputable.

539 U.S., at 415.

The Court went on to find that the President's power to displace state law through claims settlements did not support preemption in *Medellín* and upheld the state law despite the conflict with the President's policy. Note, however, that *Medellín* concerned the application of Texas's criminal laws to a Mexican citizen resident in Texas for a crime committed in Texas. What are its implications, if any, for the preemption of state laws with transnational effects?

4. ***Zschernig* and "Field" Preemption.** In *Zschernig v. Miller*, discussed in *Garamendi* and *Movsesian*, there were no executive agreements and the executive branch

did not oppose the challenged state law. The Court nonetheless found the statute invalid, in a holding applied in *Movsesian* and in *Von Saher v. Norton Simon Museum*, 592 F.3d 954 (9th Cir. 2010) (the case quoted at length in *Movsesian*). What is its constitutional basis? What does it mean to say that a subject is "field preempted"? According to *Movsesian*, how is this different from *Garamendi*?

Von Saher was a suit seeking to reclaim from a museum in California artwork wrongfully seized from the plaintiff by Nazi Germany and later acquired by the museum; the challenged statute sought to facilitate such suits in California. The majority held that the subject was field preempted, focusing principally on the fact that the statute extended the statute of limitations for suits based on Holocaust-era thefts; the court thus saw it as an attempt to provide relief for wartime injuries, a matter entrusted to the federal government. Judge Pregerson dissented, arguing:

> Where a State acts within its "traditional competence," the Supreme Court has suggested that conflict preemption, not field preemption, is the appropriate doctrine. *Am. Ins. Ass'n v. Garamendi*, 539 U.S. 396, 420 n. 11 (2003). *Garamendi* counsels that field preemption would apply "[i]f a State were simply to take a position on a matter of foreign policy with no serious claim to be addressing a traditional state responsibility. . . ." *Id.* That is not the case here.
>
> It is undisputed that property is traditionally regulated by the State. The majority acknowledges that California has a legitimate interest in regulating museums and galleries, and that [the challenged statute] "addresses the problem of Nazi-looted art currently hanging on the walls of the state's museums and galleries." However, the majority goes on to hold that because Section 354.3 applies to any museum or gallery, "California has created a world-wide forum for the resolution of Holocaust restitution claims," and that the State is therefore acting outside the scope of its traditional interests.
>
> The majority reads the statute far too broadly. A reasonable reading of "any museum or gallery" would limit Section 354.3 to entities subject to the jurisdiction of the State of California. Because California has a "serious claim to be addressing a traditional state responsibility," it is clear that *Garamendi* requires us to apply conflict preemption, not field preemption.
>
> Here, Appellee, a museum located in California, acquired stolen property in 1971. Appellant now seeks to recover that property. I fail to see how a California statute allowing such recovery intrudes on the federal government's power to make and resolve war.
>
> As the majority correctly holds, Section 354.3 does not conflict with federal policy. However, California has acted within its traditional competence, and field preemption should not apply.

Could a similar argument be made in *Movsesian*?

Gingery v. City of Glendale, 831 F.3d 1222 (9th Cir. 2017), rejected a *Zschernig*-based challenge to a statue, which Glendale placed in a public park, commemorating Korean "comfort women" kidnapped and abused by Japanese forces in World War II. According to the plaintiff, the statue interfered with foreign affairs. As the court explained:

> For several decades, Japan and South Korea have engaged in a heated and politically sensitive debate concerning historical responsibility for the

Comfort Women. South Korea has urged Japan to redress grievances relating to the Comfort Women. Japan denies responsibility for the recruitment of the Comfort Women and asserts that, in any event, all World War II-related claims, including those related to the Comfort Women, were resolved pursuant to post-war treaties between Japan and the allied nations. According to Plaintiffs' complaint, the United States has generally "avoid[ed] taking sides" and encouraged Japan and South Korea to resolve the dispute through "further government-to-government negotiations." . . .

Plaintiffs . . . claim that the monument interferes with the federal government's foreign affairs power and violates the Supremacy Clause. Plaintiffs' complaint further alleges that by installing the monument, Glendale "has taken a position in the contentious and politically-sensitive international debate concerning the proper historical treatment of the former comfort women." In Plaintiffs' view, Glendale's monument disrupts the federal government's foreign policy of nonintervention and encouragement of peaceful resolution of the Comfort Women dispute.

The court rejected this claim:

Applying the doctrine of field preemption, we have found that a state or local government is more likely to exceed the limits of its power when it creates remedial schemes or regulations to address matters of foreign affairs. In *Von Saher v. Norton Simon Museum of Art*, 592 F.3d 954 (9th Cir. 2010), for example, we held that a California statute, which extended the statute of limitations for civil actions to recover looted Holocaust-era artwork, was preempted because the statute would often require courts to review the reparation decisions of foreign nations, and thus intruded on the federal government's power "to make and resolve war." *Id.* at 965-68. More recently, in *Movsesian*, our Court, sitting en banc, concluded that a California statute, which vested California courts with jurisdiction n over certain insurance claims brought by "Armenian genocide victim[s]" and extended the statute of limitations for those claims, intruded on the field of foreign affairs. 670 F.3d at 1076-77. We explained that the California statute not only "expresses a distinct political point of view on a specific matter of foreign policy," but also "subject[s] foreign insurance companies to lawsuits in California" and would require courts applying the statute to engage in "a highly politicized inquiry into the conduct of a foreign nation." *Id.* at 1076.

What we have *not* considered, however, is the extent to which a state or local government may address foreign affairs through expressive displays or events, rather than through remedies or regulations. . . . Under the circumstances of this case, we conclude that it does not.

First, Glendale's establishment of a public monument to advocate against "violations of human rights" is well within the traditional responsibilities of state and local governments. . . . [C]ities, counties, and states have a long tradition of issuing pronouncements, proclamations, and statements of principle on a wide range of matters of public interest, including other matters subject to preemption, such as foreign policy and immigration. For example, local governments have established memorials for victims of the Holocaust and the Armenian genocide, and leaders of local governments have publicly taken positions on matters of foreign affairs, from South African apartheid in the 1980s to the recent actions of Boko Haram. Here, by dedicating a local monument to the plight of the Comfort Women in World War II, Glendale has joined a long list of other American cities that have likewise used public monuments to express their views on events that occurred beyond our borders. . . .

Second, even if Glendale were acting outside an area of traditional state responsibility, Plaintiffs have not plausibly alleged that Glendale's actions intrude[] on the federal government's foreign affairs power. To intrude on the federal government's foreign affairs power, a state's action must have more than some incidental or indirect effect on foreign affairs. While Plaintiffs broadly assert that the monument threatens to negatively affect U.S. foreign relations with Japan, Plaintiffs do not support this assertion with specific allegations that Glendale's actions have had, or are likely to have, any appreciable effect on foreign affairs. At most, Plaintiffs allege that various Japanese officials have expressed disapproval of the monument. However, Plaintiffs have not further alleged that this disapproval has in any way affected relations between the United States and Japan. In addition, Plaintiffs do not allege that the federal government has expressed any view on the monument — much less complained of interference with its diplomatic agenda. Thus, Plaintiffs have failed to plausibly allege that Glendale's installation of the monument has had more than some incidental or indirect effect on foreign affairs.

Moreover, in contrast to state actions we have found preempted, Glendale has taken no action that would affect the legal rights and responsibilities of any individuals or foreign governments. . . . Rather, by erecting a symbolic display commemorating what it views as a historical tragedy, Glendale has appropriately exercised the expressive powers of a local government and stopped short of interfering with the federal government's foreign affairs power.

5. **Foreign Affairs and Drafting Issues.** Was the problem with the statutes in *Movsesian* and *Von Saher* simply the way the statutes were worded? After *Movsesian*, what might the California legislature do to assist Armenian victims' recovery and avoid the foreign affairs doctrine? Would other doctrines related to foreign affairs be potential barriers to recovery? Indeed, is the problem in these cases that these were new causes of action? In other words, had these causes of action been based on state common law, would there be similar intrusion of foreign affairs? After *Von Saher*, the California legislature did revise the statute on stolen artwork; it dropped the reference to the Holocaust and simply extended the statute of limitations for suing to recover any stolen work of art. In *Cassirer v. Thyssen-Bornemisza Collection Foundation*, 737 F.3d 613 (9th Cir. 2013), the court upheld the revised statute against a field preemption challenge, distinguishing the prior holding in *Von Saher* on the ground that the revised statute did not "on its face" refer to matters implicating foreign affairs. In a further appeal in the *Von Saher* case, a divided panel upheld the revised statute against a conflict preemption challenge. *See Von Saher v. Norton Simon Museum*, 754 F.3d 712 (9th Cir. 2014). The *Von Saher* majority specifically distinguished *Garamendi* on the ground that

> [h]ere, however, there is no Holocaust-specific legislation at issue. Instead, Von Saher brings claims pursuant to a state statute of general applicability. Also unlike *Garamendi*, Von Saher seeks relief from an American museum that had no connection to the wartime injustices. . . .

Does this make sense? Is the previous specific statute substantially more problematic for foreign affairs than the revised statute?

6. **Role of the Executive Branch.** In dissent in the second *Von Saher* case, Judge Wardlaw relied heavily on a prior statement of U.S. foreign policy by the executive branch:

> The United States has articulated the foreign policy applicable to the very artwork and transactions at issue here. When Von Saher petitioned for certiorari from our court's decision rejecting her claims under Cal. Civ. Proc. Code § 354.3 on preemption grounds, the Supreme Court invited the Solicitor General to express the position of the United States on the question there presented. . . .
>
> The United States explained that . . . [a]fter World War II, the United States determined that it would return private property expropriated by the Nazis to its country of origin — that is, "externally" — rather than to its private owners. In turn, the country of origin was responsible for returning the property to its lawful owners through "internal" restitution proceedings. A central purpose of this policy was to avoid entangling the United States in difficult, long-lasting disputes over private ownership. . . .
>
> Thus, the policy of the United States, as expressed in its Supreme Court brief, is that World War II property claims may not be litigated in U.S. courts if the property was "subject" or "potentially subject" to an adequate internal restitution process in its country of origin.

The majority responded that "[w]e . . . do not find convincing the [United States'] position — presented in a brief in a different iteration of this case that raised different arguments, that involved different sources of law and that seems to have misunderstood some of the facts essential to our resolution of this appeal." How deferential should courts be to the federal executive branch in these cases? What are the potential problems with deferring? What are the potential problems with not deferring?

7. **Human Rights Cases in State Court.** International human rights cases brought under the federal Alien Tort Statute (ATS) (see Chapter 2) often also involve parallel claims under state law. After the Supreme Court's 2013 decision in *Kiobel v. Royal Dutch Petroleum Corp.* limiting ATS claims to those that "touch and concern" the territory of the United States (excerpted in Chapter 2), there may be much greater focus on international human rights claims in state courts and under state law. Are there constitutional problems with bringing *Kiobel*-type claims under state law? (Recall that *Kiobel* involved British/Dutch defendants sued for alleged acts in Nigeria, with the plaintiffs being Nigerian citizens who subsequently moved to the United States.) *See* Donald Earl Childress III, *The Alien Tort Statute, Federalism and the Next Wave of Transnational Litigation*, 100 Geo. L.J. 709 (2012).

8. **The Dormant Foreign Commerce Clause Doctrine.** In domestic matters, the dormant foreign commerce clause doctrine precludes certain state regulations of interstate commerce even in the absence of federal legislation. This doctrine is said to arise from Congress's power to regulate interstate commerce, granted by Article I, Section 8 of the Constitution. Generally, it precludes state laws (i) where the state law discriminates against interstate commerce; or

(ii) where the state law unduly burdens interstate commerce. A parallel doctrine applies to foreign commerce, as a result of Congress's parallel power to "regulate Commerce with foreign nations." In *Japan Line, Ltd. v. County of Los Angeles*, 441 U.S. 434 (1979), the Court invalidated the county's tax on shipping containers used exclusively in foreign commerce and present only temporarily at the port of Los Angeles. In doing so, it indicated that the dormant foreign commerce clause doctrine was more demanding than its interstate counterpart:

> [A] state tax on the instrumentalities of foreign commerce may impair federal uniformity in an area where federal uniformity is essential. Foreign commerce is preeminently a matter of national concern. In international relations and with respect to foreign intercourse and trade the people of the United States act through a single government with unified and adequate national power.
>
> Although the Constitution, Art. I, § 8, cl. 3, grants Congress power to regulate commerce "with foreign Nations" and "among the several States" in parallel phrases, there is evidence that the Founders intended the scope of the foreign commerce power to be the greater. Cases of this Court, stressing the need for uniformity in treating with other nations, echo this distinction. In approving state taxes on the instrumentalities of interstate commerce, the Court consistently has distinguished oceangoing traffic; these cases reflect an awareness that the taxation of foreign commerce may necessitate a uniform national rule.

However, subsequent cases have often declined to invalidate state laws affecting foreign commerce so long as they are not discriminatory or unduly burdensome. *E.g., Itel Containers International Corp. v. Huddleston*, 507 U.S. 60 (1993) (upholding a Tennessee tax that applied equally to containers used in domestic and foreign commerce); *Pacific Merchant Shipping Association v. Goldstene*, 639 F.3d 1154 (9th Cir. 2011) (upholding state environmental regulations of ocean-going ships and observing that the "even-handed and generally applicable [state regulations] also do not appear to discriminate against any out-of-state interests. We therefore are not presented with an example of state economic protectionism or favoritism."); *Cavel International Inc. v. Madigan*, 500 F.3d 551 (7th Cir. 2007) (upholding generally applicable state ban on slaughtering horses for human consumption, as challenged under the dormant foreign commerce clause by a producer that exported all of its horse meat to Europe). *Compare Piazza's Seafood World LLC v. Odom*, 448 F.3d 744 (5th Cir. 2006) (invalidating under the dormant foreign commerce clause doctrine a Louisiana product-labeling statute that specified "'Catfish' shall mean only those species within the family *Ictaluridae* . . . and grown in the United States of America").

1. As a lawyer in the United States, suppose your client wishes to sue an entity affiliated with a foreign government for breach of contract (assume foreign sovereign immunity is not an issue). To what extent are the doctrines discussed in this chapter likely to pose barriers to a U.S. court hearing the case? What specifically would you need to know about the client's claim to decide if the act of state doctrine might be a problem? What considerations, if any, might raise a political question? Under what circumstances might the doctrines discussed in *Garamendi* and *Zschernig/Movsesian* be a problem? How, if at all, are these considerations related to each other?

2. Now suppose that the potential defendant in the above breach-of-contract suit is a purely private corporation. Are the barriers to suit from the doctrines in this chapter eliminated? Under what circumstances might they not be?

3. Now suppose that your client wants to sue a private corporation for human rights violations arising out of that corporation's involvement with a foreign government. Are the barriers likely to be greater or lesser than in Question 1?

4. What are the policies underlying the various foreign affairs doctrines discussed in this chapter? What constitutional concerns and institutional competence concerns animate these doctrines? Do the doctrines serve similar or different purposes? What trade-offs do these doctrines entail? Should courts dismiss potentially valid legal claims because they implicate foreign policy? How else, if at all, might parties vindicate their legal rights if their claims are dismissed based on these doctrines?

CHAPTER 13

TRANSNATIONAL DISCOVERY

After a plaintiff meets the challenges associated with effecting service of process, establishing jurisdiction, and surviving a motion to dismiss, the next significant step in a transnational case is conducting discovery. A lawyer should realize that discovery is a key component in any case. First, the prospect of discovery can put significant pressure on parties to settle a case given the costs of discovery and the fact that no litigants wish to have their actions investigated by an opposing party. Second, discovery helps plaintiffs establish factual disputes to survive summary judgment. Third, if a case proceeds to trial, discovery provides the building blocks for proving the plaintiff's case. But discovery is not only for plaintiffs. It can be an important tool for defendants seeking facts to support defenses and counterclaims.

Let's begin with a brief review of what you may have learned in civil procedure. In the United States, discovery is largely initiated and conducted by the parties to the litigation. The Federal Rules of Civil Procedure (FRCP) allow extensive discovery and grant parties broad access to information their adversaries have in their possession or control that is relevant to a dispute. Under Rule 26(b)(1), "[p]arties may obtain discovery regarding any nonprivileged matter that is relevant to any party's claim or defense and proportional to the needs of the case." Information can even be requested if the party making the request does not know that the information exists or cannot describe it with specificity. Importantly, relevant material need not be admissible at trial under the rules of evidence, but rather simply must be calculated to lead to the discovery of admissible evidence. For good cause, a court may expand discovery to cover any matter relevant to the subject matter involved in the action. Discovery can be limited to prevent undue burden or cost to the parties under Rule 26(b)(2)(C). Even with these limitations, U.S. discovery is quite broad. Unlike discovery in most other nations, it is largely driven by the parties with little direct court supervision. Courts become involved in the discovery process typically through motions for protective orders pursuant to Rule 26(c), which protect parties from inappropriate discovery, or motions to compel filed pursuant to Rule 37, which provide sanctions for a party's failure to comply with an appropriate discovery request.

In civil law nations, in contrast, discovery is generally conducted by the trial judge and evidence taking by the litigants is not permitted. Likewise, the scope of discovery tends to be more limited than in the United States. Some nations consider U.S.-style discovery to be too expansive and burdensome on the parties. Consequently, U.S. discovery is not always viewed favorably in other nations and can give rise to tensions when evidence is being gathered abroad. In light of this, the United States initiated negotiations for a Convention on the Taking of Evidence Abroad in Civil and Commercial Matters (the Hague Evidence Convention) in 1968, and the Convention entered into force for the United States in 1972. We discuss the Convention below in Section B.

As you work through these materials, think about some big picture questions: What is it about U.S. rules of litigation that might have made the U.S. approach to discovery generally broader than that in other nations? Note that the rules of pleading in FRCP Rule 8 require only a "short and plain statement" of a plaintiff's claim for relief or a defendant's defenses, whereas more extensive and detailed pleading is typically required in other nations. What might be the relationship between the pleading standards and discovery standards in legal systems?

In what follows, we examine (1) how discovery is conducted under the Federal Rules (Section A), (2) how discovery is conducted under the Hague Evidence Convention (Section B), (3) how to conduct discovery when there are conflicts with foreign law (Section C), and (4) discovery in aid of foreign proceedings (Section D).

A. Conducting Transnational Discovery Under the Federal Rules

Before reading what follows, refresh your memory of discovery by reading FRCP Rules 26-37, which are available at https://www.uscourts.gov/rules-policies. We now describe how evidence may be collected abroad under the Federal Rules. Pay close attention to how the Federal Rules treat parties and nonparties. (Reminder: If the litigation is in state court, you would use the rules of that state.)

Litigants generally rely on four types of discovery: depositions via oral examination, requests for production of documents, interrogatories, and requests to admit.

Depositions are oral examinations of another party where the person being deposed is placed under oath and questioned by counsel for the party that requested the deposition. *See* Rule 30. During the deposition, there is an opportunity for counsel for the person being deposed to object to the questions. *Id.* In addition to deposing another party, a party may request a subpoena to depose any other person and require that person to produce documentary and other evidence. *See* Rule 45.

Requests for production. A party may require any other party to produce documents and to permit inspection of electronically stored information and intangible things in possession or control of the party to which the request is addressed. *See* Rule 34. For instance, a request may be styled as follows: "All statements and communications of any and all witnesses including any and all statements of Plaintiffs and Defendants, including taped recordings, whether transcribed or not, as well as written statements."

Interrogatories are written questions sent by one party to another party that must be answered under oath. *See* Rule 33. For example, "Identify all persons having knowledge or believed to have knowledge of the truth of the facts and averments set forth in the Complaint and Answer. With respect to each person identified, state concisely the facts that person is aware of, when and how the facts were obtained, and identify any document evidencing said person's knowledge. Identify all comments, written or oral, you have had with these individuals."

Requests for admission are written requests made to another party to admit certain facts, thus doing away with the need to prove them at trial. *See* Rule 36. For example, "Admit that Plaintiff was employed by the Defendant during the relevant time period and was treated and characterized as an employee by Defendant during that time."

How does the availability of each of these methods change in transnational cases? As you will see, the answer depends substantially on whether discovery is being sought from a party or a nonparty.

1. **Depositions.** Under Rule 28(b), depositions may be taken in foreign nations by any of the following methods: (1) pursuant to an applicable treaty or convention; (2) pursuant to a letter of request (whether or not it is a letter rogatory); (3) on notice before a person authorized to administer oaths in the place where the deposition is held, either under the law of that nation or U.S. law; or (4) before a person commissioned by the court. We will discuss conducting depositions pursuant to the Hague Evidence Convention in Section B below. The other methods are discussed in what follows.

   Letters of Request (sometimes called *letters rogatory*) are formal communications sent by one court where an action is pending to a court in a foreign nation. These are sometimes sent via the U.S. State Department or a consular office, and they request the aid of a foreign court in taking evidence from a witness within the foreign court's jurisdiction. Once a deposition is taken the foreign court will send a transcript or summary of the testimony to the requesting court. According to the State Department, letters rogatory are "a cumbersome, time consuming mechanism which should not be used unless there is no alternative." U.S. Department of State Circular, *Obtaining Evidence Abroad, available at* https://travel.state.gov/content/travel/en/legal/travel-legal-considerations/internl-judicial-asst/obtaining-evidence.html.*

   Depositions on notice are only available if the deponent agrees to be deposed or the party has the power to compel the deponent to appear. *Depositions before a commissioner* are similar to depositions on notice, but the deposition occurs before an appointed individual or consular office,

---

* Recall from Chapter 9 that letters rogatory are also sometimes used to transmit transnational service of process.

subject to a U.S. district court order designating a particular individual as a commissioner.

Under Rule 30 "a party may take the testimony of any person, including a party, by deposition upon oral examination without leave of court." Rule 30 applies regardless of whether the deponent is located in a foreign nation. Thus, any of the deposition methods specified by Rule 28(b) are available for party deponents, and the foreign party must submit to the deposition or be subject to court sanctions pursuant to Rule 37.

Similar to depositions of foreign party witnesses, any of Rule 28(b)'s methods can be used for taking the deposition of a foreign nonparty who agrees to be deposed. With respect to depositions of foreign nonparties who do not agree to be deposed, a party largely must rely on the letters rogatory process or the Hague Evidence Convention, discussed below. This is because foreign nonparties are typically not within the *subpoena* power of U.S. courts, unlike nonparty witnesses within the United States, nor are they vulnerable to discovery sanctions, as are party witnesses.

Courts have wide discretion to determine the time and place of the deposition. Plaintiffs generally are required to submit to depositions in the district in which they brought suit, although exceptions are sometimes made if doing so would present significant physical, financial, or other hardship. Similarly, a defendant's deposition is usually conducted in the district in which he or she resides. In choosing the location of third-party depositions, courts typically weigh the convenience of the deponent heavily.

Despite the fact that a U.S. court will accept deposition testimony under any of Rule 28(b)'s methods, the availability of these methods is nonetheless limited by and subject to the law of the foreign nation where the deposition is being conducted. Many foreign nations prohibit or restrict U.S. depositions in their territory. For example, in many civil law nations the judge — not counsel — conducts the examination of witnesses. In some nations "counsel" refers only to local counsel, and U.S. lawyers may be unable to attend evidence-taking sessions. Moreover, witnesses may not be examined under oath, and the proceedings may be recorded by a written summary, not a verbatim transcript. Even foreign nations that usually allow depositions within their territory may object to involuntary depositions.

Information about foreign restrictions on U.S. depositions may be obtained on a nation-by-nation basis from the U.S. State Department, the appropriate embassy abroad, or foreign local counsel. If a deponent is willing to cooperate, a party could consider taking the deposition in a nearby nation that does not restrict U.S. depositions or conducting the deposition by telephone.

Consider the differences between taking a party's deposition and taking a nonparty's deposition in transnational cases. How would you proceed for a party's deposition? How would you proceed for a nonparty deposition?

Practice pointer: As a general matter, counsel should pay close attention to a nation's particular restrictions because conducting depositions abroad in violation of foreign law may subject counsel to foreign criminal or civil penalties.

2. **Production of Documents.** Under Rule 34, a party to U.S. litigation can request that another party produce any relevant documents that are in the possession, custody, or control of that party. If a party does not voluntarily comply, Rule 45(a)(1)(C) permits the U.S. court to issue a *subpoena* (a court order) directing the party to produce "designated books, documents or tangible things in the possession, custody, or control of that person." The FRCP's Advisory Committee Notes clarify that "the person subject to the *subpoena* is required to produce materials in that person's control whether or not the materials are located within the district or within the territory within which the *subpoena* can be served." Thus, Rule 45 provides a means to obtain a party's documents even if they are located abroad.

　　Obtaining a nonparty's documents may be more difficult. If a nonparty voluntarily complies with a request for information, then discovery of that nonparty's documents located abroad can also proceed under Rule 34(c). If a nonparty does not voluntarily comply, Rule 45 permits a *subpoena* to produce documents or tangible things in the possession, custody, or control of a person, if the nonparty is within the *subpoena* power of the court. Thus, in some circumstances, Rule 45 provides a means to obtain a nonparty's documents abroad.

　　But often a nonparty will not be within the U.S. court's *subpoena* power. In such circumstances, the Federal Rules are of limited value and foreign judicial assistance is required. As described above, foreign judicial assistance can be obtained through a letter rogatory, a formal request by the courts of one nation to the courts of another for assistance in performing judicial acts. A letter rogatory may request that the foreign court receiving the letter compel a person within the court's jurisdiction to provide documents to the foreign court, which in turn forwards the documents to the requesting court. As the State Department website quoted above indicates, the use of letters rogatory is frequently cumbersome and time-consuming. Absent treaty commitments, foreign courts are under no obligation to execute them, and their processing frequently is delayed by poor diplomatic relations, bureaucratic inertia, and conflicts with public policy.

3. **Interrogatories and Requests for Admission.** As noted, Rule 33 and Rule 36 authorize written interrogatories and requests to admit to be served, expressly limiting their application to parties to the litigation. Interrogatories must be answered under oath based on information available to the party. Look closely at Rules 33 and 36. Are there any limits to using them in transnational cases?

　　In sum, transnational discovery under the Federal Rules is relatively straightforward when discovery is sought of another party. Nonparty discovery, on the other hand, presents significant challenges under the Federal Rules when the nonparty is located abroad.

B. Conducting Discovery Under the Hague Evidence Convention

　　We now turn to an overview of the Convention on the Taking of Evidence Abroad in Civil and Commercial Matters (the Hague Evidence Convention). (Note: Don't confuse this convention with the Hague Service Convention discussed in Chapter 9.) The Hague Evidence Convention was adopted by the Hague Conference on Private International Law in 1970, and it is now in effect among the United States and over 60 other nations — not a large number, but one that includes, for example, Germany, China, Russia, France, Italy, Australia, Korea, Mexico, and India. Some prominent nations are not parties, including Japan, Indonesia, Thailand, Canada, Egypt, and most nations in Africa and the Middle East. The Hague Evidence Convention provides a framework for cooperation among its parties on transnational discovery. The text of the Convention, and information about its parties, is available at the website of the Hague Conference on Private International Law, http://www.hcch.net/index_en.php?act=conventions .text&cid=82.

The first case below asks whether and when the Hague Evidence Convention overrides the Federal Rules in transnational cases. Subsequent cases examine the mechanics of discovery under the Convention.

Société Nationale Industrielle Aérospatiale v. United States District Court for the Southern District of Iowa

482 U.S. 522 (1987)

Justice STEVENS delivered the opinion of the Court.

The United States, the Republic of France, and 15 other Nations have acceded to the Hague Convention on the Taking of Evidence Abroad in Civil or Commercial Matters, opened for signature, Mar. 18, 1970, 23 U.S.T. 2555, T.I.A.S. No. 7444. This Convention — sometimes referred to as the "Hague Convention" or the "Evidence Convention" — prescribes certain procedures by which a judicial authority in one contracting state may request evidence located in another contracting state. The question presented in this case concerns the extent to which a federal district court must employ the procedures set forth in the Convention when litigants seek answers to interrogatories, the production of documents, and admissions from a French adversary over whom the court has personal jurisdiction.

I

The two petitioners are corporations owned by the Republic of France. They are engaged in the business of designing, manufacturing, and marketing aircraft. One of their planes, the "Rallye," was allegedly advertised in American aviation publications as "the World's safest and most economical STOL plane." On August 19, 1980, a Rallye crashed in Iowa, injuring the pilot and a passenger. Dennis Jones, John George, and Rosa George brought separate suits based upon this accident in the United States District Court for the Southern District of Iowa, alleging that petitioners had manufactured and sold a defective plane and that they were guilty of negligence and breach of warranty. Petitioners answered the complaints, apparently without questioning the jurisdiction of the District Court. With the parties' consent, the cases were consolidated and referred to a Magistrate. See 28 U.S.C. § 636(c)(1).

Initial discovery was conducted by both sides pursuant to the Federal Rules of Civil Procedure without objection. When plaintiffs served a second request for the production of documents pursuant to Rule 34, a set of interrogatories pursuant to Rule 33, and requests for admission pursuant to Rule 36, however, petitioners filed a motion for a protective order. The motion alleged that because petitioners are "French corporations, and the discovery sought can only be found in a foreign state, namely France," the Hague Convention dictated the exclusive procedures that must be followed for pretrial discovery. In addition, the motion stated that under French penal law, the petitioners could not respond to discovery requests that did not comply with the Convention.

. . .

III

In arguing their entitlement to a protective order, petitioners correctly assert that both the discovery rules set forth in the Federal Rules of Civil Procedure and the Hague Convention are the law of the United States. This observation, however, does not dispose of the question before us; we must analyze the interaction between these two bodies of federal law. Initially, we note that at least four different interpretations of the relationship between the federal discovery rules and the Hague Convention are possible. Two of these interpretations assume that the Hague Convention by its terms dictates the extent to which it supplants normal discovery rules. First, the Hague Convention might be read as requiring its use to the exclusion of any other discovery procedures whenever evidence located abroad is sought for use in an American court. Second, the Hague Convention might be interpreted to require first, but not exclusive, use of its procedures. Two other interpretations assume that international comity, rather than the obligations created by the treaty, should guide judicial resort to the Hague Convention. Third, then, the Convention might be viewed as establishing a supplemental set of discovery procedures, strictly optional under treaty law, to which concerns of comity nevertheless require first resort by American courts in all cases. Fourth, the treaty may be viewed as an undertaking among sovereigns to facilitate discovery to which an American court should resort when it deems that course of action appropriate, after considering the situations of the parties before it as well as the interests of the concerned foreign state.

In interpreting an international treaty, we are mindful that it is "in the nature of a contract between nations," *Trans World Airlines, Inc. v. Franklin Mint Corp.*, 466 U.S. 243, 253 (1984), to which "[g]eneral rules of construction apply." *Id.*, at 262. We therefore begin "with the text of the treaty and the context in which the written words are used." *Air France v. Saks*, 470 U.S. 392, 397 (1985). The treaty's history, "the negotiations, and the practical construction adopted by the parties" may also be relevant. *Id.*, at 396.

We reject the first two of the possible interpretations as inconsistent with the language and negotiating history of the Hague Convention. The preamble of the Convention specifies its purpose "to facilitate the transmission and execution of Letters of Request" and to "improve mutual judicial co-operation in civil or commercial matters." 23 U.S.T., at 2557, T.I.A.S. No. 7444. The preamble does not speak in mandatory terms which would purport to describe the procedures for all permissible transnational discovery and exclude all other existing practices. The text of the Evidence Convention itself does not modify the law of any contracting state, require any contracting state to use the Convention procedures, either in requesting evidence or in responding to such requests, or compel any contracting state to change its own evidence-gathering procedures.

The Convention contains three chapters. Chapter I, entitled "Letters of Requests," and chapter II, entitled "Taking of Evidence by Diplomatic Officers, Consular Agents and Commissioners," both use permissive rather than mandatory language. Thus, Article 1 provides that a judicial authority in one contracting state "may" forward a letter of request to the competent authority in another contracting state for the purpose of obtaining evidence. Similarly, Articles 15, 16, and 17 provide that diplomatic officers, consular agents, and commissioners "may . . . without compulsion," take evidence under certain conditions. The absence of any command that a contracting state must use Convention procedures when they are not needed is conspicuous.

Two of the Articles in chapter III, entitled "General Clauses," buttress our conclusion that the Convention was intended as a permissive supplement, not a pre-emptive replacement, for other means of obtaining evidence located abroad. Article 23 expressly authorizes a contracting state to declare that it will not execute any letter of request in aid of pretrial discovery of documents in a common-law country. Surely, if the Convention had been intended to replace completely the broad discovery powers that the common-law courts in the United States previously exercised over foreign litigants subject to their jurisdiction, it would have been most anomalous for the common-law contracting parties to agree to Article 23, which enables a contracting party to revoke its consent to the treaty's procedures for pretrial discovery. In the absence of explicit textual support, we are unable to accept the hypothesis that the common-law contracting states abjured recourse to all pre-existing discovery procedures at the same time that they accepted the possibility that a contracting party could unilaterally abrogate even the Convention's procedures. Moreover, Article 27 plainly states that the Convention does not prevent a contracting state from using more liberal methods of rendering evidence than those authorized by the Convention. Thus, the text of the Evidence Convention, as well as the history of its proposal and ratification by the United States, unambiguously supports the conclusion that it was intended to establish optional procedures that would facilitate the taking of evidence abroad.

An interpretation of the Hague Convention as the exclusive means for obtaining evidence located abroad would effectively subject every American court hearing a case involving a national of a contracting state to the internal laws of that state. Interrogatories and document requests are staples of international commercial litigation, no less than of other suits, yet a rule of exclusivity would subordinate the court's supervision of even the most routine of these pretrial proceedings to the actions or, equally, to the inactions of foreign judicial authorities. . . .

We conclude accordingly that the Hague Convention did not deprive the District Court of the jurisdiction it otherwise possessed to order a foreign national party before it to produce evidence physically located within a signatory nation.

. . .

V

Petitioners contend that even if the Hague Convention's procedures are not mandatory, this Court should adopt a rule requiring that American litigants first resort to those procedures before initiating any discovery pursuant to the normal methods of the Federal Rules of Civil Procedure. . . . It is well known that the scope of American discovery is often significantly broader than is permitted in other jurisdictions, and we are satisfied that foreign tribunals will recognize that the final decision on the evidence to be used in litigation conducted in American courts must be made by those courts. We therefore do not believe that an American court should refuse to make use of Convention procedures because of a concern that it may ultimately find it necessary to order the production of evidence that a foreign tribunal permitted a party to withhold.

Nevertheless, we cannot accept petitioners' invitation to announce a new rule of law that would require first resort to Convention procedures whenever discovery is sought from a foreign litigant. Assuming, without deciding, that we have the lawmaking power to do so, we are convinced that such a general rule would be unwise. In many situations the Letter of Request procedure authorized by the Convention would be unduly time consuming and expensive, as well as less certain to produce needed evidence than direct use of the Federal Rules. A rule of first resort in all cases would therefore be inconsistent with the overriding interest in the "just, speedy, and inexpensive determination" of litigation in our courts. See Fed. Rule Civ. Proc. 1.

Petitioners argue that a rule of first resort is necessary to accord respect to the sovereignty of states in which evidence is located. It is true that the process of obtaining evidence in a civil-law jurisdiction is normally conducted by a judicial officer rather than by private attorneys. Petitioners contend that if performed on French soil, for example, by an unauthorized person, such evidence-gathering might violate the "judicial sovereignty" of the host nation. Because it is only through the Convention that civil-law nations have given their consent to evidence-gathering activities within their borders, petitioners argue, we have a duty to employ those procedures whenever they are available. We find that argument unpersuasive. If such a duty were to be inferred from the adoption of the Convention itself, we believe it would have been described in the text of that document. Moreover, the concept of international comity requires in this context a more particularized analysis of the respective interests of the foreign nation and the requesting nation than petitioners' proposed general rule would generate. We therefore decline to hold as a blanket matter that comity requires resort to Hague Evidence Convention procedures without prior scrutiny in each case of the particular facts, sovereign interests, and likelihood that resort to those procedures will prove effective.

Some discovery procedures are much more "intrusive" than others. In this case, for example, an interrogatory asking petitioners to identify the pilots who flew flight tests in the Rallye before it was certified for flight by the Federal Aviation Administration, or a request to admit that petitioners authorized certain advertising in a particular magazine, is certainly less intrusive than a request to produce all of the "design specifications, line drawings and engineering plans and all engineering change orders and plans and all drawings concerning the leading edge slats for the Rallye type aircraft manufactured by the Defendants." Even if a court might be persuaded that a particular document request was too burdensome or too "intrusive" to be granted in full, with or without an appropriate protective order, it might well refuse to insist upon the use of Convention procedures before requiring responses to simple interrogatories or requests for admissions. The exact line between reasonableness and unreasonableness in each case must be drawn by the trial court, based on its knowledge of the case and of the claims and interests of the parties and the governments whose statutes and policies they invoke.

American courts, in supervising pretrial proceedings, should exercise special vigilance to protect foreign litigants from the danger that unnecessary, or unduly burdensome, discovery may place them in a disadvantageous position. Judicial supervision of discovery should always seek to minimize its costs and inconvenience and to prevent improper uses of discovery requests. When it is necessary to seek evidence abroad, however, the district court must supervise pretrial proceedings particularly closely to prevent discovery abuses. For example, the additional cost of transportation of documents or witnesses to or from foreign locations may increase the danger that discovery may be sought for the improper purpose of motivating settlement, rather than finding relevant and probative evidence. Objections to "abusive" discovery that foreign litigants advance should therefore receive the most careful consideration. In addition, we have long recognized the demands of comity in suits involving foreign states, either as parties or as sovereigns with a coordinate interest in the litigation. See *Hilton v. Guyot*, 159 U.S. 113 (1895). American courts should therefore take care to demonstrate due respect for any special problem confronted by the foreign litigant on account of its nationality or the location of its operations, and for any sovereign interest expressed by a foreign state. We do not articulate specific rules to guide this delicate task of adjudication.

VI

In the case before us, the Magistrate and the Court of Appeals correctly refused to grant the broad protective order that petitioners requested. The Court of Appeals erred, however, in stating that the Evidence Convention does not apply to the pending discovery demands. This holding may be read as indicating that the Convention procedures are not even an option that is open to the District Court. It must be recalled, however, that the Convention's specification of duties in executing states creates corresponding rights in requesting states; holding that the Convention does not apply in this situation would deprive domestic litigants of access to evidence through treaty procedures to which the contracting states have assented. Moreover, such a rule would deny the foreign litigant a full and fair opportunity to demonstrate appropriate reasons for employing Convention procedures in the first instance, for some aspects of the discovery process.

Accordingly, the judgment of the Court of Appeals is vacated, and the case is remanded for further proceedings consistent with this opinion.

It is so ordered.

[The opinion of Justice Blackmun, joined by Justices Brennan, Marshall, and O'Connor, concurring in part and dissenting in part, is omitted.]

NOTES AND QUESTIONS

1. **Application of the Convention.** In light of the Court's opinion, when does the Hague Evidence Convention apply and what does it require? Is this the right way to read the Convention? Under the Court's reading, what is the point of the Convention if litigants can use the Federal Rules instead? Under what circumstances will a party have a choice between the Convention and the Federal Rules, and what factors might you consider when making the choice?

2. **Practice After *Aérospatiale*.** Following the Court's decision, the general rule is that discovery can be taken through the Federal Rules even if the material to be produced is located abroad. *See, e.g., In re Automotive Refinishing Paint Antitrust Litig.*, 358 F.3d 288, 299 (3d Cir. 2004). In most cases, therefore, a lawyer will follow the Federal Rules when discovery is sought from a party. (Recall: Why would this be a litigant's preference?) When discovery is sought from a nonparty located in a nation that is a party to the Convention, recourse must be made to the Convention. (Recall: What would happen when evidence is located in a nation that is not party to the Convention?)

The Hague Convention has two mechanisms for discovery: letters of request submitted to a Central Authority and taking of evidence by diplomatic officers or commissioners.

Letters of Request are the most frequent type of discovery under the Hague Evidence Convention. They can be used for depositions, interrogatories, or requests for documents. Broadly speaking, most parties to the Convention have agreed to allow some form of discovery of documents and testimony. Document discovery under the Convention is by means of a Letter of Request, issued by the court where the action is pending and transmitted to the "Central Authority" of the jurisdiction where the discovery is to be conducted. The Central Authority is then responsible for transmitting the request to the appropriate judicial body for a response. *See* Arts. 1 & 2. Deposition testimony may also be obtained by means of a Letter of Request to the nation where the witness is located. *Id.*, Art. 3. Each of the Convention parties must establish a Central Authority responsible for accepting and processing Letters of Request from other contracting States. Where the evidence requested consists of deposition testimony, a Letter of Request can lead to the testimony being taken in a proceeding under the normal evidentiary rules of the nation where the witness is located. *Id.*, Arts. 15-22.

In the alternative, the Convention also provides procedures for the **taking of testimony in front of a diplomatic or consular officer** of the nation where the action is pending, or by a commissioner specially appointed by the court in which the action is pending.

Nations that are parties to the Hague Evidence Convention may make reservations and declarations limiting its provisions. For example, nations may opt out of the provisions allowing diplomatic or consular officers or special commissioners to take testimony, in which case a litigant seeking testimony must rely on the procedural rules of the foreign jurisdiction. Nations may also use declarations and reservations to specify requirements for and limits on the type of discovery requests they will entertain.

Most importantly, Article 23 of the Convention specifically permits a country to "declare that it will not execute Letters of Request issued for the purpose of obtaining pre-trial discovery of documents as known in Common Law countries." A large number of countries (including some common law countries) have made such a declaration. Although this exception is expressly limited to the pre-trial discovery of documents, most foreign nations that have invoked the reservation apply it to oral testimony as well. What does this mean, and how will it affect U.S. litigants?

As with the Hague Service Convention discussed in Chapter 9, the Convention has a "status table" that shows what countries are parties to the Convention and what declarations and reservations they have made. *See* https://www.hcch .net/en/instruments/conventions/status-table/?cid=82. For what purposes would a U.S. lawyer need to consult the status table? Suppose you are a U.S. lawyer seeking discovery in Australia, Japan, Mexico, and Morocco. Consult the status table. What does it tell you for each of these countries, and how does that affect your discovery planning?

The Convention contains several requirements restricting its applicability. First, both the requesting and requested persons or entities must be domiciled in countries that are parties to the Convention. Second, the Convention applies only to "civil or commercial matters." These terms are not defined in the Convention's text, and there is little consensus as to their meaning. Third, the Convention applies only to evidence sought for use in a "judicial proceeding." This may suggest that it cannot be used by arbitral panels or administrative agencies conducting investigations.

We now explore in more detail the methods for collection of evidence under the Hague Evidence Convention. As discussed, the Convention provides for the collection of evidence by letter of request, diplomatic or consular officer, or appointed commissioner.

Letters of Request. The requesting country must issue a Letter of Request to the Central Authority of the country where the evidence sought is located. The requested country then "executes [the] Letter of Request [pursuant to] . . . its own law." Art. 2. Because discovery procedures in foreign nations can vary widely from those in the United States, this provision can have a profound effect on the manner in which evidence is obtained. Thus, to reconcile these differences in evidence-taking methods, Article 9 requires nations to apply special evidence-taking procedures if requested, subject to two exceptions: Nations need not follow procedures that are (1) incompatible with their domestic law or are (2) impossible to perform because of practical difficulties.

Under the Convention, the Central Authority may refuse to implement a Letter of Request if it concludes that the request does not comply with the Convention. In that case, the Central Authority must "inform the authority of the State of origin which transmitted the Letter of Request, specifying the objections to the Letter." Art. 5. Examples of noncompliance include if the matter is not civil or commercial, as required by Article 1; if the request does not relate to judicial proceedings per Article 1; if the Letter does not comply with the form and content set forth in Articles 3 and 4 of the Convention (including any relevant declarations and reservations of the requested country); or if the request seeks the pre-trial discovery of documents and the country has filed an Article 23 reservation. In addition, a country may refuse a Letter of Request if "in the state of execution the execution of the Letter does not fall within the functions of the judiciary" or if "the State addressed considers that its sovereignty or security would be prejudiced thereby." Art. 12.

The Convention expressly precludes countries from refusing to implement requests on the grounds that that their domestic law would have exclusive subject matter jurisdiction over the action or that their domestic law would not recognize such a cause of action. However, a person subject to a foreign discovery request may refuse to give evidence if that person has a privilege or duty to refuse to give the evidence under domestic law.

There is no specific timeframe for processing Letters of Request under the Convention. Rather, the Convention provides that countries must execute them "expeditiously." Art. 9. This frequently creates problems for U.S. litigants trying to comply with U.S. discovery schedules.

Diplomatic and Consular Officers and Appointed Commissioners. These methods are not frequently used because of their limitations and requirements, and they usually are appropriate only when a person is providing evidence voluntarily. For example, Article 15 authorizes consuls to take evidence from nationals of the consul's home country pursuant to the following requirements: (1) the consul cannot use compulsion; (2) member countries may require that consuls take evidence only after obtaining permission to do so from local authorities; and (3) the consul may take evidence only for use in proceedings that have actually "commenced" (as opposed to those that are merely "contemplated").

Article 16 authorizes consuls to take evidence from nationals of the nation in which the consul is stationed. In addition to the requirements of Article 15, Article 16 states that prior approval by local authorities is necessary unless the country has filed a declaration permitting Article 16 evidence-taking without prior approval, and few countries have made such a declaration. Article 18 allows countries to declare that foreign consuls and commissioners may seek coercive orders from local authorities to compel evidence, but few countries have filed such an unconditional declaration.

Having provided some background on the Federal Rules and the Hague Evidence Convention, we now explore through the following cases how the two discovery regimes interact.

Costa v. Kerzner Int'l Resorts, Inc.

277 F.R.D. 468 (S.D. Fla. 2011)

BARRY S. SELTZER, United States Magistrate Judge.

THIS CAUSE is before the Court on Plaintiff's Motion and Incorporated Memorandum of Law in Support of Her Motion to Compel and was referred to the undersigned pursuant to 28 U.S.C. § 636. Specifically, Plaintiff Jennifer Costa ("Plaintiff") has filed a motion pursuant to Rules 26, 33 and 34 of the Federal Rules of Civil Procedure and Southern District of Florida Local Rules 7.1 and 26.1, to compel Defendants Kerzner International Resorts, Inc. ("Kerzner Resorts"), Kerzner International North America, Inc. ("Kerzner North America"), Kerzner International Marketing, Inc. ("Kerzner Marketing"), and PIV Inc., d/b/a Destination Atlantis ("PIV") to (1) produce documents responsive to each of Plaintiff's Document Requests (except Number 13); and (2) supplement their responses to Plaintiff's Interrogatories Nos. 2, 3, 6, 7 and 10, with documents and information in the possession, custody, or control of Defendants' affiliated corporations Kerzner International Limited ("Kerzner International"), Kerzner International Bahamas Limited ("Kerzner Bahamas"), and Island Hotel Company Ltd. ("Island Hotel") (collectively the "Bahamian Affiliates"). Plaintiff further seeks an award of attorneys' fees in connection with her motion. At issue is the scope of Plaintiff's Document Requests and Interrogatories; specifically, whether the reach of Fed. R. Civ. P. 33 and 34 extends to documents and information in the physical possession of Defendants' Bahamian Affiliates. The Court having considered the briefed Motion and being otherwise fully advised, it is hereby ORDERED that the Motion is GRANTED in PART as set forth below.

Background

This case is about the collection and distribution of a "mandatory housekeeping gratuity and utility service fee" that Defendants allegedly charged members of the proposed class in connection with their stay at the Atlantis Resort in the Bahamas. Plaintiff alleges that the imposition of this charge is unfair and deceptive because it is not entirely given to housekeepers as a "gratuity" or used to pay utilities, but is instead deceptively used for other (undisclosed) purposes.

. . . Defendants objected to the majority of Plaintiff's Requests for Production and Interrogatories on the basis that they call for documents and information allegedly not in Defendants' possession, custody, or control but instead in the possession, custody, or control of their Bahamian Affiliates.

Plaintiff thereafter filed the instant motion to compel, arguing that information and documents in the possession of a defendant's corporate affiliates are deemed to be in that defendant's control for purposes of Federal Rules of Civil Procedure 26,

33 and 34, particularly where, as Plaintiff alleges, the non-party affiliated corporations are intimately connected to, and enjoy the benefits of, the transaction at issue, and have a substantial stake in the outcome of the instant litigation. Defendants oppose Plaintiff's Motion. They contend that they should not be compelled to produce documents and information from their Bahamian Affiliates because they lack the requisite control; they further contend that Plaintiff should avail herself of the Hague Convention procedures for acquiring discovery from foreign entities.

Discussion

Federal Rule of Civil Procedure 34(a) governs the production of documents in civil matters. Pursuant to Rule 34(a), a party must produce documents in response to a request for production where those documents are "in the responding party's possession, custody, or control[.]" Fed. R. Civ. P. 34(a). Whether documents are in a parties control under Rule 34 is broadly construed. "Control," therefore, does not require that a party have legal ownership or actual physical possession of the documents at issue; indeed, documents have been considered to be under a party's control (for discovery purposes) when that party has the right, authority, or practical ability to obtain the materials sought on demand.

. . .

In determining whether a party has control over documents and information in the possession of nonparty affiliates, the Court must look to: (1) the corporate structure of the party and the nonparties; (2) the nonparties' connection to the transaction at issue in the litigation; and (3) the degree to which the nonparties benefit from the outcome of the litigation. "Numerous courts have addressed the concept of 'control' as between corporate entities; virtually all of the published decisions have required production by the nonparty corporation." *Mt. Hawley Ins. Co. v. Felman Prod., Inc.*, 269 F.R.D. 609, 617 (S.D. W. Va. 2010). Here, each relevant factor militates in favor of granting Plaintiff's motion to compel.

As to the first factor, Defendants and their Bahamian Affiliates are all wholly owned by one entity (Kerzner Holdings Limited), part of a unified corporate structure. Courts have consistently held that "control" exists where the party and its related nonparty affiliate are owned by the same individual. Furthermore, a subsidiary has access to and control over documents held by a foreign parent corporation, particularly when there is a close working relationship on a common transaction and the subsidiary could easily obtain the documents when it is in its interest to do so.

It is also apparent that there are financial and operational interactions between Defendants and their Bahamian Affiliates. Defendants Kerzner Resorts and PIV state that they transfer the charges and fees ostensibly collected for housekeeping gratuities and utility payments to Island Hotel. Thus, the companies from which Plaintiff is seeking discovery share commonality in their corporate structure and operations sufficient to require Defendants to produce all responsive documents in the possession, custody, or control of their Bahamian Affiliates.

. . .

As to the second factor, the Bahamian Affiliates are directly connected to the transactions at issue here. In response to Plaintiff's discovery requests relating to the "mandatory housekeeping gratuities and utility service fees," Defendants stated that "such sums are transferred to the Island Hotel Company" or that they "distribute" the fee to Island Hotel. Furthermore, it appears that cooperation between Defendants and their Bahamian Affiliates is indispensable for the completion of the transaction: Defendants impose and collect the "mandatory housekeeping gratuity" and the Bahamian Affiliates distribute those funds.

In *Cooper Industries, Inc. v. British Aerospace*, the court held that the defendant was obligated to produce documents in the possession of an affiliated British company, focusing on the party's likely access to documents in the ordinary course of business. 102 F.R.D. at 919-20. Opining that "it is inconceivable that defendant would not have access to these documents and the ability to obtain them for its usual business," the court held:

> The fact that the documents are situated in a foreign country does not bar their discovery. . . . Defendant cannot be allowed to shield crucial documents from discovery by parties with whom it has dealt in the United States merely by storing them with its affiliate abroad . . . if defendant could so easily evade discovery, every United States company would have a foreign affiliate for storing sensitive documents.

Id. at 920. Given their established corporate and transactional connections, it is similarly unlikely that Defendants do not have access to and the ability to obtain documents and information in the possession of their Bahamian Affiliates.

As to the third factor, as the parent company of Defendants and their Bahamian Affiliates, Kerzner International (and by extension its subsidiaries), has a direct financial interest in the outcome of the litigation, as it may ultimately be responsible for damages to the Class. Plaintiff, therefore, has sufficiently demonstrated that Defendants "control" the requested documents and information in the possession, custody, or control of their Bahamian Affiliates.

And finally, the Court is not persuaded that Plaintiff must first resort to the Hague Convention to obtain the requested discovery from Defendants. The Hague Convention on Taking Evidence Abroad provides procedures for judicial authorities of one signatory country to use in requesting evidence located in another signatory country. In *Société Nationale Industrielle Aérospatiale v. U.S. Dist. Court for S. Dist. of Iowa*, 482 U.S. 522 (1987), the Supreme Court addressed the interaction between the procedures provided for by the Hague Convention and the Federal Rules of Civil Procedure. The Supreme Court explained that the Hague Convention "was intended as a permissive supplement, not a preemptive replacement, for other means of obtaining evidence located abroad." *Id.* at 536. The Supreme Court rejected the precise argument advanced by Defendants here that parties must resort to Hague Convention procedures first, prior to utilizing the procedures made available by the Federal Rules of Civil Procedure.

. . .

Conclusion

Accordingly, . . . Plaintiff's Motion is GRANTED to the extent that Defendants shall provide within thirty (30) days of the issuance of this Order all documents that are in the possession of Defendants' Bahamian Affiliates . . . and . . . shall supplement their responses to Plaintiff's Interrogatories Nos. 2, 3, 6, 7 and 10, contained within Plaintiff's First Set of Interrogatories to Defendants, with information in the possession of Defendants' Bahamian Affiliates.

NOTES AND QUESTIONS

1. **Motions to Compel.** *Costa* resolves a motion to compel production of documents and responses to interrogatories. As you may recall from civil procedure, civil discovery in the United States is largely party-driven. Courts only tend to become involved when one party refuses to turn over materials or make responses that the other party believes are required under the Federal Rules. That refusal leads to a motion to compel and (if the motion is granted) a court order to the other party to comply with the discovery requests.
2. **Practice Under the Federal Rules.** Why does the question of custody or control matter? Why does the plaintiff in *Costa* want to establish that the documents are under the U.S. defendant's custody or control? What would happen otherwise? Why can't the U.S. court require the Bahamian affiliate to turn over the materials?
3. **The Convention versus the Federal Rules.** The court in *Costa* explains that, according to the Supreme Court, first resort need not be made to the Hague Evidence Convention. Is that correct? Why does the application of the Convention matter? Would it make any difference in how the case is resolved? Are there practical reasons for the plaintiff to forgo using the Convention in favor of the Federal Rules?

Let's now take a look at what happens when the Hague Evidence Convention is used.

Pronova BioPharma Norge A.S. v. Teva Pharmaceuticals USA, Inc.

708 F. Supp. 2d 450 (D. Del. 2010)

MARY PAT THYNGE, United States Magistrate Judge.

I. Background

In this patent infringement case, defendants Apotex Inc. and Apotex Corp. ("Apotex"), Par Pharmaceutical, Inc. and Par Pharmaceutical Companies, Inc. ("Par"), and Teva Pharmaceuticals USA, Inc. ("Teva") move for issuance of Letters of Request for international judicial assistance pursuant to the Hague

Evidence Convention. Plaintiff Pronova BioPharma Norge AS ("Pronova") claims that defendants' Abbreviated New Drug Applications ("ANDA") for a generic version of GlaxoSmithKline's LOVAZA® pharmaceutical product infringe its patents, specifically U.S. Patent Nos. 5,502,077 ("the '077 patent") and 5,656,667 ("the '667 patent"). Defendants maintain that their ANDAs do not infringe Pronova's patents and that the '077 and '667 patents are invalid and unenforceable. The defendants seek to obtain discovery from the inventors of the '077 and '667 patents and from several individuals who filed declarations in support of patentability during the prosecutions of those two patents. These inventors and declarants from whom discovery is presently sought reside in either Norway or Sweden.

II. Legal Standard

. . . The United States, Sweden, and Norway are contracting states under the Hague Evidence Convention. Letters of Request are one method of taking evidence pursuant to the Convention. Upon receipt of a Letter of Request, which must provide specific information regarding the lawsuit and the information sought to be discovered, the signatory state "shall [then] apply the appropriate measure of compulsion" as is customary "for the execution of orders issued by the authorities of its own country." Individuals to whom a Letter of Request is directed have the right to refuse to give evidence to the extent they are protected by a privilege under either the law of the State of execution or the State of origin.

Discussion

. . . In this case, both parties agree that Letters of Request should be used. The parties' briefing makes clear that the inventors and declarants subject to the defendants' motion are not parties to the lawsuit, have not voluntarily subjected themselves to discovery, are citizens of either Norway or Sweden, and are not otherwise subject to the jurisdiction of this court. Under these circumstances, it is appropriate to turn to the Hague Evidence Convention.

Pronova opposes only "certain details" set out in defendants' proposed Letters of Request. In its answer, Pronova provides, "Should Pronova be able to agree on the substance of the Letters of request with Defendants, Pronova would agree to join the Defendants in their motion to issue the Letters of Request." Pronova argues that the defendants' Letters of Request are inappropriate to the extent they (1) "contain requests for clearly privileged information"; (2) "contain misleading, argumentative, and/or unfounded statements"; (3) are "unreasonably broad and include requests for information not relevant and/or not reasonably likely to be within the personal knowledge of the specified individual"; (4) "call for legal conclusions from those not qualified to make them"; (5) "request documents with no foundation of existence"; and (6) "improperly request that the deponents prepare for the deposition by going through relevant documents in advance of the deposition." The defendants characterize Pronova's objections to their motion as mere attempts to inject United States procedural law where it is not required under the Hague Convention.

The court finds unpersuasive Pronova's objections to the defendants' Letters of Request based on its perception that the defendants' requests are misleading, argumentative, overly broad, otherwise of improper form, or inappropriately call for legal conclusions. If the defendants' requests suffer from such maladies under the laws of Norway or Sweden, then the requests will presumably be narrowed by the appropriate judicial authorities in those countries. . . . Equally unpersuasive is Pronova's objection based on what it characterizes as the defendants' request for documents with "no foundation of existence." As defendants argue, they cannot know exactly what specific information each witness has, and to the extent that a particular witness does not have the information requested, that witness may so state.

The court is also not convinced that the defendants must revise their Letters of Request to clarify that they will not inquire into matters which are subject to the attorney-client or any other applicable privilege, or that they will take the most restrictive view of privilege applicable, whether it be under United States, Norwegian, or Swedish law. Pronova asserts that the defendants' Letters of Request require such revisions. As the defendants point out, however, Article 3 of the Hague Evidence Convention provides that "[a] Letter *may* also mention any information necessary for the application of Article 11," and Article 11 of the Hague Evidence Convention reads:

> In the execution of a Letter of Request the person concerned may refuse to give evidence in so far as he has a privilege or duty to refuse to give the evidence —
>
> a) under the law of the State of execution; or
> b) under the law of the State of origin, and the privilege or duty has been specified in the Letter, or, at the instance of the requested authority, has been otherwise confirmed to that authority by the requesting authority.

A Contracting State may declare that, in addition, it will respect privileges and duties existing under the law of States other than the State of origin and the State of execution, to the extent specified in that declaration.

Article 11 does not dictate that the inventors and declarants to whom the defendants direct their Letters of Request need be apprised of the above right to refuse to give evidence. Under Article 11, these individuals may avail themselves of the privilege provided in this country and in the executing country. These individuals may also obtain counsel. In fact, Pronova's answering brief indicates that eight of the ten individuals to whom the defendants direct their Letters of Request have agreed to be represented in this matter by Pronova's counsel. The court is confident that Pronova's counsel will not forget, in its future representation of these individuals, to express its own views on privilege and, if necessary, to seek this court's opinion with respect to those views.

. . .

IT IS ORDERED that . . . The defendants' motion to issue Letters of Request for international judicial assistance pursuant to the Hague Evidence Convention is GRANTED. . . .

NOTES AND QUESTIONS

1. **Inability to Use the Federal Rules.** According to the court in *Pronova*, "[t]he parties' briefing makes clear that the inventors and declarants subject to the defendants' motion are not parties to the lawsuit, have not voluntarily subjected themselves to discovery, are citizens of either Norway or Sweden, and are not otherwise subject to the jurisdiction of this court. Under these circumstances, it is appropriate to turn to the Hague Evidence Convention." Why do these circumstances prevent the applicability of the Federal Rules? Why is the Convention appropriate?

2. **Limits to Discovery Under the Convention.** Note that the laws of the nation where the evidence is sought might limit the request. Why would the Hague Evidence Convention adopt this approach? Note also that the privilege law of the foreign nation (known as the executing nation) may be applicable to the declarants. Note further that the Central Authority of the executing nation may find the request defective in various respects. If that happens, what is the requesting party's recourse? Are you beginning to see why a requesting party might want to use the Federal Rules?

3. **Practice: Drafting a Letter of Request.** As a party seeking evidence under the Convention, how would you draft the request? Would you make a broad or narrow request for documents? Would you ask open-ended or specific questions? What are the competing considerations? Remember that it may be difficult to make follow-up requests or ask follow-up questions. What if you ask for a document that you are confident the foreign person has, but the response is that no such document is in the person's possession — what can you do next, if anything?

In re Urethane Antitrust Litigation

267 F.R.D. 361 (D. Kan. 2010)

JAMES P. O'HARA, United States Magistrate Judge.

This multidistrict litigation consists of class-action and direct-action lawsuits in which plaintiffs claim defendants engaged in unlawful price fixing and market-allocation conspiracies with respect to polyether polyol products in violation of the Sherman Antitrust Act, 15 U.S.C. § 1. The parties have filed cross-motions for the issuance of so-called letters of request pursuant to the Hague Convention and Fed. R. Civ. P. 28(b), to obtain evidence from certain witnesses in Germany. Plaintiffs' motion seeks the issuance of letters to the appropriate German authorities to secure the testimony of two former employees and one current employee of former-defendant Bayer. The motion is accompanied by drafts of the letters that plaintiffs request, each of which includes a list of questions to be posed to the particular witness. Defendants state that they "do not object in principle to the examination of the three foreign witnesses," but contend plaintiffs should first "make a showing that the witnesses will testify rather than assert testimonial privileges." If the court decides the letters of request should issue, then defendants' cross-motion seeks to modify the letters drafted by plaintiffs to (1) exclude certain of the examination questions plaintiffs propose, (2) add examination questions defendants propose, and (3) add procedural requests to the German authorities.

I. Background

. . .

Plaintiffs, who are direct purchasers of polyether polyol products, claim the defendant manufacturers conspired to fix, raise, maintain, and stabilize the prices at which their products were sold, and to allocate customers and markets for their products. Bayer was a defendant in this action until it settled the claims against it in 2006. As part of the settlement agreement, Bayer agreed to cooperate with plaintiffs and to identify persons with information regarding the liability of non-settling defendants, alleged co-conspirators.

According to plaintiffs, Bayer has identified three individuals who held senior positions at Bayer during the conspiracy period as possessing information relevant to this litigation. The three individuals are Christian Buhse, a former vice president who was in charge of Bayer's global sales and pricing of TDI (toluene diisocyanate); Werner Spinner, a former member of Bayer AG's board of management; and Dr. Dennis McCullough, Bayer AG's global product manager for MDI (diphenylmethane diisocyanate). According to Bayer, these men had multiple meetings with competitors in which prices, price increases, market conditions, and customer allocations were discussed. Plaintiffs state that all of these witnesses presently reside in North Rhine-Westphalia, Germany, making resort to the Hague Convention appropriate for obtaining their testimony.

II. Appropriateness of Issuing Letters of Request

Fed. R. Civ. P. 28(b) governs the taking of depositions in a foreign country. It provides that a foreign deposition may be taken "under a letter of request," which a court may issue "on appropriate terms after an application and notice of it." . . . The Hague Convention, of which both the United States and Germany are signatories, provides the mechanism for gathering evidence abroad through the issuance of a letter of request. Resort to using the procedures of the Hague Convention is particularly appropriate when, as here, a litigant seeks to depose a foreign non-party who is not subject to the court's jurisdiction.

There is no dispute that the three potential witnesses in Germany possess knowledge relevant to the claims and defenses in this case. Defendants argue, however, that the court should not issue the letters of request unless plaintiffs show that the witnesses actually will testify, rather than assert testimonial privileges.[12]

Defendants cite no persuasive authority, and the court can find none, for the proposition that a party seeking foreign assistance under the Hague Convention is required to show that the evidence sought will actually be attained.

Plaintiffs have shown that Messrs. Buhse, Spinner, and McCullough likely have knowledge that goes to the heart of the claims and defenses in this litigation. And defendants have failed to show good reason why plaintiffs' application for the issuance of letters of request should be denied. Thus, the court will issue the letters.

III. Contents of the Letters of Request

Defendants' cross-motion for issuance of letters of request asserts that the content of the letters drafted by plaintiffs should be revised. First, defendants argue that the list of "questions to be put to the persons to be examined," set forth pursuant to Article 3(f) of the Hague Convention, should be modified. Defendants assert that some of plaintiffs' questions seek evidence that would not be admitted at trial based on hearsay or other grounds. Defendants ask the court to exclude from the letters of request all questions that seek answers that would be inadmissible at trial.

The court respectfully declines defendants' invitation to pre-screen the questions to determine whether they will elicit admissible testimony. While it is true that the Hague Convention governs the use of letters of request to obtain "evidence," defendants have presented no authority to support their assertion that all such evidence must be admissible. . . .

Although the court will not parse the questions, the court notes that plaintiffs have voluntarily revised their list of questions and withdrawn some exhibits in order to address the concerns raised by defendants. The letters issued by the court will reflect these amendments.

Second, defendants request that the letters include additional exhibits and questions prepared by defendants. Plaintiffs do not object to this request. Thus, the letters issued by the court will include defendants' additional questions and exhibits.

Third, defendants ask that the letters of request include defendants' German designee alongside plaintiffs' German designee in paragraph 14. This request is granted, and defendants' German designee will be included in paragraph 14.

Fourth, defendants ask the court to modify the procedural-requests sections of the letters drafted by plaintiffs. The Hague Convention provides that the judicial authority executing a letter of request "shall apply its own law as to the methods

---

12. Article 11 of the Hague Convention permits a person being questioned "to refuse to give evidence insofar as he has a privilege or a duty to refuse to give the evidence" under the law of either the state of origin (i.e., the United States) of the state of execution (i.e., Germany).

and procedures to be followed," but "will follow a request of the requesting authority that a special method or procedure be followed, unless this is incompatible with the internal [law or practice and procedure of Germany]." Citing this provision, plaintiffs set forth a number of procedural requests in paragraph 13 of their proposed letters. These requests include permitting a U.S. court reporter to make a verbatim record of the witnesses' examinations and permitting counsel to ask additional questions following the witnesses' responses to the pre-set questions.

Defendants state they have no objection to plaintiffs' procedural requests, but move for the inclusion of additional special procedural requests. Specifically, defendants ask the court to include a request that the parties be permitted to "conduct the examinations of the witnesses, or at a minimum, allow counsel to conduct a cross-examination of the witnesses." Plaintiffs do not oppose this request. Germany's Response to the 2008 Hague Conference Questionnaire states that, under the German Code of Civil Procedure, the German court will permit a witness to "present his perceptions on the subject on which evidence is to be given in summary form" and then will "interrogate witnesses to complete the statement." Thereafter, "it is primarily the parties' lawyers who have the right to directly question witnesses." Although this right is usually exercised "by submitting questions to the witness," Germany's Response goes on to state that "the party may also be permitted by the court to interrogate the witness directly." The German courts do not permit cross-examination, however. Based on Germany's Response, the court will include in the letters the special request that the parties be permitted to interrogate the witnesses directly. The court believes it is probably futile to ask the German courts to permit the parties to cross-examine the witnesses. But since this request is unopposed, the court nonetheless will include it in the letters.

Finally, defendants request that the letters include a reference to potential testimonial privileges and that the German court advise the witnesses of "any applicable testimonial privileges." The court acknowledges that Articles 3 and 11(b) of the Hague Convention contemplate identification of potential privileges under U.S. law. Thus, in Section 16 of the letters, the court will specify the potential applicable privileges under U.S. law identified by the parties: the attorney-client privilege, and the privilege against self incrimination as conferred by the Fifth Amendment to the U.S. Constitution. The court will not, however, include a special "procedural" request that the German courts advise the witnesses of particular, "applicable," privileges. This request would go beyond mere procedure and in effect would require the German court to make substantive legal rulings on which testimonial privileges applied, before such privileges were even asserted (if at all) by the witnesses. Likewise, the court will not include in the letters defendants' purportedly "procedural" request that the German court ask certain proposed questions in the event a witness asserts a testimonial privilege. Again, the court is unpersuaded this special request is the type of procedural request contemplated by the Hague Convention.

Plaintiffs identify in their reply brief an additional special procedural request they want included in the letters: "That, if the German court decides to limit the oral examinations, *e.g.*, to a specific amount of time or a specific number of questions, the examination be divided equally between plaintiffs' questions and defendants' questions." The court finds this to be a fair procedural request and will include it in the letters.

In consideration of the foregoing,

IT IS HEREBY ORDERED:

1. Plaintiffs' motion for the issuance of letters of request is granted.
2. Defendants' cross-motion for the issuance of letters of request is granted in part and denied in part.
3. Plaintiffs shall confer in good faith with defendants to prepare final versions of the letters of request that incorporate the rulings made herein and shall submit those letters, in WordPerfect format, to the chambers of the undersigned judge by March 2, 2010.

NOTES AND QUESTIONS

1. **From Doctrine to Practice.** Why did it matter that the persons from whom the testimony is sought might assert a testimonial privilege? In what situations might a court choose *not* to issue Letters of Request? Why do you think the court declined to revise the drafted Letters of Request? Note how drafting and executing Letters of Request is a fine balancing act between a liberalized discovery process in the United States and differing views of discovery abroad. Does the Hague Convention strike the right balance?
2. **Foreign Law.** Note how the law of the executing nation, here Germany, comes into play. How does German law differ from U.S. law? The court agrees to include information on U.S. testimonial privilege, but not German privilege law. Why?

C. Discovery that Conflicts with Foreign Law

We now turn to a significant complication encountered in transnational discovery: What if the foreign nation does not permit the evidence to be subject to discovery? This problem sometimes arises in the form of so-called blocking statutes — statutes adopted by one nation to prevent compliance with another nation's discovery rules when those rules are deemed to be excessively expansive.

Strauss v. Credit Lyonnais, S.A.

242 F.R.D. 199 (E.D.N.Y. 2007)

MATSUMOTO, United States Magistrate Judge.

. . .

Plaintiffs are individuals and estates, survivors and heirs of individuals who were injured or killed in thirteen separate terrorist attacks, allegedly perpetrated by [the Islamic Resistance Movement ("HAMAS")] in Israel between March 28, 2002 and August 19, 2003. Plaintiffs allege that Credit Lyonnais is a financial institution incorporated and headquartered in France. Plaintiffs further allege that Credit Lyonnais maintains bank accounts in France for Le Comite de Bienfaisance et de Secours aux Palestinians ("CBSP"), and that although CBSP describes itself as a charitable organization, it is part of HAMAS's fundraising infrastructure. . . .

On June 30, 2006, plaintiffs served Credit Lyonnais with their First Request for the Production of Documents. [Plaintiffs sought information relating to CBSP's accounts with Credit Lyonnais]. . . .

In response, Credit Lyonnais objected to . . . plaintiffs' Document Requests . . . on the grounds that, *inter alia*, the requests, seek the disclosure of commercial and financial information in violation of Article 1 bis of French law No. 68-678, which prohibits such disclosure in connection with a foreign judicial proceeding, except pursuant to an enforceable international treaty or agreement. Under Article 1 bis, [Credit Lyonnais] would be exposed to liability under French law unless disclosure proceeds in accordance with the Convention of 18 March 1970 on the Taking of Evidence Abroad in Civil or Commercial Matters (the "Hague Convention"), to which France and the United States are parties. Such liability would be avoided by following Hague Convention procedures, which should therefore be followed here.

. . .

Plaintiffs now seek to compel Credit Lyonnais to respond. . . .

In determining whether to compel production of documents located abroad from foreign parties, courts in the Second Circuit consider the following five factors elucidated by the Supreme Court in [*Société Nationale Industrielle Aérospatiale*] and set forth in Restatement of Foreign Relations Law of the United States § 442(1)(c):

> (1) the importance to the . . . litigation of the documents or other information requested;
> (2) the degree of specificity of the request;
> (3) whether the information originated in the United States;
> (4) the availability of alternative means of securing the information; and
> (5) the extent to which noncompliance with the request would undermine important interests of the United States, or compliance with the request would undermine the important interests of the state where the information is located.
> . . .

1. The Requested Information Is Crucial to the Litigation

. . .

In this case, plaintiffs seek documents and information revealing Credit Lyonnais's knowledge of CBSP's alleged terrorist connections and the extent of the bank's financial services in support of CBSP's alleged terrorist acts. Indeed, Credit Lyonnais concedes that "the documents and information sought by plaintiffs are undeniably of potential importance to the outcome of this litigation." . . .

Given plaintiffs' allegations regarding Credit Lyonnais's provision of financial services to CBSP for more than thirteen years, including accepting deposits from and/or distributing funds to alleged terrorist organizations on behalf of CBSP, the court finds that the discovery sought is both relevant and crucial to the litigation of plaintiffs' claims. . . .

2. The Discovery Requests Are Narrowly Tailored

. . .

Here, the court finds that the requested discovery is relevant, vital and narrowly tailored to the litigation. . . . Plaintiffs' discovery requests are sufficiently focused on the vital issues in this case: whether and to what extent Credit Lyonnais knowingly provided "material support and resources" . . . and/or "financial services" to a terrorist organization. Plaintiffs' discovery requests seek, *inter alia*, documentation of the relationship between defendant and CBSP, the nature and extent of the services that defendant provided to CBSP, the collection or distribution of funds by Credit Lyonnais that may have been used by CBSP and/or its associates to support terrorism, and Credit Lyonnais's knowledge of CBSP's alleged terrorist connections. . . .

3. Availability of Alternative Methods: Plaintiffs Are Not Required to Seek Discovery Initially or Exclusively Through the Hague Convention

. . . The court notes that plaintiffs do not have direct or ready access to Credit Lyonnais's records through means other than discovery demands. Only Credit Lyonnais can provide plaintiffs with responses to their requested discovery.

Credit Lyonnais argues that plaintiffs "may be able to obtain the discovery they seek through letters of request pursuant to the Hague Convention. . . ."

The United States Supreme Court, in *Aerospatiale*, determined that parties seeking discovery need not resort to the Hague Convention as their first and exclusive means for securing foreign discovery. . . . The Court . . . found that "the Hague Convention [does] not deprive the District Court of the jurisdiction it otherwise possessed to order a foreign national party before it to produce evidence physically located within a signatory nation." . . . Addressing the applicability of French blocking statutes, the Court continued,

> It is clear that American courts are not required to adhere blindly to the directives of [a foreign blocking statute]. Indeed, the language of the statute, if taken literally, would appear to represent an extraordinary exercise of legislative jurisdiction by the Republic of France over a United States district judge, forbidding him or her to order any discovery from a party of French nationality, even simple requests for admissions or interrogatories that the party could respond to on the basis of personal knowledge. . . . Extraterritorial assertions of jurisdiction are not one-sided.

Id.

Therefore, plaintiffs in this case need not seek discovery initially or exclusively through the Hague Convention, but, instead, may appropriately seek from this court an order compelling discovery. . . .

4. The Mutual Interests of the United States and France in Combating Terrorism Outweigh the French Interest, If Any, Regarding the Disputed Discovery

. . .

Axiomatically, the United States has a substantial interest in fully and fairly adjudicating matters before its courts. When that interest is combined with the United States's goals of combating terrorism, it is elevated to nearly its highest point. . . .

The legislative history of the [Antiterrorism Act], Executive Orders signed by two United States Presidents, and the participation by the United States in international treaties and an international task force, reveal this country's profound and compelling interest in combating terrorism at every level, including disrupting the financial underpinnings of terrorist networks. . . .

Furthermore, the United States has consistently demonstrated its commitment to combating terrorist financing and to enlisting the help of foreign nations. In furtherance of that goal, the United States and other nations, including France, have committed to international cooperation. Both the United States and France are signatories to the United Nations's International Convention for the Suppression of the Financing of Terrorism, which recommends that nations "adopt[] effective measures for the prevention of the financing of terrorism. . . ." Both countries are also members of the Financial Action Task Force ("FATF"), which likewise seeks international cooperation in combating terrorist financing.

Thus, France has demonstrated its common national interests with the United States in thwarting terrorist financing by signing and joining the same convention and task force. . . .

Pursuant to Rst. § 442, the court should also weigh "the extent to which . . . compliance with the [discovery] request would undermine the important interests of the state where the information is located." . . .

Comment (c) to Rst. § 442 provides guidance for this analysis:

> In making the necessary determination of foreign interests under Subsection (1)(c), a court or agency in the United States should take into account[,] . . . expressions of interest by the foreign state, as contrasted with expressions by the parties; . . . the significance of disclosure in the regulation by the foreign state of the activity in question; . . . indications of the foreign state's concern for confidentiality prior to the controversy in connection with which the information is sought . . . [and] the long-term interests of the United States generally in international cooperation in law enforcement and judicial assistance, in joint approach to problems of common concern, in giving effect to formal or informal international agreements, and in orderly international relations.
>
> . . .

As an initial matter, the court notes that the French government has failed to respond to Credit Lyonnais's three attempts to contact it for guidance in this case. Likewise, CBSP, whose accounts were closed by Credit Lyonnais in 2002 and 2003, has not demonstrated any interest in preserving the confidentiality of its now inactive bank account records. As of the date of this order, there is no indication in the record that CBSP has responded substantively to the bank's repeated attempts at contact. The court presumes that if either the French government or CBSP objected to the production by Credit Lyonnais of information regarding CBSP's accounts, they would have so stated. Although CBSP's disinterest in protecting its rights to bank secrecy may not constitute a waiver of that right, CBSP's lack of response demonstrates a lack of vigilance and interest in preserving its right to financial secrecy. Similarly, where the French government's interests in its bank secrecy and other laws potentially affecting discovery are not asserted, the court need not give weight to those interests.

Notwithstanding the absence of any articulated interest by the French government, Credit Lyonnais asserts, "France has an obvious and undeniable national interest in protecting bank customer privacy and enforcing its internal banking, money laundering and terrorism laws, as well as its laws regarding criminal investigations." . . .

Defendant's expert, however, does not indicate whether civil and criminal liability is likely if defendant were to comply with an order of this court that the requested discovery be provided. . . .

. . . Courts have noted . . . that there is no significant risk of prosecution for violations of the French blocking statute. Moreover, as discussed below, France has pledged to participate with the international community in combating terrorist financing by signing the United Nations International Convention for the Suppression of the Financing of Terrorism and joining the FATF, both of which emphasize the importance of international cooperation. Those "international agreements" mandate disclosure of bank customer information to signatory countries, and thus arguably provide an exception to French Criminal Code 410-1.

. . .

In addition, and most importantly, France, like the United States, also has expressed and demonstrated a profound and compelling interest in eliminating terrorist financing. That France has an interest in eradicating the financing of terrorism by imposing monitoring and reporting obligations on its banks regarding customers who finance, or may be suspected of financing, terrorist acts around the world, is established by the fact that France has signed international treaties that mandate such monitoring and disclosure and explicitly direct the member countries to cooperate in legal proceedings against suspected terrorist financing groups. . . .

Accordingly, ordering Credit Lyonnais to provide plaintiffs with discovery would not "undermine the important interests of the state where the information is located," but rather, enforce them. . . .

5. Credit Lyonnais Will Not Face Substantial Hardship by Complying with Plaintiffs' Requests

In addition to the five factors prescribed in the Restatement, . . . courts may also consider the hardship a foreign party might suffer if compelled to respond to a discovery order issued by a federal court in the United States.

Credit Lyonnais argues that, because the "French laws prohibiting [Credit Lyonnais's] production of the discovery sought by plaintiffs are valid and enforceable," it would face substantial hardship by complying with plaintiffs' requests. The bank "and its personnel would incur substantial civil, administrative and criminal liability — including fines, imprisonment and the prospect of lawsuits — if they were to violate those laws. . . ." Credit Lyonnais also asserts that it would "suffer enormous professional and reputational hardship if it betrayed its customer's confidence by disclosing the customer's protected information in violation of French bank secrecy laws." Glaringly absent from the submission by Credit Lyonnais is any indication that civil or criminal prosecutions by the French government or civil suits by CBSP are likely, rather than mere possibilities.

. . .

[I]n [*United States v. First National City Bank*, 396 F.2d 897, 905 (2d Cir. 1968)], the court examined the likelihood that the German bank would suffer significant civil penalties, but found both that the chance was "slight and speculative" and that the bank had "a number of valid defenses." The court also noted that the German government had not "expressed any view on this case or indicated that, under the circumstances presented here, enforcement of the subpoena would violate German public policy or embarrass German-American relations." *Id.* at 904.

The prospect that the foreign litigant would face criminal penalties rather than civil liabilities weighs in favor of the objecting party. . . .

Although Credit Lyonnais has demonstrated that French bank secrecy laws have been enforced, the bank has failed to demonstrate that either CBSP or the French government would likely seek to sanction the bank for complying with a United States court order compelling disclosure of documents and information regarding CBSP's accounts. CBSP has shown no interest in protecting, much less asserting, its privacy right, as established by its lack of response to Credit Lyonnais's two letters. . . . [T]he French government has failed to submit any objections to producing the requested information, in response to three inquiries by Credit Lyonnais. Despite Credit Lyonnais's assertions that the "professional and reputational consequences" would be severe if it "betrayed its customer's confidence," . . . the FATF, of which France is a member, has warned financial institutions that they could be exposed "to significant reputational, operational and legal risk" if they engage in business relationships with "high risk" customers such as charities collecting funds related to terrorist activities.

Furthermore, . . . the court entered a confidentiality order in this case, which further lessens Credit Lyonnais's potential hardship. . . .

Credit Lyonnais has not demonstrated any likelihood that it will be pursued civilly or criminally if it responds to plaintiffs' discovery requests, particularly where the French interest in preventing terrorist financing through monitoring and reporting is so clearly demonstrated, and neither France nor CBSP have indicated that it objects to the bank responding to plaintiffs' discovery. . . .

Accordingly, by *June 25, 2007*, Credit Lyonnais shall produce all documents responsive to plaintiffs' Document Requests and respond to plaintiffs' Requests for Admissions and Related Interrogatories. . . .

SO ORDERED.

NOTES AND QUESTIONS

1. **Compelled Violations of Foreign Law.** Is it fair for a U.S. court to require a foreign entity to violate the laws of its own nation? The plaintiffs are requesting information that is in the possession of a French company in France. French law prohibits turning over that information. Why would France have such a law? Why might U.S. courts think it important to disregard foreign law under some circumstances? Why not have a rule that foreign laws can never be a barrier to legitimate discovery requests in the United States?

2. **The Balancing Test.** The court in *Strauss* adopts a balancing test derived from prior cases and the *Restatement (Third) of Foreign Relations Law*. Does the test identify the correct factors? Does it favor U.S. interests over French interests? Does the court in *Strauss* apply it correctly? What seem to be the critical facts in *Strauss*? What facts might change to lead to a different result?

3. **Practice: Resisting Discovery Requests in Violation of Foreign Law.** As attorney for a foreign defendant, what would you do to prepare an objection to a discovery request in violation of foreign law? What if your objection is unsuccessful? What options did Credit Lyonnais have in the *Strauss* case after the court entered a motion to compel? What do you think Credit Lyonnais did?

4. **Facts in Which a Motion to Compel Was Rejected.** In *Reinsurance Co. of America, Inc. v. Adminisratia Asigurarilor de Stat*, 902 F.2d 1275 (7th Cir. 1990), plaintiffs sought postjudgment discovery to identify the assets of the defendant, a Romanian company against which it had obtained a judgment. The defendant objected on the grounds that the discovery would violate Romanian state secrets laws. The district court refused to grant a motion to compel and the court of appeals affirmed. According to the court:

> Initially, we must balance the "vital national interests" of both the United States and Romania. We approach this task with some misgivings. As Judge Marshall of the Northern District of Illinois noted, "the judiciary has little expertise, or perhaps even authority to evaluate the economic and social policies of a foreign country." *In re Uranium Antitrust Litigation*, 480 F. Supp. 1138, 1148 (N.D. Ill. 1979). Moreover, when allegedly considering only "vital national interests," we are left with the rather ridiculous assignment of determining which competing national interest is the more vital.
>
> Whatever the semantic difficulties of our test, the courts of the United States undoubtedly have a vital interest in providing a forum for the final resolution of disputes and for enforcing these judgments. This rather general interest, however, is not as compelling as those interests implicated in . . . cases cited by [plaintiff]. For instance, in *Graco, Inc. v. Kremlin, Inc.*, 101 F.R.D. 503 (N.D. Ill. 1984), the court held that the United States had a compelling interest in ensuring that its patent laws were not undermined by a French blocking statute. Similarly, vital interests are involved when a commercial dispute implicates the integrity of American antitrust laws, *see e.g. In re Uranium Antitrust Litigation*, 480 F. Supp. at 1149. When the United States itself is a party in the litigation, the national interest involved may become compelling. Thus, enforcement of the tax laws and security laws have been considered compelling

national interests. In the case at hand, though, we are presented with a private dispute between two reinsurance corporations. The disputed materials are the subject of a post-judgment interrogatory request and not vital to the case-in-chief. While there is unquestionably a vital national interest in protecting the finality of judgments and meaningfully enforcing these decisions, this interest alone does not rise to the level of those found in these earlier cases.

Against this, we must weigh on the opposing side of the balance the Romanian interest in protecting its state and so-called "service" secrets. Given the scope of its protective laws and the strict penalties it imposes for any violation, Romania places a high price on this secrecy. Unlike a blocking statute, Romania's law appears to be directed at domestic affairs rather than merely protecting Romanian corporations from foreign discovery requests. *Cf. Compagnie Francaise D'Assurance v. Phillips Petroleum Co.*, 105 F.R.D. 16, 30 (S.D.N.Y. 1984) (French blocking statute "never expected nor intended to be enforced against French subjects but was intended rather to provide them with tactical weapons and bargaining chips in foreign courts."); *Graco*, 101 F.R.D. at 508 ("The Blocking Statute obviously is a manifestation of French displeasure with American pre-trial discovery procedures."). Given this choice between the relative interests of Romania in its national secrecy and the American interest in enforcing its judicial decisions, we have determined that Romania's, at least on the facts before us, appears to be the more immediate and compelling.

Is this discussion consistent with *Strauss*? Why do the two cases come out differently? What else might you want to know about the facts in *Reinsurance Co.*?

5. **Cases in Which a Motion to Compel Was Granted.** In *Richmark Corp. v. Timber Falling Consultants*, 959 F.2d 1468 (9th Cir. 1992), a case somewhat similar to *Reinsurance Co.* in which plaintiff sought postjudgment discovery of the assets of a Chinese company, the court acknowledged that because

> [the defendant] is likely to face criminal prosecution in [China] for complying with the United States court order, that fact constitutes a weighty excuse for nonproduction. In this case, [defendant] has in fact been ordered by the Chinese government to withhold the information, and has been told that it will bear the "legal consequences" of disclosing the information. [Defendant] therefore seems to be placed in a difficult position, between the Scylla of contempt sanctions and the Charybdis of possible criminal prosecution.

Nonetheless, the court of appeals held that the defendant was responsible for its predicament, because it could pay the judgment against it and thus avoid the need to disclose its assets. As a result, it upheld the district court's order compelling disclosure as well as substantial contempt sanctions against the defendant for refusing to comply with the district court's order. Is that fair? What if the discovery had been part of the merits of the case?

In *In re Air Cargo Shipping Services Antitrust Litigation*, 2010 WL 2976220 (E.D.N.Y. 2010), the court ordered discovery in violation of South African law, concluding:

> Comparing the national interests at stake, the United States interest in enforcing antitrust laws through private civil actions is one of fundamental importance

to this country's effort to encourage and maintain a competitive economy. The South African interest in enforcing the blocking statute at issue here, on the other hand, is entitled to less deference since it is not a substantive rule of law at variance with the law of the United States, but rather one whose primary purpose is to protect its citizens from discovery obligations in foreign courts.

The possibility that [the defendant] will suffer hardship in complying with a discovery order is speculative at best. Although the defendant cites the prospect of criminal sanctions if it violates the blocking statute, it has cited no instance in which such sanctions have ever been imposed.

How do these facts compare with the facts in *Strauss, Richmark*, and *Reinsurance Co.?*

6. **The Legal Test(s).** For a recent discussion of the issues that arise when there is a conflict between the Federal Rules of Civil Procedure and a foreign "blocking statute," consider *In re: Xarelto (Rivaroxaban) Products Liability Litigation*, 2016 WL 3923873 (E.D. La. 2016). There, a group of plaintiffs claimed injury from the manufacture, sale, distribution, and use of the medication Xarelto, an anti-coagulant used for a variety of blood-thinning medical purposes. During discovery, one party, Bayer, objected to the production of personnel files on the grounds that production of such data would constitute a violation of the German Data Protection Act.

The district court explained the state of the law as follows:

> In the wake of *Société Nationale*, courts have devised numerous mechanisms for performing the Court's unarticulated "comity analysis." Some courts use a three-factor test. For example, the District of Connecticut examines whether: "(1) the examination of the particular facts of the case, particularly with regard to the nature of the discovery requested; (2) the sovereign interests in issue; and (3) the likelihood that the [foreign discovery] procedures will prove effective." Others, such as the Second Circuit, have used a four-factor test, examining "(i) the competing interests of the nations whose laws are in conflict; (ii) the hardship that compliance would impose on the party or witness from whom discovery is sought; (iii) the importance to the litigation of the information and documents requested; and (iv) the good faith of the party resisting discovery." *But see Strauss v. Credit Lyonnais, S.A.*, 242 F.R.D. 199 (E.D.N.Y. 2007) (applying the five factors of the Restatement (Third) of the Law of Foreign Relations as well as two additional factors).
>
> The majority of lower courts, however, perform the five-factor test used in the Restatement (Third) of the Law of Foreign Relations § 442 (Am. Law Inst. 1987) (the "Third Restatement"), citing the Court's favorable reference to the Third Restatement in a footnote in *Société Nationale*. Under the Third Restatement, a court in deciding whether to order the production of information protected by a blocking statute should consider:
>
>> the importance to the . . . litigation of the documents or other information requested; the degree of specificity of the request; whether the information originated in the United States; the availability of alternative means of securing the information; and the extent to which noncompliance with the request would undermine important interests of the United States, or compliance with the request would undermine important interests of the state where the information is located.

Restatement (Third) of Foreign Relations Law § 442 (Am. Law Inst. 1987). These five factors expand to seven in the Ninth Circuit. Relying on *Société Nationale*'s holding that the Third Restatement's factors are not exhaustive, the Ninth Circuit also considers "[1] the extent and the nature of the hardship that inconsistent enforcement would impose upon the person, and [2] the extent to which enforcement by action of either state can reasonably be expected to achieve compliance with the rule prescribed by that state."

One year after the Supreme Court's holding in *Société Nationale*, the Fifth Circuit adopted a three-factor comity analysis. "The district court is only directed to determine whether [foreign discovery procedures] are appropriate after 'scrutiny in each case of the particular facts, sovereign interests, and likelihood that resort to these procedures would prove effective.'" The Fifth Circuit's formulation of the comity analysis emphasizes the sovereignty interests of foreign states. In particular, the circuit court found that district courts should "consider, with due caution, that many foreign countries, particularly civil law countries, do not subscribe to our open-ended views regarding pretrial discovery, and in some cases may even be offended by our pretrial procedures." *Id.* The *Anschuetz* opinion does not cite the Third Restatement.

Despite the *Anschuetz* court's adoption of a three-factor comity analysis, district courts in the Fifth Circuit routinely use the five-factor test of the Third Restatement.

Is this helpful? How do you advise a client? How do you proceed as an attorney?

D. Discovery in Aid of Foreign Proceedings

Our discussion thus far has concerned the question of what happens when a party to a U.S. lawsuit wishes to obtain evidence abroad. Below we consider the question of what happens when an individual involved in a foreign proceeding wishes to obtain discovery in the United States. Such assistance is governed by the following statute, as interpreted in the cases that follow.

28 U.S.C. § 1782

Assistance to foreign and international tribunals and to litigants before such tribunals

(a) The district court of the district in which a person resides or is found may order him to give his testimony or statement or to produce a document or other thing for use in a proceeding in a foreign or international tribunal, including criminal investigations conducted before formal accusation. The order may be made pursuant to a letter rogatory issued, or request made, by a foreign or international tribunal or upon the application of any interested person and may direct that the testimony or statement be given, or the document or other thing be produced, before a person appointed by the court. . . . A person may not be compelled to give his testimony or statement or to produce a document or other thing in violation of any legally applicable privilege.

(b) This chapter does not preclude a person within the United States from voluntarily giving his testimony or statement, or producing a document or other thing, for use in a proceeding in a foreign or international tribunal before any person and in any manner acceptable to him.

Intel Corp. v. Advanced Micro Devices, Inc.

542 U.S. 241 (2004)

Justice GINSBURG delivered the opinion of the Court.

This case concerns the authority of federal district courts to assist in the production of evidence for use in a foreign or international tribunal. In the matter before us, respondent Advanced Micro Devices, Inc. (AMD), filed an antitrust complaint against petitioner Intel Corporation (Intel) with the Directorate-General for Competition (DG-Competition) of the Commission of the European Communities (European Commission or Commission). In pursuit of that complaint, AMD applied to the United States District Court for the Northern District of California, invoking 28 U.S.C. § 1782(a), for an order requiring Intel to produce potentially relevant documents. Section 1782(a) provides that a federal district court "may order" a person "resid[ing]" or "found" in the district to give testimony or produce documents "for use in a proceeding in a foreign or international tribunal . . . upon the application of any interested person."

Concluding that § 1782(a) did not authorize the requested discovery, the District Court denied AMD's application. The Court of Appeals for the Ninth Circuit reversed that determination and remanded the case, instructing the District Court to rule on the merits of AMD's application. In accord with the Court of Appeals, we hold that the District Court had authority under § 1782(a) to entertain AMD's discovery request. The statute, we rule, does not categorically bar the assistance AMD seeks: (1) A complainant before the European Commission, such as AMD, qualifies as an "interested person" within § 1782(a)'s compass; (2) the Commission is a § 1782(a) "tribunal" when it acts as a first-instance decisionmaker; (3) the "proceeding" for which discovery is sought under § 1782(a) must be in reasonable contemplation, but need not be "pending" or "imminent"; and (4) § 1782(a) contains no threshold requirement that evidence sought from a federal district court would be discoverable under the law governing the foreign proceeding. We caution, however, that § 1782(a) authorizes, but does not require, a federal district court to provide judicial assistance to foreign or international tribunals or to "interested person[s]" in proceedings abroad. Whether such assistance is appropriate in this case is a question yet unresolved. To guide the District Court on remand, we suggest considerations relevant to the disposition of that question.

I

. . .

AMD and Intel are worldwide competitors in the microprocessor industry. In October 2000, AMD filed an antitrust complaint with the DG-Competition of the European Commission. . . . The DG-Competition, operating under the Commission's aegis, is the European Union's primary antitrust law enforcer. . . .

AMD's complaint alleged that Intel, in violation of European competition law, had abused its dominant position in the European market through loyalty rebates, exclusive purchasing agreements with manufacturers and retailers, price discrimination, and standard-setting cartels. AMD recommended that the DG-Competition seek discovery of documents Intel had produced in a private antitrust suit, titled *Intergraph Corp. v. Intel Corp.*, brought in a Federal District Court in Alabama. After the DG-Competition declined to seek judicial assistance in the United States, AMD, pursuant to § 1782(a), petitioned the District Court for the Northern District of California for an order directing Intel to produce documents discovered in the *Intergraph* litigation and on file in the federal court in Alabama. AMD asserted that it sought the materials in connection with the complaint it had filed with the European Commission.

. . .

The Court of Appeals rejected Intel's argument that § 1782(a) called for a threshold showing that the documents AMD sought in the California federal court would have been discoverable by AMD in the European Commission investigation had those documents been located within the Union. Acknowledging that other Courts of Appeals had construed § 1782(a) to include a "foreign-discoverability" rule, the Ninth Circuit found "nothing in the plain language or legislative history of Section 1782, including its 1964 and 1996 amendments, to require a threshold showing [by] the party seeking discovery that what is sought be discoverable in the foreign proceeding". A foreign-discoverability threshold, the Court of Appeals added, would disserve § 1782(a)'s twin aims of "providing efficient assistance to participants in international litigation and encouraging foreign countries by example to provide similar assistance to our courts."

. . .

We granted certiorari in view of the division among the Circuits on the question whether § 1782(a) contains a foreign-discoverability requirement. We now hold that § 1782(a) does not impose such a requirement. We also granted review on two other questions. First, does § 1782(a) make discovery available to complainants, such as AMD, who do not have the status of private "litigants" and are not sovereign agents? Second, must a "proceeding" before a foreign "tribunal" be "pending" or at least "imminent" for an applicant to invoke § 1782(a) successfully? Answering "yes" to the first question and "no" to the second, we affirm the Ninth Circuit's judgment.

II

To place this case in context, we sketch briefly how the European Commission, acting through the DG-Competition, enforces European competition laws and regulations. The DG-Competition's "overriding responsibility" is to conduct investigations into alleged violations of the European Union's competition prescriptions. On receipt of a complaint or *sua sponte*, the DG-Competition conducts a preliminary investigation. In that investigation, the DG-Competition may take into account information provided by a complainant, and it may seek information directly from the target of the complaint. Ultimately, DG-Competition's preliminary investigation results in a formal written decision whether to pursue the complaint. If [the DG-Competition] declines to proceed, that decision is subject to judicial review by the Court of First Instance and, ultimately, by the court of last resort for European Union matters, the Court of Justice for the European Communities (European Court of Justice).

If the DG-Competition decides to pursue the complaint, it typically serves the target of the investigation with a formal "statement of objections" and advises the target of its intention to recommend a decision finding that the target has violated European competition law. The target is entitled to a hearing before an independent officer, who provides a report to the DG-Competition. Once the DG-Competition has made its recommendation, the European Commission may dismiss the complaint, or issue a decision finding infringement and imposing penalties. The Commission's final action dismissing the complaint or holding the target liable is subject to review in the Court of First Instance and the European Court of Justice.

Although lacking formal "party" or "litigant" status in Commission proceedings, the complainant has significant procedural rights. Most prominently, the complainant may submit to the DG-Competition information in support of its allegations, and may seek judicial review of the Commission's disposition of a complaint.

III

As in all statutory construction cases, we begin with the language of the statute. The language of § 1782(a), confirmed by its context, our examination satisfies us, warrants this conclusion: The statute authorizes, but does not require, a federal district court to provide assistance to a complainant in a European Commission proceeding that leads to a dispositive ruling, *i.e.*, a final administrative action both responsive to the complaint and reviewable in court. Accordingly, we reject the categorical limitations Intel would place on the statute's reach.

A

We turn first to Intel's contention that the catalog of "interested person[s]" authorized to apply for judicial assistance under § 1782(a) includes only "litigants, foreign sovereigns, and the designated agents of those sovereigns," and excludes AMD, a mere complainant before the Commission, accorded only "limited rights."

Highlighting § 1782's caption, "[a]ssistance to foreign and international tribunals and to *litigants* before such tribunals," Intel urges that the statutory phrase "any interested person" should be read, correspondingly, to reach only "litigants."

The caption of a statute, this Court has cautioned, "cannot undo or limit that which the [statute's] text makes plain." *Trainmen v. Baltimore & Ohio R. Co.*, 331 U.S. 519, 529 (1947). The text of § 1782(a), "upon the application of any interested person," plainly reaches beyond the universe of persons designated "litigant." No doubt litigants are included among, and may be the most common example of, the "interested person [s]" who may invoke § 1782; we read § 1782's caption to convey no more.

The complainant who triggers a European Commission investigation has a significant role in the process. As earlier observed, in addition to prompting an investigation, the complainant has the right to submit information for the DG-Competition's consideration, and may proceed to court if the Commission discontinues the investigation or dismisses the complaint. . . .

B

We next consider whether the assistance in obtaining documents here sought by an "interested person" meets the specification "for use in a foreign or international tribunal." Beyond question the reviewing authorities, both the Court of First Instance and the European Court of Justice, qualify as tribunals. But those courts are not proof-taking instances. Their review is limited to the record before the Commission. Hence, AMD could "use" evidence in the reviewing courts only by submitting it to the Commission in the current, investigative stage.

Moreover, when Congress established the Commission on International Rules of Judicial Procedure in 1958, it instructed the Rules Commission to recommend procedural revisions "for the rendering of assistance to foreign courts *and quasi-judicial agencies.*" § 2, 72 Stat. 1743 (emphasis added). Section 1782 had previously referred to "any judicial proceeding." The Rules Commission's draft, which Congress adopted, replaced that term with "a proceeding in a foreign or international tribunal." Congress understood that change to "provid[e] the possibility of U.S. judicial assistance in connection with [administrative and quasi-judicial proceedings abroad]." S. Rep. No. 1580, at 7-8, U.S. Code Cong. & Admin. News 1964, pp. 3782, 3788; see Smit, International Litigation 1026-1027, and nn. 71, 73 ("[t]he term 'tribunal' . . . includes investigating magistrates, administrative and arbitral tribunals, and quasi-judicial agencies, as well as conventional civil, commercial, criminal, and administrative courts"; in addition to affording assistance in cases before the European Court of Justice, § 1782, as revised in 1964, "permits the rendition of proper aid in proceedings before the [European] Commission in which the Commission exercises quasi-judicial powers"). See also European Commission *Amicus Curiae* 9 ("[W]hen the Commission acts on DG Competition's final recommendation . . . the investigative function blur[s] into decisionmaking."). We have no warrant to exclude the European Commission, to the extent that it acts as a first-instance decision-maker, from § 1782(a)'s ambit.

C

Intel also urges that AMD's complaint has not progressed beyond the investigative stage; therefore, no adjudicative action is currently or even imminently on the Commission's agenda.

Section 1782(a) does not limit the provision of judicial assistance to "pending" adjudicative proceedings. In 1964, when Congress eliminated the requirement that a proceeding be "judicial," Congress also deleted the requirement that a proceeding be "pending." "When Congress acts to amend a statute, we presume it intends its amendment to have real and substantial effect." *Stone v. INS*, 514 U.S. 386, 397 (1995). The legislative history of the 1964 revision is in sync; it reflects Congress' recognition that judicial assistance would be available "whether the foreign or international proceeding *or investigation* is of a criminal, civil, administrative, or other nature." S. Rep. No. 1580, at 9, U.S. Code Cong. & Admin. News 1964, pp. 3782, 3789 (emphasis added).

. . .

In short, we reject the view . . . that § 1782 comes into play only when adjudicative proceedings are "pending" or "imminent." . . . Instead, we hold that § 1782(a) requires only that a dispositive ruling by the Commission, reviewable by the European courts, be within reasonable contemplation.

D

We take up next the foreign-discoverability rule on which lower courts have divided: Does § 1782(a) categorically bar a district court from ordering production of documents when the foreign tribunal or the "interested person" would not be able to obtain the documents if they were located in the foreign jurisdiction?

We note at the outset, and count it significant, that § 1782(a) expressly shields privileged material: ". . . Beyond shielding material safeguarded by an applicable privilege, however, nothing in the text of § 1782 limits a district court's production-order authority to materials that could be discovered in the foreign jurisdiction if the materials were located there.

. . .

Intel raises two policy concerns in support of a foreign-discoverability limitation on § 1782(a) aid — avoiding offense to foreign governments, and maintaining parity between litigants. While comity and parity concerns may be important as touchstones for a district court's exercise of discretion in particular cases, they do not permit our insertion of a generally applicable foreign-discoverability rule into the text of § 1782(a).

We question whether foreign governments would in fact be offended by a domestic prescription permitting, but not requiring, judicial assistance. A foreign nation may limit discovery within its domain for reasons peculiar to its own legal practices, culture, or traditions — reasons that do not necessarily signal objection to aid from United States federal courts. . . . When the foreign tribunal would readily accept relevant information discovered in the United States, application of a foreign-discoverability rule would be senseless. The rule in that situation would serve only to thwart § 1782(a)'s objective to assist foreign tribunals in obtaining relevant information that the tribunals may find useful but, for reasons having no bearing on international comity, they cannot obtain under their own laws.

Concerns about maintaining parity among adversaries in litigation likewise do not provide a sound basis for a cross-the-board foreign-discoverability rule. When information is sought by an "interested person," a district court could condition relief upon that person's reciprocal exchange of information. Moreover, the foreign tribunal can place conditions on its acceptance of the information to maintain whatever measure of parity it concludes is appropriate.

We also reject Intel's suggestion that a § 1782(a) applicant must show that United States law would allow discovery in domestic litigation analogous to the foreign proceeding. Section 1782 is a provision for assistance to tribunals abroad. It does not direct United States courts to engage in comparative analysis to determine whether analogous proceedings exist here. Comparisons of that order can be fraught with danger. For example, we have in the United States no close analogue to the European Commission regime under which AMD is not free to mount its own case in the Court of First Instance or the European Court of Justice, but can participate only as complainant, an "interested person," in Commission-steered proceedings.

IV

As earlier emphasized, a district court is not required to grant a § 1782(a) discovery application simply because it has the authority to do so.

First, when the person from whom discovery is sought is a participant in the foreign proceeding (as Intel is here), the need for § 1782(a) aid generally is not as apparent as it ordinarily is when evidence is sought from a nonparticipant in the matter arising abroad. A foreign tribunal has jurisdiction over those appearing before it, and can itself order them to produce evidence. In contrast, nonparticipants in the foreign proceeding may be outside the foreign tribunal's jurisdictional reach; hence, their evidence, available in the United States, may be unobtainable absent § 1782(a) aid.

Second, . . . a court presented with a § 1782(a) request may take into account the nature of the foreign tribunal, the character of the proceedings underway abroad, and the receptivity of the foreign government or the court or agency abroad to U.S. federal-court judicial assistance. Further, the grounds Intel urged for categorical limitations on § 1782(a)'s scope may be relevant in determining whether a discovery order should be granted in a particular case. Specifically, a district court could consider whether the § 1782(a) request conceals an attempt to circumvent foreign proof-gathering restrictions or other policies of a foreign country or the United States. Also, unduly intrusive or burdensome requests may be rejected or trimmed.

. . .

For the reasons stated, the judgment of the Court of Appeals for the Ninth Circuit is

Affirmed.

[A dissenting opinion of Justice Breyer is omitted.]

NOTES AND QUESTIONS

1. **Policy.** Why would Congress pass § 1782? What would happen in the absence of the statute?
2. **Practice.** What factors guide a court in applying § 1782? What persons are entitled to avail themselves of § 1782? What qualifies as a "proceeding" in light of this case's reasoning? What impact does discoverability have on the application of the statute? What is the district court supposed to do on remand?
3. **Judicial Assistance and International Arbitration.** Under § 1782, there is uncertainty whether arbitral tribunals qualify as "foreign and international tribunal[s]." Most recent judicial decisions have concluded that the statute applies to international arbitral proceedings, although there remains a split of authority in the courts of appeals. *E.g., Servotronics, Inc. v. Boeing Co.,* 954 F.3d 209 (4th Cir. 2020) (§ 1782 discovery is available for use in private commercial arbitration in the United Kingdom); *In re Application of Chevron Corp.,* 633 F.3d 153 (3d Cir. 2011) (§ 1782 discovery is available for use in investment arbitrations); *Republic of Kazakhstan v. Biedermann Int'l,* 168 F.3d 880 (5th Cir. 1999) (§ 1782 does not cover private international arbitrations). Consider the text and policy of the statute. The Court in *Intel* suggested but did not decide that arbitral panels are included. *But see* In re Gao, 2020 WL 3816098 (2d Cir. 2020) (adhering to prior circuit precedent excluding arbitral panels after *Intel*). Which is the better view?

REVIEW NOTES AND QUESTIONS

1. As a lawyer in the United States, what would be your flowchart for discovery of evidence abroad? When would you use the Federal Rules? When would you use the Hague Evidence Convention? When is discovery of evidence abroad going to be relatively easy? When is it going to be especially difficult?
2. How does the existence of foreign laws prohibiting disclosure of certain information complicate discovery of evidence abroad? How would you explain (quickly) to a U.S. client the impact of a foreign law prohibiting disclosure on that client's ability to gain access to information located abroad? What important facts would you need to know?
3. In addition to discovery as part of U.S. litigation, foreign parties may also have access to evidence in the United States through § 1782. How would you explain to a non-U.S. client the procedure for obtaining such evidence and the likelihood of success?

TABLE OF CASES

Principal cases are indicated by italics.

Index